Winner's Electoral College Vote %	Winner's Popular Vote %	Congress	House		Senate	
			Majority Party	**Minority Party**	**Majority Party**	**Minority Party**
**	No popular vote	1st	38 Admin †	26 Opp	17 Admin	9 Opp
		2nd	37 Fed ††	33 Dem-R	16 Fed	13 Dem-R
**	No popular vote	3rd	57 Dem-R	48 Fed	17 Fed	13 Dem-R
		4th	54 Fed	52 Dem-R	19 Fed	13 Dem-R
**	No popular vote	5th	58 Fed	48 Dem-R	20 Fed	12 Dem-R
		6th	64 Fed	42 Dem-R	19 Fed	13 Dem-R
HR**	No popular vote	7th	69 Dem-R	36 Fed	18 Dem-R	13 Fed
		8th	402 Dem-R	39 Fed	25 Dem-R	9 Fed
92.0	No popular vote	9th	116 Dem-R	25 Fed	27 Dem-R	7 Fed
		10th	118 Dem-R	24 Fed	28 Dem-R	6 Fed
69.7	No popular vote	11th	94 Dem-R	48 Fed	28 Dem-R	6 Fed
		12th	108 Dem-R	36 Fed	30 Dem-R	6 Fed
59.0	No popular vote	13th	112 Dem-R	68 Fed	27 Dem-R	9 Fed
		14th	117 Dem-R	65 Fed	25 Dem-R	11 Fed
84.3	No popular vote	15th	141 Dem-R	42 Fed	34 Dem-R	10 Fed
		16th	156 Dem-R	27 Fed	35 Dem-R	7 Fed
99.5	No popular vote	17th	158 Dem-R	25 Fed	44 Dem-R	4 Fed
		18th	187 Dem-R	26 Fed	44 Dem-R	4 Fed
HR	39.1 †††	19th	105 Admin	97 Dem-J	26 Admin	20 Dem-J
		20th	119 Dem-J	94 Admin	28 Dem-J	20 Admin
68.2	56.0	21st	139 Dem	74 Nat R	26 Dem	22 Nat R
		22nd	141 Dem	58 Nat R	25 Dem	21 Nat R
76.6	54.5	23rd	147 Dem	53 AntiMas	20 Dem	20 Nat R
		24th	145 Dem	98 Whig	27 Dem	25 Whig
57.8	50.9	25th	108 Dem	107 Whig	30 Dem	18 Whig
		26th	124 Dem	118 Whig	28 Dem	22 Whig
79.6	52.9					
–	52.9	27th	133 Whig	102 Dem	28 Whig	22 Dem
		28th	142 Dem	79 Whig	28 Whig	25 Dem
61.8	49.6	29th	143 Dem	77 Whig	31 Dem	25 Whig
		30th	115 Whig	108 Dem	36 Dem	21 Whig
56.2	47.3	31st	112 Dem	109 Whig	35 Dem	25 Whig
–	–	32nd	140 Dem	88 Whig	35 Dem	24 Whig
85.8	50.9	33rd	159 Dem	71 Whig	38 Dem	22 Whig
		34th	108 Rep	83 Dem	40 Dem	15 Rep
58.8	45.6	35th	118 Dem	92 Rep	36 Dem	20 Rep
		36th	114 Rep	92 Dem	36 Dem	26 Rep
59.4	39.8	37th	105 Rep	43 Dem	31 Rep	10 Dem
		38th	102 Rep	75 Dem	36 Rep	9 Dem
91.0	55.2					
–	–	39th	149 Union	42 Dem	42 Union	10 Dem
		40th	143 Rep	49 Dem	42 Rep	11 Dem
72.8	52.7	41st	149 Rep	63 Dem	56 Rep	11 Dem
		42nd	134 Rep	104 Dem	52 Rep	17 Dem
81.9	55.6	43rd	194 Rep	92 Dem	49 Rep	19 Dem
		44th	169 Rep	109 Dem	45 Rep	29 Dem
50.1	47.9 †††	45th	153 Dem	140 Rep	39 Rep	36 Dem
		46th	149 Dem	130 Rep	42 Dem	33 Rep
58.0	48.3	47th	147 Rep	135 Dem	37 Rep	37 Dem
–	–	48th	197 Dem	118 Rep	38 Rep	36 Dem
54.6	48.5	49th	183 Dem	140 Rep	43 Rep	34 Dem
		50th	169 Dem	152 Rep	39 Rep	37 Dem

Source for election data: Svend Peterson, *A Statistical History of American Presidential Elections.* New York: Frederick Ungar Publishing, 1963. Updates: Richard Scammon, *America Votes* 19. Washington D.C.: Congressional Quarterly, 1991; *Congressional Quarterly Weekly Report,* Nov. 7, 1992, p. 3552.

Abbreviations:

Admin = Administration supporters
AntiMas = Anti-Masonic
Dem = Democratic
Dem-R = Democratic-Republican
Fed = Federalist

Dem-J = Jacksonian Democrats
Nat R = National Republican
Opp = Opponents of administration
Rep = Republican
Union = Unionist

TENTH EDITION

AMERICAN GOVERNMENT

SUSAN WELCH
The Pennsylvania State University

JOHN GRUHL
University of Nebraska–Lincoln

JOHN COMER
University of Nebraska–Lincoln

SUSAN M. RIGDON
University of Illinois at Urbana–Champaign

THOMSON
✴
WADSWORTH™

Australia • Canada • Mexico • Singapore • Spain
United Kingdom • United States

American Government, Tenth Edition

Susan Welch, John Gruhl, John Comer, Susan M. Rigdon

Publisher: *Clark Baxter*
Executive Editor: *David Tatom*
Senior Development Editor: *Stacey Sims*
Assistant Editor: *Rebecca Green*
Editorial Assistant: *Cheryl Lee*
Technology Project Manager: *Michelle Vardeman*
Senior Marketing Manager: *Janise Fry*
Marketing Assistant: *Teresa Jessen*
Senior Project Manager, Editorial Production: *Kimberly Adams*
Executive Art Director: *Maria Epes*
Print Buyer: *Judy Inouye*

Permissions Editor: *Chelsea Junget*
Production Service: *Orr Book Services*
Text Designer: *Carolyn Deacy*
Photo Researcher: *Image Quest*
Copy Editor: *Bruce Emmer and Linda Marousek*
Cover Designer: *Brian Salisbury*
Cover Image: *Getty Images*
Cover Printer: *Transcontinental Printing/Interglobe*
Compositor: *G&S Typesetters*
Printer: *Transcontinental Printing/Interglobe*

Printed in Canada
1 2 3 4 5 6 7 09 08 07 06 05

For more information about our products, contact us at:
Thomson Learning Academic Resource Center
1-800-423-0563

For permission to use material from this text or product, submit a request online at **http://www.thomsonrights.com**. Any additional questions about permissions can be submitted by email to **thomsonrights@thomson.com**.

Library of Congress Control Number: 2005922389

Student Edition: ISBN 0-534-64768-5
Instructor's Edition: ISBN 0-495-00186-4

Thomson Higher Education
10 Davis Drive
Belmont, CA 94002-3098
USA

Asia (including India)
Thomson Learning
5 Shenton Way
#01-01 UIC Building
Singapore 068808

Australia/New Zealand
Thomson Learning Australia
102 Dodds Street
Southbank, Victoria 3006
Australia

Canada
Thomson Nelson
1120 Birchmount Road
Toronto, Ontario M1K 5G4
Canada

UK/Europe/Middle East/Africa
Thomson Learning
High Holborn House
50–51 Bedford Row
London WC1R 4LR
United Kingdom

Latin America
Thomson Learning
Seneca, 53
Colonia Polanco
11560 Mexico
D.F. Mexico

Spain (including Portugal)
Thomson Paraninfo
Calle Magallanes, 25
28015 Madrid, Spain

BRIEF CONTENTS

PART ONE

The American System

1 The American People 2

2 The Constitution 28

3 Federalism and the Growth of Government 58

PART TWO

Links between People and Government

4 Public Opinion 88

5 News Media 118

6 Interest Groups 160

7 Political Parties 198

8 Elections 234

9 Money and Politics 284

PART THREE

Institutions

10 Congress 314

11 The Presidency 354

12 The Bureaucracy 396

13 The Judiciary 428

PART FOUR

Civil Liberties and Rights

14 Civil Liberties 462

15 Civil Rights 506

PART FIVE

Public Policies

16 Economic Policy 554

17 Social Welfare and Health Policy 588

18 Regulation and Environmental Policy 618

19 Foreign Policy 652

CONTENTS

Preface xii

About the Authors xix

PART ONE

The American System

CHAPTER 1

The American People 2

YOU ARE THERE *Who, Me? 3*

A Demographic Profile 6
  Immigration and Ethnic Diversity 6
TERRORISM, POLITICS, AND POLICY
Immigration: Is the Door Still Open? 8
  *Immigration and Political Cleavage 10   Religious
  Diversity 10   Economic and Demographic
  Diversity 11   Diversity and Identity Politics 12*
AMERICAN DIVERSITY
Census and Sensibility 14

Political Culture 16
  *The Significance of Political Culture 16   Learning
  Political Culture 16*

The Core Values 17
  *Individual Liberty 18   Political Equality 18
  Majority Rule 19   Minority Rights 19   Economic
  Rights 19*

The American Citizen 20
  *Democracy in a Republic 20   Political Participation 20
  Who Has the Power? 23*

Conclusion: Is Government Responsive? 24

EPILOGUE *Who, Me? 25*

  *Key Terms 26   Further Reading 26   For Viewing 26
  Electronic Resources 27   InfoTrac College Edition 27
  American Government Resources 27*

CHAPTER 2

The Constitution 28

YOU ARE THERE *The Case of the Confidential Tapes 29*

The Articles of Confederation 31
  *National Government Problems 31   State Government
  Problems 32*
AMERICAN DIVERSITY
Founding Mothers 33

The Constitution 33
  *The Constitutional Convention 33   Features of the
  Constitution 36   Motives of the Founders 41
  Ratification of the Constitution 43   Changing the
  Constitution 45*
TERRORISM, POLITICS, AND POLICY
Interrogating Terrorists 46

**Impact of the Civil War and the Great
  Depression 48**
  *The Civil War and Reconstruction 48   The Great
  Depression and the New Deal 51   A Combination of
  Constitutions 53*

**Conclusion: Does the Constitution Make the
  Government Responsive? 53**

EPILOGUE *The President Complies in the Case of the
Confidential Tapes 55*

  *Key Terms 57   Further Reading 57   For Viewing 57
  Electronic Resources 57   InfoTrac College Edition 57
  American Government Resources 57*

CHAPTER 3

Federalism and the Growth of Government 58

YOU ARE THERE *Should Nevada Become the Country's Nuclear Waste Dump?* 59

Federal and Unitary Systems 61
Federal Systems 61   Unitary Systems 62   Why Choose Federalism? 62

The Political Bases of American Federalism 62
Political Benefits of Federalism 63   Political Costs of Federalism 63   Political Culture and Federalism 64

The Constitutional Bases of Federalism 65
Major Features of American Federalism 65 Interpretations of the Constitutional Provisions 66

Federalism and the Growth of Government 68
Small-Scale Government 68   The Civil War 68
Government as a "Bully Pulpit" 68   The New Deal and World War II 69   Social Justice and the Great Society 71   New Federalism 71   The New New Federalism 72   A Return to State-Centered Federalism? 72

The Practice of Federalism 77
Federal-State Relations 77
TERRORISM, POLITICS, AND POLICY
The State's Role in National Defense 78
Interstate Relations 81   State-Local Relations 82

People, States, and the Federal Government 83

Conclusion: Does Federalism Make Government More Responsive? 84

EPILOGUE *Nevada Continues to Fight 85*

Key Terms 86   Further Reading 86   For Viewing 86 Electronic Resources 86   InfoTrac College Edition 87 American Government Resources 87

PART TWO

Links between People and Government

CHAPTER 4

Public Opinion 88

YOU ARE THERE *How Can the President Maintain Popularity and Help Republican Candidates?* 89

Nature of Public Opinion 90

Formation of Public Opinion 91
Agents of Political Socialization 93   Impact of Political Socialization 96

Measuring Public Opinion 97
Early Polling Efforts 97
TERRORISM, POLITICS, AND POLICY
9/11 Shapes Public Opinion, But Only for a While 98 Emergence of Scientific Polling 98   Polls and Politics 99   Knowledge and Information 104
POPULAR CULTURE AND POLITICS
Politics as a Joke 105

Ideology 106
Social Welfare and the Proper Role of Government 108 Social Issues 109   Race 109   Political Tolerance 112 Trust in Government 113

Conclusion: Is Government Responsive to Public Opinion? 115

EPILOGUE *President Bush Ties the Economy to the War on Terrorism 116*

Key Terms 117   Further Reading 117   For Viewing 117   Electronic Resources 117   InfoTrac College Edition 117   American Government Resources 117

CHAPTER 5

News Media 118

YOU ARE THERE *Should You Torpedo the Admiral?* 119

The Media State 120
Roles of the Media 121   Concentration of the Media 122   Atomization of the Media 124

Relationship between the Media and Politicians 127
Symbiotic Relationship 127   Adversarial Relationship 131   Relationship between the Media and Recent Administrations 133   Relationship between the Media and Congress 136   Relationship between the Media and the Supreme Court 136   Relationship between the Media and the Military 136

Bias of the Media 138
Political Bias 138
Commercial Bias 145

AMERICAN DIVERSITY
Color and the Clicker 146

Impact of the Media on Politics 150
  *Impact on the Public Agenda 150   Impact on Political
  Parties and Elections 151 Impact on Public Opinion
  153*
TERRORISM, POLITICS, AND POLICY
The CNN of the Middle East 154

Conclusion: Are the Media Responsive? 156

EPILOGUE *Evans Pursued the Admiral 158*

  *Key Terms 159   Further Reading 159   For Viewing
  159   Electronic Resources 159   InfoTrac College
  Edition 159   American Government Resources 159*

CHAPTER 6
Interest Groups 160

YOU ARE THERE *Do You Support the Bush Prescription
Drug Proposal? 161*

Group Formation 163
  *Why Interest Groups Form 163   Why People Join
  164   Which People Join 165   Have Americans
  Stopped Joining? 163*

Types of Interest Groups 165
  Private Interest Groups 166
TERRORISM, POLITICS, AND POLICY
Feeding Frenzy 170
  Public Interest Groups 172
AMERICAN DIVERSITY
The Origin of Gay and Lesbian Rights Groups 175

Strategies of Interest Groups 180

Tactics of Interest Groups 180
  Direct Lobbying Techniques 181
POPULAR CULTURE AND POLITICS
Celebrities and Interest Groups 183
  *Indirect Lobbying Techniques: Going Public 185
  Building Coalitions 189*

Success of Interest Groups 191
  Resources 191   Competition and Goals 192

**Conclusion: Do Interest Groups Help Make
Government Responsive? 193**

EPILOGUE *AAPR Backs the Bush Administration's Drug
Plan for Seniors 195*

  *Key Terms 196   Further Reading 196   For Viewing
  196   Electronic Resources 196   InfoTrac College
  Edition 197   American Government Resources 197*

CHAPTER 7
Political Parties 198

YOU ARE THERE *Should You Violate the Rules of Congress
to Win a Partisan Victory? 199*

Characteristics of Political Parties 201
  *Purpose of Political Parties 201   The American Party
  System 202*

The Rise of American Political Parties 206
  *The Founders and Political Parties 206   Birth of
  Political Parties 206   Development of Mass Parties
  206   Why Parties Are Important to American
  Democracy 207*

Party Realignments 208
  *Rise of the Republicans and the Golden Age
  of Parties 209   Progressive Politics and the Weakening
  of Parties 210   Rise of the Democratic Party 212
  Party Identification Today 213*

Decline of Parties 218
  *Dimunition of Party Functions 218   Erosion of
  Support for Parties 219*

Resurgence of Parties 220
  *Important Remaining Functions of Parties 220   Party
  Influence on Policymaking 221*

Party Organization 222
  *National Party Organization 222   State and Local
  Party Organizations 223*

Parties and Voting 223
  Party Identification 223
TERRORISM, POLITICS, AND POLICY
Bipartisanship for a While 224
POPULAR CULTURE AND POLITICS
Parties on the Web 227
  *Candidate Evaluations 228   Issues 228   Parties,
  Candidates, and Issues 229*

**Conclusion: Do Political Parties Make Government
More Responsive? 229**

EPILOGUE *Hastert Breaks the Rules and Wins
the Vote 231*

  *Key Terms 232   Further Reading 232   For Viewing
  232   Electronic Resources 232   InfoTrac College
  Edition 233   American Government Resource 233*

CHAPTER 8
Elections 234

YOU ARE THERE *Should You Go to Iowa? 235*

The American Electorate 237
    Early Limits on Voting Rights 237 Blacks and the Right to Vote 237 The Voting Rights Act and Redistricting 239
AMERICAN DIVERSITY
Blacks and Hispanics in Office 240
    Women and the Right to Vote 242 Young People and the Right to Vote 243 Felons and the Right to Vote 243 Election Reform and New Threats to Voting Rights 243

Voter Turnout 246
    Political Activism in the Nineteenth Century 246 Progressive Reforms 246
AMERICAN DIVERSITY
Women in Office 247
POPULAR CULTURE AND POLITICS
Rock the Vote or Mock the Vote? 248
    Recent Turnout 249 Who Does Not Vote? 250 Why Turnout Is Low 251

Other Campaign Participation 255

Presidential Nominating Campaigns 255
    Who Runs for President and Why? 256 How a Candidate Wins the Nomination 256
AMERICAN DIVERSITY
Can an African American Be Elected President? 257
    Presidential Caucuses and Conventions 259 Presidential Primaries 259 Reforming the Nomination Process 260 The National Conventions 261 Independent and Third-Party Nominees 264

The General Election Campaign 264
    Campaign Organization 264 Campaign Strategies 265 Campaign Communication 268
TERRORISM, POLITICS, AND POLICY
Terrorism as an Election Issue 269
    The Electoral College 273 Campaign Funding 276

The Permanent Campaign 276

Congressional Campaigns 277
    Incumbents: Unsafe at Any Margin? 277 Challengers 278 Campaigns 279 Voting for Congress 279

Conclusion: Do Elections Make Government Responsive? 279

EPILOGUE *Kerry Makes Iowa a Priority 281*

    Key Terms 282 Further Reading 282 For Viewing 282 Electronic Resources 282 InfoTrac College Edition 283 American Government Resources 283

CHAPTER 9
Money and Politics 284

YOU ARE THERE *Should You Vote to Regulate? 285*

Money and Politics in America's Past 287
    Money in Nineteenth-Century American Politics 288 Early Reforms 289

Regulating Money in Modern Campaigns 289
    Issues in Campaign Finance Reform 290 Modern Attempts at Reform 290 Regulating the Costs of Campaigns and Public Financing 292 Contribution Limits and Ways to Avoid Them 292 Independent Spending 296
POPULAR CULTURE AND POLITICS
How the Swift Boat Ad Became a National News Story 297
    Disclosure 297 Campaign Finance Reform and the 2004 Election 297 Is Real Reform Possible? 298

The Impact of Campaign Money 299
    Does the Campaign Finance System Deter Good Candidates? 299 Does Money Win Elections? 300 Does Money Buy Favorable Policies? 301 Does Our Campaign Finance System Encourage Extortion? 305
AMERICAN DIVERSITY
Direct Contributors in the 2004 Presidential Campaign 306
    Campaign Money and Public Cynicism 306

Conflicts of Interest 307

Are There Democratic and Republican Kinds of Corruption? 309

Conclusion: Does the Influence of Money Make Government Less Responsive? 309

EPILOGUE *Schumer Discourages Tighter Accounting Regulations 311*

    Key Terms 313 Further Reading 313 For Viewing 313 Electronic Resources 313 InfoTrac College Edition 313 American Government Resources 313

CHAPTER 10

Congress 314

YOU ARE THERE *Should You Run for the Party Leadership? 315*

Members and Constituencies 316
Members 316 Constituencies 318 Congress as a
Representative Body 319
AMERICAN DIVERSITY
Congress Is Not a Cross Section of America 320
The Advantages of Incumbency 323

How Congress Is Organized 326
The Evolution of Congressional Organization 326
Contemporary Leadership Positions 328 Committees
331 Staff and Support Agencies 333
TERRORISM, POLITICS, AND POLICY
Continuity in Government 334

What Congress Does 335
Lawmaking 336 Oversight 339 Budget Making
341

Members on the Job 342
Negotiating the Informal System 342 Making
Alliances 344 Using the Media 345 Balancing the
Work 346

Congress and the Public 346

Conclusion: Is Congress Responsive? 348

EPILOGUE *Pelosi Cracks the Whip 351*

Key Terms 352 Further Reading 352 For Viewing
352 Electronic Resources 352 InfoTrac College
Edition 352 American Government Resources 353

CHAPTER 11

The Presidency 354

YOU ARE THERE *Should You Resign the Presidency
or Stay and Fight? 355*

Development and Growth of the Presidency 358

Qualifications and Tenure 359
Eligibility 359 Pay and Perks 360 Tenure and
Succession 360

Powers and Responsibilities 361
Chief Executive: Administrative Duties 362 Chief of
State: Representing the Nation 362 Chief Diplomat:

Statesmanship 363 Commander in Chief: Military
Leadership 364

Presidential Staff 364
Executive Office of the President 365 White House
Office 365 Office of the Vice President 369

Presidential Leadership 370
The President and His Party 371 The President and
Congress 371 Executive Leadership 379 The
President and the Public 381
TERRORISM, POLITICS, AND POLICY
*National Crises and the Expansion of Presidential
Powers 382*
The President and Public Opinion 387
The Ebb and Flow of Presidential Power 388

Presidential Reputation 389
Presidential Character 390 Goals and Vision 391

Conclusion: Is the Presidency Responsive? 392

EPILOGUE *Clinton Stays and Fights 393*

Key Terms 394 Further Reading 394 For Viewing
394 Electronic Resources 394 InfoTrac College
Edition 395 American Government Resources 395

CHAPTER 12

The Bureaucracy 396

YOU ARE THERE *Should You Blow the Whistle
on the FBI? 397*

The Nature of Bureaucracies 399
AMERICAN DIVERSITY
Women and Minorities in the Civil Service 400
Goals 401 Performance Standards 402
Openness 403
TERRORISM, POLITICS, AND POLICY
Veil of Secrecy 404

Growth of the Federal Bureaucracy 406
Why the Bureaucracy Has Grown 406 Controlling
Growth 407 Agencies within the Federal
Bureaucracy 408

What Bureaucracies Do 411
Administering Policy 411 Making Policy 412
Regulation 413 Data Collection and Analysis 413

Politics and Professional Standards 414
The Merit System 414 Neutral Competence 415

Overseeing the Bureaucracy 417
President 417 Congress 420 Courts 421 Interest
Groups and Individuals 421

Conclusion: Is the Bureaucracy Responsive? 423

EPILOGUE Edmonds Blows the Whistle 424

Key Terms 426 Further Reading 426 For Viewing
426 Electronic Resources 426 InfoTrac College
Edition 426 American Government Resources 427

CHAPTER 13
The Judiciary 428

YOU ARE THERE Do You Plunge into the Political
Thicket? 429

Development of the Courts' Role in Government 431
Founding to the Civil War 432 Civil War to the
Great Depression 435 Great Depression to the Present
436 The Next Era 437

Courts 438
Structure of the Courts 438 Jurisdiction of the
Courts 438
TERRORISM, POLITICS, AND POLICY
Surveillance Court 439

Judges 439
Selection of Judges 439

AMERICAN DIVERSITY
Do Women Judges Make a Difference? 443
Tenure of Judges 445 Qualifications of Judges 445
Independence of Judges 446

Access to the Courts 446
Wealth Discrimination in Access 446 Interest
Groups Help in Access 448 Proceeding through the
Courts 448

Deciding Cases 449
Interpreting Statutes 449 Interpreting the Constitution
450 Restraint and Activism 450 Following
Precedents 452 Making Law 453 Deciding Cases at
the Supreme Court 453

The Power of the Courts 456
Use of Judicial Review 456 Use of Political Checks
against the Courts 456

Conclusion: Are the Courts Responsive? 457

EPILOGUE O'Connor Plunges into the Political
Thicket 458

Key Terms 460 Further Reading 460 For Viewing
461 Electronic Resources 461 InfoTrac College
Edition 461 American Government Resources 461

PART FOUR

Civil Liberties and Rights

CHAPTER 14
Civil Liberties 462

YOU ARE THERE Do You Challenge the President
in Wartime? 463

The Constitution and the Bill of Rights 465
Individual Rights in the Constitution 465 The Bill of
Rights 465

Freedom of Expression 467
Freedom of Speech 467
TERRORISM, POLITICS, AND POLICY
The USA Patriot Act 470

Freedom of Association 474
Freedom of the Press 475 Libel and Obscenity 477

Freedom of Religion 479
Free Exercise of Religion 480 Establishment of
Religion 482

Rights of Criminal Defendants 486
Search and Seizure 488 Self-Incrimination 489
Counsel 490 Jury Trial 491 Cruel and Unusual
Punishment 491 Rights in Theory and in Practice
492

Right to Privacy 492
Birth Control 492 Abortion 492 Homosexuality
498 Right to Die 501

Conclusion: Are the Courts Responsive in Interpreting
Civil Liberties? 502

EPILOGUE Federal Courts Can Hear Detention
Suits 503

Key Terms 504 Further Reading 504 For Viewing
504 Electronic Resources 505 InfoTrac College
Edition 505 American Government Resources 505

CHAPTER 15

Civil Rights 506

YOU ARE THERE *Friend or Foe? 507*

Race Discrimination 508
   Discrimination against African Americans 508
AMERICAN DIVERSITY
Black Masters 509
   *Overcoming Discrimination against African
   Americans 513*

Continuing Discrimination against African
   Americans 521
TERRORISM, POLITICS, AND POLICY
Profiling of Arabs? 528

Improving Conditions for African Americans? 528
*Discrimination against Hispanics 531   Discrimination
against Native Americans 535*

Sex Discrimination 538
   *Discrimination against Women 538   Discrimination
   against Men 546*

Affirmative Action 547
   In Employment 547   In College Admissions 548

Conclusion: Is Government Responsive in Granting
   Civil Rights? 550

EPILOGUE *Exclusion of Japanese Is Upheld 551*

   *Key Terms 552   Further Reading 552   For Viewing
   552   Electronic Resources 552   InfoTrac College
   Edition 553   American Government Resources 553*

PART FIVE

Public Policies

CHAPTER 16

Economic Policy 554

YOU ARE THERE *Can the Country Afford a Permanent
Tax Cut? 555*

Types of Economics Systems 557
   *Capitalism 557   Socialism and Communism 557
   Mixed Economies 557*

Government and the Economy 558
   *Popular Expectations 559   Economic Problems 560
   Economic Tools 561   Using Economic Policy to
   Achieve Political Goals 565*

Current Issues 567
   *Tax Reform 567   Income Distribution 571   Deficit
   and Debt 574*
TERRORISM, POLITICS, AND POLICY
Taxing and Spending Policies during Wartime 576

Economic Growth and Job Creation 580

Conclusion: Is Our Economic Policy Responsive? 583

EPILOGUE *Murray Says No to a Permanent Tax Cut 585*

   *Key Terms 586   Further Reading 586   For Viewing
   586   Electronic Resources 586   InfoTrac College
   Edition 587   American Government Resources 587*

CHAPTER 17

*Social Welfare and Health
Policy 588*

YOU ARE THERE *Should the Government Subsidize
Corporate Farming? 589*

The Political and Legal Bases of Social Welfare
   Policies 591

The Evolution of Social Welfare Policies 592

Income Support Programs 593
   *Retirees and Their Dependents 593   The Poor 595
   Farmers 599   Veterans 601   The Impact of Income
   Support Programs 601*

Health Care Programs 601
   *Health Care for Seniors 601   Health Care for the Poor
   and Disabled 602   Health Care for Veterans 603*

Subsidized Services 603
   Education 603   Housing 603   Agriculture 605

Tax Subsidies 606
   Corporations 606   Families and Homeowners 608

Current Issues 608
   *Health Care 608   Social Security 611   Reforming
   Aid to the Poor 613*

Conclusion: Are Social Welfare Programs
Responsive? 615

EPILOGUE *Hutchinson Votes to Subsidize Big Farmers* 616

Key Terms 616   Further Reading 616   For Viewing
617   Electronic Resources 617   InfoTrac College
Edition 617   American Government Resources 617

CHAPTER 18

Regulation and Environmental Policy 618

YOU ARE THERE *Do You Belong Inside Government, or Outside?* 619

Reasons for Regulation 621
Damage to Common Property 621   Inefficient
Competition 622   Lack of Necessary Coordination 623
Unacceptable Inequities 623

Kinds of Regulation 624

The Regulatory Process 625
Writing Regulations 625   Regulatory Oversight 628
Implementing and Enforcing Regulations 629

Cycles of Regulation 631
Deregulation 631   Reregulation 632   Deregulation:
The Current Round 633   Keeping Pace with
Change 636

Regulatory Politics and Environmental Protection 637
Evolution of Government's Role 638   Implementing
Environmental Regulations 639
TERRORISM, POLITICS, AND POLICY
Cleaning Up Nuclear Waste 642
Science, Policy, and Environmental Politics 643

Benefits and Costs of Regulation 646

Conclusion: Is Regulatory Policy Responsive? 647

EPILOGUE *Schaeffer Resigns to Work outside Government* 649

Key Terms 649   Further Reading 649   For Viewing
650   Electronic Resources 650   InfoTrac College
Edition 651   American Government Resources 651

CHAPTER 19

Foreign Policy 652

YOU ARE THERE *Should You Give the President a Blank
Check to Invade Iraq?* 653

Foreign Policy Goals 655

TERRORISM, POLITICS, AND POLICY
Fighting the War at Home 657

Making Foreign Policy in a Democracy 658
The President and His Inner Circle 658   Specialists
660   Congress 661   Interest Groups and Lobbyists
662   Public Opinion 663

Changing Approaches to U.S. Foreign Policy 664
Isolationism 664   Containment 666   Détente 671
Cold Ware Revival and Death 672   Merchant
Diplomacy and Multilateralism 673   Homeland
Security and Preemption 674

Instruments of Foreign Policy 676
Diplomacy 676   Intelligence Gathering 677   Military
Instruments 678   Economic Instruments 681

Defining Security in the Global Age 685

Conclusion: Is Our Foreign Policy Responsive? 687

EPILOGUE *Lugar Votes to Fill in Some of the Blanks* 688

Key Terms 689   Further Reading 689   For Viewing
689   Electronic Resources 690   InfoTrac College
Edition 691   American Government Resources 691

APPENDIX A

The Declaration of Independence 692

APPENDIX B

Constitution of the United States of America 694

APPENDIX C

Federalist Paper 10 703

APPENDIX D

Federalist Paper 51 706

APPENDIX E

Abraham Lincoln's Gettysburg Address 708

Notes 709

Glossary 744

Index 753

PREFACE

Students voted at a higher rate in 2004 than they have in decades, spurred by efforts of both parties and many independent organizations to "Rock the Vote" and get young people to the polls. This heightened participation was a culmination of a tough and bitter election campaign, which itself followed a period of unusual turmoil in American politics. The confusion of the 2000 election, where George W. Bush, who lost the popular vote and perhaps even the electoral college vote, had Florida been tallied correctly, won the presidency and immediately began to pursue a conservative, even radical, agenda. The president brought a deeply divided country together for a few months following the horrific attack on the World Trade Center and the Pentagon, but then divided it again with the decision to go to war in Iraq.

The bitterly fought 2004 election reflected the same cleavages as in 2000 and left many of those who voted for the Democrats feeling that not only had they lost the election, they had lost a country. And many of those who voted for the Republicans woke up on November 3 believing that, at last, they had the mandate to change or even reverse many of the nation's long standing policies, from social security to abortion rights.

Yet, those who understand American politics know that it's difficult to bring about massive changes quickly. It's unlikely that the future is as bleak as the Democrats predict, or as rosy as the Republicans envision. The American system has so many checks and balances that a transitory popular majority can be frustrated.

We hope the students reading this book will come to understand these principles of our government. We hope to reinforce for students who have taken an interest in government why government is important, exciting, and controversial. And for those students who have not yet become involved, we hope we can show them why it is in their interest to learn about government and participate in it. We believe an introductory course succeeds if most students develop an understanding of major ideas, an interest in learning more about American government, and an ability to begin to understand and evaluate the news they hear about American political issues.

Although a firm grounding in the essential "nuts and bolts" of American government is crucial, other approaches are helpful in motivating students' interest in government. We offer the essentials of American government, but we also want the student to understand why (and sometimes how) these important features have evolved, their impact on government and individuals, and why they are controversial (if they are) and worth learning about. For example, we prefer that students leave the course remembering why government tries to regulate corporations, how it does so, and the political factors that lead to stronger or weaker regulations rather than specific regulatory acts. The latter will change or soon be forgotten, but understanding the "whys" will help the student understand the issues long after the course is over.

We have also tried to interest students by describing and discussing the impact of various features of government. For example, students who do not understand why learning about voter registration laws is important may "see the light" when they understand the link between such laws and low voter turnout.

Therefore, a particular emphasis throughout the book is on the *impact* of government: how individual features of government affect its responsiveness to different groups (in Lasswell's terms, "Who gets what and why?"). We realize that nothing in American politics is simple; rarely does one feature of government produce, by itself, a clear outcome. Nevertheless, we think that students will be more willing to learn about government if they see some relationships between how government operates and the impact it has on them as American citizens.

The Organization and Contents of the Book

While the basic organization of American government books is fairly standard, our text has a unique chapter on money and politics and a half-chapter on environmental politics. Other features include a civil rights chapter that integrates a thorough treatment of constitutional issues concerning minorities and women, a discussion of the civil rights and women's rights movements, and contemporary research on the political status of these groups. We include in this chapter the special legal problems of Hispanics and Native Americans.

Substantive policy chapters reinforce the emphasis on the impact of government action. The chapter on social welfare and health policy now includes major sections on types of policies: income support programs, health care programs, other subsidized services (including education, insurance, mortgages, and agriculture), and tax subsidies. A chapter on economic policymaking complements the section on budgeting found in the chapter on Congress. The treatment of economic policy highlights the relationship between politics and the economy, and it should help the student better understand issues such as the deficit, inflation, and unemployment. We have refocused this chapter to give more attention to economic policy choices that bedevil our policy makers in the areas of tax reform, the deficit, income redistribution, and economic growth. The chapter on regulation emphasizes the underlying rationale for regulation and its problems and benefits, with special emphasis on environmental regulation.

The chapter on foreign policy places current foreign policy issues in the context of the history of our foreign policy aims, especially since World War II, and features new issues arising from the post–9/11 world.

Some instructors will prefer not to use any of the policy chapters. The book stands as a whole without them, as many policy examples are integrated into the rest of the text. Different combinations of the policy chapters may also be used, as each chapter is independent.

The organization of the book is straightforward. After material on democracy, the Constitution, and federalism, the book covers linkages, including money and politics, then institutions, and finally policy. Civil liberties and rights are treated after the chapter on the judiciary.

But the book is flexible enough that instructors can modify the order of the chapters. Some instructors will prefer to cover institutions before process. Others may prefer to discuss civil liberties and rights when discussion the Constitution.

Changes in the Tenth Edition

The attack on 9/11, terrorism and its effects on policy and politics, the war on Iraq, and the divisive 2004 election campaign provide new issues of interest for analysts of American government. We explore these recent phenomena in light of the fundamentals about American government that students should learn.

We explore the impact of terrorism on American politics and policy in a new feature, "Terrorism, Politics, and Policy." Here we examine the medium term effects of the war on terrorism on issues ranging from privacy rights to immigration policy. The war on terrorism has also buttressed governmental and presidential power, and we explore this in most chapters, including the presidency, the courts, and civil liberties.

While still covering the strange outcome of the 2000 election, we also provide significant coverage of the 2004 campaign and election, including the Democratic primary, the record of young people in the election, and the election outcomes. Increasing concerns over voting rights are also a subject of new treatment in the elections chapter.

A new feature explores politics and popular culture. How does politics insinuate itself into modern culture, from the Internet to entertainment? And how do politicians use the trappings of popular culture to make their cases? As another reflection of popular culture, we have added to every chapter a "For Viewing" section to call attention to a few movies, old and new, documentaries, dramas, and comedies that reflect the themes and subjects of the chapter.

The text of every chapter has been substantially revised. Throughout we have also replaced photos and cartoons to complement the new material and to give students a chance to learn through graphic as well as textual material. As always, we have updated the judiciary, civil liberties, and civil rights chapters to incorporate new Supreme Court decisions. Expanded treatment of gay rights appears in the chapters on interest groups and civil rights. Of course, all the policy chapters have been revised to reflect new public policy developments. The foreign policy chapter contains a substantial discussion of U.S. policy toward Iraq.

We are delighted to have the opportunity to write this tenth edition and to improve the text further in ways suggested by our students and readers. We have been extremely pleased by the reaction of instructors and students to our first nine editions. We were especially gratified to have won three times the American Government Textbook Award from the Women's Caucus for Political Science of the American Political Science Association.

Special Features

Student interest and analytic abilities grow when confronted with a clash of views about important issues. Today there is much discussion about how to stimulate the critical thinking abilities of students. Beginning with the first edition, our text has provided features especially designed to do this by involving students in the controversies—and excitement—of American politics.

You Are There

Each chapter opens with a scenario called "You Are There." In a page or two, the student reads about a real-life political dilemma faced by a public official or a private citizen involved in a controversial issue. Students are asked to put themselves in that individual's shoes, to weigh the pros and cons, and to decide what should be done. The instructor may want to poll the entire class and use the "You Are There" as a basis for class discussion. In the "Epilogue" at the end of the chapter, we reveal the actual decision and discuss it in light of the ideas presented in the chapter.

Nearly two-thirds of the "You Are There" features in this edition are new. They focus on contemporary topics such as the decision by AARP to support President Bush's proposal for a drug benefit under Medicare (Chapter 6), the decision of Senator Kerry to give priority to the Iowa caucuses in his fight for the Democratic nomination (Chapter 8), the decision by Representative Nancy Pelosi to run for the Democratic leadership position in the House (Chapter 10), the actions of a whistleblower in the FBI (Chapter 12), and the rulings by the Supreme Court on the legality of the detentions at Guantanamo Bay (Chapter 14).

Terrorism, Politics, and Policy

Each of these new features highlights an issue posed by 9/11 and its aftermath that is relevant to the chapter's subject. For example, in the introductory chapter, we feature the impact of 9/11 on immigration policy; in the interest group chapter, we discuss how lobbyists used 9/11 to further their existing agendas; in the bureaucracy chapter, we explore government's new emphasis on secrecy; in the presidency chapter, we address the tendency for presidential power to expand during national crises; in the judiciary chapter we explain the little known surveillance court, which approves the government's surveillance requests; in the civil liberties chapter, we examine the Patriot Act; and in the regulation and environmental policy chapter, we focus on the safety of our own nuclear weapons in a time of terrorism.

American Diversity

In many chapters, "American Diversity" boxes illustrate the impact of the social diversity of the American population on political life. These boxes help students understand how a variety of backgrounds and attitudes shapes views of politics and positions on issues.

Boxes

In each chapter, several boxes highlighting interesting aspects of American politics draw the students into the material. Many illustrate how government and politics really work in a particular situation—how a corporation lobbies for government benefits, how a seemingly powerless group is able to organize for political action, how interest groups solicit money by mail, and how political polls are done—while others highlight features of government that may be of particular interest to students—how ethnicity shapes voting behavior and how teen pregnancies and abortions affect the abortion debate.

Other Features

Several other features also help students organize their study.

Key Terms

Key terms are boldfaced within the text and listed at the end of each chapter and in the glossary.

Further Reading

A brief, annotated list of further readings contains works that might be useful to a student doing research or looking for additional material.

For Viewing

A brief, annotated list of films, both commercial and documentary, that are interesting to a student after reading the chapter.

Electronic Resources

Each chapter lists addresses of particularly interesting or useful sites on the Internet that relate directly to the topics covered in the chapter.

InfoTrac College Edition®

At the end of each chapter are lists of suggested topic related articles that they can access in InfoTrac College Edition's extensive online library of important political science and other popular sources.

American Government Resources

A reminder for students to visit the Wadsworth American Government Resources Web site, with its many helpful tools, appears at the end of each chapter.

Ancillaries for Instructors

NEW!

Multimedia Manager for Political Science: A Microsoft® PowerPoint® Link Tool

An advanced PowerPoint presentation tool containing text-specific lecture outlines, figures, and images that allows instructors to deliver dynamic lectures quickly. In addition, it provides the flexibility to customize each presentation by editing what we have provided or by adding a personal collection of slides, videos, and animations. This instructor's resource provides a wealth of materials available electronically, including the full Instructor's Manual, Test Bank in ExamView and Word, the Video Case Study Instructor's Manual, and additional American Government tables and figures to incorporate into your lectures.

CNN® Today Videos for American Government

Six volumes of three- to six-minute video clips on relevant political issues. They serve as great lecture or discussion launchers. On VHS or DVD.

America's New War: CNN Looks at Terrorism

Free to qualified adopters, this great discussion starter includes sixteen two- to five-minute segments on terrorist attacks on U.S. targets around the world.

Video Case Studies for American Government

Free to adopters, this award-winning video contains twelve case studies on the debate on recent policy issues, such as affirmative action. Each case ends with questions designed to spark classroom discussion.

Wadsworth Political Science Video Library

So many exciting new videos...so many great ways to enrich your lectures and spark discussion of the material in this text. Your Wadsworth/Thomson representative will be happy to provide details on our video policy by adoption size.

Ancillaries for Instructors and Students

Thomson Wadsworth is proud to offer both discipline- and book-specific web resources for both instructors and students.
Visit http://politicalscience.wadsworth.com for access to:

Open and available to any user! **Political Science Homepage,** containing:

- Online catalog for our titles
- Monthly features, including in the News, Current Events Quiz, Updates on the War on Terror, and the Election 2004 mini-site.
- Opposing Viewpoints Resource Center
- Web links
- Public opinion poll
- PoliSci careers
- Calendar of events
- Meet the political science team

Open and available to any user! The **American Government Resource Center,** containing:

- Internet exercises
- InfoTrac College Edition readers
- InfoTrac College Edition exercises
- Participation activities

Adopting Instructors Only receive password-protected access to:

- 🔒 Electronic version of the Instructor's Manual.
- 🔒 Microsoft PowerPoint lecture presentations
- 🔒 Access to the Opposing Viewpoints Resource Center
- 🔒 A downloadable in-class simulation, "Responding to Terror"
- 🔒 NewsEdge, a live news feed updated every 15 minutes

Students receive access to the following book-specific resources. Note that those resources marked with a picture of a lock are password-protected. Students receive their password for FREE with every new copy of the text. Please note that the Instructor password will provide access to student supplements as well.

🔒 American PoliticsNow self-assessment

🔒 NEW! "You Are There!" interactive simulations

🔒 NEW! Interactive Timelines

🔒 Video Case Studies

🔒 MicroCase® Exercises

🔒 InfoTrac College Edition readers

🔒 InfoTrac College Edition exercises

🔒 Internet activities that expand on the "American Diversity" and "Politics and Popular Culture" features from the text

- Learning objectives
- Chapter outlines
- Chapter summaries
- Key terms
- Flash cards with audio
- Crossword puzzles
- Glossary
- Book-specific interactive exercises
- Interactive quizzing

Opposing Viewpoints Resource Center . . . For Pro and Con Debates

Expose your students to various sides of today's most compelling issues with this dynamic online library of current events topics—the facts, as well as the arguments of each topic's proponents and detractors. For a nominal fee, the Opposing Viewpoints Resource Center is available for convenient packaging with each copy of this book. For a demonstration, please visit http://www.gale.com/opposingviewpoints/.

InfoTrac® College Edition with InfoMarks™

Available as a FREE bundle! **Not sold separately.** When you adopt this text and request InfoTrac College Edition, you and your students gain FREE anytime, anywhere access to so many reliable resources! This fully searchable database offers more than 20 years' worth of full-text articles (not abstracts) from almost 5,000 diverse sources. NEW! Your subscription now includes instant access to virtual readers drawing from the vast InfoTrac College Edition library and hand selected to work with your book. Check the Book Companion Website for availability of IntoTrac College edition virtual readers. Students also have instant access to

InfoWrite, which includes guides to writing research papers, grammar, and "critical thinking" guidelines. For a tour of InfoTrac, visit http://www.infotrac-college.com/ and select the "User Demo." Journals subject to change. Restrictions apply.

JoinIn™ on TurningPoint® CD-ROM

Allows you to transform your classroom and assess your students' progress with instant in-class quizzes and polls. JoinIn lets you pose book-specific questions and display students' answers seamlessly within the Microsoft PowerPoint slides of your own lecture.

WebTutor™

Takes your course beyond classroom boundaries! Rich with content for your American government course, this Web-based teaching and learning tool includes course management, study/mastery, and communication tools. Use WebTutor to provide virtual office hours, post your syllabus and tract student progress with WebTutor's quizzing material. For students, WebTutor offers real-time access to interactive online tutorials and simulations, practice quizzes, and Web links—all correlated to *American Government* and *Understanding American Government*. Available in WebCT and Blackboard.

Student Resources

Study Guide

Features a chapter summary, key terms, and fill-in-the blank, true/false, multiple-choice, and short essay questions.

NEW!

American Government: Using MicroCase ExplorIt, Ninth Edition

Windows-compatible package that includes a CD-ROM and workbook. Students make their own decisions about the issues as they analyze and interpret current NES and GSS data.

American Government: Readings and Responses

By Monica Bauer. A wonderful collection of readings from prominent writers, plus "Chat Room" conversations with students who debate the topics in the readings.

9/11: The Giant Awakens

By Jeremy Meyer. Focuses on how the American political *system* is responding to the challenges posed by the 9/11 attacks.

Critical Thinking and American Government, Second Edition

By Kent M. Brudney, John J. Carver, and Mark E. Weber. Provides information and exercises that help students hone the skills necessary for interpreting and analyzing American government issues.

Thinking Globally, Acting Locally

By John Soares. Designed to help students get involved and become active citizens. Topics include tips for writing letters to the editor, volunteering, how to change laws, and registering to vote.

American Government Internet Activities, Third Edition

Contains activities for all major topics in the text. Students are asked to surf the Web to obtain answers to thought-provoking questions.

An Introduction to Critical Thinking and Writing in American Politics

Introduces a number of critical thinking and writing techniques, helping students make better use of the information they receive in class and in the text.

InfoTrac College Edition Student Guide for Political Science

Helps students make the most of the InfoTrac database available with their textbook, including suggested keyword search terms for political science.

The Handbook of Selected Court Cases

Includes more than thirty Supreme Court cases.

The Handbook of Selected Legislation and Other Documents

Features excerpts from twelve laws passed by the U.S. Congress that have had a significant impact on American politics.

Acknowledgments

We would like to thank the many people who have aided and sustained us during the lengthy course of this project.

We first want to thank Michael Steinman, our original co-author and original primary author of chapters 1, 11, and 12, who helped plan this book and continued his co-authorship for several editions. The shape of the book still reflects his insights and efforts. Then, we thank Margery Ambrosius and Jan Vermeer for their intellectual contributions to this book through their co-authorship in previous editions. Our current and former University of Nebraska and Penn State colleagues have been most tolerant and helpful. We thank them all. In particular, we appreciate the assistance of John Hibbing, Philip Dyer, Robert Miewald, Beth Thiess-Morse, Louis Picard, John Peters, David Rapkin, Peter Maslowski, David Forsythe, W. Randy Newell, and Steven Daniels, who provided us with data, bibliographic information, and other insights that we have used here. We are especially grateful to Philip Dyer, Alan Booth, Louis Picard, Robert Miewald, and John Hibbing, who read one or more chapters and saved us from a variety of errors. Susan Welch's Penn State colleagues Ron Filippelli and Ray Lombra have been a source of encouragement, support, and many interesting political insights.

We are also grateful to the many other readers of our manuscript and earlier editions of the book, as listed here. Without their assistance the book would have been less accurate, less complete, and less lively. And thanks too to those instructors who have used the book and relayed their comments and suggestions to us. Our students at the University of Nebraska have also provided invaluable reactions to previous editions.

Others, too, have been of great assistance to us. John Soares and Lauren Holland provided essential service and help in producing the ancillary materials for the book.

Several people at Wadsworth Publishing also deserve our thanks. Clark Baxter has been a continual source of encouragement and optimism from the beginning of the first edition through the beginning of the ninth. David Tatom has been his able replacement. We are greatly in debt to Carolyn Deacy who designed this edition of the book.

REVIEWERS OF THE NEW EDITION

Bethany Barratt, *Roosevelt University;* Kent M. Brudney, *Cuesta Community College;* Mark A. Cichock, *University of Texas at Arlington;* Timothy Howard, *North Harris College;* Michael Graham, *San Francisco State University;* Alan C. Melchior, *Florida International University*

REVIEWERS OF PREVIOUS EDITONS

Alan Abramowitz, *State University of New York at Stony Brook;* Larry Adams, *Baruch College— City University of New York;* Danny M. Adkison, *Oklahoma State University;* James Alt, *Harvard University;* Margery Marzahn Ambrosius, *Kansas State University;* Kevin Bailey, *North Harris Community College;* Kennette M. Benedict,

ABOUT THE AUTHORS

SUSAN WELCH received her A.B. and Ph.D. degrees from the University of Illinois at Urbana-Champaign. She is currently Dean of the College of Liberal Arts and Professor of Political Science at The Pennsylvania State University. Her teaching and research areas include legislatures, state and urban politics, and women and minorities in politics. She has edited the *American Politics Quarterly*.

JOHN GRUHL, a Professor of Political Science, received his A.B. from DePauw University in Greencastle, Indiana, and his Ph.D. from the University of California at Santa Barbara. Since joining the University of Nebraska faculty in 1976, he has taught and researched in the areas of judicial process, criminal justice, and civil rights and liberties. He won University of Nebraska campus-wide and system-wide distinguished teaching awards and has become a charter member of the University's Academy of Distinguished Teachers.

JOHN COMER is a Professor of Political Science at the University of Nebraska. He received his A.B. in political science from Miami University of Ohio in 1965 and his Ph.D. from the Ohio State University in 1971. His teaching and research focus on interest groups, public opinion, voting behavior, and political parties.

SUSAN RIGDON received A.B. and Ph.D. degrees in political science from the University of Illinois in 1966 and 1971. She has taught American Government at several institutions in the United States and China, and has other teaching and research interests in foreign policy, comparative government, and political development. She is a Research Associate in Anthropology at the University of Illinois at Urbana-Champaign.

CHAPTER 1

THE AMERICAN PEOPLE

Elementary students in Brentwood, California, where the multicultural present looks like America's future.

© Steve Schapiro

A Demographic Profile

    Immigration and Ethnic Diversity

    Immigration and Political Cleavage

    Religious Diversity

    Economic and Demographic Diversity

    Diversity and Identity Politics

Political Culture

    The Significance of Political Culture

    Learning Political Culture

The Core Values

    Individual Liberty

    Political Equality

    Majority Rule

    Minority Rights

    Economic Rights

The American Citizen

    Democracy in a Republic

    Political Participation

    Who Has the Power?

Conclusion: Is Government Responsive?

Who, Me?

In the opening section of each chapter in this book, you will be asked to step into the shoes of decision makers and to analyze, based on the circumstances, how you think the person should react. The epilogue to each chapter provides the actual outcome of the decision-maker's dilemma.

The first decision maker you are asked to be is, well, *you*. The decision is whether to vote in the 2004 presidential election. (Those of you who were too young to vote can analyze the decision you would have made had you been old enough).

The 2004 election is one of the most fiercely fought elections in recent history. The public is polarized. The 74 percent gap between the favorable ratings given George W. Bush by Republicans and Democrats is the greatest for any president dating back to the early 1950s, when political polling started.[1]

In typical presidential elections, most people do not pay much attention until after Labor Day, in September. But not this election. By July, most people had made up their minds. Only about one in five voters said they were "persuadable" in July, compared to about one-third in earlier elections. Crowds for candidates were bigger than usual, and political contributions much higher than usual.[2] Journalists remarked on the emotional involvement of those who attended political rallies. Many people think this is the most important election in their lifetimes.

Many groups are busy registering voters and trying to persuade them to vote. This not only includes those working directly for the candidates and parties but also a lively variety of other groups: the San Francisco band Aphrodesia, on a Just Vote tour, cruising in a vegetable oil-powered van to urge young people to vote; the Paddle for the Presidency drive featuring young college graduates canoeing the Mississippi carrying the "get out the vote" message; rappers, including Sean "P. Diddy" Combs with his "Vote or Die" T-shirt, encouraging youth to vote; a women's group targeting one thousand beauty salons in key states, hoping to increase the turnout of single women; and strip club owners encouraging dancers to whisper, "Are you registered?" to clients.[3] Most of these drives focused on Democrats; as a spokeswoman for the College Republican National Committee commented, "There must be some pretty hardcore conservatives who've put together some fun activities, but I just can't really think of any."[4] Republican get-out-the-vote efforts were, however, assisted by hundreds of conservative churches working to register their congregations.

Why this effort? Americans generally vote in lower numbers than their counterparts in other democratic societies. Despite the fact that tens of thousands of Americans have died defending freedom here and

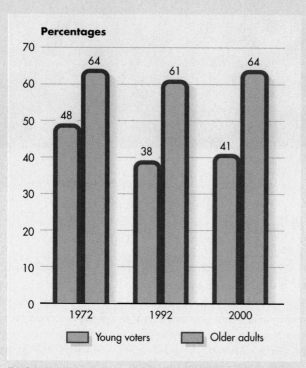

Percentages

	1972	1992	2000
Young voters	48	38	41
Older adults	64	61	64

Young voters · Older adults

FIGURE 1 ■ **Young People Vote Less** *The turnout gap between the youngest and older adults is huge. In 2004, the youth voting rate rose substantially from 2000, but the large gap remained because older voters also turned in record numbers. All figures are from self-report data and higher than official rates for youth and older adults.*
SOURCE: U.S. Census Bureau, "Voting and Registration in the Election," *Current Population Reports,* Series P20 (Washington, D.C.: Government Printing Office, various years).

abroad, only about half of us bother to vote.

And young people are far less likely to vote than their elders (see Figure 1). In 2000, one of the closest presidential elections in modern times, only 45 percent of Americans aged eighteen to twenty-five had registered, and only 32 percent voted.[5] These proportions are far less than the 64 percent of all Americans who are registered and 55 percent who vote. The highest voting rates are among seniors, two-thirds of whom typically vote.

Compared to others in the eighteen-to-twenty-five age bracket, college students *do* express more interest in participation; during the 2004 presidential primaries, 62 percent of college students said they intended to vote in the November election.[6] This upsurge of interest in politics was especially evident

in Howard Dean's Internet-based campaign, much of which was organized and run by college students. The war in Iraq also increased young people's interest in politics. Yet in a poll conducted just after the primary season ended, 43 percent of American college students said that politics has little or no relevance.[7]

So do you vote? You know that elected officials, especially the president, do make a difference in a number of things that are relevant to you: your college tuition if you attend a public school, the amount of student aid you can receive, whether you or a friend will be sent to Iraq or other places where the United States is fighting, whether those troops will be draftees or volunteers, whether you or your sister or wife can get a safe and legal abortion, and whether the government

will create more jobs when the economy lags. You know it is no coincidence that government services for older Americans, who vote at high levels are better than for members of other age groups.

You feel a sense of obligation, too. Participation is integral to the concept on which our form of government is founded. Voting is a cornerstone of our freedom. People risked and even lost their lives in the civil rights struggle so African Americans could vote, and many lost their lives in this cause. Winning voting rights for women was a long, hard struggle too, and women suffragists were beaten and tortured in at least one American prison.[8]

This is a huge country—economically, ethnically, and religiously diverse and becoming more so every year. There will always be divergent views and therefore competing interests trying to shape government policy. If you opt out, and candidates are elected and policies made that you disagree with, quite frankly, you will not have much basis for complaint. Government will become less and less responsive to the public.

But it is hard to stay interested in politics. You look at the news and see dog-eat-dog, negative campaigning, character attacks, investigations into the most intimate aspects of the lives of public figures, gridlock caused by party conflict in Congress and state legislatures, and huge campaign donations buying access to candidates or officials. And you think that Groucho Marx's observation that "politics is the art of finding trouble everywhere, diagnosing it incorrectly, and applying the wrong remedy" makes a lot of sense.

You worry that your vote will not make a difference, so why bother. Maybe it makes no difference who wins. Sometimes you think that, after all, government works: your mail comes, your grandparents' Social Security checks arrive on time, your state issued you a driver's license, the roads are paved, the bridges and dams hold up, the schools are open, and we have a large military establishment, local

law enforcement, a great-looking capital city, and a massive infrastructure. America has social stability and a well-functioning economy. Government is

doing the basics. Why should you get involved in politics?

So do you vote or not? And why do you make the decision you do?

Americans take pride in their form of government but express ambivalence toward the political process. We cherish the Declaration of Independence and the Constitution and love the symbols of democracy. We visit Washington, D.C., to marvel at the Washington Monument, the Jefferson and Lincoln Memorials, the Capitol, and the White House. We show these symbols of our democracy to our children, hoping they will learn to revere them too.

But at the same time that we point with pride to the documents and symbols of American democracy, we often seem unwilling to accept the realities of democratic practice or to spend the time it takes to familiarize ourselves with candidates and issues.[9] We are impatient with the slow pace at which government deals with the nation's problems. We refer to debates over issues as quarrels or "bickering"; we call compromises "selling out"; we too readily label conflict as mere self-interest and tag interest groups and political parties as "*special* interests." In other words, we love the concept of democracy but hate the rough and tumble, the give and take, and the conflict of democracy in action.[10]

Despite the conflict in our political life, Americans are members of one community. We are parties to a single legal contract, the Constitution, and are all equally subject to the protections and obligations of a common set of laws. We also share an economic system, and although the Constitution has little to say about its nature, our government is deeply implicated in its successes and failures. In fact, government's role in managing the economy is sufficient to link the level of confidence we have in government to how well the economy is doing or, at minimum, to how well we are doing. Our economic well-being also affects how much we participate and how much access we have to policymakers.

It is part of the American political character to fear any concentration of power that threatens individual liberty and hence to be suspicious of government for its potential to concentrate and misuse power. Yet in arguing for the ratification of the Constitution in 1789, John Jay wrote, "Nothing is more certain than the indispensable necessity of Government."[11] Why is government indispensable? Because even though government *can* be a threat to individual liberty, there is no way to guarantee liberty without the protections and constraints that government and the rule of law can provide. The Preamble to the Constitution identifies other governmental

functions—to form a union among the disparate states, to establish a system of justice, to maintain social order, to promote the general welfare of the people, and to defend against external threats. How far its authority extends in fulfilling any of these tasks is the topic of an eternal debate about the proper role of government in a system of constitutionally restricted powers. This debate in turn encompasses much of what is at stake in the political process.

If government is the instrument for forging one interest out of many in order to legislate and to speak for the country as a whole in matters of national interest, then **politics** is a means through which individual and group interests compete to shape government's impact on society's problems and goals. In political science, the term *politics* encompasses a much wider spectrum than actions directed toward government policy; it applies to all power relationships and to attempts to influence the distribution of resources in the private sphere as well as the public. But in this text we are concerned with politics as it affects competition for and performance in government office and efforts to influence policy made by government officials.

In their attempts to shape policy, individuals and groups compete through political parties and many other extragovernmental organizations, but politics is more than competition. While private organizations such as parties and interest groups do exist primarily to give voice to competing interests, government's role is to mediate among them, resolve conflicting points of view, and formulate policies that represent a collective view. Thus politics is also essential to the art of governing. This is why more than two thousand years ago, Aristotle wrote that politics is the most noble endeavor in which people can engage, partly because it helps individuals know themselves and partly because it forces individuals to relate to others. Through political participation, individuals pursue their own needs and interests, but not without consideration for the needs of other citizens. In other words, it is through politics that we learn to balance our own needs and interests against the good of the political community as a whole.

Today, Americans are less inclined to share Aristotle's conception of politics than the cynical view of novelist Gore Vidal that "who collects what money from whom in order to spend on what is all there is to politics."[12] Yet the high ideals of our founders and the be-

Immigrants crowd a New York City neighborhood in 1890.

liefs in democracy that we claim to cherish are about far more than who collects what to spend where. This book describes how people, politics, government, and the economy come together to form the "American system." We discuss how these relationships might change as we move through the twenty-first century and as we face new threats to our national security as evidenced by the events of September 11, 2001.

This chapter begins the discussion by profiling the American people, identifying the political values we share, and describing how they are expressed in our form of government. It also briefly describes how democracy, when practiced by people who are ethnically, economically, and religiously diverse and scattered across a vast and varied landscape, is destined to be characterized as much by competition and conflict as by cooperation and community. All of these topics will be developed in greater detail in later chapters.

A Demographic Profile

When the poet Walt Whitman wrote, "Here is not merely a nation but a teeming Nation of nations," he said a lot about our country and its politics.[13] It is a cliché, yet true, that the United States is a land of immigrants, peopled by individuals from all over the world. Americans are a conglomeration of religions, races, ethnicities, cultural traditions, and socioeconomic groups —what one historian calls "a collision of histories."[14]

Immigration and Ethnic Diversity

Long before Europeans arrived, the population of North America was characterized by cultural diversity. Anthropologists are still debating the timing and points of origin of the first inhabitants, but many probably arrived by crossing a land bridge from Asia thousands of years ago. Although sometimes characterized by a single term such as "Indians" or "Native Americans," they went on to found many different civilizations, both agricultural and hunting-gathering. Their nations were competitive and at times at war, and their differences were substantial enough to doom eighteenth-century efforts to form pan-Indian alliances against European colonization.[15] Today, the U.S. Census Bureau recognizes 562 different tribes, many fewer than three hundred years ago, but still suggestive of the wide array of cultures that predated European settlement.

The umbrella term *European* is itself somewhat deceptive in that European settlers emigrated from countries that not only differed linguistically, religiously, and politically but also had often been at war with one another. Migrants carried some of these conflicts with them to America. Because the colonies were ruled from England and its language and culture were dominant, we tend to think of early Americans as Anglos and Protestants. But the earliest European settlers of the southeastern and southwestern territories were more likely to be Roman Catholics from France and Spain than Anglo-Protestants. And over time, Germany, a distinctly non-Anglo country and one evenly split between Catholics and Protestants, provided more immigrants to America than England. By preference, or to avoid discrimination by earlier-arriving or more dominant settlers, immigrants often self-segregated into territories (Puritans in Massachusetts, Quakers in Pennsylvania and Rhode Island, Catholics in Maryland), which later became states. These different beliefs and traditions contributed to the rise of distinctive local cultures and to the varying character of state governments and politics.

Like Europeans, Africans, too, came from a huge continent that encompassed many languages, cultures, and religions. Even though the European slave trade was concentrated in coastal areas of Africa, the men and women forcibly removed to the Americas did not share a common tradition. But their experience in the American colonies united most in a common condition as noncitizens lacking all political and economic rights.

The ethnic and racial composition of the American population broadened further in the mid- to late nineteenth century as new waves of settlers came from southern and eastern Europe, China, and Japan, as well as Ireland and Germany. They included large numbers of Roman, Eastern, and Russian Orthodox Catholics; Jews; and some Buddhists. Immigration continued at high levels into the twentieth century before peaking in the decade 1905–1914, when more than ten million immigrants entered the country (see Figure 2).

Not all immigrants who came stayed. In addition to deportations, about 30 percent of those who arrived between 1900 to 1990 returned voluntarily to their home countries. For a few years during the Great Depression of the 1930s, more people left the United States than entered.[16] Then, following the peak years of the second decade through the end of World War II, a deliberate effort was made to slow the rate of new arrivals. It

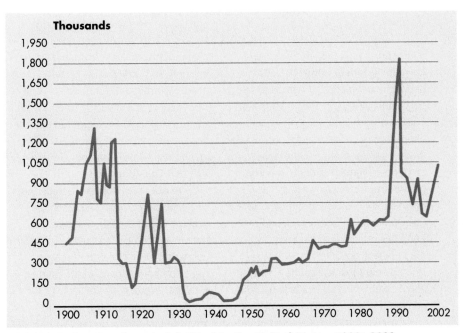

FIGURE 2 ■ Immigrants Admitted to the United States, 1900–2002
SOURCE: 2002 *Yearbook of Immigration Statistics*, Chart A, 5 (*www.uscis.gov*)

IMMIGRATION: IS THE DOOR STILL OPEN?

Terrorism is now accepted as an ongoing threat to our national security presented by groups—acting alone or in concert with an international network—who are violently opposed to U.S. policies abroad and to the reach of American culture. Though our system did not change "radically" or "forever," as some immediate pundits proclaimed, public recognition of this new danger has garnered support for policy changes necessary to enhance national security that might not have won approval or even been considered before the terrorist attacks of September 11, 2001. The threat of new attacks has created a climate of fear, and that fear can be used to achieve political objectives unrelated to security. This is especially true if fear becomes pervasive and a majority of people feel vulnerable and in need of government protection.

Now, with some distance from the events of 9/11, we are better able to sort out some of the politics from the substance of the policy response. The bipartisan commission investigating why the 9/11 terrorist attacks were not detected and prevented concluded that there were "deep institutional failings within our government" over a long period. In the "Terrorism, Politics, and Policy" boxes, we discuss ways in which 9/11 and the subsequent "war on terrorism" declared by the Bush administration have affected both the content of policy and the way government works. We also will see how government has attempted to address or sought to ignore those "deep institutional failings." In this chapter, where we are profiling the American people, we ask if the door to immigrants is as open as it was before 9/11.

We see ourselves as a community of people joined by a common commitment to the pursuit of opportunity, individual liberty, and government of, by, and for the people. But who, other than those born into it, can join this community? Are we really a refuge for political and religious dissidents and the economically downtrodden, as it says in the Emma Lazarus poem engraved on the Statue of Liberty? "Give me your tired, your poor, your huddled masses yearning to breathe free." But the "golden door," in reality, is open to only some of those who dream of settling in the United States. Thus, rules have been established to determine who will be granted an immigration visa, refugee status, and residency in the United States. Few Americans argue with the proposition that the government has the right to police its borders, but there are always disagreements over the standards regulating admission. Over time, the "golden door" has widened and narrowed, depending on the wishes of Congress.

The United States has restricted immigration since 1798, when Congress gave the president power to deport people he deemed "dangerous to the peace and safety" of the country. An 1807 law prohibited the migration or "importation" of people for purposes of slavery. Immigration within the western hemisphere remained open, but immigration from East Asia was virtually shut down by an 1882 law prohibiting further immigration from China and the 1907 "Gentleman's Agreement" with the Japanese government, which restricted new Japanese to the Hawaiian Islands. Between the 1920s and 1960s, immigration was open mainly to the European countries represented in the

American population at the time of the 1910 census, thereby favoring British, German, and northern Europeans while penalizing southern and eastern Europeans. Laws passed through the end of World War II added new categories of people prohibited entry, including anarchists and revolutionaries, members of communist parties, alcoholics, individuals with contagious diseases, and others deemed undesirable.

After the 1960s civil rights movement led to the removal of the old quota system, the door opened to people of every race, religion, and nationality. To ensure that people from all parts of the world have a chance to apply, the U.S. Citizenship and Immigration Services (USCIS) division of the Department of Homeland Security (formerly known as the Immigration and Naturalization Service, or INS) divides the world into regions and assigns annual quotas to countries within each region. Applicants who fit into newly created political categories were also singled out for preferential treatment. During the Cold War, for example, virtually everyone fleeing a communist country, including several million Cubans, Russians, Eastern Europeans, Vietnamese, Cambodians, and Laotians, were allowed in. Thousands of Chinese students were granted permanent residency under an amnesty following the 1989 Tiananmen Square massacre in Beijing.

The door was opened so wide that by 1991, immigration surpassed the peak period at the beginning of the twentieth century. But then immigration policy tightened because of fears of large numbers of immigrants coupled with the recession of the early 1990s and the increasing fear of terrorism after the first attack on the World Trade

Center in 1993. In 1996, Congress passed laws that made the detention and deportation of illegal entrants without judicial review much easier—paving the way for the post–9/11 crackdown—and the federal courts ruled that the INS the agency then in charge of enforcing immigration law, could revoke the citizenship of any naturalized American who has lied about a criminal record on an immigration application.[1] In 1997 and 1998, the INS set new records for deportations. Although in 2001 the Bush administration did propose giving amnesty to an estimated three million Mexican workers living here illegally, the terrorist attacks of 9/11 stopped that initiative.

Immigration policy was a focus of post–9/11 investigations. One of the many unhappy findings was that some perpetrators of the attacks had entered the country legally on tourist or student visas and overstayed their departure dates. The knowledge that a tiny fraction of foreigners living in our midst came for the express purpose of doing harm led to immediate changes in immigration enforcement. Although overstaying visas is an everyday occurrence in the United States, hundreds of Arab and Muslim men who had violated their visas were detained for questioning, and many were deported.[2] A hold was placed on immigration and visa applications from Middle Eastern and other predominantly Muslim countries, and applicants were subjected to extensive background checks.

Immigration, for the first time in our history, has become an overt national security policy concern. In 2003, the INS was reorganized as the USCIS within the new Department of Homeland Security. People seeking asylum are no longer as free to come into the country through Canada, and airborne drones with night-vision equipment now patrol the U.S.–Mexican border. Those who cross that border frequently—and possibly those coming from Canada as well—will be required to present biometric identity cards (laser visas). In addition, the USCIS requires that all men entering the country from certain North African and Middle Eastern countries on any kind of visa be fingerprinted and photographed. It has extended this procedure to all tourists from the twenty-one (mainly) European countries who can enter the U.S. These new measures reflect the view of the independent commission investigating 9/11 that travel documents must now be seen as weapons when put in the hands of individuals who want to enter the country under false pretenses.

Some of the most stringent new rules apply to people entering the United States on student visas because some never show up for their classes, and many overstay their visas or use them as a first step to permanent residency. The new mandatory background checks kept thousands of foreign students from beginning their classes in the fall of 2002 and continue to do so. When foreign students do arrive, their universities are required to verify their enrollments and report on their academic status to the USCIS.

Despite complaints from universities about declining graduate student enrollments and from U.S. businesses that they have lost billions of dollars because of delays or denials of visas to their foreign associates, the stricter procedures have done nothing to slow either legal or illegal immigration. The percentage of foreign-born in the population was higher in 2002 than in 2000. Even though 300,000 foreign-borns voluntarily return to their home countries annually, almost one-third as many people (350,000) continue to enter the country *illegally* as enter *legally* each year.[3] Tougher background checks, however, have decreased the number of people entering the country under the family preference quota and cut applications from those seeking asylum in the United States.[4] Refugees and those seeking asylum have been hardest hit, with thousands being held in U.S. jails and prisons with no criminal charge.[5]

A large majority of Americans support more stringent scrutiny of visa applications, including those that target specific religious or nationality groups, and a bare majority opposed Bush's proposal to give amnesty to Mexican workers living here illegally.[6] But there is no evidence yet to suggest that Americans consider *legal* immigration a high-priority issue or that they want to return to the era of restricting immigration on the basis of national origin.

1. A summary of changes in laws governing the entry of refugees and asylees and in numbers admitted can be found in the U.S. Office of Immigration Statistics, *2002 Yearbook of Immigration Statistics,* "Refugees" (Washington, D.C.: Department of Homeland Security, 2003), tab. D, 50 (uscis.gov).
2. Ibid., tab. 49; and "Enforcement," tab. 174. About 150,000 people were refused admission or deported in 2002, about three-quarters for criminal violations.
3. Office of Immigration Statistics, *2002 Yearbook,* "Immigrants," tabs. 6, 7.
4. Ibid., "Estimates," tab. 2; U.S. Office of Immigration Statistics, *2003 Executive Summary on Illegal Resident Population* (Washington, D.C.: Department of Homeland Security, 2003).
5. "The Persecuted in Chains," (Editorial), *The New York Times,* September 25, 2004.
6. ABC News Poll, January 11, 2004 (www.abcnews.com).

was not until the decade 1987–1996 that immigration reached its peak level to date (see Figure 2).

In 2003, 11.5 percent of all residents of the United States were foreign-born,[17] less than the 15 percent in the peak year 1910 but three times as many as in 1970.[18] These new Americans are far more varied in national origin than those who arrived prior to the 1970s. In 1910, the overwhelming majority of foreign-born in the United States had emigrated from Canada and Europe, whereas in 2000 over half of the foreign-born had emigrated from Central and South America and another one-quarter from Asian countries. Today, more of the new arrivals were born in Mexico than any other country, followed by persons born in India and China.[19] This shift in nationality of immigrants was the result of a change in immigration law in 1965 that ended nationality restrictions that had been in place since the 1920s. They were replaced with a preference system that targets family reunification and specific job skills. During the past thirty years, this system has undergone considerable tinkering, including an amnesty that gave permanent residency to 2.6 million illegal residents between 1989 and 1992, but the priority system remains in place despite post–9/11 policy changes. (See the box "Terrorism, Politics, and Policy" on the previous two pages).

When permanent residents become citizens—and one-third of all Americans who are foreign-born *are* naturalized U.S. citizens—all immediate members of their families living outside the United States automatically qualify for residency visas. In 2002, family-sponsored individuals accounted for 63 percent of all legal immigrants admitted.[20] This ensures that current trends in the ethnic diversification of the American population will continue and explains why Hispanics, who accounted for less than 7 percent of the population in the 1990 census, are now nearly 13 percent of the population and America's largest ethnic minority.

Immigration and Political Cleavage

There have always been some native-born Americans who fear economic competition from newcomers or perceive non-English-speaking people or anyone with different traditions and religious practices as a cultural threat. So antiforeign, or nativist, sentiments have been common throughout our history. These sentiments usually are greatest when immigration levels are high. That is why strong nativist sentiments influenced the politics of the mid-1800s, the 1920s, and the 1990s. Some of the most intense political cleavages have arisen between older and new immigrants.

The wave of immigration produced by Ireland's potato famine in the 1840s created a fever of anti-Irish and anti-Catholic sentiment, which found expression in the Know-Nothing Party. Patriotic fervor during World War I produced hostility toward Americans of German ancestry, and the Russian Revolution led to the "Red Scare" of the 1920s and the deportation of many Russian and Eastern European immigrants. During World War II, Japanese Americans were targeted as potential collaborators with Japan, had their property confiscated, and were imprisoned in camps under military guard (discussed further in Chapter 14).

After the high tide of immigration from Latin America and Asia in the 1990s, Republican presidential candidate Patrick Buchanan argued that the arrival of so many non-Europeans would "submerge" and dilute our "predominantly Caucasian Western society" and our European heritage.[21] In the same period, a newspaper criticized immigrants who "bring with them their non-Christian Third World cultures, poverty-mindedness and a tendency toward crime."[22] These characterizations are little different from those made against earlier waves of Eastern European, Irish, and Jewish immigrants. But they also obscure certain demographic truths. The country that is the single biggest contributor of new Americans—Mexico—is Western, Christian, and of mixed European heritage, as were most earlier arrivals. The majority of Muslims in the United States are African Americans, whereas more than half of all Arab Americans, who are much more recent arrivals, are Christian, not Muslim.

Although each generation of immigrants has faced resentment from preceding generations, each has contributed to the building of America. Early European immigrants settled the eastern seaboard and pushed west to open the frontier. Africans' slave labor helped build the South's economy. Germans helped develop the Midwest into an agricultural heartland, while Irish, Italian, Polish, and Russian newcomers provided labor for America's industrial revolution and turned many cities into huge metropolises. Chinese immigrants helped build the transcontinental railroad linking East and West, and Japanese and Hispanics helped California become our top food producer. More recently, young Chinese and Indian immigrants have figured prominently in high-tech industries, and older Indian immigrants dominate the motel business in the United States. All immigrant groups have gone on from their initial roles to play a fuller part in American life.

Religious Diversity

Voltaire, the great French philosopher, once wrote that a nation with one church will have oppression; with two, civil war; with a hundred, freedom.[23] We know that many of our earliest settlers—French Huguenots,

German Anabaptists, British Methodists, Catholics, and Quakers—came here to escape religious intolerance in Europe. Nevertheless, few who emigrated to the Americas expected to live in an areligious state. Once here, however, many found it necessary to establish separate communities to ensure freedom for their form of religious practice. "New Jersey, Pennsylvania, and Maryland were conceived and established as 'plantations of religion'" that gave state protection to specific religious groups.[24] Rhode Island was founded by the religious dissident Roger Williams who, after being expelled from Massachusetts's Puritan society, bought land from the Narragansett Indians and founded a colony for other religious outcasts.[25]

With independence, the United States disassociated itself not just from the government of England but from its state religion, the Anglican church, which was (and is today) headed by the monarch. Some at the Constitutional Convention wanted to name the Episcopalian church, the newly independent Anglican church in the United States, as the state religion, but most knew that in a country of wide religious diversity, such a Constitution would never be ratified. But six of the thirteen original states did establish an official religion, and some levied a religious tax, while leaving it to individual taxpayers to designate which church would receive their tax payments. State religions were not disestablished in Connecticut, Massachusetts, or New Jersey until the nineteenth century, and even then, some courts considered Christian teachings an integral part of common law.[26]

Despite the diversity in religious practice, instruction and textbooks in public schools drew much of their content from the Protestant Bible. School officials maintained that instruction was "nonsectarian," but their reluctance to remove blatantly anti-Catholic material led to the creation of Catholic church-run schools, which remain today the major alternative to public schools. Occasionally, religious differences led to violence, as in Philadelphia's Bible riots of 1843, when Protestants burned down a Catholic school and thirteen people were killed.[27]

The Know-Nothing Party won popularity during this period by spreading fear of a Catholic takeover. Catholic-Protestant conflict lasted well into the twentieth century, could be intense, and sometimes trumped ethnicity. In the small farm community of Carroll, Iowa, for example, German and other Protestants joined forces against allied German and Irish Catholics, passing "puritan Sunday" laws that prohibited Catholic church dances, singing parties, and serving alcohol on the Sabbath.[28] The Philadelphia church burnings targeted only Irish Catholic churches, not those of the older American German Catholic population.

The Library Company of Philadelphia

A Catholic church burns in the Philadelphia church burnings of 1843. Insistence that Catholic children read the Protestant King James version of the Bible, coupled with anti-Catholic material in some schools and Protestant fears of increasing numbers of Catholic immigrants, led to violence. Both Protestants and Catholics were killed.

These anecdotes from the distant past are a reminder that being "all white and all Christian" did not spare communities from exclusionary or repressive assimilationist tactics or violence against those of a different ancestry or religion. Claims that our political unity is being undermined by ethnic and religious diversity are hardly new.

America's religious profile is changing along with its ethnic makeup. Although a large majority (83 percent) still identify as Christians, Americans now claim affiliation with an estimated sixteen hundred different religions and denominations, including three million Jews, one million Buddhists, 750,000 Hindus, and one to three million Muslims.[29] To some observers, these figures represent the potential for social fragmentation; but a proliferation of religious affiliations may both bolster liberty and serve as its measure.

Economic and Demographic Diversity

Diversity involves more than differences in national origin and religious affiliation. Where people settle, what they do for a living, how much they earn, when they were born, and how long they have been here are all potential bases for political difference, and over time these factors are probably more important than religion or country of origin.

Although racial and ethnic cleavages have garnered much of the attention throughout our history, economic diversity is at least as important. We may think of

America as a land of opportunity, but most people who are born poor in the United States stay poor. Opportunities knock harder and more often for those who are born into the upper and middle classes. And although our society is not as class conscious as many others, our personal economic situations play an important part in shaping our views toward politics and our role in the process. Most people who are poor, for example, do not vote, but those who do vote tend to vote Democratic. Most well-off Americans do vote, and they vote in larger numbers for Republicans than for Democrats.

Regional and residential differences can also be important, especially since they often intertwine with economic interests. Farmers in California and the Midwest, for example, are more likely than city dwellers to be supportive of farm subsidy legislation. City dwellers may be far more enthusiastic about federal laws creating national parks or wilderness areas than the western ranchers who use the land to graze their livestock. The classic and most costly example of regional conflict in our history was the division between South and North over the right of southern states to secede from the Union in order to maintain a regional economic system rooted in slavery. Although in that case, economic and political disparities led to the bloodiest conflict in our history, regional diversity usually results in no more than political difference. However, in the face of growing income inequality and the residential segregation of gated communities, there is the danger that residential separation will lead to the political indifference of the well-off to the needs of poor neighborhoods.

Age differences, too, can affect political orientation. The needs and interests of older citizens are substantially different from those of young adults. The United States, like Canada and Western Europe, has an aging population; in 2002, one in eight Americans was sixty-five or older. A greater percentage of Americans in this age bracket than in any other age group voted in the 2000 election, and their interest groups are among the most powerful in the country. This fact has made economic security and health care for senior citizens high-priority policy issues, even while the number of children living in poverty is increasing.

Diversity and Identity Politics

There is nothing new or strange about organizing around difference. Up to a point, it is common sense. How we are situated in the world in terms of power, money, geography, race, ethnicity, age, and religion affects our perceptions of the world. As a result, people tend to define society's problems differently and have conflicting views about what government should do about them. Reconciling differences is what the political process is for.

Why, when the American population has always been so heterogeneous, does diversity seem to have so much more meaning in contemporary political life? The reason in part is that although society was diverse in the early decades of the Republic, the political spectrum was narrow, and the majority of citizens were excluded from participation. Those granted full rights of participation varied from state to state, but two groups —women and African American men, with the exception of a small number of free black men living in the North—were comprehensively shut out after the ratification of the Constitution, as were some unpropertied white men.

Diversity's scope for expression has been greatly broadened through the slow expansion of the electorate and the opening up of the political system. This process (discussed in Chapter 8) included the extension of voting rights to African American men and, almost fifty years later, to all women. About the same time, citizenship was granted to American Indians and to residents of Puerto Rico, whose country had been incorporated as a U.S. territory after the Spanish-American War in 1898. Due to restrictions in state voting laws, full Native American suffrage was not achieved until 1948 and full black suffrage not until the 1960s, but the voting and politically active public has been becoming gradually more heterogeneous since the 1920s.

Two later developments—the federal government's adoption of race, gender, and ethnic preference programs, beginning in the Nixon administration, and the wave of immigration from Asia and Latin America in the 1980s and 1990s—have increased the importance of diversity in American politics.

As government adopted affirmative action policies to compensate for historical discrimination (see Chapter 15), an individual's race, gender, or ethnicity took on added political importance. The use of such factors to influence the division of public resources has given rise to **identity politics.** This is the practice of organizing on the basis of one's ethnic or racial identity, sex, or sexual orientation to compete for public resources and to influence public policy.[30]

Paradoxically, identity politics has intensified during a period in which racial and ethnic boundaries are beginning to blur. (See the box "Census and Sensibility" on page 14) Among white ethnic groups, so much intermarriage has occurred that many people cannot identify their ancestry. Although 93 percent of whites and blacks still marry within-group, a third of all Hispanic and Asian marriages are mixed.[31] By the 1990 census, one hundred million Americans could name no

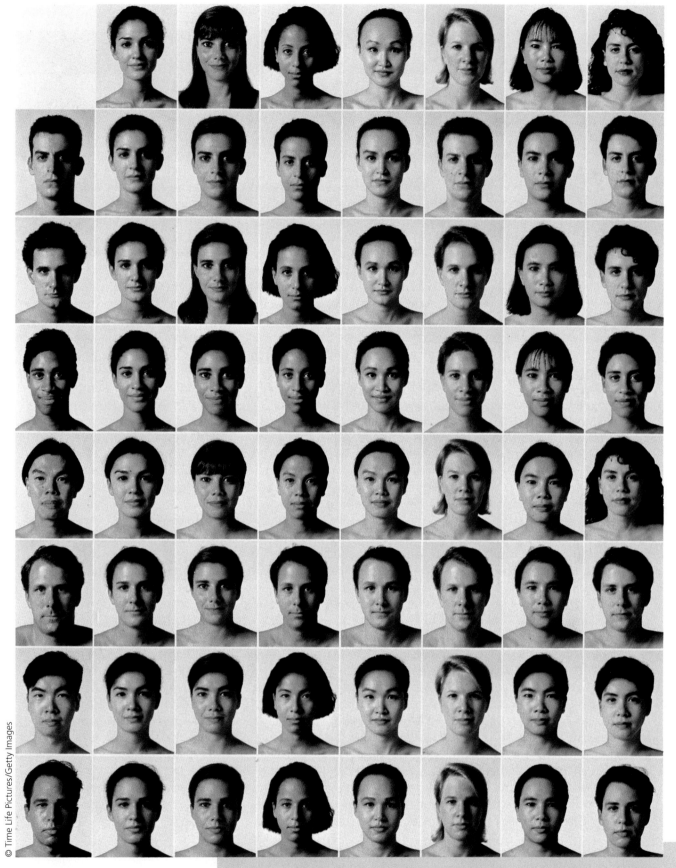

America is more a melting pot than ever, with increasing population diversity and increasing rates of intermarriage among different racial and ethnic groups. This computer-generated matrix from Time magazine reflects the changing faces of America. The intersection of each column and row shows the possible features of the offspring if the people along the top and left edges were to marry.

CENSUS AND SENSIBILITY

Every ten years, the U.S. government takes a census of the American population. This should be a fairly straightforward statistical procedure, but it has often been a contentious political issue. This is largely because the census does much more than establish the size and geographical distribution of the population; its findings have important political and economic consequences. Of special significance are the figures that reflect the racial and ethnic breakdown of the population. These data have become essential for implementation of the Voting Rights Act and court rulings stemming from the modern civil rights movement, as well as for "a smorgasbord of set-asides and entitlements and affirmative-action programs."[1] Thus today, unlike the past, the collection of information on the racial heritage of Americans has greater significance for *inclusion* than for exclusion.

Racial categories have been used since the first census was taken in 1790, when Americans were identified as "white males," "white females," "other" (free black men and women, for example, and Indians living off reservations), and "slaves" (not a racial category, but since only people of African descent were enslaved, *slave* became synonymous with *black*). Some states classified as "black" people with as little as one thirty-second African ancestry (one black great-great-grandparent), thereby consigning them to political and economic exclusion. In the late nineteen and early twentieth centuries, special mixed white and black categories sometimes appeared, including in 1890, categories of "quadroon" and "octoroon," signifying one-fourth and one-eighth

black ancestry, respectively. "Chinese" and "American Indian" became census categories in 1860; "Japanese" was added in 1870, and other "Asian races" in 1910. Mexicans were "whites" in the 1920 census, a separate racial category in 1930, and by the 1950 census reabsorbed into the white category.

From this it should be apparent that there has been little consistency in race and color classifications in the United States. The designations reflect "common or social usage" rather than scientifically determined biological differences. Moreover, through the 1950 census, race was established solely by the census taker's observation, which usually resulted in people of mixed heritage being counted as "other." One government study showed that 6 percent of people considering themselves black, one-third who considered themselves Asian, and 70 percent of those who considered themselves American Indian were recorded as white by survey researchers. A study of infant deaths showed that many infants were classified by a different race at death than on their birth certificates.

The 1980 census was the first in which an individual's ethnicity and race were established entirely by self-classification.[2] But in the 1990 census, each person had to choose from one of four racial groups—"black," "white," "American Indian or Native Alaskan," or "Asian or Pacific Islander"—and also, where applicable, to claim a Hispanic or Latino ethnic heritage. Complaints about this classificatory scheme intensified as immigration and interracial marriage increased the number of multiracial Americans, many of whom now

object to defining their heritage by a single census category. The archetypal representative of this dilemma is golf pro Tiger Woods, who describes himself as a "Cablinasian," a person of white ("Caucasian"), African, American Indian, and Asian ancestry. Why, Woods said, should he be asked to identify himself with only one part of his ancestry, and how would he decide which one to choose?[3] Another example is former Secretary of State Colin Powell, a first-generation American born to immigrants from Jamaica, who is generally considered in American society as an African American and whom President Clinton often held up as a model for affirmative action. We do not know which box or boxes Secretary Powell checked on his census form, but we do know that his maternal grandmother was a Scot and that in 2004 his family was issued a Scottish family crest.

In response to complaints about limited options for self-identification, the 2000 census offered five racial categories (Native Hawaiians and Pacific Islanders were split off from Asians) while retaining the Hispanic ethnic designation. A "multiracial" category was rejected in favor of letting each person check more than one box—even if that meant, as in the case of Tiger Woods, selecting four. The new method permits up to sixty-three variations in reporting race and ethnicity. While allowing more Americans to identify their ancestry accurately, the multiple-response option created new problems. In the analysis of the 2000 census data, someone had to decide whether to count the multiple box checkers more than once, divide them into fractions, or just assign them to a single racial category. This may sound ridiculous, but it is a very real problem for the Census Bureau. Laws guaranteeing equal access and representation have meant, in practice, that the racial or ethnic composition of the population affects who is admitted to universities, how the boundaries of legislative districts are drawn, whether school districts need to submit desegregation plans, and whether minorities are adequately represented among workers hired on federally funded projects and among business owners receiving federal contracts.

The new categories are therefore of great concern to interest groups representing American minorities. The National Association for the Advancement of Colored People (NAACP), for example, worried that an undercount of African Americans would lead to a decrease in the opportunities it worked for decades to win because people who would have been classified as black under the old "one drop of blood" standard could be counted as white or Asian if they self-identified as multiracial on their census form. One NAACP official said, "Let those mixed-race people check all the boxes they want—but *count* them as black."[4] A Hispanic American organization asked that "Hispanic" be categorized as a race rather than an ethnicity, and the Arab American Institute requested that a special protected category be created for people of Middle Eastern ancestry. An official of an Asian American interest group said she opposed the multiple-choice approach because racial and ethnic data are collected for a reason, and "if you can't tabulate it, you've undermined the ability of the federal government to provide information that will help set policy and help ensure that the civil rights laws are effectively enforced. That is the bottom line."[5] A member of the House committee that oversees the Census Bureau put it more bluntly: "The numbers drive the dollars."[6]

In the end, only 6.8 million, or 2.4 percent, of all Americans self-identified as multiracial in the 2000 census, slightly higher than predicted but far below the actual numbers of Americans with multiracial heritage.[7] Many Hispanics have mixed-race ancestry—white and African, Asian, or Native American—and by some estimates as many as 75 percent of all African Americans are mixed white-black.[8] One survey found that one-third of African Americans believe that blacks are not a single race.[9] Once seemingly clear notions of "race" as African, Caucasian, or Asian are becoming confused as we become an increasingly multiracial society. Almost half of both black and white respondents to a poll said that the U.S. census, like Canada's, should not collect information on race at all.[10]

1. Lawrence Wright, "One Drop of Blood," *New Yorker,* July 25, 1994, 47.
2. Campbell J. Gibson and Emily Lennon, *Historical Census Statistics on the Foreign-Born Population of the United States, 1850–1990* (Washington, D.C.: U.S. Census Bureau, 1999), 9.
3. Rochelle L. Stanfield, "Multiple Choice," *National Journal,* November 22, 1997, 2352–2355.
4. Ibid., 2355.
5. Ibid.
6. Representative Thomas C. Sawyer (D-Ohio), quoted in Wright, "One Drop of Blood," 47.
7. "Politics of Identity Resurface with Census," *Champaign-Urbana News-Gazette,* March 25, 2001, B8.
8. Ibid.
9. Tom Morganthau, "What Color Is Black?" *Newsweek,* February 13, 1995, 64.
10. Ibid.

Whatever our race or national origin, and despite differences that divide us, Americans are united under one flag and one set of political ideas.

specific ancestry or reported multiple ancestries.[32] Should this pattern continue, the majority of residents in the United States by 2050 will be of mixed race.[33]

Political Culture

In recent years, *diversity* has become a political catchword and has been raised to the level of a civic virtue. Yet our national motto is *"E Pluribus Unum"*—"Out of Many, One"—referring to the union of many states and the molding of one people from many traditions. There is a popular saying that Americans are people of many cultures united by a single idea. But what is that single idea, and is it, however fundamental, sufficient to form a political culture? A **political culture** is a shared body of values and beliefs that shapes perception and attitudes toward politics and government and in turn influences political behavior.

The Significance of Political Culture

Governments rely for their stability and vitality on the support of citizens: their identification with the country and its method of governing and their adoption of the political values and behavior necessary to sustain the system. The alternatives are for government to be ineffective or to gain obedience through force or coercion.

In a democracy, sharing a political culture does not mean that citizens must agree on specific issues or even generally on what government's role should be in dealing with the country's problems. Democracy embraces conflict and competition just as it requires cooperation and a sense of community. A basic function of government is to establish the rules under which interests can compete. So the essence of political culture is not agreement on issues but on fundamental principles and on a common perception of the *rights* and *obligations* of citizenship and the rules for participating in the political process. These shared values reduce the strains produced by our differences and allow us to compete intensely on some issues while cooperating on others.

Learning Political Culture

Whether the newly created United States of America came about by "design of Providence," was a "lucky accident," or the result of the Founders' skill in shaping a workable Constitution, it faced a problem common to all political systems: how to create a national identity among the citizenry.[34] Although American society has often been characterized as a melting pot, it has been a slow melt, and it has not happened by luck or accident. The Founders spoke of a united country, a people with common ancestry, a shared language, the same religion, and a commitment to the same political principles. From what you have read earlier in this chapter, you know this view was in some part wishful thinking. One of the most significant challenges to establishing a national political culture was the division of Americans among nearly sovereign states. It is easy to forget that not long ago, people's identity as Virginians or Pennsylvanians was much more important to them than being American. And it was not until the Civil War, under the influence of Abraham Lincoln's powerful reference at Gettysburg to the "unfinished work" of preserving the Union, that Americans began referring to the United States with the singular *is* rather than the plural *are*.[35]

Most of the Founders believed that an educated citizenry was essential to the survival of the new republic, and advocates of public education like Daniel Webster and Thomas Jefferson argued that *only* educated citizens would be able to understand public issues, elect virtuous leaders, and "sustain the delicate balance between liberty and order in the new political system."[36] As the public school system emerged, increasing emphasis was placed on the "training of citizens in patriotism, political knowledge and public affairs."[37] Although schools were then (as they are now) under local control, there was some common content in civic education around the country. By the mid–twentieth century, most elementary school children were studying current events in their *Weekly Reader* and beginning each day by reciting the Pledge of Allegiance to the flag. Many high school students are required to pass an exam on the U.S. Constitution, and perhaps their state's constitution as well, to graduate. However, civics is not one of the subject areas in which students must show proficiency under the new federal system of mandatory testing, and there is evidence that it is being increasingly neglected in favor of math, science, and English, courses that are subject to proficiency standards.[38]

Elementary and secondary schools are not the only purveyors of political culture. Much is absorbed simply by living in the country and participating in the political process. Television and newspapers also transmit a great deal of information on the rules of the game and how government and politics work in the United States.

Today, one of the most controversial issues in the debate over what is required to sustain a political culture is whether all citizens should speak a common language. But the Founders took it for granted that English would be the national language, and Daniel Webster's 1783 textbook promoting "a new national language to be spelled and pronounced differently from British English" was one of the first attempts to create an American national identity.[39] Fear of German-speaking immigrants in the early part of the twentieth century led Iowa

"I pledge allegiance to the flag . . . ": Sixth graders at P.S. 116 in New York City, October 1957.

to pass a law requiring all groups of two or more people to speak in English, even when using the telephone.[40] In the current era, when most immigration has come from non-English-speaking countries and some urban school districts teach in a hundred or more languages, twenty-seven states have passed laws establishing English as the official language.

The significance of political culture—even its definition—has long been and will continue to be a topic of debate. Some people argue that Americans are too diverse to share a common set of political values and that every country in the world, regardless of its level of development, is composed of "competing political cultures, not a single political culture."[41] While government provides rules and venues for these interests to compete, this is not the reason government exists. Unless there is some overarching commitment, some principles that take precedence over group interests, there will be no basis for political unity.

The Core Values

Our "nation of nations" is crosscut with cultural, political, and economic cleavages, but despite our sometimes overwhelming diversity, most Americans do share some basic goals and values. The words Americans use to characterize their form of government are less likely to come from the Constitution than from the second para-graph of the Declaration of Independence: "We hold these Truths to be self-evident, that all Men are created equal, that they are endowed by the Creator with certain unalienable Rights, that among these are Life, Liberty, and the Pursuit of Happiness."

These words suggest the basic assumptions, or core beliefs, on which the American system was founded: universal truths that can be known and acted on, equality before the law, belief in a higher power that transcends human law, and rights that are entitlements at birth and therefore can be neither granted nor taken away by government. The fundamental concept is liberty, especially the freedom to pursue one's livelihood and other personal goals that lead to a "happy" life.

The Declaration was primarily a political argument for separation from Great Britain, so it was concerned with the basic principles and philosophy of government.[42] Guaranteeing the rights of individuals, the Declaration postulated, was the primary reason for government to exist. Later, the Constitution reinforced the Declaration's emphasis on equality while specifying other core principles of American democracy: majority rule exercised through elected representatives and minority rights (a reference to political or religious minorities, not to racial or ethnic minorities). But unlike the Declaration, the Constitution had to deal with the practical problems of governing and of creating institutions that would protect the rights and pursuits of the individual while balancing them against the public interest. Thus whereas the Declaration is all principle, the Constitution is, of necessity, founded on political compromise.

Here we look briefly at each of the core principles of American democracy. Chapter 2 provides a more detailed description of how they are expressed in the Constitution.

Individual Liberty

Our belief in individual liberty has roots in the Judeo-Christian belief that every individual is equal and has worth before God. It has also been shaped by the works of the English philosophers Thomas Hobbes and John Locke. Briefly, they wrote that individuals give some of their rights to the government so that it can protect them from each other. Individuals then use their remaining liberties to pursue their individually defined visions of the good life. These ideas are part of social contract theory, which we discuss in Chapter 2.

Influenced by these ideas, early Americans emphasized individual liberty over other goals of government. James Madison, for example, justified the Constitution by writing that the government's job is to protect the "diversity" of interests and abilities that exists among individuals. Liberty is also reflected in our long tradition of rights, deriving from Great Britain's. Usually, these rights are framed as powers *denied* to the government —for example, the government shall not deny freedom of assembly or engage in unreasonable searches and seizures. Essentially, this means the overall right to be left alone by the government. Such individualistic values have molded popular expectations. Immigrants often came and still come to America to be their own bosses. The other side of this coin is that we are also at liberty to fail and accept the consequences. Although the opportunities for many individuals to get ahead in America are limited by prejudice and poverty, living in a so-

ciety with an explicit commitment to individual liberty can be exciting and liberating.

The commitment to liberty is not absolute however; that is, it cannot be exercised free of restrictions. This is what it means to live under a constitutional government and in society with other citizens: we give up some rights for the good of all and to achieve the purpose for which the government was created in the first place. The kinds of restrictions that can be placed on our exercise of individual rights and liberties is another subject of those ongoing debates about what American democracy was intended to be and should be.

One of the liveliest debates in the past few decades has been that between advocates of broadening individual liberty and those who believe there has been an overemphasis on individual freedom at the expense of community interests. Many believe that our fixation on individual rights has led to declining community consciousness and a general lack of civility. They advocate revitalizing the concept of citizenship, including the responsibilities to participate in public life and renewed emphasis on "shaping the qualities of character that self-government requires."[43] They call their program *communitarianism* and claim that it is much closer to the Founders' republican conception of freedom than the modern liberal celebration of the unencumbered individual is.

Political Equality

The Judeo-Christian belief that all people are equal in the eyes of God reflects one type of equality, but it led logically to other types, such as political equality. The ancient Greek emphasis on the opportunity and responsibility of all citizens to participate in ruling their city-states also contributed to our notion of political equality. Thus the Declaration of Independence proclaims that "all Men are created equal." This does not mean

"We can't come to an agreement about how to fix your car, Mr. Simons. Sometimes that's the way things happen in a democracy."

that all people are born with equal talents or abilities. It means that all citizens are born with equal standing before government and are entitled to equal rights.

In the early years of our country, however, as in the ancient Greek city-states, full rights of citizenship were conferred only on those thought to have the intellectual and moral judgment to act in the public interest. This wisdom could be acquired from experience in the public arena, such as through one's work, not just by formal education. In both Greece and the United States, such thinking denied political rights to slaves, who were believed incapable of independent judgment, and women, whose knowledge was seen as limited to the private or domestic sphere. This left a deep tension between the religious view that sees each individual as equal and the secular concept of differential political rights. Over time, this conflict was resolved in favor of the inherent worth of every individual and hence the political equality of all.

Americans have long considered themselves relatively equal politically and socially, if not economically. At minimum, they believe that they are inherently equal, even when equality cannot be realized in the political arena. Alexis de Tocqueville, a perceptive Frenchman who traveled through the United States in the 1830s, observed that Americans felt more equal to one another than Europeans did. He attributed this feeling to the absence of a hereditary monarchy and aristocracy in this country. There was no tradition in America of looking up to royalty and aristocrats as one's "betters."[44]

A belief in political equality leads to **popular sovereignty,** or rule by the people. Lincoln expressed this concept when he spoke of "government of the people, by the people and for the people." If individuals are equal, no one person or small group has the right to rule others. Instead, the people collectively rule themselves. And so we arrive at our form of government, a **democracy.** The word *democracy,* derived from the Greek, means "authority of the people." If all political authority resides in the people, then the people have the right to govern themselves.

Majority Rule

If political authority rests in the people collectively, and if all people are equal, then the majority should rule. That is, when there are disagreements over policies, majorities rather than minorities should decide. If individuals are equal, then policies should be determined according to the desires of the greater number. Otherwise, some individuals would be bestowed with more authority than others.

Majority rule helps provide the support necessary to control the governed. Those in the minority go along because they accept this principle and expect to be in the majority on other issues. At a minimum, the minority expects those in the majority to respect their basic rights. If these expectations are not fulfilled, the minority is less likely to accept majority rule and to tolerate majority decisions. Thus majority rule normally entails minority rights.

Minority Rights

While majority rule is important, it sometimes conflicts with minority rights. Majorities make decisions *for* "the people" but in doing so do not *become* "the people." "The people" includes members of the majority *and* members of the minority. As a result, majorities that harm minority rights diminish everyone's rights.

Sadly, as James Madison and other writers of the Constitution feared, majorities in the United States have sometimes forgotten this principle, the most egregious example being the enslavement of African Americans. At various times in our history, women and ethnic, political, and religious minorities have been denied basic rights. The idea that everyone loses when minority rights are trampled is a lesson that does not stay learned.

Economic Rights

Everyone is familiar with the idea that the American Revolution was triggered by what the colonists saw as unfair taxation and other economic burdens placed on them by the British Parliament. To a certain extent, Americans fought the Revolution to be left alone to pursue their livelihoods and to ensure that they would not have to give up any part of their wealth without their consent.

Economic freedom, specifically the right to own property, is an adjunct to our concepts of individual liberty and the "pursuit of happiness." But just as tension exists between majority and minority rights and between individual liberty and the good of all, there is also potential conflict between the political equality the Declaration avows and the property rights the Constitution protects. Inevitably, some people, through inheritance, luck, or initiative, amass more wealth and power than others and come to exercise more influence over government. The ancient Greeks feared that democracy could not tolerate extremes of wealth and poverty. They thought that a wealthy minority, out of smugness, and an impoverished minority, out of desperation, would try to act independently of the rest of the people and consequently would disregard the public interest.

Early Americans worried less about this. They thought they could create a government that would protect individual diversity, including economic disparity, and still survive. But the pursuit of political equality in a real world of great economic inequities has led government to a much greater role in regulating economic activity than the Founders anticipated.

We can see that democratic principles sometimes contradict each other. Americans have struggled for more than two centuries to reconcile practice with democratic aims and to perfect a system of government that was revolutionary for its time. We will see these contradictions many times in this book as we explore how government actually works.

The American Citizen

Supreme Court Justice Louis Brandeis once said, "The most important office in a democracy is the office of citizen."[45] That democratic principles come alive only when people participate in government is a commonly held view. This raises two basic questions: How do rules for participation affect the level of participation, and how willing and prepared to participate is the average citizen?

Democracy in a Republic

One fundamental given that sets limits on citizen participation is that our form of government is an **indirect democracy,** also known as a **republic.** Citizens do not pass laws or make policy; they select policymakers to make decisions for them. It is members of Congress, not individual citizens, who vote bills into law. These officials are not rulers or independent agents but representatives of the people who draw their authority from a constitution sanctioned by the people. This contrasts with a **direct democracy,** in which citizens vote on most issues and legislate for themselves. In the United States, forms of direct democracy exist only at the state and local levels. The best example is the town meeting, which has been the form of governance of many New England towns for over 350 years. Although town meetings today are often attended by relatively small numbers of citizens, they still offer one of the few opportunities people have to govern themselves directly. Citizens attending town meetings make their own decisions (for example, whether to put parking meters on the main street) and elect officers to enforce them (such as the police chief and city clerk). Another form of direct democracy, the initiative, allows proposed legislation that has been initiated by members of the public (either individuals or interest groups) to be placed on a statewide election ballot if enough voters sign petitions supporting the proposal. If an initiative receives a majority of votes, it can, under some state constitutions, become law, allowing citizens to legislate directly. (More information on the initiative can be found in Chapter 3.)

As with many provisions in the U.S. Constitution, there are different ways to interpret what the Founders intended in choosing the republican form of government. Some people emphasize the impracticality of a direct democracy for any but a small citizenry, such as a town or a city-state. How could people from thirteen states meet to legislate for the country as a whole? Or how could so many individuals ever reach the compromises reflected in the final wording of most legislation? In this interpretation, the Founders never considered direct democracy because it was impracticable. Other interpreters of the Founders' intentions place more emphasis on the fear of popular rule, and there is no doubt that some Founders thought of direct democracy as something closer to mob rule. Specific provisions in the Constitution, such as those for suffrage, which was deferred to the states, and selection of government officials, allowing only House members to be directly elected, suggests that fear of direct democracy was a significant, if not primary, reason for selection of the republican form.

Given that the republican form of government does delegate decision-making authority to a limited group of officials, what must citizens contribute to the political process to make our government function democratically? The Founders did not leave many instructions for citizens. Obviously, they expected that some of the citizens ruled eligible by their states would vote; expected some would stand for office; and most would come to the defense of the country in emergencies (although service was not compulsory). We can also deduce that they expected that the small part of the electorate who voted would need to spend some time becoming acquainted with issues, which explains the Founders' support for education. Beyond that, however, little was said.

Political Participation

If you rented one of the classic movies about American government, you would likely see a story about a handful of idealistic elected officials who, with backing from the mass of equally idealistic citizens, triumph over complacent, jaded, or corrupt politicians. These stories reflect what is sometimes called our "self-belief," our belief in the efficacy of our system of government and our fitness to govern ourselves. If our political process worked the way moviemakers, philosophers, and model builders think it should—and many Americans think it does—the majority of the public would be well informed, would discuss public affairs regularly, would let public officials know what we think, and would vote. In other words, most citizens would be committed to learning about and participating in government. And if you were to read most American government textbooks written before World War II, that is how the functioning of our democracy would have been described. However, as more rigorous methods were applied to polling and survey studies, researchers discovered that far fewer citizens take advantage of their democratic rights than old theories and models predicted. For example, voting is the easiest way to participate in politics and the least costly in terms of time and energy. Yet slightly more than half of all eligible Americans vote in presidential elections, far fewer in non-presidential-year elections, and fewer still in local elections. Instead of being motivated to participate in politics as in a model democracy, most Americans are little involved. Only a tiny minority are activists who take full advantage of opportunities to participate. In fact, one-fifth of the electorate do nothing at all political; they do not even discuss politics.[46]

Why Don't Americans Participate?

Why does the reality of political participation fall short of theorists' expectations, popular views of democracy, and our own self-belief? One explanation is that many Americans do not participate because they are turned off by, among other things, long political campaigns in which sound bites and negative campaigning replace meaningful dialogue about issues.[47] One academic interpretation, popularized in a book called *Bowling Alone,* is that many Americans are no longer the social animals they once were because technology has allowed us to build little islands of self-sufficiency for ourselves in our homes. We are no longer dependent on public events or group activities and are less interested in being part of any club or community, including the civic community. In short, we still bowl, but we bowl alone.[48]

Other long-standing explanations focus not on how the individual relates to the whole but on specific variables—class, income, race, ethnicity, and age—that affect the rate of political participation. Those who participate tend to be better educated and to have more money and more leisure time. Many poor adults are single heads of families with little spare time for political activity or money for transportation and baby-sitters. As a result, they have fewer opportunities to be drawn into political action through such associations and in turn have no strong organizations to promote their political participation.

Race and ethnicity explain political participation, too, but not as well. Overall, African Americans and Hispanics participate less than others, but this is due primarily to average lower education and income levels. At each education and income level, African Americans and Hispanics participate at about the same rates as non-Hispanic whites.

Age also explains participation in politics. Young people participate much less than their elders. The middle-aged are more likely to be established in a career and family life and have more time and money to devote to political activities, and seniors are likely to be retired, have more leisure time, and be better informed than young adults.

Can We Be Democratic without Participation?

The overall low participation level and the different rates of participation by people of various incomes, races, and ethnicities throw some kinks into our image of how a democracy should function. Majorities cannot rule, minority rights may go unprotected, and the plurality of interests across income, racial, ethnic, and regional lines may not be reflected in policy when most people do not take advantage of their right to vote or try to influence government by other means.[49] What it comes down to is that elected officials are being chosen by wealthier and better-educated Americans. It should not surprise us then that these officials are more likely to share the perspectives of those who elect them than the views of the less well-off and less educated who do not vote.

The fundamental need for our form of democracy to prevail is that each of us should win some of the time and no one should be a "permanent loser."[50] But can this happen if we do not participate? Some say yes, because our country has thousands of interest groups organized around the broadest range of issues, and their leaders and paid staff carry the membership's views to decision makers. Even if many do not participate individually, enough Americans belong to interest groups to ensure that government ultimately hears everyone.[51] In this view, democracy works because the constant competition among interest groups produces a kind of balance in which no group loses so often that it stops competing. As long as individuals continue to believe that they will win a future election or policy debate, they continue to participate and to accept compromise. But this multiplicity of interests can also encourage elected officials to avoid making major policy changes for fear of upsetting the existing balance of interests and their political bases of support.

Is Interest Group Democracy Really Democracy?

Interest group democracy is a kind of participation by double proxy, with citizens essentially hiring private representatives to take their interests to their elected representatives. Some scholars argue that this is one explanation for lower citizen participation: if interest group leaders can do a better job of getting what they want for them than they could do themselves, why does the average person need to participate?[52] But this assumes that democracy can be measured just as well by policy outcomes (who gets what, when, and how) as by the quality and levels of citizen participation. The pluralist model of how we can maintain a democracy with low participation levels has parallels in the theory that capitalism works because an "invisible hand" is continuously readjusting the market and moving it toward the greatest efficiencies in production and consumption. Similarly, in our democracy, groups can be seen as competing in a marketplace of ideas, interests, and political objectives under rules that ensure a distribution of policy victories across the great majority of the electorate, thus preventing any one group from becoming permanent losers. If policies *were* made in this way, it would allow the greater good to be served with an economy of participation.

As Chapter 6 will show, however, many people and issues do fall through the cracks of interest group representation. The poor are especially unlikely to be organized or to have sufficient resources to fight political battles. As unions have shrunk in influence, working-class Americans also have less of a voice in government than before. In addition, there is no guarantee that every issue can be resolved through competition to influence decision makers.

If competition is between well-organized groups with intensely held issue positions—such as on abortion and gun control—it may be difficult or impossible to reach a policy outcome that satisfies anyone. And if the competition is between one side with massive resources and another side that is barely organized—as in the awarding of tax benefits to special industries and companies—the policy outcomes are not in accord with public preferences. Moreover, effective power in a group or organization, no matter what its size, can and sometimes does gravitate to a few in leadership positions.[53] In fact, interest groups do create their own elites by establishing permanent organizations with paid staff and leadership; this arrangement creates the potential for an issue gap between leaders and the rank and file. As the professional staff spend more time with decision makers and develop ties to public officials, they may come to see group interests differently than the rank-and-file membership. When this happens, membership in an interest group is no longer a guarantee that one's views will be accurately represented to decision makers.

Some social scientists and sociologists argue that just as interest groups can become the captives of an out-of-touch leadership, so can agencies of government. Leaders of interest groups and heads of some of the most powerful government offices and departments can ne-

gotiate with one another to serve their joint interests instead of those of group members or the public good. For example, the CEO of the AARP (American Association for Retired People), one of the most powerful interest groups in the country, lobbied hard to gain passage of a prescription drug bill for seniors that many AARP members regarded as a sellout of the their interests. (See "You Are There" in Chapter 6.) Similarly, almost everyone is familiar with the accusation that members of Congress have become captives of special interests. The desire most members of Congress have to retain their seats, combined with the extremely high cost of running for office, has led many to find common cause with campaign donors, putting big donors' policy demands above the needs of their constituents and the public interest.

Participation and the Elites

Another aspect of this view of the diluted power of the citizenry comes from political scientists, who remind us that our government does not operate in a vacuum, separate from the economy. They argue that because the influence and decision-making power crucial to the public interest is not entirely invested in the offices of government, we cannot understand how our political system functions or measure how democratic it is by looking only at the public sector. There is also a private sector that includes many of the country's most important decision makers, such as heads of major corporations and media moguls. Students of government read little about this private power structure, according to these arguments, because most political science textbooks describe and explain only policies made in the more visible public sector, where interest group competition is evident and often intense. But out of public view, business operates as a parallel power system, in which executives, financial officers, and corporate board members make decisions that affect the welfare of all Americans and then use their vast resources to influence the outcome of public policy as well.[54] One political scientist has tried to demonstrate that a group of powerful decision makers (a power elite)—the holders of a few top jobs in major corporations, universities, foundations, media outlets, and the most powerful agencies of government, such as the Department of Defense—dominate governmental decision making.[55] In this interpretation of our democracy, relatively few people share the most powerful jobs and make the most important economic and political decisions, decisions that favor their own interests and help retain their grip on power.

Basically these arguments that a small number of decision makers have taken authority from the general public warn us that the great majority of interest groups

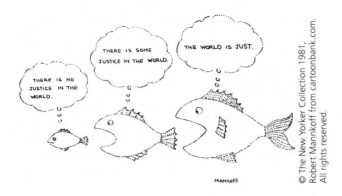

are competing for only part of the pie, and a small part at that. In this view of how American democracy works, there are groups and classes of individuals—those with little or no access to decision makers in the public or private sector—who are in fact permanent losers. The corollary is that no true democracy exists where citizens do not inform themselves, engage more actively in the political process, and take decision-making power back into their hands or the hands of representatives they elect and hold accountable.

But not everyone who believes that decision making is concentrated in the hands of a small number of elites believes that this is a bad thing or against the public interest. In contrast to the conception of a malignant power elite who conspire against reform and in support of policies that will keep economic and political power in their hands, others argue that during the past century there have been groups of elites who acted primarily to promote the general welfare rather than their own interests. This view holds that without the academics and intellectuals from the Ivy League, think tanks, and foundations like the Brookings Institution and the Ford Foundation, we would not have had the sweeping social welfare and redistributive policies of Franklin Roosevelt's New Deal or the War on Poverty legislation of the Kennedy and Johnson administrations. Elites are often best situated to win these battles, the argument maintains, because they occupy "a position of independence, between the wealthy and the people, prepared to curb the excesses of either." [56]

Who Has the Power?

We can condense all of these arguments into what is perhaps the most central question in the study of any form of government: "Who has the power?" In what offices or institutions, and in which people, is power vested?

The argument that our government is run by the few rather than the many continues to find credibility with the public. Opinion polls that ask whether government is "run by a few big interests looking out for themselves or run for the benefit of all" invariably find

only a minority of the public who believe it is being run for the benefit of all. As one newspaper columnist put it, "All the evidence suggests that when Americans look at Washington they see a conniving bunch of hustlers playing an insider's game at the expense of the nation." [57] This may be due in part to the very real role that big money plays in elections and the legislative process. But it is also a fact that it is often hard to know what *really* is going on in Washington and easy to be frustrated when the process yields outcomes we do not like. It is misleading, however, to think that a few powerful people determine everything. America's diversity produces too many different interests and opinions to permit this. Both governmental authority and political power are dispersed among local, state, and federal decision makers as well as across the private sector in corporate boardrooms and the leadership councils of interest groups and trade unions. And today, with electronic media—e-mail and the Internet in particular—it is very difficult for any handful of decision makers to control access to information. Furthermore, there is abundant evidence that these decision makers are often in competition with one another so that getting legislation passed requires compromises that give each group some of what it wants.

Thousands of lobbyists work in Washington, and they are not all working for the same handful of interests. Groups like the AARP, the National Council of State Legislatures, and farmers', teachers', and trade unions represent significant segments of the population. Rather than a clique of elites running the government, on many issues we have interest groups sufficiently powerful to exercise a de facto veto on issues affecting them. This suggests a system stymied by a kind of "hyperpluralism," with so many organized interests competing to influence policy that it is difficult to find common ground to work out solutions to problems. The close ties many groups have to congressional committees and subcommittees considering legislation allow them to stop policy ideas they dislike. And modern technology heightens their impact. A witness to congressional hearings on tax reform reported that lobbyists used cellular phones to produce floods of protest by phone or fax the instant anyone even *thought* about something they opposed. [58] So many powerful groups with clout exist that attempts to alter the status quo or change national priorities are extremely difficult. Presidents Carter, Reagan, and Clinton found this out when they tried to make major changes in energy, budget, and health care policy, respectively. The Clinton White House tried to work with over eleven hundred interest groups on health care reform, to no avail. [59] Efforts to bring about major changes in national domestic priorities are extremely difficult. It is telling that one of the most sweeping recent changes in entrenched policy was the overhaul of the welfare system, a reform whose impact will be felt primarily by the poorest and least politically active Americans.

The difficulties created by interest group vetoes often contribute to gridlock and what one observer calls the "blame game."[60] Gridlock occurs when policies are not enacted or administered effectively because the president and Congress cannot agree on what to do. Politicians representing different interests often blame each other for this inaction, playing the blame game, when they see that gridlock is likely to keep them from getting what they want. The blame game encourages elected officials to distrust each other and furthers public cynicism about government's responsiveness and effectiveness.

Given the presence of many strong groups and their veto opportunities, passing a law means fashioning compromises out of competing group views.[61] In addition to being slow, the process often leads to vaguely worded laws giving actual policymaking authority to bureaucrats who work less visibly with interest group help. In effect, agencies and interest groups, not Congress, often legislate. Thus chemical industry lobbyists help write regulations on hazardous waste, oil companies help write energy policy, and military contractors help the Pentagon write weapons contracts.

The growth of bureaucratic policymaking makes our democracy even more indirect than the writers of the Constitution intended. Most citizens do not have the time to monitor the actions of the president and 535 members of Congress organized into almost two hundred committees and subcommittees and more than one hundred federal agencies. The leaders of major interest groups can, and this gives them considerable power. The possibility that these leaders may be relatively independent of their rank-and-file memberships makes them even more important. These views challenge the claim that ours is a democracy because competition among interest groups eventually results in governments' responding to the needs of all citizens, despite low levels of participation by Americans in the lowest income and education groups. They suggest a hybrid explanation of American democracy, stressing the clout of more powerful groups, whose leaders may belong to a larger, more diversified elite. Nevertheless, theories about a small group of clubby, conspiring power elites are useful because they remind us that tremendous inequalities of resources exist, enabling some individuals and groups to influence government more than others. Interest groups do not represent everyone, especially the poor, the working class, and the politically disinterested.

In the government the Founders designed, power was dispersed across branches and levels of government and between the voting public (at the time a small minority) and their representatives. They did not concern themselves with power exercised through the private sector, and in an overwhelmingly agrarian country, economic power did not rest in the hands of a small number of corporate leaders. Today, with universal suffrage and many more officials subject to direct election, there is more power to be exercised directly by the people than at the end of the eighteenth century. To say that many choose not to exercise their power is not the same as saying that a group of powerful people has wrested it from them.

Just as the Founders disagreed over how much participation was needed in a republic, so scholars of government argue over how much it really matters whether most people participate. The most important factor, some argue, is not the number of voters or the quality of participation but that elections for government office should be truly competitive.[62] Others say that the essence of democracy is having political and governmental leaders who deliberate on public policy in such a way as to make it possible for the public to participate in decision making.[63] From these different ideas about what it means to be democratic, it is clear that it is difficult at times not only to see who has the power but also to agree on who should have it.

Conclusion: Is Government Responsive?

Our Constitution created a republic, a form of government in which the people rule indirectly and are dependent on representatives to meet their policy demands as well as the country's most fundamental needs (national security and an infrastructure to support the economy, for example). This book is organized around the theme of government responsiveness: evaluations of how effectively, and on what bases, elected representatives and other officials act on popular demands and fulfill basic government functions. But in this first chapter,

"Remember when people had only themselves to blame?"

we have also looked at the people's relation to and responsibility for government. So perhaps it is fair to ask ourselves how we measure up as citizens.

Americans love the idea that the average person has a say in government, yet half of us do not vote, even in presidential elections. As we rallied behind the war on terrorism, however, we did express less cynicism about government; 69 percent said they had a "much more" or "somewhat more favorable" view of government after 9/11. But there was little more interest in participation, nor did our leaders ask for any sacrifice from most Americans. Almost 60 percent of respondents thought it was possible to be patriotic without getting involved in political or civic life.[64] More than four-fifths of Americans did this by displaying the flag on their vehicles, clothing, or homes in the weeks after 9/11.[65] Flag waving and support for military efforts abroad may be essential to national survival and personal identifications, but they have little to do with what makes the country a democracy.

Why do Americans like their government on paper but act as if they dislike participating in it? Has government failed? Are the laws it enacts not what the people want? Is it the fault of the media, emphasizing mostly the negative side of government? Are average citizens actually shut out of the process? Or is the problem really the fault of citizens and not government at all? In a 1999 poll asking, "What's wrong with government?"

special interests were first mentioned, then the media, elected officials, and political parties.[66] No one blamed the voters. In the same poll, eight out of ten respondents said they believed government will be as important or more important in improving people's lives in this century as it has been in the past. If this is what we believe, then dropping out of the political process because we think it is futile or controlled by special interests is like cutting off our noses to spite our faces.

Although each person is not equally well situated to influence policymakers, more avenues for political participation are available now than ever before. The number of organized interests and their effectiveness in making their views known have multiplied so dramatically that government officials are besieged by a cacophony of views. We have argued that this is a necessary component of an indirect democracy serving a large and diverse nation. American government is characterized by conflict and compromise because Americans do not agree on either the nature of the problems we face or the solutions to them. If we all agreed, there would be no need for debate, bargaining, compromise, or delays. In the coming chapters, we will examine the major institutions and processes of our republic, describe their evolution since the Founding, and take up some of the arguments on how they might be reformed to make government more efficient, more just, and more democratic.

EPILOGUE

Who, Me?

his is the only epilogue in which we cannot tell you the outcome of the decision-making process. But we can speculate. Based on past elections, there was only about a 50 percent chance that you cast your vote in the 2004 presidential election—and that chance was much less if you are under twenty-five years of age. The razor-thin 2000 election margin illustrated that the participation and vote of every citizen can be crucial, and whether for this reason, or because the 2004 election was one of the most intensely fought races in years, the higher level of interest during the primaries did translate into higher voter turnout among young

people in the general election. However, because turnout went up virtually across the board—to almost 60 percent of the electorate—the share of under-30 voters stayed at 17 percent, just where it had been in 2000. Fifty-five percent of the young adult vote went to John Kerry and 44 percent to George Bush. Will the higher turnout level among younger voters be sustained in coming elections which may not be so hotly contested or the public so politically polarized?

Collectively, Americans have been accused of practicing "couch potato politics," refusing to accept the responsibilities of national citizenship.[67] Most of us, even those

who are highly dissatisfied with the way government works, do not want a king, a dictator, or an emperor to make decisions for us. Indeed, democracy assumes that majorities control government, and indirect democracy assumes that citizens control their representatives. This means that people need to get up off their couches and participate. Even after 9/11, when Americans were talking about a new kind of patriotism, only 48 percent believed that Americans were now more willing to "put themselves on the line to improve politics."[68] This was borne out when studies showed that whereas attitudes toward government became somewhat more positive, civic behavior increased only marginally.[69]

About their unwillingness to get involved in issue debates or the electoral process, Americans often say, "It's all politics." *Of course it is!* Issue debates and elections are political because the competition to determine what policy will be is essential to government. Politics is inescapable because divergence of interests is unavoidable. Politics is necessary to govern a democratic society. Ignoring politics and the institutions that represent the people to government, such as political parties and interest groups, will not eliminate politics. Rather, it would eliminate the most effective way yet developed for the public to influence government's decisions.

Key Terms

politics

identity politics

political culture

popular sovereignty

democracy

indirect democracy

republic

direct democracy

Further Reading

Joyce Appleby, *Inheriting the Revolution* (Cambridge, Mass.: Harvard University Press, 2000). A historian looks at what the first generation of Americans made of their new government and how they invented a new culture and identity. Special emphasis is given to the rise of a community of free black Americans.

Edward Countryman, *Americans: Collision of Histories* (New York: Hill & Wang, 1996). A historian traces the history of the dominant ethnic groups in America from 1600 to 1900. He argues that the very different experiences of Native, African, and European Americans mean that there is no unified American history and no one "type" who can be identified as American.

Robert A. Dahl, *How Democratic Is the American Constitution?* (New Haven, Conn.: Yale University Press, 2001). This slim and wonderfully written book is drawn from lectures delivered at Yale by one of the country's leading political scientists. He discusses how little the framers knew—and how little there was to know at the time from historical experience—about real democracies and republics. He then looks at major features of the U.S. Constitution and discusses the limitations they place on achieving full democracy.

John B. Judis, *The Paradox of American Democracy: Elites, Special Interests, and the Betrayal of Public Trust* (New York: Pantheon, 1999). A counterargument to the malignant interpretation of elitism, this book attributes the twentieth century's great waves of reform and social welfare legislation to small groups of Ivy League and think tank elites.

Harold Lasswell, *Politics: Who Gets What, When, How* (New York: New World, 1958). This is a classic treatment of some very practical political problems.

Pauline Maier, *American Scripture: The Making of the Declaration of Independence* (New York: Knopf, 1997). A historian offers a revisionist view of the importance of the Declaration by arguing that its language was not original but rather was almost identical in content to that of ninety other declarations written in the colonies at the same time. Given the widespread agreement on language and principles in all these documents, she judges the Declaration "an expression of the American mind."

Michael J. Sandel, *Democracy's Discontent: America in Search of a Public Philosophy* (Cambridge, Mass.: Harvard University Press, 1996). A political theorist argues that American politics is "ill-equipped to allay discontent" over the unraveling moral fabric of the country and suggests that one reason is the supremacy of individual rights over community interests.

For Viewing

Gentlemen's Agreement, (1947) A film starring Gregory Peck that illustrates the so-called polite anti-Semitism prevalent in the United States, even in the years following the Allied victory over Nazism and its regime of terror against the Jews. Based on Harper Lee's Pulitzer Prize–winning book, *To Kill a Mockingbird* (coincidentally also starring Gregory Peck) is the story of race relations in a southern town in the 1930s, focusing on the trial of a black man for murder and the white attorney who defends him. Both of these films, with their white, non-Jewish main character, are indicative of how cautiously any treatment of anti-Semitism and racism had to be handled in the mainstream media at the time.

Hester Street (1974) An Oscar-nominated film about the problems of assimilation for Orthodox Jewish immigrants, especially women. Set in 1896 New York and filmed in grainy black and white, it has great period atmosphere.

There are many documentaries available, most made for public and cable television, that trace the history of America's ethnic minorities. Here are just four:

The Native Americans (1994) A five-volume video series produced by the Turner Broadcasting System for television. Each fifty-minute video deals with the peoples of a specific region of the country: the Plains, the southwest, southeast, the northwest and northeast.

Africans' America (1998) A four–volume video series made by WGBH (Boston) for public television. Begins with a history of the slave trade in 1450 and runs to present day.

The Irish Americans (1998) a four–volume video series made by Disney Studios for television. The history of the Irish in America is traced from the first wave of emigration during the 1840s potato famine to present.

Italians in America (1998) A two-volume video series made for A&E's History Channel. It traces Italian American history from the first period of heavy immigration in the late nineteenth century to recent years.

 ## Electronic Resources

In each chapter, we will provide a few Internet addresses for particularly useful or interesting sites relevant to the chapter. Today, you can access information, including statistics and information about public officials, that was formerly accessible only in libraries. Unlike library call numbers, however, Internet addresses sometimes change.

www.firstgov.gov
This is a central federal government site providing comprehensive links to government Web pages, including those for all branches of government, federal agencies and commissions, and important policy areas.

www.fedstats.gov
This is the primary link to all federal statistics.

www.census.gov
This is the primary source for results of the 2000 census.

uscis.gov
This site of the U.S. Citizenship and Immigration Services leads you to the text of immigration law, official statistics on immigration flows to the United States, and analytical reports on immigration trends.

lcweb.loc.gov/exhibits/religion
This source provides a wealth of information on the role of religion in the founding of the American republic and on the relationship between organized religion and the state governments. It contains many original documents on the relationship between church and state.

 ## InfoTrac College Edition

Search for the following articles in the InfoTrac database:

Champlin, Dell P., and Janet T. Knoedler. "Embedded Economies, Democracy, and the Public Interest," *Journal of Economic Issues* (December 2004).

Grosswiler, Paul. "Historical Hopes, Media Fears, and the Electronic Town Meeting Concept: Where Technology Meets Democracy or Demagogy?" *Journal of Communication Inquiry* (April 1998).

McWilliams, Wilson C. "Democracy as Means and End," *Social Policy* (Summer 2002).

Sneider, Daniel. "An Election Isn't the Same Thing as Democracy," *San Jose Mercury News* via *Knight-Ridder/Tribune News Service* (January 12, 2005).

For more articles, enter:

"democracy" in the Subject Guide;

"direct democracy" in Keywords.

 ## American Government Resources

Visit the Government Foundations section of the Wadsworth American Government Resources Web site (politicalscience.wadsworth.com/amgov/) for a variety of tools to help you explore American democracy further. Included are simulations, video clips, Microcase exercises, and a wealth of other activities.

CHAPTER 2

THE CONSTITUTION

Soon after their deaths, the Founders were venerated by the people. Here George Washington is pictured ascending to heaven.

The Articles of Confederation

    National Government Problems

    State Government Problems

The Constitution

    The Constitutional Convention

    Features of the Constitution

    Motives of the Founders

    Ratification of the Constitution

    Changing the Constitution

Impact of the Civil War and the Great Depression

    The Civil War and Reconstruction

    The Great Depression and the New Deal

    A Combination of Constitutions

Conclusion: Does the Constitution Make the Government Responsive?

The Case of the Confidential Tapes

n June 1972, a security guard for the Watergate building in Washington, D.C., noticed that tape had been placed across the latch of a door to keep it from locking. The guard peeled off the tape. When he made his rounds later, he noticed that more tape had been placed across the latch. He called the police.

The police encountered five burglars in the headquarters of the Democratic National Committee. Wearing surgical gloves and carrying tear gas guns, photographic equipment, and electronic gear, they had been installing wiretaps on the Democratic Party's phones.

No one expected this break-in to lead to the White House. The *Washington Post* assigned two young reporters who usually covered local matters to the story. But the unlikely pair—Bob Woodward, a Yale graduate, and Carl Bernstein, a college dropout—were ambitious, and they uncovered a series of bizarre connections. The burglars had links to President Richard Nixon's Committee to Reelect the President (CREEP).

The administration dismissed the break-in as the work of overzealous underlings. Even the press called it a "caper." Indeed, it was hard to imagine that high officials in the administration could be responsible. In public opinion polls, Nixon enjoyed an enormous lead, almost 20 percent, over the various Democrats vying for their party's nomination to challenge him in the fall election. Risky tactics seemed unnecessary.

But Woodward and Bernstein discovered that White House staff members had engaged in other criminal and unethical actions to sabotage the Democrats' campaign. They had forged letters accusing some of the Democrats' candidates of homosexual acts. Later they had obtained and publicized psychiatric records, causing the Democrats' vice presidential nominee to resign.

In the November election, Nixon won handily, but the revelations forced his two top aides to resign and prompted the Senate to establish a special committee to investigate what was being called the **Watergate scandal.** When investigators happened to ask a lower-level aide to the president whether there was a taping device in the Oval Office, he said, "I was hoping you fellows wouldn't ask me about that." Then he revealed what only a handful of aides had known—that Nixon had secretly tape-recorded conversations in nine locations in the White House, the Executive Office Building across the street, and Camp David in Maryland. Nixon had intended to create a comprehensive record of his presidency to demonstrate his greatness.[1]

The tapes could confirm or refute charges of White House complicity in the break-in and cover-up, but Nixon refused to release them. The special prosecutor filed suit to

Washington Post *reporters Carl Bernstein* (left) *and Bob Woodward uncovered the Watergate scandal.*

force Nixon to do so, and a federal trial court ordered him to do so. After the federal appeals court affirmed the trial court's decision, Nixon demanded that his attorney general fire the special prosecutor. The attorney general and deputy attorney general both refused and resigned in protest. Then the third-ranking official in the Justice Department, Robert Bork, fired the special prosecutor. (Bork would later be nominated to the Supreme Court—unsuccessfully, as it turned out—by President Reagan.)

The public furor over this so-called Saturday Night Massacre was so intense that Nixon finally did release some tapes. But one crucial tape contained a mysterious eighteen-minute gap that a presidential aide speculated was caused by "some sinister force."

To mollify critics, Nixon appointed a new special prosecutor, Leon Jaworski. After his investigation, Jaworski presented evidence to a grand jury that indicted seven of the president's aides for the cover-up, specifically for obstruction of justice, and even named the president as an "unindicted coconspirator."

The House Judiciary Committee considered impeaching the president, and Jaworski subpoenaed more tapes. Nixon issued edited transcripts of the conversations but not the tapes themselves. As a compromise, he proposed that one person listen to the tapes—a senator who was seventy-two years old and hard of hearing. Frustrated, Jaworski went to the court, which ordered Nixon to release the tapes. When Nixon refused, Jaworski appealed directly to the Supreme Court.

You are Chief Justice Warren Burger, appointed to the Court by President Nixon in 1969 partly because of your calls for more law and order. Three of your brethren were also appointed by Nixon. In the case of *United States* v. *Nixon,* the question you face could lead to a grave constitutional showdown with the president. Special Prosecutor Jaworski claims that he needs the tapes because they contain evidence pertaining to the upcoming trial of the presi-

dent's aides indicted for the cover-up. Without all relevant evidence, which possibly could vindicate the aides, the trial court might not convict them.

President Nixon claims he has executive privilege—authority to withhold information from the courts and Congress. Although the Constitution does not mention such a privilege, Nixon contends that the privilege is inherent in the powers of the presidency. Without it, presidents could not guarantee confidentiality in conversations with other officials or even foreign leaders. This could make it difficult for them to govern.

You have few precedents to guide you. Many past presidents exercised executive privilege when pressed for information by Congress. In these instances, Congress ordinarily acquiesced rather than sued for the information, so the courts did not rule on the existence of the privilege. Once, in 1953, the Eisenhower administration invoked the privilege, and the Supreme Court upheld the claim. However, that case involved national security.[2]

In addition to considering the merits of the opposing sides, you also need to consider the extent of the Supreme Court's power. The Court lacks strong means to enforce its rulings. It has to rely on its authority as the highest interpreter of the law in the country. Therefore, if the Court orders Nixon to relinquish the tapes and Nixon refuses, there would be little the Court could do. His refusal would show future officials they could disregard your orders with impunity.

In this high-stakes contest, do you and your brethren on the Court order Nixon to turn over the tapes, or do you accept his claim of executive privilege?

Early settlers came to America for different reasons. Some came to escape religious persecution, others to establish their own religious orthodoxy. Some came to get rich, others to avoid debtors' prison. Some came to make money for their families or employers in the Old World, others to flee the closed society of that world. Some came as free persons, others as indentured servants or slaves. Few came to practice self-government. Yet the desire for self-government was evident from the beginning.[3] The settlers who arrived in Jamestown in 1607 established the first representative assembly in America. The Pilgrims, who reached Plymouth in 1620, drew up the Mayflower Compact in which they vowed to "solemnly & mutually in the presence of God, and one of another, covenant and combine our selves together into a civill body politick." They pledged to establish laws for "the generall good of the colonie" and in return promised "all due submission and obedience."[4]

During the next century and a half, the colonies adopted constitutions and elected representative assemblies. Of course, the colonies lived under British rule; they had to accept the appointment of royal governors and the presence of British troops. But a vast ocean separated the two continents. At such a distance, Britain could not wield the control it might at closer reach. Consequently, it granted the colonies a measure of autonomy, with which they practiced a degree of self-government.

These early efforts toward self-government led to conflict with the mother government. In 1774, the colonies established the Continental Congress to coordinate their actions. Within months, the conflict reached flashpoint, and the Congress urged the colonies to form their own governments. In 1776, the Congress adopted the Declaration of Independence.

After six years of war, the Americans accepted the British surrender. At the time it seemed they had met their biggest test. Yet they would find fomenting a revolution easier than fashioning a government, and drafting a declaration of independence easier than crafting a constitution.

The Articles of Confederation

Even before the war ended, the Continental Congress passed a constitution, and in 1781 the states ratified it. This first constitution, the **Articles of Confederation,** formed a "league of friendship" among the states. As a confederation, it allowed each state to retain its "sovereignty" and "independence." That is, it made the states supreme over the federal government.

Under the Articles, however, Americans would face problems with both their national and state governments.

National Government Problems

The Articles of Confederation established a Congress, a legislative body with one house in which each state had one vote. But they strictly limited the powers that Congress could exercise, and they provided no executive or judicial branch.

The Articles reflected the colonial experience under the British government. The leaders feared a powerful central government with a powerful executive like a king. They thought such a government would be too strong and too distant to guarantee individual liberty. Furthermore, the Articles reflected a lack of national identity among the people. Most did not view themselves as Americans yet. As Edmund Randolph remarked, "I am not really an American, I am a Virginian."[5] (And George Washington worried that Kentuckians would join Spain.[6]) Consequently, the leaders established a very decentralized government that left most authority to the states.

The Articles satisfied many people. Most residents were small farmers, and although many of them sank into debt during the depression that followed the war, they felt they could get the state governments to help them. They realized they could not influence a distant central government as readily.

But the Articles frustrated bankers, merchants, manufacturers, and others in the upper classes. They envisioned a great commercial empire replacing the agricultural society that existed in the late eighteenth century. More than local trade, they wanted national and even international trade. For this they needed uniform laws,

Although the Articles of Confederation gave the federal government authority to print money, the states circulated their own currencies as well.

stable money, sound credit, and enforceable debt collection. They needed a strong central government that could protect them against debtors and against state governments sympathetic to debtors. The Articles provided neither the foreign security nor the domestic climate necessary to nourish these requisites of a commercial empire.

After the war, the army disbanded, leaving the country vulnerable to hostile forces surrounding it. Britain maintained outposts with troops in the Northwest Territory (today's Midwest), in violation of the peace treaty, and an army in Canada. Spain, which had occupied Florida and California for a long time and had claimed the Mississippi River valley as a result of a treaty before the war, posed a threat. Barbary pirates from North Africa seized American ships and sailors.

Congress could not raise an army, because it could not draft individuals directly, or finance an army, because it could not tax individuals directly. Instead, it had to ask the states for soldiers and money. The states, however, were not always sympathetic to the problems of the distant government. And although Congress could make treaties with foreign countries, the states made (or broke) treaties independently of Congress. Without the ability to establish a credible army or negotiate a binding treaty, the government could not get the British troops to leave American soil. Nor could it get the British government to ease restrictions on shipping or the Spanish government to permit navigation on the Mississippi River.[7]

In addition to an inability to confront foreign threats, the Articles demonstrated an inability to cope with domestic crises. The country bore a heavy war debt that brought the government close to bankruptcy. Since Congress could not tax individuals directly, it could not shore up the shaky government.

The states competed with each other for commercial advantage. As independent governments, they imposed tariffs on goods from other states. The tariffs slowed the growth of businesses.

In short, the government under the Articles of Confederation seemed too decentralized to ensure either peace or prosperity. The Articles, one leader concluded, gave Congress the privilege of asking for everything while reserving to each state the prerogative of granting nothing.[8] A similar situation exists today in the United Nations, which must rely on the goodwill of member countries to furnish troops for its peacekeeping forces and dues for its operating expenses.[9]

State Government Problems

Other conflicts arose closer to home. State constitutions adopted during the American Revolution made the state legislatures more representative than the colonial legislatures had been. Most state legislatures also began to hold elections every year. The result was heightened interest among candidates and turnover among legislators. In the eyes of national leaders, there was much pandering to voters and horse trading by politicians as various factions vied for control. The process seemed up for grabs. According to the Vermont Council of Censors, laws were "altered—realtered—made better—made worse; and kept in such a fluctuating position that persons in civil commission scarce know what is law."[10] In short, state governments were experiencing more democracy than any other governments in the world at the time. National leaders, stunned by the changes in the few years since the Revolution, considered this development an "excess of democracy."

Moreover, state constitutions made the legislative branch the most powerful. Some state legislatures began to dominate the other branches, and national leaders called them "tyrannical."

The national leaders, most of whom were wealthy and many of whom were creditors, pointed to the laws passed in some states that relieved debtors of some of their obligations. The farmers who were in debt pressed the legislatures for relief that would slow or shrink the payments owed to their creditors. Some legislatures granted such relief.

While these laws worried the leaders, **Shays's Rebellion** in western Massachusetts in 1786 and 1787 scared them. Boston merchants who had loaned Massachusetts money during the war insisted on being repaid in full so that they could trade with foreign merchants. The state levied steep taxes that many farmers could not pay during the hard times. The law authorized foreclosure—sale of the farmers' property to recover unpaid taxes—and jail for the debtors. The law essentially transferred wealth from the farmers to the merchants. The farmers protested the legislature's refusal to grant any relief from the law. Bands of farmers blocked the entrances to courthouses where judges were scheduled to hear cases calling for foreclosure and jail. Led by Daniel Shays, some marched to the Springfield arsenal to seize weapons. Although they were defeated by the militia, their sympathizers were victorious in the next election, and the legislature did provide some relief from the law.

Both the revolt and the legislature's change in policy frightened the wealthy. To them it raised the specter of mob rule. Nathaniel Gorham, the president of the Continental Congress and a prominent merchant, wrote Prince Henry of Prussia, announcing "the failure of our free institutions" and asking whether the prince would agree to become king of America (the prince declined).[11] Just months after the uprising, Congress approved a convention for "the sole and express purpose of revising the Articles of Confederation."

To a significant extent, then, the debate at the time reflected a conflict between two competing visions of

FOUNDING MOTHERS

Charles Francis Adams, a grandson of President John Adams and Abigail Adams, declared in 1840, "The heroism of the females of the Revolution has gone from memory with the generation that witnessed it, and nothing, absolutely nothing remains upon the ear of the young of the present day."[1] That statement is still true today; in the volumes written about the revolutionary and Constitution-making eras, much is said of the "Founding Fathers" and very little about the "Founding Mothers." Although no women were at the Constitutional Convention, in many other ways women contributed significantly to the political ferment of the time. The political role of women during the Constitution-making era was probably greater than it would be again for a century.

Before the Revolutionary War, women were active in encouraging opposition to the British. Groups of women, some called the "daughters of liberty," led boycotts of British goods as part of the protest campaign against taxation without representation. A few women were political pamphleteers, helping increase public sentiment for independence. One of those pamphlet writers, Mercy Otis Warren, of Massa-

chusetts, was thought to be the first person to urge the Massachusetts delegates to the Continental Congress to vote for separation from Britain.[2] Throughout the period before and after the Revolution, Warren shared her political ideas in personal correspondence with leading statesmen of the time, such as John Adams and Thomas Jefferson. Later she wrote a three-volume history of the American Revolution.

Many women were part of the American army during the battles for independence. Most filled traditional women's roles as cooks, seamstresses, and nurses, but some disguised themselves as men (this was before a military bureaucracy mandated preenlistment physical exams) and fought in battle. One such woman, wounded in action in 1776, is the only Revolutionary War veteran buried at West Point. Still other women fought to defend their homes using hatchets, farm implements, and pots of boiling lye in addition to muskets.

Following independence, some women continued an active political role. Mercy Warren, for example, campaigned against the proposed Constitution because she felt it was not democratic enough.

Independence did not bring an improvement in the political rights of

A SOCIETY of PATRIOTIC LADIES, AT EDENTON in NORTH CAROLINA.

This English political cartoon satirizes a gathering of leading women of North Carolina who drew up a resolution to boycott taxed English goods and tea.

women. In fact, after adoption of the Constitution, some women lost the right to vote. It would be another century before the rights of women would become a full-fledged part of our national political agenda.

1. Quoted in Linda Grant De Pauw and Conover Hunt, *Remember the Ladies* (New York: Viking, 1976), 9.
2. Alice Felt Tyler, *Freedom's Ferment* (New York: Harper & Row, 1962).

---

the future American political economy—agricultural or commercial.[12] Most leaders espoused the latter, and the combination of national problems and state problems prompted them to push for a new government.[13]

The Constitution

The Constitutional Convention

The Setting

The **Constitutional Convention** convened in Philadelphia, then the country's largest city, in 1787. The Industrial Revolution was sweeping Europe and begin-

ning to reach this continent. The first American cotton mill opened in Massachusetts, and the first American steamboat plied the Delaware River.

State legislatures chose seventy-four delegates to the convention; fifty-five attended. They met at the Pennsylvania State House—now Independence Hall—in the same room where many of them had signed the Declaration of Independence eleven years earlier. Delegates came from every state except Rhode Island, whose farmers and debtors feared that the convention would weaken states' powers to relieve debtors of their debts. All the delegates were men (see the box "Founding Mothers").

The delegates were distinguished by their education, experience, and enlightenment. Benjamin Franklin, of

Pennsylvania, was the best-known American in the world. He had been a printer, scientist, and diplomat. At eighty-one, he was also the oldest delegate. George Washington, of Virginia, was the most respected American in the country. As the commander of the revolutionary army, he was a national hero. He was chosen to preside over the convention. The presence of men like Franklin and Washington gave the convention legitimacy.

The delegates quickly determined that the Articles of Confederation were beyond repair. Rather than revise them, as instructed by Congress, the delegates decided to start over and draft a new constitution.[14]

The Predicament

The delegates came to the convention because they complained about a government that was too weak. Yet the Americans had fought their revolution because they chafed under a government that was too strong. "The nation lived in a nearly constant alternation of fears that it would cease being a nation altogether or become too much of one."[15] People feared both anarchy and tyranny.

This predicament was made clear by the diversity of opinions among the leaders. At one extreme was Patrick Henry, of Virginia, who had been a firebrand of the Revolution. He feared that the government would become too strong, perhaps even become a monarchy, in reaction to the current problems with the Articles. He said he "smelt a rat" and did not attend the convention. At the other extreme was Alexander Hamilton, of New York, who had been an aide to General Washington during the war and had seen the government's inability to supply and pay its own troops. Ever since, he had called for a stronger national government. He wanted one that could veto the laws of the state governments. He also wanted one person to serve as chief executive for life and others to serve as senators for life. He did attend the convention but, finding little agreement with his proposals, participated infrequently.

In between were the likes of James Madison, of Virginia. Small and frail, timid and self-conscious as a speaker, he was nonetheless an intelligent and savvy politician. He had operated behind the scenes to organize the convention and to secure Washington's attendance. (He announced that Washington would attend without asking Washington first. Washington, who was in retirement, had not planned to attend and only reluctantly agreed to do so because of the expectation that he would.[16]) Madison, who had studied other countries' governments, had secretly drafted a plan for a new government, one that was a total departure from the government under the Articles and one that would set the agenda for the convention. During the convention, Madison was "up to his ears in politics, advising, per-

suading, softening the harsh word, playing down this difficulty and exaggerating that, engaging in debate, harsh controversy, polemics, and sly maneuver."[17] In the end, his views more than anyone else's would prevail, and he would be known as the Father of the Constitution.[18] Even today, he is esteemed as "our greatest political scientist" by the dean of American political scientists, Robert Dahl.[19]

Consensus

Despite disagreements, the delegates did see eye to eye on the most fundamental issues. They agreed that the government should be a **republic**—a form of government that derives its power from the people and whose officials are accountable to the people. The term more specifically refers to an indirect democracy, in which the people vote for at least some of the officials who represent them. The delegates did not seriously consider any other form of government. Only Hamilton suggested a monarchy, and only one delegate suggested an aristocracy.[20]

They also agreed that the national government should be stronger than before. At the same time, they thought the government should be limited, with checks to prevent it from exercising too much power. They agreed that the national government should have three separate branches—legislative, executive, and judicial—to exercise separate powers. They thought that both the legislative and executive branches should be strong.

Conflict

Although there was considerable agreement over the fundamental principles and elemental structure of the new government, the delegates quarreled about the specific provisions concerning representation, slavery, and trade.

Representation Sharp conflict was expressed between delegates from large states and those from small states regarding representation. Large states sought a strong central government that they could control; small states feared a government that would control them.

When the convention began, Edmund Randolph introduced the Virginia Plan, drafted by Madison. According to this plan, the central government would be strong. The legislature would have more power than under the Articles of Confederation, and a national executive and national judiciary also would have considerable power. The legislature would be divided into two houses, with representation based on population in each.

But delegates from the small states calculated that the three largest states—Pennsylvania, Virginia, and Massachusetts—would have a majority of the representatives and could control the legislature. These delegates countered with the New Jersey Plan, introduced by William

Paterson. According to this plan, the legislature would consist of one house, with representation by states, which would have one vote each. This was exactly the same as the structure of Congress under the Articles, also designed to prevent the largest states from controlling the legislature.

To complicate matters, some states claimed vast territories to their west, increasing the fears of other states that such expansion would make the frontier states even larger.

James Wilson, of Pennsylvania, asked for whom they were forming a government—"for men, or for the imaginary beings called states?"[21] But delegates from the small states would not budge. Gunning Bedford, of Delaware, threatened that the small states would leave the government and align themselves with a European country instead. "If the large states insist on representation according to population, the small ones will find some foreign ally of more honor and good faith, who will take them by the hand and do them justice."[22]

The convention deadlocked. George Washington wrote that he almost despaired of reaching agreement. To ease tensions, Benjamin Franklin suggested that the delegates begin each day with a prayer, but they could not agree on this either; Alexander Hamilton insisted they did not need "foreign aid."

Faced with the possibility that the convention would disband without a constitution, the delegates compromised. Delegates from Connecticut and other states proposed a plan in which the legislature, or Congress, would have two houses. In one, the House of Representatives, representation would be based on population, and members would be elected by voters. In the other, the Senate, representation would be by states, and members would be selected by state legislatures. Presumably, the large states would dominate the for-

mer, the small states the latter. The delegates narrowly approved this **Great Compromise,** or Connecticut Compromise. Delegates from the large states still objected, but those from the small states made it clear that such a compromise was necessary for their agreement and, in turn, their states' ratification. The large states, though, did extract a concession that all taxing and spending bills must originate in the house in which representation was based on population. This provision would allow the large states to take the initiative on these important measures. The compromise has been called "great" because it not only resolved this critical issue but paved the way for resolution of other issues.

This decision began a pattern that continues to this day. When officials face implacable differences, they try to compromise, but the process is not easy, and a resolution is not inevitable. It is an apt choice of words to say that officials "hammer out" a compromise; it is not a coincidence that we use *hammer* rather than a softer metaphor.

Slavery In addition to conflict between large states and small states over representation, conflict emerged between northern states and southern states over slavery, trade, and taxation.

With representation in one house based on population, the delegates had to decide how to apportion the seats. They agreed that Indians would not count as part of the population but differed about slaves. Delegates from the South, where slaves made up one-third of the population, wanted slaves to count fully in order to boost the number of their representatives. They argued that their use of slaves produced wealth that benefited the entire nation. Delegates from the North, where most states had outlawed slavery or at least the slave trade after

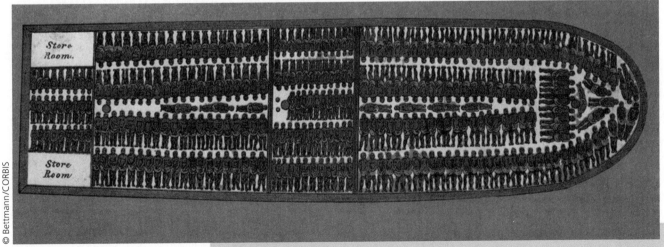

This plan of a slave ship shows the overcrowding that led to inhumane conditions, rampant disease, and high mortality.

the Revolution, did not want slaves to count at all. Gouverneur Morris, of Pennsylvania, said the southerners' position

> comes to this: that the inhabitant of Georgia and South Carolina who goes to the coast of Africa, and in defiance of the most sacred laws of humanity tears away his fellow creatures from their dearest connections and damns them to the most cruel bondages, shall have more votes in a government instituted for the protection of the rights of mankind than the citizen of Pennsylvania or New Jersey who views with a laudable horror so nefarious a practice.[23]

Others pointed out that slaves were not considered persons when it came to rights such as voting. Nevertheless, southerners asserted that they would not support a constitution if slaves were not counted at least partially. In the **Three-fifths Compromise,** the delegates agreed that three-fifths of the slaves would be counted in apportioning the seats.

This compromise expanded the political power of the people who were oppressing the slaves. The votes of southern whites became worth more than those of northerners in electing members to the House of Representatives and also in electing presidents (because the number of presidential electors was based on membership in Congress). Between 1788 and 1860, nine of the fifteen presidents, including all five who served two terms, were slaveowners.[24]

Southerners pushed through two other provisions addressing slavery. One forbade Congress from banning the importation of slaves before 1808; another required free states to return escaped slaves to their owners in slave states. In these provisions, southerners won most of what they wanted; even the provision permitting Congress to ban the importation of slaves in 1808 was little limitation because by then planters would have enough slaves to fulfill their needs by natural population increases rather than importation. In return, northerners, who represented shippers, got authority for Congress to regulate commerce by a simple majority rather than a two-thirds majority. Thus northerners conceded these two provisions reinforcing slavery in order to benefit shippers.[25]

Yet the framers were embarrassed by the hypocrisy of claiming to have been enslaved by the British while allowing enslavement of blacks. Their embarrassment is reflected in their language. The three provisions reinforcing slavery never mention "slavery" or "slaves"; one gingerly refers to "free persons" and "other persons."

Slavery was the most divisive issue at the convention. As Madison noted, "The real difference of interests lay, not between the large and small, but between the northern and southern states. The institution of slavery and its consequences formed the line of discrimination."[26] The unwillingness to tackle the slavery issue more directly

has been called the "Greatest Compromise" by one political scientist.[27] But an attempt to abolish slavery would have caused the five southern states to refuse to ratify the Constitution.

Trade and Taxation Slavery also underlay a compromise on trade and taxation. With a manufacturing economy, northerners sought protection for their businesses. In particular, they wanted a tax on manufactured goods imported from Britain. Without a tax, these goods would be cheaper than northern goods; but with a tax, northern goods would be more competitive—and prices for southern consumers more expensive. With an agricultural economy, southerners sought free trade for their plantations. They wanted a guarantee that no tax would be levied on agricultural products exported to Britain. Such a tax would make their products less competitive abroad and, they worried, amount to an indirect tax on slavery—the labor responsible for the products. The delegates compromised by allowing Congress to tax imported goods but not exported ones. Tariffs on imported goods would become a point of controversy between the North and South in the years leading up to the Civil War.

After seventeen weeks of debate, the Constitution was ready. On September 17, 1787, thirty-nine of the original fifty-five delegates signed it. Some delegates had left when they saw the direction the convention was taking, and three others refused to sign, feeling that the Constitution gave too much authority to the national government. Most of the rest were not entirely happy with the result (even Madison, who was most responsible for the content of the document, was despondent that his plan for a national legislature was compromised by having one house with representation by states), but they thought it was the best they could do.

Features of the Constitution

William Gladstone, a British prime minister in the nineteenth century, said the American Constitution was "the most wonderful work ever struck off at a given time by the brain and purpose of man."[28] To see why it was unique, it is necessary to examine its major features.

A Republic

The Founders distinguished between a democracy and a republic. For them, a "democracy" meant a **direct democracy,** which permits citizens to vote on most issues, and a "republic" meant an **indirect democracy,** which allows citizens to vote for their representatives, who make governmental policies.

The Founders opposed a direct democracy for the whole country. Many individual towns in New England had a direct democracy (and some still do), but these communities were small and manageable. Some city-

During the Constitutional Convention, Benjamin Franklin wondered whether the carving on the back of George Washington's chair showed the sun coming up or going down. After the delegates agreed to the Constitution, he observed, "Now . . . I have the happiness to know that it is a rising and not a setting sun."

states of ancient Greece and medieval Europe had a direct democracy, but they could not sustain it. The Founders thought a large country would have even less ability to do so because people could not be brought together in one place to act. They also believed that human nature was such that people could not withstand the passions of the moment and would be swayed by a demagogue to take unwise action. Eventually, democracy would collapse into tyranny. "Remember," John Adams wrote, "democracy never lasts long. It soon wastes, exhausts, and murders itself. There never was a democracy yet that did not commit suicide."[29]

The Founders favored a republic, because they believed that the government should be based on the consent of the people, and in particular an indirect democracy, because they believed that the people should have some voice in choosing their officials. So the Founders provided that the people would elect representatives to the House and that the state legislators, themselves elected by the people, would select senators from their state and also the members of the Electoral College, the electors for each state who would choose the president. In this way, the people would have a voice but one partially filtered through their presumably wiser representatives.

The Founders' views reflect their ambivalence about the people. Rationally, they believed in popular sovereignty, but emotionally, they feared it. New England clergyman Jeremy Belknap voiced their ambivalence when he declared, "Let it stand as a principle that government originates from the people; but let the people be taught . . . that they are not able to govern themselves."[30]

The Founders would have been aghast at the recent proliferation of such experiments in democracy as initiatives and referenda, which allow voters to adopt public policies, or recall elections, which allow voters to replace elected officials with new officials before their terms expire. The Founders distrusted mass popularity as a means to good government.

The Founders considered a democracy radical and a republic only slightly less radical. Because they believed that the country could not maintain a democracy, they worried that it might not be able to maintain a republic either. It is said that when the Constitutional Convention ended, Benjamin Franklin was approached by a woman who asked, "Well, Doctor, what have we got, a republic or a monarchy?" Franklin responded, "A republic, Madam, if you can keep it."

Fragmentation of Power

Other countries assumed that a government must have a concentration of power to be strong enough to govern. However, when the Founders made our national government more powerful than it had been under the Articles of Confederation, they feared that they also had made it more capable of oppression, and so they fragmented its power.

The Founders believed that people were selfish, coveting more and more property, and that leaders lusted after more and more power. They assumed that human nature was unchangeable. Madison speculated, "If men were angels, no government would be necessary." "Alas," he added, "men are not angels." Therefore, "in framing a government which is to be administered by men over men, the great difficulty lies in this: you must first enable the government to control the governed; and in the next place oblige it to control itself."[31] (Madison's views are reflected in *Federalist Papers* 10 and 51, reprinted at the back of this book.) The Founders decided that the way to oblige the government to control itself was to structure it so as to prevent any one leader, group of leaders, or factions of people from exercising power over more than a small part of it. Thus the Founders fragmented government's power. This is reflected in three concepts they built into the structure of government: federalism, separation of powers, and checks and balances.

Federalism The first division of power was between the national government and the state governments. This division of power is called **federalism.** Foreign governments had been "unitary"; that is, the central government wielded all authority. At the other extreme, the U.S. government under the Articles of Confederation had been "confederal"; the state governments wielded almost all authority. The Founders wanted a strong national government, but they also wanted, or at least realized they would have to accept, reasonably

After slavery was abolished and the right to vote was extended to racial minorities and women, the equal representation of states in the Senate was perhaps the most undemocratic aspect left in the Constitution.[1]

Because each state gets two senators regardless of its population, small or sparsely populated rural states enjoy disproportionate representation relative to their size. California, the most populous state, and Wyoming, the least populous state, have equal representation, although California has seventy times more people. Therefore, voters in California have one-seventieth as much representation, or power, in the Senate as voters in Wyoming have. Is this fair?

The equal representation of states in the Senate is not the result of some grand theory of government. As explained in the text, it was a major concession to the small states to maintain their allegiance to the country and to obtain their support for the Constitution. At least at that time, people identified more closely with their state than with the nation as a whole. Today, our mass society, mass media, and transportation networks weaken these ties and strengthen our sense of national identity.

Do the people in small states have special needs to protect that would justify their greater representation? The Constitution, including the Bill of Rights and later amendments, guarantees fundamental rights. Federal laws and court decisions preserve various rights. Federalism, which splits power between the national government and the state governments, provides states with more authority than they would have in nonfederal systems. Do the people in small states have additional needs to protect beyond these? If so, what are they? And are these needs greater than the needs of other people who do not get extra representation, such as the people who are short or fat or disabled, or the people who have been the victims of widespread discrimination, such as African Americans or Native Americans?

What if a similar rationale were applied to African Americans? If the 12 percent of Americans who are black had as many senators representing them as the 12 percent of Americans who live in our smallest states have representing them, the Senate would include forty-four black senators. Would this seem fair?

Yet even if most Americans decide that the equal representation in the Senate is unfair and undemocratic, it is unlikely they could change it. The Constitution stipulates, "No state, without its consent, shall be deprived of its equal suffrage in the Senate."[2] Further, Article 5, which addresses amendments, limits amendments in two categories. The provision regarding the importation of slaves could not be amended until 1808, and the provision regarding the representation in the Senate cannot be amended ever.

Some constitutional scholars suggest that an amendment repealing this provision could be adopted first and an amendment altering the representation itself could be adopted next. Other scholars think the courts would not tolerate this obvious subterfuge of the Founders' intentions.[3]

Regardless, it is a moot point, because amendment of the Constitution requires ratification by three-fourths of the states. Just thirteen states can block an amendment favored by the rest of the country. The thirteen small-

---

strong state governments as well. They invented a federal system as a compromise between the unitary and confederal systems. (Chapter 3 explains these types of government further.)

They even incorporated federalism into the national government by stipulating that one house of Congress, the Senate, would be based on the states. It would have two senators from each state regardless of the state's population. This would protect the interests of the states—especially the small states, which would be dwarfed in a house based on population. This would therefore give power to small states disproportionate to their population.

Separation of Powers The second division of power was within the national government. The power to make, administer, and judge the laws was split into three branches: legislative, executive, and judicial (see Figure 1). In the legislative branch, the power was split further into two houses. This **separation of powers** contrasts with the parliamentary system in most developed democracies, in which the legislature is supreme. In parliamentary systems, both executive and judicial officials are drawn from the legislature and are responsible to it. There is no separation of powers. (If the United States had a parliamentary system in the mid-1990s, consider the possibility: Newt Gingrich [R-Ga.] would have been our head of government.) Madison expressed the American view of such an arrangement when he said that "the accumulation of all powers, legislative, executive, and judiciary, in the same hands . . . may justly be pronounced the very definition of tyranny."[32] (Note, however, that parliamentary systems are no more tyrannous than other systems.)

To reinforce the separation of powers, officials of the three branches were chosen by different means. Representatives were elected by the people (at that time mostly white men who owned property), senators were se-

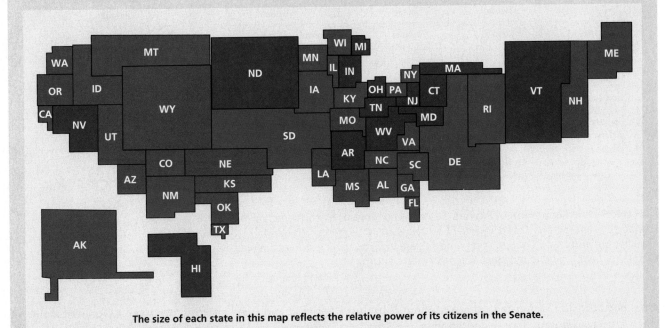

The size of each state in this map reflects the relative power of its citizens in the Senate.

Source: Michael Lind, "75 Stars," *Mother Jones* (January-February 1998), p. 130. Reprinted with permission.

est states, with only 5 percent of the nation's population, thus can thwart the wishes of the thirty-seven largest states, with 95 percent of the nation's people.

1. Most information in this box is from Robert A. Dahl, *How Democratic Is the American Constitution?* (New Haven, Conn.: Yale University Press, 2001).
2. This provision is reinforced by Article 4, which stipulates that "no . . . state shall be formed by the junction of two or more states, or parts of states, without the consent of . . . the states concerned." Thus small states cannot be forced to combine as a way to reduce their representation.
3. J. W. Peltason, *Corwin and Peltason's Understanding the Constitution,* 9th ed. (New York: Holt, Rinehart and Winston, 1982), 113. For a creative alternative, see Michael Lind, "75 Stars," *Mother Jones* (January-February 1998), 44–49.

lected by the state legislatures, and the president was selected by the Electoral College, whose members were selected by the states. Only federal judges were chosen by officials in the other branches. They were nominated by the president and confirmed by the Senate. Once appointed, however, they were allowed to serve for "good behavior"—essentially life—so they had much independence. (Since the Constitution was written, the Seventeenth Amendment has provided for election of senators by the people, and the state legislatures have provided for election of members of the Electoral College by the people.)

Officials of the branches were also chosen at different times. Representatives were given a two-year term, senators a six-year term (with one-third of them up for reelection every two years), and the president a four-year term. These staggered terms would make it less likely that temporary passions in society would bring about a massive switch of officials or policies.

The Senate was designed to act as a conservative brake on the House, due to senators' selection by state legislatures and their longer terms. After returning from France, Thomas Jefferson met with George Washington over breakfast. Jefferson protested the establishment of a legislature with two houses. Washington supposedly asked, "Why did you pour that coffee into your saucer?" "To cool it," Jefferson replied. Similarly, Washington explained, "We pour legislation into the senatorial saucer to cool it."[33]

Separation of powers creates the opportunity for **divided government.** Rather than one political party controlling both elected branches, one party might win the presidency while the other party wins a majority of seats in one or both houses of Congress. Divided government has been common throughout the nation's history. Since the emergence of the Democratic and Republican party system (1856), it has occurred as a result of two of every five elections.[34] Since World War II,

Branch:	Legislative Congress		Executive Presidency	Judicial Federal Courts
	House	Senate	President	Judges
Officials chosen by:	People	People, (originally, state legislatures)	Electoral College, whose members are chosen by the people (originally, by state legislatures)	President, with advice and consent of Senate
For term of:	2 years	6 years	4 years	Life
To represent primarily:	Common people	Wealthy people	All people	Constitution
	Large states	Small states		

FIGURE 1 ■ Separation of Powers *Separation of powers, as envisioned by the Founders, means not only that government functions are to be performed by different branches but also that officials of these branches are to be chosen by different people, for different terms, and to represent different constituencies.*

it has been the dominant mode of government.[35] In this way, American voters have added another element to Madison's concept of separation of powers.

Checks and Balances To guarantee separation of powers, the Founders built in overlapping powers called **checks and balances** (see Figure 2). Madison suggested that "the great security against a gradual concentration of the several powers in the same department consists in giving those who administer each department the necessary constitutional means and personal motives to resist encroachments by the others. . . . *Ambition must be made to counteract ambition.*"[36] To that end, each branch was given some authority over the others. If one branch abused its power, the others could use their checks to thwart it.

Thus rather than a simple system of separation of powers, ours is a complex, even contradictory, system of both separation of powers and checks and balances. The principle of separation of powers gives each branch its own sphere of authority, but the system of checks and balances allows each branch to intrude into the other branches' spheres. For example, because of separation of powers, Congress makes the laws; but due to checks and balances, the president can veto them, and the courts can rule them unconstitutional. In these ways, all three branches are involved in legislating. One political scientist calls ours "a government of separated institutions competing for shared powers."[37]

With federalism, separation of powers, and checks and balances, the Founders expected conflict. They invited the parts of government to struggle against each other to limit any part's ability to dominate the rest. The Founders hoped for "balanced government." The na-

tional and state governments would represent different interests, and the branches within the national government would represent different interests. The House would represent the "common" people and the large states; the Senate, the wealthy people and the small states; the president, all the people; and the Supreme Court, the Constitution. The parts of government would have to compromise to get anything accomplished. Although each part would struggle for more power, it could not accumulate enough to dominate the others. Eventually, it would have to compromise and accept policies that would be in the interest of all of the parts and their constituencies. Paradoxically, then, the Founders expected narrow conflict to produce broader harmony.

Undemocratic Features

The Founders left undemocratic features in the Constitution that later generations would have to deal with.[38] In various ways, the Founders denied the people the right to participate in their government and denied some groups equal treatment by their government. As explained, the Constitution did not forbid slavery or even permit Congress to forbid it for over two decades. In fact, the Three-Fifths Compromise institutionalized slavery and increased the political power of slaveholders. Further, the Constitution did not guarantee the right to vote, allowing states to exclude African Americans, Native Americans, other minorities, and women. The Founders established the Electoral College to prevent the people from choosing the president. Even with the advent of popular election of the electors, the Electoral College still allows the election of a presidential candidate who did not receive the most popular votes. The Founders stipulated that state legislatures would choose the senators to prevent the people from choosing them. By giving each state two seats in the Senate, the Founders gave disproportionate power to the people who happen to live in small states (as explained in the box "The Undemocratic Senate on page 38").

The Founders included these features partly because of their need for political compromise and partly because of their view that the people could not be trusted. The people were seen as an unruly mob threatening stable, orderly government. As later history would show, however, the Founders exaggerated the dangers of popular majorities. When Americans became more egalitarian in the decades following the adoption of the Constitution, they demanded a greater role for the average person. One political scientist concluded that if the Constitution had been written in 1820 instead of 1787, it would have been a very different, and more democratic, document.[39]

Motives of the Founders

To understand the Constitution better, it is useful to consider the motives of the Founders. Were they selfless patriots, sharing their wisdom and experience? Or were they selfish property owners, protecting their interests?

First consider the people who migrated to America. Some came for religious reasons. Their religious beliefs put them at odds with many people in their native country. They were denied privileges or penalized or, occasionally, persecuted. Usually they were adherents of Protestant sects rather than members of established churches like the Church of England or the Roman Catholic church. As such, they were more suspicious of governmental authority and religious authority than those who remained in the Old World. They were "runaways from authority."[40] Others came for economic reasons. Whether poor or well-to-do, they saw America as the land of economic opportunity. They sought to improve their status, acquiring property and perhaps even becoming wealthy. Although they were not as suspicious of established authority, they were opposed to active government. More government meant more taxes, which meant less money in their pockets. So both groups of people who migrated to America had reasons to prefer limited government.[41] They would pass down their beliefs to their descendants.

Now consider the philosophical ideas, political experience, and economic interests that more directly influenced the Founders.

Philosophical Ideas

The Founders were well-educated intellectuals who incorporated philosophical ideas into the Constitution. At a time when the average person did not dream of going

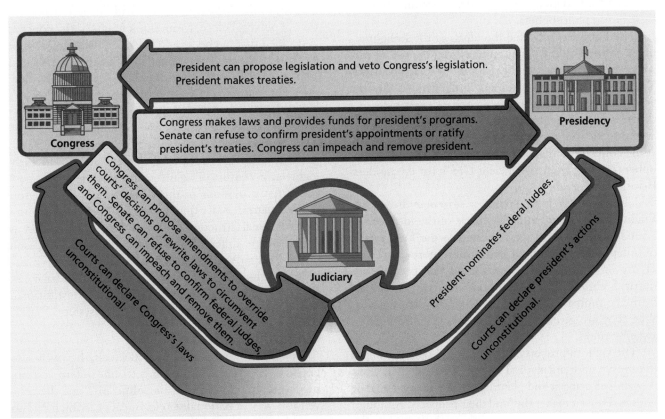

FIGURE 2 ■ Checks and Balances *Most of the major checks and balances between the three branches are explicit in the Constitution, although some are not. For example, the courts' power to declare congressional laws or presidential actions unconstitutional—their power of "judicial review"—is not mentioned.*

"Religious freedom is my immediate goal, but my long-range plan is to go into real estate."

to college, a majority of the Founders were college graduates. As learned men, they shared a common library of writers and philosophers.

The Founders reflected the ideals of the Enlightenment, a pattern of thought emphasizing the use of reason, rather than tradition or religion, to solve problems. They studied past governments to determine why the governments had failed in the hope that they could apply these lessons to the present.

From all accounts, they engaged in a level of debate at the convention that was rare in politics, citing philosophers ranging from the ancient Greeks to the modern British and French.

The views of John Locke, a seventeenth-century English philosopher, underlay many of the ideas of the Founders. In fact, his views permeate the Declaration of Independence and the Constitution more than those of any other person. Locke believed that people have **natural rights.** These rights are inherent; they exist from the moment people are born. They are unalienable; they are given by God, so they cannot be taken away by rulers.

The right to property, according to Locke, is one of the most important natural rights. When people work the land, clearing it and planting it, they mix their labor with it. This act makes the land their property. Although Americans had gotten their land through theft from the Indians or through luck from their ancestors (who had

gotten it for little or nothing by a royal grant in colonial times), in this view the important thing is what they do with their land. Farmers start with dirt and grasses and trees, and they create productive land. Some, due to greater effort or better luck, accumulate more property and create more wealth than others. Thus the right to property results in significant inequality of wealth. Yet Locke thought it would lead to greater productivity for society.[42] This view of property appealed to Americans, who saw such abundant land in the new country.

In addition to his views on the rights of the people, Locke wrote about the relationship between the people and their government. He maintained that the people come together to form a government through a **social contract**—an implied agreement between the people and their government—that establishes a **limited government,** strong enough to protect their rights but not so strong as to threaten these rights. This government should not act without the consent of the governed. To make its decisions, this government should follow majority rule. (Locke never resolved the conflict between majority rule and natural rights—that is, between majority rule and the rights for those who disagree with the majority.)

The views of Charles de Montesquieu, an eighteenth-century French philosopher, also influenced the debate at the convention and the provisions of the Constitution. Although others had suggested separation of powers before, Montesquieu refined the concept and added that of checks and balances. Referring to him as "the celebrated Montesquieu," the Founders cited him more than any other thinker.[43] (Presumably, they cited him more than Locke because by this time Locke's views had so permeated American society that the Founders considered them just "common sense."[44])

The principles of the system of mechanics formulated by Isaac Newton, a late seventeenth- and early eighteenth-century English mathematician, also pervaded the provisions of the Constitution. As Newton viewed nature as a machine, so the Founders saw the constitutional structure as a machine, with different parts having different functions and balancing each other. Newton's principle of action and reaction is manifested in the Founders' system of checks and balances. Both the natural environment and the constitutional structure were viewed as self-regulating systems.[45]

Political Experience

Although the Founders were intellectuals, they were also practical politicians. According to one interpretation, they were "superb democratic politicians," and the convention was "a nationalist reform caucus which had to operate with great delicacy and skill in a political cosmos full of enemies."[46]

The Founders brought extensive political experience to the convention: eight had signed the Declaration of Independence; thirty-nine had served in Congress; seven had been governors; many had held other state offices; some had helped write their state constitutions. The framers drew on this experience. For example, while they cited Montesquieu in discussing separation of powers, they also referred to the experience of colonial and state governments that already had some separation of powers.[47]

As practical politicians, "no matter what their private dreams might be, they had to take home an acceptable package and defend it—and their own political futures—against predictable attack."[48] So they compromised the difficult issues and ducked the stickiest ones. Ultimately, they pieced together a document that allowed each delegate to return home and announce that his state had won something.

Economic Interests

Although the Founders were intellectuals and practical politicians, they also represented an elite that sought to protect its property from the masses. The delegates to the Constitutional Convention were an elite. They included prosperous planters, manufacturers, shippers, and lawyers. About one-third were slave owners. Most came from families of prominence and married into other families of prominence. Not all were wealthy, but most were at least well-to-do. Only one, a delegate from Georgia, was a yeoman farmer like most men in the country. In short, "this was a convention of the well-bred, the well-fed, the well-read, and the well-wed."[49]

The Founders championed the right to property. The promise of land and perhaps riches enticed most immigrants to come to America.[50] A desire for freedom from arbitrary taxes and trade restrictions spurred some colonists to fight in the Revolution.[51] And the inability of the government under the Articles of Confederation to provide a healthy economy prompted the Founders

to convene the Constitutional Convention. They apparently agreed with Madison that "the first object of government" is to protect property.[52]

They worried that a democratic government, responding to popular pressures, might appropriate their property or impose high taxes to help less wealthy people. They wanted a government that could resist such populism. Yet the Founders' emphasis on property was not as elitist as it might seem. Land was plentiful, and with westward expansion, even more would be available. Already most men were middle-class farmers who owned some property. Many who owned no property could foresee the day when they would, so most wanted to protect property.

The Founders diverged from the farmers in their vision to create a national commercial economy in place of the small-scale agricultural economy. Toward this end, the Founders desired to protect other property in addition to land, such as wealth and credit. Of the fifty-five delegates, forty were owners of government bonds that had depreciated under the Articles, and twenty-four were moneylenders.[53] So the delegates included provisions to protect commerce, including imports and exports, contracts, and debts, and provisions to regulate currency, bankruptcy, and taxes.[54] (See the box "Constitutional Provisions Protecting Property" on the next page).

Political scientists and historians disagree about which of these three influences on the Founders—philosophical, political, or economic—was most important. Actually, the influences are difficult to separate because they reinforce each other; the framers' ideas point to the same sort of constitution that their political experience and economic interests do.[55]

Ratification of the Constitution

The Constitution specified that ratification would occur through conventions in the states and that the document would take effect with the approval of just nine states. These procedures were illegal. According to the Articles of Confederation, which was still in effect, any changes had to be approved by all thirteen states. However, the framers feared that the Constitution would not be supported in some states.

Indeed, ratification was uncertain. Many people opposed the Constitution, and a lively campaign against it appeared in newspapers, pamphlets, and mass meetings.

Knowing opponents would charge them with setting up a national government to dominate the state governments, those who supported the Constitution ingeniously adopted the name **Federalists** to emphasize a real division of power between the national and state governments. They dubbed their opponents

© Tom Myer, San Francisco Chronicle.

Constitutional Provisions Protecting Property

Numerous constitutional provisions, some obvious and others not, were designed to protect property:

Provision	Effect
"The Times, Places and Manner of holding Elections for Senators and Representatives, shall be prescribed in each State by the Legislature thereof."	Allows states to set property qualifications to vote.
"The Congress shall have Power . . . To coin Money."	Centralizes currency.
"No State shall . . . emit bills of credit."	Prevents states from printing paper money.
"Congress shall have Power . . . To establish uniform Laws on the subject of Bankruptcies."	Prevents states from relieving debtors of the obligation to pay.
"The Congress shall have Power . . . To regulate Commerce . . . among the several States."	Centralizes commerce regulation and thereby establishes a national economy.
"No State shall . . . pass any . . . Law impairing the Obligation of Contracts."	Prevents states from relieving debtors of the obligation to pay and thereby establishes stable business arrangements.
"The United States shall guarantee to every State [protection] against domestic Violence."	Protects states from debtor uprisings.
"The Congress shall have Power . . . To provide for calling forth the Militia to execute the Laws of the Union, suppress insurrections."	Protects creditors from debtor uprisings.

Anti-Federalists to imply that their opponents did not want a division of power between the governments. (See the box "The *Federalist Papers*.")

The Anti-Federalists faulted the Constitution for lacking a bill of rights. The Constitution did contain some protection for individual rights, such as the provision that the writ of habeas corpus, which protects against arbitrary arrest and detention, cannot be suspended except during rebellion or invasion, and the provision that a criminal defendant has a right to a jury trial. But the framers made no effort to include most rights that the people believed they had because most states already included a bill of rights in their constitutions. The framers also thought that by fragmenting power, no branch could become strong enough to deny individual rights. Yet critics demanded provisions protecting various rights of criminal defendants and freedom of the press. In response, the Federalists promised to propose amendments guaranteeing these rights as soon as the government began.

The Anti-Federalists also criticized the Constitution for other reasons. Localists at heart, they were wary of entrusting power to officials far away. They correctly claimed that republics historically worked only in small geographical areas where the population was more homogeneous and the officials were closer to the people. They worried that the central government, to function effectively, would accumulate too much power and the presidency would become a monarchy or Congress an aristocracy. One delegate to the Massachusetts convention blasted the Federalists:

These lawyers, and men of learning and moneyed men, that talk so finely, and gloss over matters so smoothly, to make us poor illiterate people swallow down the pill, expect to get into Congress themselves; they expect to . . . get all the power and all the money into their own hands, and then they will swallow up all us little folks . . . just as the whale swallowed up Jonah![56]

But the Anti-Federalists had no alternative plan. They were divided; some wanted to amend the Articles of Confederation, while others wanted to reject both the Articles and the Constitution in favor of some yet undetermined form of government. Their lack of unity on an alternative was instrumental in their inability to win support.[57]

Within six months, nine states had ratified the new Constitution, allowing the new government, with George Washington as president, to begin in 1788. Within one year, the four remaining states approved the Constitution.

Although this process might seem unremarkable today, this marked the first time that a nation had proposed a new government and then asked the people to approve or reject it. And the process occurred with little violence or coercion. As a constitutional historian observed, "The losers were not jailed, hanged, or politically disabled. They did not boycott, take up arms, or go into exile. They continued, as before, to be full and free citizens, but now living in a new republic."[58]

Out of the great debate over ratification came a series of essays considered the premier example of American political philosophy. Known collectively as *The Federalist Papers*, these essays were written by Alexander Hamilton, James Madison, and John Jay. At the urging of Hamilton,[1] the authors wrote eighty-five essays that appeared in New York newspapers during the ratification debates there. The authors tried to convince delegates to the convention to vote for ratification.

In the fashion of the time, the essays were published anonymously—using the pseudonym "Publius" (Latin for "Public Man"). The papers were so unified in their language and arguments that few of the authors' contemporaries could identify whose pen was at work. Given the debates and compromises at the Constitutional Convention, one political scientist speculated that the framers who read the essays "must have discovered with some surprise what a coherent and well-thought-out document they had prepared."[2]

Despite the unity of the papers, political scientists have identified the authors of individual ones. Hamilton wrote most of those describing the defects of the Articles of Confederation, Madison most of those explaining the structure of the new government, including the famous essays 10 and 51 (reprinted at the back of this book). Before he fell ill, Jay, who was secretary of foreign affairs at the time, wrote a few concerning foreign policy.

Actually, there is little evidence that the essays swayed any of the delegates. Yet they have endured because readers see them as an original source of political thinking, as a useful guide to the intentions of the framers, and because judges consult them when they interpret various provisions of the Constitution.

1. Although Hamilton worried that the Constitution would not establish a strong enough government—he called it "a frail and worthless fabric"—he thought it was preferable to the Articles, which he despised. Thus he saw his role like that of "a lawyer obliged to mount his most brilliant defense on behalf of a dubious client." Joseph J. Ellis, "The Big Man," *New Yorker,* October 29, 2001, 80.
2. John P. Roche, ed., *Origins of American Political Thought* (New York: Harper & Row, 1967), 163.

Changing the Constitution

The framers expected their document to last; Madison wrote, "We have framed a constitution that will probably be still around when there are 196 million people."[59] Yet because the framers realized it would need some changes, they drafted a Constitution that can be changed either formally by amendment or informally by judicial interpretation or political practice. In doing so, they left a legacy for later governments. "The example of changing a Constitution, by assembling the wise men of the state, instead of assembling armies," Jefferson noted, "will be worth as much to the world as the former examples we had given them."[60]

By Constitutional Amendment

That the Articles of Confederation could be amended only by a unanimous vote of the states posed an almost insurmountable barrier to any change at all. The framers of the Constitution made sure that this experience would not repeat itself. Yet they did not make amendment easy; the procedures, while not requiring unanimity, do require widespread agreement. More than nine thousand amendments have been proposed in Congress, but only twenty-seven (including the ten in the Bill of Rights) have been adopted.[61]

Procedures The procedures for amendment entail action by both the national government and the state governments. Amendments can be proposed in either of two ways: by a two-thirds vote of both houses of Congress or by a national convention called by Congress at the request of two-thirds of the state legislatures. Congress then specifies which way amendments must be ratified—either by three-fourths of the state legislatures or by ratifying conventions in three-fourths of the states. Among these avenues, the usual route has been proposal by Congress and ratification by state legislatures.

Amendments In the first Congress under the Constitution, the Federalists fulfilled their promise to support a bill of rights. Madison drafted twelve amendments, Congress proposed them, and the states ratified ten of them in 1791. This **Bill of Rights** includes freedom of expression and conviction—speech, press, assembly, and religion (First Amendment). It also includes numerous rights for those accused of crimes—protection against unreasonable searches and seizures (Fourth), protection against compulsory self-incrimination (Fifth), guarantee of due process of law (Fifth), the right to counsel and a jury trial in criminal cases (Sixth), and protection against excessive bail and fines and against cruel and unusual punishment (Eighth). It also includes the right to a jury trial in civil cases (Seventh). (For examination of a current issue involving the Fifth Amendment, see the box "Interrogating Terrorists" on the following page).

The war on terrorism, like past wars, raises questions about the viability of constitutional rights. Can we wage effective war and still maintain civil liberties? Americans have accepted restricted access to government buildings and heightened screening at airports, but these policies are more of an inconvenience than a threat to civil liberties. Would Americans accept other policies that would curtail civil liberties? Should they?

Consider the problem of interrogating terrorist suspects. Under our law, when police interrogate criminal suspects, they must advise the suspects of their rights to remain silent and to have legal counsel, and they must stop the questioning whenever the suspects express a desire to exercise these rights. Any statements by the suspects are supposed to be voluntary rather than coerced. Although routine police interrogation of criminal suspects is often successful even with these restrictions (as Chapter 14 explains), interrogation of terrorist suspects, especially if they are religious extremists, is more difficult. Terrorists are committed to their cause and steeled to their death, often seeking "martyrdom." They are usually well educated, physically fit, and emotionally sturdy. They usually live without the emotional attachments and material comforts that others enjoy, so they are not tempted by such inducements as money, jobs, lenient sentences, and new identities in the witness protection program.

Some people have suggested torture to make them talk.[1] (One law professor has called for "torture warrants," akin to search warrants.) Although torture is repulsive, is it justified if there is a "ticking time bomb" and lives can be saved? Is it justified if there is only a possible future attack that might be thwarted? Or is it justified in every scenario involving potential terrorists?

Torture, which is generally defined as acts that intentionally inflict "severe pain or suffering, whether physical or mental," is contrary to international law.[2] It is also contrary to our standards of human dignity. In addition to legal and philosophical objections to torture, its use poses practical problems. Officials might get the wrong person. Officials might force a suspect to say what they want to hear even if it is not true. Then they have unreliable information. Officials might use brutal methods that damage or kill a suspect. In fact, American interrogators killed at least three men while questioning them in Afghanistan and Iraq.[3]

American officials deny that they use torture. They admit instead to using what they call "stress and duress" or what others call "torture lite." Prisoners may be locked, naked and wet, in a cold cubicle in which they cannot stand, sit, or lie comfortably. They have to kneel or squat. They might be hooded to keep them in the dark and disoriented. Or they might be subjected to bright lights and loud noise—reportedly a combination of heavy metal music and the theme songs from kids' shows, such as the "Barney" song—to keep them awake. If they happen to doze, they will be awakened roughly. They may be beaten. They will be fed irregularly. With their food, they may be drugged, perhaps with a mixture of marijuana and sodium pentothal ("truth serum") to lower their inhibitions and methamphetamines to make them talk so fast that they cannot think to lie. Then, after being "softened up," they will be interrogated.

This "stress and duress" process, according to an American official, is "not pulling out fingernails, but it's pretty brutal."[4] Some of these techniques violate international law, but the Bush administration claims they do not constitute torture. In fact, after the 9/11 attacks, the administration began secretly redefining torture and revising our policy toward torture to authorize methods that had not been allowed before.[5]

For terrorist suspects considered especially important, the United States has arranged with other countries to interrogate the prisoners for us. In a procedure called "rendition," the United States seizes suspects in foreign countries and whisks them away to other countries whose intelligence services have ties with the Central Intelligence Agency (CIA). Islamic extremists have been seized from countries in Africa, Asia, and the Balkans and taken to countries such as Egypt, Jordan, Morocco, Saudi Arabia, and Syria, where torture is practiced. "We don't kick the [expletive] out of them," an American official said. "We send them to other countries so *they* can kick the [expletive] out of them."[6] The transfers have been made in secret, using unmarked planes in remote corners of airports, at night. The transfers have ignored legal formalities, such as extradition procedures, and have even defied national laws. Six suspects were taken from Bosnia even though the Bosnian supreme court had ordered them released. The secrecy reduces court battles and minimizes the publicity that could tip off suspects' comrades or inflame public opinion, especially where the government feels threatened by rebellious groups with numerous sympathizers. An official in Indonesia, which has the world's largest Muslim population, said, "We can't be seen cooperating too closely with the United States."[7] Although the United States first arranged for rendition in 1993, since September 11, 2001, according to one American official, it is happening "all the time" now.[8]

So what should the United States do when officials want to interrogate terrorist suspects? Follow the procedures that American police use on criminal

Secretary of Defense Donald Rumsfeld authorized the use of military dogs to scare Iraqi prisoners at the Abu Ghraib prison outside Baghdad. This photo was taken by an American soldier. The next photo, among the photos taken by the soldier, shows the prisoner on the ground, bleeding from dog bites.

suspects? Use "stress and duress" or "torture lite" techniques? Practice torture itself? Or arrange for rendition so that other countries will engage in torture for us?

Should we forsake our principles and violate international law? Although the strictures of international law might seem binding at times, they are in our self-interest in the long run. If we follow international law, it is more likely that other countries will feel obligated to follow it when they capture our soldiers. If we forsake our principles and violate international law, would we take a step backward in the progress of Western civilization? Would we risk becoming like the people who devalue life and disregard law, who are our enemies? Or are these concerns beside the point during war? Are extreme methods justified during war? Supreme Court Justice Robert Jackson once observed that "the Constitution is not a suicide pact."[9] He could have said the same about international law.

But if extreme methods are justified during war, when is a war like the war on terrorism over? The terrorists are not a formal army and do not represent a particular country. They do not have a single leader. Terrorist attacks, by one group or another, are likely to continue for many years. Once we start, when will we stop?

And once we use these methods against suspected terrorists, will we extend them to other enemies? Already, the "stress and duress" and "torture lite" techniques first used against suspected terrorists have been used against suspected insurgents in Iraq who have no connection to al-Qaeda. In fact, many arrestees have no connection to Iraqi insurgents either. Whenever an attack occurs, American soldiers round up the men in the area, subject them all to rough interrogation, and try to weed out the ones who are innocent.[10] Intelligence officers have estimated that 70 to 90 percent of the men who have been arrested and interrogated have been in-

nocent.[11] Thus, thousands have been subjected to "stress and duress" and "torture lite" techniques. Once the techniques were practiced elsewhere, the military could not resist employing them in Iraq.

1. An especially useful article, which provided some information for this box, is Mark Bowden, "The Dark Art of Interrogation," *Atlantic Monthly,* October 2003, 51–76.
2. According to the United Nations Convention against Torture. Torture violates both treaty law, to which the United States is a party, and customary law, which is binding on all states. A permanent international criminal court to try persons for war crimes was established in 2002. Although President George W. Bush unsigned the treaty that President Clinton had signed to bind the United States to this court, Americans accused of committing war crimes in countries that are signatories can be tried by this court. In Iraq, the administration authorized the CIA and the military to keep "dozens" of detainees, and "perhaps up to 100" of them, off the official rosters to hide them from International Red Cross inspectors. These "ghost detainees" could then be interrogated without any monitoring. This practice also violates international law. Eric Schmitt and Douglas Jehl, "Prison Scandal: Army Says C.I.A. Hid More Iraqis Than It Claimed," *New York Times*, September 10, 2004; "A Failure of Accountability," *Washington Post National Weekly Edition*, September 6–12, 2004, 24.
3. Bowden, "Dark Art," 56.
4. Jodie Morse, "How Do We Make Him Talk?" *Time,* April 15, 2002, 92.
5. Amanda Ripley, "Redefining Torture," *Time,* June 21, 2004, 49–50; Neil A. Lewis and Eric Schmitt, "Lawyers Decided Bans on Torture Didn't Bind Bush," *New York Times,* June 8, 2004, 1.
6. Dana Priest and Barton Gellman, "U.S. Decries Abuse but Defends Interrogations; 'Stress and Duress' Tactics Used on Terrorism Suspects Held in Secret Overseas Facilities," *Washington Post,* December 26, 2002, A1.
7. Rajiv Chandrasekaran and Peter Finn, "Interrogating Terrorist Suspects 'in a Way We Can't Do on U.S. Soil,'" *Washington Post,* March 12, 2002, A1.
8. Ibid.
9. This summary of Justice Jackson's observation has become a popular catchphrase. Jackson's actual words, written in his dissent to the Supreme Court decision in *Terminiello* v. *City of Chicago* (337 U.S. 1, 4–5, 1949), were as follows: "There is danger that, if the court does not temper its doctrinaire logic with a little practical wisdom, it will convert the constitutional Bill of Rights into a suicide pact."
10. Marketplace," NPR, May 5, 2004.
11. Rajiv Chandrasekaran and Scott Wilson, "Many in Prison in Error," *Lincoln Journal Star (Washington Post)*, May 11, 2004.

Two amendments in the Bill of Rights grew out of the colonial experience with Great Britain—the right to bear arms to form a militia (Second) and the right not to have soldiers quartered in homes during peacetime (Third). The Bill of Rights also includes two general amendments—a statement that the listing of these rights does not mean these are the only ones people have (Ninth) and a statement that the powers not given to the national government are reserved to the states (Tenth).

Among the other seventeen amendments to the Constitution, the strongest theme is the expansion of citizenship rights:[62]

- Abolition of slavery (Thirteenth, 1865)
- Equal protection, due process of law (Fourteenth, 1868)
- Right to vote for black men (Fifteenth, 1870)
- Direct election of senators (Seventeenth, 1913)
- Right to vote for women (Nineteenth, 1920)
- Right to vote in presidential elections for District of Columbia residents (Twenty-third, 1960)
- Abolition of poll tax in federal elections (Twenty-fourth, 1964)
- Right to vote for persons eighteen and older (Twenty-sixth, 1971)

In recent decades, two amendments proposed by Congress were not ratified by the states. One would have provided equal rights for women (this amendment is discussed in Chapter 15), and the other would have given congressional representation to the District of Columbia, as though it were a state.

These and other recent amendments have had time limits for ratification—usually seven years—set by Congress. But an amendment preventing members of Congress from giving themselves a midterm pay raise, written by Madison and passed by Congress in 1789, had no time limit. When Michigan ratified it in 1992, it reached the three-fourths mark and became the Twenty-seventh Amendment.

Although the Constitution expressly provides for change by amendment, its ambiguity about some subjects and silence about others virtually guarantee change by interpretation and practice as well.

By Judicial Interpretation

If there is disagreement about what the Constitution means, who is to interpret it? Although the Constitution does not say, the judicial branch has taken on this role. To decide disputes before them, the courts must determine what the relevant provisions of the Constitution mean. By saying that the provisions mean one thing rather than another, the courts can, in effect, change the Constitution. Woodrow Wilson called the Supreme Court "a constitutional convention in continuous session." The Court has interpreted the Constitution in ways that bring about the same results as new amendments. (Chapters 13, 14, and 15 provide many examples.)

By Political Practice

Political practice has accounted for some very important changes. These include the rise of political parties and the demise of the Electoral College as an independent body. They also include the development of the cabinet to advise the president and the development of the committee system to operate the two houses of Congress. (Chapters 7, 8, and 10 explain these changes.)

The Founders would be surprised to learn that only seventeen amendments, aside from the Bill of Rights, have been adopted in over two hundred years. In part this is due to their wisdom, but in part it is due to changes in judicial interpretation and political practice, which have combined to create a "living Constitution."

Impact of the Civil War and the Great Depression

The two most significant events in the history of the United States since its founding were the Civil War in the 1860s and the Great Depression in the 1930s. These two events had such an important impact on the Constitution that it would be inadequate, even inaccurate, for us to refer only to the Founders when we explain the Constitution.[63]

Here we will briefly sketch the impact of the Civil War and the Great Depression on the Constitution. Later chapters will further elaborate on these developments.

The Civil War and Reconstruction

The Civil War, from 1861 through 1865, and Reconstruction, from the end of the war through 1876, constituted a "second American Revolution."[64] After all the bullets and bayonets, the bloodletting and scorched earth, more than six hundred thousand soldiers lay in graves—one of every seven men between the ages of fifteen and thirty—and parts of the South lay in waste. The North's victory preserved the Union, but it did far more than this: it also altered the Constitution—in the minds of the people and in formal amendments to the document.

Although the North's leader, President Abraham Lincoln, a Republican, held views that would be considered racist today (he believed that black people were inherently inferior and that they should emigrate from

This view of the remains of Richmond, Virginia, conveys the destructiveness of the Civil War.

the United States),[65] he despised slavery because it deprived persons of their unalienable rights to life, liberty, and the pursuit of happiness promised by the Declaration of Independence. But efforts to abolish slavery were constrained by the political climate, and Lincoln was a practical politician. Before the war, he was willing to allow slavery to continue in the southern states, though not to extend into any new state, and he was concerned only to preserve the Union. But after one year of the war, he decided that these goals were too limited.[66] Abolitionist sentiment was spreading in the North, providing Lincoln with the opportunity to lead efforts to abolish slavery as well as preserve the Union. In the process, he helped reinvent America.

The Emancipation Proclamation

The **Emancipation Proclamation** offered the promise of a new constitution. President Lincoln announced it in September 1862 and ordered it to take effect in January 1863. The document proclaimed that the slaves "shall be . . . forever free" in the Confederate states where the Union army was not in control. Its language limited its sweep, for it exempted those parts of the Confederate states where the Union army was in control and also the slave states that remained loyal to the Union (Delaware, Kentucky, Maryland, and Missouri).

And despite its language, it could not be enforced in the parts of the Confederate states where the Union army was not in control. Thus as a legal document, the proclamation was problematic. However, as a symbolic measure, it was successful. The proclamation made clear that the war was not just to preserve the Union anymore but to abolish slavery as well. The announcement captured people's imagination. Between the announcement and the date it was to take effect, the proclamation created so much suspense, according to one historian, that "it had assumed the significance of one of the great documents of all times."[67] When slaves heard about it, many left their plantations, and some joined the Union army. The result sowed confusion in the South and denied a reliable labor force for the region.[68]

The Gettysburg Address

President Lincoln's **Gettysburg Address** became the preamble of the new constitution.[69] The battle at Gettysburg, Pennsylvania, in 1863, was a Union victory and the turning point in the Civil War. Lincoln was invited to deliver "a few appropriate remarks" during the dedication of the battlefield where many had fallen. Lincoln was not the main speaker, and his speech was not long. While the main speaker took two hours, explaining the battle and reciting the names of the leaders and even some of their soldiers, Lincoln took two minutes to give a 268-word speech. (He spoke so briefly that the photographer, with his clumsy equipment and its slow exposure, failed to get a single photograph.) Lincoln used the occasion to advance his ideal of equality.

He began: "Four score and seven [eighty-seven] years ago our fathers brought forth on this continent a new nation, conceived in liberty and dedicated to the proposition that all men are created equal." Here Lincoln referred not to the Constitution of 1787 but to the Declaration of Independence of 1776. For Lincoln, the Constitution had abandoned the principle of equality that the Declaration had promised. He sought to resurrect this principle.

Lincoln did not mention slavery or the Emancipation Proclamation, which were divisive. A shrewd politician, he wanted people to focus on the Declaration, which was revered.

Lincoln concluded by addressing "the great task remaining before us . . . that we here highly resolve that these dead shall not have died in vain, that this nation, under God, shall have a new birth of freedom, and that government of the people, by the people, for the people shall not perish from the earth." This phrase, which Lincoln made famous, was borrowed from a speaker at an antislavery convention.[70] It depicted a government elected by all the people, to serve all the people.[71] Lincoln's conclusion reinforced his introduction; both emphasized equality.

Although his speech was brief, Lincoln used the word *nation* five times, including the phrase "a new nation" once. His purpose was not to encourage support for the Union but to urge people to think of the nation as a whole, its identity now forged in a bloody war of brother against brother, rather than as simply a collection of individual states with their own interests.[72]

Thus the president essentially added the Declaration's promise of equality to the Constitution, and he substituted his vision of a unified nation for the Founders' precarious arrangement of a balance of power between the nation and the states. According to one historian, "He performed one of the most daring acts of open-air sleight-of-hand ever witnessed by the unsuspecting. . . . The crowd departed with a new thing in its ideological luggage, that new constitution Lincoln had substituted for the one they brought with them."[73]

The Gettysburg Address was heard by an audience of perhaps fifteen thousand, but its language was spread through word of mouth and newspapers and eventually by politicians and teachers. It was read and repeated, and sometimes memorized, by generations of schoolchildren. Although some critics at the time perceived what Lincoln was attempting—the *Chicago Times* quoted the Constitution to the president and charged him with betraying the document he swore to uphold—most citizens came to accept Lincoln's addition. His speech, which has been called "the best political address" in the country's history, thus became "the secular prayer of the postbellum American Republic."[74] (The speech is reprinted in Appendix E at the back of this book.)

The Reconstruction Amendments

If the Gettysburg Address became the preamble of the new constitution, the **Reconstruction Amendments** became its body. These three amendments, adopted from 1865 through 1870, began to implement the promise of equality and the vision of a unified nation rather than a collection of individual states.

The Thirteenth Amendment abolished slavery, essentially constitutionalizing the Emancipation Proclamation. This amendment focused on the wrongs committed by private persons. As such, it reflected a new perspective toward government—not as a threat to people's liberties, as in the original Constitution and the Bill of Rights, but as a guarantor of people's freedom. Whereas the original Constitution and the Bill of Rights are preoccupied with freedom from government, the Thirteenth Amendment is concerned with freedom from exploitation by other persons.

The Fourteenth Amendment declared that all persons born or naturalized in the United States are citizens, overturning the Supreme Court's ruling before the Civil War that blacks, whether slave or free, could not be citizens.[75] The Fourteenth Amendment also included the equal protection clause, which requires states to treat persons equally, and the due process clause, which requires states to treat persons fairly. The equal protection clause would become the primary legal means to end discrimination, and the due process clause would become the primary legal means to give persons the full benefit of the Bill of Rights.[76] This amendment, one legal scholar observes, was "a revolutionary change. The states were no longer the autonomous sovereigns that they thought they were when they claimed the right of secession. They were now, in fact, servants of their people. [They] existed to guarantee due process and equal justice for all."[77]

The Fifteenth Amendment extended the right to vote to blacks. Because women could not vote at the time, the amendment essentially provided the right to vote to black men. This amendment initiated a trend of democratizing the Constitution by extending the right to vote; five later amendments expanded that right even further.

As important as the substantive content of these amendments was a procedural provision authorizing Congress to enforce them. ("Congress shall have power to enforce this article by appropriate legislation.") That is, the amendments gave Congress broad power, beyond that granted in the original Constitution, to pass new laws to implement the amendments. Consequently, the federal government would come to oversee and even intervene in the policies of state and local governments to make sure that these governments did not disregard the guarantees of the amendments. These amendments thus marked the start of a trend of federalizing the Constitution by increasing the power of Congress.[78] Five later amendments also included this provision.

President Lincoln initiated the Thirteenth Amendment, and the Radical Republicans who controlled Congress after Lincoln's assassination initiated the Fourteenth and Fifteenth Amendments. There was a passionate national debate. Ultimately, the public supported the amendments. Although most Americans, northerners as well as southerners, were racists, many were inspired by Lincoln or propelled by the war to support greater equality. They elected and reelected supporters of the amendments to Congress.[79]

The net results of the Reconstruction Amendments were to promote equality and to shift power from the states to the federal government.

During Reconstruction, the Union army occupied the South and enforced the amendments and congressional laws implementing them. But white southerners resisted, and eventually white northerners grew weary of the struggle. At the same time, there was a desire for healing between the two regions and lingering feelings for continuity with the past. In 1876, the two national political parties, the Democrats and the Republicans, struck a deal to withdraw the Union army and to allow the southern states to govern themselves again. The entrenched attitudes of white southerners prompted them to establish segregation and discrimination in place of slavery, thus preventing blacks from enjoying their new rights. As a result, the new constitution would not really be enforced until the 1950s and 1960s, when the civil rights movement, Supreme Court rulings, presidential initiatives, and congressional acts would converge to give effect to the ideal of racial equality. In the meantime, the new constitution would lay, in our collective conscious, as an unfulfilled promise, occasionally emerging to foster greater equality.[80]

The Great Depression and the New Deal

The Great Depression began when the stock market crashed in 1929. Wealthy people lost their investments, and business activity declined. Ordinary people lost their jobs, with a quarter of them becoming unemployed. Investors lost their savings when many banks collapsed. President Franklin Roosevelt, a Democrat, was elected in 1932. He initiated an ambitious program, heralded as "a new deal for the American people," to stimulate the economy and to help the people who were

suffering. His program and his administration came to be known as the **New Deal.**

This era also altered the Constitution—not by formal amendments but through Supreme Court rulings and political practice. In the process, it changed the minds of the people.[81] As a result, we replaced our small, limited government, as envisioned by the Founders, with a big, activist government.

Supreme Court Rulings

In the late nineteenth and early twentieth centuries, a *laissez-faire* economic philosophy was popular in this country and was reflected in governmental policies. According to this philosophy, government should not interfere in the economy (*laissez-faire* is French for "leave it alone"). Although government could *aid* businesses, at least it should not *regulate* them.[82] People who believed this philosophy thought it would create a robust and efficient economy. The industrialization of the time, producing an array of new products for consumers and an increase in personal wealth for owners, seemed to confirm their expectations. But it also led to negative consequences, especially for employees, who were forced to labor in harsh, even dangerous, conditions for long hours and little pay. Many pressed government to address these problems. But when Congress and state legislatures passed laws to regulate child labor, maximum hours of work, and minimum wages for work, the Supreme Court, following the traditional philosophy, usually declared the laws unconstitutional. When Congress passed laws to implement President Roosevelt's recovery program, a majority of the Court often declared these laws unconstitutional as well. The impasse reached a climax in 1935 and 1936 when the Court invalidated twelve laws that had been proposed by the president and passed by Congress. The Court's resistance made clear that the New Deal reforms were not simply fine-tuning governmental policy toward the economy but were overhauling it.[83] In response to the Court's resistance, members of Congress introduced thirty-nine constitutional amendments to reverse the Court's rulings.

After Roosevelt was resoundingly reelected in 1936, intense pressure from the president, Congress, and the public prompted two justices who had voted against government regulation of business to switch sides and vote for such regulation in 1937.[84] One case clearly illustrates the Court's about-face. Farmers had produced crop surpluses, which drove down the prices. The government sought to reduce the surpluses in order to drive up the prices. One small farmer in Ohio was allowed by the Department of Agriculture, under a law passed by Congress, to plant eleven acres of wheat, but he chose to plant twenty-three acres. When he was cited for violating the law, he said that it should not apply to him because his farm was very small. He did not sell much

During the Depression, many people who lost their job lost their ability to put food on the table. Breadlines and soup kitchens were common. Here the unemployed wait for coffee and doughnuts at one of fifty-two relief kitchens in New York City in 1934.

of the wheat—his family and farm animals consumed most of it—so he said he did not affect market prices. But now, after the switch in 1937, the Court ruled unanimously against him.[85] Thus the Court allowed the government to extend its reach far beyond what was thought permissible just a few years before.

These transformative rulings created a "constitutional revolution."[86] They took the place of formal amendments to the Constitution, which were no longer necessary once the Court acquiesced to the policies of the president and Congress. As a result, government could regulate businesses when the public believed that regulation would be beneficial.

Political Practice

Before the Depression, Washington, D.C., had been "a sleepy southern town," in the eyes of reporters.[87] When Roosevelt took office, he was uncertain exactly what to do, but he was willing to experiment, and he did believe he had a mandate from the people, who had rejected the incumbent president, Herbert Hoover, and his administration. Roosevelt's personality and his ambitious ideas attracted many more people—hundreds of thousands of people—some simply relieved to find a job, but others excited to work for the government. These reformers brought new ideas, even radical ideas, that

would receive consideration and perhaps acceptance in the depths of the Depression. As federal efforts to provide relief and regulation spread throughout the country, many other people got jobs in federal offices outside Washington.

Within six years of Roosevelt's taking office, the number of federal workers in the District of Columbia had more than doubled,[88] the number of federal workers in the country had almost doubled, and the size of the federal budget had almost doubled.[89] In the process, the scope of the federal government had expanded tremendously. In short, we got big government and activist government in just a handful of years. These changes were so dramatic that one political scientist has said they created a "second American republic."[90]

Roosevelt's exuberance and experimentation had given people hope. As the country gradually pulled out of the Depression (though the country would not fully recover until the economic activity generated by World War II provided the final boost), people gave Roosevelt credit, electing him to an unprecedented four terms and returning Democrats to Congress to support him.[91] Ever since, Americans, albeit to different degrees, have expected the government to tackle society's problems. While sometimes mouthing the language of the Founders—for example, Thomas Jefferson's assertion,

"That government is best which governs least"—they have for the most part accepted the reality of the government that was expanded during the Depression.[92]

These changes during the Depression would lay the foundation for the government of the 1960s, which would promote the equality advanced during the Civil War. Without a powerful government pushing for change, the entrenched attitudes supporting segregation and discrimination would not have been overcome.

A Combination of Constitutions

As a result of President Lincoln and the Radical Republicans in the 1860s and 1870s and President Roosevelt and the New Deal Democrats in the 1930s and 1940s, our government is very different from the one the Founders bequeathed us.[93] Later generations of Americans made the eighteenth-century Constitution work in the nineteenth century and then they made it work in the twentieth century—by remaking that Constitution. Changes in the nineteenth century added the concept of equality and elevated the national government over the state governments. Changes in the twentieth century transformed a relatively small, limited government into a very large, activist government.

The original Constitution and the remade Constitution reflect competing visions. Should we emphasize liberty or equality? Should we demand individuals to solve their own problems or ask government to help them? Americans have not reconciled these visions. Sometimes we cling to the Founders' Constitution; other times we embrace the post–Civil War and post-Depression Constitution. In political debates, politicians, commentators, or citizens take positions without articulating, perhaps without even realizing, that these positions hark back to the Founders' Constitution, while opponents espouse views that rely on the post–Civil War and post-Depression Constitution. Thus the two constitutions coexist, sometimes uneasily, in our minds and in government policies.[94] As a consequence of our history, then, we actually have a combination of constitutions.

Conclusion: Does the Constitution Make the Government Responsive?

The Constitution established a government that has survived for over two centuries. In this document, the Founders set forth a mechanism to govern a vast territory and to provide for majority rule while allowing minority rights. This government has enabled more people to live in liberty and in prosperity than the people of any nation before or since.[95]

Americans have been grateful, venerating the Founders and embracing the Constitution as a secular Bible. Citizens consult it for guidance and cite it for support at the same time they debate the meaning of its provisions.

Despite its status as a political icon, however, the Constitution has been copied by few countries.[96] Although provisions of the Bill of Rights, such as freedom of speech, and of the Fourteenth Amendment, such as the equal protection clause, have been adopted by other countries,[97] the structure of our government has been less popular. Among the twenty-two democratic countries that have remained stable since 1950,[98] only five others have a federal system with significant power at the state level, only three others have a bicameral legislature with significant power in both houses, and only four others have one house with equal representation for the states regardless of their population. No others have a presidential system, and only two others have a judicial system that exercises judicial review of national legislation.[99] Our Constitution and governmental structure are seen more as a reflection of historical factors and political compromises than as a desirable form of government.

The Founders left important problems unresolved for succeeding generations. Most notable was slavery and the treatment of African Americans. Also troublesome was the uncertain relationship between the nation and the states. As we have seen, later Americans would have to resolve these problems, and in the process they, too, would contribute to the Constitution. Succeeding generations remade the Constitution most noticeably in the wake of the Civil War and the Great Depression, and they remade it more than many Americans realize.

But most of the original Constitution remains. We have kept the basic structure of government and the underlying fragmentation of power. The combination of federalism, separation of powers, and checks and balances, along with the unique method for choosing the president, make our government perhaps "the most intricate ever devised."[100] It is also perhaps "the most opaque . . . , confusing, and difficult to understand."[101]

The structure of government and fragmentation of power challenge citizens to hold their leaders accountable. If you disapprove of some policy, whom do you hold accountable in the next election—the president, the Senate, the House of Representatives, the unelected judges, or the state governments? Usually there is divided responsibility, resulting in less accountability.

Of course, the Founders sought a government that would be responsive to the people only to a limited extent. The Constitution created a republic, which granted the people the right to elect some representatives who would make their laws. In this way, the people had more say in government than people in other countries enjoyed at the time. Yet the Constitution was expected to filter the public's passions and purify their selfish desires. Thus the original Constitution allowed citizens to vote only for members of the House of Representatives—not for members of the Senate or the president. Further, it fragmented power, so a single group could not capture and control the entire government.

Various changes to our Constitution, whether by amendment, interpretation, or practice, have expanded opportunities for participation in government. But the changes have done little to modify the structure of our government or its fragmentation of power.

This configuration has prevented many abuses of power, although it has not always worked. During the Vietnam War and the Iraq war, for example, one branch —the presidency—exercised vast power while the others acquiesced.

This configuration has also provided the opportunity for one branch to pick up the slack when the others became sluggish. The overlapping of powers ensured by checks and balances allows every branch to act on virtually every issue it wants to. In the 1950s, President Eisenhower and Congress were reluctant to push for civil rights, but the Supreme Court did so by declaring segregation unconstitutional.

But the system's very advantage has become its primary disadvantage. In their efforts to fragment power so that no branch could accumulate too much, the Founders divided power to the point where the branches sometimes cannot wield enough. In their efforts to build a government that requires a national majority to act, they built one that allows a small minority to block action. This problem has become increasingly acute as society has become increasingly complex. Like a mechanical device that operates only when all of its parts function in harmony, the system moves only when there is consensus or compromise. Consensus is rare in a large, heterogeneous society; compromise is common, but it requires more time as well as the realization by competing interests that they cannot achieve what they want without compromise. Even then, compromise often results in only a partial solution.

At best, the system moves inefficiently and incrementally; at worst, it moves hardly at all. The Constitution has established a government that is slow to respond to change. "By intent," one political scientist noted, "the U.S. government works within a set of limits designed to prevent it from working too well."[102] Thus the system tends to preserve the status quo and to respond to the groups that benefit from the status quo.

Although the changes made in the wake of the Depression brought us big, activist government, they did not negate all of our historical aversion to such government. We still have more limited government than other advanced industrialized countries. Contrary to what many Americans believe, our taxes are lower and governmental policies in numerous areas, such as health care, welfare, and transportation, are less ambitious.[103] This, of course, limits our ability to address our problems.

Yet some political scientists believe the American people actually prefer a system that is hard to move. Because the people are suspicious of government, they may be reluctant to let one party dominate it and use it to advance that party's policies. In surveys, many people —a quarter to a third of those polled—say they think it is good for one party to control the presidency and the other to control Congress.[104] In presidential and congressional elections, more than a quarter of the voters often split their ticket between the two parties.[105] As a result, between 1968 and 2004, opposing parties controlled the executive branch and at least one house in the legislative branch for all but eight years.

Such divided government reinforces the fragmentation of power in a way that makes it difficult, if not impossible, for citizens to pin responsibility on particular officials and parties for the decisions and policies of government. "If no individual or institution possesses the authority to act without the consent of everybody else in the room, then nobody is ever at fault if anything goes wrong. Congress can blame the president, the president can blame the Congress or the Supreme Court, the Supreme Court can blame the Mexicans or the weather in Ohio."[106] If citizens cannot determine who is responsible for what, they cannot hold those individuals accountable and make them responsive.

The President Complies in the Case of the Confidential Tapes

hief Justice Warren Burger announced the unanimous decision in the case of *United States* v. *Nixon*: the president must turn over the tapes.[107] The Court acknowledged the existence of executive privilege in general but rejected it in this situation because another court needed the information for an upcoming trial and because the information did not relate to national security.

The Court emphasized that courts would determine the legitimacy of claims of executive privilege,[108] not presidents, as Nixon wanted. Because of the separation of powers, Nixon argued, neither the judicial nor the legislative branch should involve itself in this executive decision.

However, this president, who as a high school student in Whittier, California, had won a prize from the Kiwanis Club for the best oration on the Constitution, ignored the system of checks and balances, which limits the separation of powers. In this case, checks and balances authorized the courts to conduct criminal trials of the president's

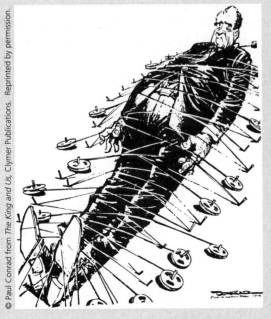

© Paul Conrad from *The King and Us*, Clymer Publications. Reprinted by permission.

aides and Congress to conduct impeachment proceedings against the president. To do so, the courts and Congress needed the information on the tapes.

Within days of the Court's decision, the House Judiciary Committee passed three articles of impeachment. These charged Nixon with obstruction of justice, by covering up a crime; defiance of the committee's subpoenas for the tapes; and abuse of power. (The committee also considered an article of impeachment for cheating on his income taxes, but members decided that this was a personal matter, rather than a governmental matter, and as such not appropriate for impeachment.[109])

Despite the charges, some Republicans maintained that there was no "smoking gun"—no clear evidence of crimes. They branded the impeachment effort as strictly political.

Regardless, Nixon's support in Congress dwindled, and he found himself caught between a rock and a hard place: Releasing the tapes would furnish more evidence for impeachment, but not releasing them would spur impeachment. He reportedly considered disregarding the decision, but after twelve days of weighing his options, he complied with the order.

Releasing the tapes did reveal a smoking gun. Although the tapes did not show that Nixon had participated in planning the break-in, they did show that he had participated in covering it up. When the burglars blackmailed the administration, Nixon approved paying them hush money. He ordered the

head of his reelection committee to "stonewall it" and "cover up." He and an aide formulated a plan to have the CIA thwart the FBI in its investigation of the scandal. When his top aides were subpoenaed to appear before the grand jury, he encouraged them to lie. (Years later, one aide to Nixon claimed that the president himself had ordered the break-in.[110])

In addition to this evidence of crimes, the tapes revealed profanity, vulgarity, and derogatory remarks about women, Catholics, Jews, blacks, Hispanics, and various other ethnic groups. ("The Italians . . . they're not like us . . . they smell different, they look different, act different. . . . Of course, the trouble is . . . you can't find one that is honest."[111]) Such language repelled the public and undercut the image Nixon had tried to project.

As his presidency came collapsing around him, White House insiders began telling people privately that Nixon was dazed, like a "wind-up doll" or a "madman." They said that he was drinking heavily, "going bananas," talking to portraits of past presidents, and showing other signs of cracking under the strain. Some worried that he was considering suicide. One day, he said to his chief of staff, General Alexander Haig, "You fellows, in your business [the army], you have a way of handling problems like this. Somebody leaves a pistol in the drawer." He paused and then added sadly, "I don't have a pistol." Afterward, Haig notified Nixon's doctors and had Nixon's sleeping pills and tranquilizers taken away.[112]

When it became clear that public opinion would force the House to impeach him and the Senate to remove him, Nixon decided to resign. On August 9, 1974—just seventeen days after the Supreme Court's ruling—he became the first American president to do so. Vice President Gerald Ford became the new president.

Although the smoking gun had been found, some people thought Nixon should not have been driven from office. But Watergate was not just a break-in. It was a series of acts, more than can be detailed here, to subvert the Constitution and democratic elections. As the magnitude of these acts came to light, Nixon lost some support. Then, as the cover-up of these acts came to light, he lost even more support. He had campaigned for the presidency on a platform calling for "law and order" and had sworn an oath promising to "take care that the laws be faithfully executed." When Watergate revelations appeared in the media, he had proclaimed his innocence. Ultimately, the hypocrisy and the lying became too much for the public to stomach. Nixon could no longer lead the public he had misled for so long.

Despite depression and cynicism about the scandal, many people saw that the system had worked as it was supposed to. The Founders had divided power to make it difficult for any one branch to amass too much. In the face of the president's efforts to exercise vast power, the courts, with their orders to turn over the tapes, and Congress, with its Senate Watergate Committee hearings and House Judiciary Committee impeachment proceedings, checked the president's abuse of power. In addition, the media, through extensive publicity, first prompted and then reinforced the actions of the courts and Congress. However, although the system worked, it worked slowly. More than two years, more than half of the president's term in office, lapsed between the break-in and the resignation.

When the affair was over, twenty-one of the president's men were convicted and sentenced to prison for their Watergate crimes. Except for one, a burglar who was most uncooperative and who served fifty-two months (G. Gordon Liddy, who now hosts a radio talk show), the men served from four to twelve months. Nixon, who could have and probably would have been prosecuted after leaving office, received a pardon from President Ford before any prosecution could begin.

Nine years after the resignation, the security guard who had discovered the break-in was convicted for shoplifting in Augusta, Georgia. Unemployed, he had stolen a pair of shoes for his son. Unlike the president's men, he received the maximum sentence—twelve months for the $12 shoes.

Congress passed a law mandating that other, unreleased tapes and documents be turned over to the National Archives, which was to make public any that related to Watergate or had "general historic significance." The archives has slowly released these materials. On one tape, Nixon is heard remarking to his chief of staff, "I always wondered about that taping equipment, but I'm damn glad we have it, aren't you?"[113]

Not only does Nixon's voice remain, but the effects of Watergate linger. The public has become less trustful of government officials, and the media have become more suspicious of them. The parties have become more aware of the benefits of a scandal involving their opponents. In the wake of Watergate, the Democrats captured the White House and gained many seats in Congress. These results have prompted both parties to point accusing fingers and to launch congressional investigations—though only against members of the other party—even when the alleged transgressions have been far less serious than those in Watergate. Thus Watergate contributed to the culture of scandal that afflicts American politics today.

To learn more about executive privilege and _United States_ v. _Nixon,_ go to this chapter's "You Are There" exercises on the text Web site.

Key Terms

Watergate scandal	checks and balances
Articles of Confederation	natural rights
Shays's Rebellion	social contract
Constitutional Convention	limited government
republic	Federalists
Great Compromise	Anti-Federalists
Three-Fifths Compromise	*Federalist Papers*
direct democracy	Bill of Rights
indirect democracy	Emancipation Proclamation
federalism	Gettysburg Address
separation of powers	Reconstruction Amendments
divided government	New Deal

Further Reading

Leonard W. Levy, ed., *Essays on the Making of the Constitution* (New York: Oxford University Press, 1969). These essays address the question "Was the Constitution an undemocratic document framed and ratified by an undemocratic minority for an undemocratic society?"

David McCullough, *John Adams* (New York: Simon & Schuster, 2001). A readable biography of the revolutionary stalwart and our second president.

Clinton Rossiter, *1787: The Grand Convention* (New York: Macmillan, 1966). A lively account of the Constitutional Convention and the ratification campaign.

Theodore H. White, *Breach of Faith* (New York: Atheneum, 1975). A chronicle of the Watergate scandal as a Greek tragedy in which actors on both sides behaved in such ways as to fulfill their destinies.

Bob Woodward and Carl Bernstein, *All the President's Men* (New York: Simon & Schuster, 1974). A riveting account of journalistic sleuthing by the two reporters who broke the Watergate story.

For Viewing

All the President's Men. (1976) See Robert Redford and Dustin Hoffman play "Woodward and Bernstein."

Electronic Resources

lcweb.loc.gov/exhibits/declara/declara4.html
At this site, you can learn more about how the Declaration of Independence was written and see a special Library of Congress exhibit on it.

www.nwbuildnet.com/nwbn/usconstitutionsearch. html
Even the Constitution has a home page. Here it is, with links to other historical documents and to PBS Project Democracy.

www.usconstitution.net
This Constitution page with interesting links was originally set up by a political science student as a class project.

InfoTrac College Edition

Search for the following articles in the InfoTrac database:

Hammons, Christopher W. "Was James Madison Wrong? Rethinking the American Preference for Short, Framework-Oriented Constitutions," *American Political Science Review* (December 1999).

Nicgorski ,Walter. "The Moral Crisis: Lessons from the Founding—Is Moral Relativism Compatible with American Constitutional Democracy?" *World and I* (Feburary 2003).

Rakove, Jack N. "Judicial Power in the Constitutional Theory of James Madison," *William and Mary Law Review* (March 2002).

Slonim, Shlomo. "The Federalist Papers and the Bill of Rights," *Constitutional Commentary* (Spring 2003).

For more articles, enter:

"James Madison" in the Subject Guide;

"United States Constitution" in the Subject Guide;

"Articles of Confederation" in Keywords.

American Government Resources

Visit the Government Foundations section of the Wadsworth American Government Resources Web site (politicalscience.wadsworth.com/amgov/) for a variety of tools to help you explore the Constitution further. Included are simulations, video clips, Microcase exercises, and a wealth of other activities.

CHAPTER 3

FEDERALISM AND THE GROWTH OF GOVERNMENT

During disasters, federal and state agencies come to the aid of local rescue agencies.

AP/ Wide World Photos

Federal and Unitary Systems

Federal Systems

Unitary Systems

Why Choose Federalism?

The Political Bases of American Federalism

Political Benefits of Federalism

Political Costs of Federalism

Political Culture and Federalism

The Constitutional Bases of Federalism

Major Features of American Federalism

Interpretations of the Constitutional Provisions

Federalism and the Growth of Government

Small-Scale Government

The Civil War

Government as a "Bully Pulpit"

The New Deal and World War II

Social Justice and the Great Society

New Federalism

The New New Federalism

A Return to State-Centered Federalism?

The Practice of Federalism

Federal-State Relations

Interstate Relations

State-Local Relations

People, States, and the Federal Government

Conclusion: Does Federalism Make Government More Responsive?

Should Nevada Become the Country's Nuclear Waste Dump?

ou are Kenny C. Guinn, Republican governor of Nevada. Since you were elected in 1998, you have been fighting attempts by the federal government to build a national nuclear waste storage facility at Yucca Mountain, a former bomb-testing site in your state. After several years of lobbying and filing lawsuits, you have failed to stop Congress and President Bush from approving development of the site. Now you have to decide whether to stop fighting Washington and accept the plan or to continue the battle through court challenges and by finding allies to bolster the position of a small state with few electoral votes.[1]

The U.S. Department of Energy (DoE) is proposing to move 77,000 tons of nuclear waste to the storage site, waste that will remain radioactive for as long as *twenty-four thousand years.* Nevada's opposition to this plan dates back to 1987, when Congress first identified Yucca Mountain, an area of rocky hills and valleys and low rainfall, as the best place to store waste and spent fuel from the country's nuclear power plants and nuclear weapons programs. The waste is currently stored at 111 temporary sites in thirty-nine states, and Congress wants it all moved to a single, secure, and permanent repository. The nuclear industry, too, is eager to have the waste it produces moved away from the plants and stored at a

distant site at taxpayer expense, and it has lobbied heavily to get approval for the Yucca Mountain facility.

You are convinced that building a nuclear waste storage facility at Yucca Mountain presents dangers both for public health and the state's economy. Nevada is a small but fast-growing state with two million residents, and Las Vegas is the fastest-growing metropolitan area in the country. Seventy-five percent of the state's population is in Las Vegas and its suburbs, 90 miles away from the proposed waste site. With the storage of that much dangerous waste so close to Las Vegas, an earthquake or accident, however small, could create a disaster. Even if there were no contamination, the scare could reduce the tourist trade on which the state relies so heavily.

Seventy percent of Nevadans agree with you. When it comes to nuclear waste storage, everyone raises the NIMBY battle cry ("not in my backyard"). No one wants to be located next to a site that holds material that will be radioactive for millennia. The congressional delegation, the state legislature, the mayor of Las Vegas, the state medical and firefighters' associations, the PTA, the tourism commission, and the commission on nuclear projects all oppose building a national waste facility in Nevada.[2] They are skeptical that Yucca Mountain is the best location and suspect that it may just

Marge Detraz of Caliente is among the 70 percent of Nevadans who oppose building a nuclear waste storage facility in their state. The government proposes to use her town as the rail transfer station for spent nuclear fuel.

be the most politically acceptable site. In fact, it was the only area to which the DoE gave serious consideration.

Many Nevadans have that "been there, done that" feeling. During the Cold War, virtually all the atomic and nuclear weapons testing carried out within the continental United States was done in Utah and Nevada. Even now the Pentagon (Defense Department) plans to test a new tactical nuclear weapon in Nevada.

Even in the 1950s, when the states were far less populated than they are today, residents exposed to radioactive fallout suffered the health effects for decades afterward—the full extent came to light only upon declassification of documents in the 1980s and 1990s.[3] These revelations are still fresh in people's minds. Of course, there is a huge difference in the risk factor of exposure to fallout from atmospheric and underground weapons testing, on the one hand, and living in proximity to radioactive waste sealed in casks and cement a thousand feet below ground, on the other. But Nevadans will have to live with the risks.

A relative newcomer to the state, you took up these concerns and made Yucca Mountain a major issue in both your gubernatorial campaigns. A retired teacher and school superintendent, you became interim president of the University of Nevada–Las Vegas when it was

trying to rebound from a basketball scandal. By donating your salary to the school scholarship fund, you became a civic hero, and soon a local pundit was referring to you as "The Anointed One," the natural successor to the incumbent, term-limited governor, even though you had never held elective office. In your campaigns, you repeatedly promised Nevadans that you would do anything you could to prevent a permanent, or even a temporary, nuclear waste storage site from being built in the state. You even supported cutting off the water supply necessary to construct the site, saying you would assess a fine of $1 million per gallon.[4]

Despite the state's overwhelming opposition to the plan, Congress gave the DoE the go-ahead to build the facility. But until 2001, Nevada had high-placed allies in Washington to thwart Congress. During his two presidential campaigns, Bill Clinton told Nevadans he would veto any plan to designate Yucca Mountain as the storage site, and he did. Presidential candidate Al Gore promised the same in 2000, and George W. Bush had said he, too, would oppose it until scientific study proved it safe. But once in office, your fellow Republican, President Bush, approved the plan, saying that evidence indicated that Yucca Mountain was the best and safest site for the facility. You were livid, but the provisions of the legislation

gave you, as governor, a chance to veto the plan. You did, and then the state filed four suits in federal court to overturn Washington's decision. But Bush asked Congress to approve it over your veto, something that could be done with a majority vote in each chamber.

Still you did not give up. You went to Washington to stop the override. In testimony before Congress, you argued that although the Nuclear Regulatory Commission had conducted extensive research, it still does not know enough about the suitability of the terrain. You also argued that it would be dangerous to transport thousands of tons of radioactive material across the country, especially in an era when the government is warning about the inevitability of more terrorist attacks. Shipments will pass through or near more than a hundred cities and come within half a mile of 145 million people. And a special rail line costing nearly $1 billion will have to be built through Nevada to carry the waste shipments to the Yucca site. And after all that, you reminded Congress, the repository will be too small; it will take only twenty-five years to fill what is intended to be the sole national repository. And by that time, the existing temporary sites near power plants would have produced fifty thousand additional tons of waste.[5] Nevertheless, Congress overrode your veto.

You rejected advice to use the decision as a way to bargain for state benefits. You want experts to revisit the scientific evidence and declare that it makes no sense to transport nuclear waste across the country to a site that may not be geologically stable. "We will not bargain, we will not negotiate, we will not waver in our determined opposition to Yucca Mountain. Today we lost a battle, but we will win the war."[6] Tough talk, and it helped you win reelection in 2002 with 68 percent of the vote.

But maybe you should compromise or concede. You do not like challenging a decision of a president from your own party, and you do not doubt the need for a solution to the waste problem.

Can the state afford to go on spending millions on advertising, legal bills, and lobbying on what looks like a hopeless cause? Yours is a tiny state with a part-time legislature and limited resources.[7] With budget shortfalls everywhere, there are many needs that the state is not meeting. Your congressional delegation consists of just two Democrats and two Republicans. That is not much to take on Washington, let alone the powerful lobbyists the nuclear industry has hired.

You are also being lobbied by a group representing Nevadans who believe that at this point what the state prefers is irrelevant because the facility is a done deal. They urge you to make the best of it and give you a long list of benefits you could negotiate for as the price for ending your opposition: fees for storage, more funding for highways, rights to draw more water from the Colorado River, and the return to state ownership of federally held land in

Nevada.[8] In addition, they point out, the waste site will reportedly bring as many as two thousand new jobs to the state.

You must choose your next course of action. Should you continue to fight, hire more lobbyists and environmental experts, or perhaps take this to higher courts? Or is it time to stop fighting Washington, accept the decision of Congress and President Bush, and get the most out of it you can for the state?

Since Independence, the states and the national government have wrangled over how power should be divided between them. The victory of the Union over secessionist states in the Civil War (1861–1865) determined that the Union was indivisible and that the states could not nullify federal law or the Constitution. But the war settled little else about the federal relationship.

Today, because of the sheer size and complexity of our country, its role in world affairs, and our expanded expectations of government, we live in a nation with a strong central government. Yet we continue to disagree about just how strong it should be. Most Americans say they want small government, but they also want a government powerful enough to keep the peace abroad and to meet their needs at home. So over the past seventy years, when states could not or would not respond to calls for government action, Americans have turned to Washington to legislate across a broad spectrum of policy, all the while claiming to believe that state governments are more responsive to them than the federal government. Because Americans are predisposed to suspect big government, it is easy for critics to decry its growth and accuse Congress of creating programs that are too large, too expensive, and too intrusive on the rights of the states. These critics, however, never mention that over the past twenty-five years, the size of state governments has doubled while the number of federal employees has fallen (see Figure 1). These contradictions are perhaps inevitable in a government created, run, and elected by people who have never agreed on the proper distribution of power within a federal system.

In this chapter, we will look at the politics behind the choice of federalism as our form of government, the constitutional provisions that define it, and how the federal distribution of power has changed over time through federal court rulings and through practice. Finally, we look at some of the day-to-day mechanics of state and national cooperation in our federal republic.

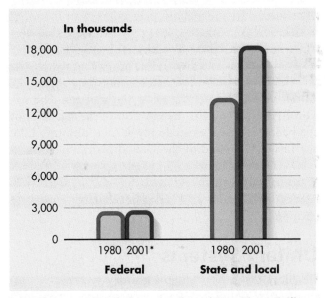

In thousands

FIGURE 1 ■ Number of Full- and Part-Time Civilian Employees in the Federal and State Governments, 1980 and 2001.

*Latest figures available.

SOURCE: U.S. Census Bureau, *Statistical Abstract of the United States, 2003* (Washington, D.C.: Government Printing Office, 2004), tab. 468.

Federal and Unitary Systems

Federal Systems

The term **federalism** describes a system in which power is constitutionally divided between a central government and subnational or local governments. In the United States, the subnational governments are the states. Nations that have federal systems—Germany, Canada, India, Brazil, and Mexico, for example—vary greatly in their basic economic and political characteristics. They are similar only in that each has a written constitution allocating some powers to the national and some to the subnational governments.

In American federalism, both levels of government receive their grants of power from a higher authority—the will of the people (popular sovereignty) as expressed in the Constitution. In other words, federalism divides something—sovereignty—that is theoretically indivisible. This is the source of some of the conflict over jurisdiction that inevitably arises between levels of government. Making arrangements even more complex, the powers granted to each level are not necessarily exclusive. Both national and state governments have the power to tax, regulate, and provide benefits. And because each level of government is sovereign in its own right, neither can dissolve the other.

In contrast, in a **confederal system,** the central government has only those powers given to it by the subnational governments; it cannot act directly on citizens, and it can be dissolved by the states that created it. The first American government, established by the Articles of Confederation, was a confederal system in which all sovereignty was vested in the states. The national government was the creation of the states—not the people—and it existed only at their pleasure. Like the first government of the United States, the United Nations is an example of a confederal system. The lack of central authority in such systems makes them basically unworkable as governmental arrangements for modern nations.

Unitary Systems

In contrast to federalism, in a **unitary system,** the national government creates subnational governments and gives them only those powers it wants them to have. Thus the national government is supreme. In Britain, for example, the national government can give or take away any power previously delegated to the subnational governments, and it can even abolish them, as it did with some city governments in the 1980s. In unitary Sweden, the national parliament abolished 90 percent of its local governments between 1952 and 1975.

In the United States, the fifty states are each unitary with respect to their local governments. Cities, counties, townships, and school districts can be altered or even eliminated by state governments. Yet every state is (and is required to be by the U.S. Constitution) a republic—that is, a representative democracy. So the difference between unitary and federal systems is not at all related to the distinction between democracy and authoritarianism. Some unitary systems are among the most democratic in the world (Britain and Sweden); others are authoritarian (Egypt and China). And while some federal systems are democracies (Canada, Mexico, Germany, India), others are authoritarian (the former Soviet Union and the former Yugoslavia).

It is also inaccurate to classify federal systems as decentralized and unitary systems as centralized. All modern governments have to delegate some power because a central government, even in a unitary system, cannot run every local service or deal directly with every local problem.

Why Choose Federalism?

Except for a few loosely organized leagues or confederations of states, there were no federal governments before the United States was created. Yet by the 1960s, as much as half the world's territory was governed by federalism.[9] Some new nations created after World War II chose federalism because they, like the American colonies, were trying to unite diverse states or territories into a single country. Federal systems are often ethnically, linguistically, religiously, or racially diverse (though not always—Germany is relatively homogeneous, for example). Agreeing to divide power among levels of government may be the only way to unite people who have strong motivation to live apart.

The power-sharing arrangements in federal governments often do not work, and many have failed. In some cases, there were not enough shared values to hold a nation together. Sometimes too much power was invested in the central government, and sometimes too little. Pakistan split from India and Bangladesh from Pakistan; Yugoslavia, the Soviet Union, and Czechoslovakia ceased to exist, and their constituent republics became independent countries. There have been failed secessionist movements in Nigeria, Canada, Mexico, the United States, and many other nations.

The Political Bases of American Federalism

The Founders of the United States did not choose federalism as an ideal form of government or as a principle in itself; the few historical examples held little to recommend it as a form appropriate to the American situation. They had to write from scratch a document that would accommodate the political reality of their loose compact of states. Although at least one delegate to the Constitutional Convention proposed abolishing the states to create a unitary system, few took this option seriously.[10] This required finding a compromise that could satisfy those who thought only strong central government could work and those who thought the union could be preserved only if the individual state governments retained most of the authority they had under the Articles of Confederation. The Founders proposed a dual form of government, a compromise between the *national* form (a strong central government) favored by some delegates and the *confederal* form (a league of states) favored by others. In arguing for its ratification, James Madison defended the Constitution in just this way, saying it would create a government that was partly national and partly federal.[11] Although today we refer to the government in Washington as the "federal" government, the Founders referred to the government they created by the type of democracy it was—a republic. The word *federal* does not appear in the Constitution.

Political Benefits of Federalism

The division of power between the national and state governments was one politically attractive feature of federalism for those delegates who worried about the center gaining advantage over the states. But with federalism's provisions for accommodating national diversity also came a means for limiting the authority of government in general. Madison explained how this would work. In *Federalist Paper* 10, he asserted that it is inevitable that "factions"—groups of citizens seeking some goal contrary to the rights of other citizens or to the well-being of the whole country—would threaten the national stability. To cure the **"mischiefs of faction,"** Madison said, government has either to remove the causes of factionalism or to control its effects. The first option, Madison believed, was unrealistic because it would require the impossible: changing human nature. It also would require taking away freedom by outlawing opinions and strictly regulating behavior. People inevitably have different ideas and beliefs, and government, he thought, should not try to prevent this.

Because the causes of faction could not be removed without placing too many restrictions on freedom, its effects had to be controlled by a properly constructed government. If a faction were less than a majority, Madison believed it could be controlled through majority rule, the majority defeating the minority faction. If the faction were a majority, however, a greater problem arose, but one for which Madison had an answer.

To control a majority faction, one had only to limit the ability of a majority to carry out its wishes. Madison believed this was impossible in a small democracy, where there is little to check a majority determined to do something. But in a large federalist system, there are many checks on a majority faction—more interests competing with each other and large distances to separate those who might scheme to deprive others of liberty. As Madison noted, "The influence of factious leaders may kindle a flame within their particular States, but

James Madison.

will be unable to spread a general conflagration through the other States." Having many states and having them spread over a large territory would serve as major checks against majority tyranny. Madison's argument in *Federalist Paper* 10 (reprinted in Appendix C at the back of this book) remains among the most influential works of American political theory.

Perhaps the benefit of the federal arrangement can be best understood by the adage "politics is the art of the possible." The division of power made the Union possible. It allowed states their differences, ceded control over local affairs, and in the process protected against both an abusive central government and the tyranny of factions.

Political Costs of Federalism

If the division of power made the Union possible, what are the drawbacks of such division? One disadvantage is that allegiance to the Union can falter if too much value is placed on accommodation of state or regional differences. The Union can also erode if the differences among the states become more important than their commitment to common principles. The United States faced secessionist threats almost immediately after its creation—by southern states when the Federalists (under John Adams) were in power and by New England states when the anti-federalists (under Jefferson) were in power. Secession was averted in part by the fear of external threats but mainly by key political leaders' commitment to make the Union work.

The constitutional provisions protecting the rights and individuality of the states were meant to accommodate what has been called our "psychology of localism."[12] Although we are now a more mobile and a more nation-oriented people than we were in the eighteenth and nineteenth centuries, we retain enough local allegiance to tilt our federal system toward decentralization and fragmentation. Indeed, federalism "creates separate, self-sustaining centers of power, privilege and profit which may be sought and defended as desirable in themselves."[13] In part, federalism is *intended* to do this, but if taken too far, it can prevent coherence and unity on major policy issues. Even when there is need for national policy—whether on energy, the environment, health care, or even national defense—members of Congress may still base their votes primarily on local interests (see Chapter 10).

Political Culture and Federalism

Despite a national media, franchises and chains bringing the same products to all parts of the country, and transportation systems that can carry us across the nation in a few hours, there are still significant differences among the states—that is, something more than Texans preferring chili and New Englanders clam chowder. States *want* to be different from one another. Each has its own constitution, flag, motto, and symbols of state, not to mention its very own official state bird and flower. Each state is basically a political actor competing for a share of the nation's resources. Just as individuals organize around identity issues, states compete with one another on the basis of their distinctive profiles.

When we refer to the Midwest, the Southwest, New England, or the Deep South, certain images immediately come to mind, not just of geographical areas but of lifestyles and political orientations. Partisan preferences, ideology, and political style continue to vary along regional lines. Individual states have developed sufficiently different political styles and attitudes that Republican strategists, for example, would never run the same kind of election campaign for a candidate in New York as they would for one in Idaho. For the same reason, candidates for national office change the points of emphasis in their stump speeches as they move from state to state.

We have defined *political culture* as a shared body of values and beliefs that shapes perceptions and attitudes toward politics and government and influences behavior. For much of the twentieth century, the United States was said to have three geographically based political subcultures—three distinctive ways of looking at and participating in politics.[14] The tendency of people in New England and the Upper Midwest to view

politics as a way of improving life and to believe in their obligation to participate was labeled a *moralistic* political culture. In the *individualistic* political culture, said to be typical of the industrial Midwest and the East, the ultimate objective of politics was not to create a better life for all but to get benefits for oneself and one's group. In the *traditionalistic* political culture, associated with the states of the Deep South, politics was seen not as a way to further the public good but as a way to maintain the status quo, and little value was placed on participation.

Today, traces of these patterns remain, but much has changed. The Deep South, for example, having been the site of intense political mobilization during the modern civil rights movement, is now a center of significant grassroots activity, especially among religious conservatives. The economic transformation of the United States from an industry- and agriculture-based economy to a high-tech and service economy also has had an inevitable impact on political culture. And the mobility of the American population means that fewer people are likely to have a political orientation as strongly rooted in a state or regional identity as in earlier decades. Every year, about one in seven Americans move, one-third of those from one state to another.[15] Only 25 percent of Nevadans were born in Nevada, for example. Mass communication, especially television and the Internet, has also had a leveling effect on some regional differences.

This is not to suggest that the three archetypal political subcultures have been completely homogenized. The country is just as diverse as ever; indeed, it is ethnically and racially more diverse. The fact that immigrants tend to settle in clusters in a handful of states and big cities helps shape regional differences. Patterns of dispersion of African Americans, Hispanics, and Asians also overlay regional differences and shape distinctive state profiles. In New Mexico, for instance, 42 percent of the population is of Hispanic origin, while in Maine, less than 1 percent of the population is Hispanic. In Mississippi, African Americans make up over 36 percent of the population; in Vermont, 0.5 percent. In Florida, almost as many people are over age sixty-five (18 percent of the population) as are under seventeen (22 percent), but in Utah, young people outnumber senior citizens more than four to one. And in Mississippi, annual per capita income is only 51 percent of what it is in Connecticut ($20,993 versus $40,640).[16]

These disparities make for different politics in the states. The priorities of older people (health care, for instance) are different from those of younger people (financial aid for education, for example). In states with larger numbers of Hispanics and African Americans, civil rights issues are more salient than in states with predominantly white populations. And states such as Mississippi, West Virginia, and Arkansas, whose citizens are poorer than those in the rest of the country, face greater demands for services and have correspondingly fewer resources to provide them.

States also vary in where they fit on the conservative-liberal continuum. One factor in determining a state's place along this continuum is religious affiliation because a few Christian denominations have distinct political orientations. Southern Baptists, who comprise 11 percent of all American Christians and who live predominantly in southern states, vote overwhelming Republican, as do most evangelical Christians. Jewish Americans tend to be more liberal and vote Democratic, and the Jewish vote is concentrated in several states, especially New York, Florida, and California.

Though "liberalism" and "conservatism" can have many meanings, two rough measures are how much a state spends on education and health care and how restrictive or lenient its policies are toward gambling and crime.[17] The map in Figure 2 illustrates the results of grouping states in this way. The differences among the states can be explained by the kind of political culture the state has and by how "liberal" or "conservative" (see Chapter 4) each state's citizens are. Policies and laws enacted by state legislatures reflect the different views and social and economic circumstances of their citizens.

Thus state boundaries mean something beyond identifying the place where you register to vote. In policy areas as diverse as economic development, taxation, welfare, and regulation of personal morality (gambling and prostitution, for example), states vary widely. Federal-ism, even with a strong national government, provides sufficient autonomy for states to adopt and maintain policies consistent with their own political cultures.

The Constitutional Bases of Federalism

Major Features of American Federalism

As we saw in Chapter 2, the Founders were unsure how to solve the problem of national versus state powers. Although they saw federalism as one way to limit government power by dividing it, they were creating a new form of federalism.

One thing almost all delegates could agree on was the need for a central government that was stronger than that provided for in the Articles of Confederation. But they never agreed on how much of their sovereignty the individual states would have to surrender to achieve a stronger national government. The Constitution assigned some powers, set limits on the exercise of others, but did so with an ambiguity and economy of wording that made the document acceptable to both advocates of a strong national government and supporters of states' rights.

Strengthening National Government

Two powers the Founders knew were necessary to the creation of a stronger national government were the right to tax without the permission of the states and the authority to make foreign and domestic policy without the states' consent. Granting Congress the authority to tax and to regulate interstate commerce gave tremendous power to the national government and made it far more independent of the will of the state governments than it had been under the Articles. But the Constitution also assigned Congress many general duties, granting it authority to make all laws **"necessary and proper"** for carrying out its specific powers. This is sometimes called the **implied powers clause** because the federal courts soon interpreted its vague wording to mean that Congress could legislate in almost any area it wished. This greatly expanded the reach of the national government.

The Founders' decision to make the presidency independent of Congress and the state legislatures also strengthened the federal government by giving the occupant a base from which to exercise independent national leadership. The president's role as commander in chief and principal executor of the laws of the United States further enlarged national powers.

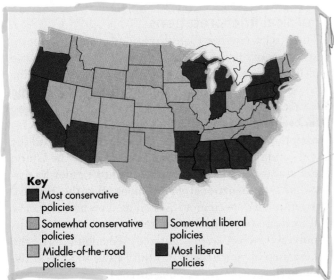

Key
- ■ Most conservative policies
- ■ Somewhat conservative policies
- ■ Middle-of-the-road policies
- ■ Somewhat liberal policies
- ■ Most liberal policies

FIGURE 2 ■ States Categorized by How Liberal or Conservative Their Policies Are

SOURCE: Robert S. Erikson, Gerald C. Wright, and John McIver, *Statehouse Democracy: Public Opinion and Policy in the American States* (New York: Cambridge University Press, 1993), tab. 4.2.

Finally, the **supremacy clause** established the predominance of the national government over the states. It says that treaties, the Constitution, and "laws made in pursuance thereof" are to be the supreme law of the land whenever they come into conflict with state laws or state actions. Furthermore, when there is a difference of opinion as to whether state actions are in conflict with the Constitution or federal law, the matter is to be decided at the national level.[18] The Constitution did not specify the individual or institution that would make these decisions, but the federal courts assumed that role during the tenure of Chief Justice Marshall. (This is discussed at length in Chapter 13.)

The significance of the supremacy clause took some time to emerge. This was because the delegates to the Constitutional Convention were not in agreement on whether they were there as *representatives of their states* (the view of many southerners) or as *representatives of the people* of their states (the view of many New Englanders).[19] This meant there was no initial consensus on who created, and therefore who could abolish or withdraw from, the new government. Was government simply the creation of the states, as the wording of Article VII makes it seem, or was it the creation of the people, as the Preamble seems to say? Individuals may continue to disagree over what the Founders intended, but the primacy of the supremacy clause was fixed by the Union victory in the Civil War.

Restricting Powers of State Governments

In addition to the categorical limitation placed on state rule making by the supremacy clause, the Constitution also identifies specific actions that states cannot take because they are reserved for the national government. States cannot enter into treaties, keep standing armies or navies, make war, print or coin money, or levy import or export taxes. These prohibitions reaffirmed that with respect to foreign policy and interstate commerce, sovereignty was vested in the national government.

The Constitution also prohibits states from infringing on certain rights of individuals. For example, a state cannot pass an *ex post facto* ("after the fact") law making an action a crime and then punish citizens who committed the "crime" before it was made illegal.

Limiting Powers of the National Government

The most important general restriction on the power of the national government with respect to the states is contained in the **Tenth Amendment.** It reserves to the states and to the people those powers not granted by the Constitution to the national government. At the time it was written, the understanding of this wording was that the national government would have only those powers specifically assigned to it in the Constitution. It

was added as a separate amendment in the Bill of Rights just in case this point was not clear in the body of the Constitution. But the broad construction of Congress's "necessary and proper" powers, established by many federal court rulings over the decades, weakened the Tenth Amendment. Yet the wording remains open to more restrictive interpretations, and since the 1990s, the federal courts have breathed new life into this amendment.[20] (See "A Return to State-Centered Federalism?" later in this chapter.)

Two other limits on national powers include the Ninth Amendment, which states that the enumeration of certain individual rights in the Constitution and the Bill of Rights cannot be read to mean the people do not retain other rights. And Article IV of the Constitution limits the national government by specifically prohibiting it from altering or abolishing existing states.

Interpretations of the Constitutional Provisions

Having reached agreement on a division of powers, the Founders left vague the details of how the nation-state relationship would work. Given the disagreements among its authors, the Constitution might never have been ratified if it had contained specifics on the practice of federalism. In fact, agreement might never have been reached on a final document, so great was the gulf between those who thought they were creating a nation—an indivisible union—and those who thought they were writing a contract between states. These competing views are the source of what still today is the biggest disagreement about our constitutional system.[21]

Political Interpretations

Those who saw the Constitution as written by representatives of the people, and ratified by the people, were inclined to view the national government as the supreme power in the federal relationship. Alexander Hamilton clearly articulated this view of **nation-centered federalism** in the *Federalist Papers*. This interpretation accepts that the Constitution grants many powers to the states and recognizes that they existed before the Union and are sovereign in the sense that they cannot be dissolved by the national government. But the national government's sovereignty is seen as supreme in that its ultimate responsibility is to preserve the Union and its indivisibility.[22] Nation-centered federalism was the view used by northerners to justify a war to prevent the southern states from seceding in 1861.

Opponents of the Hamiltonian interpretation, including many from the South, argued that because the Constitution recognized the states' existence as sovereign entities before the creation of the Union, the form our system was to take was **state-centered federalism,** giving precedence to state sovereignty over that of the national government or the Union. They cited the Tenth Amendment's limiting the powers granted to Congress to those specifically mentioned in Article I and to Madison's words in *Federalist Paper* 45: "The powers delegated . . . to the federal government are few and defined. Those which are to remain in the state governments are numerous and indefinite." In this view, any attempt by Congress to go beyond these explicitly listed powers violated state authority.

In justifying their secession from the Union, southerners held to the extreme version of state-centered federalism: that the Constitution had been written by representatives of the states, not the people. In their view, if the states had created the Union, they could dissolve it.

The Constitution can also be interpreted as having created a government in which the division of power leaves neither level dominant over the other. In this view—**dual federalism**—the Constitution created a system in which the national government and the states each have separate grants of power, with each supreme in its own sphere. In this interpretation of the division of powers, sovereignty is not just divided but divided in such a way as to leave both levels of government essentially equal. The differences between levels derive from their separate jurisdictions, not from inequality of power. Madison's description, in *Federalist Paper* 39, of the government created by the Constitution as a hybrid of national and federal forms provides one basis for this interpretation.

Over the years, the dominant interpretations of power sharing in our form of federalism have shifted among the nation-centered, state-centered, and dual views. Interpretations reflect changing federal court composition, economic conditions, the philosophies of those in the executive and legislative branches, and changing public demands. Overall, there has been a general trend away from state-centered and toward nation-centered federalism, but significant shorter-term shifts have occurred back toward the states.

Early Judicial Interpretations

Very soon after the Constitution was ratified, the federal courts became the arbiters of the Constitution. John Marshall, chief justice of the United States from 1801 to 1835, was a Federalist, a firm believer in the need for a strong national government, and the decisions of his Court supported this view.

The Marshall-led Supreme Court established the legal bases for the supremacy of national authority over the states. Among the Court's most important rulings were that decisions of the state courts could be overturned by the federal courts and, in the case of **McCulloch v. Maryland,** that the implied powers given Congress in the Constitution could be broadly interpreted. The

McCulloch decision said that the "necessary and proper" clause in Article I implied that Congress has the right to make all laws necessary to carry out its Constitutional powers.

The *McCulloch* case grew out of a dispute over the establishment of a national bank. Because the Constitution does not explicitly grant Congress the authority to charter banks, many people thought Congress may have been infringing on rights the Constitution left to the states. Ironically, it was John Calhoun, later to become the leading states' rights advocate, who introduced a bill to charter the Bank of the United States.

Once established, the bank was immediately unpopular because it competed with smaller banks operating under state laws and because some of its branches engaged in reckless and even fraudulent practices. When the government of Maryland levied a tax on the currency issued by the Baltimore branch of the bank, the constitutionality of the bank was called into question, and a case was brought to the Supreme Court.

Marshall's ruling in *McCulloch* v. *Maryland* in 1819 was one of the most influential of any Supreme Court decision for the fate of the federal relationship.[23] Pronouncing the tax unconstitutional, Marshall wrote that "the power to tax involves the power to destroy." The states should not have the power to destroy the bank, he stated, because the bank was "necessary and proper" to carry out Congress's powers to collect taxes, borrow money, regulate commerce, and raise an army. Marshall argued that if the goal of the legislation is legitimate and constitutional, "all means which are appropriate, which are plainly adapted to that end, which are not prohibited, but consistent with the letter and spirit of the Constitution, are constitutional."

Thus Marshall interpreted "necessary" quite loosely. The bank was probably not necessary, but it was "useful." This interpretation of the implied powers clause allowed Congress, and thus the national government, to wield much more authority than the Constitution gave it explicitly. Although there was some negative reaction ("A deadly blow has been struck at the Sovereignty of the States," decried one Baltimore newspaper[24]), the Court maintained its strong nation-centered position as long as Marshall was chief justice.

In 1836, with a new chief justice, the Court began to interpret the Tenth Amendment as a strict limitation on federal powers, holding that powers to provide for public health, safety, and order were *exclusively* powers of the state governments, not of the national government. This dual federalism interpretation eroded some of the nation-centered federal interpretations of the Marshall Court while continuing to uphold the rights of the federal courts to interpret the Constitution.

There have since been many Court rulings on the division of power between Washington and the states, but these early rulings set the pattern for what would be shifting interpretations of how the Constitution distributes power between levels of government.

Federalism and the Growth of Government

One indication of how dominant the national government has become in the public consciousness is the conflation of "federal" with "national." It is a confusing but now common usage to say "federal government" when referring to the national government. In just over two hundred years, the national government has grown from a few hundred people with relatively limited impact on the residents of thirteen small states to a government employing several millions, affecting the daily lives of 290 million people in fifty states and billions of people beyond our borders. The transformation to a large, complex nation inevitably changed the way our federal system functions. Territorial expansion, war, economic crises, expansion of government function, and the political philosophies of presidents have changed federalism.

Small-Scale Government

At the same time the courts were interpreting national powers broadly, the national government was exercising its powers on a rather small scale. The federal government had only one thousand employees in the administration of George Washington, and this number had increased only to thirty-three thousand by the presidency of James Buchanan seventy years later. The national government also raised relatively little revenue, most of it from import-export and excise taxes. But state governments were also small and had limited functions. There were only a few federal-state cooperative activities. For example, the federal government gave land to the states to support education and participated in joint federal-state-private ventures, such as canal-building projects initiated by the states.

Thus the first fifty years were characterized by the growth of nation-centered federalism in legal doctrine, by small-scale state and national government in practice, and the beginning of intergovernmental cooperation. But the groundwork for the growth of government was laid by Jefferson's purchase of the Louisiana Territory, which extended the nation's borders from the Atlantic to the Pacific Ocean. Once the country was set on an expansionist course, more units of government and a bigger bureaucracy were inevitable.

The Civil War

The next great impetus to the growth of government came with the Civil War; wartime almost always expands the power of the national over lower levels of government. Lincoln assumed extraordinary powers for the presidency during the war, and its outcome, of course, reaffirmed the supremacy clause and guaranteed that there would be only one national government in the continental United States. Northerners saw their Civil War victory as a severe blow to state-centered federalism, but southerners continued to see the Union, in which they were forcibly retained, as one governed by a state-centered form of federalism.

Government as a "Bully Pulpit"

In the decades following the war, vast urbanization and industrialization took place throughout the United States. Living and working conditions for many city dwellers were appalling. Adults as well as children who moved into the cities often took jobs in sweatshops—factories where they worked long hours in unsafe conditions for low pay.

Spurred by revelations of these unsafe and degrading conditions, states and sometimes Congress tried to regulate working conditions, working hours, and pay through such means as child labor and industrial safety laws. Beginning in the 1880s, a conservative Supreme Court used the dual federalism doctrine to rule unconstitutional many federal attempts to regulate. But it often ruled that the states had overstepped their powers as well, displaying more of an antigovernment, probusiness stance than a commitment to dual federalism. From 1874 to 1937, the Supreme Court found fifty federal and four hundred state laws unconstitutional.[25] Before the Civil War, in contrast, the Court overturned only two congressional and sixty state laws.

At the same time that the Court was limiting both state and national action in regulating business and industry, both levels of government were slowly expanding. Republican Theodore Roosevelt's presidency (1901–1909) was a time of tremendous government activism. He saw his office as a "bully pulpit" from which to advocate for the improvement of living and working conditions of average Americans, environmental protection, and the regulation of big business, especially its corrupting influence on state legislatures. These years saw a flood of new legislation and regulatory activity, and Roosevelt's concept of government as advocate for the average citizen changed the direction and purpose of government at the beginning of the twentieth century.

During this period, the revenues of both the national and state governments grew—the United States

Theodore (Teddy) Roosevelt (left) rode into the presidency determined to use government to improve working conditions, eliminate business corruption, and preserve national resources. Thirty-two years later, his cousin, Franklin Delano Roosevelt (FDR), used his unbridled confidence and public support for his New Deal to greatly expand the role of the federal government.

through an income tax, made legal by an amendment to the Constitution ratified in 1913. Many states and localities levied gasoline and cigarette taxes and raised property taxes, and some states adopted income taxes. Federal support for state programs also grew through land and cash grants given by the federal government to the states.[26] By the late 1920s, however, most governmental functions still rested primarily in state and local hands. The states were clearly the dominant partner in providing most services, from health and sanitation to police and fire protection; the federal government provided few direct services to individuals. The Great Depression caused a dramatic shift in this arrangement.

The New Deal and World War II

To grasp the scope of the changes that have taken place in our federal structure since 1930, consider the report of a sociologist who studied community life in Muncie, Indiana.[27] In 1924, the federal government in Muncie was symbolized by little more than the post office and the American flag. Now, two-thirds of the households in Muncie depend in part on federal funds—federal employment, Social Security and other income support, veterans' benefits, student scholarships and loans, Medicare and Medicaid, and many other smaller programs.

In large part, the Great Depression brought about these changes. When the stock market crashed in 1929, wealthy people became poor overnight. In the depths of the Depression, one-fourth of the workforce was unemployed, and banks failed daily. Unlike today, there was no systematic national program of relief for the unemployed then—no unemployment compensation, no food stamps, no welfare, nothing to help put food on the table and pay the rent. Millions of Americans were hungry, homeless, and hopeless. States and localities, which had the responsibility for providing relief to the poor, were overwhelmed; they did not have the funds or organizational resources to cope with the millions needing help. And private charities did not have enough resources to assume the burden.

Franklin Roosevelt took office on March 4, 1933. He immediately sent to Congress a group of legislative proposals, many of which Congress passed within the first hundred days of the new administration. Roosevelt's program, known as the New Deal, enlarged the role of the federal government. Shown in the photo are civilians employed in the Works Progress Administration (WPA), a New Deal agency that built schools, roads, airports, bridges, and post offices throughout the country in the 1930s. The agency was successful in putting millions of unemployed Americans to work and at the same time upgrading the nation's public buildings and infrastructure.

The magnitude of the economic crisis led to the election of Democrat Franklin Delano Roosevelt in 1932. During his first two terms, he formulated, and Congress passed, a program called the **New Deal.** Its purpose was to stimulate economic recovery and aid those who were unemployed, hungry, and in ill health. New Deal legislation regulated many activities of business and labor, set up a welfare system, and began large-scale federal-state cooperation in funding and administering programs through federal grants-in-aid. Grants-in-aid provided federal money to states (and occasionally to local governments) to initiate programs that targeted categories of needy people—the aged poor or the unemployed, for example.

These measures had strong popular support, although they were opposed by many business and conservative groups and initially by the Supreme Court. But after Roosevelt's reelection in 1936, the Court became more favorable toward New Deal legislation, and the retirement of two conservative judges shortly thereafter ensured that the Court would be sympathetic to the New Deal (see Chapter 13 for more on the Court and the New Deal).

The Court decisions approving New Deal legislation were, in a sense, a return to the nation-centered federalism of John Marshall's day. But although the Supreme Court upheld much of the New Deal, it also approved more sweeping *state* regulations of business and labor than had the less activist pre–New Deal Court. Thus the change in Court philosophy did not enlarge the federal role at the expense of the powers of the states; *it enlarged the powers of both state and federal government.* In doing so, the Court was responding to the public's preference for government to play a larger role in helping people cope with the crises stemming from the Great Depression.

The Court's rulings dealt a blow to the limited government imagined by the Founders because their sanction of greater federal involvement with states and localities led to changes in patterns of taxing and spending. As Figure 3 indicates, the federal share of spending for domestic needs (exclusive of military spending) nearly tripled, from 17 percent in 1929, before the New Deal, to 47 percent in 1939. The states' share of overall government spending stayed constant, but it increased dramatically in absolute terms, given the huge increase in total public sector spending. The federal government raised more revenue and passed some of it down to states and localities in the form of grants-in-aid to fund unemployment compensation, emergency welfare, and distribution of farm surpluses to the needy and for free school lunches, among other programs. However, local governments' share of overall spending dropped by half, reflecting the greater responsibilities assumed at the state and national level.

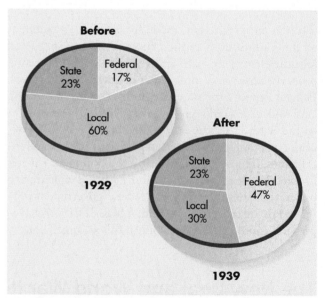

FIGURE 3 ■ **Share of Nonmilitary Spending by the Federal, State, and Local Governments before and after the Passage of New Deal Legislation**

SOURCE: Advisory Commission on Intergovernmental Relations, *Significant Features of Fiscal Federalism* (Washington, D.C.: Government Printing Office, 1979), 7.

Other New Deal policies that directly affected everyday life included new regulations on banks and working conditions, federal redistributive programs designed to protect the poor (Aid to Dependent Children), and social insurance for the elderly poor, retired, and disabled (Social Security). Overall, the New Deal brought a dramatic change in the relationship between the national government and its citizens, making it both more personal and more interdependent.

During the years that followed, increases in federal aid to the states were incremental but steady, and the aid came to carry conditions, or "strings." For example, local administrators of Aid to Dependent Children programs had to be hired on a merit system, not on the basis of political or personal connections. Construction funds for highways could be spent only on highways whose designs met professional standards, not just handed off to contractors friendly to state politicians. This was another step toward weakening the patronage system in state bureaucracies.

The other major event influencing the growth of the national government during this era was World War II. As the war brought the United States out of the Depression, Congress rolled back many of FDR's aid programs, but this could not stop the growth of government. FDR had assumed—as Lincoln had during the Civil War—extraordinary powers to meet the emergencies of wartime, including price controls, rationing, and the suspension of some civil liberties. Spending on armaments and the military gave a tremendous boost to the economy, and defense spending has remained an important element of many states' economies ever since.

Social Justice and the Great Society

By the 1950s, some public officials had become uneasy about the growing size of the federal government and its involvement in so many state and local programs. Yet under President Dwight D. Eisenhower, a Republican concerned about the growth of federal involvement, many new federal grants-in-aid to the states were added, ranging from the massively expensive interstate highway program to college programs in science, engineering, and languages. Federal grant-in-aid spending nearly tripled during his administration (1952–1960). Although worried about the impact of military expenditures on the economy, Eisenhower accepted the United States' post–World War II role in world affairs and did little to reduce military spending.

The size of federal programs exploded in the 1960s. The momentum for change came from the growing number of movements for social justice and racial equality, especially the civil rights movement. Most of the

new programs adopted were initiated by President Lyndon Johnson's massive social welfare program called the Great Society. During the Johnson administration (1963–1968), the federal government began funding work in domains that were formerly state and local preserves, such as law enforcement, urban mass transit, public education, and fire protection. Johnson's concept of federalism was born in the New Deal era. Like Roosevelt, Johnson was a Democrat, and his was a centralizing approach in which program areas were identified by, funded from, and monitored at the national level while allowing states and localities a say on which projects got funded. A new feature of the Great Society era was the increasing number of grants that went directly to localities, bypassing states. City and other local officials, believing that state legislatures were unresponsive to their interests, now demanded, and got, direct federal support.

From 1960 to 1968, as the number of federal programs grew, federal aid more than tripled, and state and local governments became increasingly dependent on federal funding.[28] Whereas state spending had been just 4 percent of gross domestic product (GDP) in 1961, under the Great Society programs it rose to 7 percent of GDP in 1971, but much of this increase was due to additional federal aid, not to the states' own resources.[29] The vast increase in programs and the multiplying requirements and conditions of the grants made federal aid ever more complex. State and local officials soon felt hamstrung by the increasingly burdensome regulations.

New Federalism

When Republican Richard Nixon (1969–1974) came into office, he wanted to make government "more effective as well as more efficient." Nixon took a managerial rather than ideological approach to streamlining the cumbersome structure created by the profusion of Great Society programs. He saw a messy bureaucratic problem and an overconcentration of decision making at the federal level, and he tried to find a solution through more efficient management.[30]

Nixon's plan had two primary elements. One was to consolidate the several hundred grant programs into six major functional areas. Instead of trying to micromanage hundreds of types of grants from the federal level, Washington would make block grants to the states and localities and leave it to them to determine how to fund programs in these functional areas. This greater leeway in how to spend grant money gave local officials more opportunity to target projects to local needs. It also meant administrative streamlining at the federal level.

The second major aspect of Nixon's **new federalism** was general revenue sharing. Under this program, tax money paid into the federal government was returned to the states to fund local projects and services. It was a way of encouraging state activism in the hope that it would decrease the need for federal programs. The main restriction on use was that money had to be spent consistent with federal civil rights and equal opportunity laws.

In contrast to Nixon's managerial approach, the new federalism of Republican Ronald Reagan (1981–1988) had a more ideological purpose, which he made clear in his first inaugural address: "Government is not the solution to our problems," he said. "Government is the problem." Reagan said he was seeking a "quiet revolution" to bring people closer to government. Thus his new federalism was aimed at reducing the power and influence of government rather than at improving intergovernmental management and effectiveness. Instead of seeing block grants as a way to encourage states to provide services the federal government would fund, Reagan saw them as a step toward ending all federal involvement in these program areas. He opposed general revenue sharing and ended that program.

Cuts in federal funding for state and local programs had the pragmatic effect of reducing the size of the budget deficits created by Reagan's increased military spending. But even this had an ideological tinge, because driving up the deficits with military spending reduced the government's domestic capabilities. Reagan's new federalism was rooted not so much in state-centered or dual federalism as it was in his opposition to government in general. Reagan's ultimate goal was to reduce the role of government (except for national defense) at all levels and increase reliance on private markets and institutions.[31] This approach—cutting federal spending on local and state programs to downsize government at all levels—has been called *instrumental federalism,* in contrast with Nixon's "rationalizing" approach, in which making government more efficient and effective was an end in itself.

While Reagan had an ideological commitment to smaller government, he had no significant programmatic approach to achieve it, and he was often more preoccupied with the Cold War than with his domestic programs. In fact, the size and expenditures of the federal government grew during his administration, and states gained few new powers. Reagan took a more indirect approach to rolling back government power by slowing enforcement or blocking implementation of rules he thought were an abuse of federal power.

The New New Federalism

Like Reagan, Democrat Bill Clinton (1993–2000) came to office with a wary view of Washington and a commitment to working in partnership with governors.

Clinton was a multiterm governor from a southern state (Arkansas) where the states' rights tradition held sway. Reforming state-federal relations had been a special interest when, as governor, he chaired both the national organization of governors and a reform group within the Democratic Party. Except in the area of civil rights policy, Clinton claimed to be a supporter of states' rights.

Clinton was not an advocate of state-centered federalism or smaller government for its own sake. But he was committed to the idea of the "states as laboratories" (earlier articulated by Justice Louis Brandeis)—that is, as places for policy experimentation. He used the phrase frequently, wrote it into executive orders, and eventually based his welfare, health care, and education policies around it.[32] From 1994 through the end of his administration, Clinton and congressional Republicans supported policies that delegated more powers to the states. Overall, Clinton's federalism policies were much closer to Nixon's than to Reagan's in that both Clinton and Nixon were primarily interested in "rationalizing intergovernmental relations" and making government more efficient.

The return of powers to make and implement policy to subunits or lower levels of government from a higher level is called **devolution.** Clinton did not support a wholesale surrender of policymaking authority because the federal government still told the states that they had to provide services. But Clinton did embrace the devolutionary trend by adopting a more deferential stance toward the states in implementing federal rules and regulations, especially regulations on business and the environment. (See the discussion of unfunded mandates in the "Conflict" section later in this chapter.)

Clinton's actions were shaped by both his own beliefs and the fact that during most of Clinton's term, Republicans held a majority in Congress. The Gingrich Republicans—named for the speaker of the House, Newt Gingrich, and his conservative Republican allies—on the other hand, shared Reagan's view of government and put forward a legislative program for downsizing the federal government. Returning power to the state and local levels and "rethinking the entire structure of American society, and . . . American government" was their goal.[33]

A Return to State-Centered Federalism?

The fervid support of the Gingrich Republicans for a smaller national government and more power to the states, Clinton's qualified acceptance of both, and a series of Supreme Court rulings that favored state immunity from federal rules suggested that by the time George W. Bush took office, the country was headed toward a more state-centered form of federalism. This final section on the growth of government looks at current views of the federal relationship.

President

Clinton favored delegating rule implementation to state agencies, but he insisted on the right of federal agencies to set national standards, such as for clean air and water and consumer and worker safety. During his last months in office, Clinton imposed a number of such standards by executive order. Bush, like Clinton, came to the presidency from the governorship of a southern state (Texas), but unlike Clinton, Bush advocated returning power to the states. Within months of taking office, Bush reversed many of the Clinton executive orders, including standards for arsenic levels in water, pollutants in the air, and health and safety in the workplace. In addition, he issued a new order making it harder for federal officials to overrule state decisions. The attitude of the Bush administration to the nation-state division of power might be best summarized by a close adviser's description of an ideal government as one "cut 'down to the size where we can drown it in the bathtub'."[34]

But in fact Bush has sent mixed signals on state-centered federalism. While being an advocate for devolution in domestic policymaking, especially regulatory policy, Bush has an expansive view of the powers of the president and the national armed forces. He also wanted a less open government and issued orders limiting public access to information about the workings of the national government. His support for expanding the role of the states in making and implementing welfare policy was countered by his intervention in public education to impose mandatory national testing on local school systems. (See the "Providing a Spare" box.) Even in the area of business regulation, Bush has sometimes butted heads with governors, most of whom want to regulate the distribution of electric power in their states. Bush argued that state regulation was inefficient and called for the construction of a national distribution system for electrical power.

Supreme Court

For more than a decade, the rulings of the Supreme Court have shown a trend toward empowering the states at the expense of the national government. Between 1992 and 2002, it handed down seven key decisions that restrict Congress's ability to impose rules and regulations on state governments and prevent litigants from bypassing state courts to seek remedies in federal courts. In a 1995 decision, the Court ruled for the first time since the New Deal that Congress had exceeded its authority to regulate interstate commerce. Although the rulings do not try to reinterpret or limit the areas in which Congress can legislate, the Court has overturned a number of obligations Congress had placed on the states to implement federal laws. Once the thinking of the Court's majority was known, dozens of other federalism suits were filed by those who want to limit Congress's ability to extend federal laws to state jurisdictions. For example, these suits have been successful in preventing a disabled person alleging a workplace violation of his civil rights as guaranteed under the Americans with Disabilities Act from suing his employer in a state court.

The current Court's interpretation of federal relations has been summarized as "rights without remedies," or one that permits Congress to confer rights on citizens but not to tell the states how to enforce them. The four dissenting justices say that recent decisions giving states immunity from federal rules are the "result of a fundamentally flawed understanding of the role of the states within the federal system" and that they intend to go on dissenting in all cases where this principle of state immunity is applied by the Court's majority.[35]

But the Supreme Court, like the White House and Congress, swings between support for states' rights and the exercise of federal authority. In 2000, during a high tide of rulings in defense of states' rights, the Court intervened in the recount of votes cast by Floridians in the presidential election, overruling the Florida Supreme Court. (Elections, whether for national, state, or local office, are the jurisdiction of the states, not the federal government.) This federal intervention, in a partisan 5–4 ruling that applied only to this election, determined that Bush would get the state's electoral votes, thus deciding the outcome of the presidential election. (See "You Are There" in Chapter 13.)

Congress

Despite its support for devolution, Congress appears to have few advocates of pure state-centered federalism. While willing to delegate some authority, Congress continues to supersede the states in rule making whenever it thinks it necessary. In recent years, bills have been introduced to supplant state laws on drunk driving with a national standard, allow property owners to bypass state courts and go directly to federal courts to protest local zoning laws, and override state laws on late-term abortions, medical use of marijuana, and assisted suicides.[36] In 1998, Congress used its power to regulate interstate commerce to impose a three-year moratorium on state taxation of e-commerce and other Internet activity. States claimed it would cost them $20 billion in lost revenue.[37] Even after twenty states had negotiated interstate tax collection agreements and lobbied hard for lifting the ban, Congress renewed it in 2002 and again in 2004, when most states were facing serious declines in revenue and budget deficits.

Few people argue that the states could do a better job than Washington providing for the national defense. But there is sharp disagreement over which level of government can make other policies more efficiently and effectively. In practice, this issue is rarely decided on principle. Sometimes one level of government fails at a certain task and so it gets reassigned to another level. Or as one cynic put it, for those times when "we have wrecked one level of government, the Founding Fathers had the foresight to provide a spare."[1]

Most people are pragmatic, favoring policies that work, no matter who runs the program. This can be illustrated by a look at two policy areas: the much-maligned federal welfare program, administration of which has been put in the hands of the states, and state- and locally managed public education, for which the federal government is assuming increasing responsibility. These examples illustrate how, for political and pragmatic reasons, state and national levels shift the burden for policy-making and implementation.

Welfare: The Feds Step Back

By the 1990s, many Americans saw welfare policy as a bungled federal program that was pouring billions of dollars annually into subsidized income and health support programs while doing little to help decrease recipients' need for them. Welfare programs were always jointly funded and implemented by Washington and the states and localities, with much of the administration at the county level. But the federal government got all the criticism because Congress authorized the programs.

In Arkansas, Bill Clinton, like many other governors, wanted control over welfare because of rising costs, the increasing number of services mandated from Washington, and poor program performance. Clinton made this an issue in his 1992 presidential campaign, and when he was elected, he found Congress sympathetic to reform. So in 1996, Congress, with Clinton's approval, devolved welfare programs on the states. The federal government would continue to mandate services and provide grants to pay for them, but the states would decide how to provide the services and how to meet the time limits set on eligibility. This new approach was meant to rationalize the administrative process by giving states more autonomy over a program they had long been implementing. But it was also smart politics because it transferred accountability to the level where most administrative decisions were being made.

A major feature of the reform was that all able-bodied applicants for welfare were supposed to work full- or part-time to remain eligible for benefits. The booming economy of the late 1990s gave all states a leg up in making welfare reform work. The millions of new jobs created helped many welfare recipients leave the rolls for full-time employment as employers scrambled to find workers and were willing to train those who didn't have it.

But it is arguable whether state control over welfare programs has made them more efficient, less expensive, or more responsive to local needs. In Wisconsin, the initial costs actually rose because of that state's intensive approach to reintegrating the unemployed in the job market. So many new programs were created they were described as a "mini–New Deal."[2] But in other states, many qualified children and poor families went without health insurance or food stamps after the reform because their state governments did not spend all the money allocated by Congress or diverted it to other programs favored by the middle class.[3]

Five years after the reform, the average number of welfare recipients who were working ranged from 20 to 30 percent. Most of those workers had high school diplomas or some additional education. Then a recession set in and states faced having to train the less skilled to find jobs at a time when unemployment was rising, state revenues were in freefall, and many new jobs did not pay enough to meet basic expenses and pay for child care. More than thirty states have since had to cut funding for training and assistance programs or subsidies and cash benefits, but the Bush administration is planning an expansion of state authority over welfare programs.[4]

Education: The Feds Step In

While the federal government has reduced its role in welfare, it has increased its role in education. Elementary and secondary education have been locally controlled since the earliest days of the Republic. In those early years, when communities were often segregated by religious or other sectarian beliefs, rural people especially feared government interference in their districts. They wanted to be free to develop local schools to conform with local beliefs.[5]

The common school movement eventually put most public school education in the hands of professionals, but policymaking remained with local school boards and state officials.[6] Fifty years ago, we had over 100,000 school districts; today we still have about 13,500, each making its own decisions on what students need to know and how to measure their performance.

There has never been an attempt to organize these thousands of districts into a national system. Even the creation of the cabinet-level Office of Education by the Carter administration in 1979 was controversial. Republican opponents saw it as one more step toward co-opting this quintessential local responsibility.

But during the 1990s, a general rumbling about the failure of public schools grew to a roar. American schoolchildren consistently scored well below their peers in other industrialized countries in science and math skills. Employers believed that the level and type of training offered in high schools was inappropriate for a labor market transformed by globalization, high technology, and the need for good communication skills. In addition, there was a general feeling among the public that schools were lax in teaching character and too tolerant of misbehavior, drug use, truancy, and even violence.

Washington began to take notice and for more than a decade tinkered with various kinds of reforms: a voluntary national curriculum, an idea from the George H. Bush administration; Clinton's idea of a voluntary national testing system; and a Republican-backed school choice program, which was enacted by Congress.[7] This was a voucher program that allowed tax dollars to help pay tuition for children in privately run schools. This encouraged the creation of new private schools, known as charter schools, to compete with the public schools (the assumption being that competition would force the public schools to improve in order to retain their students). Almost all school districts responded to the growing criticism, trying to improve performance and develop their own systems of standards-based testing. But public confidence that localities could fix the broken system appeared to be waning.

George W. Bush then proposed federal intervention through a system of mandatory testing under his 2001 "Leave No Child Behind" program. Instead of pushing for national standards or a standardized curriculum, Bush recommended mandatory testing in English, math, and science for every child, beginning in the third grade. Every state was ordered to develop its own system of standards-based reform by 2006; by 2014, all students must meet those standards. Success is measured by the students' ability to pass the standards-based tests devised by their school districts. There is *no national standard*. The program also requires teachers to show proficiency in the specific subjects they teach.

Thus the Bush program imposes a national rule for testing and a core set of subjects, but it allows localities considerable flexibility in how they measure proficiency. However, this is the most significant federal intervention in local education yet. Although school districts can still set their curricula and devise their own tests, they have far less autonomy in deciding how the school day is spent. A large part of every teacher's effort must be devoted to preparing students to pass tests in the core subjects. If the minimum number of students fail to pass and a school is labeled as "failing," federal dollars for running the testing program could be lost, and parents could opt to transfer their children to another school. If enough pupils are lost, a school could even be closed.

It is too early to know what impact the national testing system will have on the quality of education, but the concentration on math and science has led to declining performance in other areas of study, such as the social sciences.[8] And implementation of the program has frustrated many teachers and administrators with its added costs and emphasis on test preparation. The core subject measure of school performance and teacher proficiency does not allow for the great variations in school districts. Many urban schools are filled with non-English-speaking students who cannot perform well in the lower grades on English-language tests. Small rural schools frequently employ teachers who must cover many subjects and are not able to show proficiency in all. Yet when schools are labeled as "failing," they must pay for special tutors and for additional teacher training, money most districts do not have.

Yet Congress has never appropriated all of the funding authorized for No Child Left Behind. State governments, which already pick up 90 percent of the costs for public schools, are having trouble finding money for the extra services.[9] In 2003, with one school in four deemed to be failing, the government began issuing mass exemptions.[10]

The Utah House passed a law authorizing noncompliance with any

(continued)

provision of the act that the federal government did not fund. Public willingness, even eagerness, to have the federal government get involved in public education and to have state governments assume responsibility for welfare policy illustrates the politics of policymaking in a federal system. Clinton, an advocate of nation-centered federalism, devolved welfare policy to the states, and Bush, an advocate of state-centered federalism, intervened in education, the most localized of all policy areas. In both cases, action was taken for political, not philosophical or ideological, reasons. There was a widespread demand for action, and policymakers wanted to be responsive. But the public was not clamoring for either centralization or devolution. People want policy that works, by whatever level of government can make it work.

1. John D. Donahue, "The Disunited States," *Atlantic Monthly*, May 1997, 20.
2. Gary Wills, "The War between the States . . . and Washington," *New York Times Magazine*, July 5, 1998, 27.
3. "States Sitting on Unspent Welfare Funds, Group Says," *Champaign-Urbana News-Gazette*, February 24, 2000, A-4; "Audit: States Denying Medicaid," *Champaign-Urbana News-Gazette*, December 15, 1999, A6; Robert Pear, "Cash to Ensure Health Coverage for the Poor Goes Unused," *New York Times*, May 21, 2000, 22.
4. Corine Hegland, "Nickel-and-Diming," *National Journal*, August 9, 2003, 2545; "Shifting Responsibility to the States," *CQ Weekly*, April 10, 2004, 853.
5. Carl F. Kaestle, "Introduction to Part One: The Common Schools," in *School: The Story of American Public Education*, ed. Sarah Mondale and Sarah B. Patton (Boston: Beacon Press, 2001), 15.
6. David Tyack, "Introduction" in *School*, 4.
7. James Traub, "The Test Mess," *New York Times Magazine*, April 7, 2002, 48.
8. Brian Friel, "Don't Know Much about History," *National Journal*, August 2, 2003, 2500–2501.
9. Corine Hegland, "Learning Subtraction," *National Journal*, August 9, 2003, 2542–2543.
10. Sam Dillon, "U. S. Set to Ease Some Provisions of School Law," *New York Times*, March 14, 2004, 1, 21.

One member of Congress said of his colleagues that they "don't really believe in states' rights; they believe in deciding the issue at whatever level of government they think will do it their way. They want to be Thomas Jefferson on Monday, Wednesday and Friday and Alexander Hamilton on Tuesday and Thursday and Saturday."[38] That is why there is no sustained momentum toward giving power to the states.

The States

States are key players in the federal relationship, not just entities that are acted on. All states make important policies affecting their citizens' lives, and the policy preferences of each state's citizens and officials influence the balance of power between Washington and the state capitals. For example, some states have been very supportive of publicly funded social insurance and mass transit programs and the taxes needed to pay for them, while others are committed to limited state action and no income taxes.

Recent decades have witnessed increased state activism in part because of the public's expectations of government and Washington's refusal or inability to satisfy them. During the Reagan years, there was an ideological commitment to reducing the scope of government in every area but national security. Yet those years of tax cutting and increased spending on defense left spiraling budget deficits and imposed fiscal restraints that made it difficult for the Clinton administration or Congress to propose new initiatives or to fund existing programs. The Vietnam War and the Watergate, Iran-Contra, and Clinton scandals all contributed to increased partisanship and gridlock at the federal level and to declining trust among the public. State governments began looking less often to Washington, instead launching their own policy initiatives.

In the 1990s, the states experimented with charter schools and vouchers for private schools, rolled back affirmative action and bilingual programs, looked at new ways to try to teach religion in schools, and adopted a variety of crime laws such as mandatory sentencing, three-strikes laws, and victims' compensation. A few states adopted term limits and tax caps and passed their own campaign financing laws. Some placed restrictions on gay rights, while others passed laws strengthening those rights, granting health benefits to gay partners, and a few states recognized the right to same-sex marriages. After gaining control over welfare, the states experimented with many different job training and work programs.[39] In addition, they became more bold in challenging or refusing to enforce federal regulations affecting business and the environment and in one case refused to implement federal gun laws.

State activism increased during the George W. Bush administration as Washington continued its retreat from many policy areas and became preoccupied with the war on terrorism. While Congress was stalemated on how to handle the cloning issue, twenty-two state legislatures took up their own anticloning bills.[40] As the Bush administration was rolling back regulation, the states began reregulating, especially in the areas of consumer and worker safety. Some state legislatures outlawed predatory lending.[41] Some passed "no call" laws limiting tele-marketing that proved so popular that Congress rushed to approve a national do-not-call register. One lawyer called the amount of new state legislation on workplace conditions—electronic monitoring of workers, child labor laws, right to breast-feed—"mind-boggling."[42] On the use of genetic testing in hiring, for example, twenty-one states had already passed laws protecting workers from use of such tests by their employer before Congress even held hearings.[43] Thirty-four states enacted some form of equal-pay legislation, and almost half of all states in 2002 were considering laws to raise the minimum wage above the national level. Interest groups, seeing the trend, are shifting their effort toward the states. Some of the largest have lobbying operations in all fifty states.

It is important to remember that through all these policy changes, nothing has changed in the constitutional relationship between the national and state governments. Authority delegated can be taken back by the center. This is where the divergence of views occurs among contemporary supporters of devolution. Advocates of state-centered and dual federalism believe Washington has only surrendered powers that by right belong to the states, whereas the nonideological supporters of devolution see it as a practical measure to bring more efficiency to policymaking and implementation.

But devolution carries no guarantee of greater efficiency or responsiveness. States are not bureaucracy free. Collectively, state and local governments account for 86 percent of all civilian governmental employees, 33 percent of all governmental spending, and about 12 percent of GDP.[44]

Neither is devolution a guarantee of greater responsiveness to the public. States operate outside the spotlight of the national media, and in some states, media coverage is quite limited. State officials' work is less well known, and so in some ways, state officials are less accountable to the citizens than national officials. In some states, lobbyists and special interests are as at least as powerful as those in Washington.

The Practice of Federalism

Today's federalism is a mixture of cooperation and conflict. One expert calls it "competitive federalism" because states and the federal government are competing for leadership of the nation's domestic policy.[45] At the same time, Washington and the fifty states cooperate to carry out the day-to-day work of government.

Federal-State Relations

Given the large number of governments in the United States (see Table 1), cooperation is essential. The term **cooperative federalism** describes the day-to-day joint activities and continuing cooperation among federal, state, and local officials in carrying out the business of government: distributing payments to farmers, providing welfare services, planning highways, organizing centers for the elderly, and carrying out all the functions that the national and state governments jointly fund and organize. It also refers to informal cooperation in locating criminals, tracking down the source of contagious diseases, and many other activities.

One example of informal but intensive cooperation is the Centers for Disease Control and Prevention in Atlanta, which helps state and local governments meet health emergencies and prevent the spread of contagious diseases. National and state police and other crime-fighting agencies share data on crimes and criminals. The federal government and the states also jointly regulate in many areas, including occupational safety and the environment. Today, state agencies are responsible for 90 percent of all environmental enforcement actions.[46] And since the 2001 terrorist attacks, there is increased reliance on state resources to help with national defense. (See the box "The States' Role in National Defense.")

To help pay for essential services provided by state and local governments, the federal government returns tax revenues to states (see Figure 4 on page 80). Mass transit, community development, and unemployment compensation are good examples. Despite some

| TABLE 1 | **Number of Government Units in the United States** |

Part of the reason that intergovernmental relations in the United States are so complex is that there are so many units of government. Though the number of school districts has decreased dramatically since World War II and the number of townships has declined slowly, the number of "special districts"—created for a single purpose, such as parks, airports, or flood control management—continues to grow.

Year	States	Counties	Municipalities	Townships and Towns	School Districts	Special Districts*
1942	48	3,050	16,220	18,919	108,579	8,299
2002†	50	3,034	19,429	16,504	13,506	35,052

*Includes natural resource, fire protection, housing, and community development districts.
†Latest figures available. The Census Bureau takes a count of governmental units every five years, in years ending in 2 and 7.
SOURCE: U.S. Census Bureau, *Statistical Abstract of the United States, 2003* (Washington, D.C.: Government Printing Office, 2004), tab. 431.

THE STATES' ROLE IN NATIONAL DEFENSE

Because the tactics of today's terrorists involve attacking from within, targeting infrastructure, and causing as many civilian deaths as possible, the cooperation of all levels and areas of government is essential to both prevent and respond to attacks. The federal-, state-, and local-level efforts to cope with the events of 9/11 demonstrated that procedures to facilitate cooperation among agencies were woefully inadequate, due to incompatible communications technology, inaccessible databases, and unintegrated command structures. After the creation of the Homeland Security Department in 2002, its secretary, Tom Ridge, assigned governors the responsibility for coordinating security planning at the state and local levels. Since then, every governor has appointed a state director of homeland security.[1] Homeland security has been a major strain on state and localities budgets and activities.

Although the security role for the states has been enhanced, it is not new. State and federal governments have been collaborating on national defense since the first years of the Republic. Every state has a militia provided for by Article I and the Second Amendment of the U.S. Constitution, as well as by each state's constitution. In the early days, when there was no standing army, the state militia provided most of the troops for the Revolution, the frontier wars, and the War of 1812. In fact, the militias were the recipients of the first grant-in-aid ever given by Congress to the states.[2]

Known as the National Guard since 1933, the militias are still jointly funded by Washington and the states. Governors serve as commanders in chief and appoint officers, replaced by the president only when units are activated for national service. Each state determines how members of its Guard are recruited. (You may want to look at your state constitution to see what your obligations are.) The United States is the only advanced industrial country with a military establishment that has dual national and state sources of command and loyalty.

Today, most people still associate the National Guard with state and local affairs rather than national defense—emergency assistance in times of natural disasters such as floods and forest fires or as a supplement to local and state police forces in times of social unrest. President have nationalized (or threatened to nationalize) the Guard in some states to enforce federal law, as Dwight Eisenhower did to enforce school integration in Little Rock, Arkansas, and John Kennedy did to end racial segregation at the University of Mississippi, but they are still thought of as local resources. Yet in the past fifteen years, the Guard has in fact become a source of ready reserves for the U.S. armed forces. Thousands of men and women from National Guard units served in the Persian Gulf War and afterward policed the no-fly zones in Iraq. In combination with other reserve units, National Guard troops outnumbered regular army personnel in peacekeeping

missions in the Balkans and made up 40 percent of all troops on the ground in Iraq in 2004.[3]

With the largest call-up of the National Guard since World War II—more than 300,000 Guard members have been put on active duty since 9/11—the impact on state resources has been heavy, especially in states like Idaho, where 62 percent of the Guard was deployed to Iraq. Not all states were hit that hard, but governors complained to Congress and the Pentagon that they "were facing severe manpower shortages in guarding prisoners, fighting wildfires, preparing for hurricanes and floods and policing the streets."[4] Oregon was left with half its usual number of firefighters during the hot, dry summer of 2004, while California's fire and forestry officials found themselves without some of the Blackhawk helicopters it normally borrows from the Guard for firefighting because the choppers were needed in Iraq.

Governors also have had to respond to the needs of troopers' families, especially those whose main wage earners had their tours of duty extended multiple times. National Guard families, unlike those of the regular military, do not receive medical benefits. Some states tried to help with these costs and to provide other kinds of assistance, such as "college tuition and housing assistance for the children of those killed in the war."[5]

With these new demands on their resources, state governments are looking for more help from Washington. While

inefficiency, federal funding has succeeded in helping state and local governments meet real needs. Along the way, the performance standards and regulations attached to the grants have increased the professionalism of state and local bureaucrats.

State also receive indirect aid from the federal government in the form of deductions for individual taxpayers. When reporting income to the Internal Revenue Service, residents of all states are allowed to deduct the amount of income, real estate, and personal property

vice, and other federal, state, and local law enforcement agencies.[9]

As the state and local responsibilities continue to expand, the mayor of Baltimore said that homeland security has become a "new unfunded mandate called 'the common defense.'"[10]

1. Visit your state's home page and link to its Department of Homeland Security (it may be under Emergency Management Services). You will see security alerts and information on what is being done locally to prepare for terrorist attacks.
2. On the creation and evolution of state militias, see William H. Riker, *Soldiers of the States* (Washington, D.C.: Public Affairs Press, 1957).
3. Sydney J. Freedberg, "Weekend Warriors No More," *National Journal,* June 8, 2002, 1690–1698; George Cahlink, "The National Guard Changes Its Stripes," *National Journal,* April 24, 2004, 1271.
4. Sarah Kershaw, "Governors Tell of War's Impact on Local Needs," *New York Times,* July 20, 2004, 1.
5. Katherine Q. Seelye, "As War Toll Rises, Governors Face Delicate Decisions," *New York Times,* June 9, 2004, A14.
6. Raymond Hernandez, "New York Sees a Silver Lining in the Orange Alert," *New York Times,* February 23, 2003, WK3.
7. Siobhan Gorman, "Homeland Security's 'Intractable Problem,'" *National Journal,* August 8, 2003, 2548; Martin Kady II, "Localities Get the Bill for Beefed-Up Security," *CQ Weekly,* April 10, 2004, 852. Check your state's homeland security Web site and you will probably find an online form for cities to request reimbursement for the extra costs for emergency security measures.
8. "Report: States, Cities Don't Feel Informed Enough on Terror," *Champaign-Urbana News-Gazette,* August 28, 2003, A3; Siobhan Gorman, "On Guard, but How Well?" *National Journal,* March 6, 2004, 702.
9. David Johnston and Douglas Jehl, "CIA Sends Terror Experts to Tell Small Towns of Risk," *New York Times,* July 18, 2004, 13.
10. Martin O'Malley, quoted in Gorman, "Homeland Security's 'Intractable Problem,'" 2548.

the federal government has stressed the fundamental importance of the "first responders"—firefighters, police, medical technicians, and hazmat (hazardous materials) specialists—funds to pay them have actually been cut. The federal government says it is not its place to hire police or firefighters, only to pay for homeland security training and equipment. This leaves states with greatly enlarged responsibilities at a time when shortfalls in state budgets have caused a number of cities to cut the size of their police and fire departments. During the first eighteen months after 9/11, cities reported spending more than $2.5 billion on homeland security with no federal reimbursement.[6] It costs city governments collectively about $70 million

to pay for the extra security measures every week that the Homeland Security Department has the country on a heightened alert.[7]

Local officials want better intelligence as well as more money. Federal intelligence officials have been loath to share intelligence for fear that local officials would disclose classified information.[8] But this relationship is now changing, and the CIA, which has historically had little contact with local agencies and by law is not allowed to collect domestic intelligence, is sending agents to brief city and other local officials on terrorism. Eighty joint terrorism task forces have been set up around the country to coordinate the work of the FBI, Homeland Security, Secret Ser-

taxes they paid to their states and localities. This is counted as aid to the states because it lowers federal revenue by billions of dollars each year while leaving more money to be spent in the states.

Conflict

There is always some element of conflict present in federal–state relations; it is inherent in the division of powers between the two levels of government. Among the most constant thorns in the side of state governments

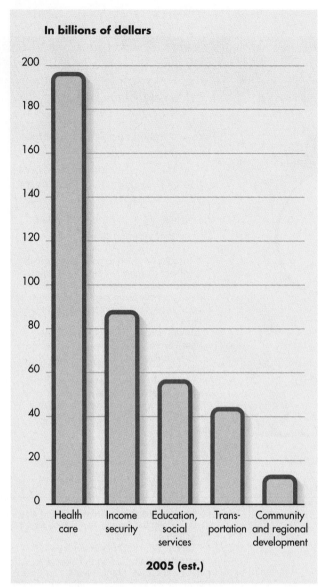

In billions of dollars

FIGURE 4 ■ **What Does the Federal Government Give the States Money to Do?** *Ninety-two percent of the estimated $401.5 billion the federal government is sending back to the states in 2005 is for programs in these areas.*

Source: "Historical Tables," *Budget of the United States, Fiscal Year 2005* (Washington, D.C.: Government Printing Office, 2004), tab. 12.2.

are **unfunded mandates,** laws or regulations imposed on the states unaccompanied by sufficient funding to implement them. For example, Congress has made it mandatory for states to deduct child support from the wages of parents who fall behind on payments and from the paychecks of fathers of children whose mothers are on welfare.[47] The administrative costs incurred in carrying out such mandates are substantial, yet states that fail to enforce them risk losing federal contributions to their welfare funds.

Implementation of federal environmental regulations also imposes heavy costs, although some states have imposed higher standards on themselves (such as for clean air) than the federal government has. Other federal laws order states and localities to make alterations to public buildings, sidewalks, and transportation facilities to ensure that they are accessible to people with disabilities. States are also required to educate the children of illegal immigrants and to pay for emergency health care for them; these costs have become so staggering in the states with the highest numbers of illegal residents that governors have sued the federal government for reimbursement.

The financial burden of unfunded mandates led state and local officials to join together to mount a national campaign to restrict their use. Congress passed a bill reforming procedures under which unfunded or underfunded mandates, especially regulatory mandates, are sent to the states, but it stopped short of prohibiting them. The federal government is required to provide information on the costs of implementing laws and rules before Congress or an executive branch agency, such as the Environmental Protection Agency, can adopt them. Federal agencies are required to consult with states and localities before imposing mandates and to adopt regulations that impose the smallest burden for implementation.[48] But unfunded mandates roll on under Democrats and Republicans alike: George W. Bush's "No Child Left Behind" education reform and Homeland Security's imposition of an array of new law enforcement and disaster preparation functions on state and localities are two recent examples.

Another source of national-state friction is the management of federally owned land—military bases, weapons facilities, and national park and wilderness areas. Twenty-seven percent of all land within the United States is held by the federal government, the majority in western states. Few Americans are against national parks or national defense, but in those states where half or more of the land is federally owned, state governments often do not have the control they would like to have over the state's natural resources. Usually the friction is over economic exploitation of resources in park land, but sometimes states object to activities they believe put their populations at risk—radioactivity from weapons production or the testing and storage of nuclear waste (as described in "You Are There" at the start of this chapter).

States and Localities as Lobbyists

Lobbying is a crucial part of the relationship between the states and the federal government. The importance of federal money to states and localities and the need for coordination between federal and state bureaucracies have stimulated the organization of groups of state and local officials, such as the National Conference of State Legislatures, the National League of Cities, and the

American Public Welfare Association. These groups lobby for favorable legislation for states and localities and work with federal agencies to ensure that new regulations are implemented in a way that is acceptable to the states. Most of these organizations have multimillion-dollar budgets and employ sizable staffs. Many individual states and cities have their own Washington lobbyists, who appear to have some positive effect on increasing federal aid.[49]

But why should states lobby when they are all represented by their elected representatives in the House and Senate? Lobbying organizations have the capability to contact large numbers of members at the same time. Moreover, the members of a state's congressional delegation may belong to different parties than state leaders, or they may not agree with state leaders—as, for example, when Congress waived state sales tax on e-commerce. Or a state may have an urban majority while its congressional delegation is closer in views to rural and suburban residents. But mainly states hire lobbyists because there is a lot at stake.

The Assembly on Federal Issues, the group that coordinates the lobbying of the National Conference of State Legislatures, monitors bills under consideration by every major committee in Congress. The groups looks especially for any new provisions that would undercut state laws, have an impact on state revenue, or tie the hands of state officials in some policy area. For example, some states are concerned about the free-trade agreements Congress has approved. Many states are big exporters, and if Congress says that certain countries are exempt from paying import taxes, it could affect the competitiveness of a state's businesses and ultimately the state's revenues. So states lobby in large part to maintain maximum control over their legislative, regulatory, and taxing authority.

Interstate Relations

Constitutional Relationship

Dealing with Washington is not the only problem in intergovernmental relations that the states face. State governments must also work with one another. The Constitution established rules governing some aspects of interstate relationships. One important provision is the **full faith and credit clause,** which requires states to recognize contracts made in other states. The Constitution also provides that if a fugitive from justice flees from one state to another, the suspect, once captured, will be extradited (sent back) to the state with jurisdiction.

Normally, meeting full faith and credit requirements is rather routine. However, politics vary from state to state, and occasionally for one state to honor the laws of another can be controversial. A historical example is the Fugitive Slave Act, which required the authorities in every state to return escaped slaves to their owners. This is something abolitionists living in free states were loath to do yet bound to do by the Constitution.

More recently, marriage contracts have become an issue. Some opponents to gay marriage have argued that under the full faith and credit rule, a gay marriage contracted in one state would have to be recognized by every state. When Vermont became the first state to register same-sex unions, it set off a controversy in other states worried about having to extend to gay partners the same legal status and rights (health, retirement, and inheritance benefits) as married heterosexual couples. In response, Congress passed the Defense of Marriage Act, which gave every state the right not to recognize same-sex marriages conducted in other states. But when the Massachusetts Supreme Court ruled that it was unconstitutional for officials in that state to deny gay partners marriage licenses on the grounds that it was equivalent to denying a civil right granted to heterosexuals, the controversy deepened. After a few states began issuing marriage licenses to gay couples, officials in states that did not want to honor these contracts appealed to the Bush administration to support an amendment to the U.S. Constitution that would define marriage as a contract between a man and a woman.

Voluntary Cooperation

All governors have to deal with a set of common problems such as resource management, education, fostering economic growth, taxation, crime, and prison systems, in addition to managing their relationships with Washington. The Governors Conference, which meets annually, was formed to facilitate information sharing and cooperation among the governors of all states.

Most state-to-state interaction is informal and voluntary; state officials consult with and borrow ideas from one another. Sometimes states enter into formal agreements, called *interstate compacts,* to deal with a shared problem—operating a port or allocating water from a river basin, for example. In fact, access to water supplies, for residential and industrial use, is one of the most common areas of state cooperation and conflict. Some states have agreements exempting citizens of neighboring states who have taken up temporary residence from paying local income taxes.

Interstate Competition

There has always been competition among the states due to cultural, political, and regional differences as well as economic competition among themselves and for aid from the federal government.

Changing economic patterns and an overall loss of economic competitiveness by the United States in the world market have stimulated vigorous competition among the states to attract new businesses and jobs. Governors market their states to prospective new businesses by touting lower taxes, a better climate, a more skilled or better educated workforce, and less government regulation than other states competing for the same business. Most states are willing to give tax subsidies and other financial incentives to companies willing to relocate. Critics believe that these offers erode a state's tax base and have little impact on most business relocation decisions, and there is some evidence to support that view.[50] Nevertheless, without offering tax breaks or deferments or other subsidies, most states feel at a competitive disadvantage in recruiting new businesses.

The tax burden may be one factor in individuals' decisions on where to settle, and the absence of an income tax is a benefit trumpeted by nine states. One estimate is that during the 1990s, almost three million people relocated to states without income taxes. Between 1990 and 2000, the overall population growth in the forty-one states that have income taxes was 11 percent, while in the nine states that have none, it was 22 percent.[51] But this relationship is not consistent for every state, and it may reflect other factors influencing resettlement, such as climate. Furthermore, if taxes are so low that the quality of schools and public services are affected, they will almost certainly be a disincentive to both population growth and business relocation.

One certain prerequisite for business and population growth is an ample water supply, and given our shrinking resources, maintaining or increasing water flow into and out of states is a high-priority issue, especially for states that do not have large bodies of water within their boundaries. These are the everyday issues that governors and other state officials are continuously negotiating. How much water should New York state officials agree to be taken from upstate farmers for urban dwellers or for use in New Jersey and Connecticut? The waters of the Upper Colorado are shared by four states and those of the Lower Colorado by three others. So rural residents of Colorado constantly struggle to keep ever more water from being channeled from the Colorado River to meet the needs of fast-growing metropolitan areas in other states.

As the federal government continues to devolve responsibilities to the states, and as federal aid has grown as a percentage of state spending, competition among states to get ever larger shares of that aid has increased. States with powerful members in their congressional delegations usually fare better than others in the share of federal tax dollars returned to their home districts. And smaller states at times find common interest in voting as a bloc in the Senate to prevent the largest states from getting a share of aid in proportion to their population. This has been true even with respect to homeland security funding, in which the more populous and higher-risk states like New York have found themselves outvoted by smaller states in attempts to win funding proportionate to their larger populations and greater chance of attack.[52]

State-Local Relations

The relationship of states to their localities—counties, cities, and special districts—is another important feature of contemporary federalism. All but fifty-one of 87,575 government units in the United States exist below the level of state government (see Table 1). These relationships are defined by state constitutions; they are not dealt with in the federal Constitution, and states differ in the autonomy they grant to their localities. Some state constitutions grant **home rule** to local governments, giving them considerable autonomy in such matters as setting tax rates, regulating land use, and choosing their form of local government. Cities of dif-

AP/Wide World Photos

From 2000 to 2004, states went from record-breaking surpluses to a collective budget gap of $84 billion. The decline in both state and federal aid to police and fire departments led to forced cuts across the country. This fire station in Revere, Massachusetts, was one of the many forced to close.

ferent sizes may have different degrees of autonomy, depending on the state. And in some states, counties are given the power to create levels of government below them. In Illinois, for example, each county can decide whether to establish township governments or do without them.

Although states cannot be altered or dissolved by the national government, localities are just creatures of their states. Yet some of the same problems that affect national-state relations also affect state-local relations. City and county officials often wish for more authority and fewer mandates from the state capitol.

People, States, and the Federal Government

One of the most important elements in the federal relationship is the people. In a system with power divided among levels of government and responsibilities divided among thousands of governmental units, where do the people fit? How do they elect and communicate with all these officials and get them to be responsive?

It is often claimed that people feel closer to their state than to the national government. At the state level, the argument goes, government and its decision makers are nearby and more accessible to the voters, more likely to have a sense of their public mood, and consequently more responsive to their specific preferences. This is important because economic conditions and political culture vary from state to state, resulting in different policy preferences. Moreover, local officials may have a better grasp of local conditions and therefore be better situated to shape policy to fit these preferences.

Are state governments more responsive to the people? State governments are undeniably smaller than the national government. Although the United States has more than 290 million residents, nine states have populations under a million. (At the other end of the spectrum, 42 percent of all Americans live in states with more than ten million residents.) But smaller does not make for greater familiarity; the average person is not necessarily better informed about state and local officials than national ones. As indicated, most local candidates and officeholders get far less media exposure than national candidates, partly because there are so many of them. Voter turnout rates for local and state elections suggest that there is less interest in state and local than in national government.

And if the basic premise about size and distance is correct, then people should be even closer to local government than to state government. There is no evidence that this is true either. There are layers of local government, some with taxing authority, such as townships,

special districts, or planning agencies, that Americans know little about. And although most Americans know about school districts and city councils, voter turnout is much lower in elections for those bodies than in state and federal elections, and public knowledge about most of these officials is very low.

One indication that Americans neither feel especially close to state and local governments nor feel that those governments are responsive to them was the increasing use of the ballot initiative throughout the 1990s. Interest groups tried to bypass not only Congress but state legislatures by getting policy questions placed on state ballots and having them decided directly by voters. Doing an end run around their state and local elected representatives, voters approved initiatives that killed state laws on affirmative action, sanctioned medical use of marijuana, imposed limits on campaign spending and contributions, expanded casino gambling, and gave adopted children the right to know the names of their biological parents. About 40 percent of all initiatives in these years became law, whereas only a tiny percentage of bills submitted to legislatures get passed into law.[53]

But laws passed through initiatives can be confusing. One year, California's citizens had to wade through a 222-page pamphlet outlining ballot choices. In San Francisco, facing a ballot with more than one hundred items, voters passed one proposition for public financing of campaigns while simultaneously passing another measure outlawing it.[54]

Moreover, lobbyists have substantial clout in most state legislatures because these bodies operate far out of the media spotlight in most states. An estimated 18 to 25 percent of all state legislators do not abide by conflict-of-interest laws.[55] They regulate businesses in which they have an interest, and they have financial ties to lobbyists. Forty-five percent of Louisianans thought the state was so corrupt that a vote for change would not make a difference. On a scale of 1 to 10 for trustworthiness, Louisianans gave their state leaders a 5.5.[56]

Big interests influence voting on initiatives, too. Huge sums of money flow into states from outside organizations to support or defeat initiatives. When an initiative to undo a gay rights law was put on the ballot in Maine, for example, money from national antigay organizations poured in to defeat it.

Still, some see the move toward greater state autonomy and more direct democracy as taking us nearer to the Founders' ideal of a government closer to the people. But the increasing use of grassroots initiatives is not a move toward the kind of government the Founders envisioned. The Founders established a system of checks on popular passions.[57] Indeed, the Founders feared policymaking getting too close to the people and government being too responsive to popular demands. They saw the potential for overheating the political process through too much direct democracy, which is why they chose an indirect or republican form of democracy and a federal division of power. The issue is how to keep a balance in these divisions sufficient to prevent a tyranny of factions while maintaining a sense of national unity and purpose.

Conclusion: Does Federalism Make Government More Responsive?

Our Founders probably did not foresee a national government that would surpass the states in power and scope of action in domestic policy. Yet one of the paradoxes of our system is that as the national government has gained extraordinary power, so have the states and localities. All levels of government are stronger than in the eighteenth century. Federal power *and* state power have grown hand in hand.

It is foolish to pretend to know how the Founders might deal with our complex federal system. However, many of them were astute politicians who would undoubtedly recognize that our system had to evolve along with population and territorial growth and social and economic change. Americans have supported the continuous growth and expansion of the country, but they have continued to believe that there is something more true or sacred about small and local government. This paradox appeared early in our history: Thomas Jefferson called his election a revolution, abolished all internal taxes, and set about making government as small, simple, and informal as possible. He tried to keep the United States out of war in Europe and closed down ports and foreign trade but soon found he needed federal policing to enforce his policy.[58] He also had an ex-

pansionist vision and, with or without formal authority, purchased the Louisiana Territory, instantly setting the country down the road from a small coastal nation to a vast continental empire in which his idea of small agrarian republic would no longer be possible.

Today, across the United States, our beliefs in democracy, freedom, and equality bind us together. In many ways, we are becoming more alike as rapid transportation, television and other forms of instant communication, fast-food franchises, hotel chains, and other nationwide businesses diminish regional distinctions. But to say that Alabama is more like New York than it used to be is certainly not to say they are alike. Our federal system helps us accommodate regional differences by allowing both state and federal governments a role in policymaking.

Is such a complex system responsive? It is very responsive in that groups and individuals whose demands are rejected at one level of government can go to another level. The federal system creates multiple points of access, each with power to satisfy political demands by making policy rejected at another level.

Yet many Americans still believe that government cannot be trusted and is not sufficiently responsive. But Americans are not enamored of state governments either, as indicated by the increasing use of ballot initiatives to bypass both national and local legislators.

In polls conducted in the months immediately following the 2001 terrorist attacks, Americans viewed government more favorably, especially its ability to deal with foreign policy issues.[59] Most still preferred "smaller government," but there was an increase in those favoring larger government with many services.[60] But by summer 2002, the polls indicated a return to normally higher levels of mistrust.[61] In some ways, that should make the Founders happy: There must be enough confidence in government for it to function and the Union to hold, yet there must be enough suspicion of government to prevent the abuse of power.

Nevada Continues to Fight

overnor Guinn fought on. The Nevada Protection Fund he set up to raise money for the legal fight hired high-powered lobbyists, including former chiefs of staff in the Clinton and Reagan administrations. It also paid for a video on the safety risks and possible real estate impact in the forty-three states through which trains carrying radioactive waste would pass. They sent copies to 1,500 local chambers of commerce and 222 TV stations.[62] Guinn even threatened to stand in front of trains carrying waste into the state. The issue drew the attention of CBS's *60 Minutes,* and soon other states declared that they did not want trains full of radioactive waste passing through their cities.

Guinn took the only legal recourse left to him after President Bush and Congress overrode his veto: he appealed to the federal court. Up to this point, he said, politics had prevailed over science. But in the courts, the "playing field is level and Nevada's factual, scientific arguments will be heard by impartial judges," where there will still be a chance to hold the DoE accountable for its "unsound decisions."[63]

In 2004, a U.S. appeals court handed down a mixed decision: it ruled that the federal government did have the constitutional authority to develop Yucca Mountain as a national repository for nuclear waste over the state's opposition, but it also ruled that the DoE had set safety standards too low. This gave Governor Guinn's campaign new life because contesting safety standards could delay the project for years.

The 2004 election also brought new support. Democrat Bill Clinton's promise to veto Yucca Mountain had helped him carry the Republican state in both 1992 and 1996. Now with the Court's ruling coming just weeks before the 2004 nominating conventions and the presidential race still a dead heat, the Democrats added a plank to their platform opposing the Yucca Mountain site. Their presidential candidate John Kerry said, if elected, he would stop the project.

Yucca Mountain illustrates several of the countless paradoxes and ironies in the federal relationship. One can be found in Nevada's attorney general's suing the federal government for money to pay its legal fees to fight the federal government and in the state's requesting funds from both the DoE and the Nuclear Regulatory Commission (NRC) to pay the lawyers who will be making the case against the DoE- and NRC-endorsed safety standards.[64]

Second, no recent president has been a greater rhetorical supporter of ceding power to the states than George W. Bush or more critical of how the federal government has exercised its control over public lands in western states. Yet Bush had no difficulty going against the wishes of Nevada's governor, state legislature, almost every important organization and interest group, and 70 percent of the population when he supported the Yucca repository. And John Kerry, a consistent supporter of federal control over the use of public lands, lent his support to the state of Nevada.

Third, the fight over where to put nuclear waste is an example of the limited power of a small state when it has to go up against Washington alone. When small states band together on a common issue, they can consistently outvote much more populous states in the Senate. However, on this issue, the NIMBY sentiment is much stronger than the fraternity among small states. The politics of the fight were summarized this way by one of Nevada's former senators: "The reaction here is that Nevada got screwed because it's a small state with little representation in Congress." The battle over the Yucca facility was just one more blow to the self-esteem of a small state, he lamented.[65]

It would be hard to refute the senator's assessment. With only two votes, Nevada does not have much to bargain with in the House. In the Senate, however, Nevada's own Harry Reid who took over the Democratic leadership in 2005, threatened to hold up all of President Bush's nominees until the Senate confirmed a former Reid staffer as a member of the NRC, the very agency that would be ruling on the final safety standards.

Finally, Guinn's dilemma was a common one for governors of western states, where the federal government owns anywhere from 50 to 80 percent of the land. Governors spend a good deal of time lobbying Washington to gain greater control over use of public lands and resources within their borders. States are in nearly continuous negotiations with federal agencies that are trying to protect national parkland or a wilderness area from ranchers and farmers seeking water or grazing rights or from businesses seeking mining or drilling rights. All of whom want to use public lands for private gain. Guinn's fight was different only in that safety issues were added to the mix.

Yucca Mountain, then, also illustrates a fundamental issue of democracy. When we say "majority rules," what majority do we mean? In the United States, a national majority, as expressed through the wishes of the president and Congress, can usually override a local majority, even on an opinion held as strongly as the Yucca Mountain repository. In many regulatory decisions, the national majority does in fact overrule a local majority, especially as in this case, where the federal government overrode state authority to use public land in what it judged to be the national interest.

Key Terms

federalism

confederal system

unitary system

"mischiefs of faction"

"necessary and proper"

implied powers clause

supremacy clause

Tenth Amendment

nation-centered federalism

state-centered federalism

dual federalism

McCulloch v. *Maryland*

New Deal

new federalism

devolution

cooperative federalism

unfunded mandates

full faith and credit clause

home rule

Further Reading

David S. Broder, *Democracy Derailed: Initiative Campaigns and the Power of Money* (New York: Harcourt Brace, 2000). A senior Washington correspondent and nationally syndicated columnist takes a look at the rise in use of the ballot initiative to legislate and explains why he believes it is a threat to our republican form of government.

Federalist Papers 39 and 23–25. Read Madison's description of the relationship between state and national governments in essay 39; then compare it to Alexander Hamilton's arguments for a strong national government in essays 23–25. You will see why we are still arguing over federalism.

John Ferejohn and Barry R. Weingast, eds., *The New Federalism: Can the States Be Trusted?* (Stanford, Calif.: Hoover Institution Press, 1997). Seven scholars of federalism look at interstate competition to attract new business and how the states are handling welfare reform and environmental regulation.

John W. Kingdon, *America the Unusual* (New York: St. Martin's/Worth, 1999). The essays in this slim volume summarize what American federalism looks like today and how it got that way.

Forrest McDonald, *States' Rights and the Union: Imperium in Imperio, 1776–1876* (Lawrence: University Press of Kansas, 2000). A historian recounts how the states' right concept evolved from Independence through the post–Civil War years.

John T. Noonan Jr., *Narrowing the Nation's Power: The Supreme Court Sides with the States* (Berkeley: University of California Press, 2002). A former federal judge and law and philosophy professor examines recent federalism rulings and explains why he thinks the Supreme Court

has taken a mistakenly narrow view of congressional authority.

Jeffrey Pressman and Aaron Wildavsky, *Implementation* (Berkeley: University of California Press, 1973). This classic looks at the difficulties of translating federal laws into working programs when dealing with a multiplicity of state and local governments.

John Steinbeck, *The Grapes of Wrath* (New York: Viking, 1939). This celebrated novel vividly portrays the dire conditions that set the stage for the New Deal.

For Viewing

The Civil War (1990) This widely acclaimed series of documentary films took longer to make than the actual Civil War lasted. It provides great insight into the issues of the war, how the war created a new nation, and the relationship between politics and war.

The Grapes of Wrath (1940) Steinbeck's novel is movingly translated to the big screen. Henry Fonda's portrayal of the everyman, Joad, is one of the iconic performances of twentieth-century film.

You Can't Take it with You (1938) Now for something really different, the feel-good side of the Great Depression. This screwball comedy won the 1938 Best Picture Oscar and is about a family of eccentrics so happy they do not seem to realize they are poor or that there is a depression. It's message is both anti–classism and anti–big government. A few years later, as the country headed into WWII, movies took on a much more nationalistic and progovernment tone.

Electronic Resources

www.ncsl.org

The National Council of State Legislatures promotes reform and increased efficiency in state legislatures, helps facilitate interstate cooperation, and lobbies for state issues. Its home page provides information about current issues of relevance to states and links to the home pages of all state legislatures.

www.fema.gov

The home page of the Federal Emergency Management Agency contains reports on cooperation with states and localities to manage current and past natural disasters and other emergencies. It provides a summary of FEMA's involvement in the response to the terrorist attacks of September 11, 2001.

www.dhs.gov

At the Web site for the new Department of Homeland Security, you can read about the division of responsibility for homeland secu-

rity among national, state, and local governments. It contains a link to your state's homeland security department.

InfoTrac College Edition

Search for the following articles in the InfoTrac database:

Bagchi, Amaresh. "Rethinking Federalism: Changing Power Relations Between the Center and the States," *Publius* (Fall 2003).

Conlan, Timothy J., and Francois Vergniole de Chantal. "The Rehnquist Court and Contemporary American Federalism," *Political Science Quarterly* (Summer 2001).

Stuntz, William J. "Terrorism, Federalism, and Police Misconduct," *Harvard Journal of Law and Public Policy* (Spring 2002).

Yenor, Scott. "Rossum, Ralph, Federalism, the Supreme Court, and the Seventeenth Amendment: The Irony of Constitutional Democracy," *Perspectives on Political Science* (Spring 2002).

For more articles, enter:

"federalism" in the Subject Guide;

"states' rights" in the Subject Guide.

American Government Resources

Visit the Government Foundations section of the Wadsworth American Government Resources Web site (politicalscience. wadsworth.com/amgov/) for a variety of tools to help you explore federalism and the growth of government further. Included are simulations, video clips, Microcase exercises, and a wealth of other activities.

CHAPTER 4

PUBLIC OPINION

In early 2003, tens of thousands of people crowded the Mall in Washington, D.C. to protest the possibility of America invading Iraq.

Charles Ommanney/ Contact Press

Nature of Public Opinion

Formation of Public Opinion

Agents of Political Socialization

Impact of Political Socialization

Measuring Public Opinion

Early Polling Efforts

Emergence of Scientific Polling

Polls and Politics

Knowledge and Information

Ideology

Social Welfare and the Proper Role of Government

Social Issues

Race

Political Tolerance

Trust in Government

Conclusion: Is Government Responsive to Public Opinion?

How Can the President Maintain Popularity and Help Republican Candidates?

t is January 2002 and you are George W. Bush, planning your upcoming State of the Union address. The address is part of a political strategy to maintain your popularity, help your party in the fall election, position yourself for your own re-election in 2004, and secure your favored domestic policies from Congress where the Senate is controlled by the Democrats. This is your first major speech to Congress and the nation since you addressed both shortly after the terrorist attacks on September 11, 2001.

In the months since, events have seemed to go well. While Osama bin Laden has avoided capture, the war in Afghanistan has, at least temporarily, succeeded in routing the Taliban and al-Qaeda. The war has showcased American military power and discredited those who warned against the dangers of military action in that part of the world. While it will take the continued presence of the United States and other military forces to ensure its survival, a new Afghani government has been established. You have support from many European allies, including France and Great Britain, and several countries in the region have supported your efforts, allowing the U.S. military to launch attacks from within their borders.

While diminished somewhat since the weeks following 9/11, patriotic feelings continue to run high, and the nation seems united more than it has been in a long time. Polls show that the overwhelming majority of Americans believe the war is going well and approve of your actions taken at home to combat terrorism.[1] Your job rating, reflected in the polls, was in the mid-50s prior to 9/11 and then jumped to the high 80s immediately after and reached 92 percent in October, the highest ever recorded by a president.[2] At the moment, your ratings are at a very high 83 percent, and your job approval has been higher for a longer period of time than for any president since Franklin D. Roosevelt.[3]

Your success in combating terrorism has also helped you and your party on domestic issues even though a significant number of Americans are worried. For example, only three in ten think the economy is healthy. Seven out of ten believe that the collapse of the Enron Corporation, a major institution whose value plunged to almost zero after revelations of phony bookkeeping, is a sign of deeper problems with American financial and economic institutions. There are calls for you and Vice President Richard Cheney to disclose meetings and correspondence the vice president and others had with Enron officials, a major bankroller of your campaign. At the same time, majorities approve of your handling of the economy, environment, and education. Sixty-two percent trust you more than the congressional Democrats to address problems facing the nation. More voters say they will vote Republican in the 2002 congressional elections than Democratic.[4]

The war has also helped increase support among groups of voters who supported Al Gore in the last election.[5] American women have been drawn by your message of hardship and discrimination facing Afghani women. Minorities have responded positively to your calls for tolerance toward Muslims. Republicans who supported Senator John McCain for president over you in the Republican primaries are impressed with your call for humanitarian aid as part of the battle plan in war-torn Afghanistan. The highly divisive 2000 election is a distant memory for most Americans.

Your call for national unity in the face of 9/11 has also put Democrats on the defensive. Not wishing to appear unpatriotic, the Democrats in Congress have supported you on the war and are reluctant to challenge you on domestic issues. For the moment, you have the advantage. You realize, however, that things can change quickly as the threat of terrorism recedes and other issues come to the fore. You recall the very strong job ratings of your father, George H. W. Bush, in January 1991, when as president he approved a military strike against Iraq (the Gulf War). Even though the military action was largely successful, by June of the same year his perceived slowness in dealing with a sagging economy led to a dra-

matic drop in his popularity. The following year he lost his reelection to Bill Clinton. Friends have noticed that this experience made a deep impression on you. Obviously, you hope to avoid a similar fate. What can you do to maintain the support of the American people?

Recognizing the increasing concern of Americans with the economy, one strategy is to make it the major focus of your address. If it does not improve, it will be an issue in the November 2002 elections. You certainly want to be seen as someone who cares about the struggles of average Americans. However, the strategy has risks. Should you focus on the economy, and it does not improve, you will give the Democrats an issue to use against you. The Democrats will become more critical as the 2002 elections approach, even if the economy improves, and they will take you to task if it does not. Your standing in the polls is likely to drop, inviting still more criticism and reducing prospects of winning support in Congress for your domestic policy goals. You and the party are likely to suffer, perhaps losing control of the nearly evenly divided House of Representatives, losing seats in the Senate, as well as reducing your reelection prospects in 2004.

Another tactic is to remain focused on terrorism. Concern for safety may keep Americans fixated on security. You have told them many times to prepare for a long war. You have identified an international terrorist network with operatives in dozens of countries, including the United States. Your approval

ratings to date are based on your success in Afghanistan and dealing with terrorism. Why shift from an issue that has brought success? If Americans are worried about terrorism, they may forget about their economic woes. Besides, you may be able to play on patriotic sentiments that will cut you some slack on the economy, particularly if you can link the economy to the war. You are likely to be no worse off should the strategy fail then if you shift attention to the economy. And if you succeed, it may provide the popular support for your other domestic initiatives. You are also likely to keep the Democrats off-balance, concerned that they will appear unpatriotic if they are too critical.

But this approach, too, has risks. The tendency of Americans to "rally around the flag" and support the president in military crises is generally temporary, decreasing as the conflict continues. Your father learned this in the Gulf War. Nor do you want to be accused of ignoring the domestic needs of the country, and surely you will if the economy continues its slide. The public's attention may be largely focused on terrorism, but economic woes strike personally and are unlikely to be overlooked by those who lose jobs or whose employers' financial situations seem shaky.

What do you do? Do you draw attention to the economic needs of the nation or keep the nation focused on war and defeating terrorism?

Public opinion is often contradictory. The public is hostile toward political leaders for failing to respond to their needs, yet, at the same time, complains that leaders simply follow the latest polls. Many are angry with the government. They do not trust it; they think it is too big and spends too much money. Yet, they like the services it provides, and very few are willing to cut spending to eliminate services or programs that benefit them.

This chapter explores public opinion to better understand these contradictions. It describes how public opinion is formed and measured, discusses the pattern of

public opinion on some important issues, and assesses the extent to which government is responsive to public opinion. Because political science is primarily interested in opinions that affect government, these are the focus of attention in this chapter.

Nature of Public Opinion

Public opinion can be defined as the collection of individual opinions toward issues or objects of general interest—that is, those that concern a significant number of people. It can be positive or negative. That is, people can have positive feelings about something, or they can have negative feelings. This is the property of direction. Generally, public opinion is mixed. On any issue or person, some people are positive, others negative. Intensity reflects the strength of public opinion. The public may have rather weak feelings about an issue or feel quite strongly about it. Intense opinions often drive behavior. Many people opposed the invasion of Iraq, for example, but only the most intense people protested it in the streets.

Public opinion is not very intense on most issues. A small minority may feel intensely about an issue, but a majority rarely does. Opinions also vary in stability. Some constantly change, while others never do. Stable opinions are often intense, grounded in a great deal of information, some of it accurate, but some quite likely inaccurate.

Feelings of attachment to American political parties tend to be stable, while opinions toward candidates and public officials, particularly high profile ones like the president, fluctuate in response to changing events and circumstances. President George W. Bush began his presidency with 60 percent of the public approving the job he was doing. This rose to 90 percent shortly after 9/11, and has dropped steadily since. It is not uncom-

mon for a president's job approval to decline over the course of his term. Confronting serious problems, in Bush's case the economy and the war in Iraq, drives approval down. Opinions can also fluctuate when voters know little about a candidate. Polls following the party nominating conventions in 1992 showed Clinton's margins over George H. W. Bush seesawing back and forth from day-to-day. Most voters didn't know enough about Clinton to form a stable opinion. They would see something on television or read something in the press favorable to Clinton and report a preference for him, and then see something unfavorable and shift back to Bush.[6]

Formation of Public Opinion

People learn and develop opinions about government and politics through the process of **political socialization.** As with learning in other spheres, individuals learn about politics by being exposed to new information supplied or filtered through parents, peers, schools, the media, political leaders, and the community. These **agents of political socialization** are what introduce each new generation to the rights and expectations of citizenship

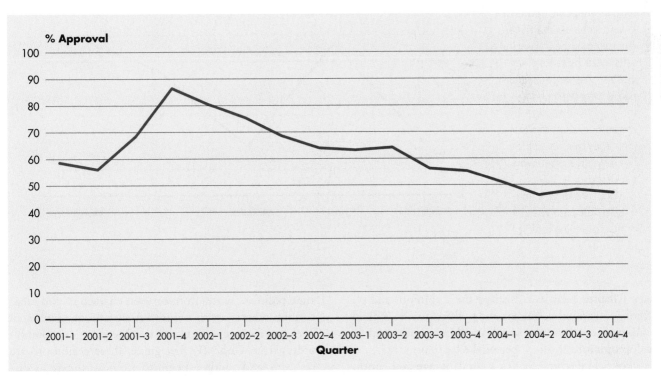

FIGURE 1 ■ George W. Bush's Approval Ratings Peaked after 9/11, then Declined Steadily

SOURCE: Gallup Poll Tuesday Briefing, April 13, 2004. Update www.pollingreport.com/bushjob.htm.
"2001–1" means first quarter of 2001, that is January through March. Second quarter scores average April through June ratings, third quarter July through September, and fourth quarter, October to December. These are nationwide polls with sample sizes of 1,000–1,200 and a margin of error of 3 percent.

While all issues have a moral element, those that are primarily moral issues have the greatest potential to divide. Slavery was a moral issue that almost destroyed the nation. In the first decades of the twentieth century, prohibition—banning the sale of alcoholic beverages—was a divisive moral issue.

Abortion emerged as a moral issue in the 1970s and remains so today. While Americans are highly supportive of abortion when the health and safety of the mother is a concern, they are quite divided when the issue is ending an unwanted pregnancy.

In the 1990s, the rights of gays and lesbians became a moral issue. While a majority of Americans have endorsed equal rights with respect to job opportunities for some time, it has only been since 1999 that a majority accepts that homosexual relations between consenting adults should be legal. About 60 percent accept this view today. Allowing homosexual couples to form civil unions and enjoy some of the same rights as married couples has gained support. However, the nation continues to be evenly divided on this. In 1996, 67 percent opposed such unions. In 2003, 49 percent opposed them. But only about one-third of the public favors allowing same-sex marriages. The ruling of the Massachusetts State Supreme Court in 2004 that same-sex marriages were legal under the state's constitution and the authorization of those marriages by a few localities may have produced a backlash.

Opinions on gay and lesbian rights are in a state of flux, changing rapidly and responding to events. While it is unlikely that a majority of Americans will accept the term "marriage" to describe homosexual unions in the short run, they are likely to continue to favor the cautious extension of basic rights to homosexuals, including the right to form civil unions. Increasing acceptance of gays and lesbians is driven to a large extent by their greater visibility and openness. Seven out of ten Americans report knowing someone who is gay or lesbian. With that knowledge comes tolerance: only a small minority are now troubled by the prospect of a homosexual teaching their elementary-school-age child, for example.

The trend toward greater tolerance is indicated by the fact that the younger generations are much more tolerant than the older generations. Thus, as the older generations pass from the scene, public opinion is likely to change.

Sources: Gallup Poll, May 15, 2003; "Same-Sex Marriage and Civil Unions," Religious Tolerance.org, "Gays getting more acceptance as they're more open, poll says,"; Lincoln-Journal Star, April 11, 2004. See also "Status of Gay Marriages and Civil Unions," report prepared from Gallup and other national polling data on Ontario Consultants on Religious Tolerance, www.religioustolerance.org/hom_poll5.htm.

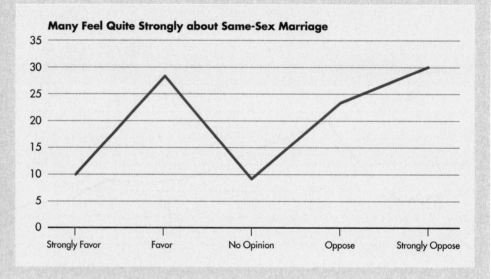

Many Feel Quite Strongly about Same-Sex Marriage

(see Chapter 1) as well as shape their opinions and positions toward officeholders and political issues. Individuals, particularly adults, also learn about politics and develop opinions through personal experiences.

Political learning begins at an early age and continues throughout life. In young children, learning is influenced by reasoning capacity and expectations.[7] When parents encourage, learning begins earlier and proceeds more quickly. Preschoolers are unable to distinguish political from nonpolitical objects. Some are unable to separate political figures from cartoon characters, and some confuse religion with politics. A significant number of five- and six-year-olds report that the president takes his orders from God.[8] By first grade, these confusions are resolved, and children begin to see government as distinct and unique.[9]

However, the inability to understand abstract concepts or complex institutions means the conception of government is limited. Most identify government with the president.[10] Children can recognize the president—

they see him on television—and understand that he is the leader of the nation much like the parent is the leader of the family. Experiences with parents and other adults provide children with a basis for understanding their relationship with authority figures with whom they have no contact.[11] Feelings toward parents are generalized to the president. Typically, children describe the president as good and helpful[12] and view him as more powerful than he really is.[13]

Older children are introduced to political ideas and political institutions in school and through the media. Their concept of government broadens to include Congress, the act of voting, and ideas such as freedom and democracy. The positive view of government reflected in feelings toward the president gives way to more complex and realistic images. The process can be accelerated by political events and the reaction of others to them. Children were much less positive toward the president and government in the 1970s than in the 1960s. The Watergate scandal in 1973 lowered both adults' and children's evaluations of the president.[14] The Clinton sexual scandals and the impeachment proceedings of 1998, however, had no impact on adult evaluations of the president and government, and presumably none on children. The approval ratings of the president reached record levels, and confidence in the executive branch remained unchanged from the year before.[15]

Even when scandal lowers children's evaluations of government, the effect may not last. The negative feelings of children during Watergate diminished as they aged.[16] In adolescence, political understanding expands still further. Children discuss politics with family and friends. By the middle teens, their positions on issues develop.[17] Some fifteen- and sixteen-year-olds develop opinions that resemble those of adults. While they begin to recognize faults in the system, they still believe the United States is the best country in the world. They rate the country low in limiting violence and fostering political morality but high in providing educational opportunities, a good standard of living, and science and technology.[18] For most, the positive feelings toward government learned earlier are reinforced.

In adulthood, opinions toward specific personalities and policies develop, and political activity becomes more serious. While most Americans revere the country and do not want to change the system, they tend to be cynical and distrustful of political leaders. Some of this negative feeling grows out of Americans' dislike of conflict and partisanship in politics.[19] Some is caused by media coverage, which not only highlights conflict, but also often exaggerates it. At the same time, the media are committed to and supportive of the American system.[20] Americans may get angry with their government, but, except for the Civil War, it has never boiled over to produce violent political change.

Critical comments about government and political leaders sharply declined after 9/11, but that cessation was short-lived. Most Americans felt gratitude toward the brave souls—many of whom lost their lives—who courageously marched to aid those under attack. Yet, except for those who were called to serve in the armed forces or who were able to volunteer to help in the World Trade Center cleanup, Americans were not asked to translate these positive feelings into action. Though commentators on 9/11 and immediately afterward predicted that nothing would ever be the same, for most Americans life did return to normal quickly and with it, skepticism toward government.

Agents of Political Socialization

It is the agents of political socialization—principally the family and schools—that are responsible for ensuring that each new generation of Americans resembles those generations that have come before.

Family

Children are not born little Democrats or Republicans. Most learn these allegiances from family. Families are particularly important in shaping the opinions of children because of strong emotional ties and exclusive control during the early years.

The family influences opinions in several ways. Parents share their opinions directly with children, who often adopt those opinions. They say or do things that children imitate. Children overhear parents' comments about the political parties and adopt them as their own. Children also transfer feelings they hold of parents to political objects. When children harbor negative feelings toward their parents, they are more likely to be negative toward the president.[21] The family shapes the personality of the child. A child who is encouraged to speak up at home is likely to do so in public. Children also inherit their social and economic position from their parents, which influences not only how they view themselves, but also how they view the world and how the world views them. A child from a wealthy family begins with advantages and opportunities that a child from a poor family can only dream about.

Children are more likely to reflect their parents' views when these views are clearly communicated and important. Parents often, if unintentionally, convey how they feel about political parties during election campaigns and children pick it up. Other opinions are less likely to be communicated to children. Seventy percent of high school seniors were able to correctly identify the party of their parents, while no more than 36 percent could identify their parents' opinion on other issues.[22]

However, even where parental influence is strong, it is not immutable. As young adults leave their parents' circle, agreement between their opinions, includ-

© Robin Nelson/Black Star

This boy, at a white supremacist rally, likely was socialized in these views by his parents.

the flag, and he felt strongly that the United States was the best country in the world. This child illustrates the importance of the school in political socialization and how values and symbols of government are explicitly taught in American schools, as they are in schools in every nation.[25]

While we do not understand exactly which aspects of formal schooling influence political opinions, there is little doubt that education and years of formal schooling —the skills it provides and experiences it represents— make a difference. People who have more education are more interested in and knowledgeable about politics.[26] They are also more likely to participate in politics and to be politically tolerant.[27]

Yet education does not seem to lead to a greater appreciation of the real workings of democracy; that is, a form of government where there are disagreements typically resolved through bargaining and compromise.[28] Education does not prepare citizens for how democracy works in practice, or how to recognize that disagreement is fundamental to democratic processes, or how to build positive feelings toward these processes.

How do the schools influence the political opinions of children? Schools promote patriotic rituals. They often begin each day with the Pledge of Allegiance, and include patriotic songs and programs in many activities. In the lower grades, children celebrate national holidays such as Presidents' Day and Thanksgiving and learn the history and symbols associated with them. Involvement in such activities fosters love and respect of country.

In the upper grades, mock elections, conventions, and student government introduce students to the operation of government. School clubs operate with democratic procedures and reinforce the concepts of voting and majority rule. The state of Illinois let the state's elementary-school children vote to select the official state animal, fish, and tree, conveying the message that voting is the way issues are decided.

Textbooks often foster commitment to government and the status quo. Those used in elementary grades emphasize compliance with authority and the need to be a "good" citizen. Even textbooks in advanced grades present idealized versions of the way government works and exaggerate the role of citizens in holding public officials accountable and in shaping public policy.

Textbooks are less likely, however, to emphasize the need for citizens to uphold democratic values such as participating in politics and tolerating others' views. Nor do they help students understand that conflicts and differences of opinion are inevitable in a large and diverse society and that the role of politics is to address and resolve these disagreements.

The number of civics courses taken in high school improves students' knowledge of government and politics and fosters beliefs that government pays attention to

ing party allegiance, and those of their parents, declines. New agents and experiences come into play.[23] Even among younger children, parental influence may not be as strong as in the past. Parents no longer have exclusive control during a child's preschool years, and the number of households with both parents working or with a single parent who works means less contact with parents. Others can be expected to fill this void. Today, schools often deal with problems the family dealt with in the past. While parental influence may be declining, whether or not one is raised in the traditional two-parent family or one with a single parent has little or no impact on important political opinions and political behavior.[24]

School

A child of our acquaintance who came to the United States at the age of five could not speak English and did not know the name of his new country. After a few months of kindergarten, he knew that George Washington and Abraham Lincoln were good presidents, he was able to recount stories of the pilgrims, he could draw

Children say the Pledge of Allegiance.

people and that elections are important in holding government responsible. Courses during the senior year are particularly important. That is when students are ready to make the transition to adulthood and when government and politics are likely to be more meaningful.[29]

Reading habits and language skills are also important to democratic citizenship. Reading, a skill learned in school but often nurtured at home, is related to interest in politics, knowledge of public affairs, political participation, and political tolerance. Those who spend time reading are more likely to reflect attributes of democratic citizenship than those who do not.[30] Proficiency with language is important, too, as language is the mechanism for communicating and assessing information and evaluating new ideas and arguments.[31] Teachers as role models also contribute in significant ways. Perceptions that school administrators and teachers are fair are linked with expressions of trust toward other people.[32]

In sum, the major impact of kindergarten through high school seems to be that it creates "good" citizens —citizens who accept political authority and the institutions of government and who also limit their political activities to the conventional and routine such as voting in elections. In this way, elementary and secondary education serves government and the status quo in ways that the dominant interests in society prefer. Schools are not

particularly effective at fostering political participation and commitment to democratic values. Nor do they provide students with the skills to critically assess social, political, and economic structures that reveal the root causes of problems and strategies for dealing with injustice and effecting political change.[33] In this regard, the failure of schools is often attributed to the "hidden curriculum."[34] Schools are not democratic institutions where students are encouraged to participate in a meaningful way. Indeed, most schools foster a climate averse to controversy. Such an environment is unlikely to produce active and engaged citizens

The impact of college often broadens students' perspectives and leads to greater understanding of the world around them. They become more open and tolerant. They become less rigid and bound by tradition. Few go to college to be influenced in this way. Many go in anticipation of a well-paying job. Some attend because their parents insist or because everyone else is going. No one goes seeking a more liberal approach to life, but this is often the result.[35] College students are more liberal than the population as a whole, and the longer they are in college, the more liberal they become. Seniors are more liberal than freshmen, and graduate students are more liberal than undergraduates.

Some argue that college professors indoctrinate students. A Carnegie Commission survey showed that 64 percent of the social science faculty in the nation's colleges identify themselves as liberal, and only 20 percent regard themselves as conservative. However, faculty in other fields are less liberal. For example, only 30 percent of the business faculty identify themselves as liberal.

During the height of the Vietnam War (1968–1971), students were more likely to identify themselves as liberal than students before or after the war. During the same period, the outlook of college faculty changed very little. Thus students are not simply a reflection of their college teachers. At large universities, where the largest percentage of students attend, the environment is sufficiently diverse to reinforce many points of view. Moreover, it is college that provides students with the self-confidence and independence that enables them to resist indoctrination.[36]

After the Vietnam War, the proportion of students identifying themselves as liberals declined significantly. However, recently liberalism has grown again, and in 2003 was at its highest level since the Vietnam War.[37] However, more college freshmen are moderates than liberals.[38]

On issues, college freshmen look much like the population as a whole, liberal on some issues but conservative on others. They are liberal in wanting the government to do more to control the sale of handguns, provide national health care to cover everyone's medical costs, guarantee homosexuals the right to have mari-

TABLE 1	Opinions of College Freshmen
The federal government should do more to control the sale of handguns.	76%
There is too much concern in the courts for the rights of criminals.	61
Same-sex couples should have the right to legal marital status.	59
Abortion should be legal.	55
Wealthy people should pay a larger share of taxes than they do now.	53
Marijuana should be legalized.	39
Federal military spending should be increased.	38
The death penalty should be abolished.	33
It is important to have laws prohibiting homosexual relationships.	26
Racial discrimination is no longer a major problem in America.	22

Source: "Attitudes and Characteristics of Freshmen," *Chronicle of Higher Education*, August 27, 2004, 19.

tal unions, and in believing that racial discrimination remains a problem. They are conservative in attitudes about crime: majorities wish to retain the death penalty and believe that the courts show too much concern for the rights of criminals. Small majorities favor prochoice, affirmative action, and taxing the rich more (see Table 1). During the past few years, freshmen have become slightly more liberal in their opinions as well as in their self-identification.[39]

The most distinctive characteristic of college freshmen in recent years has been their low interest in politics.[40] In many respects, the political apathy that has gripped adults is also reflected in college freshmen. However, since 2001, there has been a slight increase, but the 22 percent who report frequently talking about politics is far less than the high of 60 percent in 1968.[41]

In spite of declining political interest, recent college freshmen have increased their participation in organized demonstrations and volunteer work. In 2004, nearly half reported participating in a demonstration during the year, and more than 80 percent reported volunteering. Increased volunteerism reflects the growing trend of community service requirements for high school graduation (and in that sense is not really "volunteerism"). Rising levels of activism and involvement may mean increased level of civic participation in the future as these college students graduate and establish themselves.

Peers

In many instances, peers simply reinforce the opinions of the family or school. When there is a conflict between peer and parental socialization, peers sometimes win but only on issues of special relevance to youth. For example, peer influence is more important than family influence on the issue of whether eighteen-year-olds should be allowed to vote, but parental influence appears to be more significant with respect to partisanship and vote choice.[42] Peers have the most influence when the peer group is attractive to the individual and when the individual spends time with the group. With growing numbers of single-parent families and working parents, parental influence may be diminishing and friends and associates may be taking on greater importance for adults.

Mass Media

The primary effect of the media on children is to increase their level of information about politics. The primary effect on adults is to influence what they think about—that is, the issues, events, and personalities they pay attention to.[43] The media also influence opinions about issues and individuals; in recent years, the media have reflected a high degree of cynicism and negativism toward political leaders. Research shows that changes in public opinion tend to follow sentiments expressed by television news commentators.[44] The impact of the media is explored in more detail in Chapter 5.

Adult Socialization

Not all political socialization occurs in the preadult years. Opinions develop and change throughout life as one experiences new and different things. Marriage, divorce, unemployment, a new job, or a move to a new location can affect political opinions.[45]

Economic, political, and social events have the potential to change the way Americans think about politics. Many hard hit by the Great Depression were drawn to politics seeking help. Most, voting for the first time, cast their ballot for the Democrats in 1932 and have voted Democratic ever since. World War II and the attack on Pearl Harbor shaped the opinions of a generation of Americans. The Vietnam War moved many college students to the streets in protest and some to reject their country and travel to Canada to avoid the draft. In contrast, the short-term impact of the terrorist attacks on the Pentagon and the World Trade Center pushed the public closer to government, but the impact soon dissolved (see the box "9/11 Shapes Public Opinion, but Only for a While" on page 98).[46]

Impact of Political Socialization

Each new generation of Americans is socialized to a large extent by those preceding it. In many ways, each new generation will look and act much like the one that came before it. In this sense, political socialization represents a stabilizing and conserving influence. Typically, it leads to support for and compliance with government and the social order. Although many disagree with particular government policies, few question the basic structure of government.

Yet the impact of political socialization is not the same for all groups of people. The socialization experiences of poor rural children are different from those of rich suburban ones. In the 1970s and the 1980s, children from low-income families were more cynical about government; black children felt less able to influence government and were less inclined to trust it.[47] These differences, especially those linked to race, are reflected in the slightly greater trust in government by white adults.

Measuring Public Opinion

Public opinion is typically measured by asking individuals to answer questions in a survey or poll. Before polls, other techniques were employed that are still used today along with polls. Elected officials consider the opinions of people who talk to them or write or e-mail them; journalists gauge public opinion by talking selectively to individuals; letters written to newspaper editors or newspaper editorials are a measure of public opinion. Protests and demonstrations also reflect public opinion. All of these techniques provide an incomplete picture, however. Letters or messages to public officials and newspapers are more likely to come from people with extreme opinions[48] or from those with writing skills—that is, people with more education. Nor will opinions culled from a few conversations match the pattern of opinion for the nation as a whole or even a single state. Editorial opinion is even less likely to provide an accurate picture of public opinion because most newspaper publishers tend to be conservative, and this view is often reflected in their editorials. In most presidential elections in the twentieth century, newspapers favored the Republican candidate by about three to one.[49] However, John Kerry had an edge in 2004, besting Bush 212 to 199. Newspapers endorsing Kerry had a circulation of twenty-two million, Bush sixteen million.[50]

Using polls to measure public opinion may shift public opinion from being an expression of the public to a creation of the pollsters.[51] Prior to the use of polls, people who wanted to be heard had to write letters, deliver speeches, or organize protests. Today, pollsters initiate the expression of public opinion by conducting a poll. Rather than focus on what the public is concerned about, polls concentrate on what pollsters and their sponsors are most interested in. For this reason, many issues of public importance may never become the subject of a poll.

Polling remains, however, the only accurate way to assess what the nation as a whole thinks about political issues and personalities. In this sense, polls are the best measure of public opinion, but they are not perfect.

Early Polling Efforts

The first attempts to measure popular sentiments on a large scale were the **straw polls** (or unscientific polls) developed by newspapers in the nineteenth century.[52] In 1824, the *Harrisburg Pennsylvanian,* in perhaps the first poll assessing candidate preferences, sent reporters to check on support for the four presidential contenders that year. In July, the paper reported that Andrew Jackson was the popular choice over John Quincy Adams, Henry Clay, and William H. Crawford. Jackson also received the most votes in the election, but John Quincy Adams was elected president after the contest was decided by the House of Representatives. Toward the end of the nineteenth century, the *New York Herald* regularly tried to forecast election outcomes in local, state, and national races. During presidential election years, the paper collected estimates from reporters and political leaders across the country and predicted the Electoral College vote by state.

Straw polls are still employed today. Some newspapers have interviewers who ask adults at shopping malls and other locations for their voting preferences. Some have readers return coupons printed in the papers. Television and radio stations often ask questions and provide two telephone numbers for listeners to call—one for yes, one for no. Many news media run Internet polls. After each presidential debate, for example, some local and national media invite people to cast a vote on their Internet site. Preferences are electronically recorded and tabulated, but are in no way a random sample of the public.

No straw poll is scientifically valid, in the sense that it provides an accurate and reliable reading of public opinion, though such polls may spark interest in the subject of the poll on the part of the public. The major problem is that there is no way to ensure that the sample of individuals giving opinions is representative of the larger population. Generally, it is not.

The famed *Literary Digest* poll is a good example. The magazine conducted polls of presidential preferences between 1916 and 1936. As many as eighteen million ballots were mailed out to persons drawn from telephone directories and automobile registration lists. Although the purpose was less to measure public opinion than to boost subscriptions, the *Literary Digest* did have a pretty good record. It had predicted the winners in 1924, 1928, and 1932. In 1936, however, the magazine predicted Alfred Landon would win, but Frank-

9/11 SHAPES PUBLIC OPINION, BUT ONLY FOR A WHILE

Nothing since World War II has moved public opinion more dramatically than the events of 9/11. Before the terrorist attacks, many Americans considered government unimportant and irrelevant to their lives. With the fall of the Soviet Union (the nation's principal antagonist for nearly four decades), a booming economy and surging stock market during the 1990s, and a constant barrage of negative commentary about the government from the media and politicians who found it useful for their careers, many Americans felt that government was not necessary to their security and well-being. In 2000, one-third felt it unimportant who was elected president, and over 80 percent believed it unimportant to listen to the president's State of the Union address. But the attacks of 9/11 altered people's perceptions. From the ashes of the World Trade Center and Pentagon sprang a new feeling of patriotism and an increased level of trust and favorable feelings toward the national government.

Flag sales soared and millions of people bought pins, ties, bumper stickers, and other objects displaying the flag. Athletes wore flags on their uniforms, and audiences sang the national anthem more frequently.

Suddenly, what the president had to say was important. Fifty-four percent, more than twice as many as the year before, found the president's State of the Union address in January 2002 especially important. Eighty-two percent, compared with just 50 percent the year before, had a favorable view of the national government. Trust in government, hovering at 30 percent for most of the decade, nearly doubled following the attacks.[1] The public standing of the president and Congress similarly surged. There was an elevated sense that citizens needed the national government, at least to provide protection at home and wage war abroad. As someone remarked, "The only persons going up the stairs of the World Trade Center while everyone else was going down were government officials. The events

brought home the fact that the government does important work."[2]

The changed attitudes toward government and a greater sense of national unity on the part of elected officials and the public at large lead to endless pronouncements that America would be forever changed. Like Pearl Harbor, some saw 9/11 permanently changing the way Americans relate to each other, their government, and their communities.

While it's only natural that such feelings subside with time, the spirit of 9/11 faded quickly. Church attendance, increasing in the immediate post–9/11 weeks, fell back after only one month. Calls to military recruiters increased but not actual enlistments. A call for mobilization and sacrifice from the president might have kept the spirit alive, but his advice to Americans was "Live your lives, hug your children."[3] Go shopping was the call. "Your continued participation and confidence in the American economy would be appreciated."

In his 2002 State of Union address, he proposed several programs

lin D. Roosevelt won by a landslide. The erroneous prediction ended the magazine's polling, and in 1938 the *Literary Digest* went out of business.

Why did the *Literary Digest* miss in 1936? The sample was biased. Owners of telephones and automobiles in the depths of the Great Depression were disproportionately middle- and upper-income people who were more likely to vote for Landon, the Republican, than lower-income Americans were.[53] Since the sample was drawn from telephone directories and auto registrations, lower-income people were significantly underrepresented.

Emergence of Scientific Polling

Scientific polling began after World War I, inspired by the new field of business known as marketing research. After the war, demand for consumer goods rose, and American businesses, no longer engaged in the produc-

tion of war materials, turned to satisfying consumer demand. Businesses used marketing research to identify what consumers wanted and, perhaps more important, how products should be packaged so consumers would buy them. The American Tobacco Company changed from a green to a white package during World War II because it found that a white package was more attractive to women smokers.[54]

The application of mathematical principles of probability was also important to the development of scientific polling. To determine the frequency of defects in manufactured products, inspectors made estimates on the basis of a few randomly selected items, called a "sample." It was a simple matter to extend the practice to individuals, and draw conclusions regarding a large population based on findings from a smaller randomly selected sample.

In the early 1930s, George Gallup and several oth-

"But first our national anthem."

Bent on taking advantage of 9/11 to push his partisan conservative domestic agenda rather than to bring the country together around moderate programs, the president alienated Democrats. Franklin D. Roosevelt unified the nation during World War II with policies that had broad appeal. George W. Bush and the Republicans in Congress did the opposite. The result has been that public sentiments toward government have fallen back to where they were before 9/11. The only remaining effects are reflected in the high number of Americans afraid to fly (43 percent), enter skyscrapers (30 percent), or enter crowded public places (33 percent).

1. Alexander Stille, "Suddenly, Americans Trust Uncle Sam," *New York Times,* November 3, 2001, online article.
2. "Public Opinion Six Months Later," Pew Research Center for the People and the Press, news release, March 7, 2002.
3. Benjamin Wallace-Wells, "Mourning Has Broken," *Washington Monthly,* October 2003, 16–18.

to expand national service (e.g., USA Freedom Corps) and American youth responded, signing up in record numbers. But the bill never made it into law, and existing programs haven't been funded as Republicans and Democrats in Congress could not come together.

ers, using probability-based sampling techniques, began polling opinions on a wide scale. In 1936, Gallup predicted that the *Literary Digest* would be wrong and that Roosevelt would be reelected with 55.7 percent of the vote. Though Gallup underestimated Roosevelt's actual vote, accurately predicting the outcome lent credibility to probability-based polls.

Increasingly, government used polls. In 1940, Roosevelt became the first president to use polls on a regular basis, employing a social scientist to measure trends in public opinion toward the war in Europe.

Polls and Politics

Most major American universities have a unit that does survey research, and there are hundreds of commercial marketing research firms, private pollsters, and newspaper polls. For politicians, polls have become what the Oracle of Delphi was to the ancient Greeks and Merlin was to King Arthur—a divine source of wisdom. During the budget debate between President Clinton and congressional Republicans, Republicans used polls that told them that promising to "put the government on a diet" would be popular in the upcoming 1996 election. Polls directed Clinton to counter by accusing the Republicans of trying to cut Medicare. When the media wanted to make sense of the debate, they conducted more polls.[55]

Beginning in the 1960s, presidents increasingly turned to polls to assess the public's thinking on issues.[56] None, however, can match the extent to which President Clinton relied on polls during his presidency. He spent more on polling than all previous administrations combined and tested every significant policy idea and the language to promote it.[57] Following the 1994 elections in which Democrats lost control of both the House

This gimmick may have attracted customers, but it was not a scientific way to measure opinion about President Clinton's impeachment.

© Todd Yates/The Facts, Clute, Texas

and Senate, Clinton vowed never again to be out of step with the public.[58] Weekly polls shaped his centrist message, leading to his reelection in 1996. If polls showed a position to be popular, Clinton was likely to adopt it as his own. He embraced welfare reform, a Republican idea opposed by Democrats in Congress and liberals in his administration, partly because it was popular.[59] A White House poll in 1997 suggested that Americans preferred using the budget surplus to bolster Social Security rather than administer a Republican-preferred tax cut. In his State of the Union address, he called on Congress to "save Social Security first." Clinton would also quickly withdraw when polls showed an issue to be unpopular. A proposal allowing needle exchanges to check the spread of AIDS was pulled an hour before it was to be announced because a poll revealed it to be politically risky. Clinton even used polls to select a vacation spot.[60] Rather than vacation on Martha's Vineyard and play golf, Clinton went hiking in the Rockies instead, having been told by a consultant that golf was a Republican sport and that the voters he needed to win were campers.

Of course, Clinton did not always adopt positions because they were popular. He bucked public opinion and many leaders of his own party in his support for NAFTA (the North American Free Trade Agreement) and was again out of step with public opinion in his support for a multibillion-dollar bailout when the Mexican peso collapsed. He also defied public opinion in sending troops to Bosnia. To his surprise, his standing in the polls rose.[61]

Mindful of the negative publicity Clinton received as one who would not move without a poll, George W.

Doubting the Holocaust?

A major problem for pollsters is designing questions that accurately measure opinions. "Do you agree that it's not the case that a few words don't make a lot of difference in a poll question?" What? This question with a double negative is difficult to understand. Results from asking that question would be unreliable. Poorly worded questions, such as those with double negatives, can confuse the public and lead pollsters to draw the wrong conclusions.

The point was illustrated in a poll to find out the proportion of Americans who doubt that the *Holocaust* (the mass murder of millions of Jews by the Nazis in World War II) happened. The survey asked the following question: "As you know, the term Holocaust usually refers to the killing of millions of Jews in Nazi death camps during World War II. Does it seem possible or does it seem impossible to you that the Nazi extermination of the Jews never happened?" The results: 22 percent said it was possible that the Holocaust never happened; another 12 percent were not sure. The conclusion: About one-third of the country either doubted the Holocaust occurred or were uncertain.

Since no reputable historian or anyone with the slightest knowledge of world affairs denies that the Holocaust happened, this "finding" was shocking. Commentators reflected on how the public could be so ill informed regarding a major event, not just of the twentieth century, but of recorded history.

But the wording of the question was the culprit. Another version asked, "Does it seem possible to you that the Nazi extermination of Jews never happened, or do you feel certain that it happened?" This time only 1 percent said it was possible the Holocaust never happened. Eight percent were unsure and 90 percent said they were certain it happened.

Why the difference? A study of thirteen polls with estimates of Holocaust doubters from 1 to 46 percent found that high estimates resulted from confusing language. In the above question, to express that the Holocaust happened, one had to respond "impossible" that it "never happened." Confusing language produced exactly the opposite of what people actually believed.

What do Americans really know about the Holocaust? Nine out of ten have heard of the Holocaust; two-thirds are able to identify it correctly. In 1992, knowledge of the Holocaust increased with publicity surrounding the opening of the Holocaust Museum in Washington, D.C., and the release of the Academy Award–winning movie *Schindler's List*.

SOURCE: Richard Morin, "From Confusing Questions, Confusing Answers," *Washington Post National Weekly Edition,* July 18, 1994, 37.

Bush leaves the impression that he doesn't do polls.[62] When asked by a former Clinton press secretary at an informal luncheon what polls showed regarding public warnings of nonspecific terrorist threats, Bush responded, "In this White House, we don't poll on something as important as national security."[63]

But, of course, the Bush administration does poll. While Bush's spending on polls during his first year did not match Clinton's, Bush's pollster toils in the background to find the words and phrases to sell Bush's policies to the public. In a speech pushing the privatization of Social Security, Bush avoided that phrase, opting instead for terms such as "retirement security," "choice," and "opportunity." The goal is to find poll-tested phrases that can be used to sell the public on the idea. Similarly, Bush's energy plan was described as "balanced" and "comprehensive" and one that relies on "modern" methods to prevent environmental damage. "School choice," "death tax," and "wealth-generating private accounts" are other poll-tested phrases designed to push an agenda with limited appeal. For example, if voters knew that "death taxes" were taxes only on the very wealthiest Americans, they would probably not argue they should be repealed. Yet the term "death tax" implies that we all face it.

While Clinton relied on polls to find policies with broad public support, Bush relies on them to package and camouflage policies favored by his conservative base to make them more attractive to mainstream voters.[64] "Crafted-talk," as it is called, enables politicians to move away from the center and cater to the somewhat more extremist views of their base yet at the same time appear mainstream.[65]

Polls by news organizations have also increased. The number of network-sponsored tracking polls, in which a small number of people are polled on successive evenings throughout a campaign in order to assess changes in the level of voter support, exploded in 2000. Originally used in campaigns to assess the effectiveness of political ads, ABC was the first to use tracking polls in the New Hampshire presidential primary in 1984 to assess the growing strength of Democratic presidential candidate Gary Hart. Based on small samples, no more than two hundred, networks were reluctant to air their results until CNN did so in 1988. In 2000, virtually every news organization of any size featured daily tracking polls.[66] Tracking polls monitor the movement of candidates during the campaign, who is gaining and who is falling behind. This horse race aspect of the campaign makes a good story and attracts viewers.

The ease of conducting polls explains, in part, their increasing use. Pollsters can conduct a poll at a moment's notice and have results within a few hours. This ease often leads to abuse. On clearly defined issues where the public has thought about something carefully and holds strong views, such as the vote in tomorrow's election,

a well-designed poll can provide an accurate picture of the public's views. All eight of the election eve polls in the 1996 presidential election predicted the winner. One got it exactly right, finding Clinton with a 9 percent advantage over Bob Dole. The president's actual margin of victory was 8.4 percent. The average error was 1.7 percent.[67]

In 2000, the Democratic and Republican candidates each received 48 percent of the vote, with Gore a half million votes ahead. The election proved too close to call, but all election eve polls predicted the candidates' totals within each poll's margin of error. The preelection polls in 2004, in spite of some jumping around earlier in the campaign, also had it about right in the final week. The average of fourteen of the major newspaper and network commercial polls had Kerry at 47.4 percent and Bush at 48.9 percent. The actual vote was 48 percent to 52 percent.[68]

But when the public has not thought much about an issue or where the choices are less than clearly defined, polls rarely provide a meaningful guide to what the public thinks. Poll results reflecting support for candidates seeking office for the first time often jump up and down simply because voters do not know much about the candidates.

Even when issues are well defined and opinions are fairly stable, it is increasingly difficult to obtain a sample that provides a representative picture of public opinion. Many respondents refuse to be interviewed,[69] some because they don't want to be bothered, others because they fear they'll be asked to buy something or contribute money. Nonrespondents, those who refuse to be polled or cannot be reached, number from 50 to 80 percent of those included in a sample, and these people are more likely to be better educated, more affluent, and live in suburbs rather than cities and rural areas.[70]

Another problem for pollsters is the tendency of some respondents to express an opinion when they do not have one. No one wants to appear uninformed. Some respondents volunteer an answer even though they know little or nothing about a subject. The problem is getting worse as pollsters increasingly probe topics on which the public has no opinion and on which there is little reason to believe it should. For instance, pollsters asked whether the public thought President Reagan's colon cancer was serious and whether the bloody glove fit O. J. Simpson.[71]

Although polls can unintentionally be biased because of these problems, some pollsters and politicians consciously distort poll results. Today, many pollsters come from political consulting backgrounds and poll exclusively for members of one political party. Rather than provide accurate information about public opinion, their goal is to present their client in the most favorable light.[72] A more severe problem, from the public's perspective, is pollsters who have an air of partisan

At 7:50 P.M. election night in 2000, the television networks declared Al Gore the winner in Florida. While the election was far from over, a win in Florida made it more likely that Gore would be elected president. About 9:30 P.M., the call went out from Voter News Service (VNS), the consortium that conducted exit polls for the networks, to pull back. Florida was "too close to call." At 2:15 A.M. the next morning, George W. Bush was pronounced the winner in Florida and the next president of the United States with 271 electoral votes, one more than needed. The nation waited for Gore's concession. It didn't come. Bush's lead in Florida began to erode. Sometime after 3:30 A.M., Gore's campaign manager issued a statement: "Without being certain of Florida, we cannot be certain about the election. Until the results in Florida are official, the Gore campaign continues."[1] At nearly the same moment, the networks pulled back again. Florida was too close to call.

Exit polls, a part of American elections since the 1960s, are used by television networks to project winners before all votes are counted. Voting precincts throughout a state are selected at random. As voters leave polling places in these precincts throughout the day, they are asked how they voted. These results, coupled with early but incomplete election returns and an analysis of how precincts voted in the past, are used to project winners. While each network decides for itself when to call a race, they jointly contract with VNS to reduce their costs. So the networks receive the same information at the same time, which means that they usually declare a winner within a few minutes of each other. Even so, each tries to be the

first. In the competitive news business, they scramble for bragging rights, which may lead to a larger audience.

Exit polls worked well in 1992 and 1996, but 2000 was a disaster. How did it happen? Early in the day, exit poll information seemed suspect.[2] Precincts were out of step with past performance. There was still time, however, to make adjustments, and VNS rushed to alter its statistical models. While the networks were concerned with the last-minute changes, this was not shared with viewers.[3]

Problems in calling the race reflected several factors. Predicting close races requires very large samples. VNS did not have a very large sample. Moreover, no sample could have predicted an outcome as close as 2000. A second problem was that those polled were not representative of all who cast ballots. A Tampa precinct, which weighed heavily in the initial projections, overrepresented the Gore vote.[4] In addition, absentee ballots cast before the election, which tend to be Republican, were not sampled at all. Excluding absentee ballots from exit polls will become more critical now that states make it easier to vote before election day. A third problem is that VNS relies on voting history to make predictions. Voting history is a reliable guide during periods of stability, but not when states are undergoing change. In Florida, a major influx of northerners along with a growing Hispanic population has altered Florida's political makeup, making elections less predictable.

Another problem goes to the heart of what became the election controversy in Florida. A significant number of voters in one large county intended to vote for Gore but marked their ballots in ways that led them to be counted

neutrality, yet manipulate the wording of polling questions to benefit their client's position. The results are often picked up by the news media and give the impression the public feels one way when they feel exactly the opposite.

An egregious example of misuse is the **push poll.** A pollster for Jones asks whether the person called is for John Jones, Mary Smith, or undecided in the upcoming congressional election. If the answer is Smith or undecided, the voter is asked, "If you were told that Smith's hobby is driving a high-powered sports car at dangerous speeds through residential neighborhoods to see how many children and pets she can run over, would it make a difference in your vote?" The voter is then asked her preference again. The idea is to see whether certain "information" can "push" voters away from a candidate or a neutral opinion toward the candidate favored by those doing the poll.[73] Learning the weaknesses of the opposition has always been a part of politics, but push polls

seek to manipulate opinion, they rarely focus on a candidate's issue positions, and they often distort a candidate's record and the facts.

An even more vicious tactic is to pump thousands of calls into a district or state under the guise of conducting a poll but with the intent of spreading false information about a candidate. Senator John McCain accused the Bush campaign of spreading false information in the guise of a poll in the 2000 South Carolina primary when both were seeking the Republican presidential nomination. Similarly, Bush chided McCain for using a push poll in the Michigan presidential primary. Both the push poll and the phony poll are corruptions of the political process as well as violations of polling ethics.

Even reputable polls have their downside in politics. Poor standing in the polls may discourage otherwise viable candidates from entering a race, leaving the field to others who have less chance of winning or who lack the skills necessary to govern effectively. In 2000, several pofor another candidate. They, of course, did not realize the mix-up, and told pollsters that they had voted for Gore. So they were counted as Gore voters in the exit polls, but not in the actual election.

Despite these problems, the networks might not have made incorrect projections if they had not been so preoccupied with cost cutting. Networks have been taken over by conglomerates such as Disney and General Electric, which focus on the bottom line. The reason that the networks jointly contracted with VNS was to save money. Then they reduced the budget for VNS, so it apparently sampled too few precincts.[5] Thus cost cutting made the networks vulnerable. If their single source of exit polls got it wrong, they all would get it wrong. If there had been multiple sources with separate polls and different samples, probably some would have suggested a Gore win, others a Bush win, and others that it was too close to call. Then the networks would have exercised more caution and the public would have received a more realistic picture.

The wrong calls were not merely an embarrassment to the networks. Because the networks initially called Florida for Gore ten minutes before polling places in the state's western panhandle closed, it is possible that a few Republicans on their way to vote might have turned around and gone home. Because the networks later called Florida for Bush, proclaiming him the "forty-third president," it is likely that many people around the country considered Bush the legitimate winner even when the networks decided the election was too close to call after all. Then in the postelection contest, when the two sides were struggling for public sup-

port, Gore was put in the position of appearing to try to take Bush's victory, and his presidency, away from him.

Although the networks vowed to fix the exit polls, more problems popped up during the 2004 election. The pollsters accidentally oversampled Kerry voters, apparently by oversampling women, who tend to vote more Democratic than Republican. Consequently, the exit polls showed Kerry beating Bush by a substantial margin. Although the networks refrained from reporting the results until after the voting polls were closed, some bloggers obtained the results and notified their readers—and the campaigns, which were monitoring the blogs. Bush aide Karen Hughes took the president aside and told him that he was going to lose.

After the election, some Republicans, worried that inaccurate exit poll results could affect the outcome of an election if the projections are widely publicized before the polls are closed, called for the elimination of exit polls. Some Democrats, noting the large discrepancies between the exit polls and the actual results were in states with electronic voting, feared that the electronic equipment had been tampered with.

1. Seth Mnookin, "It Happened One Night," *Brill's Content,* February 2001, 152.
2. Marvin Kalb, "TV Pays Big Price: Credibility," *Lincoln Journal-Star,* December 3, 2000, 7D; Tom Wolzien, "The Bottom Line," *Brill's Content,* February 2001, 97.
3. Mnookin, "It Happened One Night," 98.
4. Diana Owen, "Media Mayhem: Performance of the Press in Election 2000," in *Overtime! The Election 2000 Thriller,* ed. Larry J. Sabato (New York: Longman, 2002), 144.
5. Richard Morin and Claudia Deane, "Why the Florida Exit Polls Were Wrong," *Washington Post,* November 8, 2000.

tential Republican candidates passed up the presidential race when early polls suggested that George W. Bush was the odds-on favorite to win the Republican nomination. And, in an unprecedented move, in 2002, Robert Torricelli (D-N.J.) withdrew from his Senate race thirty-six days before the election when polls showed that he could not win the election (he had been censured by the Senate for his unethical conduct).

In addition, polls can have a negative effect on political campaigns. Prior to polling, the purpose of campaigns was to reveal the candidates' views on the issues and their solutions to the pressing problems of the day. Instead, polls focus attention on the electorate and what they think. Polls find out what the voters want, and the candidates develop images to suit the voters.

The ease of polling also means that judgment and leadership often give way to the sentiments expressed in public opinion polls. Politicians rarely make a decision without one. Rather than educate the public regarding

the merits of particular policies, many politicians seem to follow the polls blindly or use polls to package unpopular policies in a way that the public will find appealing.

Former senator Daniel Patrick Moynihan (D-N.Y.) decried politicians' addiction to poll results, suggesting that they had caused Congress to adopt popular causes, such as the line-item veto, that were later found by the Supreme Court to be unconstitutional. "We've lost our sense of ideas that we stand by, principles that are important to us," he said.[74]

As the number of polls, both good and bad, increases, their importance for the public and, perhaps, politicians may decline. The sheer number of polls may lead everyone to take them less seriously. Moreover, if politicians allow themselves to be driven by poll results and use them to manipulate the public, no one will gain an advantage from the information they provide.[75] Still, it is unlikely that ambitious politicians bent on winning at all costs will abandon something that may help them win.

Harry Truman exults in incorrect headlines, based on poll results and early returns, the morning after the 1948 election.

TABLE 2	Large Proportions of the Public Are Ignorant of Politics	
		Percentage Unable to Identify
Who is in Washington:		
Vice president		40
Speaker of the House		46
Their Senate representative		54
Majority leader in Senate		66
Their House representative		67
What goes on in Washington?		
That the number of federal employees decreased in last three years		72
That the government spends more on Medicare than on foreign aid		73
That the House passed a plan to balance federal budget		75
That the Senate passed a plan to balance the budget		78

Source: Richard Morin, "Tuned Out, Turned Off," *Washington Post National Weekly Edition,* February 5, 1996, 6–8.

In spite of problems and abuses, polls still provide a valuable service to the nation. If direct democracy, like the New England town meeting, is the ideal, the use of public opinion polls is about as close as the modern state is likely to get to it. Polls help interpret the meaning of elections. When voters cast their ballots for one candidate over another, all anyone knows for sure is that a majority preferred one candidate. Polls can help reveal what elections mean in terms of policy preferences and thus help make the government more responsive to voters. For example, Republicans claimed their victory in the 1994 congressional elections was an indication that voters supported the party's Contract with America. However, polls showed that most Americans had never heard of it.

Knowledge and Information

Asking citizens their opinions on matters of public policy, candidates for public office, and the operation and institutions of government presumes they possess suf-

"I used to give a damn, but now they have a patch for that."

ficient knowledge and information to form opinions and that expressions of opinion reflect real preferences. Levels of knowledge regarding some basic elements of government suggest sizable numbers of Americans do not have much information. Only one-fourth can name their two senators,[76] and only one-third can name their U.S. representative.[77] More than one-third do not know the party of their representative,[78] and 40 percent do not know which party controls Congress.[79]

Many Americans are unable to identify prominent political personalities (see Table 2). Six years after he was elected vice president, 24 percent could not identify George H. W. Bush. More people can identify television personalities than major political figures.[80] In spite of increases in education, levels of knowledge regarding politics have not changed much since the 1940s.[81]

Although Americans revere the Constitution and see it as a blueprint for democracy, many do not know what is in it. One-third think it establishes English as the country's official language, and one in six thinks it established America as a Christian nation. One-fourth cannot name a single First Amendment right, and only 6 percent can name all four.[82]

Similarly, most Americans do not keep up with what goes on in Washington, D.C. Only a small percentage of Americans can identify a single piece of legislation passed by Congress.[83]

Misperception regarding government policies is widespread, which means that many members of the public are asking to be manipulated by candidates for

POLITICS AS A JOKE

More and more Americans get some of their political news from late night comedy shows, such as *The Daily Show with Jon Stewart,* the *Late Show with David Letterman, The Tonight Show with Jay Leno,* or *Real Time with Bill Maher.* And those who watch late night comedy are actually more informed about politics and campaigns than those who do not.

Late night shows are a way candidates can become better known to the population, who see them reasonably relaxed and showing a sense of humor. Moreover, late night show emcees feature news of the day in their monologues, and during election season often focus on foibles of the candidates. The public can learn about campaign issues in a rather lighthearted and superficial way even though they would not take the time to read about politics or watch campaign ads.

One analysis of the jokes told by Leno, Letterman, and Stewart in the months before the 2004 election showed that 33 percent of jokes made by Stewart during the show's "headlines" mentioned at least one policy issue, compared to 24 percent of Leno's monologue jokes and 21 percent of Letterman's. Jokes about the candidates were balanced, with about equal numbers ribbing Kerry and Bush. The exception was Leno who told more jokes about Bush than Kerry.

Jokes about Bush tended to focus on his perceived lack of intelligence, his shirking of his National Guard duty, and the failures of his policies in Iraq and for the economy. Jokes about Kerry often focused on his tendency to see all sides of an issue (or flip-flop as his opponents called it), his rather bland and boring public persona, and his wealthy wife, Teresa Heinz Kerry.

"Kerry was here in Los Angeles. He was courting the Spanish vote by speaking Spanish. And he showed people he could be boring in two languages."—*Jay Leno*

"During the debate, Bush was asked by a lady to name three mistakes he's made. And Bush responded, this debate, the last debate, and the next debate."
— Bill Maher

"John Kerry met with Ralph Nader last week. Both sides of every issue were discussed. And then, Nader spoke."—*Jay Leno*

"And the rumor is that it'll be like the last time. Kerry will win the popular vote and Bush will win the electoral votes. And they say Americans could spend weeks not knowing who's really president, Bush or Kerry. Hey, is that so bad? We spent the last four years not really knowing who is president, Bush or Cheney".
—Jay Leno

"President Bush listed his income as $822,000. You know what John Kerry calls someone who earns $822,000? Not even worth dating."
—Jay Leno

"Bush bragged that more Iraqis say their country is on the right track than Americans say our country is on the right track. Boy, there's a campaign slogan for you—'America: More F*cked Up Than Fallujah!'"
—Bill Maher

SOURCE: "No Joke: Daily Show Viewers Follow Presidential Race," based on a survey conducted by the Annenberg Center of the University of Pennsylvania. www.business-journal.com/No JokeDailyShowViewersKnowIssues.asp. Jokes reprinted from www.newsmax.com/liners .shtml; www.politicalhumor.about.com/library/blbush2004jokes.htm; www.slick.com/jokes .html.

office. While polls showed Americans in favor of reducing the size of the federal government, most have no idea whether the size of government is growing or shrinking.[84] Most Americans feel that the country spends too much on foreign aid and think we should cut its amount, but one-half estimate foreign aid to be about fifteen times greater than it is. Asked what an appropriate spending level would be, the average answer is eight times more than the country spends.[85] In one poll, nearly half of the public had an opinion on a nonexistent Public Affairs Act of 1975. Fearing to admit that they had never heard of it, these people gave an opinion anyway, just as they would do on real policies they had never heard of.[86]

Although many may not know the basics of American government, some argue that average citizens know what they need to know to make sound political judgments.[87] Most citizens take an active interest in politics and pay attention when they have a personal stake. Eighty percent know that Congress passed a law requiring employers to provide family leave following the birth of a child or in an emergency. With the war in Iraq and a shaky economy, six in ten Americans reported giving the 2004 presidential election a lot of thought as early as February, much earlier than in 2000. Over half reported more enthusiasm for voting, up 15 percent from 2000.[88] Greater interest and concern may translate into higher turnout.

Some suggest that average Americans rely on cues to direct them to wise decisions.[89] Are things going well or are they "screwed-up?" Is a candidate running an effective campaign? If not, can one expect him or her to run the country? Can a candidate hold his or her own in debates? All are cues reflecting whether or not a candidate can handle the job.

At the same time, lack of knowledge is an impediment to holding government accountable. Those who are less politically knowledgeable find it difficult to sort through the claims and counterclaims of politicians. Some support candidates and policies that work against their self-interest. By their lack of information, they are asking to be manipulated, and they are.[90]

Politicians often contribute to citizen ignorance and misperception. They often avoid discussing issues, especially controversial ones, or worse, mislead by trumpeting suspect or false information. Eight out of ten Americans continued to believe Iraq had weapons of mass destruction in spite of none being found.[91] Nearly one-half respond that Saddam Hussein was directly involved in carrying out the 9/11 attacks with no evidence supporting such a link.[92] The Bush administration had encouraged these views, orchestrating officials' comments to assert explicitly that Iraq had weapons of mass destruction and to suggest implicitly that Iraq was linked to al-Qaeda. Even when no weapons of mass destruction were found during the war and when no significant link to al-Qaeda was found by the 9/11 Commission, the administration was reluctant to correct the record.[93]

It is hard work to stay informed. It takes time and energy. With work and family, average men and women have little time for politics. But failure to stay informed means that politicians can often ignore what the public wants.

Ideology

Average Americans hold opinions on a variety of different issues. These opinions may be consistent with each other and reflect a broader framework or worldview, what scholars call an ideology. Or they may be inconsistent and unrelated. One might, for example, express a preference for government assistance to farmers hit by hard times, but oppose it for those out of work because jobs have been outsourced to a foreign country. That might seem inconsistent because you are favoring government assistance in one case but not in another. Or, one might oppose any restrictions on an individual's right to free speech, but be quite strong in their view that government should outlaw same-sex marriage. That might seem inconsistent because you are arguing for individual freedom in one case, but not in another.

But looked at from other perspectives, maybe neither of these sets of opinions is inconsistent.

An **ideology** is a worldview that leads to a consistent and coherent set of opinions on political issues, toward political personalities, or on political parties. Most Americans are not very ideological. Yet, the major contemporary ideologies, liberalism and conservatism, do help in understanding public opinion about the major institutions of American politics and political and social conflicts in society.

Liberalism is sometimes identified by the label "left" or "left wing" and conservatism by the label "right" or "right wing." These terms date from the French National Assembly of the early nineteenth century when liberal parties occupied the left side of the chamber and conservative parties occupied the right.

Liberalism, as a framework at least since the 1930s, embodies the idea that the national government can be a constructive force to extend a helping hand to cushion the impact of economic recessions and unemployment, to improve schools, to help individuals provide health insurance for their families, and to provide for a cleaner environment and safer working conditions. Franklin D. Roosevelt's New Deal policies were liberal: they were enacted to relieve the hardships of the Great Depression, give economic security to the elderly through Social Security, and expand economic opportunities and improve the quality of life of average men and women more generally. Liberals believe that government can be used to make life better for working people and the middle classes.

Conservatism, on the other hand, encompasses the notion that the nation and economy are best served if they are free of government interference. Government is generally not seen as a constructive force, except in the area of national security. Conservatives ostensibly believe that the free market should be allowed to function, and individuals, rather than the government, are responsible for their own well-being. In a conservative ideology, government is small. Conservatives often argue that when government has to act, it should be the state or local government taking the lead rather than the more distant federal government. But modern conservatives often want government to assume the economic risk for corporations and many are happy to interfere with the free market with subsidies to favored corporations or occupations, like farmers.

Pushing the idea of activist government to cushion economic hardship, Democrats came to power in the 1930s and dominated American politics through the 1960s. There was widespread agreement—indeed, a liberal consensus—that it was the government's job to ensure that all Americans enjoyed a certain quality of life. Though the Republicans were less enthusiastic

Focus Groups: Measuring or Manipulating Public Opinion?

Few are so naive to assume that a president writes his own speeches, but most accept that his speechwriters use their own words. Not so. Increasingly, presidents, candidates, and political parties use language that is tested in focus groups before it is included in a presidential address, featured in a campaign ad, or incorporated into a party platform. A focus group is a dozen or so average men and women who are brought together to share feelings and reactions to any one of a number of things, including language. For political consultants, the task is to find words and phrases that will produce the desired reaction on the part of the public toward particular policies and political candidates. There are dozens of "word labs," but one of the more elaborate is run by Republican pollster Frank Luntz. In 2000, he produced a pocket-sized pamphlet called "Right Words" and a four-hundred-page loose-leaf binder called "A Conversation with America" for the Republican Party.

Based on his focus groups, Luntz counseled Republicans that "Department of Defense" is preferred to "Pentagon," "opportunity scholarships" to "vouchers," "tax relief" to "tax cuts," and "climate change" to "global warming." If the goal is to turn people away from a policy, he recommends linking it with the super negatives "Washington" and "IRS." In the 2004 campaign, Luntz urged Republican candidates to link Saddam Hussein with weapons of mass destruction and 9/11 at every opportunity. The strategy paid off. Many Americans still believe Saddam Hussein had weapons of mass destruction and was directly tied to 9/11 despite no evidence supporting such links.

In an effort to reach women, a group that has favored Democrats, Luntz advises invoking children. Major addresses by President Bush before the 2004 election were sprinkled with references to children along with "heart," "dream," "love," and "hope." Luntz told the party faithful that by using emotional language without changing policies, Republicans can have it all. "Like Pavlov's dogs, voters will come running if you ring the right verbal bells."[1]

Focus group participants are not selected because they are representative of a group or population. Nor are focus group questions fair and unbiased. The only requirement is for participants to feel comfortable enough with each other to share their feelings. This often means a degree of similarity with respect to race, income, education, and ideology. For example, combining blacks and whites or liberals and conservatives may limit the willingness of participants to share and restrict the give-and-take that characterizes focus groups. The objective is to identify feelings that lie below the surface, which individuals may not be aware of themselves, are seldom voiced in public, and thus are not likely to be captured in a public opinion poll.

Public opinion polls rarely reveal the depth or nuance of feeling that often rises to the surface in focus groups. These feelings are likely to come into play when people vote, and political consultants want to know which will activate a positive response to their candidates or issues.

In a typical session, Luntz begins with "I want to give you a word, and I want you to tell me how you define it. If someone said 'quality of life,' what would it mean to you?"[2] Responses come from around the room: "a comfortable living," "health care," "security," and "safety." After some discussion, he throws out, "When I say 'government,' what comes to mind?"[3] He then points a finger at participants who volunteer, "the president," "controlling," "providing security for people," "laws," "bureaucracy," "wasteful," and "liars." Another speaks up, "They could leave me alone. My company would be bigger if I had a little less law and a little more help."[4] A little less law and a little more help—interesting phrase, Luntz thinks. He asks the group, "What do you think?"[5]

Focus group participants invariably come away with a sense of empowerment, a feeling that someone is genuinely interested in how they feel. Most forget what they suspected going in—that they are being used for the modest fee they are given to participate. Political handlers and consultants are interested in how participants feel, not to make the system more responsive but to produce potent messages that will color how they react and feel toward political issues and candidates. It makes one wonder whether the phrase "Real Plans for Real People" just popped into George Bush's head or was this the brain child of a word lab? Did President Clinton "build the bridge to the twenty-first century" or did he have help?

1. Deborah Tanned, "Let Them Eat Words," *American Prospect,* September, 2003, 29–31.
2. Nicholas LeMann, "The World Lab," *New Yorker,* October 16 and 23, 2000, 107.
3. Ibid.
4. Ibid., 108.
5. Ibid.
SOURCES: Elizabeth Kolbert, "Test-Marketing a President," *New York Times Magazine,* August 30, 1992; Nicholas LeMann, "The World Lab," *New Yorker,* October 16 and 23, 2000; Deborah Tanned, "Let Them Eat Words," *American Prospect,* September, 2003.

about government intervention than were Democrats, both political parties subscribed to the view that government could help reduce the disparities between rich and poor and provide at least a minimal safety net for income and health care. Liberals embrace Social Security, Medicare, a progressive income tax, government assistance for the poor and, in different forms, working- and middle- class Americans.

Liberalism and conservatism also incorporate views about government's role toward the individual. Here ideologies get even fuzzier. For example, in recent decades it has been liberals who want to use government to maintain civil rights for minorities, and conservatives who have resisted that use of government. Southerners, particularly, many of whom were liberal regarding the role of government in providing economic security, rebelled against the idea that government would protect the rights of African Americans. This issue drove a wedge into the Democratic coalition and the ascendance of a liberal sentiment in America and helped shape the modern political landscape (for more on how this played out in political parties, see Chapter 7).

Though liberals fought to have government protect the rights of African Americans and other minorities, they are opposed to government intrusion into other personal actions. It is conservatives, not liberals, who favor government regulation of abortion and contraceptive rights and same-sex marriages, for example. In these areas, liberals want government to keep hands off, while conservatives seem to approve of big government. In keeping with his core constituency of religious conservatives, President Bush has proposed laws that would spend federal money to teach teenagers sexual abstinence and prevent states from legalizing medical uses of marijuana, as well as ban same-sex marriages

and late term abortions. So one conservative dubbed him the "nanny-in-chief" of the "nanny state."[94]

While these broad descriptions capture the core ideas of liberalism and conservatism, individual politicians, political parties, and the people reflect them only imperfectly. While Democrats are typically left of center, many take conservative positions on some issues. President Bill Clinton endorsed a major overhaul of the nation's welfare program, limiting government assistance to families in need, typically considered a conservative position. President George W. Bush, while governing mostly from the right, confounded some conservatives by proposing an expansion of the Medicare program to include a drug benefit for seniors, usually considered a liberal position. Both presidents Clinton and Bush borrowed from the other side as a way to attract moderates to support them.

Although the American people tend to be conservative on some matters and liberal on others, many lean one way or the other. A little more than a third identify themselves as conservative, and a little more than a fourth identify themselves as liberal. However, more— about 40 percent—identify themselves as moderate.[95]

Social Welfare and the Proper Role of Government

Government programs to help individuals deal with economic hardship started during the Great Depression. These included programs to provide aid to the elderly (Social Security), the unemployed, and the poor. Most Americans supported government assistance of this kind in the 1930s and support it today (see Figure 2).

Most Americans want to see the government spend more for a large variety of social programs, including

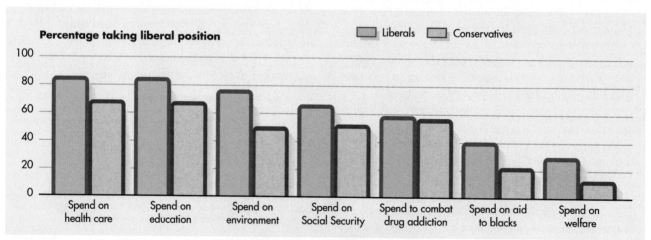

FIGURE 2 ■ Liberals and Conservatives Differ on Spending for Safety Net and Environmental Issues

SOURCE: General Social Survey, 2002 (Ns = 602 to 1,301). The proportions are those who want to increase spending on each area.

many programs for the poor. Public support is high for Social Security, assistance for child care,[96] health care, housing for the poor, increasing the minimum wage, education, and tax credits for the poor.[97]

Opinions on the poor are split. Americans appear to favor helping the poor, but they do not like "welfare," which for decades has been criticized by just about everyone, especially conservative politicians. About 60 percent would like to see food stamps more available and support a minimum income. Nearly 40 percent think the country is spending too little on the poor, while 18 percent think the country is spending too much.[98] At the same time, only one in five want to spend more on welfare,[99] which has come to mean a handout to those who don't deserve it.[100] Polls show most people supported reforms to require people on welfare to work and get off welfare after two years. Most Americans (75 percent) believe the answer to welfare is job training and are willing to pay more in the short term to provide it.

In spite of the positive sentiments toward government spending, 50 percent think their federal income taxes are too high,[101] and while support for Social Security remains high, 40 percent doubt that it will be available when they retire. More than 60 percent support the idea of setting aside a portion of their wages in a personal account and investing it in the stock market.[102] These sentiments signal a growing concern among Americans that a widely popular program is in trouble and may mean less support for it in the future. While one-half of the population would like to see lower taxes, most Americans are also concerned for the well-being of their fellow citizens and caring for the disadvantaged.

The public is generally more positive about state governments in comparison to the federal government.[103] Only 12 percent say that the federal government does the best job of spending tax dollars in an efficient and constructive manner, while 32 percent say that state governments do the best job. More than half still believe the federal government is wasteful and inefficient and controls too much of our daily lives.[104]

Figure 2 shows that liberals are more likely than conservatives to favor government spending on a variety of issues. However, only on the issue of spending for the environment do liberal and conservative opinions differ significantly, with most liberals favoring more spending to protect the environment and conservatives being almost evenly divided.

Social Issues

Social issues have often been a subject of political debate in American history. In the past few decades, examples include abortion, prayer in schools, restrictions on pornography, gay and lesbian rights, capital punish-

ment, and the role of women in society. In recent years, many of these issues have been lumped together in what some described as the "family values agenda."

Social issues represent a clash of values between those seeking to impose a set of standards on society and those who believe such things should be left to individuals to decide for themselves. Many clashes stem from the rapid social change in the 1960s and 1970s. A number of groups, including civil rights, women's, and environmental movements, challenged conventional ways of doing things. Others believed that government decisions, particularly court decisions, wrongly pushed the agenda of these groups. The Supreme Court approved the legalization of abortion, outlawed mandated prayer in school, extended rights to people accused of crimes, and raised questions about capital punishment. Aided by affirmative action, women moved into the workforce in large numbers. Homosexuals became more visible as a group and more outspoken regarding their civil rights. Some, particularly Christian conservatives, believe that these developments are evidence of social decline.

The division over values is reflected in opinions toward the Clinton impeachment. Some religious conservatives accused Clinton of subverting honesty and decency and argued that he should be removed from office; Clinton supporters accused his opponents of practicing "sexual McCarthyism" (see Chapter 14), trampling his civil liberties, and invading his privacy.[105] While most found the president's relationship with Monica Lewinsky and his denial of the relationship immoral and unethical, nearly one-half felt it was unimportant as long as he was doing a good job running the country.

Liberals see matters of religion and morality as personal, outside the scope of government. Figure 3 shows that conservatives are more willing to call on government to impose particular standards on society. Conservatives are *much* more likely than liberals to oppose unlimited rights to abortion and to believe homosexual relations are always wrong. They are somewhat more likely to support mandated prayer in public schools and the death penalty. However, they are not much different than liberals in opposing the ideas that women should stay at home rather than work outside it and opposing abortion when the mother's life is at stake.

Race

Public opinion has influenced, as well as responded to, the progress of the African American struggle for equality. Although the historical record of America's black-white relationships extends to colonial times, the polling record begins in the 1940s. Polls show white America increasingly opposed to discrimination and segregation, at least in principle.[106] In fact, the change might be characterized as revolutionary. Whereas only one-third

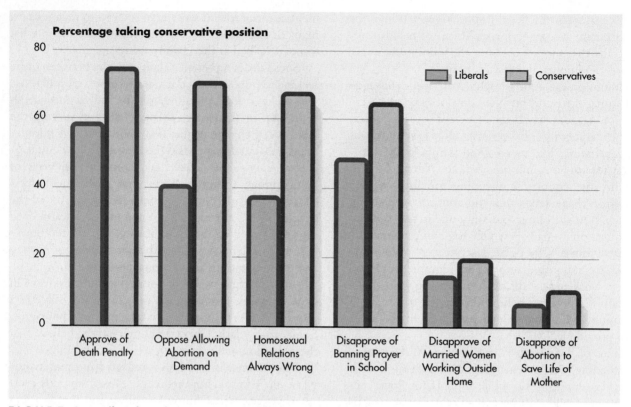

Percentage taking conservative position

Liberals | Conservatives

- Approve of Death Penalty
- Oppose Allowing Abortion on Demand
- Homosexual Relations Always Wrong
- Disapprove of Banning Prayer in School
- Disapprove of Married Women Working Outside Home
- Disapprove of Abortion to Save Life of Mother

F I G U R E 3 ■ Liberals and Conservatives Differ on Social Issues

SOURCE: General Social Survey, 2002 (Ns = 873 to 1,277). Data on married women from 1998 survey.

of whites accepted the idea of black and white children going to the same schools in 1942, in the 1980s more than 90 percent approved. Today nearly everyone approves. Over 80 percent respond that they have no objection to sending their children to schools where more than half of the students are black. Nearly two-thirds say they would not object to schools where most of the students are black.

In other areas of life, white Americans today express more equalitarian attitudes. The percentage of people believing that whites have a right to keep African Amer-

icans out of their neighborhoods has been cut in half since 1963, and a 1996 survey found that two-thirds of white Americans live in integrated neighborhoods.[107] Thirty-eight percent of whites were against laws forbidding interracial marriage in 1963; 85 percent were opposed in 1996.[108] Only 37 percent would vote for a black candidate for president in 1958; but now, 92 percent would (see Figure 4).

Although northerners continue to be more supportive of black rights than southerners, whites in both regions show increased acceptance of blacks. Clearly

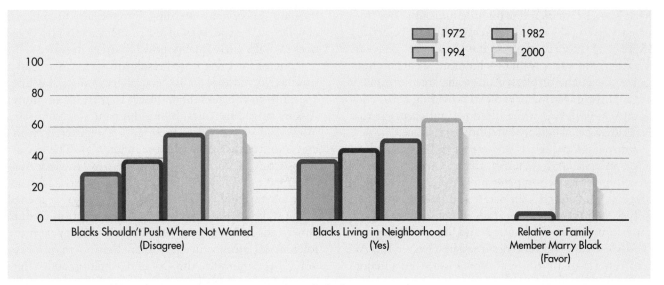

FIGURE 4 ■ **Whites Have Grown More Accepting of Blacks**

SOURCE: General Social Survey, Selected Years (N's range from 1,130 in 1990 to 2,070 in 2000). Data from whites only.

white Americans have become more accepting, but direct questioning in surveys probably exaggerates that acceptance.[109] Some people holding racist attitudes are reluctant to express them in public to an interviewer or anyone else.

Public opinion can change because individuals change or because older individuals with one set of opinions are replaced by a new generation with a different set of opinions. Changes in whites' racial opinions through the 1960s occurred for both reasons. Older whites with more stereotyped views of blacks were replaced by a younger generation who were more tolerant. At the same time, the civil rights movement promoted a reconsideration of many Americans' views about race.

Since the 1970s, most changes occurred because of the replacement of older, more prejudiced whites with younger, less prejudiced ones. Differences in socialization between those born in the 1920s and 1930s and those born in the 1950s and 1960s have led to much greater support for racial integration. More change can be expected in the future as white and black teens age and replace older Americans. For example, a majority of white adults believe the reason that blacks lag behind whites in jobs, education, and income is because they fail to take advantage of opportunities available to all rather than discrimination by whites, while a large plurality of white teens believe discrimination by whites is responsible.[110]

While white Americans accept integration, they have been much slower to accept government initiatives to achieve it. For example, though racially segregated schools often are in poor central city areas and offer inferior education, busing to achieve racial balance in schools has never had much appeal to whites. Only about one-third would support it.

Why is there a discrepancy between the increasing majorities of whites who support integration and the majorities who believe that government should not make special efforts to help minorities? In some cases, unwillingness on the part of whites to endorse government initiatives to end segregation reflects racist sentiments.[111] Although only 10 percent of white Americans respond that differences in jobs, housing, and income between whites and blacks are the result of biological differences,[112] 43 percent cling to the racist belief that it is lack of motivation and will power on the part of blacks.[113] Thus anywhere from 10 to 40 percent of white Americans harbor racist beliefs in spite of their willingness to accept blacks, live in integrated neighborhoods, and have their children attend integrated schools.

However, some whites oppose government help for blacks on principle. They object to being told what to do by government or feel government assistance for blacks is discrimination against whites. For some, government help violates their sense that individuals have a responsibility to provide for themselves.

Another reason that some white Americans are reluctant to accept government intervention is that many do not see the need. African Americans and white Americans live in very different perceptual worlds. Anywhere from 40 to 60 percent of whites believe that the average African American is as well or better off than the average white American in terms of job, income, schooling, and health care.[114] This is a direct contradiction to the reality that blacks lag behind whites on virtually every social and economic indicator. But misperceptions such as these lead many whites to reject any government effort to equalize the social and economic standing of the races. Whites who more accurately recognize the plight of black Americans are more likely to accept the government's role in providing equal education for black and white children and ensuring that blacks are treated equally by courts and police.[115]

Affirmative action has become a touchstone of racial issue polarization. A solid majority of white Americans reject affirmative action programs that give preferences to blacks.[116] Though Democrats and liberals are more likely to support affirmative action than Republicans and conservatives, many Democrats and liberals also oppose it.[117] (Affirmative action is discussed in Chapter 15.) African Americans are also split on the issue, but a majority of African Americans usually do express support for policies giving preferences to blacks in education and employment.

Most whites misperceive the reality of black Americans' lives. As the black middle class increases, whites see blacks living in their communities with job skills and income comparable to their own. Some whites are in competition with blacks for jobs, promotions, and college admission. They are unlikely to accept that blacks are worse off than whites, and government programs targeted toward blacks are likely to breed resentment.

Blacks, not unexpectedly, see things differently. A majority view themselves trailing whites in education, income, jobs, and health care, and of course this is the reality.[118] Moreover, 44 percent indicate that they personally have been denied a job or promotion because of race.[119]

What do blacks believe should be done about race discrimination? Although the polling record for blacks does not extend as far back as it does for whites, blacks have overwhelmingly endorsed integration. Nearly all blacks have responded consistently that blacks and whites should go to the same schools and that blacks have a right to live anywhere they want to live. Most blacks approve of interracial marriage (as do a majority of whites).

Like whites, African Americans have become somewhat less supportive of government initiatives. In 1964, 92 percent thought the federal government should ensure blacks fair treatment in jobs; by 1996, only 64 percent did. Support for government assistance in school integration has also declined. Some blacks fear that government initiatives will only antagonize whites. Others believe government aid hurts blacks by making them too dependent. Still others believe government is ineffective in bringing about an end to discrimination.

Unlike with many social issues, differences on racial issues between liberals and conservatives are slight. Liberals are somewhat more supportive of laws to enhance equality, but majorities of both liberals and conservatives take the pro-equality position on each issue.

One of the unexpected results of 9/11 was at least a short-term increase in interracial harmony.[120] Whites appear to trust blacks more, blacks to trust whites more; Asians trust Hispanics more, Hispanics trust Asians more, and so on. All of these groups registered an increase in trust toward each other after 9/11. The exception is the much lower degree of trust toward Arab Americans. Traditional taboos, such as interracial marriage across ethnic and racial lines, have also weakened in the wake of 9/11. Again, with the exception of Arab Americans and immigrants, Americans also appear more tolerant of ethnic diversity than they were prior to 9/11.[121] The powerful images of devastation and suffering, and the horrified and stunned reaction to them that crossed racial lines, pulled Americans together across the racial and ethnic divide like no other event since World War II.

Political Tolerance

Political tolerance is the willingness of individuals to extend procedural rights and liberties to people with whom they disagree. Tolerance is important because it allows for many elements essential to democratic government, such as freedom of speech and assembly.

J. William Fulbright, the former senator from Arkansas, once said, "Americans believe in the right to free speech until someone tries to exercise it." In other words, people are tolerant in the abstract but not when called upon to support speakers they disagree with. More than 85 percent of Americans claim to believe in free speech for all,[122] yet a classic nationwide survey conducted during the Cold War found that only 37 percent of the respondents would allow a person opposed to churches and religion to speak publicly in their communities.[123] Even fewer would permit an admitted communist to speak. More highly educated people were more tolerant than those with less education, and political elites were more tolerant than the general public.

The finding that elites were more tolerant than the general public was reassuring. After all, many elites are in a position to deprive people of rights, and elites help shape public opinion. Later studies have revealed, however, that elites are more tolerant than the general public largely because they are better educated.[124] Elites, however, do influence the opinions of the general public on civil liberties. When elites agree among themselves, the general public is more likely to reflect this consensus.[125]

More recent studies suggest that Americans have become substantially more tolerant of communists, social-

ists, and atheists.[126] However, overall levels of tolerance may not have increased that much. Today, two-thirds or more think that members of their least liked group should be banned from being president and from teaching in public schools. Many think that the group should be outlawed, indicating a high degree of intolerance.

Economic insecurity in the 1980s and early 1990s helped promote intolerance toward minorities, immigrants, and others outside the mainstream. Long before 9/11, more than 80 percent agreed that people coming to live in the United States should be restricted and controlled more than they are now.[127]

The war on terrorism has undermined public support for civil liberties and civil rights toward persons of Middle Eastern descent. Periods of stress and threat embolden public officials to take action against suspected groups, and the public generally concurs. Polls show that a majority of Americans support the government's policy to try suspected terrorists in military courts, wiretap conversations between lawyers and suspected terrorists, and detain persons traveling in the United States from the Middle East.[128] The USA PATRIOT Act (Uniting and Strengthening America by Providing Appropriate Tools Required to Intercept and Obstruct Terrorism) eroded civil liberties of average Americans, but few complained at the time, and even the name of the law was designed to quiet dissent. Under the Patriot Act, your health records, library checkout records, and student records are subject to review by the FBI without

even notifying you. Only after the horror of 9/11 began to fade did some people on both sides of the political spectrum raise their voices against these erosions.

Incidents of harassment and discrimination against Muslims in 2003 increased 70 percent over the previous year.[129] Most of these related to employment and refusal to accommodate religious practices.

Trust in Government

An important dimension of public opinion is the trust or support citizens have for their government, its institutions and officials, and their fellow citizens. With high levels of trust, citizens might do everything government demands. They would pay their taxes and, if called upon to do so, defend the government. They might also gullibly accept anything officials tell them. At low levels of trust, citizens would be skeptical; they might even disobey the law. At the lowest levels, they might try to overthrow the government or commit violent acts against it, such as those who perpetrated the Oklahoma City bombing. Thus democratic government "depends on a fine balance between trust and distrust."[130]

Public trust of government has declined significantly in the last forty years. In the early 1960s, most Americans trusted the government. A comparison of five nations—the United States, Britain, West Germany, Italy, and Mexico—found Americans to be the most positive about the responsiveness and performance of gov-

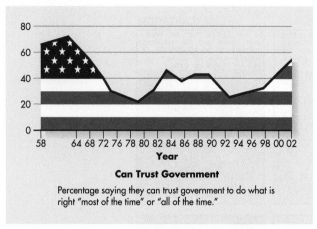

80
60
40
20
0

58   64 68 72 76 78 80 82 84 86 88 90 92 94 96 98 00 02
Year

Can Trust Government

Percentage saying they can trust government to do what is
right "most of the time" or "all of the time."

FIGURE 5 ■ **Trust in Government Declined during
the 1960s and 1970s**

SOURCE: National Election Studies, The Center for Political Studies.

ernment; 95 percent pointed to the government when asked what aspects of the nation they were proud of.[131] The picture that emerged was one of trust and confidence.

The pattern changed, however, sometime in the mid-1960s. Trust in government declined after 1964 and continued to decline through 1980 (see Figure 5). The pattern was characteristic not only of opinions toward government but all major institutions including the medical profession, big business, and mass media.

Government performance is one explanation for the decline. In the mid- to late 1960s, the nation was divided over many issues, including what to do about the war in Vietnam and the civil rights demands of blacks. Many people wanted the government to do everything possible to win the war, while others wanted an immediate withdrawal of U.S. forces; the Johnson and Nixon policies of limited and prolonged war did neither.

The civil rights struggle also divided the nation. Some wanted government to do more to speed the progress of equal rights for blacks and other minorities; others thought government was moving too fast. Government's middle course alienated both sides.[132]

Following on the heels of the Vietnam War and civil rights movement, the Watergate and related scandals roiled the nation and, after 1973, the nation experienced major economic problems: high inflation, interest rates, and unemployment. The government was little more successful in dealing with these than the problems of the 1960s. Levels of trust continued to decline.

During the first Reagan administration (1981–1984), levels of trust and confidence in government increased somewhat. People responded to an improved economy and a few foreign policy successes. Reagan's personal popularity seemed to inspire confidence in government.

However, Reagan's involvement in the Iran-Contra affair, a sense that his administration lacked compas-

sion, and popular dissatisfaction with his domestic and foreign policies diminished his appeal, and no doubt contributed to a decline in trust in his second term.[133] In the 1990s, trust remained low.[134]

Following the 1994 election, President Clinton and the Republican majority in Congress deadlocked over health care reform, welfare, and the budget deficit. Negative reaction to the Clinton sex scandal and impeachment process in 1998 did not, however, affect levels of trust. Indeed, prior to the 1998 election, trust increased.[135]

Trust continued to increase after 1998 and, as noted earlier, jumped after 9/11. Within weeks of the disaster, the number of Americans responding that they could trust the government to do what is right all or most of the time increased to 55 percent, its highest level in thirty years. Suddenly Americans felt the country was moving in the right direction, and both the president and Congress benefited from improved approval ratings. As one observer noted, "Trauma and war remind people why we have government."[136] But by July 2004, in the midst of a heated presidential campaign, the level of trust had fallen to 40 percent.[137]

Clearly, policy failures of government or the perception that government has failed affect trust in government. As citizens have become increasingly oriented to the services government provides (jobs and a high standard of living), failure to provide them or provide them at the expected level lowers trust.[138] Between 1966 and 1980, every percentage increase in unemployment lowered confidence in government by almost 3 percent.[139]

The process of government and policymaking also influences how citizens view the government.[140] Declining trust is tied to the increasing visibility of government. As Americans see the government in action, through C-SPAN and newscasts, they like and trust it less. Talking heads often interpret the give-and-take of democracy—lobbying, bargaining, negotiation, and compromise—as acts of self-interested politicians for personal gain. Since many Americans seem neither to understand nor like the workings of democracy, the more they see, the less they like.

As important as performance and process are, others factors can also play a role. Partisanship also influences trust. When Republicans are in power, Democrats and liberals are less trusting; when Democrats hold office, Republicans and conservatives are.[141]

Broad social trends also affect trust in government. Public concern with declining morality, something over which government has limited control, lowers trust.[142] Events can also boost citizens' trust in government. September 11 was neither a policy failure nor a reflection of process. It did, however, increase the importance of government to most people, and the dramatic, horrific events blotted out, for a few weeks, the kind of debate, discussion, and conflict that sours attitudes toward government.

Can anything be done to restore trust? Most of the public think the country would be better off if the nation's leaders followed public opinion more closely. Only 18 percent of Americans believe Congress would make the same decision they personally would most of the time. Most believe that the decisions of five hundred Americans selected to represent the nation would be better than the decisions of Congress. Two out of three would like public officials to consult the polls to find out what Americans think.[143]

However, these ideas are rather simplistic. Polls usually reveal a divided public, so policymakers would not have a clear direction. There is no public consensus around most important public issues, so bargaining and compromise are necessary to arrive at policy decisions.

It is conceivable that the high levels of trust evidenced in the 1950s and early 1960s were highly unusual. Perhaps the 30 to 40 percent levels of the 1980s and 1990s are the best one can hope for in a time of contentious political issues and a government that is consistently under the spotlight.

Conclusion: Is Government Responsive to Public Opinion?

We believe that in a democracy government should be responsive to the wishes of the people. Those wishes, collectively, comprise public opinion. But is government responsive? Political scientists have not had a lot of success answering this question.

The most direct way to assess whether public policy is responsive to public opinion is to compare changes in policy with changes in opinion. The largest study of this type examined several hundred public opinion surveys done between 1935 and 1979. From these surveys, the researchers culled hundreds of questions, each of which dealt with a particular policy and had been asked more than once. On more than three hundred of these questions, public opinion had changed. The authors of the study compared changes in these three hundred opinions with changes, if any, in public policy. They found agreement between opinion changes and policy changes in more than two-thirds of the opinions. Agreement was most likely when the opinion change was large and stable and when the opinion moved in a liberal direction.

The authors acknowledged that in about one-half of the cases, the policy change may have caused the opinion change, but in the other half the opinion change probably caused the policy change, or they both affected each other. Although in many instances policy was not in agreement with public opinion, on important issues, when changes in public opinion were clear-cut, policy usually became consistent with opinion.[144]

Although policy usually changes with changes in opinions, sometimes it does not. One reason is that re-election does not rest with the entire public but with the voting public, and those who vote often differ in their policy preferences from those who do not.[145] To the extent that elected public officials are responsive to voters, and voters differ from nonvoters, public policy will not reflect public opinion.

Public officials must also pay attention to the intensity of public opinion. It may be advantageous for an elected official to vote in support of a minority opinion that is intensely held. A minority with intense feelings is more likely to vote against a candidate who does not support its position than is a group with weak preferences. When elected officials are confronted with an intense minority, public policy may not reflect public opinion.

Moreover, public opinion is not the only influence on public policy, nor is it necessarily the most important. Interest groups, political parties, other institutions of government, and public officials' own preferences also influence policy, and they may or may not agree with public opinion. Where the preferences of the various influences do not agree, policy generally reflects a compromise among them.

Some observers think politicians pay too much attention to public opinion, to the point that leaders do not lead but simply follow the latest polls and are fearful of leading or of offending competing groups pulling in opposite directions. This concern is certainly valid some of the time, as we have seen, but not all of the time. Other observers are concerned that the public is being led by politicians and an increasingly intrusive and conservative 24-7 media, both of which distort the issues and blind the public to their own self-interests. However, this is a paternalistic view that assumes the public is incapable of defining its own interests if it wants to.

Finally, there is nothing sacred about public opinion. Even when a majority of the public favors a course of action, this may not be the most desirable course. This possibility led the Founders to establish a government that is insulated from public opinion. There is not always agreement between public opinion and public policy because the Founders wanted it that way. They established a federal system with a separation of powers and many checks and balances to ensure that the majority could not easily work its will. Thus one should not expect public policy to reflect public opinion perfectly. The fact that policy usually comes to reflect large and stable majorities does indicate, however, that government is responsive on some issues.

President Bush Ties the Economy to the War on Terrorism

ather than focus on one and ignore the other, the president dealt with both domestic and foreign policy as part of a "security package" devoted to dealing with the nation's economic woes and the threat of terrorism at home. He hoped to maintain popularity by keeping voters focused on his success in dealing with the continuing threat posed by terrorists around the world. He then hoped to use his standing with the public as leverage to push through a number of conservative domestic policy initiatives to deal with the economy and win support for his party in the November 2002 elections.

He opened his address with "Our nation is at war, our economy in recession, and the civilized world faces unprecedented dangers."[146] He reviewed the nation's successes in combating terrorism since 9/11 but cautioned that the war was just beginning. To keep terrorism central in the nation's consciousness, he warned that "thousands of dangerous killers, schooled in the methods of murder, often supported by outlaw regimes, are now spread throughout the world like ticking time bombs, set to go off without warning."[147] To al-Qaeda and the Taliban as targets in the war on terror, he added the nations of Iraq, Iran, and North Korea, calling them the "axis of evil."

On top of one billion dollars a month to fight the war, the president called for an additional increase in defense spending. This may have happened without 9/11 but now it was more urgent and certainly less likely to be criticized. He pointed to an impending budget deficit but justified it in terms of the war. He called on Americans to show the same resolve in defeating the recession as they showed in defeating the Taliban. His economic security was a wish list calling for good jobs, re-

liable and affordable energy, expanded trade, and tax cuts, all elements of his domestic agenda.

The speech was a success in terms of rallying the American people. His popularity hovered in the 70 percent range through the summer of 2002. But instead of using his popularity to rally the public around a moderate agenda and real sacrifices that might help in the war on terrorism and that might appeal to both parties, he used his popular standing to push his conservative agenda—for example, to roll back environmental regulation, provide more tax cuts for the wealthy, and to win support for very conservative judges. Not surprisingly, these initiatives met resistance, and political debate became more polarized.

Then as the 2002 elections grew closer, he used his popularity in a bold way, to rally support for a war against Iraq. He campaigned feverishly across the nation for Republicans, emphasizing the need to combat terror and take military action against Saddam Hussein. He portrayed Iraq as having weapons of mass destruction and links to the 9/11 terrorists. The strategy paid off in the short run as Republicans won control of both the House of Representatives and Senate providing the president with an edge to enact some of his economic agenda and to invade Iraq.

But the long-term impact of Bush's strategy was less successful. The seemingly quick victory in the invasion of Iraq turned into a prolonged occupation that some began comparing to the Vietnam War. The rationales for the war unraveled, as neither weapons of mass de-

struction or links to 9/11 terrorists were found. (The Bush administration moved away from these justifications in favor of others as it became increasingly apparent that the ostensible reasons for going to war were not valid or truthful).

Public support of the president fell with his failure to construct a moderate agenda and with the deteriorating situation in Iraq. The president's approval rating on handling the war went from 75 percent, when he declared combat operations ended, to 47 percent in September 2004. By then, nearly half of the American people thought the war was a mistake.[148] Public support for economic policies dropped as the economy failed to bounce back strongly from the recession and relatively few new jobs were created. By fall of 2004, only 40 percent approved of his handling of the economy.[149]

Yet the strategy of tying foreign and domestic issues worked for the president. Not only did he succeed in winning some of his domestic agenda, but his continued emphasis on his leadership in the war on terror overshadowed the issue of the economy in the 2004 election; and not only did he win reelection, but his party increased its strength in both the House of Representatives and the Senate.

Key Terms

public opinion

political socialization

agents of political socialization

straw polls

push poll

exit polls

ideology

liberalism

conservatism

political tolerance

Further Reading

Herbert Asher, *Polling and the Public: What Every Citizen Should Know* (Washington, D.C.: CQ Press, 2004). Asher provides an introduction to polling methodology, a discussion on the influence of polls on American politics, and advice to citizens on how to evaluate polls.

Thomas Frank, *What's the Matter with Kansas? How Conservatives Won the Heart of America* (New York: Metropolitan Books, 2004). Frank explains why many blue-collar Americans in the heartland vote against their economic interests.

Susan Herbst, *Numbered Voices: How Opinion Polling Has Shaped American Politics* (Chicago: University of Chicago Press, 1993). A historical review of the way public opinion has been measured and the way the evolution of measurement techniques has affected the definition of public opinion.

Lawrence R. Jacobs and Robert Y. Shapiro, *Politicians Don't Pander: Political Manipulation and the Loss of Democratic Responsiveness* (Chicago: University of Chicago Press, 2000). Provides an examination of how politicians use polls to craft language that will make policies that the public would likely reject acceptable to the public.

Celinda C. Lake, *Public Opinion Polling: A Handbook for Public Interest and Citizen Advocacy Groups* (Washington, D.C.: Island Press, 1987). This source includes a step-by-step treatment for lay audiences on how to conduct a public opinion poll.

Thomas E. Mann and Gary R. Orren, eds., *Media Polls and American Politics* (Washington, D.C.: Brookings Institution, 1992). Here are several essays focusing on the influence of media-conducted polls on American political institutions and elections.

Benjamin I. Page and Robert Y. Shapiro, *The Rational Public: Fifty Years of Trends in Americans' Policy Preferences* (Chicago: University of Chicago Press, 1992). Here is an examination of the influence of public opinion on public policy using public opinion polling information generated over the past fifty years.

For Viewing

Outfoxed (2004) A revealing but negative portrayal of the Republican bias of Fox news and how it shapes opinion.

12 Angry Men (1957) Shows the power of persuasion as seen in a fictional jury room.

The Oxbow Incident (1943) Demonstrates mob opinion at work.

 ## Electronic Resources

Many polling firms and media polls have home pages. Here is a sampling of some of the more reputable ones.

www.ropercenter.uconn.edu

The Roper Center Web site contains information on the current and past presidents' job performance and a listing of current Roper surveys.

www.harrisinteractive.com/harris_poll/index.asp?

The Louis Harris Center archive Web site links to current and past Harris surveys. Frequencies are available for all questions, and information can be downloaded and analyzed.

www.umich.edu/_nes/nesguide/nesguide.htm

The National Election Studies of the University of Michigan Web site provide access to the most recent national election study. This information can be analyzed online.

www.washingtonpost.com/wp-srv/politics/polls/vault/vault.htm

This site links to polls conducted by the Washington Post.

abcnews.go.com/sections/politics/PollVault/PollVault.html

The Web site links to ABC Television News surveys.

www.people-press.org

The Pew Center Web site provides recent polling information.

 ## InfoTrac College Edition

Search for the following articles in the InfoTrac database:

Irwin, Galen A., and Joop J. M. Van Holsteyn. "According to the Polls: The Influence of Opinion Polls on Expectations," *Public Opinion Quarterly* (Spring 2002).

Marshall, Randi F. "U.S. Polling Industry Tries to Regain Its Credibility with 2004 Election," *Newsday* (November 5, 2004).

Tumulty, Karen. "The Folklore of Election '04," *Time* (November 22, 2004).

Weissberg, Robert. "The Problem with Polling," *Public Interest* (Summer 2002).

For more articles, enter:

"public opinion polls" in the Subject Guide;

"political socialization" in the Subject Guide.

 ## American Government Resources

Visit the Political Behavior section of the Wadsworth American Government Resources Web site (politicalscience.wadsworth.com/amgov/) for a variety of tools to help you explore public opinion further. Included are simulations, video clips, Microcase exercises, and a wealth of other activities.

NEWS MEDIA

Admiral Mike Boorda.

The Media State

Roles of the Media

Concentration of the Media

Atomization of the Media

Relationship between the Media and Politicians

Symbiotic Relationship

Adversarial Relationship

Relationship between the Media and Recent Administrations

Relationship between the Media and Congress

Relationship between the Media and the Supreme Court

Relationship between the Media and the Military

Bias of the Media

Political Bias

Commercial Bias

Impact of the Media on Politics

Impact on the Public Agenda

Impact on Political Parties and Elections

Impact on Public Opinion

Conclusion: Are the Media Responsive?

YOU ARE THERE

Should You Torpedo the Admiral?

You are Evan Thomas, the Washington bureau chief of *Newsweek* magazine, and it is 1996. One of your contributors is proposing an exposé about an admiral who has worn medals he is not authorized to wear. The story could make a big splash in military, political, and publishing circles. You have to decide whether to pursue it.[1]

Admiral Mike Boorda is chief of naval operations (CNO)—the highest-ranking admiral in the United States Navy. The son of Ukrainian immigrants, he enlisted as a seventeen-year-old in 1956, and almost four decades later he reached the top. His appointment by President Bill Clinton broke several precedents. Boorda became the first CNO who had been an enlisted man, the first who had not graduated from the Naval Academy, and the first who was Jewish.

Boorda is devoted to his sailors. Every time he visits a ship or a base, he holds a session to respond to the sailors' questions and complaints. He tries to show the sailors that he understands their jobs. He learned how to handle the ships, from small boats to battleships, even in choppy waters, and he learned how to fly helicopters and fighter planes.

Boorda also knows how to navigate the treacherous waters of politics. He has forged ties with members of Congress and has developed skills in negotiating. Before becoming CNO, he demonstrated his talent for diplomacy by persuading UN,

NATO, and U.S. commands to work together in Bosnia. (In Sarajevo, he once slipped away from UN officials and showed up in the trenches and buildings of the Serb and Muslim fighters. To their surprise, he explained, "It's the American way. We talk to each other.")

But the admiral has come under attack from traditionalists in the navy. In the aftermath of the Tailhook convention in 1991, when several dozen women were assaulted by drunken aviators, he was expected to improve the climate for women. But when he implemented new policies developed by civilians in Washington, such as allowing women to serve on combat ships and fly combat planes and encouraging toleration of homosexuals (under the "don't ask, don't tell" policy, which will be explained in Chapter 14), he was upbraided for trying to make the policies work rather than attempting to resist them.

He has been criticized by retired admirals, who wield clout like an interest group, and by current officers for helping enlisted sailors with their problems. They say he is usurping the authority of ship and base commanders. And he has even been chastised for driving his own car rather than using a chauffeur as other admirals do. They say he is eroding the prestige of the admirals.

A former secretary of the navy in the Reagan administration who opposed women attending the Naval

Academy and serving in combat units gave a fiery speech at the academy accusing Boorda of sacrificing navy traditions for political correctness. Excerpts were printed in the *Washington Times,* a conservative newspaper, and the *San Diego Union-Tribune,* a prominent newspaper covering navy issues. Criticisms were also printed in the *Navy Times,* a newspaper circulating throughout the navy.

After two years as CNO, Boorda has been under so much pressure that he recently told his family he will not finish the two years remaining in his term.

Amid this controversy, a Washington correspondent for the National Security News Service, which, like similar organizations with a political agenda and foundation funding, locates specialized information that it passes on to bigger media, received a tip that Boorda had worn medals he might not have been authorized to wear. The correspondent contacted a friend, David Hackworth, a retired army officer who was highly decorated and who has sharply criticized the military's "medal inflation" (as some college professors have complained about grade inflation). After Hackworth had written a popular autobiography, he had been appointed a contributing editor of *Newsweek.* In competition with *Time* for readers, *Newsweek* had sought prominent people, like Hackworth, who would contribute occasional articles.

Hackworth examined photos of Boorda in his uniform and concluded that the admiral should not have worn a small *V* on two ribbons from the Vietnam War. Although he was entitled to wear the ribbons, he might not have been entitled to wear the *V,* which stands for *valor* and is reserved for troops who face fire in combat. Yet later photos of Boorda show that he stopped wearing the *V.* Still, Hackworth, who is motivated by a desire to expose wrongdoing by generals and admirals, thinks he has a story. Researching regulations at the Pentagon, he confided to some officers that he is working on a story that will bring down an admiral.

Hackworth contacted the editor of *Newsweek,* informing him of the story and telling him that it could be "a real career ender" for the admiral. The editor referred the story to you, as Washington bureau chief of the magazine, and reserved a page in the next issue if you decide to run it. You met with the correspondent for the National Security News Service, who showed the photos and explained the navy's regulations to you.

You are uneasy, wary of both the correspondent for the National Security News Service and Hackworth. Neither is a regular reporter in your bureau.

Neither, in fact, is an experienced reporter. You told a fellow editor, "There's something about this story that is too good to be true. Stories are never this neat." You consulted with a senior correspondent who specializes in national defense for the magazine. He noted that the navy's regulations concerning the *V* had changed during the war, possibly reflecting the navy's confusion over its regulations, so perhaps Boorda had not worn the *V* improperly or had not done so intentionally.

Do you run Hackworth's article exposing Boorda?

Do you first seek clarification from the navy to determine whether the *V* was actually improper? Or do you question Boorda to determine whether he was honestly mistaken? If so, do you still run the article?

If you run the article, do you balance your findings of wrongdoing with information about Boorda's contributions to the navy in his forty years of service?

Or do you reject the article, because Boorda no longer wears the *V?*

You are mindful of the competition with *Time* and realize that this story would be a real scoop and could make a big splash for *Newsweek.* You also realize that the editor has reserved a page for this story, yet you do have discretion.

A *medium* transmits something. The mass media—which include newspapers, magazines, books, radio, television, movies, records, and the Internet—transmit communications to masses of people.

Although the media do not constitute a branch of government or even an organization established to influence government, such as a political party or an interest group, they have an impact on government. In addition to providing entertainment, the media provide information about government and politics. This chapter focuses on the news media—the part of the media that delivers the news about government and politics.

The Media State

The media have developed and flourished to an extent the Founders could not have envisioned. As one political scientist noted, the media have become "pervasive . . . and atmospheric, an element of the air we breathe."[2] Without exaggeration, another observer concluded, "Ancient Sparta was a military state. John Calvin's Geneva was a religious state. Mid–nineteenth-century England was Europe's first industrial state, and the contemporary United States is the world's first media state."[3]

Americans spend more time being exposed to the media than doing anything else. In a year, according to one calculation, the average full-time worker puts in 1,824 hours on the job, 2,737 hours in bed, and

3,256 hours exposed to the media (almost nine hours a day).[4] Seventy-seven percent of adults read newspapers; the average person does so for three and a half hours a week. The average person also reads two magazines for one and a half hours a week.[5] Ninety-eight percent of American homes have a radio, and the same percentage have a television. For years, more homes had a television than had a toilet.[6] The average adult or child watches television three hours a day.[7] By the time the average child graduates from high school, he or she has spent more time in front of the tube than in class.[8] By the time the average American dies, he or she has spent one and a half years just watching television commercials.[9] With the evolution in digital technology, such as the Internet, now companies are working "to weave media and electronic communication into nearly every waking moment of our lives."[10]

The rest of this section will examine three continuing trends in journalism: the shifting roles of the media, the increasing concentration of the media, and the increasing atomization of the media.

Roles of the Media

American newspapers originated in colonial times, and political magazines appeared in the 1800s, but there were no "mass media" until the advent of broadcasting. Radio, which became popular in the 1920s, and television, which became popular in the 1950s, reached people who could not or would not read. Television became so central and influential in American life that one scholar speculated that the second half of the twentieth century will go down in history as "the age of television."[11]

Although people bought television sets to watch entertainment programs, they also began to watch newscasts. At first, the newscasts lasted only fifteen minutes and consisted solely of an anchor and a few correspondents reading the news in front of a camera. In 1963, the networks expanded the time to thirty minutes and altered the format to emphasize visual interest. These changes made the newscasts more compelling. For the first time, people said they got more political information from television than from any other source.

As television grew in popularity, newspapers waned. People did not need to read their headlines anymore, and many people did not care to read their in-depth coverage either. Newspapers have struggled for readers and advertisers, and some have folded. Since 1970, the number of adults and the number of households have increased significantly, but the circulation of daily newspapers has remained flat.[12] The percentage of regular readers has declined (from 78 percent of adults in 1970 to 54 percent in 2003).[13] The percentage of young adults who are regular readers has declined the most. (In 1966, 58 percent of first-year college students said "keeping up-to-date with political affairs" was an "essential" or "very important" goal. In 1998, only 26 percent held this view.)[14] Even after 9/11, which prompted a surge of interest in foreign affairs, readership continued to decline.[15]

Consequently, television has become the most important medium for politics. According to surveys, people pay more attention to it and put more faith in it than in other media. This makes positive coverage on television essential, and negative images on television devastating, for politicians.

While television offers more immediate and dramatic coverage, newspapers provide more thorough and thoughtful coverage. Because newspapers require more effort and provide more depth, they leave a longer-lasting impression. People remember the news they read in newspapers better than the news they watch on television.[16]

Moreover, national newspapers such as the *New York Times* and the *Washington Post,* which blanket the country with in-depth international and national news, influence opinion leaders, who in turn influence other persons.

Now the Internet is challenging the established media. It allows people to get the news when they want it and to get more news if they want it. Although the Internet is still in its infancy, already a significant number of adults, generally young and well educated, get most of their news from this source (see Table 1).

Courtesy of the National Archives, 33-SC-4899

When radio was new in the 1920s, families such as this one in Oregon gathered around the set to listen.

TABLE 1	Number of Years after Introduction to Attract Fifty Million Users
Medium	**Years**
Radio	38
Television	13
Internet	4

SOURCE: "Ticker," *Brill's Content,* March 1999, 128.

These trends will likely continue: Newspapers will lose more readers while television will lose its dominance and the Internet will gain new users.[17]

Nowadays, different media appeal to different groups. Seniors read newspapers and watch the network newscasts, while the youngest adults are more likely to surf the Web for their news. The all-news cable networks attract the least educated, and the Internet attracts the most educated. Conservatives tend to watch Fox television and listen to talk radio, while liberals tend to watch the Public Broadcasting System (PBS) and listen to National Public Radio (NPR).[18]

Concentration of the Media

Journalism is a big business. The media industry is the nation's ninth largest, ahead of the electronics industry and just behind the aerospace industry.[19]

Journalism has become a bigger business in recent decades. First, small media organizations owned by local families or local companies were taken over by chains (owning multiple newspapers, radio stations, *or* television stations) or conglomerates (owning multiple newspapers, radio stations, *and* television stations). Large media organizations were then taken over by chains or conglomerates. Finally, chains and conglomerates were bought out by larger chains and conglomerates.

Seven huge companies—Time Warner, Viacom, News Corporation, Sony, General Electric, Bertelsmann, and Disney—form the top tier of media conglomerates. Time Warner, the largest, has over eighty thousand employees and $30 billion in annual revenues. It boasts 50 percent of the online business, 20 percent of the cable television business, 18 percent of the movie business, and 16 percent of the record business in the country. It also has 160 magazines, five publishing houses, and "Looney Tunes" cartoons.[20] Twenty other companies, which are major players in one or two types of the media, form the second tier. The remaining companies form the third tier.[21]

Moreover, the seven huge companies are linked to each other. They own parts of each other and additional ventures with each other. These arrangements reduce competition, lower risks, increase profits, and at the same time erect high barriers for any upstarts that try to challenge their dominance.[22]

The long-range goal of the mergers and alliances is to control the information and entertainment markets of the future. Media conglomerates want to offer all media —newspapers, radio stations, television stations, magazines, books, movies, records, and computer services— in various formats, including through such devices as Palm Pilots, at all times of the day. Each conglomerate seeks to become the sole source of all of your news and entertainment.

An early expectation for the Internet—that it would provide unlimited diversity and offer an alternative to established media—is already being dashed as powerful conglomerates are racing to swallow their competitors and influence the government to adopt policies that will lock in their advantage.[23]

This trend toward concentration of the media is certain to continue. It will provide much more convenience, at somewhat more cost for its consumers, but it will pose problems for a democracy that relies on the media to inform its citizens. Already this trend toward concentration makes these problems apparent.

The news comes from fewer sources than it used to. Although there are tens of thousands of media entities in the United States, the numbers are misleading. Chains and conglomerates own the newspapers and magazines with most of the readers, the radio stations with most of the listeners, and the television stations with most of the viewers.[24] One media analyst, referring to the chains and conglomerates that dominate the industry now, observed, "Two dozen profit-driven companies, owned and managed by billionaires operating in barely competitive markets, account for nearly the entirety of the U.S. media culture."[25]

For example, just ten companies publish the newspapers that reach 51 percent of the readers.[26] Six companies broadcast to 42 percent of the radio audience, and five companies broadcast to 75 percent of the television audience.[27] Six companies have more than 80 percent of the cable television market. Four companies sell almost 90 percent of all music recordings, and six companies earn more than 90 percent of all film revenues.[28] One company controls over 70 percent of live music concerts in the country.[29]

Moreover, just one wire service—the Associated Press (AP)—supplies the international and national news for most newspapers. Only four radio networks— ABC, CBS, NBC, and Mutual—furnish the news for most radio stations, and only four television networks —ABC, CBS, NBC, and CNN—furnish the news for most television stations.

With fewer sources of news, there is a narrower range of views—less of a marketplace of ideas—than is healthy for a democracy. A small number of powerful people provide information—essentially, define reality —for all the rest of the people.

So far, there have been hints of political activism and censorship by these chains and conglomerates. During the Iraq war, Clear Channel Communications, the largest radio chain with over twelve hundred stations nationwide, organized prowar rallies in seven major cities.[30] Cumulus Media, the second largest radio chain, halted airplay of Dixie Chicks songs from its country stations after one member of the band criticized President Bush.[31] Comcast, the largest cable company, and CNN, owned by Time Warner, rejected peace groups' attempts to buy time for antiwar ads.[32] Sinclair Broadcast Group, the largest television chain with sixty-two stations, forbade its ABC affiliates from airing *Nightline* the night Ted Koppel read the names of military personnel killed in Iraq. The company said the show would "undermine" the efforts to fight the war.[33] Two weeks before the presidential election, it ordered all of its stations to broadcast a film in prime time accusing John Kerry of betraying American prisoners when he returned from Vietnam and testified against the war.[34] (The company modified this directive after intense criticism prompted some advertisers to pull their commercials, some viewers to threaten a boycott, some shareholders to vow a revolt, and its stock to plummet. The company said that it would produce a special incorporating parts of the film and would make this program available to the stations that chose to run it.) Sinclair, which reaches a quarter of the population, was seeking government approval to expand to other cities.[35] These instances, while relatively minor in themselves, are ominous signs for the future. It would be naive not to expect more actions by media chains and conglomerates to flex their muscles in political controversies.

In addition, there has been self-censorship when news coverage has threatened corporate interests. ABC killed a story that Disney, its owner, followed employment practices that allowed the hiring of convicted pedophiles at its parks. (Apparently ABC, as a small division of the huge company, got "mousekefear."[36]) When Michael Moore, who made the award-winning films *Roger and Me* and *Bowling for Columbine,* made *Fahrenheit 9/11,* a documentary critical of President Bush's handling of terrorism, for a company controlled by Disney, Disney prevented the company from releasing the film for fear that the film would upset the president's brother—Florida's governor—and thereby jeopardize valuable tax breaks for Disney World. (Disney later sold the film to another company that distributed it.) There has also been corporate pressure to slant the coverage. NBC aired a documentary that advocated more use of nuclear power. NBC's owner, General Electric, is a builder of nuclear power plants. NBC broadcast a report about defective bolts used in airplanes and bridges built by GE and other companies, but the references to GE were removed. When the president of NBC News complained about interference in their newscasts, the boss of GE poked a finger in his chest and shouted, "You work for GE!"[37]

Although other media might run a story killed by one organization, what if some story affects the interests of many organizations? In 1996, Congress passed the Telecommunications Act, which set aside a portion of the nation's airwaves for digital television broadcasts. Although the frequencies were valued at $70 billion, the act handed them to broadcasters free of charge. When the bill was proposed, Senator John McCain (R–Ariz.) predicted, "You will not see this story on any television or hear it on any radio broadcast because it directly affects them."[38] Indeed, during the nine months in which the bill was pending, there was little coverage of the bill or the lobbying by the broadcasters. ABC, CBS, and NBC television news shows devoted an average of just six and a half minutes to the bill and virtually none to this provision.[39] If citizens had been aware of this legislation, they might have demanded that Congress, rather than handing the broadcasters a windfall, charge the market value for the frequencies and use the $70 billion to bolster popular governmental programs.

Another problem resulting from concentration of the media is financial pressure to reduce the quality of news coverage. Media organizations are under pressure to show sizable profits each year; some are under pressure to show expanding profits each year. Media organizations are expected to match other divisions in their corporations. Corporate officers feel the heat from Wall Street analysts and major stockholders, such as managers of mutual funds, retirement funds, and insurance companies, who are more concerned with the value of the stock than the quality of the journalism. As a result, costs are cut—some reporters are let go, while others are shifted from time-consuming in-depth or investigative reporting to more superficial stories.[40] A reporter for a midsize newspaper in Illinois admitted, "If a story needs a real investment of time and money, we don't do it anymore." He lamented, "Who the hell cares about corruption in city government, anyway?"[41]

Another problem resulting from concentration of the media is a decline of local news. When a train derailed in Minot, North Dakota, and released over 200,000 gallons of ammonia, authorities tried to notify residents to avoid the area and to stay indoors. But when police called the six local commercial radio stations, nobody answered. The stations were all owned and programmed by Clear Channel, based in San Antonio, Texas.[42] By the next day, three hundred people had been hospitalized, and pets and livestock had been killed.[43]

The trend toward concentration of the media is potentially harmful for everyone but stockholders. Some observers foresee "the free-enterprise equivalent of a Ministry of Culture"[44]—the government office that regulates the media in small countries that lack a free press. In fact, the financial value of some American conglomerates is greater than the entire economy of some foreign countries whose monopolistic policies we condemn as hostile to a democratic society.

Atomization of the Media

Despite the increasing concentration of the media, a contrary trend—an atomization of the media—has also developed in recent decades. Whereas concentration has led to a national media, atomization has fragmented the influence of the national media. The major newspapers and broadcast networks have lost their dominance, while other media, some not even considered news organizations, have played a significant role in politics.

This trend is partly the result of technological changes, particularly the development of cable television and the Internet. Cable television, with a multiplicity of channels, can offer more specialization in programming.

It can provide "narrowcasting" to appeal to small segments of the audience in contrast to the networks' broadcasting to appeal to the overall audience. For example, C-SPAN covers Congress on three channels and, unlike the networks, lingers on members' speeches and committees' hearings. Even MTV covers presidential campaigns in formats to attract young viewers.

Other national cable networks cater to blacks and Hispanics. A cable system in Los Angeles and New York caters to Jews. A cable channel in California broadcasts in Chinese, one in Hawaii broadcasts in Japanese, and one in Connecticut and Massachusetts broadcasts in Portuguese. Stations in New York also provide programs in Greek, Hindi, Korean, and Russian.

Cable television can also offer twenty-four-hour news. CNN, created as a round-the-clock news network, has a large audience. Now Fox and MSNBC are challenging it.

The Internet features additional news sites. Major newspapers post their articles on Web sites before the papers themselves are delivered. Online "magazines" also address politics. During the congressional impeachment of President Clinton, one online magazine—*Salon*—revealed that the Republican representative spearheading the effort (Henry Hyde of Illinois) had had an adulterous relationship. Self-styled "journalists" even post their "news" as well. Matt Drudge offers political gossip on his own Web site, the Drudge Report, which originated in his one-bedroom apartment.[45]

With such proliferation of newscasts, the audience for the traditional nightly news has sunk to its lowest

A newsstand in Brooklyn, New York, sells sixteen Russian-language newspapers to area immigrants.

level since 1961[46]—two years before the networks attracted a mass audience by expanding the newscast and emphasizing visual interest.

The trend toward atomization of the media is also partly the result of the populist backlash against government officials and established journalists, perceived as "Washington insiders," that characterized American politics in the 1980s and 1990s. This is reflected in the popularity of radio talk shows. Many stations have such programs, and many people tune in.[47] Their numbers make talk radio a force in politics. Its middle-class audience acts as a national jury on governmental controversies.

The populist backlash also is reflected in the increasing attention paid to fringe media by the public. In the 1992 presidential campaign, the *Star,* a supermarket tabloid, published allegations by Gennifer Flowers, a former nightclub singer, that she had had a twelve-year affair with Bill Clinton while he was governor of Arkansas. The major media hesitated to repeat the *Star's* story—they had nothing but scorn for the tabloids, which, they insisted, did not practice true journalism—but within days most gave in, under the pretense of debating the propriety of reporting personal matters. Flowers then appeared on *A Current Affair,* a syndicated television show, rated Clinton as a lover on a scale from 1 to 10, and sang "Stand by Your Man." Thus Flowers did not need to take her story to the major media; she got the tabloid media to tell it and pay her for it ($150,000 from the *Star* and $25,000 from *A Current Affair*).[48]

During the impeachment of President Clinton, Larry Flynt, the publisher of *Hustler* magazine, was offended by what he considered to be hypocrisy by the president's adversaries. He offered to pay for information about any affairs that Republican leaders had. Ultimately, he published an article about an affair involving the speaker of the House designate, Robert Livingston (R–La.). Although the article appeared in his magazine, which was read by relatively few men, the revelation received publicity in other media and caused Livingston to resign.

Because the public pays attention to the fringe media more than it used to, politicians have begun to use these media. Instead of announcing their candidacy at a press conference, as politicians traditionally did, some have announced their candidacy on television talk shows. During the campaign, they have appeared on other television shows. Clinton played the saxophone on the *Arsenio Hall Show,* and Bush kissed the host on the *Oprah Winfrey Show.* Candidates swapped jokes with Jay Leno and David Letterman—and prayed they would not end up looking silly.

All this blurs the line between politics and entertainment. When Senator Bill Bradley (N.J.), campaigning for the Democratic nomination for president, appeared

at a Houston radio station that was ranked number one among men in the area, he expected to discuss his new book. Instead, the disc jockeys had two women disrobe from the waist up to report his reaction.[49]

Politicians have to be good sports, because people who pay little attention to political news do pay attention to these shows. Almost a third of adults said they get political information from late-night comedy shows; over a third of those under thirty said these shows are their *primary* source of political news.[50] So it may not be a joke when Letterman proclaims, "The road to the White House goes through me!"

Because of the expanding role of fringe media, mainstream journalists envision a shrinking role for themselves. They no longer monopolize the market of political information; they no longer control the gates through which such information must pass.

This trend toward atomization of the media has significant implications beyond its impact on the established media and their professional journalists. Although this trend makes the news more accessible to more people, it also makes the news less factual, less reliable, and less analytical.

The proliferation of news outlets and the availability of newscasts around the clock create intense competition for news stories. The media have more space or time to fill than information to fill it. So they feel pressure to find new stories or identify new angles of old stories. In addition, they use talk shows that blend news, opinion, gossip, rumor, and speculation, because these shows are cheap to produce and, if the hosts and guests are provocative, entertaining for viewers. The media can fill their time and attract an audience. But the result is a commingling of facts and nonfacts. Then these facts and nonfacts are repeated by other organizations seeking to make sure that they are not left behind. In the rush to broadcast and publish, the media put less emphasis on assessing the accuracy of the content they disseminate than they used to. The "great new sin," a veteran reporter observed, is not being inaccurate but being boring.[51]

Interest groups exploit the competition among the media and exacerbate the problem. When Vince Foster, deputy counsel for President Clinton, apparently committed suicide in a park, a right-wing group sent a fax to news organizations linking the suicide to the Whitewater land deal (a failed real estate development on which the Clintons lost money years before reaching the White House). The group passed the rumor that Foster died at an administration "safe house" and was later moved to the park. Talk show host Rush Limbaugh reported the rumor. Other talk show hosts repeated it; some added the rumor that Foster was murdered. A few financial speculators spread the rumors as a way to manipulate the stock market, prompting newspaper business sections to repeat the rumors in articles about their effect on the stock market. Thus through announcement and repetition by the media, the rumors came to seem true to many people—yet they remained just rumors (and false ones, according to three independent counsels).[52]

The mainstream media have been uncertain how to act in such situations. They are reluctant to report rumors they are unable to verify. But they fear they will lose their audience if they fail to report stories other media report. Usually, they decide to report the stories but in a different context—under the guise of addressing the political ramifications of the accusation or the journalistic ethics of publicizing it. Nevertheless, the effect is nearly the same: The accusation winds up in the mainstream media, and the public believes it. As a result, unscrupulous groups realize they can use the fringe media to manipulate the mainstream media into publicizing bogus charges. In this way, they can drag the mainstream media down to their level. President Clinton's lawyer said it reminded him of when he lived with a bunch of guys in college: Four were neat and one was a slob; by the end of the year, they were all slobs.[53]

The fringe media aggravate the problem. Their goal is entertainment and their audience is politically unsophisticated, so these media are less careful about the accuracy of the information they disseminate. Some pay for stories, possibly encouraging people to lie for the money; many sensationalize stories, possibly distorting the truth. Of course, the mainstream media are also commercial enterprises subject to the pressures of the marketplace. But they also have a tradition to uphold. Reporters at major newspapers and broadcast networks often speak of their responsibility to follow certain journalistic standards, whereas members of the fringe media sometimes reflect the views of radio talk show host Don Imus, who asserts, "The news isn't sacred to me. It's entertainment . . . designed to revel in the agony of others."[54]

The Internet aggravates the problem even more. With no editors, any person with a computer and a phone line can deliver any "fact," however erroneous, to the whole world. In 1997, Pierre Salinger, the former press secretary to President John F. Kennedy and then correspondent for ABC, asserted in a speech to an airline association that a TWA flight that crashed off the coast of Long Island had been accidentally shot down by a navy missile and that this fact was being covered up by the U.S. government. At the time, the cause of the crash was listed as "unknown," so Salinger's speech was reported prominently. When doubters asked how he had learned this, Salinger replied that he received the information from a top intelligence agent in France. Salinger had been hoodwinked. The information originated in the fertile imagination of a retired pilot in Florida who hypothesized this scenario and posted it on the Internet, where it eventually reached the intelligence agent in France.[55] (The government later determined that mechanical failure caused the crash.)

Independent Web logs—"blogs" for short—are amateur Web sites that allow any individual to convey his or her views. Blogs are an alternative to mainstream journalism, free from mainstream constraints such as objectivity and accountability. Some blogs attract tens of thousands or even hundreds of thousands of visitors per day, serving as "the voice of the little guy" in a world of media giants.[56] Blogs act like "a lens, focusing attention on an issue until it catches fire."[57] Senate Majority Leader Trent Lott (R–Miss.), at a one hundredth birthday party for Senator Strom Thurmond (R–S.C.) in 2002, made a remark seeming to praise Thurmond's past advocacy of racial segregation. Although the mainstream media ignored the remark, the blogs circulated it and kept it alive until other media eventually addressed it. Two weeks later Lott resigned his leadership position. According to one political insider, "Blogs are what talk radio was a few years ago."[58] The downside is that blogs, when conveying news rather than opinions, are more likely to be inaccurate than the mainstream media.

© Chris Buck

Web bloggers offer independent views and irreverent humor outside of the corporate media organizations. Here bloggers cover the Republican National Convention in 2004.

Meanwhile, the public is lost in this factual free-for-all. Most citizens are not well versed in the issues or very knowledgeable about the politicians. Without the help of professional journalists, many are not able to separate the blarney from the gospel truth when candidates and officials speak.

In sum, two opposite trends—concentration of the media and atomization of the media—are occurring. It is not clear how they are going to interact. Now they are developing side by side. But strong financial pressures persist, and very powerful corporations are working to dominate the media business. In the future, the huge conglomerates will probably dominate more than they do now. Independent voices from the Internet may occasionally break through on issues that have a human interest angle.

Relationship between the Media and Politicians

"Politicians live—and sometimes die—by the press. The press lives by politicians," according to a former presidential aide. "This relationship is at the center of our national life."[59]

This relationship was not always so close. President Herbert Hoover once refused to tell a reporter whether he enjoyed a baseball game he attended.[60]

But now politicians and journalists realize that they need each other. Politicians need journalists to reach the public and to receive feedback from the public. They scan the major newspapers in the morning and the network newscasts in the evening. President Lyndon Johnson watched three network newscasts on three televisions simultaneously. (Presidents Ronald Reagan, who read mostly the comics, and George W. Bush, who reads mostly the sports section, are exceptions to the rule.)[61] In turn, journalists need politicians to cover government. They seek a steady stream of fresh information to fill their news columns and newscasts.

The close relationship between the media and politicians is both a **symbiotic relationship,** meaning they use each other for their mutual advantage, and an **adversarial relationship,** meaning they fight each other.

Symbiotic Relationship

President Johnson told individual reporters, "You help me, and I'll help make you a big man in your profession." He gave exclusive interviews, told outrageous stories, and invited reporters to bunk overnight at his ranch.[62] In return, he expected favorable coverage.

Reporters get information from politicians in various ways. Some reporters are assigned to monitor beats.

Washington beats include the White House, Congress, the Supreme Court, the State Department, the Defense Department, and some other departments and agencies. Other reporters are assigned to cover specialized subjects, such as economics, energy issues, and environmental problems, which are addressed by multiple branches, departments, or agencies.

The government has press secretaries and public information officers who provide reporters with ideas and information for stories. The number of these officials is significant; one year the Defense Department employed almost fifteen hundred people just to handle press relations.[63] The Bush White House employs over fifty.[64]

The government supplies reporters with a variety of news sources, including copies of speeches, summaries of committee meetings, news releases, and news briefings about current events. Officials also grant interviews, hold press conferences, and stage "media events." The vast majority of reporters rely on these sources rather than engage in more difficult and time-consuming investigative reporting.

Interviews

Interviews show the symbiotic nature of the relationship between reporters and politicians. During the early months of the Reagan presidency, *Washington Post* writer William Greider had a series of eighteen off-the-record meetings with budget director David Stockman. Greider recounted:

> *Stockman and I were participating in a fairly routine transaction of Washington, a form of submerged communication which takes place regularly between selected members of the press and the highest officials of government. Our mutual motivation, despite our different interests, was crassly self-serving. It did not need to be spelled out between us. I would use him and he would use me. . . . I had established a valuable peephole on the inner policy debates of the new administration. And the young budget director had established a valuable connection with an important newspaper. I would get a jump on the unfolding strategies and decisions. He would be able to prod and influence the focus of our coverage, to communicate his views and positions under the cover of our "off the record" arrangement, to make known harsh assessments that a public official would not dare to voice in the more formal setting of a press conference, speech, or "on the record" interview.*[65]

Leaks

Interviews can result in **leaks**—disclosures of information that officials want to keep secret. Others in the administration, the bureaucracy, or Congress use leaks for various reasons.

Officials in the administration might leak information about a potential policy—float a trial balloon—

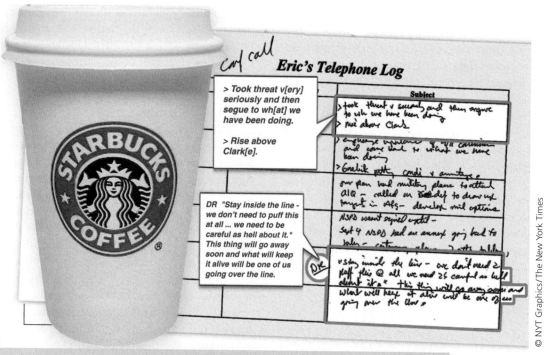

After a Pentagon aide prepared Secretary of Defense Donald Rumsfeld for a television talk show addressing accusations that the Bush administration failed to do enough to combat terrorism, the aide stopped at Starbucks, where he absent mindedly left his notes. In his "Telephone Log," Eric Ruff noted, "Emphasize importance of 9/11 commission" and "Rise above Clark" (Richard Clarke, who headed the government's anti-terrorism efforts and who criticized the administration for emphasizing Iraq rather than terrorism). The aide also left a map showing the route from the Pentagon to Rumsfeld's home.

and then gauge the reaction to it without committing themselves to it in case it is shot down. Or they might leak to prod the president or high-ranking official to take some action.[66]

They might leak to force public debates on matters that would otherwise be addressed behind closed doors. After Congress investigated the intelligence failures leading up to the terrorist attacks on September 11, 2001 someone leaked the information that the National Security Agency—the ultrasecret agency that engages in electronic surveillance around the world—had intercepted al-Qaeda messages on September 10 saying "Tomorrow is zero day" and "The match begins tomorrow" but had not translated the messages from Arabic until September 12.

Officials might leak to shift blame for mistakes or problems. When the insurgency raised doubts about the war in Iraq, officials apparently from the State Department leaked information suggesting that the Pentagon had rushed the country into war. Then officials apparently from the Pentagon leaked information claiming that the CIA had exaggerated the intelligence it located about Iraq's nuclear weapons program. Then officials apparently from the CIA leaked information indicating that the administration had distorted the intelligence

it was given about Iraq's weapons of mass destruction. Each part of the government was attempting to absolve itself of the blame for the aftermath of the war.

Officials might leak to hurt an adversary. Diplomat Joseph Wilson was sent to Niger, which exports uranium, to investigate the possibility that Iraq had sought a type of uranium used in nuclear weapons. Wilson found no evidence to support the claim. Yet President Bush included the claim, essentially as a fact, in his next State of the Union address, and others in the administration repeated it to persuade the public to support a war against Iraq. Breaking his silence, Wilson wrote an article in the *New York Times* maintaining that the administration had "twisted" the intelligence to "exaggerate" the threat. In retaliation, officials in the White House leaked the identity of Wilson's wife, Valerie Plame, who worked for the CIA. She was an analyst who had previously been an undercover spy. Although most reporters had the decency to refrain from reporting this information, Joseph Novak included it in a column and *Time* magazine placed it on its Web site. Unmasking Plame effectively ended her career as a spy and jeopardized the operations she had established and contacts she had made in foreign countries.[67] Unmasking her also makes it risky for her to travel outside the

United States. (In their zeal to play "hardball," White House officials evidently violated laws prohibiting the disclosure of classified information and of the identity of covert employees of the CIA.[68])

Officials might leak embarrassing information to help an ally or protect themselves. By leaking this information at a particular time or in a particular way, they can minimize the damage it would otherwise cause. So officials leak embarrassing information during holidays or weekends, when the news receives less attention. They leak to small or medium-size newspapers rather than to the *New York Times* or the *Washington Post* because these influential papers dislike giving prominent play to stories broken by less prestigious papers.[69] After President George H. Bush nominated Clarence Thomas to the Supreme Court, an official in the Bush administration leaked the fact that Thomas had experimented with marijuana in college. The official's purpose was to inoculate Thomas from the greater controversy that could have occurred if the press had discovered and revealed this fact closer to the confirmation vote.[70]

Most presidents are enraged by leaks. Reagan said he was "up to my keister" in leaks, and Nixon established a "plumbers" unit to wiretap aides and plug leaks once they learned who was responsible. Nevertheless, despite accusations that leaks are from low-level employees in the opposite party, most are from high-ranking officials in the same party. "The ship of state," one experienced reporter noted, "is the only kind of ship that leaks mainly from the top."[71] During the Vietnam War, President Johnson himself ordered an aide to leak the charge that steel companies were "profiteering" from the war. After an executive complained, Johnson assured him that "if I find out some damn fool aide did it, I'll fire the sonuvabitch!"[72]

Officials outside the administration might leak information about those inside the administration. Prosecutors in the independent counsel's office frequently leaked tidbits uncovered during their investigations of President Clinton. They even leaked information from grand jury testimony, which is supposed to remain secret.[73] The prosecutors' goal was to sway public opinion —create a presumption of guilt and generate a sense of momentum—against the president as his impeachment approached. Although the prosecutors apparently broke the law—a felony—the press paid little attention to this fact because the reporters were grateful to have the information.[74]

Leaks enable reporters to break a story before other media can report it. Being first to break a story is known as a **scoop.** The push for a scoop explains the rush among the networks to be the first to "call" elections. In 2000, CBS's Dan Rather announced, "Let's get one thing straight right from the get-go. . . . We would rather be last in reporting returns than to be wrong. . . .

If we say somebody has carried a state, you can pretty much take it to the bank." Yet all the networks initially called the election for Gore, then called the election for Bush, and finally decided it was too close to call for anybody. They botched it twice in the same night.

When the Supreme Court issued its decision in *Bush v. Gore,* ending the Florida recount controversy, the networks showed again that they would rather be fast than right. Under pressure to digest the decision on the steps of the Court, correspondents frantically flipped through the sixty-five-page opinion—and then issued conflicting conclusions. Rather declared, "What [the ruling] does not do is in effect deliver the presidency to George Bush."[75] Wrong again. The networks felt they could not wait a half hour for their legal consultants to read the opinion for fear that viewers would switch to some other network that was already proclaiming the result, even if erroneously.

Press Conferences

Press conferences also show the symbiotic nature of the relationship between reporters and politicians. Theodore Roosevelt, who was the first president to cultivate close ties to correspondents, started the **presidential press conference.**[76] He held occasional sessions while getting a shave. Franklin Roosevelt, who was detested by newspaper publishers, realized that the press conference could help him reach the public. He held frequent sessions around his desk and provided a steady stream of news, which editors felt obligated to publish. This news publicized his policies and his efforts to implement them at the same time that editors were writing editorials against them.

John Kennedy saw that the press conference could help him reach the public more directly if he allowed the networks to televise it live.[77] Then editors could not filter his remarks.

Of course, if a president wants to answer reporters, he can do so in private. If he wants to communicate with the public, he can do so in a formal speech without risking an embarrassing question. But he might opt for a televised conference if he performs well in front of the cameras or, like the youthful Kennedy, feels a need to demonstrate his competence to the watchful public.[78] With his intellect and wit, Kennedy excelled at the televised conference.

As a result, presidents and their aides transformed the conference into a carefully orchestrated media show. Now an administration schedules a conference when it wants to convey a message. Sometimes it even limits questions to that topic. Aides identify potential questions, and the president rehearses appropriate answers. (Former press secretaries admit that they predicted at least 90 percent of the questions asked and often the reporters who asked them.[79]) During the conference,

Henry Groskinsky, New York City

Because President Richard Nixon moved awkwardly—his gestures were out of sync with his words—he was not effective on television. He reminded some people of a marionette; one man made this doll for the president.

the president calls on the reporters he wants. Although he cannot ignore those from the major media, he can call disproportionately on those he knows will lob soft questions.

Beaming the conference to the nation results in less news than having a casual exchange around the president's desk, which used to reveal his thinking on programs and decisions. Appearing in millions of homes, the president cannot be as open and cannot allow himself to make a gaffe in front of the huge audience.

Televising the conference does not even provide much accountability, because one is scheduled when the administration wants, and nearly every aspect is scripted or predicted in advance. Televising the conference only offers an illusion of accountability.

The transformation of the conference frustrates reporters and prompts them to act as prosecutors. As one press secretary observed, they play a game of "I gotcha."[80] After Clinton's first conference, one reporter criticized him because "he didn't say a single thing he didn't mean to."[81] That is, the press could not trick him into saying something imprudent.

Still, reporters value the conference. Editors consider the president's remarks news, so the conference helps reporters do their job. It also gives them a chance

to bask in the limelight. According to a former press secretary, it gives them "fame, power in the eyes of their peers, recognition by their families, ego gratification, and lecture fees from the Storm Door and Sash Associations of the world."[82] (Business and professional associations pay well-known journalists handsome fees to speak at their annual meetings.)

Media Events

"Media events" also show the symbiotic nature of the relationship between reporters and politicians. Staged for television, these events usually pair a photo opportunity with a speech to convey a strong impression of a politician's position on an issue.

The **photo opportunity** (often simply called a "photo op") frames the politician against a backdrop that symbolizes the points the politician is trying to make. Photo ops for economic issues might use factories—bustling to represent success or abandoned to represent failure. The strategy is the same as that for advertisements of merchandise: combine the product (the politician) with the symbols in the hope that the potential buyers (the voters) will link the two.[83] In the 1996 presidential campaign, Bob Dole, who was having trouble attracting young voters, arranged for a photo op at the Rock and Roll Hall of Fame rather than at, say, the Lawrence Welk Museum.

In the run-up to the 2004 presidential election, employees of the Homeland Security Department were told to provide one homeland security photo op a month as a way to link President Bush with 9/11 and the war on terrorism.[84]

Photo ops can be misleading. To persuade people that President Bush's tax cuts, which were designed primarily to benefit wealthy taxpayers, would help working Americans, the speaker of the House, Dennis Hastert (R-Ill.), asked well-heeled lobbyists who favored the tax cuts to dress as construction workers and appear in photo ops featuring "a sea of hard hats" and signs proclaiming, "Tax Relief for Everyone." The lobbyists were urged to participate: "WE DO NEED BODIES—they must be DRESSED DOWN, appear to be REAL WORKER types, etc."[85]

The speech at a media event is not a classical oration or even a cogent address with a beginning, middle, and end. It is an informal talk that emphasizes a few key words or phrases or sentences—almost slogans, because television editors allot time only for a short **sound bite.** And the amount of time is less and less. In 1968, the average sound bite of a presidential contender on the evening news was about forty-two seconds, but in 1988, it was under ten seconds and since then has dropped to less than eight seconds.[86]

Speechwriters plan accordingly. "A lot of writers figure out how they are going to get the part they

After the initial phase of the Iraq war in May 2003, President Bush used the occasion for a dramatic photo op designed for his reelection campaign. Landing a navy jet on an aircraft carrier off the California coast, he swaggered across the deck, sporting a flight suit and backslapping the sailors. Standing under a banner that proclaimed, "Mission Accomplished," he (prematurely) announced the end of major combat in Iraq.

© Brooks Kraft/CORBIS

want onto television," a former presidential aide explained. "They think of a news lead and write around it. And if the television lights don't go on as the speaker is approaching that news lead, he skips a few paragraphs and waits until they are lit to read the key part."[87] This approach does not produce coherent speeches, but the people watching on television will not know, and the few watching in person do not matter because they are just props. But such writing does not provide either group of people with enough explanation or much inspiration.

Perhaps more than any other source of news, media events illustrate the reliance of politicians on television and of television on politicians. The head of CBS News said, "I'd like just once to have the courage to go on the air and say that such and such a candidate went to six cities today to stage six media events, none of which had anything to do with governing America."[88] Yet television fosters these events, and despite occasional swipes by correspondents, networks continue to show them.

Adversarial Relationship

Although the relationship between the media and politicians is symbiotic in some ways, it is adversarial in others. Since George Washington's administration, when conflicts developed between Federalists and Jeffersoni-

ans, the media have attacked politicians and politicians have attacked the media. During John Adams's administration, Federalists passed the Sedition Act of 1798, which prohibited much criticism of the government. Federalist officials used the act to imprison Jeffersonian editors. Not long after that, President Andrew Jackson proposed a law to allow the government to shut down "incendiary" newspapers. Even now, a former press secretary commented, "there are very few politicians who do not cherish privately the notion that there should be some regulation of the news."[89]

The conflict stems from a fundamental difference in perspectives. Politicians use the media to persuade the public to accept their policies. Politicians want the media to act as conduits, conveying their messages, exactly as they deliver them, to the public. But journalists see themselves not as conduits but as servants of the people in a democracy. They question officials and policies until the public knows enough about them to accept or reject them. According to correspondent Sam Donaldson, "My job is not to say here's the church social with the apple pie, isn't it beautiful?"[90] However, some go beyond skepticism to cynicism. In the eyes of a former presidential aide, they walk in the door "assuming that something is wrong and asking, 'What are you hiding?'"[91]

In contemporary society, information is power. The media and the government, especially the president, with the huge bureaucracy at his disposal, are the two primary sources of information. To the extent that the administration controls the flow of information, it can achieve its policy goals. To the extent that the media disseminate contradictory information, they can ensure that these policy goals will be subject to public debate.

Inevitably, politicians fall short of their goals, and many blame the media for their failures. They confuse the message and the messenger, like Tsar Peter the Great, who, when notified in 1700 that the Russian army had lost a battle, promptly ordered the messenger strangled.

When President Kennedy became upset by the *New York Times's* coverage of Vietnam, he asked the paper to transfer its correspondent out of Vietnam. (The *Times* refused.) When President Nixon became angry at major newspapers and networks, he had Vice President Spiro Agnew lash out at them. He also ordered the Department of Justice to investigate some for possible antitrust violations and the Internal Revenue Service to audit some for possible income tax violations. When aides to President George W. Bush read a *Washington Post* article questioning the truthfulness of the president's statements, they suggested that the reporter be removed from the White House beat. (The *Post* refused.[92])

However, it would be incorrect to think that the relationship between the media and politicians is usually adversarial. Normally, it is symbiotic. Although journalists like to think of themselves as adversaries who stand up to politicians, most of them rely on politicians most of the time.[93]

Yet the relationship has become more adversarial since the Vietnam War and the Watergate scandal fueled cynicism about government's performance and officials' honesty. After Watergate, Congress became more willing to launch investigations of administration officials, and reporters became more aggressive in reporting possible scandals.[94] Many reporters, according to the editor of the *Des Moines Register,* "began to feel that no journalism is worth doing unless it unseats the mighty."[95] New reporters especially began to feel this way. Senator Alan Simpson (R–Wyo.) asked the daughter of old friends what she planned to do after graduating from journalism school. "I'm going to be one of the hunters," she replied. When he asked, "What are you going to hunt?" she answered, "People like you!"[96]

With this attitude, "young reporters, without a sense of history, context, or proportion, saw scandal where none existed or at least treated any mistake, no matter how minor, as worthy of being called a 'gate.'"[97] During the Clinton years alone, reporters talked about "Filegate," "Travelgate," "Koreagate," "Troopergate," "Paulagate," and "Monicagate," as well as "Whitewatergate." Yet none of these rivaled Watergate or the Iran-Contra affair in scope or significance.

In response, politicians have restricted access for reporters out of fear that they will say something that will be used against them. In turn, reporters have complained that politicians are not accessible and that reporters cannot get the information they need to do their job.

At the same time, politicians have become more sophisticated in their efforts to **spin** the media—to portray themselves and their programs in the most favorable light, regardless of the facts, and to shade the truth. In turn, reporters have become more cynical. "They don't explicitly argue or analyze what they dislike in a political program but instead sound sneering and supercilious about the whole idea of politics."[98] This prompts politicians to increase their efforts to spin the media, which prompts reporters to escalate their comments that politicians are insincere or dishonest. And so the cycle continues.

After Vice President Al Gore announced his candidacy for president in 2000 from his family's farm in Carthage, Tennessee, ABC correspondent Diane Sawyer conducted an interview reflecting these dynamics. She began, "Are you really a country boy?" He replied, "I grew up in two places. I grew up in Washington, D.C. [as the son of a senator from Tennessee], and I grew up here. My summers were here. Christmas was here." Sawyer taunted Gore, "You mucked pigpens?" Gore answered, "I cleaned out the pigpens . . . and raised cattle and planted and plowed and harvested and took in hay." Sawyer, not satisfied, challenged Gore in an attempt to show that he was a hypocrite: "I have a test for you. Ready for a pop quiz? . . . How many plants of tobacco can you have per acre? . . . What is brucellosis? . . . What are cattle prices roughly now? . . . When a fence separates two farms, how can you tell which farm owns the fence?" By announcing from his family's farm, Gore was trying to convey his rural roots; by interviewing him in this manner, Sawyer was trying to question his sincerity.[99]

In this poisoned relationship, "the most embarrassing, humiliating thing" for a journalist, according to

"When I grow up, I hope to spoil someone's bid for the Presidency."

one, is not to have accused someone falsely but to have been perceived by one's peers as getting taken.[100] During the 1992 presidential campaign, Bush aides complimented a *New York Times* reporter for a fair article. "He looked at us like we had the plague. . . . The next thing we heard, a bunch of other reporters were grousing about [him] and accusing him of being a shill for Bush, of being 'in the tank.' By paying him a compliment we had compromised him."[101]

The increasingly adversarial relationship is also due to other factors mentioned earlier. There are so many media, with so much space to fill, that they have a voracious appetite for news and a strong incentive to compete against each other for something "new." As a result, they often magnify trivial things. And because the fringe media now play a more prominent role, and because their stories eventually appear in the mainstream media, all media pay more attention to politicians' personal shortcomings with sex, drugs, and alcohol and raise more questions about politicians' "character" than they ever used to.[102] In 1977, one of every two hundred stories on network newscasts was about a purported scandal; in 1997 (*before* the Monica Lewinsky affair was revealed), one of every seven stories was.[103]

Yet the apparent toughness usually is "a toughness of demeanor" rather than a toughness of substantive journalism.[104] Reporters exhibit tough attitudes rather than conduct thorough investigations and careful analyses. In fact, few engage in investigative journalism.[105]

After 9/11, reporters were sensitive to and even cowed by the public's fear and anger from the terrorist attacks and wide support for the Iraq war. Consequently, reporters relaxed their stance. But they became more adversarial again when the American victory in Iraq unraveled.

Relationship between the Media and Recent Administrations

Franklin Roosevelt created the model that most contemporary presidents use to communicate with the public. Newspaper publishers, who were conservative businessmen, had no use for Roosevelt and his policies. In fact, a correspondent recalled, "The publishers didn't just disagree with the New Deal. They hated it. The reporters, who liked it, had to write as though they hated it too."[106] Recognizing that he would not receive favorable coverage, Roosevelt realized that he would have to reach the public another way. He used press conferences to provide a steady stream of news about his policies and his efforts to implement them. Editors felt obligated to print this news. This tactic enabled him to override the objections of the publishers. Roosevelt also used radio talks, which he called **fireside chats,** to advocate his policies and reassure his listeners in the throes of the Depression. He had a fine voice and a superb ability to speak informally—he talked about his family, even his dog. He drew such an audience that he was offered as much airtime as he wanted (though he was shrewd enough to realize that too much would result in overexposure). This tactic enabled him to avoid the filters of editors and reporters and to take his case directly to the people.[107]

In addition, Roosevelt was the first president to seek systematic feedback from the people. He used public opinion polls to gauge people's views on his policies. Thus for him, communication was a two-way process—to the people and from the people.

Reagan Administration

Ronald Reagan refined the model. As a young man, Reagan idolized FDR, even developing an imitation with an appropriate accent and a cigarette holder.[108] As president, Reagan duplicated Roosevelt's success in using the media. Although Reagan was fuzzy on the facts about government programs and the details about his proposals, and sometimes he made bizarre assertions (once he said trees cause most air pollution), he had an uncanny ability to convey his broad themes. Reporters dubbed him the "Great Communicator."

As Roosevelt used radio, Reagan used television. By the time he reached the White House, after a long career as a movie and television star, Reagan had mastered the art of speaking and performing in front of live audiences and on camera. He had also mastered the demands of radio and television.[109] Tall, poised, and handsome, he knew exactly how to use an inflection, a gesture, or a tilt of his head to keep all eyes and ears focused on him. As a result, his speeches and even his casual comments were highly effective.

His aides knew how to make his appearances especially impressive. The administration approached its relationship with the media as "political jujitsu."[110] A jujitsu fighter tries to use the adversary's force to his or her own advantage through a clever maneuver. The administration knew that the media would cover the president extensively to fill their news columns and newscasts. An aide explained the strategy: "The media, while they won't admit it, are not in the news business; they're in entertainment. We tried to create the most entertaining, visually attractive scene to fill that box [the TV screen], so that the networks would have to use it."[111]

Aides sent advance agents days or weeks ahead of the president to prepare the "stage" for media events—the specific location, backdrops, lighting, and sound equipment. A trip to Korea was designed to show "the commander in chief on the front line against communism."

News photo of President Reagan in Korea, staged to reflect "American strength and resolve."

© Bettmann/CORBIS

The advance man went to the demilitarized zone separating North and South Korea and negotiated with the army and the Secret Service for the most photogenic setting. He demanded that the president be allowed to use the most exposed bunker, which meant that the army had to erect telephone poles and string thirty thousand yards of camouflage netting to hide Reagan from North Korean sharpshooters. The advance man also demanded that the army build camera platforms on a hill that remained exposed but offered the most dramatic angle to film Reagan surrounded by sandbags. Although the Secret Service wanted sandbags up to Reagan's neck, the advance man insisted that they be no more than four inches above his navel so that viewers would get a clear picture of the president wearing his flak jacket and demonstrating "American strength and resolve."[112]

The Reagan administration also developed the technique of highlighting a single theme with a single message for every week and every day to emphasize whatever proposal the president was pushing at the time. The administration then offered the media information and arranged appearances that reinforced that proposal. Aides strictly controlled the president. They determined "the line of the day" and instructed him what to say. He refused to answer reporters' questions about other matters, except when emerging crises necessitated his doing so. When reporters asked questions inside a building, aides frequently demanded that the television lights be shut off so that the answers could not be televised; outside they often ordered the helicopter's engines revved up so that the answers could not be heard. They did not want other remarks to overshadow the message of the

day. The strategy was to set the agenda and to prevent the media from setting it.[113]

By alternately using and avoiding the media, President Reagan's administration managed the news more than any administration previously.

Clinton Administration

In his use of the media, Clinton emulated Roosevelt and Reagan. Like Roosevelt, he tried to leapfrog journalists to reach citizens directly.[114] Like Reagan, he tried to focus on one issue at a time to shape public opinion on that issue.

Clinton was knowledgeable about policies, perhaps the most knowledgeable president ever, and he was articulate when speaking. Unlike Roosevelt and Reagan, however, Clinton was not enthralling. He lacked discipline and, as a result, talked too long and gave too many details for most listeners. He strayed from his message of the day or the week and thus blurred his focus. Consequently, many people said they did not know what he stood for or wanted to do. Yet Clinton was empathetic, conveying the feeling that he cared for others. Many people said they thought he understood the problems of people like them.

Clinton was especially effective one-on-one with reporters because of his knowledge and his charm. One network correspondent who was not a supporter said, "He is the most charming man I have ever met."[115]

But Clinton inspired visceral hatred from some opponents even before he set foot in the White House. Perhaps it was because he represented the excesses of the baby boom generation, having engaged in sexual affairs and drug use, or because his forthright and independent-minded wife, Hillary, reflected the nontraditional gender roles of that generation. Or perhaps it was because his election cast doubt on conservatives' expectations that Republicans had a lock on the White House and would continue the "Reagan revolution." For whichever reason, some conservative commentators, interest groups, and congressional investigators made a concerted effort from the very outset of his administration to undermine his presidency. They magnified minor miscues into major scandals and fed accusations and rumors, some completely unfounded, to the media.[116] The media allowed themselves to be manipulated because, owing to the atomization of the media, they were competing with other organizations and trying to fill their news columns and newscasts. They aired charges before verifying them because other organizations, including fringe media, had done so or would do so if given a chance. Also, as one reporter later acknowledged, "there's no denying that we give more coverage to stories when someone is shouting."[117]

So Clinton faced a hostile press from the start.[118] According to a joke circulating at the time, he went on a fishing trip with reporters. After their boat left the shore, Clinton realized he had left his tackle on the dock. He stepped out of the boat, walked to the shore, picked up his tackle, and returned to the boat, his feet all the while remaining on the surface of the water. The next day's headline read, "Clinton Can't Swim."[119]

As investigations into the Whitewater land deal, revelations about the president's personal life, and concerns about his party's fundraising prompted ethical questions, they dominated the news and hindered his efforts to convey his messages and accomplish his goals. The Clintons became bitter toward the media, while reporters became cynical toward the administration. They thought Clinton did not tell the truth or at least did not leave an accurate impression. They considered him "a master of lawyerly evasion."[120] So they looked for falsity or hypocrisy behind his every action or statement.

George W. Bush Administration

The Bush administration has emulated the Reagan administration in trying to manage the news by alternately using and avoiding the media.

Aides establish a message for every day and e-mail talking points to administration officials, instructing them to emphasize certain things and to avoid other topics. The president voices this message at his appearances, and backdrops bearing the message printed as a slogan reinforce it. Administration officials who are contacted by the press repeat it. All are expected to "stay on message." Otherwise, access to the president and White House officials is strictly limited. The president is made available for speeches to friendly audiences or for a few questions from a few reporters at the White House. Press conferences are rarely scheduled. Bush has held far fewer press conferences than other modern presidents.[121] In fact, in his first three years in office, he held only three prime-time solo press conferences.[122] Interviews are occasionally granted, but questions must be submitted in advance. Any reporters who displease the administration are punished by losing their access.[123] As a result of this process, according to President Reagan's aide for communications, "this is the most disciplined White House in history."[124]

When the president attended a meeting in Ireland, an Irish reporter who had submitted questions in advance was dissatisfied when the president answered in generalities. She interrupted him and pressed him for more specific answers. Unlike American reporters, she did not worry about future access to the White House.

President Bush is not comfortable in front of television cameras. Initially he shunned the role of "communicator in chief." Unlike most presidents, who used public occasions to celebrate a national accomplishment or mourn a national tragedy, Bush avoided the spotlight. When aides scheduled public appearances, he bristled.[125]

When he gave formal speeches or made informal remarks, he often looked awkward and sounded inarticulate. Reporters observed that he was "perhaps the least confident public performer of the modern presidency."[126] An aide to the previous president commented, "In the Clinton administration, we worried the president would open his zipper, and in the Bush administration, they worry the president will open his mouth."[127] As governor of Texas, Bush had worked behind the scenes and evidently expected to do the same as president.

The terrorist attacks thrust Bush into the public role he had avoided. Initially, he stumbled. On the day of the attacks, he failed to return to the White House to reassure the public from the Oval Office.[128] Later he called our task a "crusade," unintentionally linking the war against terrorism to the Crusades by European Christians against Eastern Muslims in the Middle Ages. Then, sounding like a frontier sheriff in the Wild West, he declared that Osama bin Laden was "wanted, dead or alive." But gradually Bush grew into his new role, appearing more comfortable on the national stage. At times his informal remarks touched people, and even his formal speeches sounded better. Converting "grief to anger to action,"[129] he rallied the public behind the war on terrorism and the war in Afghanistan.

Bush's strength is to speak to moral clarity. The terrorist attacks, revealing a wide chasm between good and evil, allowed Bush to talk in these terms. But September 11 was "one of history's rare unnuanced days," a presidential adviser admitted.[130] On other issues where there is less moral clarity, such as the clash between Israelis and Palestinians, Bush is less effective. His black-and-white view of the world and his "poverty of language"[131] make it difficult for him to convey any nuances in his comments and policies. (He told one senator, "I don't do nuance."[132]) On these issues, he can seem simpleminded, and he has sent confusing and contradictory messages to the public and to foreign countries affected by our policies.

Although his speechwriters are very good, Bush still stumbles when he speaks without a script. At times he forgets his train of thought, makes up words, and leaves listeners bewildered.[133] But his lack of polish does not seem to hurt him in the polls. He talks like many American men, in his tone and simple words—including the belligerence in his voice—and thus relates well to many American voters. One observer even calls him "a master of the American vernacular, that form of expression which eschews slickness and makes a virtue of the speaker's limitations."[134]

The climate created by the attacks and his popularity in the polls muted potential criticism of the president in the press. And there was no concerted effort from the left, as there was against President Clinton from the right, to undermine Bush's presidency.[135] Consequently, he received relatively gentle treatment from reporters until the occupation of Iraq fared badly and his policies toward Iraq faced sharper criticism.

Relationship between the Media and Congress

Members of Congress also use the media but have less impact. They hire their own full-time press secretary, who churns out press releases, distributes television tapes, and arranges interviews with reporters.[136] The Senate and House of Representatives provide recording studios for members and allow television cameras into committee rooms and C-SPAN into the chambers. Yet members still have trouble attracting the eye of the media. One president can be the subject of the media's focus, whereas 535 members of Congress cannot. Only a handful of powerful (or, occasionally, colorful) members receive much notice from the national media. Other members get attention from their home state or district media, but those from large urban areas with numerous representatives get little publicity or scrutiny even there.[137]

Congressional committees also try to use the media to influence public opinion. After Arizona and California voters supported initiatives on their state ballots in 1996 to allow sick people to use marijuana to control pain, the Senate Judiciary Committee held a hearing to discredit the initiatives and discourage people in other states from following their lead. The hearing, titled "A Prescription for Addiction? The Arizona and California Medical Drug Use Initiatives," included five opponents and just one proponent of marijuana use for sick people. The chair, Senator Orrin Hatch (R-Utah), opened the hearing by stating that the voters were fooled by millions of dollars spent on "stealth campaigns designed to conceal their real objective: the legalization of drugs." Hatch also asserted that marijuana has no medical value. The witnesses predicted that allowing sick people to use marijuana would result in other people using the drug and then trying harder drugs as well. All the charges are debatable, but the committee was not trying to investigate the facts; it was trying to sway public opinion.[138]

The Senate Whitewater hearings were also designed to sway public opinion. During the hearings, President Clinton talked with one of the Republican senators on the committee. "They were impugning Hillary," he recalled, "and I asked this guy, 'Do you really think my wife and I did anything wrong in this Whitewater thing?' He just started laughing. He said, 'Of course you didn't do anything wrong. That's not the point. The point of this is to make people think you did something wrong.'"[139]

Relationship between the Media and the Supreme Court

Unlike presidents and members of Congress, justices of the Supreme Court shun the media. They rarely talk to reporters, and they also forbid their law clerks from talking to the press. They try to convey the impression that they are not engaged in politics and therefore should not answer reporters' questions or concern themselves with public opinion.

As a result, the media do not cover the Supreme Court nearly as much as the presidency or Congress. Few newspapers have a full-time Court reporter; no newsmagazines or television networks do. In one recent year, only twenty-seven reporters had Court press credentials, while an estimated seventeen hundred reporters had White House press credentials.[140]

When the media do cover the Supreme Court, they focus on the rulings of the Court.[141] They seldom run stories on the personalities of the justices, and they seldom investigate or peer behind the scenes of the Court. They often ignore even relevant concerns, such as the periodic questions about the justices' health. The correspondent for *USA Today* violated the norm when he discovered that only 29 of the 394 clerks who had been hired by the current justices were minorities (and that most of these were Asians). His investigation irritated other correspondents, some of whom refused to report the story for their media.[142]

Most reporters on this beat, called "Washington's most deferential press corps,"[143] reject the role of watchdog. Consequently, the justices are shielded from both the legitimate investigation and the excessive scrutiny that officials in the other branches are subjected to. It is probably not a coincidence, then, that the public holds the Court in higher esteem than either of the other branches of government.

Relationship between the Media and the Military

During wartime, the military has tried to control media coverage to avoid the negative reports and the disturbing photographs that typified the last years of the Vietnam War. Yet severe restrictions on access and heavy censorship of stories have prompted criticism by media organizations.[144] For the Afghanistan war, the administration bought the exclusive rights to the photographic images from all private satellites so that media organizations would be unable to use any. (American taxpayers were paying private companies more than two million dollars per month to prevent them from seeing what was happening.[145]) Then the military kept the journalists at arm's length from the fighting—and even from the af-

Reporting from Iraq

"Iraq has been many things to many people: necessary war, project for democracy, quagmire without end.

"Yet for the dozens of newspaper and television reporters trying to make sense of the place, Iraq above all is a shrinking country. Village by village, block by block, the vast and challenging land that we entered in 2003 has shriveled into a medieval city-state, a grim and edgy place where the only question is how much more territory we will lose tomorrow. On some days, it seems, we are all crowded into a single room together, clutching our notebooks and watching the walls.

"What I mean, of course, is that the business of reporting in Iraq has become a terribly truncated affair, an enterprise clipped and limited by the violence all around. If the American military has its 'no-go' zones, places where it no longer sends its troops, we in the press have ours. . . . Even in areas of the capital still thought to be safe, very few reporters are still brazen enough to get out of a car, walk around and stop people at random.

"Most of us have our own store of close calls to remind us of how dangerous the streets here have become. For the newcomer, there is the video of two French reporters, kidnapped and pleading for their lives, and the list, updated regularly, of the 46 reporters killed here while doing their jobs.

"The presumption, now quaint, [is] that reporters are regarded as neutrals in armed conflicts, that they are there to record the event for history. In Iraq, this has not been true for many months. For many insurgents here, and for a fevered class of Islamic zealots, Western reporters are fair game, targets in their war.

"Here at the *New York Times,* where we have spared no expense to protect ourselves, the catalogue of hits and near-misses is long enough to chill the hardiest war correspondent: we have been shot at, kidnapped, blind-folded, held at knifepoint, held at gunpoint, detained, threatened, beaten, and chased. . . . And that's just the intentional acts. On any given day here, car bombs explode, gun battles break out, and mortar shells fall short. . . . In the writing of this essay, . . . two rockets and three mortar shells have landed close enough to shake the walls of our house.

"In my time here, I have marked significant events here, like the drafting of a new Iraqi Constitution and the formal end of the American occupation, and I have marked a number of personal ones, too.

"Oct. 27, 2003: Attacked by a mob.

"Dec. 19, 2003: Shot at.

"May 8, 2004: Followed by a car of armed men.

"Aug. 28, 2004: Detained by the Mahdi Army. 'You are the second American spy I have captured today,' the insurgent leader boasted, leading me away.

"Stepping out of my car at the scene of a suicide bombing last fall, I stepped into what appeared to be a placid crowd, only to find that it was seething and angry, blaming the Americans, as Iraqis often do, for the death and destruction all around them. The crowd surged before I and my colleagues could get back into the car.

"'Kill them!' an old man shouted. 'Kill them!'

"We barely got away. Back at the office, we counted 17 bricks inside the car, whose every window was smashed.

"In most foreign countries where I have worked, being an American was a kind of armor; the fear of messing with an American forced even the angriest zealots to take a moment to think.

"Here, that fear has vanished, and indeed, it has become its opposite. To be an American reporter in Iraq . . . is not just to be a target yourself, but it is to make a target of others, too. As a result, some Iraqis now shy away from meeting. . . . [One] asked me not to speak English in the hallway leading to his office. . . . [Another] asks that I meet his armed guards in front of a local mosque, who then drive me to his house. Better not to have an American reporter's car parked in front of his house.

"The real consequence of the mayhem here is that we reporters can no longer do our jobs in the way we hope to. Reporters are nothing more than watchers and listeners, and if we can't leave the house, the picture from Iraq, even with the help of fearless Iraqi stringers [assistants], almost inevitably will be blurry and incomplete.

"Some of my colleagues have given up. Most of the European reporters . . . are gone. And there are far fewer American reporters here than . . . just a few months ago."

SOURCE: Excerpted from Dexter Filkins, "Get Me Rewrite. Now. Bullets Are Flying." *New York Times,* October 10, 2004, WK1, 1.

termath; once the journalists were quarantined in a warehouse so that they would not see the American casualties from a stray bomb.

For the Iraq war, the military tried a new approach that promised more access for the journalists while maintaining positive coverage of the war (see the box "Reporting from Iraq"). They decided to embed the journalists into the units. Six hundred journalists ate, slept, and traveled with the soldiers and were allowed to report live. They were prohibited from providing sensitive information, such as troop locations, and they were prohibited from having anonymous interviews, which would enable military personnel to make critical comments without fear of retaliation.

The military's goals were to appease the media organizations and at the same time use them to show the technological prowess of the military and the heroic exploits of its fighters. In the process, according to an administration official, it was "important for the public to be invested in this emotionally and personally," unlike the Persian Gulf War in 1991, which was covered from a distance and looked like a "video arcade game."[146] Finally, according to an army officer, "We want you here to document the gas and the other stuff Saddam has in his arsenal. If he has it, or, God forbid, uses it, the world's not going to believe the U.S. Army. But they'll believe you."[147] (Ultimately, no chemical or biological weapons were used or discovered during the war.)

The embedded journalists provided extensive but superficial coverage.[148] The media organizations got elaborate photo ops—the war looked like fireworks displays and tank parades—and human interest stories for folks back home. But they did not provide informative coverage because each journalist was able to see only "little slices of the pie," yet their reports were run "endlessly."[149]

Other than allowing embedded journalists, the administration has limited war reporting in trivial and substantial ways. For instance, it has forbidden journalists from photographing the flag-draped coffins returning home to the United States. It has resisted requests from reporters and even from Congress, which has the power of the purse, to divulge the costs of the war. In both cases, the administration fears that publicity would diminish support for the war.

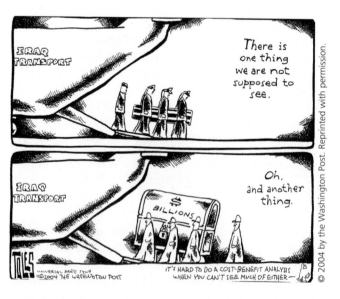

Bias of the Media

Every night, Walter Cronkite, former anchor for the *CBS Evening News,* signed off by saying, "And that's the way it is," implying that the network reported the news exactly the way it happened. It was as though the network held a huge mirror to the world and returned a perfect reflection to its viewers, without selection or distortion. But the media do not hold a mirror. They hold a searchlight that seeks and illuminates some things instead of others.[150]

From all the events that occur in the world every day, the media can report only a handful as the news of the day. Even the fat *New York Times,* whose motto is "All the News That's Fit to Print," cannot include all the news. The media must decide what events are newsworthy. When the Wright brothers invited reporters to Kitty Hawk, North Carolina, to observe the first airplane flight in 1903, none considered it newsworthy enough to cover. After the historic flight, only seven American newspapers reported it, and only two reported it on the front page.[151]

After the media decide what events to report, they must decide where to report them—on the front page or at the top of the newscast, or in a less prominent position. Then they must decide how to report them. Except for magazines, most media attempt to be "objective"; that is, they try to present facts rather than their opinions. When the facts are in dispute, they try to present the positions of both sides. They are reluctant to evaluate these positions, but when one side makes a false or misleading assertion, they must decide whether to point that out.

In making these decisions, it would be natural for journalists' attitudes to affect their coverage. As one acknowledged, a reporter writes "from what he hears and sees and how he filters it through the lens of his own experience. No reporter is a robot."[152]

Political Bias

Historically, the press was politically biased. The first papers, which were established by political parties, parroted the party line. Even the independent papers, which succeeded them, advocated one side or the other. The attitudes of publishers, editors, and reporters seeped —sometimes flooded—into their prose. But papers gradually abandoned their ardor for editorializing and adopted the practice of objectivity to retain as many of their readers as possible.

Yet the public thinks the press is still biased. Many people think the press is "out to get" the groups they identify with. Executives believe the press is out to get businesses, and laborers believe it is out to get unions. Liberals believe it is biased against liberals, and conservatives believe it is biased against conservatives. Republicans believe it is biased against Republicans, and Democrats believe it is biased against Democrats.[153]

Indeed, the public seems more critical today, when most media at least attempt to be objective, than in the past, when they did not even pretend to be. Back then, citizens could subscribe to whichever local paper reflected their own biases (without ever recognizing that the paper reflected any biases). Now, as local newspapers, radio stations, and television stations have given way to national newspapers and networks and as independently owned newspapers, radio stations, and television stations have given way to large chains and conglomerates, people have less opportunity to follow only those media that reflect their views. People who hold strong views are inevitably disappointed with this more moderate coverage. So partisans on both sides simultaneously criticize the same media for being biased.

To assess the presence and the direction of **political bias,** it is necessary to examine the differences in coverage by the advocacy media and the mainstream media; the differences in coverage of elections and of issues; and the differences in coverage of domestic policies and international policies.

Bias in the Advocacy Media

Some media do not try to be neutral. Advocacy media intentionally tilt one way or the other and seek an audience of people who share their views. Advocacy media can be found at both ends of the political spectrum, though far more are conservative than liberal.

Because conservatives perceived a liberal bias in the mainstream media, they established their own media in the 1980s and 1990s. This vocal complex includes newspapers, such as the *Wall Street Journal* (editorial page), the *Washington Times,* and the *New York Post,* various magazines, numerous radio and television talk shows, plus a network of columnists, commentators, and think tanks. These journalists, seeing themselves as part of an ideological movement, as members of the same team, are unabashedly conservative.

Their role in talk radio has been especially powerful. The rise of talk radio began in 1987 when Reagan appointees to the Federal Communications Commission (FCC) abandoned the Fairness Doctrine, which had required broadcasters to maintain editorial balance. When Congress reinstated the doctrine, President Reagan vetoed the bill, thus allowing broadcasters to cater to any audience. At the time, the daytime television audience was mostly female, while the daytime radio audience was mostly male. A gender gap emerged in political preferences as men became more conservative and women remained more liberal, and a backlash grew against feminism and affirmative action among middle-class and lower-middle-class whites. Many stations decided to capture these listeners by airing their views.

Today, more than thirteen hundred talk stations fill the airwaves, and more than a fifth of American adults consider talk radio their primary source for news.[154] The vast majority of talk shows are hosted by conservative commentators. In a week, according to one study, the forty-four top-rated stations air 312 hours of conservative programming and just five hours of liberal programming.[155] (A new liberal network, Air America Radio, began in 2004.) Popular shows are hosted by Rush Limbaugh, Sean Hannity, Bill O'Reilly, G. Gordon Liddy,[156] Oliver North, and numerous others. Limbaugh is given credit by Republicans for enabling the party to wrest control of Congress from the Democrats in 1994 and for helping George W. Bush win the presidency in 2000.[157] Now the Republican National Committee has a Radio Services Department that provides talking points to these hosts every day so that they will reinforce the message from the White House.[158]

The conservative advocacy media also include the Fox News Channel. Fox is the first television network to *narrowcast*—intentionally appeal to a narrow segment of the entire audience—rather than broadcast.[159] Owned by a conservative media mogul and operated by a former Republican consultant, Fox appeals to conservatives disenchanted with the mainstream media.[160] It presents a skewed lineup of commentators and guests that features prominent conservatives with strong personalities paired with relatively unknown liberals with relatively weak personalities. Fox also follows the talking points from the Republican National Committee. After years of critical coverage of President Clinton, now it offers fawning coverage of President Bush. Throughout its programming, the network blurs the distinction between news and commentary. For instance, when reporting on the debate over a proposal by President Bush to cut taxes, the network ran a line at the bottom of the screen urging, "Cut 'em already."[161] When reporting on Swiss protesters against the Iraq war, an anchor referred to the demonstrators as "hundreds of knuckleheads." Another referred to France, which objected to the war, as a member of the "axis of weasels." The network then ran that phrase along the bottom of the screen when reporting on France.

Fox aired relentlessly upbeat coverage of the Iraq war. Its correspondents were urged to downplay American casualties. (In a memo from a senior executive, they were instructed: "Do not fall into the easy trap of mourning the loss of U.S. lives.") They were also told to refer to marine snipers as "sharpshooters," because the word *snipers* has a negative connotation. And all along, the network questioned the patriotism of liberals and critics of the war.[162]

A former Fox correspondent said it was common to hear producers remind them, "We have to feed the core"—that is, their conservative viewers.[163] Yet the network retains a veneer of neutrality. It claims repeatedly to be "fair and balanced" and "spin free." The marketing strategy is to attract viewers by offering them conservative commentary but also the reassurance that this commentary is truth rather than opinion.[164]

Michael Moore's documentaries, such as *Fahrenheit 9/11,* also offer a combination of facts, opinions, and speculations, though from the left rather than the right. (Yet Moore does not purport to be neutral.)

The conservative media also include Christian radio networks, television organizations, and more than thirteen hundred radio and television stations.[165] These media address political issues as well as spiritual matters.

Bias in the Mainstream Media

Although the advocacy media are far more slanted, allegations of bias are leveled against the mainstream media far more often. Conservative groups and commentators, especially, claim that these media are biased toward liberal candidates and policies.[166]

Journalists for the mainstream media are not very representative of the public. They are disproportionately college-educated white males from the upper middle class. They are disproportionately urban and secular, rather than rural and religious, and they are disproportionately Democrats or independents leaning to the Democrats, rather than Republicans or independents leaning to the Republicans. Likewise, they identify themselves disproportionately as liberals rather than conservatives.[167]

Journalists who work for the most influential organizations—large newspapers, wire services, newsmagazines, and radio and television networks—are more likely to be Democrats and liberals than those who work for less prominent organizations—small newspapers and radio and television stations.[168]

Journalists in the most influential organizations are more likely than the public to support the liberal position on issues. At the same time, they support capitalism and do not think that our institutions "need overhaul."[169] Thus they are not extremely liberal.

Focusing on journalists' backgrounds and attitudes assumes that these color journalists' coverage. But several factors mitigate the effect of these traits. Most journalists chose their profession not because of a commitment to a political ideology but because of the opportunity to rub elbows with powerful people and be close to excit-ing events. "Each day brings new stories, new dramas in which journalists participate vicariously."[170] As a result, most journalists "care more about the politics of an issue than about the issue itself,"[171] so they are less likely to express their views about the issue.

In addition, mainstream organizations pressure journalists to muffle their views because of both a conviction that it is professional to do so and a desire to avoid the headaches that could arise otherwise—debates among their staffers, complaints from their local affiliates, complaints from their audience, perhaps even complaints from the White House or Congress. Sometimes media executives or editors pressure reporters because they have contrary views.[172]

Some organizations fear public perceptions of reporters' bias so much that they restrict reporters' private lives, forbidding any political activity even outside the office and on their own time.[173]

For these reasons, mainstream media do not exhibit nearly as much political bias toward candidates or policies as would be expected from journalists' backgrounds and attitudes.

To measure bias, researchers use a technique called content analysis. They scrutinize newspaper and television stories to determine whether there was an unequal amount of coverage, unequal use of favorable or unfavorable statements, or unequal use of a positive or negative tone. They consider insinuating verbs ("he conceded" rather than "he said") and pejorative adjectives ("her weak response" rather than "her response"), and for television stories, they evaluate the announcers' nonverbal communication—voice inflection, eye movement, and body language.

Bias in Elections

Researchers have examined media coverage of presidential campaigns the most and have found relatively little bias. The media typically gave the two major candidates equal attention, and they usually avoided any favorable or unfavorable statements in their news stories. They typically provided diverse views in editorials and columns, with some commentary slanting one way and other commentary slanting the opposite way. The authors of a study examining forty-six newspapers concluded that American newspapers are "fairly neutral."[174] Other studies have reached similar conclusions about various media.[175] An analysis of the data from fifty-nine studies found no significant bias in newspapers, a little (pro-Republican) bias in newsmagazines, and a little (pro-Democratic) bias on television networks.[176]

Some studies did find some bias against incumbents, front-runners, and emerging challengers.[177] For these candidates, the media apparently took their watchdog role seriously.

Overall, then, there is less bias than the public believes or the candidates feel. When candidates complain, they are usually objecting to bad news or trying to manipulate the media. The strategy is to put reporters on the defensive so that they will go easier on the candidate or harder on the opponent in the future, just as sports coaches "work the refs" over officiating calls. In the 1996 election, Bob Dole learned that reporters were considering publishing a story that he had had an extramarital affair in 1968. Although the story did not appear in the major media, Dole criticized them for being biased. Later his aide admitted that the criticism was "a preemptive strike."[178]

Yet the way in which the media cover campaigns can have different implications for different candidates. The media report the facts and the details that contribute to the facts: that one candidate is leading while the other is trailing, that one campaign is surging while the other is slipping. "We all respond like Pavlov's dogs to polls," an experienced correspondent explained.[179] This coverage has positive implications for those who are leading or surging—swaying undecided voters, galvanizing campaign workers, and attracting financial contributions—and negative implications for those who are trailing or slipping. Such coverage does not benefit one party over the other party in election after election, but it can benefit one party's candidate over the other party's candidate in a particular election.[180] People who support the losers consider such reporting biased. Journalists, however, consider it simply a reflection of reality.

Another habitual practice has different implications for different candidates. The press pays more attention to minor things that are easy to report—and easy to ridicule—than to substantive issues that are difficult to explain.[181] Hence all the emphasis on Gore's exaggerations in 2000.[182] The vice president was rebuked for saying that he and wife, Tipper, were the models for the couple in *Love Story*. In fact, he was a model for the male character but Tipper was not a model for the female character. He was made the butt of late-night comedy for claiming credit as a senator for creating the Internet—comedians cracked that he said he "invented" it (though he never used that word). In fact, he was instrumental in securing the government funding that made the Internet possible (as Newt Gingrich later acknowledged), but he did not invent it. Although reporters are willing to criticize or even ridicule candidates about minor matters, they are usually reluctant to challenge them on substantive issues. Doing so would require more knowledge about substantive policies or more nerve to draw conclusions about these policies than most reporters have.

Likewise, when covering presidential debates, the press pays more attention to style and tactics than to substantive issues—more attention to how something was said it than to what was said.[183] Reporters act more like theater critics than helpful guides to confused voters.

In the 2000 election, these tendencies rebounded to Bush's advantage. In other elections, they might benefit the Democratic candidate. These practices do not reflect bias by reporters as much as they reflect superficiality in reporting.

There are two exceptions to the generalization that overt political bias in elections is minimal. First, the media usually give short shrift to third-party candidates.[184] Ralph Nader, who first ran for president in 2000, was well known and held views partly shared by various blocs of voters, but he received scant coverage. When he held a press conference announcing his candidacy, none of the networks and few of the newspapers even reported it. When he held enthusiastic rallies on college campuses and in large coliseums, the national media virtually ignored them. Only when the election between Gore and Bush tightened and it appeared that Nader might be a spoiler did the national media pay attention. Then they focused on his potential as a spoiler rather than on his views that had attracted the crowds.[185]

Second, newspapers traditionally print editorials and columns that express opinions. In editorials before elections, papers endorse candidates. Most owners are Republican, and many influence the editorials. Since the first survey in 1932, more papers have endorsed the Republican presidential candidate, except in the elections of 1964, 1992, and 2004, when Kerry edged Bush in endorsements—212 to 199.[186]

Bias against All Candidates and Officials

Some critics charge that a general bias exists against all candidates and officials—a negative undercurrent in reporting about government, regardless of who or what is covered. President Nixon's first vice president, Spiro Agnew, called journalists "nattering nabobs of negativism." Critics believe that this bias increased after the Vietnam War and the Watergate scandal made reporters more cynical.

There seems to be considerable validity to this charge. Analyses of newspapers, magazines, and television networks show that the overwhelming majority of the stories about government are neutral.[187] However, the rest of the stories are more often negative than positive.[188]

Emphasizing the negative distorts what candidates say. In the 1996 presidential campaign, 85 percent of the candidates' comments made a positive case for the candidates, but 85 percent of the media's coverage focused on negative attacks by the candidates.[189] Emphasizing the negative also distorts what officials do. The *Washington Post* reported that Senator Robert Byrd (D-W.Va.) got the National Park Service to fund a project for his state, including the renovation of a train station—for his "personal pork barrel." "Why did the National Park Service spend $2.5 million turning a railroad station into a visitor center for a town with a population of eight?" The compelling reason—Senator Robert C. Byrd, "who glides past on Amtrak's Cardinal Limited from time to time, heading to and from his home in Sophia, a few miles south." But Byrd did not ride that train, and that train did not go to that town. Moreover, the Interior Department recommended the project; it was not "slipped" into other legislation "unwanted," as the article claimed. When the reporter was questioned, he replied with disgust, "Look, everyone knows that this is the way the world works in Washington. What's the big deal?" Indeed, this is the way things work in Washington sometimes, but apparently not this time. This article, which prompted editorials in newspapers across the country, reinforced readers' cynicism. When Byrd challenged the accuracy of the article, the paper made no effort to confirm the accuracy or correct the record.[190]

Emphasizing the negative conveys the impression that the individuals involved are unworthy of the office they seek or the one they hold. It ultimately conveys the impression that the political process itself is contemptible.[191]

Bias toward Issues

The relative lack of bias in the coverage of elections (except for the negative tone against all candidates) does not necessarily mean there is no bias in the coverage of issues. Because elections are highly visible and candidates are very sensitive about the coverage, the media might take more care to be neutral here than elsewhere.

Researchers have not examined the coverage of issues as much. Empirical studies of the coverage of several domestic issues, including abortion, school busing, and nuclear power, found a tilt toward the liberal positions.[192] Anecdotal reports of the coverage of other domestic issues, such as gay rights, gun control, capital punishment, the environment, and homelessness, also suggest some bias toward the left.[193]

At the same time, the media exaggerate crimes, drugs, and other urban pathologies that stereotype African Americans and, to a lesser extent, Hispanics.[194] In this respect, they do not reflect a bias toward the left.

Popular television programs, movies, and records often promote social ideas or trends characterized as liberal, such as diversity, multiculturalism, acceptance of racial minorities, acceptance of casual sex, and disparagement of traditional religion. (However, these media also glorify violence and possession and use of guns, which do not reflect liberal values.) Such entertainment might have as much or even more effect on individuals'

TABLE 2 Do the Media Reflect Class Bias?

Differences in opinion and income between the public and journalists suggest that the media may reflect a class bias.

Statement	Percentage of Respondents Who Agreed	
	Public	Journalists in Washington, D.C.
"President Clinton's economic plan in 1993 did not increase taxes on the wealthy enough."	72	18
"U.S. economic conditions in 1998 are 'excellent' or 'good.'"	66	92
"My household income is $50,000 or more."	34	95

SOURCE: David Croteau, "Examining the 'Liberal Media' Claim," *Fairness and Accuracy in Reporting,* June 1998; "Ticker," *Brill's Content,* October 1998, 148.

views than the news does. But this chapter focuses on the news media, not the entertainment media, which are beyond the scope of this text.

Although debates about bias revolve around liberalism and conservatism, perhaps the questions should be pointed toward class differences. An examination of the coverage of the debate over the North American Free Trade Agreement (NAFTA), drafted to ease trade between American and Canadian and Mexican companies, showed more emphasis on the benefits of free trade than on the loss of jobs that results from the treaty. Thus the media reflected the views of business more than those of workers.[195]

Analysts now suggest that on domestic issues, the most significant bias is not liberal or conservative but upper middle class over working class.[196] Such bias usually favors the liberal positions on social issues and the conservative, or business, positions on economic issues.[197] These views closely match not only the social class of most journalists but also their urban background and college education. (See Table 2.) Most journalists are "unlikely to have any idea what it means to go without health insurance, to be unable to locate affordable housing, to have their children in underfunded and dilapidated schools, to have relatives in prison or on the front lines of the military, [or] to face the threat of severe poverty."[198]

The picture on foreign policy is different than on domestic issues. The mainstream media toe the government line. Often this is the conservative position.[199]

During the Cold War, this meant harsh attacks on the Soviet Union and leftist Latin American regimes and their economic systems.[200] During the Persian Gulf

War, this meant jingoistic coverage and unquestioning acceptance of administration claims.[201] Even during the Vietnam War, often cited as an example of journalistic rejection of governmental policies, the media offered blindly positive coverage for many years and then relatively restrained criticism near the end.[202]

This bias was apparent after the 2001 terrorist attacks. For understandable reasons, the networks, featuring patriotic logos and melodramatic music, made no effort to be neutral. But some media went further. Two newspapers fired columnists after they criticized the president's delayed return to the Capitol on September 11, and cable systems yanked *Politically Incorrect* after host Bill Maher criticized the president's use of the word *cowardly* to refer to the terrorists.[203] CBS anchor Dan Rather, who prides himself on his independence, declared, "George Bush is the president. He makes the decisions and . . . wherever he wants me to line up, just tell me where." CNN's head warned the staff, "If you get on the wrong side of public opinion, you are going to get into trouble."[204] The patriotic fervor diminished media coverage and therefore public awareness of important matters, such as Arab opinion, the conflict between the Israelis and the Palestinians, and the disagreements among the countries fighting terrorism.[205]

This bias was also evident during the Iraq war. In the run-up to the war, prowar pundits dominated television talk shows, and although there were snippets of doubt and clips of protests on television newscasts, there was no substantive debate.[206] During the war, Fox and MSNBC used the administration's moniker for the war, "Operation Iraqi Freedom," and most networks used the administration's term *coalition forces*. When they used the former, they endorsed the administration's claim that this was a major motive for the war; when they used the latter, they endorsed the administration's claim that there was a broad coalition. (In fact, the war was fought by troops from the United States, with some troops from Great Britain, fewer troops from South Korea, Italy, and Poland, and token representation from other countries.)

Before the war, the media conveyed, without examination, officials' assertions that there was a link between Saddam Hussein and 9/11. For many people, this became a primary reason for the war. After the war, the

What You Watch Affects What You Believe

A majority of Americans have had serious misperceptions about important questions relating to the Iraq war, according to a study based on a series of seven polls spanning nine months. Respondents were asked whether world public opinion favored the United States's going to war, whether there was clear evidence that Saddam Hussein was working with al-Qaeda, and whether after the war weapons of mass destruction were found. (Responses to the second and third questions are shown in Figure 1.) Respondents were asked what their primary source of news is and how often they watch, listen to, or read this source. Respondents' misperceptions varied according to the media they followed. Those who watched Fox had the most misperceptions, while those who watched public television or listened to public radio had the fewest.[1] The misperceptions were not due to people's paying little attention to the news. Just the opposite: those who watched Fox more often had more misperceptions than those who watched it less often.

The results don't only suggest biased or superficial coverage by some media more than others; the results also have policy implications. Respondents' misperceptions were related to their support for the war. Those with the most misperceptions expressed the most support for the war.

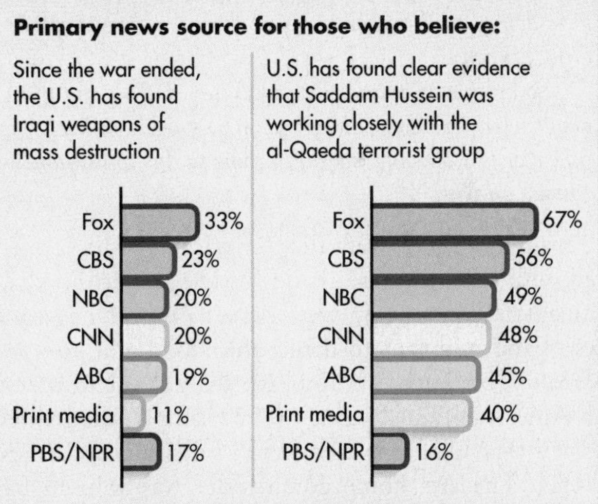

Primary news source for those who believe:

Since the war ended, the U.S. has found Iraqi weapons of mass destruction	U.S. has found clear evidence that Saddam Hussein was working closely with the al-Qaeda terrorist group
Fox 33%	Fox 67%
CBS 23%	CBS 56%
NBC 20%	NBC 49%
CNN 20%	CNN 48%
ABC 19%	ABC 45%
Print media 11%	Print media 40%
PBS/NPR 17%	PBS/NPR 16%

FIGURE 1 ■ Misperceptions and Their Origins

Source: Program on International Policy (PIPA) at the University of Maryland and Knowledge Networks. Poll of 3,334 adults, conducted January–September 2003, with a margin of error of 1.7 percent (www.knowledgenetworks.com/ganp).

1. Researchers tried to control for the possibility that people presort themselves according to ideology by comparing the same demographic groups for each source and also by comparing similar political groups—for example, they compared people who planned to vote for Bush in 2004 and watched Fox with people who planned to vote for Bush but followed other media.

president admitted that there was no known link between the two, but only three of the nation's twelve largest newspapers reported this story on the front page, and two of the papers (the *New York Post* and the *Wall Street Journal*) did not report it at all.[207]

Before the war, the media also conveyed, without examination, officials' assertions that Iraq possessed weapons of mass destruction—biological, chemical, and nuclear weapons. For many people, this, too, became a primary reason for the war (see the box "What You Watch Affects What You Believe"). After the war, the *New York Times* apologized for its coverage, particularly for its lack of scrutiny and skepticism of these claims.[208] Its apology prompted a letter to the editor that could have been sent to most American news organizations:

> *I've followed all the stories and the "spin" to create a case for war from the beginning. . . . As a university student, I sat through it and asked questions as cabinet members made their case for war. In the sixteen months leading up to my activation to fight in Iraq as a tank platoon commander, I felt that this spin was an effort to find a magic button of support with the citizenry. . . .*
>
> *So off I went, to lead my men on this quest. We fought and died holding up the soldiers' end of the democratic bargain. I lived with many of the young men fighting and dying who had such blind faith in our system of government. They felt it was just right to do what we were doing, even though many of them could not explain or justify why.*
>
> *So on this Memorial Day weekend, as I sit and think about what I've done, the people who have been hurt, the future of this ongoing tragedy, I come to this conclusion: Shame on you."*[209]

Throughout the war, the American media, compared with some European and Middle Eastern media, sanitized the war. They were slow to report negative news[210] and reluctant to depict the blood and gore— the reality of war—in both words and pictures for both Americans and Iraqis.[211] (For example, the media reported that U.S. bombers were "softening up" Iraqi defenses. The Air Force commander was amused by the phrase. "We're not softening them up," he said. "We're killing them."[212]) The media sanitized the coverage because "the dirty little secret of much war 'news' is that much of the audience wants to entrance itself into emotional surrender, and news officials want to elicit precisely that surrender."[213] Not until the aftermath of the war revealed the lack of real security in Iraq did the media offer grimmer and starker reports and photographs.

One reason the mainstream media reflect the government line on foreign policy is that they rely on government officials as the sources for most news.[214] Heavy reliance on government officials means the stories will bear their imprint. Reporters turn to officials for news because it is easy and because, ironically, they want to avoid charges of bias. Reporters believe that their peers, their superiors, and the public all consider officials as reliable sources. Ignoring them or downplaying them might be construed as showing bias against them.[215]

Because of this heavy reliance on government officials, the mainstream media focus on the debates among these officials—what "he said" versus what "she said." When there is no dissent within the government, there is little coverage by the media, even if there are alternative views in the society.[216] Journalists seem flummoxed when they cannot follow their conventional reporting practices.

Perceptions of Bias

We have seen that in the mainstream media, there is minimal bias in favor of particular candidates or parties in elections and there is some liberal bias in the coverage of domestic issues and some conservative bias in the coverage of foreign policy. Overall, however, there is far less political bias than many people believe. In particular, there is far less liberal bias than many conservatives believe.[217] Why do so many people perceive so much bias?

As noted earlier, there is some negative bias against all candidates and officials. People sense this bias against the candidates or officials on their side but don't see it against the candidates or officials on the other side. In addition, people hear aides to the candidates or officials complain about the media without realizing that the aides are simply "working the refs" rather than sincerely lodging a complaint.[218] Also, people hear the steady drumbeat from interest groups and talk shows that the media are biased against their side. Eventually, they come to believe it. They don't realize that the leaders of interest groups and hosts of talk shows are just trying to get the people riled up so that they will join the group, make a contribution, subscribe to a magazine, or listen to the show. An influential conservative admitted, "The liberal media were never that powerful, and the whole thing was often used as an excuse by conservatives for conservative failures." Yet, at the same time, he was using the claim in subscription pitches for his magazine.[219]

Strong partisans with strong views perceive more bias than average people.[220] As a result, when strong partisans on opposite sides evaluate the same stories in the same media, both groups see bias against their side, even when the stories are balanced.[221] They are certain that their side is best or correct, so they see coverage that is actually balanced as slanted because it gives their opponents more credence than they feel their opponents deserve. And although these partisans say biased coverage will not affect them, they fear that it will affect others who are less aware or astute.[222]

When strong partisans evaluate coverage that is clearly biased toward their side, they see no bias or less bias than average people.[223] They consider this coverage fair, because in their eyes it reports the "truth."

Even if people's perceptions are inaccurate reflections of media coverage, their perceptions determine which newscasts they will watch. As a result of conservatives' criticism over the years, some mainstream media have become cowed. CNN has ordered producers to include more conservatives than liberals in its stories.[224] During the 2004 presidential campaign, CBS twice postponed a documentary on the faulty intelligence about Iraq's purported weapons of mass destruction. The network said that it would show the documentary after the election, when the program could not affect the election.[225] In this climate, according to one news producer, "The main bias of journalists is the bias not to do anything that could be construed as liberal."[226]

Commercial Bias

Although the public dwells on charges of political bias, **commercial bias** is far more pervasive and significant in understanding media coverage of politics.

Reasons for Commercial Bias

Traditionally, the mainstream media believed they had a "public trust" to meet certain journalistic standards and provide the important news. Newspapers made less money than other businesses, and television news divisions consistently lost money. When *60 Minutes* first aired, the head of CBS told the creator of the show, "Make us proud."[227] The show became a hit, and in its first decade it made so much profit—more than the Chrysler Corporation did during the same years[228] —that now, the bosses tell the producers, "Make us money!"[229] This transformation of the news from an economic backwater to a profit stream has had a huge impact on the mainstream media.

As private businesses, American media, except for public broadcasting, are run for a profit. The larger their audience, the more they can charge for their advertising. A change of 1 percent in the ratings of a television news program in New York City, for example, can mean a difference of $5 million in advertising for a station in a year.[230] NBC's news division generated 40 to 50 percent of NBC's overall profit in recent years, with its entertainment and sports divisions dividing the rest.[231] Local stations' news programs also provide 40 to 50 percent of the stations' overall profit.[232] (For racial implications of the pressure to make a profit, see the box "Color and the Clicker" on the next page.)

With chains and conglomerates taking over most media, the pressure to make a sizable profit has escalated. In the 1970s, big-city newspapers expected to make a 7 or 8 percent return; today chains and conglomerates expect these papers to make a 20 percent return.[233] Corporate executives worry that financial analysts will rank them lower and mutual fund managers will unload their stock if their earnings fall below those available "from investments anywhere else in the financial universe, from a shirt factory in Thailand to the latest Internet start-up."[234]

The pressure to make a profit and the need to attract an audience shape the media's presentation of the news and lead to commercial bias. Sometimes this means that

COLOR AND THE CLICKER

Television news features African Americans in "lights-and-sirens" stories about crimes and drugs and in other stories about urban pathologies, such as single parenthood, that reinforce negative stereotypes.[1] However, television news shuns African Americans in other contexts—not just in the newscasts that focus on government officials but also in the newsmagazines, such as *Dateline, 20/20, 60 Minutes,* and *48 Hours,* that air human dramas.[2] A network staff member lamented, "Can't we do a story about day-care centers and have a black day-care owner . . . ? Why can't they be regular, normal people doing regular, normal things that aren't just associated with their ethnic backgrounds? It makes me sick."[3]

A producer working on a story about a mental disability was searching for a family who had a child with that disability. "I found a great, great upper-middle-class family in Miami, but they were black. I was told . . . : 'Find another family.'" Many network staff members have had similar experiences.

"It's a subtle thing," said one. "A story involving blacks takes longer to get approved. And if it is approved, chances are that it will sit on the shelf a long time before it gets on the air. No one ever says anything. The message gets through."

Sometimes it's not so subtle. Staffers were told by executives that a particular story was "not a good story for us" or that it would "not have broad appeal in the Midwest and in the South." Instead, they were told to feature "families with lots of blond-haired, blue-eyed children."[4]

One reporter observed, "They whisper it, like cancer: 'Is she white?'"

"'Yeah, she's white.'"

"'Are you sure?'"

"'Well, it says they are from Slovakian descent; I'm assuming.'"

"'Well, go out and check.'"

A producer on an evening newscast, working on a health series, found a story about a doctor who encouraged women to get mammograms. The doctor hauled her equipment to beauty parlors where she could test the women conveniently. But when the executive producer saw the piece, he exclaimed, "You didn't tell me that the doctor was black . . . that the people were black!" And he spiked the story.

This pattern is pervasive. A senior executive at a major network confessed, "It's our dirty little secret."

The reason? Research shows the demographic makeup of the audience for every program, and minute-by-minute ratings reveal which stories attract and keep an audience. Many middle-class whites do not want to

watch stories about either lower-class people or racial minorities. When such stories come on, these viewers click to another channel. The networks, under pressure to boast the most viewers to generate the most profits for their corporate owners, cater to the tastes of middle-class whites—the largest segment of the audience.

What appears to be racial bias by the networks is actually commercial bias, just as we have seen that what appears to be political bias by the media is usually commercial bias. But the commercial bias here has racial implications, just as the commercial bias elsewhere has political implications. As a result, television news, which could forge understanding between the races by showing sympathetic people of all colors facing common challenges, makes little effort to do so. Instead, it accepts the subtle racism of those white viewers who will not watch the same story if it portrays black folks rather than white folks.

1. Jeff Cohen, "Racial Tension," *Brill's Content,* October 1999, 54.
2. The record of *60 Minutes* is not as bad as the others, perhaps because *60 Minutes* is the only one without prime-time competition. Robert Schmidt, "Airing Race," *Brill's Content,* October 2000, 145.
3. Av Westin, "The Color of Rating," *Brill's Content,* April 2001, 84. Quotations are from this article, unless otherwise noted.
4. Schmidt, "Airing Race," 114–115.

the media deliberately print or broadcast what their advertisers want. In 2001, CBS bowed to demands by Procter & Gamble that it drop episodes of *Family Law* dealing with gun ownership, capital punishment, interfaith marriage, and abortion.[235] Sometimes the media censor themselves. Numerous magazines, in health articles, avoided references to smoking's dangers for fear of losing advertising from tobacco companies. In 2004, VH1 and MTV pulled clips of, and refused to run ads for, the documentary *Super Size Me,* which shows what

happened to a guy who ate every meal at McDonald's for a month, for fear of losing advertising from fast-food restaurants. A poll of reporters and executives found that a third admitted to avoiding stories that would embarrass an advertiser or harm the financial interests of their own organization.[236]

Usually, though, commercial bias means that the media must print or broadcast what the public wants, which is to say what the public finds entertaining. This creates a "conflict between being an honest reporter and being a member of show business," a network correspondent confessed, "and that conflict is with me every day."[237] When Dan Rather was asked why he devoted time to the demolition of O. J. Simpson's house two years after his trial, Rather answered, "Fear. . . . The fear that if we don't do it, somebody else will, and when they do it, they will get a few more readers, a few more listeners, a few more viewers than we do. The result is the 'Hollywoodization of the news.'"[238]

The dilemma is most marked for television. Many people who watch television news are not interested in politics; a majority, in fact, say that newscasts devote too much time to politics.[239] Some watch the news because they were watching another program before the news and left the television on, others because they were going to watch another program after the news and turned the television on early. Networks feel pressure "to hook them and keep them."[240]

Therefore, networks try to make the everyday world of news seem as exciting as the make-believe world they depict in their other programs. One network instructed its staff, "Every news story should, without any sacrifice of probity or responsibility, display the attributes of fiction, of drama. It should have structure and conflict, problem and denouement, rising action and falling action, a beginning, a middle and an end."[241] As one executive says, television news is "**infotainment.**"[242]

So television anchors and newscasters, hired as much or more for their appearance and personality as for their experience and ability, become show business stars. And show business stars become television anchors and newscasters. CNN hired comely detective Andrea Thompson from *NYPD Blue,* despite her lack of experience (ABC had previously hired the young actor Leonardo Di Caprio to interview President Clinton about the environment).

Consequences of Commercial Bias

The commercial bias of the media has important consequences. One is to sensationalize the news. The intentionally caused anthrax infections that occurred shortly after the 2001 terrorist attacks deserved our full attention. But the media would not let up. Even after the initial flurry of reports, they ran one overwrought account after another. *Time* magazine featured families who bought gas masks. The *Washington Post* wrote that America is "on the verge" of "public hysteria."[243] In fact, few people besides journalists panicked. In polls, large majorities expressed concern but not fear. However, the media realized that generating fear would expand their audience, forcing people to pay attention.

The emphasis on sensationalism leads to an emphasis on scandals. Since Watergate, the media have played up—blown up—other, lesser scandals. In the Clinton era, the public was subjected to saturation coverage of the Whitewater scandal[244] and extensive coverage of all the other "gates" mentioned earlier in the chapter. Perhaps there was something important in these incidents, though a succession of special prosecutors could find nothing more damning than that the president lied about having sexual relations with a White House intern named Monica Lewinsky.[245]

© Time Life Pictures/Getty Images

The media frenzy over anthrax prompted some families, like this one in Chicago, to buy gas masks.

One journalist observed:

When a scandal is breaking, talk show figures wring their hands about the "agony" of Watergate or Iran-Contra; but the truth is that journalists are happier at such moments than at any other time. The country's attention is turned toward Washington. People hang on disclosures of the latest "inside" news. Life is energizing and sweet for Washington journalists, even if the scandal of the moment is a big wheel-spinning exercise for the country as a whole.[246]

A related consequence of commercial bias is to emphasize human interest in the news. When a small boat fleeing Cuba sank, drowning eleven refugees including his mother, six-year-old Elian Gonzales survived. He was rescued by fishermen and taken to relatives in Miami, but his father wanted him returned to Cuba. The relatives and Cuban Americans in South Florida demanded that he remain there, and they provided made-for-television demonstrations for the journalists who had established round-the-clock stakeouts at the house. The plight of this boy became the story of the summer. A *Wall Street Journal* columnist wrote that "the dolphins who surrounded him like a contingent of angels pushed him upward" so that he would not drown.[247] Experts explained his presumed state of mind. Diane Sawyer, in an interview, insisted that he tell the television audience whom he really wanted to live with.

The emphasis on sensationalism and human interest includes a focus on sex. Although American newscasts do not go as far as the Bulgarian program *The Naked Truth,* which had young women disrobe as they read the news,[248] the media do dwell on sexual affairs of public officials. The escapades of President Clinton received extraordinary attention. When the allegations involving Monica Lewinsky arose, the media dropped important stories to focus on what the president did with the intern.[249] The *Los Angeles Times* assigned twenty-six reporters to examine Lewinsky's life, interviewing babysitters and kindergarten classmates.[250] The networks even interviewed one person who had eaten lunch with her three years earlier.

During the investigation by the special prosecutor, titillating details were leaked to the media and then announced to the public. There were breathless reports about phone sex, the president's cigar as a sex toy, and the intern's dress with a semen stain. There was tittering about the "distinguishing characteristics" of the president's genitals—and speculation about how this would be proved or disproved in court.

The emphasis on sensationalism and human interest also includes a focus on crime. Although the national media give crime extensive coverage, this emphasis is most apparent for the local media, where television news is, in Ralph Nader's words, "something that jerks your head up every ten seconds, whether that is shootings, robberies, sports showdowns, or dramatic weather forecasts."[251] Media consultants advise local stations how to attract the largest audience and make the most money for their corporate chain or conglomerate.[252] The saying "If it bleeds, it leads" expresses, tongue in cheek, the programming philosophy of many stations. Crime coverage fills about one-third of local newscasts.[253] A week before the presidential election of 2000, television stations in Columbus, Ohio, devoted more than twice as much time to various crimes than to the election, though the outcome was in doubt, with Ohio a key state and Columbus the state's capital.[254] (One station, however, was able to find time for an undercover investigation of a topless car wash.) A jaded reporter put it bluntly: "It doesn't matter what kind of swill you set in front of the public. As long as it's got enough sex and violence in it, they'll slurp it up."[255]

The emphasis on sensationalism and human interest leads to another consequence of commercial bias—an emphasis on controversy rather than agreement. Stories about conflict provide drama. Reporters, one admits, are "fight promoters" rather than consensus builders.[256] Reporters frame disputes as struggles between opposite camps. Thus some stories about survivors of the Holocaust include bizarre statements by people who claim that there was no plan to exterminate European Jews or that Hitler was unaware of the effort or that few Jews were ever killed. The stories present these absurd statements as though they constitute an opposing opinion that deserves a public platform.[257] With their focus on controversy, the media allow themselves to be manip-

"Luckily, none of the people inside appear to be celebrities."

ulated by people who are unscrupulous or ignorant. And with the justification that there are two sides to every story, the media promote public confusion in the process.

Once the media frame an issue as a struggle between two sides, they depict attack and counterattack, using dueling sound bites from politicians and interjecting metaphors from wars. They talk about politicians who are "targets," who are "under fire," who receive "shots across their bow." They talk about politicians who engage in "search-and-destroy missions" and who "hold back no ammunition." Occasionally, they refer to a "cease-fire," but eventually they return to a "war of attrition" with "do-or-die" battles. Ultimately, they lament the politicians who "crashed in flames."[258]

By focusing on conflict and by framing most issues as though they have two—and only two—sides, the media polarize the public. After the murderous rampage at Columbine High School in Littleton, Colorado, the public was subjected to a moronic debate about whether the incident was caused by the availability of guns in our society or by the glorification of violence in the media. The coverage prodded people to choose sides, as though it had to be one or the other and could not be a combination of the two.

So American television talk shows often pit two people against each other, representing opposite poles in the debate. In contrast, Japanese shows usually have more than two guests, thus reducing the polarization while conveying the impression that the issues are complex and might have multiple answers.[259] American shows prefer to focus on opposing extremes, because, one reporter admits, "the middle ground, the sensible center, is dismissed as too squishy, too dull, too likely to send the audience channel surfing."[260]

These practices make it harder for people to accept compromises as solutions to problems and therefore harder for politicians to forge compromises. In fact, the media belittle compromises. They portray politicians on one side as losing or "giving in" when they should have been fighting to win. Thus the media reinforce some citizens' naive belief that politicians need not and should not compromise.

Another consequence of commercial bias is to use a **game orientation** in political reporting.[261] The underlying assumption is that politics is a game and politicians, whether candidates campaigning for election or officials performing in office, are the players. The corollary to the assumption is that the players are self-centered and self-interested. They are seeking victory for themselves and defeat for their opponents and are not concerned about the consequences of their proposals or of government's policies. With this orientation, reporters highlight politicians' strategies and tactics, and they present new developments according to how these developments help some politicians and hinder others. Reporters slight the substance and impact of politicians' proposals and policies.

The game orientation appeals to journalists because it generates human interest. It offers new story lines as new information comes to light, much like a board game where "chance" cards inject unexpected scenarios and alter the players' moves and the game's outcomes.

This orientation also appeals to journalists because it is easy and relatively free from charges of partisan or ideological bias. (Stories highlight which contestants are winning, not which ones should win or what consequences might result.) Analyzing policy lacks all of these advantages for journalists.

The game orientation attracts an audience, but it breeds more cynicism. It creates the impression that politics is just a game, not an essential activity for a democratic society; that politicians are just the players, not our representatives; that politicians act just in their self-interest, not in the public interest; and that politicians' goal is just to beat others, not to make good public policy.

The assumption that politics is a game and the corollary that the players are concerned solely with their own interests leads to the conclusion that their strategies and tactics are based mostly on manipulation and deception. Journalists, casting their wary eyes on politicians, look for manipulation and deception and interpret even sincere action in those ways.

For elections, the game orientation results in what is called **horse race coverage,** with "front-runners," "dark horses," and "also-rans." An examination of presidential election coverage by metropolitan newspapers shows that the race was a staple of journalism even in the nineteenth century.[262] Other research suggests, however, that the proportion of coverage focusing on the race has been increasing in recent decades.[263]

Today, horse race coverage dominates election reporting. In 2000, about two-thirds of the reporting by newspapers, television networks, and Web sites featured the horse race, and much of the remaining reporting featured the candidates' strategies. Although there were major differences in the candidates' stands, far less reporting examined the issues or their proposals.[264]

The quintessential reflection of horse race coverage —reporting of candidates' poll standings—has increased greatly. Not only have the media reported more results of polls taken by commercial organizations, but they have also conducted more polls themselves.[265] Nowadays, coverage of polls takes more space than coverage of candidates' speeches, and it usually appears as the lead or next-to-lead story.[266]

Even after elections, the game orientation continues. When Clinton proposed a plan to overhaul the welfare system, all major newspapers focused on the political implications for his reelection; few even explained the plan, let alone its substantive implications.[267]

Commercial bias in the media leads to additional consequences for television specifically. One is to emphasize events, or those parts of events, that have visual interest. The networks have people whose job is to evaluate all film for visual appeal. Producers seek the events that promise the most action, camera operators shoot the parts of the events with the most action, and editors select the portions of the film with the most action.[268] Television thus focuses on disasters, crimes, and protests far more than they actually occur, and it displays the interesting surface rather than the underlying substance of these events—for example, the protest rather than the cause of the anger.

Another consequence of commercial bias for television is to cover the news very briefly. A half-hour newscast has only twenty-one minutes without commercials. In that time, the networks broadcast only a third as many words as the *New York Times* prints on its front page alone. Although cable television has ample time, it follows this format, too, endlessly repeating the same stories without adding new information.[269]

Television stories are short—about one minute each—because the networks think viewers' attention spans are short. Indeed, a survey found that a majority of eighteen- to thirty-four-year-olds with remote controls typically watch more than one show at once.[270] Thus networks do not allow leaders or experts to explain their thoughts about particular events or policies. Instead, networks take sound bites to illustrate what was said. Their correspondents usually do not have enough time to explain the events or policies or to provide background information about them.

A network correspondent was asked what went through his mind when he signed off each night. "Good night, dear viewer," he said. "I only hope you read the *New York Times* in the morning."[271]

When the chairman of the board of one network, in conversation with a former Reagan aide, asked what the networks could do to provide more responsible reporting, the aide answered, "Easy, . . . just eliminate ratings for news. You claim that news is not the same as entertainment. So why do you need ratings?" The chairman sighed, "Well, that's our big money-maker, the news."[272] A former network executive concluded, "Because television can make so much money doing its worst, it often can't afford to do its best."[273]

Overall, commercial bias in the media results in no coverage or superficial coverage of many important stories. This, more than any political bias, makes it difficult for citizens, particularly those who rely on television, to become well informed.

During the year before the September 11 terrorist attacks, al-Qaeda was mentioned only once on the net-

works' evening newscasts.[274] However, seven months before the airplane hijackings, a report predicting a "catastrophic attack" was issued by a government commission. A statement warning that Osama bin Laden's network was the "most immediate and serious threat" facing the country was made by the CIA director at a Senate hearing. Their dire predictions generated little interest among the media. Since the terrorist attacks, the media have paid more attention to foreign affairs, yet they continue to reflect the trends that typified news coverage before 9/11.

Impact of the Media on Politics

It is difficult to measure the impact of the media on politics. Because the media provide varied though similar coverage and reach different though overlapping audiences, it is exceedingly difficult to isolate the impact of particular media on particular groups of people. Other factors also influence people's knowledge, attitudes, and behavior toward politics. But there is considerable agreement that the media have a substantial impact on the public agenda, political parties and elections, and public opinion.[275]

Impact on the Public Agenda

The most important impact of the media is **setting the agenda**—influencing the process by which problems are considered important and solutions are proposed and debated.[276] The media publicize an issue, and people exposed to the media talk about the issue with their fellow citizens. When enough consider it important, they pressure officials to address it.[277]

The media's impact is most noticeable for dramatic events that occur suddenly. It is less noticeable for issues that evolve gradually. Watergate required months of coverage before making it onto the public agenda, and AIDS required the death of actor Rock Hudson before making it.[278]

Even for issues that evolve gradually, however, cumulative coverage by the media can have an impact. After years of extensive coverage, people told pollsters that drug use was the "most important problem" facing the country, and then they told pollsters that crime was.

Studies comparing people's views with the media coverage of these problems and with the actual rates of these activities show that people's views fluctuated more according to the media coverage than to the actual rates. When the media coverage increased, people considered the problems more serious, even when the actual rates of crime or drug use remained steady or decreased.[279]

The impact is usually greatest on people who are most interested in politics, because they are most likely

150   PART TWO ■ *Links between People and Government*

to follow the news.[280] And the impact is usually much greater for stories that appear on the front page of the newspaper or at the top of the newscast than for those buried in the back or at the end.[281] People who don't follow the news carefully often check the beginning of the newspaper or newscast for the "important" stories.

The media's power to influence the agenda has important implications. The media play a key role in deciding which problems government addresses and which it ignores. They also play a key role in increasing or decreasing politicians' ability to govern and to get reelected.

By publicizing some issues, the media create an opportunity for politicians with the authority and ability to resolve those issues. At the same time, the media create a pitfall for those who lack the power to resolve them. The Iranian seizure of the American embassy and hostages became the prominent issue in 1980. Every night, CBS's Walter Cronkite signed off, "And that's the way it is, the ___th day of American hostages in captivity." President Carter's lack of success in persuading Iranian officials to release the hostages or in directing an American invasion to rescue them cost him dearly in his reelection bid that year.

Yet the role of the media in shaping the agenda should not be overstated. Individuals' interests prompt the media to cover some things in the first place. Individuals' experiences lead them to consider other things unimportant even when the media do cover them.[282]

Moreover, politicians play an important role in shaping the agenda. For much legislation, Congress initiates action and lets the media publicize it.[283] For many issues, the president initiates action. When President Clinton launched a campaign to reduce smoking by teenagers, the media ran many stories about the problem. They could have done so years before or after, of course, but they followed the president's lead.

For elections, candidates usually establish the agenda of *policy* issues. By emphasizing issues they think will resonate with the public and reflect favorably on themselves, candidates pressure the media to cover these rather than other issues. But the media usually establish the agenda of *nonpolicy* issues, involving the candidates' personality and behavior.[284] The media are able to set the agenda for nonpolicy issues because these are more likely to catch the public's fancy.

Impact on Political Parties and Elections

The media have had an important impact on political parties and elections. In particular, they have furthered the decline of parties, encouraged new types of candidates, and influenced campaigns.

Political Parties

Political parties have declined in power, as will be addressed in Chapter 7, in large part because of the influence of the media.

In the young Republic, political parties created and controlled most newspapers. Naturally, the papers echoed the parties' views, and the journalists bowed to the parties' leaders. (The editor of one Democratic Party paper made sure a pail of fresh milk was left on the White House doorstep for President Andrew Jackson every morning, even if the editor had to deliver it himself.[285]) Nonetheless, people received much of their political information, however biased, from these papers.

When independent newspapers emerged as profit-making businesses, the party papers declined and then disappeared. Eventually, people came to receive most of their political information from independent newspapers, magazines, radio stations, and television stations. Thus people are no longer dependent on parties for their political information; they can make up their own minds about how to vote or what to support rather than rely on parties to tell them.

In other ways as well, the media, especially television, have contributed to the decline of the parties. In place of selection of the candidates by party bosses, television allows the candidates to appeal directly to the people. If the candidates win the primaries, party officials have little choice but to nominate them. In place of management of the campaign by party bosses, television appearances require new expertise, so the candidates assemble their own campaign organizations. Television advertising requires substantial money, so the candidates solicit their own financial donors. In this way, the media have supplanted the parties as the principal link between the people and their leaders.

Types of Candidates

Television has encouraged new types of candidates for national offices. No longer must candidates be experienced politicians who worked their way up over many years. Celebrities from other fields with name recognition can move into prominent positions without political experience. Jesse Ventura, a professional wrestler, was elected governor of Minnesota, and Arnold Schwarzenegger, an actor, was elected governor of California. In recent years, Congress has had an actor (Fred Grandy, R–Iowa—"Gopher" on *Love Boat*), a singer (Sonny Bono, R–Calif.), a professional baseball pitcher (Jim Bunning, R–Ky.), a professional football quarterback (Jack Kemp, R–N.Y.), a professional basketball player (Bill Bradley, D–N.J.), and two astronauts (John Glenn, D–Ohio, and Harrison Schmitt, R–N.M.). (After one term, however, Schmitt was defeated by an opponent whose slogan was "What on Earth has he ever done?") Tom Osborne, who as the former football coach at the

University of Nebraska was the best-known person in the state, got elected to Congress from a district in which he did not even live.[286]

Alternatively, unknowns with talent can achieve rapid name recognition and move into prominent positions. Jimmy Carter, who had served one term as governor of Georgia, was relatively unknown elsewhere in the country when he ran for the Democratic nomination for president in 1976. Through effective use of television, he won enough primaries that the party had to nominate him, though the leaders preferred other candidates.

At the same time that television has allowed newcomers to run, it also has imposed new requirements on candidates for national office. They must demonstrate an appealing appearance and performance on camera; they must be telegenic. President Franklin Roosevelt's body, disabled by polio and supported in a wheelchair, would not have been impressive on television. President Harry Truman's style—he was known as "Give 'em Hell Harry"—would not be impressive on television either. Although he was quite effective in whistlestop speeches, he would come across as too "hot," too intense, if

Courtesy of Franklin D. Roosevelt Library, 73-113:61

Franklin Roosevelt spent much of his life in a wheelchair, but journalists did not photograph him in it. A friend snapped this rare picture. Journalists were reluctant to photograph or write about officials' afflictions or behaviors until the Watergate scandal ushered in a new era of more personal coverage.

beamed into people's homes every day. A "cool," low-key style is more effective.

When Howard Dean finished third in the Iowa caucuses for the Democratic nomination for president in 2004, he gave a speech to rally his disappointed volunteers. He strained to be heard over the frenzy—shouting, "Yeah!"—but the mike, which was designed for television appearances in such situations, filtered out the background noise, making the speech sound like a rant and the shout sound like a scream. The reporters who were there could barely hear him, but on television, it appeared as though he had come unhinged. Film clips of "Dean's rant" were replayed on newscasts seven hundred times during the next week. The speech became the butt of comedians' jokes. Letterman called Dean a "hockey dad," and Leno called him "Mr. Rogers with rabies."[287] Although most networks later admitted overplaying the speech, the damage was done—and so was Dean's campaign.[288] His intense style was effective in person but not on television.

President Reagan was the quintessential politician for the television age. He was tall and trim with a handsome face and a reassuring voice. As a former actor, he could project his personality and convictions and deliver his lines and jokes better than any other politician. It is not an exaggeration to conclude, as one political scientist did, "Without a chance to display his infectious smile, his grandfatherly demeanor, and his 'nice guy' qualities to millions of Americans, Ronald Reagan, burdened by his image as a superannuated, intellectually lightweight movie actor with right-wing friends and ultraconservative leanings, might never have reached the presidency."[289]

Television has not created the public desire for politicians with an appealing personality. "When candidates shook hands firmly, kissed babies, and handed out cigars, the thrust was not on issues."[290] But television has exacerbated this emphasis on image.

The media have imposed other requirements on candidates for national offices. In recent decades, the intense scrutiny and constant criticism screen out those who are unwilling to relinquish most of their personal privacy and individual dignity. Candidates, of course, have always expected to sacrifice some privacy and be subjected to some criticism, but now they are expected to endure even more. One columnist wonders whether public service will attract only those with the "most brazen, least sensitive personalities."[291]

Retired Admiral Bobby Ray Inman, who had held positions in both Democratic and Republican administrations, was nominated to be secretary of defense by President Clinton. During the confirmation process, he came under attack by some senators and some newspapers. One editor told him, "Bobby, you just have to get a thicker skin. We have to write a bad story about you every day. That's our job." Although he was assured by

Howard Dean tries to rally his troops after finishing third in the Iowa caucuses in 2004.

members of both parties that he would be confirmed—the *New York Times* reported that his nomination was "unusually well received in Washington"—Inman withdrew his nomination, saying he did not want the "daily diet" of media criticism. The newspapers then turned around and criticized him for being insecure.[292]

Campaigns

The media affect nomination and election campaigns through their news and commentary and candidates' advertisements. They help set the campaign agenda, as already explained. They also inform and persuade.

The media provide information about the candidates and the issues, and they also interpret this information.[293] The public learns about the candidates and the issues[294] but in the process is influenced by the media.

Information about the candidates can have a major impact, especially at the nomination stage. In presidential elections, a party without an incumbent president running for reelection might field a dozen candidates. The media cannot cover all adequately, so they narrow the field, considering some "serious" and giving them more coverage. Once the primaries begin, they label some "winners" and others "losers," and they give the "winners" more coverage.[295] For the Democratic race in 1992, even before a single primary, the press proclaimed Clinton the front-runner, and several magazines put his picture on their covers, even though half of the public did not know who he was.[296]

By making these judgments, the media strongly influence the electoral process at this stage.[297] Because few people have formed opinions about the candi-

dates this early, they are open to impressions from the media. Therefore, when the media declare some candidates winners, they help create a bandwagon effect.[298] When they declare others losers, they make it hard for these candidates to attract contributors, volunteers, and supporters.

The media can also persuade voters directly. This influence can be seen in several ways.

Televised debates do not sway most viewers because people tend to engage in **selective perception,** which is a tendency to screen out information that contradicts their beliefs. Consequently, most people conclude that their candidate performed better.[299] However, the debates do sway some viewers, usually those who have moderate education and some interest in politics but who are not decided or at least not strongly committed to one candidate. In 1960, the debates may have convinced enough voters to cast their ballots for Kennedy that he won the election.[300]

Media commentary about the debates can also sway viewers.[301] But this effect usually does not last long; ordinarily, after the media frenzy wears off, the candidate bounces back.[302]

Newspaper endorsements of candidates apparently sway some readers, especially those with no more than a ninth- through twelfth-grade education. People with less education are less likely to read editorials, while those with more education have more sources of information and more defined ideologies to guide their decisions.[303] Even if endorsements sway only a small percentage of voters, they can determine the outcome of tight races.[304] Although endorsements have some effect on well-publicized races, such as those for president,[305] they probably have greater effect on less publicized races, such as those for state legislator or local tax assessor, because voters have little other information to guide them.

Talk radio also influences listeners. People who tune in to talk radio are more likely to turn out to vote and even to participate in campaigns.[306]

Impact on Public Opinion

Social scientists long thought that the media influenced the things people thought about but not the opinions they held about these things. Some contemporary research, however, demonstrates that the media do have a substantial impact on public opinion on things besides elections. A comparison of the networks' newscasts with the public's policy preferences in a wide variety of foreign and domestic issues shows that the media influence opinion about issues.[307] Other research shows that the media influence opinion about particular presidents.[308] They affect opinion indirectly, by providing the news and transmitting the views of various opinion leaders, as well as directly, through editorials and commentaries intended to sway opinion. (For the impact of a foreign

After the terrorist attacks of September 11, 2001, the initial reports from the Middle East showed some people rejoicing and many others voicing satisfaction that the United States got its comeuppance. This reaction raised questions about the news coverage and the American image in the Arab world.

Almost all media in Arab countries are state-run. Although they mimic American news formats, they are not independent.[1] To preserve the regime, whether a monarchy, a dictatorship, or another form of government, they are censored. Along with bland entertainment, they offer staid and sycophantic coverage of their government and its officials. They feature the formal announcements of the ministries and the comings and goings of the officials.

Then there is Al-Jazeera, a television station based in the small country of Qatar, which wields little influence in regional politics compared with Egypt and Saudi Arabia, which have controlled media. Al-Jazeera is independent and lively. It broadcasts news twenty-four hours a day, reaching viewers with private satellite dishes in twenty Arab countries. People starved for news about their country and the region tune in. The station's popularity has prompted millions of people, many of whom can barely afford basic necessities, to buy a satellite dish.[2]

Al-Jazeera began operating in 1996 after a coup in Qatar installed a young ruler who was educated in England and prepared to break from his country's conservative political traditions. Seeking a more liberal political system, with greater emphasis on voting and on educating girls, he announced the end of government censorship. He allowed the station to operate and even agreed to finance it until it became self-supporting. (Qatar, with the third largest reserve of natural gas in the world, is a wealthy country.) He promised the station its independence.[3] The station hired Arab journalists from the British Broadcasting Corporation's Arabic radio and television network. These staffers, trained in Western journalistic practices, tailored Al-Jazeera after CNN.

Al-Jazeera, whose motto is "The opinion, and the other opinion," presents competing views on topics of interest to Arabs. The station breaks taboos as it addresses issues shunned by the state-run media. In addition to examining the Palestinian *intifada* (uprising against Israel) and Western aims in the Middle East, Al-Jazeera uncovers corruption in some governments in the region. Talk shows pit fundamentalists against secularists and Iraqis against Kuwaitis, and they address topics such as polygamy among Muslims. The coverage reflects heresy according to some viewers, but the programs mirror the arguments that many Arabs have with their relatives and friends.

The station scooped the media around the world by showing film clips of Osama bin Laden talking menacingly about the September 11 attacks and future terrorist attacks against the United States. Since then it has broadcast other tapes from bin Laden. The station, unlike American media, has not sanitized its coverage of the wars in Afghanistan and Iraq. It has shown dead and injured fighters from both sides and civilian casualties as well.

The Bush administration has deplored the station's coverage. The administration has feared that broadcasting the tapes from bin Laden and showing

Arab men react to the abuse of Iraqi prisoners by American jailers at the Abu Ghraib prison outside Baghdad.

© Sungsu Cho/Polaris Images

civilian casualties inflames public opinion in the Middle East. It asked the Qatari emir to restrict the station, and it asked the station to stop broadcasting bin Laden's statements. (Both the emir and the station refused.) Then it relayed its demands more forcefully. During the war in Afghanistan, Al-Jazeera's office in Kabul was destroyed by an American missile. During the war in Iraq, Al-Jazeera's newsroom in Baghdad was leveled by another American missile and one of its correspondents was killed. On the ground, almost two dozen of Al-Jazeera's reporters and photographers were briefly jailed by the American military.[4] Although the U.S. government publicly insists that it has not targeted Al-Jazeera, the pattern of attacks is hard to ignore.[5]

Whether Al-Jazeera is balanced or biased is the subject of debate among Western observers. During the wars in Afghanistan and Iraq, the station has seemed skeptical of American aims.[6] But much that American officials complain about—airing competing views, sampling the opinions of ordinary people—reflect standard Western journalistic practices. In fact, some coverage, such as film clips of bin Laden, was duplicated by Western television networks.

It does seem clear that the station supports the Palestinian side in the struggle with Israel. Although the station conducts interviews with Israeli officials, which other Arab media avoid, it highlights Israeli attacks on Palestinians more than Palestinian attacks on Israelis. It shows graphic images of Palestinian victims and reports personal details about their lives, thus stirring the emotions of Arab viewers. It refers to Palestinian suicide bombers as "martyrs," thereby jus-

tifying their actions. In these ways, it reflects the perspective of its audience, just as American media reflect the perspective of their audience. Arabs believe that American media are biased toward Israel's side, depicting Palestinian attacks more than Israeli attacks and referring to Israeli assassinations of Palestinian activists as "targeted killings."[7] A CBS executive acknowledges, "You could argue that Al-Jazeera is too pro-Mideast or pro-Arab, but our news organizations are all pro-Western."[8]

Already Al-Jazeera has had a major impact in the Middle East. By attracting so many viewers, it has set the standard for television news in the region, prodding state-run media to loosen up. At the same time, by criticizing authoritarian Arab rulers, it has infuriated these leaders, who fear instability in their countries. Some governments have recalled their ambassador to Qatar to protest Al-Jazeera's coverage of their policies. Other governments have closed Al-Jazeera's bureaus in their countries or denied visas to Al-Jazeera's reporters seeking entry into their countries. Algeria's government turned off the electricity in its capital city to prevent residents from seeing a program about their country.

Besides infuriating the Arab leaders, the station has inflamed the Arab masses, especially in the struggle between the Palestinians and the Israelis. This has worried the rulers who are trying to walk a line between appeasing their own citizens without antagonizing the United States.

In the long run, Al-Jazeera may have a significant impact in promoting the rights of Arab women and, most obviously, the right to a free press. In the

process, it might help nourish a sense of freedom and a desire for democracy among Arab people. Ironically, then, while galvanizing Arab radicalism on particular issues, Al-Jazeera could be promoting Western values in other ways.

Yet the U.S. government has been slow to realize the influence and the potential of Al-Jazeera. American officials, while solicitous of the views of Arab leaders of friendly states, have ignored Arab opinion on the street. They have especially ignored the opinion of Arab youths, who, due to a population bubble in most countries, are numerous and approaching a future where they will find few jobs and face considerable frustration. They will be ripe for exploitation by extremists. Our officials have been slow to realize that our country was, is, and will be embroiled in a propaganda war for the hearts and minds of Arab people. After the military battles conclude, the media war will continue.

1. A United Nations report ranks the media in these Arab countries as the least independent in the world. Nadia Abou El-Magd, "Fifty Years after Revolution, Arabs Ponder Nasser's Legacy," *Lincoln Journal-Star,* July 22, 2002. There is a large independent television station in Lebanon.
2. Mohammed El-Nawawy and Adel Iskandar, *Al-Jazeera: How the Free Arab News Network Scooped the World and Changed the Middle East* (Boulder, Colo.: Westview Press, 2002), 46.
3. Apparently sensitive to this unusual arrangement, the station practices self-censorship in covering its host country and government. Ibid., 199–200.
4. Christian Parenti, "Al-Jazeera Goes to Jail," *Nation,* March 29, 2004, 20–23.
5. The Bush administration claimed that it was a mistake, but the location of the office was well known and the building was easily identified.
6. For example, see Fouad Ajami, "What the Muslim World Is Watching," *New York Times Magazine,* November 18, 2001, 48.
7. For development of this view, see El-Nawawy and Iskandar, *Al-Jazeera,* 175–196.
8. Ibid., 182.

Although the Bush administration imposed restrictions on the debates that diminished the opportunity for any candor or spontaneity, presidential debates remain high-risk political theater. In the first debate in the 2004 campaign, President Bush performed poorly—scowling, clenching his jaw, and flashing his temper—and squandered a significant lead over Senator Kerry.

© Jim Young/Reuters/Corbis

haps even despair, toward government and officials. Indeed, according to a 1995 survey, the public is even more cynical than journalists themselves. Seventy-seven percent of the public gave government officials a low rating for honesty and ethics, while only 40 percent of the journalists did.[311] Most of the public believed that politicians could "never" be trusted to do the right thing. Yet the journalists saw the American political process as "a flawed but basically decent means of reconciling different points of view and solving collective problems."[312] They apparently report in a more cynical fashion than they actually feel because of the conventions of contemporary journalism. But the public, while deploring these practices, evidently sees them as reflections of reality. So cynical coverage by the press leads to even more cynical attitudes in the citizenry.[313]

The cynical attitudes have important implications for politics. They probably reduce satisfaction with candidates and officials and reduce turnout in elections. At the same time, they probably increase votes for "outsiders" who present themselves as "nonpoliticians."

Thus, one writer observes, "the press, which in the long run cannot survive if people lose interest in politics, is acting as if its purpose was to guarantee that people are repelled by public life."[314]

Conclusion: Are the Media Responsive?

To make a profit, the media have to be responsive to the people. They present the news they think the people want. Because they believe the majority desire entertainment, or at least diversion, rather than education, they structure the news toward this end.[315] For the majority who want entertainment, national and local television and radio provide it. For the minority who want education, the better newspapers and magazines provide it. Public radio, with its morning and evening newscasts, and public television, with its nightly newscast, also provide quality coverage. In addition, Web sites on the Internet provide news on demand. The media offer something for everyone.

When officials or citizens get upset with the media, they pointedly ask, "Who elected you?" Journalists reply that the people—their readers or listeners or viewers—"elected" them by paying attention to their news columns or newscasts.

To say that the media are responsive, however, is not to say that they perform well. Giving the people what they want most is not necessarily serving the country best. "This business of giving people what they want is a dope pusher's argument," says a former president of NBC News. "News is something people don't know

television network on public opinion, see the box "The CNN of the Middle East." on page 154.)

Many people speculate that the media's coverage has contributed to the public's cynicism toward government in recent decades. The media's coverage has undermined the public's perception of the integrity of government and officials not just by reporting real shortcomings of programs and administrators but also by engaging in several of the practices already addressed in this chapter. The negative bias in coverage of all candidates and officials undermines them directly, and the game orientation undermines them more subtly. The emphasis on conflict, though intriguing the public, at the same time polarizes and alienates the public. The practice of objectivity—reporting what he said versus what she said without evaluating the truth of either—passes along some false statements and some misleading ones and confuses the public.[309] Many people complain, "The media? You can't believe anything they say."

Some researchers have concluded that the result of these practices is to foster **media malaise** among the public.[310] This is a feeling of cynicism and distrust, per-

they're interested in until they hear about it. The job of a journalist is to take what's important and make it interesting."[316]

Instead, the media personalize and dramatize the news. The result is to simplify the news. Superficial coverage of complex events leaves the public unable to understand these events and ultimately unable to force the government to be responsive.

The media give us the big hype—"Hey, listen to this! Here's something new you can't miss!" They reflect a crisis *du jour* mentality in which everything is important but ultimately nothing is important. Almost any political development is important for a day or a week or occasionally a month. But almost no political development is important for long. The headlines and the stories clamoring for attention go by in such a blur that after a while they all become a jumble for many people. They leave no sense of what's actually a crisis, what's only a problem, what's merely an irritant, and what's truly trivial.[317]

Thus most news coverage is episodic, presenting an event as a single, idiosyncratic occurrence, rather than thematic, presenting the event as an example of a larger pattern. For instance, a story might focus on a hungry person rather than on malnutrition as a national problem. Episodic coverage is more common because it is more entertaining—dramatic, with human interest—than thematic coverage. But episodic coverage makes it hard for people to see the connection between the problems in society and the actions of government. Then the people do not hold their leaders accountable for addressing or resolving the problems.[318]

Although the media give the people what they want, the people criticize the media. Almost two-thirds tell pollsters that the media "don't get the facts straight."[319] Actually, the media usually do get the facts straight, but the nature of their reporting confuses people rather than enlightens them. Almost three-fourths tell pollsters that the media get in the way of society's efforts to solve its problems. Only one-fourth say that the media help solve the problems.[320]

People rank reporters the lowest in public esteem of any profession (lower even than lawyers).[321] People also express less support for freedom of the press. Even before the 2001 terrorist attacks, a majority said the press has too much freedom. In fact, a majority went so far as to say that the media should not be allowed to endorse or criticize political candidates, and a third went further to say that the media should not be allowed to publish a story without government approval.[322] Thus at the same time the media are competing to give people what they want, their practices are alienating people.

The media's desperation is aggravated by a declining interest in politics and a decreasing number of people who read newspapers or watch newscasts. Although the public is better educated now than in the 1960s, it is less likely to follow the news and less able to answer questions about the government.[323] People under thirty-five especially reflect these trends. To retain their shrinking audience, many newspapers and newscasts have revamped their formats to replace hard news with soft features. If this process continues, it will have disturbing implications. Citizens who are not aware of the news or who do not understand it cannot fulfill their role in a democracy.

The problem is circular, as one political scientist points out:

Americans need high-quality journalism to become sophisticated citizens, but news organizations need an audience of sophisticated citizens for the organizations to produce high-quality journalism and still generate profits. "Because most members of the public know and care relatively little about government, they neither seek nor understand high-quality political reporting and analysis. With limited demand for first-rate journalism, most news organizations cannot afford to supply it, and because they do not supply it, most Americans have no practical source of the information necessary to become politically sophisticated."[324]

Individual journalists are aware of the shortcomings of contemporary journalism but pessimistic about their ability to improve the coverage. Because of commercial pressures, they are experiencing low morale in newsrooms across the country.[325]

Nevertheless, we should not lose sight of the fact that the American media, despite their shortcomings, provide very fast and relatively accurate reports of events. They also probe wrongdoing in society. Thus they serve as a check on government in many situations. As a former government official noted, "Think how much chicanery dies on the drawing board when someone says, 'We'd better not do that; what if the press finds out?'"[326]

Evans Pursued the Admiral

You decided to meet with Admiral Boorda to confront him with your allegations and give him an opportunity to respond. But you did not want to give him much warning, so you did not tell his office why you wanted to meet other than that you were preparing a story about the admiral. Two hours before the meeting, Boorda's aide called for more information. Then you revealed the purpose. Later you explained, "If you go in too soon, the navy can counterattack, and the opposition gets the story."[327]

After you revealed the purpose of the meeting, Boorda's aides checked with navy officials about the ribbons. A previous secretary of the navy had questioned why admirals wore so many ribbons. When the navy investigated its 257 admirals, it found that many wore ribbons, including the *V*, who technically should not have. Apparently, the navy's practice of awarding ribbons deviated from its regulations. When Boorda was informed last year that he should not have worn the *V*, he took it off. "It was an honest mistake," he commented to an aide. He has not worn it since then.

After Boorda learned the purpose of the meeting, he went home for lunch. He typed a letter to his wife and another to the sailors. He said to the sailors:

What I am about to do is not very smart but it is right for me. You see, I have asked you to do the right thing, to care for and take care of each other and to stand up for what

is good and correct. All of these things require honor, courage and commitment to our . . . core values.

I am about to be accused of wearing combat devices on two ribbons I earned during sea tours in Viet Nam. It turns out I didn't really rate them. When I found out I was wrong I immediately took them off but it was really too late. I don't expect any reporters to believe I could make an honest mistake and you may or may not believe it yourselves.

That is up to you and isn't all that important now anyway. I've made it not matter in the big scheme of things because I love our navy so much, and you who are the heart and soul of our navy, that I couldn't bear to bring dishonor to you. . . .

Finally, for those who want to tear our navy down, I guess I've given them plenty to write about for a while. But I will soon be forgotten.

You, our great navy people, will live on. I am proud of you. I am proud to have led you if only for a short time. I wish I had done it better.

Then Boorda went out to his garden and shot himself in the chest. At his funeral, Boorda was hailed as "the sailors' sailor." In Washington, however, he was criticized by some for having "thin skin." Yet as one columnist observed, "Thin skin is the only kind of skin human beings come with."[328]

Newsweek's efforts to pursue the story did not reflect political bias

against the navy or the admiral or the changes he was implementing. (Other critics of Boorda did have political motives—their opposition to new policies that challenged navy traditions.) *Newsweek's* efforts instead reflected commercial bias. The magazine was trying to attract more readers by running provocative articles by prominent writers.

Of course, *Newsweek* had not even run the article when Boorda decided to kill himself. A columnist for *Newsweek* pointed out, "It is possible [that Boorda] could have moved the story in a different direction, or talked the magazine out of publishing anything on the matter at all."[329] Evidently Boorda, who had considerable experience with the press, did not think this was likely.

No doubt *Newsweek's* editors were as surprised as other people when Boorda killed himself. They were just trying to do their jobs. Yet their behavior reflects journalists' mind-set that public officials are not motivated by a desire to serve the public but to advance their careers or enhance their power. Moreover, journalists see public officials as insincere. With this mind-set, journalists look for wrongdoing and seek to expose it. Essentially, journalists consider officials fair game for relentless attack.[330]

To learn more about the nature of the Boorda incident and its aftermath, go to this chapter's "You Are There" exercises on the text Web site.

Key Terms

symbiotic relationship	political bias
adversarial relationship	commercial bias
leaks	infotainment
scoop	game orientation
presidential press conference	horse race coverage
photo op	setting the agenda
sound bite	selective perception
spin	media malaise
fireside chats	

Further Reading

Timothy Crouse, *The Boys on the Bus* (New York: Random House, 1972). This irreverent account of press coverage of the 1972 presidential campaign focuses on the reporters rather than on the candidates.

Beth J. Harpaz, *The Girls in the Van: Covering Hillary* (New York: St. Martin's Press, 2001). This is an account of press coverage of Hillary Clinton's Senate campaign.

Marvin Kalb, *One Scandalous Story: Clinton, Lewinsky, and Thirteen Days That Tarnished American Journalism* (New York: Free Press, 2001). As the scandal unfolded, the press abandoned its standards.

Howard Kurtz, *Spin Cycle: Inside the Clinton Propaganda Machine* (New York: Free Press, 1998). Kurtz puts the spotlight on the Clinton administration's press operation.

John R. MacArthur, *Second Front: Censorship and Propaganda in the Gulf War* (New York: Hill & Wang, 1992). Media coverage of the war is raked over the coals in this searing critique.

Joe McGinniss, *The Selling of the President, 1968* (New York: Simon & Schuster, 1969). McGinniss provides an account of the often comical efforts by Richard Nixon's advisers to transform him into a media-friendly candidate.

For Viewing

All the President's Men (1976) See Robert Redford and Dustin Hoffman play Woodward and Bernstein.

Journeys with George (2002) This film focuses on George W. Bush's 2000 campaign from the perspective of a journalist traveling with the campaign.

Outfoxed (2004) A revealing but negative portrayal of the Republican bias of Fox news and how it shapes opinion.

Electronic Resources

www.nytimes.com
The New York Times *Web site offers in-depth reports on international and national affairs.*

www.washingtonpost.com
The Washington Post *Web site provides political news from the nation's capital.*

www.sfgate.com
The San Francisco Chronicle *has been described as an "oasis of attitude" in the world of news.*

www.alternet.org
This alternative journalism site presents news and opinion not found in most other media outlets.

www.slate.com
Slate *is a "Webzine" featuring columns and wit and perhaps the best media analysis on the Web.*

www.ajr.org
A variety of stories about the media are provided by the University of Maryland College of Journalism.

www.fair.org
This watchdog site keeps an eye on the media.

http://english.aljazeera.net/HomePage
News, in English, from alJazeera.

InfoTrac College Edition

Search for the following articles in the InfoTrac database:

Bresler, Robert J. "Media Bias and the Culture Wars," *USA Today Magazine* (July 2004).

Kunkel, Thomas, and Gene Roberts. "Leaving Readers Behind: The Age of Corporate Newspapering," *American Journalism Review* (May 2001).

O'Brien, Meredith, "A Growing Divide: War Coverage Has Pushed Press Values and the Public's Values Even Farther Apart," *Quill* (January 2002).

Sutter, Daniel. "Advertising and Political Bias in the Meida: The Market for Criticism of the Market Economy," *The American Journal of Economics and Sociology* (July 2002).

For more articles, enter:

"mass media" in the Subject Guide;

"press" in the Subject Guide;

"elections" in the Subject Guide, and then go to subdivision "media coverage."

American Government Resources

Visit the Political Behavior section of the Wadsworth American Government Resources Web site (politicalscience. wadsworth.com/amgov/) for a variety of tools to help you explore news media further. Included are simulations, video clips, Microcase exercises, and a wealth of other activities.

CHAPTER 6

INTEREST GROUPS

This woman takes a six-hour bus ride to Canada to save $1,400 on a six-month supply of her prescription drug.

Group Formation

Why Interest Groups Form

Why People Join

Which People Join

Have Americans Stopped Joining?

Types of Interest Groups

Private Interest Groups

Public Interest Groups

Strategies of Interest Groups

Tactics of Interest Groups

Direct Lobbying Techniques

Indirect Lobbying Techniques: Going Public

Building Coalitions

Success of Interest Groups

Resources

Competition and Goals

Conclusion: Do Interest Groups Help Make Government Responsive?

Do You Support the Bush Prescription Drug Proposal?

You are William Novelli, CEO of AARP, formerly the American Association of Retired Persons. You joined AARP in 2000 after being president of the Campaign for Tobacco-Free Kids, a group that tried to limit the influence of tobacco companies on children. You have also worked for CARE, an international relief organization helping the poor in Africa, Asia, and Latin America. Before that, you had a career in public relations. You consider yourself an independent voter, though in the past you worked in Richard Nixon's election campaign and have some ties to Newt Gingrich, the former Republican speaker of the House. Indeed, you wrote an introduction to a book he wrote, *Saving Lives and Saving Money,* a scathing critique of the current health insurance system.

You head an active and influential organization. Founded in 1958 to provide health insurance to the elderly, AARP, with 45 million members, is the nation's largest interest group and one of its most powerful. With eighteen hundred employees, eighteen full-time lobbyists, and a budget of more than $760 million, AARP is a potent political force. Its lobbying effort is directed at preserving and expanding government benefits for the elderly. For the modest fee of $12.50, anyone over age fifty can join, help support the organization's lobbying effort, and have access to its numerous benefits, including low-cost prescription drugs.

AARP's clout has been demonstrated many times; as President Reagan's budget director once lamented after beating a hasty retreat following a tidal wave of AARP–generated protest, "These are people who have plenty of time on their hands, who are well organized, who vote regularly, and they are a massive political force." [1] In addition to lobbying, AARP's influence is exercised by flooding Congress with letters, phone calls, faxes, and e-mails. There is no congressional district where AARP is not at least fifty thousand strong.[2]

The influence of AARP and the tendency of the elderly to vote in high numbers means that programs for the elderly (primarily Social Security and Medicare, the government-funded health insurance program for individuals over age sixty-five) account for about one-third of the federal budget. Politicians are reluctant to cut them, preferring to cut other programs with a less vocal and less activist constituency. Being tagged a "granny-basher" is something most elected officials prefer to avoid. Drug prices are a key issue for seniors and one your organization has long been concerned about. The average American over sixty-five years old spends more than $3,000 a year for drugs.[3] And costs continue to escalate; the cost of name-brand drugs most used by seniors increased 28 percent between 2000 and 2003, far more than the overall rate of inflation.[4] Both political parties declare their support for a program to provide help for the elderly with these bills, but until now the parties have been unable to agree on what exactly needs to be done.

President Bush, like his opponent Al Gore, campaigned in 2000 with a pledge to do something about the issue. In his 2003 State of the Union address, the president proposed a $400 billion prescription drug benefit. The plan is complex and would not fully roll out until 2006. Seniors and some low-income people would be eligible to purchase a card entitling them to discounts on both prescription and generic drugs. Then, starting in 2006, they would pay a monthly fee for prescriptions. They can have a plan through Medicare—the government-run program—or through private insurance plans. The proposal offers large government subsidies to private insurance companies to encourage them to offer a drug benefit. The proposal also contains a provision forbidding Medicare to use its considerable purchasing power to get cheaper drugs for the elderly.

Initially, the president hoped to couple prescription benefits with a requirement that seniors must join private health insurance plans for their prescription drugs. This is in keeping with conservative Republican plans to reduce the size of government, especially the nonmilitary- and nonsecurity-related parts of government. For example, in education, they support school vouchers, allowing tax funds to support childrens' attending private schools, as a way to replace support for public schools. Similarly, reducing Medicare is a goal of conservatives. And in this prescription plan, moving seniors out of Medicare drug plans into private insurance plans and providing billions of dollars for private insurers would reduce government and subsidize an industry that provides generous support for Republican candidates. In

the previous election, pharmaceutical companies spent more than $20 million on congressional races, four-fifths of it to help Republicans. In addition, they ran a $17 million television ad campaign in support of Republican candidates who favored letting private companies provide drug benefits.[5]

But this extreme proposal did not have enough support to pass, so the current proposal gives seniors a choice between Medicare and private plans.

The president's approach, if successful, would fulfill his campaign pledge. Still, although almost everyone wants to help seniors with their high drug bills, this proposal has a good chance of being defeated. It is opposed by most Democrats and many very conservative Republicans.

While supportive of a new drug benefit for the elderly, the Democrats point out that for some people, this new bill would provide less coverage than they already have through existing Medicare programs. It also provides nearly as large a subsidy for drug manufacturers as for the elderly.

Democrats are also strongly opposed to limiting Medicare's ability to act on behalf of seniors to drive prices down. Medicare could have a huge impact on the costs of drugs, but under this law, it is forbidden to use its clout. This remarkable provision wastes tax dollars and reflects the influence that drug manufacturers have in Congress. Indeed, drug companies did a lot to buy this concession, as noted above.

Democrats also fear that the plan might put Medicare at risk as insurance companies siphon off the nation's healthiest seniors, guaranteeing providers huge profits, while the government is left covering the sickest and most costly.

Some conservative Republicans are also wary, but for different reasons. They are committed to reducing the size of government and wonder why a fellow conservative is proposing this huge expansion of Medicare. Though they see how eventually it might erode Medicare, this plan expands govern-

ment and adds significantly to the growing budget deficit.

In this contested situation, AARP can play a crucial role. The administration's proposal may win approval in Congress without AARP's endorsement. But should AARP oppose it, it seems doomed to failure.

At first blush, your choice seems obvious. New government support to help the elderly with their drug bills has been high on the AARP agenda. Though not all of the money will be spent on drugs for the elderly, a lot of it will. Moreover, AARP is itself a prescription drug vendor. A new government-funded benefit is likely to provide millions of dollars to the organization as group members secure their prescription drugs through health insurance provided by the organization. Offering such a benefit to members may also help in recruiting new ones who wish to take advantage of AARP's prescription services.

However, what seems like an obvious choice may not be in the long-term interest of seniors. Medicare is vital to seniors, and government subsidies to private insurers might undermine Medicare. Should it be weakened or, worse yet, ended, the only option for seniors will be private health insurance, where the marketplace determines the scope and cost of coverage and many seniors could not afford to have insurance at all. Nor does the plan deal with the rising cost of drugs.

Your members, like the Democrats, are quite concerned with the giveaway to drug companies by banning Medicare from bargaining to lower costs. This restriction will make private insurance more attractive, as it can provide cheaper drugs, at least initially, because of the large subsidies provided in the Bush plan.

Moreover, many of your members are already purchasing drugs from countries where they are cheaper, such as Canada. This bill forbids that, unless approved by the secretary of Health and Human Services.

What appears on first examination

In the United States, everything from fruits to nuts is organized. From apple growers to filbert producers, nearly every interest has an organization to represent it. These organizations touch every aspect of our lives; members of the American College of Obstetrics and Gynecology bring us into the world, and members of the National Funeral Directors Association usher us out.

Organizations that try to achieve at least some of their goals with government assistance are **interest groups.** Fruit and nut growers want government subsidies and protection from imported products; doctors and funeral directors want to be free of government controls.

The efforts of interest groups to influence government is called **lobbying.** Lobbying may involve direct contact between a lobbyist—or consultant or lawyer, as they prefer to be called—and a government official, or it may involve indirect action, such as attempts to sway public opinion, which in turn influences officials.

People organize and lobby because these are ways for them to enhance their influence. As one lobbyist remarked, "The modern government is huge, pervasive, intrusive into everybody's life. If you just let things take their course and don't get involved in the game, you get trampled on."[6]

The Founders feared the harmful effects of interest groups. They did not, however, believe in trying to limit the ability of people to organize and speak out. Rather, Madison and the other Founders tried to cure "the mischiefs of faction" through government institutions that separated powers among the branches and between state and national government and provided ways for the different parts of government to check each other. In that way, no one faction could override the interests of others.

Many analysts believe that these checks no longer work; they see "special interests" manipulating government for their own good, contrary to the interests of society as a whole.[7] They argue that everyone is represented in Washington but the people.

Yet others argue that special interests are often representing some important public group. AARP, for example, represents millions of Americans.

Do interest groups undermine the people's interests? Or do they make government more responsive by giving people greater representation in the political process? These are the difficult questions explored in this chapter.

Group Formation

Throughout most of its history, America has been a nation of joiners. As early as the 1830s, the Frenchman Alexis de Tocqueville, who traveled in America, noted the tendency of Americans to join groups: "In no country in the world has the principle of association been more successfully used or applied to a greater multitude of objects than in America."[8] Even now, Americans are more likely than citizens of other countries to belong to groups.[9] Compared to most countries, the United States is racially, religiously, and ethnically diverse. These differences give rise to different interests and views on public issues and often lead to the formation of groups that express these views.[10]

Groups also organize in the United States because they can. The freedom to speak, assemble, and petition government, guaranteed in the First Amendment to the Constitution, facilitates group formation. Without such freedom, only groups favored by government or those with members willing to risk punishment should they speak out against government are likely to exist.

Federalism also encourages the formation of groups. Because state and local governments have significant authority, groups often organize at these levels as well as the national level to promote and protect their interests.

Why Interest Groups Form

The formation of interest groups occurs in waves.[11] In some periods it is rapid and extensive, while at other times it is slow or nonexistent.

Social and economic stress often account for these surges.[12] The stress of the Revolutionary War produced groups for and against independence. Slavery in the decades before the Civil War led to the formation of groups on both sides of the issue. After the Civil War, rapid industrialization led to the formation of trade unions and business associations. Economic problems in agriculture spurred the development of farm groups.

In 1773, a group of colonists organized to protest British taxes on tea by throwing tea into Boston Harbor. In 1989, groups organized to protest a congressional pay increase by sending tea bags to their representatives in Washington.

The greatest surge in group formation occurred between 1900 and 1920. Stimulated by the shocks of industrialization, urbanization, immigration, and the government's response to them, the United States Chamber of Commerce, American Farm Bureau Federation, National Association for the Advancement of Colored People (NAACP), and countless others were formed.[13]

The 1960s and 1970s witnessed another interest group explosion, directed primarily toward Washington. As the national government expanded in power and influence in the post–World War II period, it increasingly became the center of interest group efforts to satisfy demands for favorable public policy. Spurred by the success of civil rights and war protest movements in the 1960s, other groups representing racial minorities, women, consumers, the poor, the elderly, and the environment were organized. Business groups surged in the late 1970s in response to the success of consumer and environmental groups in pushing government to regulate business activity.[14]

Technological changes also accelerate group formation. A national network of railroads and the telegraph contributed to the surge in the early 1900s. In the 1960s and 1970s, computer-generated direct mail made it easier to raise money, recruit members, and push them to action. Between 1960 and 1980, the number of groups increased by 60 percent and the number sending representatives to Washington doubled.[15] In the 1990s, the spread of personal computers and the growth of the Internet facilitated communication between people with an endless variety of narrow interests. The Internet is particularly useful for those wishing to organize citizens, groups on a low budget.[16] It's also useful for groups outside the mainstream who wish to operate anonymously. Members and sympathizers of militia groups spread throughout the country, often in remote locations and with few resources, can communicate, keep each other informed, and provide social support for extreme and often outrageous views.

The government is also important to group formation. Government efforts to deal with problems often prompt the organization of groups opposed to such efforts.[17] In addition, government provides direct financial assistance to some groups, particularly nonprofit organizations. Groups as diverse as the American Council of Education, the National Governors Association, and the National Council of Senior Citizens obtain a large percentage of their funds through federal grants and contracts.[18]

Group organizers also play a role in group formation. These entrepreneurs often come from established groups.[19] They gain experience and then strike out on their own. Many civil rights activists of the 1950s and early 1960s founded new organizations in the late 1960s. Some used their skills to organize groups against the war in Vietnam and later to organize groups for women's rights and environmental causes.[20] Thus the formation of one group often opens the door to the formation of others.

Why People Join

Some people join a group because of the group's political goals or cause. But many join for economic and social reasons.[21] Some groups offer monetary benefits to members such as discounted prices for goods and services. The large nonfarm membership of the Farm Bureau is often attributed to the cut-rate insurance policies offered through the organization.[22] In addition to discount drugs and medicines, AARP provides health, home, and auto insurance; a motor club; a travel service; investment counseling; and several magazines. These services attract members and generate millions of dollars for the organization. In an effort to recruit new members and reach an increasingly diverse population as well as generate additional advertising revenue from its publications, AARP distributes several versions of its mainline magazine targeted to different age groups, the latest aimed at those forty-five to fifty-five years of age.[23]

Because members pay dues, thereby providing groups with resources to accomplish their goals and to enhance their influence with government, most groups provide a mix of benefits in an effort to maximize their membership. The National Rifle Association (NRA) lobbies against gun regulation and control. Some people join for this reason. Others join to secure other NRA services: *The American Rifleman* (a monthly magazine), a hunter's information service, low-cost firearm insurance, membership in local gun clubs, and shooting competitions.[24] Still others join because they enjoy associating with fellow gun enthusiasts.

Some people join groups because they are coerced. In some states, lawyers must join the state bar association to practice law.

Which People Join

Not all people are equally likely to join groups. Those with higher incomes and education are more likely to belong. They can afford membership dues, have free time necessary to take part, and have the social and intellectual skills that facilitate group participation. They also appear more attractive to many groups and therefore are more apt to be recruited. Whites more often belong to groups than blacks, but mostly because of their higher average income and education.[25]

Have Americans Stopped Joining?

Americans used to join groups at rates much higher than citizens of other democracies. But Americans are less likely to join groups than they were a few decades ago. This current trend was documented in a widely publicized book, *Bowling Alone*.[26]

What does bowling have to do with politics? The common thread is the dwindling membership in organized groups: declining church membership and church-related activities; the falloff in labor union membership, once the most common organizational affiliation among American workers; the decreasing membership in the PTA; and significantly diminished membership in league bowling.

If declining group membership reflected only a loss of revenue from the pizza and beer consumed by bowling leagues, only the owners of bowling alleys would care. However, the decline in league bowling and other group memberships parallels the loss of close personal relationships that foster discussion of public issues and trust among citizens, which are important to a vibrant democracy. Involvement in groups teaches people how to run meetings, handle money, keep records, and participate in group discussions. It exposes members to the workings of representative democracy and reinforces the ideals of good citizenship, such as the need to obey laws, engage in public discussion, and vote.[27]

Some people argue that the decline in membership in organized groups is not a serious problem because informal social ties provide the same opportunity to interact and discuss issues.[28] For example, people may not join bowling leagues, but they visit with others when they attend their children's soccer games. Yet being part of an organized group provides a network of associates that casual contact does not.

People today claim that they are busier than ever before and that between their work and family life, they have little time for other things. Women's lives, in particular, have changed over the past generation, with most women now in the paid workforce while still carrying the largest share of household and child-raising duties. Women used to be the backbone of most local civic, religious, political, and educational groups, but working women now have far less time to devote to such volunteer activities.

Although formal membership in voluntary organizations has decreased, membership, if one can call it that, in professionally managed issue advocacy groups is increasing.[29] The only link of members to the organization, however, is the occasional check they send to support the organization's activities.[30] They contribute to the cause but do not interact with other members. Although these organizations can be successful politically, the benefits of social interaction are lost. Members do not discuss and share information that helps in discerning one's real stake in public affairs and politics.

Some observers argue that television has replaced membership in groups as a preferred leisure-time activity. Even busy people usually find time to watch TV. But even though TV can be educational as well as entertaining, it provides no opportunity for discussion; information, if one can call it that, flows in one direction.

Types of Interest Groups

Interest groups come in all sizes. Some have large memberships, such as the American Federation of Labor–Congress of Industrial Organizations (AFL-CIO) with 13 million members. Others have small memberships, such as the Mushroom Growers Association with fourteen. Some have no members at all.

Corporations have managers and stockholders but not members in the traditional sense. They act as interest groups when they lobby government.[31] Some groups, such as the Children's Defense Fund (CDF), have no members and lobby government on behalf of others.[32] Founded in 1973 and funded from private donations, the CDF represents the interests of children.

Some interest groups are formally organized, with appointed or elected leaders, regular meetings, and dues-paying members. Others have no leaders and few prescribed rules.

Groups that solicit money from private individuals have "checkbook members" who contribute money but have no say in what the group does or how their contributions are spent. Many **political action committees (PACs)** and so-called 527 organizations that sponsor political advertisements, such as the Media Fund and MoveOn.org, operate in this way (see Chapter 9). They raise money through direct mail and the Internet and spend it on political ads for and against issues or political candidates. Decisions are made by the group's leaders with no accountability to anyone, other than contributors' decisions not to contribute in the future.

Thus interest groups can be distinguished according to their membership and their organizational structure. They can also be distinguished by their goals. Some groups pursue economic goals, primarily for the benefit of their members. Others pursue political goals or causes that have consequences for all or at least consequences that are not limited to members of the group.

Private Interest Groups

Private interest groups seek economic benefits for their members or clients. Examples include business, labor, and agriculture.

Business

With the declining power of unions, business organizations are the most numerous and among the most powerful interest groups in Washington (see Figure 1). Politics is now essentially a confrontation between business and government.[33] Business seeks to maximize profit, whereas government, at least sometimes, works to protect workers and consumers from the unfettered effects

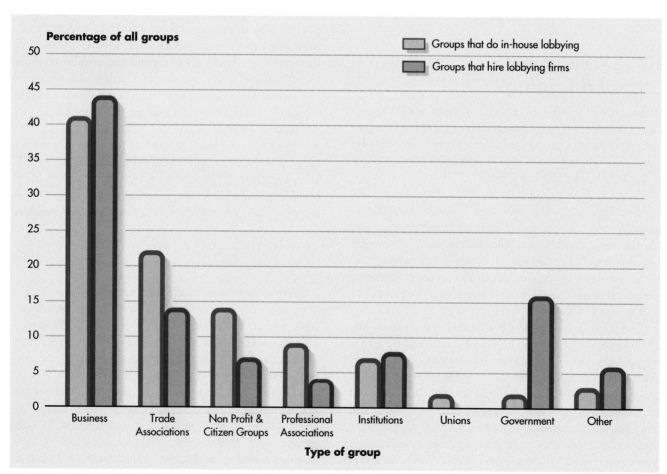

FIGURE 1 ■ **Contemporary Interest Groups** *Business interests dominate the modern interest group system. This graph categorizes 2,810 groups that maintain an office in Washington, D.C., and 6,601 groups that lobby there.*

SOURCE: Frank R. Baumgartner and Beth L. Leech, "Interest Niches and Policy Bandwagons: Patterns of Interest Group Involvement in National Politics," *Journal of Politics* 63 (November, 2001): 1191-1213. Data are based on filing reports with the government. Those identified as hiring lobbying firms represent only those with no in-house lobbyists.

of profit-seeking businesses through regulation of wages, safety standards, and certain kinds of monopolistic practices, among other interventions.

Today, however, there is little confrontation between business and government. Although the Republican Party has long favored business, in recent years the Democrat Party has also.[34] Regardless of who occupies the White House or which party controls Congress, business has generally done well. This reflects in part the disincentives in a capitalist economy for politicians of any persuasion to antagonize business, which is so important to the nation's economic success.[35] If the economy falters, politicians get blamed. Rather than do something to undermine business confidence, politicians are inclined to do what business wants. Democratic support also reflects business's financial contribution to Democratic candidates; the election of moderate and conservative Democrats like Bill Clinton, who are generally sympathetic to business; and a general climate of opinion, fostered by the media, that favors business over labor.

During the past twenty years, business has had numerous successes in rolling back government regulation. Three examples will illustrate. Deregulation of accounting and a loosening of other financial standards led directly to the scandals of Enron and many other companies in the early years of the new century, involving the looting of company employees and shareholders for the personal enrichment of top executives (see Chapter 8). The Bush administration has also unraveled a number of environmental regulations, leaving businesses freer to pollute. In 2004, the administration also put in place new rules reducing the obligations of businesses to pay overtime wages to their workers, a measure enthusiastically endorsed by business lobbies. In a deal struck in the House, Democrats succeeded in amending an appropriations bill to prevent the rules from taking effect, but President Bush threatened to veto the measure unless the new rules on overtime pay were restored. (See the boxes "Pills, Power, and Politics" on page 168 and "Feeding Frenzy" on page 170 for details of businesses' effort to win favors from Congress.)

Labor

Organized labor is a principal competitor with business but runs a distant second in influence and continues to lose ground. Although the United States has many labor unions, the AFL-CIO, a confederation of trade and industrial unions, is the most important politically. It has a staff of several hundred and some of the most skillful lobbyists in Washington. It channels money to political candidates, chiefly Democrats, through its political action committee. In the 2004 general election, it spent nearly $45 million on campaign literature, phone banks

to get out the vote, television issue ads, and voter registration.[36] Furthermore, tens of thousands of union members canvassed door-to-door, particularly important in the swing states.

Declining membership is the major challenge facing labor and the principal reason for its loss of influence over the years.[37] Only 13 percent of the workforce belongs to a union, down from 20 percent in 1983 and 35 percent in 1955 (see Figure 2). Some of this reflects the union's own lack of effort at recruiting new members and divisions within the labor movement over whether to use its scarce resources in organizing or serving members.[38] It also reflects the intimidating and illegal acts of employers directed toward employee efforts to unionize. From 1992 and 1997, some 125,000 employees lost their jobs for supporting a union.[39] Such acts are rarely prosecuted, and in the rare case of conviction, penalties are minimal. Where employers refrain from illegal practices—namely, in the public sector (teachers and government workers)—union membership has increased. The antiunion message of business communicated through the largely antiunion media has also succeeded in convincing many people that unions are something working men and women do not need.[40] Despite this, a majority of Americans approve of unions. Most report sympathy for the side of unions in labor disputes. However, only about a third would like to see the power and influence of unions increased.[41]

The decline of unions has led to lowered wages, directly because strong unions gain higher wages for their own workers and also indirectly because having high-wage workers puts pressure on nonunion employees to keep wages high. The wage gap is wide; in 2003, unionized blue-collar workers averaged more than $30 an hour, while nonunionized workers averaged $18.[42] The weakness of unions and declining pressure on wages can be illustrated by the fact that unlike in previous economic cycles, the end of the 2001 recession brought more growth in corporate profits than in wages and benefits for workers.[43]

The decline in unions has also weakened the more progressive or liberal part of the political process, for unions lobbied not only for rights for their own workers and other workers but also for other causes. They provided significant support for the civil rights movement and have fought to expand government support for health care, to name only two important issues.

Population shifts have also hurt unions. States in the South and Southwest, where antiunion sentiment is strong, have grown in population and representation in Congress. Unions have therefore had a less sympathetic ear among the nation's lawmakers. Global competition and government's unwillingness to protect American workers has also hurt unions. Fearful of losing their jobs

There is no lobby in Washington as large, as powerful, or as well financed as the pharmaceutical industry. Battle-tested over the years involving a number of health care issues going back to the creation of the Medicare program in the 1960s, the industry spent $177 million lobbying government in 1999–2000 and another $20 million in campaign contributions. Lobbying expenditures outdistanced its nearest rivals, the insurance and telecommunications industries, by $50 million. Given their political clout, it is no surprise that drug companies are the most profitable of any among the largest corporations in America.[1]

In the K Street corridor, home to Washington's most famous lobbying and law firms, there are 134 firms on the drug industry's payroll; half are either former members of Congress or former congressional staff members and government employees. For example, Bristol-Myers Squibb, manufacturer of a popular cholesterol-lowering drug and one for the treatment of diabetes, employs fifteen firms with fifty-seven lobbyists, including several former prominent Republican and Democratic members of Congress.

Why should the nation's manufacturers of pills require so much firepower in Washington? In a word, profits. An important issue is protecting drug patents that give manufacturers monopoly control for a period of time, usually twenty years. Exclusive rights to make and market a drug mean billions of dollars for the manufacturer. Having a monopoly means that the industry can charge users who need the drug very high prices.

Once the patent period is over and other companies can manufacture and sell the drug, competition drives the cost of that drug down by as much as 80 percent. Naturally, drug companies try to extend their patents, either by making minor refinements or by lobbying Congress. William Nixon, chief executive of the Generic Pharmaceutical Association, which battles the big drug companies, says the companies will do "everything to maintain their monopoly."[2]

Of course, there is a legitimate argument for why the pharmaceutical industry wants to maintain its monopoly. No company will invest in development of new drugs if it does not have the exclusive right to sell them over an extended period of time. Drug companies sponsor a great deal of research, and only a very small portion of it results in a commercially successful product. So maintaining for

as long as possible exclusive rights to sell the drugs that are commercially successful is important. Drug companies point out that generic drug companies can sell their drugs more cheaply because they haven't invested in the research that went into developing the drug.

Take Claritin, for example. If you suffer from hay fever or other allergies, you have probably taken it. Manufactured by Schering-Plough, income from sales of Claritin last year totaled $2.3 billion, paid by consumers and their insurance companies. The company spent $7.9 million in a recent year lobbying Congress. High on its lobbying priority was extending its patent on Claritin.

However, after several years of pressuring Congress to extend its patent and spending millions in the process, Schering-Plough announced that the medication would be available over the counter; that is, without a prescription and at half the cost. Why the shift?

First, the company was having little success in getting Congress to extend its patent. Insurance companies tired of paying higher costs for the drug and competing companies wanting to tap into the lucrative allergy drug market were pressuring in the opposite direction. There was also concern that continuing double-digit increases in the cost of drugs and the perception that drug companies are concerned only with profits might lead to the imposition of government controls.

But perhaps the most important factor was that Schering-Plough was about to launch a new prescription drug, Clarinex, to fill the market void left by Claritin. They could get a head start on marketing Claritin as an over-the-counter drug while preparing to sell the new drug at premium prices.

When each of us purchases a prescription drug, we are only interested in whether it makes us feel better. But even hay fever drugs have political ramifications, and those ramifications have a big impact on how much we pay for that cure.

1. "Pharmaceutical Industry Ranks as Most Profitable Industry—Again," *Public Citizen,* April 18, 2002, www.citizen.org/pressroom/release.cfm?ID=1088.
2. Leslie Wayne and Melody Petersen, "A Muscular Lobby Rolls Up Its Sleeves," *New York Times,* November 4, 2001, BU1, BU13; Charles Babcock, "An Ad Campaign That's Nothing to Sneeze At," *Washington Post National Weekly Edition,* November 8, 1999, 30.

or putting an employer at a disadvantage in a competitive market, members are reluctant to strike, and without the threat of strikes, there is little reason to heed labor's demands or for employees to consider joining unions.

In an effort to expand membership, unions have reached out to the low-wage service sector and professions. Labor won a major victory in 1999 when 75,000 nursing home employees voted to be represented by the Service Employees International Union, making it the

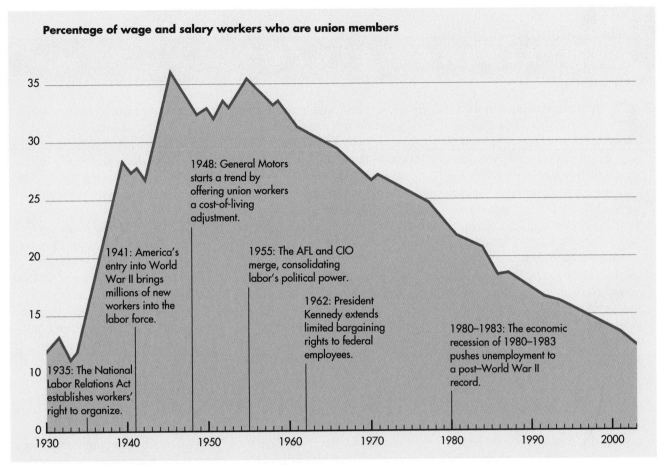

Percentage of wage and salary workers who are union members

1948: General Motors starts a trend by offering union workers a cost-of-living adjustment.

1941: America's entry into World War II brings millions of new workers into the labor force.

1955: The AFL and CIO merge, consolidating labor's political power.

1962: President Kennedy extends limited bargaining rights to federal employees.

1980–1983: The economic recession of 1980–1983 pushes unemployment to a post–World War II record.

1935: The National Labor Relations Act establishes workers' right to organize.

FIGURE 2 ■ Union Membership in the United States

SOURCE: U.S. Census Bureau, *Statistical Abstract of the United States,* online at www.census.gov/prod/www/statistical-abstract-02.html.

third-largest union in the nation.[44] Efforts proceed to organize computer specialists in areas like Silicon Valley.[45] Doctors employed by HMOs as well as those in private practice are organizing.[46] Graduate teaching assistants at the nation's major universities are unionizing over wages and working conditions.[47] Even some undergraduates are organizing.[48]

To try to enhance labor's influence, the AFL–CIO has enrolled a half million members in a new nonpartisan advocacy group, Working America. The goal is to bring nonunion and union members together in promoting issues of common concern. The group will draw on members to communicate with lawmakers via e-mails, letters, and phone calls.[49]

Agriculture

The American farm population is declining, but agricultural organizations are still important in agricultural policymaking. Agricultural interests are represented by a number of general and specialized groups. Most support government subsidies to help farmers, although a few oppose subsidies.

The American Farm Bureau Federation, the largest of the general-interest groups, began when the federal government established the agricultural extension service to educate farmers on new farming techniques. To encourage cooperation with local agents, the government offered grants to states that organized county farm bureaus. In the early part of the twentieth century, these local bureaus gradually evolved into a national organization.

Despite its roots, the Farm Bureau is a conservative organization dominated by wealthy farmers with large landholdings. Although it opposes government aid in other sectors of the economy, it favors government subsidies to farmers, many of whom are Farm Bureau members and involved in corporate-owned and -operated farms.

The National Farmers' Union, considerably smaller than the Farm Bureau, represents small farming interests. It supports government subsidies but wants them targeted to preserve small family farms. The American Agriculture Movement (AAM) began as a protest movement in the mid-1970s and, like the Farmers' Union, addresses issues that benefit small farmers and ranchers.[50]

Along with the general-interest groups, hundreds of commodity organizations promote specific products and operate much like business trade associations. Examples

FEEDING FRENZY

Efforts of special interests to secure benefits from government do not stop because of a national tragedy. The efforts are simply refocused to take advantage of the situation.

In the wake of September 11, 2001, scores of Washington lobbyists, trade associations, interest groups, and members of Congress pleading for special interests rushed to repackage their demands in patriotic wrapping. While not new to Washington politics, post–9/11 may represent a new low in trying to exploit a national disaster for personal and private gain. PBS television producer Bill Moyers put it this way: "It didn't take long for wartime opportunists—the mercenaries of Washington, the lobbyists, lawyers, and political fundraisers—to crawl out of their offices on K Street to grab what they can for their clients." [1]

It began with the nation's airline industry. By September 22, the government had given the airlines a sweet deal: $5 billion in cash, plus another $10 billion in loan guarantees. The airlines also won protection from lawsuits arising from the attacks, which would have cost them billions more. Former Secretary of Labor Robert Reich has pointed out that the bailout exceeds the combined value of all America's major airlines: United, American, Delta, Northwest, US Airways, America West, and Continental.[2] Of course, American taxpayers received no ownership in the airlines for their sizable investment. In the blink of an eye and with virtually no debate, Congress approved the measure for an industry in which several carriers were near bankruptcy before 9/11. (And less then three years later, at least two of these airlines were bankrupt again).

Following on the heels of the airline bailout, the insurance industry pressed the Bush administration to shift liability for future terrorist attacks to the federal government. It also sought to have claims confined to the federal court in Manhattan rather than reviewed in state courts, where judges would more likely approve punitive damages potentially in the billions. If the White House refused, the industry warned it would cease to cover future terrorist attacks and bring the country's economy to a standstill.

The request was not a hard sell to the administration. Insurance companies spent $1.6 million to elect George Bush in 2000. The industry also had friends in Congress after donating $20 million in soft money to both Republicans and Democrats. By October 12, the White House had outlined a plan whereby taxpayers would cover all but $12 billion of the first $100 billion in future claims. In November, the House approved the Terrorism Risk Protection Act; however, the plan stalled in the Democrat-controlled Senate.

Others picked up the strategy of the airline and insurance industries. Steel lobbied for direct subsidies as well as restrictions on imports of less costly foreign steel. The Democratic senator from West Virginia, Jay Rockefeller, made the case. "Without steel, we cannot guarantee our national security." [3] Carl Levin, the Democratic senator from Michigan, went a bit further. "Our weapons are made of steel." Before a group of cheering steelworkers, he shouted, "We go to war with what you make." [4] "Absolute baloney" was the response of a researcher at a Washington think tank. "One or two steel mills could provide all the steel needed for defense." [5] Of course, Rockefeller's and Levin's views may have been tainted by the $2.7 million the steel producers contributed to Democratic candidates in 2000. The president eventually approved restrictions on steel imports at a tremendous cost to U.S. taxpayers and opening the U.S. to retaliation by European countries. The restrictions were ultimately lifted following a finding of the World Trade Organization that they violated free-trade agreements.

The $167 billion farm subsidy labeled the Agricultural Act of 2001 became the Farm Security Act of 2001 following 9/11. On September 24, Capitol Hill was deluged with letters from growers of twenty federally subsidized commodities with the message that "food production is vital to the national interest." [6] Like steel, the growers pumped $58 million into the 2000 elections. The measure passed the House in October 291 to 120 and was later signed into law by the president.

Manufacturers of traffic signs, barricades, and other equipment wanted their share too. In an effort to bolster federal highway safety spending, a spokesman argued that increased spending for traffic-routing devices would help motorists flee cities faster and more safely during terrorist attacks. The American Bus Association, representing a thousand private companies providing intercity bus service, had been lobbying for $400 million to improve bus security and safety. After 9/11, the association maintained that it would help companies retain drivers who had come to fear potential terrorist attacks.

A capital gains tax cut was marketed as a national security initiative by the National Taxpayers Union. According to the association, a reduction in capital gains taxes would "revitalize the sagging economy and bring new revenues to Washington—aiding our war against terrorism." [7] Having succeeded in winning $135 million to shore up public beaches, the American Shore and Beach

Preservation Association sought additional funds arguing that "America needs to make a major commitment to its energy and water infrastructure, both for security and economic reasons." [8] Lobbyists also sought a $10 million subsidy for bison producers because, as they put it, the fear of terrorism drove patrons from the fancy restaurants that serve bison steaks and burgers.

Flight schools, operators of skydiving companies, manufacturers of small aircraft, and owners of small airports seeking compensation for business lost since the attacks also bellied up to the trough. Ethanol producers proposed blending its product with gasoline to check the nation's dependence on foreign oil. Travel agents sought $4 billion, arguing that without travel agencies, the nation's travel industry could not survive. Date growers in California petitioned the White House and Pentagon to buy dates and include them in food packages being dropped into Afghanistan. They argued that dates would be a real treat for the Afghans during Ramadan (a Muslim holy period). [9]

Of course, none of these groups were asking for anything different from what they sought before 9/11. But 9/11 offered an opportunity to provide a stronger argument for their causes. One lobbyist expressed what many were thinking: "What happened was a tragedy certainly, but there are opportunities. We're in business. This is not a charity." [10] A member of Congress captured the view of many lawmakers and lobbyists by saying, "It's an open grab bag, so let's grab." [11]

Perhaps the biggest grab was the economic stimulus package put forth by House Republicans. The measure would allow companies to write off expenses they hadn't yet incurred, take advantage of loopholes to avoid paying any taxes at all, and receive rebates on taxes they paid going back to 1986. The estimated stimulus effect was zero, but the lobbyist pushing it claimed it was his patriotic duty to bolster the bottom line of the nation's wealthiest corporations. Largely written by corporate lobbyists, the measure failed to win approval.

"Lobbyists are in the business of asking for things," says a researcher at the conservative Heritage Foundation. "And they adjust their message to whatever they think will sell. Right now it's national security, economic stimulus, and disaster relief, and so they link what they want to one of those—better yet all three." [12]

In earlier wars, war profiteering, making money on a war, was considered shady and unpatriotic and sometimes even illegal. Perhaps because no one is being asked to sacrifice in the war against terror except the soldiers and their families, war profiteering in this war is seen as nothing at all to be ashamed of and, indeed, practically patriotic.

"Pardon me, but could you tell us where the public trough is?"

1. Bill Hogan, "Star-Spangled Lobbyists," *Mother Jones,* March-April 2002, 59–63.
2. Alan Guebert, "Lugar's Proposal Calls Groups' Bluff," *Lincoln Journal-Star,* October 21, 2001.
3. Hogan, "Star-Spangled Lobbyists."
4. David E. Sanger and Joseph Kahn, "Bush's Plan to Raise Steel Tariffs Would Exempt Most Poor Nations," *New York Times,* March 4, 2002, A1, A14.
5. Hogan, "Star-Spangled Lobbyists."
6. Ibid.
7. Ibid.
8. Ibid.
9. David E. Rosenbaum, "Since Sept. 11. Lobbyists Use New Pitches for Old Pleas," *New York Times,* December 3, 2001, B1.
10. Ibid.
11. Hogan, "Star-Spangled Lobbyists."
12. Ibid.

IN MEMORY OF

IDA BRAYMAN

17 YEARS OLD

who was shot & killed by an Employer Feb. 5th 1913 during the great struggle of the Garment Workers of Rochester.

Copyrigted 1913 by U. G. W. Local 14 Rochester N. Y.

Gotham Book Mart, New York

This postcard commemorates the death of a seventeen-year-old woman murdered while striking for recognition of her union, an eight-hour day, and extra pay for overtime and holidays.

include cattle, cotton, milk, tobacco, and wool producers. Large agribusiness firms such as Cargill and Archer-Daniels-Midland (ADM) also have powerful lobbies in Washington.

Today, American agriculture is dominated by agribusiness and large corporate farms. The small farmer plays a minor role, although politicians often invoke the small farmer in pushing government subsidies for large corporate enterprises. Government spends more than $20 billion subsidizing crop production, or in some cases nonproduction, and most of those funds go to the wealthiest, largest—usually corporate—farms.[51] In most states, current farm subsidies go to 10 percent of farmers.[52]

Public Interest Groups

Public interest groups lobby for political and social causes rather than direct financial gain for their members. If they succeed, their success is shared more widely

than by members of the group. The National Taxpayers Union lobbies for reduced taxes not just for its members but for everyone who pays taxes. Amnesty International lobbies for the rights of political prisoners around the world even though none of its members are prisoners.

Although nearly all groups think of themselves as pursuing the public interest, the label in this instance applies only to those working for other than personal or corporate interests. However, "public interest" does not mean that a majority of the public necessarily favors the goals of these groups or that their goals are necessarily good for all or even most of the people.

Public interest groups increased dramatically in number and size during the late 1960s and early 1970s.[53] Now they number more than twenty-five hundred, with forty million members.[54] Several factors account for the surge. Americans became increasingly distrustful of government, which to many appeared to favor special interests over more general interests (see Chapter 4). The need for a balance between the two led many people to join these groups. Many middle-class Americans also had the financial means to support them. The new technologies mentioned earlier also made it easier to reach and mobilize prospective and existing members.

Whereas many of the public interest groups established during the 1960s and 1970s were "shoestring" operations staffed by idealistic social reformers with few professional skills, many of today's public interest organizations have larger budgets and memberships and a cadre of professionals—attorneys, management consultants, direct-mail fundraisers, and communication directors—handling day-to-day operations and seeking to influence government with a variety of strategies and tactics.[55]

Multiple-Issue Groups

We can classify public interest groups as being multiple- or single-issue groups. Multiple-issue groups are, by definition, involved with a range of issues. Single-issue groups have a narrower focus. This section deals with multiple-issue groups.

Women's Groups Groups advocating women's equality range from large, mass-based organizations interested in a broad array of issues to smaller groups with more specific and narrow interests.

The National Organization for Women (NOW), the largest women's group, with 250,000 members, has chapters in each state.[56] Funded chiefly by membership dues, it conducts research and lobbies at the national, state, and local levels in a number of policy areas including reproductive freedom and economic rights.

EMILY's List—EMILY stands for Early Money Is Like Yeast (it makes the "dough" rise)—is an organiza-

The first wave of women's organizations campaigned for women's right to vote. Here some twenty thousand marchers parade for women's rights in New York City in 1917.

© Bettmann/CORBIS

tion that recruits, trains, and funds pro-choice Democratic women to run for public office. Since its founding in 1985, it has helped elect eleven women to the Senate, fifty-five to the House, and seven as state governors. In 2002, the group contributed $9.3 million to candidates and another $10 million mobilizing women voters in key battleground states.[57] The National Women's Political Caucus differs from EMILY's List in that it works for the election of women regardless of their stands on particular issues.

With only sixteen hundred members, the Independent Women's Forum is a conservative counter to NOW.[58] It opposes government programs to achieve sexual equality, such as programs directed toward raising the performance of girls in public schools, arguing that it is boys who consistently underperform. It also opposes extending civil rights laws to cover discrimination against women's athletic programs in colleges and universities (see Chapter 15).

Religious Groups A majority of Americans are affiliated to some degree with an organized religious group, and the political arms of those groups are an important part of the interest group panorama in Washington. The National Council of Churches, representing liberal Protestant denominations, argues for civil and human rights, including abortion rights. Catholic groups are active in the antiabortion and antinuclear movements. Jewish groups have lobbied for liberal causes and the nation of Israel. Muslim groups lobby for an anti-Israel Middle East policy and are advocates for fair treatment of Muslims in the United States.[59]

Evangelical Protestant denominations—the Christian right—are the most potent religious force in American politics.[60] They oppose abortion, divorce, homosexuality, and women's rights and push their agenda through schools, newspapers, magazines, radio and television, and thousands of politically mobilized churches.[61] One evangelical lobby group is the Christian Coalition, developed in the 1980s by a television evangelist, Pat Robertson, who sought the Republican presidential nomination in 1988.[62] While ostensibly a religious group, the Christian Coalition is heavily involved in politics and closely linked to the Republican Party, where by the early 1990s its members were in the majority in many state and local party organizations.[63] Robertson and fellow television preacher Jerry Falwell were outspoken critics of President Clinton during the impeachment process, calling on him to resign and asking Christians to send money to make it happen.[64]

Conservative Christians helped deliver the Republican presidential nomination to George W. Bush in 2000 by mobilizing its followers in opposition to his Republican rival, John McCain. And they helped deliver the presidential election to Bush in 2004.

Still, the sway of organized conservative Christian groups may have peaked.[65] Robertson no longer heads the Christian Coalition, and the group's budget is a fraction of what it once was. Some people in the movement are disillusioned that political activity has produced so little and feel used by the Republican Party. Abortion is still legal. Creationism is excluded from the public school curriculum. The move to ban gay marriage failed in Congress. Nor are these things likely to change. Nationwide, some social attitudes are becoming more liberal. Mindful that time is against him, Falwell told would-be contributors that they needed to push the conservative family-oriented social agenda to take advantage of Bush's popularity.[66]

In recent years, Jews and evangelical Christians have found common ground in their support for Israel.[67] Conservative Christians see modern Israel as the fulfillment of biblical prophesy, signaling that the Final Judgment is near.[68] Republican operatives have used support from Christian groups for Israel to try to coax American Jews away from their traditional Democratic loyalties.[69]

The Interfaith Alliance and the Clergy Leadership Network are groups of mainline Protestants that counter the message and political activity of the Christian Coalition and other conservative religious groups.[70] These groups put greater weight on the Christian doctrines of helping the less fortunate and working for peace than on the social issues, like abortion and gay rights, that have mobilized the evangelical groups.[71]

The Freedom from Religion Foundation speaks for the estimated 14 percent of the American people who are atheists. Its goal is to make the "unbelievers'" voice loud and clear in public discourse. The organization assisted the plaintiff in a lawsuit challenging the inclusion of the words "under God" in the Pledge of Allegiance. (The U.S. Supreme Court threw the case out on a technicality.[72])

Racial and Ethnic Groups Groups promoting the civil rights of racial and ethnic groups have been an important part of American history. Chapter 15 discusses these groups and their role in the civil rights movement. Groups representing the interests of African Americans, such as the NAACP, the Congress for Racial Equality (CORE), and the Urban League, pressed for equal rights for black Americans and eventually won

major changes in the law and ultimately the treatment of minorities.

Hispanics and American Indians also have organized groups representing them. Though the roots of Hispanic American political groups date from the late nineteenth century, the longest-existing organization, the League of United Latin American Citizens (LULAC), was founded in 1927 to combat discrimination against Mexican Americans. Another prominent group, the Mexican American Legal Defense and Educational Fund (MALDEF), pursues litigation challenging discriminatory practices—for example, the creation of election districts unfavorable to Hispanic voters.

Groups supporting the rights of Native Americans have focused on the improvement of the educational and income status of American Indians and for equal treatment. More recently, some have fought against school mascots that use American Indian tribal names and, especially, symbols or demeaning images and names ("Redskins," for example).

Gays and Lesbians Gays and lesbians are represented by the Human Rights Campaign, the Gay and Lesbian Alliance Against Defamation (GLAAD), and Lambda Defense Fund, among many other groups (see the box "The Origins of Gay and Lesbian Rights Groups"). Each of these groups has worked in the courts and in the political and policy arenas.

One of the most important current issues is the right of homosexuals to marry. The Human Rights Campaign and other gay and lesbian advocacy groups make substantial donations to fight proposed state legislation that would define marriage as a bond exclusively between a man and a woman. And these organizations are fighting the battle in the courts. Gay and Lesbian Advocates and Defenders (GLAD), a New England legal rights organization, filed a lawsuit challenging the constitutionality of Vermont's exclusion of gay and lesbian couples from the institution of civil marriage. The state's supreme court upheld the challenge, and the state legislature ultimately extended same-sex couples all the legal benefits of marriage without granting the label. A similar lawsuit in Massachusetts ended that state's exclusion. Inspired by these decisions, local officials in a few other states began to grant marriage licenses to same-sex couples. Although these have been invalidated, it will be difficult to go back. Hoping to do so, under pressure from conservative Christian groups, the Bush administration proposed but Congress rejected a constitutional amendment banning same-sex marriages. However, eleven states approved bans on same-sex marriage and some approved bans on civil unions in the 2004 elections.

The Lambda Defense Fund also represents gay and lesbian young people who have been discriminated

THE ORIGIN OF GAY AND LESBIAN RIGHTS GROUPS

Gay and lesbian rights organizations developed around 1950. At this time, homosexuals largely kept their sexual orientation private and, on the rare occasions when it came to public attention, were characterized as deviates. Being known as a homosexual could mean loss of a job and public humiliation (as it still does in the military). For that reason, gays and lesbians were extremely vulnerable to blackmail and to police harassment. As an example of public attitudes toward gays in that era, in 1954, following a raid on a gay bar, a Miami newspaper story title read "Perverts Seized in Bar Raid." Even in 1965, New York's liquor authority declared that a meeting of three or more homosexuals in a bar was reason enough for the bar to lose its license.[1] In New York City, then as now a city of more liberal attitudes than many other places, until 1965, police entrapment of homosexuals was common (police in plain clothes hung around bars waiting for a proposition and then made an arrest), and discrimination in most city hiring was abolished only in 1967 and in the fire and police departments not until well after that.

During these years, as for many decades before, gays and lesbians focused primarily on how to avoid and survive persecution.[2] The first group with national scope organized to speak for the rights of homosexuals was the Mattachine Society, founded in 1950 to help raise political consciousness among gays and to fight the persecution of gays as part of the antiCommunist blacklisting in the 1950s. But the Mattachine Society was small, had branches in only a few cities, and dwindled in importance in a few years, especially when it was discovered that some leaders were communists.

Homosexuals continued to be ostracized by most of American society until 1969, widely recognized as the beginning of the modern gay rights movement thanks to a police raid at the Stonewall, a seedy bar in Greenwich Village, New York. Rumored to be owned by the Mafia and operating without a liquor license, with many underage customers, and as a dope hangout, the Stonewall, a private club, was a popular meeting place for a diverse group of gay men, "including drag queens, hippies, street people, and uptown boys slumming."[3] That summer, the New York City police were engaged in a crackdown on illegal bars, focusing mostly on those frequented by gay men, Latinos, and blacks. Several gay bars had already been raided without incident before the Stonewall, but each raid heightened the anger and desperation felt in the gay community.

A small police unit entered the Stonewall at 3 A.M. and cited the employees for selling liquor without a license. The customers were asked to leave and formed a peaceful crowd outside. But after a police van arrived to take away those arrested, the crowd grew hostile and began to throw things—first coins, then cans and bottles, and then larger items. The police took refuge in the club, but the hostile and increasingly angry crowd pressed to break in, and the police drew their weapons.[4] Soon lighter fluid and a match were thrown inside the building and a fire started, but loss of life was avoided when more police reinforcements arrived.

The crowd, obviously feeling empowered by its attempt to finally fight back, then moved down the street shouting "gay power" and celebrating their newfound strength and solidarity (though some were injured and others had been arrested, no one was seriously hurt). The next few nights, other crowds gathered to demonstrate for gay rights, and the police were summoned on at least two occasions.

After several days, the unrest ended, and the collective sense of protest and injustice were transformed into an organization, the Gay Liberation Front. Its original founders were determined to use radical political means to fight discrimination against homosexuals. Not long after, politically moderate gays and lesbians broke from the Gay Liberation Front to form the Gay Activist Alliance. Later other groups evolved that used mainstream politics, legal challenges, and peaceful protest activities to support the cause of equality for gays and lesbians. By the early 1970s, gay pride parades, usually held in late June to commemorate the anniversary of the Stonewall raid, were common in major cities, and gay rights organizations were actively working across the land.

Changes in the status of homosexuals soon followed. In 1973, the American Psychiatric Association removed homosexuality from its list of mental disorders. Then, in the early 1980s, the tragedy of AIDS focused media attention on the gay community and brought public awareness to the issue of discrimination against gays. Entertainers and celebrities who acknowledged their homosexuality, and in some instances suffered from AIDS, raised public consciousness even more. With increasing public exposure to gay people, American society began to recognize that gays are not very different from everyone else.

1. Robert Amsel, "Back to Our Future? A Walk on the Wild Side of Stonewall," www.gay astrology.com/stonwall.shtml (excerpted from *Advocate,* September 19, 1987).
2. The source for much of this discussion is Eric Marcus, *Making History: The Struggle for Gay and Lesbian Equal Rights, 1945–1990* (New York: HarperCollins, 1992); see also Jeffrey Schmalz, "Gay Politics Goes Mainstream," *New York Times Magazine,* October 11, 1992, 18ff.
3. Amsel, "Back to Our Future?"
4. An eyewitness account of all of this was provided by a *Village Voice* reporter, Howard Smith; ibid.

against or harassed in school and is working to help educate legislators, school officials, and teachers about the challenges these youth face. Although gays and lesbians have gained many legal rights and much acceptance, they are far from fully equal. Bill Clinton's public position on gay issues was mixed, but he ended the federal policy treating gays as security risks and invited gay activists to the White House. The implicit message was that gays are part of the American community, have legitimate concerns, and are accepted as full participants in political life. Despite having endorsed a constitutional amendment banning gay marriage, George W. Bush has appointed openly gay people to high-profile positions in the White House[73] and invited the Log Cabin Republicans, a gay advocacy group, to the White House for a policy briefing, reversing the 1996 decision of Republican presidential nominee Bob Dole, who returned a campaign contribution from the group. However, Republicans used the fight against gay rights to rally their political base in 2004.

Although gays can be discharged from the military and gays in most states can be fired from their jobs or evicted from their rental houses or apartments if their

sexual orientation becomes known, society has grown more tolerant and understanding. Eight out of ten Americans think discrimination in jobs and housing against gays and lesbians is wrong. Forty percent approve civil unions.[74] Gays and lesbians in the federal workforce and a dozen states are protected from job discrimination.[75] The issue for gay Americans is simply wanting to be free of discrimination and enjoy the rights guaranteed other Americans, including access to spousal health and death benefits provided by employers. The desire for economic equality is justification for legitimizing same-sex marriage, although the economic issues can be resolved without taking this step.

Transgender issues are sometimes linked with those of gays and lesbians, though they are not the same. Generally, transgender refers to individuals for whom their assigned gender on the basis of biology is different from the gender they would assign to themselves. GenderPAC, which stands for Gender Public Advocacy Coalition, works to protect everyone's right to be free of gender stereotypes.[76] GenderPAC has a number of corporate supporters, and its Congressional Gala drew two hundred people to hear an address by Colorado congresswomen Diana DeGette.[77]

Old and Young While the population of the nation as a whole has tripled since 1900, the number of elderly has increased eightfold. Today, persons over sixty-five constitute nearly 13 percent of the population. Several groups, sometimes called the "gray lobby," represent their interests. The most prominent of these is AARP, the group featured in "You Are There" at the start of this chapter.

To counterbalance the power of the gray lobby, a number of groups such as Americans for Generational Equity and the Children's Defense Fund represent the interests of young people, but they are small and not powerful by comparison. Part of this is because of the obvious fact that children cannot vote. Part is also that providing help for the elderly, who have most likely worked all their lives and are no longer able to do so, is more politically palatable than providing help for children whose parents are presumably in their prime wage-earning years. Thus aid for children becomes entangled with attitudes about welfare and helping poverty-stricken adults, and thus advocating for children's interests is not as easy as looking out for the interests of the elderly.

Young adults have no national organization representing their interests, though they have interests in common. Young workers have interests in the minimum wage and health insurance for low-wage workers. College students have an interest in reducing tuition costs and expenses associated with a university education (see the box "Hey, Kid! Have I Got a Deal for

AP/Wide World Photos

Mary Bonauto, a lawyer with Gay and Lesbian Advocates and Defenders (GLAD), brought the lawsuit that led to the legalization of civil unions in Vermont and then another that resulted in the legalization of same-sex marriage in Massachusetts.

Tuition rates are soaring, and many students borrow money to cover the cost. In 2002–2003, over six million borrowed $44 billion under federal student loan programs. Colleges offer one of two programs. Students either borrow directly from the government (the direct student loan program) or go through a private lender (the Federal Family Education Loan Program). The latter is a sweet deal for colleges and lenders but not for students.

Private lenders loan students money for college at a fixed interest rate, set by Congress above the lender's cost and conventional rates. If, however, interest rates should rise, rather than allowing the lender to lose money, the government—in other words, the American taxpayer—makes up the difference. Should students default and not repay the loan, the government covers the loss.

The direct student loan program makes 22 cents for every $100 borrowed, whereas the use of private lenders costs the government $12.80 for every $100 borrowed. One doesn't need a college education to recognize that direct loans are a better deal for American taxpayers. The direct-loan program not only saves money—indeed, the program generates income—but also costs students less by forcing private lenders to compete with the government program where interest on the borrowed money is less. We have the private lender program because of the political clout of lending institutions.

Established in 1993, the direct-loan program quickly captured a third of the student loan business and appeared on its way to dominating the market as more and more schools flocked to it. However, with billions at stake, private lenders fought back. The industry, led by Sallie Mae, the biggest player in the student loan business, attacked on two fronts. It stepped up its lobbying in Washington and began wining and dining schools.

On the lobbying front, it persuaded Congress to raise interest rates on loans and forgo a planned interest rate reduction. Students paid more, and the industry used the profits to induce schools to abandon the direct-loan program in favor of loans from private lenders. Lobbying was greased with campaign contributions to both Democrats and Republicans, particularly key members sitting on committees that oversee student loans, as well as "soft money" donations to the political parties.

The direct loans are unpopular with Republican conservatives, who believe that private lenders should handle the job, and Sallie Mae and the industry did not have to work too hard to convince the Bush administration that direct loans were not the way to go. Former representatives from the industry, clearly antagonistic to the direct-loan program, were appointed to oversee it. The administration ceased promoting the program to colleges and even proposed selling the loans the government already held to private lenders. That idea was abandoned when critics accused the administration of wanting to gut the program.

The second front targeted the schools themselves. Profits generated from interest charged to students were used to fund free meals, drinks, golf outings, and sailboat cruises for financial aid administrators. At Tuskegee University, Sallie Mae offered to provide free loan counseling for students and software for the financial aid office. The financial aid officer volunteered, "I have only praise for Sallie Mae. They are making sure we have what we need."

It was Sallie Mae who created "opportunity loans." Outside the federal loan program, Sallie Mae agrees to lend money to any student approved by a school. Why would Sallie Mae take on all the risk of lending to students when there is a government program that assumes the risk for them? Opportunity loans are available only if a school promises to leave the direct-loan program and push Sallie Mae's federally backed loan program to students. Colleges like opportunity funds because they keep enrollment up and tuition coming in.

Sallie Mae and others have also pushed "school as lender" schemes that generate a nice return for the schools and huge profits for the industry. Lenders make millions of dollars available to schools, which in turn lend the money to graduate students. The loans are then sold back to the lenders at a profit for the schools. In exchange, schools agree to drop out of the direct-loan program and route its undergraduate loan business exclusively to the lenders. Some argue that the arrangement is a conflict of interest, as colleges stand to gain with the more loans they approve.

Under the circumstances, can colleges be expected to do what is best for their students? Sixty-two colleges and universities have dropped out of the direct-loan program since 2000, and the list is growing. Sallie Mae says it has won over $1 billion in loan business from former direct-loan schools. The shift from direct loans to private lenders is costing American taxpayers as much as $250 million a year.

How one feels about this issue depends on what one thinks the goal of a student loan program should be. Should the goals include being a profit center for lending institutions? Or should it be to provide loans at the lowest cost to students and the taxpayer? Check out which loan program your school has, and think about this issue when that first payment on your college loan comes due.

SOURCE: Adapted from Megan Barnett, Julian E. Barnes, and Danielle Knight, "Big Money on Campus," *U.S. News and World Report,* October 27, 2003, 30–32, 35–40.

You"). Both have interests in various age minimums for activities as diverse as drinking and signing certain kinds of contracts.

Environmental Groups Environmental groups are another example of multiple-issue groups. Earth Day 1970 marked the beginning of the environmental movement in the United States. Spurred by an oil spill in California, what was to be a "teach-in" on college campuses mushroomed into a day of national environmental awareness with an estimated twenty million Americans taking part. A minority movement in the 1970s, the environmental lobby today is large and active, and its values are supported by most Americans.[78]

Some environmental groups, such as the National Audubon Society, the Sierra Club, and the Natural Resources Defense Council, have permanent offices in Washington with highly skilled professionals who carry out a full range of lobbying activities.[79] Groups such as Greenpeace, Earth First!, and the Sea Shepherds shun conventional lobbying approaches and are more confrontational. They seek a "green cultural revolution."

Local citizen groups have also organized in support of local environmental concerns such as the location of toxic or nuclear waste dumps. Citizens, skeptical of government and corporate claims that such facilities are safe, want them located elsewhere.[80]

Like other groups, the environmental movement has divisions within it. Some environmentalists do not want to compromise with business on any issues. Many groups rejected a Clinton administration proposal that would have allowed heavier-polluting utilities to purchase emission rights from less polluting ones while gradually moving toward lower pollution over time.

Others argue that the key to reducing pollution is to work with industry to find solutions and accept small steps toward a better environment. They argue that when a business is persuaded to make a small environmentally friendly change, others in the industry often follow out of fear that consumers will punish them if they don't, leading to real progress.[81]

Conservative Republicans generally oppose environmental regulations, arguing that businesses should be allowed to regulate themselves. The election of George W. Bush saw the reversal of many Clinton-era environmental regulations such as the prohibition of road building in national forests, the use of snowmobiles in national parks, and restrictions on companies mining for gold and other minerals on public lands.[82] Many of the changes have been justified on national security grounds, though this seems a stretch for many issues. In spite of the administration's national security argument to open up the Alaskan wildlife refuge to oil exploration, environmentalists opposed it, and the measure was defeated in the Senate. However, following his reelec-

tion, President Bush, with larger majorities in both the House and Senate, has indicated an interest in revisiting this issue.

Single-Issue Groups

Single-issue groups pursue noneconomic goals but are distinguished by their intense concern for a single issue and reluctance to compromise. We will illustrate with a few prominent examples.

The National Rifle Association is one example. Members are passionate in their opposition to gun control. Although a majority of Americans have supported gun control for years, the NRA has successfully lobbied Congress to prevent most gun control measures. The group has members in every congressional district that can be mobilized on behalf of the group's goals.

Antigun sentiment is growing as more and more Americans respond to increasing gun violence that touches cities, suburbs, and small towns. Demonstrations such as the Mother's Day march on Washington in 2000, at which nearly one million mothers gathered to hear speeches from celebrities and victims of gun violence, reflect the growing level of intensity among the population at large for what the marchers called sensible gun laws. Nonetheless, the antigun movement is not making much of an impact in Congress, and the NRA has a powerful ally in the Bush administration.

Fearful that the 2000 election of Democratic candidate Al Gore would mean gun control, the NRA waged an all-out effort to defeat him, pumping $15 million into the election campaign, making a major effort to register its members to vote, and training members in grassroots organizing. Many commentators attributed Gore's defeat in West Virginia, traditionally a Democratic state, to the anti–gun control vote there.

The NRA considered Bush a close ally, and he has proved them right. After he secured the Republican nomination, a high-ranking official boasted at an NRA

"If you still want to belong to an organization dedicated to killing Americans, there's always the tobacco lobby."

gathering that a Bush win would mean direct access to the Oval Office.[83] Although this was an exaggeration, the Bush Justice Department, led by Attorney General John Ashcroft, filed two briefs before the Supreme Court in cases involving gun regulation, arguing that the Second Amendment protects the right of individuals to keep and bear arms rather than a right that is tied to the nation's need to maintain an armed militia.[84] The administration's position reverses sixty years of government policy. The NRA, which featured a picture of Ashcroft on its magazine a year ago and called him "a breath of fresh air to freedom-loving gun owners," lauded the decision.[85] The Violence Policy Center, a gun control group, chided the decision, adding that the Justice Department "has shown a willingness to throw red meat at the gun lobby and put its political agenda above its institutional obligations."[86]

The NRA's latest effort is legislation prohibiting lawsuits against gunmakers who manufacture and dealers who sell guns used in crimes. Spurred on by success in suing tobacco companies, local and state governments hope to sue manufacturers and dealers to recover police and health care costs incurred as a result of gun violence.[87] It has also opposed the renewal of the decade-old ban on assault weapons, semiautomatic rifles. Possession of those weapons became legal again when Congress failed to renew the ban in 2004.

In a continuing effort, as the organization says, to keep guns in the hand of law-abiding citizens, it posted an extensive enemies list on its Web site. Among those listed were the Children's Defense Fund, the U.S. Catholic Conference, the YMCA, the Kansas City Chiefs, Hallmark Cards, Walter Cronkite, and Doug Flutie.[88]

Another example of single-interest groups is pro-choice and pro-life groups focused on abortion. The National Right to Life Committee seeks a constitutional amendment banning all abortions. Recognizing the unlikelihood of this, it has pushed for restrictions on abortion at the state level, such as laws requiring waiting periods and parental consent for minors. Many of these have been adopted. The antiabortion movement, including Right to Life, rallied around Republican efforts in Congress to ban late-term abortions (Right to Life groups call them partial-birth abortions) and to make it a separate offense to harm a fetus in a federal crime committed against a pregnant women. Both were approved by Congress and signed by the president. The late-term abortion ban was subsequently struck down by the courts because it had no provision to allow such abortions to save the life of the mother. The Bush White House vowed to continue to fight for the law.

While many in the pro-life movement have given up hope of outlawing abortion, working instead to reduce the number of abortions by more modest changes in the law,[89] the Army of God, a militant antiabortion group,

Pro-life demonstrators march past the Supreme Court on the anniversary of Roe v. Wade *which legalized abortions.*

marked the thirtieth anniversary of *Roe* v. *Wade,* the Supreme Court's 1973 decision upholding a woman's right to abortion, by celebrating the murder of Dr. Barnett Slepian, an abortion provider in Buffalo, slain in 1998. The group's Web site encouraged supporters to attend a march outside the clinic were Slepian worked to support the man who confessed to the killing.[90]

Violence against abortion doctors and clinics has declined, owing in part to a judgment against an antiabortion coalition responsible for Web postings of the names, addresses, and license plate numbers of doctors who perform abortions.[91] The Court agreed with pro-choice advocates that the action, dubbed the "Nuremberg Files," was designed to threaten and intimidate doctors and likely to lead to violence. The plaintiffs were awarded compensatory damages.[92]

Members of the National Abortion Rights Action League and Planned Parenthood are fervently committed to protecting women's right to choose. Often identified with abortion rights, Planned Parenthood also advocates for access to birth control, sex education in schools, and quality reproductive health care for women. Using the theme that Americans want abortion to be safe and legal, the group uses newspaper ads, congressional testimony, a Web site, mailings, and local educational efforts to get the message out. In April 2004, the group mobilized more than a million people to march in the nation's capital protesting attacks on women's reproductive rights.[93]

Single-issue groups have increased in recent decades. Some people view this with alarm. When groups form around highly emotional issues and are unwilling to compromise, the system can't deal with them and the

Pro-choice advocates form a human corridor to protect patients and workers entering a clinic in Buffalo, New York.

© Lynn Johnson/Aurora

extensions of Medicare and prescription drug benefits. Sometimes they want the president to make new policies through executive action or change the way current laws are enforced, as when business groups lobby the Bush administration to roll back environmental protections adopted during the Clinton administration. Sometimes groups lobby the bureaucracy to win new contracts for services, as Halliburton and other companies who wanted to do business in Iraq did. And sometimes groups turn to the courts to get new policy. Before civil rights groups could muster support in Congress in the 1960s, for example, they were able to get the courts to strike down old laws requiring segregation and, in essence, promulgate new policy. In all of these strategies, groups work to initiate some new law or action.

But sometimes groups want to prevent action rather than initiate it. For example, abortion rights groups lobby Congress and the president not to adopt new antiabortion laws. Groups favoring the status quo in enforcement of a policy might lobby administrative agencies not to change the policy, thus preserving the status quo. For example, proponents of women's equality in higher education have lobbied against weakening the rules requiring equity in support for women's and men's athletics. Or groups might file lawsuits to declare a new policy illegal or unconstitutional. For example, when pro-choice groups could not stop the passage of the ban on late-term abortions, they filed suit in court against the enforcement of that new law.

Usually it is easier to prevent new laws than to get new laws, because there are so many points in the policymaking process where new ideas can be killed. New laws can be stopped in Congress or at the presidential level, and new regulations can be killed in the bureaucracy. And if new laws are passed or policies are adopted in the bureaucracy, the courts can kill them. The checks and balances in the American system favor the status quo.

A final strategy for groups is to effect change by influencing appointments. If you can manage to get a member or supporter of your group into a key bureaucratic position or appointed to the courts, you have an ally the next time you try to influence policy.

issues continue to boil,[94] consuming time and energy of policymakers at the expense of broader issues that may be more important.

On the other hand, single-issue groups have always been part of politics.[95] These groups may even be beneficial because they represent interests that may not be well represented in Congress. Fears about single-issue groups may result from the groups' own exaggerated claims of influence, their heavy media coverage, and in the case of some, their confrontational tactics.

Strategies of Interest Groups

Interest groups use a variety of strategies. Sometimes they are interested in initiating action. For example, they might work toward getting new laws passed and signed by the president, as when AARP has lobbied for

Tactics of Interest Groups

To carry out their strategic goals, interest groups engage in a variety of tactics. Some tactics seek to influence policymakers directly, while others seek to mold public opinion and influence policymakers indirectly. Some do both. Others that have little chance of succeeding using conventional techniques sometimes turn to protest. Some interest groups form broad coalitions to maximize their influence.

Direct Lobbying Techniques

Direct lobbying involves personal encounters with a lobbyist. Some lobbyists are volunteers; others are permanent, salaried employees of the groups they represent; and others are contract lobbyists, "hired guns" who represent any individual or group willing to pay for the service. Contract lobbyists include the numerous Washington lawyers affiliated with the city's most prestigious law firms. Many have worked in government, allowing them to boast of contacts with and access to public officials to plead their clients' cases. Some lobbying is done by corporate CEOs and some by public officials themselves. The president's cabinet and advisers lobby Congress, and although one may not think of it as lobbying, members of Congress talk to and attempt to persuade their colleagues. Average citizens may occasionally visit their elected representatives and lay out their concerns.

Most law firms, corporations, and trade associations find it useful to have some lobbyists in their employ who are Republicans and some who are Democrats. This ensures access to the elected members of both parties. It also means that groups are able to continue doing business in Washington without interruption when control of government shifts from one party to another (see the box "K Street Makeover").

Making Personal Contacts

Making personal contacts in an office or informal setting is a very effective lobbying technique. Direct contact is not particularly expensive—a lobbyist is likely to be already on the payroll—and personal communication is most effective. Concerns and questions can be dealt with on the spot, and an appeal can be tailored to those concerns.

As personal contact with members of Congress or their staffs has become more difficult, some lobbyists are turning to electronic mail. Although e-mail is no substitute for a personal visit, only lobbyists with strong personal relationships developed over years can be assured of

K Street Makeover

The bipartisan complexion of the K Street corridor in Washington, home to lobbyists representing the nation's largest corporations and trade groups, may be diminishing, especially if the Republicans continue to control both the White House and Congress. Republicans are fighting interest groups who hedge their bets by employing lobbyists with links to both political parties. Republican leaders want to replace corporate lobbyists who are Democrats with Republicans. The goal is to not simply to ensure that lobbyists are Republican but to ensure that lobbyists are loyal first and foremost to the Republican Party.

The plan, dubbed the "K Street strategy," had its beginning with the Republican takeover of Congress in the mid-1990s. Shortly after conservatives under Speaker Newt Gingrich solidified their hold in the House, they turned their attention to the core of Washington lobbyists. In 1995, House Republican leader Tom DeLay compiled a list of the four hundred largest contributors to the parties. Lobbyists were summoned to his office one by one and shown their name in either the "friendly" or "unfriendly" column, the latter reserved for those who contributed to Democrats. He later told the *Washington Post,* "If you want to play in our revolution, you have to live by our rules."

Not content with strong-arming lobbyists, DeLay later met with CEOs from several large companies. He told them that Democratic lobbyists would have to go. Not unexpectedly, most, several who were Republican, reacted negatively to the "shakedown." With Clinton in the White House and treating business very well, the Republicans overreached.

However, with the election of George W. Bush in 2000, new life was breathed into the plan. With the Republicans in complete control of the government, the effort to give K Street a decidedly Republican look is working. From DeLay's staff alone, so-called graduates of the DeLay school, a dozen or more have moved to lobby and trade association positions since 2000. Moreover, the near parity in giving by corporations to the political parties during the 1990s has shifted so that now two are Republicans to every one Democrat.

The impact of this is to further solidify Republican control of the government. Is it illegal or unethical? Probably not. Democrats can lament it, but they can change it only when they regain power in one of the houses of Congress or the presidency. Meanwhile, private corporations gain more benefits and in turn provide more campaign and lobbying resources to ensure that the party remains in power.

The arrangement would make any turn-of-the-twentieth-century machine politician green with envy (see Chapter 7). Like the old machines, the party channels taxpayers' dollars and other favors to clients who kick back a portion, enabling the party to win a majority and remain in power. Long ago, we reformed the conditions that supported the party machines. But these oversight mechanisms do not work very well when one party controls all mechanisms of government.

Source: Adapted from Nicholas Confessore, "Welcome to the Machine: How the GOP Disciplined K Street and Made Bush Supreme," *Washington Monthly,* July-August 2003, 31–37.

a personal audience. For those lacking such ties, e-mail may serve as a substitute.[96]

Lobbyists know that contacting every legislator is unnecessary. Contacting key legislators—party leaders, those sitting on committees of particular interest, and staff serving those committees—is crucial.[97] Conventional wisdom suggests that only legislators who support a group's position or are known to be undecided should be contacted directly.[98] Putting undue pressure on opponents may hurt prospects for working in the future on other issues. (Other important rules that lobbyists have learned to follow are noted in the box "The Ten Commandments of Lobbying.")

Successful lobbying is based on friendship. As a former chair of the House Budget Committee put it, "The most effective lobbyists here are the ones you don't think of as lobbyists." Referring to one prominent Washington lobbyist, he said, "I don't think of him as a lobbyist. He's almost a constituent, or a friend." Barbara Boxer, then a Democratic representative from California, referring to the same gentleman, described him as "a lovely, wonderful guy. In the whole time I've known him, he's never asked me to vote for anything." At a gathering, she joked that he's almost "a member of the family."[99]

Direct personal contact was the strategy of the airline industry in seeking government aid following 9/11. Senator Peter Fitzgerald (R–Ill.), the only senator to vote against the $15 billion aid package, remarked, "The airline industry made a full-court press to convince Congress that giving them billions in taxpayer cash was the only way to save the republic."[100] Twenty-seven in-house lobbyists and several hired guns from forty-two Washington firms, including former White House aides, cabinet secretaries, retired members of Congress, and former Republican National Party Chair Haley Barbour, went to work. The CEOs and board members of several airlines also pitched in. One lobbyist remarked, "It was the most high-level surgical strike that I have ever seen."[101]

Rather than pursue the usual path of congressional lawmaking, committee hearings, and floor debate—which would have delayed action, allowing opposition to form, and undercut the effort—the airlines targeted a few congressional and administration leaders. "Their tactic was to bring all their top people to meet with top people in government and to say the sky is falling."[102] The result, as Representative George Miller (D–Calif.) put it, was that "the big dog got the bone."[103]

Providing Expertise

All groups or their lobbyists communicate information to public officials. However, some are known for their expertise and the accurate and reliable information they

"Mr. Speaker, will the gentleman from Small Firearms yield the floor to the gentleman from Big Tobacco?"

The Ten Commandments of Lobbying

I   Thou shalt speak only the truth, and speak it clearly and succinctly; on two pages and in fifteen-second sound bites.

II   Thou shalt translate the rustle of thy grassroots into letters, phone calls, and personal visits.

III Thou shalt not underestimate thy opponent, for he surely packeth a rabbit punch.

IV   Help thy friends with reelection; but in victory, dwelleth not on the power of thy PAC.

V   Thou shalt know thy issue and believe in it, but be ready to compromise; half a loaf will feed some of thy people.

VI   Runneth not out of patience, if thou cannot harvest this year, the next session may be bountiful.

VII Love thy neighbor; thou wilst need him for a coalition.

VIII Study arithmetic, that thou may count noses. If thou can count 51, rejoice. Thou shalt win in the Senate.

IX   Honor the hardworking staff, for they prepare the position papers for the members.

X   Be humble in victory, for thy bill may yet be vetoed.

SOURCE: Ernest Wittenberg and Elisabeth Wittenberg, *How to Win in Washington* (Cambridge, Mass.: Blackwell, 1989), 16.

CELEBRITIES AND INTEREST GROUPS

The link between politics and entertainment grows ever closer in the Internet age. One way that the two intersect is the use of celebrities as the public face and often chief fundraisers for particular causes. Movie, television, and sports personalities are increasingly offering their time and financial support to various causes. One popular cause is the fight against deadly diseases. Sometimes celebrities are victims of the particular disease or have lost a friend or loved one to the disease. Sometimes the celebrities have no more knowledge of the issue than anyone else, but their celebrity status is immensely helpful to the cause because it brings media and public attention to it.

Celebrities sometimes found their own interest groups, and sometimes they link up with an existing group. Celebrities support interest group activity in a variety of ways: often they are called on to testify before congressional committees, an event that immediately draws members, the press, and an audience to the hearings. Usually they support their cause by raising money and often become official spokespersons for the cause. Michael J. Fox, himself stricken with Parkinson's disease, has become a high-profile advocate for research to find its causes and cures. Though at first he kept his disability to himself, he later recognized that thanks to his visibility, he could be helpful to others as well as himself: "The time for quietly soldiering on is through." [1] Similarly, after Christopher Reeve was thrown from a horse, sustaining damage to his spinal cord causing paralysis, he dedicated his life to promoting research into spinal cord injuries. The foundation he established quickly raised more money than the American Paralysis Association had raised in the thirteen years previously. AIDS research and the plight of AIDS victims moved strongly into the public consciousness in the 1980s when celebrities ranging from Elizabeth Taylor to Magic Johnson spoke on behalf of the victims of AIDS.

Sometimes celebrities are active on behalf of their own economic interests too, and like members of other groups, they are not always in agreement. A few musicians, such as Lars Ulrich, the drummer for Metallica, testified before a congressional committee in support of the recording industry's fight against illegal downloading of music from the Internet. But a number of others, including Alanis Morissette, Courtney Love, and the Byrds' Robert McGuinn, argued against the recording industry.

1. Wolf Blitzer, "The Impact of Celebrity Fundraising," CNN, September 29, 1999, www.cnn.com/showbiz/movies/9909/29/celeb.fundraising.

---

provide. Public Citizen, founded by Ralph Nader, is an example. In recent years, it has lobbied against the erosion of government regulations dealing with clean air and water, safe drugs, food, and the workplace. It has also worked to limit corporate gifts, such as fancy vacations, to members of Congress and to enact campaign finance reform (see Chapter 9).

Lobbyists often draft legislation. A legislator may ask a lobbyist known to be an expert in an area to draft a bill, or both may work together in drafting legislation. Sometimes interest groups will take it upon themselves to draft legislation and ask a sympathetic legislator to introduce it. General Electric drafted a tax reform measure that saved it millions in taxes. In an effort to tap the flow of federal money following 9/11, drug and biotechnology companies supplied Congress with the precise legislative language required to provide them with what they wanted.[104] Biotechnology firms wanted to be absolved of any claims from injuries caused by vaccines produced to protect people from biological terrorism. Drug companies wanted the Food and Drug Administration to waive review procedures when called on to supply drugs in an emergency.

Sometimes star power can substitute for expertise (see the box "Celebrities and Interest Groups").

Testifying at Hearings

Testifying at congressional hearings establishes a group's credentials as a "player" in a policy area and communicates to the people it represents that those on the payroll in Washington are doing their job. It also provides free publicity. Testifying has its own rules and norms. A Washington lobbyist responsible for prepping witnesses to testify, asked to name the most important piece of advice he could give, cited the Boy Scouts' motto: "Be prepared." Other tips include these:

- Keep it short. No one has an hour to listen to you. Don't read your statement. Good salespeople know the product and can talk to you about it.

- Don't be arrogant. Some witnesses are short with members because they believe committee members don't understand their business. Most members of Congress don't care about your business; they are going to make a decision based on what they hear.

- Don't guess. If you don't know the answer to a question, say so and promise to supply the answer later.

- Don't be hokey, but illustrate whenever possible. It is easier to focus on a wrecked fender in a hearing room than to visualize a set of statistics.[105]

Not everything that happens at a hearing is spontaneous. A lobbyist might ask a sympathetic legislator to raise a question that the lobbyist is prepared to answer or to indicate in advance what questions will be asked.

Giving Money

Lobbyists want access to policymakers, and giving money is a way to guarantee this. A longtime financial backer of Ronald Reagan said that having a dialogue with a politician is fine, "but with a little money they hear you better."[106] A Democrat commented in a similar vein, "Who do members of Congress see? They'll certainly see the one who gives the money. It's hard to say no to someone who gives you $5,000."[107]

Groups, including businesses and unions, set up PACs to give money to political campaigns. The number of PACs has grown dramatically since the mid-1970s, along with the amount of money they contribute. (PACs and the role of money in politics are discussed in Chapter 9.)

Lobbying the Bureaucracy

The battle is not over when a bill is passed. Lobbyists must also influence bureaucrats who implement policy. Regulations outlawing sex discrimination in colleges and universities were drafted in the Department of Education with little specific direction from Congress. Although the legislation was passed in 1972, both women's rights groups and interests opposing them continue to lobby over the interpretation of the regulations, particularly with regard to equality between men's and women's athletics.

Bureaucrats are the targets of direct lobbying just like members of Congress. Ken Lay, former CEO of Enron, used the direct approach when he telephoned Curtis Hébert, appointed by President George W. Bush to chair the Federal Energy Commission, to let him know that Enron would continue to support him in his new job if he changed his views on electricity deregulation.[108] Lay also had access to the parties responsible for drafting the Bush administration's recommendation for the nation's energy policy. The final report included much of what Lay advocated, including finding ways to give the federal government, where Enron has substantial clout, more power over electricity transmission.[109]

Interest groups also influence who gets appointed to bureaucratic positions. By influencing the appointments to an agency, an industry or group can improve its prospects for favorable treatment by that agency.

Several examples illustrate the kinds of linkages involved. The auto industry opposed a number of President Clinton's nominees to head the National Highway Traffic Safety Administration. They felt the nominees were not sympathetic enough to the interests and concerns of the auto industry and too concerned with consumers and safety. Senator Don Nickles (R-Okla.), an ally of antiabortion groups, held up the nomination of Clinton's nominee to head the Food and Drug Administration until he was convinced she would not solicit a manufacturer for RU-486, an abortion pill.[110] Public Citizen and the Natural Resources Defense Council opposed President George W. Bush's choice to head the White House Office of Information and Regulatory Affairs out of concern that he would water down Clinton-era health and environmental safeguards. The nominee, a Harvard professor, promised to enforce current laws, even if he disagreed with them, and was confirmed.[111] Pharmaceutical manufacturers effectively vetoed Dr. Alastair Wood, a drug safety expert and early favorite of the Bush administration to head the Food and Drug Administration; drug company CEOs called the White House complaining that Wood was "too aggressive on drug safety issues."[112]

Litigating in Court

Like bureaucrats, judges also make policy. Although interest groups do not lobby judges the way they do legislators and bureaucrats, some achieve their goals by getting involved in cases and persuading the courts to rule in their favor. Although most groups do not litigate cases, some use it as their primary tactic, particularly those that lack influence with Congress and the executive branch.

Litigation has been a favorite strategy of civil rights organizations. Throughout the early part of the twentieth century, when Congress and the White House were unsympathetic to the rights of black Americans, civil rights groups fought segregation in the courts and won a series of victories, eventually leading to fuller integration (Chapter 15 provides more information on this issue). In more recent years, civil rights groups have used the courts to legitimize affirmative action, with a mixed, though largely positive, record of success.[113]

Several civil liberties organizations are pursuing court action challenging President Bush's holding suspected terrorists without giving them the right to consult an attorney or see outsiders and trying them in secrecy or in military tribunals.[114] The American Civil Liberties Union maintains that the president is making law when he has no constitutional power to do so; law-making is granted by the Constitution exclusively to Congress. Hence the president's actions violate the constitutionally established separation of powers.

Environmental groups and public interest lobbies have also turned to the courts. The Natural Resources Defense Council, along with Greenpeace, Physicians for Social Responsibility, and the Alaska Public Interest Research Group, filed suit against Bush's missile defense plan, asserting that it violates federal environmental laws.[115]

In addition to filing civil suits, groups can represent defendants in criminal cases or file "friend of the court" briefs, written arguments asking the court to decide a case a particular way.[116] Some groups use the courts to try to force their opponents to negotiate with them. Environmental groups frequently challenge developers who threaten the environment in order to delay the project, raise the costs incurred by the developers, and motivate them to negotiate with the environmental interests. The next time, developers may be more willing to make concessions beforehand to avoid lengthy and costly litigation.

Groups also try to influence the courts indirectly by lobbying the Senate to support or oppose judicial nominees. As we will see in Chapter 13, the appointment process is becoming increasingly politicized, with many groups fighting to make sure that new judges will be sympathetic to their causes or at least neutral.

Indirect Lobbying Techniques: Going Public

Traditionally, lobbyists for the most part employed direct lobbying techniques—providing information, advice, and occasionally pressure. More recently, interest groups have been going public—mobilizing their activists and molding and activating public opinion. A study of 175 lobbying groups found that most were doing more lobbying, but the largest increases were in going public,[117] including mobilizing the grass roots to contact policymakers and taking their case to the media. Protest is another form of going public used by groups.

Mobilizing the Grass Roots

The constituency of an interest group—a group's members, those whom the group serves, friends and allies of the group, or simply those who can be mobilized whether or not they have a connection to the group —can help in promoting the cause or voting for a candidate. The National Rifle Association is effective in mobilizing its members. The NRA, like many mass-membership organizations, can generate thousands of letters or calls to members of Congress in a short period

of time. Calls from irate NRA members led one senator to remark, "I'd rather be a deer in hunting season than run afoul of the NRA crowd."[118]

Conservative Christian minister Jerry Falwell activated his "gospel grapevine" to flood the White House and Congress in opposition to President Clinton's plan to lift the ban on homosexuals in the military. Warning of a new radical homosexual rights agenda, Falwell urged viewers of his *Old Time Gospel Hour* to call and register their opinions.

Senator John McCain (R-Ariz.), a sponsor of antitobacco legislation, was swamped with letters from members of the National Smokers Alliance, an organization funded by the tobacco companies.[119] Senator Tom Harkin (D-Iowa) was surprised to receive hundreds of letters opposing his antitobacco position, strangely enough from only one small region in his state. The mystery was solved when Harkin learned that all the letters came from employees of a Kraft food plant, owned by RJ Reynolds, the tobacco company.[120]

Appeals to write or phone policymakers often exaggerate the severity of the concern and the strength of the opposition. To move members, groups suggest that a monstrous adversary or a catastrophic defeat is confronting group members.

How to Mobilize To be effective, letters and phone calls must appear spontaneous and sincere. Groups often provide sample letters to aid constituents, but these are not as convincing as those written in a constituent's own words. Campaigns producing postcards with pre-printed messages or facilitating online petitions or identical messages are seldom effective. While members of Congress often enlist organizations to mobilize constituents in support of legislation, many members are turned off by the flood of mail and calls they receive. As one lobbyist put it, "Members of Congress hate it when you call in the dogs."[121]

Grassroots lobbying was the hallmark of the successful effort to defeat President Clinton's health care reform proposal in 1994. Cigarette companies, drug manufacturers, health insurance agents, physicians, and hospital administrators mobilized their employees, clients, and friends to contact their representatives urging them to kill the measure.[122] Pressure of this kind can provide members of Congress in both parties with a reason to buck the president. As one lobbyist put it, "If done well, a member of Congress summoned to the Oval Office can turn to the president and say, 'I can't go with you on this, Mr. President, because I promised the people in my district.'"[123]

The nature of grassroots lobbying has changed in the past decade. Almost all groups, particularly those with resources, use it as part of an overall lobbying strategy.

With e-mail and faxes, it is easy to inform supporters to communicate with elected officials. Many groups have Web sites that not only provide information but also invite browsers to send e-mail messages to public officials. Some sites provide the message; others suggest talking points. Use of the Web saves time and money in recruiting letter writers and checking on follow through. Because e-mails and letters often come from constituents, members of Congress pay some attention to them. Of course, a flood of e-mails with basically the same message is no more persuasive than mass postcard campaigns.

Third-Party Involvement Dozens of public relations firms assist groups in mobilizing their constituency, if there is one, or manufacturing the appearance of one, if there is not. Washington firms in the business of producing "citizen movements" on demand advertise specialties such as "development of third-party allies," "grassroots mobilization and recruitment," and "grasstops lobbying."[124] ("Grasstops lobbying" involves identifying the person or persons that a member of Congress cannot say no to—a chief donor, campaign manager, political counselor, or adviser—and persuading them to persuade the member to go along with the group.) In many respects, grassroots lobbying resembles a presidential election campaign, involving a number of specialists: a pollster to assess citizen opinion, a media consultant to produce and test-market television ads, a communications adviser to enlist journalists to write stories and editorials, think tanks to provide supporting research, a recruiter to enlist local and community leaders, a Washington lobbyist to push the idea with members of Congress, and a legal expert to draft legislation. The grassroots industry spends nearly $1 billion a year putting a "public look" on private interests.[125]

The strategy of massaging constituents and marshaling public opinion has become the method of choice for business lobbies and corporations. Relying on influential lobbyists with connections to party leaders and influential congressional committee chairs no longer works. Power is too dispersed. Today, you "send in the armies, ships, tanks, aircraft, infantry, Democrats and Republicans, grassroots specialists, and people with special relationships to members."[126]

Technology and Mobilization The Internet is becoming indispensable in attempts to activate individuals with no connection other than their position for or against a candidate or a cause. MoveOn.org, a left-leaning Web site with an e-mail list of 1.8 million, can with the click of a mouse send hundreds of thousands of messages hurtling toward Washington. Citizens opposed

AP/ Wide World Photos

The founders of MoveOn.org, Wes Boyd and Joan Blakes, run the organization from their Berkeley California home.

to electronic voting were invited to sign a petition to the president and members of Congress admonishing them to require a paper ballot backup in the 2004 election. Citizens could sign a petition demanding that Congress censure the president for lying to the American people about Iraq's weapons of mass destruction. In the 2004 campaign, the founders of MoveOn.org, husband and wife Wes Boyd and Joan Blades, electronically solicited millions of dollars to air anti-Bush commercials in key battleground states.[127]

Another example of what some refer to as Internet democracy was the so-called Virtual March on Washington, staged by Win without War, a coalition of antiwar groups including MoveOn.org. On February 25, 2003, hundreds of thousand of antiwar messages flooded congressional offices, their timing coordinated electronically to avoid tying up the telephone lines.[128]

Grass Roots and Democracy Does grassroots lobbying enhance democracy or undermine it? Insiders are convinced that their efforts mobilize real people with genuine and sincere interests, whether they are members, employees, or simply isolated individuals identified by polling and research. Senator Carl Levin (D-Mich.) has a different view. "When public relations firms are paid to generate calls, it creates a distorted picture of public opinion. When a member gets 50 phone calls, what he doesn't know is that 950 other people were contacted and said no way."[129]

Mobilizing the Vote Groups also work hard to get their members and supporters to the polls on election day. Electing a sympathetic member to Congress, not to mention a president, is more effective in the long run than relying on a continuing effort to mobilize constituents. Many groups worked hard to get their supporters to the polls in the recent presidential elections because of the anticipated closeness of the results.[130] In 2000, labor unions in closely contested states made an effort to reach all of their current and retired members by phone or through the mail. The AFL-CIO had a Web site capable of producing fliers comparing the candidates on the major issues. The flier, with a personal message from the local union official, could be printed and mailed within a day. At get-out-the-vote rallies, NRA president Charlton Heston called the 2000 election "the most important since the Civil War." If Gore won, he continued, his Supreme Court will "hammer your gun rights into oblivion." As one journalist concluded, in an election where there are no great crises or burning issues, how do you get people to vote? The answer, "Scare the hell out of them."[131]

Molding Public and Elite Opinion

Groups use public relations techniques to shape public opinion as well as the opinions of policymakers. Ads in newspapers and magazines and on radio and television supply information, foster an image, or promote a particular policy; sometimes they do all three. Tobacco companies spent a record $40 million to defeat anti-tobacco legislation in 1998. Lockheed Martin, a defense contractor, tried to persuade Congress to purchase the company's F-22 fighter jet with an ad appearing in several publications widely read by members. The ad featured a postcard on a black background. On the card, dated June 18, 2007, a wife and mother writes home telling her husband and son not to worry because "those F-22s upstairs" are "ruling the sky." Across the bottom of the ad is the caption "One day in the future, someone you love may be depending on the F-22." According to the company, the ad was an attempt to give a human dimension to an issue that is often shrouded in Pentagon jargon and mind-numbing statistics. But Senator Dale Bumpers (D-Ark.) accused the firm of pandering to the emotions of lawmakers.[132]

On occasion, groups will fabricate information. ExxonMobil is alleged to have distorted the debate on global warming by generating bogus reports and funding scientists who supported the corporation's point of view but who were not experts in the field of climatology and whose research was not reviewed by scholars in the field.[133] Conclusions by the Environmental Protection Agency in June 2002 that global warming is a significant problem discredit ExxonMobil's view that it is not. Of course, by themselves ads are unlikely to move policymakers to action or shift public opinion dramatically in the short run. They are most effective in combination with other tactics. The EPA's experts and recommendations were undermined by the Bush administration's rejection of their conclusions.

Groups may stage events such as rallies or pickets to attract media coverage to their cause. During the apartheid era in South Africa (when blacks and whites were strictly segregated), opponents of segregation won considerable attention by organizing picketing and protesting outside the South African embassy in Washington, D.C. The action was especially effective because members of Congress, community leaders, and other celebrities participated. Arrests of members of Congress for trespassing kept the issue in the spotlight.

Framing the terms of a debate can be crucial in winning public support. People and groups arguing in favor of tort reform (limiting damages the courts can award to individuals injured in auto accidents, air disasters, unsuccessful surgeries, and other mishaps) focus on the few outrageously large settlements for seemingly minor injuries. Those arguing against reform focus on the poor widows left penniless after being permanently injured by the careless and willful behavior of large corporations.[134]

Hoping to influence public opinion, interest groups also rate members of Congress. Groups choose votes crucial to their concerns or votes reflecting a liberal or conservative orientation. They count how many times a member has voted with the group's interests, calculate a score, and publicize it to their members. The ultimate objective is to defeat candidates who consistently vote against them. Such ratings have little impact unless the group uses other tactics to target opponents.

Protest and Civil Disobedience

Groups that lack access or hold unpopular positions can protest. In the fall of 1999, representatives from more than five hundred groups joined forces in protesting the World Trade Organization (WTO) at its meeting in Seattle.[135] The WTO represents 135 countries with authority to force countries to change their labor, environmental, and human rights laws that restrict trade among countries. In addition to high-profile labor unions and environmental groups, the demonstration drew less well-known organizations such as the Ruckus Society, a group that provides training in nonviolent protest, and the Raging Grannies, a human rights organization. The protesters accused the WTO of responding more to the profit needs of international corporations than to the needs of the environment, working men and women, the poor, and native peoples. The Sierra Club and the Steelworkers held a Seattle tea party with the slogan "No Globalization without Representation." Following their Boston forebears, they tossed steel imported from China, hormone-treated beef, and other goods they view as tainted by WTO decisions into the sea.[136] Taking a page from Vietnam War protests, the groups staged a number of activities, including teach-ins, concerts, and mock trials of corporations. Hundreds of protesters formed a human chain around Seattle's exhibition center, the site of the meeting, demanding that the WTO cancel the debt owed by the world's poorest nations. The protest ended in violence, and several hundred protesters were arrested and jailed.

Peaceful but illegal protest activity, in which those involved allow themselves to be arrested and punished, is known as **civil disobedience.** Greenpeace, the environmental and peace group, practices civil disobedience. The organization got its start in 1971 when a group of environmentalists and peace activists sent two boats named *Greenpeace* to Amchitka Island near Alaska to protest a U.S. underground nuclear weapon test. Although the boats failed to reach the island, the publicity generated by the affair led Washington to cancel the test.

Since its founding, Greenpeace has staged a number of protests. Thirteen activists protested the dumping of toxic wastes by lowering themselves from a New York bridge, preventing barges from carrying wastes out to sea. Members placed themselves in the path of a harpoon to protect endangered whales. Others parachuted over coal-powered plants to protest acid rain. More recently, Greenpeace has moved away from dramatic confrontations, although four protesters chained themselves to a Canadian cargo ship in 1999, maintaining that it was loaded with paper from rain forest trees, and activists from seven countries delayed a U.S. missile defense test by rafting into an area beneath the rocket's flight path.[137] The goal of such encounters is to generate publicity in the hope of energizing the general public.

Once protest organizations get a hearing—that is, once they find someone in government who is willing to listen—they often shift to an inside strategy, working with those in power rather than against them. They drop the "yelling and screaming" for more conventional lobbying techniques. Moreover, it is increasingly difficult to draw media coverage to another story of protesters willing to risk life and limb in the interest of preserving or preventing something, and it is publicity that makes such activities effective. The first time, protests are front-page news. The second time, they are buried inside, if they are covered at all.

Benefits and Costs of Protest

Protest can generate awareness of an issue, but to be successful, it must influence mass or elite opinion. Often it is the first step in a long struggle that takes years to resolve. Sometimes it leads to hostility against the protesters. Antiwar protest by college students in the 1960s and 1970s angered not only government officials, who targeted the leaders for harassment, but also many ordinary citizens. In the early years of the women's movement, the media derisively labeled many female protesters "bra burners," annoyed by their insistence that the undergarment was an unnecessary accoutrement imposed on women by men.

Extended protests are difficult because they demand great skill on the part of leaders and sacrifices from followers. Continued participation, essential to success, robs those involved of a normal life. It can mean jail, physical harm, or even death and requires discipline to refrain from violence, even as leaders and followers are targeted for violence.

The civil rights movement provides the best example

Greenpeace activists hurl plastic bottles toward the Coca-Cola plant in Buenos Aires, Argentina to protest the company's disposal of its non-biodegradable bottles.

AP/ Wide World Photos

of successful protest in twentieth-century America. By peacefully demonstrating against legalized segregation in the South, black and some white protesters drew the nation's attention to the discrepancy between the American values of equality and democracy and the southern laws that kept blacks separated from whites in every aspect of life. Protesters used tactics such as sit-ins, marches, and boycotts. Confrontations with authorities often won protesters national attention and public support, which eventually led to change. (See the box "Organizing Protest: The Montgomery Bus Boycott.")

All tactics can be effective; however, some lend themselves to particular groups more than others. Business groups with great financial resources can pay skillful lobbyists and donate to political campaigns. Labor unions with large memberships can help candidates canvass and get out the vote. Some groups can enlist the public because of the "goodness" of their cause. Where individuals and groups are excluded and prevented from participating, they can protest.

Violence

Occasionally groups turn to violence to achieve their goals. In the late nineteenth century and well into the twentieth, the Ku Klux Klan targeted African Americans and their supporters for death and destruction. In the early twentieth century, company-financed strikebreakers attacked and killed workers seeking to unionize. In the period following the legalization of abortion, "pro-life" antiabortion activists burned abortion clinics and murdered abortion providers. In 1995, right-wing militants blew up the Alfred P. Murrah Federal Building in Oklahoma City, killing 168. Violence is the tactic of people with extreme views who are willing to take extreme measures to achieve what are often personal rather than group goals.

Building Coalitions

Coalitions consist of two or more interest groups that have joined together to achieve a particular goal. Coalitions can be large or small, and they can focus on many issues or just one. Groups can join together to use direct tactics or indirect, going-public ones.

For example, Kingsford charcoal, 7-Eleven stores, and several amusement parks and lawn and garden centers joined the Daylight Saving Time Coalition to lobby Congress to extend daylight saving time. All wanted additional evening daylight hours for the users of their products and services: Kingsford for barbecuers, 7-Eleven stores for those who prefer to drive or stop for

Culver Pictures

In 1920, a horse-drawn cart loaded with dynamite exploded on Wall Street, killing forty people. No one was ever charged with the murders, which were thought to be the work of anarchists. Though anarchists were against capitalism and big business, most of the victims were clerks and secretaries, not Wall Street bankers.

a snack during daylight, amusement parks to attract customers who will stay longer, and lawn and garden centers so that people would have more time to work in their yards. Extending the daylight hours would mean higher profits for all.

Large coalitions formed around the health care reform issue during Clinton's administration. The AFL-CIO, American Airlines, Chrysler Corporation, the American College of Physicians, the League of Women Voters, and others supported health care reform, while the American Conservative Union, United Seniors Union, Citizens for a Sound Economy, and National Taxpayers Union joined a coalition against it.[138] Following the 2000 election, a coalition of corporations and business groups pressured Congress and the White House to rescind regulations issued by the Clinton administration to protect workers from repetitive-motion injuries in the workplace.[139]

Large coalitions demonstrate broad support for an issue, important in persuading lawmakers. They can also

The 1955 Montgomery, Alabama, bus boycott was the first successful civil rights protest, and it brought its twenty-six-year-old leader, Dr. Martin Luther King, Jr., to national prominence. Montgomery, like most southern cities, required blacks to sit in the back of public buses, reserving the front seats for whites. The dividing line between the two was a "no man's land" where blacks could sit if there were no whites. If whites needed the seats, blacks had to give them up and move to the back.

One afternoon, Rosa Parks, a seamstress at a local department store and a leader in the local chapter of the National Association for the Advancement of Colored People (NAACP), boarded the bus to go home. The bus was filled, and when a white man boarded, the driver called on the four blacks behind the whites to move to the back. Three got up and moved, but Parks, tired from a long day and of the injustice of always having to move for white people, said she did not have to move because she was in "no man's land." Under a law that gave him the authority to enforce segregation, the bus driver arrested her.

That evening, a group of black women professors at the black state college in Montgomery, led by Jo Ann Robinson, drafted a letter of protest. They called on blacks to stay off the buses on Monday to protest the arrest. They worked through the night making thirty-five thousand copies of their letter to distribute to Montgomery's black residents. Fearful for their jobs and concerned that the state would cut funds to the black college if it became

Rosa Parks is fingerprinted in Montgomery, Alabama, after her arrest for refusing to give up her seat on the bus to a white man. Her refusal triggered a boycott of the city buses by blacks that became the first successful civil disobedience action in the civil rights movement and made Parks a hero to black and white Americans alike.

known that they had used state facilities to produce the letter, they worked quickly and quietly.

The following day, black leaders met and agreed to the boycott. More leaflets were drafted calling on blacks to stay off the buses on Monday. On Sunday, black ministers encouraged their members to support the boycott, and on

take advantage of each group's strength. One group may be adept at grassroots lobbying, another at public relations. One may have lots of money, another a lot of members.[140]

The growth of coalitions in recent years reflects a number of changes in policymaking.[141] Issues are increasingly complex, and legislation to deal with them typically affects a variety of interests, making coalitions an effective strategy. Changes in technology make it easier for groups to communicate with one another. The number of interest groups is also larger than it used to be, especially the number of public interest groups. Many such groups have limited resources, and coalitions help them stretch their lobbying efforts. Some "black hat" business groups with image problems seek to associate themselves with "white hat" organizations ranging from labor unions to consumer groups.[142] Coalitions

help political parties garner majorities at the various stages of the legislative process.

Coalitions vary in their duration—some are short term, while others are permanent. Coalitions involved with the health care issue remained intact only until the Clinton plan was dead. Coalitions supporting and opposing NAFTA ceased to exist when Congress approved the measure.

On the other hand, the Leadership Conference on Civil Rights is a permanent coalition of 180 civil rights, ethnic, religious, and other groups. They work to pass civil rights legislation, fight the watering down of civil rights laws, and ensure that judicial appointees are in favor of civil rights. Unlike short-term coalitions, permanent ones need to be sensitive to how their actions affect coalition members. Some issues may be avoided because they are likely to drive some coalition members

Monday, 90 percent of the blacks walked to work, rode in black-owned taxis, or shared rides in private cars. The boycott inspired confidence and pride in the black community and signaled a subtle change in the opinions of blacks toward race relations. This was obvious when, as nervous white police looked on, hundreds of blacks jammed the courthouse to see that Rosa Parks was safely released after her formal conviction. And it was obvious later that evening at a mass rally when Martin Luther King, J., cried out, "There comes a time when people get tired of being trampled over by the iron feet of oppression. There comes a time when people get tired of being pushed out of the glittering sunlight of life's July, and left standing amidst the piercing chill of an Alpine November." After noting that the glory of American democracy is the right to protest, King appealed to the strong religious faith of the crowd: "If we are wrong, God Almighty is wrong. . . . If we are wrong, Jesus of Nazareth was merely a utopian dreamer. . . . If we are wrong, justice is a lie." These words and this speech established King as a charismatic leader for the civil rights movement.

In light of its initial success, the boycott was extended. Each successive day was a trial for blacks and their leaders. Thousands had to find a way to get to work, and leaders struggled to keep a massive carpool going. However, each evening's rally built up morale for the next day's boycott. Later the rallies became prayer services, as the black community prayed for strength to keep on walking, for courage to remain nonviolent, and for divine guidance for their oppressors.

The city bus line was losing money. City leaders urged more whites to ride the buses to make up lost revenue, but few did. Recognizing that the boycott could not go on forever, black leaders agreed to end it if the rules regarding the seating of blacks in "no man's land" were relaxed. Erroneously thinking that they were on the verge of breaking the boycott, the city leaders refused. Police began to harass carpoolers and to issue bogus tickets for trumped-up violations. Then the city leaders issued an ultimatum: Settle or face arrest. A white grand jury indicted more than one hundred boycott leaders for the alleged crime of organizing the protest. In the spirit of nonviolence, the black leaders, including King, surrendered.

The decision to arrest the leaders proved to be the turning point of the boycott. The editor of the local white paper said it was "the dumbest act that has ever been done in Montgomery." With the mass arrests, the boycott finally received national attention. Reporters from all over the world streamed into Montgomery to cover the story. The publicity brought public and financial support. The arrests caused the boycott to become a national event and made its leader, Martin Luther King, Jr., a national figure. A year later, the U.S. Supreme Court declared Alabama's local and state laws requiring segregation in buses unconstitutional, and only after the city complied with the Court's order was the boycott ended.

SOURCES: Taylor Branch, *Parting the Waters: America in the King Years* (New York: Simon & Schuster, 1988), ch. 4 and 5; Juan Williams, *Eyes on the Prize* (New York: Viking, 1987).

away. When, however, a coalition like the Leadership Conference is united, it can be formidable.

Coordination among PACs in channeling money to political candidates is a form of coalition. Business PACs, for example, take their lead from the Business Industry Political Action Committee (BIPAC). Information is shared on candidates' issue positions, likelihood of winning, and need for funding.

Success of Interest Groups

Although no interest group gets everything it wants from government, some are more successful than others. Politics is not a game of chance, where luck determines winners and losers. Knowing what to do and how to do it—strategy and tactics—is important, as are resources, competition, and goals.

Resources

Although large size does not guarantee success, large groups have advantages. They can get attention by claiming to speak for large numbers of people or by threatening to mobilize large numbers of people if their demands are ignored. Part of the airlines' success in securing a government bailout was the thousands of employees spread throughout the nation who were threatened with layoffs.

Location is also important. Because organized labor is concentrated in the Northeast, it has less influence in other parts of the country, diminishing its influence in Congress. The Chamber of Commerce, on the other hand, has members throughout the country, enhancing its influence.

Well-educated members are an advantage, as they

are more likely than those with less education to communicate with public officials and contribute to lobbying efforts.

Group cohesion and intensity are also advantages. Public officials are unlikely to respond to a group if it cannot agree on what it wants or if it does not appear to feel very strongly about its position. In recent years, the NAACP has suffered from disagreements among its leaders. Some members believe that the organization should be more accommodating and work within the system. Others feel that it should be more aggressive and confrontational. Some are pushing to work with more radical groups like Louis Farrakhan's Nation of Islam, while others want to limit the group to working with moderate and mainstream civil rights organizations. Conflicts such as these undermine cohesion and diminish the likelihood of success.

A large market share is another advantage. **Market share** refers to the number of members in a group compared to its potential membership. For years, the American Medical Association enrolled a substantial majority (70 percent or more) of the nation's doctors and wielded a lot of clout. As its market share declined, so did its influence.

Money is important. It is the key to mounting a complete lobbying effort, retaining skilled lobbyists, gaining access to elected officials through campaign contributions, purchasing advertising, and mobilizing the grass roots through mailings and other contact.

Knowledge is a major resource. Policy experts are more apt to get the attention of public officials. Knowing how things get done in Washington is also important, which is why many groups employ former members of Congress and people who held positions in the executive branch as lobbyists.

Few members of Congress return to their roots once their political careers are over. Most move into high-paying positions with the dozens of law firms in Washington that lobby the government. When Bob Dole resigned from the Senate in 1995 to run for president, he indicated that if he lost the presidency, he would have no place to go but back to his hometown of Russell, Kansas. If he had done that, he would have been quite unusual. Indeed, Dole went to work for a firm that includes former senator and treasury secretary Lloyd Bentsen and former Senate majority leader George Mitchell. The firm refers to Dole and the others as our "rock stars." Dole's job is to "make rain," which means recruiting clients who will bring in millions of dollars for his firm's 168 other lawyers and lobbyists.[143]

Being key to the administration's goals is also a resource that can be used successfully. After 9/11, many groups sought to position themselves as important to fighting terrorism, even though their relevance was remote at best.

Finally, public image is important. A negative public image often troubles new, change-oriented groups, such as the animal rights movement. Many of the country's traditional interest groups, big business, and organized labor also suffer from a poor image, being viewed as too powerful and self-serving. A poll revealed that only 37 percent of Americans trusted union leaders to tell the truth and 43 percent trusted business leaders to do so—and this poll was taken before the stream of revelations about corporate misdeeds in spring 2002.[144]

Few groups are blessed with all resources, but the more resources a group has, the better its chances of getting what it wants from the government.

Competition and Goals

Success also depends on group competition and goals. Whether in organized athletics, chess tournaments, or politics, many people are successful because they faced weak opponents. Supporters of gun control have public opinion on their side, but their main lobbying group, the National Council to Control Handguns, has a membership and budget that are only a fraction of the NRA's. Used-car dealers successfully lobbied against the "lemon law," which would have required them to tell customers of any defects in cars. Few lobbyists represented the other side. Such mismatches often occur on highly technical issues where one side has more expertise or the public has little interest (or both). Some corporations have no opponents at all in lobbying for government contracts, regulatory waivers, and government subsidies.[145] Such benefits cost taxpayers billions of dollars, but they are never mobilized in opposition. The accountancy profession's opposition to regulations that would have made corporations' financial dealings more transparent had few opponents until Enron's financial dishonesty and auditor Arthur Andersen's complicity in it were revealed.

When a group competes with other groups of nearly equal resources, the outcome is often a compromise or a stalemate. The Clean Air Act was not rewritten for years because the auto industry, which wanted a weaker law, and the environmental lobby, which wanted a tougher one, were about equal in strength. The increased clout of environmental forces finally led to a strengthening of the law in 1990.

Groups that work to preserve the status quo are generally more successful than groups promoting change; it is usually easier to prevent government action than to bring it about. Separation of powers among the Congress, executive branch, and the courts; checks and balances between and among the branches; and division of authority between the states and national government provide interest groups with numerous points in the political process to exercise influence. Groups wishing to change policy have to persuade officials throughout the political process to go along; groups opposed to change only have to persuade officials at one point in the process. Groups promoting change must win over the House, Senate, White House, bureaucracy, and courts; groups against change need convince only one of them.

Groups are more likely to be successful in securing very narrow and specific benefits than they are in promoting broad policy changes. For example, corporations are concerned with broad policy issues, but they are more likely to be successful in obtaining exemptions from major policy initiatives than they are in winning or losing on the policy itself. The tax code is riddled with exemptions for specific corporations; the beneficiaries are rarely identified by name. The 1986 changes in the tax code contained an exemption for Phillips Petroleum, identified in the bill as a "corporation incorporated on June 13, 1917, which has its principal place of business in Bartlesville, Oklahoma."[146] Phillips was not concerned about the basic tax changes because it would not be affected by them. Such exemptions are unlikely to receive media attention or become controversial. In this way, politicians are able to satisfy a major interest group without risking hostile public reaction.

Conclusion: Do Interest Groups Help Make Government Responsive?

Indeed they do. The nation is simply too large and diverse to expect that citizens and their myriad concerns will be represented by elected officials alone. Interest groups represent the views and opinions of members, constituents, clients, and individuals who can be mobilized on behalf of an issue—or some combination thereof—and communicate them to elected officials.

However, interest groups do not represent all interests or all interests equally. In 1960, E. E. Schattschneider described the pressure system, the totality of interest groups in Washington, as small in terms of members and biased toward business and the wealthy. By his count, no more than fifteen hundred groups existed, and more than 50 percent represented either corporations or trade or business associations.[147] Few groups represented consumers, taxpayers, the environment, women, or minorities.

Though environmental, women's, and consumer groups are more powerful than in 1960, labor unions are considerably less powerful. Business interests still dominate the pressure system, and the imbalance between business and nonbusiness interests is greater today than it was in 1960. Nearly two-thirds of the groups in Washington at last count represented either corporations or trade associations. Groups representing nonbusiness interests were less than 10 percent and were only 5 percent of those that lobby. Labor traditionally formed a strong, albeit not equal, counterbalance to business, but the organizational strength and clout of labor has declined, as we have noted. Moreover, the Democratic Party, also traditionally aligned with labor, has shifted its policies somewhat as it seeks to appeal to the big donors who finance its campaigns and the middle-class voters who are now its core constituency.

For those who argue that America is a pluralist society where all interests are represented, Schattschneider's observation from 1960 remains valid today: "The flaw in the pluralist heaven is that the angelic chorus sings with an upper class accent."[148]

Another political analyst has commented that "more

and more of the weight of influence in Washington comes from interest groups, not voters."[149] And interest groups by and large reflect the interests of business.

How is it that interest groups have greater influence in Washington than voters? After all, America is a democracy, and elected officials have to stand for election. Voters determine who wins. One answer is the growing and continuing disparity in wealth that allows those with money to provide candidates of both political parties greater and greater resources. Those resources enable officeholders to stay in power and, more important, to define the agenda—the issues that become the focus of attention. Consequently, average people increasingly believe that the political arena does not deliver much for them.[150]

This is not to say that working- and middle-class Americans, or at least some of them, do not benefit from policies favoring the interests of business. Business provides jobs. However, a system in which business interests must compete on a more equal basis with the interests of labor and other nonbusiness groups is likely to be more sensitive to the needs of average men and women, to consumers, and to all of us who share a common environment.

How can we preserve the constitutional rights of interest groups to form and petition government and still keep government responsive to the needs of citizens? Recognizing and correcting imbalances in the political power of interests in society is not simple or easy. One would not expect interests currently enjoying an advantage to give it up. Reformers have for decades battled to limit financial contributions of interest groups to candidates (a topic we will discuss in greater detail in Chapter 9). None have been very effective in restoring balance to American politics.

AARP Backs the Bush Administration's Prescription Drug Plan for Seniors

CEO Bill Novelli and his AARP supported the Bush prescription drug proposal. Not only did the organization support the initiative, it committed $7 million in advertising to promote it.[151] In an interview, Novelli said, "While not a perfect bill, America's seniors cannot wait for perfect." He acknowledged that the Bush plan was a beginning, which AARP would work to improve in the future.[152]

AARP's members reacted swiftly, strongly, and negatively. Said one, "This is the biggest sellout of any organization that purports to represent seniors." Another remarked, "I just canceled my membership a little while ago. I'm sure thousands more will be doing the same."[153] Nearly all the calls received by the organization were negative. Seemingly surprised by the reaction of the members, Novelli admitted, "We're catching hell for it."[154]

Only 18 percent of AARP members agreed with the decision, and an estimated sixty thousand dropped their membership because of it.[155] Of course, sixty thousand resignations in an organization of 45 million is not a major hit, but Novelli mourned the loss. "We work hard to recruit and retain members. It hurts."[156] The organization hurried to get on the right side of its membership by joining with Democrats in Congress to support the importation of cheaper drugs from Canada.[157]

Opponents of the prescription drug plan charged AARP with supporting a bill that will make seniors worse off in the long run. Many questioned Novelli's motives and pointed to his ties with Newt Gingrich.[158] Gingrich had argued that Medicare should "wither on the vine." When asked if he agreed, Novelli's response was, "We at AARP have no intention of letting Medicare wither."[159] However, Novelli has staffed the organization with former Republican operatives supportive of market solutions to health care issues, solutions out of favor with the AARP membership but in tune with Gingrich Republicans.

Others accused him of putting profit ahead of the health care of AARP members. Even though the organization is likely to reap significant financial gain as it markets drugs to members, Novelli contended that there is no connection between the products AARP sells and the policy positions it endorses.[160]

Novelli argued that the decision was made in part in recognition of the fact that many of AARP's members and potential members are younger baby boomers.[161] He and his board made the calculation that the baby boom generation would be supportive of this partial measure, even though the older constituents were very much in opposition.

Novelli's choice, whatever the motives, weakened AARP by taking a position counter to the vast majority of its members. Mass organizations can do this, because in the short run, leaders are not very accountable to members. But if AARP is to have clout with the elected officials it is trying to influence, it needs to show that it is acting on behalf of members who are ready to follow its lead, whether in support or opposition to policies and public officials. If leaders become isolated from followers, much of the clout of the organization will disappear.

Novelli may have decided that AARP needed to establish a working relationship with the Republicans and that supporting the bill was one way to do it. Indeed, the House leadership crowed about its support from AARP, and Gingrich argued that now the Republicans could appeal to the elderly as "never before."[162]

AP/Wide World Photos

An AARP member burns her membership card to protest AARP's endorsement of the Bush administration's prescription drug plan.

Key Terms

interest groups

lobbying

political action committees (PACs)

private interest groups

public interest groups

single-issue groups

civil disobedience

coalitions

market share

Further Reading

Jeffrey H. Birnbaum, *The Lobbyists: How Influence Peddlers Get Their Way in Washington* (New York: Times Books, 1993). Birnbaum presents an insightful study of lobbyists' activities surrounding major issues considered by Congress in the 1989–1990 session.

Osha Gray Davidson, *The NRA and the Battle for Gun Control* (Ames: University of Iowa Press, 1998). How the battles over gun control are fought in Congress becomes clear in this useful account.

Katherine Neckerman, ed., *Social Inequality* (New York: Russell Sage Foundation, 2004). This book of readings addresses the causes and consequences of income inequality in the United States.

MoveOn.org, *Fifty Ways to Love Your Country: How to Find Your Political Voice and Be a Catalyst for Change* (Makawao, Hawaii: Inner Ocean, 2004). MoveOn.org is a citizen's group dedicated to empowering the average person. Though the tips in the book are mostly written by liberal activists, they are just as relevant to conservatives looking to get involved in their community and society.

Michael Pertschuk, *Giant Killers* (New York: Norton, 1986). Low-budget lobbies can sometimes defeat the big guys through superior organization, tactics, and luck.

E. E. Schattschneider, *The Semi-Sovereign People* (New York: Holt, 1975). This classical work explains how interest group politics benefit business and corporate interests by limiting the involvement of citizens in the political process.

For Viewing

This is an eclectic group of films showing in some cases groups at work and in other cases the conditions that gave rise to group advocacy.

Bowling for Columbine (2002) Michael Moore asks provocative questions about the causes of gun violence in American society.

The Children's Hour (1962) This film is dated but still interesting for showing the stigma faced by gays and lesbians in that era and the inability of people to discuss the issue of homosexuality publicly.

Eyes on the Prize (1987, 1990) This acclaimed fourteen-part documentary on the civil rights movement was originally presented as two series broadcast on PBS.

The Murder of Emmett Till (2003) The murder of a fourteen-year-old black boy in Mississippi in 1954 won national attention and was one of the sparks that ignited the modern civil rights movement.

Norma Rae (1979) A woman faces a dangerous uphill battle promoting unionization in the workplace.

On the Waterfront (1954) The hero of this award-winning film (Marlon Brando) fights corruption in the longshoreman's union in the 1950s.

Salt of the Earth (1954) Based on a true event, this film portrays the struggle of Mexican American workers striving for parity with white workers in a zinc-mining company. The film was banned by Congress for its "leftist" sympathies in a time of intense antiCommunism.

Stonewall (1995) This film is a partly fictional account of the Stonewall raids that launched the gay rights movement.

 Electronic Resources

www.csuchico.edu/~kcfount
This Web site lists interest groups that lobby in Washington, arranged by the focus of the group (religion, older Americans, tax reform, women, and so on) and with an indication of each group's prominence.

www.atr.org/pdffiles/021004K–Street_trade.pdf
This Web site reports the results of the K Street Project (many interest groups have headquarters on or near K Street in Washington, D.C.) and identifies numerous lobbies and lobbyists along with their party affiliation, Washington contacts, and political contributions.

Most of the organizations discussed in the chapter have their own home pages. Here is a sampling:

www.aflcio.org/home.html
The home page of the largest union in America, the AFL-CIO, contains official union documents and press releases, news on issues important to the labor movement, a link to information on high corporate executive salaries in the United States, and links to other labor-related groups.

www.nam.org
The National Association of Manufacturers' Web page contains material similar to that on the AFL-CIO page but from a business perspective.

www.fb.com
The Farm Bureau's Web page contains similar information from the perspective of the more prosperous and conservative sector of agriculture, along with updates on the weather and a menu where you can register your favorite summertime activities.

www.moveon.org
MoveOn.org is an organization that promotes a liberal agenda. It was deeply involved in the Democratic presidential campaign in 2004.

www.cc.org

The Christian Coalition is a conservative grassroots political organization for people of faith interested in promoting issues associated with the Christian right.

www.thirdwavefoundation.org

The Third Wave Foundation is the only national activist philanthropic organization for young women. The organization supports and involves young women in a broad range of movements, including campaigning for a living wage, environmental protection, and reproductive rights.

www.aarp.org

AARP maintains an excellent Web site. It allows you to learn about AARP's position and congressional testimony on issues affecting the elderly and to review the myriad of benefits offered by the organization, along with much more.

www.apsanet.org

Use the American Political Science Association's home page to find out about the organization to which your professor might belong.

 ## InfoTrac College Edition

Search for the following articles in the InfoTrac database:

Blakeslee, Nate. "A Naked Emperor Disrobed: Or, How Enron Did Texas," *The Nation* (March 4, 2002).

Golden, Marissa Martino. "Interest Groups in the Rule-Making Process: Who Participates? Whose Voices Get Heard?" *Journal of Public Administration Research and Theory* (April 1998).

Kramer, Staci D. "The 527 Factor: It's Big in State Races, Too: Sixty Outside Groups- and Counting-Make Their Dollars Felt in Campaigns," *The Christian Science Monitor* (September 23, 2004).

Nicholson-Crotty, Sean, and Jill Nicholson-Crotty. "Interest Group Influence on Managerial Priorities in Public Organizations," *Journal of Public Administration Research and Theory* (October 2004).

For more articles, enter:

"pressure groups" in the Subject Guide;

"lobbying" in the Subject Guide;

"lobbyists" in the Subject Guide.

 ## American Government Resources

Visit the Political Behavior section of the Wadsworth American Government Resources Web site (politicalscience. wadsworth.com/amgov/) for a variety of tools to help you explore interest groups further. Included are simulations, video clips, Microcase exercises, and a wealth of other activities.

CHAPTER 7

POLITICAL PARTIES

REUTERS/ John Gress / Landov

Delegate Christina Butts of Iowa holds up a light at the Democratic National Convention in 2004.

Characteristics of Political Parties
Purposes of Political Parties
The American Party System

The Rise of American Political Parties
The Founders and Political Parties
Birth of Political Parties
Development of Mass Parties
Why Parties Are Important to American Democracy

Party Realignments
Rise of the Republicans and the Golden Age of Parties
Progressive Politics and the Weakening of Parties
Rise of the Democratic Party
Party Identification Today

Decline of Parties
Dimunition of Party Functions
Erosion of Support for Parties

Resurgence of Parties
Important Remaining Functions of Parties
Party Influence on Policymaking

Party Organization
National Party Organization
State and Local Party Organizations

Parties and Voting
Party Identification
Candidate Evaluations
Issues
Parties, Candidates, and Issues

Conclusion: Do Political Parties Make Government More Responsive?

Should You Violate the Rules of Congress to Win a Partisan Victory?

t is 2003, and you are the speaker of the House of Representatives, Dennis Hastert. Elected to the House from the fourteenth district in north central Illinois, you were selected speaker by your Republican colleagues in your sixth term, a relatively fast rise to the top job. As party whip following the Republican takeover of the House in 1994, you were able to push the party line without making your colleagues feel pressured. Your friendly, low-key demeanor is quite a change from the hard-driving style of your predecessor, Newt Gingrich (R-Ga.).[1] You won the job when the controversial Gingrich suddenly resigned after Republican midterm election losses in 1998. The party needed someone in a hurry, someone acceptable to most party members. You fit the bill.

The Republicans control the presidency and both houses of Congress. With complete control of the apparatus of national government, your party would seem to be in a strong position to implement its conservative policy agenda.[2] However, your House majority is slim. Currently, there are 229 Republicans and 204 Democrats. And there are hard feelings in Congress. Some of the 2002 congressional election races were bitter. The Bush administration claimed that opponents to its homeland security measure were more interested in special interests than they were in protecting the American people.[3] In the Georgia Senate race, Senator Max Cleland, a triple amputee as a result of Vietnam War wounds, was labeled unpatriotic by his successful Republican opponent for criticizing the war in Iraq and portrayed as aiding Osama bin Laden and Saddam Hussein.

And of course, Democrats resent that George Bush is president despite his having lost the popular vote in the 2000 election. So even though you control Congress and the presidency, such things as the small majority in Congress, the hard-fought recent elections, and the closeness of the presidential race reflect how evenly party support is split among the public at large.

Your party is pushing a conservative agenda notwithstanding the divided mind of the public. A key piece of legislation in that agenda is a bill to add prescription drug coverage to Medicare. President Bush pledged in 2000 to do something about the high cost of drugs for the nation's senior citizens, and in his 2003 State of the Union address, he proposed a $400 billion prescription drug benefit. Not only would passage satisfy a campaign promise, but it would also be attractive to older Americans, who now constitute about 25 percent of voters in presidential elections. It would also steal an issue that has traditionally favored Democrats.

Bush's initial plan coupled the prescription benefit with a requirement that seniors abandon Medicare, the government-run health insurance program for those over age sixty-five, and join private health insurance plans. Although it is unusual for a conservative Republican president to push for a new and costly government program, the president's approach, if successful, would not only boost his reelection prospects but also offer a private sector alternative to seniors. This had the potential to lure them away from the popular government-run Medicare program and destroy Medicare, a goal of many conservative Republicans since Medicare's inception in the 1960s.

Although almost everyone in Congress, Republicans and Democrats alike, seems to favor doing something about prescription drug benefits, this proposal has also generated many opponents. Normally, the Democrats would support the expansion of Medicare. The Medicare program was instituted in 1965 by Democratic president Lyndon Johnson and the Democrat-controlled Congress, though it also had support from a majority of Republicans. A popular piece of legislation, Medicare has helped millions of elderly Americans obtain health care. But this current prescription legislation is opposed by most Democrats because by forcing seniors into private companies, it threatens the future of Medicare. They would prefer to expand Medicare, not compete with it. Moreover, Democrats strongly oppose the portion of the the bill containing provisions that would forbid Medicare from using its tremendous purchasing power to lower drug prices. Democrats decry this Republican gift to the pharmaceutical industry, a big supporter of Republican candidates, and the extra costs it will incur.

About twenty-five Republican conservatives also oppose the bill. They are philosophically committed to reducing the size of government and are concerned with the large expansion of an already very costly program. They may believe that the bill will weaken Medicare in the long run, but in the short run, it will require a huge government expenditure.

As the legislation moved through Congress, passage seemed unlikely.

However, by gradually making concessions, Republican leaders began winning over their own as well as some Democrats in both the House and the Senate. This major overhaul of one of the nation's largest and most successful government programs appeared to be following the path similar to the legislation that originally established Medicare, gradually building a bipartisan coalition that would ensure passage. Liberal Democratic Senator Edward Kennedy of Massachusetts urged his colleagues early on to support a compromise fashioned in the Senate to allow private insurers to administer the drug benefit but allow the basic Medicare program to remain as is.[4]

And some compromises were made. So the bill has some solid support but apparently not enough. Although forcing seniors into private health plans was taken out of the bill, most Republicans still support it and most Democrats still oppose it.

It is your job as speaker to win support in the House for its approval. You schedule a vote for a Friday night, November 21. Shortly before the vote, you think the bill's chances are "tenuous." You will lose some conservatives, and not many Democrats are going to support the bill. Finally, at 3 A.M., the legislator then presiding over the session calls for a fifteen-minute vote. That means, following congressional rules and norms, that the representatives have fifteen minutes in which to vote. Rarely are the time rules violated, and then only by a few minutes.

The vote is taken, and supporters of the bill number only 215, mostly Republicans, compared to the 219 opponents, mostly Democrats. Clearly, the bill is about to be rejected and the administration would suffer a major defeat. Or would it?

If you want to try to save the bill, you have to violate the rules and allow voting to continue by trying to persuade some of the no voters to vote yes. This violation of House norms would be considered outrageous by the Democrats, but is the only way to win.

The majority party in Congress has always dominated legislative action, but

the minority has typically been treated with respect, allowed to make its case and to participate in lawmaking according to long-standing rules of procedure, even if its initiatives were doomed to failure for lack of support.[5] If you follow the rules when you are in the majority, you expect the other party to follow the rules when it has gained the majority. Just as in football, you can tackle a runner but not kick him in the shins, in legislative bodies there are clearly defined rules that both sides abide by. And you are mindful of these norms. They allow business to be conducted even though members disagree with one another.

These norms have a long history. As vice president, charged with the constitutional responsibility of presiding over the Senate, Thomas Jefferson suggested that senators not address each other by name, impugn one another's motives, or disparage one another's states.[6] Over its long existence, Congress has adopted many more formal and informal rules that define how members treat each other and how the majority and minority should work together to conduct the nation's business.

The tradition of closing the vote after everyone has had a chance to vote is a long-standing one. In fact, when the Democratic speaker in the late 1980s held the vote open once for an extra twenty minutes, Republicans complained vehemently and for years after cited it as an example of the Democratic majority's abuse of power. But since taking control of the House in 1995, the Republicans have held the vote open at least a dozen times, but for short periods of time.[7]

To follow the tradition of closing the vote when time is up means dealing the administration a blow. So what do you do? Do you violate these long-standing rules, keep the vote open, and try to twist some arms to get no votes to become yes votes? Or do you concede defeat and try to rework the bill to build stronger support for it, knowing that this would be seen as a major defeat for the administration and that the Democrats will use this against your party in next year's elections?

George Washington warned against the "baneful" effects of parties and described them as the people's worst enemies. More recently, a respected political scientist, E. E. Schattschneider, argued that "political parties created democracy and that democracy was impossible without them."[8] The public echoes these contradictory views. Many believe that parties create conflict where none exists, yet most identify with one of the two major parties.[9]

These same feelings exist among candidates for office. They often bypass political parties by establishing their own personal campaign organizations and raising their own campaign funds. If elected, they sometimes do not follow the party line. At the same time, candidates for national and state offices are nominated in the name of political parties. They rely on parties for assistance, and they have little chance of winning unless they are Democrats or Republicans.

This chapter examines American political parties to see why they are important and why many people believe that if they become less important and less effective, government will be less accountable to the people.

Characteristics of Political Parties

Political parties are a major link between people and government. They provide a way for the public to have a say in who serves in government and what policies government chooses. Political parties are organizations that seek to control government by recruiting, nominating, and electing members to public office. They consist of three interrelated components: (1) citizens who see themselves as belonging to the party, (2) officeholders who are elected or appointed in the name of the party, and (3) the **party organization,** "professionals" who run the party organization and party activities at the national, state, and local levels (see Figure 1).[10]

Purposes of Political Parties

Many voters feel an attachment to a political party. For some, this develops early in life as they observe and model their parents. For others, it stems from an impor-

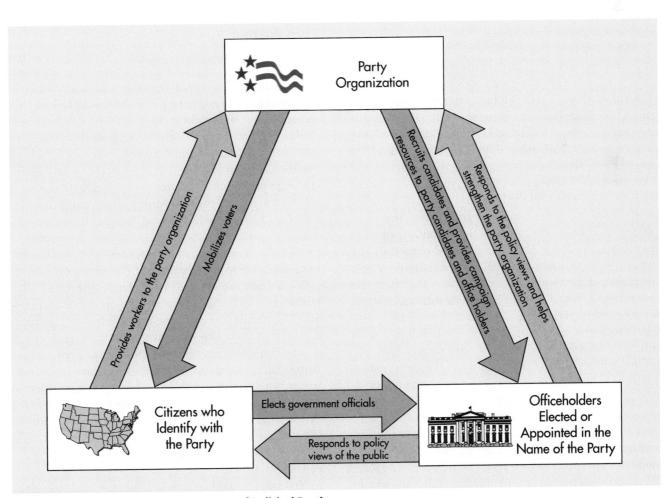

FIGURE 1 ■ The Three Components of Political Parties

tant political event. When called on to vote, many simply vote their party attachment. For those with little or no knowledge of candidates or issues, who pay little attention to political campaigns, this makes sense. Campaigns may not clarify differences between the candidates and parties very well, if at all, and issue positions are often complex and difficult for the average voter to grasp. Political parties, on the other hand, do have a history that reflects a fairly consistent approach to public policy issues. Since the 1930s, the Democratic Party has favored a redistributive approach to dealing with many of the nation's problems—that is, using the government's power to tax, spend, and regulate to implement programs to provide income support (Social Security), social services (Medicare), clean up the environment, and undertake other actions that the majority of the public seems to want. The Republican Party is more likely to oppose government programs for those ends and to favor a smaller government, which the public also seems to want. However, Republicans believe in big government when it comes to lifestyle and morality issues, such as abortion and gay marriage. They favor government action to prohibit these kinds of personal choices, whereas the Democrats want to keep government out. For example, the Republican Party would make abortion illegal and the Democratic Party would allow it under most conditions.

Most voters recognize these differences. Knowing that a candidate belongs to a party is a clue, although an imperfect one, to the candidate's stand on a broader range of issues such as health care, energy, abortion, and gay rights. Voters can take some solace in knowing that they do not need to study each candidate's position on such issues, a difficult and time-consuming task, but simply know which party a candidate is associated with. The party label serves as a general guideline on where the candidate stands on the issues of the day. When citizens choose between competing parties for control of government, they have a general understanding of what their choice will mean for the policy direction of the nation. Without the party label, where citizens see just the names of the candidates on the ballot, they have the monumental task of finding out where candidates stand on issues. Should they succeed at this, they remain clueless as to how a candidate, once elected, will join with others in forming a coalition to govern and how the person is likely to vote on major issues. Without political parties, voting and its impact on government policy become a lottery that average people may win, but the chances are much greater that they will lose.

Parties also play an important role in organizing and operating government; they formulate policy options and ultimately decide which to support or oppose. When political parties represent individuals from widely different backgrounds and interests, they aid society by aggregating and mediating conflicts and contributing to political and social stability.

In spite of the parties' role in making democracy work for average men and women, most Americans see them as part of the mess in Washington. Many hold them responsible for the government's inability to solve the nation's problems and feel that partisan differences are meaningless squabbles designed to secure political advantage. (*Partisan* implies attachment to one party or another; strong partisans have strong positive feelings about their party). Many feel that political parties create differences where none exist rather than reflecting real and legitimate differences in approaches to solving the nation's problems.

In fact, if political parties should suddenly disappear, the conflicts over how to use the nation's limited resources would still exist, narrow special interests would have a free hand, and the interests of average men and women would suffer.

The American Party System

There are many different political party systems around the world. The American party system is characterized by some intriguing and even rare qualities.

Two Parties

First, the American party system is a **two-party system.** Only two parties win seats in Congress, and only two parties compete effectively for the presidency. The development and persistence of two parties is rare among the nations of the world.

In Western Europe, **multiparty systems** are the rule. Italy has nine national parties and several regional parties; Germany has five national parties. Great Britain, although predominantly a two-party system, has several significant minor parties. Multiparty systems are also found in Canada, which has three parties, and Israel, which has more than twenty.

Why do we have just two parties? The most common explanation is the nature of American elections.[11] Officeholders are elected from **single-member districts** in which the voting results are **winner-take-all.** This means that only one individual is elected from a district or stare, the individual who receives the most votes. This contrasts with **proportional representation** (PR), in which officeholders are elected from multimember districts and the number of seats awarded to each party in each district is equal to the percentage of the total the party receives in the district. Thus in PR systems, representation in the national legislature is roughly proportional to the popular vote each party receives nationwide.

In single-member-district, winner-take-all elections, only the major parties have much chance of winning legislative seats. With little hope of winning office, minor parties tend to die or merge with one of the major parties. However, where seats are awarded in proportion to the vote, even a modest showing in an election—15 percent or less—may win a seat in the national assembly. In PR systems, even parties representing only a small proportion of the electorate have voices in the legislature to speak in support of their policy positions and bases for mounting future campaigns.

Although the nature of elections influences the number of parties, the number of parties also influences the conduct of elections. Where there are only two parties, they have strong incentives to conduct elections in a way that undermines the development and growth of other parties.[12] For example, although the court eventually struck them down, Democrats and Republicans long supported laws that made it difficult for other parties to get their candidates placed on election ballots, requiring them to secure tens of thousands of signatures in order to qualify.

Fragmentation

The federal system, with its fragmentation of power among local, state, and national governments, leads to fragmentation within parties. State and local parties have their own resources and power bases separate from those of the national party, and the interests of state and local parties are often at odds with those of the national party.

Power is also fragmented at each level. At the national level, power is shared among the three branches of government. Control of the party is also shared. The president shares power within his party with members of his party in Congress. Control of the opposition is shared between the party's members in the House and the Senate. The national party organization may also seek a role, especially for the party that lacks control of the White House. Each of these agents has its own interests and stake in manipulating and using the party for its own ends. This is reflected in the difficult time that presidents often have in winning support for their policies among their own party members in Congress. For example, Democrats in Congress broke with President Clinton on the Clinton-negotiated North American Free Trade Agreement (NAFTA). Two of the top three Democratic leaders in each chamber led the opposition. Clinton succeeded on the strength of Republican support. Several recent Bush initiatives ran into Republican opposition. For example, some party members, alarmed at the rising federal deficit, split with the president on his budget in the run-up to the 2004 election.

On some issues, members of Congress simply have to go their own way. To be reelected, they only need to satisfy a plurality of the voters in their district or state, not the president or the party. When President Clinton considered a gas tax increase to reduce the deficit, Sen-

ator Herbert Kohl (D-Wisc.) told him that the increase could be no more than 4.3 cents per gallon. Clinton had to accept Kohl's figure because the bill's outcome was in doubt and the president needed Kohl's vote. Kohl won election in his own right and was only obligated to the people of Wisconsin, not the president or the party. Similarly, President Bush and Republican leaders in Congress bowed to demands of Republicans in Congress from rural states to provide greater financial aid to rural hospitals as the price for their support on the prescription drug bill. Unwillingness to follow the president or party leads to fragmentation.

However, party members are not entirely free agents. The pull of party is strong, and members normally support the legislative program of a president of their party. As we will see later, members of the House and Senate support the president most of the time.[13]

Moderation

Major American political parties tend toward moderation at least in their appeals to voters in national elections. The reason is that most voters cluster at or near the middle in their preferences for dealing with the nation's problems (see Figure 2). To win their votes, parties direct their campaigns to the middle. Historically, American political parties have been more interested in winning public office than in maintaining ideological purity and have been willing to sacrifice ideological principle in order to win. While parties avoid the extremes in their campaign appeals, both the Democratic and Republican parties have their elements—left of center in the Democratic Party and right of center in the Republican Party—that pull them toward the extremes. These tendencies are stronger in the Republican Party (though what is considered extreme is different to different people). Elected officeholders also tend to be more extreme than their rank-and-file supporters in the electorate, creating a tension between the personal predilections of officeholders and the preferences of voters.[14]

The desire to win directs parties to nominate moderate candidates for the presidency or for ideological candidates, when they are nominated, to obscure their issue positions or move to the middle. Ronald Reagan, when running for reelection, embraced a conciliatory stance toward the Soviet Union in contrast to his earlier antagonistic posture. Bill Clinton became a "new kind" of Democrat, embracing many of the Republicans' ideas. The implication was that unlike those in the past who catered to minorities and special interests, he would deal with the problems of all Americans. As soon as his nomination as the Republican presidential candidate was secure in 2000, George W. Bush beat a hasty retreat from his conservative rhetoric in the South Carolina primary. Thereafter, he avoided discussing issues such as abortion that would identify him with the right and focused on

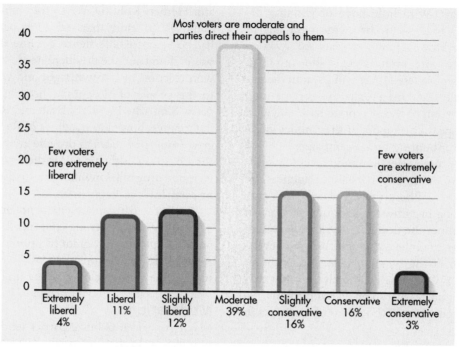

FIGURE 2 ▪ **Where the Voters Are** *The labels indicate how the voters characterize themselves. Political parties aim their campaigns at the middle because that is where most voters say they stand.*

SOURCE: Data from General Social Survey, 2002.

more centrist issues such as education, health care, and Social Security. Once in office, Bush moved back to the right to reward his ideologically conservative base by, among other things, appointing conservative John Ashcroft attorney general, backing tax cuts for the rich, and moving to undo as much government regulation as he could.

In the run-up to the 2004 election, Bush's position on gay marriage was an effort to satisfy his very conservative base. At the same time, he tried to reestablish his image as a "compassionate conservative" from the 2000 campaign by emphasizing elements of his policies that have broader appeal, such as the "No Child Left Behind" education program that increased child tax credits, and his prescription drug plan for seniors.[15]

Minor Parties in American Politics

Sometimes called "third parties," minor parties are as varied as the causes they represent. Some are one-issue parties, like the American Know-Nothing Party (1856), which ran on a platform opposing immigrants and Catholics, and the Prohibition Party (1869 to the present), which campaigns to ban the sale of alcoholic beverages.

Other parties advocate radical change. Economic protest parties, such as the Populists in 1892, occasionally appear when economic conditions are bad and disappear when the economy improves. Since the 1920s, the Communist Party USA has espoused the adoption of a communist system.

Some parties are simply candidates who failed to receive their party's nomination and decided to go it alone. In 1968, Alabama's segregationist governor, George Wallace, split from the Democratic Party to run for president as the candidate of the conservative American Independent Party. Though he had significant public support, the small number of votes he garnered did not influence the election's outcome.

Ross Perot's third-party candidacy in 1992 had no association with either party. He simply decided to run. His willingness to use his personal fortune to fund his campaign, including buying large blocks of expensive television time, made him a highly visible alternative to the major-party candidates. Perot would have floundered quickly and with little notice if not for his capacity to buy hours of national TV time. Although he polled 19 percent of the vote, quite extraordinary for a minor party, his candidacy did not influence the election outcome either, as he siphoned support away from both national parties.

Ralph Nader, the consumer advocate, ran in 2000 and again in 2004. In 2000, he was the nominee of the Green Party, an offshoot of the antinuclear and environmental movements. He campaigned on checking the influence of big business in government and received 3 percent of the vote, well below the average of minor parties historically but large enough to deny Al Gore the presidency.[16] In both the 2000 and 2004 campaigns, Nader argued that both major party candidates were pawns of corporate America, equally likely to do its bidding. On one level, the charge seems absurd. On important domestic issues, the Bush presidency has significantly differed in orientation from the national Democrats and presumably a Gore and Kerry presidency. Still, Clinton's embrace of several traditional Republican policies such as welfare reform and free trade and the willingness of congressional Democrats to go along with deregulation of accounting firms, energy policy, and other corporate activities alienated many Nader supporters. They hoped to send a message against what one Nader supporter termed "money-polluted politics, battery-operated candidates, and policies that provide government welfare to corporations." The message had little appeal in 2000 and even less in 2004.[17]

Barriers to Minor Party Success

Minor parties face many obstacles in trying to establish themselves. State laws, for example, present obstacles to minor-party and independent candidates seeking to get on the ballot, and federal laws make it difficult to secure public funding for third-party presidential candidates.

There are also psychological barriers. Minor-party and independent candidates confront the long-standing loyalty that most Americans feel toward the major parties. Even when third-party or independent candidates are preferred, many voters are reluctant to cast a vote for them, believing that there is little chance they can win. And the major parties encourage that view, reminding voters not to "waste their vote" by voting for a candidate who cannot win. Major parties also remind voters that a vote for a third-party candidate may contribute to the victory of their least preferred candidate, which happened to many Nader supporters in 2000. Most Nader supporters preferred Gore to Bush. In some closely contested states, the 2000 Nader vote was substantially larger than the Bush-Gore margin. Thus in a few states, the Nader vote gave the state to Bush, as in Florida, where Bush's 537-vote margin was far exceeded by Nader's 97,000 votes.

Democrats feared that Nader could take enough votes in 2004 to cost their candidate, John Kerry, the election. Some Republicans obviously hoped so, because a significant portion of Nader's financial support came from large donors to Bush.[18] Nader polled, however, less than 1 percent of the vote and was not a factor.

Because voters don't think third-party candidates can win, such candidates also have difficulty raising funds and attracting media attention. Financial contributors are loath to donate to a candidate who is unlikely to win. Limited media coverage weakens the attractiveness and the fundraising capacity of third-party candidates.[19]

Practical barriers to third-party and independent candidates also exist. It is difficult for third parties to recruit qualified and experienced candidates, most of whom recognize that they are most likely to win if they run as major-party candidates.

Third parties also suffer from having their ideas co-opted by the major parties. Major parties are quick to back ideas that have voter appeal. Once a major party adopts an idea, the need for a third-party alternative is eliminated. Perot's strong stand on the need to eliminate the budget deficit in the 1992 campaign was at least partly responsible for the major parties' renewed efforts to deal with it.

Finally, third-party and independent candidates have done well only in elections when the nation has faced significant social and economic problems that the parties failed to deal with. Low support for third-party candidates in 2000 no doubt reflected a strong economy and a nation at peace. Recognizable policy differences between the major party candidates in 2004 and the threat that a third-party vote might result in one's least preferred candidate winning lowered support even more.

Because third-party and independent candidates cannot win the presidency, their movements rarely extend beyond the defeat of their candidate. Perot was able to overcome this by spending his own money. His "United We Stand America" movement from the 1992 campaign became the Reform Party in 1996. But without Perot's financial support, Pat Buchanan, the party's nominee in 2000, received less than 1 percent of the popular vote.

In spite of the difficulties third parties face, many Americans say they want to see an alternative to the major parties. That support seems rather fanciful, however. Over half of all Americans have indicated in various

Ralph Nader

polls that the nation needs a third party, but few have ever voted for a third-party candidate.

The Rise of American Political Parties

Most Americans think of the Democratic and Republican parties as more or less permanent fixtures, and indeed they have been around a long time. The Democratic Party evolved from the Jacksonian Democrats in 1832, and the Republican Party was founded in 1854.

The Founders and Political Parties

The Founders had little use for political parties. Many saw them as a threat and hoped to check their development in the new nation. They hoped instead, perhaps unrealistically, to govern by consensus and realized that political parties would make this impossible. There was also concern that parties would pursue narrow self-interests at the expense of the common good. As independent thinkers, others feared that parties would impose a mindless uniformity, cutting off the capacity of individuals to think for themselves.[20]

In *Federalist Paper* 10, James Madison wrote of political parties and interest groups pursuing selfish interests. John Adams dreaded what he considered the greatest political evil, the formation of rival political parties.

Given the Founders' misgivings, it's not surprising that the Constitution does not mention political parties. Nevertheless, it created a government in which parties, or something like them, were inevitable. When the Founders established popular elections as the mechanism for selecting some political leaders, an agency for organizing and mobilizing supporters became a necessity. Despite their fears, Jefferson and Madison founded America's first political party.

Birth of Political Parties

With George Washington's unanimous election to the presidency in 1788, it appeared that the nation could be governed by consensus. But differences of opinion soon arose. Alexander Hamilton, Washington's secretary of the treasury, supported a strong national government. He and his supporters in Congress, who called themselves Federalists, were opposed by Thomas Jefferson, secretary of state, who feared a strong central government. The conflict led Jefferson to challenge John Adams for the presidency in 1796. Jefferson lost but set about recruiting political operatives in each of the states to mobilize support on his behalf. Newspapers were es-

The factors that led to the formation of the first political parties were already vying with each other in George Washington's administration. *Thomas Jefferson (standing at left) and Alexander Hamilton (second from right) are pictured here with Washington (far right).*

© The Granger Collection, New York

tablished to get out the message. On the strength of his new national party, Jefferson ran for the presidency in 1800 and won. His success established the value of a political party.

By Jefferson's second term, more than 90 percent of members of Congress were either Federalists or Jeffersonians (later called Jeffersonian Republicans) and consistently voted in support of their party's position.[21]

Development of Mass Parties

From 1815 to 1824, the so-called Era of Good Feeling, Jeffersonian Republicans, with little competition, won all presidential elections and majorities in the House and Senate. However, the party split in 1824. In the first year that an official popular vote was recorded, Andrew Jackson won the popular vote, polling slightly over 150,000 votes, but John Quincy Adams, polling only 100,000 votes, was elected president by the House of Representatives when neither candidate received a majority in the Electoral College.

The size of the popular electorate increased fivefold between 1824 and 1828, when more than one million votes were cast. Jackson and the Democrats won that election. (The National Republicans, who later became the Whigs, were the other party that grew out of the Jeffersonian Republicans' split.) Opponents of Jackson deplored his reaching out and mobilizing the masses. He was called a "barbarian," and his election in 1828 was derided as "the howl of raving democracy."[22] Jackson's popular appeal and the organizational effort of his party brought large numbers to the polls for the first time. Building on the efforts of Jefferson, Jackson introduced the idea of a political party with a large and loyal following among rank-and-file voters.

Jackson, like Jefferson, saw the strength of American democracy in the common person. His administration ushered in a number of changes that fostered participation in government by average Americans. Property ownership was lifted as a qualification for voting, and the franchise was extended to all adult white males. Popular elections rather than state legislatures became the mechanism for selecting the Electoral College, and party conventions, with representatives from every state and locality, became the mode for nominating presidential candidates. The closed and narrow congressional caucus (the party's elected members in Congress) that was used to nominate presidential candidates prior to 1828 gave way to the open, broader, and more participatory national presidential nominating convention.

By 1840, the size of the electorate had doubled again.[23]

Why Parties Are Important to American Democracy

Political parties became important in American politics early in the nineteenth century. But today, many Americans, especially young adults, are cynical about political parties. Indeed, there is much reason to be, as our political leaders sometimes appear to be without principles, pandering to special interests and acting in their own interests rather than those of the people. Against some absolute standard of goodness, they fall short. Yet if we observe the business world, we also see corporate executives without principles or ethics, stealing billions from their shareholders and employees to feather their own nests. We deplore and distrust this behavior, but we do not usually say that we should therefore get rid of corporations. Instead we support punishment for the wrongdoers and reform to strengthen accountability of the corporate executives. And that, we would argue, is how we should look at political parties. They need re-

"A LIVE JACKASS KICKING A DEAD LION."
And such a Lion! and such a Jackass!

© The Granger Collection, New York

THE THIRD-TERM PANIC.

In 1828, opponents of Andrew Jackson called him a jackass (left). Political cartoonists and journalists began to use the donkey to symbolize Jackson and the Democratic Party. In the 1870s, Thomas Nast popularized the donkey as a symbol of the party in his cartoons and originated the elephant as a symbol of the Republican Party. His 1874 cartoon (right) showed the Democratic donkey dressed as a lion frightening the other animals of the jungle, including the Republican elephant.

form and improvement, but they serve valuable functions. It is hard to imagine how we could have a democracy without them.

Parties developed in our system despite the Founders' initial dislike of them, and they persist despite their warts and problems because they offer a way for the public to participate in politics and a way to increase accountability of elected officials to the public. In other words, they offer a way to make our system democratic.

What do parties do, and why are they essential to democracy? First, they help provide political information to the population. Much of what we know about politics and government comes from political parties and the candidates they support. In the old days, this information was usually provided by word of mouth through door-to-door campaigning or in rallies and meetings. Today, we still have rallies, door-to-door campaigning, and campaign brochures, but these efforts are supplemented by advertisements in the media, especially television. As annoying as these ads can be, they help focus people's attention on government and policy issues.

Second, parties choose candidates for office or devise means by which the party faithful choose party candidates. In the nineteenth century and throughout much of the twentieth, party leaders themselves chose candidates from among their own workers. Party workers who did well were tapped for higher jobs, and if they did well there, they continued to rise. Party leaders knew the people they chose to run for office and had interests in making sure those they tapped for office could do the job.

Third, parties helped their candidates get elected. In the nineteenth and early twentieth centuries, the party organization planned and carried out the campaigns. It arranged visits by the candidate to communities and organized campaign rallies. Sometimes, it was the campaign workers who traveled around the country while the candidate himself stayed home. In 1856, James Buchanan, the Democratic candidate for president, spent the campaign at his home in Pennsylvania and, with the help of one assistant, answered the mail and received visitors while his campaign workers traveled around the country mobilizing Democratic voters.

Fourth, party members who were elected worked to carry out the party's policies. By electing enough members of the party to legislative and executive positions, parties could carry out some of the promises they made in their campaigns. The more of its nominees they elected, the better able they were to make good on their promises. And if they were able to control both the legislative and executive branches, they had a very good chance of being able to fulfill their pledges. The party then linked the two branches of government and therefore could overcome the fragmentation of our separation-of-powers system.

Fifth, by providing information, choosing candidates, getting them elected, and working to carry out their promises, parties make government responsive. Through these mechanisms, parties offer a way to give average people some political power. Warren Buffett or Bill Gates or Oprah Winfrey or the president of any large coporation, to choose a few examples, can easily have political access and political power without joining a party. Their wealth, corporate ties, or fame would give them immediate access to any political decision maker, should they want it. But most of us do not have that kind of clout. We are not influential enough individually to wield political power and to counter the influence of the wealthy, the well connected, and the special interests. If average individuals are to have any power, they need to join together, though the auspices of a political party, to influence government. The dean of American political scientists recently commented, "we can be pretty sure that a country wholly without competitive parties is a country without democracy."[24]

In fact, strong parties are the best counterweight to special interests. One might think of it as a teeter-totter. When parties are up, special interests are down, and vice versa. Therefore, political parties offer a counterbalance to the influence of special-interest groups. Special-interest groups also represent a group of people, business or labor or environmental advocates, or the gun lobby, for example. But by definition, they represent a narrower group of people than political parties do. Parties represent a broad spectrum of people and offer the average person a chance to combat the clout of special interests.

Individually, citizens have little power, but collectively, through political parties, they can elect officeholders who will do their bidding and in the process influence government. Although the existence of competitive political parties is no guarantee that average men and women will prevail in directing the course of government, the people will most assuredly fail without them.[25] This is one reason why Schattschneider believed democracy was impossible without political parties.

Party Realignments

Parties and what is called the **party system** have changed many times since the Jacksonian era. We can characterize different eras of the party systems by the competitive balance between the parties. Old parties die and new ones arise, and dominant parties may become less popular while the less dominant ones grow in strength. There have been periods when one party has dominated American politics and won most elections and periods when neither party has dominated, with control of government divided between the parties or shifting back and forth

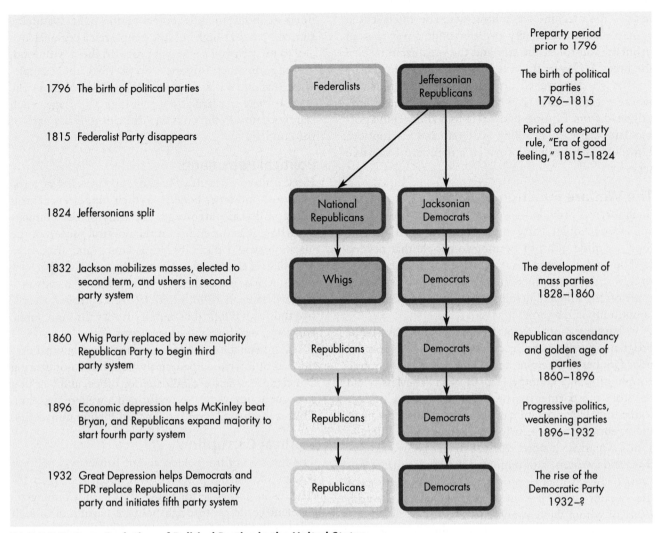

1796 The birth of political parties

1815 Federalist Party disappears

1824 Jeffersonians split

1832 Jackson mobilizes masses, elected to second term, and ushers in second party system

1860 Whig Party replaced by new majority Republican Party to begin third party system

1896 Economic depression helps McKinley beat Bryan, and Republicans expand majority to start fourth party system

1932 Great Depression helps Democrats and FDR replace Republicans as majority party and initiates fifth party system

Preparty period prior to 1796

The birth of political parties 1796–1815

Period of one-party rule, "Era of good feeling," 1815–1824

The development of mass parties 1828–1860

Republican ascendancy and golden age of parties 1860–1896

Progressive politics, weakening parties 1896–1932

The rise of the Democratic Party 1932–?

Federalists | Jeffersonian Republicans | National Republicans | Jacksonian Democrats | Whigs | Democrats | Republicans | Democrats

FIGURE 3 ■ **Evolution of Political Parties in the United States**

between them. Massive shifts in party loyalty among the voters that usher in a period of party dominance are called **realignments.** There have been several party realignments in American history, giving rise to the five party systems identified in Figure 3.

At the same time, the party system has changed its strength over time. Parties grew to be very powerful in the late nineteenth century and have declined somewhat in influence since then. Periods of dominance have followed major upheavals in American society, such as the Civil War and the Great Depression, when a majority of voters turned to one of the parties in search of an answer to the crisis.

Rise of the Republicans and the Golden Age of Parties

The mass party system lasted until 1860, when the conflict over slavery brought a new party alignment. Abolitionists and proslavery factions split the Whig Party, the principal opposition to the Democrats in the second party system. By 1860, the Whigs had disappeared and a new Republican Party (not directly related to the Jeffersonians of an earlier era) emerged. The Republicans (also known as the Grand Old Party, or GOP), reflecting abolitionist sentiment, nominated Abraham Lincoln for president. Northern Democrats who opposed slavery joined with Republicans in establishing a new dominant political party. In the decade following the Civil War (1861–1865), Republicans usually won the presidency and controlled Congress. After 1876, elections were close, and the parties were evenly matched in Congress.

Parties reached the high point of their influence in American politics during this period. Local and state party leaders had exclusive control over nominations for political offices. Voters were mobilized in elections by powerful local party organizations that could dispense favors in exchange for support.

Political Machines

These powerful **political machines** began to flourish during this period, and the last of them did not disappear until the middle of the twentieth century. At the head of the machine was a boss, who also often served as mayor and directed city government in a way so as to maintain control of the city and the organization. (See the box "A Day in the Life of a Machine Politician.")

The machine relied on the votes of the poor and working class, many of whom had only recently immigrated from Europe. Most accounts of machine politics are negative, dwelling on graft and corruption. However, the machine provided a number of valuable services.

The Welfare Function of Parties

Such services provided a welfare system for immigrants and poor people. Party organizations would provide food, clothing, jobs, or housing to people that needed it. The party workers were a kind of welcome wagon to new immigrants, meeting them on the dock as they came off the ship and helping them settle into their new community and nation.

With no national welfare system or other assistance programs, parties were crucial in providing support for poor families and helping them integrate into their new community and country. Tip O'Neill (D-Mass.) told the story of a former mayor of Boston, James Curley, a leader in the Democratic organization in Boston early in the twentieth century, who one winter called Filene's, a local department store, told the owner he needed five thousand sweaters, and reminded the owner that it was time to reassess Filene's property. Of course, Curley got the sweaters, which went to poor people in Boston, many of whom were immigrants.

Party machines did not do favors out of a spirit of altruism. They did favors because they expected other favors in return. As this little example indicates, the party organization provided poor people with sweaters and in return would expect their votes and loyalty. The party and its elected officials gave Filene's and other cooperating businesses a break when it came to regulation and in return expected some goods and services that could be used both to help the poor and in many cases to enrich the party leaders themselves. As New York's machine boss George Washington Plunkitt once said, "If a family is burned out, I don't ask whether they are Republicans or Democrats. . . . I just get quarters for them, buy clothes for them if their clothes were burned up and fix them up 'til they get things runnin' again. It's philanthropy, but it's politics too—mighty good politics. Who can tell me how many votes one of these fires brings me?"[26]

Thus in the absence of Social Security, welfare, food programs, and other government safety nets, party organizations provided a helping hand for newcomers to find jobs and housing. In return, immigrants developed loyalties to the parties and also became participants in politics. On election day, thousands of party workers went house to house to take voters to the polls. Naturally, turnout was very high because people felt a personal loyalty to the political party that provided them with food, housing, or other assistance. So in 1896, for example, voter turnout was estimated at 90 percent of those eligible to vote, particularly astonishing in an age when transportation to the polls was difficult in many parts of the country.

Political Patronage

Party leaders, once in office, openly awarded government jobs and other benefits to their supporters. This is called **political patronage.** An army of city employees whose jobs depended on the political success of the machine would dutifully bring family and friends to the polls on election day. One of the last of the big-city bosses, Mayor Richard J. Daley, head of the Chicago machine during the 1960s and 1970s, controlled thirty-five thousand public jobs and, indirectly through public contracts, ten thousand private ones.[27]

In this era, then, in addition to the functions that parties had of informing people about politics, nominating and campaigning for candidates for office, and working to enact policy, they also performed a welfare function. This strengthened their influence in their communities.

Political Corruption

The flip side of the golden age of parties was political corruption. Parties provided jobs, food, and other incentives in exchange for votes. Businesses gained government contracts through political payoffs. Although many people benefited from the arrangements, which helped generations of newcomers assimilate into the nation, others saw them as a perversion of the democratic process.

Progressive Politics and the Weakening of Parties

A realignment brought about a reaction against the party machines. The election of 1896 ushered in this alignment. Midwest farmers hard hit by poor economic conditions turned to the Democrats and William Jennings Bryan. Southerners, still feeling the sting of civil war and outrage at Lincoln and the Republicans, joined Bryan in his crusade against the banks and corporations of the Northeast that were financially squeezing ranchers and farmers. A fundamentalist Christian, Bryan also played on a growing concern with the rising number of Catholic immigrants flooding the nation's largest cities. His appeal, however, did not attract enough voters to win the election against the Republican candidate, William McKinley. And, in fact, more voters shifted to the Republican party, ushering in a period of Republican dominance.

George Washington Plunkitt was a ward leader in the infamous Tammany Hall machine, the Democratic Party organization that governed New York City for seven decades in the late nineteenth and early twentieth centuries. Although Plunkitt was on the city payroll, he did not have a free ride. The demands of his job were exhausting. Providing needed services to his constituents, he had opportunities to build support for the party. Today, government programs available to all citizens provide these services regardless of whether or not they support a political party with their votes. Although parties no longer provide the services Plunkitt delivered to his constituents, they reward their benefactors just the same, with tax breaks, government contracts, and laws that enrich some at the expense of others. Entries from Plunkitt's diary illustrate the difficult tasks he faced each day.

2:00 A.M. Aroused from sleep by a bartender who asked me to go to the police station and bail out a saloon keeper who had been arrested for violating the excise law. Furnished bail and returned to bed at three o'clock.

6:00 A.M. Awakened by fire engines. Hastened to the scene of the fire . . . found several tenants who had been burned out, took them to a hotel, supplied them with clothes, fed them, and arranged temporary quarters for them.

8:30 A.M. Went to the police court to secure the discharge of six "drunks," my constituents, by a timely word to the judge. Paid the fines of two.

9:00 A.M. Appeared in the municipal district court to direct one of my district captains to act as counsel for a widow about to be dispossessed. . . . Paid the rent of a poor family and gave them a dollar for food.

11:00 A.M. At home again. "Fixed" the troubles of four men waiting for me: one discharged by the Metropolitan Railway for neglect of duty; another wanted a job on the road; the third on the subway; and the fourth was looking for work with a gas company.

3:00 P.M. Attended the funeral of an Italian. Hurried back for the funeral of a Hebrew constituent. Went conspicuously to the front both in the Catholic church and the synagogue.

7:00 P.M. Went to district headquarters to preside over a meeting of election district captains, submitted lists of all the voters in their districts and told who were in need, who were in trouble, who might be won over [to Tammany] and how.

8:00 P.M. Went to a church fair. Took chances on everything, bought ice cream for the young girls and the children, kissed the little ones, flattered their mothers, and took the fathers out for something down at the corner.

9:00 P.M. At the clubhouse again. Spent $10 for a church excursion. Bought tickets for a baseball game. Listened to the complaints of a dozen pushcart peddlers who said they were being persecuted by the police. Promised to go to police headquarters in the morning and see about it.

10:30 P.M. Attended a Hebrew wedding reception and dance. Had previously sent a handsome wedding present to the bride.

12:00 A.M. In bed.

Source: Alistair Cooke, Alistair Cooke's America (New York: Knopf, 1973), 290–291; adapted from William L. Riordon, Plunkitt of Tammany Hall (New York Dutton, 1963), 91–93.

George Washington Plunkitt holds forth in his unofficial office, a bootblack stand at the New York County Court House.

During this period, the **Progressive movement** gained strength, chiefly among middle-class Americans concerned with the corruption of the big-city political machines. The movement championed a number of changes designed to wrest control from political machines and the lower-class immigrants they served. These reforms did reduce corruption in politics, but they also seriously weakened the power of political parties.

Changes included voter registration, the secret ballot, primary elections, and the introduction of merit systems. Voter registration made it difficult for parties to stuff ballot boxes with fraudulent votes, and the secret ballot prevented the party from knowing how citizens actually voted. Most devastating of all, the party lost control of nominations for public office. No longer able to tap someone in the private confines of a smoked-filled back room, nominations became the responsibility of voters in primary elections. Adopted initially in Wisconsin in 1903, the direct primary, as it was called, spread to virtually every state in the Union. The introduction of merit systems based government hiring on competence rather than party affiliation. Merit systems greatly reduced patronage in the awarding of jobs and contracts and thus robbed the party of resources needed to maintain the organization.

Although the Progressives never captured the presidency, these ideas did win favor with large numbers of Americans and were enacted into law in every state. Political parties were weakened, with reduced capacity to mobilize voters and use government to meet the needs of those who supported them. Adoption of the reforms did not, however, bring an end to political organization and influence. But the nature of politics changed as well—established, native-born, middle-class economic interests increased their influence.

Despite the relative weakening of the power of new immigrant groups, the sheer numbers of new Americans continued to give them political clout, especially in the large cities of the Northeast and Midwest. In the 1920s, Republican support in the nation's cities declined as the party failed to respond to the plight of poor immigrants residing there. The Republican majority in Congress limited the growth of the immigrant population by enacting quotas for immigrants from Southern and Eastern Europe, at that time the largest source of immigrants. The number of immigrants dropped sharply from more than 1.2 million in 1910 to less than 150,000 by 1920.

Rise of the Democratic Party

These conditions set the stage of a new realignment. When the country was rocked by the worldwide economic Great Depression in the 1930s, poor people, immigrants, black Americans, and working people turned to the Democrats. The election of Franklin Delano

Until the 1890s, there was no pretense of secrecy in voting. Each party's ballot was a different color. Voters chose their party's ballot, like this Republican ballot used in the 1888 Indiana elections, and placed it in a clear glass-sided ballot box. Vote buying in the 1888 election and the growing strength of party reform movements led to widespread adoption of the secret ballot over the next four years.

Roosevelt in 1932 marked the beginning of a new party alignment.

Roosevelt's **New Deal coalition,** composed of city dwellers, blue-collar workers, Catholic and Jewish immigrants, blacks, and southerners, elected him to an unprecedented four terms. Elements of the coalition were held together in the 1930s and 1940s, initially because of their common economic plight, then because of mobilization for World War II, and throughout by Roosevelt's personality and political skill.

After Roosevelt's death in 1945, the coalition began to unravel. The uneasy alliance between, on the one hand, the traditional Southern Democrats, conservative and eager to maintain racial segregation and traditional racial norms, and on the other hand, the more liberal northern urban, African American, and working people began to fray. Even though the Democrats continued to dominate Congress from the end of World War II through the mid-1990s, they had much less success in winning the presidency. Democrats have won the White House only three times since Lyndon Johnson's victory in 1964.

The Republicans won the presidency in 1952 and 1956 by nominating a popular war hero, General Dwight Eisenhower. Although the Democrats regained the White House in 1960, the civil rights movement, which saw the South move away from the party in 1964, and the Vietnam War, which split the party, cost the party victories in 1968 and 1972.[28] The Democrats have been successful by nominating southerners, first Georgia governor Jimmy Carter in 1976, then Bill Clinton, governor of Arkansas, in 1992 and 1996. In between, Democratic candidates lost to the very popular Ronald Reagan and his successor and former vice president George H. W. Bush. Al Gore, the Democratic nominee in 2000, Clinton's vice president, and former Tennessee senator, won the popular vote but lost in the Electoral College when the Supreme Court ended a recount effort in Florida that resulted in George W. Bush's winning the presidency. Bush succeeded in winning both the popular and electoral vote in 2004.

Party Identification Today

Party identification is a psychological link that individuals feel toward a party; no formal or organization membership is implied.[29] A majority of Americans identify with a political party. In 2003, 34 percent identified as Democrats, 30 percent as Republicans, and the rest as independents or supporters of another party.[30] Chapter 4 discussed how individuals develop party identification early in childhood. But party identification can also change as a person's life situation changes, as when moving to a new job or community, or in response to changes in national political or economic conditions.

It is these social issues that promote realignments. Realignments of the past have been characterized by compelling issues that fractured the major parties.[31] Before 1860, it was slavery. It divided the Democrats and destroyed the Whigs. In 1932, it was the economy. It pushed many Republicans and new voters to the Demo-

cratic New Deal coalition. Political pundits have been awaiting another realignment for decades. Kevin Phillips wrote of an emerging Republican majority in 1969.[32] That majority has yet to evolve, at least not on the scale Phillips envisioned or as Republicans hoped.

But some partisan changes have occurred. Today's partisan identities reflect changes in the New Deal party configurations that have occured since the realignment of 1932. These include, most prominently (1) a party realignment in the South, which has moved from solidly Democratic to predominantly Republican; (2) declining allegiance of some other New Deal coalition members to the Democratic Party; (3) the growth of Democratic loyalty among some formerly Republican groups; (4) the changing partisan effect of religion; (5) the uncertain partisanship of Latinos and Asians, "new" groups in the electorate; and (6) the growing ideological division between the parties. (Table 1 outlines the partisan identities of a variety of demographic groups.)

Southern Realignment

In the 1960s, the realignment issue was not the economy or war; it was race, and it took root in the South. The change in party identification among white southerners is the main reason that polls have shown a decline in Democratic loyalties nationwide.

After the Civil War (1861–1865) and until 1964, the Republicans took pride in being the "party of Lincoln," the party that ended slavery. Until the New Deal era, most African Americans voted Republican. And the Southern Democratic Party was the party of whites, supporting racist policies. But these positions have been reversed in the southern party realignment.

Roosevelt's administration worked only cautiously to improve the status of African Americans, though some progress was made. But after World War II, Roosevelt's

TABLE 1 Characteristics of Republican, Independents, and Democrats

	Republican	Independent	Democrat
Total	30	36	34
Age 18–25	7	18	16
26–30	10	13	7
31–50	52	40	39
51–65	18	18	21
Over 65	13	11	17
Less than high school	11	15	15
High school graduate	29	35	35
Some college	29	27	29
College graduate	34	22	21
Men	46	45	43
Women	54	55	57
Married	73	51	61
Widowed, Divorced, Separated	15	21	15
Never married	10	29	23
White	86	77	62
Hispanic	5	6	8
African American	2	8	21
Native American	0	1	1
Asian American	2	2	2
Mixed race	6	6	7
Protestant	63	50	57
Catholic	29	27	27
Jewish	1	1	3
None	6	18	10
Attended religious services	79	59	68
Under $15,000	5	10	14
$15,000–$35,000	20	23	24
$35,000–$50,000	15	21	16
$50,000–$85,000	34	27	28
Over $85,000	23	18	15
Family member belongs to a union	10	24	22
Employment:			
Working	64	65	73
Retired	12	12	14
Unemployed	4	12	5
Homemaker	9	3	2
Conservative	76	33	21
Moderate	18	37	31
Liberal	6	30	48

Source: NES, 2002, N=1, 511.

Democratic successor, Harry Truman, ordered the integration of the military. This move drew intense criticism in the South. Then, in 1948, the Democratic platform proposed new civil rights legislation. That led Strom Thurmond, a Democratic governor of South Carolina, and some other southern convention delegates to bolt the Democratic Party. They formed a breakaway third party, the States' Rights Party, commonly called the Dixiecrats. With that party label, Thurman ran for president against Truman, and the Dixiecrats carried four Deep South states. Although the Dixiecrats returned to the Democratic Party by 1952, southern discomfort with the Democrats grew in the 1950s when northern Democrats supported modest civil rights legislation. But at that time, so did many Republicans.

The movement of southern conservatives to the Republican Party gained momentum when Democratic president Lyndon Johnson supported and the Democratic-controlled Congress passed the landmark Civil Rights Act of 1964. This legislation, also supported by many Republicans, including the Republican leadership, gave African Americans the right to be served in restaurants, stay in motels, go to movie theaters, and make use of any facility serving the public. The bill was strongly opposed throughout the white South because it undermined the traditional white supremacy and segregation of the region. At the time he signed the bill, Johnson commented that this act would deliver the South to the Republicans for the next fifty years. And sure enough, Barry Goldwater, the Republican presidential nominee running against Johnson in 1964, denounced the Civil Rights Act as an affront to "states' rights." Though Goldwater himself seemed not to have a racial motive, and he believed strongly in states' rights in areas that had nothing to do with race, some of his advisers and other Republican leaders in the South used his opposition to appeal to the segregationist vote. His anti–Civil Rights Act speech, delivered a couple of weeks before the election, was widely disseminated in the South,[33] and his support for "states' rights" was read as code for letting the South maintain its segregated racial system. He did better in the Deep South than any other Republican presidential candidate had to that time.

Later, Richard Nixon institutionalized the Republican's "southern strategy," continuing to appeal to white voters in the South using racial code words such as "states' rights," "law and order," and "welfare," with the implication that "states' rights" meant shutting out African Americans and that "law and order" meant quelling African American criminals and rioters. After taping a campaign ad stressing "law and order in our schools," he said to his aides, "Yep, this hits it right on the nose. . . . It's all about law and order and the damn Negro–Puerto Rican groups out there."[34] This southern strategy was further enhanced by Ronald Reagan, who opened his presidential campaign by making a states' rights speech

Strom Thurmond broke with the Democratic party to run for president in 1948 on the Dixiecrat segregation ticket. Senate leader and fellow Republican Trent Lott congratulates him on his accomplishments on his 100th birthday.

in Philadelphia, Mississippi, where three civil rights workers had been brutally murdered by local citizens with assistance and cover-up provided by local law enforcement officials, one of the most notorious crimes of the civil rights era (see Chapter 15). Reagan also talked about "welfare queens"—a thinly veiled reference to black women who presumably were living the high life while on welfare.

The most famous political ad of the 1988 presidential campaign was a TV commercial sponsored by the Republicans. It linked the Democratic presidential candidate, Michael Dukakis, to a black felon, Willie Horton, whom Dukakis, as governor of Massachusetts, had, in accordance with the state's policy, allowed to go on a weekend furlough. While on that furlough, Horton raped a white woman. When the ad began to run, George H. W. Bush, the Republican candidate, began to rise in the polls. The link between the Democrats and black criminals was apparently deliberate. The ad and the reaction to it were so powerful that after the election, people who were questioned about what they recalled about the campaign mentioned "Bush, Dukakis, and Willie Horton."[35]

The Republicans' racial strategy was normally conducted carefully and only with code words. Rarely did public officials openly use racial epithets or praise segregation, as politicians of both parties did for generations before the Civil Rights Act. But in 2002, Trent Lott, the Republican Senate majority leader from Mississippi, disregarded these norms when on the occasion of the hundredth birthday of Strom Thurmond, the Dixiecrat candidate for president in 1948 who later switched to the Republican Party, he declared that his state was proud to

have voted for Strom Thurmond's ticket. "And if the rest of the country had followed our lead," he continued, "we wouldn't have had all these problems over the years either." Lott later apologized, and the public condemnation, including a rebuke by George W. Bush, caused him to resign his leadership position.

The southern strategy has been very successful. Since 1968, Republicans have carried the South in all presidential elections, except when southerner Jimmy Carter was the Democratic candidate in 1976. Even then, a majority of white southerners voted for the Republican, Gerald Ford. White southerners have increasingly voted Republican in congressional and state races too. Since 1994, they have cast the majority of their votes for Republicans.

Currently, eight of twelve southern governors are Republican, as are a vast majority of southern senators. The GOP is less advantaged in the House, holding over half the seats from the southern states. Of course, black southerners consistently support the Democrats and are the backbone of the Southern Democratic Party.[36]

This realignment certainly does not mean that all or even most southern white Republicans are racist or that all or most southern Republican officials are. It does, however, mean that the Republicans have strategically used a conservative and sometimes implicitly racist approach to race-related issues to build their dominance in the South, just as the Democrats did for generations before them.

The shift of conservative white southerners to the Republican Party not only makes the South more Republican but also makes the Republican Party more conservative and the party system more ideological. Con-

The glowering face of criminal Willie Horton, featured in a Republican TV commercial linking the criminal to the Democratic candidate, Michael Dukakis, became one of the most memorable images of the 1988 presidential campaign.

servative southern Republicans are more conservative, on the whole, than the Democrats they replaced, and they are, on the whole, more conservative than northern Republicans. Their conservative voice has shifted the balance of power in the South and among Republican officials in a conservative direction. At the same time, the Democratic Party became more liberal as the number of conservative Democrats shrank. Moreover, with African Americans as full participants in the political processes of the South, Southern Democratic public officials tend to be more liberal than the earlier generation of Southern Democratic elected officials, who were elected largely (or in some cases only) by a white electorate.

Declining Democratic Loyalty of Other New Deal Coalition Groups

Although a realignment has occurred in the South, the same cannot be said for the nation as a whole. Yet changing issues and circumstances and the fading memory of the Depression have led to other changes.

Blue-collar white ethnic minorities, many of them Catholic, were at the heart of Roosevelt's Democratic coalition.[37] But in the last quarter of the twentieth century, these groups found the Democrats much less attractive.[38] With the success of the New Deal and the economic security it provided, in some elections blue-collar workers felt free to focus on other issues, such as the Vietnam War, crime, race, and so-called family values.

Ronald Reagan captured many blue-collar votes. However, the GOP was unable to establish a lasting and permanent link with blue-collar workers. When economic times turned bad for blue-collar workers, they again turned to the Democrats, supporting Clinton in 1992 and 1996.

Growing Democratic Support among Some Former Republican Groups

Whereas blue-collar workers are less Democratic today then they used to be, other groups are more Democratic in their leanings. In the New Deal party configuration, the more affluent, better-educated, and white-collar workers voted predominantly Republican. But the relationship between income and party allegiance has weakened considerably and in some instances reversed. Many well-educated professionals (lawyers, doctors, scientists, and academics) have found a new home in the Democratic Party, where they are supportive of Democratic initiatives to make health care more affordable, preserve the environment, and guarantee abortion rights.[39] In 2000, Al Gore did quite well in the nation's most affluent communities, winning better than 70 percent of the vote in some.[40] Other white-collar workers are also somewhat less Republican than before, especially public service workers. Many of them are sympathetic to Democratic Party efforts to retain, if not expand, the government's role in providing services and dealing with the nation's problems.

If anything, women were, traditionally, slightly more politically conservative than men. Now women are increasingly voting Democratic. Though stay-at-home moms are slightly likely to be Republican, working women and unmarried women are disproportionately Democrats.[41] Women seem to be attracted to the Democrats not because of their stand on women's issues such as abortion rights but rather because of their support for human service initiatives like education, Social Security, and health insurance. Women are disproportionately the caregivers in our society, and they like the idea that government will give families a hand when needed. Women are also less attracted than men to support for war and military spending.[42]

Religion as a Factor Shaping Party Identity

Religion helped shape the New Deal coalition in that Catholics and Jews, many of them immigrants or children of immigrants, tended to be Democrats. Protestants tended to be Republicans. As cultural and social issues gained strength relative to economic ones, this cleavage has declined and a new religious cleavage has emerged. Today, the cleavage is between those who are very religious and those who are not. Church attendance is more highly correlated with partisanship than either income or education is. Among weekly churchgoers, Bush won

80 percent of the vote in 2000. Among those who never attend, Gore won 60 percent.[43] Although the number of nonreligious Americans appears to be growing, most Americans still claim to be quite religious.

The link between religiosity and partisanship probably lies in the support that the Republicans articulate for positions against homosexuality and abortion and in favor of prayer in schools and other public places, along with similar issues that are sometimes lumped together under the banner "traditional values." Many of the very religious regret and oppose the drift toward a more secular society. They believe that American society is becoming less moral, and they see political activism as a way to combat this slide.

Uncertain Partisanship of New Demographic Groups

Latinos and Asians are growing portions of the electorate. Although both Latinos and Asians have lived in the United States for generations, many current residents are from families of recent immigrants (with the important exception of "old" Latino populations in the Southwest, who predated Anglo settlement in America). As relative newcomers, they have not been part of the party histories we have described, and both parties are working to win their loyalties.

Both Latinos and Asians are divided among specific ethnic groups. Cuban Americans and Mexican Americans, for example, are both "Hispanic" but have very different histories and cultures. Latinos, except for Cuban Americans, have traditionally voted Democratic. Asians, again fragmented among many different groups, from Chinese to Pakistani, have been Republican but have become more Democratic in recent elections.

Both parties are reaching out to these groups and hope to win them over. The Bush administration has made a concerted effort to woo Hispanic voters. Bush has given his weekly radio address in Spanish, has developed a high-profile friendly relationship with the president of Mexico, and before 9/11 even suggested that illegal Mexican immigrants be granted legal status. Given the growth of the Latino population, especially in the Southwest, winning the allegiance of significant numbers of Hispanics is crucial to the Republicans' remaining competitive in states like California and Texas.

Ideological Parties

The New Deal party configuration consisted of two parties that were each quite ideologically heterogeneous. Although the Democrats were, on balance, more liberal than the Republicans, the Democratic Party included southern conservatives as well as northern liberals, and the Republicans included liberals too, though they were called "moderate Republicans." We have already shown that as a result of the southern Republican realignment,

each party is now more ideologically homogeneous than it used to be. Republicans are mostly individuals of conservative bent, while Democrats consist largely of people who are more liberal (although most Democrats do not call themselves liberals). Independents generally fall in between Republicans and Democrats, though some hold more radical beliefs.

Even though Republicans tend to be conservative, the Republican Party represents an uneasy coalition of traditional conservatives, motivated primarily by a desire to minimize government intervention in business activity, and new conservatives, motivated primarily by a desire to institutionalize their religious and moral values. Called the Religious Right, these new conservatives look to government to check personal behaviors they find objectionable, such as abortion and same-sex marriage. The Republican factions originally united in their hate for communism and their support for Ronald Reagan. But the disintegration of the Soviet Union and the departure of Reagan left them with less in common.[44]

In many state party organizations (discussed later in the chapter), the Religious Right has considerable influence in recruiting candidates to run for office and shaping the policy direction of the party in the state. Since the 1992 Republican National Convention, the right has avoided open confrontation with the shrinking group

The Republican Party has tried to pull blue-collar workers away from their traditional home in the Democratic Party. As president, Ronald Reagan was especially effective in luring these voters.

of moderate Republican officeholders, and national party leaders have stressed issues such as lower taxes and smaller government, on which both agree. Candidates from the right, except in rural areas and the South, often avoid broadcasting positions that alienate moderates. Instead, they spread the word quietly through the churches. However, in 2004, they highlighted their position on same-sex marriage, more than their position on abortion, because most voters opposed same-sex marriage (unlike abortion). Indeed, they used the specter of same-sex marriage as a rallying cry to get like-minded voters to the polls.

The Democrats are divided in different ways. Some want to emphasize their liberal roots by appealing to working men and women and denouncing Republican support for big business and wealthy taxpayers. Others want the party to appeal to moderates who want lower taxes, less government, and more local control.[45] Bill Clinton directed his appeal toward the middle, angering many liberal Democrats in Congress. Clinton, who opened his second inaugural address with the statement, "The era of big government is over," thought it political suicide for him and the party to continue pushing a liberal agenda. As one of his aides put it, "We can't define ourselves as the party of government."[46] The party needs both its liberal base and the moderate middle to be successful. Both Al Gore and John Kerry sought to appeal to moderates in their presidential campaigns, but they were also vocal in their opposition to the Republican strategies of massive tax cuts for the wealthy.

Decline of Parties

Although political parties are alive and well, their role has shrunk since their heyday in the late nineteenth and early twentieth centuries. Parties were strong then because they played a myriad of essential roles unduplicated by other agencies and individuals: they provided welfare, jobs, and information; nominated candidates and got them elected; and organized governance. One reason for their diminished role is that other groups have stepped in to fill many of the roles that parties formerly played.

Dimunition of Party Functions

Welfare

The welfare function that parties played in helping new immigrants and other poor people obtain food, housing, and jobs and be assimilated into American culture has been largely superseded by many government programs put in place in the twentieth century, ranging from Social Security to Medicare to food stamps. When economic hardship strikes, individuals can now obtain assistance from the government, so they do not need parties to provide it. Those who are hungry can apply for food stamps, and laid-off workers can apply for unemployment compensation. Schools also play a role in providing assistance to immigrant children (and sometimes their parents) who need to learn English and become assimilated to American ways.

The ability of political parties to provide jobs has also been restricted. The adoption of merit hiring in government service (for more on that, see Chapter 12) means that once elected to office, party leaders cannot just hire their supporters through patronage. Of course, some patronage jobs do exist, such as agency heads and a small number of other positions, but it is risky to put nonqualified people in high-profile jobs. (Obvious patronage jobs at the national level are certain ambassadorships, often given to big contributors to the president's campaign fund.) Of course, the adoption of merit-based hiring has been, on balance, a good thing. We want government employees to be qualified, not just friends and supporters of those elected to office. Merit appointment also reduces the opportunities for corruption and kickbacks. And merit appointment is fairer as a way of selecting those to be hired. It's not just who you know but also what you can do that is supposed to matter in merit systems.

Information

Parties also lost control over information. In the mass media age, most people get their news from newspapers and television. Most national news media strive for balance (see Chapter 8); none are controlled by political parties.

Nominations and Campaigns

Most significant, perhaps, is that parties have lost control over their ability to select nominees for office. As we noted earlier, the introduction of primary elections turned nominations over to whomever the party's electorate chose. The national parties still hold nominating conventions, but the parties' nominees have been chosen long before the convention through presidential primaries held in most states. The winner of these contests almost invariably becomes the party's nominee. Conventions are, in some ways, superfluous, but they continue to serve the function of publicizing the nominees and rallying party supporters.

Parties also play a diminished role in actually electing their candidates. Parties certainly play some role: they help finance campaigns, provide advisers and strategists, and help publicize candidates. National party leaders will often campaign for newcomers or fellow party members in tight races. However, nowadays candidates

In the days before polling and primaries, delegates to the party's presidential nominating convention selected the party's nominee for president. Delegates at the 1924 Democratic convention, shown here, required 103 ballots over the course of two weeks to nominate John Davis for president. He lost to Calvin Coolidge and faded into obscurity.

hire their own campaign managers, pollsters, media experts, computer gurus, event organizers, and all the other essential components of a modern campaign. They still seek advice from party leaders and often hire experts who have worked for other successful party members, but it is the candidate's choices that prevail and the candidate's funds that pay for the campaign team.

Governing

Paying for campaign experts and for media to publicize the candidate costs money. Though parties raise tens of millions of dollars for their candidates, others also provide significant funds. Corporations give to both parties, though in larger amounts to Republicans. Labor unions give primarily to Democrats. Special interests ranging from pro-gun lobbies to environmental groups give to candidates of both parties. By providing such financing, corporations, unions, and special-interest groups buy access to the candidates. So when public officials seek to govern, they owe loyalties not just to their political parties but also to the corporations, unions, and special interests that financed them.

Erosion of Support for Parties

Because parties do not play the roles they used to, people understandably believe that parties are less important then they used to be. The term **dealignment** has often

been used to refer to the diminished relevance of the parties.

Increase in Independents and Split-Ticket Voters

There are several indicators of dealignment. One is a decline in the strength of party allegiance in the general population. The proportion identifying themselves as either strong Democrats or strong Republicans has fallen, though not by much.[47] The number calling themselves independents has risen from less than 15 percent in 1960 to more than 40 percent in 2000.[48] The tendency for younger rather than older Americans to identify as independent means that the electorate may become even more independent as older Americans die. On the other hand, a highly partisan environment may diminish the number of independents, forcing people to take sides. (Just as plausibly, however, it could drive more people to the center if they become disgusted with bitter partisanship battles.)

Split-ticket voting is another indication of dealignment. Split-ticket voting is the term for voting for a member of one party for one office and another party for a different office, such as for the Republican presidential candidate but a Democratic House candidate. Ticket splitting is much more common than in the 1950s (see Figure 4).[49] Voters who split their ticket indicate

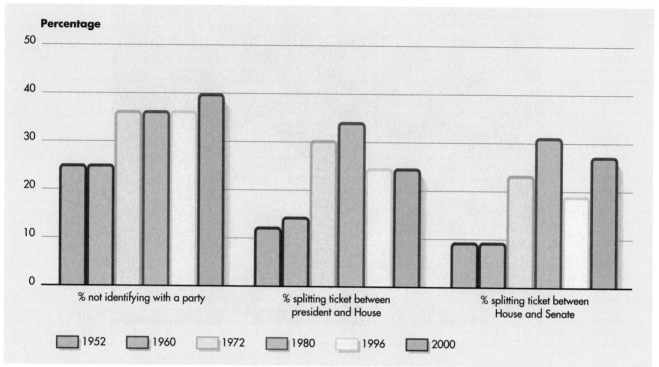

Percentage

% not identifying with a party

% splitting ticket between
president and House

% splitting ticket between
House and Senate

☐ 1952 ☐ 1960 ☐ 1972 ☐ 1980 ☐ 1996 ☐ 2000

FIGURE 4 ▪ Is Partisanship Reemerging?

SOURCE: National Election Studies, Center for Political Studies, University of Michigan, 1952–2000 (www.umich.edu/~nes).

that personalities, issues, or something other than partisanship drives their vote.

Disinterest in Parties

Another sign of dealignment is disinterest in the parties. The number of Americans who say there is nothing they like or dislike about either the Democratic or Republican Party has increased.[50] Parties are simply not reaching many voters.[51] Another indication of disinterest is low turnout in elections (see Chapter 8).

The failure of Americans to identify with political parties, the increasing incidence of split-ticket voting, and low voter turnout are all signs of loosening party ties.[52] And as party ties grow weaker, the capacity of Americans to hold government accountable diminishes and the influence of special-interest groups increases.[53]

Resurgence of Parties

We have painted a rather bleak picture of the decline of American parties during the past century. Parties are weaker than they were a century ago. Yet it is clear from the news that we hear every day that parties are far from dead. They still perform vital functions. And in fact, they have been experiencing something of a resurgence over the past twenty years. Partisanship in the national gov-

ernment has increased in the past decade, and the near parity between the parties in their electoral strength and the 2004 election process have reengaged many formerly apathetic voters.

Important Remaining Functions of Parties

Though parties no longer provide much welfare, public officials have become mediators between the public and the bureaucracy. Each year, hundreds of thousands of people ask their state legislator, member of Congress, or local council member to intervene on their behalf with the bureaucracy: to find out what happened to a missing Social Security check, to intervene to cut the time to process a visa application, or even to get a government job. Elected officials are quite interested in providing these intermediary services, and their success becomes part of the record that they, and their party, run on.

Information

Parties no longer have party newspapers, but they have become increasingly involved in providing information to their supporters on the Web, through direct mail, and on radio and television. During congressional and presidential campaigns, party supporters can expect to receive weekly or sometimes even more frequent communication from the national, state, and local party organizations and congressional campaign committees. Most of this is focused on soliciting donations, but these letters and messages also provide information about issues and candidates, portraying the party in a favorable light and denigrating the other party.

Nominations

Parties do not control nominations for national offices anymore and usually have little clout at the state level. But for many state and local offices, party leaders take the lead in encouraging qualified individuals to run for office and then provide them with an unofficial or official party endorsement and support. Party leaders often encourage and support promising candidates to run for Congress too. Once these candidates are nominated in primaries, the parties provide support in various ways. The amount of support depends on the office and the strength of the party in that area. But the national campaign organizations will provide candidates they believe have a chance to win with significant financial assistance, access to a variety of services (media consultants, for example), and opportunities to participate in seminars and workshops to get advice about running a successful campaign. Although the party does not have a monopoly on these resources anymore, the national campaign organizations are increasingly well financed and have much to offer candidates.

Governance

Parties are increasingly important in governance. Parties have important organizational and leadership functions in Congress. The majority in each chamber controls the agenda—it decides what issues will be debated and voted on. The majority also controls what happens in committees, where the work of Congress is done. The party also links the president with the members of his party in Congress. The president's party supports his policies substantially more often than the opposition. In 2003, Republicans in the Senate and House supported George W. Bush 94 and 89 percent of the time, respectively, while Senate Democrats supported him 48 percent of the time and House Democrats, a scant 26 percent.[54]

Thus important legislation is often a contest between the Republican and Democratic visions of the right policy choice. Though most Americans deplore the heightened party wrangling now occurring, the clear partisan divisions make it easier to hold elected officials responsible. Voting for one party rather than the other has definite policy consequences. Assuming that voters know the general positions of the parties when they cast their votes, legislative voting along party lines increases the prospects for popular control of government. For example, given that the Republican Party's official position is pro-life and the Democratic Party's position is pro-choice, a vote for a Republican candidate will typically mean support for a pro-life position. Should the Republicans win a majority, they would try to enact a pro-life position into law. They might not succeed immediately, but if they have a strong enough majority and hold it for long enough, eventually they could.

This is sometimes called **responsible party government.** The term implies a choice between parties, voters who comprehend that choice, and elected officials who vote for their party's position.

Great Britain is often cited as an example of responsible party government. Political parties are heavily involved in developing, articulating, and implementing public policy. If elected party members defect too often from the party's position, party leaders can deny them the right to stand for reelection as the party's candidates.

American political parties do not always conform to this model. They do not always offer clear and contrasting policy positions. Even when they do, party leaders have only limited authority to force their elected members to accept the party's position. However, in recent years, Democrats and Republicans have been more likely to accept their party's positions due to the increased ideological homogeneity of the parties.

The problem with the responsible party government model is when neither party has a clear majority. Then, instead of legislation, we find stalemate. However, when neither party has a clear majority, it probably means that Americans themselves are evenly divided and there is no firm mandate for officials to act on.

Party Influence on Policymaking

These party differences are reflected in partisan voting in Congress, which has increased dramatically since the 1980s.[55] To a large degree, this results from the realignment in the South. The days of white conservative Democrats who voted with the Republicans almost as often as with their own party are almost over.[56] As white conservatives have moved into the Republican Party, districts with conservative white majorities are much more likely to elect Republicans than conservative Democrats. Districts with large numbers of black voters are more likely than before to elect African Americans or moderate or liberal white Democrats. Thus voting patterns of representatives from the South now divide along party lines as they do in the North.[57]

It also reflects Republican control of both houses of Congress. A number of conservative Republicans committed to a very conservative agenda were elected in

1994. Eager to retain control of Congress, moderate incumbent Republicans embraced their conservative program to show voters that the party could enact legislation and govern effectively.[58] Moderate Democrats, on the other hand, did not support the GOP's agenda, and the gap between the parties increased.

Moderate Republicans have come under intense pressure from the White House to support George W. Bush and his party's conservative agenda. Senator Olympia Snow of Maine and other moderates in the Senate are routinely summoned to the White House and lobbied by both the president and the vice president. Although presidents have always pressured members of Congress, the tactics of the administration and its allies are designed to make individuals who deviate from the party uncomfortable. For her unwillingness to support a Bush tax cut higher than $350 billion, Snow was trashed by the *Wall Street Journal* and identified on the Web site Republican in Name Only, sponsored by the conservative Club for Growth.[59]

Party line voting in recent decades has been increasing and is likely to remain high. Each party has a distinct vision it is trying to implement. During the Bush administration, on issues in which majorities in each party opposed each other, House Republican's support for the party's position averaged better than 90 percent. Democrats were somewhat less unified, supporting their party's position in the mid–80 percent range. Party support in the Senate was similar (see Figure 5).[60] Only the war on terror managed to bring the parties together—fleetingly, as it turned out (see the box "Bipartisanship for a While" on page 224).

It is hard to imagine a higher rate of partisanship within our existing system of separation of powers.

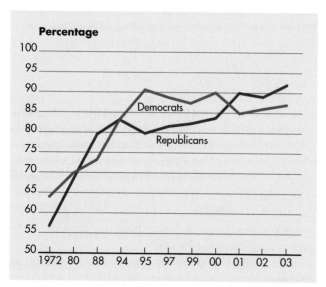

FIGURE 5 ■ Party Unity in Congressional Voting

Lower levels await a president who is committed to trying to build bridges across partisan lines and a minority party willing to work with the president.

Party Organization

Political parties consist of the partisans among the public and the party's officeholders. But behind the scenes is the third component of political parties, the party organization. Described as hollow shells in the 1950s and l960s, the national party organizations are stronger today than they have been since the early twentieth century. Behind their success is a steady flow of cash from corporations, interest groups, and unions.

The major levels of party organization—national, state, and local—coincide with political units responsible for administering elections. Within local parties, there are further subdivisions. The precinct is usually the smallest unit. Several precincts comprise a ward or district; several wards comprise a city or county. Each lower-level organization feeds into the next higher level.

Although party organization seems hierarchical (organized from the top down), it is not. Party organization is a layered structure with each layer linked to, but independent of, the others. Higher levels cannot dictate to or impose penalties on lower levels to ensure compliance. Party organization is only loosely connected with the party in government, in contrast with the British system, where party leaders in Parliament maintain a tight grip on the party organization.

National Party Organization

The **national party chair** heads each national party organization, called the **national committee.** The president appoints the chair of his party; this task falls to the national committee of the opposition party. The national party chair is a low-profile position, and the person who serves is generally not very visible to the public, though occasionally there are exceptions. If you know that in 2004, Terry McAuliffe was the Democratic National Committee chairman and Ed Gillespie the Republican National Committee Chairman, you are well informed indeed. The primary function of party chairs these days is to raise money, but they also make public appearances and issue press releases to represent the party.[61] When a party is out of office, the party chair is often the spokesperson for the party.

Although the national committees are the primary governing institutions of the Democratic and Republican parties, they seldom meet, and it is the national chair and the permanent staff who are the de facto national organization. The national committees do choose the site of their party's national convention and establish the formula for determining how many delegates each state receives.

National committee members are selected from each state using a variety of methods established by each state party. Whereas states are represented equally on the Republican National Committee (RNC), the Democratic National Committee (DNC) awards states additional seats based on population and support for Democratic candidates in elections. The DNC also includes the party's leaders in Congress, the leaders of several state and local Democratic organizations, and representatives from elements of the party that are often underrepresented on the committee, including blacks, Hispanics, and young adults.

Both major parties also have House and Senate campaign committees, which have grown in influence owing to their ability to raise and distribute campaign funds to their party's candidates for Congress.[62] The National Republican Senatorial Committee and the National Republican Congressional Committee together raised more than $100 million for the 2002 congressional elections, and their counterpart Democratic committees raised nearly $60 million.[63] New campaign finance laws have not stemmed the fundraising, which attained even higher levels in 2004 (see Chapter 9).[64]

The increasing capacity of the national party organizations to offer candidates assistance in their campaigns may be responsible for the rising level of party voting in Congress. Members of Congress no doubt do feel beholden to the national party and perhaps a commitment to support party positions. At the same time, members are less beholden to state and local parties. Thus national party organizations are growing in influence at the expense of state and local parties.[65] The national parties are even communicating directly with voters via the Internet (see the box "Parties on the Web" on page 227). The close link between the national party organizations and the parties in Congress moves us closer to the responsible party government model.

State and Local Party Organizations

Party organizations also exists at the state and local levels. There are chairs and committees to direct the activities of the party activists at these levels too. In some communities, parties may be so weak and unimportant that there is little party organization. Because of this, someone who wants to become active in the party organization only has to show up at party meetings and be willing to work. Earlier, we discussed the historical po-

litical machines in large urban areas. Today, these organizations are generally weak, though some, as in Chicago, retain some power.

Parties and Voting

Just how important are parties in shaping individual voting behavior? For sixty years, political scientists have argued about how voters make their choices among parties, issues, and personalities. Political scientist Stanley Kelley has argued that voters go through a simple process in deciding how to vote. They add up the things they like about each candidate and party, and they vote for the candidate with the highest number of "likes." If there is a tie, they vote on the basis of their party identification, if they have one. If they do not, they abstain. On the basis of this simple idea, Kelley explains more than 85 percent of the variation in voting choice.[66]

In making these calculations, then, voters consider three things:

- The party of the candidate, which has a great effect on how the voter views everything else about the person
- The candidate's personality, style, and appearance
- The issue stands of the candidate and the party

Despite considerable disagreement as to exactly how each of these is weighted in voters' minds, political scientists can offer some general conclusions.

Party Identification

Party identification is probably the most important factor influencing a person's vote: Democrats tend to vote for Democrats and Republicans for Republicans. This is true from the top of the ticket down to the bottom. Party preference influences how a voter perceives a candidate's personality and issue stance. For some people, party identification is their only source of information about candidates, and they vote on the basis of it alone.

Though partisan loyalties are not as strong as in the early twentieth century, they are still a powerful predictor of the vote. Even though there are more independents today and more people who vote contrary to their partisan loyalties than there used to be, if you are guessing how a person will vote, the best single bit of information to have is the person's party identification. In 2000, for example, among those who went to the polls, 86 percent of all Democrats voted for Gore and 91 percent of all Republicans voted for Bush.[67] These

BIPARTISANSHIP FOR A WHILE

In his 2000 election campaign, George W. Bush urged an end to the bitter partisan conflicts that characterized the Clinton years. He promised a fresh approach, seeking cooperation and building consensus with Democrats in Congress. Bush had worked cooperatively with the Democrats when he was governor of Texas. But Texas is not Washington. The Democratic Party in Texas is generally quite conservative, and as in all states, the day-to-day workings of the legislature and state government are not covered by a national media driven to feature the conflicts that divide the parties.

Thus few believed it possible that a bipartisan spirit would take hold in Washington. The parties have major disagreements about policy, disagreements that reflect differences of opinion in the public, ranging from health care to the Middle East. Moreover, Democrats were unlikely to forget the treatment of Bill Clinton by Republicans in Congress during his presidency. Many conservative Republicans hated Clinton in a way that went beyond partisanship. In addition to his policies, many objected to his personal life. Investigations of his financial dealings before becoming president dogged his presidency, and the Monica Lewinsky scandal and impeachment drove the division even deeper. Talk radio, with the occasional Republican member of Congress as a guest, filled the airways with Bill and Hillary's real and alleged wrongdoings.

The 2000 election was extremely partisan, and the outcome, decided by the U.S. Supreme Court, was a bitter pill for the Democrats to swallow, for their candidate had won the popular vote. Many Democrats, including some in Congress, believed that Gore did win the election, and were it not for Republican-appointed justices on the Supreme Court, Gore would be sitting in the White House instead of Bush. However, the Democrats accepted the verdict and hoped that indeed the new president would be a conciliator.

In spite of Bush's early efforts to establish personal relations with congressional leaders of both parties, the tone quickly turned sour. Despite his lack of any mandate from the voters, he decided to govern from the right rather than the center. His appointments and much of his legislative agenda were directed toward pleasing his conservative base rather than reflecting his moderate tone in the campaign and the closeness of the election. And the Republican leadership in Congress seemed to give up on the idea, if they ever had it, of moving toward the center, now that the party controlled both the presidency and the House.

Then came the terrorist attacks of September 11, 2001. Suddenly, "United We Stand" became the theme. In a moment, the usual political calculations were swept aside. The Senate voted 98–0 authorizing the president to use "all necessary and appropriate force" against those involved in the attack. The House followed 420–1. Singing the "Battle Hymn of the Republic," Democrats and Republicans joined hands in the Capitol. Commentators spoke of an end to partisanship and division in American society, of a new era with the nation pulling and working together. In spite of Bush's tainted election and an evenly divided Congress, bipartisanship had arrived. Democrats rallied to support the president. Of course, this response was bolstered by the president's overwhelming popular support, as his approval ratings soared over 90 percent.

But politics is politics, and real differences about policy do not disappear because of a national disaster. The president saw an opportunity to push his domestic agenda in the guise of fighting terrorism (see "You Are There" in Chapter 4), and Democrats began to complain about that. Standing outside the Capitol on September 25, 2001, House Democrats admonished the president that wartime deference would not extend beyond proposals to combat terrorism. The terrorist-induced infusion of bipartisanship lasted exactly forty-three days, by one count, from September 11 to October 24.

Yet that judgment was more superficial than real. On a whole range of policy alternatives, for months Democrats seemed afraid to challenge the president. They were fearful that the public would think they were "soft on terrorism," and the Republicans were quick to bandy those charges, even against a decorated Vietnam veteran, Senator Max Cleland (D-Ga.), who lost three limbs in that war. Most Democrats willingly signed on to support the USA PATRIOT Act, which gave investigatory agencies more power than ever before to snoop into people's private lives, de-

party support proportions were similar in the 1998 and 2002 off-year elections. Similarly, a CNN poll in the spring of 2004 showed that 97 percent of Democrats and of Republicans intended to vote for their party's nominee.[68]

How do people get to be Republicans and Democrats? Socioeconomic class is a very important predictor of the vote: the lower the income, the more likely to vote Democrat. But this general rule is crosscut with distinctive ethnic and religious patterns (we use

tain the accused without the usual due process procedures, and in general tip the balance between freedom and security heavily toward the latter. Democrats were hesitant to criticize the administration for the conduct of the war on terrorism even when it seemed to go badly, for failing to pursue al-Qaeda in Afghanistan, and for undertaking a military invasion of Iraq. Most Democrats were reluctant to criticize the president's plans to attack Iraq, even though the evidence linking Iraq and 9/11 was nonexistent. Indeed, most Democrats signed on to give the president authority to attack Iraq.

Growing public disenchantment as the Iraqi war began to drag on seemed to give the Democratic leaders renewed courage to speak out again, not just on the war but on domestic issues too. After all, bipartisanship had been pretty much a one-way street, with Democrats supporting the Bush program and little reciprocity from the Republicans moving toward the Democrats. Indeed, showing Republican disdain for bipartisanship, Dick Armey, the former House Republican majority leader, described bipartisanship as "another name for date rape." The Democrats began to realize that they had been victimized.[1]

Democratic activists among the rank and file were increasingly unhappy with the Democratic leadership's failure to provide alternatives to the president. The candidacy of Howard Dean for president galvanized many rank-and-file Democrats who were angry that their representatives in Congress had appeared cowed not by terrorists but by George

W. Bush. Dean's statement that he was running from "the Democratic wing of the Democratic party"[2] won thunderous applause at campaign rallies and galvanized many Democrats to turn out to vote in the primaries. Democratic turnout in the early 2004 primaries was at near-record highs, and anger toward the president grew among Democratic activists.

We are in a period of intense partisanship. Partisan voting in Congress was near all-time highs in 2003. By mid-2004, almost all Americans had made up their minds about their choice in the November presidential election, far earlier than normal. People either loved the president or despised him. Few were in between. One Democratic leader from California remarked that "the other team has a player we all hate, and we're going to take it out on that team in the field."[3] A Republican countered, "Hey, you're picking on my brother here. . . . Back off or I'll punch you in the nose." Vice President Cheney broke with Senate decorum and publicly used a strong vulgarity in cursing a Democratic senator on the Senate floor. A pollster reported that "we've become two warring nations" as incivility spread from Washington to the rest of the country.[4]

Another pollster measured this partisan intensity. Adding the proportion of Democrats who strongly disapproved of Bush to the percentage of Republicans who strongly approve of him, he calculated an "intensity rate" of 137 percent. This rate is significantly higher than that of Bill Clinton (92 percent), himself a polarizing figure, and nearly

double the rate for Clinton's predecessor, George H. W. Bush.[5]

The short run of bipartisanship should not be a surprise. Disagreements are inevitable in a democratic society, and it is through political parties that they are resolved. Bipartisanship has serious defects. When individuals are afraid or unwilling to challenge the prevailing view, the nation is likely fall victim to bad decisions. Looking back, it appears that the USA PATRIOT Act was an extreme reaction to 9/11 and that the war in Iraq was a diversion from the central objective of rooting out terrorism. If the Democrats had been less hesitant to challenge the president as these policies were worked out, and if the Republicans had not eagerly grabbed the "soft on terrorism" charge against Democrats critical of President Bush, it is possible that compromise solutions would have been better, had wider support, and created a less hateful environment for the 2004 election. Bipartisanship plays well in campaign speeches, but it is partisanship that serves the interests of a diverse nation.

1. Paul Glastris, "Perverse Polarity," *Washington Monthly,* June 2004, 23.
2. A phrase credited to the late Paul Wellstone, Democratic senator from Minnesota.
3. Miles Benson, "Campaign Incites '2 Warring Nations,' *Harrisburg Patriot-News,* July 11, 2004.
4. Ibid.
5. Ibid.
SOURCES: Helen Dewar, "United They Stand," *Washington Post National Weekly Edition,* November 26, 2001, 14; Karen Foerstel, "Congress and the President: A Recalibration of Power," *CQ Weekly,* September 29, 2001, 2248–2251; David S. Broder, "Fighting over the Economy" *Washington Post National Weekly Edition,* November 5, 2001, 4.

ethnic here to refer to differences of national origin and race).

For example, Jews are much more likely to vote Democratic than other whites of similar income. On the whole, they have a higher-than-average income, yet in both 1996 and 2000, over three-fourths of Jewish voters voted Democratic. As a group, they were exceeded in their Democratic allegiance only by blacks.[69]

Catholics used to be predominantly Democratic. They still are, but not as consistently. Though a majority

"This year I'm not getting involved in any complicated issues. I'm just voting my straight ethnic prejudices."

of Catholics voted for Reagan in 1980 and 1984, they returned to the Democratic fold in the 1990s. They favored Clinton by significant margins but gave Gore only a small plurality.

African Americans are probably the most distinctive group politically. About 90 percent voted Democratic in 2000; this is a higher proportion than Democrats who voted for Clinton.

Hispanics—who, like blacks, also have lower-than-average incomes—are not as universally Democratic as blacks and have voted Republican in significant numbers. Nevertheless, almost three-quarters voted Democratic in recent congressional elections and two-thirds for recent Democratic presidential candidates. Among Hispanics, Cuban Americans are much more likely to be Republican than either Mexican Americans or Puerto Ricans. Many are refugees or descendants of refugees from Castro's Cuba and are intensely anticommunist.

The voting behavior of Asian Americans has been much less thoroughly studied than that of other groups (because until recently they were quite a small group). In 1992 and 1996, their voting patterns resembled those of whites, with a small plurality in favor of the Republican candidates, but in 1998 and 2000, a strong majority of Asian Americans voted Democratic.

White Protestants generally give a majority of their vote to the Republicans and have done so for decades. Evangelical Protestants (such as Southern Baptists and

Republicans have allied themselves with conservative Christians, especially church-going Protestant evangelicals. George W. Bush uses their language.

Republicans have tried to woo Catholics away from their traditional Democratic allegiance. President Bush has made numerous overtures to Catholic leaders.

PARTIES ON THE WEB

During the course of a decade, the Internet has become a ubiquitous part of popular culture. Individuals chat with friends, sell possessions, peruse books and magazines, do their holiday shopping, and keep up with their favorite sports teams, all on the Web. It is not surprising, then, that the Internet has become an important medium for politics.

The Web is now a powerful tool in the arsenal of political parties.[1] In a no-holds-barred fight to win control of Congress, both parties constantly upgrade their congressional sites with better messages, better artwork, and more sophisticated technology. The new technology allows the parties to communicate with their activists. Overnight they can send millions of e-mails on a particular issue, at minimal cost. Fundraising on the Net has proved to be even more effective than via traditional mail solicitations.

The GOP hopes to put everything it does online. The party calculates that more Republican than Democratic voters are online. It also wants to bypass the mainstream media, which it feels add their own spin when it comes to getting the party's message out.

The Democratic presidential contenders demonstrated the power of the Web in their 2004 campaign. The Democrats believed they could tap the average person using the Web and thereby solicit hundreds of thousands of small donations. And they were right. Howard Dean, a leading contender in the 2004 primaries, used the Internet to raise mil-

lions of dollars from small contributors, leading other candidates to rethink the potential of the Web as means of generating campaign funds.[2] Nominee John Kerry used the Web to raise over $100 million, much of it in small donations, between the time he sought the nomination and the Democratic convention in late July. His Web solicitations, coupled with "personalized" e-mails to supporters and donors, galvanized the Democratic faithful.

The public was also able to link to each party's presidential nominating convention via the Web. Each site was linked to the candidates' main themes, including Spanish-language versions, ways for citizens to volunteer, and well-produced position statements on issues. The most prominent feature at each site was a little box that popped up on the screen asking for donations. Democrats could even participate and register their opinions on the party's platform. Each party also set up sites critical of the other party's presidential candidate.

Here is a list of useful political Web sites in operation at the time this book went to press:

White House	www.whitehouse.gov
Republican National Committee	www.rnc.org
Democratic National Committee	www.democrats.org
National Republican Senatorial Committee	www.nrsc.org
Democratic Senatorial Campaign Committee	www.dscc.org
National Republican Congressional Committee	www.nrcc.org
Democratic Congressional Campaign Committee	www.dccc.org
Republican House Conference	www.gop.gov
Conservative news and information	www.townhall.com
Liberal news and information	www.epn.org
Link to the minor parties involved in U.S. politics	www.politicalindex.com/sect8.htm
Green Party, USA	www.greenparty.org

1. Neil Munro, "The New Wired Politics," *National Journal*, April 22, 2000, 1260–1263.
2. J. P. Gownder, "An Online Revolution?" *Washington Post National Weekly Edition*, July 6, 2003, 23.

members of the Assembly of God) are much more likely to vote for Republicans than mainline Protestants (such as Episcopalians or Presbyterians). However, as for other groups, income differences and the degree of commitment to religion can influence how Protestants vote.

Ethnicity and religion are important in determining the vote because they serve as shorthand for many other factors that influence political behavior—class, historical treatment by society, and basic culture and values. Jews are predominantly Democratic, for example, because as a persecuted minority throughout much of their history, they have learned to identify with the underdog, even when their own economic circumstances move them into the middle or upper class. Catholics were sometimes discriminated against too; this discrimination and their working-class status propelled them to the party of Roosevelt. As Catholics have moved into the middle class and as tolerance toward Catholics has grown, Catholics, like Protestants, have tended to vote according to their income.

Candidate Evaluations

Candidates' personalities and styles have had more impact since television has become voters' major source of information about elections. Reagan's popularity in 1984 is an example of the influence of a candidate and his personality. The perceived competence and integrity of candidates are other facets of candidate evaluation. Voters are less likely to support candidates who do not seem capable of handling the job, regardless of their issue positions. Jimmy Carter suffered in 1980 because of negative evaluations of his competence and leadership among voters.

Clinton's popularity puzzled observers. Many voters did not like his evasions and his adulterous behavior, but they voted for him anyway. During the impeachment debates, many journalists expressed amazement that Clinton's popularity remained high. The public, more than journalists, seemed to be able to separate his public and private roles. The public continued to support him because they felt he was doing a good job as president, not because they admired him personally.

Personality was important in the 2004 campaign. John Kerry seemed unable to connect with people and uncomfortable on the campaign trail. At times, he appeared to be going through the motions, playing a role. In answering questions, he often provided lengthy and detailed responses. George Bush, on the other hand, seemed more at ease, comfortable working the crowd. His responses were often truncated and general. However, both candidates' performances in the first debate raised questions about the accuracy of these characterizations. Kerry appeared calm and at ease, his answers crisp and concise. Bush seemed impatient and snarly. Regardless, the image of Kerry as an effete, somewhat snobbish, Boston patrician who was out of touch with average Americans dogged him throughout the campaign.

Issues

Issues are a third factor influencing the vote. Although Americans are probably more likely to vote on issues now than they were in the 1950s, issues influence only some of the voters some of the time. In 1984 and 1988, for example, voters' issue positions overall were closer to the positions of Mondale and Dukakis than to Reagan and Bush, yet the latter won. In 2000, voters saw themselves as much closer to Gore than Bush on the issues.[70]

Although other factors also influence voters, many do cast issue votes. To cast an issue vote, voters have to be informed about issues and have opinions. In recent elections, more than 80 percent of the public could take a position on issues such as government spending, military spending, women's rights, and relations with Russia.[71] Knowledge about these issues may have been vague, but individuals were able to understand the issues enough to define their own general positions.

Also, for voters to cast issue votes, candidates must have detectable policy differences. A substantial minority of voters are able to detect some differences among presidential candidates.[72]

Issue voting occurs when individuals correctly identify the positions of the candidates and their own position and cast a consistent vote. In every election since 1972, more than 70 percent of those who met those two conditions cast issue votes.[73] Issues with the highest proportion of issue voting were those that typically divided Republicans and Democrats, such as government spending, military spending, and government aid to the unemployed and minorities. However, because many in the electorate were unable to define both their own and the candidates' positions on each issue, the proportion of the total electorate that can be said to cast an "issue vote" is usually less than 40 percent, and for some issues it is much less.[74] Abortion is another issue on which voters cast issue-related votes. In 1996, for example, about 60 percent of the voters cast issue-related votes on abortion. Of those voters (who had a position and also knew the candidates' position), 15 percent of those who opposed abortion under any conditions voted for Clinton, a supporter of abortion rights, compared with 81 percent of those who believed that abortion should be a matter of personal choice.[75]

Issue voting may be mostly an evaluation of the current incumbents. If voters like the way incumbents, or the incumbent's party, have handled the job in general or in certain areas—the economy or foreign policy, for example—they will vote accordingly, even without much knowledge about the specifics of the issues.

Voting on the basis of past performance is called **retrospective voting.** There is good evidence that many people do this, especially according to economic conditions.[76] Voters support incumbents if national income is growing in the months preceding the election. Since World War II, the incumbent party has won a presidential election only once when the growth rate

TABLE 2	Voting as a Reflection of One's View of the Economy		
Voters Who Believe That the Policies of the Federal Government Have Made the Nation's Economy:	Percentage Who Voted for the Incumbent Party Nominee		
	1984	1992	1996
Better	84	79	82
Same	52	49	52
Worse	23	29	32

was less than 3 percent (Eisenhower in 1956) and lost only twice when it was more than 3 percent (Ford in 1976 and Gore in 2000). Unemployment and inflation seem to have less consistent effects on voting, and economic conditions two or three years before the election have little impact on voting.[77]

Table 2 shows the relationship of the presidential vote to beliefs about whether federal policies have made the nation better or worse off. Those who believe the nation is better off are considerably more likely to vote for the incumbent presidential party than others. The same general pattern holds true if the question focuses on individual economic success rather than national prosperity.

President Bush was defeated in 1992 when the economy stagnated; on the other hand, Clinton's re-election in 1996 was assisted by the booming economy. In fact, political scientists believe that economic growth in the months before the election is one of the best predictors of election results. For that reason, many were perplexed by the close 2000 election and sought to explain it in terms of Gore's poor campaign. Other pundits, though, thought perhaps that the economy had been so good for so long that people took good times for granted.[78]

Parties, Candidates, and Issues

All three factors—parties, candidates, and issues—clearly matter. Party loyalties are especially important because they help shape our views about issues and candidates. However, if issues and candidates did not matter, the Democrats would have won every presidential election since the New Deal. Republican victories suggest that they often have had more attractive candidates (as in 1952, 1956, 1980, and 1984) or issue positions (in 1972 and in some respects in 1980). However, the Democrats' partisan advantage shrank throughout the 1980s. Though there are still more registered Democrats than Republicans in the United States, the margin is modest, and the number of independents is large.

Party loyalty, candidate evaluations, and issues are

important factors in congressional elections just as in presidential ones. We will discuss congressional voting in detail in Chapter 9.

Conclusion: Do Political Parties Make Government More Responsive?

Although the Founders initially opposed the idea of political parties, some later turned to parties when they began to have serious differences of opinion about public policies. They recognized that their ideas could prevail if they aligned with others who agreed with them and together elected a majority in government. Then, as now, parties were a vehicle to organize a stable majority.

Parties are also a way for average Americans to influence government policy. Making government more accountable to voters is the major contribution of political parties to democratic government. Political parties provide an easily identifiable majority, at least in two-party systems, that voters can blame when things go wrong and reward when things go right and in the process turn public policy in the direction they prefer.

Although American political parties may not always perform exactly as described, Americans have an interest in maintaining strong and viable political parties. Without them, voters would be confronted with a hopelessly confusing array of candidates and have no idea of how a vote for any one of them will influence government policy. Without parties, the media, campaign consultants, lobbying groups, big donors, and self-financed wealthy candidates would play an even larger role in politics than they do now.

There is no doubt that parties are weaker than they were a century ago. They have, however, experienced a resurgence in the past two or three decades in several important ways. The movement of voters toward independence and the erosion of party attachments appear to have reached an end. The proportion of voters claiming partisan allegiance has grown slightly after steady declines since the 1960s. Split-ticket voting peaked in 1992 but has since declined (see Figure 4).

Party loyalty among officeholders is also stronger. Party cohesion in Congress has increased. With the demise of the Southern Democratic conservatives, the Democratic Party is much more homogeneous. Many members of both parties are more dependent on the national party committees for campaign support than they were a decade ago. Both of these trends have contributed to the increase in party voting and support for the president by his own party.

Finally, national party organizations have become much more powerful. Their activities are fueled by their ability to raise and spend large amounts of money. New campaign finance laws might channel the flow, but they are unlikely to reduce it significantly (for more on this topic, see Chapter 9).

Although parties still compete for influence with interest groups, pollsters, campaign consultants, and the media, it is often funds raised by the national parties that buy the polling, campaign consultation, and media time. Both presidential and congressional candidates need the national party organizations to aid in raising revenue and providing other services.

Each component of American political parties—partisans in the electorate, officeholders, and party organization—has shown significant signs of revitalization. Each party has its core of supporters, seeking to achieve the party's goals, but neither has come up with a program that has appeal and energizes a wide cross section of the American people. This, of course, is the role that Schattschneider saw for political parties and led him to reflect on the inevitability and necessity of parties for American democracy.

Hastert Breaks the Rules and Wins the Vote

Speaker Dennis Hastert decided to hold the vote open so that he and other members of the House leadership could persuade, or pressure, some of the twenty-five Republicans who voted no to change their vote to yes. For nearly three hours, Hastert and his colleagues worked over negative voters. At one point, Hastert and Bill Thomas (R–Calif.) stood on either side of Nick Smith (R–Mich.) while the president talked to Smith on his cell phone. But Smith stuck to his no vote.[79] Later Smith reported that he had been offered $100,000 in financial support for his son's congressional campaign if he would vote yes (he later recanted the charge.)

Jo Ann Emerson (R–Mo.) left the floor to avoid being hassled about her no vote. She later returned to the floor but went to the Democratic side and hid behind a bannister to avoid being identified.

Finally, supporters of the bill spread the word to other conservatives that if the bill failed, Democrats would force a vote on another version of the bill (it is unlikely, though possible, that they could have been able to muster the support to have the bill reconsidered). With this rumor in mind, several of the conservatives voting no caucused while the president lobbied one of them on his cell phone. Nearly three hours after the vote, C. L. Otter (R–Id.) and Trent Franks (R–Ariz.) changed their votes, and with the vote of a third Republican who had switched an hour before, the bill was passed.[80]

Democrats were furious. Their House leader, Nancy Pelosi (D–Calif.), asserted that the Republicans won illegitimately, "Florida-style."[81] The nonpartisan *Congressional Weekly* labeled this the House Republicans "win at all cost" strategy.[82]

The impact of the measure on the health care of seniors and the Medicare program will not be known for some time. Many of its provisions do not take effect until 2006, 2007, and 2010. But the controversies did not wait until then. Drug company stocks soared immediately after passage of the bill as drug companies (and their investors) anticipated new revenues. Then the press revealed that the real cost of the measure was more than $100 billion than the administration had announced. A key government actuary had calculated the true cost while the bill was being considered but was told by the director of Medicare that he would be fired if he revealed this.

This episode reveals the extreme partisanship of the current era of American politics. In recent years, congressional norms of civility have frayed as a tide of partisan conflict has swamped some traditional courtesies. To be sure, conditions today are a far cry from the unpleasantness of the nineteenth century, when senators on occasion physically attacked one another. But Republicans complained rightly and bitterly in the early 1990s about the long-time Democratic majority shutting them out, pledging never to do that

if they gained a majority. And for a few years, they stuck to the rules. But beginning about 2000, they began to shut Democrats out of the policy process in unprecedented ways. Democrats were barred from conference committees that traditionally met to work out differences between House and Senate bills, they were shut out of informal consultations with the administration to try to develop bipartisan support for bills, and their representation on important committees was reduced.

In this case, the president and party leadership supressed relevant information and violated long-standing House norms to win this vote. Having done so, and because they control the presidency, the bureaucracy, and Congress, it seems naive to expect that there will not be retaliation when the Democrats win back control of one of these units. Aside from partisan conflict, Americans interested in policies based on factual evidence were the losers here when congressional representatives, both Democrats and Republicans, cast their vote based on a vastly deflated cost figure. That transgression is a bad omen for honesty in government.

Thus in counting the wins and losses from this policymaking episode, the Republicans won the vote and saw their policy enacted into law. What will be the costs of violating long-standing House rules and providing inaccurate information? The verdict on that will have to wait.

Key Terms

party organization

two-party system

multiparty system

single-member districts

winner-take-all

proportional representation

party system

realignment

political machine

political patronage

Progressive movement

New Deal coalition

party identification

dealignment

split-ticket voting

responsible party government

national party chair

national committee

issue voting

retrospective voting

Further Reading

David Brooks, ed., *Backward and Forward: The New Conservative Writing* (New York: Vintage, 1996). This is a collection of combative, often funny essays from the political right. The authors lampoon various liberal beliefs, showing that conservatism is as much about personality as about ideology.

James Carville, *We're Right, They're Wrong: A Handbook for Spirited Progressives* (New York: Random House, 1996). In this book, President Clinton's chief campaign adviser and one of Washington's most prominent Democratic strategists responds to the Republicans' platform during the 1992 and 1996 elections. Carville includes such features as the Republicans' "Biggest Lies" and "Most Expensive Boondoggles."

Congressional Quarterly, *National Party Conventions, 1831–1996* (Washington, D.C.: CQ Press, 1997). All you ever wanted to know about each party's national nominating conventions, including lists of keynote speakers, platforms, delegate selection rules, and nominees.

David J. Gillespie, *Politics at the Periphery: Third Parties in Two-Party America* (Columbia: University of South Carolina Press, 1993). This work provides both a historical review of the roles played by third parties in American politics and a look at the impact of recent third parties on election outcomes.

Stanley B. Greenberg, *Middle-Class Dreams: The Politics and Power of the New American Majority* (New York: Times Books, 1990). President Clinton's adviser looks at the radical shape of American politics today and contends that both political parties have betrayed the middle class.

Edwin O'Connor, *The Last Hurrah* (New York: Bantam, 1957). A warm, intimate novel set in Boston in the 1950s that contrasts the old-style party election campaigns with new media-oriented ones.

William L. Riordon, *Plunkitt of Tammany Hall* (New York: Dutton, 1963). This book preserves a series of witty talks given by a ward boss of New York City's Democratic Party machine. A slice of Americana, the book discusses "honest graft" and other aspects of "practical politics"

and in the process demonstrates why political machines flourished.

Mike Royko, *Boss: Richard J. Daley of Chicago* (New York: New American Library, 1971). This is an intriguing account of how the Chicago political machine operated under Mayor Richard J. Daley, who served from 1955 until his death in 1976.

Larry Sabato, *The Party's Just Begun* (Glenview, Ill.: Scott, Foresman, 1988). Sabato provides an overview of the American party system, explaining why we need it, what it does, and how we can make it work better.

Ruy Teixeria and Joel Rogers, *Why the White Working Class Still Matters* (New York: Basic Books, 2000). These authors explain why it is necessary to gain the support of the white working class in order to put together a strong party coalition and what each party can do to succeed at it.

For Viewing

The Last Hurrah (1958) based on the novel of the same name listed in Further Reading.

Tanner: A Political Fable (1988) Filmmaker Robert Altman and Pulitzer Prize–winning cartoonist Garry Trudeau are creators of this mock-documentary television miniseries, which profiles a fictitious presidential candidate on the campaign trail and sheds a revelatory light on America's political process and landscape.

Last Man Standing—Politics Texas Style (2004) The film profiles a race for the Texas state legislature and reviews many of the forces at work in national politics: multicultural and urban Texas of the future that leans democratic and ascendant Republicans of the suburbs and in politically active churches.

Electronic Resources

See the Web sites listed in the "Parties on the Web" box on page 227.

www.whitehouse.gov
The White House

www.rnc.org
Republican National Committee

www.democrats.org
Democratic National Committee

www.nrsc.org
National Republican Senatorial Committee

www.dscc.org
Democratic Senatorial Campaign Committee

www.nrcc.org
National Republican Congressional Committee

www.dccc.org
Democratic Congressional Campaign Committee

www.gop.gov
Republican House Conference

www.townhall.com
Conservative News and Information

www.epn.org
Liberal News and Information

www.politicalindex.com/sect8.htm
Link to the minor parties involved in U.S. politics

www.greenparty.org
Green Party, USA

 InfoTrac College Edition

Search for the following articles in the InfoTrac database:

Ceasar, James W. "A New GOP?" *Public Interest* (Fall 2004).

Galston, William A. "Democrats Adrift?" *Public Interest* (Fall 2004).

Lord, Lewis. "The Full Strom: Strom Thurmond and the History of Southern Politics," *U.S. News & World Report,* September 17, 2001.

Schecter, Cliff. "Extremely Motivated: The Republican Party's March to the Right," *Fordham Urban Law Journal,* April 2002.

For more articles, enter the following:

"Republican Party" in the Subject Guide;

"Democratic Party" in the Subject Guide;

"third parties" in the Subject Guide.

 American Government Resources

Visit the Political Behavior section of the Wadsworth American Government Resources Web site (politicalscience. wadsworth.com/amgov) for a variety of tools to help you explore political parties further. Included are simulations, video clips, Microcase exercises, and a wealth of other activities.

Senator John F. Kerry (D-Mass.) appeared hopelessly behind frontrunner Howard Dean, former governor of Vermont, in the race for the Democratic presidential nomination, as they headed into the Iowa caucuses in January of 2004.

The American Electorate

  Early Limits on Voting Rights

  Blacks and the Right to Vote

  The Voting Rights Act and Redistricting

  Women and the Right to Vote

  Young People and the Right to Vote

  Felons and the Right to Vote

  Election Reform and New Threats to Voting Rights

Voter Turnout

  Political Activism in the Nineteenth Century

  Progressive Reforms

  Recent Turnout

  Who Does Not Vote?

  Why Turnout Is Low

Other Campaign Participation

Presidential Nominating Campaigns

  Who Runs for President and Why?

  How a Candidate Wins the Nomination

  Presidential Caucuses and Conventions

  Presidential Primaries

  Reforming the Nomination Process

  The National Conventions

  Independent and Third-Party Nominees

The General Election Campaign

  Campaign Organization

  Campaign Strategies

  Campaign Communication

  The Electoral College

  Campaign Funding

The Permanent Campaign

Congressional Campaigns

  Incumbents: Unsafe at Any Margin?

  Challengers

  Campaigns

  Voting for Congress

Conclusion: Do Elections Make Government Responsive?

Should You Go to Iowa?

You are John F. Kerry, U.S. Senator from Massachusetts. It is late 2003 and you are running for the Democratic nomination for president. Your chances to win the nomination look bleak. You are trailing far behind in the polls. The frontrunner is Howard Dean, former governor of Vermont, who has mobilized tens of thousands of Democrats around the country with his strong attacks on the Bush administration and the status quo. But it's a crowded field of candidates, and others also have some support: Senator Joe Lieberman (D-Conn.), Al Gore's 2000 running mate, appeals to the more conservative wing of the party; Richard Gephardt (D-Mo.), has strong labor support; John Edwards (D-S.C.), another fellow senator, is popular in the South; Al Sharpton, a political activist in New York City, is trying to rally the votes of African Americans; Carol Mosely Braun, former U.S. senator from Illinois, is attempting to gain some traction for her campaign; and finally Wesley Clark, a retired general, is appealing to many looking for a new face and a fresh perspective.

You have been in politics a long time, but are not well known. On your father's side, you are the grandson of Jewish immigrants from Czechoslovakia who converted to Catholicism before coming to America and who, like many immigrants, chose an anglicized name randomly (reportedly, in their case they chose Kerry after looking at a map of Ire-

land). On your mother's side, you are the grandson of early settlers to America, including the first governor of Massachusetts, and through that side of the family, you grew up having a financially secure upper-middle-class life. You graduated from Yale, but unlike most Ivy League graduates of the Vietnam era (including George W. Bush), you chose active military service over extended deferments, a comfortable berth in the National Guard, or an escape to Canada. During your tour in Vietnam, you were wounded three times and received two medals for bravery. When you returned to the States, you spoke out against the Vietnam War in strong terms. Your testimony to Congress was highly publicized and started your political career.

But after twenty years in the U.S. Senate, your presidential candidacy is going nowhere. The Dean campaign has blown you and other candidates out of the water. Dean is billed as an insurgent, protesting the establishment Democrats in Congress and in the national party leadership who had failed to provide a substantive, vocal opposition to the policies of the Bush administration. Dean proudly announces that he is representing "the Democratic wing of the Democratic party," and thousands of Democrats, thirsting for a real opposition to the Republicans, rally to him.

Many Democrats are outraged by the fact that George W. Bush is president at all, given that Al Gore won the popular vote in 2000. (A popular bumper sticker urges "Re-defeat Bush"). They are sick and tired of congressional Democrats rolling over and supporting the president on policies that do not represent the mainstream Democrats. And many, though far from all, are against the U.S. invasion of Iraq, particularly the way it was handled, with a largely go-it-alone policy.

Dean, a former governor of Vermont who did not have to vote on the Iraq issue, galvanized many of the party's activists with his attacks on the war and on the president. As one observer said, Dean "made some Democrats proud to be Democrats again." [1] In addition to mobilizing Democrats, he brought thousands of new people, especially young people, into the political process through his active Internet campaign. Supporters from all over the country met virtually through blogs, and Internet contacts have whipped up enthusiasm for the Dean candidacy.

The first contest of the presidential election season is in the Iowa caucuses, this year scheduled for January 19. In these caucuses, people from all over Iowa meet in homes, schools, public buildings, and elsewhere to decide who will represent them at the national conventions later in the summer. Citizens gather with others in their precinct, listen to each other's speeches, and then vote for a candidate. The candidates receiving the most votes win delegates for later county and state conventions. The number of delegates is proportional to the vote that the candidate received at the caucuses (assuming the candidate got at least 15 percent).

Though the turnout is usually only a small proportion of the state's registered Democrats, it is small town democracy in action. Each precinct chooses its delegates. Some might be pledged to you, others to Howard Dean, others to the other candidates in the race, and some might be undecided. The candidate who wins the most pledged delegates decided in the caucuses is the "winner," and will receive massive media attention, new do-

nations, and a boost for the next week's New Hampshire primary. Because it is the first event of the season, the media coverage is intense, and a victory in the caucus produces the first momentum for one candidate or another in the season.

The caucus format requires excellent organization. Each candidate needs to be able to identify supporters and then make sure they get them to their precinct caucus meetings. The organization's leadership must be skillful in knowing who the supporters are and in keeping in touch with them to make sure that they actually turn out. Voters are ranked by precinct workers from 1 to 5, with 1s being sure supporters and 5s being sure for the other candidate. The Dean organization was confident it had enough 1s and 2s to carry the caucuses.

The Dean organization has thousands of eager volunteers, including many from out of state. Thousands of supporters donated millions of dollars, mostly smaller donations and many raised by Internet solicitations of supporters from all over the country. Although most of the Dean volunteers are amateurs who know little about political organization, the so-called "Deanie Babies," the leadership is more experienced, their projections rosy, and their efforts well publicized.[2] Dean's campaign manager speaks constantly to the press touting Dean, the movement behind Dean, and Dean's campaign organization. Most of the media now believe that Dean will win the Iowa caucuses. Indeed, many in the press believe that Dean campaign is a juggernaut that might just roll through Iowa and take the nomination, too.

In contrast, your campaign is not going well. You lag behind Dean in New Hampshire. Your polls show you far behind in Iowa, behind not only Dean, but also lagging behind Gephardt, from the neighboring state of Missouri. The Iowa governor tells you that you have "a solid lock on a distant third."[3]

You have built a campaign organi-

zation in Iowa, and it has been operating for several months. You have a great statewide campaign manager and considerable enthusiasm for you among a few people. But the campaign has not taken off and you have not provided your organization in Iowa with many resources. Your fundraising has lagged in the face of the Dean momentum. You are spending much of your resources in New Hampshire, where you thought you had a better chance than in Iowa because of your regional ties. Yet, some of your advisers tell you that Dean is not as strong as he looks in Iowa, and that you should take a shot at challenging him there.

Now you must decide what to do to revive your lagging campaign. You had been annointed by the press and the Democratic establishment as the frontrunner before Dean gained momentum. Now, in a complete turn of events, you could be eliminated from the race before the primary season even begins.

One choice is to redouble your effort in New Hampshire, where you know the territory well. But if you do that and do not win, you are probably finished. You had counted on an easy victory there, being from a neighboring state. But Dean is ahead there, too, and he is also a regional favorite, being from another of New Hampshire's neighboring states. New Hampshire will be risky, and if you give it priority you must win or be finished. If you cannot win in a New England state, you will be even weaker than you are now.

Another choice is to make Iowa the major focus for the next three months, gambling that a strong finish there will give you the press coverage, fundraising abilities, and momentum you need in New Hampshire. You might be considered a success in Iowa even if you finish second, since Dean seems to have such an overwhelming lead. After all, New Hampshire is your home turf, but Iowa is not. There are no expectations that you will win there.

But Iowa is also risky. You do not know if your personality and issues will

Americans have fought and died in wars to preserve the rights of citizens to choose their leaders through democratic elections. Some have even died here at home, trying to exercise these rights. Despite this, most Americans take these important rights for granted; about half do not bother to vote even in presidential elections, and fewer still participate in other ways.

Moreover, the process by which we choose our leaders, especially the president, has been sharply criticized in recent years. Critics charge that election campaigns are meaningless and offer little information to the voters, that candidates pander to the most ill-informed and mean-spirited citizens, and that public relations and campaign spending, not positions on issues or strength of character, determine the winners. Then in 2000, it also became apparent that some voters' votes were not counted even when they went to the polls, largely due to defects in the election process itself.

In this chapter, we analyze why voting is important to a democracy and why, despite its importance, so few do it. Then we examine political campaigns and elections to see how they affect the kinds of leaders and policies we have. We will see that the lack of participation by many reinforces the government's responsiveness to those who do participate, especially those who are well organized.

The American Electorate

During the more than two centuries since the Constitution was written, two important developments have altered the right to vote, termed **suffrage.** First, suffrage gradually has been extended to include almost all citizens aged eighteen or over. Second, deciding who may vote now lies largely in the hands of the federal government. The electorate has been widened mostly through constitutional amendments, congressional acts, and Supreme Court decisions.

Early Limits on Voting Rights

Although the Declaration of Independence states that "all men are created equal," at the time of the Constitution and shortly thereafter, the central political right of voting was denied to most Americans. States decided who would be granted suffrage. In some, only an estimated 10 percent of the white males could vote, whereas in others 80 percent could.[4]

Controversial property qualifications for voting existed in many states. Some argued that only those with an economic stake in society should have a say in political life. But critics of the property requirement repeated a story of Tom Paine's:

You require that a man shall have $60 worth of property, or he shall not vote. Very well . . . here is a man who today owns a jackass, and the jackass is worth $60. Today the man is a voter and he goes to the polls and deposits his vote. Tomorrow the jackass dies. The next day the man comes to vote without his jackass and he cannot vote at all. Now tell me, which was the voter, the man or the jackass?[5]

Because the Constitution gave states the power to regulate suffrage, the elimination of property requirements was a gradual process. By the 1820s, most were gone, although some lingered to midcentury.

In some states, religious tests also were applied. A voter had to be a member of the "established" church or could not be a member of certain religions (such as Roman Catholicism or Judaism). However, religious tests disappeared even more quickly than property qualifications.

By the time of the Civil War, state action had expanded the rights of white men. However, neither slaves, Indians, nor free southern blacks could vote, although northern blacks could in a few states.[6] Women's voting rights were confined to local elections in a few states.[7]

Blacks and the Right to Vote

The Civil War began the long, slow, and often violent process of expanding the rights of blacks to full citizenship. Between 1865 and 1870, three amendments were passed to give political rights to former slaves and other blacks. One, the Fifteenth Amendment, prohibited the denial of voting rights on the basis of race and thus gave the right to vote to black men.

For a short time following the ratification of this amendment, a northern military presence in the South and close monitoring of southern politics enabled blacks to vote and hold office in the South, where 90 percent of all blacks lived. During this **Reconstruction** period, two southern blacks were elected to the Senate and fourteen were elected to the House of Representatives between 1869 and 1876.

Although blacks did not dominate politics or even receive a proportional share of offices, whites saw

Four of the men shown in this 1870 poster with Frederick Douglass (center) served in Congress: Hiram Revels in the Senate and Benjamin Turner, Josiah T. Walls, and Joseph Rainey in the House. Also pictured are writer William Wells Brown and Bishop Richard Allen, founder of the African Methodist Episcopal Church.

Library of Congress

blacks' political activities as a threat to their own dominance. White southerners began to prevent blacks from voting through intimidation that ranged from mob violence and lynchings to economic sanctions against blacks who attempted to vote.

Northerners tolerated these methods, both violent and nonviolent. The northern public and political leaders had lost interest in the fate of blacks or had simply grown tired of the struggle. In 1876, a compromise ended Reconstruction. In the wake of the disputed 1876 presidential election, southern Democrats agreed to support Republican Rutherford B. Hayes for president in return for an end to the northern military presence in the South and a hands-off policy toward activities there.

By the end of the nineteenth century, blacks were effectively disfranchised in all of the South. The last southern black member of Congress served to 1901. Another would not be elected until 1972.

Southern constitutions and laws legitimized the loss of black voting rights. **Literacy tests** were often re-quired, supposedly to make sure voters could read and write and thus evaluate political information. Most blacks, who had been denied education, were illiterate. Many whites also were illiterate, but fewer were barred from voting. Local election registrars exercised nearly complete discretion in deciding who had to take the test and how to administer and evaluate it. Educated blacks often were asked for legal interpretations of obscure constitutional provisions, which few could provide.

Some laws had exemptions that whites were allowed to take advantage of. An "understanding clause" exempted those who could not read and write but who could explain sections of the federal or state constitution to the satisfaction of the examiner, and a "good moral character clause" exempted those with such character. Again, local election registrars exercised discretion in deciding who understood the Constitution and who had good character. Finally, the **grandfather clause** exempted those whose grandfathers had the right to vote before 1867—that is, before blacks could legally vote in the South.

The **poll tax** also deprived blacks of voting rights. The tax, though only a couple of dollars, was often a sizable portion of working people's monthly income. In some states, individuals had to pay not only for the present election, but also for every past election in which they were eligible to vote but did not.

In the **white primary,** blacks were barred from voting in primary elections, where party nominees were chosen. Because the Democrats always won the general elections, the real contests were in the Democratic primaries. The states justified excluding blacks on the grounds that political parties were private rather than government organizations and thus could discriminate just as private clubs or individuals could.

Less formal means were also used to exclude blacks from voting. Registrars often closed their offices when blacks tried to register, or whites threatened blacks with the loss of jobs or housing if they tried to vote. Polling places were sometimes located far from black neighborhoods or were moved at the last minute without notifying potential voters. If these means failed, whites threatened or practiced violence. In one election in Mobile, Alabama, whites wheeled a cannon to a polling place and aimed it at about one thousand blacks lined up to vote.

The treatment of blacks by the southern establishment was summarized on the floor of the Senate by South Carolina Senator Benjamin ("Pitchfork Ben") Tillman, who served from 1895 to 1918. As he put it, "We took the government away. We stuffed ballot boxes. We shot them. We are not ashamed of it."[8]

Over time, the Supreme Court and Congress outlawed the "legal" barriers to black voting in the South.

Blacks line up to vote in Peachtree, Alabama, after enactment of the Voting Rights Act of 1965.

The Court invalidated the grandfather clause in 1915 and the white primary in 1944. Through the Twenty-fourth Amendment, Congress abolished the poll tax for federal elections in 1964, and the Court invalidated the tax for state elections in 1966.[9] But threats of physical violence and economic reprisals still kept most southern blacks from voting. Although many blacks in the urban areas of the rim South (such as Florida, North Carolina, Tennessee, and Texas) could and did vote, those in the rural South and most in the Deep South could not; in 1960, black voter registration ranged from 5 to 40 percent in southern states.[10] (See the box titled "Blacks and Hispanics in Office.")

The Voting Rights Act and Redistricting

Despite our shameful history of depriving African Americans the right to vote, today black voting rates approach those of whites. In the Deep South, much of this dramatic change was brought about by the 1965 passage of the **Voting Rights Act (VRA),** which made it illegal to interfere with anyone's right to vote. The act abolished the use of literacy tests, and, most important, it sent federal voter registrars into counties where less than 50 percent of the voting age population (black and white) was registered. The premise of this requirement was that if so few had registered, there must be serious barriers to registration. Registrars were sent

to all of Alabama, Mississippi, South Carolina, and Louisiana, substantial parts of North Carolina, and scattered counties in six other states.[11]

Any changes in election procedures had to be approved by the Department of Justice or the U.S. District Court for the District of Columbia. States or counties had to show a clean record of not discriminating for ten years before they could escape this supervision. Those who sought to deter blacks from voting through intimidation now had to face the force of the federal government.

Though black registration had been increasing in the rim South due to voter registration and education projects, the impact of the VRA in the Deep South was dramatic.[12] Within a year after federal registrars were sent, hundreds of thousands of southern blacks were registered, radically changing the nature of southern politics. In the most extreme case, Mississippi registration of blacks zoomed from 7 to 41 percent. In Alabama, the black electorate doubled in four years.

Due to these increases, not only have dozens of blacks been elected, but white politicians must now court black voters to get elected. Even the late George Wallace, the segregationist Alabama governor who had opposed the civil rights movement in the 1960s, eagerly sought black votes in the 1970s and 1980s.

The VRA was renewed and expanded in 1970, 1975, and 1982. It now covers more states and other minorities, such as Hispanics, Asians, Native Americans,

BLACKS AND HISPANICS IN OFFICE

Before the Voting Rights Act (VRA) in 1965, few African Americans held major public office. Only a handful were members of Congress, and few were state legislators, mayors of major cities, or other important political officers. Following the VRA, southern blacks began to have the political clout to elect members of their own race to office for the first time and northern blacks began to increase their influence, winning races in districts where blacks were not always majorities. Progress, slow to be sure, has occurred; in 1970, there were only 179 blacks holding state and national legislative seats; by 2001, the number had more than tripled, to 633. Only one African American has ever won a governor's seat in modern times, Virginia's Douglas Wilder. In 2004, the first U.S. Senate race with blacks running as both major party candidates occurred in Illinois. Barack Obama won the race and became the only current African American member of the U.S. Senate and only the third to hold a Senate seat in the modern era.

Richard Hatcher, who became mayor of Gary, Indiana in 1968, was the first African American mayor of a major U.S. city. By 2004, 530 African Americans served as black mayors in northern and southern cities, more than forty of them in cities of fifty thousand and more and many in communities where blacks are far less than half the population. Nationally, the number of black officeholders has increased from an estimated 1,200 in 1969 to more than 9,000 in 2001. Although this is far from proportional representation, it is a dramatic increase.

Hispanics, too, have improved their representation in political office. From a total of little more than three thousand Hispanic public officials in 1985, their numbers by 2001 had grown to about 4,400, including more than two hundred state-elected legislators and executives.

In sum, though progress is slow, African Americans and Hispanics, like other ethnic groups, are achieving political power through elections. As a sign of their increased numbers and influence, both Hispanic and black elected officials are forming their own organizations to share ideas and plans.

SOURCE: *Statistical Abstract of the United States 2003* (Washington, D.C.: Government Printing Office, 2001), Tables 408 and 417; Web site of the National Council of Black Mayors, Inc, www.blackmayors.org.

---

and Eskimos, and thus serves as a basic protection for minority voting rights. For example, states must provide bilingual ballots in counties in which 5 percent or more of the population does not speak English.

The VRA dramatically changed the face of the electorate in the South and then later in other parts of the nation. Given the success of the VRA and faced with an expanded black electorate, some white officials in areas of large black populations used new means to diminish the political clout of African Americans. Their technique was **gerrymandering.** (See the box titled "Racial Gerrymandering.") Through devices that political scientists call **"cracking, stacking, and packing,"** districts were drawn to minimize black representation depending on the size and configuration of the black and white populations. *Cracking* divides significant, concentrated black populations into two or more districts so that none will have a black majority; *stacking* combines a large black population with an even greater white population; and *packing* puts a huge black population into one district rather than two, where blacks might otherwise approach a majority in each.

Initially, the Supreme Court was reluctant to find these practices illegal without specific proof that their intent was to discriminate against black voters.[13] But in 1982, congressional revision of the VRA required states with large minority populations to draw boundaries in ways to increase the probabilities that minorities will win seats. The focus of the voting rights legislation then turned from protecting the right of suffrage to trying to ensure that voting rights result in the election of African American and other minority officeholders. With this new statute as an indication of congressional intent, the Court then did strike down districting in North Carolina as inappropriately diluting black voting power.[14]

After the 1990 census, eleven new **majority-minority districts** were created for blacks and six for Hispanics. All but one were actually won by blacks and Hispanics in the 1992 election. Partly as a result of this redistricting, blacks were elected to Congress for the first time since Reconstruction in Alabama, Florida, North Carolina, South Carolina, and Virginia. Hispanics were elected for the first time ever in Illinois and New Jersey. In all, thirty-nine blacks and nineteen Hispanics were elected to Congress, a dramatic increase from the twenty-five blacks and ten Hispanics serving before the 1992 election.[15]

However, after this post-1990 redistricting, which used extensive gerrymandering to create the majority-minority districts, some white voters challenged their legality. In a series of cases, the Supreme Court then ruled that racial gerrymandering, the drawing of district lines specifically to concentrate racial minorities to try to ensure the election of minority representatives, is as constitutionally suspect as the drawing of district lines to diffuse minority electoral strength.[16] To the surprise of many, despite the consequent redrawing of several majority-minority districts after the 1994 election, the African American incumbents were still able to win re-election in 1996 and after.

Creating majority-minority districts has affected the partisan composition of some southern states. Black voters were redistricted from solid Democratic districts to create new majority black districts. This left their old districts with Republican majorities and helped Republicans get their first victories in eighteen congressional districts in the 1994 elections.

Racial Gerrymandering

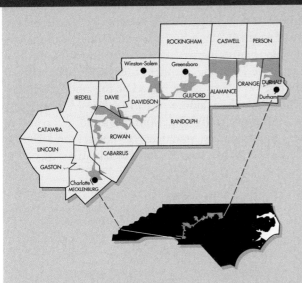

This North Carolina district (the Twelfth), shown on the maps, was drawn by its state legislature after the 1990 census to create a black majority district, and voters elected an African American in 1992. North Carolina, which is about 20 percent African American, had not elected a black representative to Congress since 1898. The state's seats, now twelve, went to whites because the black population was (and remains) relatively scattered. After redistricting in 1992, voters elected two African Americans from the twelve districts.

This Twelfth District snaked through parts of ten counties and seven of the former congressional districts as it followed Interstate 85. The district was 160 miles long and, in places, no wider than the highway cor-

ridor and, in other places, not quite this wide—the northbound and southbound lanes were in different districts. One legislator famously remarked, "if you drove down the interstate with both car doors open, you'd kill most of the people in the district." The bizarre shape was the result of the legislature's efforts to create the majority-minority district while also protecting white incumbents in other districts. Despite its strange shape, the district had some homogeneity: it was an urban district, drawing from the black populations of Charlotte, Winston-Salem, Greensboro, and Durham.

The majority of the Supreme Court, declaring the districting illegal, called the district "so irregular" and "so bizarre" that it can be understood "only as an effort to segregate the races for purposes of voting, without regard for traditional districting principles and without sufficiently compelling justification." [1] North Carolina tried redrawing its districts twice more before the Court was satisfied.

The practice of drawing strangely shaped districts to fulfill political objectives, called *gerrymandering,* is hardly

new in American politics. The name originated in 1812 when the Massachusetts legislature carved out a district that historian John Fiske said had a "dragon-like contour." When painter Gilbert Stuart saw the misshapen district, he drew in a head, wings, and claws and exclaimed, "That will do for a salamander!" Editor Benjamin Russell replied, "Better say Gerrymander," after Elbridge Gerry, then governor of Massachusetts.[2] Since then, gerrymandering has been widely used by politicians to benefit their own political parties, and today is used not only to try to create districts with majority minorities, but also to protect legislative incumbents by drawing districts that include their fellow partisans and minimize the number of the opposite party.

1. 125 L.Ed.2d 525–526, 1993.
2. *Guide to Congress,* 2d ed. (Washington, D.C.: Congressional Quarterly Inc., 1976), 563; *Congressional Quarterly,* "The Race to Capitol Hill," February 29, 1992, 103–105. OTHER SOURCES: Charles Mahtesian, "Blacks' Political Hopes Boosted by Newly Redrawn Districts," *Congressional Quarterly Weekly Report,* April 25, 1992, 1087; Bruce E. Cain, "Voting Rights and Democratic Theory toward a Color-Blind Society?" *Brookings Review* (Winter 1992), 46–50; Carol M. Swain, "The Voting Rights Act: Some Unintended Consequences," *Brookings Review* (Winter 1992), 51; Douglas Amy, *Real Choices/New Voices: The Case for Proportional Representation Elections in the United States* (New York: Columbia University Press, 1993); John Gruhl and Susan Welch, "Representation and Race Conscious Districting," paper presented at the American Political Science Association meeting, August 2002.

Women and the Right to Vote

When property ownership defined the right to vote, women property owners could vote in some places. When property requirements were removed, suffrage came to be seen as only a male right. Women's right to vote was reintroduced in the 1820s in Tennessee school board elections.[17] From that time on, women had the vote in some places, usually only at the local level or for particular kinds of elections.

The national movement for women's suffrage did not gain momentum until after the Civil War. Before and during that war, many women helped lead the campaign to abolish slavery and establish full political rights for blacks. When black men got the right to vote after the Civil War, some women saw the paradox in their working to enfranchise these men when they themselves lacked the right to vote. Led by Susan B. Anthony, Elizabeth Cady Stanton, and others, they lobbied Congress and the state legislatures for voting rights for women.

The first suffrage bill was introduced in Congress in 1868 and each year thereafter until 1893. Most members were strong in their condemnation of women as potential voters. One senator claimed that if women could hold political views different from their husbands, it would make "every home a hell on earth."[18]

When Wyoming applied to join the Union in 1889, it had already granted women the right to vote. Congress initially tried to bar Wyoming from the Union for that reason, but then relented when the Wyoming territorial legislature declared, "We will remain out of the Union one hundred years rather than come in without the women." Still, by 1910, women had complete suffrage rights in only four western states.

Powerful interests opposed suffrage for women. Liquor interests feared that women voters would press for prohibition because many women had been active in the temperance (antiliquor) movement. Other businesses feared that suffrage would lead to reforms to improve working conditions for women and children. Southern whites feared that it would lead to voting by black women and then by black men. Political bosses feared that women would favor political reform. The Catholic Church opposed it as contrary to the proper role of women. According to some people, suffrage was a revolt against nature. Pregnant women might lose their babies, nursing mothers their milk, and women might grow beards or be raped at the polls (then frequently located in saloons or barber shops).[19] Others argued less hysterically that women should be protected from the unsavory practices of politics and should confine themselves to their traditional duties.

Women's contributions to the war effort during World War I helped lead to the ratification of the women's suffrage amendment in 1920. Here Broadway chorus women train as Home Guards during the war.

Brown Brothers

About 1910, however, the women's suffrage movement was reenergized, in part by ideas and tactics borrowed from the British women's suffrage movement. A new generation of leaders, including Alice Paul and Carrie Chapman Catt, began to lobby more vigorously, reach out to the working class, and engage in protest marches and picketing, all new features of American politics. In 1917, the National Women's Party organized around-the-clock picketing of the White House; their arrest and subsequent torture through beatings and forced feedings embarrassed the administration and won the movement some support. These incidents, plus contributions by women to the war effort during World War I, led to the adoption of the Nineteenth Amendment guaranteeing women the right to vote in 1920. Although only 37 percent of eligible women voted in the 1920 presidential election, as the habit of voting spread, women's voting rates equaled those of men. (See the box "Women in Office." on page 247)

Young People and the Right to Vote

Federal constitutional and legislative changes extended the franchise to young adults. Before 1971, almost all states required a voting age of nineteen or more. The service of eighteen-year-olds in the Vietnam War brought protests that if these men were old enough to die for their country, they were old enough to vote. Yielding to these arguments and to the general recognition that young people were better educated than in the past, Congress adopted and the states ratified the Twenty-sixth Amendment giving eighteen-year-olds the right to vote. As we will see, however, young people are a lot less likely to vote than other groups.

Felons and the Right to Vote

The restriction of felons' rights to vote is an exception to the general liberalization of the right to vote. Seven states, including Florida and three other southern states with large black populations,[20] bar felons (those convicted of serious crimes) from voting forever. In some states, these laws stem from Reconstruction era laws targeted to reduce the voting power of blacks. Most other states bar them while serving time, or when they are on parole or probation, but then restore their voting rights.

In Florida, an estimated 525,000 people, most of them poor and black, were barred from voting in 2000 because of committing a prior felony.[21] Nationally, more than five million people are prevented from voting by felony convictions, including one in seven black men (in Alabama, one in three black men are barred).[22] Analyses of the impacts of these laws suggest they have had a significant effect in putting conservative Republicans in office in states with large black populations.[23]

Some might argue that we should not worry about the voting rights of felons. Loss of voting rights might be seen as part of their punishment. However, most felons barred from voting have served their time and returned to society. Many times they were convicted as young people and have been law-abiding citizens for years or even decades since. Moreover, this particular punishment does not really seem to fit the crime.

In sum, only convicted felons, the mentally incapable, noncitizens, and those not meeting minimal residence requirements are legally barred from voting now. Voting has become an essential right of citizenship, except for felons, rather than a privilege just for those qualified by birth or property.

Electoral Reform and New Threats to Voting Rights

In recent elections, new threats to voting rights, especially voting rights of African Americans, have occurred. The most widely publicized problems were in the 2000 election. Months after the presidential election that saw Al Gore win the popular vote but George W. Bush win the electoral vote and the presidency, half of the electorate thought that the outcome was unfair or downright crooked. (See the box titled "'A Perfect Storm:' The 2000 Election.") Many African Americans, who believed they were systematically disenfranchised by the way the election was run in Florida, were especially outraged. One of ten votes in largely African American precincts in Florida were thrown out as invalid, compared to one of thirty-seven in white precincts, significantly reducing the Democratic vote and changing the outcome of the presidential election.[24]

Voter Reform Legislation

The 2000 election revealed a number of problems with our electoral system. (The problems had existed for a long time, but in a close election they become more crucial). Many areas had voting equipment that not only was old, but also did not work well, resulting in many votes not being counted. Most of these were punch-card systems where voters use a penlike stylus to punch holes in the ballot in places reflecting their candidate choices. As we saw in Florida, sometimes the holes were not completely made, casting doubt on the voters' intentions. Many states had unclear laws governing procedures for recounts and challenges to voter eligibility.

To deal with some of these issues, Congress passed electoral reform legislation in 2002. This new legislation offered states funding to buy new, modern voting equipment; mandated statewide registration lists; and required states to train poll workers, post a list of voters' rights in

The 2000 election will be remembered as the election won by the candidate, George W. Bush, who got fewer votes than his rival, Al Gore, and the election decided by the United States Supreme Court (more on the Court's role in Chapter 13). The division in the Electoral College was very close, and the decision rested on the outcome in Florida where election mismanagement, partisan politics, and unavoidable human error came together to create chaos in a closely divided race.

Election Day exit polls of Florida voters showed Gore winning by a small margin. But after first declaring Gore the winner, the networks declared Bush the winner, and then in the early morning hours decided it was too close to call. The election hung in the balance (the media performance on election night 2000 is explained in Chapter 5). Bush had a tiny lead of just several hundred ballots.

Confusion reigned in the days afterward. The press and election observers reported several problems, some of them serious. Thousands of Gore votes were lost because of the strange "butterfly" ballot configuration in Palm Beach County, a heavily Democratic liberal county. The odd format, designed by the supervisor of elections in the county, made it difficult for some voters to determine which punch hole corresponded to which presidential candidate. (It was labeled the "butterfly ballot" because candidate names appeared on both sides of a row of vertical punch holes rather than only on one side, which is the standard, less confusing format; see the photo.) Even though the problem was recognized early on Election Day by some distraught voters leaving the polling places, there was no way that local election officials felt they could fix the problem then.

More than three thousand voters pushed the hole registering a vote for

Patrick Buchanan, to the right of Gore's name on the ballot. This is particularly ironic because the areas of Palm Beach County casting the most votes for Buchanan were those inhabited by mostly elderly Jewish voters, the least likely group to support Buchanan, who is thought to be anti-Semitic. As one elderly Jewish woman exclaimed after mistakenly voting for Buchanan, "I would rather have had a colonoscopy than vote for that son-of-a-bitch Buchanan."[1]

Nearly three thousand voted for Gore and the socialist candidate whose punch hole was underneath Gore, apparently thinking they voted for Joseph Lieberman, Gore's vice presidential running mate, whose name was under Gore's. (Bush lost about 1,600 votes from those who voted for him and Buchanan.) While some spoiled ballots are normal in every election, this erratic pattern in one county was a result of the badly designed ballot. But there was nothing the Gore campaign could do. The ballot was designed by a Democratic supervisor of elections who made the candidates' names larger so elderly voters could read them easier. But the larger typeface actually made the format harder to understand. Nevertheless, a sample ballot had been printed in the local newspapers before the election, as is required in many states. Clearly there was no intention to deceive any voters.

There was also a problem with overseas ballots. Americans overseas have the right to vote. They must ask for a ballot before the election and mail it by the day of the election, but the ballot does not need to be received by local officials until ten days after the election. (This time allows for mail delays.) There are strict rules about how these ballots are to be certified to avoid vote fraud: for example, the ballots have to have legible overseas postmarks showing the ballot was cast on

or before election day and the voters had to have registered in advance. But hundreds of these ballots came in without postmarks or with U.S. postmarks, from voters who were not registered, or that lacked a witness. Many military personnel must have decided to vote after the election when the outcome appeared uncertain, and some may have been persuaded to do so by partisan groups.

After the election, Gore and the Democrats pursued a conservative strategy to deal with these problems that likely cost him the election. Nothing could be done about the butterfly ballot problem save a revote, and nothing in Florida law allowed that. To deal with tens of thousands of incompletely punched cards throughout the state, Gore asked only for a recount in four strongly Democratic counties. Later, after the Bush campaign sued to stop the recount, Gore did challenge Bush to have a recount in every county, but he did not file suit to accomplish it.[2] Finally, when the Florida Supreme Court mandated a recount in every county, so much time had elapsed that the U.S. Supreme Court threw up its hands and gave the election to Bush (see Chapter 13 for the description of the U.S. Supreme Court's controversial actions).

The biggest mistake of the Democrats was not to challenge the overseas votes, even the hundreds that were patently illegal under Florida laws. Indeed, 680 were flawed, including nearly two hundred with U.S. postmarks, indicating that they had been mailed from within the country rather than from overseas; 344 were late, illegible, or missing postmarks; and even thirty-eight reflected double voting by nineteen voters.[3] Clearly, the local election judges would have thrown these out had Democratic Party representatives challenged them. But they did not, out of a timid concern about not wanting to appear against voting rights of overseas armed forces personnel, even fraudulent ones. As a consequence of the illegal military ballots alone, Gore lost Florida by 537 votes when his Election Day margin was 202 votes.[4]

The Bush postelection campaign was more skillful and more aggressive. At one point the Bush campaign even organized a demonstration to intimidate election officials in Miami-Dade County to stop conducting a recount they were in the middle of. Demonstrators barged into the building, yelling and pounding on doors. Photos from that event showed that many of the "demonstrators" were staffers in conservative congressional Republican offices who had been sent to Florida to do this, though at the time the election officials recounting the ballot did not know that. The demonstration succeeded in getting the officials to halt the recount.

The Bush campaign was also more aggressive in persuading election officials how to treat overseas ballots. Republican representatives urged election officials in Democratic-majority counties to follow the law in handling overseas ballots, so illegal ballots would not be counted; in Republican counties, they urged election officials to disregard the law, so illegal ballots would be counted. (There is nothing illegal or even immoral about Republican supporters doing this, but the election officials should not have caved, and the Democratic representatives should have argued that the laws be followed.) Meanwhile, Democratic representatives, fearing a public backlash, did not try to counter Republican efforts. As a result, Florida officials accepted hundreds of overseas absentee ballots that failed to comply with state laws."[5]

In addition, the Bush campaign had strong political allies in Florida. Not only was Bush's brother the governor,

but the secretary of state, who oversees the election system, was co-chair of Bush's Florida campaign. Making little effort to appear nonpartisan, at every opportunity she ruled in favor of the Bush campaign and forced the Gore campaign to go to court to obtain recounts and redress.

Time also worked in favor of the Bush campaign, as it held a narrow lead throughout the postelection day period and because it knew that the deadline for certifying Florida's electors would put pressure on the courts to stop the recount. Thus, the Bush campaign used delaying tactics to slow and stop the recounts.

The outcome of this election will long be argued. It is likely true that a bare majority of Florida voters, in fact, favored Gore.[6] Systematic analyses have proven that the Buchanan vote was inflated by at least 2,500 votes intended for Gore in Palm Beach County.[7] As one commentator noted, "No election analyst will say with a straight face that the butterfly design didn't cost Al Gore the presidency."[8]

Of course, the overseas ballot contributed, too, by an unknown amount. That is, we know how many ballots were illegal, but we don't know for sure their distribution between Bush and Gore. Nearly two-thirds of the 2,400 overseas ballots counted after November 7 were for Bush. Two independent scholars argue that the probability is about 99 percent that Gore would have won if the invalid overseas ballots were handled properly and a statewide recount was allowed under any reasonable standard for counting chads.[9]

The confusion surrounding the 2000 election outcome highlights an important aspect of our electoral process: state law and local policies determine the mechanics of presidential elections. In this election, these me-

chanics also were important in determining the winner. The 2000 election brought into stark relief the problems that shoddy election procedures can create. Former president and Nobel Peace Prize winner Jimmy Carter, who, through his Carter Center now works for peace and social justice around the world, is often invited to monitor elections in Asia and Africa and to attest to their fairness. He remarked, "I was really taken aback and embarrassed by what happened in Florida. If we were invited to go into a foreign country to monitor the election, and they had similar standards and procedures, we would refuse to participate at all."[10]

1. Quoted in Alan M. Dershowitz, *Supreme Injustice: How the High Court Hijacked Election 2000* (New York: Oxford University Press, 2001), 25.
2. Hendrik Hertzberg, "Up for the Count," *New Yorker,* December 18, 2000, 41.
3. Kosuke Imai and Gary King, "Did Illegally Counted Overseas Absentee Ballots Decide the 2000 U.S. Presidential Election?" available at gking.Harvard.edu.
4. Ibid.
5. David Barstow and Don Van Natta Jr., "How Bush Took Florida: Mining the Overseas Absentee Vote," *New York Times,* July 15, 2001, available at www.nytimes.com/2001/07/15/www.national/15ball.
6. Ibid.
7. Jonathan Wand, Kenneth Shotts, Jasjeet Sekhon, Walter R. Mebane, Jr., Michael Herron, and Henry Brady, "The Butterfly Did It: The Aberrant Vote for Buchanan in Palm Beach," *American Political Science Review* 95 (2001), 793–809. They examined the Palm Beach Buchanan vote in relation to all other counties in the United States to the absentee ballots (which did not use the butterfly format) in Palm Beach County, precinct-level data, and individual ballots.
8. Tom Fiedler, "The Perfect Storm," in *Overtime! The Election 2000 Thriller,* ed. Larry J. Sabato (New York: Longman, 2002), 8.
9. Imal and King, 3.
10. Jimmy Carter, quoted from *NPR* in Kéllia Ramares's special report "House Strikes Truth from the Record," *Online Journal,* July 23, 2004. You can find the full Ramares article at www.onlinejournal.com/Special_Reports/072304Ramares/072304ramares.html.

each polling place, and allow voters whose names do not appear on the precinct lists to cast a provisional ballot, which can be accepted or challenged later.

This legislation did bring about some positive changes. Though the president proposed and Congress appropriated only about one-twentieth of the money needed to buy new voting machines, many areas did buy new electronic machines that work like ATMs, responding to touches on the screen.[25] Many states enacted new standards for counts and recounts.

Problems with Voting Machines

Most technical experts, and many others, are fearful that some of the new electronic machines are open to fraud. One information-security expert argues that one particular system was "so deficient in security it could be compromised by a bright teenager intent on hacking an election."[26] The reason is that in most of the new machines there is no paper backup. Your vote for X could be counted as a vote for Y and you would never know it. The fact that the CEO of the company that manufactures the most popular electronic machine (an estimated seventy-five thousand are in use) is a strong Republican supporter and a Bush pioneer heightened the fears by both technical specialists and conspiracy theorists that the machines were rigged in some areas. Many of these machines were used in Ohio, and the CEO, in an embarrassing Republican fundraising letter, promised to "deliver Ohio to Bush."[27] In fact, Ohio did go for Bush and there were significant voting machine problems, but Bush's margin, more than one hundred thousand, was significantly larger than questionable ballots.

To deal with concerns about the potential for electronic systems to be rigged, California has required precincts to offer voters a choice of a paper ballot or an electronic one, and a proposed law to require paper backup for all these machines is on the ballot in California.[28]

About half the states are still using punch card machines, those that were at the center of the 2000 Florida election issues. With only a little funding from Congress, these states could not afford to replace the punch-card machines.

Inaccurate Lists

The statewide voter list requirement has also spawned problems. Most states have asked for a postponement for compiling their statewide databases. Of those that moved ahead with the lists, some, in updating lists, purged voters in a way that appears partisan. Florida, in trying to update its voter lists, purged twenty-two thousand black voters (largely Democratic) from the voter registration lists, but only sixty-one Hispanics (who, in Florida, are more likely than blacks to be Republicans). Florida officials admitted a mistake, and claimed it was accidental. Others point out that state officials had known the process was tainted.[29] But with

Republicans controlling the Florida state government, the president's brother (Jeb Bush) serving as governor, and the U.S. Attorney General's office as part of the Bush administration, it is unlikely that there will be a serious investigation.

Conservatives in several other swing states also pushed for significant purging of the lists and higher requirements for voting before the 2004 election. By making it more difficult to vote, these new laws may disproportionately affect low-income people, minorities and nonminorities, who have lower turnout rates even when voting is not made more difficult.

Months before the 2004 elections, both parties accused the other of trying to steal the election. Though there were problems, including more votes cast for Bush than there were voters in a couple of places, in general the worst fears proved exaggerated. The biggest problem in the election appeared to be the lack of adequate numbers of machines and poll workers in many places, especially in poorer areas.

Voter Turnout

Paradoxically, as the *right* to vote has expanded, the proportion of eligible citizens *actually* voting has contracted.

Political Activism in the Nineteenth Century

In 1896, an estimated 750,000 people—5 percent of all voters—took train excursions to visit presidential candidate William McKinley at his Ohio home during the campaign.[30] This amazing figure is but one indication of the high level of intense political interest and activity in the late nineteenth century.

In those days, politics was an active, not a spectator, sport. People voted at high rates, as much as 80 percent in the 1840 presidential election,[31] and they were very partisan. They thought independents were corrupt and ready to sell their votes to the highest bidder. In colonial America, voters usually voted by voice. By the mid-nineteenth century, most states used paper ballots. Elaborate and well-organized parties printed and distributed the ballots. Voters, after being coached by party leaders, simply dropped their party's ballot into the box. **Split-ticket voting,** that is, voting for candidates from different parties for different offices, and secrecy in making one's choice were impossible.

Progressive Reforms

The **Progressive reforms** of the late nineteenth and early twentieth centuries brought radical changes to election politics. Progressive reformers, largely professional and upper middle class, sought to eliminate cor-

Even before women were given the right to vote nationally, they held political office. Women officeholders in colonial America were rare but not unknown. In 1715, for example, the Pennsylvania Assembly appointed a woman as tax collector.[1]

Elizabeth Cady Stanton, probably the first woman candidate for Congress, received twenty-four votes when she ran in 1866.[2] It was not until 1916 that the first woman member of Congress, Jeannette Rankin (R-Mont.), was actually elected. In 1872, Victoria Claflin Woodhull ran for president on the Equal Rights Party ticket teamed with abolitionist Frederick Douglass for vice president.

More than one-hundred thousand women now hold elective office, but many of these offices are minor. Inroads by women into major national offices have been slow. Geraldine Ferraro's 1984 vice presidential candidacy was historic, but not victorious. In recent years, women have only gradually increased their membership in Congress. But in the 1992 elections, women candidates won striking increases in national legislative offices. Women have continued to gain seats and, after 2002, numbered 14 percent of each house of Congress. About 80 percent of the female senators and two-thirds of the female House of Representatives members are Democrats.[3]

Real progress has also been made in state and local governments. Women

"Nothing against Rudy, I just feel that a woman would be instinctively better on dairy issues."

hold 25 percent of all statewide elective offices, although only five women are governors (but seventeen women are lieutenant governors). In 1969, only 4 percent of the state legislators were women; today 22 percent are. However, the rates of increase have slowed in recent years with only a 2 percent growth in the past decade.[4] The proportion ranges widely, from 9 percent in South Carolina to 37 percent in Washington, where electing women state legislators is obviously quite common.

More than 20 percent of the city council seats in medium and large cities are now occupied by women and 15 percent are mayors of America's one hundred largest cities. Women are twice as likely to be found on school boards, however, where they make up 40 percent of the members.

Does it make a difference in terms of policy to have women officeholders rather than men? Behavioral studies of women members of Congress and other legislative bodies indicate that they are, on the whole, more liberal than men.[5] Women tend to give issues relating to women, children, and the family higher priority than male legislators do.[6] Women are also less likely to be involved in corrupt activities.

More and more women are getting graduate and professional education and working outside the home. These changes, coupled with increased public support for women taking an active role in politics, suggest that the trend toward more women in public office will continue.

1. Joseph J. Kelley, *Pennsylvania: The Colonial Years* (Garden City, N.Y.: Doubleday, 1980), 143.
2. Elisabeth Griffin, *In Her Own Right* (New York: Oxford University Press, 1983).
3. Data are from Center for the American Woman and Politics, National Information Bank on Women in Public Office, Rutgers University, www.rci.rutgers.edu/~cawp/pdf/elective.pdf.
4. Kira Sanbonmatsu, *Democrats, Republicans, and the Politics of Women's Place* (Ann Arbor: University of Michigan Press, 2002).
5. Susan Welch, "Are Women More Liberal Than Men in the U.S. Congress?" *Legislative Studies Quarterly* 10 (1985), 125–134.
6. Sue Thomas and Susan Welch, "The Impact of Gender on Activities and Priorities of State Legislators," *Western Political Quarterly* 44 (1991), 445–456.

ruption from politics and voting. But they also meant to eliminate the influence of the lower classes, many of them recent immigrants. These two goals went hand in hand, because the lower classes were seen as the cause of corruption in politics.

The Progressive movement was responsible for several reforms: primary elections, voter registration laws, secret ballots, nonpartisan ballots (without party labels), and the denial of voting rights for aliens, which removed a major constituency of the urban party machines. The movement also introduced the merit system for public employment to reduce favoritism and payoffs in hiring.

The reforms, adopted by some states at the end of the nineteenth century and by others much later, were

ROCK THE VOTE OR MOCK THE VOTE?

The 2004 presidential election race was considered a dead heat during much of the campaign season; every political group scoured the hustings for undecided and new voters. Young voters, those eighteen to twenty-four, were prime targets. Campaign organizations used both traditional means and icons of popular culture to attract these new voters.

Many young voters are disaffected by politics.[1] Most candidates for national office are older and much more inclined to target their campaign messages toward middle-aged and older voters who turn out in far greater numbers than young voters.[2] One twenty-something said about the 2000 presidential race: "I feel like if you are not sixty-five-years old and don't have arthritis, these candidates have nothing to say to you."[3]

The feeling of being left out stimulated the marketing of a T-shirt in 2004 (designed by a twenty-five-year-old Yale graduate) with the logo *Only Old People Vote.* The marketer was immediately bombarded by outraged activists from groups like Punk Voter who were trying to get young people registered before the 2004 election. The company explained that it only meant to "highlight the growing gap between politicians' platforms and the concerns of young people," so it did stop marketing the shirt.[4]

Some credit young people with recognizing, better than older people, that the political system is broken and registering their judgment on what they see as a meaningless process.[5] Others argue that young people are mostly ignored, and when they are not, they will turn out at the polls in percentages as high as any other demographic group. For example, Representative Tammy Baldwin (D-Wisc.), four-term incumbent from the congressional district that is the home of the University of Wisconsin and several other colleges, got so many student voters to the polls that her election was called a "youthquake." The turnout was so high that some polling places ran out of ballots, and students waited in line up to two hours for more ballots.[6]

Baldwin had several things going for her: she was a Madison native, a University alum, and still in her thirties when she first ran. She is also the first openly gay candidate to have won election to the House. But in addition to that, Baldwin found that getting out the youth vote is pretty much like turning out the vote among any other age group—grassroots organization and outreach. Baldwin's campaign organization established a presence in every residence hall and dormitory, complete with captains and floor leaders. She made campaign signs small enough to fit in dorm windows and, with student volunteers, printed her name in chalk on campus sidewalks. She devoted a large portion of her campaign funds to reach students through ads on MTV and *Ally McBeal.* Of the three thousand precinct walkers she recruited, more than half were students.[7]

Like most members of the House, Baldwin spends more than half of her days in the district, attending constituent functions and participating in campus events, such as helping students move into their dorms at the opening of the school year. She knocks on dorm doors and eats with students in the dining halls. She has ties to youth-oriented groups such as CHAOS (Changing Our

largely effective in cleaning up politics. But the reformers also achieved, to a very large extent, their goal of eliminating the lower classes from politics. Taking away most of the reason for the existence of the political parties—choosing candidates and printing and distributing ballots—caused the party organization to decline, which, in turn, produced a decline in political interest and activity on the part of the electorate. Without strong parties to mobilize voters, only the most interested and motivated participated. The new restrictions on voting meant that voters had to invest more time, energy, and thought in voting. They had to think about the election months in advance and travel to city hall to register. As a consequence, politics began to be a spectator activity. Voter turnout declined sharply after the turn of the century.

Turnout figures from the nineteenth century are not entirely reliable and not exactly comparable with today's figures. In the days before voter registration, many aliens could vote, and some people voted twice. In some instances, more people voted in a state election than lived there! Nevertheless, it is generally agreed that turnout was very high in the nineteenth century and that it has diminished substantially; it dropped from more than 77 percent from 1840 to 1896 to 54 percent in the 1920 to 1932 era, when the Progressive reforms were largely in place. During the New Deal era, when the Democratic Party mobilized new groups of voters,

State), the New Voters Project, and a networking organization for young professionals.

To overcome the "voting is for old people" syndrome, her campaign platforms directly target student issues, including the cost of health care, the draft, and rising tuition and fees. Her Web site has a student page with links to information on financial aid, student loans, and tax tips for parents of college students.

Although the 10 percent student composition of her constituency is not typical, Baldwin has shown that young people will participate in large numbers if targeted. In fact, the Democratic National Committee asked her to help prepare a "tool kit" for mobilizing the youth vote. In the 2004 presidential primaries Howard Dean demonstrated, as Baldwin has in her House races, that young people will participate in large numbers if they are enthusiastic about a candidate and if the candidate is actually speaking to what concerns them.

In addition to these traditional means of getting out the vote, during 2004, college campuses experienced new attempts to interest students in the election and get them to register. In addition to Rock the Vote, other action groups formed to keep young people in the campaign after Dean's departure, including Declare Yourself, the Hip-Hop Summit Action Network, Get Out Her Vote (targeted to young women on campus), Music for America, and the World Wrestling Entertainment's Smack-Down Your Vote. Some of these organizations sponsored rock concerts at popular campus venues, and the parties recruited celebrities popular with young people like Arnold Schwarzenegger (for the Republicans) and Michael Moore and Howard Dean (for the Democrats) to visit campuses.

The turnout of young people was much higher in 2004 than for many years, and presumably some of that was due to these "get out the vote" efforts. Perhaps, as one observer noted, those who are trying to get young people to the polls should take a lesson from the "Just Say No" anti drug campaign. "The campaign only started to have an impact when it dropped that slogan and just tried to scare the shit out of people. Maybe we should stop trying to make voting cool. We should just show kids what happens when they don't. In other words, we need to get them to watch the news." [8]

1. Thomas E. Patterson, *The Vanishing Voter* (New York: Knopf, 2002), 87–88.
2. Amy Goldstein and Richard Morin, "The Squeaky Wheel Gets the Grease," *Washington Post National Weekly Edition,* October 28–November 3, 34.
3. Steven Hill and Rashad Robinson, "Demography vs. Democracy: Young People Feel Left Out of the Political Process," *Los Angeles Times,* November 5, 2002. Posted by the Youth Vote Coalition (www.youthvote.org/news/newsdetail.cfm?newsid=6). The survey cited was conducted by Harvard University.
4. Editorial, "Voting is Not Just for Old People," *Daily Skiff* (newspaper of Texas Christian University), February 27, 2004 (www.skiff.tcu.edu/2004/spring/Issues/02/27/vote.html).
5. Hill and Robinson, "Demography vs. Democracy: Young People Feel Left Out of the Political Process," 2.
6. Heidi Pauken, "The Students' Rep," *American Prospect* 14 (2003), A23.
7. Ibid, A22.
8. Ann Marie Cox, "Pimping the Vote," *In These Times,* May 13, 2004 (www.inthesetimes.com/site/main/article/pimping_the_vote), online article.
OTHER SOURCES: Phone interview with Representative Tammy Baldwin, September 1, 2004; Young Chang, "T-Shirt's Sassy Slogan Riles Some Voters," *Seattle Times,* March 2, 2004. Special thanks to Jerilyn Goodman.

turnout rose again, but it has never achieved anything close to the levels of the nineteenth century.

Recent Turnout

Between 1964 and 2000, turnout in presidential elections slowly declined, from 62 percent to 52 percent. That is, only half of all citizens voted in recent elections. This means that only one-fourth of the potential voters actually vote for the winning candidate.[32]

The turnout for off-year congressional elections is even lower. It has not exceeded 45 percent since World War II, and in 1998 it was 42 percent.[33] Only in Minnesota did more than half of the voters turn out. Turnout in primary elections is far lower still, sometimes as low as 10 percent.

Although nations count their turnouts differently, it is clear that Americans vote in much lower proportions than citizens of other Western democracies. Only Switzerland, which relatively recently gave women the right to vote (in 1971), approximates our low turnout levels.

Within the United States, turnout varies greatly among the states. In the 2000 presidential election, for example, 70 percent of Minnesota's citizens voted, but only 43 percent of Hawaii's did.[34] Turnout tends to be lower in the South and higher in the northern Plains and Mountain states.[35]

© Getty Images

AP/ Wide World Photos

People over sixty-five have the highest voting turnout of any age group. Granny Haddock, aged ninety-four, walked across America in 1999 urging electoral reform. In 2004, many groups worked to increase voting by young people, as P. Diddy's t-shirt suggests.

These differences suggest that not only are there certain kinds of people who are unwilling to vote, but also there are also certain kinds of laws and political traditions that depress voter turnout.

Who Does Not Vote?

Before we can explain why some people do not vote, we need to see who the nonvoters are. The most important thing to remember is that voting is related to education, income, and occupation—that is, to socioeconomic class. For example, if you are a college graduate, the chances are about 70 percent that you will vote; if you have less than a high school education, the chances are less than half that.[36] Differences between higher- and lower-income people are also quite large and growing. Although voting among all groups of Americans has declined in the past forty years, the proportion of college-educated persons who participated fell by less than 10 percent, while that of high school–educated persons dropped by nearly 20 percent. Education apparently is linked to voting because those with more years of education are more interested in, and knowledgeable about, politics.

Though many people take it for granted that those in the working class vote at lower rates than those in the middle and upper classes, in the United States these differences are far wider than in other nations[37] and far greater than in nineteenth-century America. So there appears to be something unique about the contemporary American political system that inhibits voting participation of all citizens, but particularly those whose income and educational level are below the average.

Voting is also much more common among older people than younger people. In 1972, the first presidential election when all eighteen- to twenty-year-olds were eligible, less than half of young voters turned out, and even that small turnout has declined precipitously since (see Chapter 1, Figure 1). Even in 2004, when voter turnout among young people rose significantly, so did voting among older people, leaving the same gap. Often young people complain that senior citizens have more political clout than they do. There are a number of reasons for that, but it starts with the ballot box and the low turnout of young people. (See the box titled "Rock the Vote or Mock the Vote." on page 248.)

Young people are volunteering in their communities in record numbers.[38] So why the low voting rates? Young people's initial tendency to vote is positively influenced by their parents' education and political engagement and by their own high school experiences and going on to college. Later in life, getting married, establishing a stable residence, and becoming active in the community are important to continuing their voting habits.[39]

Thus, low turnouts may reflect many who grew up in homes where there was a low interest in government and the news, so they did not learn that politics are important.[40] Poor civic education in some schools may leave young people with no sense of civic obligation and little knowledge of issues or how politics really work. Then too, like many of their elders, some young people cannot discern significant differences between the two major political parties. Many also believe that the candidates do not address issues of primary concern to young people.

Low voter turnout is also a product of the high degree of mobility of young adults; they change their residences frequently and do not have time or do not take time to figure out how and where to register. Many young people are preoccupied with major life changes—going to college, leaving home, beginning their first full-time job, getting married, and starting a family.

If registered at all, the registration place may be in their hometowns, far away from their college or other current residence. Often voter registration officials in college towns do not want students to vote, fearing that they will challenge local norms and ways of doing things, and do everything possible to deter them. During the 2004 election season, a county district attorney threatened to prosecute students from Prairie View A&M University if they tried to register. When students filed suit, the attorney apologized. A Fox station in Tucson, Arizona quoted a local election official that University of Arizona students who lived in dorms and tried to register might be committing a crime.[41] More typically, election officials make it difficult for students to vote by not putting polling places on campus and not trying to get students registered.

Why Turnout Is Low

There are a number of other possible reasons more Americans, especially low-income and young Americans, do not vote.

Satisfaction among Nonvoters

One reason sometimes given for low rates of voter turnout is that nonvoters are satisfied; failing to vote is a passive form of consent to what government is doing.[42] This argument falls flat on two counts. First, voter turnout has decreased in an era when public trust in government has decreased, not increased. Levels of trust and voter turnout both started declining after 1964. Second, voter turnout is lower precisely among those groups of citizens who have the least reason to be con-

tent, not those who have the most reason to be so. If staying at home on Election Day were an indication of satisfaction, one would expect turnout to be lower among the well off, not among the working class and the poor.

Voters Are "Turned Off" by Political Campaigns

About one-third of a nonvoting group in the 1990 election, when asked why they did not vote, gave reasons suggesting they were disgusted with politics.[43] In explaining low turnout, analysts often point to the hateful advertising, attacks on other candidates, candidates who do not tell the truth about their positions, incessant polling, and lack of thoughtful media coverage.[44]

These analyses surely contain some grains of truth, but how many? After all, people who are most likely to pay attention to the media, watch the ads, hear about the polls, and follow the campaigns are the most likely to vote, not the least. It is possible that the increasingly media-oriented campaigns have decreased overall turnout during the past generation (and we will have more to say about these campaigns later in the chapter). In fact, turnout is inversely related to media spending; the more the candidates spend, the lower the turnout. Moreover, voters who watch negative political ads are less likely to vote or to feel their vote counts.[45] But negative advertising does not affect turnout much, if at all,[46] and negative advertising and other media attention cannot explain the class bias in nonvoting.

In addition to the *quality* of the campaigns, some people think turnout has declined because our elections are so frequent, campaigns last so long, and so many offices are contested that the public becomes bored, confused, or cynical.[47] At the presidential level, the sheer quantity of coverage, much of it focused repetitively on "who's winning," may simply bore people. Moreover, the continual public opinion polling and the widely publicized results may lead some to believe they don't need to vote. To the extent that people feel their votes do not count, the close election in 2000 may change some minds.

At the local level, voters elect so many officeholders, all the way down to weed and mosquito control commissioners, that many have no idea for whom or what they are voting. This proliferation of elective offices, thought by some to promote democracy and popular control, may promote only voter confusion and alienation. The problem is compounded because elections for different offices are held at different times. For example, most states have decided to hold elections for governor in nonpresidential election years. This decision probably reduces presidential election turnout by 7 percent and may reduce by one-third the number of those who vote for governor in those states.[48]

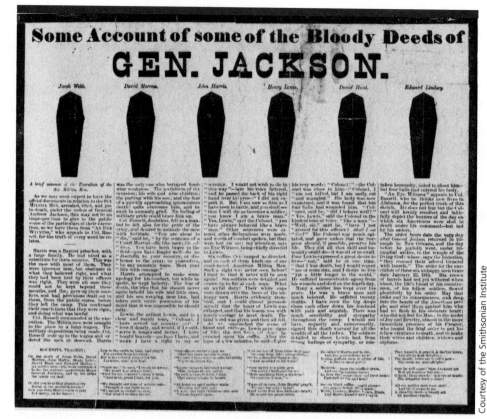

Courtesy of the Smithsonian Institute

In this chapter, there are eight photos, each marked with a blue band along the top, that illustrate American campaign tactics throughout the years. In this photo from the 1828 campaign, Andrew Jackson's opponents accused him of executing soldiers he commanded (as symbolized by the coffins). Jackson won anyway.

Primary elections also affect turnout. One estimate is that holding primary campaigns diminishes the general election turnout by 5 percent.[49]

By contrast, in Britain the time between calling an election (by the current government) and the actual election is only a month. On May 9, 2001, Prime Minister Tony Blair called the election, and on June 7, 2001, it was held. All campaigning was done during that time. There are no primaries. Moreover, as in most other parliamentary democracies, British citizens vote only for their representative in Parliament and (at one other time) for their local representative. Voters are not faced with choices for a myriad of offices they barely recognize.

Lack of Social Rootedness

Turnout is low partially because of what one analyst has called lack of "social rootedness."[50] Middle age, marriage, and residential stability lead to rootedness in one's community. Americans move around, marry late, and get divorced more than those in other nations. Mobility alone may reduce voting by as much as 9 percent. However, American turnout is still low even taking into account these factors.

Barriers to Registration

Most other democracies have nonpersonal systems of voter registration. That is, the state or parties are responsible for registering voters. Voter registrars go door-to-door to register voters, or voters are registered automatically when they pay taxes or receive public services. Consequently, almost everyone is registered to vote.

The United States puts the responsibility for registration on the individual, and that is a major impediment to voting. Only about 70 percent of U.S. citizens are registered.[51] About one-quarter of nonvoters surveyed in 1990 indicated they did not vote because it was too difficult. As one commentator put it, "The United States is the only major democracy where government assumes no responsibility for helping citizens cope with voter registration procedures."[52] Difficult registration procedures have a special impact on low-income Americans, who were 17 percent less likely to vote in states with difficult registration procedures than in other states.[53]

Given that states are laboratories—some things are tried in one state, other approaches tried in another— we know that some registration procedures encourage people to register and vote and others do not. One estimate is that voter turnout would be 9 percent higher if all states' procedures were similar to those of states that try to facilitate voter registration.[54]

Some states make it more convenient to register by having registration periods lasting up to Election Day (most states require registration at least twenty-five days before the election). This innovation, though only used in a few states, increases registration rates.[55] Other ways to facilitate registration include neighborhood registration instead of one central county office, registration by mail, registration offices open in the evenings and Saturday, and a policy of not purging voters from the registration lists who fail to vote.

In other jurisdictions, voter registrars do not provide these options, *plus* they actually try to hinder groups working to increase registration. They may refuse to allow volunteers to register voters outside the registration office.[56] As we have seen, several states have attempted to intimidate minority voters from registering and voting. In fact, the states with the highest barriers to voting tend to be states with the largest minority populations. Other new voters sometimes are challenged, too. In Ohio, in the 2004 elections, Republicans filed challenges to thirty-five thousand newly registered voters. Even if all were declared eligible to vote, the threat of challenge deters some voters from going to the polls. After the election, several groups challenged the honesty of the Ohio elections, citing malfunctioning voting machines and inoperable voting machines in several black precincts in Cleveland.

Some states regularly purge the registration lists of voters who fail to vote. They are fearful that people have moved, reregistered, and will vote twice. Sometimes less high-minded motives are at work, and this tactic is used to disenfranchise lower income and minority voters. This practice means that sometimes voters who think they are registered find they are not when they arrive at their polling places.

To increase registration, a national law allows people to register at public offices, such as welfare offices and the Department of Motor Vehicles (for this reason it is called the **motor voter law**). Similar plans had increased registration in the twenty-nine states that had these policies before the federal government did.[57] The law led to the greatest expansion of voter registration in American history; five million new voters registered,[58] but it has not increased actual turnout.[59]

A related proposal suggests that change-of-address cards filed with the post office be accompanied by cards that go to the voting registration offices in the voter's former residence and new residence. Registration in the new residence would be automatic. The proposal would also reduce election fraud by removing from voting rosters the names of residents who move.[60]

Postregistration Laws Can Influence Turnout

States could also encourage voting for those who are already registered. For example, some states mail sample ballots and information about where to vote to registered voters. Others open the polls very early and keep them open until 9 P.M. or later. Still others allow voters to vote with absentee ballots, even if they are not planning to be absent from their home on Election Day. These practices make a significant difference in how many people turn out to vote, and the effect is particularly great for those who have less education or who are younger.[61] Some of the mystery is taken from the voting process when voters learn what the ballot looks like and where they go to vote, and their convenience is increased if they can vote before their family, job, or classes need their attention in the morning or after the dinner hour in the evening.

Absentee balloting makes voting something that can be done at the voter's convenience. One observer remarked, "A revolution is taking place. The concept of Election Day is history. Now it's just the final day to vote."[62] Though this is clearly an overstatement, almost all Oregon voters vote before Election Day, perhaps a harbinger of the future for other states. Indeed, half the states, including most of those west of the Mississippi, provide for unrestricted absentee voting. Twenty states, most of them in the west and south and including many of those who also provide unrestricted absentee voting, allow voters to cast votes in the county clerk's office two to three weeks before the election.[63] It is not yet clear whether ballot security is the same for these early votes, however.

In 2004, both parties made aggressive efforts to reach these early voters, though clearly having many people vote long before Election Day complicates campaign strategies. For example, in Iowa, voting started forty days before Election Day, and 140,000 ballots had been requested by then.[64] To reach these voters, parties must begin television advertising and flyer mailing much earlier. At the same time, they can track each of these voters more carefully to make sure they have voted. Early voters may also be unable to account for last minute news, and of course, early voters do not have the same protections of privacy as those voting on Election Day.

Failures of Parties to Mobilize Voters

Traditionally, political parties mobilized voters to turn out. In the 1980s and 1990s, the effectiveness of parties doing this declined. They spent more time raising funds than mobilizing voters.[65] The failure of parties to mobilize voters is another reason for low voter turnout, especially among the working class and poor. Because of their low income, a majority of nonvoters are Democrats. If mobilized, they would probably vote for Democrats, but not to the degree many Republicans fear. In many elections, the preferences of nonvoters have simply reflected the preferences of voters.[66]

In 2004, both parties returned to their traditional mobilization function. Both put much emphasis on registering voters and getting them to the polls. Both parties used increasingly sophisticated technology to link information about each party supporter with neighborhood information. Each party communicated with its core supporters via e-mail, and frequently urged them to register and vote.

Both parties have developed sophisticated databases recording individuals' residential location, gender, education, race, homeowner status, and many other variables. The Democratic National Committee has 166 million voters in its database; the Republicans have an even larger and similarly sophisticated database. The parties use these databases to communicate and to target where they might best be able to mobilize potential voters to go to the polls and vote their way.[67]

In 2004, nonparty organizations such as Americans Coming Together (ACT), MoveOn.org, evangelical religious groups, and others also worked hard to increase registration and voting. Though some of these organizations were nonpartisan, many were focused on getting out either the Democratic or Republican vote.

In the past, Republicans have been most fearful of general get-out-the-vote efforts, because the Republicans have no interest in mobilizing lower- and lower-middle class voters. But even some Democrats are wary. The party has embraced social and economic policies that attracted many middle-class and some business groups. The goals of these groups sometimes conflict with those of the working class and poor, and the party's leaders do not want to threaten these constituencies.[68] However, increasing voter turnout has now become a partisan issue, with most Democrats backing state attempts to increase turnout (as they did with the "motor voter" plan) and most Republicans opposing these attempts. States with the highest turnout tend to have active and liberal Democratic parties, giving voters a choice and thus a motive to vote.

In 2004, conventional wisdom about turnout was challenged. Though the Democrats waged a tremendously effective voter turnout campaign, the Republicans were even more successful. Together, voter turnout efforts yielded the highest turnout since 1960.

Voting as a Rational Calculation of Costs and Benefits

Nonvoting may also be the result of a rational calculation of the costs and benefits of voting. Economist Anthony Downs argues that people vote when they believe the perceived benefits of voting are greater than the costs.[69] If a voter sees a difference between the parties or candidates and favors one party's position over the other, that voter has a reason to vote and can expect some benefit from doing so. For that reason, people who are highly partisan vote more than those less attached to a party, and people with a strong sense of political efficacy, the belief they can influence government, vote more than others.

Voters who see no difference between the candidates or parties, however, may believe that voting is not worth the effort it takes and that it is more rational to abstain. In fact, 40 percent of nonvoters in 1990 gave only the excuse that they were "too busy," suggesting a large degree of apathy.[70] Nevertheless, some people will vote even if they think there is no difference between the candidates because they have a sense of civic duty, a belief that their responsibilities as citizens include voting. Most voters feel gratified that they have done their duties as citizens. In fact, more voters give this as an explanation for voting than any other reason, including the opportunity to influence policy.[71]

Downs assumes that the costs of voting are minimal, but, in reality, for many people the time, expense, and possible embarrassment of trying to register are greater than the perceived benefits of voting. This is especially true for lower-income people who perceive that neither party is attentive to their interests. Moreover, they are especially vulnerable to a climate where voters are being challenged at the polls over their right to vote. That is why it is crucial that either the state or the parties provide services to help voters gain information about voting and even (in the case of parties) provide assistance in getting to the polls. It is also possible that the frequency, length, and media orientation of campaigns lowers the perceived benefits of voting for people of all incomes by trivializing the election and emphasizing the negative.

Some analysts believe that voter turnout in the United States will not increase substantially until one of

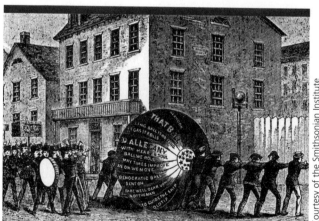

Courtesy of the Smithsonian Institute

From this 1840 Whig campaign gimmick came the phrase "keep the ball rolling."

the political parties works to mobilize the traditional nonvoters through policies that appeal to them. For example, Roosevelt's New Deal mobilized thousands of new voters. If voters believe they have a reason to vote, then their calculation of the benefits of voting increases relative to the costs.

Other Campaign Participation

We have seen that only about half of all Americans vote in presidential elections, and even fewer vote in off-year congressional races. Still fewer participate actively in political campaigns. For example, in a recent year, about one-quarter of the population said that they worked for a party or candidate. About an equal proportion claimed that they contributed money to a party or a candidate. Smaller proportions attended political meetings or actually belonged to a political club.

Unlike voting, rates of participation in campaigns have not declined over the past twenty years. This suggests that people are about as political as they always have been, but that something about elections themselves has decreased voter turnout. Indeed, more people give money to candidates and parties than they used to, probably because, unlike twenty years ago, candidates and parties now use mass mailings and the Internet to solicit funds from supporters.[72] Hundreds of thousands of potential donors can be reached in a very short time.

Just as there is a strong class basis to voting, there is also a strong class basis to participation in campaign activities.[73] Those with more education and income are more likely to participate. Those with some college education actually increased their participation over the past twenty years, whereas those with less than a high school education decreased theirs. Thus, the class bias in participation, as in voting alone, has increased.[74]

Gender, race, age, and regional differences in participation also appear. Even taking education into account, men usually participate slightly more than women, whites somewhat more than blacks, older people more than younger people, and southerners more than northerners. But these differences change over time. Young people participated more than their elders, and blacks more than whites, during the late 1960s and early 1970s.[75] The civil rights and anti–Vietnam War movements drew many young and black people into political activity.

Presidential Nominating Campaigns

Many Americans believe in the Horatio Alger myth, which states that with hard work anyone can achieve great success. This myth has its parallel in politics, where it is sometimes said that any child can grow up to be president. In fact, only a few run for that office, and even fewer are elected.

In the nineteenth century, politics involved most people, and political parades and festivities were common. Here a torchlight parade honors Grover Cleveland in Buffalo in the late 1880s.

Who Runs for President and Why?

In deciding whether to run for president, individuals consider such things as the costs and risks of running and the probabilities of winning.[76] Most people have little chance of being president: they are unknown to the public; they do not have the financial resources or contacts to raise the money needed for a national campaign; they have jobs they could not leave to run a serious campaign; and their friends would probably ridicule them for even thinking of such a thing.

But a few people are in a different position. Take, for instance, a hypothetical U.S. senator from Massachusetts or a governor of Texas. By their vote-gathering ability in a large state, they have demonstrated some possibility that they could win. Their decision to run might hinge on considerations such as whether they think they could raise the money necessary to run a campaign, whether they are willing to sacrifice a good portion of their private life and their privacy for a few years, whether they have an embarrassing skeleton in the closet that would be discovered and lead to humiliation, and whether they would lose the office they currently hold if they ran and lost.

These calculations are real. Most candidates for president are, in fact, senators or governors.[77] In recent decades, governors (George W. Bush, Bill Clinton, Ronald Reagan, and Jimmy Carter) have been more successful than senators (George McGovern, Robert Dole, and John Kerry). Vice presidents also frequently run, but until George H. Bush's victory in 1988, they had not been successful in this century.

Why do candidates run? An obvious reason is to gain the power and prestige of the presidency. But they may have other goals as well, such as to gain support for a particular policy or set of ideas. Ronald Reagan, for example, clearly wanted to be president in part to spread his conservative ideology. Jesse Jackson wanted to be president in part to help those at the bottom of the social ladder. (See the box titled "Can an African American Be Elected President?" for views on electing an African American president one day.) Eugene McCarthy ran in 1968 to challenge Lyndon Johnson's Vietnam policy.

Sometimes candidates run to gain name recognition and publicity for the next election. Most successful candidates in recent years have run before. George H. Bush lost the nomination in 1980 before being elected in 1988; Ronald Reagan lost in 1976 before his victory in 1980; Richard Nixon lost in 1960 before winning in 1968.

Sometimes candidates run for the presidency to be considered for the vice presidency, probably viewing it as an eventual stepping-stone to the presidency. But only occasionally, such as when Reagan chose Bush in 1980 or Kennedy chose Johnson in 1960, do presidential candidates choose one of their defeated opponents to run as a vice presidential candidate.

How a Candidate Wins the Nomination

The nominating process is crucial in deciding who eventually gets elected. Boss Tweed once said, "I don't care who does the electing, so long as I get to do the nominating."[78] American presidential candidates are nominated through a process that includes the general public, the financial supporters of each party, and other party leaders.

Over time, voters and fundraisers have gained more power at the expense of party leaders. Presidential candidates try to win a majority of delegates at their party's national nominating convention in the summer preceding the November election. Delegates to those conventions are elected in state caucuses, conventions, and primaries. Candidates must campaign to win the support of those who attend caucuses and conventions and of primary voters.

Courtesy of the Smithsonian Institute

Soliciting votes by giving speeches and making appearances was once considered beneath the dignity of the presidential office. William Jennings Bryan was the first presidential candidate to break this tradition. In 1896, he traveled more than eighteen thousand miles and made more than six hundred speeches in an effort to win voters. One observer noted that he was "begging for the presidency as a tramp might beg for a pie." Although Bryan lost the election to William McKinley, his approach to campaigning became the standard. This photo illustrates how the term stump speech, *used to refer to candidates' boilerplate campaign speeches, may have developed.*

CAN AN AFRICAN AMERICAN BE ELECTED PRESIDENT?

Will the American presidency continue to be held only by white, non-Jewish males? Can an African American or a woman ever be elected?

These questions sound familiar. In 1960, some doubted that a Catholic could ever be elected president. At that time, only 71 percent of all voters said they would vote for a Catholic for president.[1] The only previous major-party Catholic candidate, Alfred Smith, had been soundly defeated by Herbert Hoover in 1928. But in 1960, John F. Kennedy was elected and that barrier was broken. In 2004, John Kerry's Catholicism did not seem to be an issue except for very conservative members of his own church, who disdained his position on abortion and gay rights. The candidacy of Joseph Lieberman, an orthodox Jew, for vice president on the 2000 Democratic ticket was widely applauded.

But race has been a more pronounced cleavage in American society than religion. Racism persists, and race influences all kinds of political debates, from welfare reform to the all-volunteer military. The party realignment that has occurred in the South is shaped by racial as well as class issues. A majority of white southerners, resentful of the Democratic Party's support of the civil rights struggle, has turned to the Republican Party.

Among campaigns during the past twenty years, race was probably most important in the 1988 campaign. It surfaced when the Republicans succeeded in tying Democratic candidate Michael Dukakis to Willie Horton, an African American convict who raped a

woman while on furlough from prison. It also came up when Jesse Jackson's prominence in the Democratic Party was highlighted and made to seem somehow illegitimate and frightening. A campaign letter from the California Republican Party asked, "Why is it so urgent you decide now? Here are two [reasons]." Below the letter were two photos, one of Bush and Reagan, the other of Jackson and Dukakis. "If [Dukakis] is elected to the White House," it continued, "Jesse Jackson is sure to be swept into power on his coattails."[2]

This is not to say that all of those who voted against Jackson in the primaries or against the Democrats in the general election were racists. Jackson had no experience holding office and is identified with the most liberal wing of the Democratic Party.

Race seemed less important in 1996 when Colin Powell, an African American former chair of the Joint Chiefs of Staff

(the nation's highest military post) and former secretary of state, was considered a strong presidential candidate. Many from both parties were quite disappointed when he chose not to run.

As the figure shows, only 6 to 7 percent of the public say they would not vote for a black or a woman who was their party's nominee, and a slightly lower proportion say they would not vote for a Jew. Although 6 to 7 percent is enough to make a difference in a close race, many more people today say they would vote for a black, Jew, or woman than said they would vote for a Catholic in 1960. John Kennedy's victory suggests that 6 or 7 percent is not an insurmountable barrier.

1. Barry Sussman, "A Black or Woman Does Better Today Than a Catholic in '60," *Washington Post National Weekly Edition,* November 21, 1983, 42.
2. "Though This Be Meanness, Yet There Is a Method in It," *Washington Post National Weekly Edition,* October 10, 1988, 26.

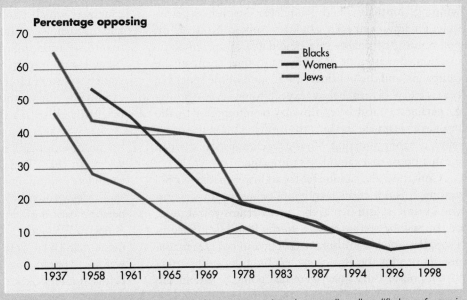

SOURCE: Gallup Polls. The question asked was, "If your party nominated a generally well-qualified man for president and he happened to be a black [Jew], would you vote for him?" or "If your party nominated a woman for president, would you vote for her if she were qualified for the job?" No questions were asked about African Americans until 1958. The "1961" data for blacks are from 1963. The 1994 and 1996 data are from the NORC's General Social Surveys. No data are available after 1996 for blacks, after 1998 for women, and after 1987 for Jews.

Normally, candidates formally announce their candidacies in the year preceding the presidential election year. Then their aim is to persist and survive the long primary and caucus season that begins in January of election year and continues until only one candidate is left. Candidates use a number of methods to try to maximize their chances of survival. They carefully choose the primaries they will enter and to which they will devote their resources. Candidates must enter enough primaries so they are seen as national, not regional, candidates, but they cannot possibly devote time and resources to every primary or caucus. Especially important are the early events—the Iowa caucus and the New Hampshire primary—and the larger state primaries.

Candidates try hard to raise substantial amounts of money early. A large war chest can mark a candidate as unbeatable. George W. Bush started strong in the 2000 primaries because he had raised millions more than all his opponents combined. Candidates also try to survive by establishing themselves as *the* candidate for a particular policy or other constituency. In 2000, Gary Bauer and Steve Forbes each tried to combat their better-known opponents by trying to win the loyalties of the new Christian Right within the Republican Party. They were unsuccessful in enlisting enough of these voters to offset Bush's head start. In 2004, Richard Gephardt tried to appeal to the union vote and Al Sharpton tried to rally African Americans to his cause, but neither was very successful.

To compete successfully, candidates also need considerable media coverage. They must convince reporters that they are serious candidates with a real chance of winning. Journalists and candidates establish expectations for how well each candidate should do based on poll results, the quality of a candidate's campaign organization, the amount of money and time spent in the campaign, and the political complexion of the state. If a candidate performs below expectations, even though garnering the most votes, this may be interpreted by the press as a weakness and hurt the campaign. On the other hand, a strong showing when expectations are low can mean a boost to a candidate's campaign.

Consequently, candidates try to lower media expectations. It is not enough to win a primary; you have to win by at least as much as the media claims you should, or you will be seen as a loser. In the Republican race in 1988, Pat Robertson's organizers tried to counter media predictions for the Iowa caucuses by urging supporters to tell pollsters that they were not going to attend the caucuses. Because pollsters do not count people who do not plan to vote, this tactic could result in an artificially low prediction—and then a surprisingly high vote.[79] (Robertson did poorly anyway.)

Sometimes even losers are portrayed as winners if they do better than expected. For example, in 1968 in the New Hampshire primary, antiwar candidate Senator Eugene McCarthy won 40 percent of the vote against President Johnson, who had become increasingly unpopular because of the Vietnam War. Although McCarthy did not win, he did much better than expected, and the press interpreted the vote as a repudiation of Johnson's leadership. Bill Clinton finished second in the New Hampshire primary in 1992, but because the top vote getter (Paul E. Tsongas) was from neighboring Massachusetts, Clinton's second place finish was considered a victory. Coming far from behind, he pronounced himself "the comeback kid," a designation that became the story of the primary. Said one journalist, "Clinton's New Hampshire abracadabra remains . . . the furriest, plumpest rabbit any politician has ever pulled out of the battered New Hampshire hat."[80] In the modern era of primary elections, Clinton is the only president not to have won the New Hampshire primary.

In sum, the primary season is a game among the media, the candidates, and the voters, with the candidates trying to raise voter enthusiasm and lower media expectations simultaneously. One commentator has called the political reporters, consultants, and pollsters "the expectorate," the group who decides whether the candidate has done well enough.[81]

The common wisdom about presidential primaries is that the key ingredient is "momentum." That is, a candidate needs to win early, or at least do better than expected, to gain momentum, and then keep winning to maintain momentum. The "expectorate" needs to pronounce him a winner. In 1976, Jimmy Carter, then an unknown governor from Georgia, won the Iowa caucuses, which attracted tremendous media attention and, in turn, led to further primary wins and eventually the nomination. John Kerry, by winning Iowa and then New Hampshire in the 2004 Democratic primaries, gained so much momentum that he knocked the other candidates out of the race very quickly, in what was originally billed as a tightly contested race.

Early in the primary season, candidates try to find the position, slogan, or idea that will appeal to the most voters. In 1984, Ronald Reagan presented himself as the candidate embodying traditional America. As one of his staff aides wrote in a campaign memo, "Paint RR as the personification of all that is right with, or heroized by, America."[82] George W. Bush capitalized on the sentiment that Bill Clinton's standard of personal morality was low, portraying himself as someone who would bring morality back to the White House.

Candidates must avoid making a big mistake or, worse yet, being caught covering up a mistake or untruth. Edmund Muskie's front-running candidacy ground to a halt in 1972 when he cried at a public appearance while denouncing a newspaper attack on his wife. Gary Hart's 1988 candidacy collapsed when the media discovered that his marriage did not prevent him from having an affair with another women. He compounded the damage by lying. The Muskie incident was taken by the media and public to indicate that he could not handle the stress of a campaign or, by inference, the presidency. The Hart incident raised questions about his character and honesty. In contrast, during the primary campaign, Clinton admitted his marriage was not perfect, but did not flaunt ongoing affairs. (The Monica Lewinsky scandal occurred after he was in the White House and was already a popular president.)

Incumbent presidents seeking renomination do not have the same problems as their challengers. Incumbents usually have token or no opposition in the primaries. No incumbent who sought renomination was denied it in the twentieth century.

In addition to these general strategies, candidates must deal specifically with the particular demands of caucuses, conventions, and primaries.

Presidential Caucuses and Conventions

Some states employ caucuses and conventions to select delegates to attend presidential nominating conventions. In 1992, one or both parties in sixteen states selected delegates in caucuses.

The Iowa caucuses, except for their timing and newsworthiness, are similar to those in other states. Iowa, as the first state to hold its caucuses, normally gets the most attention. Thousands of representatives of the media cover these caucuses, which have gained importance beyond what one would normally expect for a small state. Although only a handful of delegates to the national convention are at stake, a win with the nation's political pros watching can establish a candidate as a serious contender and attract further media attention and financial donations necessary to continue the campaign.

Presidential Primaries

Delegates to presidential nominating conventions are also selected in direct primaries, sometimes called **presidential preference primaries.** In these elections, governed by state laws and national party rules, voters indicate a preference for a presidential candidate, for delegates committed to a candidate, or both. Some states have preference primaries, but delegates are actually selected in conventions. These primaries are often called "beauty contests" because they are meaningless in terms of winning delegates, though they can be important in showing popular support. Like other primaries, presidential primaries can be open or closed.

Until 1968, presidential preference primaries usually played an insignificant role in presidential nominations.

Wendell Willkie, Republican presidential candidate in 1940, rides into Elmwood, Indiana. In the days before television, motorcades allowed large numbers of people to see the candidates and were a way for the candidates to generate enthusiasm among the voters.

Only a handful of states employed primaries to select delegates. The conventional wisdom was that primary victories could not guarantee nomination, but a loss would spell sure defeat.

The insignificance of most primaries was illustrated in 1968 by Vice President Hubert Humphrey's ability to win the party's nomination without winning a single primary. Humphrey was able to win the nomination because a majority of the delegates to the convention in 1968 were selected through party caucuses and conventions, where party leaders supportive of Humphrey had considerable influence.

Humphrey's nomination severely divided the Democratic Party. Many constituencies within the party, particularly those opposed to the Vietnam War, were hostile to Humphrey and believed that the nomination was controlled by party elites out of touch with the preferences of rank-and-file Democrats.

Delegate Selection Reform

In response, the Democratic Party changed delegate selection procedures to make delegates more representative of Democratic voters. One change established quotas for blacks, women, and young people to reflect the groups' percentages in each state's population. These reforms significantly increased minority and female representation in the 1972 convention and, quite unexpectedly, made the primary the preferred method of nomination. Criteria of openness and representativeness

could be more easily satisfied through primary selection. In recent years, more than 70 percent of the Democratic delegates were chosen in primaries.

The Democrats have replaced quotas for minorities with guidelines urging minority involvement in party affairs. However, the quota remains that half the delegates must be women.

The Democratic Party reforms diminished the participation of party and elected officials. Critics felt that this weakened the party and increased the probability of nominating a candidate who could not work with party leaders. To fix this problem and help ensure that the party's nominee would be someone who could work with other elected officials within the party, since 1984, 15 to 20 percent of the delegates have been "superdelegates" appointed from among members of Congress and other party and public officials.

The Republican Party has not felt as much pressure to reform its delegate selection procedures. Republicans have tried to eliminate discrimination and increase participation in the selection process.

Reforming the Nomination Process

Each election year political observers discuss changing the presidential nomination process. They correctly complain that primaries tend to weaken political parties

The train "whistle-stop" campaign was a staple of many presidential races. Here President Harry Truman gives a speech from the back of a train in 1948.

and have very low, unrepresentative turnouts. More-over, the current system gives disproportionate influence to two small states, Iowa and New Hampshire, that come first in the process. Voters in most other states do not get to see most candidates; they have already been weeded out by the time the April, May, and June primaries occur. Moreover, some charge that the media has too much influence in the current system. The press exaggerates the victories of the winners and makes the losers seem weaker than they actually are.

There are two advantages of giving disproportionate influence to small states that select their delegates early. Only in these first small states do candidates come in contact with voters on a very personal basis. In large states, the primaries are strictly media events. One estimate was that candidates in contested races might spend as much as one thousand days, collectively, in Iowa, far beyond what any candidate could do in later primaries. In the 1996 campaign, one of every five New Hampshire voters had met a presidential candidate. In large states, most voters go through their entire lives without ever meeting a presidential candidate.[83] This personal attention is illustrated in this anecdote from the 1988 Iowa caucus where Democratic presidential candidate Bruce Babbitt reported that one caucus participant, a tropical fish hobbyist, said he would deliver his vote to Babbitt if he could tell him the "pH and sediment density of the Congo River at its mouth." Babbitt assigned a staffer to look into the question.[84]

Having small states at the beginning of the primary season also allows candidates to test their popularity without spending millions of dollars. Those who are successful could then attract funds for the larger, more expensive races. This system gives little-known candidates a better chance than most alternative arrangements would give.

Several large states—California, New York, Texas, Florida, and Illinois—have moved their primaries earlier into the primary season to increase their influence on the nominating process. And, on **Super Tuesday,** most southern states hold their primaries simultaneously. Nonetheless, the impact of the Iowa caucuses and New Hampshire primaries remain. They are still a launching point for candidates who want to demonstrate their appeal to voters and donors alike.

Some observers are glad that we no longer have the "smoke-filled rooms" where party bosses chose nominees. Nevertheless, the primary system has weakened political parties, and the small primary electorate is unrepresentative of the general public. Indeed, these voters might be less representative of the public than the party bosses who met in smoke-filled rooms. And they know less about the nominees than the party bosses did. But the days when party leaders could anoint the nominees are probably gone forever.

"I'd love to join you for pancakes, Mr. Kerry, But Dick Cheney is here mowing the lawn and John Edwards is on his way over to give me a foot massage."

The National Conventions

Once selected, delegates attend their party's national nominating convention in the summer before the November election. Changes in party rules have reduced the convention's role from an arena where powerful party leaders came together and determined the party's nominee to a body that ratifies a choice based on the outcome of the primaries and caucuses.

In the "old" days, often many ballots were necessary before a winner emerged. In 1924, it took the Democrats 103 ballots to nominate John W. Davis. Now nominees are selected on the first ballot. In most election years, some experts predict a close nomination race, which would force the decision to be made at the convention. But in fact, the recent national party conventions served the purposes they have served for more than fifty years: to endorse the nominee and his choice for vice president, to construct a party platform, to whip up enthusiasm for the ticket among party loyalists, and to present the party favorably to the national viewing audience. Thus even without the nomination job, national conventions give meaning to the notion of a national party.

Before 1972, delegates were predominantly white and male. After 1972, the percentage of delegates who were black, women, and under thirty increased substantially. In 2004, 50 percent of the Democratic and 43 percent of the Republican delegates were women; 18 percent of the Democratic and 6 percent of the Republican delegates were black. (Only 2 percent of Republican voters are black and 28 percent of Democratic voters are.) Similarly, Democratic delegates are much more likely to be Latino and very slightly more likely to be Asian than are Republican delegates.[85]

Compared to the population, delegates to national party conventions are well educated and well off financially. Delegates also tend to be more ideologically extreme than each party's rank and file. Democratic delegates are generally more liberal and Republican del-

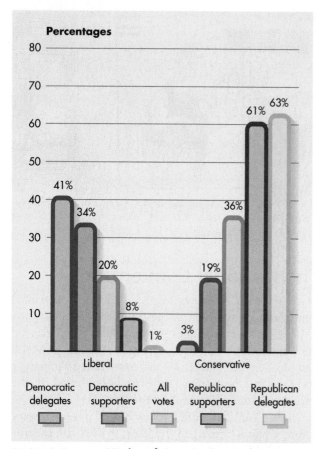

Percentages

41%	34%		36%	61% 63%

Liberal   Conservative

Democratic delegates | Democratic supporters | All votes | Republican supporters | Republican delegates

FIGURE 1 ■ National Convention Delegates Are More Ideologically Extreme Than Rank-and-File Members

SOURCE: Data are from delegate and public surveys reported in *New York Times*, August 29, 2004, 13.

egates more conservative than their party's supporters and the public in general (see Figure 1).

The Activities of the Convention

National party conventions are full of color and portray at least a semblance of excitement. They are a montage of balloons, placards, and demonstrations. Candidates and their lieutenants scurry in search of uncommitted delegates. Behind-the-scenes negotiators try to work out differences among factions of the party. Journalists are everywhere covering everything from the trivial to the momentous. The keynote address reviews the party's glorious past, speaks to a promising future, and levels attacks, usually relatively gentle, on the opposition. Each candidate is placed in nomination by a party notable who reviews the candidate's background and experience. The roll call of the states ratifies the party's choice, and on the last night delegates cheer the acceptance speeches of the presidential and vice presidential nominees. Those who contested the nomination often join the nominees on the platform at the end in a display of party unity.

Aside from these very visible aspects, each conven-

tion has three central committees, which, at times, can be important. The *credentials committee* reviews any challenges that may arise regarding the right of specific delegates to participate. The *rules committee* formulates convention and party rules, such as those governing delegate selection. The *platform committee* drafts the party's platform. The contents of the platform can generate conflict. For example, in 1968 the Democrats fought bitterly over a platform provision calling for an end to the Vietnam War. The failure of the party's nominee, Hubert Humphrey, to support the provision led many antiwar Democrats to sit out the election. After supporting the Equal Rights Amendment for years, the Republicans split over it and did not endorse it in their 1980s platforms. The abortion issue has spurred quarrels at some recent Republican conventions.

Apart from being important symbols of the direction the party wants to take, do platforms mean anything? Surprisingly, amid the platitudes, more than half of the platforms contain pledges regarding proposed future actions, and most of those pledges are fulfilled.[86] Platforms do provide observant voters with information about what the party will do if elected.

Overall, the function of the conventions might best be summarized by the comment, "Conventions are now like bar mitzvahs. They are rites of passage. But rites of passage are very important in society. The guy is changing from a politician and a candidate to one of the two people who are going to be president for sure; it gives them a certain majesty."[87]

The Media and the Convention

Before 1932, nominees did not attend the convention. Acceptance of the nomination took place sometime afterward in a special ceremony. Franklin D. Roosevelt broke with tradition in 1932 and presented his acceptance speech to the convention and to a nationwide radio audience; he did not want to lose an opportunity to deliver his message to the American people. The Republicans did not follow his example until 1944. Since then, both parties' conventions have closed with the acceptance speeches of the presidential and vice presidential nominees.

With the beginning of radio coverage in 1924 and television coverage in 1940, the conventions have become media events. In 2004, there were six times as many media representatives as delegates at the conventions.[88] The parties try to put on a show they hope will attract voters to their candidates. Polls usually show the party's candidate doing better during and after the party's convention, called the "convention bounce," though the effect does not last long.

Major addresses, such as the acceptance speech, are planned for peak viewing hours. Any potentially disruptive credential and platform proceedings (and there have been few in recent years) are scheduled for non–prime time hours. Conventions have become tightly organized and highly orchestrated affairs where little is left to chance. The stakes are too high.

In the past, party leaders did not, or could not, exercise as much control, however. When there are deep cleavages in the party, it may be impossible to prevent them from surfacing at the convention during prime time. The classic late–twentieth century example is the 1968 Democratic Convention. It was filled with conflict—conflict inside the convention between the supporters of Hubert Humphrey and opponents of the Johnson policies on the Vietnam War and conflict outside the convention on the streets of Chicago between antiwar demonstrators and the Chicago police. Television covered both events, associating the division in the convention with the turmoil outside, and dimmed Humphrey's chances of winning the election.

In recent years, with the nomination settled well in advance of the convention and few vociferous floor fights over platforms, the conventions have been less dramatic and suspenseful. Consequently, the major networks are no longer showing them "gavel to gavel," leaving that coverage to public television or specialty cable networks such as CNN and C-SPAN. The major networks showed only a few prime-time events of each 2004 national convention: the keynote speech; an occasional speech by a party luminary, such as President Clinton at the Democratic convention, and Arnold Schwarzenegger, governor of California, at the Republican one; the vice presidential acceptance speech; and the presidential acceptance speech. This limited coverage is the logical outcome of the successful attempt of party leaders to control the conventions. If there's no controversy, there's no media attention.

Selecting a Vice Presidential Nominee

Selection of a vice presidential candidate normally is done by the party's presidential nominee and then merely ratified at the convention, although in 1956, Democratic presidential nominee Adlai Stevenson broke with tradition and left the decision to the convention.

Presidential candidates usually select a vice presidential nominee who can balance the ticket. What exactly does "balance" mean? A careful analysis of vice presidential choices of both parties since 1940 revealed that presidential candidates tend to balance the ticket in terms of age—choosing a running mate from a different age cohort, as John Kerry did with John Edwards.[89] Those with little Washington experience usually balance the ticket by choosing a Washington insider as a running mate (as, in 1992, outsider Clinton did by choosing Gore and, as in 2000, outsider George W. Bush did by choosing Richard Cheney). However, Washington insiders tend to choose other insiders, as

when Robert Dole chose insider Jack Kemp in 1996 and insider John Kerry chose insider John Edwards in 2004. Although common wisdom also suggests that presidential candidates balance the ticket in terms of region (e.g., John F. Kennedy from Massachusetts chose Texan Lyndon Johnson in 1960) or ideology (e.g., the more liberal Michael Dukakis chose the more conservative Lloyd Bentsen in 1988), this happens only occasionally.[90] In 2004, both presidential candidates had running mates whose ideologies were similar to their own.

Gender traditionally has not been part of a ticket-balancing effort, but since Walter Mondale's historic choice of Geraldine Ferraro in 1984, women are sometimes among those given consideration.

The most important factor, however, is choosing a vice presidential running mate from a large state—the larger, the better.[91] Presidential candidates believe that choosing a vice presidential candidate from a large state will help win that state in the November election. In fact, this is not true; the added advantage of a vice presidential candidate in his or her home state is less than 1 percent, and the bigger the state, the less the advantage.[92] About one-third of the vice presidential candidates since 1960, including John Edwards, did not even carry their home state.[93] Both Bush and Kerry ignored the large state potential in choosing their running mate. In his 2004 debate with John Edwards, Richard Cheney even joked about his home state's, Wyoming, miniscule contribution to the Electoral College totals (Wyoming has 3 votes out of the total 535).

Do vice presidential choices affect the election outcome? In most cases, no.

© Jonathan Torgovnik

John Edwards's skills as a campaigner led John Kerry to choose him as his running mate in 2004.

...before the greatest audience ever...

MORE THAN 70,000,000 VOTERS!

These Tips Tell How Your Behavior Can Win Democratic Votes From Our TV Audience...

We're Playing To The World's Greatest Audience—SHOW WHAT A GREAT PARTY WE ARE!

Courtesy of the Smithsonian Institute

In the 1950s, at the dawn of the television age, Democratic Party leaders instruct their delegates how to behave on camera.

Independent and Third-Party Nominees

Independent and third-party candidates are part of every presidential campaign. Most of these candidates are invisible to all except for the most avid political devotee. But in recent elections, strong independent candidates have emerged with some frequency, such as George Wallace in 1968, John Anderson in 1980, Ross Perot in 1992 and 1996, and Ralph Nader in 2000. The Perot candidacies were visible both because he had money to finance his campaigns and because he ran in an era when voters identified less strongly with parties and expressed more dissatisfaction with politics as usual. Though many people thought Perot might have an impact on the election, he did not. Nader did have an effect in 2000, however. His nearly one hundred thousand votes in Florida far exceeded the razor-slim Bush final margin, to take just one example. Though Pat Buchanan took some conservative votes away from Bush, too, his totals were far less than those of Nader's.

It is not easy for independent candidates to get on the ballot. State laws control access to the ballot, and Democratic and Republican legislators and governors make those laws. Thus, the candidates of the Democratic and Republican Parties are automatically placed on the ballot in all fifty states, but independent candidates must demonstrate significant support to get on the ballot through petitions signed by voters. In 2004, Nader tried and failed to get on the ballots in several states, though he was successful in Florida, Minnesota, and Wisconsin, among the swing states. In Pennsylvania, his supporters submitted petitions with the required number of signatures. However, the judge hearing the appeal against Nader commented that the Nader supporters "shock[ed] the conscience of the court . . . . In addition to Mickey Mouse, Fred Flintstone, John Kerry, and . . . Ralph Nader, there were thousands of names created at random." Therefore, Nader was not allowed on the Pennsylvania ballot.[94]

The General Election Campaign

We take it for granted that the election campaign is what determines who wins and it does have a modest effect.[95] But consider this: only twice since 1952 has the candidate who was ahead in the polls in July, before the national conventions, lost the election. Those years were 1988 when Dukakis led and 2000 when Al Gore led (and since Gore won the popular vote, perhaps his case is only a partial exception to the rule).[96] This suggests that although campaigns can make a difference, a lot of other factors determine who is elected.

Campaign Organization

Staffing the campaign organization is crucial, not only to get talented people, but also to get those with considerable national campaign experience and a variety of perspectives. In 1984 and 1988, the Republicans had the advantage in national campaign experience, but in the 1990s, the advantage shifted to the Democrats. In 2004, both teams had considerable experience, given many of Kerry's advisors were old Clinton advisors, though the Republican team was much more cohesive.

The candidate's own personal organization is only one part of the overall campaign organization. The national party organization and state parties also have some responsibilities, including the very important functions of registering potential party voters and getting them to the polls, as well as trying to make sure that the presidential candidate's local appearances will help the party's congressional and state candidates. Party organizations are also crucial in raising funds after the conventions, when direct fundraising by candidates is no longer legal (see Chapter 9).

Campaign Strategies

Developing a strategy is an important element of a presidential campaign. But every strategy is surrounded by uncertainty, and even political pros cannot always predict the impact of a particular strategy.

Candidates seek to do three things: mobilize those who are already loyal to them and their party, persuade independent voters that they are the best candidate, and try to convert the opposition. Most candidates emphasize mobilizing their own voters. Democrats have to work harder at this than Republicans because Democratic voters often do not vote and are more likely to vote for the other party than are Republicans.

Both parties must try to persuade independent voters because independents are the swing voters; their votes determine the outcome. In 1964, when Johnson trounced Republican Goldwater, 80 percent of Republicans voted for Goldwater. In 2000, 86 percent of the Democrats voted for Gore, in the most partisan election in recent history. In these and other cases, it was the independent voters who determined the outcomes.

The crucial strategic question is where to allocate resources of time and money: where to campaign, where to buy media time and how much to buy, and where to spend money helping local organizations.

Allocating Resources among States

Candidates must always remember that they have to win a majority of the Electoral College vote (see "The Electoral College" section later in this chapter). The most populous states, with the largest number of electoral votes, are vital. Prime targets are those large states that could go to either party, such as, in 2004, Ohio, Pennsylvania, and of course Florida. In recent years, candidates have been increasingly sophisticated about where to use their limited resources. Thus in the 2004 presidential campaign, there was little advertising or activity in several of the largest states—California, Illinois, New York, and Texas—because the first three were considered sure Kerry states and the last a sure Bush state. Instead, the campaign focused mostly on the so-called **battleground states** (or **swing states**) where the results were in doubt, not just the large states of Ohio, Pennsylvania, and Florida, but medium-sized states like Wisconsin and Iowa and even smaller states like New Mexico with its five electoral votes and New Hampshire with four. As one indicator of attention, President Bush visited Pennsylvania eighteen times during the campaign and Senator Kerry visited it twenty-two times. Ohio was John Kerry's most frequent stop (with twenty-six visits), and it was second for George W.

Bush (with seventeen visits). Relatives of the candidates, entertainers, and party luminaries who campaigned for the candidates also focused on these swing states.

In focusing on swing states, candidates are attempting to expand their existing bases of support. Most of the Rocky Mountain states have been solidly Republican in their presidential loyalties. Republicans must build on this base and their strength in the South by carrying some of the large eastern or midwestern industrial states to win.

Democrats have a strategic problem given the solid Rocky Mountain and Southern Republican bloc. Between the end of Reconstruction (in 1877) and 1948, the South was solidly Democratic. Since 1976, the Democrats have consistently lost the South, as we discussed in Chapter 7. Some strategists have urged the Democrats to win back the South by choosing more conservative candidates. Others argued for a strategy to win without the South, aiming for the industrial states of the East and Midwest along with California and a few other states of the West. This was Clinton's winning strategy, although he did win three southern states in each election. (This strategy was also used successfully by the Republicans between the 1870s and the 1920s, when they were able to capture the White House regularly without ever winning a southern state.)

Red States and Blue States

Popular parlance often refers to the solid Republican states as "red" states and the solid Democratic states as "blue" states, probably because TV networks use red and blue to depict them on election night maps. Figure 2 illustrates the red states and blue states as well as the results of the 2004 election.

Though the press tends to discuss the red states and blue states as if they were fixed in concrete, of course they are not. There are a core of states that, in recent years, have voted solidly Republican and a core that have voted consistently Democratic, but many states change their majorities from one election to another. However, only one state (New Hampshire) voted Republican in 2000 but Democratic in 2004, and two states (New Mexico and Iowa) voted Democratic in 2000 but Republican in 2004.

The media and many political consultants also portray the people who live in the red states and blue states as very different, with red staters being conservative, gun toting, and religious, and the blue staters being liberal, less supportive of the military, and not religious at all. Said one, "the red states get redder, the blue states get bluer, and the political map of the United States takes on the coloration of the Civil War."[97] One of Bush's top advisors commented, "You've got 80 percent to 90 percent of the country that look at each other like they are on separate planets."[98]

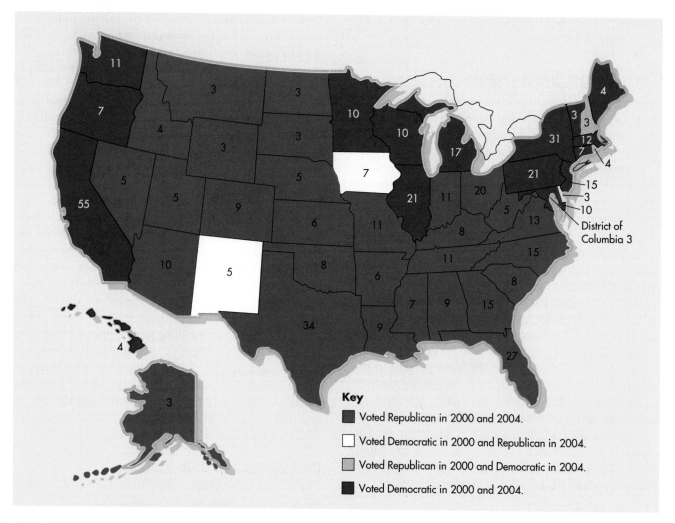

Key

- ■ Voted Republican in 2000 and 2004.
- □ Voted Democratic in 2000 and Republican in 2004.
- ▨ Voted Republican in 2000 and Democratic in 2004.
- ■ Voted Democratic in 2000 and 2004.

FIGURE 2 ■ **Party Strength Displays Geographic Patterns** *The numbers inside the states indicate electoral votes, out of a total of 538.*

SOURCE: Richard Scammon and Alice McGilliaray, *American Votes* 19 (Washington, D.C.: Congressional Quarterly, 1991), 9–13; *Congressional Quarterly Reports,* November 7, 1992, 3549.

It is true that red states tend to be more rural and blue states more urban. Moreover, voters in red states are more likely to be Protestant and born-again Christians.[99] Yet, as Barack Obama (D-Ill.) so eloquently stated at the Democratic National Convention, "We worship an awesome God in the Blue States, and we don't like federal agents poking around our libraries in the Red States. We coach Little League in the Blue States and have gay friends in the Red States. There are patriots who opposed the war in Iraq and patriots who supported it. We are one people, all of us pledging allegiance to the [S]tars and [S]tripes, all of us defending the United States of America."

And a careful examination of survey data also shows that voters in the red states and blue states are not that different. Voters in red states are slightly more conservative than those in the blue states, but the differences, for the most part, are relatively small. Similar propor-

tions of individuals in both kinds of states agree that religion should be kept out of politics. Majorities in the red states usually are on the same side as majorities in the blue states. Figure 3 describes several examples of how people in red and blue states feel about several issues.

Red state and blue state voters differ most in their religious values. In recent elections, most of the very religious Americans have voted Republican and most of the less religious have voted Democratic.

After the 2004 election, many in the media pointed to "moral values" as the reason for George W. Bush's victory. They drew this from an exit poll showing that "moral values" was the explanation most often given by voters choosing Bush. And, indeed, he captured the votes of most of those who disapproved of abortion and gay rights, while Kerry won overwhelming support from those most concerned about the economy and

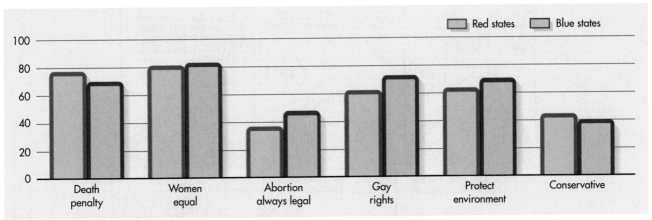

FIGURE 3 ■ **Red- and Blue-State Voters Have Similar Opinions on Many Controversial Issues** *These are proportions of voters who 1) favor the death penalty; 2) believe in an equal women's role; 3) believe abortion should be legal under all conditions; 4) oppose discrimination against gays and lesbians; 5) believe we should do whatever it takes to protect the environment; and 6) see themselves as conservative.*
SOURCE: 2002 Pew National Survey reported in Fiorina, 2005.

health care. However, more considered analysis showed that moral values were no more likely cited in the 2004 election than in the previous two elections. Moreover, when voters were allowed to say what their main concerns were (instead of being shown a list), they were much more likely to mention war and terrorism than moral values. And one-fourth to one-third of those mentioning moral values voted for Kerry.

If red states and blue states are not different, why does our political environment feel so polarized? One reason is that those we elect to office are polarized.[100] Most are nominated in primaries, and primaries are dominated by the more extreme members of their parties. Only 15 percent of the public votes in primary elections, and these are the most partisan voters. With little competition in most congressional districts, the more extreme and polarized views are not effectively challenged. Then, too, the campaign finance system may contribute to the polarized atmosphere by rewarding those candidates whose allegiance to a single issue or cause is most fierce.

Second, the media contributes to the polarization. With the proliferation of cable channels, talk radio shows, and the Internet, the public can hear the news only from media they agree with. The moderating effect of having three national networks, whose newscasts were not targeted toward any one audience, has nearly disappeared.

With our public officials generally representing the more extreme views in their party, and the media emphasizing those views and suggesting that those who disagree are un-American, it is not so surprising that our debate has become more polarized despite the fact that the average American is not extreme.

Creating Images

Largely through the media, candidates try to create a favorable image and portray the opponent in an unfavorable way. The George H. Bush campaign was remarkably successful at creating a negative image for Dukakis in 1988; Dukakis was unsuccessful in either creating a positive image for himself or reinforcing Bush's negative image.

In 1992, the Bush campaign struggled to create both a positive image for the president and a negative image for Clinton. Bush could not find a focus for redefining himself, and his efforts to define a negative image for Clinton had limited success. The Clinton team had learned from the Dukakis debacle. They answered every attack Bush made, but, at the same time, they stayed focused on their own campaign message.

In 2000, George W. Bush used his warm personality to establish a positive image despite the concerns many voters had about his abilities. Voters were comfortable with Gore's abilities, but had reservations about his personality. Moreover, after eight years of Clintonian evasions and lies about personal issues, Gore's exaggerations may have seemed too much like those of Clinton.

In 2004, Bush tried to define himself as a resolute war leader and define Kerry as a "flip-flopper" with no principled positions. Kerry, in turn, painted Bush as an arrogant person unwilling to listen to criticisms or admit failures.

Issues can also be the basis for an appeal to voters. Democrats traditionally have used the "pocketbook" issues, arguing that economic times are better when Democrats are in the White House. In 2004, though, the Iraq war and the war on terrorism were the predominant issues of the campaign (see the box titled

"Terrorism as an Election Issue"). Though Kerry sought to turn attention to domestic issues, such as lack of health insurance, unemployment, and environmental degradation, the campaign was fought largely on the issue of who would be the stronger leader in a dangerous world. And the results indicated that those voters concerned about this issue voted strongly for Bush.

Issue appeals are usually general, and often candidates do not offer a clear-cut choice even on the most important controversies of the time. For example, the 1968 presidential election offered voters little choice on Vietnam policy, because the positions of candidates Nixon and Humphrey appeared very similar.[101] Voters who wanted to end the war by withdrawing and others who wanted to escalate the war had no real choice of candidates. In 2004, the situation was similar with neither candidate offering an option to withdraw from Iraq, though Kerry appeared more willing to declare Iraq a failed venture.

Ideally, the major campaign themes and strategies have been put into place by the end of the summer, but these themes and strategies are revised and updated on a daily, sometimes hourly, basis as the campaign progresses. Decisions are made not only by the candidate and the campaign manager, but also by a staff of key advisers that includes media experts and pollsters. Sophisticated polling techniques are used to produce daily reports on shifts in public opinion across the nation and in particular regions. Campaign trips are modified or scratched as the candidate's organization sees new opportunities. And media events can be planned to complement the paid advertising the candidate runs.

Campaign Communication

Candidates use multiple ways of communicating with their supporters and with the millions of swing voters who might vote either way. Campaign advertising, appearances on television, candidate debates, mass mailings, and electronic communication are all part of campaign communication. They inform, they help set the campaign agenda, and they help persuade voters.[102] In Chapter 5, we discussed these effects generally; here we discuss some effects related specifically to campaigns.

Media Advertising

Paid advertisements allow candidates to focus on points most favorable to their cause or to portray their opponents in the most negative light. In 2004, the presidential candidates and associated groups spent more than $1 billion on advertising in an attempt to sway public opinion.[103]

Television ads were first used in the 1952 campaign. One, linking the Democratic Truman administration to the unpopular Korean War, showed two soldiers in combat talking about the futility of war. Then one of the soldiers is hit and dies. The other one exposes himself to the enemy and is also killed. The announcer's voice says, "Vote Republican."[104] Today's ads are shorter and less melodramatic, but still appeal to emotions. One classic example was the 1984 Reagan ad, depicting his policies as putting the country on the road to greatness again ("It's morning in America").[105] Many of these historic ads are available for viewing online at www .movingimage.us.

When the nation is at war or is threatened by an external enemy, there is almost always a "rally 'round the flag" effect. For the moment, anyway, citizens put aside partisan differences to provide a common front to a threatening enemy. The Gulf War in 1991 led President George H. Bush's public opinion ratings to skyrocket as the public supported the war. No president has had a bigger and more prolonged rally, however, than George W. Bush after the events of 9/11. In this case, America was attacked on its own soil, and millions of Americans witnessed through television the horrifying events that caused the death of almost three thousand people. Within a few days, Bush's public support rose to more than 90 percent, and it stayed near there for months. The president, whose very legitimacy was questioned by many because of the way he won the 2000 election and his reputation of having a shaky grasp on issues, suddenly became the articulate spokesperson for a united America.

Immediately after 9/11, the administration's policies seemed to win the approval of the vast majority of Americans, stunned by the suddenness and violence of the attacks on the World Trade Towers and the Pentagon. The tremendous popularity of the president made it difficult to ask questions about tactics, let alone challenge fundamental policies. Even routine legislative matters, such as subsidies for airlines or crops, became entangled with 9/11 patriotic fervor (as we saw in Chapter 6) as supporters of this or that policy announced that it was vital to America's security. In turn, the Democrats vowed their support for the war.

It is not surprising, then, that the events of 9/11 affected the 2002 congressional campaigns. Candidates of both parties attempted to wrap themselves in the flag and identify with the war on terrorism. Republicans were effusive in their praise of President Bush. Some Republicans encouraged the view that questions about the success of the war or the way we were fighting it were dangerous to our fighting troops, if not downright treasonous. The president implied that congressional Democrats were not interested in the security of America when they did not pass a resolution quickly enough giving him a free hand to invade Iraq.

Though most Democrats seemed afraid to challenge the president on his handling of the war, Republicans used the war in attempts to unseat Democratic House and Senate incumbents in the 2002 election. Senator Tom Harkin's (D-Iowa) unsuccessful opponent, House Republican Greg Ganske, pointed out that Harkin had opposed a constitutional amendment to ban flag burning. Said Ganske, "America has a renewed sense of patriotism and a renewed appreciation for our American flag. Not everyone agrees."[1] An Iowa Republican leader accused Harkin of "trying to make America's war on terrorism a partisan issue."[2]

Norm Coleman, the challenger to liberal senator Paul Wellstone (D-Minn.), took him to task for having voted against increased military spending before 9/11 and again when Wellstone opposed invading Iraq. After Wellstone was killed in a plane crash a few days before the election, Coleman won. The Republican opponent of Senator Tim Johnson (D-S.Dak.) accused Johnson of

voting consistently against the B-2 bomber and national missile defense system (again, before 9/11). The attack backfired, and Johnson won when his supporters ran an ad showing his son, an army sergeant, fighting in Afghanistan. Saxby Chambliss, the Republican opponent of Senator Max Cleland (D-Ga.) accused Cleland of breaking his oath to defend America by voting in favor of a chemical weapons treaty. This accusation offended even some Republicans who knew that Senator Cleland, a Vietnam veteran, had lost both legs and an arm in that war. Nonetheless, with George W. Bush's support, Chambliss won.

By the middle of 2002, Democrats began to state more openly that the war on terrorism was not going well. Then the United States invaded Iraq. The seemingly quick military success turned into a prolonged conflict that seemed to radicalize Iraqis who, at first, welcomed the toppling of Saddam Hussein. By 2004, the protracted military action in Iraq led to significant opposition and renewed determination of the Democrats to oust the president.

Patriotic rallying-'round-the-flag can, over time, turn to public hostility against wars that America does not win, as Presidents Johnson and Truman learned to their sorrow. This seems especially true when the president politicizes the war, as Bush did in 2002 and 2003. But even if he had not, the fears of an Iraqi quagmire would have stimulated opposition.

1. Helen Dewar, "War on Terror Colors the Battle for Congress," *Washington Post,* July 5, 2002, A1.
2. Ibid.

There is both an art and a science to campaign ads. Most political ads are quite short, thirty or sixty seconds in length. Campaigns are sophisticated in where they place ads. Selections of television shows and media markets are important. For example, in 2004, President Bush ran many of his ads on crime shows like *Law and Order* and *NYPD Blue* because he thought there would be an audience of conservative men sympathetic to Republican appeals watching those shows. The Kerry campaign ran more ads on shows with more appeal to women, such as *Judge Judy* and *Oprah,* and to younger and older men, such as the *Late Show with David Letterman*.[106] Kerry also advertised more on shows with African American stars. Both campaigns spent a lot to advertise on morning news shows and popular daytime shows like *Dr. Phil*.[107]

Both campaigns focused on the battleground states and wasted little of their advertising budget on states already thought to be sure for one candidate.[108] But within the battleground states, the Bush campaign focused more on the rural and outer suburban areas than did the Kerry campaign.

Campaigns also have to decide what combination to run of positive ads, touting their own programs; negative ads, attacking their opponents; and response ads, responding to opponents' charges. Today, media ads can be added and deleted as polls reflect their impact. Negative ads were more prominent in the 2004 election than in the recent past. At least in the early stages, the Bush campaign ran far more negative ads than the Kerry campaign. About three-fourths of Bush's ads through the early summer were negative ads, while only about one-fourth of Kerry's ads were.[109] It is likely true that the proportions for both candidates rose as Election Day drew nearer.

This high level of negativity is unusual for an incumbent, but probably reflected his low approval ratings. Strong front-runners tend to stay positive.[110] The 2004 election was so close that both sides made liberal use of negative ads. However, many were run not by the candidates themselves, but by advocacy groups.

Negative ads do provide some helpful information about issues, supplementing media news coverage, which focuses heavily on personalities, conflicts, and the "horse race" aspect of campaigns.[111] Negative ads tend to reinforce previous inclinations. So, if you believed in 2004 that the president had made a mess of Iraq, then you are more likely to believe an ad charging him with that; if you thought Kerry was a flip-flopper, you were more open to negative ads on that point. Republicans and independents find negative ads more believable than Democrats do, perhaps because Republicans and independents are more cynical about politics and government to begin with.

Many negative ads contain some grain of truth, though not always. Kerry did vote for many tax in-

creases, but not as many as the Republicans charged. Hundreds of thousands of jobs were lost during the Bush administration, but not as many as the Democrats claimed. The war in Iraq had not cost $200 million by September 2004 as the Democrats claimed, but it did by December. Still, there is little evidence, for example, that negative ads increase voter cynicism or depress turnout significantly.

However, many negative ads are simply false, such as charges that Kerry would raise the gas tax by fifty cents or that he claimed that all U.S. troops were responsible for the misconduct of a few at Abu Ghraib prison. Among the most discussed negative ads in 2004 were those of the Swift Boat Veterans for Truth. The group attacked Kerry's war record. (Kerry, as a young Naval lieutenant, commanded a "swift boat" in the Vietnam War, and won medals for heroism as well as for his wounds.) The Swift Boat veterans did not serve with Kerry, and several were angry with him for returning from Vietnam and opposing the war. The Kerry campaign was slow to respond to these August ads, and lost ground in the polls during this period despite the fact that independent reexaminations of the record found nothing to substantiate the Swift Boat veterans' ad claims.

After the Swift Boat fiasco, Kerry began responding immediately to other negative ads. Technology allows opposition candidate's ads to be evaluated continuously and new ads prepared immediately to counter attacks that might be having an impact. For example, one day in October, the Kerry campaign learned that President Bush had just charged that Kerry would "weaken America and make the world more dangerous." Within three hours, the Kerry campaign had made an ad accusing Bush of "desperately attacking" Kerry. By late afternoon, the script and video were sent to reporters.[112] Often new response ads are targeted as much to the media as to the public and are only run a few times. The Bush campaign had a similar instant-response operation.

After the first debate, the Bush campaign immediately ran an ad focusing on Kerry's comment about a "global test," and implied that Kerry would not defend the United States without allies' approval. The Kerry campaign immediately struck back stating "George Bush lost the debate. Now he's lying about it" and repeated Kerry's statement about the president always having the right to make a preemptive strike. The Kerry ad ran only in a few cities and on the cable networks where the Bush ad ran.[113]

The Kerry campaign ran some negative ads of its own, raising fears that the Republicans would undermine Social Security with a privatization plan (which Bush then endorsed after the election). Some campaign advisers believe negative ads are very effective, even though most people say they do not like them.[114] One campaign advisor said, "People won't pay any attention [to positive ads]. Better to knock your opponent's head off."[115] And polls show that negative ads can sometimes have a dramatic short-term effect on a candidate's standing. The Bush campaign outspent the Gore campaign near the end of the 2000 campaign and might have shifted the balance in a few key states.

Historians tell us that negative campaigning is as American as apple pie. When Thomas Jefferson faced John Adams in 1796, a Federalist editorial called Jefferson "mean spirited, low-lived . . . the son of a half-breed Indian squaw" and prophesized that if he were elected, "[m]urder, robbery, rape, adultery and incest will be openly taught and practiced."[116] When Andrew Jackson ran for president in 1832, his mother was called a prostitute, his father a mulatto (someone of mixed races, black and white), his wife a profligate woman, and himself a bigamist.[117] A British observer of American elections in 1888 described them as a "tempest of invective and calumny . . . imagine all the accusations brought against all the candidates for the 670 seats in the English Parliament concentrated on one man, and read . . . daily for three months."[118]

Checks do exist on negative campaigns.[119] One check is the press, which could point out errors of fact. In recent campaigns, many in the press have tried to do this, but often end up simply giving more attention to the negative messages.[120] In 2004, fact checkers were more active and many papers ran critiques of the truthfulness of ads (and statements in debates). The voters, who might become outraged, are another check. The third check is the candidate under attack, who in most cases will strike back. Both candidates were aggressive in countering negative ads in 2004.

Campaigns are expensive because they rely so heavily on the media to get the candidate's message to the voters. As one observer argued, "Today's presidential campaign is essentially a mass-media campaign. It is not that the mass media entirely determine what happens. . . . [b]ut it is no exaggeration to say that, for the large majority of voters, the campaign has little reality apart from the media version."[121]

Television Appearances and Media Events

Increasingly, candidates are getting free publicity by appearing on various television shows. In earlier elections, candidates appeared only on "serious" shows, like the Sunday morning talk shows where candidates would be interviewed by one or more members of the press. Now it is increasingly common for candidates to appear in more informal, sometimes humorous, settings such as late night talk shows or comedy shows. The candidates hope to use these settings to show voters that they are approachable and down to earth. It also gives candidates a chance to poke fun at their own foibles, and thus possibly defuse opponents' attacks.

National television appearances might be the only sight that voters in a majority of states ever get of the

© Brooks Kraft/CORBIS

In 2004, George W. Bush campaigned on his role as commander in chief and was often photographed with the military.

candidates. Given the increasing sophistication of the campaigns, most television and radio ads never appear in states that are solid for one candidate for another. Although voters in battleground states might consider it a blessing to not have to listen to campaign ads, voters in nonbattleground states may feel less connected to the campaign.

Candidates also try to use the media to their advantage by staging media events that allow them to be photographed doing and saying noncontroversial things in front of enthusiastic crowds and patriotic symbols. Candidates spend most of their time going from media market to media market, hoping to get both national and local coverage.[122] Vice presidential candidates often appear in the smaller media markets, while the presidential contenders hit the major metro areas. In 1988, George H. Bush almost literally wrapped himself in the flag, frequently "pledging allegiance," until negative media reaction led his advisers to realize that they were overdoing it.

Televised Debates

Candidates also use televised debates as part of their media campaigns. In 1960, Kennedy challenged Nixon to debate during their presidential campaigns. Nixon did

Families all across the country gathered in front of their TVs to watch the first televised presidential debates in 1960, featuring Senator John F. Kennedy (D-Mass.) and Vice President Richard Nixon (R-Calif.).

not want to debate because as vice president he was already known and ahead in the polls. He remembered his first election to the House of Representatives when he challenged the incumbent to debate and, on the basis of his performance, won the election. Afterward he said the incumbent was a "damn fool" to debate. Nevertheless, Nixon did agree to debate, and when the two contenders squared off, presidential debates were televised to millions of homes across the country for the first time.

Nixon dutifully answered reporters' questions and rebutted Kennedy's assertions. But Kennedy came to project an image. He sought to demonstrate his vigor, to compensate for his youth and inexperience. He also sought to contrast his attractive appearance and personality with Nixon's. So he quickly answered reporters' specific questions and then directly addressed viewers about his general goals.

Kennedy's strategy worked. He appealed to people and convinced them that his youth and inexperience would not pose problems. While Kennedy remained calm, Nixon became very nervous. He smiled at inappropriate moments, his eyes darted back and forth, he had a five-o'clock shadow that gave him a somewhat sinister look, and beads of sweat rolled down his face.

According to public opinion polls, people who saw the debates thought that Kennedy performed better in three of the four. (The only debate in which they thought Nixon performed better was the one in which the candidates were not in the same studio side-by-side. They were in separate cities, and with this arrangement Nixon was less nervous.) Yet people who heard the debates on radio did not think Kennedy performed as well. They were not influenced by the visual contrast between the candidates. Clearly, television made the difference.

No more presidential debates were held for sixteen years. The candidates who were ahead did not want to risk their lead. But in 1976, President Ford decided to debate Carter, and in 1980, President Carter decided to debate Reagan. Both incumbents were in trouble, and they thought they needed to debate to win. Although President Reagan was far ahead in 1984, he decided to debate Mondale because he did not want to seem afraid. By agreeing to debate, he solidified the precedent begun anew in 1976. In 2000, the low expectation by the media for Bush's performance, coupled with his congenial, personal style, helped him hold his own or even win the debates in the view of many, even though the debates revealed his limited grasp of issues and his misstatements. Gore's mannerisms seemed stiff and even phony to many, particularly in the first debate. And the press, in an attempt to be fair, mentioned more about Gore's body language than it did Bush's misstatements of fact.

Because candidates have different strengths, each campaign wants a debate format that builds on its candidate's strengths. The "debate about debates" has become as predictable a part of campaigns as the debates themselves. Representatives of candidates debate the number of debates, the formats, the topics to be covered, the size of the audience, even the size and shape of the podia. The 2004 debates were governed by a thirty-two-page set of rules agreed to by the candidates' representatives.

In 2004, those negotiating for Bush argued that the first debate should be about foreign policy, ostensibly Bush's strength. He thought he could easily show Kerry to have an uncertain grasp and a vacillating policy. Instead, Kerry looked assured and confident and attacked Bush's foreign policy mistakes throughout the debate. When cameras focused on Bush listening to Kerry, he looked surly and angry at being attacked. And when Bush had chances to respond, he was not able to consistently offer a coherent and articulate defense of his policies. Consequently, though Kerry had been trailing in the polls before the debate, his performance in this first debate narrowed the gap.

Postdebate analyses focused on the fact that Bush had been so confident before the debate that he did not prepare much. Moreover, Bush was not used to direct criticism of his policies. Within the White House, criticism was not welcomed, and on the campaign trail, Bush usually spoke only to handpicked Republican supporters, whose tough questions tended to be about whether he liked broccoli or what he felt about his legacy.[123] Thus, he did not have much recent experience facing criticism nor with presenting a serious counter argument to it. The ridicule and dismissiveness that he used in his campaign stump speeches did not work well when faced with a real-life opponent making real-life arguments on stage.

The President prepared more for the second and third debates and looked more confident and pleasant. However, most people thought that Kerry bested Bush in those debates, too, but only by a small margin.

E-Campaigning

Increasingly, candidates are relying on electronic communication to keep supporters informed about the campaign and the issues, to raise money, and to solicit volunteer activity. The contemporary candidacy would not be complete without an Internet address to provide information on policies, report recent speeches, offer opportunities to send messages to the candidates, and encourage browsers to volunteer. Some sites offer opportunities to register to vote.

The presidential campaigns have moved beyond rather static Web sites to e-mail lists that keep the campaign in close contact with its key supporters. In the 2004 election, the Kerry campaign had more than two million supporters on its e-mail lists, and the Republicans reportedly had as many as six million.

With the touch of a button, e-mail allows campaigns to communicate with hundreds of thousands of people, making them feel like insiders and encouraging their continued support and allegiance (see the box titled "You've Got Mail"). These e-mail messages supplement the use of direct postal mailings, which are more expensive and less responsive to breaking events. An e-mail can be prepared and sent in a few hours, a direct mailing takes days or longer.

The Electoral College

All planning for the campaign has to take into account the peculiar American institution of the **Electoral College.** In the United States, we do not have a direct election of the president. Though Al Gore had more than five hundred thousand more votes than George W. Bush in 2000, he lost the election.

The Way the System Works

What counts is the popular vote in each state, because that vote determines which candidate will receive the state's electoral votes. Each state has as many electors as its total representation in Congress (House plus Senate) (see Figure 2). The smallest states (and the District of Columbia) have three, whereas the largest state—California—has fifty-five. Voters choose electors of the Electoral College. The election is not decided until these electors gather in each state capitol in December after the presidential election to cast their votes for president and vice president.

With the exception of Maine and Nebraska, which divide some of their Electoral College votes according to who wins in each congressional district, all of each state's electoral votes go to the candidate winning the most votes in that state. If one candidate wins a majority (270) of the electors voting across the United States, then the election is decided. If the electoral vote is tied, or if no candidate wins a majority, then the election is decided in the House of Representatives, where each state has one vote and a majority is necessary to win. This has not happened since 1824, when John Quincy Adams was chosen. If voting in the Electoral College for the vice president does not yield a majority, the Senate chooses the vice president, with each senator having one vote. If it should get to that stage, the largest and smallest states would have equal weight, a very undemocratic procedure.

In an attempt to assess and compare the frequency, content, and effectiveness of candidates' electronic mailings, one of the authors of this book enrolled on the e-mail lists of both candidates in the 2004 presidential election. Enrolling was easy; it only required going to the Web sites and filling out a simple form.

Table 1 summarizes the scope of the e-mailing over a seventy day period from the conclusion of the Democratic convention through the Republican convention and all four debates.

There were both similarities and differences in the candidates' uses of e-mail. Both wrote more than once every other day (the Democrats more than the Republicans), exhorted their supporters to register to vote, then later in the period to volunteer to help register others to vote. Both asked their supporters to volunteer for other tasks, including hosting house parties during the conventions and the debates and participating in trying to spin the message after the debates. Several times the Kerry e-mails asked supporters to sign petitions protesting some Republican act, such as the ties between the ostensibly independent group organizing the anti-Kerry Swift Boat ads and the Republican party. Both occasionally used family members and other celebrities to send messages; Laura Bush and the Bush daughters and Arnold Schwarzenegger for the Republicans; and Teresa Heinz Kerry, John Edwards, and Hillary Clinton for the Democrats.

But there were also striking differences in the way the two campaigns used their electronic messages; this reflected the different context of the campaigns. The Bush campaign was well funded by corporate contributors, the Democrats relied more heavily on small donors. Hence, more than 40 percent of the Kerry e-mails asked for money, while only about 10 percent of the Republican messages did.

Kerry needed to become better known, even to Democratic activists, so he sent a string of e-mails early in this time period outlining his views on various issues. The president was already well known to his closest supporters and did not lay out his platform or programs in any systematic way except to send the text of his acceptance speech from the Republican Convention.

The Bush campaign, as viewed through the lenses of this e-mail traffic, seemed low key during the first part of these seventy days. While the Kerry campaign was asking for money and volunteer activity, many of the Bush e-mails were asking supporters to go on online chats to visit with celebrities, relatives of the candidates, and campaign organizers. The Bush campaign also directed their supporters to read certain new books, books that, of course, had only the most laudatory things to say about the president and his policies. Perhaps the Bush campaign was already up and running and did not need additional volunteer activity or money at that time. It did want to keep its supporters engaged, so it

substituted these other opportunities for campaign involvement.

The Kerry campaign provided none of these opportunities for online chats or book suggestions. There was more of a sense of urgency, as the campaign continually asked for money and for volunteer effort. Before the first debate, the Kerry campaign urged its supporters to participate in online polls and chat groups after the debate and gave them several Web addresses to check. The Bush campaign did not do so. Then in a backhanded acknowledgement of Kerry's success in the first debate and the postdebate spin, the Republicans announced in an e-mail later in the week that "Senator Kerry demonstrated he was serious about winning an election while President Bush demonstrated he was serious about winning a war."[1] By the second debate, the Bush campaign also was urging its supporters to vote in online polls and write letters to the editor.

As the seventy days went on, especially after Kerry's success in the first debate, the Bush campaign attacked Kerry and the Democrats more frequently and called on supporters for volunteer work more often. For their part, the Kerry campaign continued with its frequent requests for money and time and it, too, had some attack messages.

Several ads by both campaigns attacked the policy positions of the other. And about 20 percent of each were sharper, attacking the other candidate or organization for lies, distor-

Strategic Implications

The campaign strategies that candidates use are shaped by the Electoral College system. That is why states like New York and California had few political ads and visits by the campaigns. Their votes were considered to be safe for John Kerry, so neither Bush nor Kerry paid attention to the state. Without an Electoral College system, both Bush and Kerry would have spent much more time in those states given the huge populations in these states.

But the small states that tend to favor the existing system did not receive much attention either. The safe Republican states in the prairies, the South, and the Great Plains were ignored, too, by Bush as well as Kerry.

TABLE 1	Content of Candidates' and Parties' E-Mails, 2004 Presidential Election		
		Republicans	Democrats
Number of:			
E-mails sent		43	51
Requests for financial donations		5	21
Requests to volunteer in traditional campaign tasks like canvassing and calling potential voters		8	17
Number of requests to sign petitions, write newspapers, host a party to watch the debate or convention, and participate in other ways		9	11
Information about the issues of the campaign		5	10
Reports on progress of the campaign		1	2
Requests to read books or participate in online chats with election experts, celebrities, and other information gathering activities		11	0
Appeals to register and vote		3	8
Negative, nonpolicy attacks on opposition		9	10
Other		3	0

Source: Based on research by author Susan Welch for 70 days of the campaign.

tions, and extremism. Half of the Kerry negative attacks were responses to the Republican-linked "Swift Boat Veterans for Truth" ads questioning his courage and patriotism (see Chapter 6). Typical was this message from Mary Beth Cahill, Kerry's campaign manager, "We knew it was coming: the Bush campaign and several allied right-wing groups are using August to launch a vicious smear attack against John Kerry." And Cahill later in the month, "George Bush and his Republican friends have become so desperate that they are returning to their old tricks—whenever a campaign is going badly, they smear the record of a Vietnam veteran. They did it to John McCain in 2000, to Max Cleland in 2002, and now they are doing it to John Kerry." In September, the Democratic National Committee ac-

cused Bush of lying about his National Guard duty.[2]

The Bush campaign's negative attacks focused more on tying the Democrats to the far left wing and to unaccountable groups. Stated Bush's campaign manager Ken Mehlman in this August message, "We don't have shadowy groups doing our bidding." And Ed Gillespie, chair of the Republican National Committee added two weeks later, "Any mention of John Kerry's votes for higher taxes and against vital weapons programs will be met with the worst kind of personal attacks. Such desperation is unbecoming of American Presidential politics . . . " He followed later in the month with the charge, "The Democratic party [is becoming] more liberal, more angry, and more hate filled."[3]

Whether used to raise money, solicit volunteers, attack opponents, or lift the morale and fighting spirit of the candidates' core supporters, clearly e-mail has found an important place in campaign communication. It increases the candidates' abilities to have immediate communication and respond strategically to the imperatives of the developing campaigns. This technology is here to stay in political campaigns.

1. October 2, 2004.
2. Messages of August 11, August 21, and September 10.
3. Messages of August 28, September 8, and September 18.

Rationale and Outcomes of the Electoral College

The Founders neither wanted nor envisioned a popular election of the president; selection of the president was placed in the hands of state elites, the electors. The Founders assumed that the Electoral College would have considerable power, with each elector exercising independent judgment and choosing from among a large number of candidates. They did not foresee the development of political parties or the development of a political climate where the popular vote is seen as the source of legitimacy for a candidate. In practice, as state parties developed, the electors became part of the party process, pledged to party candidates. Thus electors usually rubber-stamp the choice of voters in each state rather than exercise their own judgment.

A discrepancy between the Electoral College and the popular vote outcome occurred three times in the nineteenth century (1824, 1876, and 1888). However, after more than a century of presidential elections whose outcome was known once the popular vote was tallied, and since the principle of "one person one vote" has become enshrined in law and political culture, the American public has become used to thinking of elections as an expression of the will of the people.

When the 2000 election yielded an Electoral College winner who had not won the popular vote, there were immediate calls for the elimination or reform of the Electoral College system. However, these calls went nowhere, and the Electoral College remains.

Possible Reforms

Over the years, several proposed reforms have been considered. One reform would be to abolish the Electoral College altogether and leave the choice of president to the popular vote because direct election is a more understandable system. However, supporters of a popular vote system disagree over whether we should have a runoff election if no candidate wins a majority. When the election is close and there are third-party candidates who get more than a token vote, some runoff system might be necessary.

Even though one might think support for a popular election would be overwhelming given the democratic values of our society, it is not. The Electoral College is based on states, so it encourages campaigns designed to win "states." In this sense, it reinforces the federal system. People in small states support it because their electoral votes are a larger proportion of the Electoral College than their actual votes are as a proportion of all votes.

On the other hand, many political and legal experts believe the Electoral College system gives greater weight to a vote cast in a large state; a one-vote margin in Pennsylvania, for example, yields twenty-one votes for the winning candidate compared to only three votes in North Dakota. So it is more important to get that extra vote in Pennsylvania. Therefore, candidates focus their campaigns in, and appeals to, the large states with tight races.

An even more undemocratic feature of the Electoral College is that not all states require their electors to cast their votes for the candidates who won the state vote. The **faithless elector** is one who casts his or her vote for a personal choice, even someone who was not on the ballot. Even though the intent of the Founders was to allow electors to cast their votes any way desired, today, reformers have proposed that, in our more democratic era, electors should be bound by the wishes of the voters in their states. It is true that no faithless elector has ever made a difference in the outcome of an election, but in the 2000 election, as few as three faithless electors could have made a difference.

Another target of reform is the requirement that, if the electoral vote is tied, the presidential choice is to be thrown to the House of Representatives. There is no expectation that each state's House delegation will vote for the presidential candidate that its state's voters chose; rather, states will follow the majority party in their House delegation. In this process, Alaska will carry the same clout as California. This is a very undemocratic feature of the process, and would probably cause a crisis if actually used to elect a candidate with a minority of the popular vote.

Campaign Funding

Success in raising money is one of the keys to a successful political campaign. Although some of the money for presidential campaigns comes from public funds, much is raised privately. In Chapter 9 we will discuss campaign funding and its impact on politics.

The Permanent Campaign

The **permanent campaign** is a term coined by political scientists to describe the current state of American electoral politics.[124] During each election cycle, the time between the completion of one election and the beginning of the next gets shorter and shorter. By summer 2005, only a few months after Bush's re-election, candidates will already be busy visiting New Hampshire and other early primary states, assembling field operations, hiring consultants and fundraisers, and commissioning polls. No longer does the election campaign start in the election year; now it is nearly a four-year process.

Several factors are responsible for this change, some political and some technological. The political process has changed a great deal during the past twenty years. Primaries have become the chief means by which candidates get nominated, and parties have shrunk in importance in the nominating process. The necessity to win primaries in different regions of the nation means that potential candidates must start early to become known to key political figures, and ultimately to the voting public, in these states. In the "old days," candidates only had to woo party leaders, a process which, though not easy, was much less public and much less expensive than campaigning for primary victories.

Technology has also contributed to the permanent campaign. Certainly, in comparison to the turn of the twentieth century, transportation and communications technology have revolutionized campaigns. Then travel was by rail, ship, or horse, and candidates could not simply dart about the country spending the morning in New York and the afternoon in Seattle. Telephone communication was primitive, and there were no radios or televisions. The idea of potential candidates spending four years publicly campaigning for office under these conditions would have been ludicrous.

But even in comparison with only thirty years ago, the media and information technology have revolutionized campaigning and thus have contributed to the permanent campaign. Modern computer and telephone technology enable the media and private organizations to take the pulse of the public through opinion polls almost continually. As polls have become more common, they have become a source of fascination by the media (and as pollsters have discovered that the media's appetite for polls is nearly insatiable, polls have proliferated). Whereas in the 1950s polls were rarely done and poll results were rarely discussed in media coverage of elections, by the 1980s hundreds of stories about each election campaign focused on poll results. Indeed, much of the media coverage of the campaign focuses on exactly that (see Chapter 5 for more on this topic). In 2004, many news outlets carried daily polls during the last couple of months of the campaign. Thus, candidates must pay attention to how well they do in the polls, which means they must begin campaigning early to earn name recognition by the public.

And, more generally, the fact that campaigns have become media events means that candidates must begin early to establish themselves as worthy of media attention. Until candidates have organizations, fundraisers, and pollsters, the media does not take them seriously. Nor would it be very rational to do otherwise, because a modern campaign cannot succeed without these things.

All of these factors—the decline of the party organizations and the increased importance of primaries, the growth of polling, and the overwhelming role the media now play in campaigns—have contributed to the perpetual motion that modern elections have become. These trends seem irreversible. Only the rolling back of the primary system would seem to make much difference, and that change is highly unlikely.

Congressional Campaigns

Because reelection is an important objective for almost all members of Congress and *the* most important objective for many, members work at being reelected throughout their terms.[125] Most are successful, though senators are not as secure as members of the House.

Incumbents: Unsafe at Any Margin?

Most members are reelected even if they have not done that much for their home districts.[126] Indeed, one Republican member remarked, "Let's face it, you have to be a bozo to lose this job."[127] Still, incumbents believe the best way to ensure victory is to be so good at serving the home district, so successful in getting money for their districts, and so well known to the voters that no serious rival will want to run. Incumbents hope potential rivals will bide their time and wait for a better year or run for some other office.[128]

Given the advantages of office that incumbents have, in name recognition and in favors they can do their constituents (for more on this point, see Chapter 10), you may wonder why they worry about losing. But worry they do. One political scientist proclaimed that members feel "unsafe at any margin."[129] No matter how big their last victory, they worry that their next campaign will bring defeat. And despite the high reelection rate of incumbents, a few do lose. This fear prompts members to spend even more of their energies preparing for the next campaign.

For the most part, this fear is misplaced. Turnover in Congress comes primarily from those who decide not to run. Even in the anti-incumbent elections of 1994, only 10 percent of House incumbents lost (all of them Democrats). In 2000, only 2 percent did, and in 2004, less than 2 percent did. In the 2004 elections, only about three dozen of the 435 seats were even competitive.

The advantages of incumbency are becoming larger. State legislative majorities in 2001 drew most House districts in ways to make sure their fellow partisans had the safest seats possible. Mostly, they protected incumbents of their own party, but in doing so created safe seats for the other party, too. The only states to have many competitive seats were where district drawing was taken out of the hands of the legislature and placed in nonpartisan hands; Iowa is the best example. This gerrymandering has significant consequences for our democracy because it is primarily through elections that we hold public officials accountable.

House members really do have to offend their constituencies to lose. Senators are somewhat more vulnerable. Most senators are also reelected, but the probabilities of defeat are higher than for the House. In the late 1970s and early 1980s, it was not uncommon for a third of the senators running to be defeated. Those proportions have decreased, but in 2000, 21 percent of senators running lost. Even so, the electoral benefit of incumbency still exists for the great majority of candidates who choose to run for reelection.[130]

For example, in 2004, only nine of the thirty-three Senate seats were even seriously contested, in most cases where the incumbents had retired. But only one incumbent lost, Tom Daschle (D–S.Dak.), the Senate majority leader. In the other seats, the incumbent has so much money that the challenger cannot really get into the race. For example, George Voinovich (R–Ohio) raised more than $4 million while his Democratic opponent had less than $100,000 late in the campaign. Similarly, Harry Reid (D–Nev.) had raised more than $3 million, his opponent less than $20,000. Obviously, challengers cannot run effective races with these kinds of disadvantages.[131]

Challengers

Another reason for the uneasiness of incumbents is that as their media and public relations sophistication has grown, so has that of their challengers. Still, without the advantages of incumbents' free mailing privileges and other opportunities to become well known to constituents, challengers have a difficult time. The best advice to someone who wants to be a member of Congress is to find an open seat.

To beat an incumbent, challengers need money. The more they spend, the more likely they are to win. In recent House campaigns, a challenger needed to spend at least one million dollars to have even a one in four chance of winning—and the cost continues to rise.[132] Spending is important for challengers because they must make themselves known in a positive way, and they must suggest that something is wrong with the incum-

bent. Usually, challengers will charge incumbents with ignoring the district, being absent from committee hearings or floor votes, being too liberal or too conservative, or voting incorrectly on a key issue. Sometimes, of course, the incumbent has been involved in a scandal, which offers a ready target for the challenger.[133]

Sometimes challengers will try unusual tactics to make themselves known. Tom Harkin (D–Iowa) worked in a series of blue-collar jobs when running for the House to show people in his district that he understood their problems. Meanwhile, he got a lot of free publicity.

Senate challengers have a better chance than House challengers (see Figure 4). One reason is that Senate seats are bigger prizes and so attract stronger candidates. Then, too, in a statewide constituency there is a larger pool of challengers to draw on. Because they are often former governors or members of the House with a statewide reputation, Senate challengers are better known than House challengers.[134] One analysis of this showed that about 80 percent of voters recognized the name of the person running against their incumbent senator; less than 60 percent recognized the challenger to their House incumbent.[135]

Another reason Senate challengers have greater success is that most incumbents have not had personal contact with as high a proportion of voters as a representative due to the much greater number of people they represent. Also there is a wider range of views and demands to satisfy in their larger and more heterogeneous constituencies.[136] Senators from the largest states have about a six- or seven-point electoral disadvantage compared to senators from the smallest states. Senators from

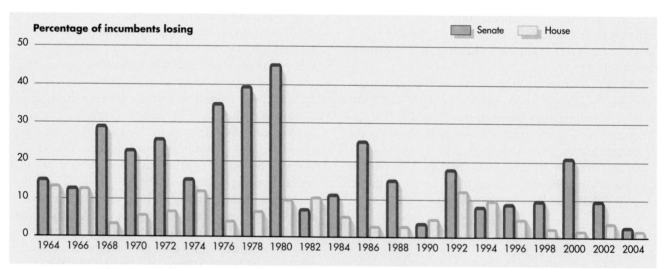

FIGURE 4 ■ House Incumbents Have Had Secure Jobs in Recent Years *In the 1980s and 1990s, more House incumbents lost in the reapportionment years (1982 and 1992); in the 1970s, most lost in 1974, the Watergate year. In the 1960s, reapportionment occurred both before the 1964 and 1966 election. Senate results do not reflect this cycle because, of course, there is no redistricting of the Senate constituencies. Each senator represents the whole state.*
SOURCE: *Statistical Abstract of the United States 2004.*

the smallest states do about as well in retaining their seats as House members from their states.[137]

Campaigns

In the nineteenth century, political parties organized congressional and presidential campaigns, and the candidates had relatively little to do. Today, however, congressional as well as presidential campaigns are candidate centered.

Congressional candidates usually hire the staff, raise the money, and organize their own campaigns. They may recruit campaign workers from local political parties; interest groups they belong to; unions, church, civic, or other voluntary organizations; or they may simply turn to friends and acquaintances.[138]

Political parties do have a significant role, however. National and local parties also recruit potential candidates. Presidents make personal appeals to fellow party members who they think can run strong races, and national campaign committees also recruit aggressively. Said one Democratic congressional campaign chair, "I'm not looking for liberals or conservatives. That's not my bag. I'm looking for winners."[139] Parties redouble their efforts when, as in recent elections, control of Congress is at stake. Besides, if candidates are not closely linked to parties then, once elected, they are not as indebted to their party nor as obligated to reflect party views. Recognizing this, national parties have increasingly provided services to congressional candidates—helping them manage their campaigns, develop issues, advertise, raise money, and conduct opinion polls. National party organizations give substantial sums of money to congressional candidates.

Congressional Media Campaigns

To wage a serious campaign, the challenger or a contender for an open seat must wage a media campaign. Candidates hire media consultants and specialists in polling, advertising, and fundraising. The old-style politician who might have been effective in small groups but who cannot appear poised and articulate on television has given way to someone who can project an attractive television image. Candidates are elected on the basis of their media skills, which may not be the same skills as those needed to be a good lawmaker.

Campaign Money

The old adage says, "Half the money spent on campaigns is wasted. The trouble is, we don't know which half." This bromide helps explain why congressional campaigns are expensive. There is a kind of "campaign arms race" as each candidate tries to do what the other candidate does and a little more, escalating costs year by year. In the next chapter, we review some of the escalating costs of running a winning House or Senate campaign.

Voting for Congress

In Chapter 7, we reviewed the impact of parties, issues, and candidates on voting choices. The same factors influence voting choices in congressional races.

Party loyalty, candidate evaluations, and issues are important factors in congressional elections just as in presidential ones.[140] Party loyalty is even more important for congressional than for presidential elections because congressional elections are less visible, so more people base their vote on party identification. Incumbency is also much more important than in presidential races. The result is that increasingly, since about 1960, voters have split their tickets in voting for presidential and congressional candidates. Ronald Reagan faced a Democratic majority in each house, while Bill Clinton had to deal with a Republican majority in both houses during his second term.

Normally, the party of a winning presidential candidate gains seats during a presidential election year and loses a number of seats in the midterm election. This maintains a sort of equilibrium in party control of Congress.[141] In most recent elections, these losses have been modest. In 1998, the Democrats actually gained five seats in the House and lost no seats in the Senate. The same pattern was true in 2002 when George Bush's incumbent Republican Party gained two Senate and six House seats.

To some extent, midterm election results are a referendum on how well citizens think the president is doing. In 1998, Clinton was given credit for the economic good times the country was experiencing, and in 2002 voters rewarded the Republicans for Bush's strong antiterrorist stance. The percentage of the total vote for congressional candidates that went to Democrats in 1996 and in 1998 was within a percentage point of the vote Clinton won in 1996. (In 2000, though George W. Bush won the presidency, the Democrats gained five Senate seats while losing two in the House.)

Conclusion: Do Elections Make Government Responsive?

Although election campaigns are far less successful in mobilizing voters and ensuring a high turnout today than they were in the past century, in a democracy, we expect elections to allow us to control government. Through them we can "throw the rascals out" and bring in new faces with better ideas, or so we think. But other than to change the party that controls government, do elections make a difference?

In the popular press, we hear a lot about "mandates."

A president with a **mandate** is one who is clearly directed by the voters to take some particular course of action—reduce taxes or begin arms control talks, for example. George W. Bush won a majority in 2004. Did he have a mandate? If so, what for? The largest proportions of the public, 41 percent, were concerned about national security issues, mainly the war in Iraq and terrorism.[142] Most of those voted for Bush, but about one-third of Kerry voters thought this was the most important issue, too. So does that mean the president has a mandate to stay in Iraq until we "win," however we define a win, or is there a mandate to withdraw once elections are held? Or just to do what he thinks best?

And how about on domestic issues? More than 25 percent of voters reported that economic issues were the most important to them, and another 11 percent said domestic issues, like health care and Social Security, were. Most voters concerned about domestic and economic issues favored Kerry, though some of Bush's supporters also thought this was most important. So Bush does not have a mandate on these issues, but as president will, of course, have to deal with these crucial issues. Only about 10 percent said "cultural" issues were most important to them, and two-thirds of those voted for Bush.[143]

Did Bush have a mandate? Like most things in politics, the answer is not simple. Sometimes elections have an effect on policy, but often their effects are not clear-cut. In close elections, few would argue that there is a mandate. In 2000, voters favored the Democratic policy positions and did so in a time of peace and prosperity. A plurality gave their votes to Gore. Yet, Bush became president and acted as though his narrow Electoral College victory was a mandate in support of his foreign policies and conservative domestic policies.

It is primarily political parties that translate the mix of various issues into government action because voters' issue positions influence their party loyalties and their candidate evaluations. Over time, a rough agreement usually develops between public attitudes and policies.[144] A vote for the candidate of one's own party is usually a reflection of agreement on at least some important issues. Once in office, the party in government helps sort out the issues for which there is a broad public mandate from those for which there is not.

Elections that appear to be mandates can become "mandates for disaster." More than one observer has pointed out that every twentieth-century president who won the election by 60 percent or more of the popular vote soon encountered serious political trouble. After his landslide in 1920, Warren Harding had his Teapot Dome scandal involving government corruption. Emboldened by his 1936 triumph, Franklin D. Roosevelt tried to pack the Supreme Court and was resoundingly defeated on that issue. Lyndon Johnson won by a landslide in 1964 and was soon mired in Vietnam. Richard Nixon smashed George McGovern in 1972 but then had to resign because of Watergate. Ronald Reagan's resounding victory in 1984 (a shade less than 60 percent) was followed by the blunders of the Iran-Contra affair. Of these presidents, only Roosevelt was able to recover fully from his political misfortune. Reagan regained his personal popularity but seemed to have little influence on policy after Iran-Contra. One recent observer has argued that these disasters come because "the euphoria induced by overwhelming support at the polls evidently loosens the president's grip on reality."[145]

Elections can point out new directions for government and allow citizens to make it responsive to their needs, but the fact that many individuals do not vote means that the new directions may not reflect either the needs or wishes of the public. If election turnout falls too far, the legitimacy of elections may be threatened. People may come to believe that election results do not reflect the wishes of the majority. For this reason, the increase in turnout in 2004 should hearten all of us. If elections promote government responsiveness to those who participate in them, higher turnouts help increase responsiveness.

On the other hand, if we believe in democracy, we should be concerned about the decline in competitiveness of congressional elections. Essentially, in most states, state legislative majorities have had the capacity to determine election outcomes, including their own seats, for a decade. While the power to redistrict has always been in state legislative hands, the power and precision of new technology makes this power even greater. This is a significant challenge to responsiveness.

Kerry Makes Iowa a Priority

Kerry decided to gamble everything on a vigorous campaign in Iowa. He mortgaged his house to raise money, recruited a top political operative and sent him to Iowa, and began to woo the state's Democratic electorate. As the Kerry campaign stated, "The road to New Hampshire is through Iowa."

Obviously, his efforts paid off. Kerry's skilled campaign staff discovered that the Howard Dean "juggernaut" was less than met the eye. Dean's 1s (the sure votes) were not firm, and his hyped campaign organization was much less skillful than advertised. Dean's surge of out-of-state young volunteers who poured into Iowa a few days before the election were untrained, resented by Iowans, and a burden on the Dean staff in the last few days of the campaign. Kerry's organization was built on local Democratic activists and organizers. Neighbors recruited neighbors.

Kerry's organization gathered lists of veterans in Iowa and enlisted their support. A turning point came when the man whose life Kerry saved in Vietnam made a surprise appearance and told his story. This appearance invigorated Kerry workers, won national media attention, and gave the Kerry candidacy a huge lift.

On caucus night, Kerry not only beat Dean overall, but he beat him among Dean's supposed core constituencies, young voters and Internet users. Kerry credited his campaign manager for the come-from-behind victory: "He works quietly behind the scenes like the [W]izard of Oz behind the curtain. . . ."[146]

In the end, it was Howard Dean who finished a distant third. Though Democrats later credited him for mobilizing Democratic activists and young people who had been turned off by politics, he did not have the organization or perhaps the experience to win the nomination. He raised the enthusiasm and hopes of Democrats, but then when they saw that George W. Bush might be defeated, they turned to Kerry as the man most likely to beat him. Many Democratic bumper stickers in Iowa reflected this reality when they declared, "Dated Dean, Married Kerry."

From Iowa, Kerry went on to take New Hampshire, and then win a string of other primaries. Dean soon dropped out of the race and later endorsed Kerry. Instead of a contentious primary season, the spring soon became a lovefest, with Kerry's opponents uniting to fight George W. Bush. And Kerry himself reflected, "Sometimes you have to go out and make your own breaks and make the fight. Iowa is the fight I chose."[147]

Key Terms

suffrage

Reconstruction

literacy tests

grandfather clause

poll tax

white primary

Voting Rights Act (VRA)

gerrymandering

cracking, stacking, and
packing

majority-minority districts

split-ticket voting

Progressive reforms

motor voter law

presidential preference
primaries

Super Tuesday

battleground states
(swing states)

Electoral College

faithless elector

permanent campaign

mandate

Further Reading

Stephen Ansolabehere and Shanto Iyengar, *Going Negative* (New York: Free Press, 1996). Two political scientists report the results of their research on the impact of negative television ads on voters and voting.

Taylor Branch, *Parting the Waters: America in the King Years, 1954–63* (New York: Simon and Schuster, 1988). An excellent, readable account that illustrates the impact of political protest in changing America's race laws and, to a considerable extent, its attitudes about race.

Evan Cornog and Richard Whalen, *Hats in the Ring: An Illustrated History of American Presidential Campaigns* (New York: Random House, 2000). Here is an entertaining look at presidential campaigns, including many photos, cartoons, prints, and anecdotes along with factual information.

Robert Darcy, Susan Welch, and Janet Clark, *Women, Elections, and Representation* (Lincoln: University of Nebraska Press, 1994). An examination of the potential barriers faced by women candidates.

Kathleen Hall Jamieson, *Packaging the Presidency: A History and Criticism of Presidential Campaign Advertising* (New York: Oxford University Press, 1984). The history and impact of presidential campaign advertising.

David A. Kaplan, *The Accidental President: How 413 Lawyers, 9 Supreme Court Justices, and 5,963,110 Floridians (Give or Take a Few) Landed George W. Bush in the White House* (New York: Morrow, 2001). A humorous look behind the scenes of the Bush and Gore organizations fighting for the 2000 election after Election Day.

Zachary Karabell, *The Last Campaign: How Harry Truman Won the 1948 Election* (New York: Knopf, 2000). The story of the Truman-Dewey 1948 campaign that some campaign experts believe was the best in the second half of the twentieth century.

Thomas E. Patterson, *The Vanishing Voter* (New York: Knopf, 2002). A political scientist blames candidates, parties, the media, and the public themselves for low turnouts and makes some suggestions for change.

Joe Trippi, *The Revolution Will Not be Televised: Democracy, the Internet, and the Overthrow of Everything* (New York: Regan Books, 2004). Howard Dean's campaign manager explains how the Internet changed campaigning.

Theodore H. White, *The Making of the President,* 4 vols.: *1960, 1964, 1968,* and *1972* (New York: Atheneum, 1961, 1965, 1969, 1973). Journalistic accounts of presidential elections from 1960 to 1972. White was the first journalist to travel with the candidates and give an inside view of campaign strategy.

For Viewing

Fahrenheit 9/11 (2004) Like it or hate it, this Michael Moore film, with its harsh critique of President Bush's handling of the war on terrorism and the war in Iraq, won both critical acclaim and a place in the campaign of 2004. The Republicans countered with several videos, probably the best being *George W. Bush: Faith in the White House.* This DVD portrays Bush as something akin to God's representative on earth, and was being specifically targeted to be the counter to *Fahrenheit 9/11.* Reportedly, three hundred thousand copies were distributed to churches.

The Candidate (1972) This film starring Robert Redford features a candidate for the Senate who finds that as his chances of success increase, his ability to tell the truth as he sees it decreases.

Primary (1960) A documentary that reports on John F. Kennedy and Hubert Humphrey contesting for the 1960 Democratic party nomination. This film started the trend of close film coverage of presidential candidates. You will probably be startled by the primitive technology compared to today.

The War Room (1963) This documentary features Bill Clinton's campaign.

Journeys with George (2000) This film focuses on George W. Bush's 2000 campaign from the perspective of a journalist traveling with the campaign.

🌐 Electronic Resources

Most congressional and many state candidates have Web sites that provide news about the candidates, issues, how to vote, and related matters.

www.democrats.org/party and www.rnc.org
Links to the Democratic National Committee and the Republican National Committee. Each of these pages contains information about the campaign organizations of the two national parties.

www.Movingimage.us
Check out historical and contemporary campaign commercials on this site.

www.washingtonpost.com
The Washington Post *covers national politics and elections more thoroughly than any other newspaper.*

www.rockthevote.com/home.php
Rock the Vote encourages young voters to register and vote and provides nonpartisan information about campaigns and issues.

 ## InfoTrac College Edition

Search for the following articles in the InfoTrac database:

Pitney Jr., John J. "Chad All Over," *Reason* (August 2001).

Walsh, Kenneth T. "In the Homestretch, Hitting His Stride,"*U.S. News & World Report* (November 6, 2000).

Wattenberg, Martin P. "Elections: Was the 2000 Presidential Election Fair? An Analysis of Comparative and Retrospective Survey Data," *Presidential Studies Quarterly* (December 2003).

Wlezien, Christopher. "Presidential Election Polls in 2000: A Study in Dynamics," *Presidential Studies Quarterly* (March 2003).

For more articles, enter

"Democratic Party" in the Subject Guide;

"Republican Party" in the Subject Guide;

"third parties" in the Subject Guide.

 ## American Government Resources

Visit the Political Behavior section of the Wadsworth American Government Resources Web site (politicalscience.wadsworth.com/amgov) for a variety of tools to help you explore elections further. Included are simulations, video clips, Microcase exercises, and a wealth of other activities.

CHAPTER 9

MONEY AND POLITICS

Initiated by Howard Dean in his Democratic primary campaign, Internet fundraising became a major new development in the 2004 presidential election.

Money and Politics in America's Past

Money in Nineteenth-Century American Politics

Early Reforms

Regulating Money in Modern Campaigns

Issues in Campaign Finance Reform

Modern Attempts at Reform

Regulating the Costs of Campaigns and Public Financing

Contribution Limits and Ways to Avoid Them

Independent Spending

Disclosure

Campaign Finance Reform and the 2004 Election

Is Real Reform Possible?

The Impact of Campaign Money

Does the Campaign Finance System Deter Good Candidates?

Does Money Win Elections?

Does Money Buy Favorable Policies?

Does Our Campaign Finance System Encourage Extortion?

Campaign Money and Public Cynicism

Conflicts of Interest

Are There Democratic and Republican Kinds of Corruption?

Conclusion: Does the Influence of Money Make Government Less Responsive?

Should You Vote to Regulate?

t is 2000, and you are Charles Schumer, a Democratic senator from New York. You are weighing a proposed rule to restrict potentially corrupt practices in the financial industry. Elected to public office immediately after graduating from Harvard Law School, you have served in the New York state assembly, the U.S. House of Representatives, and now the U.S. Senate.[1] Though a relatively junior senator, you are highly visible. As a member of the House, you were known both for your legislative activism and success and for your nose for publicity. Bob Dole once joked that "the most dangerous place in Washington was in between Schumer and a television camera."[2] In 1998, you won a Senate seat, beating a popular incumbent in the most expensive Senate race ever waged until then.

Given your New York constituency, it is not surprising that you have a liberal voting record, strongly supporting gun control and abortion rights, for example. On the other hand, one of your special interests is the financial services industry—that is, banks, savings and loans, brokerage houses, and related financial institutions—and there you have established a less liberal record, voting frequently to lighten government regulation. In this, you are mindful of your constituency. New York City is the heart of the nation's and the world's financial system, so legislation and regulations affecting the financial industry are of keen interest to many of your most influential constituents.

In both the House and the Senate, you served as a member of the Banking, Housing, and Urban Affairs Committee, which oversees the Securities and Exchange Commission (SEC), the federal agency that regulates the stock exchange. Your seat on the Banking Committee makes you an important person to people in the financial industry and corporate America. They reflect this importance through generous campaign contributions, an important factor given the cost of running statewide races in New York.

During the past decade, Congress has been busy deregulating the financial services industry, giving banks, savings and loans, insurance companies, and investment bankers more flexibility to do business with each other and to compete for business normally handled by other sectors of the financial industry. Deregulation has also meant that federal oversight has been reduced and protection for consumers and investors weakened.

Because the New York financial world is part of your constituency, you have supported legislation to deregulate much of the financial services industry. A few years ago, as a member of the House, you joined the Republican majority in voting to strip investors of their rights to sue companies, overriding President Clinton's veto and removing a big check on corporate criminals.[3]

Now Arthur Levitt, chair of the SEC, proposes to tighten regulations involving auditing firms. Auditing firms are increasingly providing consulting services for companies that they are auditing. Levitt believes that there was an increasing chance that auditors' reports were being corrupted. Indeed, in a speech in 1998, he complained of "accounting hocus-pocus" by corporations and their auditors.[4]

The reason is the obvious potential for conflict of interest. Auditors in firms that have lucrative consulting contracts with corporations they are auditing may feel that they can't come down hard on suspicious accounting practices. As consulting becomes increasingly important to the top accounting firms, their independence is more and more compromised. By the late 1990s, big accounting firms were making more from consulting than from their auditing business.

Because of these conflicts, Levitt wants the SEC to pass a rule requiring firms to choose between being auditors of corporations and being consultants for them. In the complex world of corporate finance, accounting principles govern how profits are calculated. Auditors, hired by the company boards of directors but with ostensible independence from the company, are charged with investigating adherence to these accounting principles and then certifying that they have been met. Certifying that the company's books are accurate ensures investors and potential investors that the finances of the corporation are as portrayed. And favorable reports reassure investors and allow the corporation's stock to continue increasing in value, whereas unfavorable reports worry investors and prompt them to unload their stock in the corporation, causing its value to decline. As the economy boomed in the 1990s, pressure increased on corporations to boost their earnings and thus benefit from the high-flying stock market. A rosy earnings picture was among the factors that drove stocks to record highs.

One way to increase earnings is to increase revenue and cut costs; the other way is to cook the books. And indeed, the demand to show stockholders large profits put pressure on auditors to certify that the healthy financial pictures that corporations painted were accurate even when they were not. By the end of the 1990s, the SEC regulators began to find that accountants were not holding corporations to the appropriate standards for calculating profits and losses; indeed, in some cases they were participating in outright fraud.

The SEC argued that lax oversight could have catastrophic consequences if a business overstated its earnings and investors invested their money on the basis of this false information. When the truth was uncovered, stock prices would plummet, and investors would lose some or all of their investments in the business. Moreover, if one large corporation's unethical accounting practices were uncovered, other companies could suffer as mistrust would dampen investors' willingness to invest in stocks. In a nutshell, poor accounting practices, as dry and boring as they might seem, could threaten our capitalist system.

The rule that Levitt and the SEC proposes is not legislation; it does not need to be passed by Congress. But before it makes a rule, the SEC wants to get support from the various constituencies the agency serves. In particular, the members of the Banking Committee have considerable clout with the SEC. The committee has oversight power for the SEC, giving them power to reward the agency through favorable budget recommendations or to make the lives of the officials of the SEC miserable in various ways, such as by holding hearings, demanding information, failing to endorse the president's recommendations for high-level appointments to the agency, proposing unfavorable legislation affecting the agency (such as reducing its jurisdiction), and cutting its budget. And committee members have an influence on the larger membership of Congress when it comes to budgets affecting the SEC.

The SEC would like to have your support for this proposed rule because you are an influential Democrat on the Banking Committee. What is your response? Do you support this regulation or not?

Your first instinct is to oppose the rule. You have generally supported deregulation of the financial industry, and the new rule would mean more regulation, not less. Moreover, the accounting lobby has mobilized to oppose the rule. This is a lobby with significant clout. It helped persuade Congress to shield companies and their auditors from suits by stockholders, the legislation that you supported against the opposition of the SEC and President Clinton. Now the accountants' lobby has hired high-powered lawyers and is working to persuade individual members to lobby the SEC against the bill. The lobbyists are even helping draft letters that members of Congress can send to the SEC.

These lobbyists have access to you and other influential members of Congress because you have worked together over the years on legislation of interest to the accounting profession. Moreover, over the past few years, they have made significant contributions to your political campaigns and those of many others. In fact, you have received nearly $330,000 from the accounting lobby since 1995, more than any other member of Congress. But among the others who have received substantial contributions are the chair of the Banking Committee, Phil Gramm (R-Tex.), who received $200,000. Of course, you and your colleagues have also received campaign donations from many corporations that are also opposing this bill. One such aggressive corporation, Enron, a high-flying Texas energy company, has donated more than $70,000 to you and much more to other members.

On the other hand, among your constituents, there are certainly more investors than there are accountants and corporation executives. Yet even though some one hundred million Americans, including millions of New Yorkers, own stocks, they are not well organized as a lobby. So constituency pressure to support the rule is weak. As Levitt said, investors are "potentially the most powerful lobbying force in the country, and . . . the least well organized." Investors don't stand a chance of winning in a face-off with most business interest groups that are well organized.[5]

You have heard warning signals that some firms might be acting unethically by publishing inflated earnings reports. Just last year, one of the nation's largest accounting firms, Ernst & Young,

agreed to pay over $300 million to shareholders who blamed the firm for misleading profit statements by a large corporation it had audited. Ernst & Young claimed it was the victim of fraud by the company but paid anyway.[6] Obviously, you have no interest in seeing scandal overtake the accounting industry or corporate America; this would hurt the country and would certainly hurt New York's economy. Levitt's rule might help prevent such scandal.

Whatever you decide on the proposed rule, your position will be immediately known to the accounting lobby and to the large corporations who do

not want the rule to be adopted. Your position is not so likely to be known by unorganized groups in favor of the rule or by most of your constituents. Most will never know unless corrupt auditing practices cause a corporation's stock to plunge and the investors—including your constituents—to lose their money. Then they might blame you. But of course, this scenario might never occur. Public interest in this rule is weak. Short of some scandal, it will remain weak. This fight is mostly an "inside the Beltway battle" between the head of the SEC and the big accounting firms.[7]

What do you do and why?

Former speaker of the House of Representatives Tip O'Neill once said, "There are four parts to any campaign. The candidate, the issues . . . , the campaign organization, and the money. Without money you can forget the other three."[8] Conventional wisdom holds that "money is the mother's milk of politics." But we are not sure whether that milk is tainted or pure. On the one hand, without money, candidates or people with new political ideas could never become known in our massive and complex society. Television spreads names and ideas almost instantaneously, so having money to buy television time means that your ideas will be heard. In that sense, money contributes to open political debate.

On the other hand, money can be a corrupting influence on politics. At the least, it can buy access to decision makers. At the worst, it can buy decisions. Money allows some points of view to be trumpeted while others are forced to whisper. Some candidates or groups can afford to spend hundreds of thousands of dollars for each prime-time minute of national television or for prestigious Washington law firms to lobby; others can afford only Web pages and letters. Money increases inequities in political life.

Money, then, leads to a dilemma in politics. In our largely capitalist society, we expect substantial differences in wealth and income. In most cases, we see nothing wrong when individuals of great wealth are able to buy goods and services that others cannot afford. But in politics, many people feel uneasy when high-income individuals or well-bankrolled groups are able to buy political favors. We feel so uneasy that we have outlawed certain kinds of buying of political favors, such as politicians paying voters for their votes or interest groups paying politicians and bureaucrats for their support.

But we are also uneasy about placing other limits on the influence of money. Many people feel that individuals or groups should be allowed to contribute as much money to candidates as they want and that candidates should be permitted to buy as much media time to get their point of view across as they want and can afford. This view holds that contributing money and buying media time are forms of constitutionally guaranteed freedom of speech. The opposite view says that these practices distort the democratic process.

These issues are growing more important as the cost of political campaigns increases. In 2000, candidates at all levels spent $4 billion, and that number increased in 2004. Only a fraction came from public funds. So it is not surprising that political candidates scramble for money. Campaign finance laws seek to limit the amounts individuals and groups can give to candidates and establish procedures to track those donations. Journalists and other analysts also try to determine what the donors received in return for their gifts.

In this chapter, we first focus on the development of laws that regulate how money can influence politics, then turn to the role and impact of money in elections, and finally briefly examine conflicts of interest on the part of decision makers in Congress and the executive branch.

Money and Politics in America's Past

Concern about the illegitimate influence of money on politics is older than the Republic. In 1699, after asking how campaign money could be regulated, the Virginia House of Burgesses (the colony's legislature) voted to prohibit the bribing of voters.[9] In his campaign for the Virginia House of Burgesses in 1757, George Washington was accused of vote buying. He had given out twenty-eight gallons of rum, fifty gallons of rum punch, thirty-four gallons of wine, forty-six gallons of beer, and two gallons of cider. Because there were only 391 voters in his district, he had provided more than a quart and a half of beverages per voter![10]

Obviously, Washington survived these charges, and his constituents probably survived the effects of the rum and cider. But most discussions of the impact of money on politics were more sober. In his well-known analysis of controlling factions, James Madison, in *Federalist Paper* 10, recognized that "the most common and durable source of factions has been the various and unequal distribution of property." Madison went on to say that although ideally no one should be allowed to make decisions affecting his or her own self-interest, almost any subject of legislation—taxes, tariffs, debts—involves self-interest. For those making laws, "every shilling with

which they overburden the inferior number is a shilling saved to their own pockets."

Madison hoped that the design of the new nation, with the power of the government divided among the branches of government and between the nation and the states, would mean that no one interest or faction would overwhelm the others. The interest of one person or group would check the interest of another.

This view of counterbalancing interests is an optimistic one and has not always worked. Over the decades, Americans have found it necessary to make additional rules to restrict the ways that people or groups with money can try to influence policymakers.

Money in Nineteenth-Century American Politics

The influence of money on politics has shaped several epochs of American history. For example, from the earliest westward expansion of the nation, charges of graft and corruption surrounded the government's sale and giveaway of land. Indeed, the West was developed by giving land to speculators and railroads, sometimes in exchange for bribes. When Congress was debating whether to give federal land to the railroads, the lobbyists "camped in brigades around the Capitol building."[11]

The impact of money on political life probably reached its peak in the late nineteenth century, during the so-called Gilded Age after the Civil War. During that time, the United States grew from a small agrarian society to a large industrialized one. This industrialization produced great wealth in such fields as oil exploration and refining, the steel industry, and the railroad companies that were spanning the nation. This was the era of "robber barons," when the owners of giant corporations (called *trusts*) openly bought political favors.

Business contributions to campaigns and to politicians were routine. One railroad president justified the bribing of political officials by noting, "If you have to pay money to have the right thing done, it is only just and fair to do so."[12] Mark Hanna, a Republican fundraiser in the presidential election of 1896, assessed banks at a fixed percentage of their capital and also collected substantial sums from most insurance companies and large corporations.[13] However, Cornelius Vanderbilt, one of the wealthiest men of his time, refused to contribute to election campaigns, believing that it was cheaper to buy legislators after they were elected!

Not only did lobbyists bribe politicians, but politicians bribed reporters. In the 1872 presidential campaign, the Republican Party gave money to about three hundred reporters in return for favorable coverage.[14] (See the box "Honest Graft" for more on money's role in nineteenth-century politics.)

This cartoon mocks President Ulysses S. Grant's involvement in various corrupt activities. Grant (dressed in the flag suit) is shown supporting various political bosses and profiteers.

© The Granger Collection, New York

The influence of money on local politics reached a high point in the late nineteenth century. Urban machines used money to cement a complex network of businesses, voters, and political party organizations. Business payoffs to government and party officials for licenses and contracts and party payoffs to voters for their support were the norm. Graft was tolerated and even expected.

As we saw in Chapter 7, George Washington Plunkitt was a famous leader of the New York City machine known as Tammany Hall. Plunkitt, born in 1842, began life as a butcher's helper and ended up a millionaire through deals made in his role as a party leader and public official. He held a number of state and local public offices; at one point, he held four at the same time. He drew a salary for three of them simultaneously.

Plunkitt's view of graft illustrates the casual attitude about the influence of money on politics common among many of his time:

There's all the difference in the world between [honest graft and dishonest graft]. There's an honest graft, and I'm an example of how it works. I might sum up the whole thing by sayin': "I seen my opportunities and I took 'em."

Just let me explain. . . . My party's in power in the city, and it's goin' to undertake a lot of public improvements.

Well, I'm tipped off, say, that they're going to lay out a new park at a certain place. I see my opportunity and take it. I go to that place and I buy up all the land I can in the neighborhood. Then the board of this or that makes its plan public, and there is a rush to get my land, which nobody cared particular for before. Ain't it perfectly honest to charge a good price and

make a profit on my investment and foresight? Of course, it is. Well, that's honest graft.

Tammany was beat in 1901 because the people were deceived into believin' that it worked dishonest graft. . . . [They supposed that] Tammany men were robbin' the city treasury or levyin' blackmail on disorderly houses, or workin' in with the gamblers and lawbreakers. . . . Why should the Tammany leaders go into such dirty business when there is so much honest graft lyin' around?

. . . I don't own a dishonest dollar. If my worst enemy was given the job of writin' my epitaph . . . he couldn't do more than write: George W. Plunkitt. He Seen His Opportunities, and He Took 'Em.

SOURCE: William L. Riordon, *Plunkitt of Tammany Hall* (1905; repr., New York: Dutton, 1963), 3–6.

U.S. senators bought their own seats (this was before senators were elected by the public) by bribing state legislators to select them. When one member proposed that all of those who had bribed their way into the Senate be expelled, another member observed that "we might lose a quorum" if that were done.[15]

Early Reforms

Around the turn of the twentieth century, the Progressive reformers and their allies in the press, called **muckrakers,** began to attack this overt corruption. They wanted to break the financial link between business and politicians. In 1907, a law prohibited corporations and banks from making contributions to political campaigns, and a few years later, Congress mandated public reporting of campaign expenditures and set limits on campaign donations. Prohibitions against corporate giving to political campaigns were broadened over time to forbid utilities and labor unions from giving as well.

The 1920s was another era of financial scandal as stock markets rose and banks sold worthless stocks and bonds. The **Teapot Dome scandal** of 1921 stimulated further attempts to limit the influence of money on

electoral politics. The secretary of the interior in the Harding administration received almost $400,000 from two corporations that then were allowed to lease oil reserves in California and Wyoming (one of them was called the Teapot Dome). This led to the Federal Corrupt Practices Act (1925), which required the reporting of campaign contributions and expenditures.

Because none of these laws were enforced, each had only a momentary effect. Nevertheless, the reforms did seem to make open graft and bribery less acceptable and less common. Instead of outright bribes, political interests now sought to influence politicians through campaign contributions.

Regulating Money in Modern Campaigns

Waging a campaign in state or national politics is expensive. And because most funding for such campaigns is private, candidates for office must continually look for sources to fund their campaigns. At least some of

At the turn of the twentieth century, rich New Yorkers, wearing vine leaves on their heads, enjoy their wealth.

those who give money see donations as an opportunity for access and influence.

Issues in Campaign Finance Reform

Since the early 1970s, Americans have been at least intermittently concerned about the influence of campaign money on modern politics. Landmark legislation was passed in 1974 and again in 2002, and the Supreme Court has also made a number of important decisions. These laws deal primarily with five questions that are at the heart of debates about campaign finance reform:

1. Should we regulate the overall costs of political campaigns?

2. Should we fund campaigns from public funds?

3. Should we regulate the overall amount of money that individuals and groups give to candidates, called **contribution limits?**

4. Should we limit spending by independent groups and organizations who want to support their favored candidates, called **independent spending?**

5. Should we insist on **public disclosure,** requiring that the names of donors be on the public record?

Modern Attempts at Reform

Reforms of the 1970s

Prompted by the increasing use of television in campaigns and the rising cost of buying television time, Congress passed a law regulating spending on advertis-

ing in 1971. The law limited the amount that candidates could donate to their own campaigns and required candidates to disclose the names and addresses of donors of more than $100.

In the course of the Watergate investigations (see Chapter 2), it became clear that corporations were not abiding by these restrictions. Several corporations secretly funded President Nixon's reelection campaign. For example, Nixon's Justice Department negotiated a settlement favorable to the ITT Corporation in a pending legal dispute soon after an ITT subsidiary gave the Republican National Committee $400,000.[16] Altogether, twenty-one individuals and fourteen corporations were indicted for illegal campaign contributions, mostly but not entirely to the Nixon reelection campaign.

In response to these scandals, Congress again attempted to regulate campaign financing. New legislation was passed in 1974. The objectives of the 1974 law were to limit spending, to make the campaign finance system more open by disclosing the names of donors, and to force candidates to be less reliant on a few big donors. Thus the law called for public financing of presidential campaigns and limited overall candidate expenditures; limited the contributions of individuals, committees, national parties, and political action groups to campaigns for federal office; required donors' identities to be disclosed; and prohibited cash contributions of more than $100. The act also established the bipartisan **Federal Election Commission** (FEC) to enforce the law. The 1974 act also imposed limits on independent spending, spending by groups not under the control of

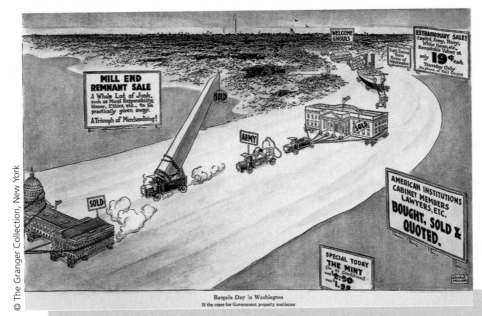

Warren G. Harding, one of the least successful presidents, could not say no to his friends. This failure led to the Teapot Dome scandal.

candidates. These limits were immediately ruled unconstitutional and no longer apply.

Because of the importance of money in campaigns, both elected officials and individuals and groups who want something from the officials found ways to get around the campaign finance laws. The Supreme Court also found several provisions unconstitutional. Indeed, by the 1990s, the 1974 campaign finance law no longer had any practical effect except for the disclosure mandates.

McCain-Feingold Act

By the early 1990s, calls for reforms became deafening. Journalists, public interest groups, and ordinary citizens in public opinion polls called on Congress for new regulations to limit the flow of private funds to candidates. They worried that public confidence in government was being eroded by the close connection between wealthy special interests and elected officials. Reformers favored the public financing of the 1974 act and the disclosure provisions but wanted much tighter control over donations and spending.

In the 2000 presidential campaign, Arizona Republican John McCain, the challenger to the front-runner, George W. Bush, in the 2000 presidential primaries, made campaign finance reform a major issue. His candidacy withered and died. Al Gore, the Democratic presidential candidate, supported campaign finance reform but did not make it one of his central issues. With the election of Bush, an opponent of campaign reform, change was seemingly postponed for several more years.

But in 2002, when the Enron collapse made it all too obvious that Enron money had bought at least a decade of lax corporate regulation, campaign reform received a new impetus.

Efforts for reform were led by McCain and another Senate maverick, Russ Feingold (D-Wisc.). In 2002, after extensive negotiations and polls showing strong public support for reform, Congress passed, and the president signed, a new campaign finance law, the Bipartisan Campaign Finance Reform Act (usually referred to as the **McCain-Feingold Act** after its sponsors). The Democrats voted overwhelmingly in favor of

the bill and the Republicans against it, but enough Republicans crossed party lines to pass the bill. This law had its first effect in the 2004 elections.

We can examine the politics and impact of the 1974 and 2002 legislation in terms of the five issues enumerated earlier.

Regulating the Cost of Campaigns and Public Funding

In 1976, the Supreme Court knocked huge holes in the 1974 law when it struck down spending limits except in presidential elections that were publicly funded.[17] Because spending often goes to buy advertising, the Court argued that spending restrictions violated individuals' First Amendment right of free speech. Spending in a campaign enables candidates to get their message out. Giving money is a form of expression protected by the Constitution.

Consequently, spending limits still do apply in presidential races, but only if candidates accept public funds. At the primary stage, presidential candidates may get up to $19 million in funds and are subject to a $45 million spending limit (the money comes from a voluntary checkoff of $3 on individuals' tax returns; the spending limit increases each year to take inflation into account). Candidates who do not accept public funding can spend as much as they can raise. In 2004, George W. Bush, John Kerry, and Howard Dean decided not to accept public money, so they had no spending limits at all at the primary stage.[18]

Once candidates receive their parties' nominations, public funding pays them each about $75 million for the general election campaign (also adjusted each election for inflation), and they can accept several million more from their party's national committee. At this point, fundraising is supposed to be officially over for the candidates. However, this prohibition does not limit other groups from raising and spending money to sway public opinion and thereby help their favored candidate.

Contribution Limits and Ways to Avoid Them

In addition to limiting candidate spending, the 1974 law also tried to limit individual and group contributions to candidates and campaigns. The Court upheld these limits. And the McCain-Feingold Act increased the limits set by the 1974 act in order to keep up with inflation. Individuals can now give $2,000 per candidate per election. Upward adjustments were also made in donations to national party committees ($25,000) and to state or local committees ($10,000). The overall aggregate donations permitted rose from $25,000 per year to $95,000 over a two-year election cycle (the odd-numbered year before each federal election and the election year itself). Limits on contributions by political action committees to candidates and parties were not changed.

Because of the legal restrictions of direct donations to candidates and campaigns, along with the prohibition of **soft money** (donations given to political

"It says here that you gave a lot of money to both parties and neither expected nor received anything in return. Very nice, but we'll have to put you in the crazy section."

parties ostensibly for uses other than campaigning), the McCain-Feingold law gave impetus to Internet fundraising, trying to attract small direct contributions from people who are not fat cats. The Democrats took an early lead in this effort, led first by Howard Dean, the Democratic front-runner in the early primary season, and then by John Kerry. The Dean campaign quickly realized the potential of the Internet to link his supporters with the campaign and with each other. Tens of thousands of his supporters were in constant contact with the campaign through e-mail and were regularly solicited for funds. Seeing the success that Dean was having through the Internet, Kerry's staff advised him to mention his Web address in his Iowa victory speech. This mention resulted in an instantaneous tenfold increase in hits on Kerry's Web site. After he won the Super Tuesday primaries, he took in $2.6 million in a single day.[19] Enough funds were raised by both Dean and Kerry in the primary season to allow both to reject public funding for their campaigns.

By the end of the 2004 campaign, millions of citizens were on the e-mail lists of one or both parties, and tens of millions of dollars were raised from them. This helped balance the role of the fat cats in the 2004 election.

But the fat cats had other places to play. The limits on direct contributions were negated in other ways through four huge loopholes: PACs, soft money, 527 groups, and independent spending.

Political Action Committees

Although the 1974 legislation and the McCain-Feingold Act limited group contributions to candidates, it did not limit individuals' contributions to groups. This loophole was originally created by a little-noticed provision of the 1974 law reaffirming the right of unions and corporations to establish **political action committees (PACs)** using voluntary contributions. Funded from dues and "voluntary" contributions from members in the case of labor unions and "voluntary" contributions from employees in the case of businesses, PACs contributed to political campaigns of candidates seen as friendly to the interests of the organization or likely to hold powerful positions that could affect the interests of the organization. Labor unions were the first to establish PACs; businesses soon followed suit, and today many groups with interests affected by government have their own PACs.

Now that there were limitations on the amount of money individuals could give to campaigns, PACs became the vehicle by which individuals could channel more money to their favorite candidates. Individuals could give a limited amount directly to candidates and then give $5,000 to each of several PACs, which could

in turn give it to candidates.[20] The funding activities of PACs differ greatly. Although there are more than four thousand such organizations, about one-third do not contribute to any candidates, and only four hundred or so give more than $100,000 in total.

Business and trade PACs predominate (trade PACS include groups of professionals, such as the American Veterinary Medical Association PAC, or groups of industries, such the American Wind Energy Association, and producers, such as the National Pork Producers Council Pork PAC).

PACs differ in the targets of their donations, but some patterns are clear. PACs show a distinct preference for Republicans in the presidential races and for incumbents—Republicans or Democrats—in congressional races (see Figure 2). PACs usually want to give to the candidate they believe will win so that they will have access to a policymaker. Enron's PAC donations are illustrative of spending patterns. It supported substantially more Republicans than Democrats but also funded Democrats on key committees, including Charles Schumer.

Although the majority of PACs are business related and are ideologically much more sympathetic to the Republicans, PACs before 1994 gave predominantly to the Democrats because they were the majority party. When the Republicans gained control of both houses of Congress, they began receiving the majority of PAC donations.

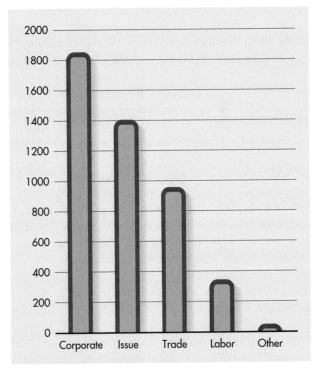

FIGURE 1 ■ Types of PACs Reflect Dominance of Business in American Politics

SOURCE: The data are number of PACS of each type Data from 2002. Edward Zuckerman, *The Almanac of Federal PACs: 2004–05* (Hedgesville, W. Va.: Amward Publications, Inc., 2004).

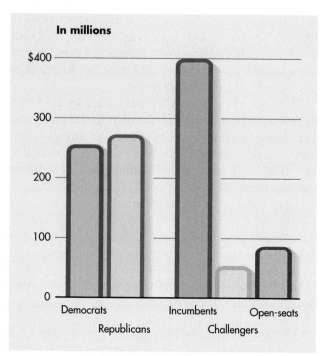

In millions

**FIGURE 2 ■ Recipients of Political Action Commit-
tee Donations in the 2001–2002 Election Cycle** *PACs give
overwhelmingly to incumbents. The donations charted here
were to House and Senate candidates.*
SOURCE: U.S. Census Bureau, *Statistical Abstract of the United States, 2005*
(Washington, D.C.: Government Printing Office, 2004), tab. 41b. Open
seats are those races without an uncumbent.

What criteria aside from incumbency and party
guide PAC donations?[21] Most PACs give money to
members in districts where the PACs have a substantial
interest, such as a large number of union members for a
union PAC or a large factory for a corporate PAC. Enron focused much of its support on Democrats in Texas,
where Enron was headquartered. And Enron's substantial support for Bush was partly due to his powerful position as Texas governor before he became president.

PACs also target contributions to members of key
congressional committees. For example, PACs organized by defense contractors give disproportionately to
members who serve on the Armed Services Committees, which have a big role in deciding what weapons to
purchase. Unions and shipping companies involved in
the maritime industry give large sums to those on the
House Merchant Marine and Fisheries Committee and
its Senate counterpart, the Commerce, Science, and
Transportation Committee.[22] Members of congressional committees that specialize in tax law (Ways and
Means, Finance) and business regulations (Commerce)
receive generous contributions from business PACs.[23]

Women's PACs, including EMILY's List, one of the
biggest-spending PACs, are unusual in focusing most of
their money on nonincumbents. Their goal is to get
more women elected, which often means supporting
nonincumbents with strong chances of winning.

Soft Money

Soft money provided the largest loophole in the 1974
campaign funding regulation. Soft money was exempted from limitations of the 1974 act because it was
not to be used for campaigns. Instead, it is supposed to
be used for such "party-building" activities as national
party conventions, voter registration drives, direct mailings, polling, issue ads, and advertisements for nonfederal party candidates. Donors who wanted to give more
than their legal federal maximum could give soft money
to national party committees. Some of those funds were
channeled to state parties, which spend under even less
stringent state regulations.

In reality, most soft money was spent by independent groups for national television advertisements for
the parties' candidates. In 2000, the Democrats' ads
prominently featured Gore and the Republicans' Bush.
As Robert Dole, the Republicans' 1996 presidential candidate, explained about an ad financed by soft money
that spent fifty-six seconds dealing with his life and four
seconds on the issues, "It never says that I'm running for
President. I hope that it's fairly obvious since I'm the
only one in the picture."[24]

The campaign finance reform system evolved, in
other words, in a way that made direct campaign contribution limits irrelevant because the soft money loophole allowed people with money to spend as much as
they want. By 2000, the growth of soft money signaled
to everyone not in solitary confinement that the campaign finance regulations dealing with contributions to
candidates and parties were totally unrealistic. Parties
and candidates were raising millions, flaunting the spirit
if not the letter of the campaign finance laws. Not only
were millions being raised, they were raised by overtly
offering access to the candidates in return for donations.
Though criticisms of Clinton's exploitation of the presidential office for fundraising were a staple of the 2000
Republican campaign, once in office, the Republicans
offered their big donors a chance to "dine with diplomats and embassy officials and discuss international affairs at one of Washington's famous embassies."[25] Later
the Republicans, capitalizing on a national tragedy, gave,
in exchange for a donation, photos of George W. Bush
calling Vice President Cheney on September 11, 2001
(see the box "The President as Chief Fundraiser" on the
next page). Naturally, the Democrats called it "a strategy to use the war for political gain."[26]

527 Groups

The McCain-Feingold Act closed part of the soft
money loophole, banning soft money contributions to
national political parties. However, it left a huge loop-

Following the 1996 elections, the Lincoln Bedroom in the White House became a staple of editorial writers and late night comedians. To raise soft money for the Democratic National Committee and thus for his campaign, President Bill Clinton had invited big donors to the White House to have coffee with him and, in some cases, to stay overnight. These and other revelations about fundraising practices prompted new calls for campaign finance reform and cries of outrage from Republicans. Said George W. Bush, "Will we use the White House . . . as a fundraising mechanism—in other words, you give money and you get to sleep in the Lincoln Bedroom? The answer is no."[1]

Once in office, the Bush administration just as blatantly exploited his office for partisan fundraising as the president invited big donors to dine with diplomats at an embassy and meet with cabinet officials.[2] Indeed, Bush and his organization are by far the biggest fundraisers ever among political candidates. They have used their close connections to industry to raise staggering amounts from corporate executives eager to have high-level access to the president and his team.

His top fundraising volunteers are given names of honor: the Pioneers are those who have raised $100,000 for the campaign, the Rangers, have raised $200,000, and the Super Rangers have raised $300,000. One fundraising expert provided a lively description: "Carole Bionda darted through the halls of the Capital Hilton, armed with a red-white-and-blue tote bag bulging with checks made out to Bush-Cheney '04. Three hundred executives from the nation's most influential construction firms were meeting at the hotel. . . . As the executives split up into regional

caucuses, she ran from room to room, pitting South against East, West against Midwest" in a competition to see who could donate the most.[3]

In three days, Bionda raised $147,000 from the construction executives. This was easy because the Bush administration had gotten rid of regulations that would have improved working and safety conditions at construction sites, which would have cost construction companies more, and other regulations that would have denied government contracts to big polluters.

The Bush-Cheney fundraising organization set as a target $200 million in 2004, most of it expected to come via organized fundraising like this. Each Pioneer, Ranger, or Super Ranger has a number, and all donations through that person are tracked by that number. Results are posted on the Web, and competition between fundraisers is encouraged.

Large donors are given perks, such as photos with the president or the first lady, Laura Bush. More substantively, after the 2000 elections, 104 of the 246 Pioneer fundraisers received government jobs. Four were named cabinet secretaries—Tom Ridge, Don Evans, Elaine Chao, and Alphonso Jackson—and twenty-two received ambassadorships, including one found guilty of swindling his business partners for $1 million.[4]

For some, access is more important than jobs. More than half the 2000 Pioneers were heads of companies and another 20 percent were lobbyists.[5] Executives and lobbyists for the financial and real estate world, energy, construction, and transportation were well represented in this elite group.

Did the Bush administration deregulate specifically because it received

campaign funds from big construction and other regulated industries? Probably not; conservative Republicans prefer to let business regulate itself and would favor deregulation independent of contributions. Did construction executives give money to the Bush campaign specifically to thank the administration for relaxing regulations and allowing them to make even more money? We do not know. Did they give the funds in the hope and expectation of future policies loosening regulations? Again, no one knows for sure, but that is a reasonable expectation.

It is difficult to point out the exact cause and effect of these close ties between donors and public officials. Even if all that is being bought and sold is access, access is worth something. If access did not influence policy, most people would not be trying to buy it. Even if no favors were exchanged for money and nothing illegal transpired, many Americans find these activities unethical and unbecoming a president. Indeed, the most troubling activities are the ones that are apparently legal. Unless voters elect members of Congress who agree, campaign finance activities will continue to provide material for cartoonists and comedians, embarrassment for public officials, and ultimately loss of public trust in both business and politics.

1. Mike Allen, "Does an Embassy Trump the Lincoln Bedroom?" *Washington Post National Weekly Edition,* May 7, 2001, 14.
2. Ibid.
3. Barry Yeoman, "Bush's Bagmen," *Rolling Stone,* March 10, 2004, www.rollingstone.com/politics/story/_/id/5940033. See also Thomas Byrne Edsall, Sarah Cohen, and James Grimaldi, "Pioneers Fill War Chest, Then Capitalize," *Washington Post,* May 16, 2004, A1.
4. Edsall, Cohen, and Grimaldi, "Pioneers Fill War Chest," A1.
5. Ibid.

"Some of it is soft and some of it is hard, but the main thing is that all of it is money."

and those who funded them were often large donors to the opposition party. They were technically independent but in reality closely linked to the candidates.

Independent Spending

Independent spending by other (nonpolitical) groups is unregulated. In 1985, the Supreme Court ruled that PACs could spend unlimited amounts working on behalf of issues or candidates, publicly funded or not, as long as they do not give funds directly to parties or candidates.[27] The Court assumed that this spending would be meaningfully independent. However, "independent" spending is often done by organized groups with indirect links to the candidate. Thus interest groups, through their PACs, can spend as much as they want as long as they are not actually campaigning for a candidate. Instead, they engage in "issues advocacy," usually targeted to promoting a particular candidate or party. The Court's rule to judge whether an ad is a campaign ad is whether it uses language such as "vote for" or "vote against." However, this is a meaningless criterion because only a small proportion (4 percent) of ads sponsored by the candidates themselves use these phrases.[28]

Thus anyone not officially part of a campaign or national party, such as 527 groups and PACs, can spend as much as they want. However, to be independent and to escape regulation, they cannot be officially linked to a candidate or party, nor can they endorse a candidate or party.

The 527 groups illustrate these relationships. The Media Fund, run by a former Clinton White House adviser, ran television ads throughout the primary campaign. One featured a shot of a factory with the voice pointing out that "it's true that George W. Bush has created more jobs. Unfortunately, . . ." The camera then reveals that the factory is in China, and the voice announces that most of the new jobs were in places like China.[29] The ad did not endorse Kerry but clearly worked in his interest.

The Republicans had even more effective 527 groups. One of the most visible was the so-called Swift Boat Veterans for Truth. Led by an ex-veteran who first opposed Kerry in the 1970s, financed largely by Bush supporters and advised by an attorney who was an official in the Bush campaign (who resigned when this tie was revealed) but technically independent of the Bush campaign, the group waged a scurrilous attack on Kerry's war record. (Kerry, as a young Navy lieutenant, commanded a "swift boat" in the Vietnam War and won medals for heroism as well as three Purple Hearts for his wounds.) The Swift Boat Veterans did not serve with Kerry, but were on other ships at the same time or on Kerry's ship at a different time. Several were angry at

hole allowing soft money contributions to various independent groups as well as to state and local parties.

Because the Republicans had traditionally raised much more hard money than Democrats, whereas Democrats relied more on soft money, McCain-Feingold hurt the Democrats more than the Republicans. So the Democrats took the lead in exploiting the loophole created when McCain-Feingold banned soft money contributions to the national parties but did not ban soft money contributions to private groups.

Big donors gave to old or new so-called **527 groups,** named after the provision in the tax code authorizing them. Three of the most visible Democratic groups were MoveOn.org Voter Fund, the Media Fund, and America Coming Together (ACT), focusing on voter registration and involvement in addition to supporting Democratic candidates. These tax-exempt groups, and many others on both sides of the partisan divide, collected unregulated money from supporters of the candidates and then used that money to fund television advertisements promoting their candidates. One prominent Democratic donor gave $20 million to start MoveOn.org. Neither fundraising nor expenditures of groups like MoveOn.org are limited by the McCain-Feingold law as long as the groups are independent of the campaigns and do not endorse candidates. They can, however, bash the opposing candidate. The organizers of these 527 groups were often important party activists,

HOW THE SWIFT BOAT AD BECAME A NATIONAL NEWS STORY

The original Swift Boat Veterans for Truth ad was run only in a few local spots. Its metamorphosis from local ad to dominating news story for a few weeks illustrates how news is disseminated today.

The ad and the charges against John Kerry were first publicized by conservative "bloggers" who write news stories on the Web. Bloggers mix fact and opinion and are not subject to the same kinds of standards as regular newspaper reporters. They made no attempt to discern the truth or falsity of any of the charges by seeking official records or interviewing people who were actually there. Talk radio, mostly dominated by conservatives too, picked up the story. Again, they had no interest in looking at the factual basis for the story. Opinions

about opinions are the staple of talk radio. Then Fox, the largely Republican television channel, began to publicize it and other cable news stations picked it up too. Meanwhile, some major Bush contributors donated more funds so that the ad could be run nationally and frequently.

By this time, the story was everywhere and the mainstream media—the networks and the national press—began to cover it. Although by this time the major media began investigating and presenting the facts about Kerry's war record, the story had already developed a life of its own.

Kerry and his supporters realized that they had made a strategic mistake not countering the story when it first came out. They had looked at the small

local ad buys and assumed that everyone would realize that the ad was not truthful but did not factor in how stories spread via new modes of communication. This was an incredibly naive view of both the political and information environments.

The story did continue to play among conservative audiences. The men behind the ad published a book, *Unfit for Command,* with Regnery Press, a publisher of popular conservative political books, and it enjoyed huge sales during the election season. The book reprised the points of the original Swift Boat ad and added accusations of treachery, treason, and murder conspiracies to the mix.

him for returning from Vietnam and subsequently opposing the war.

Though their claims were found to be largely untrue as documented by both official military records and the people on Kerry's ship, the ads gained national publicity for several weeks (see the box "How the Swift Boat Ad Became a National News Story") and were effective in weakening Kerry's campaign at a crucial period. They undermined a central premise of his campaign, that his service in Vietnam was an important element in his fitness to serve as president today. These ads did not endorse Bush but clearly worked in his interest.

Disclosure

The Supreme Court upheld the provisions of the 1974 campaign finance reform act that mandate disclosure of contributions. The Federal Election Commission provides public reports on who has given money to whom. Through this part of the law, journalists and the public can see what private interests are contributing and who the beneficiaries of their contributions are. This is one aspect of the legislation that has been effective. Financers of 527 groups must also be disclosed.

Campaign Finance Reform and the 2004 Election

John Kerry raised more money than any presidential challenger has ever raised, and George W. Bush raised more in 2004 than his record-breaking total in 2000. These are the totals regulated by legislation. However, the money raised through loopholes also skyrocketed in 2004, and the total spending in the presidential campaign is estimated to be as much as $2 billion.

Loopholes were gladly opened by the Federal Election Commission, responsible for overseeing the campaign finance laws. The FEC immediately adopted rules to weaken the impact of the reforms. Several of the commission members, an equal number of Democrats and Republicans, were appointed precisely because they did not favor tough finance rule.

After all, John McCain himself says, "Money is like water: it finds cracks in the wall."[30] In a democracy, it is hard to find ways of restricting the flow of private resources into political campaigns. We can be appalled by the lies in ads trashing one or the other of the candidates; the 527 groups, like candidates, are held to no standard of truthfulness. Unlike candidates, they are not really held accountable either. That is the public's and media's responsibility. Since the ads would not appear if they were not effective, perhaps it is we, the voters, who need a higher standard of evaluation of these ads. As long as people are free to form groups and express their opinions, it will be impossible to shut down groups who want to express their opinions, based on facts, fantasy, or a combination of the two, through ads.

Is Real Reform Possible?

Opposition to Reform

There are many reasons why we do not get more serious campaign finance reform. Some individuals, on both sides of the liberal-conservative divide, oppose even trying to get private money out of campaigns. They think prohibitions on private giving are a violation of free speech. Some emphasize that individuals should have the right to spend as much as they wish on the candidate of their choice. Others believe that private groups should be able to run as many advertisements as they want in support of their views.[31] Still others oppose reform because they dislike government regulation.

Most elected officials are not big fans of campaign finance reform either. They do not want to tie their own hands by limiting their abilities to raise funds from friendly interest groups. After all, when one party starts spending money in a close race, the impulse is for the other party to match or exceed it, a kind of campaign finance arms race. In a close contest, both sides want to do everything possible to win, and a few extra hundreds of thousands of dollars might indeed make the difference.

Powerful interest groups with money to spend also resist reform. Though reform would save them money in the short run, many big interests believe that their clout with key elected officials in getting favorable legislation is worth what they donate and much more. Major areas of business—including "pharmaceuticals, mining, oil and gas, defense, commercial banking and accounting—have basically made a decision to back the GOP."[32] Democrats, in turn, have the strong support of unions, the entertainment industry, and trial lawyers. As one observer has pointed out, these divisions reflect the ideological divisions of the parties.[33] These groups are not eager to upset the status quo of campaign finance.

Suggestions for Reform

Still, the unappetizing spectacle of wealthy donors, both individuals and corporations, receiving political favors from those they supported keeps the idea of reform alive. Several kinds of ideas have been proposed.

One proposal might avoid the pitfalls of the attempts to limit soft money by mandating that radio and TV stations grant free time to the candidates. This proposal focuses on reducing the cost of campaigns and hence the need to have so many private donors.

Why should the media be asked to donate time? Because radio and television stations have free use of the public airwaves and use that gift to make considerable profit. In what Bob Dole called "a giant corporate welfare program," Congress in 1996 gave away even more airwave space to facilitate the transition to digital technology.[34] The United States is the only country that does not provide some free television time to political candidates.[35]

Moreover, a large part of the cost of campaigns is buying media ads. Political ads on television cost nearly $1 billion in the 2000 election and are expected to top $1.5 billion in 2004, as the presidential campaigns bought more ads earlier in the race.[36] Nearly 10 percent of TV profit is earned through political ads, which are stations' third-largest advertising category, bigger than, for example, fast-food or movie ads.[37] A New York television station sales manager, contemplating the media ads from the 2000 Hillary Clinton–Rudy Giuliani Senate race exulted, "It's like Santa Claus came."[38]

In light of the fact that the public provides the airwaves free to broadcasters who in turn profit from campaign spending, a panel of broadcasters and reformers are asking stations to donate five minutes of free airtime each day for thirty days before the elections for political discussions among national, state, and local candidates for office. Five minutes a day sounds rather minimal, but currently the major networks broadcast each evening less than one-half minute of candidate dialogue, and local stations offer less.[39] Only twenty of the nation's thirteen hundred commercial television stations agreed to meet this standard in the 2000 election, and the proposal was opposed by the National Association of Broadcasters (NAB), fearing lost revenue.

The NAB lobbied hard and succeeded in defeating another proposal to force stations to offer political candidates their least expensive advertising rates. This proposal passed the Senate but was killed in the House. We can expect other proposals dealing with media costs to be on the reform agenda because it is unlikely that we can stem the flow of money into campaigns without curbing the costs of the campaigns themselves.

Free or reduced-price media would dramatically reduce the costs of campaigns. Unless it was combined with public financing, it would not eliminate private gifts or affect outside groups' playing a role in campaigns.

A second idea is more public financing. Public financing seeks to limit the overall cost of the campaign and eliminate the need for private donations and the special access that comes with them. Currently, the presidential campaigns have such financing, but it does not begin to cover campaign costs. As noted earlier, the presidential candidates together receive $150 million for the general election, and several million more goes to primary candidates who agree not to raise private funds. However, this is a small fraction of the costs of presidential campaigns. Some people have even proposed extending public financing to congressional elections.

About half the states have some public financing for state legislative or judicial candidates, several in conjunction with spending limits. But it seems unlikely that a major expansion of public funding for national candidates will be adopted anytime soon.[40] Opposition to government spending, public dissatisfaction with political campaigns, and the uncertainty that such a plan would really work to limit private money in politics all militate against it. And even if the official campaigns were funded, public funding does not solve the problem, if it is a problem, of independent organizations' collecting funds and promoting candidates.

A third reform idea is to allow unlimited giving but keep the identity of the givers secret from the recipients. This proposal focuses on the unsavory relationship between money given and favors sought. Thus people would give as much as they want, but it would be channeled to candidates through an organization that would keep the donations anonymous. Some people, who give out of ideological and partisan conviction, would still give, but others might not give if they could not use the fact of their giving as leverage. Of course, anyone could tell a candidate that he or she gave, but the candidate would have no way of knowing who did and who did not.

A fourth suggestion for reform is to amend the Constitution, allowing Congress to limit free speech in the area of campaign finance. Such an amendment would prohibit groups from running any issue or attack ads during the run-up to the election (ads in favor of specific candidates are already prohibited). Assuming that part of free speech rights is the right to pay to have your speech heard, this would be a major blow to free speech and the rights guaranteed by the First Amendment to the Constitution. This would seem to have little or no chance of passage.

Most Americans find the campaign finance system distasteful and believe that big interests with big money have special access, a perception that is true. However, there is no agreement, even among the turned-off public, on what the right solutions are. Public financing, media donation of time, and overall limitations on the costs of campaigns seem possible, but none of the reforms address the fundamental issue of spending by groups who have opinions about candidates and issues.

Whatever the problems with the current system, we should be careful not to contrast it with an idealized version of the past. After all, over one hundred years ago, Mark Twain observed, "It could probably be shown by facts and figures that there is no distinctly native American criminal class except Congress."[41] Big interests have always had influence and access in Washington. The ways in which they exercise that influence are different now. In some ways, this influence is more open because the campaign finance reforms have made public the organizations working for special interests and the money they spend doing it. Thirty years ago, we would not have known how much each member of Congress received from each lobbying group; today we do.

The Impact of Campaign Money

We have discussed several aspects of money in elections: how much there is, who contributes it, and how they do so. Now we turn to the question of what difference campaign money makes. An obvious question is whether money influences the outcomes of elections. But we will also focus on three other kinds of potential effects of money and the way it is raised: the recruitment of good candidates, the policy decisions of elected leaders, and the cynicism of the public.

Does the Campaign Finance System Deter Good Candidates?

When John Glenn, an unsuccessful Democratic candidate in 1984, was asked whether running for president had been worthwhile despite his defeat, Glenn replied, "My family was humiliated. I got myself whipped. I gained 16 pounds. And I'm more than $2.5 million in debt. Except for that, it was wonderful."[42] In 1998, nearing the end of his career, Glenn remarked in a similar vein, "I'd rather wrestle a gorilla than ask anyone for another 50 cents."[43]

Other presidential candidates have lamented the difficulties and humiliations of having to raise money; Jack Kemp, Richard Cheney, and Dan Quayle, all potential 1996 presidential candidates, bowed out early in 1995, indicating that the magnitude of necessary fundraising was one reason. In 2000, George W. Bush's huge campaign war chest deterred several potential candidates from entering the race. Bush raised $94 million in the primary season and spurned federal matching funds; his next-best-financed competitor, John McCain, raised $45 million, including federal matching funds. Others, such as Elizabeth Dole, dropped out after losing early primaries partly because of the impossibility of matching Bush's funding levels (she had raised

Oliphant Copyright © 1990. Universal Press Syndicate. Reprinted with permission.

only $5 million).[44] Bush had raised and spent more money before the first primary than Bob Dole did in his entire 1996 election campaign.[45]

The necessity of raising a lot of money deters congressional candidates, too. As one leading congressional scholar noted, "Raising money is, by consensus, the most unpleasant part of a campaign. Many candidates find it demeaning to ask people for money and are uncomfortable with the implications of accepting it."[46] As one senator commented, "I never imagined how much of my personal time would be spent on fundraising. . . . I do not think a candidate for the U.S. Senate should have to sit in a motel room in Goldendale, Washington, at 6 in the morning and spend three hours on the phone talking to political action committees."[47] And once elected, many new members of Congress are surprised and chagrined to find that they must begin raising funds for their next campaign almost before they are sworn into office.

Does Money Win Elections?

Money helps win elections. It's not the only factor, of course. Many candidates have tried and failed to "buy" elections with their own money. But money certainly aids in getting the candidate's message out.

Looking first at presidential elections, the evidence is mixed as to the impact of money on winning presidential primaries. Primaries are the crucial elections that lead to each party's nomination. Some candidates are never considered serious contenders because they do not have sufficient money to mount a large campaign. In that sense, money is crucial.

In primaries, candidates of each party run against others of their party to achieve the nomination. Most primary candidates start out with little name recogni-

tion. Moreover, candidates cannot count on party loyalty to win votes. In primaries, voters choose among candidates of their own party; that is, Republican voters have to choose among Republicans rather than between a Republican and a Democrat. For both those reasons, money is crucial to increase candidate visibility.

Primary candidates who appear to be doing well generally attract money.[48] "Doing well" includes favorable media coverage that suggests the candidate is gaining popularity and momentum. Actual success in early primaries also stimulates giving. Money, in turn, allows further purchases of media ads to become known in the next primaries. However, in 2000, George Bush lost the first primary but used his huge lead in fundraising to pummel his chief opponent with hard-hitting ads in subsequent primaries.

Other things being equal, spending does influence voting in primaries. Money appears to be a necessary condition for primary victory, although not sufficient by itself. One analysis suggests that every 1 percent increase in spending buys $\frac{1}{3}$ percent more votes.[49] Money is most important in multicandidate races, as is often typical early in the primary season when candidates are seeking to distinguish themselves from other little-known contenders.[50] Money is less important in two-candidate primary contests, often the situation late in the primary season when one candidate has emerged as a front-runner.

By the time presidential candidates are nominated, they have already spent a great deal of money. The name recognition achieved during the primaries and at the national conventions carries into the general election campaign. Presidential candidates receive extensive free media coverage in news stories. The amount that they spend after the convention is less likely to be as crucial. This is just as well for the health of the two-party system, because if money determined elections, the Republicans would have won every presidential election since World War II. However, of the presidential elections lost by the Democrats during that time, probably only the election of 1968 between Richard Nixon and Hubert Humphrey and possibly the Gore-Bush 2000 election were close enough that they might have turned out differently had the Democrats been able to spend more.[51] When the elections are close, as in 1968, the Republicans definitely have the advantage by having more money.[52] However, the Democrats are catching up; they have been increasingly aggressive in raising soft money and in 2004 were not significantly behind in fundraising, counting 527 groups.

In congressional races, incumbents usually start with a huge advantage. Some analysts estimate that their advantage is about 5 percent of the vote just by virtue of being incumbents.[53] Their name is recognized by many, if not most, of their constituents. And as incumbents, they are able to raise money early to finance their campaigns. In many cases, the incumbents' huge war chests deter potentially strong challengers from even entering the race.[54] Challengers know that they must raise considerable money to fund media ads even to be competitive. Thus the ability of challengers to raise and spend money is crucial to any chance of success in the election.

But incumbent fundraising and spending are also important. Fundraising is important early in the campaign to deter potential opponents. And campaign spending is important, especially for relatively new members of Congress. That is because those who have served only a few terms are less well known than more senior incumbents and thus are considered vulnerable.[55] Of course, incumbents tend to spend the most when they have the toughest opponent. In general, as challengers spend more, so do incumbents.[56]

Most of the time, the person who spends the most to win a congressional seat wins. In 2002, for example, the biggest spender won about 80 percent of Senate races. Most of these winners were incumbents, and the link between spending and victory is also a link between incumbency and victory. The average incumbent is able to raise significantly more money than challengers. In 2002, for example, House incumbents raised about $1 million, four times what their challengers raised. The average Senate incumbent outspent his or her opponent by more than 2 to 1.[57]

Sometimes the biggest spender loses, but the relative rarity of this occurrence only highlights the general link between spending and victory. In probably the most publicized Senate race of 2000, in an open-seat contest in New York, Hillary Clinton won by a large margin over Congressman Rick Lazio, despite being outspent by more than $10 million in one of the most expensive races ever (in total, the candidates spent nearly $70 mil-

lion). But Clinton was well known before she ran her first TV ad, so she did not have to spend money just to become visible.

Does Money Buy Favorable Policies?

As we have seen, donors are not a random cross section of the public. Money usually buys access, and that access is by the wealthiest segment of the population, whose views on public issues, especially economic issues, are more conservative than the larger population.

In recent years, corporate interests have pushed hard to deregulate and to lower taxes and have used substantial gifts to help gain access to rule makers. The accounting industry, for example, in the early 1990s helped fund more than three hundred congressional races, including both Democrats and Republicans, and spent $2 million for lobbyists. This clout led to Congress passing a law erasing liability for accountants and lawyers aiding and abetting securities fraud. Though President Clinton vetoed the law, his veto was overridden.[58] The law provided a disincentive for auditors to uphold strict accounting standards and removed a tool by which stockholders could hold companies accountable. Enron money bought considerable access (See the box "Buying Energy and Influence" on the next page).

If money buys access, does it also buy votes? Both anecdotal and systematic evidence suggest that money does buy votes, although only under some conditions.

Money is not likely to buy votes on issues that are highly publicized, because legislators' constituents usually have strong views on these issues and legislators feel pressured to follow them.[59] For the same reason, money is less likely to buy roll-call votes on the floor of each house than votes in committees. The former are public and recorded; the latter are not as visible to the public. Compared to their activity on the floor, in committees, legislators with PAC support are more active in speaking and negotiating on behalf of the PAC's positions and offering amendments that reflect these positions.[60]

Money is also not likely to buy votes on moral issues, because legislators themselves often have firm views on these issues. These sorts of issues (abortion, gay rights, and school prayer, for example) also tend to be publicized.

But most matters that come to a vote are neither highly publicized nor moral issues. Most are relatively technical matters that constituents and legislators do not care as strongly about as PACs do. For these, members are susceptible. The deregulation of the accounting and energy industries was done when the public had no interest. "You can't buy a Congressman for $50,000. But you can buy his vote," a member admitted. "It's done on a regular basis."[61]

"No company in America did more to help George W. Bush get elected president than Enron." So reports the *Wall Street Journal*.[1] Enron's CEO, Kenneth Lay, was "the biggest sugar daddy in Bush's political career."[2] During Enron's heyday, its funds helped elect friendly lawmakers, mostly Republicans but also many Democrats; gain access at the highest levels; and buy loosened regulation and favorable tax policies. It made billions of dollars and benefited greatly from government deregulation of the energy industry. In the end, when Enron crashed, though, its substantial influence was not enough to get the government to bail it out.

This seeming contradiction illustrates well the point that money is most influential when the public is not paying attention. Most congressional legislation does not get featured on the evening news or in local papers. It is subject mostly to "inside the Beltway" battles. It is often dry, seemingly affecting only a few companies or groups of individuals. On such issues, the influence of well-organized and powerful lobbies can greatly profit the beneficiary corporations or groups.

But on well-publicized issues, those that CNN, the nightly news, and the local papers are featuring, it is more difficult for money to have the dominant influence. Thus a Bush aide spoke of the Enron affair as a "tribute to American capitalism" because the government let the company fail.[3] This point of view, of course, ignores what went on before and after Enron failed, including the enrichment of a few at the expense of workers and investors, the loss of public and investor con-

fidence in the truthfulness of corporate financial statements, and later the power crisis in California, which cost California taxpayers and consumers billions.

What did Enron give, and what did it get in return? Though the full story is unlikely ever to be known, we do know that Enron gave, from 1989 to 2001, nearly $6 million to parties and candidates, three-fourths of it to Republicans.[4] Enron's generosity include gifts from its executives and other employees, corporate soft money gifts, and gifts from Enron's PAC, funded by contributions by individual Enron employees. Fundraising for the PAC was done by high-level executives who kept track of who gave and who did not. In 1999, Kenneth Lay himself sent letters asking for contributions for the Bush campaign. One employee recalls a "menacing reference" to her husband's job and felt compelled to give even though she had not decided whether she favored Bush.[5]

Separate from corporate gifts, Lay and his wife donated more than $600,000 to the campaigns of George W. Bush, beginning when he first ran for Texas governor and including $325,000 in 2000.[6] Lay also raised millions of dollars for the Bush campaigns. Their connection was close. Bush used Enron's planes during the Republican primaries in 2000 to fly staff and even his parents. An Enron jet flew former president George H. W. Bush to his son's inauguration in January 2001, and a $100,000 donation from Lay helped fund the inaugural expenses.

But Enron also bought access to top Democrats. When Bill Clinton de-

feated George H. W. Bush in 1992, Lay began contributing to the Democrats. Enron gave nearly as much in soft money to Democrats as to Republicans in the 2000 election.[7] Enron may have provided funds for nearly half of all members of the House and three-fourth of the senators.[8]

Enron also spent lavishly to influence public opinion. It provided handsome consulting fees (up to $50,000 a year) for high-level journalists, think tank leaders, and others to spend a couple of days a year at Enron talking about political issues and Enron.

What favors did Enron get from politicians? Enron profited from Democrats. In 1992, the Democratic-majority Congress approved an energy bill that set the stage for Enron's growth, and later Clinton took an interest in a large Enron project in India. In 1997, Lay met with President Clinton, Vice President Al Gore, and other administration officials to discuss the U.S. position at the Kyoto global warming conference.[9]

But Enron profited even more consistently from its Republican ties. For example, when Bush was governor, he signed an energy deregulation bill that opened lucrative markets for Enron. He established a panel that acted in secret to grant exemptions allowing power plants to exceed legal pollution limits, and Enron got several of these exemptions.[10] When Bush arrived in Washington, D.C., he rolled back efforts to crack down on American corporations' use of offshore banks (banks set up in the Caribbean, for example, to help U.S. firms—and others such as drug

One survey of members found that about one-fifth admit that political contributions have affected their votes on occasion, and another one-third are not sure.[62] Analysis of voting has revealed that contributions from the AFL-CIO affected voting on the minimum wage legislation and contributions from the trucking interests

led senators to vote against deregulation of trucking. Senators facing reelection the year in which the vote was taken were most susceptible.[63] Voting is also related to donations in such disparate areas as minimum wage legislation, gun control, and billboard regulation.[64]

One classic, well-studied example concerns used-car

Former Enron employees revised the company's block E logo to reflect the company's unscrupulous practices.

sion, the government agency that was Enron's regulator.[13] This seems to be a first, allowing the parties to be regulated to be involved so directly with the choice of the regulator.

Enron's investment in public officials over a dozen years did not in the end save the firm from bankruptcy. But as one observer said, "Money allowed the Enron leadership to come to town. . . . Everyone says they didn't get anything. . . . But if you look back over the last five years, what they did get was no oversight." [14]

1. "Enron Lessons: Big Political Giving Wins Firms a Hearing, Doesn't Assure Aid," *Wall Street Journal,* January 15, 2002, 1 ff.
2. Howard Fineman and Michael Isikoff, "Light's Out: Enron's Failed Power Play," *Newsweek,* January 21, 2002, 15.
3. Paul Krugman, "A System Corrupted," *New York Times,* January 18, 2002, A25.
4. Richard Stevenson and Jeff Gerth, "Web of Safeguards Failed as Enron Fell," *New York Times,* January 20, 2002, 1.
5. Joe Stephens, "Hard Money, Strong Arms, and the 'Matrix,'" *Washington Post National Weekly Edition,* February 18, 2002, 11.
6. Dan Morgan, "Enron's Cash Was Good for Democrats, Too," *Washington Post National Weekly Edition,* January 21, 2002, 12.
7. Ibid.
8. Ibid.
9. These examples are from ibid.
10. "Enron Lessons"; Bob Port, "Bush, Lay Friendship Is Study of Mutual Benefit," *Lincoln Journal-Star,* February 4, 2002.
11. Molly Ivins, "Free-Range Markets: How Enron 'Aggressive Accounting Practiced' the Bank," *Fort Worth Star-Telegram,* January 29, 2002.
12. Michael Weisskopf and Adam Zagorin, "Getting the Ear of Dick Cheney," *Time,* February 11, 2002, 15.
13. Jonathan Alter, "Which Boot Will Drop Next?" *Newsweek,* February 4, 2002, 25.
14. Ibid.

dealers—evade American tax and criminal laws), a move of great benefit to Enron, which reportedly had eight hundred offshore accounts. As a consequence of this and other creativity, Enron avoided paying a single penny in U.S. taxes in four of its last five years.[11]

Bush also established an energy policy task force headed by his vice president, Dick Cheney. The task force, meeting in secret and whose membership and agenda have never been released, reportedly included Kenneth Lay and other lobbyists for the utility and energy industries, the past and present chair of the Republican Party, the secretary of energy, and other administration officials. The past Republican chair, Haley Barbour, at about the same time was lobbying utilities for large campaign contributions.[12] It is not surprising that the task force recommended a weakening of a major clean-air rule opposed by the utilities and the energy industry. It also endorsed increasing coal and nuclear power. The General Accountability Office is suing, on behalf of the public, to obtain information about the membership and proceedings of the task force.

Another benefit of Enron's access was that Kenneth Lay was allowed to "interview" candidates for positions on the Federal Energy Regulatory Commis-

legislation. Auto dealers spent $675,000 in the 1980 congressional elections. This investment seemed to pay off in 1982 when Congress voted against a rule requiring dealers to inform prospective buyers of any known defects in used cars. The senators who opposed the measure received twice as much money from the auto dealers' PAC as those who voted for it. In the House, those who opposed the measure received on average of five times as much money as those who voted for it. Almost 85 percent of the representatives opposing the legislation had received PAC money.[65]

The relationship between PAC money and votes still

existed even when the party and ideology of the members were taken into account. For conservatives, who might have voted against requiring auto dealers to list defects anyway, PAC contributions made only a marginal difference in their voting; but for liberals, PAC money substantially raised the probability that they would vote with the used-car dealers. "'Of course it was money,' one House member said. . . . 'Why else would they vote for used-car dealers?'"[66]

The relationship between PAC contributions and voting should not be exaggerated, however.[67] Even on these low-visibility votes, a member's party and ideology are important. The constituency interests of members are also key factors explaining votes. For example, members with many union workers in their districts are going to vote for those interests regardless of how much or little they get in PAC contributions.[68] Members without these constituents, though, may be more swayed by PAC contributions.

Money can do even more than help buy votes; it can buy influence with the executive branch too. Presidential candidates tend to have widely publicized views, and their actions as president are subject to intense scrutiny and publicity. Once in office, presidents need donors less than donors need them, thus making the leverage of a campaign donation uncertain. Contributors are sometimes disappointed, as steel baron Henry Frick, a major contributor to the campaign of Teddy Roosevelt, was: "We bought the son of a bitch," Frick complained, "but he did not stay bought."[69]

However, on actions not widely visible to the public, donors can help shape policy. The Bush fundraising success is partly based on support from the oil and gas industries. Their reward has been deregulation of both accounting and financial requirements and environmental standards. The Enron scandal was only the tip of the iceberg. Contractors who received billions of dollars of contracts in Iraq and Afghanistan had donated generously to the Bush campaign. The director of the Center for Public Integrity commented that there is a "stench of political favoritism and cronyism surrounding the contracting process in both Iraq and Afghanistan."[70]

Analyses of large donors to and fundraisers for the 1992 George H. Bush campaign reveal that many were given special favors or benefits from the federal government. The Department of Labor reduced a proposed fine by nearly 90 percent against a large sugar farmer who gave $200,000 to the campaign.[71] President Clinton created a furor when on his last day in office, he pardoned the fugitive ex-husband of a major campaign donor, Denise Rich. Rich had contributed generously to the Democratic Party and later to the Clinton presidential library.[72]

While it is impossible to prove a cause-and-effect relationship in these cases, clearly large donors who expect favorable treatment have plenty of precedents to lead them to that conclusion. As the leader of a watchdog group noted, "The point is, we're not just electing politicians. . . . We're also electing their patrons and their priorities."[73]

The influence of big money in presidential campaigns probably makes both parties more conservative. The biggest contributors to the Republicans in the last few presidential elections have been some of the most conservative people in that party. The big-money contributors to the Democrats are, on the whole, less liberal than the mainstream of the party.

Some Democratic House leaders were surprised when members said they could not vote against a capital gains tax cut (which would benefit the wealthy) because it would anger their business contributors. Said one member, "I get elected by voters. I get financed by contributors. Voters don't care about this; contributors do."[74]

Large contributions to presidential campaigns often lead to appointments to public office, especially ambassadorships. The **spoils system,** the practice of rewarding jobs to supporters, has been with us since at least the time of Andrew Jackson, so it cannot be blamed on modern PACs and soft money.

Beyond the specific policies and appointments that reflect the influence of big money, we can step back and look at the bigger picture. Public policy helps shape the distribution of income in our society through taxation, the regulation of corporations and unions, and many other ways. During the past quarter century, the rich have gotten a lot richer and almost everyone else has struggled to maintain what they have. The wealthiest 1 percent of Americans now own 47.3 percent of all the country's wealth. In 1980, the richest 5 percent of Americans had 14.6 percent of all income; by 2001, they had 21 percent. The rest of the top 20 percent of wealthiest Americans also gained. But everyone else lost.[75]

Turning from shares of income to income that we actually spend, Table 1 provides an eye-opening look. Between 1970 and 2000, before the Bush administration, the average income of the bottom 90 percent of Americans fell by $25 in real terms (that is, adjusted for inflation), while the average income of the top 10 percent grew by tens of thousands and even more staggering amounts. The tax cut policies of the current Bush administration have increased the inequities since 2000 as higher unemployment and tax cuts directed primarily at the wealthiest Americans further skewed income.

We can look at income and wealth data in different ways, using different years of comparison, but each supports the same general conclusion that the income gap is increasing. In addition, during the past twenty-five years, regulation of corporations has been weakened,

| TABLE 1 | The Rich Are Getting Richer | | | | | | |

Pretax incomes*

	Bottom 90%	90 to 95	95 to 99	99 to 99.5	99.5 to 99.9	99.9 to 99.99	Top 13,400 Households
1970	$ 27,060	$ 80,148	$ 115,472	$ 202,792	$ 317,582	$ 722,480	$ 3,641,285
2000	$ 27,035	$ 103,860	$ 178,067	$ 384,192	$ 777,450	$ 3,049,226	$ 23,969,767
Percentage Change	−0.1%	29.6%	54.2%	89.5%	144.8%	322.0%	558.3%

*In 2000 dollars
Source: David Cay Johnston, *Perfectly Legal* (New York: Portfolio, 2003). Data from Thomas Piketty and Emmanuel Saez.

health insurance has decreased for millions of Americans, and other holes in our social safety net have been enlarged.

It would be inaccurate to charge the campaign finance system and the policies they have bought with all of these rising inequities. However, it would be shocking if the tens of millions of dollars flowing to the campaign coffers of our elected officials and the consequent increased access and influence of the wealthiest and most powerful interests in society did not have an impact on public policy and the distribution of wealth.

Does Our Campaign Finance System Encourage Extortion?

PAC, corporation, and union contributions to campaigns are products of mutual need. Special interests need access to and votes of members of Congress and the president, and elected officials need (or think they need) large sums of money to win elections. Thus donations are useful to officials and to the donors (see the box "Direct Contributors in the 2004 Presidential Campaign" on the following page to see to whom individual contributors donated in 2004).

Although special interests try to buy access and sometimes votes, members of Congress are not simply victims of greedy PACs and corporations. Indeed, as one observer remarked, "There may be no question that the money flowing into campaign coffers is a crime. But there is a question whether the crime is bribery of public officials or extortion of private interests."[76]

Members themselves are aggressive in soliciting for donations. They fear defeat in the next election and think that raising a lot of money can protect them. Senators, for example, must raise more than $18,000 each week during all six years of their term to fund an average-cost winning reelection campaign. A senator from a populous, high-cost state needs to raise even more. Many incumbents raise millions even when they face little-known opponents.

Until the 1960s, most fundraising by members of Congress was done in their home districts because

members did not want their constituents to think they were influenced by Washington lobbyists. That has changed dramatically. Today, the majority of PAC funds are raised in Washington.[77] Members of Congress continually hold fundraisers to which dozens of lobbyists for PACs are invited. Well-known lobbyists get hundreds of invitations to congressional fundraisers every year.[78] Indeed, the number of these events is so large that a private company sells a special monthly newsletter listing all of them.

Pressure on corporations and unions is unrelenting. Some members keep lists of PACs that have given to them on their desks as an implicit indication that it is those groups that will have access. Others play one PAC off against another. Tom DeLay (R-Tex.), the majority whip in the House, is called "The Hammer" for his success at strong-arming potential donors. He offers lobbyists and corporate interests an open *quid pro quo:* They give, and they get to help develop Republican strategy and interests and shape legislation that Republican leaders will support.[79] (In 2003, he went further and offered a Republican House member an endorsement for his son's race for Congress if the House member would vote with DeLay—an offer that the Ethics Committee deemed a violation of House rules.)

Not all of the fundraisers are for campaign contributions, but all involve putting the arm on lobbyists. A fundraiser titled "Salute to the President Pro Tempore" was designed to "honor the career and public service" of Ted Stevens (R-Alaska). The funds were to go to Stevens's foundation to benefit Alaska and thus were both tax exempt (campaign contributions are taxable) and not subject to the limitations of campaign finance laws. But Alaskans at the fundraiser were in short supply. The invitation list included most Washington lobbyists who were concerned about the legislation their groups have pending before the Senate Appropriations Committee, of which Stevens is the chair. And the foundation apparently consists of a former staff member in Stevens's office who is his campaign treasurer too.

In recent years, some corporations, including General Motors, Ameritech, and Monsanto, have said that

DIRECT CONTRIBUTORS IN THE 2004 PRESIDENTIAL CAMPAIGN

Direct contributors to the Democratic and Republican parties are very different, reflecting a diversity in the population that goes beyond race and gender. One group studied the tendency of members of different professions to support George W. Bush and John Kerry; their patterns of giving are reflected in the following table.[1]

Group	Ratio of Donations, Bush to Kerry
Corporate CEOs	5–1
Social workers	1–14
Actors	1–19
Authors	1–38
Journalists	1–93
Librarians	1–223

As far as other groups are concerned, Kerry won strong support in the gay and Jewish communities. Bush's major fundraisers tend to be heavily in the agribusiness, energy, construction, and transportation industries.

1. "Redefining Democratic Fundraising," *Washington Post*, July 24, 2004, A01.

they do not intend to give more political contributions. Companies such as this should favor campaign finance regulation, which could provide a defense to fundraising pressure.[80]

Campaign Money and Public Cynicism

We have seen repeatedly that public confidence and trust in government have diminished greatly over time. Indeed, most of the public believes that most individuals in government are out to feather their own nests (see Table 2) and that many are crooks. Some of the reasons for this low trust have nothing to do with money. But public trust was certainly affected by the Watergate scandal in the 1970s, and it is likely that revelations about big-money lobbying activity reinforce public cynicism and lack of confidence.

American elections are funded, for the most part, by private money. It is therefore not surprising that candidates turn to people who have money to help with that funding. It is also not surprising that the current system alienates voters. Even if we believe that no votes are actually bought, the appearance of conflicts of interest that permeates the existing system and clearly disturbs the public should give pause to those interested in the health of our political system.

Walter Lippmann, a famous American journalist, once said that American attitudes about corruption alternate between "fits and starts of unsuspecting complacency and violent suspicion."[81] We think nothing is wrong, and then we think everything is wrong. So it is with our views of campaign money. For several years after the 1974 reforms, we thought things were going along pretty well. More recently, many people have be-

come convinced that the nation is in terrible jeopardy because of the influence of money. This fear is compounded because money has helped bring about regulatory lapses, which in turn have been partly responsible for failures to check the dishonesty of many corporations, which in turn has led to eroding confidence in corporate America. So beyond leading Americans to grow cynical about government, the campaign finance system has indirectly helped lead to a loss of confidence in business too.

Elected officials appear to be more afraid of being without campaign donations than they are that the campaign finance system will further erode confidence in the system. Ideologically, Democrats are more sympathetic to limiting the influence of big money, but practically, Democratic incumbents are heavily dependent on their PAC "fixes." Thus neither party has much incentive to support campaign finance reform, despite the fact that the public is repelled by the existing system.

Perhaps the public recognizes that a culture of greed cannot sustain itself forever. The two clearest examples

TABLE 2	Public Opinion Is Cynical about Government	

Statement	Percentage of People Agreeing That They Have a Great Deal of Confidence in . . .
Confidence	
The military	36%
The church	26%
The presidency	23%
Congress	11%
Big business	7%

Statement	Percentage of people who believe . . .
Accountability	
Government is run by a few big interests	64%
Government is run for the benefit of all the people	28%

NOTE: 2% had no opinion on the first poll and 8% were unsure on the second poll.

SOURCES: Gallup poll of 1,002 adults nationwide, margin of error = 3%, May 21–23, 2004; and CBS News and *New York Times* poll of 955 adults nationwide; margin of error = 3%, July 11–15, 2004; both polls online at www.pollingreport.com/institut.htm.

of rampant corruption in the American political and business systems suggest that they end unhappily. In both cases, at the end of the Gilded Age and the Roaring Twenties, they ended with the failure of thousands of banks and companies and with unemployment and despair.

As Figure 3 shows, support for change is overwhelming in the general public. The 2002 bill did not go as far in reform as most voters seem to want. However, it is unlikely that any reform is going to be able to limit the impact of private money as long as our election system relies on private support rather than public financing or limitation of spending. Campaign finance reform continues to wait for its champions who can rally sustained public interest and support around a realistic new finance system.

Conflicts of Interest

In addition to money's influence on political campaigns and policymaking, it also leads to **conflicts of interest,** situations in which officials face making decisions that directly affect their own personal livelihood or interest. The campaign contribution system we have just described presents a huge conflict of interest. Presidents and members of Congress make decisions about policies affecting people who give them campaign money. But

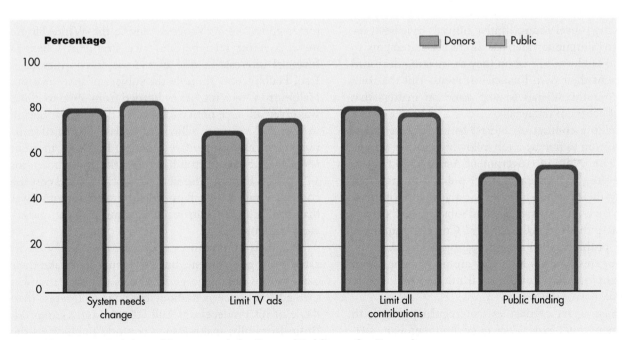

FIGURE 3 ■ Opinion of Donors and the General Public on the Campaign Finance System *Donors and the public agree that the system needs to be fixed. The bars show the percentage of respondents agreeing with various proposals suggested in a nationwide* Washington Post *survey.*

SOURCE: Ruth Marcus and Charles Babcock, "Feeding the Election Machine," *Washington Post National Weekly Edition,* February 17, 1997, 10.

conflicts of interest are not confined to decisions involving campaign money. As James Madison noted, almost every decision involves potential conflicts of interest. Decisions made by presidents, bureaucrats, and members of Congress can affect their personal financial interests (including stocks, bonds, and other investments).

Despite periodic attempts to limit conflicts of interest, violations of ethics codes still occur in Congress and in the executive branch. In 1981, six House members and one senator were convicted in an FBI undercover operation known as Abscam. Five were even videotaped accepting cash bribes. Incidents of blatant bribery such as this are rare, but conflicts of interests are more common. They are harder to deal with, however, because the issues are not clear-cut.

It is difficult to untangle the effects of personal financial interests, constituency interests, and party loyalties. For example, most people on the Agriculture Committee have agribusiness interests and represent districts with large agricultural interests. If those members vote in favor of agricultural interests, they are voting both for their own interests and those of their constituents. And they are likely to think that they are advancing the national interest at the same time. It appears that the impact of these personal interests on voting is fairly small once constituency interests are taken into account.[82]

In the executive branch, decision makers operate under much less direct public and media scrutiny. Yet they, too, may be acting on matters that affect their personal economic position. Since the Carter administration, all high-level administrative officials have been required to file public financial disclosure statements to allow the public to see when they are making decisions that benefit their own financial interests. But the rules do not require officials to step aside on matters that would affect them financially.

It is also a conflict of interest to use one's government position to line up a job following a public service career. The Ethics in Government Act of 1978 tries to regulate this. The act bars former public servants from lobbying their former agencies for a year and, on matters in which they "personally and substantially" participated as public officials, for life. Current employees also are prohibited from participating in decisions affecting interests with which they are negotiating about future employment. But the act is not very stringently enforced.

Because many companies that regularly deal with government think experience in government is an asset, especially experience in the agency that regulates the company's activities, many officials take well-paying jobs in the industry they came to know while in government. Critics call this the "revolving door," referring to the movement of people from government service to the private sector and sometimes back again.

Using a government job to line up lucrative private employment can also involve **influence peddling,** using one's access to powerful people to make money. Former high government officials can and do use their access to former colleagues to win jobs representing clients in business or labor. A well-publicized case of influence peddling was that of Michael Deaver, the deputy chief of staff and one of President Reagan's closest advisers during his first term. Deaver left government, immediately set up a public relations and lobbying firm, and began soliciting clients largely on the basis of his close relationship with the president.[83]

Conflicts of interest and influence peddling are bipartisan phenomena. Such accusations swirled around the Clinton White House, although no high official was convicted of illegal acts in office. But both President Clinton and First Lady Hillary Clinton were accused of conflicts of interest in the long-running investigation of the Whitewater affair (an investment scheme in which they had participated years earlier), but they were never found guilty of anything. A number of Clinton administration members, including a cabinet secretary, Mike Espy, left office under an ethical cloud relating to conflicts of interest and interest peddling.

George W. Bush came to Washington saying that the ethical standards of his administration would be higher than those of the Clinton White House, but if anything, influence peddling seems to be greater than ever. In some cases, corporate interests have been part of secret policymaking processes inside the White House in ways never seen before. Vice President Cheney's financial interests in one of the major contractors in Iraq, Halliburton, are now the subject of investigation. Halliburton, which Cheney headed from 1995 to 2000, was given advance notice to plan for the postwar period in Iraq and received billions of dollars' worth of contracts without competitive bidding. In 2004, an audit revealed that Halliburton had billed the government for $4.3 billion in reimbursement for work that had cost the company only $1.8 billion (Halliburton's response was that conditions in Iraq made keeping up with paperwork difficult).

Conflicts of interest can never be completely eradicated from government, but presidents can make their expectations clear. George W. Bush's administration has seemed less concerned about conflicts of interest than those of his predecessors, Bill Clinton and George H. Bush. Ironically, making such conflicts public runs the risk of reinforcing public perceptions of lower ethical standards in government than elsewhere in society. However, recent revelations of dishonesty and greed in the corporate world illustrate clearly that people in government are probably neither more nor less ethical than those in business, labor, or other parts of the private sector (and public confidence in big business is as low as in Congress, see Table 2).

Are There Democratic and Republican Kinds of Corruption?

Some observers have pointed out that although both Democrats and Republicans have ethical lapses, the kinds of ethics problems they have are quite different. Corrupt Democrats steal. They accept bribes and improper campaign donations, divert public funds to their own pocket, and seek personal financial aggrandizement. This style of corruption is reminiscent of the "honest graft" of the big-city political machines (see the box "Honest Graft" earlier in the chapter). Although some Republicans also steal—for example, former vice president Spiro Agnew, who pleaded no contest to charges of kickbacks, bribery, and extortion, and former representative Joseph McDade (R-Pa.), who was convicted of bribery and racketeering—most of these sorts of scandals have involved Democrats. Examples include Daniel Rostenkowski (D-Ill.), former chair of the House Ways and Means Committee, convicted of corrupt acts involving mail fraud, and Robert Torricelli (D-N.J.), censured by his Senate colleagues for accepting gifts from lobbyists.

Republican ethical failings tend to be related to the use of government for improper means. President Nixon's Watergate scandal involved trying to use the powers of government to punish his personal enemies and then lying about it. He also ordered Cambodia to be bombed and tried to keep it a secret. President Reagan tried to subvert the constitutional powers of Congress by secretly selling arms to Iran and supplying weapons to rebels in Nicaragua, both expressly against the law. Although Democratic presidents have also been guilty of misuse of government power (for example, President Johnson lied about alleged attacks by the North Vietnamese on an American ship to justify getting the United States more deeply involved in the Vietnam War, and President Kennedy ordered the FBI to wiretap Martin Luther King, Jr.), subverting government seems more a Republican style of corruption.

Why do these differences exist? They could be coincidental, of course. But one Democrat argued that these differences were tied to the class basis of the parties: "The lower classes steal; the upper classes defraud." A prominent Republican had a different view: "Most Republicans are contemptuous of government; few Democrats are." Whatever the reason, these examples suggest that partisanship extends to more than presidential preferences.

Conclusion: Does the Influence of Money Make Government Less Responsive?

The influence of money in American politics is a perennial source of concern to those who want to live up to the democratic ideals of political equality and popular sovereignty. Our democratic values tell us that government should represent all, the poor as well as the rich, and that everyone should have an equal chance to influence government. We know that in the real world, things do not work this way. We tolerate much inequality in access because that seems to be the way the world works in the private as well as in the public sphere, because everyone is not equally interested in influencing government, and because for most people the effort of changing this pattern would be greater than the benefits gained.

Nevertheless, our reaction to the influence of money seems to be cyclical. We tolerate it; then when stories of inside deals, influence peddling, and buying access and even votes become too frequent, we act to do something about it. We then slip back into apathy until the next cycle comes along.[84]

In recent history, the low point of the use of money to buy access was probably during the Watergate scandals associated with the 1972 election. We then reacted strongly to those scandals by passing new laws and cleaning up our campaign finance system. But as the years went by, we found ways to get around the laws until they became nearly meaningless with the important exception that we know how much money is being given to candidates. Now it appears we are in another era of growing concern over ethical standards in government, and the 2002 campaign finance reforms are one indication of that.

We should not think of our times as the low point in government morality. In political campaigns, big money is certainly less influential than it was a century ago. Campaign funding disclosure legislation means that the public can at least know who is buying influence.

Some commentators believe that the standards of public conduct decreased during the 1980s and have remained low. But although conflicts of interest and

I'M WRITING A FUND-RAISING LETTER.

THE SECRET TO GETTING DONATIONS IS TO DEPICT EVERYONE WHO DISAGREES WITH YOU AS THE ENEMY. THEN YOU EXPLAIN HOW THEY'RE SYSTEMATICALLY WORKING TO DESTROY EVERYTHING YOU HOLD DEAR.

IT'S A WAR OF VALUES! RATIONAL DISCUSSION IS HOPELESS! COMPROMISE IS UNTHINKABLE! OUR ONLY HOPE IS WELL-FUNDED ANTAGONISM, SO WE NEED YOUR MONEY TO KEEP UP THE FIGHT!

HOW CYNICALLY UNCONSTRUCTIVE. / ENMITY SELLS.

influence peddling in government may shock some, they reflect the ethical standards of the larger society. Making money in any way possible seems to be the hallmark of modern times, the age of "pinstriped outlaws." In the 1980s and 1990s, numerous Wall Street bankers bought and sold illegal insider tips, savings and loan officers looted their institutions of millions of dollars, military contractors cheated government, and many other executives made millions in shady deals that were just this side of legality. One businessman lamented, "We are all embarrassed by events that make the *Wall Street Journal* read more like the *Police Gazette*."[85]

The new millennium did not change things much. Many business leaders have also seemed intent on making their fast buck, regardless of the ethics or legality of their actions. Corporate leaders falsifying corporate income and plundering corporate funds for personal gain while shareholders lose their investments have been common occurrences in the new century. A prominent CEO remarked, "In my lifetime, American business has never been under such scrutiny, and to be blunt, much of it deserved. You pick up the paper, and you want to cry."[86]

We should also not exaggerate the amount of money involved in politics. Corporations spend much more to attract consumers than politicians spend to attract voters. We reported that the cost of the presidential campaigns in 2004 could be as much as $2 billion. This is an extremely large sum until we compare it to the $4.7 billion a year that Americans spend on laundry detergent or the $1 billion a month that car companies spend selling their wares or the $1 billion that the federal government spends every few hours.[87] It is not the amount of money in politics as much as its possible effects that concern us.

But the effects of money are hard to pin down. It is difficult to measure exactly the influence of money on political outcomes. Money sometimes influences votes and policies. Campaign contributions have some impact on voting in Congress. Money seems to have moved both parties toward more conservative policies. Money in politics is no doubt responsible for the increased in-

equality between the rich and poor. But at some times, especially when the public is paying attention, money appears to have little impact.

We do not know exactly how presidential candidates might be influenced by huge campaign donations or whether bureaucrats are using promises of future jobs as trade-offs for current favors. We think that good candidates are hindered or deterred from running by a shortage of money or even just by the knowledge that they need to raise big money, but it is difficult to measure exactly how many. Even though money is very tangible, its influence sometimes is quite intangible.

To the extent that money has an impact, it limits the responsiveness of government to the average citizen. It causes some policymakers to be more responsive to the big interests than to the average person. This does not mean, though, that those with the most money always win. Organization and a sense of the public interest can sometimes defeat even big money.

In designing laws to regulate the use of money in political life, perhaps the best that reformers can reasonably hope for is a system in which public officials who want to be honest will not feel under pressure to be influenced by money. Certainly, there will always be a few "bad apples," and no political system can protect us completely from them. It should be enough to design rules and structures that ensure that people of average honesty who serve in public office are rewarded for putting the public interest, rather than their private interests, first. Our current laws, especially our congressional campaign finance laws, do not always do that. The penalties we suffer are less in politicians stealing from the public till (relatively little of this occurs, certainly in comparison with the stealing that has been revealed in corporate America). They are more in the loss of public trust, an increasing alienation from government, and anger at politicians who seem to be putting their interests before the public interest. Perhaps, then, even a largely symbolic effort by our legislators to limit the influence of money on the political process is important, because it sends the signal that they are aware of and accountable to public concerns.

Schumer Discourages Tighter Accounting Regulations

enator Schumer joined many of his colleagues on the Senate and House banking committees in urging the SEC not to impose this tighter regulation on the accounting industry. Collectively, the members of Congress who wrote to the SEC arguing against this new regulation had received more than $3.5 million in campaign donations from the accounting industry. Eleven of the fourteen senators writing the SEC against the proposed regulation were on the Banking, Housing, and Urban Affairs Committee. And most of the House members who wrote were on the parallel House committees that oversee the SEC.

Schumer's comments were more moderate than some, but he challenged the assumption that consulting conflicts with auditing responsibilities. The rule was never adopted, though a watered-down version requiring auditing firms to disclose their consulting relationships was put in place. Levitt left the SEC at the end of President Clinton's term. He was replaced by a Bush appointee with close ties to the accounting profession (he had been the attorney representing the auditing industry in early lobbying for decreasing the liability of accounting firms when companies were charged with securities fraud).

Perhaps we would have heard little more about the SEC's failure to approve this rule, at least not so soon, if it had not been for the failure of Enron. Enron was a $100 billion-a-year Texas-based energy trading company, number 7 on the *Fortune* 500 and one of America's most admired and visible companies. After an announcement that its earnings had been vastly overstated, possibly by more than $1 billion, its stock plummeted to almost nothing

and it declared bankruptcy. Enron's auditor, Arthur Andersen, had overlooked Enron's inflated earnings and illicit ways of hiding debt. Before the announcement that Enron was bankrupt instead of making excellent profits, Arthur Andersen attested that Enron's internal accounting system "was adequate to provide reasonable assurance as to the reliability of financial statements" and that the financial reports of Enron "present fairly, in all material respects, the financial condition of the company." [88]

Enron executives who had advance knowledge of the announcement that earnings were inflated sold their stock before the announcement and made millions (Kenneth Lay, the CEO, had made $103 million in the year before the bankruptcy; seven others made more than $5 million; and the top

AP/ Wide World Photos

Former Enron CEO Kenneth Lay is led away in handcuffs.

one hundred executives made $300 million). Lower-level Enron employees, many of whose pension plans were invested heavily in Enron, collectively lost millions, many of them their life savings. Enron had forbidden its employees to sell their Enron stock invested in company pension plans, insisting that all was well, until the stock had plummeted to 26 cents a share. Ordinary investors, likewise in the dark about the financial shenanigans, also found their stock worthless.

The consequences of Enron's criminal behavior went far beyond its shareholders. Later the public learned that Enron deliberately manipulated electricity markets, one of the major reasons for the California power crisis in 2000–2001 and the rise in prices there.

Individuals had invested in Enron because they believed it was a profitable company. They believed it was a profitable company because one of the nation's largest accounting firms, Arthur Andersen, attested that it was profitable. It did so despite Enron's obvious violations of basic accounting principles and despite the fact that the directors of the corporation were asked to waive ethics rules at least twice so that officers of the company could become partners in one of Enron's many phony companies and subsidiaries.

Arthur Andersen did $27 million of consulting business with Enron on top of its $25 million auditing contract. Would Andersen have been less likely to go along with these shady practices if Schumer and his Senate colleagues had supported the rule that Arthur Levitt proposed forbidding auditing firms to do consulting business? It's quite possible that it would have.

Technically, Schumer and the other recipients of donations from accounting or energy firms who led the fight against regulation did nothing that was illegal. But it is hard to call the system anything but corrupt if powerful institutions can buy their way free of government regulations at the expense of consumers, employees, and stockholders. Securities regulatory agencies were underfunded and overworked, as well as partially declawed, by a Congress eager to deregulate. And other parts of the regulatory system had been corrupted too. Corporate boards of directors turned their head away from shady practices— some because they were too busy, others because they didn't want to sacrifice their lucrative positions on the board. Securities analysts evaluating Enron and other companies and making recommendations to the public to buy Enron stock made money on those stock transactions. Everyone got in on the deal but the public and the employees.

Capitalism depends on a set of institutions, some private and some governmental. As one economist pointed out, "None of the checks and balances that were supposed to prevent insider abuses worked; the supposedly independent players were compromised. Arthur Andersen was told of these concerns, but . . . gave Enron a free pass . . . and the regulators were nowhere to be seen, partly because politicians with personal ties to Enron . . . took care to exempt Enron from regulation."[89]

Our entire financial system, the stock market, and the health of American business rests on the assumption that investors have accurate information about the profitability of companies as they make their decisions to buy or sell. When they don't, when companies lie about their profits, and when both private accounting firms and government regulators look the other way, the capitalist system itself is threatened.[90] As one columnist declared luridly, "Enron is a cancer on capitalism . . . . The disease may be in the nodes of the marketplace, poisoning the rest of the financial system."[91]

After the Enron shenanigans came to light, other companies began to reveal that their earnings were not as reported. In fact, between 1997 and 2002, nearly one thousand companies restated their earnings, indicating that the original figures they published were incorrect.[92] The SEC investigated fraud and other criminal activity at numerous well-known companies such as Xerox and others less well known such as Qwest, WorldCom, Global Crossing, Tyco, Adelphia, Waste Management, MicroStrategy, and Halliburton, all of which found their names in the headlines as examples of firms that had grossly exaggerated their profits.[93] The press has been particularly interested in Halliburton, whose CEO was Dick Cheney, now vice president; the SEC charged that it falsely inflated its income statements by as much as $100 million a year, again certified as appropriate by Arthur Andersen.[94]

After Schumer learned of the extent of the Enron fiasco and its effect on its former employees, the senator, like many others who had accepted campaign donations from the now pariah firms, decided to donate his contributions from Arthur Andersen and from Enron to a fund for former Enron employees.

Under strong pressure from the media and public, in the summer of 2002, Congress did pass a new corporate accountability law (known as the Sarbanes-Oxley Act, after its sponsors) that mandates new, higher penalties for those who violate laws on corporate accounting and related practices. But immediately after it was passed and signed by the president, when the public's attention turned away from this issue, the accounting and corporate lobbies and allies in Congress, including Oxley himself, went to work to try to undermine the new law.[95]

After all, laws mean little unless they are effectively implemented.

Accounting regulation, like many other kinds of regulation, is generally of little interest to the public. But when Enron and other companies crashed, taking the life savings of thousands with them, suddenly the public became temporarily very interested. But now that the public's attention has waned, Schumer and others are free to work again on behalf of those with whom they have strong financial ties. Whether new regulations are implemented or ignored will depend on whether the public's attention can be refocused on the issue.

 To learn more about the troubles of the accounting industry and efforts to reform it, go to this chapter's "You Are There" exercises on the text Web site.

Key Terms

muckrakers
Teapot Dome scandal
contribution limits
independent spending
public disclosure
Federal Election Commission
McCain-Feingold Act
soft money
political action committees (PACs)
527 groups
spoils system
conflicts of interest
influence peddling

Further Reading

Bruce Ackerman and Ian Ayres, *Voting with Dollars* (New Haven, Conn.: Yale University Press, 2002). The authors propose a novel way of financing political campaigns through "patriot dollars," donations from the public at large, given anonymously.

Jeffrey H. Birnbaum, *The Money Men* (New York: Times Books, 2000). The real scandal in Washington isn't what's illegal; it is what is legal. This book follows the money in a very readable way.

Larry J. Sabato and Glenn Simpson, *Dirty Little Secrets: The Persistence of Corruption in American Politics* (New York: Times Books, 1996). The authors take a close look at corruption in politics.

Bradley Smith, *Unfree Speech: The Folly of Campaign Finance Reform* (Princeton, N.J.: Princeton University Press, 2001). Smith, once nominated to the FEC, argues that restricting campaign donations is unconstitutional and ineffective besides.

For Viewing

Bigger than Enron (2002) This *Frontline* documentary from PBS on how the failure of congressional and regulatory oversight led to corporate fraud can be viewed online at www.pbs.org/frontline.

 Electronic Resources

www.commoncause.org
This is the home page of Common Cause, the public interest group whose major focus is reforming the campaign finance system. Linked to the page are the group's reports tracking relevant legislation, periodic reports on campaign spending, coverage of the Enron and accounting scandals, and reports on financial ties of those voting against major regulatory legislation such as the tobacco bill.

www.pbs.org/wgbh/pages/frontline/president
The home page for the PBS special So You Want to Buy a President *contains much useful information on how much is contributed and who the contributors are.*

www.fec.gov/index.html
The Federal Election Commission does not have much regulatory power, but it does publish useful reports of campaign spending. This page describes election rules and links to FEC reports on campaign spending and on voter turnout.

www.politics.com
This Web site provides links to news stories and polls and allows you to see who in your neighborhood (or any other, by ZIP code) gave to which campaigns.

www.enron.com/corp
Enron's site now featuring bankruptcy news and advice for laid-off workers.

InfoTrac College Edition

Search for the following articles in the InfoTrac database:

Adkins, Randall E., and Andrew J. Dowdle. "The Money Primary: What Influences the Outcome of Pre-primary Presidential Nomination Fundraising?" *Presidential Studies Quarterly* (June 2002).

Faucheux, Ron. "New Campaign Law: Whose Ox?" *Campaigns and Elections* (July 2002).

Phelps, Douglas H. Phelps. "Leveling the Playing Field," *National Civic Review* (Summer 2004).

Tumulty, Karen, and Michael Weisskopf. "What $6 Million Can Buy: Connection between George W. Bush and Enron." *Time* (January 28, 2002).

For more articles, enter

"campaign finance reform" in the Subject Guide;

"campaign funds" in the Subject Guide, and then go to subdivision "analysis";

"campaign funds" in the Subject Guide, and then go to subdivision "finance".

American Government Resources

Visit the Political Behavior section of the Wadsworth American Government Resources Web site (politicalscience. wadsworth.com/amgov) for a variety of tools to help you explore money and politics further. Included are simulations, video clips, Microcase exercises, and a wealth of other activities.

CHAPTER 10

CONGRESS

Scott J. Ferrell / Congressional Quarterly, Inc.

Speaker of the House Dennis Hastert (R-Ill.) and Minority Leader Nancy Pelosi (D-Calif.) reflect the bitter partisanship that has characterized the House of Representatives in recent years by rarely voting on the same side and, in the case of Hastert, rarely consulting Pelosi.

Members and Constituencies

Members

Constituencies

Congress as a Representative Body

The Advantages of Incumbency

How Congress Is Organized

The Evolution of Congressional Organization

Contemporary Leadership Positions

Committees

Staff and Support Agencies

What Congress Does

Lawmaking

Oversight

Budget Making

Members on the Job

Negotiating the Informal System

Making Alliances

Using the Media

Balancing the Work

Congress and the Public

Conclusion: Is Congress Responsive?

Should You Run for the Party Leadership?

ou are Nancy Pelosi, seven-term Democratic incumbent in the House of Representatives. It is January 2001, and the newly elected Congress is now in session. Although you won your reelection in California's 8th district in a landslide, as you have done for the last several elections, the 2000 congressional elections were very disappointing for your party. It again failed to regain a majority in the House.

You are trying to decide whether to make a bid to become minority whip of the House Democratic Caucus, the second highest leadership position in the minority party. A woman has never been a serious contender for the position, let alone held it. (The current whip, David Bonoir, gave up his House seat to run for governor of Michigan.) As whip, you would be an important leader within the party, participating in shaping the Democratic strategies and priorities in the House and working with other leaders to make sure that Democrats vote in accord with Democratic priorities.

The whip is chosen by a vote of all Democratic members of the House. You expect stiff opposition from Steny Hoyer (D-Md.), the assistant whip who, as the next in line to Bonior, should have the inside track. He has chaired the party caucus, is a veteran legislator, and has been campaigning hard for the position. He also has what some see as an advantage: he is somewhat more conservative than you are.

In recent years, the Democratic Party's rank and file have been moving toward the center and more and more voters have been registering as Republicans and Independents. Some in your party reason that they have to present a moderate alternative to the growing conservatism of the Republicans and also to present a more conciliatory image in the conduct of House business to counter a Republican leadership that is aggressively partisan. You disagree with that position. You think the party may be in danger of losing its sense of what it has stood for since the New Deal years of FDR. You say you want to cut Democrats loose and let them be free to be Democrats.

You know Democratic Party history from the inside out. You were to the manner born; your father was a ward leader in Baltimore's Little Italy, served four terms in the House, and then for twelve years was the mayor of Baltimore. You grew up in a household where constituents congregated, political discussions dominated, and grassroots politics was a crucial part of life.

You remained active in politics after moving to California, where you married and stayed at home to raise five children. The delay may have put you on a later career track, but you gained organizational and people skills from having five children in six years.[1] On the side, you did precinct work and organized and hosted fundraisers for California Democrats. You rose to chair the

California state Democratic committee and were chief planner of the 1984 Democratic national convention. Then in 1987, with your children grown, you were asked by the congressional incumbent, who was dying, to run for her seat. You had a lot of chits to call in from your years of electioneering and fundraising, and you won easily.

Conservative journals have labeled you a "latte liberal," and the press has picked it up, prefacing your name with "liberal" so consistently that it is as if your name is actually Liberal Nancy Pelosi. Your district, which includes San Francisco, is indeed one of the most liberal constituencies in the United States.[2] But you have never had a latte in your life, and you call yourself a "nonmenacing progressive Democrat."[3]

One of the first issues you took up when you entered Congress was human rights; as the most persistent ally of Chinese dissident students after the Tiananmen Massacre in 1989, you helped win an amnesty that allowed them to stay in the United States. You have consistently linked China's trading privileges with the United States to improvements in the Chinese human rights record, at some risk of alienating substantial numbers of Chinese American businesspeople in your district. You do not see this as liberal or conservative any more than your support for veterans' and workers' rights, environmental protection, or funding for AIDS research.

During your years in the House, you have not been just an advocate for your constituency or a specialist on a few issues. Your ace in the hole has been fundraising. You have traveled around the country recruiting candidates to run in the primaries, promising to help them raise the money they will need, and succeeding at doing so. In the 2000 elections, you raised more than $3 million for your colleagues' campaigns. And now you know that regardless of the minority whip votes that have been promised to Steny Hoyer, you have your own IOUs out there too.

Should you go for the whip position? On the one hand, you could hang back, support Hoyer's candidacy, and wait in the wings to succeed him as whip if he becomes caucus leader. Hoyer has been your friend and ally in the House. There will be more leadership opportunities soon, as rumors circulate that Dick Gephardt (D-Mo.), the Democratic minority leader, will give up his seat to run for president. That might get you into the whip's position without having to go up against a well-liked colleague and risk creating the impression that there is a left-center split in the caucus at a time when party unity is extremely important.

On the other hand, you think there are good reasons to bid for the position. You want to be part of the leadership and help set strategy. You can feel Democratic caucus morale sinking by the day as the Republicans pass legislation over Democratic opposition, sometimes without even consulting them. You think that aggressive leadership is needed to get the party back on the winning track. And you feel strongly that more women and minorities are needed in the leadership. Women now make up 20 percent of the Democratic delegation in the House; why shouldn't a woman be in the top leadership group?

What do you do? Should you run for whip or "wait your turn"?

The Founders clearly intended Congress to be the dominant branch of government. They laid out its role and powers in Article I, and their discussion takes up almost half the document. Through its formal powers, Madison believed, Congress would dominate the presidency because it alone had "access to the pockets of the people." But Congress has not always been first in the hearts of the people, nor has it always been the most respected or trusted branch of government. On the other hand, most people like their own representatives and senators, at least well enough to return them to office at impressively high rates.

In this chapter, we look at the current composition of Congress and ask how representative a body it is. We describe how Congress is organized and how it carries out its constitutional responsibilities, then look at how individual members carry out their duties in Washington and their districts and what makes them so popular back home that they usually get reelected. Finally, we look at Congress's relationship to the other branches of government and to the public. To understand Congress, one must also understand the process by which members are elected, a topic covered in Chapter 8.

Members and Constituencies

Members

Alexis de Tocqueville was not impressed with the status of members of Congress, noting that they were "almost all obscure individuals, village lawyers, men in trades, or even persons belonging to the lower class." His view was shared by another European visitor, Charles Dickens, who was shocked in 1842 to find Congress full of tobacco spitters who committed "cowardly attacks upon opponents" and seemed to be guilty of "aiding and abetting every bad inclination in the popular mind."[4] However one views their behavior, members of Congress were not then, and are not now, a cross section of

*In its early years, Washington, D.C., was described as "a miserable little swamp."
When this photo was taken in 1882, it still retained the look and feel of a small town.*

the American public. But they are a more diverse group than the membership of Congresses of the eighteenth and nineteenth centuries ever were or thought they should be.

Who Can Serve?

The Constitution places few formal restrictions on membership in Congress. One must be twenty-five years old to serve in the House and thirty in the Senate. One must have been a citizen for at least seven years to be elected to the House and nine years to be elected to the Senate. Members must reside in the states from which they were elected, but House members need not reside in their own districts. As a practical matter, however, it is highly unlikely that voters will elect a person to represent their district who is not from the district or who does not maintain a residence there.

Local identity is not as significant a factor in Senate races; national figures like Robert Kennedy and Hillary Rodham Clinton, who established in-state residency within weeks or months of the election, both ran successful campaigns in New York. It is more difficult to run in another state if the state is less cosmopolitan or the candidate is not already well known, as was the case in 2004 when Maryland resident Alan Keyes ran for, and lost, a U.S. Senate seat in Illinois.

Length of Service

Every member of the House stands for election every two years, while senators serve six-year terms, with one-third of the membership standing for election every two years. Although the Articles of Confederation did set a limit on the number of terms a representative could serve, the Constitution placed no cap on how many times an individual can be elected to the House or Senate. Perhaps the Founders thought that no one would want to serve more than a few terms. In the late eighteenth and early nineteenth centuries, leaving one's home to serve in Congress was considered a great sacrifice. Washington was a muddy swamp, with debris-filled streets, farm animals running loose, and transportation so poor almost no one got home during a session. In fact, during Congress's first forty years, 41 percent of House members, on average, dropped out every two years, and in the early 1900s, the median length of service for a representative was still only five years.[5]

But as Washington became a power center and a much more livable and accessible city, members were more receptive to longer periods of service. In the 1910s and 1920s, power in the House became less centralized, and individuals were able to build personal power bases. And as seats went uncontested in the one-party South, more legislators became career politicians, spending thirty and even forty years in Congress. These long-serving members began to dominate committee work and to control the legislative agenda. Although they by no means comprised a majority of Congress, they were probably foremost in the minds of those Americans who began to see government as increasingly unresponsive to the public.

Term Limits

During the height of public anger with government in the 1990s, there was a nationwide move to limit the number of terms that state and national legislators could serve. By 1995, over 70 percent of the survey respondents said they favored term limits.[6] Though Congress narrowly defeated term-limit legislation, in twenty-three of twenty-four states that allow ballot initiatives, voters adopted term limits for their members of Congress and state legislators.

Some supporters of term limits were influenced by the mid-nineteenth-century image of "citizen lawmakers" who set aside their personal business for a few years to attend to the public's business and then return home. Most supporters believed that by not having to worry constantly about getting reelected, legislators would be free to consider the "public interest," not "special interests," and would have no desire to build personal empires. Others also saw term limits as a way to weaken the power of government by having a more rapid turnover in the membership of Congress and state legislatures.

Opponents believed that term limits would weaken Congress at the expense of the special interests and the federal bureaucracy and president. Legislators would be relative novices compared to much more experienced lobbyists and bureaucrats.

This debate subsided when in 1995, in a 5–4 vote, the Supreme Court held term limits for members of Congress unconstitutional. The majority argued that permitting individual states to have diverse qualifications for Congress would "result in a patchwork of state qualifications, undermining the uniformity and national character that the framers envisioned and sought to ensure."[7] By adding to the qualifications spelled out in the Constitution (age and citizenship), the Court ruled that states were in effect "amending" the Constitution. By definition, then, such laws would be unconstitutional because the Constitution can be amended only through the processes of adoption and ratification it specifies, not by state or congressional laws.

By the late 1990s, enthusiasm for term limits in the state legislatures had waned, and measures to weaken or repeal term limits were pending in ten states. In 2001, Idaho became the first state to repeal term limits, and others have since followed.

Tenure

For a short time in the 1990s, turnover in Congress did increase. In 2001–2002, almost two-thirds of all House members had served ten years or less.[8] Now this trend is in reverse. The committees that draw district lines are creating more and more "safe districts," whose members are serving longer. The 108th Congress (2003–2004) had only 53 first-termers, down from 110 a decade earlier,[9] and the number of freshmen in the current Congress is significantly lower, only 40. In fact, in 2004, only about 30 House races were truly competitive.[10]

Constituencies

The district a member of Congress represents is called a **constituency.** The term is used to refer to both the area within the electoral boundaries and its residents. There are two senators from each state, so each senator's constituency is the entire state and all its residents. Most states have multiple House districts, though six states (Alaska, Delaware, North Dakota, South Dakota, Vermont, and Wyoming) have populations so small that they are allotted only a single seat in the House of Representatives. For those states, the constituency for the House member is also the entire state. Except for those six states, every House district must have (in accordance with the one-person, one-vote rule) roughly the same number of residents, so the number of districts in each state depends on its total population.

Except in single-district states, the geographic size of a constituency is determined by the distribution of the population within the state. In states with large urban populations, several districts may exist within a single city. The logistics of campaigning are thus very different for a representative from Manhattan, whose district can be measured in a few square miles, and one from Wyoming, who must cover the entire state.

Reapportionment

Initially, the House of Representatives had fifty-nine members, but as the nation grew and more states joined the Union, the size of the House increased too. Since 1910, it has had 435 members, except in the 1950s, when seats were temporarily added for Alaska and Hawaii. Every ten years, in a process called **reapportionment,** the 435 seats are allocated to the states based on the latest census. Since the first Congress, the number of constituents each House member represents has grown from 30,000 to roughly 650,000.

Within a constant 435-seat House, states with fast-growing populations gain seats, while those with slow-growing or declining populations lose seats. Since World War II, population movement in the United States has been toward the South, West, and Southwest and away from the Midwest and Northeast. This has been reflected in the allocation of House seats. For example, from 1950 through 2000, California gained twenty-three seats and New York lost fourteen. Illinois, Wisconsin, Pennsylvania, and Ohio lost House seats after the 2000 census, while Arizona, California, Colorado, Florida, Georgia, Nevada, and Texas gained them.

Redistricting

States that gain or lose seats and states whose population shifts within the state must redraw their district boundaries, a process called **redistricting.** This is always a hot political issue. The precise boundaries of a district determines the election prospects of candidates and parties. In fact, districts are normally drawn to benefit the party in control of the state legislature. A district whose boundaries are devised to maximize the political advantage of a party or a racial group is known as a **gerrymander** (see also Chapter 8). Majority parties in state legislatures persist in securing political advantage by drawing bizarrely shaped districts while still complying with the Supreme Court ruling that all congressional districts be approximately equal in population.

Before 1960, states were often reluctant to redistrict their state legislative and congressional boundaries to conform to population changes within the state for fear that doing so would endanger incumbents and threaten rural areas whose populations were declining. After decades without reapportioning, some legislative districts in urban areas had as much as nineteen times the population of rural districts.

When state legislatures, frequently dominated by rural representatives, still refused to reapportion themselves, the Supreme Court, in *Baker* v. *Carr* (1962), issued the first in a series of rulings forcing states to reapportion their legislative districts.[11] Two years later, the Court required congressional districts to be approximately equal in population, thus mandating the principle of "one person, one vote."[12] As a result, most states had to redraw district lines, some more than once, during the 1960s. These decisions fueled heated controversy, including a proposed constitutional amendment to overturn them. But after a while, the principle of one person, one vote came to be widely accepted.

Because of the important role state legislatures play in the redistricting process, the 2000 state legislative elections were crucial for both parties. In the early 1980s, Democratic-controlled state legislatures were able to help Democratic candidates in states such as California by drawing lines that concentrated Republican strength in a few areas and created districts with small Democratic majorities.[13] After the 1990 state legislative elections, which gave Republicans more clout, many states drew boundaries favoring Republicans, a factor in the Republicans' victories in 1994.

The 2000 election left sixteen state legislatures under Democratic control, eighteen in Republican hands, and fifteen states with divided control. The split was so close in Illinois that the decision on whether the Republican- or the Democratic-drawn redistricting map would go into effect was decided by drawing a name of out of a hat to determine whether a Democrat or a Republican would be added to the committee to break the deadlock. A Democrat won, and his party's map was approved.

As we explained in Chapter 8, the sophistication of the software used to measure voting patterns to the block level means that legislators can determine the outcome of most districts throughout the decade. This is a serious problem for democratic accountability. Fair and competitive elections are the primary way the public controls government.

The redistricting process has been very important to underrepresented minorities. As we saw in Chapter 8, before the 1992 election, redistricting produced eleven new districts with black majorities and six with Hispanic majorities; all but one were won by blacks and Hispanics. However, the Supreme Court has since ruled that although race may be taken into consideration, it cannot be the primary basis for creating districts.[14]

Congress as a Representative Body

What Does Representative Mean?

To take the measure of how representative Congress is, we first have to establish what "representation" means. During the Revolutionary War, John Adams said that any legislature to be created under a new government "should be an exact portrait, in miniature, of the people at large, as it should think, feel, reason, and act like them."[15] Benjamin Franklin said simply that Congress should be a mirror of the people. These statements leave unresolved what has priority in representation. Is it more important, for example, for Congress to look like a demographic cross section of the public or for the policies it advances to reflect constituent issue positions? And in what situations can elected representatives use their delegated authority to act as their conscience dictates, to do what they believe is right or in the national interest, even if not supported by a majority of their constituents?

To have a Congress that reflects the demographic mix is one where descriptive representation is high. This kind of representation is not rooted in what legislators do but rather on their personal characteristics— what they *are* or *are like*.[16] The rise of identity politics has increased demands for a Congress that better reflects the country's demographic profile, and so today it is more likely than ever that a predominantly Hispanic, white, or African American congressional district will be represented by a member of the corresponding ethnicity or race. But Congress is far from representative in this way (see the box "Congress Is Not a Cross Section of America").

For the first century of the Republic, the possibility of having citizen-legislators who were a cross section of the general public was just a romantic notion. Only certain landed, business, or professional white men could even think about running for Congress. It was not until 1920 (with ratification of the Nineteenth Amendment, grant-

CONGRESS IS NOT A CROSS SECTION OF AMERICA

Congress is not now, and never has been, a cross section of the American population (see Table 1). The citizens who serve in Congress are still disproportionately white and male: white non-Hispanic males, who make up about 37 percent of the total population, currently hold about 72 percent of the seats in the House of Representatives and 83 percent of the seats in the Senate.

Women make up 51 percent of the nation's population but only about 15 percent of the Senate and of the House. They are the most underrepresented demographic group; four states (Iowa, Delaware, Vermont, and New Hampshire) have never elected a woman to Congress.[1] Most states do send at least one female representative, however, and California's delegation has twenty women, including both senators (accounting for one-third of all women in Congress).

Hispanic, Asian, and African Americans are also below parity with their numbers in the population. The fastest-growing immigrant group, Asian Indians, are represented for the first time in the 109th Congress [Bobby Jindal, (R-La.)].

Congress is also not representative of the range of political or religious views among the general public. Although only 62 percent of the public identifies with the two major parties, Republicans and Democrats hold almost

TABLE 1 Members of the 109th Congress: Not a Cross Section of the Public (2005–2007)

	Population (%)	House *(%)	Senate (%)
Women	51	15	14
African American	13	9	1
Hispanic	13	5	2
Asian Pacific	4	0.7	2
American Indian	0.7	0.3	0
Lawyer	0.3	37	58
Blue Collar	30	1	0
Millionaires	0.7	27[†]	40[†]
Foreign Born	11.5	2**	0**
Median Age	35	55	60
Protestant	51[†]	62	56
Catholic	25[†]	29	24
Jewish	2.6[†]	6	11
Mormon	1.3[†]	3	5
Muslim	1–2[†]	0	0

*Does not include nonvoting members from Puerto Rico, Guam, Samoa, the Virgin Islands, or the District of Columbia.
**Does not include those born abroad of American parents, such as John McCain.
†Estimates; members need only report income and assets within a broad dollar range; the U.S. Census does not collect data on religion. Congressional affiliates are by self-declaration; will not add up to 100 percent because ten members specified no affiliation or others than those listed.

all the seats in Congress. Christianity and Judaism account for virtually all religious affiliations declared by members, though these groups find adherents among only about 87 percent of the population.

Members are much better off financially than the average householder: about 30 percent are millionaires, and a number are multimillionaires.[2] They also

tend to rank well above average in education; nearly all have college degrees, and a majority have graduate or professional degrees (mostly law, but also PhDs, MDs, and one dentist). Although blue-collar workers constitute nearly one-third of the working population, only ten congressional members in 2004 claimed blue-collar backgrounds.[3]

ing women the right to vote) that a majority of Americans could vote, and most of them, realistically, could not stand for office. Although federal barriers to African American male suffrage had been removed in the nineteenth century, state laws prevented most from voting until the 1960s. Today, although adults in all economic categories can meet the minimum requirements needed to stand for office, the demands of the nomination and

selection process, especially campaign costs, limit the number of people who can reasonably choose to run.

"Acting For" Representation

If Congress still has a way to go to look like the American public, does it "think, feel, reason, and act" like them? The "acting for" conceptualization of representation holds that the legislator is not just standing in for

The most common occupational background of congressional members has been the law. But this pattern is beginning to change as legislative careers have become more demanding. Today it is difficult for an attorney to maintain a law practice and also serve as a legislator. Ethics laws requiring financial disclosure and information about client relations have also discouraged practicing attorneys from running for congressional office. Whereas the Senate is still dominated by lawyers, there are now more House members with backgrounds in business and real estate than in the law. But in this era of high technology, such fields as engineering and science are barely represented in Congress.

Another dent in the citizen-legislator ideal has been the presence of "dynasty" families (the Adamses, Harrisons, Lodges, Kennedys, and Bushes). In the 107th Congress (2000–2001), seventy-seven members were relatives of elected officials at some level of government, and in the 108th, there were three pairs of siblings and twenty-six members whose parents had also served in Congress.[4]

Members of the Senate are even less a cross section of the American population than the House, but the Senate was established to represent a different set of interests—those of the states—and was not intended to be a mirror of the people. Representation in the Senate is not based on the one-person, one-vote

The Sanchez sisters—Loretta (left) and Linda—serve in the House of Representatives as Democrats representing two districts in Southern California.

standard but on a one-state, two-vote standard. This structure allows for the overrepresentation of the interests of low-population states and the underrepresentation of the interests of the larger, more urban, and more ethnically and racially diverse states. Senators must still define and represent state interests in the aggregate, not just those of a specific group or district. This is less complicated for senators from more socially and economically homogeneous, low-population states such as Nebraska and Wyoming than for senators from much larger and more diverse populations and economies like New York and California.

1. A list of all women who have served in the House can be found at www.loc/gov/thomas; those who have served in the Senate can be found at www.senate.gov/artandhistory/history/common/briefing/women_senators.htm.
2. These are estimates drawn from members' financial disclosure statements, which are do not provide exact figures on income. Members need only report income and assets within a broad dollar range. A few members do, however, release their tax statements. A good Web site for tracking the pay and perks of members of Congress is that of the nonprofit, nonpartisan Center for Public Integrity (www.publicintegrity.org).
3. *CQ's Politics in America, 2004: The 108th Congress* (Washington, D.C.: CQ Press, 2003), vi.
4. Ibid., 1133. Eleven of the twenty-six whose mother or father served in Congress directly succeeded their parent.

others but acting "in behalf of," "in the interest of," and "as the agent of" the members of the constituency.[17]

Part of the reason why there has been interest in having Congress look like America is that there is a relationship between a person's sex, race, ethnicity, income, and religion and that person's position on issues. Historically, the political conditions of women and minorities have differed from those of white men to the degree that today women, African Americans, Hispanics, and Asian Americans are seen as *national* constituencies with distinct issue priorities. House members now organize around these identities so as to represent national constituencies as well as their home districts (see "Making Alliances" later in this chapter). Poor people and blue-collar workers are other groups who have sent few of their numbers to Congress and yet often have

Barack Obama (D-Ill.) is the only African American in the Senate and just the third since Reconstruction.

different positions than the lawyers and professionals who dominate the legislature.

But does it make a difference? For instance, do women really represent their constituents differently from their male colleagues? There is no guarantee that any one woman (or African American or Mexican American) will represent women (or blacks or Hispanics) collectively better than, say, a white man; there is no rule that a millionaire will not look out for the interests of blue-collar workers or that a Christian or Jew will not care about the civil rights of a Muslim. But as women, blacks, Hispanics, and Asians increase their presence in Congress, so does the likelihood that the issues of greatest concern to them will be heard. Imagine a Congress made up not of wealthy males but of blue-collar females. It is hard to imagine that the legislation coming out of that Congress would be the same as it currently is. Of course, we cannot test that speculation; nevertheless, in the 1993–1994 session, which brought twenty-two new women members to the fore, Congress passed a record sixty-six bills of special importance to women. That nearly equaled the number of such bills passed in the entire previous decade.[18] So it does seem that there is a relationship between descriptive representation and the likelihood that legislation will be representative of the wishes of the broadest segment of the electorate.

One simple measure of "acting for" representation is party identification. In 2003, the American public was split evenly among Independents, Democrats, and Republicans, but this was not reflected in the composition of Congress (see Figure 1).[19] Republicans and Democrats hold 99.7 percent of the seats. There are only two Independents in Congress, one each in the House and the Senate, and they caucus with the Democrats. Due to the winner-take-all electoral system, minor party identifiers (Greens, Libertarians, the Reform Party, socialist and other labor parties), who now account for 6 to 7 percent of all voters, have no representation in Congress, except when their position on an issue overlaps with that of one of the two major parties. This compares to parliamentary systems based on proportional representation, which mandate that any party receiving a certain minimum of the votes case—depending on the country, usually 1 to 5 percent—receive a proportionate number of seats in the legislature.

Another measure of "acting for" representation is a legislator's voting record. By casting hundreds of votes each year, members try to represent the interests of their constituencies, bring benefits to the district, and in the process win support for reelection. Members must consider what benefits their districts as a whole as well as the needs of subgroups within the district, such as party voters, socioeconomic groups, and personal supporters.[20] Overall, if districts are filled with farmers, the members must represent farmers, whether or not they know anything about farming. Representatives of districts with large universities must be sensitive to the reactions of students and professors even if they personally think academics have pointed heads.

For members to act as their constituents would if they were making policy themselves, pursue policies they favor, and vote as they would on issues requires that members keep in close touch with the home district. And in fact most members do spend about half of each year in their districts. On the whole, the member's issue positions are usually not far from those of his or her party or the majority of the constituency *that votes*. But members are more likely to share the issue position of constituents when the issue is important to constituents and when their opinions are strongly held. Since constituents are often uninformed, divided, or apathetic and most votes in Congress are on bills the electorate knows little about, members can vote their personal issue preferences, with their party, or with those constituents or donors who most forcibly make their positions known.

Constituents are becoming more active in communicating with their legislators, flooding them with faxes, e-mails, poll results, and mailgrams, often stimulated as a result of radio or television talk shows or interest groups mobilizing their memberships. These communicative individuals, however, are often not representative of the majority in a member's constituency and tend to hold their positions with greater intensity than

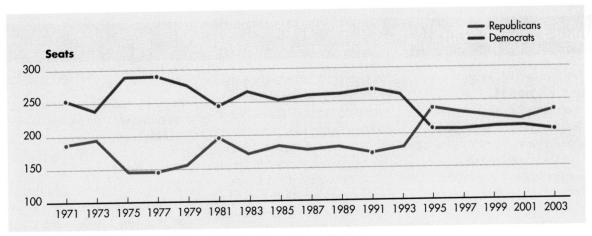

FIGURE 1 ■ Makeup of the House of Representatives, by Party, 1971–2003 *Representation of the two major parties in the House has been much more equal since 1995 than in earlier decades but other parties have been shut out.*

NOTE: Figures are for the first day of each Congress and do not include Independents or vacant seats.

SOURCE: *Congressional Quarterly Weekly Review,* April 3, 2004, 790.

the average voter. As we saw in Chapter 4, Congress is more likely to respond to those with intensely held views. And Congress itself has become more extreme in its views than the public in general. Republican members have become more conservative and Democrats more liberal, even though one in four Americans still identifies as a "moderate."

The Advantages of Incumbency

Because reelection is an important objective for almost all members of Congress and the most important objective for many, much of the work members do throughout their term is targeted at getting reelected. Most incumbents are successful, though Senate seats are not as secure as House seats. Nevertheless, few members take anything for granted, and they use the many advantages of incumbency to keep themselves in office.

Before they even take the oath of office, newly elected representatives are given an introduction to the advantages of incumbency. At meetings arranged by the Democratic and Republican leadership and by the House Administrative Committee, new members learn about free mailing privileges, computers and software to help them target letters to specialized groups of constituents, facilities to make videotapes and audiotapes to send to hometown media, and other "perks" designed to keep members in touch with their constituencies and, not coincidentally, to help win reelection (see the box "Pay and Perks of Office" on the next page).

Incumbents win because they are better known than nonincumbents. Voters have seen their representatives and senators on television or received mail from them, and they can give a general rating of their perfor-

mance.[21] Although most voters can correctly identify their representatives and senators as liberal or conservative, only a small minority know how these legislators voted on any issue.[22] Therefore, incumbents have the advantage of name recognition without the disadvantage of having voters know how they actually cast their votes on most pieces of legislation.

Incumbents' high level of public recognition is not so surprising given that members of Congress spend much of their time and energy looking for and using opportunities to make themselves known to their constituents. Members spend half or more of their days in their district, making an average of thirty-five trips home a year—at taxpayers' expense.[23] To accommodate these trips, the House operates, as business allows, on a three-day week, Tuesday through Thursday, allowing legislators four-day weekends in the home district. The Senate operates on a five-day week but takes off every fourth week to make longer home visits possible.

Casework

Arguably the main advantage of incumbency is the opportunity that being in office gives representatives to perform services and do favors for their constituents. Members send constituents calendars, U.S. flags that have flown over the Capitol, and publications of the federal government. This is one of the best ways members of Congress have to make themselves known in their districts and to create a kind of patron-client relationship. You will not read about this in the Constitution, where the duties of Congress are defined. But in practice, electoral politics has meant that members must spend a great deal of their time serving the specific interests of their districts, which are not necessarily

The first members of Congress made $6 a day, which paid for boarding-house accommodations, firewood, candles, their meals, and a mileage allowance for travel to and from the capital.[1] Today members receive a handsome salary indexed to inflation, a generous benefits package including full medical and dental care, and money for office, staff, mailing, and travel. The cost of funding Congress in 2005 will be more than $4 billion.[2]

Personal Benefits of Serving in Congress

Salary

Congress has indexed its salaries to inflation so that members no longer have to vote each session on salary increases. Now they vote only if a member brings a motion to reject the automatic increase. Salaries have increased from $90,000 in 1989 to $158,100 in 2004. This puts members of Congress among the top 5 percent of American wage earners, and the figure does not include members' income from other sources.[3] Salaries of congressional leaders are somewhat higher; the speaker of the House earns about $195,000.

Health Care

For a modest monthly premium, members can opt for a first-class private health care plan or care at one of two military hospitals. Taxpayers spend millions more each year to keep a doctor and staff on site at the Capitol's Wellness Center.

Pensions

All members of Congress are required to pay Social Security taxes, but they also have 401(k) plans and a generous federal pension program that is adjusted each year for inflation. We do not know exactly how generous the pension is because specific dollar amounts are not reported to the public. In general, the longest-serving members—those retiring with several decades of service—receive about 75 percent of their salaries. This amounted to slightly less than $100,000 per year for those retiring in 2000.[4] But for the average member, who serves many fewer years, pensions might range from $47,000 to $51,000 a year. If Congress voted to convert its pension system to the same kind of cash balance plan many members are advocating for American workers, the value of their pensions would drop by as much as 60 percent.[5]

Benefits That Help Reelection Chances

Office and Clerical Support

Representatives are authorized to hire up to eighteen staff members, and they receive an allowance for office space and furniture in their home district. Senators' staff budgets vary with the population of their states. The average size of a Senator's personal staff is about 34 full-time workers.

Travel and Mailing Allowances

Members receive an allowance for travel to and from their districts, adjusted according to their distance from Washington. Their mailing allowance (franking privilege) covers the cost of mailings to constituents; its value has been estimated as equivalent to $350,000 in campaign contributions.

Studio Access

Television and radio recording studios are provided for preparing ads and sound bites for the news.

Other Perks

- Free parking on Capitol Hill, on Washington streets, and at airports
- Subsidized meals in the Senate and House dining rooms
- Fitness centers and swimming pools
- Child-care center
- Free car washes
- Taxpayer-subsidized travel abroad
- Pagers, e-mail accounts, and Internet access

A Final Benefit

Taxpayers fund life insurance policies and a death benefit equal to a year's salary for each member of Congress. And if a legislator so desires, the sergeant-at-arms will arrange for an undertaker to plan the member's final journey.

1. *Per diem* and travel allowances for the first members were verified in 2002 when Senate custodial staff found an eighteenth-century ledger with payment accounts.
2. *Budget of the United States, Fiscal 2005* (Washington, D.C.: Government Printing Office, 2004), 19–32. The Web site of the Center for Public Integrity (www.publicintegrity.org) is excellent for tracking congressional pay and benefits.
3. *Now with Bill Moyers,* Public Broadcasting System, July 2, 2004, www.pbs.org/now.
4. "$100,000 Pension Set for Some Lawmakers," *Champaign-Urbana News-Gazette,* December 31, 1997, C-8.
5. *Now,* July 2, 2004.

synonymous with the interests of the nation as a whole. Members take this aspect of their representational responsibilities very seriously because it is their own constituents who will reelect them—or not.

Collectively, the House and Senate receive close to one hundred million pieces of mail each year, and even more e-mail messages.[24] The work of answering questions and doing personal favors for constituents who write or call for help is called **constituency service** or **casework.** More than 30 percent of senators' staffs and almost half of all representatives' staffs are located in their home state or district offices to better serve constituents.[25]

Congressional staff function as red-tape cutters for everyone from elderly citizens having difficulties with Social Security to small-town mayors trying to get federal grants for new sewer systems. They provide information to students working on term papers, people looking for federal jobs, citizens puzzled about which federal agency to ask for assistance, or residents trying to get information about a relative in the military. Typically, responsibility for mediating with federal agencies is divided among the casework staffers by issue area, allowing them to specialize and resolve constituents' problems—passports, immigration, Social Security payments, and the like—more efficiently.

Of course, not all casework is directed toward winning reelection. Some members say they enjoy their casework more than their policy roles, perhaps because the results of casework are more immediate and tangible. Individually, they may have limited power in trying to get important legislation passed, but in dealing with a constituent's problems, their power is much greater because of their clout with bureaucrats. A phone call or letter to a federal agency will bring attention to the constituent's problem. And casework does allow members to build nonpartisan and seemingly nonpolitical ties with their constituents.

Mailing Privileges

For the 109th Congress, taxpayers will provide more than a half billion dollars for office and franking expenses (mailing costs).[26] The franking privilege is a great asset of incumbency because it allows members to write their constituents without paying for postage out of pocket or using campaign funds. (The frank is a facsimile of the member's signature, and it works like metered mail, with the frank appearing where the stamp would be.) It is not free; the Postal Service records all franked mail and sends Congress a bill at the end of each year. That means that the cost of the frank goes up with each postal increase. Its main advantage is helping each member increase name recognition (and newly elected members can begin using the frank immediately, even before they are sworn in). The frank cannot be used to send personal correspondence to constituents or to ask them for their vote or a campaign contribution, but members can send out newsletters that inform constituents of their work for the district or to survey constituents' issue positions. Much of the time, however, the frank is used to send constituents material they have requested, such as government forms or publications, and this too increases a member's name recognition.

Media Advantage

In addition to regular mailings, members use increasingly sophisticated production equipment and technology to make television and radio shows to send home. Constituents may see or hear stories about their representatives on local television and radio news programs produced in congressional studios by the representatives' own staff and paid for out of campaign or party funds. Members like to tape themselves at committee meetings asking questions or being referred to as "Mr. (or Madam) Chairman" (many members chair at least a subcommittee). The tape then is edited to a thirty-second sound bite and sent to local television stations. Often stations run these productions as news features without telling their viewers that they are essentially self-promotion pieces prepared by the members. Congressional staffers also write press releases about accomplishments of their bosses and fax them to local newspapers, which often print them as written.

Fundraising

Media access enhances another advantage of incumbency—the opportunity to raise funds from the hundreds of political action committees (PACs) that populate Washington. Eager to gain access to members of Congress, PACs make fundraising much easier for incumbents than challengers, as we pointed out in Chapter 9.

Committee assignments are also extremely important in fundraising. If a member wins a seat on one of the powerful "juice" committees—one that considers legislation important to big money interests—the chances of attracting large campaign donations are greatly increased.

Pork Barrel Funding

Incumbents can gain the attention of or curry favor with constituents by obtaining funds for special projects, new programs, buildings, or other public works that bring jobs, benefits, and business to their districts or states. Such benefits are sometimes defined as "federal spending with a ZIP code attached"[27] but are best known as **pork barrel** projects. A pork feature of virtually every annual budget is money for yet another bomber, fighter plane, weapon, or military construction project the Pentagon has not requested. Universities are also perennial winners in the pork sweepstakes; in 2001, representatives whose districts include a college or university obtained almost $1.7 billion in funding for campus projects.[28]

Citizens Against Government Waste (CAGW), which publishes an annual "Pig Book" and gives an "oinker of the month" award, estimated that about $30 billion was spent on pork in the 2004 election year.[29] Even after tax cuts, the recession, and the cost of the war on terrorism produced federal budget deficits of

Although most experts believe that our largest cities are the most likely targets of terrorism, pork barrel politics has spread homeland security funds to every congressional district. Here firefighters don hazardous materials suits to protect against a chemical attack in Casper, Wyoming.

historic levels, Congress still approved well over ten thousand pork barrel projects, including $200,000 for recreation improvements in North Pole, Alaska, and $100,000 for the renovation of a Coca-Cola building in Georgia.[30] A last-minute addition to the bill that gave a tax break to native Alaskan whalers led some lawmakers to call the bill "a study in grease, pork and blubber."[31] This is why CAGW's spending alert system (which mimics Homeland Security's color-coded graph) registers "low" only when Congress is in recess.

Because members consider pork barrel projects crucial to their reelection chances, there is little support in Congress for eliminating projects most know to be unwise or wasteful. David Stockman, director of the Office of Management and Budget during the Reagan administration, observed, "There's no such thing as a fiscal conservative when it comes to his district."[32] Liberals and conservatives, Democrats and Republicans, protect these kinds of projects. Former Senator Alfonse D'Amato (R-N.Y.), who identified himself as a fiscal conservative, was called "Senator Pothole" for his ability to win highway and transportation projects for New York. And the biggest pork producers of all—not surprisingly—are the most senior and most powerful members of budget and appropriations committees.

How Congress Is Organized

An institution with 535 voting members that must make thousands of policy decisions every year without benefit of a unified leadership is an institution not likely to work quickly or efficiently. Like all organizations, legislatures need some structure to be able to accomplish their purposes. Congress does have both a leadership system and a committee structure, but each is organized along party lines. Alongside this partisan organization exist many other groups—caucuses, coalitions, work and study groups, and task forces—whose membership cuts across party lines or reflects the division of interests within party caucuses. Some of this micro-organizing is a means of bypassing the committee system that dominates Congress's legislative and oversight functions.

The Evolution of Congressional Organization

The Constitution calls for the members of the House of Representatives to select a **speaker of the House** to act as its presiding officer and for the vice president of the United States to serve as president (or presiding officer) of the Senate. But the Constitution does not say any-

Vitriolic exchanges are not a new phenomenon in Congress. Shown here is a fight in the House of Representatives in 1798. After Rep. Matthew Lyon (Vt.) spit on Rep. Roger Griswold (Conn.) and the House refused to expel Lyon, Griswold attacked Lyon with a cane. Lyon defended himself with fire tongs as other members of Congress looked on—with some amusement, it seems.

thing about the powers of these officials, nor does it require any further internal organization. So little about the speaker is specified in the Constitution that it is not even required that he be a member of the House.

The first House, meeting in New York in 1789, had slow and cumbersome procedures. For its first several sessions, Congress's legislative work was accomplished by appointing ad hoc committees. By the Third Congress, there were about 350 committees, and the system had become too unwieldy. Soon permanent committees were created, each with continuing responsibilities in one area, such as taxes or trade.[33]

As parties developed, the selection of the speaker became a partisan matter, and the speaker became as much a party leader as a legislative manager. The seventh Speaker, Henry Clay (Whig-Ky.), who served ten of the years between 1811 and 1825, transformed the speakership from a ceremonial office to one of real leadership. To maintain party loyalty and discipline, he used his powers to appoint committee members and chairs. Under Clay's leadership, the House was the dominant branch, but its influence declined when it, like the rest of government, could not cope with the divisiveness of the slavery issue. By 1856, it took 133 ballots to elect a speaker. Many physical fights broke out on the House floor; duels were held outside.[34]

The Senate, a smaller body than the House, was less tangled in procedures, less rulebound, and more effective in its operation. Its influence rose as visitors packed the Senate gallery to hear the great debates over slavery waged by Daniel Webster (Mass.), John C. Calhoun (S.C.), and Clay (who had moved from the House). During this era, senators were elected by state legislatures, not directly by the people. Thus they had strong local party ties and often used their influence to get presidential appointments for home state party members. But the Senate, too, became ineffective as the nation moved toward civil war. Senators carried arms to protect themselves as debates over slavery turned to violence.

After the Civil War, with the presidency weakened by the impeachment of Andrew Johnson, strong party leadership reemerged in the House, and a period of congressional government began. Speaker Thomas Reed (R-Me.), nicknamed "The Czar" by his colleagues, assumed the authority to name members and chairs of committees and to chair the **Rules Committee,** which decided which bills were to come to the floor for debate. A major consequence of the speaker's extensive powers was increased party discipline. Members who voted against their party might be punished by a loss of committee assignments or chairmanships.

At the same time, both the House and the Senate became more professional. The emergence of national problems and an aggressive Congress made a congressional career more prestigious. Prior to the Civil War, membership turnover was high; members of the House served an average of only one term, senators, only four years. After the war, the strengthening of parties and the growth of the one-party South, where Democrats controlled virtually all elective offices, made reelection easier, thus offering the possibility of a congressional career.

This desire for permanent careers in the House produced an interest in reform. Members wanted a chance at choice committee seats and did not want to be controlled by the speaker. Resistance against the dictatorial practices of Reed and his successor, Joseph Cannon (R-Ill.), grew. Cannon, more conservative than many of his fellow Republicans, used his powers to block legislation he disliked, to punish those who opposed him, and even to refuse to recognize members who wished to speak. In 1910, there was a revolt against "Cannonism," which had become a synonym for the arbitrary wielding of the speaker's powers.

The membership voted to remove the speaker from the Rules Committee and to strip him of his authority to appoint committees and their chairs. The revolt weakened party influence. Party discipline could no longer be maintained by the speaker's punishment of members through loss of committee assignments. And it gave committees and their chairs a great deal of independence from leadership influence.

The Senate also was undergoing a major reform. As part of the Progressive movement, pressure began to build for the direct popular election of senators. The election of senators by state legislatures had made many senators pawns of special interests—the big monopolistic corporations (called "trusts") and railroads. In a day when millionaires were not as common as now, the Senate was referred to as the "Millionaires' Club."

Not surprisingly, the Senate first refused to consider a constitutional amendment providing for its direct election, although in some states popular balloting on senatorial candidates took place anyway. Finally, under the threat of a call for a constitutional convention, which many members of Congress feared might lead to other changes in the Constitution, a direct-election amendment was passed in the House and Senate in 1912 and ratified by the states a year later.

These reforms of the early twentieth century dispersed power in both the House and the Senate and weakened leadership. House members no longer feared the kind of retribution levied by Speaker Cannon on members who deviated from party positions. In the Senate, popular elections made senators responsive to the diverse interests of the electorate rather than to party leaders.

Contemporary Leadership Positions

The modern leadership of Congress cannot be understood from reading the Constitution. Not only is the speaker now a party leader as well as the House leader, but none of the secondary leadership positions in the House and none of the current top posts in the Senate are provided for in Article I. This is because they came into being with political parties, and the Founders did not anticipate parties or take them into account. There were no party organizations in Congress when it first met.

Speaker of the House

The leaders in each party are selected by its party caucus, all of its members meeting (sitting in caucus) to conduct party business. **Party caucus** refers both to party meetings and to the party members collectively. The House Republican Caucus, for example, consists of all Republicans serving in the House, and the Democratic Caucus consists of all Democratic members, plus the lone Independent, who chooses to caucus with them. The full House must vote on the speaker, of course, but it is a straight party line vote, so the real selection is made in the majority party's caucus. The speaker is typically someone who has served in the House a long time and is usually a skilled parliamentarian and an ideological moderate. The institutional task of the speaker is to act as presiding officer and to see that legislation moves through the House. He (so far all speakers have been men) is also second in line to succeed to the presidency, after the vice president. The speaker's partisan task is to secure the passage of measures preferred by his party. By tradition, the speaker does not cast a vote on most bills before the House, participating only on "symbolic or party-defining issues."[35]

Trying to win partisan support is often difficult, but the speaker has some rewards and punishments to dispense for loyalty and disloyalty. He influences committee assignments, which committees will be given jurisdiction over complex bills, what bills will come to the House floor for a vote, and how his party's congressional campaign funds are allocated. He also decides who will be recognized to speak on the floor of the House and whether motions are relevant. He has the authority to appoint members to conference and select committees, and he controls some material benefits, such as the assignment of extra office space. He also has the power to name the chair of the Rules Committee and all of his party's members on the committee. Despite these formal powers, the speaker must be persuasive to be effective.

In modern times, the only speaker to attempt the level of control of the strong speakers Reed and Cannon was Newt Gingrich (R-Ga.), elected speaker in 1995. Gingrich had been the intellectual and tactical leader of

House Majority Leader, Tom Delay of Texas, exerts control over his Republican members and the House's agenda.

AP/ Wide World Photos

conservative House Republicans. Although a sixteen-year veteran of the House, his only formal prior leadership service had been as a whip; he had never had the chance to chair a committee or even a subcommittee because the Republicans were in the minority during his prespeaker years. Like other speakers who were too controlling, Gingrich met with rebellion in his own party and had to fight back a challenge to his leadership in his third year. Gingrich's demands for party discipline in support of a national legislative program (the so-called Contract with America) left many members with too little flexibility to respond to their constituencies and risked their chances for reelection. This is one reason that an ideological moderate with a conciliatory manner is often sought for the speaker's position.

Dennis Hastert (R-Ill.), Gingrich's successor in 1999, came to the leadership more in the mold of a traditional speaker. He was from the mainstream of the party and a mediator and persuader rather than the kind of agenda-driven leader who uses a heavy hand to enforce party discipline. In his first year, Hastert had only a five-vote margin to work with, the smallest majority in fifty years. He said then that his approach to the speakership was to "do things in regular order" and "not to throw his weight around." His low-key approach had its disadvantages with the public. After several years on the job, few people knew anything about him, and those who did gave him lower approval ratings than they gave House Republicans.[36] This was not so important because a speaker does not need public approval to be successful; he needs to have good working relationships with his colleagues so that he can see his party's bills through to passage. However, after the Republicans won the White House and regained control of the Senate in the 2000 elections, Hastert became a much more forceful leader.

Party Leadership Positions

The party leadership in the House includes a majority leader, a minority leader, and majority and minority whips. The **majority leader** is second in command to the speaker, and the **minority leader** is, as the name suggests, the leader of the minority party. **Whips** originated in the British House of Commons, where they were named after the "whipper in," the rider who keeps the hounds together in a fox hunt. This aptly describes the whips' role in Congress. Party whips try to maintain contact with party members, determine which way they are leaning on votes, and attempt to gain their support. Assisting the majority and minority whips are a number of deputy and assistant whips who keep tabs on their assigned state delegations.

Party organization in the House also includes committees that assign party members to standing committees, discuss policy issues, plan legislative and campaign strategies, and allocate funds to party members running for reelection.

Senate Leadership

The Senate has no leader comparable to the speaker of the House. The vice president of the United States is formally the presiding officer but in reality attends infrequently and has relatively little power. Richard Cheney, however, has been an active presence on Capitol Hill during his tenure as vice president. When sitting as Senate president, the vice president is allowed to cast the tie-breaking vote in those rare instances when the Senate is evenly split. The Senate has an elected president pro tempore, by tradition the senior member of the majority party. It is an honorific post with few duties except to preside over the Senate in the absence of the vice president. In practice, during the conduct of routine day-to-day business, presiding duties are divided among junior senators. This releases the senior member from boring work while giving the Senate's newest members a chance to learn the rules and procedures.

The position of Senate majority leader was not created until 1911 and has often been held by individuals of no particular distinction in their parties. The office has none of the speakership's potential for control of chamber proceedings. A congressional watcher once said the majority leader "is often more a coat-check attendant than a maitre d' or chef."[37] The instances of powerful majority leaders are few, the most notable being Lyndon Johnson (D-Tex.). He assumed office at a time when the Democrats had a slim hold on the Senate, giving him an opportunity to exercise his extraordinary

As Senate majority leader, Lyndon Johnson (left), shown here with Sen. Theodore Green (D-R.I.), "used physical persuasion in addition to intellectual and moral appeals. He was hard on other people's coat lapels." If the man he was trying to persuade was shorter than Johnson, "he was inclined to move up close and lean over the subject of his persuasive efforts." When dealing with a taller man, Johnson "would come at him from below, somewhat like a badger." Quotes are from Eugene McCarthy, Up 'til Now *(New York: Harcourt, 1987).*

powers of personal persuasion to keep party members in line on key votes. Johnson's reputation was made through a combination of personality and mastery of the legislative process (he had been an aide to the House speaker and served in the House before election to the Senate). There is nothing inherent in the office to give a majority leader the power Johnson had, and no one has had it since.

The Senate majority leader is a spokesperson for his party's legislative agenda and is supposed to help line up members' votes on key issues. But procedurally, the Senate is a free-for-all compared to the House, with "every man and woman for him- or herself."[38] Unlike the speaker, the majority leader cannot control the terms under which a bill is considered on the floor, since rules are assigned by unanimous consent in the Senate, and he has little power to stop a filibuster—endless talk by a member in an attempt to block legislation. This means that a majority leader needs to do much more than keep his own party in line to keep legislation moving through the Senate.

The leader can influence the general atmosphere of deliberation in the Senate by adopting an approach to working with the minority party that is either conciliatory or partisan. When Robert Dole left the Senate to run for president in 1996, Republicans selected Trent Lott (R-Miss.) to replace him as majority leader. In con-

trast to Dole, who worked very much in the conciliatory, clubby style common to the Senate, Lott chose a rather aggressively partisan approach closer to the leadership style of Newt Gingrich, who was then House speaker. But Lott's partisanship was less strident because Gingrich's style would never be accepted in the more egalitarian atmosphere of the Senate. Lott's successor, Bill Frist (R-Tenn.), was a heart surgeon with little political experience and a less combative style. But he was a close ally of George W. Bush and, like Speaker Hastert, became much more partisan in style under pressure from the administration to maintain party discipline on key votes.

The Senate minority leader's job is similar to that of the majority leader in that its effectiveness depends on a limited package of incentives and procedural ploys to enforce party discipline. As minority leader, Tom Daschle (D-S.D.), who had served as Senate majority leader before Frist, had a less aggressively partisan or confrontational style in his dealings with the press and the public but was no less partisan behind the scenes. But Daschle's leadership was complicated by his home base being a heavily Republican state and he was defeated in 2004. His successor, Harry Reid (D-Nev.,) is also from a largely Republican state and may face the same limitations in speaking out for an increasingly liberal Democratic membership for fear of endangering his own reelection.

Both parties also elect assistant floor leaders and whips to help maintain party discipline. These are important, if not essential, positions for working one's way into the top leadership in both the House and the Senate.

Committees

Much of the work of Congress is done in committees. Observers of American politics take this for granted, yet the power of legislative committees is rare among Western democracies. In Britain, for example, committees cannot offer amendments that change the substance of a bill. In our Congress, the substance of a bill can be changed in committee even after its passage in both chambers.

The division of labor provided by committees and subcommittees enables Congress to consider a vast number of bills each year. If every member had to review every measure in detail, it would be impossible to deal with the current workload. Instead, most bills are killed in committee, leaving many fewer for each member to evaluate before a floor vote. Committees also help members develop specializations. Members who remain on the same committee for some time gain expertise and are less dependent on professional staff and executive agencies for background information.

Standing Committees

Today there are nineteen **standing committees** in the House and sixteen in the Senate. Each deals with a different subject matter, such as finance or education or agriculture. Each has a number of subcommittees, totaling seventy-five in the House and sixty-eight in the Senate.[39] Nearly all legislation introduced in Congress is referred to a standing committee and then to a subcommittee. Subcommittees may hold public hearings to give interested parties a chance to speak for or against a bill. They also hold **markup** sessions to provide an opportunity for the committee to rewrite the bill. Following markup, the bill is sent to the full committee, which may also hold hearings. If approved there, it goes to the full House or Senate.

The number of seats on any committee can change from one session to another as party caucuses try to satisfy as many of their members' preferences as possible. Standing committees vary in size from nine to seventy-five members in the House and from twelve to twenty-eight in the Senate. Party ratios—the number of Democrats relative to Republicans on each committee—are determined by the majority party in the House and negotiated by the leadership of both parties in the Senate. The ratios are generally set in rough proportion to party membership in the particular chamber, but the majority party gives itself a disproportionate number of seats on several key committees to ensure control.

When the Senate was evenly divided at 50–50 in the early months after the 2000 election, the negotiations were particularly hard fought, with Republicans arguing that Vice President Cheney's role as presiding officer and his ability to cast a tie-breaking vote gave them a *de facto* majority and entitled them to chair all committees. When Senator James Jeffords (I-Vt.) left the Republican Party to become an Independent and vote with the Democrats, the Democrats gained a majority, the chairs were turned over to Democrats, and the ratio of seats on all committees were renegotiated. This was done all over again when the Republicans regained the majority in 2003.

Committee Membership

Committees are essential not only to the legislative process but also for building a power base within Congress, attracting campaign donors, gaining the influence and name recognition needed for reelection, and perhaps even higher office. New members and members seeking committee changes express their preferences to their party's selection committee. The party tries to accommodate members' requests for assignments that will be most beneficial to their constituencies, but there is some self-selection by seniority. Historically, junior members did not ask for the most prestigious posts, but this tradition has broken down as freshmen have become bolder in their requests and even receive instruction in how to get the assignments they want. And if there are freshmen members whose reelection races are likely to be tough or whom the party leadership believes have the potential to be future leaders, those members will likely be given helpful committee assignments. For example, Barack Obama, thought to be a future Democratic star, was given a position on the influential Foreign Relations Committee.

The committees dealing with appropriations, taxes, and finance are always sought after because having a say in the allocation of money and how the tax burden falls on individuals and businesses gives members power and enhances their ability to help their home district. These are sometime called "juice committees" because of the advantage they give members in squeezing interested parties for campaign contributions. Most members also want committee assignments that let them tell constituents they are working on problems of the district. Members from rural districts, for example, seek seats on the agriculture committees.

The practice of filling committees with representatives whose districts have an especially strong economic interest in its work makes committees rather parochial in their outlook. It also encourages costly and wasteful legislation; if committee members' constituents benefit from programs under their jurisdiction, committee members have no incentive to eliminate them or pare them back. This is one of the biggest weaknesses in the committee system.[40]

Committees are also often filled with members who have financial interests in the businesses they make policies for. Most members who sit on the banking committees own bank stock, many on agriculture committees own agribusiness stock, and those on the armed services committees hold stock in defense industries.[41] Phil Gramm, the ranking Republican on the Senate Banking Committee and instrumental in deregulating the banking industry in the 1990s, gave up his Senate seat in 2003 to become an investment banker.

Media coverage is another criterion important in deciding committee preference. The work of some committees is more likely to be covered by television. Committees scrambled to hold attention-getting hearings on the new Department of Homeland Security and corporate fraud in 2002 and on 9/11 failures and the reorganization of intelligence agencies in 2004. Getting on the right committee is important to those who want to become nationally known. When a journalist once asked Senator Joseph Biden (D-Del.) why he was so newsworthy, Biden replied, "It's the committees, of course." Biden had served on the three committees with the greatest media exposure.

Committee Chairs

The chair is usually the most influential member of a committee. Chairs have the authority to call meetings, set agendas, and control committee staff and funds. In addition, chairs have strong substantive knowledge of the matters that come before their committees, and this, too, is a source of influence.

Historically, the member of the majority party with the longest service on a committee became its chair by the so-called **seniority rule.** The rule was adopted to protect committee members from powerful speakers of the House, who often used their authority to award committee chairs to friends and allies. Under the iron-clad seniority rule, chairs may have been senile, alcoholic, or personally disliked by every member of the committee, but if they had served the longest and their party had a majority in the House, they became chairs.

Many members believed the custom of seniority led to chairs who were dictatorial and out of step with the rest of their party. In response to those complaints, in the early 1970s both parties agreed that the seniority rule no longer had to be followed. Since then, the Committee on Committees in the Republican caucus and the Steering and Policy Committee in the Democratic caucus have recommended chairs in addition to assigning committee seats. All members of each party caucus vote on these recommendations by secret ballot, although in some cases the result is a foregone conclusion. In the House, the speaker has power to name members to the Rules Committee and to appoint or recommend

the chairs of the most powerful committees. Speaker Hastert, after initial reluctance, now weighs in on who should serve as chair, just as Newt Gingrich did.

Some members prefer this method because they believe it can prevent potentially damaging intraparty fights over who will chair important committees, just as the seniority principle did. At the same time, it reduces the likelihood of producing the kind of autocratic chairs who were common under the seniority rule.

The end of the automatic seniority rule also brought a change in the behavior of senior members. Before 1975, committee chairs were less supportive of their party than other party members in roll-call votes.[42] They could go their own way with impunity because their powerful positions were guaranteed. Since 1975, committee chairs have been much more likely than other members to vote with their party. They have an incentive to be party loyalists if they want to keep their jobs. The same pattern holds true of those who are second, third, and fourth in seniority on each committee. Senior party members are now much less likely to deviate from their party's position. In that sense, the reforms have strengthened party influence in Congress. At the same time, it has led to a greater concentration of power as it has gravitated away from committees and to the leadership.

Subcommittees

Each standing committee is divided into subcommittees with jurisdiction over part of the committee's area of responsibility. The House International Relations Committee, for example, has six subcommittees—one each for the geographic areas of Africa, East Asia and the Pacific, the Western Hemisphere, the Middle East and South Asia, and Europe, and the sixth for international operations (trade) and human rights.

In the days of the seniority rule, standing committee chairs chose the subcommittee chairs and controlled subcommittees' jurisdiction, budget, and staff. Since 1974, each House subcommittee operates semi-independently of the parent committee. Similar changes took place in the Senate.

These reforms, sometimes called the "subcommittee bill of rights," allowed more members, especially newer members, to share in important decisions. In this way, they made Congress more democratic. But by diffusing power, they also made it less efficient because the very number of subcommittees contributed to government gridlock. Complex legislation might be sent to several subcommittees, each with its own interests and jurisdiction. For example, seven different House committees managed the 1990 clean air bill. When the House had to meet in conference with the Senate to work out a unified version, the House ended up sending 140 members.[43]

Under the Republican majority in the House, standing committee chairs reasserted control over their subcommittees. In 1999, new rules were adopted to streamline the legislative process and reduce the number of subcommittees. All but a few House committees were limited to five subcommittees (excluding oversight), and House members were permitted to serve on no more than four subcommittees. No restrictions were placed on the number of subcommittees in the Senate, but senators are not supposed to sit on more than five.[44] These reforms have not ended the problem of overlapping jurisdictions. When President George W. Bush proposed establishing the cabinet-level Department of Homeland Security, for example, twelve House committees were involved in marking up the bill.

One of the most significant rule changes under the Republican majority was the three-term limit on service as a committee chair. Opponents argue that term limits punish experience and weaken oversight as chairs are forced out just when they have become familiar with the operations of the agencies they oversee.[45] An attempt to repeal term limits for chairs was defeated in 2001, but each member is now allowed to serve six years as ranking member in addition to three terms as chair.

Select and Special Committees

There are a few other types of congressional committees. *Select* or *special committees* are typically organized on a temporary basis to investigate a specific problem or to hold hearings and issue a report on special problems that arise, such as Watergate or intelligence agency failures prior to 9/11. These committees are disbanded when their work is completed. The exceptions are the House and the Senate Select Committees on Intelligence and the Senate Select Committee on Ethics, which are in effect permanent committees. In 2003, the House added the Select Committee on Homeland Security.

Other Committees

Joint committees include members from both houses, with the chair alternating between a House and Senate member. There are four permanent joint committees, two of which study budgetary and tax policy. The other two administer institutions affiliated with Congress, such as the Library of Congress.

The most notable committees with joint membership are the conference committees appointed whenever the Senate and the House pass different versions of the same bill. Members from the committees that managed the bill in their respective chambers work out a single version for the full membership to vote on. Conference committees are dissolved after the compromise version is agreed on. Their work is discussed in greater detail in the section on lawmaking.

Task Forces

The traffic jams and turf wars surrounding much committee work have led members of Congress with strong interests in particular areas to look for ways to bypass the committee structure. This is a major reason for the use of a task force or ad hoc committee to study major issues and draft legislation.[46] Task forces have existed in the House for decades, used by Democratic and Republican leaders alike, usually to get around foot-dragging committees. Currently, the House has a dozen task forces, about half working on issues as important as Medicare, AIDS, and drug policy.

Task forces achieved their greatest visibility when Gingrich was speaker, when they became a vehicle for his "adhocracy" approach of aggressively pursuing a legislative agenda and moving it through the legislative process as fast as possible. To do that, the speaker sometimes bypassed committees, handpicking members for a task force to draft bills such as a Republican version of Medicare reform. Democrats used the same strategy to bypass Ways and Means to write a welfare reform bill. But the most significant contribution of the task force has been writing bills that offer an alternative to what the relevant standing committees are likely to produce and doing it more quickly.

The use of a task force does have some advantages. It can overcome the paralysis that results from the divided partisan control of Congress and the presidency. Direct negotiations between the White House and congressional leaders can sometimes break long-standing deadlocks. On the other hand, task forces bypass mechanisms for accountability to the public and to most rank-and-file members. Bills are written without formal hearings or the opportunity to point out any potential pitfalls and problems of the legislation. Rank-and-file members often face having to vote on a huge package of legislation about which they know only what they read in the newspaper.

This is happening increasingly. In late 2004, the House was embarrassed when it passed an appropriation bill that few had read. Someone had stuck in a provision allowing an individual's tax return to be viewed by members of Congress. A staff member confessed to adding it, and red-faced members removed it.

The general impact of task forces under Gingrich was to weaken the power of standing committees and their chairs. However, with Hastert as speaker, committee chairs receive much more deference, and task forces have declined in importance.

Staff and Support Agencies

Congress encompasses not only elected representatives but also a staff of more than twenty thousand, not including individuals employed in support positions such as security and maintenance. The cost of running Congress exceeds $4 billion if the costs of affiliated agencies such as the Library of Congress are included.[47] As large as this may seem, staff size has been falling since the early

The airplane that passengers forced hijackers to crash in the Pennsylvania countryside on September 11, 2001, was believed headed to Washington to slam into either the White House or the Capitol building. The White House is protected against such attacks in ways the Capitol is not. Safeguards include antiaircraft artillery on the White House roof and bunkers nearby for speedy evacuation. In addition, since the Cold War, drills have been conducted for loading the president and designated key officials onto planes and keeping them aloft during an attack. And if all this fails, the Constitution provides a line of succession to the presidency and vice presidency (see Chapter 11).

In the early weeks after 9/11, the White House assembled a shadow government at a secret location outside Washington. These one hundred or so officials, including Vice President Dick Cheney, were to provide continuity in government in the event that high-level executive branch officials were killed in a subsequent attack on Washington.[1]

No similar provisions were made for Congress, even though it is legally the heart of representative government and even though the Capitol building, with its large cupola and fewer fortifications, has always been more vulnerable than the White House. But no one wants the seat of a popularly elected government to look like an armed camp. Historically, the main arrangement for the physical safety of members of Congress during an enemy attack has been their evacuation from Washington to a bunker in the hills of West Virginia.

What would have happened if the plane had hit the Capitol and killed or maimed dozens or even a few hundred members of Congress? While Congress was beginning to grapple with that possibility, it faced a variation on the dilemma when anthrax spores sent through the mail contaminated its offices. Speaker Dennis Hastert (R-Ill.) decided to shut down the House, the first closure in its history. Senate Majority Leader Tom Daschle (D-S.D.) kept the Senate in operation, but members had to evacuate much of their meeting space while the areas were checked for anthrax exposure and decontaminated where necessary.

In a time of national emergency, continuity in leadership is essential both to respond to the crisis and to prevent chaos. Who would make decisions on measures necessary to respond to and recover from a major terrorist attack? In the first nine months after 9/11, for example,

Susana Raab Photography

When anthrax contaminated House offices, Gary Ackerman (D-N.Y.) set up an office outside.

Congress passed a great deal of legislation providing funds for disaster relief, or-

1990s, when Democrats made a 10 percent reduction. Much larger reductions were made in 1995 when Republicans assumed control. Still, Congress hires far more staff than any other legislative body.

Today the committee staff alone are equal in number to the entire congressional staff in 1947. But Congress cannot serve its proper role as a check on the executive branch if it does not have its own information base. To this end, staff in support agencies carry out various research functions. The Government Accountability Office (GAO) checks on the efficiency and effectiveness of executive agencies, the Congressional Re-

search Service conducts studies of public issues and does specific research at the request of members, the Office of Technology Assessment provides long-range analyses of the effects of new and existing technology, and the Congressional Budget Office provides the expertise and support for Congress's budgeting job.

To research difficult problems, members can call on the seven hundred full-time congressional research staffers in the Library of Congress. These researchers have issue specializations and contacts with experts in the academic world, in all the relevant federal agencies, and with the interest groups that lobby on behalf of

dering new security measures in mass transport and public facilities, authorizing the manufacture and stockpiling of antidotes in the event of a bioterrorism attack, and appropriating money for recruiting and training special personnel and the acquisition of new weapons systems. Congress also had to conduct normal daily business. Having a functioning government visibly carrying out day-to-day business as well as taking necessary defense measures is essential for maintaining public order and social stability in times of crisis. To plan for such emergencies, both the House and the Senate established Continuity Committees.

The committees dealt with such areas of legal ambiguity as how and where a dislocated Congress would conduct its business. The Constitution stipulates that neither chamber of Congress can meet away from its usual place of business unless it is approved by the other chamber. This may be a minor technicality in an emergency, but the reality is that Congress had no fixed backup office or assembly space. One is now under construction.

Another legal uncertainty was whether a regrouped Congress could conduct official business if it did not meet the constitutional standard for a quorum. A legal quorum has come to be defined as half of the living membership, but if more than half of Congress were incapacitated but not dead, would any action Congress took be legal?[2] And how would the dead be replaced? The Constitution allows governors to appoint temporary successors to Senate seats, but House members who have died can be replaced only by special elections.

It took two and a half years after 9/11 for legislation on replacement of House members to reach a floor vote. The new law sets a forty-five-day limit for special elections to fill House seats whenever more than one hundred are declared vacant by the speaker.[3] Members resisted the call for speedier replacement by appointment on the grounds that this would subvert the Founders' intention that one chamber was to be "the people's house." In any case, replacement by appointment rather than election could not be done by simple law; it would require amending the Constitution.

In addition to filling in the legal loopholes, Congress dealt with some of the practical problems as well, such as how the two chambers would stay in communication should an evacuation of the Capitol or the city occur. Evacuation drills and simulation exercises were planned to prepare for quick and orderly departure. All senators were given personal digital assistants (PDAs) and had their whip pagers—the devices that call them to the floor when a vote is pending—connected to a police notification system. Key congressional staff have been designated for evacuation, too, and provided with "fly-away" kits with all the materials and equipment needed to conduct legislative business. In addition, provisions were made to include members of the press in the evacuation and perhaps even a mobile recording studio. The secretary of the Senate said, "The press has got to be there because the American people need to know that their government is functioning."[4]

1. A comprehensive source for reviewing congressional proceedings on these issues is the "Continuity of Congress" site created by the American Enterprise Institute at www .aeipoliticalcorner.org/continuity.htm. It includes the texts of and hearings on proposed constitutional amendments and new legislation, as well as links to dozens of newspaper and journal articles on the subject.
2. This issue is discussed by Norman Ornstein in "Preparing for the Unthinkable: Bush's 'Shadow Government' Plan Is a Start—but Only a Start," *Wall Street Journal,* March 11, 2002, and "What If Congress Were Obliterated? Good Question," *Roll Call,* October 4, 2002.
3. Susan Ferrechio, "House Rise above Discord to Pass Continuity of Congress Bill," *Congressional Quarterly Weekly Report,* April 24, 2004, 961; *Congressional Record,* April 22, 2004.
4. This quote and other material in the paragraph are drawn from Mark Preston, "Senate Plans Disaster Drill," *Roll Call,* May 16, 2002.

these issues. No member of Congress would have the time to develop this kind of expertise, yet without it, competent legislation could not be written, and Congress would not have the background it needs to challenge facts and figures presented in communications from the executive branch.

What Congress Does

The importance of Congress is reflected in the major, explicit constitutional powers the Founders gave it: to lay and collect taxes, coin money, declare war and raise and support a military, and regulate commerce with foreign governments and among the states. Essentially, most of the named powers the Constitution gives to the national government were given to Congress. (See the box "Continuity in Government" for a discussion of plans to keep Congress functioning after a terrorist attack.) These and other powers specifically mentioned in the Constitution are called the *enumerated powers* of Congress.

Congress also has *implied powers;* that is, it is permitted to make all the laws "necessary and proper" to carry out its enumerated powers. Although the Founders did not necessarily foresee it, this tremendous grant of power covers almost every conceivable area of human activity.

Lawmaking

In each congressional session in the past decade, between six thousand and nine thousand bills and resolutions have been introduced. Less than 10 percent of these measures pass, and most die in committee. Of those passed, many are noncontroversial, including the so-called "sense of the chamber" measures, such as resolutions congratulating the winners of the Super Bowl and taking note of the death of singer Ray Charles, or very specific bills such as for the naming of a federal courthouse. A number of the bills passed each year are private; they resolve an issue an individual or private party has with the government, such as citizenship status or a monetary claim. Our concern is with public bills, those that become laws affecting the general public.

Turning a bill into a law is like running an obstacle course. Because of the need to win a majority at each stage, the end result is almost always a compromise. That does not mean a compromise of all interests but only of those that manage to play a role in shaping a particular bill. The formal steps by which a bill becomes a law are important but do not reveal the bargaining and trade-offs at every step in the process. Opponents of a bill have an advantage because it is easier to defeat a bill than to pass one.

Submission and Referral

Bills may be introduced in either the House or the Senate, except for tax measures (which according to the Constitution must be initiated in the House) and appropriations bills (which by tradition are introduced in the House). This reflects the Founders' belief that the chamber directly elected by the people should control the purse strings.

Although the president initiates about half of all legislation passed, only members of Congress can introduce bills. Interest groups, constituents, or the president must find a congressional sponsor for a proposed bill.[48]

After a bill's introduction, it is referred to a standing committee by the speaker of the House or the presiding officer in the Senate. The content of the bill largely determines where it will go, although the speaker has some discretion, particularly over complex bills that cover more than one subject area. Many such bills are referred to more than one committee simultaneously.

Committee Action

Once the bill reaches a committee, it is assigned to the subcommittee that covers the appropriate subject area. One of the main functions of committees is to screen bills with little chance of passage. (If a committee kills a bill, there are procedures that members can use to try to get the bill to the floor, but these are used infrequently.) Bills receiving subcommittee approval go to full committee; hearings may be held at both levels.

Hearings on bills and the markup of bills are, unless otherwise specified, open to the public, although few people know about them or would have the time or opportunity to sit in. Consequently, lobbyists fill most of the hearing rooms. For critical meetings, lobbyists will hire messengers to stand in line for them, sometimes all night, and then pack the hearing room. Members who receive financial or other support from groups affected by the legislation often face intense and direct pressure to vote a particular way in committee. Sometimes lobbyists mob members as they leave the hearing room.

Scheduling and Rules

Once a House committee approves a bill, it is placed on one of four "calendars," depending on the subject matter of the bill. The Senate has just two calendars: one for private and public bills and another for treaties and nominations. Bills from each calendar are generally considered in the order in which they are reported from committee. In the House, the Rules Committee sets the terms of the debate over the bill by issuing a rule on it. The rule either limits or does not limit debate and determines whether amendments will be permitted. A rule forbidding amendments means that members have to vote yes or no on the bill; there is no chance to change it. If the committee refuses to issue a rule, the bill dies.

The Rules Committee is not as independent or as powerful as it once was. In earlier years, the committee was controlled by a coalition of conservative Democrats and Republicans who used the committee to block liberal legislative proposals, including, for decades, meaningful civil rights proposals. But the committee now functions as an arm of the majority leadership.[49] The speaker uses his majority to fashion rules to control and expedite floor action.

Because the Senate is a smaller body, it can operate with fewer rules and formal procedures (Table 2 summarizes House and Senate differences). It does not have a rules committee. A lot of work is accomplished through the use of privately negotiated unanimous consent agreements, which allow the Senate to dispense with standard rules and define terms for the debating and amendment of a specific bill. As the Senate's workload has increased and its sense of collegiality has decreased, it has become more difficult to get opponents to accept a unanimous consent agreement. A few senators can and do delay or kill important bills.

Debate and Vote

Debate on a bill is controlled by the bill managers, usually senior members of the committee that sent the bill to the full chamber. The opposition, too, has its managers who schedule opposition speeches. "Debates" are not a

TABLE 2	Important Differences between the House and Senate

HOUSE	SENATE
Constitutional Differences	
Must initiate revenue bills	Confirmation power over many major presidential appointments
Initiates impeachment and votes on impeachment bills	Tries impeached officials
Apportioned by population	Ratification power over treaties
	Two members from each state
Differences in Operation	
More centralized; procedures more formal:	Less centralized; procedures less formal:
Speaker's assignment of bills to committee hard to challenge	Assignment of bills to committee appealable
Rules Committee fairly powerful in controlling time and rules of and debate	No rules committee; limits on debate come through unanimous consent or cloture of filibuster
Nongermane amendments forbidden	Nongermane amendments permitted
Scheduling controlled by majority party	Schedule and rules negotiated between majority and minority leaders
More impersonal, less clubby	More personal
Power less evenly distributed	Power more evenly distributed
Members highly specialized	Members are generalists
Emphasizes tax and revenue policies	Has more foreign policy responsibilities
Changes in the Institution	
Power of key committees and the leadership increasing	Senate workload and partisanship increasing; informality breaking down
House procedures more efficient with less debate and fewer amendments	Members are becoming more specialized; debate and deliberation are less frequent
More organizing and bill writing outside committees	

series of fiery speeches of point and counterpoint. They are often boring recitations delivered to sparse audiences, some of whom are reading, conversing, or walking around. In the house after the time allotted for debate is over, usually no more than a day, the bill is reported for final action.

Without a unanimous consent agreement, there is no rule limiting debate in the Senate, and there are no restrictions on adding amendments. Opponents can add all sorts of irrelevant amendments to pending legislation. One senator held up an antibusing bill for eight months with 604 amendments.

The other major mechanism for delay in the Senate is the **filibuster.** This is a continuous speech made by one or more members to prevent the Senate from taking action on a bill. Before 1917, only unanimous consent could prevent an individual from talking. Today a **cloture** vote of three-fifths of the members closes or ends debate on an issue thirty hours after cloture is invoked. Then the measure must be brought to a vote.

Both liberals and conservatives use filibusters (as they do irrelevant amendments). The filibuster developed in the 1820s when the Senate was divided between slave and free states. Unlimited debate maintained the deadlock.[50] For over a century, the filibuster was used primarily to defeat civil rights legislation. It took a cloture vote to end seventy-three days of debate and get the 1964 Civil Rights Act to the floor for a vote.

During Bill Clinton's first year in office, Republicans

used the filibuster quite frequently to block proposals from the Democratic Senate majority. After Republicans took control of the Senate in 1995, Democrats returned the favor. Filibusters prevent domination and

Senator Strom Thurmond, Democrat of South Carolina, is congratulated by his wife after setting a record for the longest filibuster. He talked for 24 hours and 18 minutes to prevent a civil rights bill from being voted on in 1957. His effort was in vain, as the bill passed.

precipitous action by the majority. But by requiring sixty votes to end debate, they impede the majority's right to legislate and contribute to gridlock.[51]

When members finally cast their votes on major public bills, they are usually voting on the general aim of the bill without knowing its exact provisions. Rarely does any member read a bill in full. The texts of laws like the No Child Left Behind Act, the USA PATRIOT Act, NAFTA, and the prescription drug benefit for seniors, run from eight hundred to more than one thousand pages. The very complex Patriot Act, which had serious implications for civil liberties, was rushed through Congress in just a few weeks with virtually no member having read it.

When a measure passes, it is sent to the other chamber for action.

Conference Committee

The Constitution requires that the House and Senate pass an identical bill before it can become law, and since this rarely happens, the two versions must be reconciled. Sometimes the chamber that passed the bill last will simply send it to the other chamber for minor modifications. But if the differences between the two versions are not minor, a **conference committee** is set up to try to resolve them. The presiding officers of each chamber, in consultation with the chairs of the standing committees that considered the bill, choose the members of the committee. Both parties are represented, but there is neither a set number of conferees nor a rule requiring an equal number of seats for each chamber.

If the leaders of both parties are strongly committed to passing a version of a bill, they may negotiate the compromise themselves and essentially impose it on the committee. They may even negotiate the final version with the president to avoid a veto. These negotiations can also be planned by the White House with intent to limit the wiggle room party leaders have to negotiate compromises.

Conference committees, or the individuals in control of them, have tremendous latitude in how they resolve the differences between the House and Senate versions of a bill. One aide to the Clinton White House described these committees as "no-man's land" because there are no formal rules governing how they operate.[52] Sometimes a bill is substantially rewritten, and occasionally a bill is killed. It is even possible to add provisions to a bill that were not in the version passed by either chamber. The power of conference committees to alter bills after their passage is why they are sometimes called the "Third House" of Congress.[53]

Once the conference committee reaches an agreement, the bill goes back to each chamber, where its approval requires a majority vote. It cannot be amended at that point, so Congress must either "take it or leave it." In the Senate, however, any individual member can challenge a provision added in conference that was not related to the original bill. In practice, both House and Senate accept most conference reports because members of both parties in each chamber have participated in working out the compromise version. However, in the years of unified government—in Clinton's first years and under George W. Bush—minority parties often felt so blocked out of the negotiations that determined the final wording of a bill that they refused to sign on to conference committee reports.

Clearly, conference committees can be very influential in determining the final provisions in major legislation, yet the work they do happens almost completely out of public view. Knowing how to win a seat on a conference committee—that is, to participate in rewriting an important piece of legislation—is an essential skill for any legislator who wants to wield influence.

As should be clear from this overview of the complex legislation process, to be a successful member of Congress—to get bills passed or to keep them from being passed, to influence other members, or to rise to a position of leadership—a legislator must know how to use the inner workings of the legislative process. The conference committee is an important part of that process, as is the tactical use of a full range of parliamentary rules and procedures within the congressional system.

Presidential Action and Congressional Response

The president may sign a bill, in which case it becomes law. The president may veto it, in which case it returns to Congress with the president's objections. The president also may do nothing, and the bill will become law after ten days unless Congress adjourns during that period.

Most presidents have not used the veto lightly, but when they do, Congress does not usually override them. A two-thirds vote in each house is required to override a presidential veto. Congress voted to override only nine of former President Reagan's seventy-eight vetoes, only one of President George H. Bush's forty-six, and only two of Clinton's thirty-four.

Lawmaking by Committee

The division of labor provided by committees and subcommittees enables Congress to consider a vast number of bills each year. If every member had to review every measure in detail, it would be impossible to deal with the current workload. Instead, most bills are killed in committee, leaving many fewer for each member to evaluate before a floor vote. Committees also help members develop specializations. Members who remain on the same committee for some time gain expertise and are less dependent on professional staff and executive agencies for information.

But committee government also has disadvantages. By splitting off into subcommittees and developing expertise in a few areas, a House member runs the danger of being more responsive to narrow interests and constituencies and less responsive to national objectives when making national policy. Over time, members of congressional subcommittees develop close relationships with lobbyists for the interest groups and staff in executive branch agencies affected by their work. Over the years, these three groups—legislators, lobbyists, and bureaucrats, sometimes called an "iron triangle"—get to know each other, often come to like and respect one another, and seek to accommodate each other's interests. These personal relationships can result in favorable treatment of special-interest groups.

The division of authority and the specialization of individual members have often made it difficult for Congress to get things done. Most members of the majority party in the Senate and about half of those in the House chair committees or subcommittees. With their own bases of power, they have the potential to act independently from party leaders. This can make it difficult for the opposition party in Congress to mount a coherent alternative to the president and opens the possibility for members of the president's own party to block his initiatives.

Many of the reforms of the Gingrich era were aimed at stemming the flow of power to committees and their chairs and channeling it back to the leadership in hopes of ending gridlock and enforcing party government. The second Bush administration took this a step further by setting party policy and the legislative agenda in the White House and insisting that the congressional leadership enforce it. This has led to another kind of gridlock by causing Democrats and dissenting Republicans, frustrated by being left out of planning and negotiations, to resort to obstructionist tactics.

Oversight

As part of the checks-and-balances principle, it is Congress's responsibility to make sure that the bureaucracy is administering federal programs as Congress intended. This monitoring function is called **oversight** and has become more important as Congress continues to delegate authority to the executive branch. For a variety of reasons, Congress is not especially well equipped, motivated, or organized to carry out its oversight function. Nevertheless, it does have several tools for this purpose.

One tool is the Government Accountability Office (GAO), created in 1921 and known as the General Accounting Office until 2004. It functions as Congress's watchdog in oversight and is mostly concerned with making sure that money is used properly.

Another method of oversight, albeit not a very effective one, is committee hearings. Members can quiz representatives from agencies on the operation of their agencies, but often the hearings go into great detail about some particular problem of minor importance and neglect broader policy questions. Scheduling conflicts and the pressure of other business often mean that a member's attention is not focused on committee hearings. Nevertheless, officials in agencies view hearings as a possible source of embarrassment for their agency and spend a great deal of time preparing for them. This is especially true when Congress decides, often for political reasons, to seek maximum media coverage for hearings.

This attempt at publicity points to one of the problems with the use of these proceedings to carry out the oversight function: hearings are often held after oversight has failed. This was painfully clear after the corporate collapses of 2002—of Enron, Global Crossing, and World-Com, for example—when four Senate and three House committees held hearings in succession, all vying for media time. If Congress had not weakened the regulatory clout of the Securities and Exchange Commission, these scandals might not have occurred and some of the enormous costs to employees and investors might have been prevented. (See "You Are There" in Chapter 9 for an example.) Prominent members of oversight committees, such as Joseph Lieberman (D-Conn.) and Christopher Dodd (D-Conn.), who represent a state where some of the failed businesses were headquartered and who had received large campaign contributions from them, actively worked to prevent new regulations from being adopted. Occurring after the failures, the hearings were more aftersight than oversight but served as a way for Congress both to consider remedial measures and to make it seem like it was doing something about the problem.

The Army's top brass appear before the Senate's Armed Services Committee to answer questions about abuses at the Abu Ghraib prison in Baghdad.

The incentive of committee members to place constituent protection and the interests of big campaign donors above rule enforcement is one weakness of oversight. But the fragmentation of oversight responsibility is also a problem. There were at least seven Senate committees and six House committees with some oversight responsibility for the accounting and financial practices that led to so many industry bankruptcies in 2002. And many more committees were responsible for oversight of the defense and intelligence agencies whose failures were so widely publicized after 9/11 (see "You Are There" in Chapter 12).

Congress can also exercise its oversight function through informal means.[54] One way of doing this is to request reports on topics of interest to members or committees. In a given year, the executive branch might prepare five thousand reports for Congress.[55] Moreover, the chair and staff of the committee or subcommittee relevant to the agency's mission are consulted regularly by the agency. But one can question whether any serious oversight is exercised informally. There are few electoral or other incentives for members to become involved in the drudgery of wading through thousands of pages of reports or for doing a really thorough job in any area of oversight, at least until a crisis arises or public confidence in the economy or government institutions is threatened.

The primary means for congressional oversight is its control over the federal budget. Congress can cut or add to agencies' budgets and thereby punish or reward them for their performance. Members with authority over an agency's budget can use that power to get benefits for their constituents, and by going along with the members' wishes, agencies may stand a better chance of having their budget requests approved. There is an incentive in this relationship for congressional committees to exercise oversight, but increasingly it has failed to do so. It has allowed authorizing legislation for agencies as important as the Consumer Product Safety Commission, the U. S. Commission on Civil Rights, the Corporation for Public Broadcasting, and the Federal Election and Trade Commissions, among others, to expire. The agencies continue to function because Congress waives budget rules to provide annual funding for them without oversight by authorization committees.[56]

If Congress has received low marks for gridlock in legislating, it has been absent without leave in carrying out much of its oversight function. Many members of Congress have made the charge themselves, especially with respect to oversight of intelligence operations and defense policy and appropriations. In the wake of 9/11, the Bush administration encouraged Congress to neglect oversight in these areas by arguing that the president needed a free hand to wage the war on terrorism.

Senator Rick Santorum (R-Pa.) explained the weakening of oversight in the Republican-controlled Congress as a party preference: "Republicans don't enjoy oversight—not nearly as much as Democrats—and so . . . we don't do as much."[57] But Representative Henry Waxman (D-N.Y.) suggested that it might be more a matter of the kind of oversight the majority preferred. He cited House Republicans' willingness to take "more than 140 hours of testimony to investigate whether the Clinton White House misused its holiday card database but less than five hours of testimony regarding how the Bush administration treated Iraqi detainees."[58]

Budget Making

The topic of budget making may be dull, but without money, government cannot function. Real priorities are reflected not in rhetoric but in the budget. An increasingly large part of the job of Congress is to pass a budget. The Constitution gave budget powers to Congress, but in the 1920s, Congress delegated its authority to prepare the annual budget to the president (through the Office of Management and Budget, or OMB). In years when the president's party does not control Congress, the congressional majority produces its own budget, with priorities distinctly different from the president's.

Congress is aided in budget review by the Congressional Budget Office (CBO), which provides expertise to Congress on matters related to both the budget and the economy. Before the establishment of the CBO, members of Congress felt they were junior partners in budget making because they had to depend on information provided by the president, his budget advisers, and the OMB. Because the CBO is responsible to both parties in Congress, it provides a less politically biased set of forecasts about the budget than the administration or the leadership of either party would.

Characteristics of Budgeting

Congressional budgeting has two basic characteristics. First, the process is usually incremental; that is, budgets for the next year are usually slightly more than budgets for the current year. Normally, Congress does not radically reallocate money from one year to the next; members assume that agencies should get about what they received the previous year. This simplifies the work of all concerned. Agencies do not have to defend, or members scrutinize, all aspects of the budget. A second feature is that Congress tends to spend more in election years and in times of unemployment.

There are exceptions to these general rules, such as times of war or domestic crisis. The first budget submitted after 9/11, for example, requested a huge increase in defense spending. There are also instances of ideological budgeting. President Reagan's domestic budget cuts and increased military spending in 1981 were clearly an exception to incrementalism. The Gingrich Contract with America approach of cutting programs wholesale was another exception.

Authorizations and Appropriations

Each year, Congress passes a budget resolution that sets a dollar amount of spending for the fiscal year, but money is not appropriated in a single piece of legislation. Since the 1970s, the budget has been divided and reviewed as thirteen separate bills, each of which focuses on a different area of expenditure, such as defense. All budget legislation goes through a process similar to but more complicated than other bills. To grasp the complexity, we have to understand the distinction between budget authorizations and budget appropriations. **Authorizations** are acts that enable agencies and departments to operate, either by creating them or by authorizing their continuance. They also establish the guidelines under which the agencies operate. Although authorization bills might specify funding levels, they do not actually provide the funding. **Appropriations** are acts that give federal agencies the authority to spend the money allocated to them. Both authorization and appropriations bills must pass each house, and differences must be resolved in conference.

Typically, authorizations precede appropriations, although this is not always the case. Budgetary procedures are not defined in the Constitution but are determined by House and Senate rules, which can be, and often have been, changed. The standing committees that oversee the work of the agency or program being funded usually work out the authorizations. The House Interior and Insular Affairs Committee and the Senate Energy and National Resources Committee, for example, review the authorization of the Park Service in the Department of the Interior; the agricultural committees write authorizations for the Department of Agriculture. Close ties often exist between the agency being reviewed and the authorizing committee, which can cause proposed funding levels to be set without consideration of the overall demand on federal revenues. But the real power to limit spending rests with the House and Senate Appropriations Committees.

Each of the two Appropriations Committees has thirteen subcommittees corresponding to the thirteen functional areas into which budget allocations are divided. The Appropriations Committee assigns a spending limit for each area, and the relevant subcommittee then decides how to apportion it among the agencies in its jurisdiction. The power of those who chair appropriations subcommittees is suggested by their nickname, "The Cardinals." In reviewing an agency's proposed budget, the subcommittee is not bound to fund it at the level requested in the president's budget proposal or the authorization bill. Nor do a subcommittee's funding proposals have to be accepted by the whole committee.

Although appropriations subcommittees may develop close ties with the agencies they review, the committee as a whole does not, and it may not be as generous as its subcommittees. In the bills it sends to the floor for a vote, the Appropriations Committee can increase or cut the previous year's funding levels, or it can eliminate an agency altogether.

The House and Senate also have Budget Committees, but these are not as powerful as the Appropriations Committees. The Budget Committees have existed only since 1974 and were created to work with the CBO on big-picture issues such as economic forecasting and fiscal planning, including deficit management and controlling overall spending. The House Budget Committee prepares a budget proposal that sets out spending goals in the context of projected federal revenues. The House and Senate committees cannot enforce their guidelines, however, and spending limits are routinely violated.

During the budgetary process, committees hold hearings, but these have become a sideshow to the main event. The real decisions are made in private negotiations, and budgets are produced after months of direct negotiations among congressional leaders, their staff, administration aides, individual members, and the president. The rest of Congress is often left with a "take-it-or-leave-it" budget package laid out in the thirteen separate or several omnibus appropriations bills.

Problems with the Budget Process

Almost everyone is critical of congressional budget making. One reason is that members simply cannot agree on spending for any fiscal year; only twice since 1996 has Congress actually passed all thirteen appropriations bills.[59] Instead, under pressure as the fiscal year draws to a close, they lump spending into several omnibus bills in order to keep government operating. These cumbersome bills are difficult to decipher and make oversight by scrutiny of agency budgets very difficult.

Another problem is that Congress does not honor its own budget resolutions, which establish the amount of total spending for each fiscal year. At least ten times in the past two decades, Congress has outspent the dollar limit that it set.[60] It has also consistently violated the pay-as-you-go rule that requires all new spending to be offset by a revenue source.

Many members are troubled by the fact that for decades, Congress has been slowly ceding budget-setting power to the executive branch. White House staff typically get involved in negotiating final dollar amounts with congressional leaders, but the Bush administration took this a step further, often working out final versions of appropriations bills with the Republican leadership before conference committees ever met.

Members on the Job

This section examines how members of Congress go about the day-to-day business of legislating, budget making, oversight, and constituency service, as well as carrying out party caucus— and campaign-related activities.

Negotiating the Informal System

To be successful, representatives and senators must not only serve their constituents and get reelected but must also know how to work with their colleagues and how to maneuver within the intricate system of parliamentary rules, customs, and traditions that govern the House and Senate.

Informal Norms

First among the many lessons every new member must learn are the customary ways of interacting with colleagues both on and off the floor of Congress.[61] These **informal norms** help keep the institution running smoothly by attempting to minimize friction and allowing competition to occur within an atmosphere of civility. As in other American institutions, the norms of Congress are changing.

The Founders' velveteen breeches, frock coats, and

white wigs symbolized the drawing room gentility of their circle. It was Thomas Jefferson, the best known of the gentlemen farmers, who in 1801 wrote the foundational rules for in-chamber conduct for members of the new Congress in an effort to contain the inevitable conflict between Federalist and Anti-Federalist, abolitionist and slave owner. His notes laid the groundwork for Congress's system of informal norms.

Throughout much of the twentieth century, the most important norm was institutional loyalty, the expectation that members would respect their fellow members and Congress itself, especially their own chamber. Personal criticism of one's colleagues was to be avoided, and mutual respect was fostered by such conventions as referring to colleagues by title, such as "the distinguished senator from New York," rather than by name.

In recent years, hostility among members seems as sharp as among those delegates to the First Congress, but scholars differ on the origins of this decline in civility. Some say it dates back decades to the time Democrats had a lock on both chambers, leaving Republicans permanently aggrieved. Some say it began with Watergate—that Nixon's enemies list and Congress's impeachment hearings poisoned the atmosphere. Others tie it to the hearings on the nominations of Robert Bork and Clarence Thomas to the Supreme Court, which were notorious for their overheated exchanges and character bashing. Still others trace the decline to Newt Gingrich's tenure as party leader and speaker. He attacked his predecessor and Congress as an institution (a severe departure from the institutional-loyalty norm) and encouraged an aggressive, combative style on the floor of the House.

The growth in partisan voting, illustrated in Figure 2, gives little support to the Democratic majority or Watergate explanations, though there was a small spike in 1974, the year of those investigations, but then partisanship returned to its formerly low levels. The voting data give more support to the Bork, Thomas, and especially the Gingrich explanations, since there was some increase in partisanship in 1987, at the time of the Bork hearing; in 1992 and 1993, after the Thomas hearings; and dramatically in 1995, after Gingrich became majority leader.

It was in this climate that Republicans launched the impeachment hearings against President Clinton, leaving many Democrats wanting revenge for what they felt was an outrageous diversion of time and energy from crucial business. Under Speaker Hastert's leadership, it seemed at first that there would be a trend toward more conciliation and civility in the conduct of House business. But in 2003, the Republican leadership, reinvigorated by gains in the midterm elections and determined to tighten procedural control over the House, called in the Capitol Police to break up a meeting of Democratic members. Several months later, Hastert broke House rules by holding a vote open for three hours while he rounded up the support needed to pass a Bush administration bill.

While it is still the norm in Great Britain's House of Commons to hear members refer to one another as the

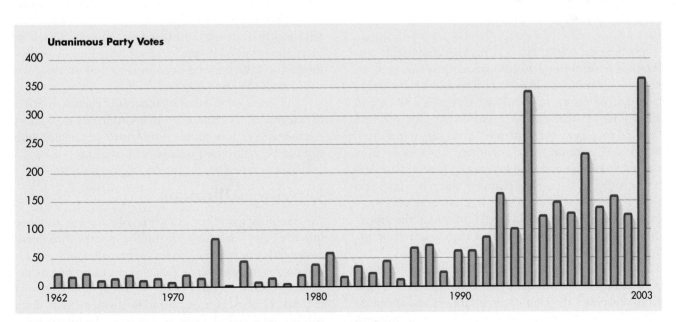

FIGURE 2 ■ Number of Unanimous Votes by Both Parties in the House and the Senate, 1962–2003 *The number of times all members of a party vote in unison on a bill or resolution is on the rise. It is a sign of hardened party lines and increasing partisanship.*

SOURCE: *Congressional Quarterly Weekly Review,* January 3, 2004, 15.

Cover Your Ears, Mr. Jefferson!

In the past several years, members of Congress have not tried to hide their contempt for Congress or its leaders:

"[Congress] is a sick institution, and . . . has no legitimate authority. . . . [It] does not represent the constitutional government. It is, in fact, a subversion of the process of free elections."—Newt Gingrich on the *MacNeil/Lehrer NewsHour*, 1989.[1]

"I've never seen such amateur leadership in all the time I've been in Congress, 21 years."—Senate Minority Whip Harry Reid (D-Nev.), on the Senate floor, in reference to Majority Leader Bill Frist.[2]

"If you kill my dog, I'll kill your cat."—Republican Majority Leader Tom DeLay.[3]

"I'm glad the children of America were asleep."—House Minority Leader Nancy Pelosi, speaking to the press about Speaker Hastert's late night hold of the vote on the prescription drug bill while he searched for votes.

"F—— you"—Vice President Richard Cheney to Senator Patrick Leahy (D-Vt.), on the Senate floor, 2004.

1. Richard E. Cohen, Kirk Victor, and David Bauman, "The State of Congress," *National Journal,* January 10, 2004, 86.
2. Sheryl Gay Stolberg, "The High Costs of Rising Incivility on Capitol Hill," *New York Times,* November 30, 2003, W-10.
3. Cohen, Victor, and Bauman, "State of Congress," 90.

"right honorable member" or "my right honorable colleague," never using personal names, today one is apt to hear much more informal and not particularly polite language when members of our Congress talk to and about one another and the institution. (See the box "Cover Your Ears, Mr. Jefferson!"). And even in today's House of Commons, the formal terms of address are a veneer, as Labour and Conservative members sit on opposite sides of a narrow chamber floor hooting and shouting epithets at their fellow Honourables. However, this is a long and well-loved tradition in the House of Commons and not a modern manifestation of increased hostility.

The only reassuring aspect of this intense degree of partisanship is that it is neither new nor destined to last. Congress passes through cycles of greater and lesser civility. Although they may be name calling now, they are not beating up or shooting at one another as members were in the years leading up to the Civil War. And Jefferson's ears were hardly virgin; a frequent target of gossip and character attacks, he could dish with the best and used paid agents to spread slander about his Federalist opponents.

Reciprocity

Reciprocity, or "logrolling," is summarized in the statement "You support my bill, and I'll support yours." Reciprocity helps each member get the votes needed to pass legislation favored in his or her district. The traditional way in which reciprocity worked was described by the late Sam Ervin, Democratic senator from tobacco-growing North Carolina: "I got to know Milt Young [then a senator from North Dakota] very well. And I told Milt, 'Milt, I would just like you to tell me how to vote about wheat and sugar beets and things like that, if you just help me out on tobacco.'"[62] Reciprocity is another informal norm that is disappearing. Open meetings, media scrutiny, stronger party leadership, and more partisan voting have made it more difficult for members to "go along" on bills unpopular in their constituency or with the party leadership.

Specialization

Tied to reciprocity is the norm of specialization. By specializing, a member can become an expert, and possibly influential, in a few policy areas. Given the scope of Congress's legislative authority, members cannot be knowledgeable in all areas, so House members especially specialize in subject areas important to their home districts or related to their committees. The leader of one freshmen class of legislators advised his new colleagues, "If you've got 20 things you want to do, see where everything is. You'll find that maybe 10 of those are already being worked on by people and that while you may be supportive in that role, you don't need to carry the ball. . . . If you try to take the lead on everything, you'll be wasting your time and re-creating the work that's already going on."[63]

The Senate's smaller membership cannot support this degree of specialization. In addition, some senators see themselves as potential presidential candidates who need to be well versed on a variety of issues.

Making Alliances

Any member who wants to get legislation passed, move into the party leadership, or run for higher office needs to develop a network of allies among colleagues. An increasingly common venue for cooperation among members, especially in the House, is the **special-interest caucus.** Caucuses are organized by members who share partisan, ideological, issue, regional, or identity interests to pool their strength in promoting shared interests and gaining passage of related legislation. Caucus size ranges from a handful to more than a hundred; almost every member belongs to at least one. The House and Senate have more than one hundred caucuses, some organized cross-chamber. Some caucuses have a narrow focus, such as those promoting bikes, bearings, boating, the wine industry, or wireless technology. Some are rooted in personal experience, such as the caucuses of Vietnam veterans and cancer survivors.

Among the most significant of the caucuses are those designed to pool the strength of women and minorities. They develop policy in key issue areas and serve national constituencies. The Caucus for Women's Issues, working across party, racial, and ethnic lines, has managed to recruit all but two House women to membership and many male colleagues as well. With a Republican and a Democrat serving as cochairs, the caucus is regarded as one of the most bipartisan in Congress. Its legislative agenda includes supportive measures for woman-owned businesses, pay equity, and women in the military.

The Black Caucus was organized in 1970 by thirteen House members determined to gain some clout. Today, with all forty-one black Democrats in the House and some of their white colleagues as members, the Black Caucus encompasses nearly one-fifth of the House Democratic Caucus. Hispanics, Asians, and Native Americans also have special-interest caucuses.

The Black Caucus has declined in influence because Republican majorities in Congress give Republicans control of the committees. The last year that the Democrats had a majority in the House, black members chaired 26 percent of all committees and many subcommittees too. But with a Republican majority, no African American chairs a committee because none is a Republican. They maintain their strength within the Democratic caucus, but a secondary party leadership position does not compare to the influence wielded by the chair of a key committee.

Prior to the 1995 Republican-led reforms that reduced administrative spending, the most important caucuses had their own office space and budgets. Today they are run out of members' offices and are supported by their office staff and budgets, just as the smallest of the caucuses have always had to operate.

Personal Friendships

In some cases, caucuses are the source of a House member's closest political allies. But with the exception of its Centrist Coalition, caucuses are not as important in the much smaller Senate. There, personal friendships might count for more than committee or caucus membership, and strong relationships of trust sometimes develop across party lines. John Kerry (D-Mass.) and John McCain (R-Ariz.), two decorated Vietnam War veterans, became friends while working together on veterans' issues. A more unusual example is the close friendship between the very liberal Senator Edward Kennedy (D-Mass.) and his very conservative counterpart former

Senator Orrin Hatch (R-Utah). In both houses, much of the work gets hammered out in personal conversations and exchanges away from official venues.

Political Action Committees

The most influential members of Congress now have their own PACs for raising campaign funds to disperse to colleagues. Hillary Rodham Clinton (D-N.Y.), a junior senator and former first lady, has been able to use her celebrity and connections to raise millions of dollars for her PAC, Friends of Hillary. By making donations to the reelection campaigns of colleagues, she can build a network of supporters whose chits she may later cash in when looking for a committee chair, leadership position, or a race for the presidency. Nancy Pelosi was able to beat out rivals for the Minority Leader position due in large part to her phenomenal ability to get campaign donations for colleagues. By the time she announced that she wanted the position, dozens of fellow House members were in her political debt. Tom DeLay, the very powerful House majority leader, also built his clout by dispensing funds.

Using the Media

Forty years ago, the workday routine in both House and Senate for resolving most issues involved bargaining with other members, lobbyists, and White House aides. Working privately, one-on-one in small groups, or in committees, members and staff discussed and debated issues, exchanged information, and planned strategies. Even though many issues are still resolved through these private channels, much has changed in the way Congress operates.

For today's members to further their goals, it is often as important to "go public," to reach beyond colleagues and to appeal directly to the larger public, as it is to engage in private negotiation.[64] **Going public** means taking an issue debate to the public through the media as Congress does when it televises floor debates and important hearings. The most media-oriented members of Congress are experts in providing short and interesting comments for the nightly network news, writing articles for major newspapers, and appearing on talk shows and as commentators on news programs.

In the early days of television, networks broadcast only important congressional proceedings, such as the McCarthy hearings and testimony on investigations into the Watergate scandal and the Iran-Contra affair. In 1979, after considerable controversy and anxiety, the House began televising its proceedings. Fearful of being overshadowed by the House, in 1986 the Senate followed suit. But today exposure comes daily on C-SPAN (the Cable Satellite Public Affairs Network), which is seen by more than twenty million viewers each week.

Senator Diane Feinstein (D-Cal.) holds a press conference to call attention to the assault weapons ban, which was scheduled to expire in 2004. Feinstein was supported by the San Francisco police department, whose chief is in the background. Despite her efforts to persuade the public, Congress refused to extend the ban.

AP/Wide World Photos

the evening newscasts, Minority Leader Richard Gephardt (D–Mo.) excoriated both the Republicans' bill and their parliamentary tactics.

Balancing the Work

Schedules

The typical senator sits on four standing committees and five subcommittees, while a House member averages two or three standing and several subcommittee assignments. These multiple assignments, in combination with party caucus work, fundraising, and visits to the district, mean that members have impossible schedules (see the box "A Day in the Life of a U.S. Senator" on page 348). At times, committees cannot obtain quorums because members are tied up with other obligations. Members attend meetings with legislative staff in tow to take notes and to consult with during hearings. If they cannot attend or have to leave for floor business or another meeting, a staffer is there to take notes and brief the member later.

Use of Staff

We already noted the huge staff available to members. Staffers do most of the background work on the complex foreign and domestic issues that cross the members' desks every day, aided when deep expertise is need by the CRS staff. Through their service, staffers gain a great deal of experience and the opportunity to create a network of contacts that can help them should they decide to run for Congress. Sixty-nine members of the 108th Congress were former congressional staffers, including Senator Durbin.[66]

Regular viewers watch twelve hours of programming per week, and though they are not a huge audience, nine out of ten C–SPAN viewers voted in the 2000 election.[65]

Two of the three C–SPAN advertisement-free channels are available with almost all basic cable service. Local television listings provide times for daily coverage of House and Senate floor proceedings as well as for committee hearings and other official business. In addition, C–SPAN covers members of Congress on the campaign trail, attending fundraisers, giving stump speeches, and chatting with constituents. Besides its unbroken coverage of events, what sets C–SPAN apart from commercial network coverage of Congress is that there is no intermediary between the viewers and the events and people they are watching. C–SPAN does not use reporters, so televised events are free of commentary and on-the-spot analysis.

The congressional leadership goes public, too. Leaders of both parties regularly call producers of television talk shows to suggest guests. They meet with the press and often have prepared statements. Before important congressional votes on key issues, the leadership plans letters to the editors of important newspapers and floor speeches designed for maximum television coverage. For example, when the Republican leadership refused to allow the Democrats to bring their bill providing prescription drug benefits to a vote before the 2000 election, the Democratic leadership organized a walkout of party members while the vote on the Republicans' version of the bill was taking place. Striding down the Capitol steps to a battery of cameras and just in time for

Congress and the Public

As we have noted, one of the most frustrating things about Congress for the average citizen is the "messiness" of the legislative process. Not only is the process of crafting laws incredibly complex, but it provides many places along the way where individual legislators and interest groups, often for seemingly (or truly) selfish motives, can exact concessions from the people who want to pass the bill. Add to that the partisan bickering, with Democrats picking a proposal apart simply because a Republican introduced it or vice versa, and casual observers throw up their hands in exasperation.

It seems that the more media exposure Congress gets, the less supportive the public is of its work. Now as never before, every step—or misstep—that members of Congress take is carried to every part of the nation. Or as one observer commented, "Modern Washington is wired for quadraphonic sound and widescreen video, flashed by fax, computer, 800 number, overnight poll, FedEx, grassroots mail, air shuttle and CNN to every citizen in every village on the continent and Hawaii too. A member's every twitch is blared to the world, thanks to C-SPAN, open meetings laws, financial-disclosure reports, and bloggers, and every misstep is logged in a database for the use of some future office seeker."[67]

Media attention is valuable, because we prize open government in a democracy. But too much is not so good, because in a heterogeneous society, we rely on compromise to achieve our public goals, and under the harsh glare of media, there are fewer opportunities to compromise and deliberate without fear of losing votes back home.

The public is intolerant of debate and discussion, often partisan and sometimes petty but at the same time reflecting the real divisions among the people. Of the three branches of government, the public has been least supportive of Congress, where the processes of democracy are exposed for all to see. None of this is surprising, of course, in a complex society where people and groups do have quite different interests and views of the world. Members themselves contribute to the poor image of Congress by belittling the institution and promising voters a change when they campaign for office.

For some years, the public gave its highest level of support to the Supreme Court, the institution that is most isolated from the public. Historically, little of the disagreement, negotiation, and compromise of the Court has taken place in public view. This has changed somewhat at the beginning of the twenty-first century with a deeply divided Court and its highly publicized split ruling that decided the 2000 presidential election (see Chapter 13). The Court lost ground to the president and Congress in approval ratings after 9/11 when the nation was rallying around its leaders in the war on terrorism (see Figure 3). But whereas President Bush's public approval ratings stayed high for months, those of Congress quickly plunged.

That being said, however, the public's attitudes about Congress are themselves conflicted. One famous political scientist once observed that Americans hate Congress but love their own member of Congress.[68] Two-thirds of the public approve of their own representatives, compared to just 41 percent who approve of Congress as a whole.[69]

The public thinks that most members of Congress care more about power than about the best interests of the nation, care more about special interests than the people, and lose touch with the people quickly after being elected. In early 2002, members of Congress placed sixteenth on a list of seventeen professions ranked by trust, one notch below business leaders. Only 42 percent of respondents said they trusted members of Congress to tell the truth.[70]

The public is not mistaken in its impression of a cozy relationship between Congress and special-interest lobbies. The U.S. Association of Former Members of Congress estimates that as many as 15 percent of ex-members become lobbyists after the one-year cooling-off period mandated by a 1989 ethics law. In 1999, fully 142 former members were registered lobbyists; others worked as "consultants" and were not required to register.[71] Even during the one-year period, a former member can work as a lobbyist as long as it is not on Capitol Hill. Within six months of resigning as speaker-elect of the House, Robert Livingston had signed up thirty-one clients for about $350,000 worth of business, more than double his annual salary as a representative. After one year, ex–House members have easy access to their former colleagues because they retain rights to use the dining room and gym and have floor privileges for life—although they are prohibited from lobbying on the floor. (The Senate has no such restrictions.)

Despite all this, the idea of Congress as a constitutionally mandated "people's house" is esteemed by the public. It is the people in Congress and the way Congress works that the public dislikes. But just over half of all voters turn out for congressional elections (less in years where the president is not being elected), and most members of the public are poorly informed about what Congress does. They are much more likely to know about ethics violations and sexual improprieties of members of Congress than they are about the legislation passed in any session. Thus the public evaluation of Congress as accomplishing "not much" or "nothing at

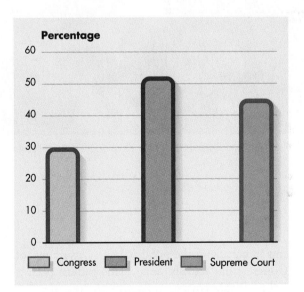

FIGURE 3 ■ Confidence in Political Institutions *Fewer Americans express "a good deal" or "a lot" of confidence in Congress than in the president or the Supreme Court.* SOURCE: Gallup Organization, poll conducted May 21–23, 2004. Sample=1002; error margin ±3.

Senator Richard Durbin is in his second term in the Senate after serving seven terms in the U.S. House and thirteen years as a legislative aide in the Illinois Senate. In the 108th Congress (2003–2004), he had the responsibility of "shaping" the weekly message for the Democractic Caucus and currently is the party whip. He sits on one of the Senate's most powerful committees, Appropriations, as well as on the Judiciary and Rules Committee. Assisting him in Washington are thirty-five staffers—legislative assistants, "legislative correspondents" who do casework, and aides assigned by the committees on which Durbin serves. As Democratic whip in the 109th Congress, he will be assigned additional staff to help with party work.

The days chronicled here show how the senator must divide his time among his legislative and budget-making responsibilities (committee and floor time), party caucus work, fundraising, and constituency service.

A Day in Washington
Tuesday, June 22, 2004

8:00 A.M.—Durbin meets with members of the Illinois congressional delegation over breakfast in the Senate dining room to discuss various state projects in appropriations bills.

9:00 A.M.—Meets with fellow members of the Democratic Senate leadership team.

9:47 A.M.—The Senate convenes. The Democratic leadership has de-

cided to press the issue of Halliburton's overbilling the U.S. government. Durbin goes to the floor where Minority Leader Tom Daschle delivers the Halliburton remarks. Later in the morning, Durbin speaks in support of an amendment to require Attorney General John Ashcroft to turn over all documents relevant to the treatment of Iraqi prisoners held at Abu Ghraib. He stays for the vote on this and other amendments.

10:00 A.M.—While he is still on the Senate floor, Durbin has a scheduled meeting of the appropriations subcommittee on the District of Columbia.

10:45 A.M.—Another appropriations subcommittee, on defense, is meeting to mark up the 2005 defense budget. Durbin's legislative assistant for appropriations attends, but the senator can attend only when he is free to leave the floor.

12:00 P.M.—Meets with Sen. Ben Nighthorse Campbell (R-Colo.) regarding markup of the 2005 legislative branch appropriations bill.

12:30 P.M.—Attends the weekly Democratic Caucus luncheon.

2:00 P.M.—Scheduled meeting of the Judiciary's Terrorism, Technology and Homeland Security Subcommittee, which is considering Patriot Act II. The subcommittee is hearing testimony on the subpoena and pre-

Senator Richard Durbin shares a meal with Illinois constituents serving with U.S. forces in Afghanistan.

© Tim Boyle/Getty Images

all" stems in part from the public's lack of awareness of what Congress has actually done. This pattern persists even with C-SPAN coverage and even though most local papers each week print a congressional scorecard with the voting records of local legislators.

Conclusion: Is Congress Responsive?

Congress is certainly responsive to individual constituents, but is it responsive to the policy demands of the national constituency? The pressures of elections and of constituency service seem to undermine Congress's

trial detention powers granted by the original USA PATRIOT Act. This is staffed by Durbin's legislative assistant for the judiciary.

2:15 P.M.—The senator slips out of his meeting to pose for the annual photo of all senators.

3:30 P.M.—With an assistant, Durbin attends a meeting of the full Appropriations Committee to mark up the 2005 defense appropriations bill.

4:30 P.M.—Meets with the chair of Dynergy, Inc., regarding the company's business operations in Illinois.

5:00 P.M.—Attends an event for the recipients of the Jefferson Awards for Public Service and gives a speech congratulating the winners.

5:30 P.M.—Meets with the director of the Centers for Disease Control and Prevention regarding the department's new goals and integrated operations.

6:30 P.M.—Attends a fundraiser for Senate Democratic Leader Tom Daschle.

7:30 P.M.—Attends a reception, dinner, and movie (*The Terminal*) hosted by the Motion Picture Association of America.

A Day in the District

Every Thursday night or Friday morning, Durbin flies to Illinois, returning to Washington on Monday afternoon. He also spends the Senate's monthly recess week in-state, so he is in Illinois nearly half the year. He keeps homes in both Chicago and Springfield, his hometown.

With nearly thirteen million people, Illinois is the fifth-largest state; it is more than four hundred miles long and economically diverse. It is also racially and ethnically diverse and one of the principal destinations for new immigrants. When in Illinois, the senator has nineteen staffers to assist him—ten in his Chicago office; seven in Springfield, the state capital; and two in Marion, in southern Illinois. As he travels around the state, he is accompanied by staff—outreach coordinators for the areas he visits and a press secretary. On this day, the senator is "downstate," but other days he might be in Chicago and its suburbs.

Thursday, July 1, 2004

8:40 A.M.—At Johnny's Steakhouse in Rock Island (on the Iowa border), Durbin discusses pending legislation in Congress of concern to the labor community with U.S. Rep. Lane Evans (D-Ill.) and Quad Cities labor leaders.

9:45 A.M.—Departs for the Rock Island Arsenal.

10:00 A.M.—Holds a news conference to announce $33 million in new federal funding for a series of projects at the Rock Island Arsenal. He tours the arsenal's new child care facility, built with federal funding.

11:15 A.M.—Flies to Quincy, about 150 miles to the south.

12:30 P.M.—Meets with Quincy's mayor, officials from Corporate Airlines, and community leaders over lunch to discuss the airline's most recent investment in the Quincy airport.

1:30 P.M.—Holds a news conference to announce that Corporate Airlines will be relocating its maintenance facility to the Quincy airport and creating new jobs.

2:30 P.M.—In downtown Quincy, the senator meets with agricultural and labor leaders to discuss legislation (which he sponsored) that would modernize several locks and dams on the Missouri and Illinois Rivers and allow barges to transport farm products more quickly.

3:40 P.M.—Flies back to Chicago.

6:00 P.M.—Attends a fundraiser for Barack Obama, Democratic U.S. Senate candidate from Illinois.

8:00 P.M.—Attends a book event to celebrate the release of Bill Clinton's *My Life* to benefit the Democratic National Committee.

SOURCES: Schedules provided by Sen. Richard J. Durbin's Chicago office; David Hawkings and Brian Nutting, eds., *CQ's Politics in America: The 108th Congress* (Washington, D.C.: CQ Press, 2003), 312–316; Michael Barone and Richard E. Cohen, *The Almanac of American Politics, 2004* (Washington, D.C.: National Journal, 2003), 531–533. Special thanks to Christina Angarola.

ability to focus on public policy. Pressure to be in the home district meeting constituents competes with legislators' desires to do a good job at lawmaking and to work more efficiently. The public wants Congress to be responsive to its individual needs and group interests, but then it looks down on the institution for its pork barrel politics and big spending.

Pressure to raise money for reelection campaigns incurs obligations to interest groups that may not be consistent with either the members' or the constituents' views. Indeed, congressional leaders from both parties have problems articulating a clear vision in part because so many of them have become dependent on the contributions of PACs for their campaign funding. This puts them in the position of having to support some interests that are not consistent with voters' views or interests.

The procedures and organization of Congress also give individuals and small groups opportunities to block or redirect action. This is particularly true in the Senate, where procedures allow a minority of senators to engage in unlimited debate unless sixty members vote to stop it. The fragmented committee and subcommittee structure in both houses offers many venues in which action can be killed. Political parties have been strengthened in recent years but are not strong enough to protect against the pressure of lobbyists or outraged constituents. These factors mean that Congress continues to be more responsive to individual and group interests than to national needs.

The increasing partisanship in Congress has been one of the biggest changes since the mid-1990s (see Figure 2). After the Republicans gained the majority of the House in 1995, they had a record number of unanimous votes (263). During George W. Bush's first administration, the White House intervened heavily to press its policy agenda. Though in the time after 9/11 partisanship in voting decreased, it shot up to record highs in 2003 as the legislative process became party dominated.

In contrast to the dominant tradition, the opposition was shut out of many important stages of the process, including the drafting of final versions of legislation in conference committees. This further heightened the partisan divisions, made the output of Congress less a product of compromise than in earlier years, and decreased the responsiveness of congressional action to the broader public.

Even in the best of times, Congress best represents those voters who identify with one of the two major parties; in recent years, much legislation has been the product of a single party and the group interests closest to its political base. This has complicated what was already a difficult process for the formulation of broadly responsive public policy; namely, the overweening influence of large campaign donors on voting on both sides of the aisle. It is difficult to get consistently good legislation when special interests, partisan concerns, and pork-hungry legislators dominate the lawmaking process. It is especially difficult when only the majority party is making the decisions.

Pelosi Cracks the Whip

ancy Pelosi did challenge and beat Steny Hoyer for the position of House minority whip. The risk Pelosi ran in challenging the party's next-in-line probably seemed smaller to her than to outside observers. She knew she had the votes to beat Hoyer when she announced for the position; they would come from a combination of fellow Democrats who owed her for raising money on their behalf and from others who shared her view that the party leadership had become too timid, too eager to be conciliatory, and consequently too easy for the Republicans to steamroll.

Pelosi showed that she would offer a different kind of leadership when she organized 126 Democrats to vote against the resolution giving President Bush the authority to go to war in Iraq. Minority Leader Richard Gephardt had helped write that resolution, yet Pelosi, as whip, organized more than half of the caucus to vote against it.

Having taken the plunge to challenge Hoyer, Pelosi was now next in line when Gephardt gave up the leadership after the 2002 elections to run for president in 2004. Gephardt was basically a spent force as minority leader anyway, after the Democrats lost six House seats in an off-year election.

Pelosi announced her candidacy, even though the chair of the party caucus said he would run for the position. It turned out to be a one-day campaign when Pelosi presented her opponents with a letter signed by a majority of the caucus endorsing her candidacy. One of her allies said, "It was clear what was wrong. . . . [The Democrats] had lost a sense of purpose . . . lost a sense of direction and commitment. That all had to be restored and rebuilt. Her candidacy became the vehicle by which members could see how that could be achieved."[72] Another colleague called her "our Margaret Thatcher," "tough as hell" but with a nice style.[73]

Pelosi's style was to disarm people with the congeniality of a grandmother of five, which she was. She had earned a reputation for getting both Democrats and Republicans to her office and wooing them with chocolate and fresh fruit. Her style has been to lead by consensus.

But after identifying the common ground among caucus members, Pelosi expects party loyalty. (One of her first big blows as minority leader was to see sixteen of her colleagues cross the aisle to vote with the Bush administration on a Medicare reform bill.) She said that there are "just three good rules to break with the caucus: conscience, constituents, or the Constitution."[74] She immediately set out to establish better discipline by getting the caucus to pass a rule change giving the leadership the power to name the chairs of the most powerful subcommittees in the House, something similar to what the Republican leadership had done. This would make sure that those holding these powerful positions were party loyalists. What, she asked, was the point of being part of a group whose members share issue positions if they could not stick together to achieve their common interests: "Who wants to join that club?"[75]

Pelosi's ability to speak forcefully for the party was enhanced by representing a safe district with a liberal constituency; she did not have to worry that advocating for traditional Democratic issues would alienate the folks back home, as Senate Minority Leader Harry Reid (D-Nev.) does. And a lifetime of grassroots activism and fundraising led her to refocus Democrats' energies on campaign fundamentals and away from the deep frustration they felt at the Republican leadership for shutting them out of negotiations on the final wording of legislation and blocking Democrat-sponsored bills from coming to the House floor. Pelosi told her colleagues, "It's not anything to whine about. We just have to win. No whining, just winning."[76]

There was another reason Pelosi's victory energized Democrats. When she entered the 108th Congress as minority leader, she was not just the first woman to head a congressional party caucus but also the first woman to be placed in nomination for the speakership. Because the speaker of the House is elected on a straight party vote, the nomination was a formality. But should the Democrats regain control of the House, Pelosi would, with near certainty, become the first woman to serve as speaker.

Key Terms

constituency

reapportionment

redistricting

gerrymander

constituency service

casework

pork barrel

speaker of the House

Rules Committee

party caucus

majority leader

minority leader

whips

standing committees

markup

seniority rule

filibuster

cloture

conference committee

oversight

authorizations

appropriations

informal norms

special-interest caucus

going public

Further Reading

Michael Barone and Richard E. Cohen, *The Almanac of American Politics, 2004* (Washington, D.C.: National Journal, 2003). This reference work offers background on each member, the member's district, and the member's voting record. It is revised every two years. A volume similar in format and publication schedule is *CQ's Politics in America,* compiled by the staff of *Congressional Quarterly.* The most recent edition is for the 108th Congress (Washington, D.C.: CQ Press, 2003).

Robert A. Caro, *Master of the Senate* (New York: Knopf, 2002). When you have some time on your hands, check out this monumental study of a master legislator at work. This is the second in a projected three-volume study that tracks the House and Senate career of former president Lyndon B. Johnson, arguably the most powerful Senate majority leader in U.S. history.

Roger H. Davidson and Walter J. Oleszek, *Congress and Its Members,* 9th ed. (Washington, D.C.: CQ Press, 2004). This classic general reference work on Congress is revised every few years.

Richard Fenno, *Home Style: House Members in Their Districts,* 2nd ed. (New York: Longman, 2003). This political science classic examines how House members interact with people in their districts and how this influences their political style and decision making.

Timothy Phelps and Helen Winternitz, *Capitol Games: Clarence Thomas, Anita Hill, and the Story of a Supreme Court Nomination* (New York: Hyperion, 1992). The authors take a close look at the Senate hearings on Clarence Thomas's nomination to the Supreme Court, which some observers say encouraged the current partisan atmosphere in Congress.

Nelson W. Polsby, ed., *How Congress Evolves: Social Bases of Institutional Change* (New York: Oxford University Press, 2004). Essays by congressional scholars chronicle changes in rules, procedures, and informal norms since the 1930s.

Barbara Sinclair, *Unorthodox Lawmaking: New Legislative Processes in the U. S. Congress,* 2nd ed. (Washington, D.C.: CQ Press, 2000). Sinclair examines how the legislative process is being transformed by focusing on bills that came before Congress during the Clinton administration.

For Viewing

The Congress (1989) This Ken Burns documentary traces the development of both the Capitol building and Congress as an institution, with commentary on historic leadership figures and landmark events such as the Great Compromise, the McCarthy hearings, and Watergate. It also contains clips from Frank Capra's *Mr. Smith Goes to Washington* (1939), a classic black-and-white Hollywood film that conveys an idealistic view of how Congress works. In the same vein is Otto Preminger's *Advise and Consent* (1962), which shows the triumph of principle in the Senate.

 ## Electronic Resources

thomas.loc.gov

This Web site, Thomas: Legislative Information on the Internet, links to texts of bills, the Congressional Record *(reporting entire floor debates), and committee hearings and reports. It is also a good site for obtaining information on congressional history and individual members. It contains links to all kinds of statistics about Congress and to the home pages and e-mail addresses of members. You can also link to the latest edition of* How a Bill Becomes a Law, *prepared by the House Judiciary Committee.*

www.c-span.org

This is the Web site of the cable station that covers congressional proceedings. It is a treasure trove of information on congressional history as well as current affairs. It also has an archive of frequently asked questions about Congress and resources for students of American government.

www.washingtonpost.com

This is the Web site of the Washington Post, *whose news coverage of Congress is unrivaled.*

www.cq.com

This is the Web site of Congressional Quarterly, *publisher of the most authoritative weekly review of congressional affairs.*

 ## InfoTrac College Edition

Search for the following articles in the InfoTrac database:

Bishin, Benjamin G. "Dormant Delegation: Evidence on the Conflicting Findings of Research on Legislative Representation," *Polity* (July 2004).

Bovitz, Gregory L. "Electoral Consequences of Pork-busting in the U.S. House of Representatives," *Political Science Quarterly* (Fall 2002).

Crowley, Michael. "On the Hill: Switch Hit (Jim Jeffords)," *New Republic* (December 31, 2001).

Devins, Neal. "Congress as Culprit: How Lawmakers Spurred on the Court's Anti-Congress Crusade," *Duke Law Journal* (October 2001).

For more articles, enter

"United States Congress" in the Subject Guide;

"United States Congress House" in the Subject Guide;

"United States Congress Senate" in the Subject Guide.

 American Government Resources

Visit the Government Institutions section of the Wadsworth American Government Resources Web site (politicalscience. wadsworth.com/amgov) for a variety of tools to help you explore Congress further. Included are simulations, video clips, Microcase exercises, and a wealth of other activities.

CHAPTER 11

THE PRESIDENCY

As commander in chief, George W. Bush took America into a war with Iraq. This image is comprised of photos of the first 609 American troops killed there.

Courtesy Joe Wezorek

**Development and Growth
of the Presidency**

Qualifications and Tenure
Eligibility
Pay and Perks
Tenure and Succession

Powers and Responsibilities
Chief Executive: Administrative Duties
Chief of State: Representing the Nation
Chief Diplomat: Statesmanship
Commander in Chief: Military Leadership

Presidential Staff
Executive Office of the President
White House Office
Office of the Vice President

Presidential Leadership
The President and His Party
The President and Congress
Executive Leadership
The President and the Public
The President and Public Opinion
The Ebb and Flow of Presidential Power

Presidential Reputation
Presidential Character
Goals and Vision

Conclusion: Is the Presidency Responsive?

Should You Resign the Presidency or Stay and Fight?

ou are William Jefferson Clinton, forty-second president of the United States. It is 1998, and you are facing the biggest fight of your political life. The House of Representatives has voted to open an unrestricted inquiry into possible grounds for your impeachment. You have been accused of misconduct in office for having an affair with a young White House intern and later of lying under oath in a civil suit about that relationship. Washington has been in political turmoil, the press in a feeding frenzy, and the public transfixed by the barrage of accusations flying between Congress and the White House and by one lurid media story after another. Would it be better for the country if, as Richard Nixon did when he faced the certainty of impeachment, you resigned and let Congress and the country get back to business as usual?

It has been decades since such a period of fierce partisanship has gripped the Congress. After their resounding victory at the polls in 1994, the conservative wing of the Republican Party, led by House Speaker Newt Gingrich, has been in heated battle with you and your legislative agenda. The Republican leadership has authorized so many investigations into your actions, some before you became president, that the tactic is being called the criminalization of politics. One group of Republican campaign donors even charged you with murdering your White House counsel and close friend Vince Fos-

ter.[1] After millions of taxpayer dollars were spent on legal fees and thousand of hours diverted to dealing with investigations of special counsels, no charges of wrongdoing were ever brought. Some of the charges they are lodging against you now stem from testimony given in a civil sexual harassment suit brought for alleged actions taken while you were governor of Arkansas. The suit was dismissed for lack of cause, but some of your most vocal opponents were involved in lodging the suit and paying the defendant's legal costs.

You see the looming impeachment inquiry as a simple display of power politics; the Republicans have the votes in the House of Representatives to impeach you, so they are going to do it, as Gingrich said, "because we can."[2] The House has the power of **impeachment**—that is, the authority to bring formal charges against a president (similar to an indictment in criminal proceedings) for "Treason, Bribery, or other high Crimes and Misdemeanors" (Article II of the U.S. Constitution). In an impeachment inquiry, the House holds hearings to determine whether there is sufficient evidence to impeach, and if a majority votes yes, the president is impeached and the process moves to the Senate, where a trial is held with the chief justice of the United States presiding. Conviction requires a two-thirds vote of members present in the Senate and results in removal from the presidency.

The Founders established the

impeachment option as part of the system of checks and balances, a final weapon against executive abuse of power. The procedure had been adapted from British law, where it had served, according to Jefferson (who was not present at the writing of the Constitution), as "an engine more of passion than of justice." [3] James Madison, who was present at the drafting, objected to the inclusion of the phrase "and other high crimes and misdemeanors" in the impeachment article precisely because he thought it was so vague that it could be used for political purposes. But through compromise, it was retained. [4]

Impeachment was intended to be a legal procedure for removing a president who had committed unconstitutional acts or serious criminal transgressions, not as a means for unseating a president for political or partisan reasons. The procedure is cumbersome and meant to be; the Founders did not intend for the president, as head of state and the only nationally elected official in government, to be removed from office easily.

It was precisely the fear that impeachment could become a partisan tool that led the Founders to divide indictment and removal powers between the House and the Senate. If trying the charges were left to the popularly elected House, Hamilton wrote in *Federalist Paper* 65, "there will always be the greatest danger that the decision will be regulated more by the comparative strength of parties, than by the real demonstrations of innocence or guilt."

You know that given Republican control of the House and its deeply partisan leadership, the chances that articles of impeachment will be approved are near certain. You also know that acquittal in the Senate is also a near certainty because of the two-thirds rule. The Republicans hold fifty-five seats in the Senate, so your removal would take the vote of every Republican senator and twelve Democrats as well. It is unlikely that any Democrat will cross party lines to vote for conviction.

However, before you ever get to a Senate trial, you and the country will have to endure more weeks of sensa-tionalistic press coverage; every aspect of your personal life will be dragged before the public. You know you opened the door to this political warfare by your own actions in having an affair with a White House intern. You lied to your wife and let her go on national television to defend you by saying the affair was manufactured by a right-wing conspiracy. If you do not resign, your wife and daughter will be exposed to additional humiliations. Every day, news programs run the few existing film clips that show you and the intern, Monica Lewinsky, in the same frame. Radio and television repeatedly play illegally made tapes of phone calls Lewinsky made to her friend Linda Tripp in which Lewinsky discussed the affair (it is illegal to tape conversations without the permission of those being taped). If Tripp, backed by some of your opponents, had not made the tapes and given them to a reporter, the relationship would have remained a private matter. You know you created your own problem by what you later call "my indefensible personal conduct." [5]

If you resigned, you could spare your family this ordeal and perhaps Congress would get on with governing the country instead of tying itself up with partisan investigations. You could leave office confident that the White House would be in the hands of someone ready for the job, your vice president, Al Gore. Gore, a small-state southerner like yourself, has years of Washington experience. He may not have your leadership skills or charisma, but he could pass anyone's character test, has years of service in Congress, and perhaps could get the administration back on track in pursuing its legislative agenda and foreign policy initiatives. He would have a leg up on any Republican contender if he ran as a sitting president.

But you are every bit as competitive and partisan as your Republican opponents. You had a strong first term and won reelection handily. You do not want to leave office this way, on charges that would never have been lodged against any other president and that even Republicans concede cannot

Senators Barbara Mikulski (D-Md., foreground) and Olympia Snowe (R-Me.) preceded Chief Justice William Rehnquist into the Senate chambers for the trial of President Clinton.

possibly win a conviction. You also know that your wife is at least as partisan as you are, and despite the fact that you lied and exposed her to ridicule, she will never agree to give in to your attackers. Your daughter is another story; if you do not resign, there is no way you can spare her further embarrassment.

But you have to think about what is best for the country. Things are looking pretty good, with a booming stock market, great job growth, and a budget deficit that is about to turn into a surplus. Your approval ratings have never been higher and those of Congress have seldom been lower. In the recent midterm election, your party won seats at the expense of the Republicans, and Gingrich had to resign the speakership. Now you are in the midst of Middle East peace negotiations, trying to find the right response to ethnic cleansing in Bosnia and Croatia, and being pressured by the head of the counterterrorism office, Richard Clarke, to develop a better strategy for pursuit of terrorists who have bombed U.S. embassies in Africa and the U.S.S. *Cole* off the shores of Yemen. Knowing that you will not be convicted even if impeached, maybe you should just hang on and try to concentrate on finishing these jobs.

Pharaohs, consuls, kings, queens, emperors, tsars, prime ministers, and councils of varied size served as executives in other governments before 1789. But no national government had a president, an elected executive with authority equal to and independent of a national legislature, until George Washington was elected president of the United States.

The Founders viewed their creation as a chief executive officer, someone who would serve as both a check on bills passed by Congress and the administrator of those enacted into law. He would also be head of state, chief diplomat, and commander of the armed forces. At its inception, the presidency was a not very powerful office in a fledgling country that had few international ties and virtually no standing army. The office's first occupants were drawn from among the Founders; a few of them, Washington and Jefferson especially, served with some reluctance. Nevertheless, they were willing to lend their reputations and abilities to the cause of stabilizing the new government, and as a result, they had the opportunity to influence the direction of its development.

Throughout the nineteenth century, except for the Civil War period, real power at the national level resided in Congress, so much so that Woodrow Wilson characterized the federal arrangement in the 1880s as "congressional government."[6] Thus between Andrew Jackson, early in the nineteenth century, and Franklin Roosevelt, in the middle of the twentieth, many who sought the presidency were "ordinary people, with very ordinary reputations."[7] There were powerful exceptions, such as Abraham Lincoln, Theodore Roosevelt, and Woodrow Wilson, and a few men of exceptional achievement before their presidencies, such as Ulysses Grant and Herbert Hoover, who fared badly in the White House.

Today the president of the United States is among the most powerful people in the world. By the 1970s, the scope of that power led one historian to write about an "imperial" presidency.[8] Yet most presidents since World War II have suffered reelection defeats and at times have seemed almost powerless to shape events affecting the national interest. The immensely popular war hero Dwight Eisenhower (1953–1961) was unable to buck Cold War sentiment and prevent the buildup of the military-industrial complex. John Kennedy (1961–1963), who enjoyed an extraordinary success rate in a conservative Congress, was stymied in getting civil

Howard Pyle Collection/Delaware Art Museum, Wilmington/Bridgeman Art Library

Although political scientists rank Jefferson as a great president, he did not consider the office, or his performance in it, very important. His instructions for an epitaph listed what he thought were his three main accomplishments in life: writing the Declaration of Independence and a Virginia law guaranteeing religious freedom and founding the University of Virginia. He did not include his two terms as president.

rights legislation accepted. The domestic goals of Lyndon Johnson (1963–1968), along with his chances for reelection, were derailed by a war that took Richard Nixon (1969–1974) years to end. And Nixon was forced from office because of his Watergate cover-up. Ronald Reagan (1981–1988), one of our most popular recent presidents, was so frustrated when Congress thwarted his foreign policy initiatives that he condoned illegal activities, producing the Iran-Contra scandal and a tarnished personal reputation. Gerald Ford (1974–1976), Jimmy Carter (1977–1980), and George H. Bush (1989–1992) failed to get reelected. At century's end, Bill Clinton (1993–2000) discovered that instead of an imperial presidency, the country had something closer to an "impossible" or "imperiled" presidency.[9] Although he won reelection handily, most of his domestic agenda, other than economic growth and deficit reduction, was sidetracked by one congressional investigation after another. When George W. Bush entered office in 2001, he brought with him a retinue of Washington professionals and set out to restore the presidency to its former preeminence.

In this chapter, we will consider the paradox of presidential power and presidential weakness. After describing the growth of the modern presidency, we look at the constitutional provisions, the qualifications for the office, and its responsibilities. We explain why a bureaucracy grew up around the presidency at the same time the president was becoming a more personal and accessible representative of the American people. Inevitably, the growth of the modern presidency has affected the balance of power between the executive and legislative branches, and that is another topic of this chapter.

Development and Growth of the Presidency

Although most of the Founders believed that Congress would be the predominant branch of government and described its structure and functioning first in the Constitution, over time the influence and visibility of the presidency has grown to rival and often exceed those of Congress. Americans have been lucky to get presidential leadership when we needed it: during the birth of the nation, the Civil War, and foreign crises. This implies that our needs change, that we need more government and executive leadership during crises and less at other times. Presidential power was traditionally supposed to return to its "normal" low profile after we resolved special problems.

This expectation may have been realistic before the United States became a unified country that accepted Washington as the center of governmental power. But once the nation stretched from Mexico to Canada and from the Atlantic to the Pacific, once it had a standing army, international trade aspirations, and the ambition to dominate the hemisphere, governmental power gravitated to Washington. The image of Thomas Jefferson sitting at his desk in isolation week after week conducting the presidency by personal correspondence was a quaint memory even twenty years later when Andrew Jackson was dubbed the "people's president."[10] Jackson was the first to act assertively to fulfill the popular mandate he saw in his election—the first to veto a bill because *he* did not like it. Thirty years later, Lincoln assumed extraordinary powers during the Civil War, suspending civil liberties, overturning state laws, and boldly interpreting the Constitution to say that the Union was indivisible.

Teddy Roosevelt, who has been called the "preacher militant," used the presidency in an unprecedented way to challenge corporate power and to argue for labor reform and better living conditions for average Americans. He also saw an imperial role for the United States in world politics, especially through military expansion, and led the country toward those "entangling alliances" that George Washington had warned against. Eight years after Roosevelt left office, Wilson became the first twentieth-century president to lead us into a major for-

America does not have a monarchy, but it does have political dynasties. George W. Bush, shown here with his father George H. Bush, who served as president, vice president, CIA director, and member of the House of Representatives, is also the grandson of a U.S. senator.

George Bush Presidential Library

eign involvement, World War I, and he was the first president to travel to Europe while in office.

The Great Depression and World War II led to a large expansion in the role of the national government and tremendous growth in presidential power. Franklin Delano Roosevelt (FDR) was elected president in 1932 because people thought he would help them. In his first inaugural address, he told Americans that he would ask Congress for "broad executive power" to fight the crisis, equivalent, he said, to what he might be granted if an enemy had invaded the country. The enactment of New Deal programs led to an expansion of the executive branch because new agencies had to be created and new civil servants hired. This increased the president's power by making him more important as a manager and policymaker. And after the United States entered World War II, Roosevelt assumed additional powers as a hands-on commander in chief.

Radio and television contributed significantly to the expansion of presidential power. As an integral part of national life by the 1930s, broadcasting made the news seem more immediate and compelling. Along with the wire services, it gave people a way to follow presidents and a way for presidents to "sell" their policies and provide leadership. Because it is easier to follow one person than many (as with Congress), the media helped make the presidency the focal point of national politics. With his radio broadcasts during the Great Depression, Roosevelt became a kind of national cheerleader, a one-man band of optimism, persuading the public that solutions were at hand.

Congress is not structured to provide this kind of national leadership. Its 535 members are divided into two houses and hundreds of committees and subcommittees and come from both major political parties. It is difficult for either the majority or minority leadership to develop and articulate national policy goals or to keep its members faithful to them.

Even after the fifteen years of crisis receded, FDR's successors had little opportunity to shrink the presidency. With the United States emerging from World War II as the preeminent world power and with the onset of the Cold War, Congress was willing to cede even more leadership to the president to counter the Soviet threat. Responsibilities as chief diplomat and commander in chief of the world's largest military establishment have made the president a principal actor in world politics, a platform not afforded to any other government official or institution.

Of his postwar administration, Harry Truman said, "Being president is like riding a tiger. You have to stay on or get swallowed." And thus we have today's presidency, with everyone looking to see whether the man is riding the tiger or the tiger is swallowing the man.

Qualifications and Tenure

Eligibility

The Constitution requires that a person meet only three conditions to be eligible to hold the presidency: one must be a "natural-born citizen," at least thirty-five years old, and have resided in the United States for at least fourteen years before taking office.

Historically, it also has helped to be a white male with roots in small-town America; a Protestant of English, German, or Scandinavian background; a resident of a state with a large population; and a good family man. In recent years, however, this profile has broad-

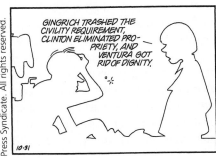

ened considerably as society has become more inclusive, the electorate more diverse, and social norms more tolerant of divorce, but gender and racial barriers remain. The nature of contemporary elections also makes it necessary that a candidate be reasonably telegenic and either independently wealthy or an outstanding fundraiser.

Pay and Perks

In return for services rendered, the Constitution authorized Congress to award the president "a Compensation," which could be neither increased nor decreased during a president's term of office. Our first seventeen presidents received an annual salary of $25,000. Grant got the first raise in 1873, a doubling to $50,000; by the time Nixon took office, the salary was $200,000, where it stayed through the end of the Clinton years. A majority of the public was not eager to see it go higher, even though by century's end the president's salary ranked 785 among those of the 800 highest-paid CEOs.[11] Supporters of a pay increase argued that the president's low salary was holding down the base pay for all other top-level officials and interfering with government recruitment. Congress agreed, and in 2001 the president's salary was bumped up to $400,000; he continues to receive $50,000 for expenses and $100,000 for travel.

In addition, there are *substantial* fringe benefits. These include living quarters in one of the world's most famous mansions, a rural retreat in Maryland (Camp David), the best health care money can buy, and fleets of cars and aircraft. After leaving office, the president is entitled to a generous pension, as well as a security detail and money for an office and staff.

Tenure and Succession

Presidents serve four-year terms. The Twenty-second Amendment limits them to serving two terms (or ten years if they complete the term of an incumbent who dies or resigns). Four presidents died in office from illness (Harrison, Taylor, Harding, and Franklin Roosevelt), and four were assassinated (Garfield, McKinley, Lincoln, and Kennedy).

Presidents can be removed from office if impeached and convicted. Only three presidents have been targets of full impeachment proceedings.[12] Andrew Johnson, who came to office on Lincoln's assassination, was a southerner who was unpopular in his own party; he was impeached by the House in a dispute over Reconstruction policies in the post–Civil War South. The Senate failed to convict by a single vote. A century later, the House Judiciary Committee voted to impeach Richard Nixon on obstruction of justice and other charges stemming from the Watergate scandal, whereupon Nixon resigned as president. Once out of office, he avoided possible indictment on criminal charges through a full

pardon granted by his successor, Gerald Ford, a move that aroused a storm of controversy at the time. In 1998, as discussed in "You Are There" at the start of this chapter, Bill Clinton became the third target of the process when the House voted to open an unrestricted inquiry into possible grounds for his impeachment.

Should a president be removed, die, resign, or become incapacitated, his replacement is provided for by the Constitution and supplemental laws. At the time the Constitution was written, it was assumed that the vice presidency would be occupied by the man who had been the runner-up in the presidential election, and the wording simply said that presidential powers "shall devolve on the Vice President." It was left to Congress to make provisions for filling the vacated vice presidency and dealing with a situation in which both the presidency and the vice presidency were vacated. When Lincoln was assassinated, there still were no provisions for replacing Vice President Andrew Johnson when he succeeded to the presidency. Had Johnson been convicted in his impeachment trial, the presidency would have gone to the president pro tempore of the Senate who was next in the line of succession according to rules in effect at the time.

Not until 1947, two years after the death of Franklin Roosevelt had put the virtually unknown Harry Truman in the White House, did Congress pass the Presidential Succession Act. It established the order of succession of federal officeholders should both the president and the vice president be unable to serve. The list begins with the speaker of the House, followed by the president pro tempore of the Senate, and then proceeds through the secretaries of the cabinet departments in the order in which the departments were created. The Succession Act has never been used because we have always had a vice president when something happened to the president. To ensure that this is always the case, the Constitution was amended in 1967.

That amendment, the Twenty-fifth, directs the president to name a vice president acceptable to majorities in the House and Senate if the vice presidency falls vacant. These provisions have been used twice. Nixon chose Gerald Ford to replace Spiro Agnew, who resigned after pleading no contest to charges of taking bribes when he was a public official in Maryland. After Nixon resigned and Ford became president, Ford named Nelson Rockefeller, the former governor of New York, as his vice president.

The Twenty-fifth Amendment also charges the vice president and a majority of the cabinet—or some other body named by Congress—to determine, in instances where there is doubt, whether the president is mentally or physically incapable of carrying out his duties. This provision was meant to provide for situations in which it is unclear who is or should be acting as president, such as when James Garfield was shot in July 1881. He did

At few times in American history have five ex-presidents been alive at the same time, let alone appeared together. This early 1990s photograph shows, from left, Richard Nixon (1969–1974), Gerald Ford (1974–1977), Jimmy Carter (1977–1981), Ronald Reagan (1981–1989), and George H. Bush (1989–1993).

not die until mid-September, and during this period he was completely unable to fulfill his duties. In 1919, Woodrow Wilson had a nervous collapse in the summer and a stroke in the fall and was partially incapacitated for seven months. No one was sure about his condition, however, because his wife restricted access to him.

Under the amendment's provisions, the vice president becomes "acting president" if the president is found mentally or physically unfit to fulfill his duties. As the title suggests, the conferral of power is temporary; the president can resume office by giving Congress written notice of his recovery. Reagan followed the spirit of this section in 1985. Before undergoing cancer surgery, he sent his vice president, George H. Bush, a letter authorizing him to act as president while Reagan was unconscious. George W. Bush took the same precaution in 2002 when he was briefly under anesthesia during a medical checkup.

If the vice president and other officials who determined the president unfit do not concur in his judgment that he has recovered, they can challenge his return to office by notifying Congress in writing. Then it falls to Congress to decide whether the president is capable of resuming his duties.

The issue of succession arose again after the terrorist attacks of 2001. Facing the possibility of an attack on Washington that might take the lives of or incapacitate everyone in the immediate line of succession, the Bush administration, just hours after the attack, activated an emergency plan established during the Eisenhower administration to provide for continuity of government in case of a nuclear attack. A shadow government of from seventy-five to one hundred senior executive branch officials (serving in a rotation system) were removed to a secret fortified location outside the capital where they lived and worked underground twenty-four hours a day. They were given responsibility for carrying on essential work if elected leaders were disabled. Bush also issued executive orders defining a line of succession in each cabinet department. As an added precaution, in the immediate months after the 9/11 attacks, Vice President Dick Cheney spent much of his time at undisclosed locations that the press referred to collectively as "the Bunker."

Powers and Responsibilities

The foundation of presidential power lies in the formal duties assigned by the Constitution. It assigns the president four major areas of responsibility: administration, representing the nation, foreign policy, and military leadership. These duties are sometimes summarized by the four "chief" titles: chief executive, chief of state, chief diplomat, and commander in chief.[13] Collectively, they represent a towering set of responsibilities.

There are three other sources of presidential authority, two of which stem from the constitutional powers given to Congress and the courts. Congress has delegated, by law, some of its authority to the president (budget making, for example), and the federal courts have used their authority to interpret the meaning of the Constitution to validate other powers necessary for presidents to fulfill their formal duties. These are called implied or inherent powers because they are seen as natural extensions of authority granted by the Constitution. A third set of powers is informal and derived from the office itself and the person who serves. These powers expand and contract with each president and are dependent on his view of the office and his will to exercise all of its powers.

Chief Executive: Administrative Duties

The president's administrative duties are assigned by Article II's charge that "Executive power shall be invested in a President." The article has few specific provisions describing the president's administrative duties, but it does invest the president with the authority to demand written reports from his "principal officers." It also directs the president to nominate the most important officers of the executive branch. He can also remove those not appointed to fixed-term positions.

The president was given power neither to create executive branch departments and agencies nor to fund them—this authority resides with Congress—so his means for controlling the bureaucracy lie in his formal powers of appointment, his implied power to remove his appointees, and his delegated authority to propose reorganizations and to make budget recommendations.

Chief of State: Representing the Nation

As the chief administrative officer, the president is the also the chief presiding officer or head of government. But in our form of republic, the head of government is also the **head of state.** This arrangement is not common among Western democracies, which treat the government as a separate entity, presided over by politicians and elected officials with partisan interests. The state is the embodiment of the nation itself—the people and their history, traditions, flag, and other symbols—and in most other nations, its representative (an elder statesman, a king or queen) is assumed to be above partisan politics. The unifying, nonpolitical nature of the role of head of state is the reason why some democracies choose to separate this office from that of head of government. The latter is usually filled by the leader of a political party (in Great Britain, for example, the prime minister), who is by definition partisan.

In the United States, the president serves in both roles. As head of government, he is the leader of a political party with a partisan agenda. But as head of state, the president serves as the official representative of the country and of all the people. His office symbolizes the collective unity and identity of the nation. The fusion of these two offices gives the American president a political advantage that leaders of other Western governments do not have. Members of Congress, the press, or the public who may attack him freely in his partisan role as head of government usually show more deference when the president is acting in his capacity as head of state. When he stands in public behind the Great Seal of the United States of America, he is not just a politician who was elected to govern but a nonpartisan representative of all the people, entrusted with the symbols, emblems, and traditions of the country.

The president's duties as head of state include serving as the official representative of the United States at a variety of state and ceremonial occasions both at home and abroad. It could be opening the baseball season; lighting the White House Christmas tree; attending the swearing in, coronation, or funeral of a foreign head of state; or serving as official greeter when a foreign leader visits this country. The head of state is also empowered to take actions that symbolize national sentiment, such as issuing proclamations to commemorate events, or making gestures that express a humane national spirit, as in the granting of reprieves and pardons to people convicted of federal crimes. The president's role as unifier

Presidents traditionally throw out the first ball of the baseball season. Shown here are, from the left, Woodrow Wilson (1913–1921), Franklin Roosevelt (1933–1945), and Dwight Eisenhower (1953–1961).

of the nation was acted out by Bill Clinton in leading the national mourning for victims of the bombing of the federal building in Oklahoma City and by George W. Bush participating in a memorial service at Washington's National Cathedral for the victims of 9/11.

As head of state, the president is required by the Constitution to report to Congress "from time to time" about the "State of the Union." He notes the successes of the past year, addresses problems, and outlines his policy agenda for the coming year. Part of the report usually deals with the mood of the country and identifies goals for maintaining or increasing national unity. Today these addresses are televised and delivered in the House of Representatives before a joint session of Congress at the start of each congressional session, in January each year. Even when presidents are mired in political controversy at the time of the speech—Nixon during the Watergate investigation or Clinton in 1998, delivering the State of the Union address just weeks after the revelation of allegations of personal wrongdoing—congressional leaders usually caution the membership to show respect to the person who is speaking in his constitutional role as head of state.

The chief-of-state role confers responsibilities but also political advantage and power. Through the power of pardon, the president can, on his own authority, erase the guilt and restore the civil rights of anyone convicted of a federal crime, except an impeached president. One of Lincoln's last acts, signed the day he was assassinated, was to pardon a Union Army deserter. Blanket pardons have been issued to Confederate Army veterans and Vietnam draft dodgers, but most presidents have used the power to clear the names of minor offenders who have served their sentences. Using it to absolve government officials or persons convicted of crimes with political overtones can evoke strong public reactions. George H. Bush discovered this when he pardoned Reagan's secretary of defense and five other officials charged with or convicted of crimes related to the Iran-Contra scandal. So did Clinton, with his last-minute pardon of a fugitive commodities trader whose ex-wife was a large donor to the Democratic Party.

Hundreds of people appeal to the president for pardons every year. Although the president is not required to consult government lawyers or other law enforcement officials before granting pardons, he usually does. The overwhelming majority of requests are vetted by Department of Justice lawyers and refused.

Chief Diplomat: Statesmanship

As head of state, the president is given ceremonial powers "to receive Ambassadors and other public Ministers." Ambassadors are individuals appointed by other nations to represent their country's interests in the United States. An ambassador must present his or her credentials to the president and have them accepted before taking up office. What appears to be a ceremonial duty has real potential for foreign policymaking. Recognition is not automatic. The power to accept or reject foreign ambassadors, by extension, gives the president the power to decide which governments the United States will recognize and which will be shut out. We did not recognize the Soviet government until sixteen years after the Bolshevik Revolution of 1917 or that of the Communist government of mainland China until more than twenty-five years after it took power.

As chief diplomat, the president also appoints ambassadors and consuls to represent us abroad, subject to Senate approval. But he frequently conducts diplomacy directly with other heads of state or governments, such as at summit conferences where leaders gather to discuss economic, trade, environmental, or arms issues. The president can negotiate treaties and trade deals, although the former must be ratified by the Senate and the latter approved by both chambers.

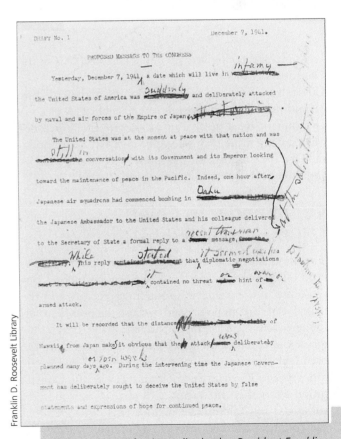

Franklin D. Roosevelt Library

As the nation's foreign policy leader, President Franklin Roosevelt edited his own speech to Congress about the Japanese attack on Pearl Harbor. He added the word that made memorable his phrase "a date which will live in infamy."

President Lincoln, as commander in chief, consults his generals at the Antietam battlefield during the Civil War. Lincoln wanted a more active role in Civil War battles, but his generals, worried for his safety, made sure he was out of harm's way whenever there was fighting.

National Archives

Some of these powers are implied in Article II of the Constitution and were acknowledged by the Supreme Court in a 1936 decision.[14] The Court said there is logic behind presidential power in foreign policy. A nation's government must be able to speak with one voice because having more than one voice could make it impossible for the government to represent its official policies and intentions to the rest of the world.

Commander in Chief: Military Leadership

The president's military authority stems from his role as head of state and his foreign policy responsibilities. Because use of the military is sometimes necessary in the conduct of foreign policy and because the president sets foreign policy goals, the Founders made him commander in chief. In doing so, they were designating the president "first general" and "first admiral," as Hamilton wrote in *Federalist Paper* 69. In this way, the Constitution established the primacy of civilian over military authority; by holding the highest rank, the president can countermand the order of any military leader who is not executing defense or war policies as established by elected officials and their appointees.

But the Founders did not want to give the president the sole power to make war. In the words of Connecticut delegate (and later representative and senator) Roger

Sherman, they believed "the Executive should be able to repel and not to commence war." The Founders feared that presidents, like the British kings from whom they had recently freed themselves, would be too eager to go to war.[15] So they gave Congress the power to declare war. James Madison expressed the view of several of the Founders when he argued that "the executive is the branch of power most interested in war and most prone to it. [The Constitution] has, accordingly, with studied care, vested the question of war in the legislature."[16] The Founders therefore set up a system of checks and balances in military affairs; the president commands the troops, but Congress has the power to declare war and to decide whether to authorize funds to pay for it. Thomas Jefferson thought this arrangement would be an "effectual check to the dog of war, by transferring the power of letting him loose from the executive to the legislative body, from those who are to spend to those who are to pay."[17]

Presidential Staff

George Washington paid a nephew out of his own pocket to be his only full-time aide, and Jefferson had only four cabinet officers to advise him. Congress did not appropriate funds for a presidential clerk until 1857, and even then Lincoln, with a staff of four, opened and answered much of the daily mail himself. The telephone was introduced in the White House in 1879, and in the 1880s Grover Cleveland was still answering it himself. Even in the early twentieth century, Woodrow Wilson typed many of his own speeches.[18] We can think back wistfully to those days, but it was not just another time but a very different country. As just one example, Jefferson oversaw a military establishment of about 6,500, whereas President Bush commands more than two million troops and sailors.

As the work of the president has expanded, staff size has exploded. Today, as presiding officer of the executive branch, the president heads, in addition to the military, a civilian bureaucracy of fifteen cabinet departments and 2.7 million civil servants (their work is described in Chapter 12). To carry out the day-to-day duties of his office, he has a large staff of policy specialists and liaisons to Congress and federal agencies.

Executive Office of the President

The bureaucracy that surrounds the modern president had its origins in the administration of Franklin Roosevelt. Because his small staff was overwhelmed by the workload of administering New Deal agencies and programs, FDR called in a team of public administration experts to help restructure his office, and in 1939 the Executive Office of the President (EOP) was created.[19]

The EOP is essentially the president's personal bureaucracy, sitting atop the executive branch and monitoring the work done in cabinet departments and agencies to see that the president's policies are carried out. Many EOP staffers are career civil servants, but the president appoints those who fill the top policymaking positions. Since FDR's administration, the EOP has been reorganized many times to reflect changing national problems and the issue priorities of individual presidents. It is not a single office but a group of offices, councils, and boards devoted to specific functional or issue areas such as national security, trade, the budget, and drug abuse (see Figure 1). The Office of Management and Budget (OMB), which has its own eight-story building, accounts for a large part of the growth in the president's bureaucracy. It is the successor agency to the Bureau of the Budget (BOB), which was created in 1921 as the primary tool for developing budget policy after Congress delegated this authority to the president. Nixon changed the name to the Office of Management and Budget to stress its function of helping the president oversee other executive branch agencies.

The EOP continued to grow in size from the 1930s to more than seventeen hundred people in George H. Bush's administration, then shrank somewhat when Clinton attempted to downsize government. The influ-

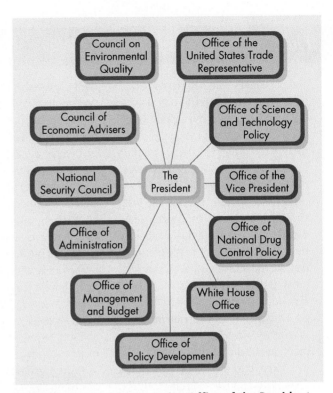

FIGURE 1 ■ The Executive Office of the President

SOURCE: Adapted from *United States Government Manual, 2003–2004* (Washington, D.C.: Government Printing Office, 2003), 87–102.

ence of other EOP heads varies with the president's issue priorities, but the head of OMB is almost always influential.[20]

White House Office

Members of the White House staff have greater influence than most advisers because the president appoints all of them, works daily with them, and tends to trust them more than others. They are often people who helped him get elected or worked for him when he held other offices. Many presidents have counted their wives among their closest advisers, and every first lady has her own office and staff within the Office of the White House. (See the box "The First Lady: A Twofer?")

Jimmy Carter and Bill Clinton are notable among recent presidents for their degree of reliance on their wives and other longtime associates. Unlike Kennedy, Nixon, Johnson, and the first George Bush, neither Carter nor Clinton had experience in Washington, and they filled their top staff positions with old friends and political operatives from their respective home states, Georgia and Arkansas. George H. Bush was a consummate Washington insider but relied heavily on his fellow Texan and longtime friend James Baker to serve on the White House staff, in the cabinet, and as his campaign manager. Of recent presidents, Ronald Reagan, who had

The president's wife has always had to walk a fine line, presiding over state social functions and being supportive of her husband without looking as though she is politically out in front of him.[1] In some ways, the concern over the influence and accountability of presidential spouses is moot. The first lady is not subject to congressional approval, but neither are the members of the White House staff or the president's close advisers outside government. But as Hillary Clinton discovered, first ladies are not immune from investigation of criminal wrongdoing, and when they serve by official appointment, as she did on the health care task force, they are subject to the same rules as other public officials. Martha Washington and Louisa Adams (wife of John Quincy Adams) were just two first ladies who felt they were in a prison, hemmed in by the limits of acceptable behavior.[2] (Louisa Adams titled her autobiography *The Adventures of a Nobody.*) Barbara Bush's chief of staff described the position as "filled with banana peels and land mines."[3]

There is no mention of a presidential spouse in the Constitution, and she has no official role or title and no salary. Yet a president's wife is definitely expected to serve as what Martha Washington called "the hostess of the nation."[4] Unmarried presidents have had to borrow a stand-in: the widower Thomas Jefferson often relied on Dolley Madison, the wife of his secretary of state.

In addition to an intense schedule of state social functions, the first lady must oversee the White House domestic staff. And it has become the custom for first ladies to identify causes, usually nonpartisan, on which they will focus special effort. Jacqueline Kennedy devoted herself to historic preservation, Lady Bird Johnson to environmental issues, Betty Ford to the creative arts and welfare of the elderly, Nancy Reagan to drug abuse prevention, Barbara and Laura Bush to literacy, and Hillary Rod-

ham Clinton to child welfare. But It was not until 1978 that Congress made formal budgetary provisions for the Office of the First Lady as an official unit within the Executive Office of the President's White House office.[5]

The visibility of the first lady increased enormously after the arrival of photography in the mid-nineteenth century; mass circulation newspapers and magazines provided new means for satisfying public curiosity about the president's private life. There was heightened interest in seeing presidents' wives in public, and early in the twentieth century, first ladies began accompanying their husbands at official functions.

With the era of television campaigns, the wives of presidential candidates began to figure much more prominently in campaign strategy. But behind the scenes, wives had long been involved. Much of the work organizing and financing Warren Harding's 1920 presidential campaign was done by his wife, Florence, which explains her widely repeated comment to her husband: "I got you the presidency; now what are you going to do with it?" Even first ladies not interested in electoral politics were used to great effect in getting votes. For example, Dwight Eisenhower considered his wife a better campaigner than he was, and Jacqueline Kennedy attained a level of popularity and celebrity that surpassed her husband's. Today it is a given that candidates for the presidency will have a spouse campaigning with them.

First ladies have been loved (Dolley Madison), feared (Abigail Adams, Edith Wilson), and both loved and feared (Eleanor Roosevelt). Dolley Madison was so highly regarded among Washington's influential that in 1844 Congress reserved a seat for her whenever she chose to attend sessions.[6] When John Adams's opponents referred to his wife as "Mrs. President," they meant something more than her marital status. Abigail Adams was an accomplished writer

with strong political opinions and not afraid to express them (for example, that women would "foment a Rebellion" if made subject to laws without representation). Her views on women's rights and other issues, coupled with the fact that her long and happy marriage to John Adams made her his principal adviser, led both supporters and opponents of the president to believe that she might have "undue" influence on policy decisions.

Edith Wilson served what she called a "stewardship" (but what others called "bedside government") during a seven-month period when her husband was disabled by a stroke.[7] She decoded classified diplomatic and military messages, encoded presidential responses, controlled access to her husband, and kept information about his condition from the public.

Although many first ladies have been political advisers to their husbands, no one did it quite so publicly, or from such an independent platform, as Eleanor Roosevelt. She held press conferences (for women journalists shut out of the president's briefings), wrote a syndicated newspaper column read by millions, and made regular radio broadcasts. She discussed policy with her husband, bombarded him with memos, and brought supporters of the causes she advocated into the White House. She served on countless committees and traveled around the world promoting racial equality, women's and social justice issues, and the war effort. After her husband's death, in later years, her efforts for human rights and international cooperation as a delegate to the United Nations earned her the title "First Lady of the World."

Mrs. Roosevelt's stature was attained under the exceptional circumstances of her husband's long tenure in the White House during a prolonged period of national crisis (the Great Depression and World War II). Furthermore, after his incapacitation from

this way made it difficult for Clinton to keep his and the nation's focus on important issues. He got so bogged down in details that his wife complained that he had become the "mechanic-in-chief."[27] In addition, his young, unruly staff and Clinton's penchant for sitting up all night with them talking issues and policy were taken by some as symptomatic of a chaotic and disorganized management style.[28] Under Clinton's second and third staff chiefs, lines of authority and communication were tightened. But his White House operation still reflected his love of policy details and an inability to maintain a schedule and stick to a few clear policy themes when communicating with the public and the media.

George W. Bush employed a near-opposite approach to management. With experience as an enforcer of political loyalties on his father's staff, and as the only president to hold an M.B.A., Bush set out to run his White House along corporate lines. He tried to delegate work along crisp lines of authority, kept to a tight schedule, and demanded complete team loyalty with no public dissent from administration policy.[29] The deeper he got into his term, as his policies played out, he found what most presidents find: that it is impossible to keep rivalries and dissident policy positions from emerging, even among close advisers.

Bush also delegated so much policy responsibility that his first secretary of the treasury said that in cabinet and private meetings, he seemed disengaged and uninformed on issues.[30] It sometimes made Bush appear to be a secondary figure in his own administration; his closest adviser, Karl Rove, gained the nickname "Bush's Brain." Bush's press staff had to work hard to remind the public that the president was in charge of the White House.

Office of the Vice President

The Office of the Vice President was made part of the EOP in 1972. Not long afterward, the vice president got his own white mansion (the former home of the chief of naval operations) when the government decided that maintaining an official residence was much less expensive than paying for the necessary security arrangements on the homes of each new vice president.[31] The vice president, paid slightly more than $200,000 in 2004, has his own budget for office and staff (housed in the old Executive Office Building adjacent to the White House) and an official airplane (*Air Force Two*).

That vice presidents have succeeded to office unexpectedly nine times (following eight presidential deaths and one resignation) may be responsible for the growing importance of the office.[32] Most recent vice presidents have been seasoned public servants with considerable experience and personal records of achievement.

That they were willing to take the job suggests that it has become more than "standby equipment," as Nelson Rockefeller once called it.

The only formal duties the vice president has are to preside over the Senate, cast tie-breaking votes, and succeed to the presidency should it be vacated. Historically, presidents gave their vice presidents little information and few opportunities to prepare for succession. Woodrow Wilson's vice president, Thomas R. Marshall, said that holding the job was like being "a man in a cataleptic fit. He cannot speak, he cannot move. He suffers no pain. He is perfectly conscious of all that goes on. But he has no part in it." Franklin Roosevelt's first vice president, John Nance Garner, was less elegant in observing that his job was not worth a "pitcher of warm piss." Harry Truman did not even know about the atomic bomb program until after Franklin Roosevelt's death, but within months he had to decide whether to use the bomb against Japan.

Until recent times, presidents had difficulty delegating important jobs to their vice presidents. One reason is that vice presidential candidates have often been chosen to balance a ticket geographically and ideologically, not because of closeness to the presidential candidate. In fact, sometimes they are electoral opponents. And once in office, some vice presidents have used the position to build an independent political base from which to run for the presidency. This has not always made them the most loyal supporters of the president's agenda.

Historically, vice presidents were asked to deal mainly with ceremonial matters or partisan activities (such as being the attack dog during the campaign, leaving his running mate free to appear more presidential). How much work and authority vice presidents have depends on the personal relationship with the president, how needy the president is for assistance, or how generous he is about sharing power. Jimmy Carter was the first president to delegate to his vice president responsibilities for day-to-day White House operations.[33] He gave Walter Mondale, who had the Washington experience Carter lacked, a White House office, scheduled weekly lunches with him, included him in all White House advisory groups and all important meetings, and asked him to lobby Congress and read the paperwork that crossed Carter's desk. Ronald Reagan, Bill Clinton, and both George Bushes added to this new tradition.

Prior to the Bush-Cheney administration, the closest working relationship between a president and vice president was undoubtedly that between Bill Clinton and Al Gore. Gore became so influential in the Clinton White House that he was referred to as a "shadow president" and his staff as a "shadow cabinet." Divisions did not surface until Gore was running his own presidential

President George W. Bush and Vice President Dick Cheney in sync.

campaign and trying to distance himself in order to establish his own identity.

Richard Cheney was already well known to George W. Bush from service in his father's administration, and he had far more administrative and Washington experience than the new president. Cheney ran Bush's transition team and chose many members of the White House staff. He headed the most important policymaking groups in the White House and was the author of its energy policy. He also created his own national security staff and worked closely on military policy with his old friend Donald Rumsfeld, secretary of defense (a position Cheney had once filled). Cheney had unprecedented access to the Oval Office, meeting the president every morning and sometimes several times more during the day. He was also deeply involved in the president's legislative strategy, using his role as Senate president and his ties to the House as an ex-member to keep a constant presence on Capitol Hill.

In fact, Cheney's influence and visibility were so great in the early months of the administration that he had to be pushed to the background so that Bush would have the chance to establish his own identity as president. To this end, Cheney stopped speaking in staff meetings when Bush was present.[34] Yet when Bush was asked to appear before the 9/11 Commission, he agreed to comply only on the condition that he and Cheney be interviewed together. Many observers continued to believe, even after he assumed a less public presence, that the far more experienced and policy-savvy Cheney was running a large part of the White House operation. This would not be surprising given Bush's preference for delegating work. And Bush could do so free of the fear that his vice president would use that power to build an organization to support his own race for the presidency. For health and other reasons, Cheney had no interest in running. However, outperforming the president and serving as his attack dog—Cheney won the nickname "Darth Vader" for his dark critiques of the opposition—does carry political liabilities for the vice president as well as the president. Midway through Bush's term, some of his supporters advocated dropping Cheney from the 2004 ticket in favor of Condoleezza Rice.

Presidential Leadership

We choose presidents who we think can be effective leaders and whose goals we share. As presidential scholar Richard Neustadt pointed out long ago, presidents need more than their formal powers to achieve these goals. They need the **power to persuade.**[35] The modern president comes into office with extensive experience in persuading the public, but presidents must be able to win over interest group leaders; newspaper and magazine publishers, reporters, and columnists; judges who hear challenges to their policies; leaders in the business community; and a majority in Congress. These policymakers and opinion elite, whom Neustadt called Washingtonians, are, in short, the people the president needs to get his policies enacted. Because the Washingtonians also need him to get what they want, a president can bargain and persuade.

The effective president is "one who seizes the center of the Washington bazaar and actively barters to build winning coalitions."[36] Presidents "remember" their friends by putting their pet projects in the budget, by campaigning for them, and by naming the people they want to public office.

In pursuit of his policy agenda, a president can use his powers to persuade the public as a means to bring pressure on a reluctant Congress, or when the public is disinterested or slow to accept, he can try to persuade Washingtonians to shape public opinion. In doing so, he has much more to rely on than his rhetorical skills. A president's powers give him considerable favors and penalties to dispense. As the chief maker of foreign policy, he can seek support from Irish, Cuban, and Jewish Americans by supporting their objectives in Northern Ireland, Cuba, and the Middle East, respectively. As *de facto* leader of his party, he can use the symbolic resources of the presidency in campaigning for candidates he supports. And as chief budget maker, he has many favors to give and withhold, including support for hundreds of pork barrel projects.

In this section, we will look at how presidents use their powers, including their powers of persuasion, to provide leadership.

The President and His Party

The fact that the president is the head of his party and chief advocate for its policy agenda is an important dimension of presidential power. As party leader, the president is an electoral adversary of members of the House and Senate who do not belong to his party. He can use his reputation and the weight of his office not only to challenge legislative priorities but also to try to unseat those who oppose them.

To improve the electoral chances of their party, presidents try to help recruit good candidates for House and Senate races. In addition, presidents help raise money by being the headliner at fundraising events and by staying on good terms with major contributors. They also send their aides around the country to help fellow Democrats or Republicans with their campaigns and sometimes even go themselves. Seeing presidents in person—seeing a little history in the making—is exciting, and they almost always draw a crowd and good media coverage. But the president usually tries to camouflage his role as party leader when trying to persuade people to support him or to vote for his party's candidates, because people are more likely to listen to a president when they see him as head of state.

Presidential partisanship has a purpose: The more members of a president's party who sit in Congress, the more support he gets for his policies. However, a president's support, when he chooses to give it, is no guarantee of electoral success for congressional candidates, especially in off-year elections (see Table 1). Since 1932, the president's party has lost an average of twenty-seven House and four Senate seats in off-year elections.

However, this trend no longer prevails, due to the increasingly safe seats brought about by the fact that almost all incumbents run for reelection, their seats are tailored to protect them, and they have a tremendous fundraising advantage. These factors help make candidates safe even when their presidential candidate loses or is unpopular at midterm. The 1998 election was the first off-year election since 1934 that the president's party had a net gain, but that feat was duplicated in 2002.

In presidential election years, the average gains for the winning presidential candidate's party in Congress are close to their losses in off-year elections, twenty in the House and three in the Senate. Again, these patterns are changing. In 1988 and 1992, the winning presidential party lost seats in Congress. In 2004, the winning presidential party gained the historical average in the Senate (three) but fell far below the historical average in the House.

The President and Congress

Predictably, the office of the president has grown along with the expansion of the country, the size of government, and the economic and military power of the United States. The Founders expected both Congress and the presidency to have significant policymaking powers and worked hard to balance these powers so that one branch did not dominate the other. Yet they described Congress and its powers first in the Constitution because they expected it to be the most influential part of government.[37] And even near the end of the nineteenth century, Woodrow Wilson described our system as congressional government. Today, observers are more likely to comment on the powers of the presidency or what some now call presidential government.[38] Yet Congress remains influential, and we should not overstate the dominance of the president in our system.

The president does have some advantages over Congress in providing leadership. He is a single voice, one

| TABLE 1 | The President's Tattered Coattails: Congressional Gains and Losses for the President's Party in Off-Year Elections |

Seats Gained or Lost by the President's Party			
Year	President	House	Senate
1934	Roosevelt (D)	+9	+10
1938	Roosevelt (D)	−71	−6
1942	Roosevelt (D)	−45	−9
1946	Truman (D)	−55	−12
1950	Truman (D)	−29	−6
1954	Eisenhower (R)	−18	−1
1958	Eisenhower (R)	−47	−13
1962	Kennedy (D)	−4	+4
1966	Johnson (D)	−47	−3
1970	Nixon (R)	−12	+2
1974	Ford (R)	−48	−3
1978	Carter (D)	−11	−3
1982	Reagan (R)	−26	0
1986	Reagan (R)	−6	−8
1990	G. H. Bush (R)	−8	−1
1994	Clinton (D)	−52	−9
1998	Clinton (D)	+5	0
2002	G. W. Bush (R)	+6	+2
Average, all off-year elections		−26	−3
Average, all presidential election years		+20	+3

SOURCES: *Congressional Quarterly Weekly Review,* various issues; Roger H. Davidson and Walter J. Oleszek, *Congress and Its Members,* 9th ed. (Washington, D.C.: CQ Press, 2004), 106.

that commands media attention. Congress has many voices, divided among party leaders, committee leaders, and others who by their personality command attention. The president can move swiftly to respond to a crisis; Congress, by its nature, moves slowly through a complex legislative process. The president represents the United States in negotiations with other nations; Congress can only react to the results of these negotiations.

It is not surprising, then, that the president has gained some powers at the expense of Congress. Many were delegated (budget making), voluntarily ceded to the president (foreign policymaking during the Cold War and then in the war against terrorism), or assumed by default through congressional inaction. What the executive branch gained was not the simple sum of what the legislative branch lost, as if the president and Congress were contestants in a zero-sum game. In many cases, the president exercised power never exercised by any branch of the national government before. Crises arise, presidential incumbents respond, and in the process they assume powers of government not yet established at the federal level. Indeed, several extraordinary extensions of presidential authority occurred in wartime or at a time of national crisis, including Lincoln's suspension of *habeas corpus* in the Civil War and, most recently, George W. Bush's authorization of military tribunals to try suspected terrorists in the absence of an act of war or a uniformed enemy.

The president has significant powers to shape legislation. This includes powers of agenda setting, persuasion in influencing the content of legislation, the veto power, and special influence in foreign and military policy.

Setting the Agenda

One way the president can achieve his legislative priorities is that he can set the agenda. As the head of a political party with an issue agenda, the president has become a chief advocate for a legislative program. Whether packaged as the Square Deal, the New Deal, the Fair Deal, the Great Society, or the New Frontier, most presidents come to office with a legislative agenda.

Agenda setting means that the president can influence what Congress and the Washingtonians are talking about. Obviously, he cannot control the agenda, as demonstrated by the Lewinsky scandal in the Clinton years, which the press, the public, and Congress apparently found much more fascinating than policy issues. But by clearly articulating his priorities and then staying on that message and working to achieve those priorities, the president has a huge influence on what Congress—and the country—is focusing on.

The president has less clout over the alternatives Congress considers to deal with the issue the president frames. For example, the president may have health insurance reform at the top of his priority list, but a hos-

tile Congress might shape it in a way that defeats the president's goals.

Budget making is an area where the president has many tools to set the agenda. The Founders gave Congress—the House of Representatives, in particular—the power of the purse. For many years, the president had a negligible role in managing executive branch budgets. Agency funding requests went to the House unreviewed and unchanged by the White House. But by the end of World War I, a general awareness had developed that a larger government required better management. In the Budget and Accounting Act of 1921, Congress delegated important priority-setting and managerial responsibilities that have given presidents so inclined the opportunity to dominate budgetary politics.

The 1921 act requires the president to give Congress estimates of how much money will be needed to run the government during the next fiscal year. The president's annual budget message contains recommendations for how much money Congress should appropriate for every program funded by the national government. Formulating the message requires the White House to examine all agency budget requests and to decide which to support or reject. This exercise allows the president and his staff to begin the annual budget debate on their own terms.

Having the OMB within the Executive Office of the President gives the president an edge in dealing with Congress on budget issues because its hundreds of experts work only for the president. Congress's nonpartisan budget office, the Congressional Budget Office (CBO), prepares budget reports that are regarded as substantially more reliable than those of the OMB, but the policy initiative lies with the OMB and the White House because they prepare the first budget draft. The annual budget is huge and hard to read and understand. Because the president presents it to Congress and the public, he has the opportunity to set the agenda and shape the debate on spending priorities.

The president also has an overwhelming advantage in shaping the foreign policy agenda. It is very difficult for Congress, with its 535 voices, to articulate coherent policy alternatives to the president's. In private, the president's advisers may advocate for conflicting policies, but most of these do not make it into the national debate, or at least not until after a policy has stalled or failed. Reasonable alternatives may never be mentioned in major media outlets, let alone debated by the public. The media did little to initiate discussion of our overall goals in the Persian Gulf or Iraq wars, choosing instead to cover troop commitments largely as a logistical challenge and a human-interest story. Reporters' acceptance of Pentagon restrictions on news gathering in the Gulf War also helped George H. Bush generate support for his policies by producing news of successful, but not unsuccessful, attacks and by concealing information describing casualties on both sides. His son's administration used a more effective tactic in embedding reporters with combat units, tipping journalistic coverage to the soldiers', rather than an independent, perspective. Journalistic coverage was limited in other ways as well, such as by refusing photographers and camera crews access to soldiers' coffins being returned from Afghanistan and Iraq.

Shaping and Passing Bills

Presidents can have considerable influence over the shape of legislation too. How active the president's personal role is, and how influential he is, depends on his involvement in policy detail, knowledge of congressional operations, and powers of persuasion. In all, twenty-four presidents have served in Congress and presumably understood how that institution works. Aside from their personal experience and knowledge, all presidents have advisers who serve as congressional liaisons; they lobby for the president's agenda and facilitate exchange of information with members of Congress on pending legislation.

Not all presidents who served in Congress were knowledgeable or effective. For example, Truman, Kennedy, and the first George Bush had short and undistinguished congressional careers, and Nixon used his short time in the House and Senate to build a national reputation rather than to sponsor legislation. In contrast, Gerald Ford and Lyndon Johnson rose to leadership positions through long years of congressional service. As a former Senate majority leader of legendary persuasiveness, Johnson is the classic example of the president as an inside dopester and congressional coalition builder. He knew how to approach members and was a masterful lobbyist.

Johnson was essentially a persuader and a deal maker, but sometimes White House staffers are more heavy-handed in seeking support. A Reagan aide described how the White House changed one senator's vote: "We just beat his brains out. We stood him in front of an open grave and told him he could jump in if he wanted" to oppose Reagan.[39] Such tactics can succeed but can also make a president look bad.

Presidents also use the prestige of their office as an instrument of persuasion. *Air Force One* is a favorite of all presidents for influencing anyone and everyone they want to sway with shows of the power of the office.

Reagan's leadership style in dealing with Congress involved going public to pressure it for support. In contrast, Clinton tried to generate congressional support for his policies by personally lobbying individual members and intermediaries such as business and union leaders and by trying to get backing in the parts of the country and the interest groups most affected by the policies. He gave interviews to journalists whose papers and magazines reached people he wanted to influence. During his administration, the final versions of many pieces of legislation were worked out in direct negotiations between conference committee leaders and White House staffers or Clinton himself. Clinton was often criticized for having so much hands-on involvement with Congress because such a strategy invests the prestige of the office in too many issues while also risking the political capital of the president himself.

George W. Bush avoided this involvement in his first years, taking positions on far fewer issues and keeping a personal distance from Congress while relying to a great extent on Vice President Cheney to handle relationships with congressional leaders. Cheney served in the House and also worked as a legislative liaison when he was a White House staffer. Bush reportedly told one senator repeatedly, "When you're talking to Dick Cheney, you're talking to me."[40] Cheney goes to Capitol Hill at least once a week to meet with the Republican caucus and has a working office there. For lobbying purposes, he also keeps an office in the House of Representatives; he is the only vice president in history to have had an office in that chamber.

The president's power to shape the budget is one of the greatest sources of friction in relations between the executive and legislative branches. Little is possible without funding, so the stakes in the budget process are high. Presidents who are little interested in the details of domestic policy, like Reagan and both Bushes, do not get maximum political leverage out of the budgetary powers Congress has delegated them. But a president whose strength lies in the mastery of detail may be able to use those powers, as Clinton did, to dominate budgetary politics and the debate over deficit reduction.

Presidents cannot always get the support they need, however. Members of Congress have their own constituencies and careers. And presidential persuasion does not always involve bargaining. Presidents also remind fellow Republicans or Democrats of the need to stick together to promote their party platform and achieve party goals. Bipartisan appeals can sometimes be effective, too, especially in foreign affairs.

Veto Power

No president has to rely solely on his persuasive powers to affect legislation. The Constitution has given the chief executive veto power over bills passed by Congress. The veto power is not listed among the president's formal powers in Article II but rather is included in Article I as a check on Congress's power to legislate.

When the president receives a bill passed by Congress, he has three options: he can sign it into law; he can veto it and send it back to Congress along with his objections; or he can take no action, in which case the bill becomes a law after ten congressional working days.

An unsigned bill returned by the president can be passed into law if two-thirds of both houses vote to override the veto. But if Congress adjourns within ten working days after sending legislation to the White House and the president chooses to pocket the bill—that is, not to act on it—the legislation dies. This option, called a **pocket veto,** is a means by which the president can kill a bill without facing an override attempt in Congress.

Given the presence of White House supporters in Congress and the president's ability to go public, mobilizing two-thirds majorities in both houses to override a veto is usually very hard. As a result, presidents can try to influence the content of bills by threatening to veto them if they do not conform to presidential wishes.

Only nine presidents, including George W. Bush in his first term, never vetoed a bill. Franklin Roosevelt holds the record with 635 vetoes in fourteen years; only 9 were overridden. Presidents who use the veto too often may appear isolated or uncooperative or may seem to be exercising negative leadership. But the fact that presidents are rarely overridden reminds us of their power when they decide that they really want something.

Divided Government

Presidential success in working with Congress is influenced strongly by whether Congress is controlled by the president's party or the opposition party. This explains why presidents usually take an active role in congressional campaigns. When one party controls the White House and another controls one or both houses of Congress, it is called **divided government.** The Founders made divided government possible by giving each branch its own powers and distinctive constituency and providing for different methods of election. This contrasts with parliamentary systems, in which voters elect members of the legislative branch, who in turn choose the head of government.

In the first half of the twentieth century, divided government did not occur very often. From 1900 to 1950, only four of twenty-six presidential and midterm elections resulted in divided government.[41] From 1952 to 2000, however, sixteen of twenty-five elections produced divided government. Even with Reagan's overwhelming victory in 1980, the Republicans captured only the Senate. Their dominance lasted until 1986, when the Democrats regained majority control. George H. Bush had to work with a Democratic Congress, and Clinton had a Republican-controlled Congress after 1994. In contrast, George W. Bush had a unified government for all but a few months of his first term.

Some observers believe that divided government is at least partly responsible for the failure to solve many of the country's important problems. The term *gridlock* has often been applied to this policy stalemate. The president presents a program and Congress does not accept

it, or Congress passes a bill and the president vetoes it. The result can be a lot of squabbling but few results. The especially bitter rivalry between the White House and Congress during the impeachments proceedings in 1998 brought legislative action to a standstill. But in times of national emergency, a divided Congress is not necessarily a barrier to action; witness the significant amount of legislation passed by Congress in the first months after 9/11 when the Senate was controlled by the Democrats.

The impact of divided versus unified government on a president's reach can be seen in the difference between the Clinton and George W. Bush administrations. Clinton worked mainly with a divided government, while Bush's has mainly been unified. Clinton's success rate in Congress plummeted to 40 percent in 1998, whereas Bush's exceeded 80 percent for most of his first term. Clinton had to modify almost all of his legislative proposals, such as welfare reform, to versions that would be accepted by Republicans. And he could not sustain any momentum in his legislative agenda because the Republican leadership tied up Congress with special investigations of the president's actions.

In contrast, during Bush's third and fourth years, Democratic legislators were virtually shut out of all negotiations on final drafts of legislation and at times not allowed to bring their own bills to a vote. Bush's congressional liaisons were involved in the drafting and rewriting of administration-proposed legislation at all stages of the process. Furthermore, congressional oversight of executive agencies, especially those involved with military, foreign, environmental, and regulatory policies, came to a near halt. From the Clinton to the Bush administration, congressional limits on the president's legislative and budgetary powers all but evaporated.

Success with Congress

Success in getting congressional support for the legislation he wants is an important indicator of the president's effectiveness with Congress. Franklin Roosevelt's ranking as one of our greatest presidents can be attributed in part to his legislative effectiveness. He was able to persuade Congress to enact much of his legislative program within the first one hundred days of his administration. Those were extraordinary times, and few presidents since have been able to match his success in Congress (see Figure 2).

Reagan's effectiveness with Congress was greatest in his first year in office, when he got Congress to approve a major tax cut and increase military spending. Economic problems produced in part by these changes and a growing public awareness that he was uninformed about White House activities led to a drop in his effectiveness with Congress during the remainder of his administration. As Figure 2 shows, Reagan's congressional

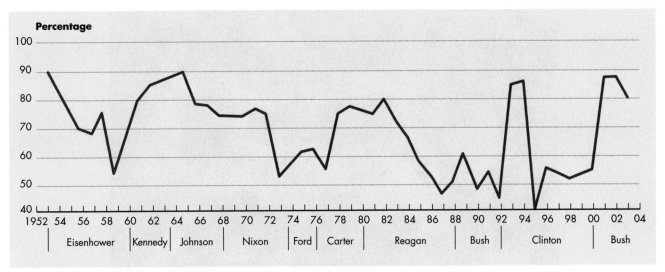

Percentage

F I G U R E 2 ■ **Presidential Success on Congressional Votes** *Presidents usually have the most success with Congress early in their first terms. This figure shows the percentage of votes that presidents have won when they took a position. Clinton's and George W. Bush's scores rank among the highest of any presidents in their first year, yet Clinton also had the two lowest in CQ's nearly fifty years of record keeping.*

SOURCE: *Congressional Quarterly Weekly Report,* January 12, 2002, 112; December 14, 2002, 3237; David Nather, "Score Belies Bush's Success," *Congressional Quarterly Weekly Report,* January 3, 2004, 18–20.

support fell after 1981 and was low compared to other presidents.

Congressional support for George H. Bush was weak throughout his term. Figure 2 shows that his first-year success with Congress was the lowest of any elected president since 1953, when scores were first computed. Bush had fewer congressional Republicans to work with than any GOP president in the twentieth century, but he even had low support among congressional Republicans. He lacked a well-articulated legislative program. He also failed to capture the public's attention with clear themes, what he once called "the vision thing." This prevented Bush from securing more congressional support, even after the Persian Gulf War, when his popularity was very high.

Clinton tried to emulate Reagan's successful first-year strategy of asking Congress to vote on a few high-priority bills. This strategy lets presidents define their positions in relatively simple terms and seek congressional support during the postelection honeymoon period, before other influences on Congress have time to make mobilizing a majority more difficult. Enjoying early success with Congress can help presidents build their professional reputations.

With both houses of Congress controlled by Democratic majorities at the outset of his administration, Clinton did not have to deal with a divided government. Despite substantial disagreements among congressional Democrats, Clinton succeeded in getting majority support for most of his early economic proposals.

His early legislative record was impressive, but it did not give him a reputation for effectiveness. It was overshadowed by the scandals that followed him into his second term and by his failure to articulate larger goals in a way that let the American people know where he wanted to lead them. In 1995 and 1998, he had the lowest success rates in Congress of any president in the second half of the century (see Figure 2).

George W. Bush's first-year success rate of 87 percent was nearly identical to that of Clinton's first year; like Clinton, he had majorities of his own party in both houses, most of the time. He achieved this by taking positions on only half as many bills as Clinton had. In addition, Bush usually took a public stand only after Congress had drafted a bill in a form likely to pass.[42] With this strategy of doing and risking far less than his predecessor, Bush equaled Clinton's success rate. He was also very successful in his second year, partly reflecting his post–9/11 public support. His success rate fell to a still impressive 79 percent in 2003.

The relationship between president and Congress is a complex one. Ultimately, how persuasive a president is with Congress in getting his legislative agenda passed is an important element of whether he will be judged a successful president.

Making Foreign and Military Policy

The president has become more powerful than Congress in foreign and defense policy. Nonetheless, the president's success in foreign policy also relies on persuasion,

Signaling the growing importance of Asia in U.S. foreign policy, Bill Clinton became the first president since Jimmy Carter to visit India, the world's second most populous country and an emerging nuclear power.

not only with members of Congress but also foreign leaders.

The president has the initiative in foreign policy through his constitutional duties in diplomacy and defense and the political imperative that the nation have a single official position when representing its policies to other countries. The president also has in foreign policy, to a greater extent than in domestic policy, access to more information than other politicians do. He can often stifle debate by citing classified or secret information from the CIA, Defense Department, State Department, and other agencies and saying, "If you knew what I knew, you would agree with me." The president can make information available on a selective basis, sharing certain material with Congress (and the public) while withholding other material. Members of Congress are at a distinct disadvantage.

This advantage was obvious in the run-up to the 2003 invasion of Iraq. The president told Congress, and had his secretary of state tell the United Nations and the rest of the world, that Iraq possessed weapons of mass destruction. He also told them that Saddam Hussein was in large part responsible for the attacks of 9/11. The public had no way of knowing that neither of these was true until much later, after the invasion revealed no weapons and investigations revealed that prewar intelligence was misused by the Bush White House. Yet the claims the Bush administration made so dominated the public discussion that even by the time of the 2004 election many Americans still believed them.

This ability to set both the issue and debate agendas gives the president a tremendous advantage in appealing for public support. There is almost always a "rally 'round the flag" effect on the public when the president takes a strong stance in foreign policy, especially if troops are involved. This advantage can be short-lived, however, as George H. Bush found after the Persian Gulf War and his son did after the quick toppling of the Iraqi government led to a prolonged insurgency. Presidents who take military action without a broad consensus need to accomplish their goals quickly or face loss of public support.

Another advantage the president has over Congress is that he can act decisively, whereas Congress must reach agreement and vote in order to act, and this takes time. If the action involves deploying troops into combat areas, Congress may hesitate to oppose the president because it fears that doing so may be seen as disloyalty to the troops and by other nations as a sign of American weakness or lack of resolve.

The president has similar advantages in military policy. A president needs to be able to act decisively in international affairs without making any prolonged or costly commitments against the public's wishes. Congress has historically served as the most important check on the president, but its power to influence military policy is limited in emergency or crisis situations.

Of the forty-two men who have served in the presidency (Grover Cleveland served two nonconsecutive terms), all but twelve have had military experience. Nine achieved the rank of general, and six were propelled to the presidency by virtue of military fame (Washington, Jackson, William Harrison, Taylor, Grant, and Eisenhower). Both Theodore and Franklin Roosevelt served as secretary of the navy, and FDR played an active role in directing the naval war against Japan. On the other hand, Lincoln led the Union through the Civil War with only brief experience in the Illinois state militia.

It is unlikely that future contenders or presidents will have the kind of military experience their predecessors had, given the absence of the draft and the rise of a volunteer military. John McCain, Bob Kerrey, John Kerry, Richard Gephardt, Robert Dole, Wesley Clark, and Al Gore are among the recent presidential contenders who have served in the regular armed forces, although Gore was a noncombatant. McCain, Kerry, Dole, and Kerrey were decorated for bravery, but this experience did not provide a steppingstone to the White House. President Carter graduated from the Naval Academy with the intention of making the military his career, but he a was nuclear engineer, not a battle commander, and his career was cut short after seven years.

No *sitting* president has ever led troops into battle, but modern weaponry has led to more presidential involvement, especially in setting limits on the scope of battle. The decisions to wage limited wars in Korea and Vietnam, for example, were based on presidential beliefs that victories over North Korea and North Vietnam were not worth risking a nuclear holocaust. Under our Constitution, decisions on goals and containing the costs and consequences of war are for elected civilian leaders to make, not the professional military.

The development of high-tech weaponry has also given presidents more military leadership opportunities. Johnson and Nixon used sophisticated communications equipment to select targets in Vietnam. In the Persian Gulf War, Bush's White House sent orders to General Norman Schwarzkopf on everything from how to stop a blockade-running Iraqi tanker to when to end combat.[43] During the Iraq war, George W. Bush said he left the strategy entirely to the military commanders, but it was an open secret that many decisions, such as the number of combat troops committed and the types of units deployed, were made by Bush's secretary of defense, Donald Rumsfeld.[44]

Despite congressional oversight of military policy, presidential power is wide ranging and has been extended to domestic affairs that presidents judged crucial to their national security goals. Historically, these powers have been exercised most extensively during wars endangering our national survival. During the Civil War, Lincoln suspended the use of writs of *habeas corpus,* seized control of some eastern railroads, and blockaded southern ports. He took these actions as commander in chief and without congressional authorization. The survival of the Union was at stake, and Lincoln believed that he had to take extraordinary measures. Because many in Congress agreed with him, he was able to do what he thought necessary.

Acting under his expansive definition of commander in chief, Franklin Roosevelt put one hundred thousand Americans of Japanese descent into camps during World War II. He had the government seize and operate more than sixty industries important to the war effort and vulnerable to union strikes. In addition, he created special agencies to control the consumption and price of gasoline, meat, shoes, and other goods.

Wars that do not threaten our national survival tend not to generate high levels of support for executive actions. When Truman had his secretary of commerce seize most of the nation's steel mills during the Korean War to keep them operating in the face of a possible labor strike, one of the steel companies took him to court. In 1952, the Supreme Court sided with the company by ruling that Truman had not exhausted other, legal remedies to the problem.[45] But Truman, a World War I infantry officer, surrendered none of his power as commander in chief. When General Douglas MacArthur, commander of U.S. and United Nations Forces in Korea, refused to carry out his orders to keep the war contained in Korea, Truman ordered him home, effectively ending his military career.

The extent of the war-making power exercised by Presidents Johnson and Nixon during the undeclared war in Vietnam inspired the 1970s characterization of the presidency as "imperial" and led Congress to take action to limit the power of the president to take unilateral military. In 1973, Congress passed the **War Powers Resolution** to limit the president's ability to commit troops to combat. It says that the president can use troops abroad under three conditions: when Congress has declared war, when Congress has given him specific authority to do so, or when an attack on the United States or its military creates a national crisis. If a president commits troops under the third condition, he is supposed to consult with Congress beforehand, if possible, and notify it within forty-eight hours afterward. Unless Congress approves the use of troops, the president must withdraw them within sixty days, or ninety days if he needs more time to protect them. Congress can pass a concurrent resolution (not subject to presidential veto) at any time ordering the president to end the use of military force.

President George W. Bush surprised the troops at Thanksgiving dinner in Iraq. As commander in chief, the president has the ability to burnish his image and capitalize on the public's desire to rally around the flag.

AP/Wide World Photos

President George H. Bush rallies the troops as the Persian Gulf War looms.

© Time Life Pictures/Getty Images

Congress passed the War Powers Resolution over Nixon's veto. He, and all presidents since, believed it violated his constitutional authority to protect the nation from military threats. Although presidents have not questioned Congress's constitutional authority to declare war, all have fought congressional involvement in the use of troops. As a result, enforcement of the act has proved difficult. For example, when George H. Bush sent troops to invade Panama in 1989, he did not even refer to the War Powers Resolution in the two-page letter he sent to Congress—sixty hours after the invasion began—justifying the invasion. He also ordered 250,000 troops to the Persian Gulf between August and November 1990 on his own authority and delayed announcing his decision to double this number until after the November elections. This kept the decision that changed our mission from defense (Operation Desert Shield) to offense (Operation Desert Storm) from coming to Congress until Bush had mobilized United States and world opinion and gained United Nations support. By the time Congress authorized using force in January 1991, the question of whether to do so was, practically speaking, already decided. The same can be said for George W. Bush's decision to invade Iraq in 2003. He reluctantly went to Congress for authorization, but the decision to invade had been made well before Congress consented.

Although the War Powers Resolution was not very effective in curtailing the president's dominance in military policy, the end of the Cold War did temporarily threaten the president's free hand in foreign policy. Without the threat of a challenging external enemy of superpower status, Congress was less willing to give the president the benefit of the doubt in major foreign policy initiatives, certainly not those involving a commitment of military forces. Clinton, the first post–Cold War president, was not able to count on congressional support even when he had committed troops, as in Bosnia and Haiti. In 2000, the Senate tried, and just narrowly failed, to use the War Powers Resolution to force Clinton to withdraw U.S. troops from the NATO contingent in Kosovo. Many of Clinton's trade and economic initiatives met with similar resistance.

Prior to 9/11, George W. Bush was already trying to recover some of the power the White House lost to Congress during the post–Cold War years. After minimal consultation with Congress, he withdrew from prior treaty agreements, including those on antimissile defense and global warming. The war on terrorism strengthened the president's power further. The shock of the first-ever attack on the U.S. mainland by a foreign enemy and the uncertainty of how to deal with a new kind of warfare resulted in Congress's giving the president a virtually free hand in planning the initial response. In a strengthened position after the attacks, Bush was successful in winning greater latitude in covert operations for intelligence agencies and regaining the "fast-track" trade authority that allows the president to negotiate trade deals that Congress can reject but cannot change.

The problem with the deference of Congress to the president in the war on terror is that it is an ill-defined war, one that, like the war on drugs and the war on crime, has no prospect of a finite end. Thus any surrender of congressional power and civil liberties could be longer-term than in America's previous wars against a defined enemy.

Executive Leadership

The one area where there is no doubt that the Founders expected the president to lead was in running the executive branch. The Founders expected Congress to make policy and the president to administer it. The president has several tools in leading the executive branch.

Appointment

The Office of Management and Budget not only proposes allocations for each department, agency, and program of the federal government but also monitors how and when executive branch agencies spend appropriated funds, their operating procedures, and the policies they develop. This gives the president another advantage over Congress, one that Reagan used to great advantage. By appointing agency and department heads who oppose policies that he opposes but that Congress has funded, the president can issue directives that effectively bring policy implementation to a halt.

Although most of the staff in the executive branch are civil service appointees, the president nominates about three thousand people to civilian positions in the State Department and other federal agencies, two-thirds of whom do not require confirmation. About one-third do require formal approval by the Senate, but only about six hundred of the most important policymaking jobs—heads of regulatory agencies, boards and commissions, cabinet secretaries and ambassadors, and federal judges, for example—receive careful review.[46] For the highest-profile positions, such as the secretaries of state and defense, televised hearings are held prior to a confirmation vote in the Senate.

For decades, it was customary for the Senate, no matter which party controlled it, to approve the president's nominations to policymaking positions on the grounds that having won the election, he is entitled to surround himself with people who can help put his policies in place. But the highly partisan context of the Senate in the last several decades has weakened this tradition somewhat. In practice, the president's freedom to name people to some positions is limited by the custom of **senatorial courtesy.** This gives senators from the president's party a virtual veto over appointments to positions, including judicial appointments, in their states. As the leader of his party, the president has a political (not governmental) obligation to help senators from his party get reelected. So he usually defers to their political needs and wishes when making federal appointments in their home states, even though doing so limits to some extent his freedom to choose.

Presidents have more latitude in nominating people to positions with national jurisdictions, such as cabinet posts and seats on regulatory boards and independent agencies. It has become customary to give preference in some appointments to people with politically useful backgrounds, such as naming a westerner secretary of the interior, a person with union ties to be labor secretary, or a close associate of the president to be attorney general. But these considerations were never confining and, as traditions, are weakening.

Removal Power

Although the power to remove appointees is not in the Constitution, presidents have it. Their power to name people they trust implies a power to remove those they find wanting, but because the power is not explicit, Congress has not always recognized it. The battle over removal powers was fought and largely won by Grover Cleveland, who on entering office in 1885 insisted on replacing many policymaking officials with his own appointees. He was challenged by the Senate, but he persevered. His persistence is credited with helping revitalize a presidency weakened by Andrew Johnson's impeachment.

In 1935, the Supreme Court refined this removal power by saying that presidents can remove appointees from purely administrative jobs but not from those with quasi-legislative and judicial responsibilities. This ruling protects many appointees, but distinguishing quasi-legislative and judicial positions from those with no policymaking authority can be subjective.[47]

There is no ambiguity, however, about a president's removal authority over people he has appointed to policymaking positions with fixed terms, such as regulatory boards and the Federal Reserve Board. Presidents *cannot* remove these people. To grant the president the power to remove federal judges would interfere with the system of checks and balances between the executive and judicial functions of government.

Of course, presidents can appoint and remove political aides and advisers on their White House staff at will; none of these appointments require Senate approval. Presidents also have wide latitude in replacing cabinet heads and some agency directors—even though these positions do require Senate confirmation—because they are seen as agents of presidential policy. This does not keep the Senate from trying at times to badger a president into firing one of his appointees, as it did repeatedly and unsuccessfully with Clinton's attorney general, Janet Reno. A president may give in for political reasons, but the Senate cannot compel him to do so.

Reorganizing Executive Branch Agencies

When the president enters office, a huge bureaucracy is already in place. Each new president has to be able to reorganize offices and agencies to fit his administrative and working style and to be consistent with the issue priorities he has set.[48] This can mean redrawing agency boundaries to promote coordination when actions overlap or duplicate each other. It may involve merging or abolishing offices or creating new ones.

Within the White House Office itself, the president has a fairly free hand to reshuffle staff and offices. But any major reorganization of government departments and agencies requires congressional approval. In the past, presidential reorganization plans went into effect absent a veto from either chamber. But approval is increasingly hard to win. Now every reorganization proposal is likely to get a thorough review in each house, and most are altered, sometimes severely.[49] When George W. Bush created the new cabinet-level Department of Homeland Security, reorganizing the jurisdictions of dozens of executive branch agencies, it required congressional approval. And because it required reassigning almost two hundred thousand federal employees, transferring funds, and authorizing new spending authority, this reorganization set up a classic turf battle, both within the bureaucracy and between the White House and Congress.

Inherent Administrative Powers

Because the Constitution charges the president with ensuring that "the laws be faithfully executed," the courts have ruled that the president has inherent power to take actions and issue orders to fulfill that duty. This gives the president the authority to issue directives or proclamations, called **executive orders,** that have the force of law and are therefore a form of legislative power residing in the executive branch. In arguing for these powers, presidents have claimed that Article II of the Constitution grants them inherent power to take whatever actions they judge to be in the nation's best interests as long as those actions are not prohibited by the Constitution or by law. The rationale is that Congress often lacks the expertise and ability to act quickly when technological or other developments require fast action and flexibility.[50] Recent examples of this use are the numerous Bush directives responding to problems created by the 9/11 attacks.[51]

The recording and numbering of executive orders did not begin until 1907, and although an effort was made to identify and retroactively number orders issued back to the Lincoln administration, it is uncertain how many have been issued over the years. Since 1946, Congress has required all executive orders, except those dealing with classified national security issues, to be published in the *Federal Register.*[52] Many of these orders have had a significant impact. Truman, for example,

used an executive order to integrate the armed forces, Kennedy to end racial discrimination in public housing, and Lyndon Johnson to require affirmative action hiring by firms with federal contracts.

Presidents more commonly use executive orders to deal with organizational problems and internal procedures, but presidents also use them to implement the provisions of treaties and legislative statutes that are ambiguously stated (perhaps deliberately) by Congress. In fact, presidents have used executive orders to make policies opposed by congressional majorities. Reagan and both Bushes used this power to ban abortion counseling in federally financed clinics and financial aid to United Nations–sponsored family planning programs. Another significant use of executive orders is to manage the controversial system for classifying government documents and withholding information from the public. (See the box "Veil of Secrecy" in Chapter 12.)

Through the exercise of this inherent power of office, the presidency has acquired significant legislative authority. But executive orders are much more easily overridden than congressional acts; a president can rescind or countermand orders issued by a predecessor, as Clinton did with foreign aid restrictions on family planning, and George W. Bush did with several of Clinton's environmental protection orders. Furthermore, the legality of executive orders can be challenged in federal court. Early in his presidency, George W. Bush ordered the posting of signs in union shops informing workers that they were not required to allow union dues to be withheld from their paychecks. A federal court ruled that this was a misuse of an executive order.

The president also has the power of **executive privilege,** the right of a president to refuse to make public some internal documents and private conversations. Since the 1970s, federal court rulings have argued that without such a privilege, a president cannot fulfill his administrative duties because he would not be able to get full and frank advice from his aides. The courts have also ruled that the power is limited in scope rather than absolute but have not defined its limits, deferring that task to Congress. Congress has also refused to specify the limits of executive privilege, leaving it to the courts to resolve each invocation of privilege that the president and Congress cannot resolve.

In the landmark ruling ordering President Nixon to turn over tape recordings of Oval Office conversations to the Watergate special prosecutor (see "You Are There" in Chapter 2), the Supreme Court did establish that executive privilege cannot be invoked to withhold evidence material to an investigation of criminal wrongdoing. Similarly, it ruled against President Clinton when he invoked the privilege to prevent an aide from testifying before a grand jury about possible criminal wrongdoing.

Teddy Roosevelt called the presidency a "bully pulpit" from which he could speak, through the press, to the people in an effort to persuade them to support his programs.

However, the courts upheld Clinton's extension of executive privilege to his conversations about political strategy with his aides and to those between his aides and the first lady, who served as his political adviser and whom the courts had already recognized as serving in a quasi-official role. In 2002, President Bush took this power a step further when Congress, in its investigation of Enron's financial collapse, subpoenaed records of Vice President Cheney's meetings with executives from energy industries. The White House, claiming that executive privilege extended to the vice president, refused to turn over most of the documents, even after being ordered to do so by a federal court.

The President and the Public

The Founders did not anticipate that the president would one day be popularly elected and accountable to the public. They envisioned a president chosen only indirectly by the people through the intermediary of the Electoral College. The evolution of a popularly elected president has been a major contributor to the development of presidential government. The president is a politician with a national constituency.

Our earliest presidents had little contact with the general public. George Washington and Thomas Jefferson averaged only three speeches a year to the public; John Adams averaged one. Adams spent eight months of his presidency at his Massachusetts home, avoiding

Congress and the need to make a decision over involvement in a war between England and France.[53]

Abraham Lincoln thought it prudent to avoid giving speeches. He told people gathered at Gettysburg the night before his famous address, "I have no speech to make. In my position it is somewhat important that I should not say foolish things. It very often happens that the only way to help it is to say nothing at all."[54] It has been many years since we have had such a diffident public speaker in the White House.

Franklin Roosevelt's fireside chats were the first presidential effort to use the media to speak directly and regularly to people in their homes. They helped make him, and his office, the most important link between people and government. In a personalized style, he began, "My friends." People gathered around their radios whenever he was on, and many felt he was talking directly to them. Whereas President Herbert Hoover had received an average of forty letters a day, Roosevelt, after beginning his so-called fireside chats, received four thousand letters a day.[55] He even received some addressed not to himself by name or position but simply to "My Friend, Washington, D.C." There has been no turning back from a president's need to forge a bond with the public.

Now when a president is not heard from frequently, the media begin to speculate about what is wrong. George W. Bush took heat from the press for giving few press conferences and for spending a total of 535 days at Camp David, his ranch in Texas, and his parents' home

NATIONAL CRISES AND THE EXPANSION OF PRESIDENTIAL POWERS

Often in wartime or crisis situations, a president demands greater latitude in exercising his powers of office in order to respond quickly to the problems the country is facing. Sometimes this demand corresponds to a president's own wishes to strengthen the office.

After the terrorist attacks of September 11, 2001, George W. Bush assumed extraordinary powers for both himself and the executive agencies he presides over, especially the Department of Justice and the newly created Department of Homeland Security. He had no reluctance in exercising these powers because he came into office with the goal of strengthening the presidency. He felt that the inherent powers of the office had eroded to "an unsettling degree over the past thirty years" and that he would use his administration to reclaim those powers. "I have an obligation to make sure that the presidency remains robust and that the legislative branch doesn't end up running the executive branch." [1]

His press secretary said Bush was especially unhappy about the president's not having enough control over budgetary matters and use of the military. But Bush was clearly worried about personal privacy as well, as any president might after witnessing the extraordinary invasion of the Clintons' personal lives during the previous administration. He told a group of schoolchildren at the end of his first year in office that the biggest

sacrifice he had made in running for the presidency was privacy. [2]

Bush was especially unhappy with the rule established by Franklin Roosevelt in 1934 that presidential papers belonged to the public rather than to the individual president. He stopped his daily habit of e-mailing his daughters and other relatives and friends because he did not want the messages to become part of the presidential record to which the public might someday have access. He did not believe that scholars or the public, or even congressional oversight committees, should have access to his personal communications or his discussions with White House staff or advisers. And shortly after taking office, he began exploring how he could use the inherent powers of office, such as executive privilege and executive orders, to bolster the presidency against congressional and public scrutiny.

After the attacks of 9/11, Bush was given an additional reason to make claims for less scrutiny of White House activities: national security. He referred to the period following the attacks as "wartime" and demanded that he be granted the right to exercise the powers of a president leading a country at war. In the past, this has given presidents a platform from which to demand that Congress rubber-stamp any action taken in the name of national security. In this and earlier chapters, we have given examples of the uses and abuses of such powers by earlier presidents:

suspension of *habeas corpus,* limits on free speech rights, and internment of American citizens without indictments or trials and confiscation of their property. Woodrow Wilson got Congress to pass a law during World War I that permitted the arrest of anyone who spoke publicly against the war or conscription. It was used to imprison third-party presidential candidate Eugene Debs for three years. The war powers that Bush proclaimed are even more dangerous today because the "war on terrorism" is not a defined war that can be won definitively; wartime might last forever, or at least until another president decides to rebalance presidential prerogatives and civil liberties.

Bush asked for, and Congress granted, authority to fight the war against terrorism as he saw fit, including committing troops to prolonged periods of combat in Afghanistan and Iraq without an act of war, permitting the indefinite detention of material witnesses to or those suspected of acts of terrorism, and establishing military tribunals that denied defendants due process or lawyer-client privilege (see Chapter 14). He was also successful in getting Congress to accept the kind of covert operations by intelligence agencies that had been outlawed in the 1970s because of abuse and lack of success. He made the director of the White House Homeland Security office answerable only to himself. When he finally bowed to congressional will to create a cabinet

in Maine during his first three years in office.[56] But how often and under what circumstances a president wants to address the public—or his staff wants him to—depends in part on his communication skills. Ronald Reagan, often called the "Great Communicator" although

he usually read from notes, spoke in public an average of two hundred times a year. Bill Clinton, considered one of the best extemporaneous speakers ever to occupy the White House, spoke in public an amazing 550 times a year.[57]

department for homeland security, he demanded that part of the budgetary and personnel authority be ceded to himself and the cabinet secretary, and he threatened to veto any bill that did not grant these powers.

Because the security threat the country faces is very real, most members of Congress went along with most of the president's demands. In the political climate created by a direct attack on the country and significant loss of lives, Congress was reluctant to exert its oversight of executive branch actions. As the Democratic chair of a powerful Senate committee said in voting for a presidential request he did not support, he did not "wish to create dissent where we need unity."[3]

Bush used this opportunity of bipartisan acquiescence to help restore other presidential initiatives he thought had been thwarted by Congress. He got money appropriated for an antimissile defense shield program that had many opponents in both parties before 9/11. Bush went on to extend the "national security" rationale to a number of situations where its application is highly questionable. A month after the attacks, he issued an executive order making public access to the papers of past presidents much more difficult to obtain (an order immediately challenged in court, but not by Congress). He also gave the attorney general broad discretion in limiting public access to any information or documents that might have national security implications.

Two months after 9/11, Bush invoked executive privilege to deny Congress access to documents on federal prosecutors' decision-making process, even in cases dating back decades. A memo to the Justice Department explaining his denial said simply, "I believe congressional access to these documents would be contrary to the national interests." He also used executive privilege to protect his vice president against congressional oversight committees investigating possible collusion with energy industry officials in writing energy legislation.[4] And Bush often refused to let his advisers testify before congressional committees, especially on foreign policy or defense matters, by pointing out that they have no obligation to do so. While it is true that his personal staff and advisers do not have a legal obligation to give testimony to Congress, they are often willing and even eager to do so, both to help Congress understand White House policy and to gain support for that policy. The president's actions led members of both parties to accuse Bush of creating a monarchical or imperial presidency "to keep Congress from overseeing the executive branch and guarding against corruption."[5]

During investigations of pre-9/11 intelligence failures, Bush resisted efforts to declassify records that would reveal how much he had been told in briefings prior to the attacks, and after many re-fusals, he finally gave in to pressure to let his national security adviser, Condoleezza Rice, give testimony before the 9/11 Commission.

Bush is one of a number of presidents who believed strongly in presidential prerogatives and the right to set policy and to function relatively freely of congressional oversight. Insistence on unchecked executive authority destroyed the presidencies of Lyndon Johnson and Richard Nixon, and FDR's reputation took a beating over such abuses as the internment of Japanese Americans and his attempt to pack the Supreme Court. When presidents use war or other national crises to justify expansion of their powers—whatever the hardships on individuals or the impact on society in the short run—the results are usually undone when the crisis eases, and the separation of powers reasserts itself. In the process of trying to make a lasting imprint on the office, presidents can do serious harm to their own legacies while the office itself gets reshaped by its next occupant.

1. Quoted in Bill Straub, "A Debate Concerning the Use or Abuse of Presidential Powers," *Champaign-Urbana News-Gazette,* May 15, 2002, B5.
2. Carl M. Cannon, "For the Record," *National Journal,* January 12, 2002, 96.
3. Quoted in Jeffrey Toobin, "Can Democrats Still Play the Game?" *New York Times,* October 28, 2001, WK13.
4. Jill Barshay, "A Closer Look at GAO vs. Cheney: Politics and Separation of Powers," *Congressional Quarterly Weekly Report,* February 2, 2002, 289–291.
5. "Bush Invokes Executive Privilege," *Champaign-Urbana News-Gazette,* December 12, 2001, A5.

Personal Presidency

Political scientist Theodore Lowi believes that since the New Deal era, we have had what he calls a **personal presidency.**[58] He argues that consciously or unconsciously, the American people have had a "new social contract" with the president since the 1930s. In return for getting more power and support from us than we give to other government officials, the president is supposed to make sure we get what we want from government. The personal presidency ties government directly

When President Franklin Roosevelt died, most Americans felt a personal loss. Here Chief Petty Officer Graham Jackson plays "Nearer My God to Thee" as the president's body is carried to the train that returned him to Washington for burial.

to the people and gives us someone to rally around during times of crisis. To the extent that it serves as a focal point for national unity, the personal presidency also contributes to our ability to achieve national goals.

Polls have consistently shown that Americans consider "leadership" very important in evaluating presidents.[59] Somewhat paradoxically in light of their fear of "big government," most people want a president who can get government to "do" things. Franklin Roosevelt was the first president to use survey data to identify public needs and to use the media to tell people that he would give them what they wanted. Making himself the major link between public opinion and government often enabled him to overcome the inertia and divisions associated with a system of fragmented powers.

However, Roosevelt's actions also revealed a cost of the personal presidency: presidents with great power often seek more. Roosevelt won reelection in 1936 by a landslide, confirming popular support for his New Deal. This led him to seek more power by trying to expand the size of an unfriendly Supreme Court so that he could appoint judges who supported him. He also tried to get local and state parties to nominate congressional candidates he favored by using federal funds as an inducement. The defeat of pro-Roosevelt congressional candidates in 1938 ruined both his plans. People did not want the Court politicized, and state and local parties wanted to pick their own nominees.

Nixon and Reagan also tried to override constitutional limitations on their power after their landslide reelections in 1972 and 1984, as evidenced in the Water-

gate and Iran-Contra scandals. George W. Bush seized on the 9/11 attacks to declare a war on terrorism and to present himself as a wartime president. He used this status to make extraordinary claims of power for the presidency and ran his reelection campaign almost entirely on his policy on fighting terrorism. The success of his presidency hinged so much on his association with this issue that a prominent foreign policy columnist said he had become "addicted to 9/11"[60] (see the box "National Crises and the Expansion of Presidential Powers").

The use of real or perceived popular mandates to amass power in the Oval Office illustrates how the rise of the personal presidency has fed the expansion of the office. Practitioners of the personal presidency have sought more power to deliver on all the promises they make to win votes and campaign donations. They get caught in a cycle of seeking more power to honor them and making even greater promises to get more power. Inevitably, most politicians promise more than they can deliver. George H. Bush promised to send astronauts to Mars, protect the environment, be the "education president," and do many other things while cutting the budget deficit without raising taxes.

After the Reagan and Bush administrations had doubled the national debt, promising *less* from government became the tactic of the personal presidency. So while Clinton also began by making promises and saying he wanted "to do it all as quick as we can," he started his second term by announcing that "the day of big government is over."[61]

Yet Clinton had his own angle on the personal presidency, an approach that is said to have "changed the very nature of what the public expects" of presidents. While deemphasizing big government, Clinton dwelt on "little initiatives," such as his proposal to adopt uniforms in public schools. These are what one of his top advisers called "kitchen table issues," problems that families deal with on a daily basis and may discuss around the kitchen table.[62] Not only was Clinton extremely adept at speaking directly to people in a conversational style, but he projected an intimate knowledge of domestic, school, and community problems that were of great concern in everyday life.

Lowi might have been right in calling the personal presidency the "victim" of democracy, but irresponsible leadership is not an inevitable consequence of the age of mass media. The separation of powers and the vote should check the short-term excesses of presidents. However, every president since the 1960s has needed and sought media exposure and has in turn had to submit to intense scrutiny by media that delve into every detail of his personal life, as well as his performance of official duties. Few people can withstand such prolonged exposure without losing public esteem. The continuous congressional and special prosecutor investigations of Bill Clinton resulted in the media's being saturated with the most graphic private and intimate details of a president's life ever revealed. "It is entirely possible," one reporter observed, "that the Clinton era will be remembered by historians primarily as the moment when the distance between the President and the public evaporated forever."[63] (For attitudes toward the presidency by its occupants, see the box "Match the Quote to the President.")

The strategy of making a direct presidential appeal to the people to gain cooperation from Congress and Washington power brokers is known as "going public."[64] The strategy includes giving prime-time television and radio addresses, holding press conferences, making speeches at events around the country, and using satellite technology to give interviews to local television stations, conventions, and other audiences. These techniques have become so important to the success of a president's policies that he is now sometimes referred to as the "salesman in chief." This suggests that more than a good argument, well constructed and presented, is at the root of persuasion; the packaging of the argument has become as important as the argument itself.

Much depends on the president's own communication skills, but he is not out there alone. Every president has a large communications staff, led by a press secretary, to get his message out. The goal is usually to set a message for the day or week and keep everyone on message. This is something at which George W. Bush's administration is especially skilled; the television audience tuning in to morning or evening news programs or talk shows on a any given day can hear administration officials delivering the same message in virtually the same words. The pressure of running such an operation is high, and most press secretaries do not stay long in their jobs. When Bush's first press secretary turned in his resignation after two years, he said he wanted to do "something more relaxing, like dismantling live nuclear weapons."[65]

Why have some presidents found going public attractive? One reason is that the weakness of party identification forces presidential candidates to appeal as widely as they can for support. Presidents also sometimes find it easier to go public than to persuade directly the interest groups, congressional committees, subcommittees, and executive agencies involved in the making and implementation of public policy.

Going public may sometimes lead presidents to emphasize public relations over results and to blame the media rather than themselves for low poll scores. For example, Nixon claimed the media had hounded him from office, Reagan said they exaggerated the importance of the Iran-Contra scandal, and Clinton complained they did not give him credit for his first-year accomplishments. "I have fought more damn battles than any president has in twenty years with the possible exception of Reagan's first budget and not gotten one damn bit of credit from the knee-jerk liberal press," Clinton said. "I am sick and tired of it, and you can put that in the damn article."[66]

George H. Bush's use of the strategy of going public in garnering support for the Persian Gulf War was very skillful. He decided to use military force soon after Iraq invaded Kuwait in August 1990. Until January, when Congress approved this option, Bush made many speeches comparing Iraq's Saddam Hussein to Hitler, condemning his use of chemical and biological weapons on his own people, and warning that Iraq would soon have nuclear weapons. Bush's efforts won more public support for using force, which in turn made congressional support more likely.

George W. Bush, widely criticized for his poor command of the language, preferred to speak more informally in venues with carefully vetted groups of political supporters, where he was highly successful. His speechwriters turned Bush's speaking limitations into a virtue by cultivating a vernacular, everyman style. Bush's speeches usually consisted of short declarative sentences, with a single point, delivered in a slow, deliberate style, stressing each syllable for effect. The average sentence length of Bush's acceptance speech at the 2000 nominating convention was less than fifteen words. This compares to the average 104 words per sentence used by William Jennings Bryan, a man considered one of the greatest political orators of the late nineteenth century.[67]

Bush needed no strategy to win popular support for the military operation against al-Qaeda's base in Afghanistan because it followed a direct attack on the United States. But in trying to rally the public behind his goal of expanding the war to Iraq, he used a tactic similar to his father's, referring to Saddam Hussein as part of an "axis of evil." When the failures of the postwar strategy for nation building began to cut into public support, the administration tried to regain that support with a single, continuously repeated message about Iraq being essential to the victory in the war on terrorism.

Spectacle Presidency

An important part of going public is being seen as well as heard. And the important part of being seen is projecting an image that conveys the president's character and style. Presidents need to "make fully realized dramatic characters out of themselves, who exist in an intimate relationship with the voting public. The character has to bear some relation to the real person . . . but it is still a genuine act of creation."[68]

If a president fails to take charge of his image (as Bill Clinton did, for example), the press will probably do it for him and in ways he will not like. Teddy Roosevelt was cast as the big-game hunter and Rough Rider, FDR as the jaunty optimist, Eisenhower as the peaceloving war hero, Kennedy as the youthful and athletic man of action and intellect. Ronald Reagan and George W. Bush were very successful in portraying themselves as dramatic characters. Reagan, an actor by profession, had little difficulty projecting an image as a rugged cowboy even though he had spent most of his life in Hollywood. Bush's persona as a Texas-style "good ole boy"—he wore cowboy boots to his inaugural and made sure the press got photographs of them—was mostly invented, and his "packaging" as a war leader was even more intentional. The staging by his press staff of the flight-suited commander in chief landing by fighter jet on an aircraft carrier and then speaking before a "mission accomplished" sign was one of the most dramatic image-creating photo opportunities in the history of the presidency.

The advantage of such bold efforts is that the visual image lingers. But that is also a disadvantage. Bush's public relations people announced the end of the war in Iraq far too soon, and the photo op came back to haunt Bush when critics later castigated him as a reckless rather than resolute war leader.

The increasing frequency of stage-managed photo ops, featuring the president in a dramatically staged event or setting, has led one scholar to proclaim the emergence of the **spectacle presidency.** He attributes this development to the "extreme personalization" of the presidency, people's excessive expectations of the president, and "the voluminous media coverage that fixes on presidents."[69] Of course, most public appearances by presidents are not intended as spectacle, although virtually all are staged.

The observation that "all politics is theater" is sometimes intended as ridicule, but settings and character presentation do matter. Few people are aware that the retiring and reticent Calvin Coolidge gave more press conferences per year than the much better packaged Franklin Roosevelt.[70] Not many people would guess that the reluctant president William Howard Taft did more trust-busting than the much more dramatic champion of the cause, Theodore Roosevelt. And the characterization of the Kennedy administration as "Camelot" left a lasting image of a tuxedoed president hosting glamorous White House galas for classical musicians and great intellects. In fact, Kennedy preferred listening to Frank Sinatra and reading Ian Fleming's James Bond books.

The President and Public Opinion

Americans pay more attention to the president than to other public officials, and we typically link government's success to the effectiveness of his leadership. Although many factors affect public opinion about presidential effectiveness, a positive image of a president's leadership skills helps protect his ratings after serious policy failures.

Many people are predisposed to support the president and to look at his overall record rather than the short term.[71] Failure on specific issues does not always produce low scores on general performance. For example, majorities of respondents simultaneously disapproved of Reagan's handling of environmental and foreign policy issues, important to them, *and* registered approval of his overall performance.

Crises called *rally events* affect presidential popularity.[72] President Clinton's approval ratings increased after the bombing of the federal building in Oklahoma City, and George W. Bush's rose by 40 points after 9/11. Public support increases significantly at such times because people do not want to undermine the president, the symbol of national unity. However, the higher levels of support produced by rally events are rarely sustained long.[73] Bush's support fell from an astounding 90 percent after 9/11 to around 50 percent by the time of the 2004 election.

Support for the first President Bush's policies toward Iraq after its invasion of Kuwait showed a similar pattern. As indicated in Figure 3, this increasing support helped raise Bush's general approval ratings from 54 percent in October 1990 to 89 percent in February 1991, a month after the invasion.[74] However, the ef-

Ronald Reagan Library

The public didn't always agree with President Reagan's policies or views, but he remained popular throughout his presidency in part because of his image as a rugged individualist.

fect of the Gulf War faded as Americans began focusing on domestic concerns, especially economic problems. Bush's approval rating fell to 33 percent by mid-1992, leading to his defeat by Clinton in November.[75]

Clinton's up-and-down scores during his first term reflected public anxiety about his leadership skills. In 1995 polls, 56 percent of Americans described Clinton as a weak president, and 80 percent expected that the Republican Congress would have more influence than Clinton on the nation's direction.[76] But Clinton was far more adept at going public than the Republican leadership, and by the end of his first term, his approval

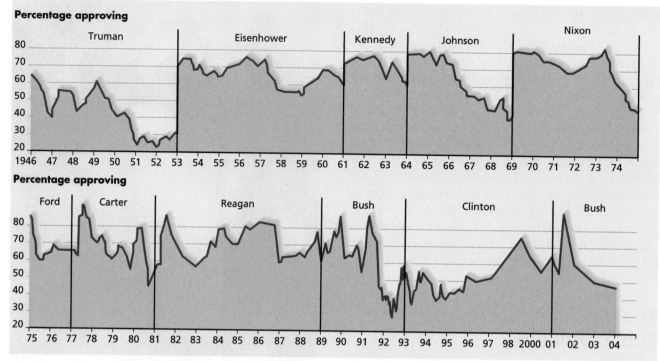

Percentage approving

Percentage approving

FIGURE 3 ■ **Presidential Popularity** *Since the end of World War II, presidential popularity has usually declined over time. Only three presidents—Eisenhower, Reagan, and Clinton—left office with ratings at a level comparable to that when they entered.*

SOURCE: Gallup polls, reported in *Public Opinion* and updated at www.gallup.com. The question asked is, "Do you approve or disapprove of the way [name of president] is handling his job as president?" The 2004 approval rating for G. W. Bush is from *New York Times*/CBS News poll data.

rating was at 53 percent and Congress was in legislative retreat.

When public anger and frustration with government are widespread, winning consistently good ratings is difficult. Although short-term crises or rally events can help a president's ratings, long-term conditions will continue to influence them more decisively. Clinton's 67 percent approval rating during the impeachment investigation may have been sparked by a public backlash against the salaciousness of congressional and media commentary, but it is more likely that he got a positive bounce from public confidence in the overall state of the economy.

The more important issue is whether a president with high approval ratings can translate them into policy successes. Reagan had only qualified success in using his popularity to get Congress to enact his legislative proposals. He relied heavily on his own appointment and budgetary powers and the issuing of executive orders to accomplish much of his agenda. The problem with this approach is that it is easily reversible by a successor. Clinton, with higher sustained approval ratings than either Reagan or George H. Bush late in their

terms and a substantial legislative agenda, was not able to translate his popular support into victories in Congress. George W. Bush used his high approval ratings to win concessions of power from Congress and to push through legislation he saw as crucial to his reelection.

The Ebb and Flow of Presidential Power

Today a person elected to the presidency is the recipient of the respect bestowed on the office itself: people stand when the president enters a room, "Hail to the Chief" is played when he appears on a dais or at ceremonial events, men and women in uniform salute him, he is surrounded by bodyguards and aides, and the media scrutinize every detail of his personal life and public performance. He is almost universally regarded as the most powerful person in the world. Yet some presidents have become so frustrated by limitations on their power that they try to overcome those limitations by exceeding their constitutional authority. The most famous example of illegal presidential action in the face of perceived frustration was Nixon's attempt to gather intelligence on his political opponents by invading their personal privacy with phone taps, break-ins, and unauthorized reviews of income tax returns and then obstructing justice by trying to cover up evidence of these acts.

Some years ago, observers of the presidency branded it the "imperial presidency" and worried that presidential power had gone too far. In the last quarter of the twentieth century, however, the power of the presidency appeared to wane. The decline began in reaction to the sometimes arrogant exercise of power during the Johnson and Nixon administrations, especially with respect to the conduct of the Vietnam War and abuses of the electoral process during Nixon's reelection campaign. Reagan's personal popularity and his conception of the presidency—emphasizing the head-of-state and symbolic roles of the office over governance—restored some of the prestige or grandeur of the presidency, but the illegalities of the Iran-Contra affair and ethics scandals involving his appointees eroded public confidence again.

The end of the Cold War also restricted the president's freedom to act unilaterally in international affairs and reduced his role as a rally figure to mobilize public opinion against foreign enemies. In domestic affairs, decades of budget deficits, the return of many responsibilities to the states, and a tendency toward downsizing national government limited how much the president could credibly promise or deliver to the American public. Under Clinton, the personal presidency seemed to be imploding. Six years of ethics investigations, a record number of special prosecutors, sensational headlines, and constant scrutiny of the first family's personal lives all contributed to the diminution of the office.

Some historians and analysts felt that Clinton's impeachment would be similar in impact to Andrew Johnson's, which weakened the presidency for the next half-century.[77] This argument is based in large part on precedents set by federal court decisions issued during the investigation. These rulings limited a president's ability to use executive privilege to deny Congress access to records of conversations he has with his advisers and to exercise attorney-client privilege to protect such records in cases in which the advice is provided by government lawyers. The court also allowed Secret Service agents to testify before grand juries about the president's activities, including his personal conduct. But perhaps most important was the court's ruling that a sitting president can be sued for private conduct that occurred before he took office. In this last decision, judges reasoned that it was unlikely that the need to defend himself in a civil suit would divert a president's time and energy from carrying out his duties. This was a colossal misjudgment insofar as the case in the sexual harassment suit brought against Clinton was concerned. It not only consumed the time and attention of the president but also diverted much of the attention of many Washingtonians. Critics of the decision wondered whether the filing of civil suits would become one more maneuver to hamstring the presidency.

However, it does not appear that these precedents have yet affected the power of the presidency. Clinton's personal conduct probably did far more damage to his professional reputation and legacy than to the office of president.[78]

George W. Bush's ability to restore power drained from the office during the Clinton years and to add to it immeasurably illustrates the elasticity of presidential power. Bush used executive privilege to shield the office from congressional and public scrutiny and his inherent legislative authority to repeal policies of the Clinton administration. He also distanced the presidency from the political fray, portraying himself as a wartime leader whose key policies were above scrutiny. It is impossible to say for certain whether he could have achieved as much of what he wanted as he did without the political climate created by the events of 9/11. But it is likely that Bush's early successes resulted from a convergence of his will to reassert the powers of the presidency and the opportunity handed to him by a national emergency to do so. Today, we have returned to concern about an overly activist president, as President Bush has wielded his expanded powers to erode individual rights, such as freedom of information and privacy, and to reduce government transparency.

Although scholars and journalists sometimes overreact to short-term events, these changing perceptions of the presidency illustrate that as conditions change, so do the ways in which presidents exercise their authority.

Presidential Reputation

Every president develops a track record of his effectiveness as a leader, what Richard Neustadt calls the president's professional reputation.[79] A president with an effective reputation has a record of getting what he wants, helping his allies, and penalizing the opposition. This reputation contributes to his continuing ability to persuade the public, Congress, and other Washingtonians. Few modern presidents were more adept at getting what they wanted from Congress than Lyndon Johnson, yet Johnson is often not ranked among the great presidents, at least not by the public. A president's professional reputation is of great importance to him while he is in office and is a commentary on his political and administrative skills. But having the ability to get what

Almost all rankings of presidents list Washington, Lincoln, and Franklin Roosevelt among the greats and Jefferson, Jackson, Theodore Roosevelt, Wilson, and Truman with the near-greats. Some presidents—Taylor, Harding, and Ford—spent such short periods in office that they are hard to rank.

In 2000, at C-SPAN's request, fifty-seven historians and presidential scholars rated the presidents on ten personal and professional qualities: economic management, moral authority, crisis leadership, public persuasion, relations with Congress, international relations, administrative skills, vision and agenda setting, pursuit of equal justice, and performance in the context of his time. Their overall ranking of the top ten and bottom five was arrived at by averaging those scores. Because scholars and the public often have different ideas about presidential reputations, C-SPAN also invited viewers to rate presidents using the same ten criteria. (See Table 2.)

Former presidents sometimes get a bounce in poll ratings: Truman, Eisenhower, Carter, and Reagan, for example, received much higher favorable ratings

TABLE 2	Presidential Rating Survey	
Historians/Presidential Scholars (57) **Top Ten (in rank order)**		**C-SPAN Viewers (1,145)** **Top Ten**
1. Abraham Lincoln		Abraham Lincoln
2. Franklin D. Roosevelt		George Washington
3. George Washington		Theodore Roosevelt
4. Theodore Roosevelt		Franklin D. Roosevelt
5. Harry S. Truman		Thomas Jefferson
6. Woodrow Wilson (13)*		Ronald Reagan (11)**
7. Thomas Jefferson		Harry S. Truman
8. John F. Kennedy (12)		Dwight D. Eisenhower
9. Dwight D. Eisenhower		James Monroe (14)
10. Lyndon B. Johnson (19)		James Madison (18)
Bottom Five		**Bottom Five**
41. William Henry Harrison		James Buchanan
40. Warren G. Harding		Warren G. Harding
39. Franklin Pierce		Franklin Pierce
38. Andrew Johnson		Andrew Johnson
37. James Buchanan		Millard Fillmore

SOURCE: C-SPAN survey, 2000. Full results at www.americanpresidents.org.
* ranking by viewers
** ranking by scholars

in retirement than they had at the end of their terms. But higher approval does not necessarily lead to a higher performance ranking; Clinton finished his term with strong approval ratings and in this C-SPAN poll was ranked in the top five on economic management and pursuit of social justice. But he finished at 21 and 36 (out of 41) in the overall ratings by scholars and viewers.

You can review the survey results at www.americanpresidents.org.

---

he wants is not the same as being able to do what is best for the country, and therefore presidents seen as highly effective in office are not always judged by history to have been great presidents.

Presidential Character

Every president comes to office with a somewhat different view of the office and its reach and, depending on personality, talents, education, experience, and ideology, varying predispositions to exercise established powers or to expand them. The study of presidential character and personality is a subfield within presidential scholarship but one we only touch on in this survey chapter.[80]

How can presidential performance be measured? Neustadt has called the presidency a "choice-making machine," and presidents who can act decisively are often well regarded. Truman epitomized the decisive style and has probably benefited from the contrast with the more waffling approaches of recent presidents who are often seen as driven by polls and focus groups. The sign inscribed "The Buck Stops Here" that Truman kept on his desk illustrated both his sense of accountability and his no-nonsense rhetoric. In historical perspective, his leadership skills have looked more impressive than they did while he was in office, and this view has helped move him to the ranks of near-great presidents. (See the box "Rating the Presidents.")

It is not always immediately clear how deep an impact a president's tenure has had on the direction of the country, and assessments of presidential performance do change over time. Truman exemplifies a president who was unpopular during his tenure and in the immediate years afterward but who left a legacy of directness, personal integrity, and decisiveness on key decisions during an extremely difficult time (the national trauma of FDR's death while we were engaged in World War II).

Scholarly assessment of Eisenhower's administration has also changed significantly. Shortly after he left office, he was judged an average president, a good and honest man with strong administrative skills but one who took few chances and lacked an overall vision for the country. In retrospect, analysts regard as level-headed and prescient both his leadership during an extremely volatile period in the nuclear arms race and his warnings about the dangers the military-industrial complex would present to the economy and our sense of national purpose.

Goals and Vision

In characterizing the role of the president, the nineteenth-century historian Henry Adams wrote that he "resembles the commander of a ship at sea. He must have a helm to grasp, a course to steer, a port to seek."[81] That is, the incumbent must have a goal, a destination toward which he is leading the nation; he must have programs and a course of action to enable the nation to get there; and he must be willing and able to use the instruments of his office to reach that goal.

Franklin Roosevelt fit the definition of a great president as a leader "of thought at times when certain ideas in the life of the nation had to be clarified."[82] This reminds us that an opportunity factor is involved in rising to the highest ranks of performance. FDR's examples of our best presidents—"Washington [embodying] the idea of the federal union, Jefferson and Jackson the idea of democracy, Lincoln union and freedom"[83]—are men who served at critical times in the country's development. These are presidents whom almost all scholars rank among our greatest, and they are associated with ideas and policies that took root and affected the course of our country.

Any concept of presidential effectiveness inevitably involves the "vision thing." A president will likely be seen as effective only if he has a clear idea of where he wants to take the country. This is why Reagan is regarded by much of the public as a more effective president than George H. Bush, a man consistently described as lacking in vision. To rank with the "greats," however, vision must be coupled with the political and administrative skills necessary to achieve it. In the scholarly

consensus, Bush was willing and able to grab the helm but was steering to no port in particular; Reagan had a fixed destination but no firm hand on the helm and insufficient knowledge or interest to steer the ship. Like Bush, Reagan had a mediocre legislative record and an abysmal fiscal record, but in the public eye, Reagan had a clear vision of what he wanted for the country. In contrast, Clinton had all the political and communication skills to steer the ship but kept changing his destination. He was unsuccessful in projecting to the public a clear and consistent vision of where the country should be headed.

It is far too early to evaluate George W. Bush's presidency, but in his early years he gave a clearer idea of what he wanted to do with the office of president than he did about where he wanted to lead the country. Early assessments were based almost entirely on how he handled the aftermath of the 9/11 attacks—both his policy response and his personal demeanor in projecting the national will. The public took his aggressive military posture as a sign of character and strong leadership and gave him high approval ratings, despite the failure of aspects of his defense policy (the war in Iraq) and weak performance on the economy and social welfare issues. He was very successful in using what he labeled a crisis situation to fend off congressional and outside scrutiny of executive branch policies and the internal workings of the White House.

Conclusion: Is the Presidency Responsive?

The presidency has become the most consistently visible office in government as well as one of the most personalized and responsive. Americans expect leadership from the president even in these days of "less" government. The presidency is responsive in that whoever holds that office has an almost direct relationship with the public. Using the media, a skillful president can tell us what he wants and attempt to shape our opinion. Through public opinion polls and the ballot box, we tell the president what we think. In this relationship, there is a danger of overresponsiveness. To remain popular, a president may seek short-term solutions to the nation's problems and neglect long-term interests. And short-term responsiveness that caters to public opinion can siphon off the attention and resources a president should be devoting to the real needs of the nation.

But most recent presidents gradually came to understand the limits of presidential power, sometimes the hard way. Indeed, the moral of the personal presidency suggests that presidents who become popular by making exaggerated promises have trouble keeping both the promises and their popularity in a system of fragmented power. The Clinton years illustrated another danger in exercising the personal presidency in the age of tabloid media: the risk of diminishing the office when scrutiny of the occupant's private life overtakes evaluation of his public role.

One of the most interesting aspects of this unusual office is its resilience and elasticity. It can be stretched and shrunk from one administration to another or even within a single administration. Each occupant is likely to make something quite different of it than his predecessor, either by the attitude and skills he brings to it or because the times force him to do so.

Clinton Stays and Fights

linton refused to go and resigned himself instead to months of legal wrangling, diversion from normal duties, and personal humiliation. In December 1998, after a $47 million investigation by Independent Counsel Kenneth Starr, the House held hearings and voted two articles of impeachment against the president for failing to execute his oath of office by obstructing justice through (1) perjuring himself in testimony about his affair with Monica Lewinsky and (2) encouraging witnesses in a federal civil rights suit to conceal evidence or give misleading testimony.[84]

It was up to the Senate, sitting as a court with the chief justice of the United States presiding, to decide whether the president should be found guilty of either or both of charges and removed from office. A small number of moderate Republicans opposed to the impeachment proceedings tried to devise an exit strategy from the trial by drafting a "finding of fact."[85] This resolution contained a list of the offenses they believed Clinton had committed but took no position on whether they warranted removal from office. Moderates said they wanted to avoid the certainty of legal terms like *guilty* and *conviction*. The drafters proposed bringing the resolution to a vote in the Senate before the vote on the formal charges. This would give those who did not believe Clinton guilty of impeachable offenses the option to censure him for misconduct while voting not guilty on the articles of impeachment. A group of moderate Democrats devised their own censure resolution, which they hoped to put to a vote after the vote on articles of impeachment.

These compromises were labeled "impeachment plus" and "conviction lite" and were brushed aside. Quite possibly, either resolution drafted by moderates could have served as an alternative to impeachment proceedings had their supporters been able to bring them to the floor before the move toward impeachment had gained momentum. But once the politics were in motion and the lines firmly drawn, partisans on either side began lining up their votes. The Republican leadership was set on Clinton's guilt and wanted a straight vote for or against conviction. At that point, the Democratic leadership, knowing the Republicans did not have the votes to convict, resisted any alternative to exoneration.

With a vote on the articles unavoidable and the nation watching via a live telecast, the senators stood at their desks as the chief justice polled them in alphabetical order: "Senators, how say you? Is the respondent, William Jefferson Clinton, guilty or not guilty?" In the end, five Republican centrists voted not guilty on the perjury charges. All forty-five Democrats voted to acquit the president on both articles.

Still, Clinton stands as the only *elected* president ever to be impeached. He was also cited for contempt and fined by a federal judge for giving misleading testimony to a grand jury. At the end of his term, Clinton made a deal with the independent counsel that any remaining charges would be dropped in exchange for his acceptance of a temporary suspension of his license to practice law in Arkansas.

As one Democratic senator said, "The Founders made it extremely hard to remove a popularly elected president." A Republican colleague agreed, saying that although everyone is entitled to an opinion of the president, impeachment is hard and "was meant to be hard."[86] One of the Republicans who voted for acquittal said, "Everything up here is very divided. There's no instrument for breaking down those walls of separateness. It is degrading to the Senate. I hear it at home. It has not gone unnoticed by the public."[87] The polls bore her out; after the House impeached Clinton, his approval ratings jumped to 73 percent while those of the Republican Party fell to 31 percent.[88] However irresponsibly they may have believed the president to have acted, the great majority of the public clearly did not believe that those acts constituted impeachable offenses. The vote in an impeachment trial must end in the president's exoneration or removal from office. It cannot be undone, and its impact on the office of the president will reverberate through history.

Key Terms

impeachment

head of state

power to persuade

pocket veto

divided government

War Powers Resolution

senatorial courtesy

executive orders

executive privilege

personal presidency

spectacle presidency

Further Reading

Anonymous [Joe Klein], *Primary Colors: A Novel of Politics* (New York: Random House, 1996). Inspired by the first Clinton presidential campaign, this is one of the most insightful and readable books on modern presidential politics and certainly the funniest.

Michael R. Beschloss, ed., *Reaching for Glory: The Secret Johnson White House Tapes, 1964–65* (New York: Simon & Schuster, 2001). The second in a series of books based on White House conversations secretly taped by President Johnson, this volume contains Johnson's private thoughts on the Vietnam War and reveals that even as he committed more men and resources to the war, he believed we could not win it.

Philip B. Kunhardt Jr., Philip B. Kunhardt III, and Peter W. Kunhardt, *The American President* (New York: Riverhead, 1999). This is a companion volume for the PBS series on the presidency. It describes all presidencies through Clinton's, grouping them by shared characteristics rather than chronologically. It also offers a marvelous pictorial history of the office and presidential families.

Richard E. Neustadt, *Presidential Power and the Modern Presidents* (New York: Free Press, 1990). This, the most cited book on the presidency, argues that presidential power is based on the ability to persuade.

Ron Suskind, *The Price of Loyalty: George W. Bush, the White House, and the Education of Paul O'Neill* (New York: Simon & Schuster, 2004). This is an "as told to" account of the Bush management style by Bush's first secretary of the treasury, Paul O'Neill.

Gary Wills, *James Madison* (New York: Penguin, 2001). This biography of one of the best-known Founders but one of our least-known presidents is one in a series of presidential biographies being published by Penguin in small-book format (about two hundred pages). Each is, or will be, written by a well-known American writer.

For Viewing

PBS, *The American President*, 2000. With commentary by presidential scholars, including Richard Neustadt, this ten-volume series groups presidents by shared characteristics, rather than chronologically or by party.

PBS, *The Presidents*, 1990–. These documentaries include family as well as political histories on the Lincolns and the Kennedys, Lyndon Johnson, Eisenhower, both Roosevelts, Truman, Reagan, Wilson, Grant, and Carter. These have been well reviewed for their balanced cover-

age and assessments. Compare these documentary treatments of presidential biographies with film treatments.

John Ford, *Young Mr. Lincoln*, 1939; Aaron Sorkin, *The American President*, 1995; Oliver Stone, *Nixon*, 2000. Stone's dark and contemporary psychological approach to presidential biography stands in stark contrast to Ford's film, one of the many idealized portrayals from Hollywood's golden era, and to Sorkin's equally romanticized treatment of a fictional president in the modern presidency.

PBS, *Abraham and Mary Lincoln: A House Divided*, 2001. This two-volume study of Abraham and Mary Todd Lincoln's marriage from the *Presidents* series offered new insights on how Mrs. Lincoln's background as the daughter of a southern slaveholding family affected her and her husband's attitudes toward the Civil War, African Americans, and white southerners.

PBS, *Eleanor*, 2000; Daniel Petrie, *Eleanor and Franklin*, 1976. The PBS documentary on Eleanor Roosevelt's role in her husband's presidency contains home movies, voice recordings, interviews with relatives, and news footage. Petrie's film, originally shown as a television miniseries, is a dramatic adaptation of Joseph Lash's book of the same title.

NBC, *The West Wing*, 1999–. This popular series is a fictionalized account of a president and his staff. The storylines often parallel the real issues facing the president and the nation.

Discovery Channel, *Watergate*, 1994. This three-volume series documents the decline of the "imperial" presidency of Richard Nixon from the break-in and burglary at the Watergate complex through the conspiracy to cover up the crime and the impeachment investigation that led to the president's resignation.

PBS, *The Jesus Factor*, 2004. This is an exploration of the role of religion in the administration of George W. Bush.

Electronic Resources

www.whitehouse.gov

The White House home page has links to the Office of the Vice President, the Office of the First Lady, the Department of Homeland Security, and all EOP offices. You can tour the White House, read presidential speeches, and e-mail the president. The link to the first lady's home page allows viewers to send e-mail, look at the work of the office, and link to biographies of each of America's first ladies.

www.historyplace.com

This site contains sound bites from speeches made by all the presidents since Franklin Roosevelt.

www.americanpresidents.org

This is C-SPAN's Peabody Award–winning Web site for historical coverage of the American presidency.

www.access.gpo.gov/usbudget

This site has a copy of the most recent federal budget. Reading the president's annual budget message is one way to find out the basic goals of his administration.

InfoTrac College Edition

Search for the following articles in the InfoTrac database:

Canes-Wrone, Brandice. "The Public Presidency, Personal Approval Ratings, and Policy Making," *Presidential Studies Quarterly* (September 2004).

Greenstein, Fred I. "The Contemporary Presidency: The Changing Leadership of George W. Bush: A Pre– and Post–9/11 Comparison," *Presidential Studies Quarterly* (June 2002).

Mayer, Jeremy D. "The Contemporary Presidency: The Presidency and Image Management: Discipline in Pursuit of Illusion," *Presidential Studies Quarterly* (September 2004).

Rose, Melody. "Losing Control: The Intraparty Consequences of Divided Government," *Presidential Studies Quarterly* (December 2001).

For more articles, enter

"George W. Bush" in the Subject Guide;

"Bill Clinton" in the Subject Guide;

"Presidential Studies Quarterly" for journal name in PowerTrac.

American Government Resources

Visit the Government Institutions section of the Wadsworth American Government Resources Web site (politicalscience. wadsworth.com/amgov) for a variety of tools to help you explore the presidency further. Included are simulations, video clips, Microcase exercises, and a wealth of other activities.

CHAPTER 12

THE BUREAUCRACY

John Stanmeyer/ VII

Turf wars and failures to communicate with each other have hampered the effectiveness of U.S. intelligence-gathering bureaucracies. Intelligence agencies have also been handicapped by their lack of success in recruiting agents to do undercover work in areas such as Peshawar, Pakistan.

Should You Blow the Whistle on the FBI?

ou are Sibel Edmonds, born in Iran, reared in Turkey, and educated in the United States. After marrying an American, you became a U.S. citizen, and nine days after the 9/11 attacks, you went to work as an FBI translator with a "top secret" security clearance. You quickly became aware of incompetence and negligence in your section of the agency. You are trying to decide if you should go public with your concerns or just keep them to yourself.

You are fluent in Turkish, Farsi (the official language of Iran), and Azerbaijani, the language of your father's birthplace. You were assigned to the Washington Field Office, the agency's largest translation department, to which information is sent from all over the country. Your job was to translate audiotapes from wiretaps and other documents on counterterrorism, counterintelligence, and criminal investigations.[1]

You had barely begun when your supervisor told you not to work so fast, to take long lunch hours and spend time with friends. He said that having a work backlog was the only way the FBI would be able to justify its request to Congress for a bigger budget and more translators. He even went so far as to erase translations from your computer files and then told you to do them over. You were surprised by these instructions because you, and almost everyone else, feel a sense of urgency about

making changes to prevent another terrorist attack.

You are aware of the criticisms of agency operations made by post–9/11 investigations. They revealed many problems, including outdated computer equipment, inadequate surveillance of visa violators, reluctance to share data with other intelligence agencies, and too few data analysts. The agency is slow and inefficient, especially in its inability to translate intelligence in a timely manner and get it to the analysts. The agency was found to be hundreds of thousands of pages behind in its translations and short of staff with the requisite language skills.

These problems were apparent to you when you first arrived. Many of the documents assigned to you had been translated at least once before by translators whose language skills were not up to the job. The agency was even sending a translator who had failed both the English- and the Turkish-language proficiency tests to the Guantanamo Bay prison camp to translate interviews with Turkish-speaking prisoners captured in Afghanistan. You complained he was not capable of doing the work, but he was sent anyway.

You also found yourself working with a woman who had ties to a Turkish organization under investigation by the FBI. You wondered how she got through the background check with a top-secret security

The Nature of Bureaucracies
Goals
Performance Standards
Openness

Growth of the Federal Bureaucracy
Why the Bureaucracy Has Grown
Controlling Growth
Agencies within the Federal Bureaucracy

What Bureaucracies Do
Administering Policy
Making Policy
Regulation
Data Collection and Analysis

Politics and Professional Standards
The Merit System
Neutral Competence

Overseeing the Bureaucracy
President
Congress
Courts
Interest Groups and Individuals

Conclusion: Is the Bureaucracy Responsive?

FBI translator Sibel Edmonds.

the FBI into the modern world, restore its reputation, or redefine its mission.

Even before 9/11, the agency was increasingly regarded as adrift and in urgent need of reform. It had weathered one foul-up after another. In a standoff with a right-wing separatist at Ruby Ridge, Idaho, an FBI sniper killed the rebel's wife. The Agency leaders narrowly escaped formal censure from the Justice Department for their handling of that case. Next came the debacle at Waco, Texas, where dozens of women and children, members of a religious cult, were killed in a fire while the agency had their compound surrounded. The agents at the site were widely regarded as having provoked the situation that led to the deaths. And in a grave lapse, the agency discovered that one of its own veteran agents, Robert Hanssen, had been spying for the Soviet Union for years. A man living far beyond his means, and whose own brother-in-law suspected him of spying, continued to pass muster at the FBI. No one knows how many agents lost their lives because of information sold by Hanssen.³ Because of these and other foul-ups, by 2001, six separate reviews of the agency were in progress.⁴

Then came September 11, and questions about the bureau's failures in fighting terrorism. A flight school administrator in Arizona had called the local FBI office to report a suspicious student who wanted to learn to take off but not to land. The agent passed that information to Washington, but there was no follow-up. One message intercepted on September 10, 2001, said,

"Tomorrow is zero hour," and another said, "The match is about to begin," but neither was translated until days after the attack because of the backlog of information and the shortage of trained personnel.⁵

When you joined the agency, its new director, Robert Mueller, was already on the defensive. Later he admitted to Congress that the agency was woefully short of intelligence analysts and that it had to borrow twenty-six from the CIA for its post–9/11 antiterrorist investigation. In the face of so many bungled operations, some members of Congress wanted to remove the agency from the Justice Department, where it has been since its creation and where career agents prefer to stay, and put it in the proposed Department of Homeland Security.

Your complaints to supervisors came in the midst of this threatened shakeup at the bureau. Some of the agents clearly think that if the FBI were given a bigger budget and allowed to hire more staff, it could resolve some of the problems; no one seems interested in listening to your complaints. If higher-ups at the agency will not listen, what can you do? Should you just ignore the problems and trust that your supervisors know what to do? Or are the problems so serious that they cannot be ignored?

One option open to you is take the problem outside the agency, to blow the whistle by sharing inside information with people in a position to take the action your supervisors refuse to take. As **whistleblowers,** individual bureaucrats can sometimes make a big difference by exposing wrongdoing in their workplace, be it mismanagement, fraud, or abuse of power. By their actions, some whistleblowers have helped remove dangerous products from the market, stopped discrimination and harassment on the job, and saved the taxpayers millions of dollars. It is also true that many of them, in return, have been fired or demoted.

You have not been on the job long, and the agency is a bastion of old boy ties and networks. Career agents are fiercely loyal to the agency and its tradi-

© Chris Kleponis/CORBIS

clearance. She was assigning all documents pertaining to the investigation to herself and marking some of them as "not pertinent" and unnecessary to translate. You reported this to a supervisor, but he said, "If you insist on this investigation, I'll make sure in no time it will turn around and become an investigation about you."² But if your suspicions are right, it would be one more stunning revelation about the bureau's failures.

Founded in 1908 to enforce federal criminal laws, the FBI has a long history, some of it inglorious. From 1924 to 1972, the agency was headed by J. Edgar Hoover, who made it into a respected organization and even an icon of popular culture. However, during his forty-eight years as director, Hoover turned the FBI into his own personal fiefdom, grossly abusing his powers by keeping personal files on presidents and members of Congress and then using the information to get what he wanted for the agency and to protect his own position. Hoover was followed by a series of political appointees, many with substantial backgrounds in criminal law, but none were able to lead

When George Wallace ran as a third-party candidate for president in 1968, he campaigned against "pointy-headed bureaucrats" in Washington making decisions that regulated good people's lives. Bureaucrats, according to Wallace, were out of touch with everyday citizens and their concerns. Wallace did not invent bureaucracy bashing, but he helped make it popular among candidates for federal office.

President Reagan never tired of talking about his dissatisfaction with big government and liked to say he preferred flying over Washington to being on the ground because from the air, government looked smaller. Presidential candidates Patrick Buchanan and Ross Perot ran for office by disparaging the people who run the government they wanted to lead. And not long after taking office, George W. Bush discounted a report on global warming "put out by the bureaucracy," implying that, given its source, it need not be taken seriously.

When these men refer to "Washington" they mean big government using too much money to do unnecessary things. These critics imply that bureaucrats are not like ordinary citizens. Rather, they are busybodies committed to expanding government's size, spending taxpayers' money, and designing regulations to make life more difficult for individuals and businesses.

To some people, the federal bureaucracy has become the symbol of big government and the embodiment of everything they dislike about it. It is seen as equivalent to a fourth branch of government—powerful, uncontrollable, and with a life of its own. In fact, the federal bureaucracy has no independent legislative authority, only that delegated by Congress, and it has no budgetary powers. The bureaucracy's official role is to implement and enforce policies made by elected officials— that is, by Congress and the president. In doing this, bureaucrats do, in some instances, make new law. But departments and agencies exist at the pleasure of Congress, which can eliminate them or trim their budgets if it does not approve of their behavior. If an agency within the bureaucracy consistently supersedes its authority, it is because Congress is intentionally letting it do so or is failing to fulfill its oversight duties.

Bureaucratic decision making is involved in so much of our lives because government has come to serve many different purposes and interests. The federal government employs butchers, truck drivers, engineers, and three-quarters of all the holders of doctorates in mathematics working in the United States. In all, it employs 2.7 million civilians who work in one hundred agencies at more than eight hundred different occupations. (The armed forces put another 2.3 million on the federal payroll.) Federal bureaucrats do crop research and soil analysis, run hospitals and utilities, fight drug trafficking, check manufacturers' claims about their products, inspect mines, develop high-tech weapons systems, send out Social Security checks, authorize Medicare payments, administer student loan programs, and regulate air traffic, to mention only a few responsibilities.

As we shall see, government bureaucrats are a lot like everyone else. They are ordinary citizens with attitudes that mirror those of their fellow citizens. Very few of these civil servants, about 16 percent, work in the Washington, D.C., metropolitan area. It may not fit your image of people pushing paper in buildings the size of the Pentagon, but the great majority of federal bureaucrats serve in offices near you; check the U.S. government listing in your telephone book and see how many branch offices of federal agencies are located in or near your hometown. (See the box "Women and Minorities in the Civil Service." on the next page)

In this chapter, we look at the evolution of the federal bureaucracy—its growth in size, function, and lawmaking powers. We describe the people who staff the bureaucracy, how they are recruited, what rules govern their work, and how Congress and the president set guidelines for the executive branch and oversee its activities. Finally, we describe ways in which the public can join in the work of monitoring the bureaucracy and have a say in the rules it makes.

The Nature of Bureaucracies

Many people automatically associate the word *bureaucracy* with the federal government. They may visualize rows of cubicles with nameless clerical workers doing monotonous work very inefficiently. Trying to cash in on this stereotype, a Virginia company once sold a

WOMEN AND MINORITIES IN THE CIVIL SERVICE

Americans expect their public bureaucracies to be open and responsive. Andrew Jackson recognized this when he opened the civil service to people of "common" origins. By putting his frontier supporters in office, he hoped to make the bureaucracy more responsive by making it more representative. In the twentieth century, the expectation that public agencies should be open to all qualified applicants gave some groups, such as Irish, Jewish, and African Americans, more job opportunities than were open to them in the private sector because of segregation and quotas.

In the past two decades, significant progress has been made in making the federal bureaucracy more reflective of American diversity. Thirty-one percent of Americans identified as minorities in the 2000 census, and that is the proportion of federal workers who were minorities in 2002.[1] African Americans are particularly well represented, being a substantially larger portion of the federal workforce (16.9 percent) than of the general population.[2] Both American Indians and Asian Americans have a slightly larger percentage of federal jobs than their population share, while Hispanics are significantly underrepresented in the federal workforce, despite an aggressive Hispanic recruitment program.[3] Women are represented almost in exact proportion as in the private sector, filling 45 percent of federal positions compared with 46 percent of private sector jobs.

The relatively good news about the overall profile of the bureaucracy fades at the top of the pay scale. Women and minority men have not yet broken completely through the "glass ceiling" that has kept them out of top management positions. Even after passage of civil rights and equal opportunity legislation, barriers did not fall because often the individuals who enforced the new regulations were opposed to the policies.

There is progress, however. Women now fill almost 30 percent of senior-grade pay positions, more than twice the share held a decade ago. Collectively, minorities hold over 16 percent of all senior positions.

Federal court rulings and out-of-court settlements in discrimination cases account for some of the improvement in upward mobility. African Americans won a suit against the Department of Education charging abuse of the system designed to promote those who took on extra work. The additional responsibilities were usually given to whites, putting them on a faster promotion track.[4] Women agents charged the FBI with a

Federal employment has opened opportunities for African Americans. Shown here are two Bureau of Engraving and Printing employees checking the quality of $20 bills. (The woman at right is holding $8,000 in printing mistakes.)

similar tactic by denying them assignment to SWAT teams, even though experience on such teams was crucial to advancement. Only when they threatened to sue did the FBI change its promotion procedures.[5]

TABLE 1	Women and Minorities as a Percentage of the Senior Federal Civil Service Workforce		
	1985	**1990**	**2002**
Women	8	12	30
African Americans	4	5	8
Hispanics	1	2	4
Asians and Pacific Islanders	1	1	3
American Indians	—	0.5	1

NOTE: Data are for employees at senior pay levels. Overall, about 1 percent of all federal employees are at this grade.
SOURCE: Office of Personnel Management, "Federal Civilian Workforce Statistics," *The Fact Book, 2003 Edition,* www.opm.gov.

1. Office of Personnel Management, *The Fact Book, 2003 Edition,* www.opm.gov, tab. 11.
2. The comparison of public and private sector employment is from "Diversity Trickles Up in Government," *Champaign-Urbana News-Gazette,* July 17, 2001, A3.
3. Ibid.; "Hispanics Sought for Federal Work Force," *Champaign-Urbana News-Gazette,* February 3, 2002, A6.
4. "Diversity Trickles Up."
5. Katherine C. Naff, "Through the Glass Ceiling: Prospects for the Advancement of Women in the Federal Civil Service," *Public Administration Review* 54 (1994), 513; for an account of discrimination against women in the FBI, see Rosemary Dew and Pat Pap, *No Backup: My Life as a Female FBI Special Agent* (New York: Carroll & Graf, 2003).

"Bureaucrat" doll as "a product of no redeeming social value. Place the Bureaucrat on a stack of papers on your desk, and he will just sit on them."[6] The problem with this joke is that the parodied traits are not necessarily common among government bureaucrats, nor are they unique to bureaucrats. All organizations except the very smallest have bureaucracies: Your college or university has one, as did your local school district; corporations, most religious denominations, and large philanthropic foundations have them, too, not to mention the Olympics, your favorite sports league, and the unions that represent the players in that league.

All these bureaucracies, public and private, share some common features. For example, all have hierarchies of authority; that is, everyone in a bureaucracy has a place in a pyramidal network of jobs, with fewer near the top and more near the bottom. Almost everyone in a bureaucracy has a boss, and except for those in the bottom tier, most have some subordinates. People advance up the hierarchy on the basis of performance or seniority, so those with more authority tend to be those with more experience and expertise.

Because of the hierarchical structure, bureaucratic behavior is not always consistent with democratic principles. Most bureaucrats are not elected, and as in any hierarchical organization, higher-level authorities can restrict the opportunity of someone lower in the pyramid to express an opinion or share expertise in the decision-making process. In their relative lack of openness, bureaucracies have the potential to restrict consumer and client access to information about their products and services and how they operate and to limit citizens' access to information about their own government. In effect, organizational tendencies, if unrestrained in a government bureaucracy, could transform "citizens" into "subordinates."[7] But our constitutional system provides checks on the power of federal bureaucrats and ways for the public to participate in decision making that few people know about or take advantage of.

Not only are government bureaucracies structurally similar to private ones, but they do the same types of work. Employees in both private and public bureaucracies perform a lot of routine tasks. Auditing expense vouchers, managing employee travel, and creating personnel systems, for example, are as routine in business firms as in public agencies. And both also have workers who are productive, honest, and efficient and others who are not. Executives in the Defense Department bought $600 toilet seats and spent more than $75 apiece for metal screws sold elsewhere for 57 cents. In the 1970s and 1980s, their private counterparts at Chrysler, Lockheed, Penn Central, and hundreds of banks and savings and loans ran their businesses into the ground, then looked to the government for bailouts or buyouts. During the 1990s, corporations such as Enron, Tyco, and

"I'm sorry, dear, but you knew I was a bureaucrat when you married me."

WorldCom paid out hundreds of millions of dollars in stock options and bonuses to executives who, in return, lied about company earnings and cost investors billions of dollars.

But there are some distinctions between private and public bureaucracies. Here we look at several.[8]

Goals

Businesses are supposed to make a profit; if they do not, they fail. Public agencies are supposed to promote the "public interest"; if they do not, they fail to serve the people who pay their salaries. Although people disagree over what the public interest is, it is not the same thing as making a profit, just as a government is not a business. This is why we have different words for these two kinds of organizations which exist for completely different reasons.

The goals of a public bureaucracy are defined by elected officials, who collectively determine what is in the public interest. They are sometimes accused of setting goals as if they were in a private bureaucracy—that is, making policies that will do well in the polls rather than those that will best serve the public. But in general, the goals set by these officials are supposed to accomplish tasks and provide services that private bureaucracies cannot. In some cases, such as providing for national security during wartime, they must do so irrespective of cost.

Some part of the public's varying perception of how well the bureaucracy does its job stems from a lack of agreement on the work it is given to do. One person's lazy, red-tape-ridden, uncaring bureaucracy is another's responsive agency. But even when unhappy with performance, Americans still expect government to provide a

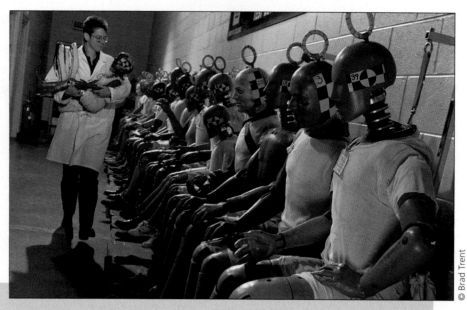

To save lives, federal regulations mandate testing autos for safety and setting safety standards. These dummies allow simulation of the impact of crashes on humans.

vast array of services, costing billions of dollars annually, from highways that accommodate high-speed cars to Social Security payments that arrive on time, from clean tap water to safe neighborhoods, from protection from foreign enemies to a cure for cancer.

Performance Standards

It is relatively easy to tell if a private organization is meeting its goals: is it profitable (ignoring for the moment fraudulent accounting)? We might dislike the chocolate-covered raisins that a candy company produces but would still consider the company successful if it made a profit selling them. We would not typically denigrate the company because it makes something we do not approve of. But we rightly use a different standard in judging government. Yet what is the appropriate standard for evaluating the performance of government if making a profit is not the goal?

One obvious method is to determine whether a public agency is efficient and cost-effective. That sounds logical, but any method of assigning dollar values to bureaucratic output must be partly subjective. It is usually easier to place a value on a commodity than on a government service. We can estimate what price to place on a chair or a house by computing the cost of constructing it. But placing a dollar value on such public goals as education or consumer safety is much harder. How many children have to die from swallowing pills and medications before government requires pharmaceutical manufacturers to use childproof caps on bottles? How many lives saved makes it worthwhile for govern-

ment to require auto manufacturers to install air bags? These are questions bureaucrats must answer on a daily basis. They are required to calculate how much a human life is worth and how productive an individual will be during his or her lifetime. Then they have to estimate the costs of putting the policies in place to protect lives, as well as to monitor and enforce the policies.

Private bureaucracies ask the same questions before their leaders decide whether it is profitable to install safer fuel tanks in cars or to remove a low-risk flaw from a child's toy. Although the federal bureaucrat, too, is always weighing costs against benefits, many people believe that the government should not use cost as the primary standard when lives are at risk.

Another way to evaluate performance is to measure waste that stems from inefficiency and corruption. This is not particularly difficult to do once exposed. It is not hard to calculate how much more an agency paid out because it failed to get competitive bids for equipment and supplies, hired more employees than necessary to do a job, contracted consultants to do imaginary work, or erred in calculating welfare payments or farm subsidies. Recently, for example, several investigations are exploring the waste caused by contracting with private companies without competitive bidding to provide services in Iraq, ranging from protecting supplies to constructing buildings. But other kinds of government "waste" are hard to measure.

Some people deem a program wasteful, no matter how well it is run, because they are opposed to its goals. Perhaps the program is providing services the taxpayer thinks inappropriate for government, or maybe it serves relatively few people at a large cost. These were the criteria many Americans used to evaluate welfare programs. Accusations of waste and fraud were common, but as a percentage of overall expenditures, there was little client fraud in the welfare program. Most criticism stemmed from opposition to the program itself and services provided at great cost to a small clientele without appropriate results.

In a less publicized example, when a government commission called it wasteful to keep open hundreds of very small post offices that served rural communities, they were not alleging fraud or mismanagement. The commission believed that the post offices cost too much for the small number of people served. To the residents of these communities, however, their post offices were a good return on their tax dollars, and paying to keep them open was more efficient than having to drive miles to a distant station.

Citizens have rarely applied this standard of waste to corporate behavior, at least not prior to our more environmentally conscious era. If a business or industry makes a profit, most people think it is a job well done, without asking whether the product or service offered is in itself wasteful. Marketing a hundred different kinds of breakfast cereal in packaging twice the size of the contents may not be an efficient use of resources, but if they sell, consumers are inclined to say, "Why not?" We may not like lime green sofas with pink stripes, but we do not consider their manufacturer wasteful for making them as long as the product is profitable.

Historically, private corporations have been able to waste more than a government agency of comparable size without the public ever taking notice. In 2001, when senior managers in the federal bureaucracy got bonuses averaging $11,000, it prompted public scrutiny of their agencies' performances.[9] When CEOs of corporations that lost money got multimillion-dollar bonuses, much of the public simply said, "Whatever the market will allow." (Some of that thinking changed when the executives were found to have committed criminal acts.)

We see government expenditures as *our* money, and we feel entitled to complain, especially since payment of that money (taxes) is not voluntary. Only recently has such a large percentage of the public invested in stock that they have begun paying attention to how private bureaucracies manage *investors'* money. Yet private investments are often made through public bureaucracies, such as a university's or a school district's pension fund, and when losses occur because of corruption or poor performance by the corporate bureaucracy, it may still be the public bureaucracy that takes much of the heat.

Openness

The openness of public bureaucracy is another feature distinguishing it from a private bureaucracy. Private firms operate with much more secrecy than public agencies do, even when private actions have a significant impact on the public. For example, tobacco companies' lack of openness—long assumed to be their right—cost the lives of many people. The courts ordered tobacco companies to open their files only after much scientific evidence on the dangers of tobacco had accumulated.

In contrast, the greater visibility, or openness, of public agencies helps make them more responsive. Only by having knowledge of both the process and the content of public decisions can interested groups and individuals express their preferences effectively. No one articulated this better than James Madison when he wrote, "A popular Government without popular information or the means of acquiring it, is but a Prologue to a Farce or a Tragedy or perhaps both. Knowledge will forever govern ignorance, and a people who mean to be their own Governors, must arm themselves with the power knowledge gives."[10]

To this end, Congress in 1813 established a system for making government documents accessible to the public by placing them in local libraries around the country. But as government grew and agencies and paper proliferated, it became harder for the public to keep track of what government was doing. In 1934, Congress passed the Federal Register Act, requiring that all government rules, regulations, and laws be published in the *Federal Register* and that all rules in their final version appear in the *Code of Federal Regulations*. (Today both are available online at www.gpoaccess.gov/fr/index.html.)

Congress went further in 1946 by passing the **Administrative Procedure Act (APA),** which provides for public participation in the rule-making process. All federal agencies must disclose their rule-making procedures and publish all regulations at least thirty days in advance of their effective date to allow time for public comment. Today citizens can often post comments on proposed rules at an agency's Web site, but it is common for public hearings to be held on controversial rules or those with wide impact. Environmental rules frequently provoke citizen reactions, with comments sometimes numbering in the tens of thousands.

Congress increased public access to the bureaucracy in another way by passing the Freedom of Information Act in 1966. As amended in 1974, **FOIA** (pronounced "foy-ya") lets any member of the public apply to an agency for access to unclassified documents in its archives. The government also puts out a handbook telling how to take advantage of this right, and every government Web site is required to have a link to its FOIA office. FOIA cannot be used to gain access to internal records such as personnel files, for example, or sensitive documents on a living person. But it can be used to get your FBI file, should you have one, or the file of a person no longer living. Requests must be made according to a formal procedure, and they must cite specific

A few months after the destruction of the World Trade Center, federal officials contacted the head of the Documents Library at the University of Illinois and told her to destroy a CD with information on the nation's largest water supplies. The library had received the CD under the federal depository library program, established in 1813 "to guarantee public access to government information by making it available free of charge." Illinois is one of 1,350 libraries designated as depositories. Facing the possibility of losing that designation, the documents librarian destroyed the CD.[1]

The water supply CD was just one of thousands of scientific and technical documents the government began removing from public release at the beginning of 2002, some from libraries and many from government Web sites. The Environmental Protection Agency, for example, deleted a database on chemicals used at industrial sites.[2] The government also asked scientists' professional associations to restrict what they publish.[3]

In the public eye, the tightening of access to public documents could be justified in the face of a palpable threat to national security. It was widely believed that one of the reasons terrorists were able to carry out their plans on September 11, 2001, was that they knew how to take advantage of the openness of American society. No one wants to make it easier for terrorists to plan new attacks by having access to detailed site information on nuclear waste dumps, nuclear power plants, or other utilities and public facilities or instructions on how to construct nuclear, biological, and chemical weapons. At the same time, most Americans do not want the fear of terrorism to destroy the openness and access to information essential to any democracy.

This is the crux of the problem. Information of interest to potential terrorists is not all that has been removed from public view. By executive order from President George W. Bush and directives from Attorney General John Ashcroft, new rules on access to all government documents and reports were put in place, reversing the openness standards established by the Clinton administration.

By executive order, Bush also reversed a Clinton policy that had prohibited thousands of department and agency heads from stamping documents "secret" on their own authority. Whereas during Clinton's presidency four times as much material had been declassified as in the previous fifteen

FOIA requires the release of documents, but sometimes the government will censor information within them. This comment was all that remained of an e-mail that the Bush administration censored before releasing.

documents. Agencies are not obligated to give "information," only to provide copies of the documents requested, if they have them and if they are not in an exempt category.

Efforts to make government agencies more open often run up against a desire to limit the distribution of critical or embarrassing information. It is the rare public or private bureaucracy that wants to reveal its failures. Thus an evaluation of FOIA found that agencies used many tactics to discourage people from seeking information, such as delaying responses to requests, charging high fees for copies of records (the State Department once charged $10 a page for copying records), and requiring detailed descriptions of documents requested.[11] The FBI once refused to expedite the release of information to a prisoner on death row who was afraid he would be executed before the information was available. The FBI's judgment that his situation did not show "exceptional need or urgency" was overruled by a federal court.[12]

As the chief executive, a president's views on the openness of agencies are also important. The president's policy on FOIA implementation is communicated to federal agencies by the attorney general at the beginning of each administration. Under Presidents Reagan and Bush Sr., federal agencies adopted a narrow reading of the act, making it more difficult to get information.[13] In contrast, President Carter banned classification of documents unless they were clearly related to national security, and President Clinton issued an executive order

years,[4] the Bush administration classified 14 million documents in 2003 alone, at a cost to taxpayers of $6.5 billion. That is $459 per memo, almost four times the cost of declassification.[5]

Bush's tightening of access to government documents, however, may owe more to the desire to strengthen the executive branch and protect federal bureaucrats and elected officials from public scrutiny than to the war on terrorism.[6] Bush came into office saying he wanted to strengthen the office of president and reduce both congressional and public oversight of the executive branch. He frequently refused to turn over White House papers to congressional oversight committees. By executive order, he applied this policy specifically to presidential papers, including his father's, which were due to be opened to the public. Vice President Cheney was a long-standing opponent of FOIA.[7]

The Bush administration's narrow definition of public access rights and the penchant for secrecy drew criticism from both conservatives and liberals. The head of the nonpartisan interest group Judicial Watch concluded that the administration's attitude was simply that "the government is not to be questioned."[8] The Cato Institute, a libertarian think tank, accused the administration of being "a law unto itself,"[9] and one of Bush's strongest supporters, Representative Dan Burton (R-Ind.), said, even while granting that every president wants to protect himself from oversight, "a veil of secrecy has descended around the administration."[10] Thomas Kean, cochair of the 9/11 Commission, said that in carrying out the investigation, "three-quarters of the classified material he reviewed . . . should not have been classified in the first place."[11]

1. Greg Kline, "Information at Risk," *Champaign-Urbana News-Gazette,* January 20, 2002, 1.
2. A list of excised material appears at www.ombwatch.org.
3. William S. Broad, "U.S. Is Tightening Rules on Keeping Scientific Secrets," *New York Times,* February 17, 2002, 1, 13.
4. Ellen Nakashima, "Frustration on the Left—and the Right," *Washington Post National Weekly Edition,* March 11, 2002, 29.
5. Eric Lichtblau, "Government by, and Secret from, the People," *New York Times,* September 5, 2004, WK5.
6. Linda Greenhouse, "A Penchant for Secrecy," *New York Times,* May 5, 2002, WK1.
7. As a presidential aide in the Ford administration, Cheney encouraged President Ford to veto the 1974 bill strengthening FOIA rights. Congress ultimately passed the bill over Ford's veto.
8. Nakashima, "Frustration."
9. Greenhouse, "Penchant for Secrecy."
10. Interview by Bill Moyers, "Behind the Freedom of Information Act," on *Now with Bill Moyers,* PBS, April 5, 2002.
11. (Senators) Trent Lott and Ron Wyden, "Hiding the Truth in a Cloud of Black Ink," *New York Times,* August 26, 2004, A27.

authorizing the declassification of most documents twenty-five years old or older. He also put a ten-year limit on the classified status of new documents unless a review had determined that they must remain secret.[14] The Clinton administration standard for access to government records had been to exempt a document from a FOIA request only if there was a "foreseeable harm" in its release.[15]

George W. Bush rolled back FOIA access, justifying the move on national security grounds. A memo from his first attorney general, John Ashcroft, to federal agencies one month after the 9/11 attacks changed the standard for release of government documents to the public. Ashcroft assured FOIA administrators that when they "decide to withhold records, in whole or in part," the Justice Department "will defend your decisions unless they lack a sound legal basis or present an unwarranted risk of adverse impact on the ability of other agencies to protect important records."[16] Thus under the Bush standard, any FOIA request denied by an agency on any "sound legal basis" can expect Justice Department backing. (See the box "Veil of Secrecy.") But that did not stop FOIA requests from tripling between 2000 and 2003, when 3.2 millions requests were submitted.[17]

There is disagreement over which public documents are subject to FOIA requests and which are exempt. The federal government, like private businesses, stores an increasing amount of information electronically. Retrieving the growing mass of information stored on computer can be easier than finding information on paper.

However, FOIA neither defined when electronic information was in the public domain nor required agencies to save and release it. The aides of George H. Bush and Clinton used e-mail extensively. The first George Bush took his aides' e-mail tapes with him when he left office and argued that they were not public property. A federal appeals court ruled that these tapes are public records and must be preserved, and they applied the same ruling to Clinton administration requests for exemption. Because of these rulings, the current Bush administration has been very cautious about exchanges of views by e-mail, and Bush himself stopped all of his own personal e-mail.

Despite the limitations of FOIA, it has enabled individuals and groups to gain important and useful information. Citizens have used it to gather injury and fatality information on defective cars, to assess dangerous infant formulas, to reveal a link between aspirin and a disease known as Reye's syndrome, to learn that J. Edgar Hoover authorized the FBI to carry out a four-year investigation of women's rights groups, and to force the Internal Revenue Service (IRS) to release a 40,000-page manual on its auditing procedures.[18] Scholars have used FOIA to retrieve thousands of documents on Cold War diplomacy, to get records of medical experiments on the effect of radioactivity conducted on unwitting subjects, and to retrieve the FBI files of anthropologists kept under surveillance during the Cold War and the McCarthy era.

Public access to records that document experiments on human subjects and surveillance of private citizens is an essential check on abuse of power by federal bureaucrats. Yet some categories of information and types of deliberation among decision makers require privacy. It is not always easy to strike the right balance between the need for privacy and openness to the public, interest groups, and the media.

Another significant law mandating openness in government is the aptly named **Sunshine Act.** Adopted in 1977, it requires that most government meetings be conducted in public and that notice of such meetings must be posted in advance. Regulatory agencies, for example, must give notice of the date, time, place, and agenda of their meetings and follow certain rules to prevent unwarranted secrecy. State governments have adopted their own sunshine laws, and today it is difficult for any public body—city council or planning commission or any of their subgroups—to meet in secret to conduct official business. Results of meetings conducted in closed, unannounced sessions are open to citizen challenge.

Growth of the Federal Bureaucracy

The Founders did not discuss the federal "bureaucracy," but they did recognize the need for an administration to carry out laws and programs. They envisioned administrators with only a little power, charged with "executive details" and "mere execution" of the law. But the growing size and complexity of society and increasing demands that government do more have dramatically changed the nature of the federal bureaucracy.

George Washington's first cabinet included only three departments and the offices of attorney general and postmaster general, all combined employing just a few hundred people. More people worked at Mount Vernon, Washington's plantation, than in his executive branch in the 1790s.[19] The Department of State had just nine employees. By 1800, the bureaucracy was still small, with only three thousand civil servants. Only the Treasury Department had much to do, collecting import and excise taxes and purchasing military supplies for an army of a few thousand. From then until 1990, the bureaucracy grew continuously, though at an uneven rate.

Why the Bureaucracy Has Grown

As we saw in Chapter 3, government, over time, responded to public wishes by creating federal agencies to

---

The Under Secretary of Energy
Washington, D.C. 20585

December, 1992

MEMORANDUM FOR SECRETARIAL OFFICERS

SUBJECT: NE/NE-60 Concurrence

Recently, memoranda have been prepared for my signature or directed to departmental offices from other departmental offices which contain statements regarding whether the direction contained in the memorandum is applicable to Naval Reactors (NE-60). Several memoranda have been incorrect in their assumption regarding the effects on NE-60, resulting in unnecessary further correspondence to correct the misunderstanding.

Applicability to NE-60 of a contemplated action is not always obvious. In many cases, the impact is either indirect or the direct impact is not appreciated due to lack of understanding of the scope of NE-60 responsibility. To avoid misunderstandings in the future, you are requested to consult NE regarding applicability statements before they are made and before memoranda are presented to me, the Secretary, or Deputy Secretary for signature.

I appreciate your attention to this matter.

Hugo Pomrehn
Hugo Pomrehn

Sometimes real examples of bureaucratic thinking are stranger than anything we might imagine. This example was reprinted in Washington Monthly. *Is it any wonder ordinary people think bureaucrats have their own language?*

assist and promote emerging economic interests of business, agriculture, and labor and more recently to provide health and economic benefits to workers, consumers, retirees, and other groups.[20] One scholar explained the bureaucracy's growth by pointing to Americans' discovery that "government can protect and assist as well as punish and repress."[21] Thus at the same time we criticize government's growth, we demand education, irrigation projects, roads, airports, job training, effective policing, consumer protection, security from terrorism, and many other services. Each of us might be willing to cut benefits for someone else, but most of us want to keep the benefits *we* have.

When new bureaucracies are created, the intent is to hold them to their original size, but most grow over time because once they are in place, additional responsibilities are assigned to them. After World War II, the Department of Defense did not return to its prewar size or scope because the Cold War gave us a new reason to support a massive military establishment. That era also created additional demands for health care and other services for veterans. The Administrative Procedure Act was passed in 1946 partly because the bureaucracy had grown so much in size and power during the Depression and World War II that Congress believed it needed to increase its oversight.[22] Bureaucracy usually grows during national crises. After the Cold War, when thoughts turned to downsizing the Defense Department, supporters of military spending found new justifications for expansion in the threat of global terrorism. Forty-five days after 9/11, Congress rushed to pass the USA PATRIOT Act (officially, the Uniting and Strengthening America by Providing Appropriate Tools Required to Intercept and Obstruct Terrorism Act) before members had even read it. That act increased both the power and the size of the federal bureaucracy. Implementation of government's extraordinary new power to wiretap, search e-mail, and gain access to library borrowing records and many business records, paper and electronic, required more personnel and increased spending. Opponents, however, are more frightened by the loss of privacy and liberty than by the increased size and cost of the bureaucracy.

Bureaucrats cannot produce growth on their own. Every agency exists because it is valuable to enough people with enough influence to sustain it. Every agency needs congressional and presidential approval of its programs, appropriations, staffing, and procedures. Sometimes government grows because the president and Congress want it to be more accountable. This often results in hiring more managers, greater inefficiency, and ironically, more difficulty in holding agencies accountable.[23]

The growth of the bureaucracy should be seen in the perspective of the overall growth of our economy and population. For example, the number of federal bureaucrats for every one thousand people in the United States decreased from sixteen in 1953 to ten in 1999.[24] We saw in Chapter 3 that the major growth in public employment in recent decades has been at the state and local levels. Over 37 percent of all government workers were federal employees in 1953; in 1999, fewer than 14 percent were.[25]

Controlling Growth

Once departments are established, their consolidation or elimination is rare. More commonly, departments become so large that they must subdivide (for example, the Department of Commerce and Labor was divided into separate departments of Labor and Commerce) or for offices and agencies to become so big or their work so important they are made into cabinet departments (Veterans Affairs, Homeland Security), where they become even larger.

Yet almost every president since Lyndon Johnson has tried to streamline or downsize the bureaucracy. Richard Nixon tried to merge seven departments into four but could not gain approval, and despite many attempts to ax the Department of Education, it is stronger than it ever has been. Jimmy Carter was a committed deregulator and a micromanager who oversaw the elimination of thousands of rules and some regulators. He unsuccessfully tried to introduce a budgeting process that would have required every agency to justify its budget every year on the basis of its success in achieving agency goals.

For all Ronald Reagan's talk against big government, it grew by over two hundred thousand employees during his administration. Although many agencies lost personnel (the biggest loser was the Department of Housing and Urban Development), others, such as Defense, Justice, and the Treasury, gained. In addition, Reagan created a new cabinet office, the Department of Veterans Affairs, from what had been an independent agency. He had entered office with a plan to wage a "war on waste," but he left office with the country another trillion dollars in debt and the Defense Department buying $600 toilet seats. The Clinton administration's initiative on "reinventing government" also attempted to reduce the size of the bureaucracy—with limited success: the number of government employees did decrease by 1.5 percent during his years in office.

There is a general assumption that size and performance are linked. So presidents often think they can establish more efficient management plans and then cut personnel. George H. Bush, for example, came into office with a plan for "total quality management," and George W. Bush, with a business administration degree, adopted a system for grading the performance of every agency. The Office of Management and Budget, which performs much of the executive branch's internal oversight, evaluated each department or agency in five management categories: personnel, competitive bidding, financial management, e-government (using technology to improve efficiency), and whether program achievements justify a budget (similar to Carter's zero-based budgeting).[26] Those who fell short or whose work was duplicated in another department were to have their budgets slashed, with the money redirected to programs that work. Almost all agencies and departments received poor or failing marks in some categories, and the OMB even gave itself a failing grade. Under this system, some agencies did receive budget cuts. However, in 2003, the Department of Defense, which got poor marks in all five categories, received its largest one-year budget increase since the Reagan era.

Despite Bush's admiration for smaller, more efficient government, the federal bureaucracy, after shrinking by almost 3 percent in the previous decade, grew by 5 percent (79,000 jobs) during his first three years in office.[27] Some of the growth was due to the war on terrorism—adding a new cabinet department and increasing defense appointments. But there was also some padding—or thickening—of the bureaucracy through the creation of new positions at the senior level in cabinet departments that have nothing to do with national security.[28] The number of people at the highest pay level more than tripled during Bush's first three years. The significance of this thickening is that it adds layers of administration to cabinet departments at a time when the efficient upward and downward flow of information within the bureaucracy has become a major issue, even a life-and-death issue, as it was in the intelligence bureaucracy in 2001. A 2004 survey showed that the new Department of Homeland Security had jumped from three to twenty-one layers of administration and had 146 senior administrative positions two years after its creation.[29]

Career civil servants are skeptical about the attempt of every administration to take on the bureaucracy and cut it down to size. One explanation of the perception gap is that there is a "natural antipathy" between presidents and career civil servants because the president is elected on his ability to articulate basic human values while "civil service is about enforcing rules and procedures and treating all citizens and issues equally." Bureaucrats are not about values in the sense that politicians use that term.[30] Reform is difficult when presidents appoint individuals to fill political leadership positions in agencies who do not stay around long enough to learn their jobs and have little chance of really reshaping their agencies. Presidents and their appointees find that reality does not always match political slogans. And presidents find that reforming the bureaucracy is much tougher than they anticipated and usually soon turn to other activities with more immediate payoffs. Thus in the view of a former OMB official, reform is mostly "three yards and a cloud of dust."[31] (See the box "What Do Bureaucrats Want Anyway? on page 410)

Agencies within the Federal Bureaucracy

The Constitution says little about the organization of the executive branch other than indicating a need for the president to have a cabinet. As government's role expanded, it became clear that a single type of organization would not be appropriate for every task assigned to the bureaucracy. Cabinet departments, for example, are headed by people who serve at the president's pleasure and are there to help carry out his policies. But other agencies must implement law without reference to an individual president's preferences. These agencies require protection from political interference, as do those established to carry out highly technical work. In this section, we review the major types of agencies in the executive branch.

Departments

Departments are organizations within the executive branch that form the president's cabinet. Their heads, called secretaries (except for the head of the Justice Department), are appointed by the president with the consent of the Senate, and they are directly responsible to the president. There are fifteen departments; the newest is Homeland Security (see Figure 1). These departments constitute the lion's share of the federal bureaucracy; the largest employer is the Defense Department, with close to 30 percent of all civil servants.

Cabinet departments exist to carry out the president's policy in specific functional areas: national security, federal law enforcement, fiscal policy, health and welfare, foreign relations, and so forth. They are staffed by career civil servants, but all top policymaking positions in each division of a department are held by presidential appointees. The fifteen cabinet departments have more than 350 such positions. Permanent staff believe that the increase in the number of appointive senior positions makes their work more difficult.

Independent Agencies

Independent agencies differ from departments in that they are usually smaller and their heads do not sit in the cabinet. Agency heads are, however, appointed by and responsible to the president. And occasionally a president does extend cabinet status to the head of an independent agency, most notably the director of the Environmental Protection Agency (EPA). Some agencies, such as the EPA, the CIA, the Social Security Adminis-

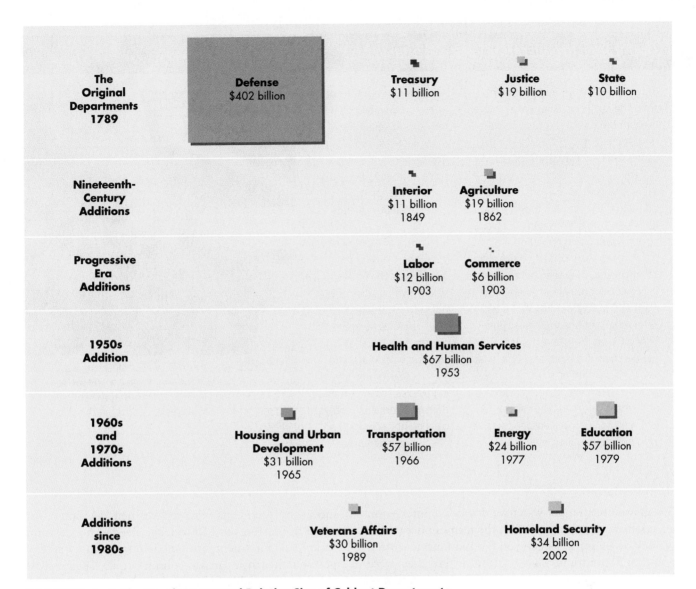

FIGURE 1 ■ The Development and Relative Size of Cabinet Departments
*Dollar figures are each department's discretionary budget for fiscal 2005. The modern
Department of Defense (1949) replaced the Departments of War (1789) and the Navy
(1798); the Justice Department (1870) replaced the Department of the Attorney General
(1789); the Commerce and Labor Departments were first established in 1903 as a
joint enterprise; and the Department of Health, Education and Welfare (1953) was divided in 1979 into the Department of Health and Human Services and the Department
of Education.*

SOURCE: "United States Budget for Fiscal Year 2005," *Manual of the United States Government, 2003–
2004* (Washington, D.C.: Government Printing Office, 2003).

tration, the Peace Corps, and the National Aeronautics
and Space Administration (NASA), are well known to
the public. Others, such as the Office of Government
Ethics, are relatively unknown.

Some independent agencies are responsible for
highly specialized areas of policy such as space exploration (NASA) or law enforcement (FBI). The people
appointed to head them usually have an appropriate
professional background, not just a political profile ac-

ceptable to the president. However, if the agency deals
with policy that has widespread impact, as the EPA and
CIA do, political credentials are likely to be the president's first consideration in naming a director.

Independent Regulatory Boards and Commissions

Although unfamiliar to most Americans, independent
agencies affect almost every aspect of our daily lives—

Bureaucrats are not much different from the rest of us. They are no more likely to favor raising taxes or government spending; they have about the same confidence as other citizens in government and other institutions, such as organized religion, business, labor, and the press, and they are about as likely as other Americans to favor or oppose busing and gun control.[1]

When civil servants do differ from other citizens, they seem more open to diversity. For example, they are more likely to say they would vote for an African American or a woman as president and less likely to accept traditional gender roles. And they are somewhat *less* likely than other Americans to approve government intrusions into people's private lives. They also are less likely to approve censoring people who hold unpopular views or laws banning pornography or interracial marriage. On only one issue are they more liable to favor "big government": they are somewhat more likely to favor wiretapping.

Federal bureaucrats, like many other Americans, are critical of their own institutions. "Having endured a decade of downsizing, two decades of bureaucratic bashing, three decades of constant reform, four decades of increasing workloads, and five decades of pay and hiring freezes," the attitudes of many federal bureaucrats do not add up to a "healthy public service."[2]

© Stefano Paltera/Gamma Presse, Inc.

Adding to their job anxieties, federal employees are sometimes on the front line of danger. A mail carrier protects herself after other postal workers were infected by anthrax spores sent through the U.S. mail in 2001.

the air we breathe, the water we drink, the interest on a bank loan, the fee at an ATM, the terms under which we buy or sell stock, labeling on food and manufactured goods and conditions in the plants where they were made, phone and mail service, and the construction of every car, train, plane, or bus we ride on.

Each independent regulatory board and commissions regulates a specific area of business or the economy. Examples include the Federal Communications Commission (FCC), which regulates the electronic media; the Securities and Exchange Commission (SEC), which makes and enforces rules regarding stocks, bonds, and securities; and the Federal Reserve System (the Fed), which sets prime interest rates and controls the amount of money in circulation. These and other regulatory agencies are designated "independent" because the work they do is supposed to be removed from politics as much as possible. Congress created the first such commission, the Interstate Commerce Commission, in 1887 to decide such things as interstate freight rates, railroad ticket prices, routes, and conditions of service.

Each of these independent regulatory boards and commissions is directed by five to ten presidential appointees. By law, each board and commission must be balanced with members of both major political parties. Appointees serve staggered terms and cannot be re-moved by presidents who dislike their decisions. Because of the technical knowledge needed for decision making, appointments are supposed to be based on expertise rather than partisan considerations. Of course, it is almost impossible for politics, in the sense of an individual's values, not to have some impact on decision making. Presidents who want less government regulation appoint commissioners who share that value. Commissioners, in turn, can then make it difficult for the professionals in the agency to carry out their regulatory mission. However, the goal of having these independent commissions is to make politics secondary to professional expertise.

Government Corporations

Government corporations are businesses run by government to provide services the public needs but that no private company will provide because they are not profitable—or were not profitable at the time government began providing the service. The first government corporation, the Tennessee Valley Authority (TVA), was created when no utility company was willing to invest in the infrastructure necessary to bring electricity to what was then a very poor, undeveloped region of the country. The TVA still supplies electricity to its part of the country.

Federal bureaucrats do not have a particularly high opinion of the political appointees who wander into their agencies for short periods (eighteen to twenty-four months on average) to fill leadership positions and quickly disappear, often without ever learning very much about what the agency is all about.[3] What most bureaucrats seem to want is for Congress and the president to stop using them as guinea pigs for their management experiments and instead to provide the tools and training they need to do their jobs right. Sixty percent of federal employees said that Congress "generally acts in ways that worsen the management of their organizations," and 41 percent said the same about the president. Overall, the attitude of federal employees is not "Show me the money" but "Let me do my job."[4]

At lower levels of the civil service, employees are especially apt to complain about their lack of access to training, and at most levels there is dissatisfaction over the lack of equipment, especially state-of-the-art computers, necessary to do their work properly and efficiently. Other major concerns are the impact of past reforms that have left many programs without sufficient personnel to carry out their work and the increasing number of positions within the bureaucracy that have been removed from civil service and made appointive. Some people believe that this has made the work of the bureaucracy too politicized. In addition, many of those at lower levels believe that there is too much bureaucracy—too many layers of administration between top and bottom, impeding

communication and making their jobs more difficult.

Bureaucrats are very hard on themselves, both their own performance and that of their agencies, citing too many people in positions they are unqualified for, especially senior people and political appointees. They want "to eliminate the 'yes' men (and women) and give responsibility back to the employees."[5]

1. Gregory B. Lewis, "In Search of the Machiavellian Milquetoasts: Comparing Attitudes of Bureaucrats and Ordinary People," *Public Administration Review* 50 (1990), 220–227.
2. Paul C. Light, "What Federal Employees Want from Reform: Reform Watch Brief No. 5," Brookings Institution, March 2002, www.brookings.edu/comm/reformwatch/rw05.htm.
3. Paul C. Light, "Fact Sheet on the Continued Thickening of Government," Brookings Institution, July 23, 2004, www.brookings.edu/views/papers/light/20040723.htm.
4. Light, "What Federal Employees Want," 10.
5. Ibid., 7.

The United States Postal Service, which was originally a cabinet department, was converted to a business operation in 1971. Formerly a government monopoly, it now has competition from UPS and FedEx, for example, for some of the services it provides. In the 1960s, when railroads were no longer willing to provide passenger service, the government created the National Railroad Passenger Corporation (Amtrak). And because no private insurance company would ever bear the risk of insuring private bank deposits, the government established a corporation to protect your savings account (the Federal Deposit Insurance Corporation). Similarly, the government is now the main purveyor of terrorism insurance because after 9/11, private firms were no longer willing to assume the risk.

Government corporations charge for their services or products, just like private firms, but their primary objective is to provide a needed service, not to make a profit. Of course, the government is quite happy if they do or if they at least break even. When a government corporation does become profitable, its assets may be sold to private businesses and the corporation closed. This is what happened with CONRAIL, the government corporation that took over rail freight and turned it back into a profitable enterprise. Some people argue that the government should privatize the unprofitable

rail passenger and postal systems, too, but the services provided are so important to the national economy that without certainty that private businesses would continue providing them indefinitely, government would have difficulty justifying the sale of their assets.

What Bureaucracies Do

Having examined forms of bureaucratic organization, we now look in greater detail at the sources of the bureaucracy's authority and the responsibilities assigned to it.

After elected officials make a law, someone must carry it out. That is the primary job of the bureaucracy. Bureaucrats convert laws passed by Congress and signed by the president into rules and actions that have an actual impact on people and things. We call this process **policy implementation.** The general process of policy implementation has two major components: administering policies and making them.

Administering Policy

Public bureaucracy's oldest job is to administer the law. To "administer" is to execute, enforce, and apply the rules that have been made either by Congress or the bureaucracy itself. Thus if policymakers decide to go to war, they must empower agencies to acquire weapons, recruit and train soldiers, and devise a winning strategy. Policymaking without administration is tantamount to having no policy at all.

Administration includes thousands of different kinds of activities. It involves writing checks to farmers who receive payments for growing—or not growing—crops, providing direct services to the public, evaluating how well programs are working, prosecuting those who try to defraud the government, and maintaining buildings and offices. For forest rangers, administration involves helping backpackers in the Grand Canyon or putting out a forest fire in northern Minnesota. For postal employees, it includes delivering the mail or repairing an automatic sorting machine.

Making Policy

Responsibility for administering policy inevitably conferred lawmaking powers on the bureaucracy. This can be illustrated with the example of the Americans with Disabilities Act (ADA). The ADA directs employers to make a "reasonable accommodation" for a competent worker with a disability that "substantially limits" a major life activity such as seeing or walking, except when this causes "undue hardship." [32]

This seemingly straightforward law is in fact extremely complex and its impact far reaching. Although the act went into effect in 1992, the Equal Employment Opportunity Commission (EEOC), which has responsibility for its implementation, is still clarifying what specific provisions in the act mean. What is the difference between a "reasonable accommodation" and an "undue hardship"? When voters want local governments to spend less, is the $2 million that Des Plaines, Illinois, had to shell out for sidewalks and curb cuts an "undue hardship" or not? [33] Will the EEOC let colleges and universities make only some classrooms and offices accessible to students and staff in wheelchairs, or must every classroom and faculty office be accessible to people with disabilities, at a cost of millions of dollars for large universities?

Answering such questions and formulating rules to implement them is *de facto* policymaking. Implementation requires disseminating the rules and negotiating interpretations with the parties who have to put them in place and enforce them. State and local counterparts of the EEOC and their clients must be informed of the rules, assisted in their attempts to use the rules, and monitored in their progress. Bills must be paid, disputes resolved, and information collected as to how successful the program is. If affected parties reject the EEOC's interpretation or the officials' implementation, the rules can be challenged in federal court. This is where almost

all disputed provisions of the ADA are being decided. Bureaucrats very often do not have the last word in determining how a policy is implemented.

The passage of thousands of complex bills like the ADA accounts for the growth in policymaking functions of public bureaucracies. Industrialization, population growth, urbanization, and profound changes in science, transportation, and communications have put problems of a more complex nature on government's agenda. The large number and technical nature of these problems, as well as policy differences among its members, have often limited Congress's ability to draft specific policy responses.

Congress often responds to this situation by enacting a general statement of goals and identifying actions that would help achieve them. Congress then delegates the power to an agency with the relevant expertise to draft specific rules that will achieve these goals. This **delegated legislative authority** empowers executive branch agencies to draft, as well as execute, specific policies. Just as the ADA left rule making to the EEOC, any tax reform legislation requires thousands of rules to be written by the IRS and the Treasury Department.

Agency-made policy is just as binding as acts of Congress because agencies make it at the direction of Congress. In strictly numerical terms, agencies make much more policy than Congress. On average, for example, executive agencies issue about seven thousand new rules and regulations a year, ten times Congress's annual production of new laws.

Many political scientists believe that Congress abdicates its authority and acts in an irresponsible manner by refusing, because of political pressures and its heavy workload, to develop specific guidelines for agencies. [34] Thus agencies are sometimes left to implement policies without much guidance from Congress beyond the bill itself. Sometimes, however, agency complaints about the ambiguities or lack of specificity in legislation are just excuses not to implement disliked policies. Often these lead to partisan conflicts, especially over regulatory policy. Republican presidents have appointed agency heads who drag their feet or outright refuse to execute regulations passed by a Democrat-controlled Congress.

Congress can send more detailed directives to agencies. But this does not prevent the political appointees who head executive branch agencies from resisting congressional directives they dislike on the grounds that they are too complex or unrealistic to follow.

In effect, the competition between the White House and Congress was extended to the bureaucracy when Congress delegated legislative authority to agencies. This competition can intensify or subside, depending on whether the president is of the same party as congressional majorities. However, the competition continues even in the Republican-dominated government of recent years.

Sometimes agencies are in the difficult position of having to satisfy competing demands. To figure out what Congress, the president, and others want, agency officials read congressional debates and testimony and talk to members of Congress, committee staffers, White House aides, lobbyists, and others. Although agencies also try to determine what the public wants, they are more likely to respond to well-organized and well-funded groups that closely monitor their actions. As a result, agency-made policy is often less responsive to the general public than to particular interests.

Regulation

A special kind of policymaking called **regulation** produces rules, standards, or guidelines conferring benefits and imposing restrictions on business conduct and economic activity. Regulations have the force of law and are made by agencies whose directors and board members are appointed by the president and whose operating procedures are generally governed by the Administrative Procedure Act. Regulatory agencies include not only independent regulatory boards and commissions but also some independent agencies, such as the Environmental Protection Agency, and some agencies within cabinet departments, such as the Food and Drug Administration (FDA) in Health and Human Services and the Office of Safety and Health Administration (OSHA) in the Labor Department.

Regulatory actions include two steps: making rules and adjudicating their enforcement. Rule making is the establishment of standards that apply to a class of individuals or businesses. Adjudication occurs when agencies try individuals or firms charged with violating standards. To do this, they use procedures that are very similar to those of courts.

Most regulations derive from laws passed by Congress that direct agencies to take actions to accomplish the goals established in the legislation. Environmental legislation, for example, requires regulatory agencies to set standards for clean air, safe disposal of toxic wastes, or safe workplaces that businesses must meet. Businesses are often allowed some flexibility in the methods used to meet the standard. But failure to comply can result in fines or other legal penalties.

Consumer protection legislation directs federal regulators to set quality or safety standards for certain types of products, such as cars, toys, food, and medical equipment. This is why there are seat belts, air bags, and shatterproof windows in cars and why materials used to make children's toys or clothing cannot be flammable or toxic.

Another form of regulation is licensing the right to own or use public properties. For example, the Federal Communications Commission licenses the publicly owned airwaves to people who own and operate radio and television stations. Regulations may also require businesses to provide information through labeling, such as the cancer warnings on cigarette packages and lists of ingredients noting fat, sugar, salt, and vitamin content on packaged food.

Data Collection and Analysis

In the course of policymaking and administration, the bureaucracy performs other functions. It collects data, as in the decennial census, and it makes information available to the public. Much of what we know about ourselves as a people comes from the government's collection of data on births and deaths, occupations and income, housing and health, crime, and many other things. A cursory glance at the annual *Statistical Abstract of the United States* shows that the government reports on everything from the incidence of abortions to the export of zinc and in between informs us how much celery we eat and how many DVDs we own.

Bureaucracy also keeps us informed about what government is doing, and the Internet is a valuable tool to assist in this function. Every federal agency has a Web site with information about its policies and programs and an e-mail link for feedback from the public. If we want to know the rules governing camping in national parks, we can call the National Park Service or go to its Web site. If we want to know the fate of a bill in Congress or how our representatives voted on it, we can find it posted on the Internet.

The bureaucracy engages in research, too. A prime example is the Department of Agriculture, which for nearly 140 years has conducted research on how to grow bigger and better crops, raise healthier animals, and transport and market products more effectively. Government researchers, such as those at the National Institutes of Health and the Centers for Disease Control and Prevention, do much of country's medical research, especially on mental health and epidemiology. Many vaccines and prescription drugs are also developed in government labs.

In addition, providing continuity is an important offshoot of the bureaucracy's activities. Presidents and members of Congress come and go, and political appointees in the bureaucracy stay an average of two years. Many barely learn their jobs by the time they leave. Career civil servants have a much deeper knowledge of their agencies' work, which can make them more productive. (For information on civil service recruitment, see the box "Wanted: Young Bureaucrats.")

The attractiveness of government service ebbs and flows over time, reflecting the ethos of the era, the number of job opportunities, and national needs. The Great Depression and World War II presented the challenge of true national crises. Many in the 1960s and 1970s generations were attracted to public service by the civil rights movement and the War on Poverty. Each generation sees somewhat differently the importance of public service and the potential for government to make positive changes in society.

During the 1980s and 1990s, there were no national crises to draw people together in a common enterprise that could be expressed through government service. People who grew up in this era seem less inclined to believe that government can make a positive difference. Indeed, young people heard a generation of politicians railing against government. In the 1990s, given the alternative lure of the booming economy and the dot-coms, young people saw government service as less attractive than the private sector. Public service took a back seat to "making as much as you can as quickly as you can." And even those who chose public service had choices outside government as the growth of nonprofit philanthropic organizations provided alternatives.

Consequently, it is not surprising that from 1990 to 2000, the average age of government employees rose from forty-two to over forty-six. The average length of service rose from thirteen to seventeen years.[1] Today the civil service employs more people in their sixties than in their twenties, and by 2008, half of the entire civil service will be eligible for retirement.[2] That would open up more than a million federal jobs—hence the urgent need to recruit young people. But the government spends little on recruitment, and most people do not even know about federal job opportunities.

Although the government cannot match private sector salaries, the civil service has well-paying jobs; the average executive branch worker makes more than $54,000, a librarian $65,000, and an astronomer about $100,000 a year, with excellent benefits.[3]

After 9/11, when trust in government rose, the numbers of Americans who said they would recommend a government career to their children rose from 30 to 39 percent. Diminished private sector job opportunities have also made federal employment more attractive, but the civil service still appears to be a job choice of last resort for many people.[4]

1. Office of Personnel Management, *The Fact Book, 2001 Edition*, www.opm.gov.
2. Nicolas Thompson, "Star Search," *Washington Monthly*, June 2003, 22.
3. Ibid., 26.
4. Paul C. Light, "What Federal Employees Want from Reform: Reform Watch Brief No. 5," Brookings Institution, March 2002), www.brookings.edu.

Politics and Professional Standards

As the part of government that implements policies made by elected officials, the bureaucracy cannot escape politics and is subject to constant lobbying. That does not mean that civil servants have the green light to implement policy in a partisan manner. Today's civil servants are governed by laws that place professional competence above political loyalties. Most Americans want fair, apolitical performance such that the quantity and quality of any government service they receive is not dependent on whether they belong to the same party as the president or their member of Congress. And most of us would prefer to have a civil engineer rather than a political crony in charge of the dam being built near our town. The chances that the engineer will get the job over the crony have improved significantly since patronage was outlawed in the federal bureaucracy.

The Merit System

For decades, American public bureaucracies were staffed under the **patronage** system, which allowed elected officials to fill administrative jobs on the basis of political loyalty rather than merit. By providing their supporters with jobs, elected officials could strengthen their political base, and many people regarded this as simply a means for government agencies to provide employment to citizens. It operated in rough accordance with the principle "To the victor belong the spoils," as the newly elected filled jobs with their own supporters. At the federal level, Andrew Jackson's presidential election in 1828 was a watershed in using the patronage system. Jackson believed that any white male citizen of average intelligence and goodwill could do a government job well. So he reversed the existing practice of naming mostly well-off people from the East Coast by appointing less well off supporters from frontier areas.

The most obvious problem with staffing the bu-

Andrew Jackson made the bureaucracy more representative of the nation's population. He also opened the doors to the White House. The guests at a White House party open to the public consumed or carried away much of a 1,400-pound cheese.

reaucracy with political supporters rather than through competitive recruitment is that jobs will go to people who are not competent to perform their duties. This became a major problem as government work became more technical and specialized. Furthermore, patronage could and frequently did lead to corruption, in particular to deal making between candidates and voters or individuals who controlled blocs of voters. Voters supported candidates who promised them jobs or other favors. Such corruption increasingly sullied city councils, state legislatures, and Congress during the 1800s.

Although patronage was affecting government performance, the influence wielded by the political machines that had grown powerful through its use kept Congress from acting until an unsuccessful job seeker assassinated President James Garfield in 1881. The Pendleton Act of 1883 established the **Civil Service Commission** to fill designated positions within the bureaucracy with people who had proved their competence in competitive examinations. Jobs under the commission's jurisdiction were part of the **merit system.** The new law also protected people holding merit positions from pressure to support or oppose particular candidates and from dismissal for political reasons.

Neutral Competence

The merit system established **neutral competence** as the professional standard for civil service employees. It requires that individuals filling merit positions be chosen for their expertise in executing policy and that they

carry out their work in a nonpartisan or neutral manner. This standard assumes that there is no Republican or Democratic way to build a sewer, collect customs duties, or fight a war. In effect, it says that partisan politics has no place in bureaucracy. It also implies that bureaucrats should not profit personally from the decisions they make.

Woodrow Wilson, a strong advocate of neutral competence, believed that bureaucrats could learn to execute policy both expertly and responsively.[35] He saw government jobs as either political or administrative in nature and felt that by knowing which was which, we could create a bureaucracy that elected officials could control. Most current observers are less sanguine about the possibility of completely separating politics from administration.[36]

The Pendleton Act authorized the president to extend merit system coverage to additional federal jobs by executive order. In 1884, the merit system covered about 10 percent of the jobs in the federal bureaucracy. Today that figure is over 75 percent, down from a high of 90 percent, as changes in civil service law exempted positions covered by other merit systems, such as the State Department's Foreign Service and the Executive Senior Service, and created more political appointments.

Even within the regular civil service, merit is not all that counts. The system favors veterans by adding a 5-point bonus to their test scores (disabled veterans get 10 points). And positioning counts as well: people already in the system are favored because they know about job openings first and may have skills identical to those in the job listing. Sometimes job descriptions are written to fit particular individuals. (Of course, this happens in private businesses as well.)

Banning patronage from federal hiring did not end partisan political activity by federal employees, so Congress passed another law expressly defining the limits on such activities. The **Hatch Act** of 1939 prohibited federal employees from active participation in partisan campaigns, even at the state and local levels. Political activities were restricted to voting, attending rallies, and having private conversations. But federal employees cannot participate in party-sponsored voter registration drives, endorse party candidates, or work for or against them in any way. These prohibitions also apply to employees of state and local government who are supported by federal funds.

The Hatch Act has always been controversial. Supporters argue that it protects the neutral competence of civil servants from partisan influences. Critics say it makes civil servants second-class citizens by denying them the First Amendment guarantees of freedom of speech and association. In 1993, Congress changed the law to allow most federal employees to hold office within a political party, to participate in political campaigns, and to raise funds for political action committees when they are not on duty. However, all employees of law enforcement and national security agencies remain under the earlier, more stringent prohibitions.[37]

The neutral competence standard prohibits bureaucrats from gaining materially from their decisions. Civil servants are supposed to make decisions based on their professional judgment and not to advance the cause of something in which they have a financial stake. For example, bureaucrats who are stockholders in chemical companies are not supposed to be making policy about chemical waste. Even if it were possible for policymakers to put self-interest aside, holding stakes in firms they regulate automatically takes on the appearance of a conflict of interest. This in turn would allow critics of a decision to challenge the regulation in court. Furthermore, the appearance of a conflict of interest undermines public confidence in government.

To better define what constitutes a conflict of interest, Congress passed the Ethics in Government Act in 1978. The act sought to prevent former public officials

© The Granger Collection, New York

When a disappointed office seeker assassinated President Garfield, that violent act alerted federal officials to the level of public anger over the use of patronage to staff the bureaucracy and led to adoption of the Pendleton Act, which required that federal employees be hired and retained on the basis of competence rather than political considerations.

with inside information from using it and their contacts to give their new employers an unfair competitive advantage. The act barred former public servants from lobbying their agencies for one year and prohibited for life lobbying on matters in which they "personally and substantially" participated as public officials. In 1989, news that former Reagan administration officials had used their government service for substantial financial gain led to the passage of a law designed to strengthen the 1978 act. These new rules had little more impact than the old ones.

President Clinton issued an executive order requiring many of his political appointees to sign a pledge that they would not lobby the agencies in which they worked for five years after leaving government and would never lobby for foreign political parties and governments. In 2002, four of Clinton's former cabinet members and other high-level political appointees, including his trade representative and the heads of the FCC and the SEC, each held multiple seats on corporate boards. It is not unthinkable that they were hired for their government contacts, although holding such positions in itself does not violate any ethics rule.

George W. Bush appointed more corporate executives to head government agencies than any other president. Some are regulating industries whose payrolls they had just left or in which they had held stock. During the corporate accounting scandals of 2001–2002, he appointed Harvey Pitt to head the Securities and Exchange Commission. Pitt is a lawyer whose main work had been to defend the very Wall Street firms he would have to regulate as SEC head. Shortly after he took office, Pitt announced that under his direction, the SEC would be "a kinder place for accountants," a statement he undoubtedly wished he had not made after the Enron scandal broke. Then Congress began asking whether he had the neutral competence necessary to toughen regulations. Public outrage over the corporate failures was so great that Pitt had to reverse his position and call for much tighter regulation of insider trading, accounting practices, and law firms that consult on corporate finance. Then he quietly worked to weaken the new rules until public pressure forced his resignation.

Sometimes the range within which bureaucrats can exercise neutral competence is severely restricted by their superiors. Agencies and department heads are political, not merit, appointees, and many are specifically charged with carrying out the programs of the president who appointed them. In addition, some of the policy that bureaucrats are implementing was made by presidential directive or executive order. EPA bureaucrats gearing up to implement Clinton's executive orders on clean water and clean air in December 2000 were required to write very different rules several months later when Bush rescinded Clinton's orders and substituted radically different policies. When an agency appears to be partisan in the way it implements, or fails to implement, congressional acts, it may be because of presidential directives or orders issued by the short-term political appointee temporarily heading the agency.

Perhaps no agency head has suffered more severe criticism for not exercising neutral competence than former CIA Director George Tenant. The day after the 9/11 attacks, President Bush made clear to the head of his counterterrorism unit and to others in his administration his interest in establishing a connection between Iraq and al-Qaeda.[38] The evidence of a connection was weak, but Bush thought an invasion of Iraq could be justified on the grounds that Saddam Hussein's arsenal of weapons of mass destruction presented an imminent threat. When he asked Tenant whether there was evidence to support his case to Congress and the public, Tenant told him it was a "slam dunk."[39] Postwar investigators found no evidence to support the claim that Iraq possessed stockpiles of weapons of mass destruction or even active programs to develop them.[40] Furthermore, many arms experts within the agency had questioned the validity of the evidence Bush used to support his case in public statements. But Tenant and higher-ups in the CIA had signed off on it.

Tenant had been a Clinton appointee whom Bush retained when he became president; Tenant's retention and reappointment were dependent on Bush's judgment of his work. Because Bush's policy preferences on Iraq were well known inside and outside the administration, most concluded that Tenant had violated his neutral competence mandate and simply told the president what he wanted to hear. Having lost credibility in Congress and with the public, Tenant was forced to resign.

Another example of a political appointee facing a decision on whether to succumb to political pressure or exercise neutral competence is presented in the box "Bureaucracy and the Fight against AIDS." In this case, the appointee chose a different route than Tenant did.

Overseeing the Bureaucracy

The principal overseers of the bureaucracy are of course the president, who heads it and appoints its top policymakers; the Senate, which holds confirmation powers; and Congress as a whole, which has authority to create, monitor, and fund agencies. Congress has also given the public a significant, if vastly underused, role, through legislation mandating openness in government.

President

The development of the bureaucracy led to demands for **executive leadership**—a central leader to set the direction of the agency and monitor its responsiveness. The president, constitutionally the chief executive, has several tools to control the bureaucracy.

Presidential Means of Control

One of the tools at the president's disposal is budgeting. Presidents can try to cut agency appropriations to limit agencies' range of actions, or they can tie conditions to appropriations to make them take specific actions. Using this strategy effectively can be difficult, but presidents may directly affect the work of regulatory agencies through their appointment powers and the use of executive orders.

A president can try to control agencies by appointing people who share his views. This is expected in the case of cabinet departments. Reagan and Bush filled health care–related positions in the Department of Health and Human Services with people who were against abortion, while Clinton filled them with people who were pro-choice. In appointments to regulatory agencies, Republican presidents tend to appoint people who favor business and Democratic presidents people who favor consumers and organized labor. Reagan chose heads for regulatory agencies such as OSHA, the Consumer Product Safety Commission, and the EPA who agreed with his goal of reducing government regulation; Clinton named a lifelong environmental activist to head the EPA.

Of course, sometimes presidential appointees, despite their being screened for issue positions, may end up representing long-standing agency policies and norms rather than the president's interests. Most appointees have less expertise and experience in agency operations than career civil servants, and some come to rely on career officials for information about agency history, procedures, and policy questions. But much depends on the president's leadership, how high a priority change in the agency is for him, and how closely he monitors a particular agency's activities and directions.

Administrative reform is a third means a president can use to increase his control over the bureaucracy. Generally, the more sweeping a president's recommendation for change, the more he must anticipate congressional and interest group resistance. For example, Reagan wanted to abolish the Departments of Education and Energy and merge the Commerce and Labor Departments, but Congress would not support him. The most audacious attempt at bureaucratic control by a modern president has been George W. Bush's reorganization of the executive branch to create the new

There is no greater health concern in the world today than AIDS (acquired immunodeficiency syndrome), a disease unknown to the medical community until the early 1980s. AIDS involves a virus (the human immunodeficiency virus, or HIV) that weakens the body's immunity, making it vulnerable to deadly infections. Other diseases claim more lives than AIDS, but many of these are curable if victims can be reached with appropriate medical care. There is no cure for AIDS, and most countries still have inadequate programs of testing, blood screening, and public education. Therefore, many people live with the disease without knowing they have it, passing their infection along to others.

AIDS was believed to be introduced in the United States by a widely traveled French tourist who happened to be homosexual. This is why the first infections were found in male homosexuals. The disease spread swiftly, taking thousands of lives before the federal government began to formulate a policy to curb the epidemic. From the victims' standpoint, the government came too late to the problem, but compared to the way the disease has been handled in many countries, our federal health bureaucracy did far better than most. Many thousands, perhaps even millions, of lives were saved through the introduction of preventive measures.

The government's first AIDS prevention program was the work of a federal bureaucrat who put professional responsibility above his political preferences. In 1986, President Ronald Reagan asked the government's top medical officer, Surgeon General C. Everett Koop, to report to him on the AIDS crisis. By that time, there were more than 35,000 cases reported in the United States, and 20,000 people had already died of the disease. An estimated 1.5 million people had been

exposed to the virus, and it was projected that there would be 270,000 full-blown cases by 1991.[1] At the time, intravenous drug users and homosexual men were at the greatest risk.[2] However, AIDS was beginning to spread among non-drug-using heterosexual men and women through contact with prostitutes and bisexuals and from blood transfusions received before the spring of 1985, when blood banks began testing for the HIV virus.

As AIDS began to spread to the general population, public anxiety increased. Americans knew little about the illness or how it was contracted. Many people thought they could be infected through social contact or just being near an infected person. Some parents tried to bar children with AIDS from the schools their children attended; some people were afraid of even indirect physical contact with an HIV-infected person and began to

worry about contamination of swimming pools and other public facilities.

The government needed a policy to address both the illness and the fear of it. Certain preventive and diagnostic steps, such as mandatory blood testing, were already required of military recruits and Foreign Service officers. But the government had to decide if testing should be extended to the public, or at least to individuals at high risk, and whether such testing should be voluntary or mandatory. The government also had to decide to if it should be involved in trying to find a treatment for the disease and a vaccine to prevent it or if most of this work should be left to the private sector.

The atmosphere surrounding AIDS policy was very politicized.[3] Social conservatives saw AIDS as a moral issue and believed it was necessary to change teens' behavior by teaching sexual abstinence in the schools. Ex-

At the height of the AIDS epidemic in the 1980s, Christian protestors displayed leaflets proclaiming that AIDS is a "plague from God."

tremists even said AIDS was a punishment for homosexuality and drug use. They pressured Surgeon General Koop to recommend mandatory testing for convicted prostitutes and intravenous drug users, venereal disease patients, immigrants, and couples seeking marriage licenses. Some wanted government to quarantine the infected to keep them from infecting others (as was done in Cuba). At least one member of Reagan's cabinet recommended a policy of mandatory notification of the spouses and past sexual partners of those who tested positive.

Public health experts rejected almost all of the politically driven recommendations as unworkable or as likely to backfire, driving people at risk to go underground to avoid being tested. They opposed mandatory notification as a violation of doctor-patient confidentiality and thought that few people would identify their sexual partners. They worried about increased social and employment discrimination against people who were infected but had not developed full-blown AIDS, as well as individuals just thought to be at risk. Health professionals also believed, given human nature, that teaching abstinence was unrealistic and therefore very risky; they recommended educating young people about "safe sex" and contraception.

Reagan was more comfortable with conservative views on AIDS. He had appointed Koop surgeon general not so much for his medical reputation but because he was a born-again Christian with conservative views on abortion and birth control. Had he relied only on his political instincts or preferences when preparing his report, Koop would have moved in the direction of the man who appointed him. But Koop was also a doctor who respected the views of health care professionals and took his responsibility to

respond to a health crisis more seriously than the political demand to remedy what some regarded as a cultural or social crisis.

Koop's report to the president emphasized prevention through public education. It also advocated voluntary over mandatory measures, which Koop could fairly argue was a more truly conservative response than the Orwellian testing, quarantine, and abstinence program advocated by some of the president's other political appointees. The report concluded that in the absence of a vaccine or cure, sex education was essential to containing the spread of AIDS and recommended adding materials explaining prevention methods to schoolchildren. In a radio broadcast, Koop called on the nation's networks to lift their self-imposed ban on condom advertising. He argued that "anyone who is sexually active should use a condom from start to finish. AIDS kills, and sexually active people have to be told this."

The most visible aspect of the government's new program was a brochure mailed to 107 million households in 1988 describing how AIDS is contracted and how to avoid it. That same year, a presidential commission and a National Academy of Sciences panel on AIDS made recommendations that echoed those in the Koop report.

Koop put his professional foot forward, exercised neutral competence, and in essence bit the political hand that fed him. Political appointees in the bureaucracy are supposed to serve the public interest just as civil servants do, but they must also be responsive to their superiors—in Koop's case, to the president. But as Koop said, "I'm not afforded the luxury of bringing ideology or morals into my job, especially with the sort of threat we have with AIDS."[4]

Koop's public education campaign changed the direction of public think-

ing and helped people see the necessity of confronting the disease head-on as a public health crisis. The campaign helped calm fears driven by ignorance of how the disease was contracted and spread. Later Koop acknowledged weaknesses in his approach, especially that health workers had been "singularly unsuccessful in penetrating the drug-addicted culture" with educational messages.[5]

By 2002, AIDS had killed almost half a million people in the United States, but that number would almost certainly have been far higher without the public education campaign and other preventive measures, including blood screening. Countries that have been in denial about AIDS or that lack public health resources to combat it have lost millions of citizens, and the death toll is still growing.

Greater public awareness also helped win support for federal funding for AIDS research. That research resulted in new drug treatments that have allowed many AIDS patients to live relatively normal, active lives for indefinite periods. Of course, not all is well; complacency and a return to unsafe practices have set in some populations, and in others, poverty places the life-prolonging drugs out of reach. Nonetheless, Koop's refusal to allow politics to compromise his professional competence saved many lives.

1. "AIDS: Who Should Be Tested?" *Newsweek*, May 11, 1987, 64–65.
2. Stephen Jay Gould, "The Exponential Spread of AIDS Underscores the Tragedy of Our Delay in Fighting One of Nature's Plagues," *New York Times Magazine*, April 19, 1987, 33.
3. "AIDS Becomes a Political Issue," *Time*, March 23, 1987, 24.
4. Quoted in Julie Kosterlitz, "Health Focus," *National Journal*, January 28, 1989, 259.
5. Lawrence K. Altman, "Who's Stricken and How: AIDS Pattern Is Shifting," *New York Times*, February 5, 1989, 1, 16. See also Sandra Panem, *The AIDS Bureaucracy* (Cambridge, Mass.: Harvard University Press, 1988).

cabinet-level Department of Homeland Security. The plan had great scope, affecting twenty-two agencies and 177,000 employees. But what made it bold was Bush's request for exemption from worker protection laws and the authority to transfer funds and personnel from agency to agency without congressional approval. In other words, he asked Congress to cede substantial budgetary and oversight powers to the White House.

The White House can also try to influence independent agencies and commissions by lobbying and mobilizing public opinion. Attempts by presidents of both parties to influence Federal Reserve Board decisions on interest rates, for example, are legion.

Strengthening Presidential Control

Despite these powers, there are many limits on the president's ability to control the bureaucracy. Given its size and complexity, the president cannot possibly control every important decision. Moreover, presidents have found it increasingly difficult to lead an executive branch containing large numbers of merit system employees deliberately insulated from presidential control. This is one reason Bush asked for exemptions from the system for many Homeland Security Department positions.

Presidential control problems escalated in the 1930s with the establishment of many new programs and agencies. In 1935, Franklin Roosevelt appointed the Brownlow Committee, named after its chair and composed of public administration specialists, to draft a statement on principles of executive leadership. Its 1937 report was very influential. At its suggestion, the Bureau of the Budget (BOB), which had been created in 1921, was put into the new Executive Office of the President to help the president manage the bureaucracy.

Perhaps the most significant development for monitoring the bureaucracy was the establishment of the Office of Management and Budget (which absorbed BOB) in the Executive Office of the President. The OMB has specific responsibility for overseeing agency performance, and it reports its findings to the public as well as the president by posting them at its Web site.

Congress also increased the president's appointive powers with a reclassification of civil service positions. The Civil Service Reform Act of 1978 replaced the Civil Service Commission with two agencies. One agency promotes executive leadership by working with the president in writing and administering civil service regulations. The other is intended to protect civil servants from violations of these regulations. It also created the Senior Executive Service (SES), positions outside the regular civil service. (In all, one-quarter of all positions in the federal bureaucracy are in exempt categories.) In addition, the act gave managers more opportu-

nity to fire incompetent subordinates and authorized bonuses and a new pay scale for managers to encourage better performance.

Despite this legislation, executive leadership is still thwarted by the difficulty of removing poor performers from the civil service. Although job security is not meant to shield public servants who do poor work, it does make firing incompetent workers difficult and time consuming. The organization of public employees into unions contributes to this, although unions also protect workers from being dismissed without grounds. The government's rate of discharging people for inefficiency, 0.01 percent a year, did not increase after the 1978 reforms, though no doubt some employees left after being threatened with dismissal or demotion. As one public employee said, "We're all like headless nails down here—once you get us in you can't get us out."[41] This attitude captures what some say is the civil service's built-in bias toward job survival rather than innovation.[42]

Agencies that have strong allies in Congress, in powerful interest groups, or in the public provide another limit to presidential leadership. Presidents have more success controlling agencies that lack strong congressional allies and domestic clientele groups, such as the Treasury and State Departments, than agencies that have such allies, such as the Social Security Administration and the Agriculture and Health and Human Services Departments. However, the increasing number of political appointees in senior positions gives the president many more opportunities to exercise his influence over agency operations, even in agencies like the EPA, which has strong bipartisan support in Congress and powerful interest groups monitoring its work.

Not all presidents have the same interest in exercising executive leadership over the bureaucracy. Although all want to appoint people to policymaking positions who are committed to a similar set of goals, the will to pressure these individuals after they have been appointed varies. The scientific community roundly criticized George W. Bush for using his appointees to redirect agency work in a way that interfered with the exercise of neutral competence and scientific integrity. The Union of Concerned Scientists charged Bush with ordering politically motivated changes in the evidence and conclusions of reports prepared by government scientists on climate change, mercury pollution, and the effectiveness of sex education in disease prevention.

Congress

Congress has the power to create, reorganize, or eliminate agencies and the ultimate instrument of control—the power of the purse strings. Much of the bureaucracy's power is delegated authority from Congress, and much of its work is implementing laws passed by Congress. Although the president has the edge in leadership through his appointment powers, Congress has greater scope for oversight and control. This is not just because of its budgetary powers but because Congress has dozens of committees (supported by a staff of thousands) to which executive agencies must report.

Just as an agency's outside allies can work to thwart presidential control, they can also limit congressional oversight. Agencies frequently work closely with certain congressional committees and interest groups for mutual support and outcomes favorable to all. (These relationships are sometimes called "iron triangles" or issue networks.) Agencies may adjust their actions to suit the preferences of the congressional committees that authorize their programs and appropriate their funds. For example, decisions by members of independent regulatory commissions are sensitive to the views of members of their congressional oversight committees. When the membership of the committees becomes more liberal or more conservative, so do the decisions regulators make.[43]

Iron triangles make oversight look less like monitoring the bureaucracy and more like collusion. Constituent service, by contrast, provides a motive for members of Congress to try to shape bureaucratic decision making. Members often try to influence agencies to take some action on behalf of constituents or in the interest of their districts. In fact, congressional staff who do casework often have their duties assigned according to the agencies they are responsible for contacting about constituent complaints. This can lead to inefficiencies when bureaucrats are pressured to help members of Congress satisfy constituent demands rather than to use neutral competence as a decision standard. It is this kind of pressure that keeps military bases open years beyond their usefulness simply because they are good for the economy of a member's district. This pressure from Congress makes it difficult for bureaucrats to act with neutral competence.

Courts

Federal courts act as another check on the bureaucracy. Judicial decisions shape agency actions by directing agencies to follow legally correct procedures. Of course, the courts cannot intercede in an agency's decision making unless some aggrieved person or corporation files a suit against the agency. Nevertheless, in almost any controversial agency action, there will be aggrieved parties and possibly some with sufficient resources to bring a court action.

The courts interpret lawmakers' intentions by deciding what congressional majorities and the president had in mind when they made a law. This can be difficult. Sometimes, in their haste, lawmakers fail to specify crucial elements of a law, or they may be unable to reach agreement on a provision and leave it ambiguous in order to get the bill passed. Lawmakers may also write a certain amount of vagueness into a law so that agencies will be able to adapt it to unknown future conditions. How the courts read a law may augment or reduce the ability of Congress and the president to influence its implementation. In the current Supreme Court, the conservative majority has increasingly used its authority to interpret the intent of congressional acts in ways that expand the Court's own powers. We discuss these issues in Chapter 13.

Regulators and other agency policymakers appear to be quite sensitive to federal court decisions. For example, when the courts overturn the National Labor Relations Board's decisions in a prolabor direction, NLRB decisions soon become more prolabor. Similarly, decisions drift the other way when courts overturn agency decisions in a probusiness direction.[44]

Interest Groups and Individuals

The public has numerous opportunities to oversee and to influence bureaucratic decision making. Most of these rights stem from laws designed to ensure openness in government.

Openness laws also extend to media access and thus provide another important check on bureaucratic abuses. But the media can also make the bureaucracy's work more difficult. Reporters like to cover conflict and bad news and are therefore usually on the lookout for stories about internal policy disputes. They may even fan the flames to make a better story.

Interest groups and their lobbyists are also part of the public. Lobbyists tend to take much greater advantage of their rights of access than the general public does, and they are the source of much of the public comment on proposed rules received by agencies. Most FOIA requests still come from businesses, interest groups, lawyers, scholars, and the media. In one year, 85 percent of the requests for information submitted to the Food and Drug Administration came from companies that it regulates. That information enabled the companies to evaluate their strategies for influencing agency decisions that affect them. Interest groups want to make sure bureaucracies adopt rules and enforcement practices they favor. An environmental group cannot rest on its laurels just because Congress has passed a law placing new safeguards on toxic waste disposal. The group's job is not over until it makes sure the EPA writes strict rules to enforce the law. Consequently, the group must lobby the regulators as well as Congress.

If an agency seems to be sabotaging the intent of Congress, interest groups can work with friendly congressional committees to put pressure on the agency to mend its ways. And interest groups can also try to rally public opinion to their side to pressure Congress or the president to do something about the agency. Environmental groups are especially skilled at this. Sometimes interest groups pressure an agency so effectively that the agency is said to be "captured."[45] This term is used most frequently for regulatory agencies thought to be controlled by the groups they are supposed to be regulating.

We know that interest groups can influence the bureaucracy, but can individual citizens too? It is difficult for an individual to influence public agencies when acting alone, but that does not mean there are no opportunities to do so. Perhaps one person posting a comment on a Web site will not change agency policy, but if all residents opposed to a decision on cleaning up a hazardous waste site in their neighborhood file comments, it can make a difference. Rules have been reversed or amended.

An individual who uses FOIA to retrieve documents that expose agency corruption or abuse can also make a difference by going public with the story. And members of the general public are increasingly taking advantage of openness laws even though the process is not made easy for those who try. A lot of paperwork is involved, some costs, and often a long wait, even though government agencies employ over five thousand administrators to process the requests.

Ordinary citizens could have a greater impact if they used all the tools that Congress has given them to oversee and to influence the bureaucracy. Individuals within the bureaucracy often have the best opportunity to monitor agency practices. Some do act as whistleblowers. Some whistleblowing is unsuccessful, but some makes a real difference. One of the most famous whistleblowers was Pentagon employee Daniel Ellsberg, who in 1968 leaked thousands of documents on the conduct of the Vietnam War to the *New York Times*. Henry Kissinger claimed that Ellsberg was the most dangerous man in the world, but Ellsberg's acts helped the public understand that the Johnson and Nixon administrations' private rationale for fighting the war were not the same as the reasons they stated in public.

That same year, Ernest Fitzgerald, an Air Force cost accountant, revealed that the Lockheed C-5A transport plane vibrated so much in flight that its wings actually fell off if they were not replaced after only two hundred hours of flying time. Saying it wanted "to save expenses"—his $32,000 salary—the Air Force reacted by firing Fitzgerald. He sued to get his job back and won, but all he got was his title, office, and pay. The Air Force gave him nothing to do, and he had to wait for a court order in 1982 before the Air Force gave him responsibilities equal to his qualifications. The wings were repaired, and the C-5A operated successfully for many years.[46] But two decades later, the Air Force was still trying to neutralize what one Pentagon veteran called "the most hated man in the Air Force" by juggling his assignments.[47]

Partly in response to experiences like this, Congress provided for an agency to protect whistleblowers in the 1978 Civil Service Reform Act. Bureaucrats who blow the whistle on mismanagement, sexual or political harassment, or other abuses of power in their agencies are protected from arbitrary firing. Private citizens can be whistleblowers, too, by suing companies with government contracts that defraud the government.[48]

Despite the legal protections, it is the rare person who will set aside cordial relations with colleagues and ambition for promotion in order to challenge the status quo. Most people, whether working in the private or the public sector, find it difficult to expose their employer's dirty laundry. And even if the law does protect their jobs, their careers may be effectively ruined. About half of all whistleblowers lose their jobs, half of those lose their homes, and half of those lose their families.[49]

Rarely does an agency publicly thank an employee for blowing the whistle, as FBI Director Robert Mueller did when Coleen Rowley went public with that agency's mishandling of a 9/11–related investigation. Rowley, a Minneapolis-based agent involved in the case of Zacarias Moussaoui, an Algerian, under indictment as the so-called twentieth hijacker, had complained to Director Mueller that a midlevel manager had thwarted her attempt to get a search warrant to go through Moussaoui's personal belongings and the contents of his computer.[50] She criticized the director for doing what FBI directors usually do when they get bad news—protecting the agency. Rowley testified before the Senate Judiciary Committee, and even if her complaints had not become public, Mueller could not just ignore them. Rowley was a twenty-one-year veteran with a law degree and an unblemished record in the agency, and Mueller went public to commend her for her actions.

But Mueller's actions were not so much an indication of changing attitudes toward whistleblowers as a measure of the trouble the agency was in with Congress. Rowley was one of three whistleblowers (another exposed accounting fraud at Enron) named by *Time* magazine when it proclaimed 2002 "The Year of the Whistleblower."

But for most whistleblowers, retaliation continues; in recent years, airport baggage screeners, border patrol agents, and the chief of the United States Park Police were disciplined or fired for reporting problems in their agencies. The most publicized case was that of Medicare's chief actuary, who was threatened with dismissal by the political appointee who heads his agency if he provided Congress with accurate numbers on the cost of the Bush administration's proposed prescription drug benefit for seniors.

Disclosure of bureaucratic failures increased after 9/11 because many individuals, like Sibel Edmonds, saw that neglected shortcomings could have serious consequences. In 2004, Congress responded by writing a new law with stronger protections for whistleblowers, including freedom from reprisal for those, like the Medicare actuary, who provide information to Congress. But the bill was strongly opposed by the Bush administration, which contended that it "unconstitutionally interferes with the president's ability to control and manage the government." [51]

Conclusion: Is the Bureaucracy Responsive?

In 2002, Congress oversaw the biggest reorganization of the federal bureaucracy in a half century when it created the Department of Homeland Security. The changes were prompted by failures in performance that helped make possible the terrorist attacks of September 11, 2001. Particular targets of the reform were intelligence and law enforcement agencies and customs and immigration services. A reporter noted that the bureaucratic morass in the Immigration and Naturalization Service was encapsulated in the title of the official put in charge of the reorganization: the "assistant deputy executive associate commissioner for immigration services." [52]

Is the federal bureaucracy an impenetrable forest or an uncontrollable fourth branch of government, as some portray it? The turf wars, miscommunication, and fragmented authority that surfaced after 9/11 certainly indicate that at least part of the federal bureaucracy is an impenetrable forest. It is not surprising that most of the agencies that failed so badly are among the least open to citizens or the media and even to congressional oversight. Those agencies continued to oppose reform even as Congress was implementing the recommendations of the 9/11 Commission to reorganize our fifteen different intelligence agencies under a single directorate to improve communication, gain more central control, and limit interagency rivalries.

But the bureaucracy as a whole is not an errant fourth branch of government. With the exception of supersecret agencies like the National Security Agency, for which Congress has forfeited much of its oversight responsibility in the interests of national security, most of the bureaucracy is subject to presidential and congressional control. Indeed, one of the by-products of the Bush administration's current attempts to increase presidential control of executive branch agencies at the expense of Congress is that it has reawakened Congress to its oversight lapses.

Our fragmented political system has created an environment of uncertainty and competition for public agencies. Bureaucrats have many bosses: a president, his appointees, Congress, and its many committees and subcommittees. In addition, numerous interest groups try to influence them. The often contradictory demands for responsiveness and neutral competence contribute to an uncertainty of expectations, too. As a result, agencies try to protect themselves by cultivating the support of congressional committees and interest groups. Even presidents have trouble influencing agencies because of these alliances. Although some presidents, such as Franklin Roosevelt and Lyndon Johnson, have occasionally rearranged the status quo, their successes in articulating a vision of national priorities are more the exception than the rule.

Then there is the issue of a vaguely defined but frequently articulated public suspicion that any bureaucracy is destined to be intransigent and inefficient. We have tried to show that some of that attitude stems from lack of consensus on what the work of government should be. If you do not like the work that Congress and the president have assigned to the bureaucracy, there is not much chance you will view the bureaucracy as responsive to your needs. If the dissatisfaction is more over how the bureaucracy does its work, there is hope that at least some areas of performance will meet with your approval. The public does have tools to influence how bureaucrats do their work, but it has many more ways to lobby Congress and the president to change the work they give the bureaucracy to do.

Despite people's negative feelings about the bureaucracy, the mail is delivered, bridges get inspected, and passports are issued. As Charles Goodsell points out, "Unmistakably, bureaucracy works most of the time." [53] It usually does what it is supposed to do.

While this still holds true for much of the bureaucracy, the investigation into INS, FBI, and CIA actions prior to September 11, 2001, made clear that these agencies had experienced catastrophic failures. While Americans' opinion of how the government was doing its job and its overall trust in government increased substantially after the attacks, there was also a more serious concern for poorly functioning government agencies.

The head of one government watchdog group summarized the feeling this way: "Before September 11 there was a bit of a blasé attitude of 'OK, the government screwed up again.' Now people see the consequences on their lives and see the necessity of government functioning well."[54]

Edmonds Blows the Whistle

fter getting no response from higher-ups in the agency to her multiple complaints about being pressured to slack off in her work, the use of ill-trained translators, and possible security lapses, Sibel Edmonds took her complaints to the Senate Judiciary Committee, the main oversight committee for the FBI. The following month, April 2002, after just six months on the job, Edmonds was fired. The letter of dismissal simply said that it was for the "convenience of the agency." Senators Patrick Leahy (D-Vt.) and Charles Grassley (R-Ia.), the chair and ranking member of the Judiciary Committee, wrote letters to the Department of Justice's inspector general and to Attorney General Ashcroft asking for an investigation into Edmonds's charges and dismissal.[55]

Edmonds got very different treatment than Colleen Rowley, who was commended for her whistleblowing. In October 2002, Edmonds was subpoenaed as a witness in a civil suit brought by survivors of 9/11 victims against the government and Saudi officials whom the suit claimed were linked to the terrorists. But Attorney General Ashcroft, at the request of FBI Director Mueller, labeled Edmonds's information a "state secret" and imposed a gag order on her. He quashed Edmonds's attempts,

CONNECTING THE DOTS

© Fiore 2002. www.markfiore.com. Reprinted with permission.

through a FOIA request, to get all documents related to her case, and he classified all materials that had been presented in previously unclassified meetings with the Senate oversight committee. When Edmonds filed a whistleblower suit against the FBI to get her job back, Ashcroft threw a blanket of secrecy over all aspects of the suit.

Although no longer free to speak about many details of her case, Edmonds went public, appearing on *60 Minutes,* where Senator Grassley said, "she's credible, and the reason I feel she's very credible is because people within the FBI have corroborated a lot of her story."[56] Edmonds did give testimony to many of the commissions investigating circumstances sur-

rounding 9/11, but her statements to the official 9/11 Commission had to be made in closed session.[57] She also spoke to the press with the other two best-known 9/11 whistleblowers, Richard Clarke and Coleen Rowley.[58]

In 2004, the Turkish translator who had been sent to Guantanamo Bay to translate prisoner interviews after flunking his language proficiency exams was still on the job, and the supervisor who had been told to slow down the pace of work was promoted. The translator with alleged ties to a foreigner under investigation by the FBI quit her job and moved to Belgium. The agency found no merit in Edmonds's charges against her, but Director Mueller later said he would have the investigation reopened. Edmonds remains fired.

In his defense of Edmonds's charges, Senator Grassley said the FBI needed to be "turned upside down."[59] And Director Mueller, when submitting his agency reorganization plan for congressional approval, said there was no longer any doubt that "we needed to fundamentally change the way we do business."[60] Yet the agency did not seem to change the way it did business. The Department of Justice inspector general reported that since 9/11, a backlog of 123,000 hours of terrorism-related interviews had accumulated waiting for translation.[61] The investigation also concluded that the bureau was within its rights to let Edmonds go but found that her allegations "were at least a contributing factor in why the FBI terminated her services."[62] The public cannot read these findings, however, because former Attorney General Ashcroft classified the entire report.

Reports show that the FBI has shifted well over a thousand agents from crime fighting and the antidrug program to work on counterterrorism. But three years after 9/11, the director reported that the new computer system that was supposed to facilitate the sharing of information and allow agents to do content searches of documents might have to be scrapped. The shortage of storage capacity in the old system automatically deleted old materials still not translated as agents fed new evidence into the system.

Although Mueller was able to keep the FBI from being divided up and incorporated into the new Department of Homeland Security by agreeing to move counterterrorism to the top of its priority list, in 2005 his agency will have to answer to the newly created director of National Intelligence.[63]

Key Terms

whistleblowers

Federal Register

Administrative Procedure
    Act (APA)

FOIA

Sunshine Act

independent agencies

policy implementation

delegated legislative authority

regulation

patronage

Civil Service Commission

merit system

neutral competence

Hatch Act

executive leadership

Further Reading

C. Fred Alford, *Whistleblowers: Broken Lives and Organizational Power* (Ithaca, N.Y.: Cornell University Press,
2001). A political science professor chronicles the impact
on the lives and careers of individuals who reported corruption and mismanagement in government agencies.

Jonathan Kwitny, *Acceptable Risks* (New York: Poseidon,
1992). Kwitny tells a fast-paced and well-written story
of two men who prodded and fought the Food and
Drug Administration to make potentially helpful medicines available to AIDS patients. It reveals the agency's
rigidity but also, ultimately, its responsiveness.

Paul C. Light, *The New Public Service* (Washington, D.C.:
Brookings Institution, 1999). If you are interested in a
career in a public bureaucracy, this is a useful handbook
written by one of the leading scholars of the U.S. Civil
Service.

George Orwell, *Nineteen Eighty-Four* (New York: Harcourt,
Brace, 1949). One of the most popular novels of the
twentieth century gives you a look at an überbureaucracy
and its intrusion into private life. It will put any complaints you might have about the federal bureaucracy
into perspective.

Mark Riebling, *Wedge: The Secret War between the FBI and the
CIA* (New York: Knopf, 1994). Riebling describes the
different jurisdictions assigned to these agencies by Congress and how this division led to destructive turf wars.

Eileen Welsome, *The Plutonium Files* (New York: Dial,
1999). This is an account of secret government medical
experiments that involved injection of radioactive plutonium into human subjects. The documents on which
it is based were retrieved through a FOIA request.

For Viewing

During J. Edgar Hoover's directorship, the FBI was a na-
tional icon, a view reflected in the TV series *I Led Three
Lives* (1953–1956), the movie version (equally fictional) *I
Was a Communist for the FBI* (1951), and movies like *The
FBI Story* (1959)—during the making of which Hoover
was on the set each day—and *Elliot Ness* (1987).

Orwell's *Nineteen Eighty-Four* was filmed and released in 1984.

October Sky (1999). Most people think of federal bureaucrats
as paper pushers, but thousands are scientists and mathematicians who work in research and development. This is

a true story of how one boy's interest in rocketry led to a
career as a NASA bureaucrat.

 Electronic Resources

www.gao.gov
*This is the site of the Government Accountability Office, the con-
gressional office that monitors the performance of executive branch
agencies.*

www.opm.gov
*At the Office of Personnel Management site, you can review tables
that reveal the composition of the federal workforce, demographics,
occupation, pay, and many other statistics.*

www.fedstats.gov
*Federal agencies collect statistics about the American population,
the economy, housing, employment, and many other areas of life.
This Web site provides a guide to finding and using those statistics,
whether they involve the mean household income of American families or last year's export trade data. The site also provides a link
to the most recent edition of the Statistical Abstract of the United
States.*

www.ombwatch.org
*This is a site set up by interest groups and private individuals to
monitor the performance of executive branch agencies. You can review agency evaluations, changes in FOIA, and other laws and
rules governing openness in government. The site maintains a lot
of information removed from government Web sites after 9/11.*

www.openthegovernment.org
*This Web site is devoted to tracking government policy on issues of
secrecy and public access to government documents. Site managers
advocate for greater openness.*

www.usajobs.opm.gov
*At this site, you can see what jobs are open in the federal govern-
ment and submit an online application.*

InfoTrac College Edition

**Search for the following articles in the InfoTrac
database:**

Agranoff, Robert, and Michael McGuire. "American
Federalism and the Search for Models of Management,"
Public Administration Review (November–December
2001).

Krauss, Elishia L. "Building a Bigger Bureaucracy: What
the Department of Homeland Security Won't Do," *The
Public Manager* (Spring 2003).

Riccucci, Norma M. "Street-level Bureaucrats and In-
trastate Variation in the Implementation of Temporary
Assistance for Needy Families Policies," *Journal of Public
Administration Research and Theory* (January 2005).

Wise, Charles R. "Election Administration in Crisis: An
Early Look at Lessons from Bush versus Gore," *Public
Administration Review* (March 2001).

For more articles, enter

"Public Administration" in the Subject Guide, and then go to subdivision "Analysis";

"Public Administration" in the Subject Guide, and then go to subdivision "Evaluation";

"Public Administration Review" for journal name in PowerTrac.

American Government Resources

Visit the Government Institutions section of the Wadsworth American Government Resources Web site (politicalscience. wadsworth.com/amgov) for a variety of tools to help you explore the bureaucracy further. Included are simulations, video clips, Microcase exercises, and a wealth of other activities.

CHAPTER 13

THE JUDICIARY

© TOUHIG SION/CORBIS SYGMA

Justice Sandra Day O'Connor

Development of the Courts' Role in Government
Founding to the Civil War
Civil War to the Great Depression
Great Depression to the Present
The Next Era

Courts
Structure of the Courts
Jurisdiction of the Courts

Judges
Selection of Judges
Tenure of Judges
Qualifications of Judges
Independence of Judges

Access to the Courts
Wealth Discrimination in Access
Interest Group Help in Access
Proceeding through the Courts

Deciding Cases
Interpreting Statutes
Interpreting the Constitution
Restraint and Activism
Following Precedents
Making Law
Deciding Cases at the Supreme Court

The Power of the Courts
Use of Judicial Review
Use of Political Checks against the Courts

Conclusion: Are the Courts Responsive?

Do You Plunge into the Political Thicket?

You are Justice Sandra Day O'Connor of the United States Supreme Court, and it is a month after the presidential election of 2000. The election is still undecided, and its outcome hinges on the results of the vote in Florida. Whichever candidate prevails in Florida will gain the state's twenty-five electoral votes and become the country's forty-third president.

The morning after the election, it appeared that Republican candidate George W. Bush had an eighteen-hundred–vote lead.[1] Because this was less than half of 1 percent of the votes cast, state law required a retabulation of the totals from the voting machines. The retabulation narrowed the gap to less than three hundred votes. The Democratic candidate, Vice President Al Gore, claiming that the machines had failed to count some votes, sought a manual recount in four strongly Democratic counties. Secretary of State Katherine Harris, who was also the cochair of the Bush campaign in Florida, tried to prevent a manual recount.[2] In the meantime, a manual recount in one of the disputed counties would, if accepted, shrink the lead to just 150 votes. It appeared that a manual recount in the remaining counties might give the lead to Gore.

The Florida Supreme Court ruled that manual recounts from the disputed counties must be accepted and, hearing a related case three weeks later, ruled that manual recounts from the entire state must

be undertaken.[3] The court set a general standard for the recounts: The counties should ascertain "the intent of the voter." The court did not specify how counties that used punch card ballots should count incomplete punches ("hanging chads" and "dimpled chads"). In these two decisions, the Florida justices interpreted the state's law, which was an incomplete and contradictory patchwork,[4] in ways that benefited Gore's campaign. Some legal scholars consider their interpretations questionable,[5] though others consider them plausible.[6] In several other cases, however, the court ruled in ways that hindered Gore's campaign.[7] Thus although the Florida justices were mostly Democratic appointees,[8] they were not clearly partisan,[9] prone to favoring one party over the other.

Candidate Bush appealed to the United States Supreme Court to stop the manual recounts ordered by the Florida Supreme Court. You have to decide whether to plunge into what a previous justice called the "political thicket" of state election law.[10]

You are a staunch Republican and an ideological conservative. You grew up on a ranch in Arizona with a father who opposed President Franklin Roosevelt's New Deal policies.

You graduated in the top 10 percent of your class at Stanford Law School but did not get hired by a law firm because you were a woman, so you became a prosecutor instead.

Bush and Gore supporters debate the election outside the Supreme Court.

After returning to Arizona, you became an assistant attorney general, then a state legislator—eventually the first woman elected majority leader of any state legislature—and then a state judge. In 1981, you were appointed to the U. S. Supreme Court—the first woman elevated to the high Court—by President Ronald Reagan.

On the conservative Rehnquist Court, you sit near the middle. There is a bloc of three archconservatives, two moderate conservatives, three moderates, and one liberal.[11] Justice Anthony Kennedy and you are the two moderate conservatives. When you two join the archconservatives, you form a majority. When you two join the other justices, you form a majority in the opposite direction. Therefore, you are usually in the majority. Last term, you wrote only one dissenting opinion.[12] As a swing justice on the Supreme Court, you may be the most powerful woman in America.

Unlike the three archconservatives, you are cautious, reluctant to sweep away precedents, even precedents you might not have voted for had you been on the Court at the time. For instance, in 1992 you voted to reaffirm the precedent of *Roe* v. *Wade,* which legalized abortion, despite demands to overturn it.[13] You expressed concern for the legitimacy of the Court if it abandoned its precedents:

The country's loss of confidence in the judiciary would be underscored by an equally certain and equally reasonable condemnation for . . . overruling unnecessarily and under pressure. . . . Unlike the political branches, a Court thus weakened could not seek to regain its position with a new mandate from the voters. . . . Like the character of an individual, the legitimacy of the Court must be earned over time.

In response to Bush's appeal, you have several choices. You could avoid this tangled thicket. The Supreme Court is not required to take the case; it has discretion. Sometimes it refuses to take a case if it thinks other branches or other levels of government should resolve the dispute.[14] Usually, in fact, it refuses to take cases that involve election outcomes.[15] It prefers elected officials, who have been chosen by the voters and are accountable to the voters when they run for reelection, to resolve these disputes rather than unelected judges.

This practice reflects *judicial restraint*—a tendency to avoid political disputes and to defer governmental policymaking to other branches. For the past half-century, conservatives have preached judicial restraint and attacked judges who they claim have practiced *judicial activism* instead. Republican candidates for president have promised to nominate as judges only individuals who have professed or demonstrated judicial restraint. The Rehnquist Court has usually echoed these views. At the same time, however, the Rehnquist Court has sometimes practiced judicial activism by invalidating federal laws.[16]

If the Court does take the case, it could allow or disallow the Florida Supreme Court's order for a statewide recount. The argument for allowing the order is based on federalism. The states have primary responsibility for conducting elections, even federal elections, and a state's supreme court has primary authority to interpret the state's law. Normally, federal officials take a hands-off approach unless the state discriminates against some group of voters, as southern states did when they denied African Americans the right to vote.

The Rehnquist Court has emphasized the role of federalism in our system and has returned more power to state governments. As a former official in all three branches of Arizona's government, you have been especially sensitive to state concerns. You have, in fact, been the leader of the Rehnquist Court's movement. Your views on federalism might incline you to avoid the case or to allow the order. Either way, the result would be the same.

The argument for disallowing the order is based on the equal protection clause of the Fourteenth Amendment.[17] This clause, added to the Constitution during Reconstruction, was designed to prevent southern governments from denying constitutional rights to former slaves. But the language in the clause is general, so the clause has been used to protect various groups of people, including other minorities, poor people, illegitimate children, and women. The Rehnquist Court has also used it to protect white men, claiming reverse discrimination, in affirmative action cases.[18]

Bush maintains that the order would deny equal protection—that is, it would foster discrimination—because it does not set specific standards for counting hanging chads and dimpled chads. For example, Broward County officials decided that dimpled chads would be counted, but Palm Beach County officials decided that dimpled chads would be counted only if there was additional evidence of the voter's intent (such as dimpled chads for other offices on the ballot too). Therefore, a small percentage of voters would not have their ballots counted the same as other voters in other counties because the standards in their county would differ from the standards in other counties. They could be Bush voters or Gore voters. There would be no intentional discrimination, and there would be no systematic pattern favoring one candidate or the other. There would be no identifiable group singled out for discriminatory treatment as there normally is in equal protection cases. Nevertheless, the absence of statewide standards for a statewide recount is troubling.

Yet courts have never insisted that manual recounts, which have occurred periodically, must use specific standards throughout the state.[19] Thirty states do not provide specific standards in their laws for manual recounts.[20] Moreover, the Rehnquist Court has shown limited concern for voting rights[21] and has downplayed equal protection. The Court has even allowed states to use capital punishment when it reflects a pattern of racial discrimination.[22] You have joined the majority of the Court in these decisions.[23]

Thus the Court's pronouncements and its precedents suggest that it will not get embroiled in this controversy. Your past behavior suggests the same. Do you follow these pronouncements and precedents in this case?

Some media commentators have expressed alarm that the election is still unresolved. The American people themselves, while arguing for one side or the other, have remained calm.

There have been no signs of unrest, no stockpiling of consumer goods, and no instability in financial markets. There have been no problems in our relations with other countries, though foreign leaders do not know which man they will have to deal with as president come January. But the situation is unsettled, and nobody knows what might happen if it drags on. Do you worry about the possibility that this high-stakes civics lesson might turn into political chaos?

Your decision could determine the outcome of the election. You realize that a manual recount might result in a Gore victory, yet you fervently hope for a Bush victory. Of course, you know that a judge is not supposed to decide cases according to the persons or parties involved.

Your decision could affect future appointments to the Court as well. President Bush would nominate very different justices than President Gore.

You have to be careful. The country is sharply divided, even polarized, over this election and its aftermath. If you make a mistake, you could exacerbate the split and also hurt the Court's legitimacy. Unlike the presidency and Congress, which derive their legitimacy primarily from the elections of their officials, the Court must derive its legitimacy primarily from the decisions of its justices. By *appearing* independent and wise, as well as by *acting* independent and wise, the justices nurture a sense of legitimacy among the people.

With these considerations in mind, what do you decide?

The public expresses more support for the Supreme Court than for the president or Congress.[24] The public dislikes the disagreements and debates and the negotiations and compromises among governmental officials, and it deplores the efforts of interest groups to influence governmental policies. These messy features of democratic government, which are visible in the executive and legislative branches, are not visible in the judicial branch. Many people conclude that they do not occur.

Indeed, many people assume that courts are nonpolitical and that judges are objective. People say we have "a government of laws, not of men." But this view is a myth. At any time in our history, "it is individuals who make, enforce, and interpret the law."[25] When judges interpret the law, they are political actors and the courts are political institutions.

Thus public support for the Supreme Court and the lower courts rests partly on false assumptions about the absence of politics in this branch. There is plenty of politics, as will be seen in each of the topics covered in this chapter—the history, structure, jurisdiction, composition, operation, and impact of the courts.

Development of the Courts' Role in Government

The Founders expected the judiciary to be the weakest branch of government. In the *Federalist Papers,* Alexander Hamilton wrote that Congress would have power to pass the laws and appropriate the money; the president would have power to execute the laws; but the courts would have "merely judgment"—that is, only power to resolve disputes in cases brought to them. In doing so, they would exercise "neither force nor will." They would not have any means to enforce decisions, and they would not use their own values to decide cases. Rather, they would simply apply the Constitution and laws as written. Consequently, the judiciary would be the "least dangerous" branch.[26]

This prediction was accurate for the early years of the Republic. The federal courts seemed inconsequential. The Supreme Court was held in such low esteem that some distinguished men refused to accept appointment to it; others accepted appointment but refused to attend sessions. The first chief justice thought the Court was "inauspicious,"[27] without enough "weight and dignity" to play an important role.[28] So he resigned to be governor of New York. The second chief justice resigned to be envoy to France.

When the nation's capital was moved to Washington, D.C., in 1801, new homes were built for Congress and the president but not for the Supreme Court. Planners considered the Court too insignificant for more than a small room in the Capitol. But the Court could not even keep this room. For decades, it would be shunted from one location to another, from the marshal's office to the clerk's office, from the clerk's home to the Capitol's cellar—a dark and damp chamber in which visitors joked that Lady Justice would not need to wear a blindfold because she could not see anyway—and from one committee room to another.[29] It would not get its own building until 1935.

However, the status of the Court began to change after the appointment of the fourth chief justice, John Marshall. Under his leadership, the Court began to develop "weight and dignity" and to play an important role in government.

The development of the courts' role in government can be shown by dividing the courts' history into three eras: from the founding to the Civil War, from the Civil War to the Great Depression, and from the Great Depression to the present.

Founding to the Civil War

The first primary issue facing the courts, in the era from the country's founding to the Civil War, was the relationship between nation and state. In addressing this issue, the Supreme Court established judicial review and national supremacy.

Judicial Review

Judicial review is the authority to declare laws or actions of government officials unconstitutional. The Constitution does not mention judicial review. At the Constitutional Convention, the idea was proposed, but it was strongly opposed by some delegates who feared that it would give too much power to the federal judges and would weaken the state governments. Proponents of the idea did not press for its inclusion because they worried that doing so might jeopardize the Constitution's ratification. Even so, they expected the federal courts to claim and use judicial review eventually. Already some state courts used it, and in the *Federalist Papers,* Hamilton said the federal courts would have authority to void laws contrary to the Constitution.[30]

The Supreme Court articulated the power of judicial review in the case of ***Marbury* v. *Madison*** in 1803.[31] The case had its origins in 1800, when the Federalist president, John Adams, was defeated in his bid for re-election by Thomas Jefferson and many Federalist members of Congress were defeated by Jeffersonians. With both the presidency and Congress lost, the Federalists tried to ensure continued control of the judiciary. The lame-duck president and lame-duck Congress added more judgeships, most of which were unnecessary. (Forty-two were for justices of the peace for the District of Columbia, which was sparsely populated.) They hoped to fill these positions with loyal Federalists before the new president and new Congress took over.

In addition, Adams named his secretary of state, John Marshall, to be chief justice. At the time, though, Marshall was still secretary of state and responsible for delivering the commissions to the new appointees.

But he ran out of time, failing to deliver four commissions for District of Columbia justices of the peace.

Supreme Court Historical Society

This portrait of William Marbury is the only portrait of a litigant owned by the Supreme Court Historical Society, testifying to the importance of the case of Marbury v. Madison.

He assumed that his successor would deliver them. But Jefferson, angry at the Federalists' efforts to pack the judiciary, told his secretary of state, James Madison, not to deliver the commissions.[32] Without the signed commissions, the appointees could not prove that they had in fact been appointed.[33]

William Marbury and the three other appointees petitioned the Supreme Court for a writ of *mandamus* (Latin for "we command"), an order that forces government officials to do something they have a duty to do. In this case, it would force Madison to deliver the commissions.

As chief justice, Marshall was in a position to rule on his administration's efforts to appoint these judges. Today this would be considered a conflict of interest, and he would be expected to disqualify himself. But at the time, people were not as troubled by such conflicts.

Marshall could issue the writ, but Jefferson would tell Madison to disobey it and the Court would be powerless to enforce it. Or Marshall could decline to issue the writ, and the Court would appear powerless to issue it. Either way, the Court would reflect weakness rather than project strength.

Marshall shrewdly found a way out of the dilemma. He interpreted a provision of a congressional statute in a questionable way and then a provision of the Constitution in a questionable way as well.[34] As a result, he could claim that the statute violated the provision of the Constitution. Therefore, the statute was unconstitutional, and the Court could not order the administration to give the commissions. Thus Marshall exercised judicial review. He wrote, in a statement that would be repeated by courts for years to come, "It is emphatically the province and duty of the judicial department to say what the law is."

Marshall justified judicial review this way: The Constitution is the supreme law of the land. If other laws contradict it, they are unconstitutional. Marshall continued: Judges decide cases, and to decide cases they have to apply the Constitution. To apply it, they have to say what it means. They can be trusted to say what it means because they take an oath to uphold it. On this point, some of Marshall's contemporaries disagreed with his reasoning. Other officials also have to follow the Constitution and also take an oath to uphold it, and they could interpret it as appropriately as judges could.

But Marshall was persuasive enough to convince many. A sly fox, he sacrificed the commissions—he could not have gotten them anyway—and established the power of judicial review instead. In doing so, with one hand he gave the Jeffersonians what they wanted, while with the other he gave the Federalists something much greater. And all along he claimed he did what the Constitution required him to do.

Chief Justice John Marshall (right) swears in President Andrew Jackson in 1829. Although Marshall's party, the Federalists, had dissolved, Marshall remained as chief justice, serving for thirty-four years.

Jefferson saw through this. He said the Constitution, in Marshall's hands, was "a thing of putty,"[35] adding that Marshall's arguments were "twistifications." But the decision did not require Jefferson to do anything, so he could not do anything but protest. Most of Jefferson's followers were satisfied with the result. They were not upset that the Court had invalidated a Federalist law, even though it had articulated judicial review to do so.

Of course, they were shortsighted because this decision laid the cornerstone for a strong judiciary. Thus a case that began as a "trivial squabble over a few petty political plums"[36] became perhaps the most important case the Court has ever decided. (See the box "The Quintessential American?" on the next page.)

National Supremacy

After *Marbury*, the Court did not declare any other congressional laws unconstitutional during Marshall's tenure, although it did declare numerous state laws unconstitutional.[37] These decisions entrenched the practice of judicial review and at the same time underlined the supremacy of the national government over the state governments.

The Court also furthered the supremacy of the national government by broadly construing the power of Congress. In *McCulloch* v. *Maryland,* discussed in Chapter 3, the Court interpreted the "necessary and proper

Thomas Jefferson is well known among Americans, with his face on the nickel and a beautiful monument in Washington. His adversary, John Marshall, is relatively unknown despite the chief justice's historic accomplishments in strengthening the Supreme Court and the national government.

Though distant cousins and Virginia natives, these two great Americans detested each other, perhaps because they were so different from each other. Jefferson was an aristocrat, broadly educated, with an interest in science and a flair for inventing things and also with an interest in architecture and a real talent for practicing it, as evidenced by Monticello, his home. He owned slaves, yet he lived beyond his means and was usually over his head in debt. Marshall, the oldest of fifteen children from a frontier family, was a self-made man. He worked hard to establish himself as a lawyer. He also tried to increase his wealth as a land speculator. By combining law and business, Marshall reflected the American fascination with these two professions.

During the Revolutionary War, Marshall served with General George Washington through the long winter at Valley Forge. He witnessed American farmers selling their food to British troops rather than to American troops who desperately needed the food, because the American army paid with worthless money. The American government under the Continental Congress was too weak to tax, so it lacked the resources to back up the money it printed. This experience would contribute to Marshall's belief in a strong central government.

After the war, Marshall gained extensive political experience. He served in the Virginia legislature, the Virginia convention for ratification of the Constitution, and the U. S. House of Representatives. As a United States minister to France, he led a delegation to negotiate a treaty between the two countries. But when the French foreign minister demanded money in exchange for an agreement, Marshall rebuffed him and returned home a hero. Outraged Americans threatened war, but Jefferson, who admired French society and fancied French finery, upbraided Marshall for antagonizing French officials.

President John Adams appointed Marshall secretary of state and, at the end of his administration, chief justice of the Supreme Court. By the time Marshall reached the Court, his political experience had sharpened his political acumen to the point where he could lead his brethren and write persuasive opinions for the Court over the opposition of other officials and political parties.

Throughout his career, Marshall dressed casually and got along well with people from all classes. He seemed as comfortable in rowdy taverns as in genteel homes. (They say that as a candidate for Congress, he provided the best whiskey on election day.) Even as chief justice, he often did the shopping for his sick wife. At the market one day, a young dandy who did not recognize him said, "Here, my man. Just take this turkey to my house," and tossed a coin. Marshall took the coin and delivered the turkey.[1]

The aristocratic Jefferson envisioned an agrarian country and championed the poor farmers who seemed at the mercy of the commercial interests of the northern cities. He spoke against efforts to strengthen the national government, which, he believed, would be controlled by these powerful interests. The self-made Marshall, however, envisioned a commercial empire and advocated a strong government that could provide a stable economy in which business could flourish. Over the years, Americans would talk like Jefferson—"That government is best which governs least" would become a perennial quotation—but they would act like Marshall, and the country would develop as Marshall envisioned far more than as Jefferson did.

In other ways, Marshall was more advanced for his times, though less successful in furthering his views. He favored equality for women and opposed efforts to drive Indian tribes off their lands. When Georgia tried by law to force the Cherokees from the state, the Supreme Court held the laws unconstitutional.[2] But Georgia ignored the ruling, and former Indian fighter President Andrew Jackson reportedly said, "John Marshall has made his decision. Now let him enforce it."

1. Robert Wernick, "Chief Justice Marshall Takes the Law in Hand," *Smithsonian,* November 1998, 159.
2. *Worcester* v. *Georgia,* 31 U.S. 515 (1832). SOURCE: Robert Wernick, "Chief Justice Marshall Takes the Law in Hand," *Smithsonian,* November 1998, 157–173.

clause" to allow Congress to legislate in many matters not mentioned in the Constitution. Then the Court narrowly construed the power of the states to regulate commerce.[38]

When President Andrew Jackson named Roger Taney to replace Marshall, proponents of a strong national government worried that Taney would undo what Marshall had done. But although Taney did not further expand national power, he upheld national supremacy and thus solidified most of Marshall's doctrine.

Yet in one case, Taney severely undermined the Court's reputation. In the *Dred Scott* case,[39] the Court jumped into the thick of the slavery conflict and declared the Missouri Compromise of 1820, which controlled slavery in the territories, unconstitutional. This was only the second time the Court had declared a congressional law unconstitutional, and it could not have come in a more controversial area or at a less opportune time. The slavery issue had polarized the nation, and the ruling polarized it further. Southerners had been disenchanted with the Court because of its emphasis on a strong national government. Now northerners became disenchanted too. The Court's prestige dropped so precipitously that it could play only a weak role for two decades. President Abraham Lincoln refused to enforce one of its rulings,[40] and Congress withdrew part of its jurisdiction.[41] As a result, the Court shied away from important issues.

The Taney Court naively thought it could resolve the clash over slavery and thereby resolve the conflict between nation and state. But no court could achieve this. It would take the Civil War to do so.[42]

Civil War to the Great Depression

With the controversy between nation and state muted, the next primary issue facing the courts was the relationship between government and business in cases involving regulation of business.

After the war, industrialization proceeded at breakneck pace, bringing not only benefits but also many problems. Some corporations abused their power over their employees, their competitors, and their custom-

ers. Although legislatures passed laws to regulate these abuses, the corporations challenged the laws in court. The Supreme Court, dominated by justices who had been lawyers for corporations, reflected the views of corporations—the *laissez-faire* attitudes of the late nineteenth and early twentieth centuries—and struck down the regulations on them.

Beginning in the 1870s, intensifying in the 1890s, and continuing in the 1900s, the Court invalidated laws that regulated child labor,[43] maximum hours of work,[44] and minimum wages for work.[45] It also discouraged employees from joining unions and unions from striking employers,[46] and it limited antitrust laws.[47] In just one decade, the Court invalidated forty-one state laws regulating railroads.[48]

In 1935 and 1936, the Court struck down twelve congressional laws,[49] nearly nullifying President Franklin Roosevelt's New Deal program to help the country recover from the Great Depression.

The Court's action precipitated another major crisis. Roosevelt was reelected resoundingly in 1936. Heady from his victory and frustrated by his lack of opportunities to appoint new justices in his first term, he retaliated against the Court by proposing what was soon labeled a **court-packing plan.** The plan would have authorized the president to nominate and the Senate to confirm a new justice for every justice over seventy who did not retire, up to a total of fifteen. At the time, there were six justices over seventy, so Roosevelt could have immediately appointed six new justices and assured himself

Although many children worked long days in unhealthy conditions, the Supreme Court declared initial laws prohibiting child labor unconstitutional. This boy worked in the coal mines in the early 1900s.

Utah State Historical Society

of a friendly Court. The plan was the dominant political issue for five months. It was debated in Congress, in newspapers, and on the radio. Public opinion was divided. Even some of Roosevelt's supporters criticized him for tampering with the Court.

Before Congress could vote on the plan, two justices who often sided with four conservative justices against New Deal legislation switched positions to side with three liberal justices for legislation. Chief Justice Charles Evans Hughes and Justice Owen Roberts apparently thought the Court would suffer if it continued to oppose the popular president and his popular programs. Indeed, it is likely that the plan would have passed if the Court had not changed. The two justices' conversion made the court-packing plan unnecessary, and Congress scuttled it. The switch was dubbed "the switch in time that saved nine."

Thus the Court resolved this issue in favor of government over business. Since then, it has permitted most efforts to regulate business.

© Dennis Brack/Black Star

Chief Justice Earl Warren, flanked by Justices Hugo Black (left) and William O. Douglas.

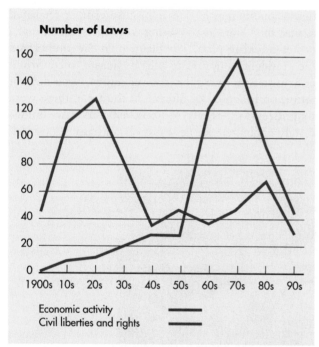

FIGURE 1 ■ **Laws Regulating Economic Activity and Restricting Civil Liberties and Rights Declared Unconstitutional by the Supreme Court since 1900** *The Supreme Court was nearly as activist in striking down laws in the 1910s, 1920s, and 1930s, as it was in the 1950s, 1960s, and 1970s. But in the former years, it was activist in economic cases (usually ones involving governmental regulation of business), whereas in the latter years, it was activist in civil liberties and rights cases.*

Source: Congressional Research Service, *The Constitution of the United States: Analysis and Interpretation* and its 1998 supplement (Washington, D.C.: U.S. Government Printing Office, 1996 and 1999); Kenneth Jose, *The Supreme Court Yearbook, 1998–1999* (Washington, D.C.: CQ Press, 2000); Lawrence Baum, *The Supreme Court,* 8th ed. (Washington, D.C.: CQ Press, 2004), 181.

Great Depression to the Present

With the controversy between government and business subdued, the next primary issue facing the courts was the relationship between government and the individual in cases involving civil liberties and rights. Often this issue featured a conflict between the majority, whose views were reflected in government policy, and a minority who challenged the policy.

Despite people's perceptions today, the courts paid little attention to civil liberties and rights historically. The courts regularly allowed their governments to ignore these rights. But the courts' lax attitude began to change when President Dwight Eisenhower, fulfilling a campaign pledge to a presidential rival, Earl Warren, appointed him chief justice. From 1953 through the 1960s, Warren led the Court more effectively than any chief justice since Marshall. The **Warren Court** (1953–1969) completely overhauled doctrine involving racial segregation, criminal defendants' rights, and reapportionment.[50] It also significantly altered doctrine involving libel, obscenity, and religion. In the process, it held many laws unconstitutional. It was more activist in civil liberties and rights cases than the Court had ever been (see Figure 1).

The Warren Court sympathized with unpopular individuals and powerless groups—alleged subversives, criminal defendants, racial minorities, and religious minorities—when they challenged governmental policies. Thus the most elite institution in our government used its power to benefit many nonelites in our society. In its sympathies, the Warren Court differed sharply from previous Courts, which historically favored the haves over the have-nots and efforts to preserve the status quo over struggles to change it.

The Warren Court's decisions brought about a backlash in the late 1960s.[51] President Richard Nixon vowed to change the direction of the Court, and in 1969 he appointed Warren Burger to be chief justice after Earl Warren retired. Then Nixon and his former vice president, President Gerald Ford, appointed four more justices when vacancies occurred. They sought to slow, halt, or even reverse the Warren Court's actions. They expected the **Burger Court** (1969–1986) to make a "constitutional counterrevolution."

But the Burger Court did not. Although it eroded some of the Warren Court's doctrine, particularly in the area of criminal defendants' rights, it left most of the rest intact. Furthermore, it advanced doctrine in two areas where the Warren Court was silent: sexual discrimination and abortion. Although it was not as committed to civil liberties and rights as the Warren Court, the Burger Court was more committed to them than any earlier Court.

Presidents Ronald Reagan and George H. W. Bush also wanted to reverse the Court's liberal doctrine. When Burger retired, Reagan elevated William Rehnquist, the most conservative associate justice, to be chief justice in 1986. Then Reagan appointed three more conservatives, and Bush appointed two more conservatives. By this time, Republican presidents had named ten justices in a row.

The election of President Bill Clinton led to the appointment of the first Democratic justices since 1967. Although these two moderates slowed any further swing to the right, the conservatives controlled the **Rehnquist Court** (1986–2005). But conflicts among the conservatives splintered the bloc. Some were bold, eager to sweep away liberal precedents and substitute conservative principles. Others were cautious, willing to uphold liberal precedents they would not have agreed to set in the first place and inclined to decide cases on narrow bases rather than on broad principles. In some terms, the former group dominated, but in other terms, the latter group dominated.[52] Overall, the Rehnquist Court, though markedly more conservative than the Burger Court, did not overturn most of the previous Courts' actions.

Yet the Rehnquist Court made some changes to legal doctrine. The conservative justices continued to erode criminal defendants' rights. They also made it harder for racial minorities to use affirmative action and

for religious minorities to follow the tenets of their religion. In two less obvious areas, the Rehnquist Court altered doctrine in more fundamental ways. It tightened access to the courts for individuals and groups trying to challenge government policies. And it limited efforts by Congress to impose new regulations on the states. The latter development is the most notable change by the Rehnquist Court.[53] In these ways, the Republican justices mirrored the views of the Republican presidents and members of Congress in the 1980s, 1990s, and early 2000s.

In sum, throughout its history, the Court's role in government has been that of a policymaker—in relationships between nation and state, government and business, and government and the individual. In the first and second eras, the Court was a solidly conservative policymaker, protecting private property rights and limiting government regulation of business; in the third era, the Court was a generally liberal policymaker, permitting government regulation of business and supporting civil liberties and rights for the individual.

It now appears that the third era is over. Although the Rehnquist Court did not interfere with most of the previous Courts' doctrine, it deemphasized individual rights (with the possible exception of freedom of speech, which will be addressed in Chapter 14), pruning them in some areas and not expanding them in others.

The Next Era

If the third era is over, what controversy will the fourth era address? We probably will not know for many years, until we can look back with more perspective than we have now, but it is interesting to speculate.

Might the fourth era focus on information technology, including computers, the software they use, and the data they store? And might it resolve disputes about which people have access to this technology, when people have access to it, and how people can use it—in short, in what ways and to what extent the government and the private sector can impose restrictions on the new technology? These questions would be similar to ones the Court answered about freedom of speech, freedom of the press, libel, and obscenity in the third era. Or perhaps the emphasis will be on privacy from all the intrusions of this new technology. The Court barely addressed invasion of privacy in the third era. (Chapter 14 explains the Court's doctrine in this area.)

Or might the fourth era focus on biotechnology? Advances in genetics herald a revolution promising the opportunity for people to live longer and for parents to choose various characteristics of their children, such as gender and eye color, and alter other characteristics, such as intelligence, personality, and athletic ability. Research even offers the possibility of cloning. Initial legal issues might involve restrictions on experiments and techniques. Once the techniques are developed, the legal issues might involve access to these procedures.

Information technology and biotechnology will experience exponential growth in the first half of the twenty-first century. Technological change, according to one scientist, "will appear to explode into infinity, at least from the limited and linear perspective of contemporary humans." This change will be "so rapid and so profound that it represents a rupture in the fabric of human history."[54] If this prediction is at all accurate, litigants and judges will be wrenched from their current preoccupations and forced to address new issues barely imagined now.

Courts

Most countries with a federal system have one national court over a system of regional courts. In contrast, the United States has a complete system of national courts side by side with complete systems of state courts, for a total of fifty-one separate systems. This setup makes litigation far more complicated than in other countries.

Structure of the Courts

The Constitution mentions only one court—a supreme court—although it allows Congress to set up additional lower courts, which it did in the Judiciary Act of 1789. The act was a compromise between Federalists, who wanted a full system of lower courts with extensive jurisdiction (authority to hear and decide cases) in order to strengthen the national government, and Jeffersonians, who wanted only a partial system of lower courts with limited jurisdiction in order to avoid strengthening the national government. The compromise established a full system of lower courts with limited jurisdiction. The peculiar result was that many federal courts were established, but they were allowed to decide very few cases. They were authorized to hear disputes involving citizens of more than one state but not disputes relating to the U.S. Constitution or laws. The state courts were permitted to hear all these cases.

In 1875, Congress granted the federal courts extensive jurisdiction. Sixteen years later, Congress created another level of courts, between the Supreme Court and the original lower courts, to complete the basic structure of the federal judiciary.

In the federal system, the **district courts** are trial courts. There are ninety-four, based on population but with at least one in each state. They have multiple judges, although a single judge or jury decides each case.

The **courts of appeals** are intermediate appellate courts. They hear cases that have been decided by the district courts but are appealed by the losers. There are twelve, based on regions of the country known as "circuits." They have numerous judges, although a panel of three judges decides each case.[55]

The Supreme Court is the ultimate appellate court. It hears cases that have been decided by the courts of appeals, district courts, or state supreme courts. (Although it can hear some cases—those involving a state or a diplomat—that have not proceeded through the lower courts first, in practice it hears nearly all of its cases on appeal.) The group of nine justices decides its cases.

The district courts conduct trials. The courts of appeals and Supreme Court do not; they do not have juries or witnesses to testify and present evidence—just lawyers for the opposing litigants. Rather than determine guilt or innocence, these courts evaluate arguments about legal questions arising in the cases.

The state judiciaries have a structure similar to the federal judiciary. In most states, though, there are two tiers of trial courts. Normally, the lower tier is for criminal cases involving minor crimes, and the upper tier is for criminal cases involving major crimes and for civil cases. In about three-fourths of the states, there are intermediate appellate courts, and in all of the states there is a supreme court (although in a few it is known by another name).

Since 1978, the federal system has also had a very special secret court of which few Americans are aware (see the box "Surveillance Court").

Jurisdiction of the Courts

As noted, **jurisdiction** is the authority to hear and decide cases. The federal courts can exercise jurisdiction over cases in which the subject involves the U.S. Constitution, statutes, or treaties; maritime law; or cases in which the litigants include the U.S. government, more than one state government, one state government and a citizen of another state, citizens of more than one state,[56] or a foreign government or citizen. The state courts exercise jurisdiction over the remaining cases. These include most criminal cases because the states have authority over most criminal matters and pass most criminal laws. Consequently, the state courts hear far more cases than the federal courts.

Despite this dividing line, some cases begin in the state courts and end in the federal courts. These involve state law and federal law, frequently a state statute and a federal constitutional right. For these cases, there are two paths from the state judiciary to the federal judiciary. One is for the litigant who lost at the state supreme court to appeal to the U.S. Supreme Court.

The other path, available only in a criminal case, is for the defendant who has exhausted all possible appeals

Behind closed doors in a windowless room in the Justice Department's basement, a highly secretive court meets. The court hears requests from the FBI for electronic surveillance of possible spies and terrorists and sometimes for physical searches of their homes and computers.

The Foreign Intelligence Surveillance Court operates like no other court in the United States. It consists of eleven district court judges handpicked by the chief justice of the Supreme Court. The members sit in panels of three judges and serve for seven years. Lawyers for the government, acting on behalf of the FBI, seek approval for electronic surveillance, much as law enforcement officers seek search warrants for routine searches from regular courts. Lawyers for the defense—the targets of the surveillance—do not appear in court to protect the secrecy of the surveillance. In fact, they are not informed, and not aware, that a case involving the defendants is being heard at all.

Congress established the court in 1978 after abuses by the Nixon administration, which itself authorized the FBI to engage in wiretapping, bugging, and other forms of electronic surveillance. The administration spied on American citizens active in the antiwar and civil rights movements, claiming that these

protesters were threats to "national security," and then tried to disrupt their organizations and harass their leaders. Despite these abuses, Congress thought the government should be allowed to engage in surveillance in genuine national security cases involving foreign agents or American citizens spying for foreign countries. Thus Congress established the court to approve or disapprove such surveillance and thereby check future administrations.

Yet because of the need for strict secrecy, the court's decisions are shielded from virtually all scrutiny. They can be appealed to the Foreign Intelligence Surveillance Court of Review, which consists of three appellate court judges, also handpicked by the chief justice. But this appellate court has heard just one case during its existence, and in this case it thwarted an effort by the trial court to check the government.

The Surveillance Court had turned down the government's requests only once while approving them some thirteen thousand times. In refusing the request in 2002, the judges identified over seventy-five cases in which the FBI had misled the court about the evidence it had to justify its requests for surveillance. When the FBI lacked sufficient evidence to obtain approval for surveillance in ordinary criminal cases—not

spying or terrorism cases—from regular courts, it tried to circumvent the law by going to the Surveillance Court, which requires less evidence to grant surveillance because of the seriousness of spying and terrorism.[1] The furious judges admonished the FBI to discontinue this practice. But the Bush administration appealed, and the Court of Review overturned the decision. The Court of Review concluded that the USA PATRIOT Act had broadened the law to allow the FBI to continue this practice after all.

Since 9/11, the number of requests for surveillance has increased each year. In 2003, it was over seventeen hundred, eclipsing the number of requests for surveillance in ordinary criminal cases to regular federal and state courts (578 and 864, respectively).[2] Thus it appears that the secret Surveillance Court will be hearing the majority of requests for surveillance, whether for spying and terrorism cases or for ordinary criminal cases, in the future as a result of 9/11.

1. John Podesta and Peter Swire, "Speaking Out about Wiretaps," *Washington Post National Weekly Edition,* September 9, 2002, 27; Seymour M. Hersh, "The Twentieth Man," *New Yorker,* September 30, 2002, 56–76.
2. Dan Eggen and Susan Schmidt, "It's a Whole New Spy Game," *Washington Post National Weekly Edition,* May 10, 2004, 29.

in the state courts to appeal to the local federal district court through a writ of **habeas corpus** ("You should have the body," the first words of the writ in Latin). This order demands that the state produce the defendant and justify his or her incarceration. If the district court decides that the state courts violated the defendant's constitutional rights, it will reverse the conviction. After the district court's decision, the losing side can try to appeal to the courts of appeals and the Supreme Court (see Figure 2).

Judges

Selection of Judges

Benjamin Franklin proposed that judges be selected by lawyers because lawyers would pick "the ablest of the profession in order to get rid of him, and share his practice among themselves."[57] The Founders rejected this unique idea, instead deciding that the president and the Senate should share the appointment power. The Con-

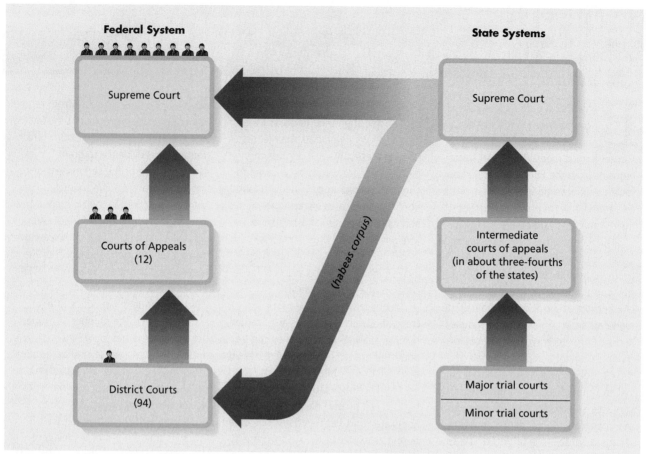

Federal System

Supreme Court

Courts of Appeals
(12)

District Courts
(94)

State Systems

Supreme Court

Intermediate
courts of appeals
(in about three-fourths
of the states)

Major trial courts

Minor trial courts

(habeas corpus)

FIGURE 2 ■ **Federal and State Court Systems** *The arrows indicate the primary avenues of appeal, and the heads indicate the usual number of judges who hear cases in the federal system.*

stitution stipulates that the president shall nominate judges and the Senate shall provide "advice and consent"—that is, recommend judges and then confirm or reject them.[58] There are no other requirements in the Constitution, although there is an unwritten requirement that judges be trained as lawyers.

The Founders expected these appointments to be based on merit rather than on politics. However, as soon as political parties developed, presidents and senators used politics as well as merit in making these appointments.

Mechanics of Selection

For the lower courts, lawyers who want to become judges try to become politically active in their party. When vacancies arise, they lobby political officials, bar association leaders, or interest group leaders in the hope that these elites will recommend them to the administration. They especially focus on their senators, who play a key role through the practice of senatorial courtesy. This tradition allows senators of the president's party to recommend, and to veto, candidates from their state for

judgeships in their state. This practice applies not only to district courts, which lie within individual states, but sometimes also to courts of appeals, which span several states. For courts of appeals, senators informally divide the seats among the states. (This practice does not apply to the Supreme Court because it has too few seats.)

Senatorial courtesy can limit the president's choices. During President Kennedy's term, the practice was ironclad. In deference to southern senators, the president, who advocated civil rights, was forced to appoint southern judges who favored segregation. One of them characterized the Supreme Court's desegregation ruling as "one of the truly regrettable decisions of all time," and another even called blacks "niggers" and "chimpanzees" in court.[59] However, senatorial courtesy is not as ironclad now as it was then. Since the 1970s, many administrations have sought certain candidates for their ideology or diversity, so they have pressured senators to cooperate. Consequently, there is more give-and-take between the senators and the president than there used to be. Nevertheless, in 1999, Senator Orin Hatch (R-Utah), chair of the Judiciary Committee, blocked all of President Clinton's nominees for six months until the president agreed to nominate one of Hatch's allies for a judgeship in Utah.

For the Supreme Court, lawyers who want to become justices try to become politically active in their party and also prominent in the legal profession. They write articles or give speeches designed to attract officials' attention. When vacancies arise, political officials, bar association leaders, and interest group leaders urge consideration of certain candidates. The administration also conducts a search for acceptable candidates. Sometimes even sitting justices make a recommendation. Chief Justice Burger recommended Harry Blackmun, a childhood pal and the best man at his wedding, and Justice Rehnquist recommended Sandra Day O'Connor, a law school classmate whom he had dated occasionally.

Once the president has chosen a candidate, he submits the nomination to the Senate, where it goes to the Judiciary Committee for hearings. Senators question the nominee about his or her judicial philosophy, and interest groups voice their concerns. If a majority of the committee consents, the nomination goes to the whole Senate. If a majority of the Senate consents, the nomination is confirmed.

The Judiciary Committee is the battleground for controversial nominations. The committee is controlled by the party that has a majority in the Senate, so the committee reflects the views of that party. If the committee confirms the nominee, normally the whole Senate will confirm the nominee. If the committee rejects the nomination, normally the nomination will die and the president will have to submit another one.

The mechanics of selection for all federal courts are similar, but the process of selection for the Supreme Court is more politicized at every stage because the Court is more powerful and visible. Its seats are fought over more intensely.

Criteria Used by Presidents

Although presidents want judges who demonstrate merit, they choose judges who meet various political criteria. Presidents normally nominate members of their party. In fact, they normally nominate active members who have served in office or contributed to candidates of the party. In the twentieth century, presidents selected members of their party 82 percent of the time (William Howard Taft) to 99 percent of the time (Woodrow Wilson).[60] This practice has become so established that senators of one party usually defer to the president and confirm the nominees of the other party.

Some presidents want judges who hold certain ideological views. President Theodore Roosevelt sought judges who opposed business monopolies and supported the rights of labor unions, and President Franklin Roosevelt sought judges who supported his New Deal policies.

President Nixon vowed to appoint judges who would change the direction of the Warren Court.

The Nixon administration was the first to recognize that it could accomplish some policy goals by selecting lower court judges as well as Supreme Court justices on the basis of ideology.[61] The Reagan administration, however, was the first to institutionalize this process and centralize it in the White House. The George H. W. Bush administration did the same. These two administrations sought judges who held conservative views and were willing to roll back the rulings of previous courts in various areas. They had candidates fill out lengthy questionnaires and then submit to daylong interviews probing their positions. They expected candidates, for example, to oppose the right to abortion, the Supreme Court's ruling establishing the right, and the Supreme Court's reasoning in the case.[62]

President George W. Bush has called for judges from the same mold as Antonin Scalia and Clarence Thomas —the most conservative justices on the conservative Rehnquist Court. His administration has followed a similar process as his father's and Reagan's and has screened candidates especially for their views on abortion, gay rights, and affirmative action.[63] These three Republican administrations have made the most systematic efforts to select judges on the basis of ideology.

Some presidents seek judges who provide more diversity on the courts. In the past, presidents chose Catholics and Jews to balance the Protestants who dominated the bench. In 1967, President Johnson chose the first black justice, Thurgood Marshall; in 1981, President Reagan chose the first woman justice, Sandra Day O'Connor. Presidents bowed to the pressure from various groups to solidify their support from these groups. Reagan, who was not an advocate of women's rights,

The Stanford Law School class of 1952 included future justices Sandra Day O'Connor (front row) and William Rehnquist (far left, back row).

pledged to appoint a woman to the Court to shore up his support among female voters. (After fulfilling this pledge, he felt no need to appoint many women to the lower federal courts.) Now Hispanics want a seat on the Supreme Court. Both parties, who see support from this growing group as crucial to future electoral success, would welcome the opportunity to appoint the first Hispanic justice.

Presidents Carter and Clinton appointed numerous women and minorities to the lower federal courts. Before Carter took office, only eight women had ever served on the federal bench.[64] Sixteen percent of Carter's appointees were women, and 21 percent were racial minorities.[65] Of Clinton's appointees, 29 percent were women and 25 percent were racial minorities.[66] These two Democratic administrations, which were not as driven by ideology, made the most concerted efforts to select judges for diversity.

President George W. Bush has also made an effort, greater than previous Republican administrations, to appoint women and minorities to the lower federal courts.[67]

Demands for diversity can reduce presidents' choices, but presidents can acquiesce to these demands and still find candidates with the desired party affiliation and ideological views. When Thurgood Marshall retired in 1991, President Bush felt obligated to nominate another black for this seat, but he wanted to nominate a conservative. He chose Clarence Thomas, a court of appeals judge. Whereas Marshall had been an ardent champion of civil rights, Thomas opposes affirmative action and other policies favored by many black leaders. Whereas Marshall was one of the most liberal justices on the Warren Court, Thomas was the most conservative justice on the Rehnquist Court, espousing a return to some positions abandoned by the Court in the 1930s. Occasionally, groups have to satisfy themselves with nothing more than the symbolic benefits from having "one of their own" on the Court. Thus many blacks get the psychological lift from having a fellow African American on the bench but not the additional satisfaction from having one who reflects their policy views. (See the box "Do Women Judges Make a Difference?")

Criteria Used by Senators

Although the Senate played a vigorous role in the appointment process in the nineteenth century, rejecting 22 of 81 presidential nominations to the Supreme Court between 1789 and 1894, it became a rubber stamp of the president's nominations in the first half of the twentieth century, rejecting only one nomination until 1968.[68] In the first half of the twentieth century, the nominees were not asked to appear at committee hearings, and their views were not scrutinized by the senators. However, the controversies over the Vietnam War

and the civil rights struggle emboldened some senators in the 1960s. In quick succession, the Senate rejected two nominations by President Johnson and two more by President Nixon. The Senate's scrutiny continued as the culture wars between traditionalists and reformers in American society—for which the strident abortion debate is only the most obvious manifestation—persisted in the decades after the 1960s. Then the Senate rejected two nominations by President Reagan.[69]

Of these six nominees, most were qualified in an objective sense.[70] Although some were accused of ethical lapses, most were rejected for ideological reasons.[71] Johnson's were deemed too liberal, while Nixon's and Reagan's were deemed too conservative.

Reagan's nomination of Robert Bork both reflected and exacerbated the tendency of the appointment process to become embroiled in the culture wars.[72] Bork had been a Yale Law School professor and, briefly, an appellate court judge. In articles and speeches, he had rejected a right to privacy, which is the basis of Court decisions allowing birth control and abortion, and he had criticized Court decisions and congressional laws advancing racial equality and sexual equality. Although Bork had legal reasons for these positions—he had not advocated that whites should discriminate against blacks, for example, only that the Court should not have forbidden them from doing so—he seemed oblivious to the practical consequences of his positions. Senator Ted Kennedy (D–Mass.) gave an inflammatory speech:

> *Robert Bork's America is a land in which women would be forced into back-alley abortions, blacks would sit at segregated lunch counters, rogue police could break down citizens' doors in midnight raids, school children could not be taught about evolution, writers and artists could be censored at the whim of the government, and the doors of the federal courts would be shut on the fingers of millions of citizens.*

Out of their fear about Bork's views, a coalition of interest groups mounted the first grassroots campaign against a judicial nomination, urging citizens to contact their senators. Bork's positions struck many Americans as extreme—one political cartoon, which appeared when daylight saving time ended in the fall, depicted Bork admonishing people, "Now, this fall remember to turn your clocks back thirty years"—and the Senate denied confirmation. This defeat, at the high-water mark of the conservative movement, signaled that moderate Americans did not want to reverse legal doctrine they considered settled (even doctrine that many had opposed when it was new). Yet conservative activists were bitterly disappointed and were vowing revenge. Two decades later, they still use this battle as a rallying cry and as a continuing justification for their efforts to influence judicial appointments.

DO WOMEN JUDGES MAKE A DIFFERENCE?

Some people argue that there should be more women judges because women are entitled to their "fair share" of all governmental offices, including judgeships. Others argue that there should be more so that women will feel that the courts represent them as well as men. Still others argue that there should be more because women hold different views than men and would therefore make different decisions.

A study of Justice Sandra Day O'Connor, the first woman on the Supreme Court, shows that although she generally votes as a conservative, she usually votes as a liberal in sex discrimination cases. Moreover, her presence on the Court apparently sensitized her male colleagues to gender issues. Most of them voted against sex discrimination more frequently after she joined the Court.[1]

Some studies find similar results for women justices on state supreme courts. Even women justices from opposite political parties support a broad array of women's rights in cases ranging from sex discrimination to child support and property settlement.[2]

But studies that compare voting patterns on issues less directly related to gender have less clear findings. Women judges appear more liberal than men in cases involving employment discrimination and racial discrimination. Perhaps the treatment they have experienced as women has made them more sympathetic to the discrimination others have faced. On the other hand, women judges do not appear more liberal or conservative than men in cases involving obscenity or criminal rights.[3]

Studies that compare the sentencing of criminal defendants in state courts find scant differences between men and women judges.[4] However, women judges do tend to sentence convicted defendants somewhat more harshly, especially black men who are repeat offenders. Apparently women judges consider these defendants more dangerous or more prone to commit new crimes after prison. Possibly women judges are influenced by the fact that these defendants are less often married and employed than other defendants.[5]

Women judges in Harris County, Texas, which includes Houston, have applied the death penalty with "greater ferocity" than their male predecessors. This county, a majority of whose judges are female, has given the death penalty to more defendants than all other states but one.[6]

But the studies comparing men and women judges find more similarities than differences. This should not be surprising, because the two sexes were subject to the same training in law school and the same socialization in the legal profession, and they became judges in the same ways as others in their jurisdiction.

Perhaps the most significant difference women judges have made has been to protect the credibility of women lawyers and witnesses. In court, men judges have occasionally made disparaging remarks about women lawyers, suggesting that they should not be in the profession—for example, calling them "lawyerettes." More frequently, male judges or lawyers have made paternalistic or personal remarks to women lawyers or witnesses, referring to them by their first name or by such terms as "young lady," "sweetie," or "honey." Or the men, in the midst of the proceedings, have commented about their perfume, clothing, or appearance.

"How does an attorney establish her authority when the judge has just described her to the entire courtroom as 'a pretty little thing'?"[7] Even if the men consider their remarks harmless compliments rather than intentional tactics, their effect is to undermine the credibility of women lawyers and witnesses in the eyes of jurors. Women judges have squelched such remarks.

1. Karen O'Connor and Jeffrey A. Segal, "Justice Sandra Day O'Connor and the Supreme Court's Reaction to Its First Female Member," in *Women, Politics, and the Constitution,* ed. Naomi B. Lynn (New York: Haworth Press, 1990), 95–104.
2. David W. Allen and Diane E. Wall, "Role Orientations and Women State Supreme Court Justices," *Judicature* 77 (1993), 156–165.
3. Sue Davis, Susan Haire, and Donald R. Songer, "Voting Behavior and Gender on the U.S. Courts of Appeals," *Judicature* 77 (1993), 129–133; Thomas G. Walker and Deborah J. Barrow, "The Diversification of the Federal Bench," *Journal of Politics* 47 (1985), 596–617.
4. John Gruhl, Cassia Spohn, and Susan Welch, "Women as Policymakers: The Case of Trial Judges," *American Journal of Political Science* 25 (1981), 308–322.
5. Darrell Steffensmeier and Chris Hebert, "Women and Men Policymakers: Does the Judge's Gender Affect the Sentencing of Criminal Defendants?" *Social Forces* 77 (1999), 1163–1196.
6. Jeffrey Toobin, "Women in Black," *New Yorker,* October 30, 2000, 48.
7. William Eich, "Gender Bias in the Courtroom: Some Participants Are More Equal than Others," *Judicature* 69 (1986), 339–343.

Observers wondered whether anyone with a record could be nominated again. Indeed, when George H. W. Bush had his first vacancy, he chose a man who had left no trail of controversial writings and speeches. David Souter, though a former New Hampshire attorney general and then a state supreme court justice, was called the "Stealth candidate" (after the bomber designed to elude radar). Souter was a private person, living alone in a house at the end of a dirt road. He had expressed few positions and made few decisions reflecting his views on constitutional doctrine. In the hearings, he refused to reveal his views. He offered a small target and won confirmation easily.

When Bush had his second vacancy, he chose a better-known conservative, Clarence Thomas, the head of the Equal Employment Opportunity Commission and then a judge on a federal court of appeals. His confirmation process became another bruising battle. The concern was over his conservative views, though much of the debate focused on allegations of sexual harassment (which will be addressed in Chapter 15). Thomas was confirmed, though only by four votes, because although most black leaders opposed him, many black citizens were pleased that a black man was nominated to replace Thurgood Marshall. This sentiment split Democratic senators, as Bush had anticipated.

When Clinton had his first vacancy, he was wary because the Republicans had vowed to avenge Bork's defeat and Thomas's near defeat. The president chose Ruth Bader Ginsburg, a court of appeals judge for thirteen years. The nomination satisfied Republicans because Ginsburg had often voted with Republicans on the bench, yet it also pleased some Democratic constituencies. Women's groups, of course, wanted more seats, and Jews, who had not had a member on the Court since 1969, also welcomed this choice.

Although Ginsburg had tied for first place in her graduating class from Columbia Law School in 1959, she was turned down for a clerkship by Justice Felix Frankfurter and for jobs by New York City law firms. The firms, just beginning to hire Jews, were not eager to hire mothers with young children either. She taught law and then served as an attorney for the American Civil Liberties Union (ACLU). In the 1970s, she argued six sex discrimination cases before the Supreme Court and won five of them.

When Clinton had his second vacancy, he was still wary of a confirmation fight, so he chose another moderate, Stephen Breyer, a judge on a federal court of appeals.

Nominations to the Supreme Court have become contentious since the 1960s partly because of the Court's activism—both liberals and conservatives have seen what the Court can do—and partly because of the divided government that has characterized our government for most years since the late 1960s. Often Republicans dominated the presidency while Democrats dominated Congress (though in the 1990s, the situation was the reverse), so both have fought over the judiciary to tip the balance. Nominations have also become contentious because of the rise of interest groups on the left and the right that scrutinize the appointments, pressuring presidents and senators on their side to nominate and vote their way.

Even nominations to the lower courts, especially to the courts of appeals, which serve as "farm teams" for future justices, have become contentious in recent decades.[73] First the Democratic Senate in the late 1980s responded to the Republican presidents' (Reagan's and Bush's) emphasis on ideology in choosing judges by blocking more nominations of conservatives than the senators had in the past. Then the Republican Senate in the 1990s retaliated against the Democratic president (Clinton) by blocking many more nominations, mostly of moderates.[74] It did not matter if the nominees were well qualified; one woman who was blocked was later appointed dean of Harvard Law School. The Republican Senate followed a pace that kept about one hundred seats vacant.[75]

Once the Republican party regained control of both the presidency and the Senate in 2003, the Democratic minority in the Senate employed the filibuster, which had previously been used to block legislation rather than appointments, against ten conservatives nominated by President George W. Bush.

This cycle of recrimination and retribution reflects the polarization of American politics today. It also demonstrates the role of interest groups. "You go out on the streets of Raleigh," Senator Jesse Helms of North Carolina once said, "and ask one hundred people: 'Do you give a damn who is on the Fourth Circuit Court of Appeals?' They'll say: 'What's that?'"[76] But political activists representing interest groups on the left and the right do know and do care, deeply, because they see the connection between the judges on the lower courts and the success of their policy goals. In elections, these political activists mobilize their party's base of voters. Thus they have influence on their party's senators, who need their enthusiastic help. They can persuade, sometimes demand, that their party's senators fight a nomination by the other party's president.[77] Then they use the controversy to enlist more members and raise more money from their supporters: "Send your contribution so that we can continue our vigilance . . . ."

Results of Selection

Judges are drawn primarily from the lower federal and state courts, the federal government, or large law firms. These established legal circles are dominated by white men, so not surprisingly, most judges have been white

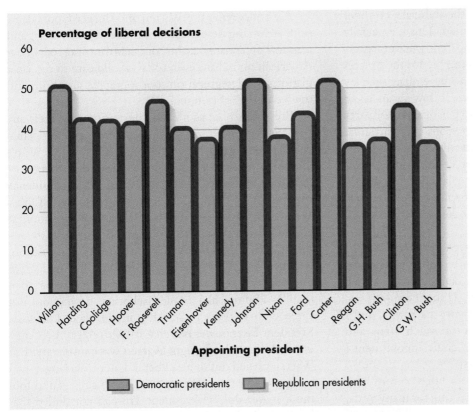

Percentage of liberal decisions

Democratic presidents

Republican presidents

FIGURE 3 ■ Percentage of Liberal Decisions Handed Down by District Court Appointees of Presidents Woodrow Wilson through George W. Bush
Appointees of Democratic and Republic presidents tend to decide cases somewhat differently.
SOURCE: Robert A. Carp, Ronald Stidham, and Kenneth L. Manning, *Judicial Process in America,* 6th ed. (Washington, D.C.: CQ Press, 2004), fig. 7-1.

men. Although recent presidents have appointed more minorities and women, the composition of the bench changes slowly because of life tenure for the judges.

Most judges have been well off; many have been quite wealthy. Seven of the current justices on the Supreme Court are millionaires (all but Kennedy and Thomas); so are 40 percent of Clinton's appointees to the lower courts, and 58 percent of Bush's.[78]

Despite the efforts to provide racial and sexual diversity, no effort has been made to represent various groups according to their proportion of the population. Throughout history, judges have come from a narrow, elite slice of society. Most have been born into families of Western European stock (especially English, Welsh, Scottish, and Irish), profess the Protestant religion (especially Episcopalian, Presbyterian, Congregationalist, and Unitarian), and are upper-middle-class or upper-class. Moreover, they have been born into families with traditions of political or even judicial service, families with prestige and connections as well as expectations for achievement.[79]

With the power to nominate judges, presidents have a tremendous opportunity to shape the courts and their decisions (see Figure 3).

Tenure of Judges

Once appointed, judges can serve for "good behavior," which means for life, unless they commit "high crimes and misdemeanors." These are not defined in the Constitution but are considered serious crimes or, possibly, political abuses. Congress can impeach and remove judges as it can presidents, but it has impeached only thirteen and removed only six. The standard of guilt—"high crimes and misdemeanors"—is vague, the punishment drastic, and the process time consuming, so Congress has been reluctant to impeach judges.

As an alternative, Congress in 1980 established other procedures to discipline lower federal court judges. Councils made up of district and appellate court judges can ask judges to resign or can prevent them from hearing cases, but they cannot actually remove them. The procedures have been used infrequently, although their existence has prompted some judges to resign before being disciplined.

Qualifications of Judges

Given the use of political criteria in selecting judges, are judges well qualified?

Political scientists who study the judiciary consider federal judges generally well qualified. This is especially true of Supreme Court justices, apparently because presidents think they will be held responsible for the justices they nominate and do not want to be embarrassed by them. Also, because presidents have so few vacancies to fill, they can confine themselves to persons of their party and political views and even to persons of a particular region, religion, race, and sex and still locate good candidates. This is less true of lower court judges. Presidents and senators (through senatorial courtesy) jointly appoint them, so both can avoid taking full responsibility for them. These judges are also less visible, so a lack of merit is not as noticeable.

Presidents do appoint some losers. President Truman put a longtime supporter on a court of appeals who was "drunk half the time "and "no damn good." When asked why he appointed the man, Truman candidly replied, "I . . . felt I owed him a favor; that's why, and I thought as a judge he couldn't do too much harm, and he didn't. . . . He wasn't the worst court appointment I ever made. By no means the worst."[80]

Sometimes presidents appoint qualified persons who later become incompetent. After serving for many years, they incur the illnesses and infirmities of old age, and perhaps one-tenth become unable to perform their job well.[81] Yet they hang on because they are allowed to serve for "good behavior." And they prevent other lawyers from filling their seats on the bench. This problem has prompted proposals for a constitutional amendment setting a term limit of eighteen years[82] or a mandatory retirement age of seventy. Either of these changes would have a substantial impact because over one-third of all Supreme Court justices have served longer than twenty years and past age seventy-five. But constitutional amendments are difficult to pass, and mandatory retirement ages are out of favor now. Further, some of the best judges have done some of their finest work late in their career.

Independence of Judges

Given the use of political criteria in selecting judges, can judges be independent on the bench? Can they decide cases as they think the law requires? Or do they feel pressure to decide cases as presidents or senators want them to?

Because judges are not dependent on presidents for renomination or senators for reconfirmation, they can be independent to a great extent. When President Nixon claimed executive privilege to keep the Watergate tapes secret, three of his appointees joined the other justices in ruling against him.[83] When President Clinton asserted presidential immunity from Paula Jones's lawsuit charging sexual harassment, both of his appointees joined the Republican justices in deciding against him.[84]

After surveying the Warren and Burger Court decisions involving desegregation, obscenity, abortion, and criminal defendants' rights, one scholar observed, "Few American politicians even today would care to run on a platform of desegregation, pornography, abortion, and the 'coddling' of criminals."[85]

Presidents have scoffed at the notion that their appointees become their pawns, even when they maintain a personal relationship (see the box "Guess Who's Coming to Dinner"). A study concluded that one-fourth of the justices deviated from their president's expectations.[86] Theodore Roosevelt placed Oliver Wendell Holmes on the Court because he thought Holmes shared his views on trusts. But in an early antitrust case, Holmes voted against Roosevelt's position, which prompted Roosevelt to declare, "I could carve out of a banana a judge with more backbone than that!"[87] Holmes had ample backbone; he just did not agree with Roosevelt's position in this case. Likewise, President Eisenhower placed Earl Warren on the Court in part because he thought Warren was a moderate. But Warren turned out to be a liberal. Later Eisenhower said his appointment of Warren was "the biggest damn fool thing I ever did."[88] President Truman concluded that "packing the Supreme Court simply can't be done. . . . I've tried it and it won't work. . . . Whenever you put a man on the Supreme Court he ceases to be your friend."[89]

Truman exaggerated, although some presidents have had trouble "packing" the courts. They have not been able to foresee the issues their appointees would face or the ways their appointees would change on the bench. Nevertheless, presidents who have made a serious effort to find candidates with similar views usually have not been disappointed.

Access to the Courts

In our litigation-prone society, many individuals and groups want courts to resolve their disputes. Whether these individuals and groups get their "day in court" depends on their case, their wealth, and the level of court involved.

Courts hear two kinds of cases. **Criminal cases** are those in which governments prosecute persons for violating laws. **Civil cases** are those in which persons sue others for denying their rights and causing them harm. Criminal defendants, of course, must appear in court. Potential civil litigants, however, often cannot get access to court.

Wealth Discrimination in Access

Although the courts are supposed to be open to all, most individuals do not have enough money to hire an attor-

As members of the Washington elite, Supreme Court justices are on the "A list" for Georgetown dinner parties. In other ways as well, they socialize with important government officials. Although the justices are granted independence from powerful politicians, their independence may be called into question when they interact.

Justice Antonin Scalia took a duck-hunting trip to Louisiana with Vice President Cheney and others in 2004. The trip was sponsored by an energy company. At the time, a case was pending before the Court that involved the vice president's energy task force, which allegedly allowed campaign contributors and energy companies to formulate the administration's energy policy. Some politicians and newspapers called for Scalia to recuse (disqualify) himself from the case, but he refused to do so—he denied having discussed the case, and he called the hunting "lousy"—and then sided with the administration in the 7–2 decision.[1] Given his views, Scalia probably would have voted this way regardless, but his participation in the case compromised his impartiality in the eyes of some people.

In the twentieth century, there were frequent contacts between justices and politicians.[2] Justice Harlan Fiske Stone took a cruise with President-elect Hoover. Then he became a member of a small group, called the "Medicine Ball Cabinet," that exercised with a medicine ball before breakfast during Hoover's term. Once Stone hit the president in the face with the ball and knocked him down. Justice Robert Jackson had been attorney general under President Franklin Roosevelt; the two continued to socialize after Roosevelt appointed him to the Court. Justice William Douglas and Roosevelt often played poker after the president named him to the Court. Presumably, neither Jackson nor Douglas discussed pending cases with the president.

Chief Justice Frederick Vinson, who had been treasury secretary under President Truman, continued to play poker with the president after being named chief justice. When Truman seized private steel mills to avert a labor strike during the Korean War, the Court ruled against him.[3] Vinson had assured the president that the Court would rule in his favor, but the chief justice was unable to deliver the votes, and the president was embarrassed. To make amends, Justice Hugo Black, who had written the Court's opinion, invited Truman to a party with the justices at Black's home. During the party, Truman turned to Black and said, "Hugo, I don't much care for your law, but by golly, this bourbon is good!"[4]

Justice Antonin Scalia (center) and Federal Reserve head Alan Greenspan socialize at the home of Secretary of Defense Donald Rumsfeld.

It is more problematic when the justices discuss policies with the president than when they merely socialize with him. Justice Abe Fortas, a close confidante of President Johnson, advised him on the Vietnam War. Chief Justice Warren Burger felt so comfortable with President Nixon that he stopped at the White House unexpectedly to congratulate him for bombing Cambodia during the Vietnam War. Yet periodically, cases involving the war or the protest against the war came to the Court.[5]

Social and political contacts between the justices and other officials are possible, perhaps even likely, because most justices have political backgrounds and were appointed by political officials for political purposes. In recent decades, however, the public has become more sensitive to conflicts of interest and to appearances of conflicts of interest.

1. *Cheney v. U.S. District Court,* 159 LEd.2d 459 (2004). For Scalia's justification for not recusing himself, see 158 LEd.2d 225 (2004).
2. The rest of this box is based substantially on Jeffrey Rosen, "The Justice Who Came to Dinner," *New York Times,* February 1, 2004, WK1.
3. *Youngstown Sheet and Tube v. Sawyer,* 343 U.S. 579 (1952).
4. Jeffrey Rosen, "The Justice Who Came to Dinner," *New York Times,* February 1, 2004, WK1.
5. Yet Burger did cast his vote against the president in the Watergate tapes case.

ney and pay the costs necessary to pursue a case. Only corporations, wealthy individuals, or seriously injured victims suing corporations or wealthy individuals do. (Seriously injured victims with a strong case can obtain an attorney by agreeing to pay the attorney a sizable portion of what they win in their suit.) In addition, a small number of poor individuals supported by legal aid programs can pursue a case.

The primary expense is paying an attorney. New lawyers in law firms charge approximately $100 an hour; established partners may charge several times that.[90] Other expenses include various fees for filing the case, summoning jurors, paying witnesses, and also lost income from missed work due to numerous meetings with the attorney and hearings in court.

Even if individuals have enough money to initiate a suit, the disparity continues in court. Those with more money can develop a full case, whereas others must proceed with a skeletal case that is far less likely to persuade judges or jurors. Our legal system, according to one judge, "is divided into two separate and unequal systems of justice: one for the rich, in which the courts take limitless time to examine, ponder, consider, and deliberate over hundreds of thousands of bits of evidence and days of testimony, and hear elaborate, endless appeals and write countless learned opinions" and one for the nonrich, in which the courts provide "turnstile justice."[91] (During the week that one judge spent conducting the preliminary hearing to determine whether there was sufficient evidence to require O. J. Simpson to stand trial for murdering his ex-wife and her friend, other judges in Los Angeles disposed of 474 preliminary hearings for less wealthy defendants.) Consequently, many individuals are discouraged from pursuing a case in the first place.

Interest Groups Help in Access

Interest groups, with more resources than most individuals, help some individuals gain access to the courts. The groups sponsor and finance these individuals' cases. Of course, the groups do not act purely out of altruism. They choose cases that they hope will advance their goals. An attorney for the American Civil Liberties Union (ACLU), which takes cases as a way to prod judges to protect constitutional rights, admitted that the criminal defendants the ACLU represents "sometimes are pretty scurvy little creatures, but what they are doesn't matter a whole hell of a lot. It's the principle that we're going to be able to use these people for that's important."

Some liberal groups—especially civil liberties organizations such as the ACLU, civil rights organizations such as the National Association for the Advancement of Colored People (NAACP), environmental groups such as the Sierra Club, and consumer and safety groups

Interest groups' financial support can cover more than their clients' legal bills. When Paula Jones sued President Clinton for sexual harassment, Jones's team, funded by conservative groups, had her made over to appear more appealing.

such as Ralph Nader's organizations—use litigation as a primary tactic. Other groups use it as an occasional tactic. In the 1980s and 1990s, some conservative groups began to use litigation as aggressively as these liberal groups. The Rutherford Institute, for example, arose to help persons who claimed that their religious rights were infringed, representing children who were forbidden from reading the Bible on the school bus or praying in the school cafeteria. The institute also funded Paula Jones's suit against President Clinton.

Interest groups have become ubiquitous in the judicial process. About half of all Supreme Court cases involve a liberal or conservative interest group,[92] and many lower court cases do as well. Even so, interest groups can help only a handful of the individuals who lack the resources to finance their cases.

Proceeding through the Courts

Cases normally start in a district court. Individuals who lose have a right to have their case decided by one higher court to determine whether there was a miscarriage of justice. They normally appeal to a court of appeals. Individuals who lose at this level have no further right to have their case decided by another court, but they can appeal to the Supreme Court. However, the Court can exercise almost unlimited discretion in choosing cases to review. No matter how important or urgent an issue seems, the Court does not have to hear it.

Litigants who appeal to the Supreme Court normally file a petition for a **writ of** *certiorari* (Latin for "made more certain"). The Court grants the writ—agrees to hear the case—if four of the nine justices vote to do so. The rationale for this "rule of four" is that a substantial number, but not necessarily a majority, of the justices should deem the case important enough to review. Generally, the Court agrees to review a case when the justices think an issue has not been resolved satisfactorily or consistently by the lower courts.

From over seven thousand petitions each year, the Court selects fewer than one hundred to hear, thus exercising considerable discretion. The oft-spoken threat "We're going to appeal all the way to the Supreme Court" is usually just bluster. Likewise, the notion that the Court is "the court of last resort" is misleading. Most cases never get beyond the district courts or courts of appeals.

That the Supreme Court grants so few writs means that the Court has tremendous power to control its docket and therefore to determine which policies to review. It also means that the lower courts have considerable power because they serve as the court of last resort for most cases.

Deciding Cases

In deciding cases, judges need to interpret statutes and the Constitution and determine whether to follow precedents. In the process, they make law.

Interpreting Statutes

In deciding cases, judges start with statutes—laws passed by legislatures. If statutes are ambiguous, judges need to interpret them in order to apply them to their cases.

When statutes are ambiguous, judges try to ascertain the legislators' intent in passing them. They scrutinize the legislators' remarks and debates. But they often find that different members said different things, even contradictory things, and most members said nothing about the provisions in question. This gives judges considerable leeway in construing statutes.

For example, Congress passed the **Americans with Disabilities Act** to protect people from discrimination in employment and public accommodations (businesses open to the public, such as stores, restaurants, hotels, and health care facilities). The act applies to people who have a "physical impairment" that "substantially limits" any of their "major life activities." The statute does not define these terms. Thus the courts have had to do so, and in the process they have determined the scope of the act.

When a dentist refused to fill a cavity for a woman with HIV, she sued, claiming discrimination under this act. The Supreme Court agreed by a 5–4 vote.[93] The majority concluded that HIV was a physical impairment, although the woman was in the early stages and was not prevented from performing any activity yet. In concluding that HIV was a physical impairment, the majority considered what life activities it would limit and how important those activities are. The majority

© Zigy Kaluzny/Getty Images/Stone

Although Congress wrote the Americans with Disabilities Act, the Supreme Court has determined what it means through the justices' interpretations of the statute.

acknowledged that HIV would limit, for example, the important life activity of reproduction, because the disease could infect her fetus if she got pregnant. (Of course, HIV would also affect other important life activities as well.) The dissenters denied that reproduction is a major life activity, and they denied that HIV in its early stages limits reproduction. They interpreted the statute to apply to repetitive activities that are essential for daily existence rather than important activities that rarely, if ever, occur in a person's life.

When twin sisters who were severely nearsighted were denied the opportunity to become global airline pilots, they sued. This time the Court ruled the opposite by a 7–2 vote.[94] Because their condition could be corrected with glasses, they were not limited in any major life activity. Although they could not get jobs as global pilots, they could get jobs as regional pilots. The majority observed that 100 million Americans have impaired vision that requires glasses (and 28 million have impaired hearing and 50 million have high blood pressure), and they concluded that Congress could not have intended the act to apply to so many people.[95]

When a woman developed carpal tunnel syndrome on the assembly line at a manufacturing plant, she sued, claiming that the company did not make the reasonable accommodation—in this situation, give her a job that did not require repetitive manual labor—that it was required to under the act. She said her condition limited

Supreme Court clerks are recent graduates of law schools, usually the top students from the most prestigious universities, who serve for one year. Each justice can hire four clerks to help read petitions asking the Court to hear new cases and to help research statutes and precedents in pending cases.

© Lynn Johnson/Aurora

her major life activities of performing manual tasks at work and at home, including lifting, sweeping, and gardening; playing with her children; and driving long distances. The Court unanimously ruled that these are not major life activities.[96] For the act to apply, the activities must be of central importance to most people's daily lives—for example, seeing, hearing, or walking.

Thus although the Court interpreted the act broadly when it covered persons with HIV, it interpreted the act narrowly when it refused to cover workers with less serious ailments. In these cases, the Court protected employers from having to make individual arrangements for many employees. From these rulings it should be evident that judges can make law when they interpret statutes.

Interpreting the Constitution

After interpreting statutes, judges determine whether they are constitutional. Or if the cases involve actions of government officials rather than statutes, judges determine whether the actions are constitutional. For either, they need to interpret the Constitution.

Compared to constitutions of other countries, our Constitution is short and therefore necessarily ambiguous. It speaks in broad principles rather than in narrow details. The Fifth Amendment states that persons shall not be "deprived of life, liberty, or property without due process of law." The Fourteenth Amendment states that persons shall not be denied "the equal protection of the laws." What is "due process of law"? "Equal protection of the laws"? Generally, the former means that people should be treated fairly and the latter means that they should be treated equally. But what is fairly?

Equally? These are broad principles that need to be interpreted in specific cases.

Sometimes the Constitution uses relative terms. The Fourth Amendment provides that persons shall be "secure . . . against unreasonable searches and seizures." What are "unreasonable" searches and seizures? At other times the Constitution uses absolute terms. These appear more clear-cut but are deceptive. The First Amendment provides that there shall be "no law . . . abridging the freedom of speech." Does "no law" mean literally no law? Then what about a law making it a crime to falsely shout "Fire!" in a crowded theater? Whether relative or absolute, the language needs to be interpreted in specific cases.

Occasionally, politicians assert that judges ought to be "strict constructionists"; that is, they ought to interpret the Constitution "strictly." This is nonsense. Judges cannot possibly interpret ambiguous language strictly.

When the language does not give sufficient guidance, some judges believe they should follow the intentions of the framers.[97] Yet these intentions are difficult to ascertain. Fifty-five delegates attended the Constitutional Convention and many more participated in state ratifying conventions. The historical sources do not indicate what most delegates thought about most provisions.[98] And of course, the delegates represented American citizens who undoubtedly had their own views.

Other judges believe they need not follow the intentions of the framers. They maintain that the Constitution was designed to be flexible and adaptable to changes in society.[99] These judges try to distill the essential meaning from the constitutional provisions and apply this meaning to contemporary situations. The Fourteenth Amendment's equal protection clause does not refer to schools, and its framers did not intend it to apply to schools. However, they did intend it to grant blacks greater equality than before, and therefore the Court applied this meaning to segregated schools. Then the Court applied it to other segregated facilities, then to other racial minorities, and then to women. In short, the Court extracted the essential meaning of equality and extended it to prohibit discrimination in many situations. In this way, the Court put into practice Chief Justice Marshall's statement that the Constitution is "intended to endure for ages to come."[100]

When judges interpret the Constitution, they exercise discretion. As former Chief Justice Charles Hughes candidly acknowledged, "We are under a constitution, but the Constitution is what the Supreme Court says it is."[101]

Restraint and Activism

All judges exercise discretion, but not all engage in policymaking to the same extent. Some, classified as restrained, are less willing to declare laws or actions of government officials unconstitutional, whereas others, classified as activist, are more willing to do so.

Restrained judges believe that the judiciary is the least democratic branch because (federal) judges are appointed for life rather than elected and reelected. Consequently, they should defer to the other branches, whose officials are elected. That is, they should accept the laws or actions of the other branches rather than substitute their own views instead. They should be wary of "government by judiciary." "Courts are not the only agency of government that must be presumed to have the capacity to govern," Justice Harlan Stone said. "For the removal of unwise laws from the statute books, appeal lies not to the courts, but to the ballot and the processes of democratic government."[102] Restrained judges also believe that the judiciary is the least capable branch because judges are generalists who lack the expertise and resources that legislators and bureaucrats use to make policy.

Restrained judges further maintain that the power to declare laws unconstitutional is more effective if it is used sparingly. Justice Louis Brandeis concluded that "the most important thing we do is not doing."[103] That is, the most important thing judges do is declare laws constitutional and thereby build up political capital for the occasional times that they declare laws unconstitutional.

Ultimately, restrained judges contend that showing appropriate deference and following proper procedures are more important than reaching desired results. When a friend taking leave of Justice Oliver Wendell Holmes one morning said, "Well, Mr. Justice, I hope you do justice today," Holmes replied, "My job is not to do justice but to follow the law." Justice Harry Blackmun, appointed by President Nixon, reflected this view in a capital punishment case:

> *I yield to no one in the depth of my distaste, antipathy, and, indeed, abhorrence for the death penalty, with all its aspects of physical distress and fear and of moral judgment exercised by finite minds. That distaste is buttressed by a belief that capital punishment serves no useful purpose that can be demonstrated. For me, it violates childhood's training and life's experiences, and is not compatible with the philosophical convictions I have been able to develop. It is antagonistic to any sense of "reverence for life." Were I a legislator, I would vote against the death penalty.*

But as a judge, he voted for it.[104]

Activist judges are less concerned with showing appropriate deference and following proper procedures. They seem more outraged at injustice. Chief Justice Earl Warren said that the courts' responsibility was "to see if justice truly has been done." He asked lawyers who emphasized technical procedures during oral arguments, "Yes, yes, yes, but is it right? Is it good?"[105]

Activist judges do not believe that the judiciary is the least democratic branch. Warren, who had served as governor of California, saw that the legislators, though elected, were often the captives of special interests. As a result of these attitudes, activist judges have a more flexible and more pragmatic view of separation of powers. District court judge Frank Johnson, who issued sweeping orders for Alabama's prisons and mental hospitals, replied to critics, "I didn't ask for any of these cases. In an ideal society, all of these . . . decisions should be made by those to whom we have entrusted these responsibilities. But when governmental institutions fail to make these . . . decisions in a manner which comports with the Constitution, the federal courts have a duty to remedy the violation."[106]

Activist judges do not believe that the power to declare laws unconstitutional is more effective if it is used sparingly. Rather, they claim that the power is enhanced if it is used frequently—essentially, they urge their colleagues to "use it or lose it"—because the public gets accustomed to it.

Thus judicial restraint and judicial activism are belief systems and role concepts that people think judges should adopt and follow when they decide cases. Some judges tend to be restrained, while others tend to be activist; most fall somewhere in between.

In response to the liberal activism of the Warren Court, conservative officials and commentators insisted that judges should adhere to judicial restraint. But as the number of conservative justices increased, a pattern of conservative activism by the Rehnquist Court emerged as well. Although the Rehnquist Court accepted some liberal laws, it struck down others, including laws implementing gun registration, affirmative action, legislative districts that help racial minorities elect their candidates, and governmental policies that help religious minorities practice their religion. The Court also invalidated a series of congressional laws affecting the states, including the Violence Against Women Act.

Indeed, conservatives and liberals have practiced restraint or activism according to the political climate at the time. In the late nineteenth and early twentieth centuries, the Court was conservative and activist; it struck down regulations on business. After the switch in the late 1930s, the Court was liberal and restrained; it upheld regulations on business. Then in the 1950s and 1960s, the Court was liberal and activist as it struck down restrictions on individual rights. Nowadays the Court sometimes is conservative and activist.

Although these are useful concepts, we should not make too much of them. It usually is more important to know whether a judge is conservative or liberal than whether the judge purports to be restrained or activist. Political science research shows that justices' votes reflect their ideology: conservative justices vote for the conservative position, and liberal justices vote for the liberal position in most cases. Sometimes justices claim to be restrained, but usually their decision—allowing a

Justice Clarence Thomas shares a laugh with his clerks in his chambers.

particular law or policy to continue—produces the conservative or liberal outcome they prefer.[107] Thus some political scientists conclude that "judicial restraint" is little more than "a cloak for the justices' policy preferences."[108] That is, it enables them to proclaim their "restraint" while actually voting on the basis of their ideology—without ever admitting this to the public. We should be skeptical when we hear judges or politicians using these terms, whether touting their "restraint" to pacify the public or deriding opponents' "activism" to inflame the public.

Following Precedents

In interpreting statutes and the Constitution, judges are expected to follow precedents established by their court or higher courts in previous cases. This is the rule of *stare decisis* (Latin for "stand by what has been decided").

When in 1962 the Supreme Court held unconstitutional a New York law that required public school students to recite a nondenominational prayer every day, the ruling became a precedent.[109] The following year, the Court held unconstitutional a Baltimore school board policy that required students to recite Bible verses.[110] The Court followed the precedent it had set the year before. In 1980, the Court held unconstitutional a Tennessee law that forced public schools to post the Ten Commandments in all classrooms.[111] Although this law differed from the previous ones in that it did not require recitation, the majority concluded that it reflected the same goal—to use the public schools to promote the Christian religion—so it violated the same principle, separation of church and state. In 1992, the Court ruled that clergy cannot offer prayers at graduation ceremonies for public schools.[112] Although this situation, too, differed from the previous ones in that it

did not occur every day at school, the majority reasoned that it, too, reflected the same goal and violated the same principle. Finally, in 2000, the Court ruled that schools cannot use, or allow clergy or students to use, the public address system to offer prayers before high school football games.[113] Thus for almost four decades, the Court followed the precedent it originally set when it initially addressed this issue.

Stare decisis provides stability in the law. If different judges decided similar cases in different ways, the law would be unpredictable, even chaotic. "Stare decisis," Justice Brandeis said, "is usually the wise policy; because in most matters it is more important that the applicable rule of law be settled than that it be settled right."[114] Stare decisis also promotes equality in the law. If dif-

Before the Supreme Court ruled that official prayers in public schools are unconstitutional, the practice was common. Here children pray in a Washington, D. C. school.

452　PART THREE ■ *Institutions*

ferent judges decided similar cases in different ways, the courts would appear discriminatory toward some litigants.

However, even when judges try to follow precedents, sometimes they have discretion in choosing which ones to follow. There might not be any that are controlling but several that are relevant, and these might point in contrary directions. In 1996, the justices weighed government regulation of indecent programming on cable television. They had precedents that governed broadcast television, telephones, and bookstores. But as Justice Breyer observed, none of these really paralleled cable television, which looks like broadcast television but uses telephone lines rather than airwaves to transmit its signals. Thus he was uncertain which precedents to use. Apparently, the others were uncertain also, as the nine justices split three ways and wrote six opinions while upholding one section and striking down two other sections of the law.[115]

Making Law

Many judges deny that they make law. They say that it is already there, that they merely "find" it or, occasionally, "interpret" it with their education and experience. They imply that they use a mechanical process. Justice Owen Roberts wrote for the majority that struck down a New Deal act in 1936:

It is sometimes said that the Court assumes a power to overrule . . . the people's representatives. This is a misconception. The Constitution is the supreme law of the land. . . . All legislation must conform to the principles it lays down. When an act of Congress is appropriately challenged in the courts as not conforming to the constitutional mandate, the judicial branch of government has only one duty—to lay . . . the Constitution . . . beside the statute . . . and to decide whether the latter squares with the former.[116]

In other words, the Constitution itself dictates the decision.

However, by now it should be apparent that judges do not use a mechanical process and that they do exercise discretion. They *do* make law—when they interpret statutes, when they interpret the Constitution, and when they determine which precedents to follow or disregard.[117]

In doing so, they reflect their own political preferences. As Justice Benjamin Cardozo said, "We may try to see things as objectively as we please. Nonetheless, we can never see them with any eyes except our own."[118] That is, judges are human beings with their own perceptions and attitudes and even prejudices. They do not, and cannot, shed these the moment they put on their robes.

But to say that judges make law is not to say that they make law as legislators do. Judges make law less directly. They make it in the process of resolving disputes brought to them. They usually make it by telling governments what they cannot do, rather than what they must do and how they must do it. And judges make law less freely. They start not with clean slates but with established principles embodied in statutes, the Constitution, and precedents. They are expected to follow these principles. If they deviate from them, they are expected to explain their reasons, and they are subjected to criticism within the legal profession.

Deciding Cases at the Supreme Court

The Supreme Court's term runs from October through June. Early in the term, the justices decide which cases to hear, and by the end of the term, they will have decided how to resolve those cases.

After the Court agrees to hear a case, litigants submit written arguments. These "briefs" identify the issues and marshal the evidence—statutes, constitutional provisions, and precedents—for their side. (The word *briefs* is a misnomer, as some run to more than one hundred pages.) Often interest groups and governments, whether federal, state, or local, submit briefs to support one side. These *amicus curiae* ("friend of the court") briefs present additional evidence or perspectives not included in the litigants' briefs. Major cases can prompt many briefs. A pair of affirmative action cases from the University of Michigan in 2003 prompted a record 102 briefs.[119]

Several weeks after receiving the briefs, the Court holds oral arguments. The justices gather in the robing room, put on their black robes, and file into the courtroom, taking their places at the half-hexagon bench. The chief justice sits in the center, with the associate justices extending out in order of seniority. The crier gavels the courtroom to attention and announces:

The Honorable, the Chief Justice and Associate Justices of the Supreme Court of the United States! Oyez, oyez, oyez! [Give ear, give ear, give ear!] All persons having business before the Honorable, the Supreme Court of the United States are admonished to draw near and give attention, for the Court is now sitting. God save the United States and this Honorable Court.

The chief justice calls the case. The lawyers present their arguments, although the justices interrupt with questions whenever they want. When Thurgood Marshall, as the counsel for the NAACP before becoming a justice, argued one school desegregation case, he was interrupted 127 times. The justices ask about the facts of the case: "What happened when the defendant . . . ?" They ask about relevant precedents that appear to support or rebut the lawyers' arguments: "Can you distinguish this case from . . . ?" They ask about hypothetical scenarios: "What if the police officer . . . ?"

Chief Justice William Rehnquist in the Court's robing room.

© JASON REED/Reuters/CORBIS

These questions help the justices determine what is at stake, how a ruling would relate to existing doctrine, and how a ruling might govern future situations. They are experienced at pinning lawyers down. Chief Justice Rehnquist, who was affable toward his colleagues, was tough on the lawyers appearing before him. When asked whether the lawyers were nervous, he replied, "I assume they're all nervous—they should be."[120] Occasionally, one faints on the spot.

The chief justice allots half an hour per side. When time expires, a red light flashes on the lectern, and the chief justice halts any lawyer who continues. Rehnquist, who valued efficiency and punctuality, cut lawyers off in midsentence when their time was up.

The oral arguments identify and clarify the major points of the case for any justices who did not read the briefs, and they assess the potential impact of the possible rulings. The oral arguments also serve as a symbol: They give litigants a chance to be heard in open court, which encourages litigants to feel that the eventual ruling is legitimate. However, the oral arguments rarely sway the justices, except occasionally when a lawyer for one side is especially effective.

The Court holds Friday conferences to make a tentative decision and assign the opinion. The decision affirms or reverses the lower court decision; it indicates who wins and who loses. The opinion explains why. It expresses principles of law and establishes precedents for the future. It tells judges on lower courts how to resolve similar cases.

A portrait of Chief Justice John Marshall presides over the conference. To ensure secrecy, no one is present but the justices. They begin with handshakes. (During his tenure, Chief Justice Marshall suggested that they begin with a drink whenever the weather was rainy. But even when it was sunny, Marshall sometimes announced, "Our jurisdiction extends over so large a territory that the doctrine of chances makes it certain that it must be raining somewhere."[121] Perhaps this accounts for his extraordinary success in persuading his colleagues to adopt his views.) Then the justices get down to business. The chief justice initiates the discussion of the case. He asserts what he thinks the issues are and how they ought to be decided, and he casts a vote. The associate justices follow in order of seniority. Although the conference traditionally featured give-and-take among the justices, discussion was perfunctory under Rehnquist, and the conference became a series of quick votes.[122]

The Court reaches a tentative decision based on these votes. If the chief justice is in the majority, he assigns the writing of the opinion to himself or another justice. If he is not in the majority, the most senior associate justice in the majority assigns it. This custom reveals the chief justice's power. Although his vote counts the same as each associate justice's vote, his authority to assign the opinion can determine what the opinion says. He knows that certain colleagues will lay down broad principles and use strong language whereas others will hew closely to specific facts of the case and use guarded language.

Before Marshall became chief justice, each justice wrote his own opinion. But Marshall realized that one opinion from the Court would carry more weight. He often convinced the other justices to forsake their opinions for his. As a result, he wrote almost half of the more than eleven hundred opinions the Court handed down during his thirty-four years. Recent chief justices have assigned most opinions—82 to 86 percent—but have written just slightly more than their share—12 to 14 percent.[123] Some Court watchers believe that Rehnquist downplayed his conservative views after he became chief justice to stay in the majority and retain control of the opinion.[124]

After the conference, the Court produces the opinion. This is the most time-consuming stage in the process. After Justice Brandeis died, researchers found in his files the thirty-seventh draft of an opinion he had written but still had not been satisfied with.

Because the justices are free to change their vote anytime until the decision is announced, the justice assigned the opinion tries to write it to command support of the justices in the original majority and possibly even some in the original minority. The writer circulates the draft among the others, who suggest revisions. The writer circulates more drafts. These go back and forth as the justices attempt to persuade or cajole, nudge or push their colleagues toward their position.

Sometimes the outcome changes between the tentative vote in the conference and the final vote in the decision. According to Justice Harry Blackmun's notes, eleven times during his last three years, one or more justices switched sides to fashion a new majority from the original minority. In the case involving graduation prayers, Justice Anthony Kennedy was writing the majority opinion to allow such prayers, but he was unable to persuade himself. He abandoned the majority and joined the minority, thus making it the eventual majority.[125]

These inner workings underscore the politicking among the justices. Justice William Brennan, a liberal activist on the Warren and Burger Courts, was a gregarious and charming Irish American who was well liked by his colleagues. After drafting an opinion, he sent his clerks to other justices' clerks to learn whether their justices had any objections. Then he tried to redraft it to satisfy them. If they still had qualms, he went to their offices and tried to persuade them. If necessary, he compromised. He didn't want "to be 100% principled and lose by one vote," a law professor observed.[126] Brennan was so adept at persuasion that some scholars consider him "the best coalition builder ever to sit on the Supreme Court."[127] In fact, some say the Warren and Burger Courts should have been called the Brennan Court.

Justice Scalia, a conservative activist on the Rehnquist Court, is a brilliant and gregarious Italian American who, when appointed by President Reagan, was expected to dominate his colleagues and become the leader of the Court. Yet he has not fulfilled this expectation. He has been brash and imprudent, appearing to take more pleasure in insulting his colleagues than in persuading them.[128] In a case in which Justice Sandra Day O'Connor, also conservative but more cautious, did not want to go as far in limiting abortion rights as he did, Scalia wrote that her arguments "cannot be taken seriously."[129] In another case in which Chief Justice Rehnquist, who usually votes with Scalia, voted opposite him, Scalia wrote that his arguments were "implausible" and suggested that any lawyer who advised his client as Rehnquist urged should be "disbarred."[130] As a result, Scalia has not been as effective in forging a consensus among conservatives as Brennan was among liberals.

Due to the maneuvering and politicking, opinions are often compromises among justices in the majority. As Justice Stone explained to a law professor who criticized one of his opinions:

I [would] have preferred to have written your opinion [rather] than the one which will actually appear in the books. Had I done so, I [would] have been in a minority of two or three, instead of a majority of six. Someone else would have written the opinion [of the Court]. . . . I proceed upon the theory . . . that the large objectives should be kept constantly in mind and reached by whatever road is open, provided only that untenable distinctions are not taken, and that I am not in the process, committed incidentally to the doctrine of which I disapprove or which would hinder the Court's coming out ultimately in the right place.[131]

If the opinion does not command the support of some justices in the original majority, they write a concurring opinion. This indicates that they agree with the decision but not the reasons for it. Meanwhile, the justices in the minority write a dissenting opinion. This indicates that they do not agree even with the decision. Both concurring and dissenting opinions weaken the force of the majority opinion. They question its validity, and they suggest that at a different time with different justices, there might be a different ruling. Chief Justice Hughes used to say that a dissenting opinion is "an appeal to the brooding spirit of the law, to the intelligence of a future day."[132]

Unlike the high courts of many other countries, which do not report any dissents, the United States Supreme Court routinely does, and the American people normally accept the existence of such disagreements about the law.[133] But too many dissents indicate a fractious Court. One-third of the Rehnquist Court's cases were decided by a 5–4 vote in 2001, possibly the highest proportion ever.[134]

Finally, the Court's print shop in its basement prints the opinions, thus preventing the leaks that might occur if the opinions were printed elsewhere. Then the Court announces its decisions and distributes the opinions in public session.

The job of a justice is unlike that of other political officials. Even after three decades of experience, Justice William Brennan often ate at his desk so he could finish his work.

"My dissenting opinion will be brief. You're all full of crap."

The Power of the Courts

Alexis de Tocqueville, the French aristocrat who traveled throughout the United States in the 1830s, observed, "Scarcely any political question arises in the United States that is not resolved, sooner or later, into a judicial question."[135] Because Americans are more inclined than others to bring suits, courts have many opportunities to wield power. The courts have been able to capitalize on these opportunities because they interpret the Constitution, which is revered by the people, and they enjoy relative (though not absolute) independence from the political pressures on the other branches.

The use of judicial review and the use of political checks against the courts reveal the extent of the power of the courts.

Use of Judicial Review

Judicial review—the authority to declare laws or actions of government officials unconstitutional—is the tool the courts use to wield power. When the courts declare a law or action unconstitutional, they not only void that law or action, but they also might put the issue on the public agenda, and they might speed up or slow down the pace of change in the government's policy.

When the Supreme Court declared Texas's abortion law unconstitutional in *Roe* v. *Wade* in 1973, the Court put the abortion issue on the public agenda.[136] It had not been a raging controversy before the decision.

The Court used judicial review as a catalyst to speed up change in the desegregation cases in the 1950s. At the time, President Eisenhower was not inclined to act, and Congress was not able to act because both houses were dominated by senior southerners who, as commit-

tee chairs, bottled up civil rights legislation. The Court broke the logjam.

The Court used judicial review as a brake to slow down change in the business regulation cases in the first third of the twentieth century. The Court delayed some policies for several decades.

Judicial review, an American contribution to government, was for years unique to this country. It is now used in numerous other countries, but not as extensively or as effectively as in the United States.

The Supreme Court alone has struck down over 150 provisions of federal laws and over 1,200 provisions of state and local laws.[137] The number of laws struck down, however, is not a true measure of the importance of judicial review. Instead, the ever-present threat of review has prevented the legislatures from enacting many laws that they feared would be struck down.

By using judicial review to play a strong role in government, the Court has contradicted the Founders' expectation that the judiciary would always be the weakest branch. Usually it has been the weakest branch, but occasionally it has been stronger. Arguably, these times include some years during the early nineteenth century, when the Court established national supremacy; the late nineteenth century and early twentieth century, when the Court thwarted efforts to regulate business; and the 1950s and 1960s, when the Court extended civil liberties and rights.

Nevertheless, the extent to which the Court has played a strong role in government should not be exaggerated. The Court has not exercised judicial review over a wide range of issues; in each of its three eras, it has exercised review over one dominant issue and paid relatively little attention to other pending issues. Moreover, the one dominant issue has always involved domestic policy. Traditionally, the Court has been reluctant to intervene in foreign policy.[138]

And when the Court has addressed an issue, it has been cautious. Of the provisions of congressional laws held unconstitutional, more than half were voided more than four years after they had been passed, and more than one-fourth were voided more than twelve years after they had been passed.[139] These laws were voided after many members of Congress who had supported them had left Congress. The Court confronted Congress when it was safer to do so.

Use of Political Checks against the Courts

Although the courts enjoy relative independence from the political pressures on the other branches, they do not have absolute independence. Because they are part of the political process, they are subject to some political checks, which limit the extent to which they can wield judicial review.

Checks by the Executive

Presidents can impose the most effective check. If they dislike judges' rulings, they can appoint new judges when vacancies occur. Many appointees remain on the bench two decades after their president has left the White House.[140] Even so, some appointees are reluctant to reverse established precedents, as Presidents Reagan and Bush discovered.

Presidents and state and local executives, such as governors and mayors and even school officials and police officers, can refuse to enforce courts' rulings. School officials have disobeyed decisions requiring desegregation and invalidating class prayers. Police officers have ignored decisions invalidating some kinds of searches and interrogations.

Yet executives who refuse to enforce courts' rulings risk losing public support, unless the public also opposes the rulings. Even President Nixon complied when the Court ordered him to turn over the incriminating Watergate tapes.

Checks by the Legislature

Congress and the state legislatures can overturn courts' rulings by adopting constitutional amendments. They have done so four times (with the Eleventh, Fourteenth, Sixteenth, and Twenty-sixth Amendments).[141] They can also overturn courts' rulings by passing new statutes.

When courts base decisions on their interpretations of statutes, or when they make decisions in the absence of statutes, legislatures can pass new statutes, with clear language, that negate the decisions. The Supreme Court ruled in 1986 that the Air Force did not have to allow an ordained rabbi to wear his yarmulke with his uniform.[142] The next year, Congress passed a statute permitting military personnel to wear some religious apparel while in uniform. From 1967 through 1990, Congress passed statutes to negate 121 Supreme Court rulings.[143]

Legislatures can refuse to implement courts' rulings, especially when money is necessary to implement them. The legislators simply do not appropriate the money.

Although these checks are the most common, Congress has invoked others, though only rarely. It can alter the structure of the lower federal courts, it can limit the appellate jurisdiction of the Supreme Court, and it can impeach and remove judges.

As a result of occasional checks or threatened checks, the courts have developed a strong sense of self-restraint to ensure self-preservation. This, more than the checks themselves, limits their use of judicial review.

Conclusion: Are the Courts Responsive?

Courts tend to reflect the views of the public. Studies comparing 185 Supreme Court rulings from the mid-1930s through the mid-1990s with public opinion polls on the same issues found that the rulings mirrored the polls in about 60 percent of the cases.[144] The justices reflected the views of the public about as often as elected officials did. Thus the justices either responded to the public or, having been appointed by political officials chosen by the public, simply reflected the views of the public as political officials did.

Research shows that citizens know little about the cases (and less about the judges; more adults can identify the character names of the Three Stooges than a single justice on the Supreme Court),[145] but they do remember controversial decisions and they do recognize broad trends. A study of public opinion toward the Supreme Court from 1966 to 1984 found that the public became more negative when the Court upheld more criminal rights and struck down more congressional statutes.[146] This opinion pressured presidents and members of Congress to appoint justices with different views. Thus these officials responded to the public, and ultimately they got the Court to respond to the public.

Although the courts are directly or indirectly responsive to the public, the Founders did not intend for them to be very responsive. The Founders gave judges life tenure so that the courts would be relatively independent of both officials and the public.

Indeed, the courts are more independent of political pressures than the other branches are. This enables them, in the words of appellate court judge Learned Hand, to stand as a bulwark against the "pressure of public panic." They can provide a "sober second thought."[147]

The courts can even protect the rights of various minorities—racial minorities, religious minorities, political dissidents, and criminal defendants—against the demands and the wrath of the majority. Chapters 14 and 15 will show how courts extended civil liberties and rights to unpopular individuals and groups who lacked clout with the executive and legislative branches and support from the public. Yet protecting the rights of these individuals and groups has historically been the exception rather than the rule. It was typical of the Warren Court era and to some extent the Burger Court era, but it was not typical of most years before and has not been typical of most years since.

The courts are part of the political process and are sensitive to others in the process, especially to the president, Congress, and the public. Although they enjoy relative independence, they are not immune to political pressure. They have therefore "learned to be a political institution and to behave accordingly" and have "seldom lagged far behind or forged far ahead" of public opinion.[148]

O'Connor Plunges into the Political Thicket

In the disputed presidential election of 2000, a majority of the Supreme Court, including Justice Sandra Day O'Connor, intervened aggressively and decisively when prudence counseled restraint.

The Court decided the case of **Bush v. Gore** and set aside the Florida Supreme Court's order for a manual recount throughout the state.[149] The Court's decision meant that Bush got Florida's electoral votes, which gave him a majority of all electoral votes. Thus the tally hassle in Tallahassee came to an end.

In a contentious case, it is desirable for the justices to be unanimous or nearly unanimous, as they were in the Watergate tapes case, which also arose from a controversy involving the presidency (see Chapter 2). Unanimity helps dispel fears that their decision is partisan. But in *Bush* v. *Gore,* the justices were sharply split, 5–4. The majority consisted of the five most conservative justices, including O'Connor, with the four moderate-to-liberal justices in the minority. The majority were all Republicans, while the minority had two Republicans and two Democrats.[150]

The majority ruled that manual recounts throughout the state denied equal protection to some voters.[151] There was no uniform standard specifying how hanging chads and dimpled chads would be counted. As a result, some voters, whom the majority assumed had improperly marked their ballots, would have their votes counted, and the voters who had properly marked their ballots would have their votes "diluted." In this reasoning, the majority ignored the mechanical limitations of some voting machines. Many voters had actually marked their ballots as they were supposed to, but the machines had not counted their votes.

The Court could have allowed Florida to set statewide standards and then proceed with the recounts, but there was limited time and no desire by the majority to let the state try such standards.[152]

By intervening, the majority was activist rather than restrained. Moreover, the majority rejected the federalism principle that allows state supreme courts to interpret state laws.[153] The justices seemed contemptuous of the Florida Supreme Court. Justice Scalia called that court's reasoning "peculiar" and "absurd."

Much public reaction to the Court's decision was strictly partisan. Bush supporters liked it because it meant that their candidate would become president. Gore supporters disliked it for the same reason. Legal scholars, however, had more concern for how the Court's decision reflected established legal doctrine and affected the Court's legitimacy.

Most legal scholars were stunned when the Court agreed to intervene in the first place.[154] They assumed that the Court would avoid this tangled thicket because it was a political dispute, it could be resolved through the political process, and the public was sharply divided. For these reasons, the Court ordinarily did avoid election controversies. But the legal scholars underestimated the intense feelings aroused on the right by this election. Around the country, political and social conservatives wanted to repudiate Gore to rebuke Clinton, who had survived their impeachment effort. Former law clerks for the conservative justices, who formed a powerful network in conservative law firms and interest groups, encouraged Bush's legal team to take the case to the Supreme Court. The clerks knew that these justices had strong feelings about this election and predicted that they would agree to hear the case.[155]

Most legal scholars also were critical of the Court's rationale for its ruling. One said it was "embarrassingly weak."[156] Even conservative scholars were baffled; one called the justices' use of the equal protection argument "weird."[157] "It was not consistent," another observed, "with anything they have done in the past twenty-five years."[158] It departed from precedents in several ways.[159] Never before had states' recount procedures been held in violation of the federal Constitution or counties' election procedures been required to be standardized by the federal courts.[160]

In our decentralized governmental system, states often deviate from other states, and counties often deviate from other counties in the same state. Even for a policy with critical consequences such as capital punishment, courts allow variations among states and among counties. A defendant convicted of murder in one part of Florida might be executed, while a defendant convicted of murder in another part of Florida might be imprisoned.[161]

Although the majority focused on the absence of statewide standards for evaluating chads, it ignored the greater problem of the absence of statewide standards for voting machines. In Florida, wealthier counties used newer machines with near-perfect counting rates, while poorer counties used older machines with spotty counting rates.[162] These variations produced a bias toward the candidates favored by the voters in wealthier counties.

Even the majority seemed uncertain about its use of the equal protection clause. The majority said its use was "limited to the present circumstances." That is, it would not serve as a precedent for future cases. Thus the majority rejected the role of precedents both in making its ruling and in following this ruling in subsequent cases involving electoral procedures. This made the majority look as if it were concerned with the outcome of this particular case rather than with the establishment of a valid principle that would govern other cases too. "Like a great spot-relief pitcher in baseball," a law professor remarked, "this equal protection argument was trotted out to do its singular job of striking out Vice President Gore and was immediately sent to the showers, never again to reappear in the game."[163]

But legal scholars were most taken aback by the willingness of the majority justices to forsake their judicial philosophies. Most people understand that the justices, like other politicians, have their own ideologies. People assume that the justices hold these ideologies sincerely and will follow them consistently. By doing so, the justices may be political but nevertheless demonstrate an integrity that comes from deciding particular cases according to their established principles rather than their preferred outcomes. Thus we would expect justices who have a strong view about, say, freedom of speech to follow that view regardless of their distaste for the individual and the expression involved in a given case. Otherwise, it would appear as though they decide cases according to the individual and the expression involved rather than the principles they hold. In *Bush* v. *Gore,* the majority justices abandoned long-held principles about judicial restraint, federalism, and

equal protection.[164] Their ruling was "wildly out of character."[165] Nearly six hundred law professors signed an open letter calling the majority justices hypocritical and devious.

As a result, the ruling appeared partisan.[166] A former law school dean, a conservative, called it "an unmistakably partisan decision without any foundation in law."[167] Legal scholars questioned whether the majority justices could have passed "the shoe-on-the-other-foot test." Would they have ruled the same way if Gore had been ahead and Bush had been seeking a recount? A senior law professor who had voted for Bush said, "I don't want to believe it. I don't want to have to tell my students to believe it. It goes against everything I've been saying and teaching for decades. But there is no escaping the conclusion that if Bush had been the one seeking the recount, at least some of the majority justices would have voted the other way."[168]

The charges of partisanship were fueled by reports that Justice O'Connor, who was seventy, was hoping for a Bush victory so that she could retire and a Republican president could appoint her successor. At an election night party, when the networks projected Gore as the winner in Florida, she exclaimed, "This is terrible!" After she left the room in disgust, her husband explained that they wanted to retire to Arizona and now would have to wait another four years.[169] Reports also indicated that Justices Kennedy and Scalia wanted to be chief justice when Rehnquist retired.[170] As Republicans, they had a chance only if the president is a Republican. In addition, Justice Scalia's two sons were working as lawyers for the Republicans' law firm in the case, and Justice Thomas's wife was already screening applicants for jobs in a Bush administration.

Despite the appearance of partisanship, we do not know whether the justices were influenced, either consciously or subconsciously, by such concerns. They might have been influenced as much or more by a fear of potential chaos. Some legal scholars defended the decision (though not its rationale), saying that it prevented a crisis by bringing the election to a relatively prompt and decisive conclusion. Thus it enabled a smooth transition to the next administration.[171]

What would have happened if the Court had not intervened? Under various scenarios, Gore would

Steve Benson/Arizona Republic. Reprinted by permission of United Media.

have won the recount. But the Republican secretary of state, who was also cochair of the Bush campaign in Florida, and the Republican governor, who was Bush's brother, probably would have refused to certify Gore's slate of electors. Then the Republican legislature probably would have submitted another slate of electors. Thus two slates of electors probably would have been sent to Congress—one pledged to Gore and one pledged to Bush. According to the Constitution, Congress would select one. The House of Representatives had a Republican majority, while the Senate, after the election, was divided, 50–50. As the current vice president, Gore might be in the position to cast the tie-breaking vote in the Senate, which could stalemate the two houses. Then the selection would revert to the governor, Bush's brother. But there would be tremendous pressure to avoid this unseemly prospect, and politicians would engage in politics—negotiating and brokering some agreement.

This scenario would be messy, as politics often is. It might polarize people further, as politics sometimes does. But it might also continue the civics lesson already in progress—about how a stable democracy deals with its electoral problems.[172] Should it be frightening to imagine that an electoral deadlock might be settled by elected officials accountable to the voters?

Whether the justices were partisan or pragmatic, they certainly were political. Of the Court's decision, the worst that can be said is that the majority disregarded the law because of their partisan feelings. The best that can be said is that the majority disregarded the law as a way to avoid chaos and maintain order.

Either way, the Court deprived the new president of the public confidence that he was elected fairly. And perhaps the Court deprived itself of the public legitimacy that it had carefully nurtured. Half of the respondents to a survey said they believed the justices were "influenced by their personal political views." A year later, after 9/11 and the surge in Bush's popularity, almost half of the respondents still said they believed Bush either "won on a technicality" or "stole the election."[173] But the decision was not as disastrous for the Court's legitimacy as some others in its history. Unlike the Dred Scott decision, *Bush* v. *Gore* was not linked to any controversy, such as slavery, that was already at a flashpoint. Unlike the business regulation cases in the 1930s, *Bush* v. *Gore* was not linked to any series of decisions that had eroded public support. It was a one-shot case. Thus large majorities said they support the Court and would obey its decisions even if they disagreed with them.[174] (Republican support increased by 20 percent; by contrast, support among Democrats dropped by 28 percent and among independents by 3 percent.)[175]

Meanwhile, Justice O'Connor decides other cases in her office, where a hand-stitched pillow offers a motto: "Maybe in error but never in doubt."[176]

To learn more about the Supreme Court's decision in *Bush* v. *Gore,* go to this chapter's "You Are There" exercises on the text Web site.

Key Terms

judicial review
Marbury v. *Madison*
court-packing plan
Warren Court
Burger Court
Rehnquist Court
district courts
courts of appeals
jurisdiction
habeas corpus

criminal cases
civil cases
writ of *certiorari*
Americans with Disabilities Act
restrained judges
activist judges
stare decisis
Bush v. *Gore*

Further Reading

Vincent Bugliosi, *No Island of Sanity:* Paula Jones *v.* Bill Clinton (New York: Ballantine, 1998). This examination of Paula Jones's Supreme Court case is interesting and readable.

Robert Chrisman and Robert L. Allen, eds., *Court of Appeal: The Black Community Speaks Out on the Racial and Sexual Politics of* Thomas *v.* Hill (New York: Ballantine, 1992). This is a collection of passionate and provocative essays by black writers reflecting on the nomination and confirmation of Justice Thomas.

Richard D. Kahlenberg, *Broken Contract* (Boston: Faber & Faber, 1992). This memoir by a student at Harvard Law School reveals a lot about law schools, the legal profession, and the nature of American law.

David M. O'Brien, *Storm Center,* 5th ed. (New York: Norton, 2000). This is a lively account of the Supreme Court and its very human justices.

LeRoy Phillips and Mark Curriden, *Contempt of Court* (New York: Faber & Faber, 1999). The authors tell the story of the Supreme Court's only criminal trial—of a Chattanooga sheriff for allowing a lynch mob to murder a defendant whose appeal was pending before the Supreme Court in 1906.

Bob Woodward and Scott Armstrong, *The Brethren* (New York: Simon & Schuster, 1979). This book takes a behind-the-scenes look at the politicking among Supreme Court justices for major cases during the 1970s.

CHAPTER 14

CIVIL LIBERTIES

Christopher Morris/VII

Detainees are incarcerated at the U.S. Naval Base in Guantanamo Bay, Cuba.

For Viewing

Gideon's Trumpet (1985). A television movie based on the true story of the criminal defendant who insisted upon receiving an attorney for his defense. Eventually, he reached the Supreme Court, which used his minor case to make a landmark ruling.

Twelve Angry Men (1957). This film demonstrates the value of a jury, as one juror tries to convince the others that the case is not as clear cut as they think.

The Ox-Bow Incident (1943). A movie based on the acclaimed novel by Walter Van Tilburg Clark, examines mob justice, in the absence of legal procedures, on the frontier.

 ## Electronic Resources

www.supremecourtus.gov
This is the Supreme Court's official site, with decisions and opinions posted the day they are announced. A similar site, operated by Cornell University, is supct.law.cornell.edu/supct/index.php.

www.oyez.nwu.edu
This site, developed by Northwestern University, has biographies of all Supreme Court justices, past and present. You can hear the marshal cry, "Oyez, oyez,"; listen to oral arguments in important cases; take a virtual tour of the Court; and search for Court decisions by subject, date, or citation.

www.courttv.com/library/supreme
Current legal news, recent court cases, and links to historical criminal cases from Court TV can all be found here.

www.law.umkc.edu/faculty/projects/ftrials/ manson/manson.html
A law professor at the University of Missouri provides information on more than thirty famous American and international trials.

 ## InfoTrac College Edition

Search for the following articles in the InfoTrac database:

Balkin, Jack M. "The Use That the Future Makes of the Past: John Marshall's Greatness and Its Lessons for Today's Supreme Court Justices," *William and Mary Law Review* (March 2002).

Lazarus, Simon. "The Most Dangerous Branch? The Supreme Court Has Been Signaling That It Will Treat Congress Roughly in the Coming Decade—but Nobody Seems to Be Paying Attention," *Atlantic Monthly* (June 2002).

Peck, Robert S. "The Role of Personality, Stare Decisis, and Liberty in the Constitutional Construction," *Perspectives on Political Science* (Summer 2004).

Sunderland, Lane V. "Introduction: The Supreme Court and the Rule of Law in the Twenty-First Century," *Perspectives on Political Science* (Summer 2004).

For more articles enter

"United States Supreme Court" in the Subject Guide;

"United States Constitution" in the Subject Guide;

"federal courts" in the Subject Guide.

 ## American Government Resources

Visit the Government Institutions section of the Wadsworth American Government Resources Web site (politicalscience. wadsworth.com/amgov) for a variety of tools to help you explore the judiciary further. Included are simulations, video clips, Microcase exercises, and a wealth of other activities.

The Constitution and the Bill of Rights

  Individual Rights in the Constitution

  The Bill of Rights

Freedom of Expression

  Freedom of Speech

  Freedom of Association

  Freedom of the Press

  Libel and Obscenity

Freedom of Religion

  Free Exercise of Religion

  Establishment of Religion

Rights of Criminal Defendants

  Search and Seizure

  Self-Incrimination

  Counsel

  Jury Trial

  Cruel and Unusual Punishment

  Rights in Theory and in Practice

Right to Privacy

  Birth Control

  Abortion

  Homosexuality

  Right to Die

Conclusion: Are the Courts Responsive in Interpreting Civil Liberties?

Do You Challenge the President in Wartime?

ou are Justice John Paul Stevens of the United States Supreme Court, which is deciding whether American courts have any jurisdiction to hear lawsuits brought by foreign men captured abroad and imprisoned at the United States Naval Base at Guantanamo Bay, Cuba.

Since the September 11, 2000, terrorist attacks, approximately 750 men from forty-four countries have been rounded up and flown to Guantanamo Bay, where they have been detained as terrorist suspects. Most have been captured in Afghanistan or Pakistan, and most have been imprisoned for over two years. Vice President Dick Cheney called them "the worst of a very bad lot." Secretary of Defense Donald Rumsfeld called them "among the most dangerous, best-trained, vicious killers on the face of the earth." [1]

It is difficult to evaluate these claims because the Bush administration has pulled a veil of secrecy over the captives. It has refused to release the names of almost all of them or to allow journalists to interview any of them. Apparently one was a driver for Osama bin Laden, and another was a bodyguard for him. But so far none has been charged with carrying out a terrorist attack. At least some were simply in the wrong place at the wrong time. They were picked up by Afghani or Pakistani tribesmen and turned over to U.S. officials in exchange for bounty money. Approximately 150 have been released and returned home.

Whether dangerous or not, all have been imprisoned without being charged, without being tried, without receiving counsel, and without gaining access to any court. [2] The administration says the remaining 600 will be detained indefinitely. And in fact, the Navy has erected new facilities, which appear more permanent, for housing and interrogating the prisoners.

The families of two Australian, two British, and twelve Kuwaiti captives have filed suit, asking American courts to determine the legality of their detention. [3] The plaintiffs have petitioned for a writ of *habeas corpus,* which criminal defendants use to challenge the legality of their confinement by the government. As explained in Chapter 13, *habeas corpus* is a traditional and integral component of English and American law, mandating that government prosecutors must produce a defendant and justify the person's incarceration to the court. The U.S. Constitution stipulates that *habeas corpus* cannot be suspended unless there is a rebellion or foreign invasion. It is further authorized by a congressional statute that grants federal courts jurisdiction to hear petitions for *habeas corpus* from anyone claiming to be held in violation of the Constitution, laws, or treaties of the United States. The statute does not distinguish between American citizens and aliens, and it does not distinguish between peacetime and wartime.

An independent dresser as well as thinker, Justice John Paul Stevens wears bow ties, which he laboriously knots by hand. When a guest at a party poked fun at him for wearing a "clip-on" bow tie, Stevens slowly unraveled his tie and then carefully retied it without saying a word.

AP/ Wide World Photos

The Supreme Court did rule that it does not apply to aliens who are outside of U.S. territory.[4] During World War II, American forces captured German soldiers in China and tried them before a military commission there. The Supreme Court did not allow the German soldiers to use *habeas corpus* to challenge their detention.

The Bush administration claims that this precedent should apply to the prisoners at Guantanamo Bay. The naval base consists of forty-five square miles of land and water along the southeastern coast of Cuba. It is a natural harbor where Christopher Columbus dropped anchor on one of his voyages to the Americas. The United States administered Cuba after the Spanish-American War in 1898 and granted Cuba independence four years later, retaining the right in a treaty to lease Guantanamo Bay as a naval refueling station. In 1934, the United States renegotiated the agreement to remain in effect as long as

the United States wants it to. The terms specify that the United States shall have complete control and jurisdiction but that Cuba shall retain "ultimate sovereignty" over the territory. The latter provision, however, is merely symbolic. When the Castro government tried to exercise its "ultimate sovereignty" by asking the United States to leave, the Navy refused to do so. Each year, the United States makes payment under the lease, but in protest Cuba refuses to cash the checks.

Except for the symbolic assertion that Cuba retains "ultimate sovereignty," Guantanamo Bay is in actuality American territory. It is like an American city with five thousand sailors and civilians. It has its own schools and local transportation, and it generates its own power and provides its own water. It has a golf course, a movie theater, and the only McDonald's in Cuba. But no one can enter or leave without the permission of the U.S. government.

The Bush administration makes a second, more sweeping claim. It insists that the president, as commander in chief, has expanded powers during wartime that the courts cannot review or question.[5] Hence the courts cannot force the government to defend the detentions or provide any rights to the detainees. The likelihood that the detentions will continue for years or even decades—because terrorism as a tactic will continue as long as people have grievances, the "war on terrorism" might never end—

makes no difference, according to the administration.

The administration also insists that international law does not apply because the detainees, as (alleged) members of al-Qaeda, do not represent an official army of an actual country, so they are "unlawful combatants." The significance of this argument is that if international law does not apply, the detainees do not have the rights normally accorded prisoners of war.

In sum, the administration maintains that the detainees have no rights —none under our Constitution or laws and none under international law. Essentially, the detainees are in a legal black hole. This may be the first time that the United States has officially held anyone outside of all legal processes.[6] "The United States," remarked one legal scholar, "has created an offshore penal colony that might as well be on the moon."[7]

Should this matter to American citizens? Some, thinking back to 9/11, might decide that a legal black hole is just fine. Others might decide that the rule of law reflects our principles and provides at least some integrity in our procedures. Or American citizens might think about their long-range self-interest: we are foreigners when we travel abroad, and we expect to be treated fairly in the countries we visit.

Nonetheless, the lower federal courts bowed to the president in this case, as most federal courts have in other cases involving various issues of the "war on terrorism." Now the Supreme Court is deciding this case.

You were appointed to the Supreme Court by President Gerald Ford in 1975. You were selected because of your merit rather than because of any ideology. As a student at Northwestern University's law school, you had the highest grades in the school's history, and as a judge on a federal appellate court in Chicago, you were well respected. Initially a moderate, you gradually became more liberal as the Supreme Court became more conservative. All along, you have been an independent thinker. Now, at eighty-four, you are the eldest member of the Court.

Should the federal courts have authority to hear cases brought by the detainees and thus review policies established by the government? Or should the Supreme Court avoid this legal can of worms? Should you defer to the president's authority in wartime, or should you challenge the president's authority and risk a constitutional confrontation if the administration refuses to follow a ruling by a lower court or the Supreme Court?

How do you decide?

Americans value their "rights." Eighteenth-century Americans believed that people had "natural rights" by virtue of being human. Given by God, not by government, the rights could not be taken away by government. Contemporary Americans do not normally use this term, but they do think about their rights much as their forebears did.

Yet Americans have a split personality toward their rights. As described in Chapter 4, most people tell pollsters they believe in various constitutional rights in the abstract, but many do not accept these rights in concrete situations. For example, most people say they believe in free speech, but many would not allow communists, socialists, or atheists to speak in public or teach in schools.

Surveys in recent years show that Americans remain divided over their support for civil liberties. Even before the terrorist attacks, many respondents were ready to ban expression that might upset other people. One-third said they would not allow a rally that might offend community members. Two-thirds said they would not allow persons to say things in public that might offend racial groups, and over one-half said they would not allow persons to say things in public that might offend religious groups. One-fifth said they would not allow newspapers to publish without government approval of the articles.[8]

After the terrorist attacks, people's opinions reflected their fears. More respondents were skeptical about the value of the First Amendment; half said the amendment "goes too far" in guaranteeing rights (49 percent in 2002, compared to 22 percent in 2000). Two-fifths said newspapers should not be allowed to "freely criticize" the government's military strategy and performance. The same proportion said professors should not be allowed to criticize the government's military policy. Half said the government should be able to monitor religious groups for security purposes even if doing so infringes on religious freedom. (However, two-fifths said, "It's more important to ensure people's constitutional rights, even if it means that some suspected terrorists are never found.")[9]

Conflicts over civil liberties and rights have dominated the courts since the Great Depression. This chapter, covering civil liberties, and the next, covering civil rights, describe how the courts have interpreted these rights and tried to resolve these conflicts. We will explain the most important rights and recount the struggles by individuals and groups to achieve them. We will see how judges act as referees between litigants, brokers among competing groups, and policymakers in the process of deciding these cases.

The Constitution and the Bill of Rights

Individual Rights in the Constitution

Although the term *civil liberties* usually refers to the rights in the Bill of Rights, a few rights are granted in the body of the Constitution. The Constitution bans religious qualifications for federal office and guarantees jury trials in federal criminal cases. It bans bills of attainder, which are legislative acts rather than judicial trials pronouncing specific persons guilty of crimes, and *ex post facto* ("after the fact") laws, which are legislative acts making some behavior illegal that was not illegal when it was done. The Constitution also prohibits suspension of the writ of *habeas corpus,* except during rebellion or invasion of the country. These rights are significant, but they by no means exhaust the rights people believed they had when the Constitution was written.

The Bill of Rights

Origin and Meaning

The Constitution originally did not include a bill of rights; the Founders did not think traditional liberties needed specific protections because federalism, separation of powers, and checks and balances would prevent the national government from becoming too powerful. But to win support for ratification, the Founders promised to adopt constitutional amendments to provide such rights. James Madison proposed twelve, Congress passed them, and in 1791 the states ratified ten of them, which came to be known as the **Bill of Rights.**[10] Of these, the first eight grant specific rights. (See the box "Civil Liberties in the Bill of Rights.") The Ninth says that the listing of these rights does not mean they are the only ones the people have, and the Tenth says that any powers not granted to the federal government are reserved for the state governments.

Civil Liberties in the Bill of Rights

- First Amendment grants
  freedom of religion
  freedom of speech, assembly, and association
  freedom of the press
- Second Amendment grants
  right to keep and bear arms
- Third Amendment forbids
  quartering soldiers in houses during peacetime
- Fourth Amendment forbids
  unreasonable searches and seizures
- Fifth Amendment grants
  right to a grand jury hearing in criminal cases
  right to due process
  forbids double jeopardy (more than one trial for the
    same offense)
  compulsory self-incrimination
  taking private property without just compensation
- Sixth Amendment grants
  right to speedy trial
  right to public trial
  right to jury trial in criminal cases
  right to cross-examine adverse witnesses
  right to present favorable witnesses
  right to counsel
- Seventh Amendment grants
  right to jury trial in civil cases
- Eighth Amendment forbids
  excessive bail and fines
  cruel and unusual punishment

The Bill of Rights provides rights against the government. According to Justice Hugo Black, it is a collection of "Thou shalt nots" directed at the government.[11] In practice, the Bill of Rights provides rights for political, religious, or racial minorities against the majority, because government policy toward civil liberties tends to reflect the views of the majority.

As explained in Chapter 2, the Founders set up a government to protect property rights for the well-to-do minority against the presumably jealous majority. Federalism, separation of powers, checks and balances, and some specific provisions of the Constitution were intended to limit the ability of the masses to curtail the rights of the elites. However, as Americans became more egalitarian and as the masses gained more opportunity to participate in politics in the nineteenth and twentieth centuries, the relative importance of property rights declined while the relative importance of other rights increased. Thus the Bill of Rights became the means to protect the fundamental rights of the have-nots of society—the unpopular, powerless minorities, with nonmainstream ideas, religions, or pigmentation—when they come in conflict with the majority.

Responsibility for interpreting the Bill of Rights generally falls on the federal courts. Because their judges are appointed for life, they are more independent from majority pressure than elected officials are.

Application

For many years, the Supreme Court applied the Bill of Rights only to the federal government, not to the state governments (or to the local governments, which are under the authority of the state governments). That is, the Court ruled that the Bill of Rights restricted only the actions of the federal government.[12]

In ruling this way, the Court followed the intentions of the Founders, who assumed that the states, being closer to the people, would be less likely to violate their liberties.[13] The Founders did not realize that the states would in fact be more likely to violate their liberties. The state governments, representing smaller, more homogeneous populations, tended to reflect majority sentiment more closely than the federal government, so they often ignored—and sometimes obliterated—the rights of political, religious, or racial minorities or of criminal defendants. When disputes arose, the state courts tended to interpret their citizens' rights narrowly.

However, starting in 1925[14] and continuing through 1972,[15] the Supreme Court gradually applied most provisions of the Bill of Rights to the states, using the Fourteenth Amendment's due process clause as justification. This clause, adopted after the Civil War to protect former slaves from their southern governments, reads, "Nor shall any state deprive any person of life, liberty, or property, without due process of law." The clause refers to states and "liberty." It is ambiguous, but the Court interpreted it to mean that states also have to provide the liberties in the Bill of Rights.

The Court has applied all but two provisions of the First and the Fourth through the Eighth Amendments to the states: the exceptions are the guarantee of a grand jury in criminal cases and guarantee of a jury trial in civil cases. In addition, the Court has established some rights not in the Bill of Rights, and it has applied these to the states, too: presumption of innocence in criminal cases, right to travel within the country, and right to privacy. Thus most provisions in the Bill of Rights, and even some not in it, now restrict the actions of both the federal and the state governments.

To see how the Court has interpreted these provisions, we will look at four major areas—freedom of expression, freedom of religion, rights of criminal defendants, and right to privacy.

Freedom of Expression

The **First Amendment** guarantees freedom of expression, which includes freedom of speech, assembly, and association, and freedom of the press. (The amendment also guarantees freedom of religion, which will be addressed in the next section.)

The amendment states that "Congress shall make no law" abridging these liberties. The language is absolute, but no justices interpret it literally.[16] They cite the example of the person who falsely shouts "Fire!" in a crowded theater and causes a stampede that injures someone. Surely, they say, the amendment does not protect this expression. So the Court needs to draw a line between expression the amendment protects and that which it does not.

Freedom of Speech

Freedom of speech, Justice Black asserted, "is the heart of our government."[17] By creating an open atmosphere, it promotes individual autonomy and self-fulfillment. By encouraging a wide variety of opinions, it furthers the advancement of knowledge and the discovery of truth. The English philosopher John Stuart Mill observed that individuals decide what is correct by comparing different views. Unpopular opinions might be true or partly true. Even if completely false, they might prompt a reevaluation of accepted opinions. By permitting citizens to form opinions and express them to others, freedom of speech helps them participate in government. It especially helps them check inefficient or corrupt government. Thus the American philosopher John Dewey remarked that "democracy begins in conversation."[18] Finally, by channeling conflict toward persuasion, freedom of speech promotes a stable society. Governments that deny freedom of speech become inflexible; they force conflict toward violence.[19]

Seditious Speech

The first controversies to test the scope of freedom of speech involved **seditious speech**—speech that encourages rebellion against the government.[20] The public becomes most opposed to seditious speech, and the government becomes most likely to prosecute individuals for such speech, during or shortly after war, when society is most sensitive about loyalty.

Numerous prosecutions came with World War I and the Russian Revolution, which brought the Communists to power in the Soviet Union in 1917. The Russian Revolution prompted the "Red Scare," in which people feared conspiracies to overthrow the U.S. government. Congress passed the Espionage Act of 1917, which prohibited interfering with military recruitment, inciting insubordination in military forces, and mailing material advocating rebellion, and the Sedition Act of 1918,

which prohibited "disloyal, profane, scurrilous, or abusive language about the form of government, Constitution, soldiers and sailors, flag or uniform of the armed forces." State legislatures passed similar laws. In short, our governments prohibited a wide range of speech.

During the war, the federal government prosecuted almost two thousand and convicted almost nine hundred persons under these acts, and the state governments prosecuted and convicted many others. They prosecuted individuals for saying that war is contrary to the teachings of Jesus, that World War I should not have been declared until after a referendum was held, and that the draft was unconstitutional. Officials even prosecuted an individual for remarking to women knitting clothes for the troops, "No soldier ever sees those socks."[21]

These cases gave the Supreme Court numerous opportunities to rule on seditious speech. In six major cases, the Court upheld the federal and state laws and affirmed the convictions of all the defendants.[22] The defendants advocated socialism or communism, and some advocated the overthrow of the government to achieve their goal. Except for one—Eugene Debs, the Socialist Party's candidate for president—the defendants did not command a large audience. Even so, the Court concluded that these defendants' speech constituted a "clear and present danger" to the government. Justice Edward

Eugene V. Debs, the Socialist Party's candidate for president, criticized American involvement in World War I and the draft. He was convicted of violating the Espionage Act and sentenced to ten years in prison. When President Warren Harding pardoned him early, Debs commented, "It is the government that should ask me for a pardon."

© Bettmann/CORBIS

Sanford wrote, "A single revolutionary spark may kindle a fire that, smoldering for a time, may burst into a sweeping and destructive conflagration."[23] In reality, there was nothing clear or present about the danger; the defendants' speech had little effect.

Society was intolerant of dissent. When Zechariah Chafee, a Harvard Law professor and leading constitutional scholar, criticized the Court's rulings, the university's administration, prompted by the Justice Department, charged him "unfit" to be a professor. He was narrowly acquitted.[24]

More prosecutions came after World War II. In 1940, Congress passed the Smith Act, which was not as broad as the World War I acts because it did not forbid criticizing the government. But it did forbid advocating overthrow of the government by force and organizing or joining individuals who advocated overthrow.

The act was used against members of the American Communist Party after the war. The uneasy alliance between the United States and the Soviet Union during the war had given way to the Cold War between the two countries. Politicians, especially Senator Joseph McCarthy (R-Wisc.), exploited the tensions. McCarthy claimed that many government officials were Communists. (He said he had a list of 205 "known Communists" in the State Department alone.) He had little evidence (and provided no list).[25] Other Republicans also accused the Democratic administration of covering for Communists. They goaded it into prosecuting members of the Communist Party so that it would not appear "soft on communism." In 1951, the Court upheld the Smith Act and affirmed the convictions of eleven top-echelon leaders of the Communist Party.[26] These leaders organized the party, and the party advocated overthrowing the government by force, but the leaders had not attempted to overthrow the government. (If they had, they clearly would have been guilty of crimes.) Even so, the Court majority concluded that they constituted a clear and present danger, and Chief Justice Fred Vinson wrote that the government does not have to "wait until the putsch is about to be executed, the plans have been laid and the signal is awaited" before it can act against the party. The minority argued that the Communist Party was not a danger. Justice William Douglas said that the party was "of little consequence. . . . Communism has been so thoroughly exposed in this country that it has been crippled as a political force. Free speech has destroyed it as an effective political party." Yet after the Court's decision, the government prosecuted and convicted almost one hundred other Communists.

However, the Cold War thawed slightly, and the Senate condemned McCarthy after he tried to bully the Army. His method was likened to witch hunts, and the tactic of making political accusations or name-calling

© Bettmann/CORBIS

At congressional hearings, Senator Joseph McCarthy identified the supposed locations of alleged Communists and "fellow travelers."

based on little or no evidence eventually came to be known as **McCarthyism.** In the meantime, two new members, including Chief Justice Earl Warren, had joined the Supreme Court. Although the public, stoked by media speculation and traveling speakers (including one who warned parent audiences that *Mad* magazine was Communist-inspired), remained fearful of communism, these developments led to a new doctrine. In a series of cases in the mid- to late 1950s and early 1960s, the Warren Court made it more difficult to convict Communists,[27] thereby incurring the wrath of the public, Congress, and President Dwight Eisenhower. In a private conversation at the White House, Eisenhower criticized the rulings. Warren asked Eisenhower what he thought the Court should have done with the Communists. Eisenhower replied, "I would kill the S.O.B.s."[28]

In addition to prosecutions under the Smith Act, the governments took other actions against the Communists. The federal government ordered them to register, and then some state governments banned them from public jobs such as teaching or private jobs such as practicing law or serving as union officers. Legislative committees held hearings to expose and humiliate them. The Court heard numerous cases involving these actions and usually ruled against the governments.

Yet the public's fear throughout the 1950s was so consuming that the government's actions extended beyond active Communists to former Communists—some Americans had dabbled with communism during the Great Depression in the 1930s—and even to individuals who had never been Communists but who were lumped together as "Commie dupes" or "comsymps"

(Communist sympathizers). Ultimately, a campaign that mandated loyalty oaths and created blacklists cost an estimated ten thousand Americans their jobs.[29]

The Vietnam War did not prompt as much fear as World Wars I and II did. Congress did not pass any comparable laws, perhaps because many people, including "respectable" people, opposed this war and also because the Court in the 1950s and 1960s had permitted more seditious speech.

Even so, the federal government took some actions against individuals and groups. Numerous conscientious objectors were imprisoned; others felt forced to flee to Canada. Many peaceful protesters were arrested. Antiwar groups were harassed by federal grand juries, and their leaders were spied on by the U.S. Army. Some prominent opponents were prosecuted for conspiring against the draft.[30] However, opposition to this war was so widespread that the government's actions did not silence the protesters' speech.

The Court developed a new doctrine for seditious speech in 1969. A Ku Klux Klan leader said at a rally in Ohio that the Klan might take "revengeance" on the president, Congress, and the Supreme Court if they

During the Cold War, Americans feared communism so much that some built bomb shelters in their yards, believing that taking refuge there would protect their family in the event of a nuclear attack.

© Time Life Pictures/Getty Images

continued "to suppress the white, Caucasian race." The leader was convicted under a statute similar to those upheld after World War I, but this time the statute was unanimously struck down by the Court.[31] The justices drew a distinction between advocacy and incitement. People can advocate—enthusiastically, even heatedly—as long as they do not incite illegal action. This doctrine protects most criticism of the government, whether at a rally, from a pulpit, or through the media, and it remains in effect today.

Thus after many years and many cases, the Court concluded that the First Amendment protects seditious speech as much as other speech. Justice Douglas noted that "the threats were often loud but always puny."[32] Even the attorney general who prosecuted the major Communist cases later admitted that the cases were "squeezed oranges. I didn't think there was much to them."[33] Nevertheless, the Court had permitted a climate of fear to overwhelm the First Amendment for many years.

The collapse of the Soviet Union and the demise of the Cold War made communism less threatening, but this doctrine remains important. After the Oklahoma City bombing in 1995, government surveillance of right-wing militia groups increased, but prosecution of the members, under terrorism laws, was limited because most of the evidence was fiery rhetoric, which is protected speech (unless it urges immediate action to violate any laws).

After the terrorist attacks in 2001, pressure to conform—to temper criticism and to support the government's response—mounted. An organization identified forty college professors with "un-American" agendas, in an effort to prod the schools to discipline and restrain their professors. (Negative reaction prompted the organization to remove the names from its Web site.)[34] A tenured professor at the University of New Mexico who cracked, "Anyone who can blow up the Pentagon gets my vote," was reprimanded, and a lawsuit demanding his termination was filed.[35] During the Iraq war, pressure to conform was linked to support for our troops. Critics were branded as "unpatriotic" and "disloyal" by conservative commentators who stoked their listeners' anger.[36] Pressure to conform was muted only when the aftermath of the war proceeded poorly and the number of critics increased sharply.

Although the government did not adopt comparable laws during the war on terrorism or the war in Iraq as it adopted during World Wars I and II, it did pass the USA PATRIOT Act, which has important implications for civil liberties. (See the box "The USA PATRIOT Act" on the next page.)

Now we will turn to other speech—nonseditious speech—to see how the Court has interpreted the First Amendment in these situations.

Forty-five days after the terrorist attacks of September 11, 2001, President Bush signed the Uniting and Strengthening America by Providing Appropriate Tools Required to Intercept and Obstruct Terrorism Act—the USA PATRIOT Act. Under pressure to act decisively, Congress passed the act in a rush —with few hearings, no committee report, and little public debate—and at a time when senators were evacuated from their offices because of anthrax contamination. Yet the act has significant implications for fighting terrorism and also for retaining civil liberties.

The act, which is 342 pages long, is a series of amendments expanding previous acts (making it difficult to research). The act focuses on domestic intelligence gathering. It establishes the foundation for unprecedented surveillance within the United States, and it shifts the FBI's primary function from solving crimes to gathering intelligence. within the United States (The CIA and other intelligence agencies gather intelligence outside the United States.)

The act includes the following provisions:

- *Information sharing:* After revelations about illegal spying and harassment of antiwar and civil rights protesters, including Martin Luther King, Jr., came to light in the 1970s, Congress erected barriers between the FBI and the CIA, preventing the agencies from sharing their information. The FBI was supposed to solve domestic crimes, while the CIA was supposed to gather foreign intelligence. And the FBI was not supposed to employ the CIA's surveillance techniques against peaceful protesters. Today such barriers could hamper efforts to nab dangerous terrorists. Because

terrorist cells can operate both inside and outside our borders, each agency could obtain useful information—the FBI inside and the CIA outside—but be unaware of the other agency's information. The Patriot Act lowers these barriers.

- *"Roving wiretaps":* An old law allowed wiretaps only on particular phones—that is, on certain numbers—known to be used by criminal suspects. Today many people use multiple phones, even disposable phones; sometimes criminals do so to avoid wiretaps. The Patriot Act allows "roving wiretaps," which authorize surveillance on all phones used by particular persons, wherever they might be.[1]

- *Electronic communications:* The Patriot Act extends surveillance to devices that identify the senders and receivers of phone calls, technology that identifies Internet sites visited and key words used in search engines, and technology that identifies header information (for example, to, from, and subject lines) in e-mail messages. Although the act does not permit surveillance of the body of e-mail messages, a related act passed three months later does encourage Internet service providers to turn over the contents of their customers' private messages.[2]

- *"Sneak-and-peek searches":* Normally, law enforcement officers are expected to knock and announce themselves when executing a search warrant at someone's home or office. This practice notifies the occupants about the search so that they can contest its legality in court afterward. They can also point out any mistakes—sometimes the officers get the wrong address—and monitor

the search in case the officers exceed the bounds prescribed by the warrant. In contrast, "sneak-and-peek searches" allow the officers to enter when no one is present and to conduct a search, usually taking photos (but occasionally seizing things). They do not need to notify the subject of the search until much later. Thus they can continue to conduct their investigation without the subject's being aware of it. Although some courts allowed these searches to a limited degree before, the Patriot Act expands their use.

- *Tangible items:* The Patriot Act lowers the standard of proof required for the FBI to obtain court orders for tangible items such as papers, documents, records, and books. These provisions encompass bookstore and library records. FBI agents can get the records of the books bought or checked out and of the Internet sites visited on library computers. (Some 9/11 terrorists communicated via library computers.) The act forbids the bookstores and libraries from notifying their patrons that they are under investigation.

The act overrides state privacy laws passed after publicity about the FBI's "Library Awareness Program" during the Cold War. From the 1960s through the 1980s, FBI agents checked the reading habits of library patrons with Eastern European accents or those suspected of left-wing leanings.

The library provisions of the Patriot Act have been among the most controversial. The American Library Association opposes them, and some librarians have rebelled against them by posting warning signs to notify their patrons that the library's records can be checked or by destroying the library's records at the end of each day.

The impact of these provisions is unclear. A survey of libraries revealed that at least 545 reported requests by federal or local law enforcement officers during the first year of the act's existence. But Attorney General John Ashcroft called the librarians "hysterical" and insisted that the act's provisions had not been used at all.[3] If the survey is accurate and the attorney general is truthful, this could mean that local officers, rather than FBI agents, made the requests or that FBI agents made the requests without invoking the legal procedures in the act and the librarians complied without demanding these legal procedures.

- *Foreign student database:* Because some 9/11 terrorists entered the country on student visas, the Patriot Act provides for monitoring foreign college students through an electronic database. When the students apply for a visa, their data is logged into the database. Then the schools are required to forward information about the students' classes each semester and activities on campus. When government officials investigate particular students, the schools are forbidden from disclosing to the students that their records have been checked. These provisions amend a privacy act adopted by Congress in the 1970s.[4]

- *Alien registration and interrogation:* Acting under authority of the Patriot Act, the U.S. Citizenship and Immigration Services (USCIS) requires male nonresident aliens who are older than sixteen and come from any of twenty-five countries, all

but one of which are Arab or Muslim, to report to its offices to be fingerprinted, photographed, and interrogated. The men must report any change of address within ten days, and they must reappear annually. If they fail to appear, they can be deported. If they appear but the interrogation uncovers immigration violations, they can be detained indefinitely and then deported under other laws.

- *Alien detentions and prosecutions:* Although the Patriot Act focuses on intelligence gathering, it contains other important provisions that enhance the government's ability to detain and prosecute aliens. Those suspected of committing a crime related to terrorism can be detained, without trial, longer than before. And those accused of providing "material support" to organizations involved in terrorism can be prosecuted more easily than before. Anyone who assists an organization involved in terrorism (as defined by the government) by soliciting money, gathering information, or providing communications, weapons, or training is guilty of providing material support, even if the person did not intend to support terrorism and even if the assistance did not actually further terrorism. Under this provision, six Yemeni Americans from New York were indicted for traveling to Afghanistan before 9/11. They claim they went solely for religious reasons. And a college professor in Florida was indicted for soliciting money for a Palestinian group.

Although some provisions of the Patriot Act are scheduled to expire in 2005, the Bush administration and con-

gressional leaders plan to extend them. The administration, in fact, claims that the act does not go far enough, and it has proposed new legislation, dubbed "Patriot II," which would allow the FBI to seek information from records or individuals without first getting approval from a court.

Already the administration and Congress have put in place a more extensive surveillance state than Americans have ever experienced before. Further terrorist attacks in the United States would almost certainly produce public anxiety and political pressure for even more pervasive intelligence gathering. Because of the intrusions into individuals' privacy, a rare alliance of civil libertarians on the left and on the right has pushed for some revisions of the Patriot Act. Yet it is difficult for anyone to evaluate the implementation and the effects of the act because this administration is unusually secretive, not only hiding its operations from potential terrorists but shielding them from congressional oversight, judicial review, and public scrutiny as well.[5]

1. The act also extends the life span of many warrants for electronic surveillance.
2. The Homeland Security Act.
3. "Some Patriot Act Powers Have Yet to Be Used," *Lincoln Journal-Star,* September 18, 2003.
4. In addition to the Patriot Act, various bureaucratic policies that affect foreign students have been revised.
5. Readers interested in researching the Patriot Act will find many articles in law journals, usually addressing one provision of the act. More succinct analyses by legal scholars and lawyers active in litigating issues raised by the act can be found in Cynthia Brown, ed., *Lost Liberties* (New York: New Press, 2003).

REMEMBER THAT LADY WHO CAME TO OUR GRADUATION AND SPOKE ABOUT CIVIL LIBERTIES?

YEAH. WE BOOED HER OFF THE STAGE.

WHAT THE HECK WERE WE THINKING?

U.S. GOVT. I.D. 450-U35

U.S. GOVT. I.D. 72-B405

Public Forum

Although people usually communicate with each other in private, speakers sometimes want more listeners and use public places where people congregate. This means that the speakers will be heard by some listeners who do not like their message or their use of public places to disseminate it, and it also means that the speakers might be disrupting the normal functions of these places.

The Court holds that individuals have a right to use public places, such as streets, sidewalks, and parks, to express their views on public issues. These places constitute the **public forum** and serve as "the poor person's printing press."

When speakers seek to use other public facilities, the Court has to determine which ones are also part of the public forum. In a series of cases, it decided that federal and state capitol grounds,[37] Supreme Court grounds,[38] and public school grounds[39] are part of the forum. It decided that blacks could protest library segregation at a public library[40] and promoters could show the rock musical *Hair* at a public theater[41] because these, too, are part of the forum.

On the other hand, the Court decided that civil rights activists could not demonstrate against jail segregation outside a jail because of the need for security[42] and that Benjamin Spock, the famous baby doctor, and other antiwar activists could not encourage opposition to the Vietnam War at an Army base because of the need for discipline in the military.[43]

Normally, only publicly owned facilities are considered part of the public forum, but the proliferation of shopping malls prompted speakers to use these privately owned facilities to reach crowds of shoppers. The Warren Court permitted them to do so, saying that shopping malls are similar to downtown shopping districts where streets and sidewalks are part of the public forum.[44] But the Burger Court overruled the Warren Court, allowing the shopping malls to prohibit speech. Thus the Burger Court emphasized property rights over First Amendment rights in this situation.[45] During the run-up to the Iraq war, a sixty-year-old man wore a T-shirt with the slogan "Give Peace a Chance" at a mall in Albany, New York. Security guards ordered him to take off the shirt or leave the mall. When he refused, he was arrested.[46]

Even in public forums, people cannot speak whenever and however they want. The Court has divided speech into three kinds—pure speech, speech plus conduct, and symbolic speech—and established doctrine for each.

Pure Speech

Pure speech is speech without any conduct (besides the speech itself). Individuals can say what they want as long as they do not cause a breach of the peace or a riot. They can use offensive language.[47] During the Vietnam War, a man walked through the corridors of the Los Angeles County courthouse wearing a jacket with the words "Fuck the Draft" emblazoned on the back. Police arrested him. The Court reversed his conviction, and seventy-two-year-old Justice John Harlan remarked that "one man's vulgarity is another's lyric."[48] People can even swear at police.[49] Before the Court's ruling in 1972, arrests for swearing were common. In the District of Columbia, for example, about ten thousand people per year were arrested for swearing, usually at police (and charged with "disorderly conduct").[50]

The media, however, cannot broadcast some offensive language. A California radio station broadcast a monologue by comedian George Carlin. Titled "Filthy Words," it lampooned society's sensitivity to seven words that "you couldn't say on the public airwaves . . . the ones you definitely wouldn't say, ever." The seven words, according to the Federal Communications Commission report, included "a four-letter word for excrement" repeated seventy times in twelve minutes. A majority of the Court ruled that although the monologue was part of a serious program on contemporary attitudes toward language, it was not protected under the First Amendment because people, including children, tuning the radio could be subjected to the language in their homes.[51] Now the FCC prohibits indecent material on noncable TV and radio between the hours of 6 A.M. and 10 P.M. and fines media that violate the ban. (The largest fines have been levied on the *Howard Stern Show* and on a New York City radio station that broadcast a tape of a couple having sex in Saint Patrick's Cathedral.)[52] Yet the Court struck down a Utah law restricting "indecent material" on cable television. The difference, apparently, is that people choose to subscribe and pay for cable television.[53]

Speech Plus Conduct

Speech plus conduct is speech combined with conduct that is intended to convey ideas—for example, a demonstration in which protesters chant slogans or carry signs with slogans (the speech) and march, picket, or sit in (the conduct).

Individuals can demonstrate, but they are subject to some restrictions. Places in the public forum are used for other purposes besides demonstrating, and individuals cannot disrupt these activities. They cannot, Justice Arthur Goldberg remarked, hold "a street meeting in the middle of Times Square at the rush hour."[54] Thus abortion protesters can demonstrate on public streets and public sidewalks near abortion clinics, and they can approach staffers and patients who come and go. But protesters cannot block access (and to ensure this, judges can order them not to come within a certain distance—for example, fifteen feet—of driveways and doorways).[55]

To help enforce the restrictions, governments can require groups to obtain a permit, which can specify the place, time, and manner of the demonstration. However, officials cannot allow one group to demonstrate but forbid another, no matter how much they dislike the group or its message. They cannot forbid the group even if they say they fear violence, unless the group actually threatens violence. In short, officials may establish restrictions to avoid disruption, but they may not use these restrictions to censor speech.

Accordingly, lower federal courts required the Chicago suburb of Skokie to permit the American Nazi Party to demonstrate in front of the town hall in 1978.[56] About forty thousand of Skokie's population of seventy thousand were Jews. Of these, hundreds survived the German Nazi concentration camps during World War II, and thousands had relatives who died in the camps. The city, in anticipation of the demonstration, passed ordinances that prohibited wearing "military-style" uniforms and distributing material that "promotes and incites hatred against persons by reason of their race, national origin, or religion." These ordinances were thinly disguised attempts to bar the demonstration, and the courts threw them out. One quoted Justice Oliver Wendell Holmes's statement that "if there is any principle of the Constitution that more imperatively calls for attachment than any other it is the principle of free thought—not free thought for those who agree with us but freedom for the thought we hate."[57]

The Rehnquist Court, however, did uphold a Milwaukee suburb's ordinance that prohibited picketing at a residence.[58] The city passed the ordinance after anti-abortionists had picketed, six times in one month, the home of a doctor who performed abortions. Although protesters can march through residential neighborhoods, the Court said, a city can prohibit them from focusing on a particular home. Thus the Court emphasized the right to privacy at home over the right to demonstrate in this situation.

Symbolic Speech

Symbolic speech is the use of symbols, rather than words, to convey ideas.

During the Vietnam War, men burned their draft cards to protest the draft and the war. This was powerful expression, and Congress tried to stifle it by passing a law prohibiting the destruction of draft cards. The Supreme Court was uncomfortable with symbolic speech and reluctant to protect it. Even Chief Justice Warren

Young men illegally burned their draft cards to protest the Vietnam War, and the Supreme Court refused to protect that action as symbolic speech.

Mary Beth Tinker, seen here with her mother and brother, wore a black armband at school to protest the Vietnam War.

© Bettmann/CORBIS

worried that this would mean that "an apparently limitless variety of conduct can be labeled 'speech.'" The Court upheld the law.[59]

One year later, however, the Court was willing to protect symbolic speech. A junior high and two senior high school students in Des Moines, Iowa, including Mary Beth Tinker, wore black armbands to protest the war. They were suspended, and they sued school officials. Public schools, Justice Abe Fortas said, "may not be enclaves of totalitarianism." They must allow students freedom of speech, providing students do not disrupt the schools.[60]

In the 1960s and 1970s, many students wore long hair or beards in violation of school policy. Some claimed they did so to protest "establishment culture." Blacks and American Indians claimed they wore Afros and braids to show racial pride. Federal courts of appeals split evenly as to whether this was symbolic speech. The Supreme Court refused to hear any of these cases, so there was no uniform law across the country.

Some individuals treated the American flag disrespectfully to protest the Vietnam War. A Massachusetts man wore a flag patch on the seat of his pants and was sentenced to six months in jail. A Washington student taped a peace symbol on a flag and then hung the flag, upside down, outside his apartment. The Court reversed both convictions.[61]

When a member of the Revolutionary Communist Youth Brigade burned an American flag outside the Republican National Convention in Dallas in 1984, the justices faced the issue of actual desecration of the flag. The Rehnquist Court surprisingly permitted this symbolic speech.[62] Two Reagan-appointed conservatives joined the three most liberal members of the Court to

forge a bare majority. The foremost free-speech advocate on the bench, Justice William Brennan, wrote that the First Amendment cannot be limited just because this form of expression offends some people. "We do not consecrate the flag by punishing its desecration, for in doing so we dilute the freedom that this cherished emblem represents." The ruling invalidated the laws of forty-eight states and the federal government.

In a dissent, Chief Justice William Rehnquist emotionally criticized the decision. He said the First Amendment should not apply because the flag is a unique national symbol. He recounted the history of "The Star-Spangled Banner" and the music of John Philip Sousa's "Stars and Stripes Forever," he quoted poems by Ralph Waldo Emerson and John Greenleaf Whittier that refer to the flag, and he discussed the role of the Pledge of Allegiance.

Civil liberties advocates praised the decision. One lawyer for the defendant said, "If free expression is to exist in this country, people must be as free to burn the flag as they are to wave it." Another said veterans should cheer the decision because it shows that the values in the Bill of Rights that they fought for are intact. Yet veterans' groups were outraged.

President George H. Bush proposed a constitutional amendment to override the decision. Members of Congress, always eager to appear patriotic, lined up in support. But some, mostly Democrats, later came out in opposition. They criticized the proposal for creating an unprecedented exception to the First Amendment. Then, instead of the proposed amendment, Congress passed a statute prohibiting flag desecration. Apparently, a majority felt that this less permanent substitute would be an adequate shield against the public's wrath. Yet in 1990, the justices, dividing the same way, declared the statute unconstitutional for the same reasons they reversed the Dallas conviction.[63] Again President Bush proposed a constitutional amendment, and congressional Republicans warned Democrats that their opposition to the amendment "would make a good thirty-second spot" for the next election, but Congress rejected the amendment. Members sensed much less pressure from the public, whose initial emotional reaction had ebbed.[64]

Freedom of Association

Although the First Amendment does not mention "association," the Supreme Court has interpreted the right to speak, assemble, and petition the government for a redress of grievances, all of which the amendment does list, to encompass a **freedom of association** for individuals to join with others to do these things. This right allows a minority to pursue interests without being prevented from doing so by the majority.

Implicit in this freedom is a right not to associate. Groups can therefore exclude individuals from their association.

The right is strongest when the organization forms for "expressive association"—that is, when it speaks, assembles, and petitions the government for a redress of grievances. The right is also strong when the organization forms for "intimate association"—that is, when it is relatively personal, selective, and small, such as a social club or a country club.

Organizations formed for expressive or intimate association can usually exclude others. The Supreme Court allowed organizers of the Saint Patrick's Day parade in Boston to exclude a group of gays, lesbians, and bisexuals.[65] Because the organizers were private individuals—the parade was not sponsored by the city—and because a parade is an expressive activity, the organizers did not have to allow any views contrary to their views. The Supreme Court also allowed the Boy Scouts of America to expel an assistant scoutmaster who is openly gay.[66] The Court concluded that the Boy Scouts is an expressive organization, which espouses various values, including its opposition to homosexuality.

The right is weakest when the organization forms for "commercial association"—that is, when it is designed to enhance business interests of its members and is relatively impersonal, unselective, and large. Organizations formed for commercial association often cannot exclude others. Their right to associate can be overridden by others' right to be free from discrimination. For example, Minnesota and California adopted laws prohibiting sex discrimination in various organizations. The Court ruled that the Jaycees (the Junior Chamber of Commerce), which was a business organization of young men, and the Rotary Club, which was a civic organization of men, could not discriminate against women in these states because the laws forbade such discrimination.[67] The right to freedom from discrimination overrode the right to freedom of association because the organizations were formed for commercial rather than expressive or intimate association.[68]

Freedom of the Press

Unlike most civil liberties cases, which pit a relatively powerless individual or group against the government, press freedom cases usually feature a more powerful publisher or broadcaster against the government. Even so, these cases still involve rights against the government.

Prior Restraint

The core of freedom of the press is freedom from **prior restraint**—censorship. If the press violates laws prohibiting, for example, libelous or obscene material, it can be punished after publishing such materials. But freedom from prior restraint means the press at least has the opportunity to disseminate the information it thinks is appropriate and the public at least has the opportunity to see this information.

Yet freedom from prior restraint is not absolute. At the height of the Vietnam War, the secretary of defense in the Johnson administration, Robert McNamara, became disenchanted with the war and ordered a thorough study of our involvement. The study, known as the Pentagon Papers, laid bare the reasons the country was embroiled—reasons not as honorable as the ones officials had given the public—and it questioned the effectiveness of military policy. The study was so revealing that McNamara remarked to a friend, "They could hang people for what's in there."[69] He printed only fifteen copies and classified them "top secret" so that few persons would see them. One of the report's thirty-six authors, Daniel Ellsberg, originally supported the war but later turned against it. Haunted by his failure to act sooner, he photocopied the papers and gave them to the *New York Times* and *Washington Post* in the hope that their publication would sway public opinion and force the government to end the war. The newspapers did publish excerpts.

Although the papers embarrassed the Kennedy and Johnson administrations, President Richard Nixon, who was in office at the time, was continuing to fight the war, and publication of the excerpts infuriated him. Meeting with his chief of staff and his national security adviser, he demanded:

> I have a project I want somebody to take. . . . This takes 18 hours a day. It takes devotion and loyalty and diligence such as you've never seen. . . . I really need a son of a bitch . . . who will work his butt off and do it dishonorably. . . . And I'll direct him myself. I know how to play this game and we're going to start playing it. . . . I want somebody just as tough as I am for a change. . . . We're up against an enemy, a conspiracy. They're using any means. We're going to use any means.[70]

This tirade set in motion the developments that eventually would culminate in the Watergate scandal.

But immediately Nixon sought injunctions to restrain the newspapers from publishing more excerpts. However, the Supreme Court refused to grant them.[71] Most justices said they would grant injunctions if publishing the papers clearly jeopardized national security. But the information in the papers was historical; its disclosure did not hinder the current war effort.[72] Thus the rule remained—no prior restraint—but exceptions were possible.

One exception occurred in 1979 when *The Progressive,* a monthly political magazine, planned to publish technical material about the design of hydrogen bombs. The article, "The H-Bomb Secret: How We Got It,

The chief of the presses of the Washington Post hails the Supreme Court's decision allowing publication of the Pentagon Papers.

Why We're Telling It," argued for open debate rather than secret classification. Although the article was not a "do-it-yourself guide," a federal district court judge concluded that it might help a medium-size nation develop a bomb sooner than it would otherwise. He prohibited the magazine from publishing the article.[73]

The Rehnquist Court did approve prior restraint in a situation far removed from national security. When journalism students at a Saint Louis high school wrote articles for their newspaper about the impact of pregnancy and of parents' divorce on teenagers, the principal deleted the articles, and three of the students sued. The Court, noting that students below the college level have fewer rights than adults, decided that officials can censor school publications.[74]

Principals have typically exercised their authority over articles covering school policies or social issues. A Colorado principal blocked an editorial criticizing his study hall policy while allowing another editorial praising it. A Texas principal banned an article about the class valedictorian who succeeded despite the death of her mother, the desertion of her father, and her own pregnancy. An editorial urging students to be more responsible about sex was censored by a Kentucky principal, who feared it could be interpreted as condoning sex, and a survey on AIDS was censored by a Maryland principal, who prohibited students from defining the term *safe sex*. A North Carolina high school newspaper was shut down and its adviser was fired because of three articles, including a satirical story about the "death" of the writer after eating a cheeseburger from the school cafeteria.

Some principals have tried to restrict their students from using the Internet to criticize school officials or policies. But like the underground newspapers of the 1960s and 1970s, Web pages created off campus (rather than in class) cannot be censored by administrators.

Web pages cannot make terrorist threats, however. A Georgia student was arrested for suggesting that the principal be shot, his daughter kidnapped, his car keyed, and its locks clogged with Superglue.

Despite these exceptions to freedom from prior restraint, the press in the United States is freer than that in Great Britain, where freedom from prior restraint began. Britain has no First Amendment and tolerates more secrecy. The government banned radio and television interviews with all members of the outlawed Irish Republican Army (IRA) and its political party, including its one representative in Parliament.[75] The French government banned the sale of a song—"Go for It, Saddam"—that criticized the West during the Persian Gulf War. The German government banned the sale of music by skinhead groups after neo-Nazi violence.

Restrictions on Gathering News

Although prior restraint is an obvious limitation on freedom of the press, restrictions on gathering news in the first place are less obvious but no less serious. They also keep news from the public.

The Burger Court denied reporters the right to keep the names of their sources confidential. In investigative reporting, reporters frequently rely on sources who demand anonymity in exchange for information. The sources might have sensitive positions in government or relations with criminals that would be jeopardized if their names were publicized. A Louisville reporter was allowed to watch persons make hashish from marijuana if he kept their names confidential. But after publication of the story, a grand jury demanded their names. When the reporter refused to reveal them, he was cited for contempt of court, and his conviction was upheld by the Supreme Court.[76] The majority said reporters' need for confidentiality is not as great as courts' need for information about crimes. So either reporters cannot guarantee anonymity to a potential source, which means they might not obtain information for an important story, or they may have to choose between breaking their promise or being cited for contempt and jailed for months.

A *Time* magazine reporter was informed by a George W. Bush administration official of the identity of a CIA secret agent. When her identity was published, her cover was blown and her career was finished. This reporter, unlike the one above, was not engaged in investigative journalism; he was used as a tool by the administration to punish an American diplomat—the husband of the agent—who criticized the Iraq war. (This incident is explained in Chapter 5.) Because it is illegal to reveal the identity of secret agents, a special prosecutor was appointed to investigate who in the administration leaked her identity. The *Time* reporter refused to answer the prosecutor's questions, so he was held in contempt of court and ordered to jail.

Invasion of Privacy

The right to a free press can conflict with an individual's desire for privacy when the press publishes personal information. The Supreme Court has permitted the press to publish factual information. For example, although a Georgia law prohibited the press from releasing the names of crime victims to spare them embarrassment, an Atlanta television station announced the name of a high school girl who was raped by six classmates and left unconscious on a neighbor's lawn to die. The girl's father sued the station, but the Court said the press needs freedom to publish information that is a matter of public record so that citizens can scrutinize the workings of the judicial system.[77]

In 1975, a man in a crowd watching President Gerald Ford noticed a woman pull out a gun. He grabbed the gun and prevented an assassination. Reporters wrote stories about this hero, including the fact that he was a homosexual. This coverage caused him considerable embarrassment and practical problems as well, so he sued. The courts sided with the press again. The man's good deed made him newsworthy, whether he wanted to be or not.[78] Persons who become newsworthy are permitted little privacy. Justice Brennan said this is a necessary evil "in a society which places a primary value on freedom of speech and of press."[79]

However, the Court has prohibited the press from sending reporters and photographers with law enforcement officers when they conduct a search or make an arrest at someone's home.[80] The Court decided that the police department's desire for good publicity and the local media's desire for interesting stories did not justify the invasion of the defendants' or residents' privacy. Entering the home and photographing the scene made these practices more intrusive than the ones allowed in other cases.

Libel and Obscenity

Despite the broad protection for freedom of the press, the Supreme Court grants much less protection for libelous and obscene material. Traditionally, the justices considered such material irrelevant to the exposition of ideas and search for truth envisioned by the framers of the First Amendment. Any benefit such material might have had was outweighed by the need to protect persons' reputations and morals. For many years, the Court allowed the states to adopt libel and obscenity laws as they saw fit.

Libel

Libel consists of printed or broadcast statements that are false and that tarnish someone's reputation. Victims are entitled to sue for money to compensate them for the harm done.

The Warren Court decided that traditional state libel laws infringed on freedom of the press too much and forced radical changes in these laws. Its landmark decision came in *New York Times* v. *Sullivan* in 1964.[81]

The *Times* ran an ad by black clergymen criticizing Montgomery, Alabama, officials for their response to racial protests. The ad contained some trivial inaccuracies, and although it did not name any officials, the commissioner of police claimed that it referred to him implicitly, and he sued. The local jury ordered the *Times* to pay him a half million dollars! The Supreme Court realized that Alabama's libel law was used to punish a detested northern newspaper for its coverage of controversial civil rights protests. The Court could not overlook the size of the award or the fact that another jury had ordered the *Times* to pay another commissioner a half million dollars for the same ad. It was apparent that traditional libel laws could be used to wreak vengeance on a critical press.

The Court ruled against the commissioner and made it more difficult for public officials to win libel suits. It said that officials must show not only that the statements about them were false but also that the statements were made with "reckless disregard for the truth." This standard gives the press some leeway to make mistakes—to print inaccurate statements—as long as the press is not careless to the point of recklessness.

This protection for the press is necessary, according to Justice Brennan, because the "central meaning of the

Leanne Tippell and Leslie Smart, two of the Saint Louis high school students who sued their school for suppressing their student newspaper story, meet with their attorney, Leslie Edwards (left).

© 2003 Bob Sacha

First Amendment" is that citizens should have the right to criticize officials' conduct. This statement prompted one legal scholar to herald the decision as "an occasion for dancing in the streets."[82]

In later cases, the Court extended this ruling to public figures—persons other than public officials who have public prominence or who thrust themselves into public controversies. It held several persons to be public figures: candidates for public office,[83] a retired general who spoke for right-wing causes,[84] a real estate developer,[85] and a university athletic director.[86] The Court reasoned that it should be more difficult for public figures, as for public officials, to win libel suits because they may influence public policy as much as public officials do. They are also newsworthy enough to get coverage to rebut any false accusations against them.[87]

In sum, the Warren Court's doctrine shifted the emphasis from protection of personal reputation to protection of press freedom.

This shift in emphasis has helped the press report the news—and consequently, helped the public learn the news—during a time when media coverage of controversial events has angered many people. Since the 1960s, individuals and groups have sued the press not primarily to gain compensation for damage to their reputation but to punish the press for its coverage. For example, a lawyer for a conservative organization that sued CBS for its depiction of the army general who commanded the U.S. military in Vietnam admitted that the organization sought the "dismantling" of the network.[88]

Although the press has an advantage in the law when public officials or figures bring suits, lawsuits are expensive to defend against. One case cost the *Washington Post* over a million dollars in legal fees just for the trial (not including the appeal).[89] This specter pressures the press to avoid controversial material. Although large news organizations can withstand the pressure, many small ones cannot. After twelve libel suits in as many years, the publisher of six weekly newspapers in suburban Philadelphia halted his papers' investigative reporting. "I found myself vigorously defending the First Amendment and watching my business go to hell," he said. "Now the communities our papers serve no longer learn about the misconduct of their officials."[90]

Obscenity

Whereas it is relatively clear what libel is and who the victim is, it is not at all clear what obscenity is and who, if anyone, the victim is. It is not even clear why the law needs to address it. Some say the law is necessary because obscenity is immoral; others say it is necessary because obscenity leads to improper behavior (although this link is uncertain). The justices themselves have disagreed, perhaps more than in any other area, and their decisions reflect this. They have been neither clear nor consistent.

The Warren Court decided that state obscenity laws restricted publication of sexual material that should be allowed. While maintaining that the First Amendment does not protect obscenity, the Court narrowed the definition of obscenity in a series of cases in the 1950s and 1960s.[91] The result was to expand the category of pornography that could be produced and sold lawfully.

The Burger Court thought that the Warren Court went too far, and it broadened the definition of obscenity in the 1970s.[92] The goal was to reduce the availability of pornography. The Burger Court defined **obscenity** as sexual material that is patently offensive to the average person in the local community and that lacks any serious literary, artistic, or scientific value. This definition revolves around the views of the average person, rather than the most tolerant or most prudish person. And it revolves around the views in the local community where the material is sold, rather than the views in Los Angeles or New York where the material often is produced and where the attitudes tend to be freewheeling. This definition remains in effect today. In practice, it is implemented by state legislatures and local juries when they pass obscenity statutes and decide obscenity cases.

Occasionally, local officials, especially the prosecutors aiming for higher office, get carried away. A prosecutor in Charlottesville, Virginia, announced that he would prosecute persons who sold *Playboy* magazine. A prosecutor in Albany, Georgia, prosecuted a theater manager who showed the movie *Carnal Knowledge*. The movie, which featured explicit language and occasional nudity, was nominated for an Academy Award as the best film of the year. When the theater manager appealed, the Burger Court reversed his conviction, announcing that local communities have discretion but not "unbridled discretion."[93] The movie, apparent from its nomination for an Academy Award, had serious artistic value.

A prosecutor in Cincinnati prosecuted the director of an art gallery for an exhibit of photographs by Robert Mapplethorpe. The homoerotic pictures, which the director called "tough, brutal, sometimes disgusting," included three showing penetration of a man's anus with various objects. Yet the prosecutor could not prove that the photographs lacked serious artistic value because the photographer had received praise from art critics and the pictures were displayed in an art gallery, so the jury acquitted the director.

Although the Court's broadened definition of obscenity should have made it easier to stanch the flow of obscenity, it has not reduced the availability of sexual material, whether obscene or lawful. Prosecutors say they actually prosecute fewer cases because people are less concerned about obscenity than they used to be, so jurors are less likely to convict.[94]

In fact, sexual material is so popular that Ameri-

The Internet enables people to get pornography in the privacy of their home without having to go to a seedy adult bookstore or movie theater and risking the embarrassment that might occur. Users can type key words into their browser and easily find their way to "Bianca's Smut Shack." Perusing pornography is one of the most common, if not the most common, recreational uses of computers. (At one university, thirteen of the forty most visited sites had names like "rec.arts.erotica.")[1] Some of this depicts sex with children or animals or other deviant practices such as bondage or sadomasochism.

Shocked by the amount and the nature of online pornography and worried about its availability to children, Congress passed a law prohibiting people from knowingly circulating "obscene" or "indecent" material online "in a manner available" to those under eighteen. Thus the law banned sexual material that would be defined, under existing law, as "obscene" and additional material that would be considered "indecent." The latter was not defined clearly.

A coalition of forty-seven groups filed suit to have the law declared unconstitutional. These included the American Civil Liberties Union (ACLU), the American Library Association, Microsoft, and America Online. The U.S. Chamber of Commerce filed a supplementary brief arguing that the law threatened multinational corporations' ability to compete globally in an age of new communications.

The new technology of the Internet has made the old laws under the First Amendment difficult to apply. What precedents should apply? Is the Internet like the print media, which have substantial freedom as long as they do not publish the narrow category of material defined as obscene? Or is the Internet more like the broadcast media, which have less freedom because they are pervasive and reach into people's homes? Or because the goal is to protect children, is the law more analogous to child pornography laws that prohibit a broader range of material than regular obscenity laws?

A lower federal court recognized that the Internet is a different medium and is in fact the most participatory speech medium yet developed. As such, the judges concluded, it should be nurtured, not stifled. In 1997, the Supreme Court, in its initial effort to apply the First Amendment to cyberspace, agreed.[2] It did not want the Internet censored more than other media. Thus it accorded the Internet as much protection as books, magazines, and newspapers (and more than radio and television). As a result, the portion of the law banning "obscene" material was upheld, while the portion banning additional "indecent" material was struck down. This portion was too broad and too ambiguous. It might lead to prosecution of people for discussing homosexuality or prison rape. It could even lead to prosecution of parents for sending their children information about birth control. Or the stiff penalties, two years in prison and a $250,000 fine, might cause people to avoid subjects they should feel free to address. Then the law would have a "chilling effect" on speech, which the First Amendment is supposed to guard against.

Although the goal of protecting children was worthy, the justices said, the result would be to prevent adults from communicating with each other because the nature of the Internet made it impossible to know who was receiving the material. Adults might be prosecuted if children were obtaining the material even though the adults were unaware that the children were doing so.

Congress passed another law, this one prohibiting people from circulating virtual child pornography, which is computer-simulated images that depict children engaged in sex. Virtual and actual child pornography can be hard to tell apart, and Congress assumed that either type leads to child abuse. But the Court invalidated the statute because virtual pornography does not involve real people, so its production harms no actual children.[3]

1. Philip Elmer-DeWitt, "On a Screen Near You: Cyberporn," *Time,* July 3, 1995, 40.
2. *Reno* v. *American Civil Liberties Union,* 138 L.Ed.2d 874 (1997).
3. *Ashcroft* v. *Free Speech Coalition,* 152 L.Ed.2d 403 (2002).

cans, according to estimates, spend between $8 billion and $10 billion a year on "adult entertainment"—videos and DVDs, cable and satellite porn, Internet porn, phone sex, peep shows, sexual magazines, and sexual toys. This amount roughly equals Hollywood's domestic box-office receipts.[95] (See the box "Regulating Cyberporn.")

Society is less tolerant of child pornography than adult pornography, however, partly because children are used in the production and partly because pedophiles, adults who molest children, are attracted to this material. Consequently, the Court has made it easier to crack down on child pornography. Material that depicts children engaged in sexual conduct, whether obscene or not, can be prohibited, and individuals who produce, distribute, or merely possess it can be prosecuted.[96]

Freedom of Religion

Some people came to America for religious liberty, but once they arrived, many did not want to grant this liberty to others. Some communities became as intolerant as the ones in the Old World from which people had fled.[97] But people came with so many religious views that the diversity gradually led to grudging tolerance, and by the time the Constitution and the Bill of Rights were adopted, support for religious liberty was fairly widespread.

Both the diversity and the tolerance are reflected in the two documents. The Constitution, unlike the Declaration of Independence, is a secular document. It does not mention "God," "Creator," "Providence," or "divine."[98] It does not claim to be a compact between the people and God (or, like some monarchies, between the rulers and God); rather, it is a compact among the people, as the Preamble underscores from its very start —"We the people . . . ."

The Bill of Rights grants freedom of religion in the First Amendment, which states, "Congress shall make no law respecting an establishment of religion, or prohibiting the free exercise thereof." These two clauses— the establishment clause and the free exercise clause— were intended to work in tandem to provide freedom for people's religions and, by implication, freedom from others' religions.

The Founders recoiled from Europeans' experience of continuous conflict and long wars fought over religious schisms. Consequently, Thomas Jefferson explained, the clauses were designed to build "a wall of separation between church and state."[99] Each would stay on its own side of the wall and not interfere or even interact with the other. **Separation of church and state** was a novel idea; according to one historian, al-

though the phrase is not in the Constitution, it was the "most revolutionary" aspect of the Constitution.[100]

Today some deeply religious people scorn the idea of separation of church and state. They think that this idea devalues the importance of religion. But the Founders did not propose separation because they considered religion less important than government. Rather, they saw it as a practical means to preserve the peace that had eluded European states. In addition, they saw it as a way to protect religion itself. Without interference by government officials, whether to hinder or to help, churches would be free to determine their dogma and establish their practices as they saw fit. They would be free to flourish. Indeed, religion is stronger in the United States than in Europe, where churches endorsed and supported by the government sit mostly empty.

Despite the Founders' intention, as society became more complex and government became more pervasive, church and state came to interact, sometimes to interfere, with each other. Inevitably, the wall began to crumble, and the courts had to devise new doctrine to keep church and state as separate as possible while still accommodating the needs of both.

Free Exercise of Religion

The **free exercise clause** allows individuals to practice their religion without government coercion. Government has occasionally restricted free exercise of religion

Amish children head for the cornfields to avoid school officials in Iowa.

directly. Early in the country's history, some states prohibited Catholics or Jews from voting or holding office, and as late as 1961, Maryland prohibited nonbelievers from holding office.[101] In the 1920s, Oregon prohibited students from attending parochial schools.[102] More recently, prisons in Illinois and Texas prohibited Black Muslims and Buddhists from receiving religious publications and using prison chapels.[103] The Supreme Court invalidated each of these restrictions.

A suburb of Miami tried to ban the Santeria religion in 1987. Santeria blends ancient African rites and Roman Catholic rituals, but its distinguishing feature is animal sacrifice. Adherents believe that animal sacrifice is necessary to win the favor of the gods, and they practice it at initiations of new members and at births, marriages, and deaths. They kill chickens, ducks, doves, pigeons, sheep, goats, and turtles. When adherents, who had practiced their religion underground since refugees from Cuba brought it to Florida in the 1950s and 1960s, announced plans to construct a church building, cultural center, museum, and school, the city passed ordinances against ritualistic animal sacrifice, essentially forbidding adherents from practicing their religion. The Court struck down the ordinances.[104] "Although the practice of animal sacrifice may seem abhorrent to some," Justice Anthony Kennedy wrote, "religious beliefs need not be acceptable, logical, consistent, or comprehensible to others in order to merit First Amendment protection."

Government has also restricted the free exercise of religion indirectly. As society has become more complex, some laws have inevitably interfered with religion, even when not designed to. The laws have usually interfered with minority religions, which do not have many members in legislatures looking out for their interests.

At first the Court distinguished between belief and action: Individuals could believe what they wanted, but they could not act accordingly if such action was against the law. In 1878, male Mormons who believed their religion required polygamy could not marry more than one woman.[105] The Court rhetorically asked, "Suppose one believed that human sacrifices were a necessary part of religious worship?" Of course, belief without action gave little protection and scant satisfaction to the individuals involved.

In the 1960s, the Warren Court recognized this problem and broadened the protection by granting exemptions to laws. A Seventh-Day Adventist who worked in a textile mill in South Carolina quit when the mill shifted from a five-day to a six-day workweek that included Saturday—her Sabbath. Unable to find another job, she applied for unemployment benefits, but the state refused to provide them. To receive them, she had to be "available" for work, and the state said she was not available because she would not accept jobs that required Saturday work. The Court ordered the state to

grant an exemption to its law.[106] The Burger Court ruled that employers need to make a reasonable effort to accommodate employees' requests to fit work schedules around their Sabbath.[107]

Amish in Wisconsin withheld their children from high school, although the law required their attendance until age sixteen. The parents sent their children to elementary and junior high school to learn basic reading, writing, and arithmetic, but they complained that high school would subject their children to worldly influences that would interfere with their semi-isolated agricultural life. The Warren Court ruled that the Amish could be exempt from the additional one to two years the law required beyond junior high school.[108]

Congress, too, has granted some exemptions. It excused the Amish from participating in the Social Security program because the Amish support their own elderly. And in every draft law, it excused conscientious objectors from participating in war.

The Court has been most reluctant to exempt individuals from paying taxes. It did not excuse either the Amish[109] or the Quakers, who as pacifists tried to withhold the portion of their income taxes that funded the military.[110] The Court worried that many other persons would try to avoid paying taxes, too.

The Rehnquist Court, which was not as sensitive to minority rights, refused to grant such exemptions.[111] The Native American church uses peyote, a hallucinogen derived from a cactus, in worship ceremonies. Members believe that the plant embodies their deity and that eating it is an act of communion. Although peyote is a controlled substance, Congress has authorized its use on Indian reservations, and almost half of the states have authorized its use off the reservations by church members. But when two members in Oregon, a state that did not allow its use off the reservations, were fired from their jobs and denied unemployment benefits for using the drug, the Court refused to grant an exemption.[112] A five-justice majority rejected the doctrine and precedents of the Warren and Burger Courts. Justice Antonin Scalia, a Catholic, admitted that denying such exemptions will put minority religions at a disadvantage but said that this is an "unavoidable consequence of democratic government." That is, denying minority rights is an inevitable and acceptable result of majority rule. This rationale, of course, could be used to emasculate not only the free exercise clause but other provisions of the Bill of Rights as well.

Although Congress overturned the particular focus of the decision, restricting Indians' use of this drug,[113] the broad implications of the decision remained. Some adherents of minority religions were not allowed to practice the tenets of their religions. Families of deceased Jews and Laotians, who reject autopsies on religious grounds, were overruled. Muslim prisoners whose religion forbids them from eating pork were refused other

Alfred Smith, fired for using peyote in religious ceremonies, challenged Oregon's law prohibiting use of the drug.

Courtesy of the National Archives

The country's religious diversity has led to demands for some exotic exemptions. Inspired by the Bible's statement that Jesus's followers "shall take up serpents" and "if they drink any deadly thing, it shall not hurt them," members of the Holiness Church of God in Jesus's Name handle snakes and drink strychnine. Some become enraptured and entranced to the point of hysteria, and occasionally some die. In 1975, the Tennessee Supreme Court forbade such practices, saying that the state has "the right to guard against the unnecessary creation of widows and orphans." However, these practices continue in some places.

© Phil Schofield

meat instead. Members of the Sikh religion, who wear turbans, had been exempted from the federal law requiring construction workers to wear hard hats, but after the decision, this exemption was rescinded.[114]

Even mainstream churches worried about the implications of the ruling, and a coalition of religious groups lobbied Congress to overturn it. Congress passed and President Bill Clinton signed an act reversing the ruling and substituting the previous doctrine. But the Rehnquist Court invalidated the act in 1997 because it challenged the justices' authority and altered their interpretation of the First Amendment without going through the process required to amend the Constitution.[115]

Establishment of Religion

Two competing traditions reflecting the role of government toward religion have led to intense conflict over the **establishment clause.** Many early settlers in America wanted government to reinforce their religion, yet the framers of the Constitution were products of the Enlightenment, which emphasized the importance of reason and deemphasized the role of organized religion. The two individuals most responsible for the religious guarantees in the First Amendment, Jefferson and Madison, feared the divisiveness of religion. They wanted separation of church and state, advocating not only freedom *of* religion for believers but freedom *from* religion for others.[116]

Early decisions by the Supreme Court usually reflected the first of these traditions. In 1892, Justice David Brewer smugly declared that "this is a Christian nation."[117] But as the country became more pluralistic, the Court moved toward the second of these traditions. Since the early 1960s, the Court has generally interpreted the establishment clause to forbid government not only from designating an official church, like the Church of England in England, which receives tax money and special privileges, but also from aiding one religion over another or even from aiding religion over nonreligion.

Courts have used the clause to resolve disputes about prayer in public schools. In 1962 and 1963, the Supreme Court issued its famous—some might say infamous—prayer rulings. New York had students recite a nondenominational prayer at the start of every day, and Pennsylvania and Baltimore had students recite the Lord's Prayer or Bible verses. The Court, with only one justice dissenting, ruled that these practices violated the establishment clause.[118] Technically, the prayers were voluntary; students could leave the room. But the Court doubted that the prayers really were voluntary. It noted that nonconforming students would face tremendous pressure from teachers and peers and that leaving the room usually connotes punishment for bad behavior. The Court therefore concluded that the prayers fostered religion. According to Justice Black, "Government in this country should stay out of the business of writing and sanctioning official prayers and leave that purely religious function to the people themselves and to those the people choose to look to for religious guidance." Although schools could teach religion as a subject, they could not promote religion.

For similar reasons, the Court ruled that Kentucky could not require public schools to post the Ten Commandments in classrooms.[119]

Many people sharply criticized the rulings. A representative from Alabama lamented, "They put the Negroes in the schools, and now they've driven God out."[120] Actually, the justices had not driven God out—students could pray on their own whenever they pleased.

Empirical studies in the years after the rulings found that prayers and Bible readings had decreased but by no means disappeared, especially in the South.[121] For example, just one of 121 districts in Tennessee fully complied. A local official said, "I saw no reason to create controversy," and another asserted, "I am of the opinion that 99 percent of the people in the United States feel as I do about the Supreme Court's decision—that it was an outrage. . . . The remaining 1 percent do not belong in this free world."[122]

Despite the passage of time, periodic news reports indicate that many schools, especially in the rural South, still use prayers or Bible readings in violation of the Court's rulings. These practices are reinforced by social pressure. In 1993, a woman whose family had moved to Pontotoc, Mississippi, to be near relatives discovered that Christian prayers were being broadcast on the intercom and the Bible was being taught in a class. When she objected, rumors circulated that she was an outside agitator paid by the ACLU to force the town to change.

One of her children said his teacher told the class that he did not believe in God, while another of her children said he kept "getting jumped" in the bathroom. Then the woman lost her job in a convenience store after customers threatened to boycott the store.[123]

News reports also indicate that schools in Kentucky and Ohio at least allowed volunteers to put the Ten Commandments inside or outside public schools in violation of the Court's ruling.[124]

Congress considered a constitutional amendment to overturn the rulings but did not pass one for several reasons. Some people support the rulings. Others support the Court and do not want to challenge its authority and thereby set a precedent for other groups on other matters.

Some religious leaders doubt that groups would ever agree on specific prayers. America's religious diversity means that the prayers would offend some students or parents. Prayers that suit Christians might not suit Jews; those that suit Jews might not suit persons of other faiths. Recent immigrants from Asia and the Middle East, practicing Buddhism, Shintoism, Taoism, and Islam, have made the country even more pluralistic. Now, according to one researcher, America's religious diversity is greater than that of any country in recorded history.[125] Thus asking students in this country to say a prayer would be like "asking the members of the United Nations to stand and sing the national anthem of one country."[126] However, many local communities are not diverse, and the majority may assume that everyone, or at least all "normal" people, share their views of religion.

In lieu of an amendment, about half of the states have passed laws providing for a "moment of silence" to begin each school day. Although the laws are ostensibly for meditation, some legislators admit they are really for

© Sylvia Plachy, photographed for the New Yorker

Muslim students in Dearborn, Michigan, reflect our religious pluralism. The Detroit area has the second-largest concentration of Arabs outside the Middle East.

Sikhs from India were sometimes mistaken for Muslims after the 9/11 attacks. One Sikh was murdered in Arizona.

prayer. Yet a majority of justices indicated that they would approve a moment of silence if students were not urged to pray.[127]

The Rehnquist Court reaffirmed and extended the prayer rulings of the Warren Court. It held that clergy cannot offer prayers at graduation ceremonies for public elementary, middle, and high schools.[128] The prayers in question were brief and nonsectarian, but the majority reasoned, "What to most believers may seem nothing more than a reasonable request that the nonbeliever respect their religious practices, in a school context may appear to the nonbeliever or dissenter to be an attempt to employ the machinery of the state to enforce a religious orthodoxy." Although attendance at the ceremony was voluntary, like participation in school prayers, the majority did not consider it truly voluntary. Justice Kennedy wrote, "Everyone knows that in our society and in our culture high school graduation is one of life's most significant occasions. . . . Graduation is a time for family and those closest to the student to celebrate success and express mutual wishes of gratitude and respect."

Although the Court's language here was emphatic, its stance on student-led prayers has been ambiguous. In 1992, the Court refused to review a federal court of appeals ruling that allowed student-led prayers at graduation ceremonies.[129] A Texas school board permitted the senior class to decide whether to have a prayer and, if so, which student to give it. The appellate court held that this policy was not precluded by the Supreme Court's ruling because the decision was not made by officials and the prayer was not offered by a clergy member, so official coercion was not present. But in 1996, the Court also refused to review a federal court of appeals

ruling from a different circuit that prohibited student-led prayers at various school events.[130] The Court's reluctance to resolve this controversy means that the ruling of each court of appeals remains but applies only to schools in its circuit and that no appellate ruling governs schools in the rest of the country.

The first appellate court's holding encouraged opponents of the Supreme Court's rulings to use the same approach to circumvent these rulings as well. Several southern states passed laws allowing student-led prayers to start each school day. Some school officials, who selected the students, let them give the prayers over the intercom. Federal courts in Alabama and Mississippi invalidated these laws because school officials were involved and because all students were required or at least pressured to listen to the prayers.

The Rehnquist Court did invalidate the use of schools' public address systems by clergy or students to give prayers at high school football games.[131] Although student attendance is voluntary, the games are official school events.

The public desire for official school prayers is fueled by a nostalgia for the less troubling times before the 1960s. As one writer perceived, the desire "doesn't have much to do with prayer anyway, but with a time, a place, an ethos that praying and pledging allegiance at the beginning of school each day represent."[132] Many people echo the feelings of a Pennsylvania school board member who said, "The country has certainly gone downhill since they took it out."[133] For these people, reinstitutionalization of school prayers would be a symbol that our society stands for appropriate values.

The public desire for official school prayers is also fueled by occasional reports of school officials who mistakenly believe that court rulings require them to forbid all forms of religious expression. Thus some confused administrators have prohibited a few students from wearing religious jewelry, reading the Bible while riding the bus, and praying before eating their lunch.[134]

In another case, the Supreme Court said that the University of Missouri at Kansas City had to make its meeting rooms available to students' religious organizations on an equal basis with other organizations, even if the religious organizations used the rooms for prayer or worship.[135] Otherwise, the university would be discriminating against religion.

After this decision, Congress passed a law that requires public high schools as well as colleges and universities to allow meetings of students' religious, philosophical, or political groups outside class hours. The Court accepted this law in 1990.[136] Justice Sandra Day O'Connor said that high school students "are likely to understand that a school does not endorse or support student speech that it merely permits on a nondiscriminatory basis." Students have established Bible clubs in one-quarter of public high schools, according to one estimate.[137] (As a result of this act, students have also established gay-straight clubs—organizations of gay and straight students who support the rights of gays, lesbians, and bisexuals—in more than seven hundred high schools.)[138] Yet students' interest in Bible clubs has not always been the driving force. Adults eager to put prayers back into the schools have often taken the initiative. Organized networks have encouraged the clubs and provided advice, workshops, and handbooks for them.

The Rehnquist Court also said that the University of Virginia had to provide funding, from students' fees, to students' religious organizations on an equal basis with other campus organizations, even if a religious organization sought the money to print a religious newspaper.[139] On the basis of this precedent, a federal court of appeals ruled that the University of South Alabama had to provide funding to a gay organization.

Despite its prayer rulings, the Court has been reluctant to invalidate traditional religious symbols. It has not questioned the motto "In God We Trust," on our coins since 1865 and paper money since 1955, or the phrase "one nation under God," in the Pledge of Allegiance since 1954.[140]

In 2002, a federal court of appeals held the phrase "under God" in the Pledge unconstitutional when recited in the public schools. The court said it promotes religion as much as if it professed that we are a nation "under Jesus" or "under Vishnu" or "under Zeus" or "under no god." It promotes Christianity and leaves out not only atheists and agnostics but believers of other deities, such as Buddhists and many Native Americans. Although the ruling was a logical extension of the prayer rulings, it was a lightning rod for the public's anger, and the Supreme Court sidestepped the issue (deciding that the student's father, an atheist, lacked authority to bring suit on the student's behalf because the

student's mother, a born-again Christian, had custody of the child after their divorce).[141]

The Burger Court upheld the display of a nativity scene on government property, at least when it is part of a broader display for the holiday season.[142] Pawtucket, Rhode Island, had a crèche, Santa Claus, sleigh with reindeer, Christmas tree, and talking wishing well. Although the nativity scene was an obvious symbol of Christianity, the Court said it was a traditional symbol of a holiday that has become secular as well as religious. Moreover, the presence of the secular decorations diluted any religious impact the nativity scene would have. A crèche by itself, however, would be impermissible.[143]

The chief justice of Alabama's supreme court had a granite marker bearing the Ten Commandments installed in Alabama's Judicial Building in the middle of the night. Lower federal courts ruled this display, which stood by itself, a violation of the establishment clause. The Supreme Court refused to hear an appeal by the chief justice in 2003. When the chief justice, defying a court order, refused to remove the 5,300-pound marker, he was suspended by his own court.

Other states have authorized displays of the Ten Commandments along with historical documents such as the Magna Carta and the Declaration of Independence in the hope that such displays will pass constitutional muster.[144]

Courts have also used the establishment clause to resolve disputes about teaching evolution in schools. In 1968, the Supreme Court invalidated Arkansas's forty-year-old law forbidding schools from teaching evolution.[145] Arkansas and Louisiana then passed laws requiring schools that teach evolution to also teach "creationism"—the biblical version of creation.[146] In 1987, the Court invalidated these laws because their purpose was to promote the fundamentalist Christian view.[147] Yet teaching evolution remains controversial.

© Time Life Pictures/Getty Images

A Christian Bible club meets in a Minneapolis high school.

A crew prepares to move a granite marker bearing the Ten Commandments from Alabama's Judicial Building after federal courts ruled that the display violated the establishment clause.

Many science teachers skip it to avoid confrontations with conservative parents and religious groups.[148]

Courts have also used the establishment clause to resolve disputes about aid to parochial schools. Historically, most parochial schools were affiliated with the Catholic Church. Protestants opposed aid to these schools because they feared growth of this church. But changes in society, beginning with the desegregation of public schools, prompted more Protestants to form their own schools.[149] Now millions of students attend either Catholic or Protestant schools, and their parents pay tuition and other expenses. Schools have asked legislatures to provide money to defray part of the costs of their nonreligious activities. Courts have had to decide whether providing the money helps religion or whether denying it hinders religion. In addition, courts have had to determine whether providing the money leads to excessive entanglement of church and state because of the monitoring required to ensure that the money is not spent for religious purposes.

The Court has upheld some types of aid[150] but has rejected most types.[151] Yet the Court, reflecting shifting coalitions of justices, has not drawn a clear line separating permissible from impermissible forms of assistance.[152]

The Rehnquist Court, reflecting its justices' greater tolerance for aid to parochial schools and perhaps the majority's Republican affiliations, narrowly upheld tuition aid, in the form of school vouchers, for some students to attend private schools, including religious ones.[153] Although this case involved only a pilot pro-

gram for Cleveland's failing schools, the ruling has been used by conservatives to push for similar programs throughout the country.[154]

Through Republican officials, conservative Christians have pushed for numerous policies and programs reflecting their beliefs. Despite legal doctrine emphasizing separation of powers, the Bush administration has sought to implement these policies and programs. It has opposed abortions, limited scientific research involving stem cells, withheld federal money from family planning organizations and efforts in the United States and abroad, and given federal money to abstinence-based sex education programs, church-run social programs for child care and drug treatment, and church-run marriage initiatives. As a result, for example, the government gave federal money to Louisiana, which funneled it to Protestant groups to teach abstinence through Bible lessons and skits and to Catholic groups to hold prayer sessions at abortion clinics.[155]

Despite ongoing tensions and frequent conflicts, the effort to separate church and state has enabled the United States to manage, and even nourish, its religious pluralism. The effort has kept many religious debates and potential religious fights out of the political arena. But today this practical arrangement is opposed by those religious conservatives who most fear the changes in modern society. They see their religion as a shield protecting their family against these changes and want their religion to be reinforced by the authority of the government.

Rights of Criminal Defendants

The Fourth, Fifth, Sixth, and Eighth Amendments provide numerous **due process** rights for criminal defendants. When the government prosecutes defendants, it must give them the process—that is, the procedures —they are due; it must be fair and "respect certain decencies of civilized conduct,"[156] even toward uncivilized people.

One defense attorney said that many of his clients "had been monsters—nothing less—who had done monstrous things. Although occasionally not guilty of the crime charged, nearly all my clients have been guilty of something."[157] Then why do we give them rights? We give criminal defendants rights because we give all individuals rights in court. As Justice Douglas observed, "respecting the dignity even of the least worthy . . . citizen raises the stature of all of us."[158]

But why do we give all individuals rights in court? We do so because we have established the **presumption of innocence.** This presumption is "not . . . a naive belief that most or even many defendants are in-

What about the Second Amendment?

Individuals and interest groups opposed to gun control cite the **Second Amendment,** which provides "the right of the people to keep and bear arms." But these opponents seldom quote the rest of the amendment, which reads in its entirety, "A well regulated militia being necessary to the security of a free state, the right of the people to keep and bear arms shall not be infringed." The amendment was adopted at a time when there was no standing army to protect people from foreign invasions, Indian uprisings, or mob riots. The language links the right to bear arms with the security of the state. The language suggests that the right belongs to each state or, if to individuals, only to individuals when they are protecting their state—that is, when they are serving in the militia of their state. At the Founding, the militia was a ragtag band of civilians in each community; today the militia is the National Guard of each state. Therefore, the amendment might be a useless anachronism if it merely allows the National Guard to have weapons.

Accordingly, the federal courts have routinely upheld gun control laws when they are challenged as violations of the Second Amendment.[1] The Supreme Court has rarely reviewed these decisions, and it has never offered a definitive interpretation of the amendment.

Conservative Chief Justice Warren Burger criticized the National Rifle Association for misleading people by insisting that the Second Amendment should prevent gun control legislation. He said the amendment "has been the subject of one of the greatest pieces of fraud—I repeat the word 'fraud'—on the American public."[2]

Yet the persistent views of the American public have prompted legal scholars to take a closer look at the adoption of the Second Amendment.[3] Some have concluded that there might be a right for individuals, separate from the right for states and National Guards, to own and use guns. Their rationale is that the original notion of a militia encompassed all individuals who had political rights, such as the rights to vote and to serve on juries—that is, all white males who owned property. Today individuals who have political rights include all adult citizens (except felons in most states). Thus the word *militia* in 1791 might mean all adult citizens today. However, this expanded view of the Second Amendment would provide a right only for individuals to own and use guns to defend their state or, possibly, their homes or themselves.[4] It would not provide a right to own and use guns for hunting or other recreational purposes because the language—"the security of a free state"—indicates that the justification for the right is just protection.[5]

"You know, if she weren't part of a well-regulated militia, I'd be a little nervous."

Even if this expanded view of the Second Amendment becomes more common—the Bush administration is the first to advocate an expanded view—it would not bar most gun control laws or proposals. The amendment refers to a "well regulated militia," making clear that arms can be regulated, as they were even in colonial times. (George Washington proposed government inspection of private arms at least twice a year.) As Justice John Paul Stevens observed, arms have "long been subject to pervasive governmental regulation because of the dangerous nature of the product and the public interest in having that danger controlled."[6]

So a huge gap remains between what many people think and what most judges and legal scholars have concluded.

1. A federal district court did make headlines in 1999 when it ruled unconstitutional a federal law prohibiting a person under a restraining order from owning a gun. This was apparently the first time a court struck down a law because the court thought it infringed on the Second Amendment.
2. Joan Biskupic, "A Second (Amendment) Look at Bearing Arms," *Washington Post National Weekly Edition,* May 15, 1995, 33.
3. For a balanced synthesis of the conflicting views, see David C. Williams, *The Mythic Meanings of the Second Amendment* (New Haven, Conn.: Yale University Press, 2003).
4. In the original debate over the proposed amendment, the framers apparently never discussed the use of firearms for personal protection. Garry Wills, *A Necessary Evil: A History of American Distrust* (New York: Simon & Schuster, 1999).
5. In addition, some argue that the amendment allows the people as a whole—not a faction of the people—to use firearms to resist government tyranny. Williams, *Mythic Meanings.*
6. *United States* v. *Thompson/Center Arms Co.,* 504 U.S. 505, 526 (1992).
Source: Except where noted, Laurence H. Tribe, *American Constitutional Law,* 3rd ed., vol. 1 (New York: Foundation Press, 2000), 894–903.

nocent, or a cavalier attitude toward crime." It reflects a mistrust of the state, as it recognizes the possibility of an overzealous prosecutor or an unfair judge. It requires the state to prove the defendant's guilt, essentially saying, "We won't take your word for it." [159] Of course, when the crime rate is high or a particular crime is heinous, many people fear the state less than the criminals. Then they want to give officials more authority and defendants fewer rights. But this is the way the people eventually lose their rights.

Search and Seizure

England fostered the notion that a family's home is its castle, but Parliament made exceptions for the American colonies. It authorized writs of assistance, which allowed customs officials to conduct general searches for goods imported by the colonists without paying taxes to the crown. The English tradition of home privacy combined with the colonists' resentment of these writs led to adoption of the Fourth Amendment, which forbids **unreasonable searches and seizures.**

One type of seizure is the arrest of a person. Police must have evidence to believe that a person committed a crime. Another type of seizure is the confiscation of illegal contraband. The general requirement is that police should get a search warrant from a judge by showing evidence that a particular thing is in a particular place.

However, the Supreme Court has made numerous exceptions to this requirement that complicate the law. These exceptions account for the vast majority of searches. If persons consent to a search, police can conduct a search without a warrant. If police see contraband in plain view, they can seize it; they do not need to close their eyes to it. If police have evidence to arrest someone, they can search both the person and the area within that person's control. If police suspect that someone is committing a crime but lack evidence to arrest the suspect, they can "stop and frisk" the person—conduct a pat-down search. If police want to search a motor vehicle (in some situations), they can do so because vehicles are mobile and could be gone by the time police got a warrant. If police face an emergency situation, with a person's life in jeopardy, they can search for weapons.

Customs and border patrol officials can search persons and things coming into the country to enforce customs and immigration laws. Airport guards can search passengers and luggage to prevent hijackings and terrorism. And prison guards can search prisoners to ensure security.

These are general principles that need to be interpreted in specific cases. The Court has tried to walk a fine line between acknowledging officials' need for evidence and individuals' need for privacy. Liberal judges

interpret these principles more broadly, and conservative judges interpret them more narrowly. Besides liberal and conservative interpretations, the law is so complex that it is often difficult to determine the legality of many searches and seizures. (See the box "When a Court Reverses a Conviction. . .")

Exclusionary Rule

To enforce search and seizure law, the Court has established the **exclusionary rule,** which bars from the courts any evidence obtained in violation of the Fourth Amendment. The rule's goal is to deter illegal conduct by police officers.

Although the Court issued the rule for federal courts in 1914,[160] it did not impose the rule on state courts until 1961. Even so, the Warren Court's decision, in the case of *Mapp* v. *Ohio,*[161] was one of its most controversial. Until this time, police in many states had ignored search and seizure law.

The decision still has not been widely accepted. The Burger Court created an exception to it. In a pair of cases, the justices allowed evidence obtained illegally to be used in court because the police had acted "in good faith." [162]

Electronic Surveillance

The Fourth Amendment traditionally applied to searches involving a physical trespass and seizures producing a tangible object. Electronic surveillance, however, does not require a physical trespass or result in a tangible object.

This posed a problem for the Supreme Court when it heard its first wiretapping case in 1928. Federal prohibition agents tapped the telephone of bootleggers by installing equipment on wires in the basement of the

When a Court Reverses a Conviction . . .

. . . the defendant does not necessarily go free. An appellate court normally only evaluates the legality of the procedures used by officials; it does not determine guilt or innocence. Therefore, when it reverses a conviction, it only indicates that officials used some illegal procedure in convicting the defendant—for example, they may have used evidence from an improper search and seizure. Then the prosecutor can retry the defendant, without this evidence, if the prosecutor thinks there is enough other evidence. Often prosecutors do retry the defendants, and frequently judges or juries reconvict them.

bootleggers' apartment building. The Court's majority rigidly adhered to its traditional doctrine, saying that this was not a search and seizure, so the agents did not need a warrant.[163]

In a classic example of keeping the Constitution up-to-date with the times, the Warren Court overruled this precedent in 1967.[164] Because electronic eavesdropping might threaten privacy as much as traditional searching, officials must get judicial authorization, similar to a warrant, to engage in such eavesdropping.

Yet judicial authorization is easy to get. In a recent four-year period, the FBI requested 2,686 wiretaps, and the courts granted all but one.[165]

Self-Incrimination

The Fifth Amendment provides that persons shall not be compelled to be witnesses against themselves—that is, to incriminate themselves. Because defendants are presumed innocent, the government must prove their guilt.

This right means that the defendants on trial do not have to take the witness stand and answer the prosecutor's questions, and neither the prosecutor nor the judge can call attention to their decision to exercise this right. Neither can suggest that the defendants must have something to hide and thereby imply that they must be guilty. (But if the defendants do take the stand and testify, they thereby waive their right, so then the prosecutor can cross-examine them and they must answer.)

This right also means that the prosecutors cannot introduce into evidence any statements or confessions from the defendants that were not voluntary. However, the meaning of "voluntary" has changed over time.

For years, law enforcement officials used physical brutality—"the third degree"—to get confessions. After 1936, when the Supreme Court ruled that confessions obtained this way were invalid,[166] officials resorted to more subtle techniques. They held suspects incommunicado so that the suspects could not notify anyone about their arrest and delayed bringing them to court so that the judge could not inform them of their rights.[167] Officials interrogated suspects for long periods of time without food or rest, in one case with alternating teams of interrogators for thirty-six hours.[168] The Court ruled that these techniques, designed to break the suspects' will, were psychological coercion, so the confessions were invalid.

The Warren Court still worried that many confessions were not truly voluntary, so it issued a landmark decision in 1966. Arizona police arrested a poor, mentally disturbed man, Ernesto Miranda, for kidnapping and raping a woman. After the woman identified him in a lineup, police interrogated him for two hours, prompting him to confess. He had not been told that he could remain silent or be represented by an attorney.

In *Miranda* v. *Arizona,* the Court decided that his confession was not truly voluntary.[169] Chief Justice Warren, himself a former district attorney, noted the tremendous advantage police have in interrogation and said that suspects needed more protection. The Court ruled that officials must advise suspects of their rights before interrogation. These came to be known as the **Miranda rights:**

- You have the right to remain silent.
- If you talk, anything you say can be used against you.
- You have the right to be represented by an attorney.
- If you cannot afford an attorney, one will be appointed for you.

The Burger and Rehnquist Courts did not require police and prosecutors to follow *Miranda* as strictly as the Warren Court did but, contrary to expectations, did not abandon it. In 2000, the Rehnquist Court reaffirmed *Miranda* by a 7–2 vote.[170]

Even with the warnings, most suspects talk anyway. Some do not understand the warnings. Others think the police, who may rattle off the warnings fast or in a monotone, give them only because they are required to, not because they actually mean them. Also, suspects in an interrogation are in a coercive atmosphere and face law enforcement tactics designed to exploit their weaknesses. Detectives are trained to persuade the suspects to talk despite the warnings. One said, "Before you ever get in there, the first thing an investigator usually thinks about is . . . how can I breeze through this *Miranda* thing so I don't set the guy off and tell him not to talk to me, song and dance it, sugarcoat it, whatever."[171] So detectives frequently lie and trick suspects.

As a result of the Miranda decision (Ernesto Miranda is pictured left), police must advise suspects of their Miranda rights to silence and counsel before interrogating them.

Counsel

The Sixth Amendment provides the **right to counsel** in criminal cases. Initially, it permitted defendants to hire an attorney to help them prepare a defense, and later it permitted defendants to have the attorney represent them at the trial. But it was no help to most defendants because they were too poor to hire an attorney.

Consequently, the Supreme Court required federal courts to furnish an attorney to all indigent defendants as long ago as 1938.[172] But most criminal cases are state cases, and although the Court required state courts to furnish an attorney in some cases, it was reluctant to impose a broad requirement on these courts.[173]

In 1963, the Warren Court accepted the appeal of Clarence Earl Gideon. Charged with breaking into a pool hall and stealing beer, wine, and change from a vending machine, Gideon asked the judge for a lawyer. The judge refused to appoint one, leaving Gideon to defend himself. The prosecutor did not have a strong case, but Gideon was not able to point out its weaknesses. He was convicted and sentenced to five years. On appeal, the Warren Court unanimously declared that Gideon was entitled to be represented by counsel.[174] Justice Black explained that "lawyers in criminal courts are necessities, not luxuries." The Court finally established a broad rule: State courts must provide an attorney to indigent defendants in felony cases.

Gideon proved the Court's point. Given a lawyer and retried, he was not reconvicted. The lawyer did the effective job defending him that he had not been able to do himself.

In 1972, the Burger Court expanded the rule: State courts must provide an attorney to indigent defendants in misdemeanor cases too, except those that result in no incarceration,[175] because misdemeanor cases as well as felony cases are too complex for the defendants to defend themselves. In 2002, the Rehnquist Court expanded the rule further, declaring that state courts must provide an attorney to indigent defendants even in cases that result in no incarceration if the defendants receive probation or a suspended sentence, which could eventually result in incarceration if the defendants fail to follow the terms of such sentence.[176]

The Supreme Court also decided that in addition to an attorney for the trial, the courts must provide an attorney for one appeal.[177]

Receiving counsel does not necessarily mean receiving effective counsel, however. Some assigned attorneys are inexperienced, some are incompetent, and most are overworked and have little time to prepare the best possible defense.

Some places make little effort to provide effective counsel, even in murder cases where capital punishment looms. In Illinois, at least thirty-three convicts on death row had been represented at trial by attorneys who were

Clarence Earl Gideon, convinced that he was denied a fair trial because he was not given an attorney, read law books in prison so that he could petition the Supreme Court for a writ of certiorari. Although he had spent much of his life in prison, he was optimistic. "I believe that each era finds an improvement in law [and] each year brings something new for the benefit of mankind. Maybe this will be one of those small steps forward."

Courtesy of the National Archives

later disbarred or suspended.[178] In Louisiana, a defendant was represented by an attorney who was living with the prosecutor in the case. In Florida, a defendant was represented by an attorney who was a deputy sheriff at the time. In Georgia, a black defendant was represented by a white attorney who had been the Imperial Wizard of the local Ku Klux Klan for fifty years.[179] Also in Georgia, an attorney was so unversed in criminal law that when he was asked to name criminal rulings he was familiar with, he could think of only one (*Miranda*).[180] In three murder cases in one recent year in Texas, defense attorneys slept through the trials. When one of these defendants appealed his conviction on the ground that he did not receive his constitutional right to counsel, the appellate court announced that "the Constitution doesn't say the lawyer has to be awake."[181] (Stung by criticism, the appellate court sat *en banc* and overruled itself. The Supreme Court refused to hear the case, thus allowing the final appellate court ruling to stand.) At least these attorneys were present. In Alabama, a defendant was represented by an attorney who failed to appear when his case was argued before the state supreme court. The defendant lost and was executed.[182]

In recent years, the issue of legal counsel for those defendants subject to the death penalty has received more scrutiny because new investigations and technologies have demonstrated definitively that dozens of people on death row were not guilty of the murder for which they were convicted and sentenced. Nonetheless, there is little effort to provide effective counsel for criminal defendants because few groups, other than lawyers' associations, urge adequate representation. Criminal defendants have no political power in our system, and the public has little sympathy for their rights.[183]

Jury Trial

The Sixth Amendment also provides the **right to a jury trial** in "serious" criminal cases. The Supreme Court has defined "serious" cases as those that could result in more than six months' incarceration.[184]

The right was adopted to prevent oppression by a "corrupt or overzealous prosecutor" or a "biased . . . or eccentric judge."[185] It has also served to limit governmental use of unpopular laws or enforcement practices. Regardless of the extent of evidence against a defendant, a jury can refuse to convict if it feels that the government has overstepped its bounds.

The jury is to be "impartial," so persons who have made up their minds before trial should be dismissed. It also is to be "a fair cross section" of the community, so no group should be systematically excluded.[186] But the jury need not be a perfect cross section and in fact need not have a single member of a particular group.[187] Most courts use voter registration lists to obtain the names of potential jurors. These lists are not truly representative because poor people do not register at the same rate as others, but courts have decided that the lists are sufficiently representative. And Congress passed and President Clinton signed the "motor voter bill," which requires drivers' license and welfare offices to offer voter registration forms. As a result, more people have registered to vote and are eligible to serve on juries.

Cruel and Unusual Punishment

The Eighth Amendment forbids **cruel and unusual punishment** but does not define it. The Supreme Court had defined it as torture or any punishment grossly disproportionate to the offense, but the Court had seldom used the provision until applying it to capital punishment in the 1970s.

Because the death penalty was used at the time the amendment was adopted and had been used ever since, it was assumed to be constitutional.[188] But the Burger Court, albeit with Chief Justice Burger and the other three Nixon appointees in dissent, held that capital punishment as it was then being administered was cruel and unusual.[189] The Court said that the laws and procedures allowed too much discretion by those who administered the punishment, and too much arbitrariness and discrimination for those who received it. The death penalty was imposed so seldom, according to Justice Potter Stewart, that it was "cruel and unusual in the same way that being struck by lightning is cruel and unusual." Yet when it was imposed, it was imposed on black defendants out of all proportion to their convictions for murder.

The decision invalidated the laws of forty states and commuted the death sentences of 629 inmates. But because the Court did not hold capital punishment cruel and unusual in principle, about three-fourths of the states adopted new laws that permitted less discretion in an effort to be less arbitrary and discriminatory.

These changes satisfied a majority of the Court, which ruled that capital punishment is not cruel and unusual for murder if administered fairly.[190] But the death penalty cannot be imposed automatically for everyone convicted of murder, for the judge or jury must consider any mitigating factors that would call for a lesser punishment.[191] Also, capital punishment cannot be imposed for rape, because it is disproportionate to that offense.[192]

The new laws have apparently reduced but not eliminated discrimination. Although past studies showed discrimination against black defendants, recent studies show discrimination against black or white defendants who murder white victims. People who affect the decision to impose the death penalty—prosecutors, defense attorneys, judges, and jurors—appear to value white lives more. Despite evidence that in Georgia those who killed whites were more than four times as likely to be given the death penalty as those who killed blacks, the Rehnquist Court, by a 5–4 vote, upheld capital punishment in the state.[193]

The new laws have not addressed an equally serious problem—inadequate representation provided to poor defendants who face the death penalty—which we discussed in conjunction with the right to counsel.

For years, most people dismissed any suggestions that innocent defendants might be put to death. They assumed that the criminal justice system used careful procedures and made no mistakes in these cases at least. However, since capital punishment was reinstated in the 1970s (with stricter procedures), one hundred inmates awaiting execution have been released because new evidence, including DNA tests, revealed their innocence. This number represents one exoneration for every seven or eight executions—a disturbing frequency for the ultimate punishment.[194] Some were the victims of sloppy or biased police or overzealous prosecutors; some were the victims of mistaken witnesses; others were the victims of emotional or prejudiced jurors. Many were the victims of inadequate representation.

Due to the patterns of racial discrimination and inadequate representation, the American Bar Association called for a moratorium on the use of capital punishment in 1997. After Illinois released its thirteenth innocent inmate from death row, most after investigations by Northwestern University journalism students, its governor announced a moratorium in 2000. Three years later, when he left office, he commuted the death sentences of 167 inmates to life in prison.

In recent years, the public has become uneasy about capital punishment. Often juries have become reluctant to impose it, instead opting for life in prison.[195]

Even the Rehnquist Court, long a staunch supporter of the death penalty, reflected the public's mood. In 2002, it ruled that states cannot execute the mentally retarded.[196] Previously, it had allowed execution of the mentally retarded, including a man who had the mental capacity of a seven-year-old and still believed in Santa Claus.[197] But now, the six-justice majority observed, there was a new "national consensus" against such executions.

Rights in Theory and in Practice

Overall, the Supreme Court has interpreted the Bill of Rights to provide an impressive list of rights for criminal defendants (although one of the significant changes from the Warren Court to the Burger and Rehnquist Courts was a decline in support for criminal defendants). Yet not all rights are available for all defendants in all places. Some trial court judges, prosecutors, and police do not comply with Supreme Court rulings. If defendants appeal to a high enough court, they will probably get their rights, but most defendants do not have the knowledge, the resources, or the perseverance to do this.

When the rights are available, most defendants do not take advantage of them. About 90 percent of criminal defendants plead guilty, and many of them do so through a **plea bargain.** This is an agreement among the prosecutor, the defense attorney, and the defendant, with the explicit or implicit approval of the judge, to reduce the charge or the sentence in exchange for a guilty plea. A plea bargain is a compromise. For officials, it saves the time, trouble, and uncertainty of a trial. For defendants, it eliminates the fear of a harsher sentence. However, it also reduces due process rights. A guilty plea waives the defendants' rights to a jury trial, at which the defendants can present their own witnesses and cross-examine the government's witnesses and at which they cannot be forced to incriminate themselves.

A guilty plea also reduces the defendants' right to counsel because it reduces their lawyers' need to prepare a defense. Consequently, most attorneys pressure their clients to forgo a trial so that the attorneys do not have to spend the time to investigate and try the case. Despite these drawbacks for due process rights, the Supreme Court allows plea bargaining, and the trial courts encourage it because the practice enables judges and attorneys to dispose of their cases quickly.[198]

Right to Privacy

Neither the Constitution nor the Bill of Rights mentions privacy. Nevertheless, the right to privacy, Justice Douglas noted, is "older than the Bill of Rights,"[199] and the framers undoubtedly assumed that people would have such a right. In fact, the framers did include amendments that reflect a concern for privacy: The First Amendment protects privacy of association; the Third, privacy of homes from quartering soldiers; the Fourth, privacy of persons and the places where they live from searches and seizures; and the Fifth, privacy of knowledge or thoughts from compulsory self-incrimination. The Supreme Court would use these to establish an explicit **right to privacy.**

So far, the Court's right-to-privacy doctrine reflects a right to autonomy—what Justice Louis Brandeis called "the right to be left alone"—more than a right to keep things confidential. As noted earlier in the chapter, the Court has been reluctant to punish the press for invading people's privacy.[200]

Birth Control

The Warren Court explicitly established a right to privacy in 1965 when it struck down a Connecticut law that prohibited distributing or using contraceptives.[201] To enforce the law, the state would have had to police people's bedrooms, and the Court said the very idea of policing married couples' bedrooms was absurd. Then the Court struck down Massachusetts and New York laws that prohibited distributing contraceptives to unmarried persons.[202] "If the right of privacy means anything," Justice William Brennan said, "it is the right of the individual, married or single, to be free from unwarranted governmental intrusion into matters so fundamentally affecting a person as the decision whether to bear or beget a child."[203]

Abortion

When twenty-one-year-old Norma McCorvey became pregnant in 1969, she was divorced and already had a five-year-old daughter, and she sought an abortion. But Texas, where she lived, prohibited abortions unless the mother's life was in danger. "No legitimate doctor in Dallas would touch me," she discovered. "I found one doctor who offered to abort me for $500. Only he didn't have a license, and I was scared to turn my body over to him. So there I was—pregnant, unmarried, unemployed, alone, and stuck."[204]

Unaware of states that permitted abortions, McCorvey put her baby up for adoption. But the state law rankled her. When she met two women attorneys who recently graduated from law school and who also disliked the law, they offered to take her case to challenge the law. She adopted the name Jane Roe to conceal her identity.

In *Roe* v. *Wade* in 1973, the Burger Court extended the right to privacy from birth control to abortion.[205] Justice Harry Blackmun surveyed the writings of doctors, theologians, and philosophers over the years and found that these thinkers do not agree when life begins. Therefore, the majority concluded that judges should not assert that life begins at any particular time, including at conception, which would make a fetus a person and abortion murder. Thus the majority omitted this factor from the equation. As a result, the majority decided that a woman's right to privacy of her body is paramount.

The Court ruled that women have a **right to abortion** during the first six months of pregnancy. States can prohibit an abortion during the last three months because the fetus becomes viable—it can live outside the womb—at this point. (However, states must allow an abortion for a woman whose life is endangered by continuing her pregnancy.) Thus the right is broad but not absolute.

The justices, as revealed in memos discovered years later, acknowledged that their division of the nine-month term was "legislative," but they saw this as a way to balance the rights of the mother in the early stages of pregnancy with the rights of the fetus in the later stages.[206]

Although *Roe* was not even the lead story in the news when it was decided, it has had an enormous impact on American politics. The Court's ruling invalidated the abortion laws of forty-nine states[207] and increased the number of abortions performed in the country (see Figure 1). It put abortion on the public agenda, and it galvanized conservative groups who saw it as a symbol of loosening social restraints at a time of rampaging social problems. Disparate groups, such as Roman Catholics and evangelical Protestants (and some Orthodox Jews), rural residents and urban ethnics, who rarely saw eye to eye, coalesced around this issue and exercised leverage within the Republican Party.

The right-to-life movement pressured presidents and senators to appoint justices and lower court judges who opposed the ruling. The movement also lobbied mem-

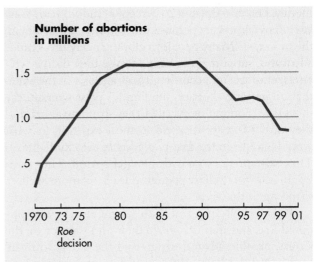

FIGURE 1 ■ **Number of Legal Abortions Performed in the United States, 1970–2000** *The number of abortions performed in the United States was increasing before the Supreme Court's Roe decision because some states had liberalized their laws. After the Roe decision, the number increased sharply but leveled off in the 1980s and declined in the 1990s.*

SOURCES: Susan Hansen, "State Implementation of Supreme Court Decisions: Abortion Rates since *Roe v. Wade*," *Journal of Politics* 42 (1980), 372–395; Stanley K. Henshaw and Ellen Blaine, *Abortion Services in the United States, Each State, and Metropolitan Areas, 1981–1982* (New York: Alan Guttmacher Institute, 1985), 64; Stanley K. Henshaw, "Characteristics of U.S. Women Having Abortions, 1982–1983," *Family Planning Perspectives* 19 (1987), 6–7; Stanley K. Henshaw, Jacqueline Darroch Forrest, and Jennifer Van Vort, "Abortion Services in the United States, 1984 and 1985," *Family Planning Perspectives* 19 (1987), 64; Alan Guttmacher Institute, *Abortion Fact Book* (New York: Alan Guttmacher Institute, 1992); "Number of Abortions at Lowest Level since '79," *Lincoln Journal-Star*, June 16, 1994; Tara Meyer, "Abortion Rate Lowest since 1976 in U.S.," *Lincoln Journal-Star*, January 4, 1997; "U.S. Abortions Continue Decline," *Lincoln Journal-Star*, January 7, 2000; Lawrence Baum, *The Supreme Court*, 8th ed. (Washington, D.C.: CQ Press, 2004), 227.

bers of Congress and state legislatures to overturn or circumvent the ruling. Although Congress refused to pass constitutional amendments banning abortions or allowing states to regulate them, Congress and state legislatures did pass statutes limiting abortions in various ways.

The Burger Court invalidated most of these statutes,[208] but it upheld a major limitation. The Medicaid program, financed jointly by the federal and state governments, had paid for abortions for poor women. As a result, the program had paid for a third of the abortions in the country each year.[209] But Congress eliminated federal funding (except when pregnancy threatens the life of the mother or is the result of rape or incest), and most state legislatures eliminated state funding. Consequently, poor women need to pay the entire cost. The Court upheld these laws, ruling that governments have no obligation to finance abortions, even if this means that some women cannot take advantage of their right to have them.[210]

For some women, these laws delay abortions, making them more risky, while the women search for the money. For an estimated 20 percent of the women, these laws deny abortions because the women cannot obtain the money.[211] Many people, including many pro-choice advocates, support these bans because they dislike welfare spending. Yet according to an analysis of the states that do provide abortion funding for poor women, the states save money. For every $1 they spend on abortions, they save $4 in welfare and medical expenses in what would have been the first two years of the child's life.[212] They save much more over a longer period. Thus public distaste for welfare spending leads to more welfare spending in this area.

Presidents Reagan and Bush sought justices who opposed *Roe,* and after they filled their fifth vacancy on the Court, pro-life advocates expected the Court to overturn it. Yet the Rehnquist Court did not overturn it.[213] In 1992, a bare majority reaffirmed the right to abortion.[214] At the same time, the majority permitted more restrictions on the right—as long as the restrictions do not place an "undue burden" on the women seeking abortions.

Therefore, the majority upheld Pennsylvania's twenty-four-hour waiting period between the time a woman indicates her desire to have an abortion and the time a doctor can perform one. Although a twenty-four-hour waiting period is not a burden for many women, it can be for poor women who live in rural areas and must travel to cities to obtain abortions. One woman in Mississippi hitchhiked and planned to sleep on outdoor furniture in the Kmart parking lot across the street until the clinic offered to pay for her motel room.[215]

A waiting period can also affect teenagers. Pro-life groups in some cities note the license numbers of cars driven to clinics by teenagers. After looking up the name and address of the family, they inform the parents in the hope that the parents will persuade or pressure the daughter to change her mind during the waiting period. (See the box "Teen Pregnancies and Abortions.")

The majority struck down Pennsylvania's requirement that a married woman notify her husband before having an abortion.[216] This was an undue burden because a woman who fears physical abuse from her husband would be deterred from seeking an abortion. Justice O'Connor wrote that a state "may not give to a man the kind of dominion over his wife that parents exercise over their children."

The Court upheld some states' requirement that unmarried minors notify their parents before having an abortion and other states' requirement that unmarried minors obtain their parents' consent before having an abortion.[217] For either requirement, if a daughter does not want to tell her parents, she can seek permission from a judge. She must convince the judge that an abortion would be in her best interest or that she is mature

enough to make the decision herself. If she is not mature enough, she must become a mother. These laws, Justice Marshall wrote in dissent, force "a young woman in an already dire situation to choose between two fundamentally unacceptable alternatives: notifying a possibly dictatorial or even abusive parent or justifying her profoundly personal decision in an intimidating judicial proceeding to a black-robed stranger."[218]

Pro-life groups advocated these laws with the expectation that they would result in fewer abortions. They believed that many teenagers would go to their parents rather than face the forbidding atmosphere of a court hearing and that their parents would persuade or pressure them not to have the abortion. Some evidence indicates that the laws have had this effect.[219]

When teenagers do go to court, they routinely get waivers in some states but not in others. The Nebraska supreme court ruled that a fifteen-year-old was too immature to decide to have an abortion because although she could discuss the consequences of keeping the baby or giving it up for adoption, discuss her philosophy of abortion, and explain the procedures involved, she was unable to explain the risks involved (even though the risks are less than those involved in giving birth).[220]

After the Rehnquist Court reaffirmed the right to abortion, pro-life groups tried to prohibit one abortion procedure, known as "intact dilation and extraction" in medicine but referred to as "partial-birth abortion" in politics—a rhetorical success of antiabortion supporters. In this procedure, a doctor delivers the fetus except for the head, punctures the skull and drains the contents, and then removes the fetus from the woman. Because the procedure is gruesome, pro-life groups used it to try to sway undecided people in the abortion debate. Numerous states passed laws banning the procedure, but the Supreme Court struck down Nebraska's law in 2000.[221] The five-justice majority said that the law was too broad—the language might ban other methods as well—and did not provide an exception for the health of the mother.

Then Congress passed a similar law for the whole country, but it did provide an exception for the life of the mother (not for the health of the mother, which would be broader). Although members expected the Supreme Court to invalidate this law as well, they passed it to mollify social conservatives and to rally these allies for upcoming nominations to the High Court.

In recent years, pro-life groups have quietly pressed state legislatures to enact extrastringent building codes for abortion clinics. These codes specify such things as the heights of ceilings, widths of hallways and doorways, dimensions of counseling rooms and recovery rooms, rates of air circulation, and the types and angles of jets in drinking fountains. (All states have construction codes for their buildings, but some new laws apply only to

Teen Pregnancies and Abortions

Of American teenagers aged fifteen to nineteen, about 10 percent become pregnant, and about 35 percent of these have an abortion. This teen pregnancy rate is higher than that of every other developed country except Russia. The high rate is apparently not because American teens are having more sex but because they are using fewer contraceptives. In European countries, contraceptives are readily available and widely encouraged.

However, the American teenage pregnancy rate has been falling. After peaking in 1990, it has dropped 28 percent since. The primary reason is not abstinence. Delayed onset of sexual activity accounts for a quarter of this decline, and increasing use of contraceptives (though still less than in other countries) accounts for three-quarters of the drop.

The teen pregnancy rate of African Americans is more than twice that of whites who are not Hispanic. The rate of Latinos is almost twice that of whites who are not Hispanics. The teen pregnancy rates also vary from region to region and state to state. The rates are highest in the South and Southwest and lowest in the North Central and Northeast regions. The conservatism of the South may prevent contraception, but it evidently does not prevent teen sex or pregnancies. On the other hand, Massachusetts, one of the most liberal states, has a rate well below average. Perhaps its liberalism fosters greater use of contraceptives.

The states with the highest teen pregnancy rates are

(1)   Nevada,

(2)   Arizona,

(3)   Mississippi,

(4)   New Mexico, and

(5)   Texas.

The states with the lowest teen pregnancy rates are

(50)   North Dakota,

(49)   Vermont,

(48)   New Hampshire,

(47)   Minnesota, and

(46)   Maine.

The American teen abortion rate is also higher than that of most other developed countries. However, the abortion *rate*, which is the number of abortions per one thousand teens, and the abortion *ratio*, which is the percentage of those teens who get pregnant who have an abortion, have both been falling. Since 1986, the abortion ratio has dropped from 46 percent to 33 percent. That is, 46 percent of teens who got pregnant in 1986 had abortions; just 33 percent did in 2000. More gave birth, perhaps because abortions became more restricted due to state laws requiring parental notification and consent or less available due to fewer providers or perhaps because single parenthood became less stigmatized. But the decline has occurred only among whites who are not Hispanic.

African Americans have the highest abortion ratio, at 41 percent, and Latinos have the lowest, at 28 percent. Whites who are not Hispanic are in between, at 34 percent.

The teen abortion rates are highest in the most urban states, where abortions are more available. The states with the highest teen abortion rates are

(1)   New Jersey,

(2)   New York,

(3)   Maryland,

(4)   California, and

(5)   Nevada.

The states with the lowest teen abortion rates are

(50)   Utah,

(49)   South Dakota,

(48)   North Dakota,

(47)   Kentucky, and

(46)   West Virginia.

For all racial and ethnic groups, older teens (eighteen to nineteen) had more pregnancies and abortions than younger teens (fifteen to seventeen) because the older teens are more sexually active.

SOURCE: Based on statistics for 2000, the most recent year for which data are available, from the Alan Guttmacher Institute, 2004.

abortion clinics.) Some codes require equipment or levels of staffing, such as a registered nurse rather than a licensed practical nurse, beyond what is normal in these clinics. Although the stated goal is health and safety, the real purpose is to drive up the clinics' expenses so they have to increase their patients' fees to the point where many women can no longer afford to have an abor-

tion.[222] When South Carolina's law, which mandates twenty-seven pages of requirements just for abortion clinics, was challenged, a lower court upheld the law and the Supreme Court refused to hear the case, thus allowing the law to stand.

Despite considerable dissatisfaction by activists on both sides of this controversy—pro-life groups are dis-

President Bush, surrounded by the congressional sponsors, signs the Partial Birth Abortion Ban Act.

appointed that the conservative Supreme Court has upheld the right to abortion while pro-choice groups are critical that it has upheld some restrictions on abortion —it is worth noting that the nonelected, nonmajoritarian Supreme Court has come closer to forging a policy reflective of public opinion than most politicians have. Polls show that the public is ambivalent. A majority believes that abortion is murder, but a two-thirds majority opposes banning it. This two-thirds majority favors letting women choose. (Over half of those who believe abortion is murder nonetheless favor letting women choose.)[223] Thus many people support the right to abortion but are uncomfortable with it and are presumably willing to permit restrictions on it. The Court's doctrine essentially articulates this position.[224]

But the Court's rulings are not necessarily the final word in this controversy, as they have not been the final word in some other controversies. Frustrated by the Court's refusal to overturn *Roe,* activists in the pro-life movement (not most of the pro-life supporters) adopted more militant tactics. First they targeted abortion clinics. Organizations such as Operation Rescue engaged in civil disobedience, blockading clinics and harassing workers and patients as they came and went. Some activists sprayed chemicals inside clinics, ruining carpets and fabrics and leaving a stench that made the clinics unusable. Such incidents occurred fifty times in one year alone.[225]

Then activists targeted doctors, nurses, and other workers of the clinics. Operation Rescue ran a training camp in Florida that instructed members how to use public records to locate personal information about clinic employees, how to tail them to their homes, and how to organize demonstrations at their homes. (The group even convinced Jane Roe of *Roe* v. *Wade* to defect to its side; see the box "Tools and Symbols.") Activists put up "Wanted" posters, with a doctor's picture, name, address, and phone number and then encouraged people to harass the doctor, the doctor's spouse, and even their children. (One thirteen-year-old was confronted in a restaurant and told that he was going to burn in hell.)[226] Letters containing powder and threats of death by anthrax were sent to over one hundred doctors and clinics, both before and after anthrax infected people in 2001. (The letters to the doctors and clinics were hoaxes.)[223] Some extremists even came out in favor of killing the doctors. One minister wrote a book— *A Time to Kill*—and marketed a bumper sticker reading "EXECUTE ABORTIONISTS—MURDERERS."[228]

In this climate, three doctors, two clinic receptionists, and one clinic volunteer were killed, and seven other doctors, employees, and volunteers were wounded.[229] Numerous clinics were firebombed.

The tactics have had their intended effect on doctors.[230] They have made the practice of providing abortions seem dangerous and undesirable. Fewer medical schools offer abortion classes, fewer hospitals provide abortion training, fewer doctors study abortion procedures, and fewer gynecologists and obstetricians, despite most being pro-choice, perform abortion operations.[231]

One pro-life leader proclaimed, "We've found the weak link is the doctor."[232] Another observed, "When

Norma McCorvey, a carnival barker, was used as a tool by pro-choice lawyers and then as a symbol fought over by both pro-choice and pro-life forces.

Young lawyers Sarah Weddington and Linda Coffee were planning to challenge antiabortion laws when they met the pregnant McCorvey, who said she had been gang-raped. She wanted an abortion, and although the lawyers knew how she could get an illegal one, they did not tell her. So she agreed to be the plaintiff in a test case, adopting the name "Jane Roe" to protect her anonymity. After signing an affidavit and approving the suit, she was not involved in the case or even informed of its progress. When the Supreme Court issued its ruling in *Roe* v. *Wade* in 1973, she learned about it from the newspapers.

After the ruling, she lived in anonymity, partly to protect her privacy and partly to conceal her lie: Her pregnancy was the result of romance rather than rape. In 1989, feeling proud of her involvement in the landmark case, she decided to go public, admitting that she was "Jane Roe." As a result, she received hate mail, found baby clothes scattered across her lawn, and was shot at through the window of her home.

Pro-choice groups considered her a useful symbol and gave her a job at an abortion clinic in Dallas. But otherwise they ignored her. Yet she had led a difficult life and craved more attention. She had been born to an alcoholic mother, was sexually abused as a teenager, married at sixteen but deserted soon after, and got hooked on drugs. She was "so spiritually needy that she ran through religions as if channel surfing." She said, with dismay, that she could not remember anyone from a pro-choice group ever calling and asking, "Good morning, Norma, are you having any trouble in your life?" Indeed, when pro-choice groups hosted a twentieth anniversary party for *Roe* v. *Wade*, they did not bother to invite her.

She felt uncomfortable with the upper-middle-class women who predominated in the movement. "I am a rough woman," she said. "I don't have a degree from Vas-

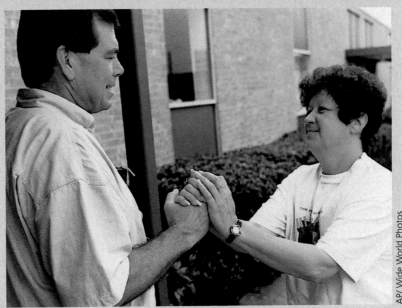

AP/Wide World Photos

Operation Rescue's Flip Benham moved Norma McCorvey—"Jane Roe" of Roe v. Wade—*to his side in the battle over abortion rights.*

sar." When Operation Rescue, a pro-life group, moved its headquarters into the same building that housed the abortion clinic where she worked, she called the organization "a pack of whores." But their charismatic leader, Flip Benham, wooed McCorvey, and she eventually warmed to him. "He doesn't make me feel bad about myself," she said.

In 1995, after watching a second-trimester abortion, she quit her job at the abortion clinic and became a volunteer for Operation Rescue. She dramatically announced that she was "pro-life." One activist gleefully remarked, "The poster child has jumped off the poster." So the woman whose case was used to further the pro-choice cause was now being used to advance the pro-life cause.

McCorvey says she wants to be "a regular person," but she has become too valuable as a public symbol in the abortion debate. Both sides, with their eyes on the ambivalent views of the people in the ideological center of the spectrum, want to use her to influence these people.

SOURCES: David Van Biema, "An Icon in Search Mode," *Time,* August 21, 1995, 36; Ellen Goodman, "Poster Child for Ambivalence," *Lincoln Journal-Star,* August 17, 1995.

you get the doctors out, you can have all the laws on the books you want and it doesn't mean a thing."[233]

Abortions remain available in most metropolitan centers but not in most rural areas. Eighty-six percent of U.S. counties, containing 32 percent of the American women aged fifteen to forty-four, have no doctor who performs abortions. Some states have only one and others have only two cities where women can obtain abortions.[234]

Despite the debate over this issue today, abortion

is not likely to fuel such contentious arguments in the future. Expanded use of contraceptives, especially the "morning-after pill," undoubtedly will occur. (The morning-after pill is considered a contraceptive by the medical profession because it prevents implantation of the zygote in the uterine wall, but it is considered an abortion drug by the Catholic church because the sperm and egg have already united.) Other pharmaceutical remedies that actually induce abortions will probably be accepted because they will seem to work more like contraceptives than abortions to most people exposed to the pictures of aborted fetuses and the descriptions of grisly procedures. These types of pills, which are feared and opposed by the pro-life movement, will eventually defuse the debate over early-term abortions. The debate over middle-term abortions, which are less common, may continue along with secondary arguments over government funding, parental consent, and other issues. The ban on late-term abortions, except when necessary to save the life of the woman, will probably remain.[235]

Homosexuality

For years, states had laws prohibiting adultery, fornication, and sodomy. Reflecting Christian doctrine, the statutes targeted various forms of nonmarital sex and nonprocreative sex (including masturbation and withdrawal prior to ejaculation).[236] After the "sexual revolution" of the 1960s, many states repealed these statutes. However, most states retained their sodomy statutes, which prohibited oral or anal sex (performed by heterosexuals or homosexuals) because of the legislators' disgust toward homosexual practices and opposition to the emerging gay rights movement.[237] Although these statutes were primarily symbolic, they were occasionally enforced against homosexuals.

The Supreme Court was reluctant to extend the right to privacy to protect homosexual practices. When police delivered a summons to the residents of a house and discovered two men violating Georgia's law, police arrested them. Although prosecutors did not file charges, one of the men sued to have the courts declare the law unconstitutional. In 1986, the Rehnquist Court, by a one-vote margin, refused to do so.[238]

However, in 2003, the Rehnquist Court, this time by a two-vote margin, reversed itself. When a neighbor phoned a false report of an armed intruder, police responded and discovered two men violating Texas's law. The men were arrested, jailed, and fined $200. The Texas courts affirmed their conviction, but in *Lawrence* v. *Texas,* the Supreme Court overturned it and invalidated the sodomy laws of the thirteen states that still had them.[239] In a broad opinion, Justice Anthony Kennedy wrote, "Liberty presumes an autonomy of self that includes freedom of thought, belief, expression, and certain intimate conduct." Therefore, homosexuals are entitled to "dignity" and "respect for their private lives." In dissent, Justice Antonin Scalia accused the majority of taking sides in the "culture war." Yet a sizable shift in public opinion had occurred in the seventeen years since the 1986 ruling.[240] As more homosexuals "came out," they gained greater acceptance from straights. Seven of ten Americans say they know someone who is gay or lesbian, and six of ten say they are sympathetic to the gay and lesbian communities. In addition, numerous states repealed their sodomy statutes after the 1986 ruling, even though the ruling allowed the states to keep the statutes. Thus in the *Lawrence* case, according to one law professor, "The Court legitimized and endorsed a cultural consensus."[241]

Although the majority in *Lawrence* said the ruling would not necessarily extend to same-sex marriages, the dissenters feared that establishing a right to privacy for homosexual practices would indeed lead to a right to marry for homosexual couples. Already there had been some attempts to create this right. Although most gay and lesbian groups, fearing a public backlash against the gay rights movement, had been reluctant to push for this right, some homosexual couples had filed lawsuits. In 1993, the Hawaii Supreme Court implied that same-sex couples had a right to marry, prompting the state's voters to amend their constitution to override their court.

The Hawaii ruling worried opponents that some states would allow same-sex marriages, which would prompt homosexual couples to marry there and then

John Lawrence (left) and Tyron Garner appealed their sodomy convictions to the Supreme Court, which invalidated state sodomy laws.

return home as married couples. Under the full faith and credit clause of the Constitution, states usually must recognize the public records and judicial proceedings of other states. Although this clause might not apply to same-sex marriages,[242] Congress adopted the Defense of Marriage Act, which forbids federal recognition of same-sex marriages and thus denies federal benefits, such as Social Security, to same-sex couples.[243] The act also allows states to disregard same-sex marriages performed in other states. Almost forty states have passed laws to do so.

Although marriage was a fantasy for most homosexuals, their lack of legal rights was a cause for concern and a source of anger. In the 1980s and 1990s, the AIDS epidemic had forced gays to recognize their legal status as they encountered problems involving health insurance, hospital visitation, disability benefits, funeral planning, and estate settling. Gays were often unable to participate fully in these life-and-death matters due to legal impediments that did not exist for married couples. In the same decades, new technology had allowed lesbians to give birth using donated sperm and gay men had begun to raise adopted children or their own born to surrogate mothers, yet gay couples realized that they did not have legal protections for their families. These developments increased the calls for legal rights commensurate with the rights of heterosexual couples.[244]

In 1999, the Vermont supreme court ruled that the state must either legalize same-sex marriages or equalize the benefits received by same-sex couples and traditional married couples. The legislature decided to equalize the benefits, such as family leave, bereavement leave, health insurance, pension benefits, and inheritance rights. To implement this policy, the legislature established "civil unions," with procedures for couples to become official partners (similar to marriage) and procedures for them to dissolve their relationship (similar to divorce). The civil unions also establish the rights to make medical decisions for a partner who is ill, visit a partner who is in the hospital, arrange the funeral and burial for a partner who dies, and receive wrongful death benefits for a partner who dies.

Although these civil unions provide most of what regular marriages provide, the unions do not apply when couples move from Vermont to other states. And they do not apply to federal benefits. By one count, 1,138 federal laws apply to married couples that do not apply to unmarried couples. Some impose responsibilities; most provide rights and benefits, such as tax breaks.[245] Also, of course, the unions do not provide the same symbolism that regular marriages do.

So the pressure for same-sex marriages continued. In 2004, the Massachusetts Supreme Judicial Court, hearing a suit brought by seven couples, ruled that same-sex

A lesbian couple in San Francisco said "I do," but the California Supreme Court said "adieu."

marriages were allowed under the state's constitution. Otherwise, same-sex couples are relegated to "a different status. . . .The history of our nation has demonstrated that separate is seldom, if ever, equal."[246] The court held that the state must authorize these marriages by 2006 (and because of constitutional procedures, the state cannot amend its constitution until 2008).

In quick succession, officials in San Francisco; Portland, Oregon; and smaller cities in New York, New Jersey, and New Mexico were inspired to issue marriage licenses to same-sex couples. State courts halted the licenses but not until thousands of beaming couples had married and posed for news photos. Although the marriages were pronounced invalid, the head of the Lambda Legal Defense and Education Fund observed, "You can't put the toothpaste back in the tube."[247]

There was an immediate backlash. Polls showed that a majority of the public opposed same-sex marriages (see Figure 2). President Bush proposed a constitutional amendment and lined up congressional sponsors. One sponsor claimed, "There is a master plan out there from those who want to destroy the institution of marriage." Another senator, comparing the threat of gay marriage to that of terrorism, called the amendment "the ultimate homeland security." An evangelist predicted that "the family as it has been known for five millennia will crumble, presaging the fall of Western civilization itself."[248] Yet there was more fire from the pulpits than there was in the pews. Evangelical leaders expressed puzzlement and frustration that there was no loud out-

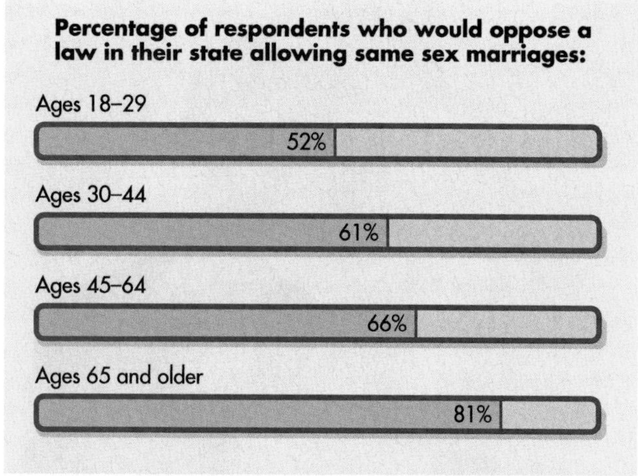

Percentage of respondents who would oppose a law in their state allowing same sex marriages:

Ages 18–29

52%

Ages 30–44

61%

Ages 45–64

66%

Ages 65 and older

81%

FIGURE 2 ■ Public Opinion toward Gay Marriage, by Age *The graph shows the percentage of respondents who would oppose a law in their state allowing same-sex marriages.*
SOURCE: National Annenberg Election Survey at the University of Pennsylvania, 2004.

cry from their faithful.[249] Many people who oppose gay marriage do not feel threatened by it. Consequently, the amendment failed to pass. Nevertheless, in the 2004 elections, voters in eleven states adopted such amendments to their state constitution, most by a wide mar-

gin. Conservatives renewed their calls for an amendment to the U.S. Constitution.

Despite many people's objections, gay rights leaders predict that once homosexuals begin to marry and straights see that "the sky doesn't fall," people will stop opposing their marriages.[250] (See the box "Constitutional Amendments to Protect the Family.")

Meanwhile, homosexuals have gained equal benefits at some workplaces. Large corporations especially have been willing to grant health care packages to same-sex couples as a way to attract and retain good workers. Some cities and states also offer these benefits.

Yet homosexuals remain vulnerable at other workplaces. In most states, employees can be fired merely for being homosexual. Although some state and local legislatures have passed laws barring discrimination in employment, housing, credit, insurance, and public accommodations, Congress rejected a bill barring discrimination in employment at the same time it passed the Defense of Marriage Act.[251]

Congress also blocked President Clinton's pledge to issue an executive order barring discrimination against homosexuals in the military.[252] Since World War II, the military has rejected recruits who admit to being homosexual and discharged troops who are found to be

Constitutional Amendments to Protect the Family

During the debate over the proposed constitutional amendment to prohibit same-sex marriages, other amendments were also proposed to protect the family against common threats to traditional marriages:

■ **Amendment XXVIII:** Both spouses shall spend at least one weekend per year doing something one spouse considers screamingly dull but the other spouse considers completely engrossing—for example, antiquing, fishing, visiting a sister who just had twins, or attending a sporting event that involves giant trucks.

■ **Amendment XXIX:** No in-law shall, in time of peace, be quartered in any house without the consent of the other spouse.

■ **Amendment XXX:** The right of the wife to chat during TV shows shall be limited to commercial breaks, provided the right of the husband to watch TV shall end after two half-hour comedies or one full-hour drama.

■ **Amendment XXXI:** The right of the husband to use the bathroom shall be contingent on his leaving it free of gleaming globs on any porcelain surface.

■ **Amendment XXXII:** The right of the wife to the bathroom shall be curtailed if the fog of scented products

becomes so thick that subsequent bathroom users leave for the construction site smelling like Shalimar.

■ **Amendment XXXIII:** In all prosecutions dealing with whether a husband forgot a "special day" or even remembered the special day but not with a "special enough" gift, said husband shall submit to a speedy and public finger wag and then the wife shall get over it.

■ **Amendment XXXIV:** Husbands shall spend at least one day a month in a Hallmark shop and not leave without a stuffed animal, card, candy box, or some combination thereof, no matter how astronomical the markup.

■ **Amendment XXXV:** Questions like "Where is the butter?" cannot be submitted without the querying spouse first walking over to the fridge, opening it, and actually looking inside.

These tongue-in-cheek proposals reflect gross gender stereotypes, yet they illustrate the sort of marital conflicts that may doom heterosexual marriages more than the existence of homosexual marriages.

SOURCE: Adapted from Lenore Skenazy, "Some Amendments We Really Need," *New York Daily News*, March 2, 2004.

homosexual. According to the military, having homosexuals in the trenches or on ships would undermine the discipline and morale essential for combat.[253] However, Western European countries, Canada, Japan, and Israel, which has a battle-tested military, all tolerate homosexuals in their services.[254]

But strident opposition from military officials and members of Congress forced President Clinton to accept a compromise, a policy called "don't ask, don't tell." The military (including the Reserves and the National Guard) is not allowed to ask questions about sexual orientation on enlistment or security questionnaires but is allowed to discharge members for statements admitting homosexuality or conduct reflecting homosexuality (or bisexuality). Such conduct is defined broadly to encompass not only sexual actions but also holding hands, dancing, or trying to marry someone of the same sex. The restrictions apply off base as well as on. They do not encompass reading gay publications, associating with gay people, frequenting gay bars or churches, or marching in gay rights parades.

The policy has not helped much. Many commanders have seemed confused, and some have been unwilling to accept the policy; they continue to ask and discharge. And the debate about the policy called attention to homosexuality, so that "everyone from private to general openly speculated about who in their unit might be gay, and as a result there are some people who've had a bull's-eye on their back."[255] In fact, more homosexuals have been discharged since the policy went into effect than beforehand.[256] Over six thousand have been booted in the past six years.[257] In the run-up to the Iraq war, even fluent Arabic speakers, who were in very short supply, were discharged.[258]

Right to Die

The Court has broadened the right to privacy to provide a limited right to die. When Nancy Cruzan's car skidded off an icy road and flipped into a ditch in 1983,

doctors were able to save her life but not her brain. She never regained consciousness. She lived in a vegetative state, similar to a coma, and was fed through a tube. Twenty-five at the time of the accident, she was expected to live another thirty years. When her parents asked the doctors to remove the tube, the hospital objected, and the state of Missouri, despite paying $130,000 a year to support her, also objected. This issue, complicated enough in itself, became entangled in other controversial issues. Pro-life groups contended that denying life support was analogous to abortion; disability groups, claiming that her condition was merely a disability, said that withholding food and water from her would lead to withholding treatment from other people with disabilities.[259]

Her parents filed suit and when the battle over her life support reached the Supreme Court, the Rehnquist Court established a limited **right to die.**[260] The justices ruled that individuals can refuse medical treatment, including food and water, even if this means they will die. But individuals must make their decision while competent and alert. They can also act in advance, preparing a "living will" or designating another person as a proxy to make the decision if they are unable to.

After the Court's decision, Cruzan's parents returned to a Missouri court with evidence that their daughter would prefer death to being kept alive by machines. Three of Cruzan's coworkers testified that they recalled conversations in which she said she never would want to live "like a vegetable." The court granted her parents' request to remove her feeding tube. She died twelve days later.

Although the legal doctrine seems clear, difficult practical problems persist. Many people do not make their desires known in advance. Approximately ten thousand people in irreversible comas now did not announce their decision beforehand.[261] Some people who do indicate their decision beforehand waver when they face death. Some doctors, who are in the habit of prolonging life even when their patients have no chance of enjoying life, resist the patients' decision. The doctors try to persuade the patients or their families not to "pull the plug."[262]

The Rehnquist Court resisted patients' pleas to extend the limited right to die to encompass a broader right to obtain assistance in committing suicide.[263] Thus the Court drew a distinction between stopping treatment and assisting suicide; individuals have a right to demand the former but not the latter. The justices seemed tentative, as is typical with an issue new to the courts. Chief Justice Rehnquist emphasized, "Our holding permits this debate to continue, as it should in a democratic society." Under the Court's doctrine, states can prohibit assisted suicide, as the majority have, or they can allow it, as Oregon has. Yet the pro-life Bush administration has challenged Oregon's law in court, claiming that states cannot allow assisted suicide.

A majority of the public favors a right to assisted suicide,[264] but conservative religious groups oppose one. They insist that people, even when facing extreme pain and no hope of recovery, should not take their life. Some ethicists worry that patients will be pressured to give up their life because of the costs, to their family or health care provider, of continuing it. The ethicists fear that a right will become a duty.

Meanwhile, the practice, even where officially illegal, is widely condoned, much as abortion was before *Roe*. Almost a fifth of the doctors who treat cancer patients in Michigan admitted in a survey that they have assisted suicide, and over half of two thousand doctors who treat AIDS patients in San Francisco also admitted that they have done so.[265]

Conclusion: Are the Courts Responsive in Interpreting Civil Liberties?

The Supreme Court has interpreted the Constitution to provide valuable civil liberties. The Warren Court in the 1950s and 1960s expanded civil liberties more than any other Court in history. It applied many provisions of the Bill of Rights to the states. It substantially broadened rights in the areas of speech, libel, obscenity, and religion. It enormously broadened rights of criminal defendants in the areas of search and seizure, self-incrimination, counsel, and jury trial. And it established a right to privacy.

Observers predicted that the Burger Court would lead a constitutional counterrevolution. However, it did not. The Burger Court in the 1970s and 1980s narrowed rights in some areas, especially for criminal defendants.

But the Court accepted the core of the Warren Court's doctrine and even extended the right to privacy to encompass abortions.

Nor did the Rehnquist Court produce a constitutional counterrevolution. It, too, narrowed rights in some areas, but it also accepted most of the Warren Court's doctrine and even extended the right to privacy to encompass homosexual practices.

The decisions by these Courts show the extent to which the Supreme Court is responsive to the people in civil liberties cases. The majority of the people support civil liberties in general but not necessarily in specific situations. The elites support civil liberties more than the masses. As the Court has expanded civil liberties, it has been more responsive to various minorities—political and religious minorities and unpopular groups such as criminal defendants—than to the majority. And it has been more responsive to the elites than to the masses.

When the Supreme Court has upheld civil liberties, it has fulfilled what many legal scholars consider the quintessential role of the highest court in a democracy —"to vindicate the constitutional rights of minorities, of dissidents, of the unrepresented, of the disenfranchised, of the unpopular." The other branches of government, whose officials are elected every two, four, or six years, are sensitive to the needs of "the majority, the politically powerful, the economically influential, and the socially popular."[266]

Because the Court was not intended to be very responsive to the majority, it was given substantial independence. Therefore, it does not have to mirror public opinion, although it cannot ignore this opinion, either. It must stay within the broad limits of this opinion, or it will be pulled back. Thus the Warren Court went too far too fast for too many people. It produced a backlash that led to the Burger and Rehnquist Courts, which were somewhat more responsive to majority opinion— and somewhat less vigilant in protecting civil liberties.

Federal Courts Can Hear Detention Suits

In the suit brought by the families of detainees at the United States Naval Base at Guantanamo Bay, Cuba, the Supreme Court ruled that the federal courts do have authority to review the legality of the detention.[267] Justice Stevens wrote the opinion for the majority of six justices.

First, the majority concluded that Guantanamo Bay is essentially American territory. Next, the justices rejected the Bush administration's position that the federal courts have no authority to review and question the president's policies in wartime. Without any stirring or provocative language, the majority rebuffed the president, telling him that he, too, must follow the rule of law. Therefore, the detainees are entitled to challenge their designation as "enemy combatants" by presenting evidence to the contrary before a federal judge or other neutral decision maker.

However, the opinion did not specify what procedures must be used. It did not even specify whether the detainees have a right to counsel or other rights. Lower federal courts and the Supreme Court will have to make these decisions as new cases come to them.

Thus the Court's ruling was a tentative step in this new era of terrorism. Although the courts will play a role, it may be a limited role. Despite rebuffing the president on the general issue, the majority acknowledged his authority to detain actual enemy combatants for the duration of the conflict. And although the detainees have a right to challenge their designation as enemy combatants, the administration is given an advantage. It merely has to present credible evidence against them. Then they have to prove that they should not be classified as enemy combatants. Essentially, they have to prove their innocence, which can be difficult to do.

The Court acted as a political institution, much like the Court of Chief Justice John Marshall did in *Marbury* v. *Madison* in 1803. There the Court articulated the new constitutional principle of judicial review, which angered President Thomas Jefferson, but the ruling did not require the president to change his behavior. Here the Court articulated an important constitutional principle, which had been articulated before but not implemented during wartime,[268] but the ruling may not require the administration to modify its policies very much. Yet like judicial review, this new principle may become more established—it may get some teeth—in the future.

The most conservative justices on the Court—Rehnquist, Scalia, and Thomas—dissented. They argued that the ruling is cumbersome and impractical and that it will reduce the government's authority and ultimately hamper the war effort. They did not acknowledge the advantages that the ruling gives to the government.

On the same day, the Court decided a similar case involving an American citizen who had been raised in Afghanistan and captured during the war against the Taliban government and who had been held in the United States. The Court ruled similarly, although the fact that the detainee was an American citizen prompted eight justices (all but Thomas) to declare that he was entitled to contest his detention and four justices to conclude that his detention was unlawful.[269] The ruling prompted the government to release the defendant because it did not have enough evidence to charge him.

After the decisions, the Bush administration interpreted the rulings as narrowly as possible. The Pentagon opened military hearings in the hope that these would satisfy the requirement to allow the detainees to appear before a federal judge or other neutral decision maker. The Pentagon denied the detainees a right to counsel. It is not clear whether the courts will consider military panels convened by the administration to be neutral decision makers or whether they will permit the denial of counsel.

These developments show that

MARGULIES
© 2004 THE RECORD NEW JERSEY
www.northjersey.com/margulies

Well, whaddyaknow! They say I'm subject to the U.S. legal system...

SUPREME COURT RULES ON GUANTANAMO DETAINEES

SUPREME COURT RULES ON GUANTANAMO DETAINEES

© Margulies 2004. Reprinted with permission.

judicial decisions are not always the last word in a political controversy. Sometimes they are only the first thrust in a long battle. Court rulings on new issues are usually tentative and ambiguous, and they reflect shifting coalitions of justices. These factors allow the officials who are supposed to comply with the rulings an opportunity to interpret them as they prefer and thus to circumvent them, as the Bush administration appears to be attempting here.

Nevertheless, although only one detainee was deemed not an "enemy combatant," 134 were released and 56 more were turned over to foreign countries (through September 2004).[270]

Key Terms

Bill of Rights	establishment clause
First Amendment	due process
freedom of speech	presumption of innocence
seditious speech	Second Amendment
McCarthyism	unreasonable searches
public forum	and seizures
pure speech	exclusionary rule
speech plus conduct	Miranda rights
symbolic speech	right to counsel
freedom of association	right to a jury trial
prior restraint	cruel and unusual punishment
libel	plea bargain
obscenity	right to privacy
separation of church and state	right to abortion
	right to die
free exercise clause	

Further Reading

Fred W. Friendly, *Minnesota Rag* (New York: Random House, 1981). Friendly provides a lively examination of the Court's first important freedom of the press case, *Near* v. *Minnesota*, in 1927.

David J. Garrow, *Liberty and Sexuality: The Right to Privacy and the Making of* Roe v. Wade (New York: Macmillan, 1994). This is an exhaustive account of the hard road to *Roe*.

Franz Kafka, *The Trial* (numerous editions, 1937). One of the great novels of the twentieth century shows, perhaps more dramatically than anything else written, what life without due process rights would be like.

James Kirby, *Fumble: Bear Bryant, Wally Butts, and the Great College Football Scandal* (New York: Dell, 1986). Think of this as law for football fans—the story of the libel suit against a national magazine for writing that the coach of Alabama and athletic director of Georgia fixed a football game between the two schools. The author, a lawyer, was hired by the Southeastern Conference to determine what really happened in the dispute.

Anthony Lewis, *Gideon's Trumpet* (New York: Vintage, 1964). This is a wonderful account of Clarence Earl Gideon's suit and the Court's landmark decision.

Patricia G. Miller, *The Worst of Times* (New York: HarperCollins, 1992). Miller presents recollections of women who had abortions before *Roe* made them legal and interviews abortionists, doctors, and police who witnessed the effects.

David Moats, *Civil Wars: A Battle for Gay Marriage* (Orlando, Fla.: Harcourt, 2004). The author traces the political battle for civil unions in Vermont.

Helen Prejean, *Dead Men Walking* (New York: Vintage, 1993). This account of capital punishment in the United States is written from the front lines.

Jonathan Rauch, *Gay Marriage: Why It Is Good for Gays, Good for Straights, and Good for America* (New York: Times Books, 2004). Presenting a conservative argument for gay marriage, the author predicts that marriage will have a greater effect on homosexuals, by imposing responsibility and conformity on them, than they will have on the institution of marriage.

Jeffrey Rosen, *The Naked Crowd: Reclaiming Security and Freedom in an Anxious Age* (New York: Random House, 2004). Rosen traces the threats to privacy posed by the combination of contemporary technology and our post–9/11 fears.

For Viewing

Atomic Café (1992). A collage of government propaganda films from the 1960s telling Americans that the atomic bomb is not a threat to their safety.

Fahrenheit 451 (1966). Based on a Ray Bradbury novel, this movie is set in a future time when the government bans books.

The Front (1976) A Woody Allen movie about a poor schlub—Allen, of course—who gets embroiled in the Hollywood blacklisting during the McCarthy era.

The Thin Blue Line, (1988) Documentary filmmaker Errol Morris uncovers the actual killer in the process of making a film about the death penalty.

The Way We Were (1973) A classic film which addresses personal relationships during the McCarthy era, and stars a younger Robert Redford and Barbra Streisand.

 **Electronic Resources**

fact.trib.com
This home page for the First Amendment, sponsored by the Casper (Wyo.) Star-Tribune has garnered a national award as one of the best online newspaper services. It provides links to First Amendment issues and Supreme Court decisions.

www.loc.gov/exhibits/religion
Information on the role of religion in the founding of the country can be found at this site, maintained by the Library of Congress.

www.perkinscoie.com
This site, maintained by a law firm, features the latest cases involving Internet legal issues.

www.aclu.org/index.html
The American Civil Liberties Union is the foremost group dedicated to protecting civil liberties through legal and political action. Its site provides links to information and position papers on many issues covered in this chapter.

www.lifeandliberty.gov
The Department of Justice presents arguments in favor of the Patriot Act.

www.bordc.org
This site makes the case for changes in the Patriot Act.

www.naral.org
This is the site for the National Abortion Rights Action League, a pro-choice group.

www.prolifeinfo.org
This site links to pro-life groups.

www.lambdalegal.org
Lambda Legal is the oldest organization fighting for full recognition of the rights of gays, lesbians, bisexuals, and transgendered individuals.

www.nra.org
The National Rifle Association maintains this site.

 InfoTrac College Edition

Search for the following articles in the InfoTrac database:

> Baker, Nancy V. "National Security Versus Civil Liberties," *Presidential Studies Quarterly* (September 2003).

> Heymann, Philip B. "Civil Liberties and Human Rights in the Aftermath of September 11," *Harvard Journal of Law & Public Policy* (Spring 2002).

> Lewis, Penney. "Rights Discourse and Assisted Suicide," *American Journal of Law and Medicine* (Spring 2001).

> O'Neil, Robert M. "Rights in Conflict: The First Amendment's Third Century," *Law and Contemporary Problems* (Spring 2002).

For more articles, enter

> "Prayer in public schools" in the Subject Guide;

> "Assisted suicide" in the Subject Guide;

> "Capital punishment" in the Subject Guide, and;

> "Gay liberation movement" in the Subject Guide.

 American Government Resources

Visit the Government Foundations section of the Wadsworth American Government Resources Web site (politicalscience.wadsworth.com/amgov) for a variety of tools to help you explore civil liberties further. Included are simulations, video clips, Microcase exercises, and a wealth of other activities.

© Justine Parsons

The civil rights movement led to the integration of some communities, such as this formerly all-white suburb in New Jersey.

Race Discrimination

Discrimination against African Americans

Overcoming Discrimination against African Americans

Continuing Discrimination against African Americans

Improving Conditions for African Americans?

Discrimination against Hispanics

Discrimination against Native Americans

Sex Discrimination

Discrimination against Women

Discrimination against Men

Affirmative Action

In Employment

In College Admissions

Conclusion: Is Government Responsive in Granting Civil Rights?

Friend or Foe?

You are Justice William Douglas, and you are facing a difficult decision during World War II. The Supreme Court is deciding the case of *Korematsu* v. *United States.* Fred Korematsu, a Japanese American, was born and raised in California. He was working as a welder when Japan bombed Pearl Harbor and drew the United States into World War II. He tried to enlist in the Army but was rejected because of ulcers. A few months later, President Franklin Roosevelt, under pressure from West Coast politicians and newspapers, issued an executive order, which Congress ratified, authorizing the secretary of war to exclude persons of Japanese ancestry from the three West Coast states and part of Arizona to prevent espionage and sabotage. Under the order, all persons of Japanese ancestry, even those with American citizenship, were required to report to assembly centers—fairgrounds, racetracks, or stockyards, from which the animals had been removed just days before. From there, they were relocated, with whatever possessions they could carry, to camps in deserts and swamps farther inland for the duration of the war. Enclosed by barbed wire and patrolled by armed guards, these detention camps resembled prisoner-of-war camps.

Korematsu did not leave with the others. He had fallen in love with an Italian American woman, and they planned to marry. He had undergone plastic surgery in an at-tempt to appear Spanish Hawaiian instead of Japanese. But the surgery was not successful, and while walking down the street in his home-town, he was identified and arrested for violating the order. He was convicted at trial, and his conviction was upheld on appeal. On further appeal, his case has reached the Supreme Court.

The government claims that the order is justified. Since the attack on Pearl Harbor and the success of Japanese forces in the Pacific, American officials have been jittery. Although they do not expect an invasion of the West Coast, they do fear espionage and sabotage. Before the war, it appeared that many Japanese Americans supported Japan's efforts to expand its territory in Asia. Some contributed money, tinfoil, and scrap metal, and a few formed an espionage ring. Intelligence agents crushed the ring but fear renewed attempts.

Already Japanese submarines have attacked American merchant ships off the West Coast, sinking two and damaging another. Officials speculate that Japanese Americans were signaling Japanese subs. (The *Los Angeles Times* even reported that Japanese American farmers might be guiding Japanese pilots to California targets: "Caps on Japanese Tomato Plants Point to Air Base.")[1]

Officials question the loyalty of Japanese Americans. Most, born here, are U.S. citizens, but they have

Japanese American boys await relocation during World War II.

a disturbing and confirming indication that such action will be taken."

Many Americans characterize Japanese Americans as rats. Some West Coast restaurants have placed signs in their windows: "This Restaurant Poisons Both Rats and Japs." Some West Coast drivers have put stickers depicting a rat with a Japanese face on their cars. A patriotic parade in New York City included a float the crowd reportedly "loved"— an eagle leading a squadron of American bombers toward a herd of yellow rats trying to escape.[3]

Korematsu claims that the order discriminates against him on the basis of his race and thereby violates his Fifth Amendment right to due process of law. As evidence, he notes that the order does not apply to persons of German or Italian ancestry. (Although the order was general, the military commander was told not to remove the many persons of Italian descent on the

West Coast. The mayor of San Francisco was Italian, and baseball star Joe DiMaggio, whose parents were aliens, was a national idol. Anyway, President Roosevelt said he was not worried about the Italians. "They are a lot of opera singers.")[4]

Korematsu also notes that there has been widespread discrimination against Asians on the West Coast. For decades, there has been talk of the "yellow peril." In 1913, Congress refused to allow more Japanese to become citizens and in 1924 refused to allow more to immigrate. The discrimination has resulted in segregated neighborhoods and schools and, in at least one city— Bakersfield—even the omission of their names from the telephone directory.

The hostility has fueled efforts to drive Japanese Americans off their productive farmland. Many Japanese, brought over as cheap laborers, worked hard enough to become successful landowners. At the outbreak of the war, according to some estimates, they grew about half of the fruits and vegetables in California, and an acre of their land was worth more than seven times the value of an acre of other farmland in the state. Consequently, competitors covet their land.

You are torn. You were appointed by President Roosevelt, yet you are strongly committed to individual rights.

What do you decide?

been granted citizenship by Japan also because of their ancestry. And they have formed semiclosed communities and adhered to Old World cultural patterns. Thousands have sent their children to Japan for several years of schooling. The American general in charge of the evacuation expressed the prevalent attitude toward them: "There isn't such a thing as a loyal Japanese."[2] He concluded that "the very fact that no sabotage has taken place to date is

The phrase *civil rights* refers to equality of rights for persons regardless of their race, sex, or ethnic background. The Declaration of Independence proclaimed that "all men are created equal." The author, Thomas Jefferson, knew that all men were not created equal in many respects, but he sought to emphasize that they should be considered equal in rights and equal before the law. This represented a break with Great Britain, where rigid classes with unequal rights existed; nobles had more rights than commoners. The Declaration's promise did not include nonwhites or women, however. So even though colonial Americans advocated equality, they envisioned it only for white men. Others gradually gained more equality, but the Declaration's promise remains unfulfilled for some.

Race Discrimination

African Americans, Hispanics, and Native Americans all have endured and continue to experience discrimination. This chapter recounts the struggle for equal rights by members of these groups.

Discrimination against African Americans

Slavery

The first Africans came to America in 1619, just twelve years after the first whites. The blacks, like many whites, initially came as indentured servants. In exchange for

BLACK MASTERS

Although most slave owners were white, some were black. William Ellison of South Carolina was one. Born a slave, he bought his freedom and then his family's by building and repairing cotton gins. Over time, he earned enough money to buy slaves and operate a plantation. With sixty slaves, Ellison ranked in the top 1 percent of all slaveholders, black or white.

Ellison was unusual, but he was not unique. In Charleston, South Carolina, alone, more than one hundred African Americans owned slaves in 1860. Most, however, owned fewer than four.

Although part of the slave-owning class, black slaveholders were not accepted as equals by whites. Ellison's family was granted a pew on the main floor of the local Episcopal church, but they had to be on their guard at all times. Failure to maintain the norms of black-white relations—acting deferentially—could mean instant punishment. And as the Civil War approached, whites trying to preserve the established order increasingly viewed free blacks, even slaveholders, as a threat. Harsher legislation regulated their lives. For example, they had to have a white

"guardian" to vouch for their character, and they had to carry special papers to prove their free status. Without these papers, they could be sold back into slavery.

Some black slaveholders showed little sign that they shared the concerns of black slaves. Indeed, Ellison freed none of his slaves.[1]

1. For an acclaimed novel exploring the moral intricacies for black slave owners, read Edward P. Jones, *The Known World* (New York: Amistad, 2003).
SOURCE: Michael Johnson and James L. Roark, *Black Masters* (New York: Norton, 1984).

---

passage across the ocean, they were bound to an employer, usually for four to seven years, and then freed. But later in the seventeenth century, the colonies passed laws requiring blacks and their children to be slaves for life.

Once slavery was established, the slave trade flourished, especially in the South. But slavery was also common in the North. There were large plantations in Connecticut, Massachusetts, and Rhode Island that shipped agricultural products to the West Indies in exchange for molasses used to make rum. (Newport, Rhode Island, had more than thirty distilleries.) There were also slaves in the cities. In the mid-1700s, New York City had more slaves than any city in the colonies except Charleston. Soon after that, however, most northern slaves were freed. By the time of the Constitutional Convention, there were sharp differences between northern and southern attitudes toward slavery.

As a result of compromises between northern and southern states, the Constitution accepted slavery. It allowed the importation of slaves until 1808, when Congress could bar further importation, and it required the return of escaped slaves to their owners.

Shortly after ratification of the Constitution, northern states officially abolished slavery. In 1808, Congress barred the importation of slaves but did not halt the practice of slavery in the South. Slavery became increasingly controversial, and abolitionists called for its end. Southerners began to question the Declaration of Independence and to repudiate its notion of natural rights, attributing this idea to Jefferson's "radicalism."[5] But by the time of the Civil War, one of every nine black people in America was free; the other eight were slaves.

The Supreme Court tried to quell the antislavery sentiment in the **Dred Scott case** in 1857.[6] Dred Scott, a slave who lived in Missouri, was taken by his owner to the free state of Illinois and the free territory of Wisconsin and, after five years, was returned to Missouri. The owner died and passed title to his wife, who moved but left Scott in the care of people in Missouri. They opposed slavery and arranged to have Scott sue his owner for his freedom. They argued that Scott's time in a free state and a free territory made him a free man even though he was brought back to a slave state. The owner, who also opposed slavery, had authority to free Scott, but she and the people caring for him sought a major court decision to keep slavery out of the territories.

In this infamous case, Chief Justice Roger Taney stated that no blacks, whether slave or free, were citizens and that they were "so far inferior that they had no rights which the white man was bound to respect." Taney could have stopped here—if Scott was not a citizen, he could not sue in federal court—but Taney continued. He declared that Congress had no power to control slavery in the territories. This meant that slavery could extend into the territories Congress already had declared free. It also raised the possibility that the states could not control slavery within their borders.[7]

By this time, slavery had become the hottest controversy in American politics, and this decision fanned the flames. It provoked vehement opposition in the North and prompted further polarization, which eventually led to the Civil War.[8] Meanwhile, Scott received his freedom from his owner. Most other slaves were not so lucky (see the box "Black Masters").

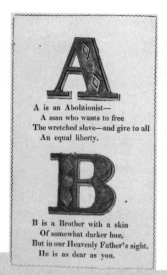

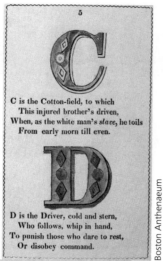

A is an Abolitionist—
A man who wants to free
The wretched slave—and give to all
An equal liberty.

B is a Brother with a skin
Of somewhat darker hue,
But in our Heavenly Father's sight,
He is as dear as you.

C is the Cotton-field, to which
This injured brother's driven,
When, as the white man's *slave*, he toils
From early morn till even.

D is the Driver, cold and stern,
Who follows, whip in hand,
To punish those who dare to rest,
Or disobey command.

Boston Anthenaeum

Slavery became a polarizing issue years before the Civil War. The Anti-Slavery Alphabet, *a children's book, was first published in 1847.*

The North's victory in the Civil War gave force to President Lincoln's Emancipation Proclamation ending slavery.[9] But blacks would find short-lived solace.

Reconstruction

After the war, Congress passed and the states ratified three constitutional amendments. The Thirteenth prohibited slavery. (In 1995, Mississippi became the last state to ratify the amendment, but of course the state's ratification was merely a symbolic action by then.) The Fourteenth granted citizenship to blacks, thus overruling the Dred Scott decision, and also granted "equal protection of the laws" and "due process of law." The **equal protection clause** would eventually become the primary guarantee that government would treat people equally. The Fifteenth gave black men the right to vote.

These amendments not only granted specific rights for African Americans but also transformed the relationship between the federal and state governments. Each amendment included a stipulation that "Congress shall have power to enforce" the provisions of the amendment. Congress did not trust the southern states to enforce constitutional provisions they had just fought a war against. This stipulation granted the federal government new power—whatever power was necessary to guarantee these rights. This new power stands in marked contrast to the Founders' original understanding that the federal government would have limited power. The Civil War and these amendments together thus constituted a constitutional revolution, as explained in Chapter 2.[10]

Congress also passed a series of Civil Rights Acts to reverse the "Black Codes" that southern states had enacted to deny the newly freed slaves legal rights.[11] These laws allowed blacks to buy, own, and sell property; to make contracts; to sue; and to serve as witnesses and jurors in court. They also allowed blacks to use public transportation, such as railroads and steamboats, and to patronize hotels and theaters.

Even so, most freed blacks faced bleak conditions. Congress rejected proposals to break up plantations and give former slaves "forty acres and a mule" or to provide aid to establish schools. Without land or education, they had to work for their former masters as hired hands or sharecroppers. Their status was not much better than it had been. Landowners designed a system to keep the former slaves dependent. They allowed sharecroppers to sell half their crop and keep the proceeds, but they paid so little, regardless of how hard the farmers worked, that the families had to borrow to tide them over the winter. The next year, they had to work for the landowner to pay off their debt. The cycle continued, year after year. And lacking education, most sharecroppers did not keep records of how much they owed and how much the landowner owed them, and many were cheated.

During the period of Reconstruction, the Union Army enforced the new amendments and acts. While the Army occupied the South, military commanders established procedures to register voters, including the newly freed slaves; hold elections; and ratify the Fourteenth Amendment. The commanders also started schools for children of the newly freed slaves. But in state after state, the South resisted, and eventually the North capitulated. After a decade, the two regions struck a deal to end what was left of Reconstruction. The 1876 presidential election between Republican Rutherford Hayes and Democrat Samuel Tilden was disputed in some states. To resolve the dispute, Republicans, most of whom were northerners, and Democrats, many of whom were southerners, agreed to a compromise: Hayes would be named president, and the remaining Union troops would be removed from the South.

The collapse of Reconstruction would limit the impact of the Civil War. In effect, the South would be allowed to nullify one result of the war—the granting of legal and political rights to blacks—in exchange for accepting two other results—preserving the Union and abolishing slavery.

In hindsight, it should not be a surprise that Reconstruction did not accomplish more. It was not easy to integrate four million former slaves into a southern society that was bitter in its defeat and weak in its economy. Northern citizens who expected progress to come smoothly were naive. When it did not come quickly, they became disillusioned. At the same time, there was a desire for healing between the two regions and lingering feelings for continuity with the past.

However understandable, public attitudes during Reconstruction thus began a recurring cycle that continues to this day: The public gets upset about the treatment of African Americans and supports some efforts to improve conditions. But the public is naive and impatient, and when the efforts do not immediately produce the expected results, the public becomes disillusioned and dissatisfied with the costs. The public's lack of sophistication and patience forces officials to put the race problem on the back burner for some future generation to pick up again.[12]

Segregation

In both the South and the North, blacks came to be segregated from whites.

Segregation in the South The reconciliation between Republicans and Democrats—northerners and southerners—was effected at the expense of blacks. Removing the troops enabled the South to govern itself again, and this enabled the South to reduce blacks to near-slave status.

Before the Civil War, slavery itself had kept blacks down. Segregation would have been inconvenient when blacks and whites needed to live and work near each other. There was no residential segregation—not in rural areas, where former slaves' shacks were intermixed with plantation mansions, and not in urban areas, where few blocks were solidly black. But after slavery, southerners established segregation as another way to keep blacks down. Initially, they did so haphazardly—one law here, another there. By the early 1900s, however, there was a pervasive pattern of **Jim Crow laws.**[13]

Jim Crow laws segregated just about everything. Some segregated blocks within neighborhoods, others neighborhoods within cities. Laws in some small towns excluded blacks altogether. Some did so explicitly; others simply established curfews that required blacks to be off the streets by 10 P.M. Laws also segregated schools, which blacks had been allowed to attend during Reconstruction, and even textbooks (black schools' texts had to be stored separately from white schools' books). Many laws segregated public accommodations, such as hotels, restaurants, bars, theaters, and transportation. At first, the laws required the races to sit in separate sections of streetcars; eventually, they required them to sit in separate cars; finally, they also forced them to sit in separate sections of waiting rooms. Other laws segregated parks, sporting events, and circuses. Laws segregated black and white checkers players in Birmingham and established districts for black and white prostitutes in New Orleans. They segregated drinking fountains, restrooms, ticket windows, entrances, and exits. They segregated the races in prisons, hospitals, and homes for the blind. They even segregated the races in death—in morgues, funeral homes, and cemeteries.

The harm from segregation was not primarily that blacks were denied access to better facilities or locations, though they were, but that they were degraded. The system of Jim Crow laws was "an officially organized degradation ceremony, repeated day after day." Segregation told blacks they were inferior and did not belong in the communities where they lived.[14]

Blacks were forced to defer to whites in informal settings as well—for instance, to move off the sidewalk when a white pedestrian approached. Failure to defer could mean punishment or even death. Blacks were "humiliated by a thousand daily reminders of their subordination."[15]

Meanwhile, northern leaders, who had championed the cause of the slaves before and during the Civil War, abandoned African Americans a decade after the war. Congress declined to pass new laws, presidents refused to enforce existing laws, and the Supreme Court gutted the constitutional amendments and Civil Rights Acts.

The Supreme Court struck down the Civil Rights Act allowing blacks to use public accommodations, including hotels, restaurants, bars, theaters, and transportation.[16] Where the Fourteenth Amendment said that "no state" shall deny equal protection, the Court interpreted this to mean that "no government" shall, but private individuals—owners of hotels, restaurants, bars, theaters, and transportation—could. The Court's interpretation might seem plausible, but it was clearly contrary to Congress's intent.[17]

Then the Court upheld segregation itself. Louisiana passed "an Act to promote the comfort of passengers," which mandated separate accommodations in trains. New Orleans black leaders sponsored a case to test the act's constitutionality. Homer Adolph Plessy bought a ticket and sat in the white car. When the conductor ordered him to move to the black car, Plessy refused. He maintained that the act was unconstitutional under the Fourteenth Amendment. In ***Plessy v. Ferguson*** in 1896, the Court disagreed, claiming that the act was not a denial of equal protection because it provided equal accommodations.[18] Thus the Court established the **separate-but-equal doctrine,** which allowed separate facilities if they were "equal." Of course, government required separate facilities only because it thought the races were not equal, but the Court brazenly commented that the act did not stamp "the colored race with a badge of inferiority" unless "the colored race chooses to put that construction on it." Only Justice John Harlan, a former Kentucky slaveholder, dissented: "Our Constitution is color-blind, and neither knows nor tolerates classes among citizens."

Three years later, the Court accepted segregation in schools.[19] A Georgia school board turned a black high school into a black elementary school. Although the board did not establish a new high school for blacks or allow them to attend the ones for whites, the Court did not object. This set a pattern in which separate but equal meant separation but not equality.

Segregation in the North Although Jim Crow laws were not as pervasive in the North as in the South, northerners imitated southerners to the point where one writer proclaimed, "The North has surrendered!"[20]

Job opportunities were better in the North. Southern blacks were sharecropping—by 1930, some 80 percent of those who farmed were still working somebody else's land[21]—and northern factories were offering jobs. Between 1915 and 1940, more than a million southern blacks headed north in the "Great Migration." But they were forced to live in black ghettos because they could not afford better housing and because they could not escape discrimination in the North either.

Denial of the Right to Vote

With the adoption of the Fifteenth Amendment, many African Americans voted and elected fellow African Americans to office during Reconstruction, but southern states began to disfranchise them in the 1890s (as explained in Chapter 8). Thus they were unable to elect black representatives or even pressure white officials to oppose segregation.

Violence

To solidify their control, whites engaged in violence against blacks. In the 1880s and 1890s, whites lynched

Lynching occurred not only in the South but also in northern cities such as Marion, Indiana, in 1930. The girls on the left hold pieces of the victims' clothing, torn off as "souvenirs."

© Bettmann/CORBIS

Reason	Number of Lynchings
Murder	5
Attempted murder	5
Manslaughter	10
Rape	9
Attempted rape	11
Burglary	3
Harboring a fugitive	1
Theft of 75 cents	1
Having a debt of $3	2
Winning a fight with a white man	1
Insulting a white man	1
Talking to white girls on the telephone	1
Being the wife or son of a rapist	2
Being the father of a boy who "jostled" white women	1
Expressing sympathy for the victim of mob violence	3

TABLE 1   Why Whites Lynched Blacks in 1907

Whites gave the following reasons for lynching blacks, who may or may not have committed the acts cited.

SOURCE: Adapted from Ray Stannard Baker, *Following the Color Line* (New York: Harper & Row, 1964), 176–177.

about one hundred blacks a year. In the 1900s, vigilante "justice" continued (see Table 1). For example, a mob in Livermore, Kentucky, dragged a black man accused of murdering a white man into a theater. The ringleaders charged admission and hanged the man. Then they permitted the audience to shoot at the swinging body—those in the balcony could fire once; those in the better seats could empty their revolvers.[22]

Lynchings often began with a false report of a white woman being sexually assaulted by a black man. Then a mob would gather and force the hapless man to endure a humiliating and excruciating ordeal. Usually they tortured him before killing him. The mob routinely castrated him, often before lynching him, and frequently hacked off his fingers and ears as well.[23]

Lynchings were not the result of a few troublemakers but were a social institution in southern society. The ritualized spectacles were used to cling to the antebellum order that had been upset by the Civil War. At the same time, lynchings were related to the increase in white women who worked outside the home at the turn of the twentieth century. As these women experienced greater independence, insecure men evidently feared that the women would become too independent, perhaps even leave them for black men. Hence the ritual of castration.[24] Through lynchings, then, white men could remain in charge—at home as well as in society—as they appeared to defend women's honor.

In 1919, twenty-five race riots erupted in six months. White mobs took over cities in the North and South, burning black neighborhoods and terrorizing black residents for days on end.[25]

In 1921, ten thousand whites burned down thirty-five blocks of Tulsa's black neighborhood. The incident that precipitated the riot was typical—a report of an assault by a black man on a white woman. The report was false, fabricated by the woman (and later retracted), but residents were inflamed by a racist newspaper and encouraged by the city's officials. Almost three hundred people were shot, burned alive, or tied to cars and dragged to death. Survivors reported corpses stacked like firewood on street corners and piled high in dump trucks.[26]

Sometimes the violence was intended to drive black families off their land. In addition to lynchings and burnings, bands of white farmers known as Whitecaps nailed notes, with a drawing of a coffin and a warning to leave or die, on the doors of black farmers. Then the cities or counties put the land up for auction or simply gave it to white families who owned adjacent land.[27] This process affected not just the black families at the time but their descendents for many generations. The black families lost wealth that is accumulating value for the white owners today, many of whom may be unaware of how the land changed hands.

The white supremacist Ku Klux Klan, which began during Reconstruction and started up again in 1915, played a major role in inflaming prejudice and terrorizing blacks. It was strong enough to dominate many southern towns and even the state governments of Oklahoma and Texas. It also made inroads into some northern states such as Indiana.

Federal officials contended that such violence was a state problem—presidents refused to speak out, and Congress refused to pass legislation making lynching a federal offense—yet state officials did nothing.

For at least the first third of the twentieth century, white supremacy reigned—in the southern states, the border states, and many of the northern states. It also pervaded the nation's capital, where President Woodrow Wilson instituted segregation in the federal government.[28] (See also the box "Passing the 'Brown Bag Test'" on the next page)

Overcoming Discrimination against African Americans

African Americans fought white supremacy primarily in three arenas: the courts, the streets, and Congress. In general, they fought in the courts first and Congress last, although as they gained momentum they increasingly fought in all three arenas at once.

The Movement in the Courts
The first goal was to convince the Supreme Court to overturn the separate-but-equal doctrine of *Plessy* v. *Ferguson.*

The NAACP In response to white violence, a group of blacks and whites founded the National Association for the Advancement of Colored People, or **NAACP,** in 1909. In its first two decades, it was led by W. E. B. Du Bois, a black sociologist. In time, it became the major organization fighting for blacks' civil rights.

Frustrated by presidential and congressional inaction and its own lack of power to force action, the NAACP decided to converge on the federal courts, which were less subject to pressures from the majority. The

Tulsa's black neighborhood after whites burned it down in 1921.

Tulsa Historical Society

Whites' preoccupation with skin color affected blacks even in their relationships with other blacks. In the early twentieth century, African Americans who wanted to join certain African American clubs and churches had to pass the "brown bag test." They had to put their hand into a brown paper bag; if what was showing was lighter in color than the bag, they were eligible for membership. A social club in Nashville had a similar test. Aspiring members had to demonstrate that their blue veins could be seen through their pale skin on the inside of their wrists.

This concern for lighter skin stemmed from the slavery era, when light-skinned blacks often brought higher prices and got better jobs as household workers than as field hands. In 1860, the census classified fully 30 percent of free blacks as "mulatto" (having some white ancestry), compared to only 10 percent of the slaves. After emancipation, lighter skin continued to be a social and economic advantage. Many blacks with darker skin used bleach, lye, or other products to lighten their color.

Although black colleges did not restrict admission to African Americans with lighter skin, in the 1930s most of their students did have lighter skin.

Sorority sisters as Fisk University, a historically black college, in 1936.

National Archives/ Harmon Collection, 200(S)-HS-1-92

They were the children of doctors, dentists, lawyers, and morticians, who themselves had lighter skin and were more successful in their communities. They were predominant among African Americans who could afford to send their children to college in those years. At college, their children took up whites' pastimes, such as cotillions and tennis, in an attempt to distinguish themselves from poor blacks and to gain acceptance from whites. (But acceptance still was not granted.) As late as the 1960s, when the slogan "Black is beautiful" became popular, the homecoming queen at Howard University usually had a light complexion.

This concern for lighter skin persists. Fashion models on *Ebony's* covers often have pale skin, and the sales of bleaching products still continue. African Americans with lighter skins have a higher socioeconomic status, and many African Americans prefer lighter-skinned mates.

SOURCE: "For Black College Students in the 1930s, Respectability and Prestige Depended on Passing the Brown Bag Test," *Journal of Blacks in Higher Education,* January 31, 1999, 119–120; Louie E. Ross, "Mate Selection Preferences Among African American College Students," *Journal of Black Studies* 27 (1997), 554–569; St. Clair Drake and Horace R. Clayton, *Black Metropolis* (New York: Harcourt, Brace, 1945); Mark Hill, "Color Differences in the Socioeconomic Statuses of African American Men," *Social Forces* 78 (2000), 1437–1460.

association assembled a cadre of lawyers, mainly from Howard University Law School, a historically black school in Washington, D.C., to bring lawsuits attacking segregation and the denial of the right to vote. In 1915, they persuaded the Supreme Court to strike down the grandfather clause (which exempted persons whose ancestors could vote from the literacy test);[29] two years later, they convinced the Court to invalidate laws prescribing residential segregation.[30] But the Court continued to allow most devices to disfranchise blacks and most efforts to segregate.

In 1938, the NAACP chose a thirty-year-old attorney, Thurgood Marshall, to head its litigation arm.[31] Marshall—whose mother had to pawn her engagement and wedding rings so that he could go to an out-of-state

law school because his in-state school, the University of Maryland, did not admit blacks—would become a tireless and courageous advocate for equal rights. (In 1946, after defending four blacks charged with attempted murder during a riot in rural Tennessee, he would narrowly escape a lynch mob.)[32]

Over the next two decades, presidents appointed more liberals to the Supreme Court. These two developments led to the NAACP's success in the courts.

Desegregation of Schools Seventeen states and the District of Columbia segregated their schools (and four other states allowed cities to segregate their schools). The states gave white students better facilities and white teachers larger salaries. Overall, they spent from two to ten times more on white schools than on black ones.[33] Few of these states had graduate schools for blacks: As late as 1950, they had fifteen engineering schools, fourteen medical schools, and five dental schools for whites and none for blacks; they had sixteen law schools for whites and five for blacks.

The NAACP's tactics were first to show that "separate but equal" really resulted in unequal schools and then to attack "separate but equal" head on, arguing that it led to unequal status.

The NAACP began by challenging segregation in graduate schools. Missouri provided no black law school but offered to reimburse blacks who went to out-of-state law schools. In 1938, the Supreme Court said the state had to provide a law school for black students.[34] Texas established a black law school that was clearly inferior to the white law school at the University of Texas. In 1950, the Court said the black school had to be made substantially equal to the white school.[35] Oklahoma allowed a black student to attend the white graduate school at the University of Oklahoma but designated a separate section of the classroom, library, and cafeteria for the student. The Court said this, too, was inadequate because it deprived the student of the exchange of views with fellow students necessary for education.[36] The Court did not invalidate the separate-but-equal doctrine in these decisions, but it made segregation almost impossible to implement in graduate schools.

The NAACP continued by challenging segregation in grade schools and high schools. Marshall filed suits in two southern states, one border state, one northern state, and the District of Columbia. The suit in the northern state was brought against Topeka, Kansas, where Linda Brown could not attend the school just four blocks from her home because it was a white school. Instead, she had to go to a school twenty-one blocks away.[37]

When the cases reached the Supreme Court, the justices were split. Although Chief Justice Fred Vinson might have had a majority to uphold the separate-but-equal doctrine, the Court put off a decision and rescheduled oral arguments for its next term. But Vinson suffered a heart attack, and President Eisenhower appointed Earl Warren to take his place. When the Court reheard the case, the president pressured his appointee to rule in favor of segregation. Eisenhower invited Warren and the attorney for the states to the White House for dinner. When the conversation turned to the segregationists, Eisenhower said, "These are not bad people. All they are concerned about is to see that their sweet little girls are not required to sit in schools alongside some big overgrown Negroes."[38] Warren not only voted against segregation but used his considerable determination and charm to persuade the other justices, some of whom had supported segregation, to vote against it too. Justice Felix Frankfurter later said Vin-

son's heart attack was "the first indication I have ever had that there is a God."[39]

In the landmark case of **Brown v. Board of Education** in 1954, the Court ruled unanimously that school segregation violated the Fourteenth Amendment's equal protection clause.[40] In the opinion, Warren asserted that separate but equal not only resulted in unequal schools but was inherently unequal because it made black children feel inferior. In overruling the *Plessy* doctrine, the Court showed how revolutionary the equal protection clause was—or could be interpreted to be. The Court required the segregated states to change their way of life to a degree unprecedented in American history. After overturning laws requiring segregation in schools, the Court overruled laws mandating segregation in other places, such as public parks, golf courses, swimming pools, auditoriums, courtrooms, and jails.[41]

In *Brown,* the Court had ordered schools to desegregate "with all deliberate speed."[42] This was a compromise between justices who thought schools should do so immediately and those who thought communities would need to do so gradually.[43] The ambiguity of the phrase, however, allowed communities to take many years to desegregate—far longer than any justices envisioned. The ruling prompted much deliberation but little speed.

The South engaged in massive resistance. The Court needed help from the other branches of government to implement its ruling but failed to get any cooperation for some time. President Eisenhower was reluctant to tell the states to change. In fact, he joined their representatives in Congress in criticizing the decision. With his position and popularity, the president could have speeded implementation by speaking out in support of the decision, yet he did not do so for more than three years. When nine black students tried to attend a white high school under a desegregation plan in Little Rock, Arkansas, the governor's and state legislature's inflammatory rhetoric against desegregation encouraged local citizens to take the law into their own hands. Finally, Eisenhower acted, sending federal troops and federalizing the state's national guard to quell the riot.

A few years later, in 1962, President Kennedy used federal marshals and paratroopers to stop violence after the governor of Mississippi blocked the door to keep James Meredith from registering at the University of Mississippi. Kennedy again sent troops when the governor of Alabama, George Wallace, proclaiming "segregation now, segregation tomorrow, segregation forever," blocked the door to keep blacks from enrolling at the University of Alabama.

After outright defiance, some states attempted to circumvent the ruling by shutting down their public schools and providing tuition grants for students to use at new private schools, which at the time could segregate.

They also provided textbooks and recreation facilities for private schools. Some white communities offered scholarships for poor white students. These efforts hindered desegregation and hurt black education because the black communities seldom had the resources to establish their own schools.

The states also tried less blatant schemes, such as "freedom of choice" plans that allowed students to choose the school they wanted to attend. Of course, virtually no whites chose a black school, and due to strong pressure from whites, few blacks chose a white school. The idea was to achieve desegregation on paper, or token desegregation in practice, in order to avoid actual desegregation. But the Court rebuffed these schemes and even forbade discrimination by private schools.[44]

To black southerners, the Court's persistence raised hopes. Chief Justice Warren, according to Thurgood Marshall, "allowed the poor Negro sharecropper to say, 'Kick me around Mr. Sheriff, kick me around Mr. County Judge, kick me around Supreme Court of my state, but there's one person I can rely on.'"[45]

To white southerners, however, the Court's rulings reflected a federal government, a distant authority, that was exercising too much control over their traditional practices. The rulings engendered bitterness. Justice Hugo Black, who was from Alabama, was shunned by former friends from the state; his son was driven from his legal practice in the state; and the justice was never sent an invitation to his fiftieth reunion at his alma mater, the University of Alabama.[46]

Despite the Court's rulings, progress was excruciatingly slow. If a school district was segregated, a group like the NAACP had to run the risks and spend the time and money to bring a suit in a federal district court. Judges in these courts reflected the views of the state or local political establishment, so the suit might not be successful. If it was, the school board would prepare a desegregation plan. Members of the school board reflected the views of the community and the pressures from the segregationists, so the plan might not be adequate. If it was, the segregationists would challenge it in a federal district court. If the court upheld the plan, the segregationists would appeal to a federal court of appeals. Judges in these courts came from the South, and they sat in Richmond and New Orleans, but they were not as tied to the state or local political establishment, and they usually decided against the segregationists. But then the segregationists could appeal to the Supreme Court. The segregationists knew they would lose sooner or later, but the process took several years, so they could delay the inevitable.

Thus the segregationists tried to resist, then to evade, and finally to delay. In this they succeeded. In 1964, a decade after *Brown,* 98 percent of all black children in the South still attended all-black schools.[47]

By this time, the mood in Congress had changed. Congress passed the Civil Rights Act of 1964, which, among other things, cut off federal aid to school districts that continued to segregate. The following year, it passed the first major program providing federal aid to education. This was the carrot at the end of the stick; school districts began to comply to get the federal money.

Finally, by 1970, only 14 percent of all black children in the South still attended all-black schools. Of course, some went to mostly black schools. Even so, the change was dramatic.

Busing *Brown* and related rulings addressed *de jure* **segregation**—segregation enforced by law. This segre-

Dorothy Counts, the first black student to attend one white high school in Charlotte, North Carolina, is escorted by her father in 1957.

© Stanley J. Forman, Pulitzer Prize, 1977

Busing led to riots in some cities, such as Boston. Here protesters assault a black man in 1976.

gation can be attacked by striking down the law. *Brown* did not address **de facto segregation**—segregation based on residential patterns—typical of northern cities and large southern cities, where most blacks live in black neighborhoods and most whites live in white neighborhoods. Students attend their neighborhood schools, which are mostly black or mostly white. This segregation is more intractable because it does not stem primarily from a law, so it cannot be eliminated by striking down a law.

Civil rights groups proposed busing some black children to schools in white neighborhoods and some white children to schools in black neighborhoods. They hoped to improve black children's education, their self-confidence and aspirations, and eventually, their college and career opportunities. They also hoped to improve black and white children's ability to get along together.

The Burger Court authorized busing within school districts—ordinarily cities. These included southern cities where there was a history of *de jure* segregation, and northern cities where there was a pattern of *de facto* segregation and evidence that school officials had located schools or assigned students in ways that perpetuated this segregation.[48]

Busing for desegregation was never extensive. In one typical year, only 4 percent of students were bused for desegregation. Far more students were bused, at public expense, to segregated public and private schools.[49]

Even so, court orders for mandatory busing ran into a wall of hostile public opinion. White parents criticized the courts sharply. Their reaction stemmed from a mixture of prejudice against blacks, bias against poor persons, fear of the crime in inner-city schools, worry about the quality of inner-city schools, and desire for the convenience of neighborhood schools. They also resented the courts for telling local governments what to do. Even some black parents opposed busing because it disrupted and complicated their children's lives. Black parents also resented the implication that their children could learn only if sitting next to white children. But other black parents favored busing because it offered the opportunity for their children to go to better schools.

Due to the opposition of white parents, busing—and publicity about it—prompted an increase in "white flight" as white families moved from the cities to the suburbs to avoid the busing in the cities.[50] This trend overlapped other trends, especially reductions in the white birthrate and increases in the nonwhite immigration rate, that altered the racial and economic composition of our big cities. As a result, there were fewer white students to balance enrollments and fewer middle-class students to provide stability in the cities' schools.

Therefore, even extensive busing could not desegregate most large cities, where blacks and other minorities together became more numerous than whites. Consequently, civil rights groups proposed busing some white children from the suburbs to the cities and some black children from the cities to the suburbs. This approach would provide enough of both races to achieve balance in both places.

The Burger Court rejected this proposal by a 5–4 vote in 1974.[51] It said that busing is not appropriate between school districts unless there is evidence of intentional segregation in both the city and its suburbs. Otherwise, such extensive busing would require too long a ride for students and too much coordination by administrators.

Although there was intentional segregation by many cities and their suburbs,[52] the evidence is not as clear-cut as that of the *de jure* segregation by the southern states, so it was difficult to satisfy the requirements laid down by the Burger Court. Consequently, the Court's ruling made busing between cities and suburbs very rare.

Thurgood Marshall, by then a Supreme Court justice, dissented and predicted that the ruling would allow "our great metropolitan areas to be divided up each into two cities—one white, the other black." Indeed, the ruling did contribute to this result. The ruling was the beginning of the end of the push to desegregate public schools in urban areas.

Busing could not accomplish all that civil rights groups and federal judges expected—or at least hoped— it could. Busing could not compensate for massive residential segregation. It could not overcome students' poverty or their parents' lack of involvement in their education. Consequently, studies of the performance of minority children bused to white schools showed disappointing results. In addition, busing furthered the deterioration of minority communities because it diminished the neighborhood schools that had helped define these communities and hold them together.

In 1991, the Rehnquist Court decided that school districts have no obligation to reduce *de facto* segregation and in fact diminished the obligation to reduce the vestiges of *de jure* segregation.[53] This ruling relieved the pressure on school districts, and by the mid-1990s, most had stopped mandatory busing. When some tried other programs to balance enrollments, the Court looked askance at these programs.[54] The rulings in the 1990s reflected none of "the moral urgency of *Brown*."[55] Instead, the justices decided that desegregation is less important than minimizing judicial involvement in education and judicial authority over local governments. In these ways, the majority of the justices mirrored the views of the Republican presidents who had appointed them.

The Movement in the Streets

After the NAACP's early successes in the courts, other blacks, and some whites, took the fight to the streets. Their bold efforts gave birth to the modern civil rights movement.

Martin Luther King, Jr., pictured with his wife, Coretta Scott King, is arrested in 1958.

© Charles Moore/Black Star

The movement came to public attention in Montgomery, Alabama, in 1955, when Rosa Parks refused to move to the back of the bus. Her refusal and arrest prompted blacks to boycott city buses. For their leader, they chose a young Baptist minister, Dr. Martin Luther King, Jr. The boycott catapulted the movement and King to national attention (as explained in Chapter 6).

King was the first charismatic leader of the movement. He formed the Southern Christian Leadership Conference (SCLC) of black clergy and adopted the tactics of Mahatma Gandhi, who had led the movement to free India from the British. The tactics included direct action, such as demonstrations and marches, and civil disobedience—intentional and public disobeying of laws considered unjust. The tactics were based on nonviolence, even when confronted with violence. This strategy was designed to draw support from whites by contrasting the morality of the movement's position with the immorality of discrimination and violence against blacks.

For a long time, some whites, focusing on civil rights leaders such as King and even fearing infiltration by foreign communists, deluded themselves into thinking that "outside agitators" were responsible for the turmoil in their communities.[56] But the movement grew from the grass roots, and it eventually shattered this delusion.

The movement spread among black students. In 1960, four students of North Carolina A&T College sat at the lunch counter in Woolworth's, one of a chain of five-and-ten-cent stores, and asked for a cup of coffee. The waitress refused to serve them, but they stayed and were arrested. On following days, as whites waved the Confederate flag and jeered, more students sat at the lunch counter. Within a year, such sit-ins occurred in more than one hundred cities.

When blacks asserted their rights, whites often reacted with violence. In 1963, King led demonstrators in

Students sit in at a lunch counter in Jackson, Mississippi.

Birmingham, Alabama, seeking desegregation of public facilities. Police unleashed dogs to attack the marchers. In 1964, King led demonstrators in Selma, Alabama, for voting rights. State troopers clubbed some marchers, and vigilantes beat and shot others.

In the summer of 1964, black and white college students mounted a voter registration drive in Mississippi. By the end of the summer, one thousand had been arrested, eighty beaten, thirty-five shot, and six killed.[57] When a black cotton farmer, who had tried to register to vote, was shot in the head in broad daylight by a white state legislator, the act was not even treated as a crime.[58]

Indeed, perpetrators of the violence usually were not apprehended or prosecuted. When they were, they usually were not convicted. Law enforcement was frequently in the hands of bigots, and juries were generally all white. The Supreme Court had struck down discrimination in choosing juries,[59] but discrimination continued through informal means.

During these years, most whites told pollsters they disliked the civil rights movement's speed and tactics: "They're pushing too fast and too hard." At the same time, most said they favored integration more than ever. And they seemed repelled by the violence. The brutality against blacks generated more support for black Americans and their cause.

The media, especially national organizations based in northern cities such as the *New York Times,* the Associated Press, and the major television networks, played a role simply by covering the conflict. The leaders of the civil rights movement staged events that captured attention, and violent racists played into their hands. As northern reporters and photographers relayed the events and violence to the nation, the movement gained public sympathy in the North. Yet the national press became as vilified as the federal government in the South. (This anger would lay the foundation for southerners' distrust of the media for their coverage of the Vietnam War and later events as well.)[60]

Although the movement's tactics worked well against southern *de jure* segregation, they did not work as well against northern *de facto* segregation or against job discrimination in either region. By the mid-1960s, progress had stalled and dissatisfaction had grown. Young blacks from the inner city, who had not been involved in the movement, questioned two of its principles: interracialism and nonviolence. As James Farmer, head of the Congress of Racial Equality (CORE), explained, they asked, "What is this we-shall-overcome, black-and-white-together stuff? I don't know of any white folks except the guy who runs that store on 125th Street in Harlem and garnishes wages and repossesses things you buy. I'd like

When three civil rights workers were murdered in Neshoba County, Mississippi, no one was indicted by the state. Later eighteen persons, including the sheriff (right) and deputy sheriff (left), were indicted by the federal government for the lesser charge of conspiracy. (There was no applicable federal law for murder.) Ultimately, seven persons, including the deputy, were convicted by the federal court.

to go upside his head. [Or] the rent collector, who bangs on the door demanding rent that we ain't got. I'd like to go upside his head."[61] These blacks criticized King and his tactics. In place of the integration advocated by King, some leaders began to call for "black power." This phrase, which implied black pride and self-reliance, meant different things to different people. To some it meant political power through the ballot box, while to others it meant economic power through ownership of their own businesses. To a few it meant violence in retaliation for violence by whites. The movement splintered further.

The Movement in Congress

As the civil rights movement expanded, it pressured presidents and members of Congress to act. Presidents Kennedy and Johnson supported civil rights but felt hamstrung by southerners in Congress who, through the seniority system, had risen to chair key committees and dominate both houses. As a result, the presidents considered civil rights leaders unreasonable and the movement a nuisance that alienated the southerners on whom the presidents had to rely. But once the movement demonstrated its strength, it was able to prod officials to act. After two hundred thousand blacks and whites marched in Washington in 1963, President Kennedy introduced civil rights legislation. His successor, President Johnson, with consummate legislative skill, forged a coalition of northern Democrats and northern Republicans to overcome southern Democrats and pass the Civil Rights Act of 1964. After one thousand blacks

and whites had been attacked and arrested in Selma, Johnson introduced and Congress passed the Voting Rights Act of 1965. Three years later, Johnson introduced and Congress passed the Civil Rights Act of 1968. Within a span of four years, Congress passed legislation prohibiting discrimination in public accommodations, employment, housing, and voting. These would become the most significant civil rights acts in history.

It is impossible to exaggerate how radically controversial these laws were. In 1964, the Republican nominee for president, Senator Barry Goldwater of Arizona, opposed the Civil Rights Act. He had been assured by two advisers—Phoenix attorney William Rehnquist and Yale professor Robert Bork—that it was unconstitutional.[62] The conservative Republican Ronald Reagan, preparing to run for California governor, also strongly opposed the act.[63] (Years later, as president, Reagan would appoint Rehnquist as Chief Justice and nominate Bork as an associate justice of the Supreme Court.)

Although President Johnson believed he was doing the right thing, he realized the political ramifications. Upon signing the first of these acts, he commented that he was handing the South to the Republican Party "for the next fifty years."[64] He was perceptive. In the next election, he became the first Democrat since the Civil War to lose the white vote in the southern states. In less than a decade, the South, which had been solidly Democratic since the Civil War, would go from the most Democratic region of the country to the most Republican.[65]

Desegregation of Public Accommodations The **Civil Rights Act of 1964** prohibits discrimination on the basis of race, color, religion, or national origin in public accommodations. This time, in contrast to its actions after the Civil War, the Court unanimously upheld the law.[66]

The act does not cover private clubs, such as country clubs, social clubs, or fraternities and sororities, on the principle that the government should not tell people with whom they may or may not associate in private. (The Court has made private schools an exception to this principle to help enforce *Brown*.)

Desegregation of Employment The Civil Rights Act of 1964 also prohibits employment discrimination on the basis of race, color, religion, national origin, or sex and (as amended) physical disability, age, or Vietnam-era veteran status. The act covers employers with fifteen or more employees and any unions.[67]

In addition to practicing blatant discrimination, some employers practiced more subtle discrimination. They required applicants to meet standards unnecessary for their jobs, a practice that hindered blacks more than whites. A high school diploma for a manual job was a common example. The Court held that standards must relate to the jobs.[68] However, standards that hindered blacks more than whites were not necessarily unlawful. Washington, D.C., required applicants for police officer to pass an exam. Although a higher percentage of blacks failed to pass, the Court said the exam related to the job.[69]

Desegregation of Housing Although the Supreme Court had struck down laws that prescribed segregation in residential areas, whites maintained segregation by making **restrictive covenants**—agreements among neighbors not to sell their houses to blacks. In 1948, the Court ruled that courts could not enforce these covenants because doing so would involve the government in discrimination.[70]

Real estate agents also played a role in segregation by practicing **steering**—showing blacks houses in black neighborhoods and whites houses in white neighborhoods. Unscrupulous real estate agents practiced **blockbusting.** After a black family bought a house in a white neighborhood, the agents would warn white families that more blacks would move in. Because of prejudice and fear that their houses' values would decline, whites would panic and sell to the agents at low prices. Then the agents would resell to blacks at higher prices. In this way, neighborhoods that might have been desegregated were instead resegregated—from all white to all black.

Banks and savings and loans also played a role. They were reluctant to lend money to blacks who wanted to buy a house in a white neighborhood. Some engaged in **redlining**—refusing to lend money to people who wanted to buy a house in a racially changing neighborhood. The lenders worried that if the buyer could not keep up with the payments, the lender would be left with a house whose value had declined.

The government also played an important role. The Veterans Administration and the Federal Housing Authority, which guaranteed loans to some buyers, were reluctant to authorize loans to blacks who tried to buy a house in a white neighborhood but were generous to whites who were fleeing the cities to buy in all-white suburbs. And the federal government, which funded low-income housing, allowed local governments to locate such housing in ghettos. In these ways, the governments helped perpetuate segregation.[71]

But the **Civil Rights Act of 1968** bans discrimination in the sale or rental of housing on the basis of race, color, religion, or national origin and (as amended) on the basis of sex, having children, or having a disability. The act covers about 80 percent of the available housing and prohibits steering, blockbusting, and redlining.

Restoration of the Right to Vote After years of skirmishing with the states, the Supreme Court and Congress barred measures designed to keep blacks from voting. The Voting Rights Act of 1965 permitted large numbers of blacks to vote for the first time (as explained in Chapter 8).

Continuing Discrimination against African Americans

African Americans have overcome much discrimination but still face some. Overt laws and blatant practices have been struck down, but subtle manifestations of old attitudes and habits persist—and in ways far more numerous and with effects far more serious than this one chapter can convey.[72] Moreover, African Americans must cope with the legacy of generations of slavery, segregation, discrimination, and for many, the effects of poverty. And they must cope with the attitudes of whites. Although few people say they want to return to the days of legal segregation, about half reject the dream of an integrated society.[73] (See the box "How Much Is White Skin Worth?" on page 525 for a hypothetical but telling response to coping with discrimination.)

Discrimination in Education

For blacks who can afford it, a great deal of desegregation has occurred in education. Affluent parents who can pay for private schools or live in better-off neighborhoods with good public schools can send their children to integrated schools. However, for most blacks in big cities, medium cities, or areas where private schools predominate, much less desegregation has occurred.

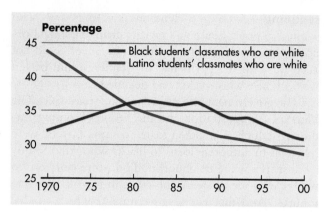

FIGURE 1 ■ **Segregation in the Public Schools, 1970–2000** *For both black and Latino students, schools are becoming increasingly segregated. The graph for black students reflects the push for desegregation through the 1970s.* SOURCE: Ellis Cose, "A Dream Deferred," *Newsweek,* May 17, 2004, 59.

Although *de jure* segregation of schools has been eliminated, *de facto* segregation remains. In fact, this segregation is getting worse. After progress in the mid-1960s and 1970s, the trend toward desegregation reversed itself in the 1980s and got worse in the 1990s. "For the first time since the *Brown* v. *Board* decision," according to one study, "we are going backwards"[74] (see Figure 1). One-third of black students attend schools that are 90 to 100 percent minority.[75]

The reversal is due to white flight to private schools and to the suburbs, leaving fewer white children, and also due to higher nonwhite birthrates and immigration rates, producing more nonwhite children. White parents intentionally look for schools with low numbers of racial minorities. Although many say they move for better schools, few ever visit the schools in either the old neighborhood or the new one before moving, and few seek out test score results. They use racial composition as a proxy for school quality. The more racial minorities, the poorer the quality, they assume.[76]

The reversal is also due to the Reagan administration's elimination of a program that offered incentives to school districts for desegregating and to the Burger and Rehnquist Courts' rejection of cross-district busing and other alternatives to balance enrollments. School districts got the message that desegregation is no longer an important national goal.[77]

As a result, only one of four students in public schools in our forty-seven largest cities is white.[78] In some cities, it is far fewer. Consequently, there is more segregation today in northern cities, where the segregation has been mostly *de facto,* than in southern cities, where the segregation had been mostly *de jure.*[79]

The persistence of *de facto* segregation and the waning of commitment to integration have led national, state,

and local officials to adopt an attitude of resignation: "We still agree with the goal of school desegregation, but it's too hard, and we're tired of it, and we give up."[80]

Reforms proposed for urban schools rarely include desegregation. Officials speak of a ghetto school that is more "efficient" or one that gets more "input" from ghetto parents or offers more "choices" for ghetto children. But the existence of segregated education as "a permanent American reality" appears to be accepted.[81]

A writer who visited many central-city classrooms and talked with students, teachers, and administrators observed that Martin Luther King was treated as

> *an icon, but his vision of a nation in which black and white kids went to school together seemed to be effaced almost entirely. Dutiful references to "The Dream" were often seen in school brochures and on wall posters in February, when "Black History" was celebrated in the public schools, but the content of the dream was treated as a closed box that could not be opened without ruining the celebration.*[82]

Indeed, many cities have a school named after King—a segregated school in a segregated neighborhood—"like a terrible joke on history," a fourteen-year-old, wise beyond her years, remarked.[83]

Many minorities have gotten so frustrated that they themselves have questioned the goal of school desegregation. Instead, they have voiced greater concern about improving the quality and safety of their schools and neighborhoods.[84]

By virtually every measure of school quality—school funding, class size, teacher credentials, teacher salaries, breadth of curriculum, number of computers, opportunities for gifted students—minority children attend worse schools[85] (see Figure 2).

Unequal Funding In areas where schools are segregated, the quality varies enormously—from "the golden to the godawful," in the words of a Missouri judge.[86] And of course, minorities are more likely to be in the "godawful" ones.

Schools are financed largely by property taxes paid by homeowners and businesses. Wealthy cities collect more in property taxes than poor ones. In modern America, this means that suburban school districts have more to spend per pupil than central-city school districts. Even though many suburbs tax their residents at a lower rate than cities do, the suburbs still bring in more revenue because their property is valued at a higher level. Thus these suburbs ask their residents to sacrifice less but still provide their children with an education that costs more.[87]

Spending-per-pupil figures do not take into account that the needs of poor children, after years of neglect

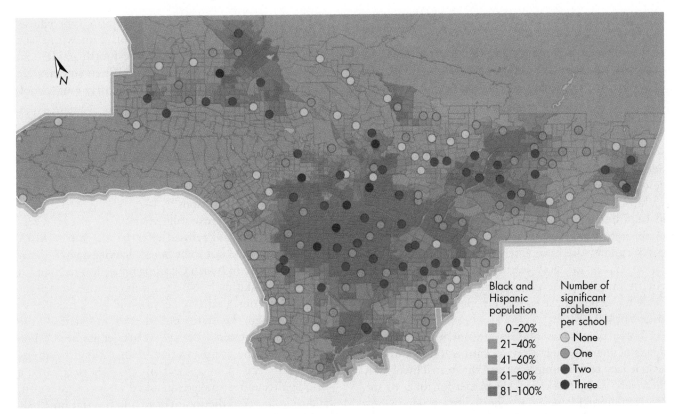

FIGURE 2 ■ Shortcomings among Schools in Los Angeles County *In Los Angeles County, schools in black and Hispanic neighborhoods have far more shortcomings than schools in white neighborhoods. A white dot represents a high school with no significant shortcomings. A gray or black dot represents a high school that has a significant shortcoming involving its teachers (less than 80 percent are certified), its curriculum (less than two-thirds of the courses prepare students for a four-year college), or its facilities (the students attend school in shifts because the buildings are so crowded, and as a result they have a shorter school year). The more shortcomings, the darker the dot. Not a single school that is 90 percent or more white and Asian has a significant shortcoming.*

SOURCE: *Atlantic Monthly*, July-August 2004, 64.

and with scores of problems at home and in the neighborhood, are greater than the needs of other children. Schools for poor children would require *more* funding to provide their students an equal education.

So many inner-city schools are bleak institutions, filthy and in disrepair. Most are overcrowded. Classes are held in hallways and former coatrooms or closets. Some cities in New Jersey that ran out of classrooms tried to rent space in vacant schools in the suburbs. But the cities were turned down because the suburbs did not want the mostly nonwhite children coming into their communities.[88]

Many inner-city schools do not have texts for all their students, up-to-date texts that are at the appropriate grade levels. Some schools cannot afford to hire science, art, music, or physical education teachers. Almost none can afford to offer competitive salaries to hire good teachers in the subjects the schools do offer. A New York City principal said he is forced to take the "tenth-best" teachers. "I thank God they're still breathing."[89]

Despite the pervasive pattern of unequal funding, cash alone would not solve all the problems. Cultural and economic factors in inner cities also restrict the quality of education available. But cash would help. According to one calculation, if New York City schools had been funded at the same level as the highest-spending suburban schools on Long Island, a typical fourth-grade class of thirty-six children would have had $200,000 more invested in the children's education in one year. The difference would have been enough to divide the class in half, hire two excellent teachers, and provide the classrooms with computers, new texts, reference books, learning games, carpets, air conditioning, and new counselors to help the children cope with problems in their environment outside school.[90]

Some states have equalized funding, but moves to do so in other states have encountered fierce opposition.

An alternative to equalized funding would be supplementary funding by states for schools in inner cities. But people's priorities run in other directions. In 1999, the Pennsylvania legislature approved $160 million of public financing for new stadiums for the Eagles and Phillies and another $160 million of public financing for new stadiums for the Steelers and Pirates, while the schools in Philadelphia and Pittsburgh languished.[91]

Second-Generation Discrimination Even where desegregation of schools has been achieved, segregation within schools exists. This "second-generation discrimination" isolates many minority students by placing them in separate programs or classes from white students. Black children are more likely to be put in special education classes for slow learners and less likely to be put in programs for gifted students. They are more likely to be put in classes for the educable mentally retarded (EMR).[92]

These facts by themselves are not necessarily evidence of second-generation discrimination, because the long legacy of discrimination and the dismal living conditions of many blacks make it harder for them to succeed in school. However, in school districts where more minorities are school board members or are administrators or teachers, less disparate treatment occurs.[93] The presence of minorities in authoritative positions apparently sensitizes white administrators or teachers to this discrimination.

Black children are also more likely to be disciplined.[94] Cultural misunderstandings between white teachers and black students—for example, misinterpretation of body language signaling respect or disrespect—and "racial paranoia" are common. One education professor observed, "We see this a lot with black boys who are cute until about the fourth grade, and then teachers start to fear them."[95] When students are suspended, they fall behind in class and may quit school.

Discrimination in Public Accommodations

Black newlyweds no longer have to spend their wedding night in a funeral parlor, as Martin Luther and Coretta Scott King did. Most businesses comply with the Civil Rights Act of 1964 prohibiting discrimination in public accommodations.[96]

However, Jim Crow still lives in some places. A restaurant in Maryland refused to serve a group of black men, who turned out to be Secret Service agents. A car rental franchise in North Carolina refused to rent cars to blacks. A gas station in North Carolina refused to sell gas to blacks. When a thirty-one-year-old black man, traveling through the state, pulled into the station, the white attendant said, "Boy, you can't get gas here." The man figured the pumps were broken. "No," the attendant said. "Boy, you can't get any gas." At that point, a black police officer pulled up, asked what was going on, and then directed the motorist to another station.[97] Although illegal, these practices persist if no one files a complaint or brings a lawsuit.

Some businesses try to circumvent the act. For instance, some restaurants give blacks poor service so they will not return. A suburban mall refused to allow city buses from Buffalo in its parking lot, although it allowed Canadian buses to bring their shoppers from across the border. Mall executives assured shopkeepers that "you'll never see an inner-city bus on the mall premises."[98]

Even some businesses that try to comply with the act have employees who treat blacks differently and embarrassingly. As one writer notes:

> You stroll into a shop to look at the merchandise, and it soon becomes clear that the clerks are keeping a watchful eye on you. Too quickly, one of them comes over to inquire what it is you might want, and then remains conspicuously close as you continue your search. It also seems that they take an unusually long time verifying your credit card. Then you and a black friend enter a restaurant, and find yourselves greeted warily, with what is obviously a more anxious reception than that given to white guests. Yes, you will be served, and your table will not necessarily be next to the kitchen. Still, you sense that they would rather you had chosen some other eating place.[99]

Because the Civil Rights Act does not apply to private clubs, many country clubs and golf clubs discriminate against blacks. One estimate is that three-fourths of these clubs have no black members, and many of the remainder have only one or a few token members.[100]

A teacher tries to teach in the hallway of an overcrowded school in the underfunded Philadelphia school system.

How Much Is White Skin Worth?

You will be visited tonight by an official you have never met. He begins by telling you he is extremely embarrassed. The organization he represents has made a mistake, something that hardly ever happens.

According to the group's records, he goes on, you were to have been born black—to another set of parents, far from where you were raised.

However, the rules being what they are, this error must be rectified, and as soon as possible. So at midnight tonight, you will become black. And this will mean not simply a darker skin but the bodily and facial features associated with African ancestry. However, inside

you will be the person you always were. Your knowledge and ideas will remain intact. But outwardly you will not be recognizable to anyone you now know.

Your visitor emphasizes that being born to the wrong parents was in no way your fault.

Consequently, his organization is prepared to offer you some reasonable recompense. Would you, he asks, care to name a sum of money you might consider appropriate? He adds that his group is by no means poor. It can be quite generous when the circumstances warrant, as they seem to in your case. He finishes by saying that the records show you are scheduled to

live another fifty years—as a black man or woman in America.

How much financial recompense would you request?

A professor who puts this parable to white college students finds that most feel $1 million per year—$50 million total—would be appropriate. This much would protect them from, and reimburse them for, the danger and discrimination they would face if they were perceived as black. In acknowledging that white skin is worth this much, the students also are admitting that treatment of the races has not been nearly equal.

SOURCE: Andrew Hacker, *Two Nations: Black and White, Separate, Hostile, Unequal* (New York: Scribner, 1992), 31–32.

Thus the business, professional, and political elites who form the membership perpetuate inequality in their circles and also send a message that discrimination is acceptable for others in society.

Discrimination in Employment

Although the Civil Rights Act of 1964 and affirmative action (discussed later in the chapter) have prompted more employers to hire and promote African Americans, discrimination remains.

Researchers sent out fictional résumés for fictional applicants in response to help-wanted ads in Boston and Chicago newspapers. They found that the fictional applicants with white-sounding names, such as Emily or Greg, received significantly more responses than the fictional applicants with black-sounding names, such as Lakisha or Jamal, even though all applicants had similar credentials.[101]

Other researchers used pairs of white and black high school graduates, matched according to their job histories and demeanors, to apply for low-skilled positions in Milwaukee. The white men admitted serving eighteen months in prison for possession of cocaine with intent to sell, while the black men had no criminal record. Nonetheless, the whites received slightly more callbacks than the blacks.[102]

Many blacks who are hired are passed over when they believe they should be promoted.[103] But discrimination at this point is more subtle and difficult to prove.

On the job, some face racial slurs in comments, notes, and graffiti. They endure an unfriendly or hostile environment.[104] Others experience negative stereotypes that question their competence and value. Upper-level executives realize that it is economically advantageous to have a diverse workforce, but some middle-level white managers and lower-level white workers interact poorly with the black employees.

Discrimination in Housing

The Civil Rights Act of 1968 prohibiting discrimination in housing has fostered some desegregation of housing, especially big apartment complexes, which are visible and therefore susceptible to pressure from civil rights groups and the government. And the act has resulted in large penalties on individuals found guilty of violations. Lawyers for fair-housing organizations say white jurors think discrimination has been eliminated—until they hear the testimony, which jars them into granting large awards.[105]

But the act is working at a snail's pace to change housing patterns. One reason is economic. Most blacks do not have enough money to buy homes in white neighborhoods. This problem is aggravated by local zoning laws designed to establish a certain type of community. Often these laws require large lots and large houses, which command high prices.

Another reason is continuing discrimination. Occasional violence and considerable social pressure discourage blacks who try to move into white neighborhoods. Actual discrimination by homeowners, real estate

© Mark Heckman

An artist in Grand Rapids, Michigan, erected this billboard to make white motorists think about how they would feel if discrimination were directed at them instead. By the next day, a racial slur had been scrawled on the billboard, and the mayor had received so many complaints that the artist had to remove the billboard.

agents, lenders, and insurers also stymies them. A study of twenty metropolitan areas, using white and minority testers responding to house and apartment ads, found that blacks who try to buy a house face discrimination 17 percent of the time, and those who try to rent an apartment do so 22 percent of the time. (These figures from 2002 are about 25 percent lower than the results from 1989, which was the last time the government had conducted this research.)[106] If callers sound black, landlords may claim that the apartment has already been rented. Most Americans can identify a telephone caller as black or white.[107]

Some real estate agents still practice steering. Many lenders apparently require extra proof that blacks will repay their home loans. The Federal Reserve Board examined over five million mortgage applications to over nine thousand financial institutions and found that applications from blacks were denied more than twice as often as those from whites with comparable incomes. As a result, applications from high-income blacks were rejected about as often as those from low-income whites.[108]

The Clinton administration proposed that the government phase out its public housing projects and give residents vouchers—government coupons—to use for any housing unit they locate on their own. The goal was to let them escape the dreary environment of the huge projects, but one consequence would be to desegregate more neighborhoods as the minorities in the projects fanned out throughout the city or possibly adjacent suburbs. Congressional Republicans blocked the proposal. Although they support the concept of vouchers—allowing individuals to choose a service rather

than having the government determine what particular service is best for them—to enable children to attend religious schools, many oppose the use of vouchers to enable minorities to move into white neighborhoods.[109]

For all these reasons, residential segregation remains pervasive in metropolitan areas. However, it is declining slowly. The 2000 census shows that people in the fast-growing suburban areas in the West and South are more likely to live in integrated neighborhoods than a decade earlier. At the same time, however, people in the stagnant "rust belt" cities in the East and Midwest are at least as likely to live in segregated neighborhoods as they were a decade earlier, partly because of continued white flight from the central cities.[110] Even middle-class blacks who escape the ghetto often end up in black neighborhoods in the suburbs of these cities.[111]

Segregation does not continue because blacks "want to live among their own kind," as some whites insist. Surveys show that only about 15 percent want to live in segregated neighborhoods, while 85 percent would prefer mixed neighborhoods. (Many say the optimal level would be about half blacks and half whites.) Blacks who say they want to live in majority-black or even half-black neighborhoods most often do so because they fear white hostility. Yet whites tend to move out, and new ones do not move in, when the concentration of blacks reaches 8 to 10 percent.[112] These very different views make integration an elusive goal, particularly because blacks make up 12 to 13 percent of the American population and a much larger percentage of some cities.

These patterns and attitudes are all the more troublesome because residential segregation, of course, leads to further school segregation.

Discrimination in Other Ways

African Americans face discrimination from police officers. The practice of **racial profiling,** which is based on the assumption that minorities, especially males, are more likely to commit crimes, especially ones involving drugs, targets minorities for stops and searches. So even without any evidence, officers stop minority drivers and search them and their vehicles.[113] Racial profiling is sometimes directed toward pedestrians and passengers in airports as well. Although police departments deny following this practice, statistics show clear evidence that disproportionate numbers of minorities are stopped and searched. Interstate 95 from Florida to New York is notorious. On I-95 through Maryland, whereas 18 percent of speeders were black, 29 percent of those stopped and 71 percent of those searched were black. On the New Jersey Turnpike, 15 percent of speeders were black, but 35 percent of the drivers pulled over were black.[114] The practice of racial profiling contributes to the tensions between minorities and police.

Now African Americans speak of the moving violation "DWB"—*driving while black.* A Chicago journalist who was stopped at least every other time he traveled through the Midwest learned not to rent flashy Mustangs or wear his beret. Others avoid tinted windshields or expensive sunglasses—any flamboyance—to avoid the cops.[115] Representative J. C. Watts (R-Okla.) was pulled over by police six times in one day in his home state.[116]

Profiling might be justified if this tactic led to the apprehension of dangerous criminals, but apparently it does not. Although minorities, especially young men, evidently do commit a larger percentage of certain crimes,[117] the profiling does not lead the police to many criminals. When police stop motorists, they find no greater evidence of crimes by minorities than by whites.[118] Some states and many counties and cities have taken steps to reduce profiling, such as recording data on every stop to see whether the police, or individual officers, are prone to profile. Yet the cops on the beat, who feel that profiling is useful, are reluctant to change their habits. (See the box "Profiling of Arabs?")

Other discrimination from police officers is less common but more serious. Sometimes officers arrest black citizens without legal cause, and occasionally they use excessive force against them. Numerous examples attest to improper beatings.[119] Sometimes officers lie while testifying against black suspects in court. As a result, even prominent African Americans say their "worst fear is to have to go before the criminal justice system."[120] It is little wonder, then, that black jurors hearing the O. J. Simpson trial and black citizens following it put less faith in the police testimony than white observers did.

Cautious parents feel obligated to teach their children how to avoid sending the wrong signals to police. Some parents urge their children not to wear street fashions and not to use cell phones, which from a distance might be mistaken as weapons. Some schools offer survival workshops for police encounters. Minority officers instruct the students what to do when they get stopped: Don't reach for an ID unless the officer asks for one; don't mumble or talk loudly; don't antagonize by asking for a badge number or threatening to file a complaint.[121]

Most blacks, even those in the upper and middle classes and those in professional occupations, face insults because of their race. Black women tell of being mistaken for hotel chambermaids. One family therapist, invited to speak at a conference, was stopped in the hallway by a white attendee who asked where the restrooms were. When the therapist appeared taken aback, the attendee said she thought the woman worked at the hotel. Although the therapist was wearing her official name tag and presenter's ribbon, the attendee did not look past her black face.[122] Black women also tell of waiting for friends in hotel lobbies and being mistaken for prostitutes by white men and police officers. A distinguished black political scientist tells of people who assume he is a butler in his own home. Black doctors tell of dressing up when they go shopping to avoid being regarded as shoplifters. But even dressing up is no guarantee. A black lawyer, a senior partner in a large law firm, arrived at work early one morning, before the doors were unlocked. As he reached for his key, a young white lawyer, a junior associate in the firm, arrived at the same time, blocked his entrance, and asked, repeatedly and demandingly, "May I help you?" The white associate had taken the black partner for an intruder.[123] Although in these encounters the insults were unintentional, the stings hurt just the same.

The accumulation of these incidents—poor service, fearful movements, disrespectful comments—which more than eight in ten blacks say they occasionally experience, has created a "black middle-class rage" among many.[124]

Overall, discrimination against African Americans continues. Whites speak of "past discrimination"—sometimes referring to slavery, sometimes to official segregation—but this phrase is misleading. Of course, there is a lot less discrimination now due to the civil rights movement, Supreme Court decisions, and congressional acts. However, there is nothing "past" about much "past discrimination."[125] The effects linger, and the discrimination itself persists.

Even when blacks point out the discrimination, some whites insist that little discrimination is left. These whites apparently assume that they know more than blacks do about what it is like to be black. Indeed, the

PROFILING OF ARABS?

Before September 11, 2001, a consensus was emerging that racial profiling by law enforcement was inappropriate. Eighty percent of the public opposed it, a bill was moving through Congress to forbid it, and the Justice Department was preparing to sue local police departments that continued to use it. After September 11, however, the public's opinion changed, and these government efforts against racial profiling were shelved. Because the attackers were all young men from Arab countries that harbor terrorist groups, the public and government officials began to ask whether profiling directed at possible terrorists might be appropriate after all.

The government has established various programs to ferret out hidden terrorists or sleeper cells.[1] These programs have focused on young men from the Middle East.

Immediately after the attacks, the government rounded up approximately twelve hundred immigrants, most from Arab or Muslim countries. They were put in solitary confinement in undisclosed locations and were detained for an indefinite time with limited access to their lawyers.

The men had been singled out because of anonymous tips or miscella-

neous information discovered by officials. One man had a book that had an ad for another book that had a photo of Osama bin Laden. Another man had materials for a correspondence course on becoming a private investigator. An Egyptian antiques dealer had made airplane reservations at the same place and about the same time as one of the hijackers. A Pakistani gas station attendant had renewed his driver's license at the same place and about the same time as another of the hijackers. The government, reeling from the attacks, cast its net widely.

Then the Justice Department sought to interview eight thousand men between the ages of eighteen and thirty-three who entered the country since 2000 from Middle Eastern countries with links to terrorist groups. FBI agents or local law enforcement officers asked them not only about their travel history but also about their religious beliefs, political views, and even their future marriage plans. Also, the Justice Department instructed the interviewers to ask the "catch-all question"—whether the individual is aware of any criminal activity, whether related to terrorism or not. Lying to a federal officer can result in deportation of a person on a visa, so an incorrect answer could have serious

consequences for an individual who was aware of, say, underage drinking or any other minor offense.

When the Justice Department asked local police departments to help conduct the interviews, some departments refused. They said the policy resembled racial profiling, which they were trying to avoid. They also worried that the interviews would jeopardize their relations with the Arabs in their community and thus hinder their efforts to gain the cooperation they might need for future investigations.

Pursuant to the USA PATRIOT Act (explained in Chapter 14), the government has also created a foreign-student database, which gathers information about foreign students from Arab or Muslim countries, and established an alien registration and interrogation program, which requires aliens from Arab or Muslim countries to report annually for fingerprinting, photographing, and questioning.

Along with these programs comes informal scrutiny and questioning as well. Federal officials have made unannounced visits to Arab or Muslim students, asking their educational plans, political views, and so on. An FBI agent told an economics professor at the University of Massachusetts that he

---

perceptual gap between blacks and whites about the existence of discrimination is one of the real barriers to making progress on the issue of race. Whites who believe nothing is wrong do not favor actions to fix what they see as a nonexistent problem.

As African Americans have become frustrated with the slow pace of progress, some have been attracted to the black separatist movement. These blacks, seeing themselves as realistic, consider integration a naive ideal from the 1950s and 1960s—an impossibility even in the future. They want to direct their energy toward building up the black community.[126] (Supreme Court Justice Clarence Thomas seems to hold this view.) But

most blacks, remaining hopeful, consider separatism premature and risky; they fear it will play into the hands of the most prejudiced whites trying to perpetuate discrimination.

Improving Conditions for African Americans?

Despite continuing discrimination, African Americans have taken great strides toward achieving equal rights. These strides have led to much better living conditions for them and to a healthier racial climate in society.

had a tip that the professor held anti-American views and he wanted the professor to explain. The professor, who is a U.S. citizen, explained that he was indeed loyal; he came to the United States from Iraq after his brother-in-law was executed by Saddam Hussein's regime. But the professor was shaken. Referring to the agent's suspicion and questions, he said, "I came to America to get away from that kind of thing."[2]

Finally, federal officials keep tabs on an unknown number of Arab men, monitoring their movements, telephone calls, e-mail messages, Internet use, and credit card charges around the clock. Local officials train a wary eye on local Arabs and on local mosques.

People assume that profiling is common at airports. However, Secretary of Transportation Norman Mineta, who as a Japanese American boy was interned during World War II, has resisted attempts to employ race-based profiling. The Federal Aviation Administration (FAA) uses an automated system for deciding which passengers to screen and which checked bags to screen because most airports cannot screen all luggage. The criteria are confidential, but they include the passenger's origin and destination and the passenger's method of buying the ticket. For example, buying a one-way ticket raises a red flag. The FAA insists that speaking Arabic, being Muslim, or wearing a veil or a beard are not factors.

Despite the government's concern about race-based profiling, some airplane passengers have complained about Arab-looking men in line or on board, and some pilots have refused to fly unless these men were ejected.

The profiling disturbs some people. One law professor said it shows that "we have decided to trade off the liberty of immigrants—particularly Arabs and Muslims—for the purported security of the majority."[3] Another observer asked, "How would you feel about the IRS auditing Italian Americans' taxes in order to deter Mafia activity?"[4]

Others believe that profiling is legitimate because of the severity of the threat. Still others justify it because the attacks did come only from young male Arabs, although they overlook the earlier Oklahoma City bombing done by a native-born American. And there is no certainty that future attacks will be carried out by Arabs. News reports, which may or may not be reliable, indicate that al-Qaeda is looking for non-Arabs who could elude detection more easily.

The alternative, at least for airports and other transportation hubs, may be to employ far more sophisticated screening systems than we use now. In fact, such systems are in development. Using a computer network to link multiple databases, they will be able to scan every passenger's travel history, living arrangements, and other personal information gleaned from driver's licenses, credit cards, magazine subscriptions, and who knows what else.[5] Such systems will be so sophisticated that they can look at many factors without considering race or ethnicity. Will they be better for this reason? Or will they be worse because they will pose a threat to the privacy of everyone? That may be the trade-off.

1. For a good analysis of this issue and its relationship to racial profiling of African Americans, see Tanya E. Coke, "Racial Profiling Post-9/11: Old Story, New Debate," in *Lost Liberties,* ed. Cynthia Brown (New York: New Press, 2003), 91–111.
2. Anthony Lewis, "First They Came for the Muslims . . . ," *American Prospect,* Spring 2003, A13.
3. David Cole, quoted in Clarence Page, "Look Who's Profiling Now," *Lincoln Journal-Star,* October 6, 2001.
4. Ibid.
5. Robert O'Harrow Jr., "Will Passenger Profiling Fly?" *Washington Post National Weekly Edition,* February 11, 2002, 29; Jeffery Rosen, "Silicon Valley's Spy Game," *New York Times Magazine,* April 14, 2002, 46.

Since the 1960s, blacks' lives have improved in most ways that can be measured.[127] Blacks have a longer life expectancy and a lower poverty rate than before. They have completed more years of education, with larger numbers attending college and graduate school. They have attained higher occupational levels—for example, tripling their proportion of the country's professionals[128]—and income levels. Many more have reached the middle class. Well over half of blacks are considered middle-class.[129] A third have moved to the suburbs,[130] and nearly half own their own homes.[131]

During the same years that blacks' lives have improved, whites' racial attitudes have also improved. Although answers to pollsters' questions cannot be accepted as perfect reflections of people's views, especially on emotional matters such as racial attitudes, the answers can be considered general indicators of these views. Polls encompassing a wide variety of racial questions show that whites' views have changed significantly (even assuming that some whites gave more socially acceptable answers than they really felt).[132]

Whites and blacks both report more social contact with members of the other race since the 1960s (see Table 2), and both report more approval of interracial dating and marriage (see Table 3). The acceptance of interracial dating and marriage is especially significant because these practices were the ultimate taboos in segregated society. Interracial couples represented the clearest breach and their potential offspring the greatest threat to continued segregation.

TABLE 2   Social Contact between Blacks and Whites since the 1960s

The percentages of respondents who say that members of the other race do the following:

	Blacks	Whites
Live in their neighborhood		
1964	66	20
1976	70	38
1994	83	61
Are friends of theirs		
1964	62	18
1976	87	50
1989	82	66
Are "good friends" of theirs		
1975	21	9
1994	78	73
Have been dinner guests in their home		
1973	39	20
1994	53	34
Attend their church		
1978	37	34
1994	61	44

SOURCE: Stephan Thernstrom and Abigail Thernstrom, *America in Black and White* (New York: Simon & Schuster, 1997), 521.

TABLE 3   Approval of Interracial Dating and Marriage since the 1960s

The following percentages of respondents say it is all right for blacks and whites to do the following:

Date	Blacks	Whites
1963	N.A.	10
1987	72	43
1994	88	65*
Marry		
1958	N.A.	4
1968	48	17
1978	66	32
1983	76	38
1994	68	45

*65 percent is the overall total; 85 percent of individuals aged eighteen to twenty-four responded in the affirmative to this question, but only 36 percent of those sixty-five and older.
N.A. = not available.
SOURCE: Stephan Thernstrom and Abigail Thernstrom, *America in Black and White* (New York: Simon & Schuster, 1997), 524–525.

Some whites, of course, remain blatant racists (perhaps from 2 to 24 percent, according to various estimates by social scientists).[133] But blatant racist behavior occurs less frequently and is condemned more quickly than before.

Even so, blacks have pessimistic views of whites' attitudes. In 1989, one-fourth of blacks believed that at least a quarter of whites were in the Ku Klux Klan; one-fourth of blacks also believed that most whites shared the views of the KKK. In 1992, two-thirds of blacks believed that about half of whites were "basically prejudiced." (Whites also believed this about whites.)[134] One sociologist estimates that despite the improvement in whites' attitudes, there are still two white racists for every African American. For socioeconomic reasons, blacks are more likely to come into contact with prejudiced whites, who live and work in closer proximity to blacks, than they are to come into contact with tolerant whites, who are more educated and more prosperous.[135] Furthermore, some blacks have not experienced the overall improvements. It would be more surprising if they were not pessimistic.

When the push for civil rights opened doors, some blacks were not in a position to pass through. About a quarter of the black population lives in poverty—two and one-half times the rate among the white population—and about a tenth, the poorest of the poor, exists in a state of economic and social "disintegration."[136] This "underclass" is trapped in a cycle of self-perpetuating problems from which it is extremely difficult to escape. These people are isolated from the rest of society and demoralized about their prospects for improvement.

The problems of the lower class and the underclass were exacerbated by economic changes that began in the 1970s and hit the poor the hardest. Good-paying manufacturing jobs in the cities—the traditional path out of poverty for immigrant groups—disappeared. Chicago lost over three hundred thousand jobs, New York over five hundred thousand.[137] Many jobs were eliminated by automation, while many others were moved to foreign countries or to the suburbs. Although service jobs increased, most were outside the cities, required more education, or paid lower wages than the manufacturing jobs had.

As a result, many black men, especially, lost their jobs and lost their ability to support a family. This led not only to pressure on intact families but also to a decrease in the number of "marriageable" black men and an increase in the number of households headed by black women.[138] The percentage of such households rose from about 20 percent of all black families in 1960 to 45 percent in 2000.[139] And 60 percent of black children live in such households. These families are among the poorest in the country (see Chapter 17).

Meanwhile, much of the black middle class fled the inner cities to the suburbs. Their migration left the ghettos with fewer healthy businesses, strong schools, or other institutions to provide stability and fewer role models to portray mainstream behavior.[140] By 1996, one Chicago ghetto with sixty-six thousand people had just one supermarket and one bank but forty-eight state-licensed lottery agents and ninety-nine state-licensed liquor stores and bars.[141] The combination of chronic unemployment in the inner cities and middle-class migration from the inner cities created an environment that offers ample opportunity and some incentive to use drugs, commit crimes, and engage in other types of antisocial behavior.

The development of crack, a cheap form of cocaine, in the mid-1980s aggravated these conditions. It led to more drug use and drug trafficking that overwhelmed whole neighborhoods. Crack ravaged the lives of users in ways that other drugs did not, and by producing steady demand by users and huge profits for dealers, it stimulated more violence.[142] The spread of AIDS, rampant among intravenous drug users, further aggravated these conditions.

Half of the victims of murder and more than half of those charged with murder are black, although the U.S. population is only 12 to 13 percent black.[143] Two-thirds of the defendants sent to state prisons for drug offenses are black. According to one study in Washington, D.C., one-fourth of black males born in the 1960s were charged with drug dealing between the ages of eighteen and twenty-four.[144] (Of course, part of this is due to harsher treatment of black drug offenders than of white ones.)

The plight of young black men is worse than that of any other group in society. A black man in Harlem had less chance of living past forty than a man in Bangladesh.[145] Moreover, by 1995, almost one of every three black men between the ages of twenty and twenty-nine was serving a criminal sentence in prison or was on probation or parole.[146] This situation, too, exacerbated the problem of marriageable men and female-headed black households.

After the riots in the 1960s, the Kerner Commission, appointed by President Johnson to examine the cause of the riots, concluded, "What white Americans have never fully understood—but what the Negro can never forget—is that white society is deeply implicated in the ghetto. White institutions created it, white institutions maintain it, and white society condones it." After the riots, however, governments did little to improve the conditions that precipitated the riots. Now the conditions in the ghettos are worse.

After the 1992 riots in Los Angeles that followed the trial of the police officers who beat Rodney King, there was more talk about improving conditions in the ghetto. But a columnist who had heard such talk before commented, "My guess is that when all is said and done, a great deal more will be said than done. The truth is we don't know any quick fixes for our urban ills and we lack the patience and resources for slow fixes."[147]

These problems are all the more difficult to resolve because the cities have lost political power as they have lost population due to white flight and black migration. In 1992, for the first time, more voters (including many blacks) lived in the suburbs than in the cities. Suburban voters do not urge action on urban problems. Sometimes, in fact, they resist action if it means an increase in their taxes or a decrease in their services.

For the black lower class, and especially for the black underclass, it is apparent that civil rights are not enough. As one black leader said, "What good is a seat in the front of the bus if you don't have the money for the fare?"[148]

But most blacks do not fall in the lower class or underclass, and most do not dwell in the inner cities. It would be a serious mistake to hold the stereotypical view that the majority reside in the inner cities and that a majority of them live in dysfunctional families filled with crackheads and prone to violence. Although black men lag behind, black women especially have vastly improved lives—academically, professionally, and financially—over the span of one generation.[149]

Discrimination against Hispanics

Hispanics, also called Latinos, are people in the United States who come from a Spanish-speaking background. Although they are frequently spoken of as a separate race, they can be of any race. Some are brown skinned, others black skinned, and still others white skinned. Many Hispanics come from an amalgam of European, African, and American Indian ancestry that makes it impossible to label them by race. Thus Hispanics should be regarded as an ethnic group and a statistical category rather than a distinct "race."

The first Hispanics came to America from Spain in the 1500s. They settled in the Southwest, and when the United States took this land from Mexico in 1848, they became U.S. citizens. Other Latinos came to America more recently (see Figure 3).

About 61 percent of Hispanics trace their ancestry to Mexico and live mainly in the Southwest, though some live in large cities in the Midwest. About 15 percent are from Puerto Rico, which is a commonwealth—a self-governing territory—of the United States. As members of the commonwealth, they are U.S. citizens. Most live in New York, Boston, Chicago, and other cities in the North. Another 6 percent are from Cuba. Following the establishment of a Communist government in Cuba in 1959, many fled to the United States and settled in South

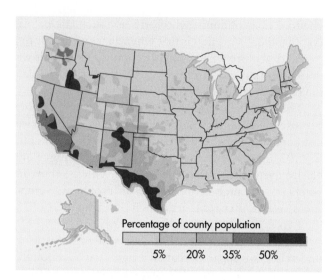

FIGURE 3 ■ **Hispanics in the United States** *Hispanics are concentrated in the Southwest and the West.*
SOURCE: Eric Schmitt, "U.S. Now More Diverse, Ethnically and Racially," *New York Times,* April 1, 2001, sec. 1, 20.

Florida. In recent years, Latinos from other Caribbean or Central American countries have immigrated to the United States to escape turmoil and oppression.

Despite the diversity of their origins, Latinos are heavily concentrated in six states. More than half live in California and Texas, where they make up one-third of the population. Already they outnumber Anglos in Los Angeles (47 percent to 29 percent) and Houston (37 percent to 31 percent).[150] Many of the rest live in Florida, New Jersey, New York, and Illinois. But there are growing pockets elsewhere.

Latinos represent over 12 percent of the U.S. population. According to the 2000 census, they have overtaken blacks as the largest minority. Already the United States has the seventh-largest Latino population in the world, and within the United States, this group, fueled by high immigration rates and birthrates, is the fastest-growing minority (growing slightly faster than Asians).

Latinos never endured slavery, but they have faced discrimination. Although numerous Latinos are Caucasian, many Puerto Ricans and Cubans have African ancestry, and many Mexicans have some Indian ancestry, so they have darker skin than non–Hispanic whites. Like blacks, Hispanics have faced discrimination in education, employment, housing, and voting.[151]

Latinos also encounter discrimination due to continuing immigration. The illegal immigrants pouring in from Mexico exacerbate hostility and discrimination against Latinos, especially in the Southwest. U.S. Border Patrol and local law enforcement officials, who cannot tell the difference between Latinos who are citizens or legal residents and those who are not, often stop them for questioning not only at the border but inland as well.

(Agents stopped the mayor of Pomona, California, more than one hundred miles from the border and ordered him to produce papers to prove that he is a legal resident.) Even if officials are well intentioned, their conduct is considered harassment by law-abiding legal residents.

Latinos also encounter discrimination from police, as African Americans do. Police use racial profiling, suspecting them of crimes involving drugs as well as illegal immigration. In Illinois, Latinos constitute 8 percent of the population but 30 percent of individuals stopped by police.[152]

Latino immigrants who are farmworkers face additional problems. Agriculture has long avoided regulations imposed on other businesses. For decades, the minimum wage law did not apply to farmworkers. Still today, they are denied the opportunity for overtime pay and the right to organize. In many states, they are excluded from workers' compensation and unemployment benefits programs. Their lack of governmental protection, coupled with their economic desperation, makes them vulnerable to unscrupulous employers. The Department of Justice is investigating over one hundred cases of involuntary servitude—slavery—and has prosecuted a half dozen from South Florida in recent years.[153]

Discrimination in Education

For years, Latino children in some areas were not allowed to attend schools at all. In other areas, they were segregated into "Mexican" schools whose quality was not comparable with that of Anglo schools.[154]

In the 1940s, Mexican American organizations asked the courts to find that Mexican Americans were "white" so that they could not be segregated. The federal courts agreed. This strategy backfired, however, after the Supreme Court declared segregation by race illegal. Many school districts achieved "integration" by combining blacks with Latinos, leaving non-Hispanic whites in separate schools.[155]

Even when admitted to schools, Latinos faced discrimination due to their language. Traditionally, teachers and administrators forbade students to speak their native Spanish to each other in school. They reprimanded, spanked, or expelled those who did. Some even anglicized students' names in class and in school records so that Jesus became Jesse and Miguel became Michael.[156]

Although *de jure* segregation has been struck down,[157] *de facto* segregation exists in cities where Latinos are concentrated due to residential segregation and white flight to the suburbs. Many Latinos attend schools with more than 90 percent minorities, and most attend schools in which more than half the students are minorities.[158]

Even where Latinos go to desegregated schools, they are often segregated within the schools. They face second-generation discrimination, though not as much as blacks.[159]

Predominantly Latino schools, like predominantly black schools, are not as well funded as other schools because they are located in poor communities that do not get as much revenue from property taxes. In San Antonio, Mexican American families were concentrated in the poorest districts, while wealthy families were concentrated in a section that was incorporated as a separate district, though it was surrounded on four sides by the rest of the city. Its property taxes financed its schools only. When Mexican American parents sued, the Burger Court ruled that the Fourteenth Amendment's equal protection clause does not require states to equalize funding between school districts.[160] The case highlighted this problem, prompting some states to equalize funding but allowing other states to maintain the status quo.

Latinos' primary problem in education, however, is the language barrier. Many are unable to speak English, causing them to fail in school and drop out of school at higher rates than other students, even African Americans. One-third of Latinos leave school at some point; one-fourth drop out in high school.[161]

Bilingual education was established to help such students. These classes use the students' native language to teach them English and also substantive subjects such as math. The goal is to transition from their native language to English. In 1968, Congress encouraged bilingual education by providing funding, and in 1974, the Supreme Court, in a case brought by Chinese parents, held that schools must teach students in a language they can understand.[162] This can be their native language, or it can be English if they have been taught English. These federal actions prompted many states to establish bilingual education programs. More than 150 languages, from Chinese to Yapese, have been offered. Because almost three-fourths of the students who do not speak English are Hispanic, Spanish is the most common.[163]

Bilingual education programs have been controversial. Latino parents want their children to learn English and to learn it well. A survey of Latinos in forty cities found that more than 90 percent thought U.S. citizens and residents should learn English.[164] A survey of Cuban Americans in south Florida found that 98 percent thought it was important for their children to read and write "perfect English."[165] And their children apparently agree. More than four-fifths of immigrant children in South Florida and more than two-thirds of those in San Diego prefer English to their familial language.[166] Latino parents and children worry that bilingual programs will delay the mastery of English. Seventy-five percent of recent immigrants, including 56 percent of Mexican immigrants, oppose these programs.[167]

In fact, bilingual programs have not worked as well in practice as they have promised in theory. Although their results are difficult to measure because the programs vary, being staffed at different levels and for different lengths of time, they have been disappointing. Perhaps these results should not be surprising, given that the programs grew partly out of political as well as pedagogical needs. Latino groups in the Southwest saw them as a way to tap into federal antipoverty funds.[168]

Indeed, the debate revolves around politics as much as education. Some Latino groups see bilingual education as a way to preserve their native language and culture. They consider it to be a component of multiculturalism. So they want it not as a temporary bridge until students learn English but as a permanent fixture through high school. Many Anglo citizens, especially those who fear the influx of immigrants, also see bilingual education as a way to preserve Latinos' native language and culture. But these Anglos discount the need for multiculturalism. Instead, they want the students to be exposed only to English so that they will be more likely to assimilate into society. Some Latino leaders accuse these Anglo citizens of "cultural genocide."[169]

For both sides, then, bilingual education is a symbolic issue. It prompts concerns, even fears, about the relative dominance of Anglo culture and Hispanic culture and about the extent to which Anglo Americans will make room for Hispanic Americans in society.

The debate is complicated by economic and bureaucratic problems in bilingual programs. Because they require more teachers and smaller classes, the programs are expensive and therefore impractical. Many schools cannot find enough teachers in the necessary languages.

Cuban Americans are more likely than other Latinos to be middle class.

Latinos Choose Anglo Names

Despite Anglos' concern that Latinos are not assimilating, Latinos are favoring Anglo names for their children. For Hispanic children born in Texas in 2002, the most popular names for boys were:

Jose

Daniel

Jonathan

David

Christopher

The most popular names for Hispanic girls born in Texas in 2002 were:

Ashley

Jennifer

Emily

Samantha

Maria

In New York City, the most popular names for Hispanic boys were:

Justin

Christopher

Kevin

Anthony

Brandon

And the most popular names in New York City for Hispanic girls were:

Ashley

Jennifer

Emily

Brianna

Samantha

SOURCE: Sam Roberts, "In a Changing Nation, Smith Is Still King," *New York Times,* July 11, 2004.

California, where half of all students in bilingual programs lived, fell twenty-one thousand teachers short in 1998.[170] Schools were unable to offer bilingual education to two-thirds of the students who were eligible.[171]

For all these reasons, California citizens voted to abolish bilingual programs in 1998. Now non-English-speaking students receive intensive immersion in English for one year and then move into regular classes. Initial research indicates that Spanish-speaking students are improving rapidly in their ability to read English and to understand other subjects taught in English.[172]

Despite the disappointing results of bilingual programs and the widespread perceptions of many Americans, current immigrants are learning English as previous waves of European immigrants learned it. Among Spanish speakers in the United States, 90 percent speak English (though 18 percent say that they do not speak it well).[173] Although about half of those who arrived as teenagers or adults do not speak English proficiently, almost all of those who arrived as young children or who are in the second generation do speak English proficiently.[174] Cuban Americans are learning it as fast or faster than any group in history.[175] Mexican Americans are learning it as they live longer in the United States. Although many of those who come for work and plan to return to Mexico do not speak English, most of those who plan to remain in the United States learn to speak more English, and almost all of their children learn to speak fluent English.[176]

The drive to learn English is so strong that only a third of Latinos born in the United States are bilingual. Most cannot speak Spanish.[177]

It is true that some immigrant communities, especially Cubans in South Florida and Mexicans in parts of the Southwest, are so large that people can survive without learning English. But most feel pressure to learn English to function in the broader society and for their children to succeed in school. Indeed, 89 percent believe that those who immigrate must learn English to succeed in the United States.[178] And most Hispanic immigrants give their children Anglo names (see the box "Latinos Choose Anglo Names").

Combating Discrimination against Hispanics

In the 1960s, Latino advocacy groups tried to imitate African American groups by using protests and other forms of direct action. The Chicano movement attempted to forge a powerful bloc from the diverse population of the Hispanic people. César Chávez successfully led a coalition of labor, civil rights, and religious groups to obtain better working conditions for migrant farmworkers in California. But few other visible national leaders or organizations emerged.

Although their birthrates and immigration rates have expanded their numbers, Latinos remain more diverse and less cohesive than blacks. Most do not even consider themselves part of a Hispanic group.[179] They identify strongly with their national origin and have little contact with Hispanics of differing ancestry. Therefore, most do not call themselves "Hispanics" or "Latinos" but rather "Mexican Americans," "Puerto Ricans," or "Cuban Americans."[180] Also, they have different legal statuses. Puerto Ricans are American citizens by birth, but many other Latinos are not citizens. And they lack a common defining experience in their background, such as slavery for blacks, to unite them.

In fact, they do not agree on a label for themselves.

Latinos are gradually improving their status. This woman toils as a migrant farmworker, but her son graduated from college and runs personnel management programs for farmers.

The traditionalists often use *Hispanic,* while the activists usually say *Latino.* Those who derive from the Iberian peninsula, which includes Spain and Portugal, tend to favor *Hispanic.* They believe that *Latino* excludes those who are not from Latin America. Those who derive from south of the border increasingly favor *Latino,* as many in California used to prefer *Chicano.*[181] (Because of this lack of agreement, our text uses the terms *Latino* and *Hispanic* interchangeably.)

But where Hispanics are highly concentrated, they are increasingly powerful at the local and state levels of government. Rather than portraying themselves as a victimized group, they are moving into the mainstream. Rather than focusing primarily on immigration issues, bilingual education, and affirmative action, they are addressing broader concerns, such as improving health care and reducing school class size. Yet Latino politicians have not shaped a common agenda, perhaps because Latino people, of diverse origins, do not share a common agenda.[182]

They are potentially powerful at the national level as well. With their huge numbers, Latinos are a coveted bloc of voters. Yet many are not citizens, and many of those who are citizens do not register and vote. Although the Latino and African American populations are nearly the same size, six million more blacks than Hispanics are registered to vote.[183] Nevertheless, the Latino voters are numerous enough to be courted. Although most, except Cuban Americans, are Democrats, the Republicans believe they need to attract more if their party hopes to win national elections in the future. The Bush administration has adopted a strategy to en-

tice them. President Bush appointed a Cuban American as secretary of the Department of Housing and Urban Development and a Mexican American as counsel to the White House. He proposed granting legal status to the Mexican immigrants illegally living in the United States now, though this proposal died a quiet death when 9/11 turned the focus to problems with illegal immigrants. And he sprinkles Spanish into his speeches before Hispanic or mixed audiences.

At the same time, Latino individuals are moving up society's ladder. More attend college and become managers and professionals. At least those who speak educated English appear to be following the pattern of earlier generations of immigrants from Southern and Eastern Europe—arriving poor, facing discrimination, but eventually working their way up. At the same time, they are also assimilating through high rates of marriage to non-Latinos.

Discrimination against Native Americans

More than two million Native Americans live in the United States. Although some are Eskimos and Aleuts from Alaska, most are Indians, representing more than 550 tribes with different histories, customs, and languages. Most are proud of their tribal heritage and prefer to be known by their tribal name, such as Cheyenne or Sioux, than by the collective terms Native Americans or Indians. About half live on reservations (see Figure 4).

Although Native Americans have faced some discrimination similar to that against blacks and Hispanics, they have endured much discrimination of a different nature.

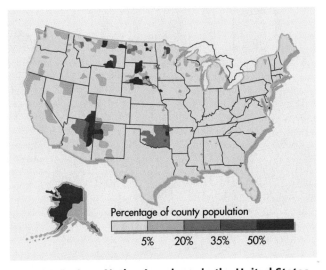

FIGURE 4 ■ Native Americans in the United States
SOURCE: Eric Schmitt, "U.S. Now More Diverse, Ethnically and Racially," *New York Times,* April 1, 2001, sec. 1, 20.

Government Policy toward Native Americans

The government's policy toward Native Americans has varied over the years, ranging from forced separation at one extreme to forced assimilation at the other.

Separation Initially, the policy was separation. For many years, people believed that the North American continent was so vast that most of its interior would remain wilderness, populated by Indians who would have ample room to live and hunt. The Constitution reflects this belief. It grants Congress authority to "regulate commerce with foreign nations, and among the several states, and with the Indian tribes." In early cases, Chief Justice John Marshall described the tribes as "dependent domestic nations."[184] They were within U.S. borders but outside its political process.

Early treaties reinforced separation by establishing boundaries between Indians and non-Indians. The government thought these boundaries were necessary for its growth, the Indians for their survival. The boundaries were intended to minimize conflict. White hunters or settlers who ventured across the boundaries could be punished as the Indians saw fit.

But as the country grew, it became increasingly difficult to contain settlers within the boundaries. Mounting pressure to push Native Americans farther west led to the Indian Removal Act of 1830, which authorized removal of tribes east of the Mississippi River and relocation on reservations west of the river. At the time, people considered the Great Plains to be the great American desert, unfit for habitation by whites but suitable for Indians. At first, removal was voluntary, but eventually it became mandatory for most and was supervised by the U.S. cavalry.

Assimilation and Citizenship As more settlers moved west, the vision of a separate Indian country far enough beyond white civilization to prevent conflict faded. In the 1880s, the government switched its policy to assimilation. Prompted by Christian churches, officials sought to "civilize" the Indians—that is, to incorporate them into the larger society, whether they wanted to be incorporated or not. In place of their traditional means of subsistence, rendered useless once the tribes were removed from their homelands, the government subdivided reservation land into small tracts and allotted these tracts to tribe members in the hope that they would turn to farming as white and black settlers had. (In the process, the government reclaimed "surplus" land and sold it to white settlers. Ultimately, the Indians lost about two-thirds of their reservation land.)[185] Bureau of Indian Affairs (BIA) agents, who supervised the reservations, tried to root out Native American ways and replace them with white dress and hairstyles, the English language, and the Christian religion. Government boarding schools separated Native American children from their families to instill these new practices.

Early in the history of the United States, Native Americans were not considered citizens but members of separate nations. Treaties made exceptions for those who married whites and for those who left their tribes and abandoned their tribal customs. But in 1890, after government policy switched to assimilation, Congress permitted some who remained with their tribes on reservations to become citizens by applying to the U.S. government. Citizenship was sometimes marked by a formal ceremony. In one, the Indian shot his last arrow and then took hold of the handles of a plow to demonstrate his assimilation.[186] After World War I, Congress granted citizenship to those who served in the military during the war, and finally, in 1924, Congress extended it to all those born in the United States.

Citizenship enabled Indians to vote and hold office, though some states effectively barred them from the polls for decades. Arizona denied them the right to vote until 1948, Utah until 1956.[187]

Tribal Restoration By the 1930s, the government recognized the negative consequences of coerced assimilation. Most Indians could speak English, but they were poorly educated in other respects. And with their traditional means of earning a living gone, most were poverty-stricken. The policy led to destruction of Native American ways without much assimilation into white society. Consequently, in 1934, Congress implemented a new policy of tribal restoration that recognized Indi-

"I love the way you make those yams. You'll have to give me the recipe before your culture is obliterated from the face of the earth."

Tom Torlino, before and after his transformation at a boarding school in Carlisle, Pennsylvania. Native Americans were shorn of their hair and clothes and trained to adopt white ways.

ans as distinct persons and tribes as autonomous entities that were encouraged to govern themselves once again. Traditional cultural and religious practices were accepted, and children, no longer forced to attend boarding schools, were taught some Indian languages.

The government even made an effort to settle claims for the wrongful taking of tribal land. For several decades, the Indian Claims Commission authorized the payment of money—not the return of property—to tribes whose land was illegally taken by the government after 1776. But the commission faced an impossible task. Most tribes had a hazy conception of land ownership and did not keep written records. How would disputed land be valued—according to the earlier subsistence living of the Indians or the later market value to farmers, ranchers, and miners? And how would religious land be valued? (Native religions focus on particular parcels of land or prominent features of the landscape, rather than on buildings such as churches or figures such as Jesus.) Ultimately, the commission authorized as much money as it thought was politically feasible, but this amounted to less than $1,000 for every Native American.[188]

Reflecting the policy of tribal restoration and the efforts of other minorities in the 1960s and 1970s, Indian interest groups became active. Indian law firms pursued cases in court, seeking to protect not only tribal independence and traditional ways but also land, mineral, and water resources. The diversity and the dispersion of the tribes—they are divided by culture and by geography, often located in the remotest and poorest parts of the country—make it difficult for them to present a united front. Nevertheless, they have been able to wrest some autonomy from the government. In particular, they have gotten more authority over the educational and social programs administered by the BIA for the tribes.[189]

In recent years, Indians have fought for the return of some tribal land and for an accounting of the money owed them for the use of their individual land held in trust by the government. In the early nineteenth century, the government took tribal land and put it in trust for the Indians. But then the government divided the land, paying individual Indians a pittance and offering the parcels to white settlers. In this way, the Indians lost most of their territory. The government held the remaining land in trust for the Indians, leasing it to ranchers, loggers, and miners who contracted with the government to use it. The government collected the rents and royalties for the Indians. But the BIA did not bother to keep accurate records or even to preserve its records. Now a class-action lawsuit, dubbed "the Indian Enron case," seeks a reckoning of the accounts and a payment to the Indians who are owed money.[190]

Some tribes are enjoying renewed vitality with the income they receive from mineral rights or gambling casinos. After a Supreme Court ruling and a congressional law in the 1980s underscored tribal sovereignty on tribal land, tribes could establish gambling casinos on reservations, even if their state did not allow casinos.[191] Almost three hundred tribes have done so, although less than a dozen have found a bonanza.[192] With their new revenues, the successful tribes have begun to buy into the political process, as other groups have done. Threatened by gambling interests in Las Vegas and Atlantic

Native Americans feel renewed cultural pride in ancient traditions but also the lure of modern technology.

© Gabe Palmer/CORBIS

City, which fear that tribal casinos will lure away potential customers, the tribes have formed their own lobby, the National Indian Gaming Association, and made their own contributions to politicians.

Overall, Native Americans enjoy renewed pride. From 1970 to 1990, according to birth and death records, the Indian population increased by 760,000. Yet according to people's self-identification for the census, this population rose by 1.4 million.[193] Evidently, many people, including those with only distant Indian ancestry, who did not wish to identify themselves as Indians in 1970 did so two decades later. Now more Indians share the views of one activist who says, "You have a federal government, state governments, and tribal governments—three sovereigns in one country. This is the civil rights movement of Native Americans."[194]

Nevertheless, Indians remain at the bottom of America's racial and ethnic ladder. They are the least educated and most unemployed group, the poorest and sickest group, with the highest rates of alcoholism and the lowest life expectancy, of any people in the country.

Sex Discrimination

Discrimination against Women

For many generations, people believed that natural differences between the sexes required them to occupy separate spheres of life. Men would dominate the public domain of work and government, while women would dominate the private domain of the home. Both domains were important, and men were considered superior in one while women were considered superior in the other. Unlike racial minorities, women were not held in disdain in every aspect of life.

Thomas Jefferson, the most egalitarian of the Founders, reflected this widespread view when he said,

"Were our state a pure democracy there would still be excluded from our deliberations women, who, to prevent deprivation of morals and ambiguity of issues, should not mix promiscuously in gatherings of men."[195] That is, women are more moral than men, so they would be corrupted by politics, but they also more irrational, so they would confuse the issues. For both reasons, they should not be involved in politics.

Women were denied the right to vote in most places, and married women were denied other rights. They did not have the right to manage property they owned before marriage, to manage wages they received from jobs, to enter into contracts, or to sue. Although some states eventually enacted laws granting women these rights, when disputes arose within families, male judges hesitated to tell other men how to treat their wives. Often, then, these rights would not exist in practice until well into the twentieth century.

Even women's citizenship was tied to their husbands'. If a foreign woman married an American man, she automatically became a United States citizen. But if an American woman married a foreign man, she automatically lost her United States citizenship. (Women's citizenship would not become independent of their husbands' until 1922, shortly after women gained the right to vote.)

Women were also barred from schools and jobs. Before the Civil War, they were not admitted to public high schools. Because they were being prepared for motherhood, education was considered unnecessary, even dangerous. According to the *Encyclopaedia Britannica* in 1800, women had smaller brains than men.[196] Education would fatigue them and possibly ruin their reproductive organs. Similarly, before the Civil War, women were not encouraged to hold jobs. Those who sought employment were shunted into jobs that were seen as extensions of the domestic domain, such as producing textiles, clothes, and shoes in sex-segregated factories.[197]

This traditional conception of gender roles created problems for women who did not fit the mold. After the Civil War, Myra Bradwell ran a private school, founded a weekly newspaper, and worked for civic organizations. She was active in the women's suffrage movement and instrumental in persuading the Illinois legislature to expand women's legal rights. But after studying law, she was denied a license to practice law solely because she was a woman. The U.S. Supreme Court upheld the Illinois policy in 1873.[198] Justice Joseph Bradley declared:

> *Law, as well as nature itself, has always recognized a wide difference in the respective spheres and destinies of man and woman. Man is, or should be, the woman's protector and defender. The natural and proper timidity*

and delicacy which belongs to the female sex evidently unfits it for many of the occupations of civil life. . . . The constitution of the family organization . . . indicates the domestic sphere as that which properly belongs to the domain and functions of womanhood. The harmony . . . of interests and views which belong, or should belong, to the family institution is repugnant to the idea of a woman adopting a distinct and independent career from that of her husband. . . . The paramount destiny and mission of woman are to fulfill the noble and benign offices of wife and mother. This is the law of the Creator. And the rules of civil society must be adapted to the general constitution of things, and cannot be based upon exceptional cases.

Sometimes it was difficult to distinguish between this separate-but-equal view and discriminatory treatment. In the 1860s and 1870s, the doctors who practiced scientific medicine formed the American Medical Association (AMA) to drive out other people who offered medical services. These people included not only hucksters and quacks but also women who served as midwives or abortionists. Although abortions had been widely available, the AMA, drawing on popular fears about the women's suffrage movement, convinced male state legislators that abortions were "a threat to social order and to male authority." The woman who seeks an abortion, the AMA explained, "becomes unmindful of the course marked out for her by Providence, she overlooks the duties imposed on her by the marriage contract. She yields to the pleasure—but shrinks from the pains and responsibilities of maternity. . . . Let not the husband of such a wife flatter himself that he possesses her affection."[199]

Sometimes the discriminatory treatment was even more blatant. The Mississippi Supreme Court acknowledged a husband's right to beat his wife.[200] Using the "rule of thumb," it claimed, a husband could not beat his wife with a weapon thicker than his thumb.

The Women's Movement

Early feminists were determined to remedy these inequities. Many had gained political and organizational experience in the abolitionist movement. It was not considered "unladylike" for women to campaign for the end of slavery because the movement was associated with religious groups. Yet women were barely tolerated by the male leaders of the movement and not allowed to participate fully in the major antislavery society. They formed their own antislavery society, but when they attended a convention of antislavery societies, they were not allowed to sit with the male delegates.

Angry at such treatment, the women held a meeting to discuss the "social, civil, and religious rights of women." This first Women's Rights Convention in

1848 adopted a declaration of rights based on the Declaration of Independence. It said, "We hold these truths to be self-evident: that all men and women are created equal." The convention also passed a resolution in favor of women's suffrage.

Following the Civil War, women who had worked in the abolitionist movement expected that women, as well as blacks, would get legal rights and voting rights. When the Fourteenth and Fifteenth Amendments did not include women, they felt betrayed and disassociated themselves from the black movement. They formed their own organizations to campaign for women's suffrage. This movement, led by Susan B. Anthony and Elizabeth Cady Stanton, succeeded in 1920, when the Nineteenth Amendment gave women the right to vote.

Then dissension developed within the women's movement. Many groups felt that passage of the Nineteenth Amendment was but a first step in the struggle for equal rights. They proposed the Equal Rights Amendment to remedy remaining inequities. Other groups felt the battle had been won. They opposed the Equal Rights Amendment, arguing that it would overturn labor laws recently enacted to protect women. Because of this dissension and the conservatism in the country, the movement became relatively dormant.[201]

The movement reemerged in the 1960s. As a result of the civil rights movement, many women recognized their own inferior status. Numerous writers sensitized more women to this. Betty Friedan published *The Feminine Mystique,* which grew out of a questionnaire she circulated at her fifteenth college reunion. The book addressed the malaise that afflicted college-educated women who had been socialized into the feminine role but who were finding it unsatisfying.[202] Friedan's manifesto became the best-selling nonfiction paperback of 1964. In 1966, Friedan and other upper-middle-class, professional women formed the National Organization for Women (NOW). They resolved "to bring women into full participation in the mainstream of American society *now.*"

Other women, also middle class but veterans of the civil rights and antiwar movements, had developed a taste for political action and gained political experience. They formed other organizations. Where NOW fought primarily for women's political and economic rights, the other organizations fought more broadly for women's liberation in all spheres of life. Together these organizations pushed the issue of discrimination against women back onto the public agenda.

Nevertheless, they were not taken seriously for some years. In 1970, *Time* magazine reported, "No one knows how many shirts lay wrinkling in laundry baskets last week as thousands of women across the country turned out for the first big demonstration of the women's liberation movement. They took over [New

York City's Fifth Avenue], providing not only protest but some of the best sidewalk ogling in years."[203]

Although the movement tried to broaden its base beyond upper-middle-class and college-educated women, it was unable to do so. The movement generated an image of privileged women who looked with disdain on other women. *Housewife* became a derisive term. Traditional women viewed the movement as being antimotherhood and antifamily and, as it became more radical in the 1970s, prolesbian. This image gave "women's liberation" a bad name, even while most women agreed with most goals of the movement.[204] This image persists. More Americans believe that extraterrestrials have visited the earth than think that the word *feminist* is a compliment.[205] (It is unclear whether this says more about Americans' attitudes toward gender equality or about our penchant for paranoid conspiracy theories.)

The Movement in Congress and the Courts

Congress initially did not take the modern women's movement seriously either. When civil rights proponents sponsored a bill to forbid racial discrimina-tion in employment, eighty-one-year-old Representative Howard Smith (D-Va.) proposed an amendment to add sex discrimination to the bill. A foe of equal rights for blacks, Smith thought his proposal so ludicrous and so radical that it would help defeat the entire bill. Indeed, during debate on the amendment, members of Congress laughed so hard that they could barely hear each other speak.[206] But the joke was on them, because the amendment, and then the entire bill, passed.

Congress later adopted legislation to forbid sex discrimination in credit and education. Congress also passed the **Equal Rights Amendment (ERA).** The amendment simply declared, "Equality of rights under the law shall not be denied or abridged by the United States or by any state on account of sex." Introduced in 1923 and every year thereafter, Congress passed the amendment in 1972.

It appeared that the amendment would zip through ratification by the states. Both parties endorsed it, and the majority of the public supported it. But after about half of the states ratified it, the amendment bogged down. Observers noted that it would make women subject to the draft and possibly combat duty. Opponents charged that it would result in unisex restrooms and ho-

During World War II, women were urged into the labor force to replace men called to war. "Rosie the Riveter" became a symbol of these women working toward the war effort. Following the war, they were told that it was patriotic to go home and give their jobs to returning veterans. The 1955 magazine cover on the right depicts the stereotypical women's role in this postwar era before the beginning of the modern women's movement.

"Some kids at school called you a feminist, Mom, but I punched them out."

mosexual rights. Legal scholars denied that it would lead to these latter consequences, but after the judicial activism of the 1950s, 1960s, and 1970s, some people distrusted the courts to interpret the amendment.

The main problem, however, proved to be the symbolism of the amendment. For many women, the ERA represented an attack on the traditional values of motherhood, the family, and the home. Early feminists emphasized equality in employment so much that they gave some women the impression that they were against these values. Traditional women sensed implicit criticism for being housewives.[207] To underscore the symbolism, women in anti-ERA groups baked bread for state legislators about to vote on ratification. Because of the symbolism, even some women who favored equality opposed the amendment itself. Although many young women supported it, fewer of their mothers and grandmothers did; and although many working women supported it, fewer housewives did. Women's organizations had not created an effective grassroots campaign to sway traditional women. Ultimately, the disaffection of many women allowed male legislators to vote according to their traditional attitudes. They did not need to worry that a strong majority of their female constituents would object.[208]

In 1980, the Republican Party became the first party not to endorse the ERA since 1940, and President Reagan became the first president not to support the amendment since Truman.

When the deadline for ratification set by Congress expired in 1982, the ERA fell three states short of approval by the necessary three-fourths—thirty-eight—of the states. Like the Nineteenth Amendment, it was not ratified primarily by southern states.

But women were beginning to win rights in court.

Courts traditionally upheld laws that limited women's participation in the public domain and occasionally even laws that diminished their standing in the private domain. As late as 1970, the Ohio supreme court held that a wife is a husband's servant with "no legally recognized feelings or rights."[209]

The Burger Court finally reversed this pattern of decisions. In 1971, for the first time, the Court struck down a law that discriminated against women,[210] heralding a long series of rulings that invalidated a variety of such laws. In these rulings, the Court used the congressional statutes and also broadened the Fourteenth Amendment's equal protection clause to apply to women as well as to racial minorities.

The change was especially apparent in a pair of cases involving the selection of jurors. For the pool of potential jurors, some states drew the names of men, but not women, from voter registration or other lists. These states allowed women to serve only if they voluntarily signed up at the courthouse. Consequently, few women served. In 1961, the Court let Florida use these procedures because the "woman is still regarded as the center of home and family life."[211] In 1975, however, the Court forbade Louisiana from using similar procedures,[212] thus overturning a precedent only fourteen years old.

The Court's rulings rejected the traditional stereotypes that men are the breadwinners and women the child rearers in society. The Court invalidated Utah's law that required divorced fathers to support their daughters until age eighteen but their sons until twenty-one.[213] The state assumed that the daughters would get married and be supported by their husbands, whereas the sons would need to get educated for their careers. But the Court noted, "No longer is the female destined solely for the home."

Employment The Civil Rights Act of 1964 forbids discrimination on the basis of both sex and race in hiring, promoting, and firing. It prohibits discrimination on the basis of sex, except where it is a "bona fide occupational qualification" for the job. The Equal Employment Opportunity Commission (EEOC), which enforces the act, interprets it broadly and accepts sex as a legitimate qualification for very few jobs, such as restroom attendants, lingerie salesclerks, models, or actors. On the other hand, employers cannot seek only males for jobs men traditionally held, such as those that entail heavy physical labor, unpleasant working conditions, late-night hours, overtime, or travel.

Some employers are reluctant to comply. For matched pairs of men and women, résumés were sent to sixty-five Philadelphia restaurants in 1995. The men were more than twice as likely to get an interview and more than five times as likely to get the job at the higher-priced restaurants than the equally qualified women were.[214]

The **Equal Pay Act** of 1963 requires that women and men receive equal pay for equal work. The act makes exceptions for merit, productivity, and seniority.

As a result of the act, the gap between what women and men earn has slowly been shrinking. For workers with the same job and experience, women earn 89 cents for every dollar men earn.[215] The gap is mostly between married women and married men. Single women and single men between the ages of twenty-one and thirty-five receive nearly equal pay. When the women get married, however, their pay starts to lag, and when they have children, it lags further, apparently because they work fewer hours due to child-care and household responsibilities.[216]

Overall, working women make less than working men primarily because they have different jobs than men, and these jobs pay much less. Traditionally, women were shunted into a small number of jobs. These "pink-collar" jobs include secretaries (98 percent are women), household workers (97 percent), child-care workers (97 percent), nurses (93 percent), bank tellers (90 percent), librarians (83 percent), elementary school teachers (83 percent), and health technicians (81 percent). In contrast, few women are carpenters (1 percent), firefighters (2 percent), mechanics (4 percent), or truck drivers (5 percent).[217]

Although the Equal Pay Act mandates equal pay for equal work, it does not require equal pay for comparable work—usually called "comparable worth." According to a personnel study in the state of Washington, maintenance carpenters and secretaries performed comparable jobs in terms of the education, skill, or other qualifications needed, but the carpenters, mostly men, made about $600 a month more than the secretaries, mostly women. In general, "men's jobs" paid about 20 percent more than comparable "women's jobs." These findings prompted unions representing government employees in the state to file a suit and demand an increase in pay for jobs held mostly by women. The federal court of appeals, in an opinion by Judge Anthony Kennedy, now on the Supreme Court, rejected comparable worth. Nevertheless, some state and city governments implemented comparable worth plans for their employees after prodding by unions and women's groups. Most private companies, however, did not adopt comparable worth because it would require them to pay many of their women employees more.

Although formal barriers against women have been lifted, informal ones remain. Women face male stereotyping. Their superiors and colleagues often assume that women are not serious about careers, will quit to have babies, are too emotional, and are not tough enough. Women also feel excluded from informal networks of communication that transact business.[218] In addition to these barriers, some women also face sexual harassment (see the box "Sexual Harassment at Work"). However, acceptance of women in executive positions is growing (see Figure 5).

Mothers with young children confront more obstacles. Their male employers and coworkers think women should be responsible for raising children but do little to accommodate the demands of child rearing. Most companies do not provide paid maternity leave, flexible schedules, or on-site day care. The United States lags far behind many other countries, ninety-eight of which grant partly paid maternity leaves for at least three months.[219] Only California provides partly paid family leaves (55 percent of a worker's wages for up to six weeks).

Congress passed and President Clinton signed a bill

FIGURE 5 ■ Acceptance of Women in the Workplace *A majority of men don't care whether their boss is a woman or a man or whether the woman they date has a higher salary than they do. Shown here are the responses of 1,302 men polled by telephone in 2004 to the following questions.*

Source: *Time,* August 23, 2004, 38.

requiring employers to grant unpaid maternity and paternity leaves. Companies must allow unpaid leaves for up to three months for workers with newborn or recently adopted children or with seriously ill family members. The act applies to companies that have fifty employees and to workers who work twenty-five hours a week for a year.[220] This covers about half of American workers.

Relatively few workers take advantage of family leaves where they are available. Most workers cannot afford to take unpaid leave. Moreover, managers often do not support such measures, and coworkers resent the additional burdens, so employees are reluctant to ask for them. At a time when many companies have laid off workers to cut costs, "If you look like you are not career oriented, you can lose your job."[221]

Mothers and fathers with young children often face unreasonable time demands from employers accustomed to hiring married men with a wife at home to rear the children, maintain the house, and run the errands. Now employers are putting the same demands on married women, especially those with professional jobs. Nobody is left to do the jobs of the housewife. Although women often continue to perform most of them, both spouses frequently feel stretched thin and stressed out.

Not surprisingly, among men with children, those who have a wife at home rise up the career ladder faster than those who have a wife working outside the home. The latter men apparently put in less "face time" at work. Executives who reach the higher rungs are "almost always" men who have a wife at home.[222] An executive of a *Fortune* 500 company, in a conversation with business professors at a southwestern university not long ago, admitted that his company still prefers to hire men married to a woman who remains at home.

So even though women have gained greater acceptance in the workplace, they—and their spouses—have not yet overcome the expectations that developed long before they were ever allowed in the workplace. And these expectations are exacerbated by Americans' glorification of work. "We glorify an all-work, all-the-time lifestyle," notes one commentator, "and then weep crocodile tears for kids whose parents are never home."[223] With new communications technology has come a perverse celebration of the "24/7 workweek" in the past decade.

Credit The Equal Credit Opportunity Act of 1974 forbids discrimination on the basis of sex or marital status in credit transactions. Historically, banks, savings and loans, credit card companies, and retail stores discriminated against women. Typically, these businesses determine how much money people can borrow according to how much they earn. Yet the lenders refused loans to single women, regardless of income, because

© Bettmann/CORBIS

Men resisted the expansion of women's athletics. The Boston Marathon was traditionally a race for men only. When the first woman tried to participate in 1967, a marathon official assaulted her.

they assumed that the women would work only until they got married and became pregnant. Likewise, the lenders did not count a wife's income as part of a couple's total income, again because they assumed that the wife's employment was temporary. Only if women were professionals or in their forties would lenders count their income the same as men's. When businesses lent money to a married couple, they put the transactions in just the husband's name. Thus when they became divorced or widowed, women had no credit record and little chance to obtain credit.

The Equal Credit Opportunity Act requires lenders to lend to single women and to count the wife's income as part of a couple's total income. It restricts lenders from asking women whether they intend to bear children. The act also requires lenders to put accounts in the names of both spouses if they request it.

Education The Education Amendments of 1972 (to the Civil Rights Act of 1964) forbid discrimination on the basis of sex in schools and colleges that receive federal aid. The amendments were prompted by discrimination against women by undergraduate and graduate colleges, especially in admissions and financial aid.

The language of the amendments, often referred to as **Title IX,** is so broad that the Department of Education, which administers them, has established rules that cover more aspects of education than their congressional supporters expected.[224] The department has used the amendments to prod institutions into employing and promoting more female teachers and administrators, opening vocational training classes to women and home economics classes to men, and offering equal athletic programs to women. If institutions do not comply, the government can cut off their federal aid.

The amendments have affected athletic programs especially. Before the amendments, schools provided

Although the Supreme Court had ruled that sexual harassment was a form of job discrimination prohibited by the Civil Rights Act of 1964,[1] and Congress had passed a law allowing victims to collect monetary damages from employers for distress, illness, or loss of their job due to harassment, there was little public awareness of the law until Clarence Thomas's confirmation hearings for appointment to the Supreme Court in 1991.

The hearings propelled sexual harassment to the forefront of social debate. For seven days the public was riveted to the televised hearings. Anita Hill's charges—that Thomas, as her supervisor at the Equal Employment Opportunity Commission, made lewd comments about her, about sex, about finding pubic hairs on Coke cans, and about watching animals have sex in films—led to many discussions around workplace water coolers.

After the hearings, more women recognized that behavior they had dismissed as merely annoying was actually harassment. The number of complaints filed with the EEOC doubled (though in recent years it has leveled off).

Courts recognize two types of sexual harassment. The most obvious is *quid pro quo,* in which a supervisor makes unwanted sexual advances and either promises good consequences (for example, a promotion) if the employee goes along or threatens bad consequences (for example, an unde-

sirable reassignment) if the employee refuses. Less obvious is creating a hostile environment that interferes with the employee's ability to do the job. To prove a hostile environment, the employee must demonstrate that the conduct was severe or persistent.

Paula Jones's suit against President Clinton was dismissed because the alleged sexual advance was considered neither severe enough nor, as a single incident, persistent enough to constitute a hostile environment. If it happened, the judge said, it was "boorish and offensive" but not technically harassment. Although many men seem to worry that innocuous comments will be classified as sexual harassment, Justice Antonin Scalia emphasized that the law did not create "a general civility code."[2]

Yet considerable confusion persists because the law is relatively recent and different courts have issued varying interpretations. In addition, employers, who can be held responsible for sexual harassment by their employees (even if the employers are unaware of the harassment), can defend themselves by having policies to prevent such conduct.[3] Some have adopted "zero tolerance" policies to insulate them from employee lawsuits. These policies are stricter than the law, and they have led to the firing of a few men who would not have been convicted under the law. For example, an executive told a woman coworker about the plot of the

Seinfeld show he had seen the night before. Seinfeld was telling his friends about a woman he met but whose name he could not remember except that it rhymed with a female body part. The coworker complained of sexual harassment, and Miller Brewing Company fired the executive, despite his nineteen years of service to the company. (When the executive sued the company, however, a mostly female jury awarded him millions of dollars for being wrongfully dismissed.)

Consultants who advise employers have observed that women in traditional female jobs, such as secretary, are more likely to be subjected to *quid pro quo* harassment from supervisors, whereas women in traditional male jobs, especially blue-collar jobs, are more likely to be subjected to hostile-environment harassment from coworkers. Hundreds of women in the Mitsubishi auto plant in Normal, Illinois, experienced incidents ranging from finding plastic penises in tool buckets to being asked their sexual habits and preferences; being called "bitches," "sluts," and "whores," rather than their names; and being grabbed by their breasts, buttocks, and genitals. Some women had their work sabotaged to make their performance seem slow and shoddy.[4]

The dynamics of sexual harassment do not revolve around sex as much as they reflect abuses of power. A supervisor, teacher, or coworker makes a

fewer sports for females than for males, and they spent far fewer dollars—for scholarships, coaches, and facilities—on women's sports. Now the department interprets the amendments to require a school either to have approximately the same percentage of female athletes as female undergraduates, to continually expand opportunities for female athletes, or to fully accommodate the interests and abilities of female students. (This last would occur if a school's female students were satisfied that it offered sufficient opportunities for them, given

their interests and abilities, even if the opportunities were not equal to those for men.)

Very few colleges meet the first requirement. To comply, most are trying to meet the second requirement by expanding the number of women's sports. But they worry that they will have to fulfill the first requirement eventually. And they fear that they will have to cap the squad size of their football team, which has the most players and costs the most money, to do so. This would lessen the imbalance in the numbers of male and female

woman feel vulnerable and thus exercises psychological dominance over her.

Consultants have observed that a very small percentage of men harass women, but these men do it a lot. One consultant has found that perhaps three to five men out of one hundred create problems, but these men might affect fifty women in the same workplace. The harassers typically feel bitter toward women or threatened by them. Some have long been bullies toward men as well as women.[5]

Surveys how that a third of female workers say they have been sexually harassed on the job.[6] After twenty-three women acknowledged in 1992 and 1993 that they had to fend off sexual advances by Senator Bob Packwood (R-Ore.), the *Washington Post* conducted a survey of women who worked as aides to members of Congress or staffers for congressional committees. It found the same results. A third of the women had been sexually harassed in the hallowed halls of Congress, and a third of these had been harassed by a member of Congress. (The others had been harassed by supervisors, coworkers, or lobbyists.)[7]

Yet few victims file formal complaints, let alone bring lawsuits, because they need their jobs. According to several studies, only 3 percent of women who have been harassed have filed formal complaints.[8] On Capitol Hill, 80 percent of the women surveyed said they would lose their job if they

did, 80 percent said they would never find another job there if they did, and 70 percent said nothing would be done to the harasser anyway.[9]

Sexual harassment can be directed toward men as well.[10] About 15 percent of male workers say they have been sexually harassed by men or women on the job.[11]

A backlash has set in, apparently because of the legal confusion in the courts and zero-tolerance policies of some employers. A majority—57 percent of men and 52 percent of women—say that "we have gone too far in making common interactions among employees into cases of sexual harassment."[12]

Defining sexual harassment too broadly jeopardizes free speech. One library employee filed a complaint against another because the other had posted an innocuous *New Yorker* cartoon in his cubicle.[13] One graduate teaching assistant filed a complaint against another because the other had placed a photograph of his wife, wearing a bikini, on his desk in their office at the University of Nebraska.

While companies and courts have been sensitive, sometimes overly sensitive, to sexual behavior, they have been callous toward the discrimination that sexual harassment law was originally intended to prevent. When women have coworkers who will not train them and will not work with them, coworkers who repeatedly subject

them to verbal abuse or obscene gestures, the women face discrimination, but the courts usually rule against them because the coworkers' behavior was not sexual. Yet these women face more discrimination than women whose sensibilities are offended by a sexual remark or an off-color joke. Some judges have interpreted the law to be puritanical toward sex but indifferent toward discrimination.[14]

1. *Mentor Savings Bank* v. *Vinson,* 91 L.Ed.2d 49 (1986).
2. *Oncale* v. *Sundowner Offshore Services,* 140 L.Ed.2d 201 (1998).
3. *Faragher* v. *Boca Raton,* 141 L.Ed.2d 662 (1998); *Burlington Industries* v. *Ellerth,* 141 L.Ed.2d 633 (1998).
4. Kirsten Downey Grimsley, Frank Swoboda, and Warren Brown, "Trouble on the Line," *Washington Post National Weekly Edition,* May 6, 1996, 6–7.
5. Kirsten Downey Grimsley, "Confronting Hard-Core Harassers," *Washington Post National Weekly Edition,* January 27, 1997, 6.
6. Richard Morin, "Think Twice before You Say Another Word," *Washington Post National Weekly Edition,* December 28, 1992, 37.
7. Richard Morin, "Jack and Jill Went up the Hill," *Washington Post National Weekly Edition,* March 1, 1993, 37.
8. Daniel Goleman, "Sexual Harassment: About Power, Not Sex," *New York Times,* October 22, 1991, B8.
9. Morin, "Jack and Jill."
10. *Oncale* v. *Sundowner Offshore Services.*
11. Janice Castro, "Sexual Harassment: A Guide," *Time,* January 20, 1992, 37.
12. John Cloud, "Sex and the Law," *Time,* March 23, 1998, 49.
13. Henry Louis Gates Jr., "Men Behaving Badly," *New Yorker,* August 18, 1997, 5.
14. For further analysis and a critique, see Jeffrey Toobin, "The Trouble with Sex," *New Yorker,* February 9, 1998, 48–55.

athletes, and it would free more money for women's teams.

Some colleges have therefore resisted enforcement of Title IX, partly because many athletic departments are struggling to make ends met and partly because it threatens deeply ingrained cultural values that are reflected in men's athletics. Administrators and boosters fear that women's sports will take money from men's sports and thereby weaken the primacy of men's athletics.

When Brown University tried to eliminate women's volleyball and gymnastics (at the same time it dropped men's golf and water polo), members of the women's teams sued. More than sixty schools filed briefs supporting Brown's decisions and criticizing the department's interpretations of Title IX. Lower courts ruled against Brown, and in 1997, the Supreme Court refused to hear the case, which left the lower courts' rulings intact. The Supreme Court's refusal signaled that the department's interpretations would remain and the schools would have to comply.

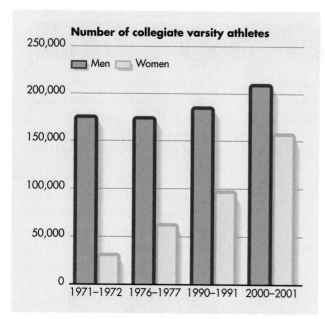

FIGURE 6 ■ Participation in Varsity Sports since Passage of Title IX *Both men's and women's participation in varsity sports has increased since passage of Title IX in 1972. Although many colleges have dropped some men's teams to make room for women's teams, more schools offer more sports than in the 1970s, so more men overall are participating, as well as a great many more women.*

SOURCE: Welch Suggs, "Title IX at 30," *Chronicle of Higher Education*, June 21, 2002, 39.

Already Title IX has had a major impact. Colleges have increased their women's teams—almost twice as many as in the early 1980s—and their female athletes—fully ten times as many as before (see Figure 6).[225] Women now make up 42 percent of all college athletes and receive 42 percent of the scholarship money (though their teams have lower coaches' salaries and operating expenses).[226]

Colleges with successful football or basketball programs have increased their women's teams the most because these sports generate revenue that funds women's sports. Colleges with no football program have also increased their women's teams. Colleges with football programs that do not generate a profit (and most do not) lag behind. They pour money into football but lack revenue from television or bowl contracts to fund women's sports.[227]

To reduce the gender imbalance, however, many colleges have eliminated low-profile men's teams, especially wrestling, gymnastics, tennis, and track. Marquette University eliminated men's wrestling even though the team was financed mostly by private donations.[228]

Title IX has also had a major impact on high schools, which have increased their girls' teams, and on American Olympic teams, which have benefited from their women's training in college.

But supporters have a broader goal in mind as well.

"If girls are socialized the way boys are to take part in sports," the editor of a women's sports magazine says, and "if boys and girls grow up with the idea that girls are strong and capable, it will change the way girls and women are viewed—by themselves and by society."[229]

Discrimination against Men

Although most sex discrimination has been directed at women, some has been directed at men. The traditional conception of gender roles has created problems for men who do not fit the standard mold.

When the Burger Court rejected stereotypes that led to discrimination against women, it also rejected some that led to discrimination against men. It invalidated Mississippi's law that barred men from one of the state's university nursing schools.[230] It also invalidated Alabama's law that allowed just women to seek alimony upon divorce.[231] Thus the Court rejected stereotypes that only women become nurses and only women are dependent on their spouses.

On the other hand, the Burger Court upheld some laws that were designed to protect women but that discriminate against men. It affirmed laws that prohibit statutory rape—intercourse with a minor, with consent—by males but not by females.[232] It also affirmed draft registration, required for males but not for females.[233] In 1980, President Carter asked Congress to reinstate draft registration, though not the draft itself, to show our "toughness" to the Soviet Union and other communist countries. He also urged Congress to include women in the program. Although Congress had admitted women to the military academies in 1975, it did not include them here. The Court upheld the law requiring registration for men only, rationalizing that registration eventually could lead to the draft and the draft eventually could lead to combat. And it insisted that most women are not capable of combat. Thus the Court accepted the stereotypes that only men initiate sex with underage partners and only men can fight in war.

In the absence of war, the most significant discrimination against men may occur in divorce cases, where the norm is to grant custody of children to mothers and require payment of support by fathers. Although courts give fathers visitation rights, they permit mothers to move miles away, making visitation difficult and sporadic. And although governments have taken steps to enforce support payments, they have done little to enforce visitation rights. This practice reflects the stereotype that fathers are capable of financing their children's upbringing but not of bringing them up themselves. The Supreme Court has ignored this problem.

The California Supreme Court, however, issued a pathbreaking ruling in 2004. It held that if a custodial parent (usually the mother) moves far away after di-

Although most single parents are women, an increasing number are men, such as this father of an eleven-year-old in Dallas.

© Brent Humphreys

vorce, custody might be shifted to the other parent (usually the father) so that the children can remain in their community. This has vast implications not only for the families after divorce but also for parents' decisions to divorce, parents' decisions to relocate, and employers' flexibility to transfer their workers.

Overall, Congress and the courts have moved steadily toward legal equality for the sexes. Women, and men, have accomplished through congressional and judicial action much of what they would have accomplished with the ERA. It is an indication of the success of the movement that young women today take their equality for granted and that they focus on their personal lives rather than see the need for further reform.

Affirmative Action

Assume there is a track meet. A black runner and a white runner start together. But the officials force the black runner to carry heavy weights, and he falls behind. Eventually, the officials realize that this is unfair, and they take the weights off. Of course, the black runner is still behind. Would this be fair? Assume now that the officials not only take the weights off but also allow him to catch up. Would this be more fair? Or would it be unfair to the white runner, who insists that the black runner's weights are not his fault?[234]

This scenario captures the dilemma of civil rights policy today. Although most race and sex discrimina-

tion has been repudiated by the courts and legislatures, the effects of past discrimination survive. Now the question is whether civil rights policy should ignore race and sex or take race and sex into account to compensate for the effects of past discrimination. That is, should the policy require nondiscrimination only or **affirmative action** as well?

Affirmative action applies to employers in hiring and promoting minorities and women, governments in reserving a portion of their contracts for businesses owned by minorities and women, and colleges and universities in admitting minorities and women.

In Employment

The Civil Rights Act of 1964, which bars discrimination in employment, does not mention affirmative action, but it does authorize the bureaucracy to make rules to help end discrimination. In 1969, the Department of Labor called for affirmative action by companies doing business with the federal government. Later, the Equal Employment Opportunities Commission called for affirmative action by governments and the Office of Education by colleges as well. Presidents from Nixon through Carter supported it with executive orders, and the Supreme Court sanctioned it in a series of cases.[235] Many state and local governments also adopted it.

Affirmative action applies most extensively to employment. It requires positive steps to ensure that qualified minorities and women receive a fair share of jobs at all levels. Just what the positive steps and the fair share should be are the subject of much controversy.

If the number of minorities and women in a company that has government contracts and is subject to affirmative action or in a government agency, at any level, is less than the number in the local labor force, the company or agency must agree to recruit more or, in serious cases, draw up an affirmative action plan. The plan must include goals to hire or promote more minorities or women and a timetable to reach these goals. If the company or agency does not reach them, it must show that it made an effort to reach them. If the company cannot satisfy the government, it can be denied future contracts (though in reality these companies are rarely penalized).

Although the requirements for affirmative action plans speak of "goals," critics charge that they really mandate quotas and that quotas amount to "reverse discrimination" and result in lower standards.[236] But affirmative action rarely requires quotas. The terms do blur; if employers are pressured to meet "goals," they might interpret "goals" to mean "quotas." But only after a finding of deliberate and systematic discrimination does affirmative action entail quotas.[237]

In addition, courts scrutinize the plans to make sure that they do not prevent all white men from being hired and promoted and that they are temporary (usually until the percentage of minority employees reaches the percentage of minority workers in the community).

Because of concern that affirmative action should not pose too great a burden on innocent individuals, the Court has struck down affirmative action in laying off workers—that is, struck down protection for minorities and women when employers pare their workforce for economic reasons. Instead, the Court has accepted the traditional practice, based on seniority, that the last hired is the first fired.[238]

Despite these limits on affirmative action, the Rehnquist Court made it more difficult for governments to adopt or require affirmative action.[239] Governments must have clear evidence of some specific discrimination, rather than the typical pattern of pervasive historical discrimination, and they must show that their programs would ameliorate the problems.

Affirmative action has helped minorities and women. White men dominate public and private institutions, and as the personnel director of a *Fortune* 500 company observed, "People tend to hire people like themselves."[240] So affirmative action has prodded them to hire more minorities and women. Companies that have government contracts and are therefore subject to affirmative action have shown more improvement in hiring minorities and women than other companies. And state and local governments, also subject to affirmative action, have shown more improvement in hiring than private companies. Companies and governments subject to affirmative action have shown even greater progress in promoting minorities and women, who had previously been kept in low-level positions.[241]

The state of Alabama, for example, made dramatic gains. After a court found that the state troopers had never employed any blacks, it ordered them to hire one new black for every new white until the force reached 25 percent black. The force became the most integrated force in the country. Faced with the threat of a similar order, other departments of the state government quickly hired more blacks at all levels.

While continuous controversy swirls around government efforts toward affirmative action, private businesses use affirmative action extensively and champion it under the name of "diversity." They have found new pools of untapped talent in overlooked groups, and they have reached new markets in these groups. Hiring more minority and female workers has led to insights that enable the corporations to sell products to more minority and female consumers.[242]

Affirmative action has helped middle-class and some lower-class blacks get jobs in government and business.[243] It has noticeably increased the number of blacks in government agencies, police departments, fire departments, construction trades, and textile companies.

It has also helped women get jobs in government and business that traditionally went only to men.

But affirmative action has not pulled blacks out of the "underclass." Many, from families that have suffered long-term poverty, experience continual unemployment because they lack the education and the skills necessary to compete for available jobs.[244] And affirmative action cannot create new jobs or better jobs, so it is not as helpful to minorities or women as a flourishing economy is.

In short, affirmative action should not be given more credit or more blame than it deserves. It has boosted some minorities and women, but it cannot help many others. It has displaced some white men, but it has not affected most others.

Yet 13 percent of white men think they lost a job or promotion because of their race, and 10 percent think they did because of their sex.[245] Many others claim they "heard about" another white man who did. Yet affirmative action is not as pervasive as many people assume.[246] Many people subconsciously view affirmative action as they do handicapped parking. When looking for a parking space in a crowded lot, numerous drivers see a handicapped space and think, "If it weren't for that space, I could park here." Of course, if the space wasn't reserved for handicapped drivers, only one other driver could park there.[247] So it is with affirmative action. Many white men think they would get a particular job if it weren't for affirmative action, but only one would. Meanwhile, the rest feel victimized by the policy.

For both sides in the controversy, affirmative action has become a symbol. For civil rights leaders, it represents fairness and real progress toward equality. For critics, it represents unfairness and an attack on individuality and merit. It is important to debate these values, but it is also important to recognize that affirmative action is neither the key public policy for racial and sexual equality nor the biggest stumbling block for individual achievement, as supporters and detractors seem to assume.

Indeed, some supporters say affirmative action reaches so few individuals that it is an attempt to achieve "racial justice on the cheap," without facing up to the greater problem of the underclass.[248]

In College Admissions

Affirmative action also applies to college and university admissions. Colleges and universities began to use affirmative action in the 1970s. Some schools used limited programs that gave a small boost to minority applicants, while other schools used extensive programs that reserved seats—essentially, they set quotas—for minority applicants. The medical school of the University of California at Davis reserved sixteen seats in its class

FROM THE DETROIT FREE PRESS

MIKE THOMPSON, COPLEY NEWS SERVICE

of one hundred students for minorities. In *University of California* v. *Bakke,* the Burger Court upheld the use of race as a factor in admissions but struck down the use of quotas (unless the school had a history of intentional discrimination in the past).

The Supreme Court would not rule on this issue again until 2003. In the meantime, voters in California and Washington and the governor of Florida mandated an end to the use of race in admissions to public universities. Federal courts of appeals in two circuits, ignoring the *Bakke* precedent, also ordered an end to the practice.

The moves against affirmative action prompted concerns that minority enrollments would plunge. Some state legislatures and universities decided not to let this happen. The Texas legislature passed a law guaranteeing admission, at the undergraduate level, to its state universities for all high school graduates in the top 10 percent of their class. The University of California Board of Regents guaranteed admission, at the undergraduate level, to at least one of the UC campuses for those in the top 4 percent.

These programs use geography instead of race; in particular, they use residential segregation, which has stymied the efforts to desegregate the schools from grade schools through high schools, as a way to diversify the universities. Minority students who performed well in their segregated schools can still get admitted to the universities, even if their schools provided a less competitive education than predominantly white schools provide.

The Texas program has lowered standards somewhat as schools have had to accept students who were in the top 10 percent of their class but who had some other weakness in their file (and reject students who fell just below the top 10 percent at more competitive schools).[249] Although both the Texas program and the California program have increased the number of minorities above the levels they would have had without the program, the number is lower than it had been with affirmative action. In the two states, Asians have been the prime beneficiaries of the demise of affirmative action. Whites have seen their admission rate dip slightly.[250]

Finally, the Rehnquist Court revisited the *Bakke* ruling in 2003. In a pair of cases from the University of Michigan, one directed at undergraduate admissions and one directed at law school admissions, five justices upheld affirmative action but only as part of a "holistic review" that gives "individualized consideration" to each application. Schools cannot use formulas that add points for minority status; they must use a more labor-intensive review.[251] The decision to uphold affirmative action came as a surprise, because the Rehnquist Court had narrowed the practice in employment cases.

Some justices may have been influenced by *amicus curiae* briefs. A record number of these—102—were prepared, most supporting affirmative action. They were filed not only by universities but also by dozens of *Fortune* 500 companies. One was filed by twenty-one retired generals and admirals, including three former superintendents of the military academies. This brief recalled the Vietnam War, when there were few minority officers and there was considerable tension between the black troops and the white officers. Since then, affirmative action has produced an integrated officer corps and consequently, a more effective military, according to the retired brass. Justice Sandra Day O'Connor, who provided the crucial fifth vote, acknowledged that selective universities—the ones that use affirmative action—train the leaders of our society and that an integrated leadership helps govern a diverse people.

Just as some white men believe that affirmative action cost them a job or promotion, some white students believe it cost them, or will cost them, a seat in the college or university of their choice. But 60 percent of colleges admit nearly all students who apply; only 20 percent are selective enough to use affirmative action much.[252] Students who apply to elite schools are more likely to lose a seat because other applicants' parents are alumni of these schools. Typically, a fifth of Harvard's students are given preferential treatment because their parents attended the school. Harvard's "legacies" are more than twice as likely to be admitted as blacks or Latinos. A similar advantage exists at other selective schools, including public schools such as the Universities of California and Virginia.[253] This advantage encourages alumni to continue donating to their school. Affirmative action may be more widespread in graduate schools, however.[254]

Conclusion: Is Government Responsive in Granting Civil Rights?

Blacks and women have made tremendous progress in obtaining civil rights since the time when a federal official who fired competent blacks could insist, "A Negro's place is in the cornfield,"[255] or employers who refused to hire women could insist, "A woman's place is in the home." The civil rights movement and the women's movement initiated the changes. They protested legal inequality and put the issue on the public agenda. As they grew and garnered support, they pressured the government. Finally, about a century after the first significant agitations for change, the government responded.

Within the government, the Supreme Court exercised decisive leadership. Historically, the Court was both activist and restrained toward blacks—whichever stance was necessary to deny their rights—and restrained toward women. But in the 1950s and 1960s, the Warren Court was activist in striking down racial segregation, and in the 1970s and 1980s, the Burger Court was activist in striking down sexual discrimination. Each may go down in history as that Court's major achievement. But the Court's rulings themselves did not guarantee the rights. Because the Court lacks the means to enforce its decisions, the president and Congress had to help overcome public resistance.

Thus the areas of racial and sexual discrimination show the power, and the limit of the power, of the courts. The Supreme Court exercised power because it articulated emerging views in society—that racial segregation or sexual discrimination by law is wrong. But the Court was unable to accomplish the changes alone. The Court has struggled, mostly in vain, to accomplish further changes in the area of racial discrimination. It has made little progress in overcoming residential segregation and the accompanying problems of school segregation and school inequality and in ameliorating the poverty that makes it difficult for many minorities to take advantage of their rights.

The changes in policy illustrate the responsiveness of the government. In its subjugation of minorities until the 1950s and its treatment of women until the 1970s, the government was responding to the majority view. When minorities and women organized to protest their status, the government began responding to them and to shifts in the majority view that their protest prompted.

In pressuring the government to respond, African Americans have benefited from being numerous, visible, and—with their common legacy of slavery, segregation, and discrimination—relatively cohesive. Their concentration in large northern cities and some southern states has helped them exercise political power. Their long legacy, though, has fostered debilitating ghetto conditions and denied them the resources to make quicker progress.

Latinos have become more numerous. Their concentration in some western and southwestern states has enabled them to influence state and local governments. Their diversity and lack of cohesiveness, however, have hindered their ability to influence the national government. The increasing size of their electoral bloc will give them more clout in coming years.

Native Americans are the smallest, most isolated, and least organized minority, so they have had the poorest success in pressuring the government.

As minority groups grow in size, they will be able to exert pressure on governments more effectively. But as minority groups expand, they will increasingly come into conflict with each other, especially when economic conditions are stagnant. Competition for scarce resources will widen the cracks in the coalition. Already there are tensions. Some blacks resent the faster progress of Latinos and Asians. These blacks say they were here before most Latinos and Asians, they suffered more and struggled longer, and so they should reap the rewards sooner. On the other hand, some Latino leaders resent the reluctance of black groups to help them with their civil rights problems.[256] Sometimes there are conflicts over issues. Occasionally, there have been riots. Blacks have rioted in Miami from frustration with the Cuban-dominated leadership. Latinos have rioted in Washington, D.C., out of anger with their lack of city services and jobs and with gerrymandering by the black power structure.

Nonminority women were never subjugated as much as minority men and women, so they have had less to overcome. Moreover, women are a majority, they vote as frequently as men, and they have well-organized and well-funded interest groups. Consequently, they have made the greatest strides toward equality.

Exclusion of Japanese Is Upheld

In *Korematsu* v. *United States*, the Supreme Court, by a 6–3 vote, upheld the order excluding 120,000 Japanese Americans from the West Coast.[257] Although Justice Douglas voted against the order in conference, he switched to the majority just before the decision was announced.[258]

The majority held that the government could take precautions to prevent espionage and sabotage during wartime, and it noted that the president and Congress agreed that the order was necessary. Thus the majority was restrained, deferring to the combined force of the other branches. These justices did not question whether officials had a valid fear of espionage or sabotage by Japanese Americans. In contrast, the minority was activist, challenging the other branches. These justices disputed the suspicions of disloyalty and suggested that discrimination against Japanese Americans led to the order.

The minority raised the specter that the Court's ruling would set a dangerous precedent. "A military order, however unconstitutional, is not apt to last longer than the military emergency," Justice Robert Jackson wrote. "But once a judicial opinion rationalizes such an order . . . the Court for all time has validated the principle of racial discrimination . . . and of transplanting American citizens. The principle then lies about like a loaded weapon ready for the hand of any authority that can bring forward a plausible claim of an urgent need."

In December 1944—two and a half years after it began the evacuation and one day before it heard the Court's decision—the military ordered the release of "loyal" Japanese Americans.

Upon their release, they discovered that the government had failed to keep its promise to protect their property. Many of their possessions, stored in warehouses, had been vandalized or stolen. Some of their homes had been taken over by strangers, and some of their land had been seized for unpaid taxes. "They did me a great wrong," Korematsu said. But he returned to live in the same town where he was arrested. "I love this country and I belong here."

Near the end of his career, Justice Douglas expressed regret that he and others in the majority had gone along with the government. The case "was ever on my conscience."[259] He did not live long enough to learn that the War Department had presented false information to the Court. The department had altered some reports and destroyed others demonstrating the loyalty of the Japanese Americans.[260] In fact, from Pearl Harbor until the end of the war, the government had no record of any incident of espionage or sabotage by a Japanese American citizen or alien in the United States.[261]

With help from the lawyer who discovered the false information, Korematsu reopened his case through a rarely used procedure available only when the original trial was tainted with prosecutorial misconduct and fraud. In 1983, a federal judge reversed his conviction.[262]

In 1988, Congress passed a law offering a public apology for the internment and $20,000 compensation to each surviving internee.[263]

After the September 11 terrorist attacks, there was renewed talk about the Japanese relocation. Should legal immigrants from countries with links to terrorist groups be rounded up and put in internment camps? A majority of Americans rejected this proposal, but nearly a third said they might accept it.[264] In 2003, Fred Korematsu filed a friend-of-the-court brief on behalf of the detainees at Guantanamo Bay.

To learn more about *Korematsu* v. *United States* and the controversy surrounding it, go to this chapter's "You Are There" exercises on the text Web site.

A Japanese relocation camp in Amache, Colorado.

Courtesy of the National Archives, NW-DNS-210-G-A753

Key Terms

Korematsu v. United States	restrictive covenants
Dred Scott case	steering
equal protection clause	blockbusting
Jim Crow laws	redlining
Plessy v. Ferguson	Civil Rights Act of 1968
separate-but-equal doctrine	racial profiling
	bilingual education
NAACP	Equal Rights Amendment (ERA)
Brown v. Board of Education	
de jure segregation	Equal Pay Act
de facto segregation	Title IX
Civil Rights Act of 1964	affirmative action

Further Reading

Edward Ball, *Slaves in the Family* (New York: Farrar, Straus & Giroux, 1998). The descendant of a plantation owner searches for the descendants of his family's slaves.

Jennifer Baumgardner and Amy Richards, *Manifest A: Young Women, Feminism, and the Future* (New York: Farrar, Straus & Giroux, 2000). The authors have created a primer on feminism for the members of Generation X.

Taylor Branch, *Parting the Waters: America in the King Years, 1954–63* (New York: Simon & Schuster, 1988). Branch provides a readable account of Martin Luther King Jr. and the first decade of the civil rights movement.

Seth Cagin and Philip Dray, *We Are Not Afraid: The Story of Goodman, Schwerner, and Chaney and the Civil Rights Campaign for Mississippi* (New York: Macmillan, 1988). This book documents an American crime committed in the steamy summer of 1964.

Veronica Chambers, *Having It All? Black Women and Success* (New York: Doubleday, 2003). This social and cultural history examines the portrayal of black women in the media, entertainment, and business worlds.

Ian Frazier, *On the Rez* (New York: Farrar, Straus & Giroux, 2000). Frazier provides a firsthand guide to life on Indian reservations.

David Halberstam, *The Children* (New York: Random House, 1998). A focus on the lives of eight students who attended college in Nashville and helped launch the civil rights movement reveals how a small group of courageous students helped transform the country.

Peter Irons, *Justice at War* (New York: Oxford University Press, 1983). The story of Fred Korematsu and other cases involving the Japanese American relocation is recounted by the attorney who uncovered the government's false information.

Randall Kennedy, *Nigger: The Strange Career of a Troublesome Word* (New York: Pantheon, 2002). An African American law professor traces the history of this most explosive word.

Gregory Howard Williams, *Life on the Color Line: The True Story of a White Boy Who Discovered He Was Black* (New York: Dutton, 1995). The life of a ten-year-old boy changed dramatically the day he learned that his father was black.

For Viewing

Eyes on the Prize (1987) This documentary series on the civil rights movement was originally made for TV.

Freedom on My Mind (1994). A documentary based on the recollections often of civil rights veterans.

Not for Ourselves Alone: The Story of Elizabeth Cady Stanton and Susan B. Anthony (1999). A Ken Burns documentary about these two remarkable women.

The Intolerable Burden (2003) A black family enrolled eight of their children in an all-white school in Mississippi in 1965 under the school district's "freedom of choice" plan. They weren't expected to do that, as this documentary shows.

The Murder of Emmett Till (2003) The Mississippi murder of a black boy from the North in 1954 was a spark that ignited the civil rights movement.

The Native Americans (1994) A five-part documentary, with each part focusing on the native peoples of the various regions of the United States.

To Kill a Mockingbird (1962) and *In the Heat of the Night* (1967) These two Hollywood blockbusters show the racial climate in the southern states in the 1950s and 1960s. Starring Gregory Peck and Sidney Poitier, respectively.

Electronic Resources

www.naacp.org
The Web site of the NAACP, the largest and oldest civil rights organization, has links to discussions of policy issues and information about the organization and its mission.

www.census.gov/statab/www
Updated annually, the Statistical Abstract of the United States provides information about the state of the American people, their incomes, family structures, occupations, and many other characteristics. It includes detailed information about individual ethnic and racial groups as well as men and women.

www.americanwest.com/pages/indians.htm
This site provides information about Native Americans and their cultures and links to various tribal home pages.

oyez.nwu.edu
You can read important civil rights cases online here, accessed by name or by topic.

wwwsecure.law.cornell.edu/topics/ civil_rights.html
This page provides much useful information regarding civil rights.

www.yforum.com
Are there questions about blacks or whites, or Latinos or Asians, that you have never understood? Post your questions and have people from those communities respond.

www.leofranklynchers.com/leofranklynchers.html
This Web site addresses the lynching of a Jew in Georgia in 1915 and documents the identity of some of those responsible.

InfoTrac College Edition

Search for the following articles in the InfoTrac database:

Bagenstos, Samuel R. "The Future of Disability Law," *Yale Law Journal* (October 2004).

Fleischmann, Andrew M. "Protecting Poor People's Right to Vote: Fully Implementing Public Assistance Provisions of the National Voter Registration Act," *National Civic Review* (Fall 2004).

Langham, Sylvia. "Sacred Cows? (The Success of the Feminist Movement and Gender Discrimination)," *Sociology Review* (February 2001).

Rubenfeld, Jed. "The Anti-Antidiscrimination Agenda (of the U.S. Supreme Court)," *Yale Law Journal* (March 2002).

For more articles, enter

"Race relations" in the Subject Guide;

"Feminism" in the Subject Guide

American Government Resources

Visit the Government Foundations section of the Wadsworth American Government Resources Web site (politicalscience.wadsworth.com/amgov) for a variety of tools to help you explore civil rights further. Included are simulations, video clips, Microcase exercises, and a wealth of other activities.

CHAPTER 16

ECONOMIC POLICY

The Internet has spawned many new businesses, including online retailers—
"e-tailers." Greater reliance on high technology spurred big productivity gains
in the 1990s.

Types of Economic Systems

Capitalism

Socialism and Communism

Mixed Economies

Government and the Economy

Popular Expectations

Economic Problems

Economic Tools

Using Economic Policy to Achieve
Political Goals

Current Issues

Tax Reform

Income Distribution

Deficit and Debt

Economic Growth and Job Creation

**Conclusion: Is Our Economic Policy
Responsive?**

Can the Country Afford a Permanent Tax Cut?

ou are Patty Murray, senior senator from Washington State. It is June 2002, and the Senate is trying to clear the deck for its summer recess. One item on the agenda is a permanent repeal of the estate tax, sometimes called the "death" tax because it is levied against inherited wealth. When a person dies, if the estate is not passed on to a spouse and if its value is $1 million or more, it is subject to a federal tax. Only the richest are subject to the estate tax; 98 percent of all estates are too small to be taxed. Half of all revenue generated by the tax comes from estates worth more than $5 million.[1]

Still, you are no fan of the estate tax. You sympathize with the Republicans' argument that the estate tax has ruined some family farms and mom-and-pop businesses.[2] So, you sponsored legislation to raise the exemption limit for farmers and small businesses and worked for partial or total repeal of the tax, just as you had promised in your campaigns. Two years ago, despite heavy opposition from your own party, you voted for a Republican bill that is now phasing out the tax over a ten-year period. But that law had a "sunset" provision—an expiration date—that will nullify the tax cut at the end of ten years if Congress does not reauthorize it. The bill you are looking at now would permanently abolish the estate tax. With control of both houses of Congress at stake in the upcoming midterm election, and President Bush's popularity riding high, the Re-

publicans are hoping to make permanent all tax cuts that were passed with time limits. The House leadership knows that some of these taxes (income, estate, marriage penalty, pension deductions, and so on) have broader support than others, so they decided to have a separate vote on each instead of presenting them in one all-or-nothing bill. They see the estate tax as the least popular of all taxes, and they believe they can get it through the Senate despite Majority Leader Tom Daschle saying he "will go all out to kill the legislation."[3]

Republicans believe they cannot lose on this issue. If enough Democrats vote with them, Republicans will get the credit for abolishing an unpopular tax; if the bill is killed, they can blame Democrats for "taxing the dead." You must decide whether to stick with your party as it heads into the election or to vote again for estate tax repeal.

You ran for the Senate as "the mom in sneakers." The daughter of a disabled veteran, you were a stay-at-home mom after college, only later returning to the workforce as a teacher. You served on the local school board and have made increased funding for education one of your major issues. You see the problems of women and children, and low- and middle-income families, especially rural families, as your special concern. In fact, you have started your own "Rural Initiative" to benefit Washington's rural residents.[4] Your state still has a number of family

"Can't we put in something about rich white guys don't have to pay taxes?"

farms and orchards, as well as many small high-tech start-ups.

But Washington State is also home to many multimillionaires, including Bill Gates and others made wealthy by the success of Microsoft. If the tax were repealed, these multimillionaires would be as free to transfer their wealth untaxed to the next generation as would the owners of family farms and businesses. However, Bill Gates's father, the president of the Gates Foundation, has repeatedly stated his support for retention of the estate tax. But for every Mr. Gates you have a constituent who says that estate taxes ruined the family farm or mom-and-pop business by forcing its sale to pay taxes.

One of the reasons the estate tax has so few active supporters is its depiction as a tax on the dead and a double billing on wealth that had been taxed during a person's lifetime. But the dead cannot be taxed, and spouses of the deceased are exempt from the tax. The loss is to heirs who in many cases did not contribute to earning the wealth. That is because most inherited wealth does not come from family farms and mom-and-pop businesses; it comes from stocks, bonds, and nonfarm real estate. At the time the phaseout bill passed two years ago, 96 percent of all farm estates were not worth enough to be subject to estate tax. And family-owned farms and businesses already have a higher exemp-

tion than other estates; if it were raised by just another half million or so, virtually no family-owned farm would ever pay an estate tax.

Most Democrats had opposed the ten-year phaseout, just as they now oppose making it permanent. They point out that eliminating the tax would benefit only the wealthiest Americans, widen the income gap, and substantially reduce federal revenues. Democrats had argued then that the best use of the surplus was to reduce the nearly $6 trillion national debt and to bolster Social Security reserves so that when the economy slowed or took a downturn, as it always does after a boom period, the federal Treasury would be prepared. There was nothing put away for an emergency. Congress had gambled on the tax cuts stimulating economic growth and generating new revenues.

But the phaseout passed in a presidential election year when the budget was in surplus and Congress was sprinkling benefits and tax breaks everywhere. Now conditions are very different: the economy is faltering, and the costs of the war against terrorism coupled with billions in lost revenue from all the tax cuts have sent the federal budget into deficit. Forty-five of the fifty state budgets are in deficit, and most states that have an inheritance tax get a percentage of the federal tax.

Revenue losses during the decade of estate-tax phaseout are expected to be $135 billion, and five times that during the following decade if the cut is made permanent—all to benefit the wealthiest 2 percent of the country.[5] And this does not count further losses from the Bush income tax cuts, also weighted toward the highest income groups, which constitute the biggest tax reduction in two decades.[6]

You are not up for reelection until

2004, so your vote on the permanent repeal will not be an issue this November. You probably could go against your party's leadership with little political fallout. You have shown that you can win without much help from the national party: in your last race, you ran eight percentage points better than Clinton had in 1996, winning Microsoft's hometown of Seattle with 63 percent of the vote. But the Senate Democrats have treated you well. You received good committee assignments, and although you are still a junior member of the Senate with only a few years' prior legislative experience in your state's senate, you were given a role in the Senate's minority leadership. After your big 1998 win, you were named vice chair of the Democratic Senatorial Campaign Committee, and now you are a deputy whip. You think that the confidence the party has shown in you might deserve, even require, loyalty on a partisan vote. And if Daschle decides to run for president in 2004, there will be openings in the Senate leadership. Going against the party on one of its bread-and-butter issues will not win you any support in the party caucus.

A vote with the Republicans will help guarantee huge revenue losses at a time of budget deficits, thereby undermining your position as a fiscal moderate and supporter of balanced budgeting. And you would be putting more money in the pockets of the wealthiest Americans, few of whom support your party. You have criticized the Republicans for offering so many new benefits without "debate on how tax cuts fit in with our long-term budget goals . . . , reducing the national debt . . . and extending the long-term solvency of Social Security and Medicare."[7] Nevertheless, you have stated your opposition to the tax countless times, and that is how you have voted every time the issue has come to the floor. Can you reverse your position now?

Do you stick with your party and call it a vote for fiscal responsibility, or do you vote for permanent repeal and defend it as support for small farms and businesses?

How do you vote?

Americans pride themselves on their free market economy. Yet when economic problems occur, they want government to do something. The degree to which government should be involved in the economy is a perennial source of conflict. Only a few people believe government should not be involved at all. Most agree that government has to levy taxes in order to pay for national security and the infrastructure (roads, bridges, rails, waterways) that make interstate commerce possible. Most also believe that businesses should not be free to use publicly owned resources for private profit without government regulation, and that government should prevent a concentration of economic power that stymies competition, fixes prices, and endangers consumer and worker safety. Despite broad consensus on points such as these, there is much honest disagreement about how far government should go in regulating the economy to stimulate or slow growth or to alter the distribution of wealth.

Types of Economic Systems

Capitalism

The role of government in the economy largely determines the kind of economic system a country has. An economy in which individuals and corporations own its capital goods or productive capacity—businesses, factories, and farms—is called a **capitalist economy,** or sometimes a free market, free enterprise economy.

In a pure capitalist economy, prices, profits, working conditions, and wages would be totally determined by private sector decisions rather than by the government. Manufacturers would sell goods at what the market could bear, pay workers as little as possible, and manufacture products as cheaply as possible, concerned with health and safety only to the extent dictated by individual morality and the necessity to maintain consumer loyalty.

The idea that a capitalist economy would promote prosperity was popularized in 1776 by the British economist Adam Smith in *The Wealth of Nations*.[8] In his view, as each person seeks to maximize his or her own economic well-being, the collective well-being is enhanced. Businesses become more efficient, sell more at lower costs, hire more workers, and hence promote the economic well-being of the workers as well as the owners. Smith spoke of the "invisible hand" of the marketplace bringing about these positive outcomes.

Socialism and Communism

Socialism, in theory, is an economic system in which a country's productive capacity is under the collective ownership and control of the people. In real socialist systems, however, it has been the state that controls capital goods and production and has the power to set wages and determine the supply of, and demand for, goods.

There have been many well-known theorists of socialism, but none so famous as Karl Marx. He was even better known for his writings on communism; perhaps this is why *socialism* is often used interchangeably with *communism*. But in theory, communism is a more advanced form of economic organization than socialism. Collectively owned economic units would also become self-governing, and the need for formal government or "the state" would disappear. No country that called itself communist ever came close to achieving this utopian goal. In fact, in those countries labeled communist, the state grew large and became increasingly more invasive in the economy and in its citizen's private lives.

At the core of the debate between capitalists and socialists is intense disagreement about how much control government should have over the economy and the consumption and work habits of its citizens. Sometimes in American public debate, one candidate will accuse another of supporting "socialism"; in this context, socialism is often just a synonym for something a person does not like, especially bigger government.

Mixed Economies

In practice, there are no pure capitalist or socialist systems, and there never have been. In the United States, for example, government owns power-generating dams, some railroads, and 27 percent of all land, and it acts as an insurer of individual and corporate assets. It has loaned money to corporations to save them from bankruptcy and it has bailed out large banks in danger of failing. In other modern societies, such as Great Britain, France, Sweden, Germany, and the former communist nations of Eastern Europe, it is not unusual for government to own airlines, television networks, and telephone systems.

"There, there it is again—the invisible hand of the marketplace giving us the finger."

Just as all capitalist nations have socialist components, socialist nations have capitalist aspects. Even before the reforms of the late 1980s, which led to socialist governments being swept away across Eastern Europe, most of these nations found it useful to tolerate or even encourage private enterprise, and some countries, such as Hungary, had quite large private economies.

Most countries, then, have a **mixed economy.** Some are more capitalist, others more socialist, but all have elements of both. Government plays a large role in the economies of most mixed systems. For example, government directly influences the behavior of business and industry through regulation and taxation. Even Adam Smith believed there was some role for government intervention in a capitalist system, such as to ensure conditions for fair competition in the marketplace.

Our own system is a mixture of private enterprise and government ownership combined with considerable government intervention through taxation and regulation (see Chapter 18). In nineteenth-century America, government involvement in the economy was much less than it is today. Initially, we moved toward a more active economic role for government because of abuses by big business in the late nineteenth century: child labor was widely used, workers were paid a pittance, filthy and unsafe working conditions (as suggested by the term *sweatshop*) led to thousands of workers' deaths from industrial accidents, food and drugs were often unsafe, and the markets for some products came to be dominated by a few large producers who controlled prices and wages. Public anger led to increased government regulation of wages, working conditions, content of food and drugs, and more.

Government also intervenes in the economy by taxing and spending. Budget policies can make the rich richer and the poor poorer, or it can make the poor better off at the expense of the rich. Most Western democracies have fairly elaborate social welfare systems that redistribute some wealth from the rich to the poor in order to provide them with a minimal standard of living. In the United States, we do less of this than do most other industrialized nations.

Despite our mixed economy, we have a very individualistic, capitalistic ethic. The idea that individuals, not government, should provide services and that government should be small influences a wide range of public policies. The belief that individuals are poor because of their own failings limits our sense of responsibility to provide support for low-income families. The idea that private business is inherently self-regulating makes it difficult to enact higher standards for worker health and safety. The belief that private profit is not only the most important goal of business, but perhaps the only one, means that those fighting to protect the environment from abuse by both industry and consumers must either defeat or find compromise with powerful lobbies.

Government and the Economy

Our Constitution specifies only a little about the nature of our economic system. It emphasizes private property rights and gives government monetary, taxation, and regulatory powers. By contrast, the governments of most other mixed and socialist economies, whether democracies or dictatorships, have constitutions that link their political system to a form of economic organization and give government major responsibilities for achieving economic goals.

Economic distinctions between capitalism and socialism are not necessarily linked to gradations in democracy. Capitalist systems are not inevitably democratic. The most democratic systems in the world are mixed economies with strong elements of capitalism (such as Sweden, Britain, and Denmark), but many capitalist systems have been undemocratic: South Africa under white rule is one example; the United States is another. The United States was capitalist well before it was a democracy. Most blacks could not vote until after the Civil War. Then Southern blacks were disenfranchised until the Voting Rights Act in 1965. Women could not vote in most places until 1920.

Some argue that evolution toward democracy is inevitable in capitalism because the economic power that individuals gain as workers and consumers will, over time, lead to their political empowerment. The same argument is made in socialist theory, although socialists do not believe that voting alone is an adequate form of empowerment.

Wherever one believes power resides, there is an undeniable tension between capitalism and democracy,

"I've noticed our tax system tends to favor bigger, meaner citizens."

just as there is between socialism and democracy. The capitalist marketplace rewards and encourages inequities that, if unchecked, threaten democratic beliefs about individual equality. For example, capitalist systems place no upper limits on the accumulation of wealth, even though wealth can be used to buy greater access to decision makers. The potential for greater exercise of influence by the wealthy weakens the concept of one person, one vote.

Socialist doctrine argues for common ownership and equality in wages, but, in practice, most socialist systems have tolerated significant disparity in the overall standard of living as well as enormous inequities in the overall distribution of power. Although socialist theory advocates democratic control by workers, in countries such as China and the former Soviet Union, the Communist Party has used its dictatorial powers to deny individual freedom.

Governments and economies are inevitably intertwined, and it is equally true that power is always dispersed among public and private institutions and the people. The nature of that relationship determines the nature of government. In systems where most power is concentrated in the government and in those where it is concentrated primarily in the hands of the corporate elite, democracy will suffer. To exist, capitalism and socialism must prevent these concentrations of power. A lopsided maldistribution of wealth eventually will produce inequality of access and the loss of any meaningful practice of political equality. This is why in democratic capitalist systems, government develops its power to regulate economic activity and continues to exercise it.

Popular Expectations

Economic cycles of boom and bust have been one of the constants of human history. Good times with rising living standards are followed by bad times when harvests are poor, economic activity slows, investment income declines, people go hungry, unemployment is rife, and living standards decline. Until modern times, governments did little to regulate these cycles, although some tried to ease the consequences of the bad times by distributing grain to people who were starving or by providing temporary shelters for the homeless. In the United States, it was not until the 1930s that government tried, through economic policies, to prevent these cycles from occurring.

The idea that government intervention could ease the boom-and-bust cycle of the economy was revolutionary. Classical economists had argued that the market would adjust itself without government action. But in democratic societies, as government became larger and more powerful, people expected government at least to try to alleviate economic problems. Since the Great Depression, government has almost always been linked in the public mind to poor performance by the economy, whether or not government's policies contributed much to the failures. It is still possible that government will

During the energy crisis of the 1970s, motorists had to wait in line to fill up. When gasoline prices soared in 2004, motorists may have thought they were paying an arm and a leg but, adjusted for inflation, gasoline was cheaper than during the 1970s crisis and consumption was basically unaffected.

In Germany in 1923, inflation was so high that a basket of money barely sufficed to buy a few groceries. This hyperinflation was caused by the German government's printing ever more money to pay penalties they were assessed by the victors of World War I. The government finally ended the inflation by issuing new currency, one unit of which was equal to one trillion of the old. This made the lifetime savings of many people worthless.

receive little or no credit for a robust economy, but the president and Congress will certainly try to take credit for it.

Government can have an impact on some of the economic problems of greatest concern to the average citizen—unemployment, interest rates and inflation, the high cost of food and gasoline, fair employment practices, minimum wage, and barriers to trade. But it cannot do as much as many people have come to expect because much of the decision-making power lies in the private sector. Still, most Americans look to the government as an ally during hard times.

Economic Problems

One of the familiar economic problems that modern government is expected to do something about is unemployment. Even in a "full employment" economy, several percent of the labor force will be out of work—people who quit their jobs to look for something better, those just entering the workforce, those unable to work, and those who do not want to work for one reason or another. But most Western countries experience periods when there are many people unemployed because the economy does not create enough jobs.

A **depression** is a period of prolonged high unemployment. During the Great Depression (1929–1939), over one-quarter of the American working population was without jobs. A second recurring economic problem is **inflation**—a condition of increasing prices dur-

ing which wages and salaries do not keep pace with the price of goods. As the dollar declines in value, there is little incentive to save and great incentive to borrow. In the late 1950s and early 1960s, inflation in the United States was quite low, as little as 2 or 3 percent a year, but the Vietnam War and the high cost of imported oil during the early 1970s stimulated a sharp rise in inflation. It was not until the 1990s that inflation returned to pre–Vietnam War levels.

Though some economists believe moderate inflation is not a bad thing,[9] many people feel threatened by it. It erodes the value of savings and gives people an incentive to consume rather than save. Bankers hate inflation because the dollar paid back to them in the future is going to be worth less than the dollar they lend today. Inflation drives interest rates up as banks charge higher and higher interest to compensate for the declining value of the dollar. Credit becomes more expensive, which makes it difficult for businesses and industries to expand. And, of course, inflation is bad because people think it is bad—they worry about it getting out of control.

A third economic problem is stagnant production—that is, the failure of the economy as a whole to produce increasing amounts of goods and services. Two or more consecutive quarters (a quarter is three months) of falling production are termed a **recession.** During the peak of the recession in 1981–1982, over 10 percent of the American workforce was unemployed, and many others had only part-time work or had simply quit looking for work. In 2001, the United States went into

Keynesians believe that government intervention can be effective both in steering the economy and in cushioning the blow to consumers of a sluggish or overheated economy. Supply-siders believe that taxing and spending for these purposes are inappropriate and inefficient uses of government powers. They believe it is better to leave as many decisions on spending and investing, and as much money as possible, in the hands of consumers.

Supply-side economics, as implemented by Reagan's economic team and continued by George H. Bush's administration (despite Bush having labeled it "voodoo economics"), led to disillusionment with the policy. It created record-smashing budget deficits. Dramatically increased spending for the military combined with small cuts in spending for social programs and the loss of billions of dollars in tax revenues left the country with $2.5 trillion of new debt.

Monetary Policy

Whereas fiscal policy affects the economy through spending and taxation decisions, **monetary policy** attempts to regulate the economy through control of short-term interest rates and the supply of money. Monetary policy is made by the Federal Reserve Board (the Fed), composed of a board of governors, twelve Federal Reserve Banks located in major cities around the country, and the Federal Open Market Committee (FOMC).[12] The FOMC meets several times a year to determine monetary policy. Since 1978, its primary mandate from Congress has been to achieve price stability and full employment (full employment is considered achieved when the unemployment rate falls somewhere between 5 and 6.5 percent).

The Federal Reserve Board is largely, but not completely, independent of the president. Fed members are appointed by the president, with Senate consent, but their terms are fourteen years. The terms are staggered in such a way that, barring resignations, the maximum number any president could appoint in a four-year term is two. Another factor that helps maintain the independence of the Fed is that it does not depend on Congress for funding; its operating costs come out of the more than $20 billion in annual interest earned on its holdings of U.S. government securities. The chair, however, serves only a four-year term, although reappointment is possible and often happens. The relatively short-term appointment opens the door to influence by Congress and the president, especially when the Fed chair wants to be reappointed. The current chair, Alan Greenspan, is an adept Washingtonian serving an unprecedented fifth term and known for his ability to cultivate members of Congress and the cabinet.[13]

The role of the Fed as governing body of the nation's central banking system is crucial. As Will Rogers once said, "There have been three great inventions since the beginning of time: fire, the wheel, and central bank-

© Matt Mendelsohn/CORBIS

Many people gave Federal Reserve Board chair Alan Greenspan much of the credit for the economic boom of the 1990s, but his reputation was dented by his easy acceptance of Bush tax cuts that led to new levels of deficit spending after 2001.

ing!" The Fed is *the* bank for the federal government; it distributes our currency, supervises and regulates some national banks, and acts as clearinghouse for many of the checks written on those banks. But from the standpoint of the overall health of the economy, its most important work is using its monetary powers to maintain a balance between demand for and supply of currency.[14]

In the nineteenth century when government spending was low and fiscal policy was not yet a major factor in the economy, "tight" money was often the main issue in elections. Today, when most people are more focused on the federal budget, you may think monetary policy is too dry a subject to bother with, but if you think of what it actually determines—interest rates and the availability of money—you will quickly see why it is important to your well-being and why it can have a dramatic impact. In 1982, for example, when the Fed tightened the money supply, forcing interest rates, unemployment, and bankruptcies up, one man entered the offices of the Fed and tried to kill its chair.[15] Other groups drew up "wanted" posters for the board members. And still others, thrown out of work or off their farms, committed suicide. When interest rates are low, as they have been in recent years, the average person (although not business) focuses less on what the Fed is doing.

Today, the chair of the Federal Reserve Board is one

of the most powerful people in the country. The chair is required by law to give testimony to Congress twice a year on monetary policy, but Greenspan, nicknamed "the Maestro," and the most visible head the Fed has ever had, averages a dozen appearances before congressional committees and fifteen public speeches each year. His comments on the state of the economy can cause the stock market to soar or plummet.

The Fed controls the supply of money in several ways. It can buy and sell hundreds of millions of dollars of treasury notes and bonds. When it buys, it pumps money into other banks; when it sells, it depletes the money reserves of the banks and thus takes money out of the economy. The Fed also changes the interest rates it charges banks to borrow its money. Low interest rates stimulate borrowing and put more money into the economy. As a last resort, the Fed can increase or decrease the amount of reserves (cash on hand) it requires banks to have. If the reserve requirement is increased, banks take money out of circulation to build up their reserves. If the reserve requirement is decreased, banks take money out of their reserves and lend it to customers, which increases the money supply.

When the Fed makes money scarce, interest rates go up, and businesses and industries find it harder to borrow money for expansion. As a result, production and inflation may slow. When the Fed allows more money into the economy, interest rates go down, making it easier for businesses to borrow for expansion. The Fed's influence grew in the 1980s as huge budget deficits limited the options available to the president and Congress to stimulate or slow the economy through taxing and spending. With little flexibility left in fiscal policy, monetary policy was the principal means for fine-tuning the economy. Even in the late 1990s, Wall Street and business continued to look on monetary policy as the primary means for stimulating growth and productivity as well as for slowing the economy when it became overheated. This is the view favored by *monetarists,* who believe that if government has to intervene in the economy, it should do so through monetary, not fiscal, policy.

Monetary policy is made primarily to protect the value of currency and ultimately to protect investors. Fiscal policy is geared more toward protecting the average consumer against unemployment and the effects of inflation (rather than toward *preventing* inflation). While many people are both investors and consumers, and while fiscal and monetary policy should be complementary and not at odds, at times they may seem to be at cross-purposes.

To see how this works, we can look at the fiscal policy of the Clinton administration and the monetary policy of the Fed under Greenspan's chairmanship. Clinton came into office with the goal of "growing" the economy and increasing the real wages of workers. Primar-

ily a politician, his eye was on the earning and buying power of the average voter. As protector of the currency, Greenspan did not want to see Clinton achieve his goals through a too-rapid expansion of the money supply or by wage increases that were too precipitous. Primarily a banker, Greenspan's eye was on investors.

During Clinton's first two years in office, the growth rate soared, 5.5 million new jobs were created, and inflation stayed at or below 3 percent. But as the unemployment rate fell toward 6 percent and then below it, the Fed began imposing a series of interest rate hikes.

Greenspan also started jawboning (see the section "Persuasion, or Jawboning" later in this chapter), trying to slow the economy and offset a rise in inflation. Although it is arguable whether the impact of monetary policy can be felt so quickly, by early 1995, the rate of growth did slow and unemployment rose for the first time in two years.

To a large extent, the concerns of the Fed and the Clinton administration should have overlapped. In an era of flat wages, workers did not want higher prices, and Clinton certainly would not have wanted to take the rap for high inflation and a devalued dollar. On the other hand (remember that expression?), most workers would rather have a job and higher prices than have no job and stable prices, especially in an era of decreased spending for welfare. And while no politician may claim to favor it, the devalued dollar can lead to more exports, and more exports can mean more jobs.

In addition to the difference in the priorities of fiscal and monetary policymakers, accountability is also an issue. If greater power to regulate the economy *has* gravitated toward monetary policymakers, it has passed into the hands of men and women who are not directly accountable to voters and who most Americans cannot identify. Adding to the Fed's lack of short-term accountability is its ability to escape openness-in-government rules that apply to other federal agencies. Some consider the Fed under Greenspan's leadership far more open than it was in the past because of the frequency of his public appearances and pronouncements on Fed policy, but Greenspan also uses his power to protect the agency from oversight. On his own authority, in reaction to a House Banking Committee demand to see transcripts of a Fed meeting, he ordered some Fed proceedings not to be taped, even though the committee was well within its oversight rights in requesting the minutes. Furthermore, Greenspan has ruled that the only transcripts of Fed meetings that will ever be available to archives, and hence to the public, will be versions edited by Fed staff.[16] It is not likely that any other agency head could exercise this kind of power with respect to Congress.

Of all federal agencies, the Fed is the most independent as well as the most powerful. In part, this stems from the fact that it never needs to go to Congress to justify a budget. But the Fed can do more with its money than pay its own operating costs. On its own authority, it can extend billions of dollars in credits and loans to businesses, other banks, and even to foreign countries. During the 1995 financial crisis in Mexico, the Clinton administration wanted to make a loan quickly to avoid the crisis spreading to other countries, but it found the Treasury without enough money and Congress unwilling to approve the loan. So Clinton went to the Fed, which used its own funds to loan Mexico $50 billion—something it can do *without* congressional approval. In this case, the initiative came from the White House, but it is part of the Fed's responsibilities to make independent decisions on loans and credits. Because it can act independently, it can act quickly, and it can have a significant impact on the economy without the public ever being aware of its actions. After 9/11, for example, the Fed, fearing a possible economic meltdown, freed up currency and extended billions of dollars in credits and loans to businesses.

Regulating Business

A third formal power government has to manage the economy is regulation. Government's constitutional and statutory authority to regulate interstate commerce, make trade policy, provide for the common welfare, and ensure equal opportunity provides broad legal ground for regulating economic activity. Government regulates the banking industry, the stock market, hiring practices, industrial pollution, food and product safety, and, through licensing and special concessions, mediates competing claims for use of public property such as the airwaves, airspace, mineral resources, and timberland. And the federal government's stewardship of millions of acres of wilderness, forest, and grazing areas and wetlands has an impact on climate and agricultural production.

The impact on market efficiency and economic growth from government regulation is one of the most controversial aspects of any administration's economic policy. The debate over how much regulation is necessary, and which economic behavior should be regulated, is usually centered on whether government action fosters or inhibits investment and economic growth and how its obligation to protect public health and safety weighs against business needs. In Chapter 9, we saw the far-flung consequences of government's deregulation of many aspects of the financial industry, and the link between regulation and campaign donations of regulated industries. Regulatory policies are so extensive and have such far-reaching effects that they are dealt with in a separate chapter (see Chapter 18).

Persuasion, or Jawboning

The government, and the president in particular, has an informal means for affecting the economy—trying to persuade businesses or individual consumers to behave in a certain way. *Jawboning,* or persuasion, can make a difference because psychological factors affect economic behavior. For example, economists recognize the importance of consumer confidence—that is, the degree of optimism individuals have about the economy. Confidence is rooted in the real performance of the economy, but sometimes there is a lag between the economy's performance and consumers' perception of its health.

A president can try to persuade businesses to expand or consumers to spend, for example, by expressing his confidence in the country's economic direction. Lyndon Johnson was extremely skillful in persuading business and labor leaders to accept his economic policies, and Kennedy and Reagan were remarkably adept at persuading both business and the public. In contrast, Carter's calls for sacrifice to meet economic problems seemed to decrease consumer confidence, and George H. Bush's inability to convince the public that the country was coming out of recession in 1992 contributed to his defeat by Clinton.

Perhaps the most impressive feats of jawboning in recent years have come from Fed chairs. However, when the economy is in a prolonged period of expansion, as it was during the 1990s, and consumer confidence is very high, the Fed chair's persuasive powers are not as strong. At those times the economy seems to run on its own momentum. In 1999, when Greenspan tried to cool what he saw as a dangerously overheated economy by accusing investors in the stock market of "irrational exuberance" and threatening new interest rate hikes, his comments produced only a short-term flurry of activity, and the stock market continued to climb.[17]

Using Economic Policy to Achieve Political Goals

Democrats and Republicans differ in their use of fiscal and regulatory policies to influence economic growth, employment, cost of living and disposable income, and consumer and environmental safety. There are fewer differences over monetary policy because, although not free from partisan influence, it is not directly controlled by elected officials. It is not uncommon for a Fed chair appointed by a Democrat to be retained by a Republican (Paul Volcker, for example), or one appointed by a Republican to be retained by a Democrat (Alan Greenspan, for example).

However, even in monetary policy, partisanship can be significant. Greenspan, a Republican, worked collaboratively with President Clinton, but his conservative Republican leanings led him to pull his punches in discussing Bush tax cuts. These tax cuts threw the economy into a massive deficit of the sort that Greenspan would have probably spoken out against had a Democrat been in office.

Historically, conservatives and Republicans have

been more tolerant of high unemployment than liberals and Democrats have been. The Democratic Party's political base has more to fear from unemployment than does the Republican base. Republicans are less tolerant than liberals and Democrats of high inflation rates. Again, the Republican base of business and finance interests is more sensitive to inflation than are working- and middle-class taxpayers. Democrats are also more supportive of government regulation for consumer and environmental protection and to correct inequities in the marketplace, while Republicans have been more supportive of tax cuts and deregulation of business. Again, these reflect the priorities of the people supporting each party.

Republicans were long considered more committed to fiscal prudence and balanced budgets than spending on health and safety and income support. In the Reagan and both Bush administrations, however, deficits ballooned and government spending increased.

The shift in spending that occurs when control of Congress changes hands shows that both parties adhere to the old adage "To the victor go the spoils." In the early 1990s when Democrats were in the majority, on average $34 million more per year was spent in Democratic congressional districts than in Republican congressional districts. After Republicans assumed control in 1995, spending shifted from urban and poor rural areas to suburban and farm counties until by 2001, $612 million more was being spent in Republican congressional districts than in Democratic congressional districts. While spending increased in all districts during these years, it rose by 52 percent in Republican districts compared to 34 percent in Democratic districts.[18]

There is little difference between parties, either in Congress or the White House, in their willingness to adjust economic policy during election years.[19] Cuts in government spending and increases in taxes reduce real personal income, so budget cuts and tax increases are unlikely in election years. And congressional spending on pork-barrel projects almost always increases in election years.

The prediction before the 2002 and 2004 elections of multiyear budget deficits did not stop Congress from proposing additional tax cuts or making permanent existing tax breaks. Democrats and Republicans vied for the leading role in providing a prescription drug benefit to seniors, who not only vote in large numbers, but also are represented by one of the country's most powerful interest groups, the AARP (formerly the American Association of Retired Persons). (See the "You Are There" sections in Chapters 6 and 7.) Congress also approved billions for pork-barrel projects and highway construction in their districts, and the districts that seemed the least likely targets received a huge proportion of the funds.

Monetary policy is also subject to election year pres-

sures. During a campaign when the economy is the central issue, there is enormous potential for politicization of the Fed despite its independence. In the summer before the 1992 election, following a jump in the unemployment rate, the Fed lowered its prime lending rate (in an attempt to increase borrowing and thus consumer and business spending). President Bush had publicly demanded such a reduction just several days earlier. His secretary of the Treasury was accused of pressuring the Fed's chair (Greenspan) to lower rates even further as a condition of his renomination for another term.[20] Although Bush denied placing any condition on Greenspan's renomination, he reportedly blamed the Fed chair for his 1992 reelection loss. But the Fed chair does not have to listen to the president.

Greenspan treated Bush's son, George W., better. Having advised Clinton throughout his administration of the need to hold down spending and end budget deficits, Greenspan was very receptive to the huge tax cuts passed in George W. Bush's administration, even though the cuts clearly contributed to huge budget deficits from 2002 through 2005. The explanation for this double standard, according to longtime Fed watchers, lay in Greenspan's politics: he was not so much an opponent of deficit spending as he was of spending for social programs—education, health, and welfare. Because higher amounts of social spending are more likely in a Democratic than Republican administration, Greenspan urged Clinton to avoid deficit spending, while later accepting Bush's increased spending on tax cuts and defense without comment. Although in private Greenspan told Bush's first Treasury Secretary Paul O'Neill that the tax cuts should have had a trigger mechanism that would have reversed them if the budget fell into deficit, he never said so publicly. Instead, in keeping with his opposition to social spending, Greenspan called for "program read-

justments" in Social Security.[21] In 2004, Bush reappointed him to a fifth term.

The economy has an impact on the vote, although it is not as simple as one might suspect. Those who have studied the impact of economic hard times on individual vote choices have reported that how people feel they are doing compared to a year or two before does have a mild influence on their presidential and congressional voting choices. If they feel things are improving, they are somewhat more likely to favor the incumbent; if they believe their financial situation is eroding, they are somewhat more likely to vote against the incumbent.

Voters are more concerned, however, with the state of the overall economy than with their own family's situation. But they do not seem to respond decisively to changes in unemployment or inflation levels. The 1994 congressional election provided evidence for this. With the economy strong and unemployment low, voters were strongly anti–status quo, expressing deep pessimism over the country's future.[22] But in 1998, after four years of economic boom, the president's party gained seats in Congress for only the second time in the twentieth century.

Some observers believe the 1990s run of prosperity changed, if only temporarily, the economy's impact at the polls. Whereas in the past, a prolonged period of low unemployment, low inflation, and rising wages would have helped incumbents, it did not give Vice President Al Gore much of a lift in his 2000 presidential campaign. He had to emphasize other issues such as "family values," income inequality, and health care to catch up to Bush in the polls. The reason, some argue, is that people were doing so well that they took continued growth and near full employment for granted. Furthermore, factors other than government policy, such as individual hard work, are given credit for the good times. It is also possible that individuals did not credit government for economic gains. If voters adopt the view that most of the credit for economic good times lies outside the White House and Congress, for example, that they themselves were responsible for their success through savvy investments or that business is responsible through productivity growth, then incumbents will gain little at the polls in times of prosperity.[23] Gore did win the popular vote in 2000, but it was far closer than it would have been had economic conditions been the deciding factor in how people cast their ballots.

In leaner times, the economy is more likely to be a campaign issue. Incumbents can easily become scapegoats, deserved or not. Much depends on where voters place the economy in the constellation of issues that concern them and who they hold accountable. Private investment and the stock market received most of the credit for the boom of the 1990s and apparently absorbed all of the blame for the crash of 2002. In that year's congressional elections, voters did not punish elected officials for the deregulation of the financial industry that led directly to corporate fraud and business failure. Republicans gained seats in both the House and Senate.

Nor did a so-so economy hurt George W. Bush's bid for reelection. During wartime, domestic policy and the economy can take a backseat, and this worked to Bush's advantage in 2004. Going into the election the economy was only in marginally better shape than in 2002 from the standpoint of job creation. Bush was the first president since Herbert Hoover to have a net loss of jobs on his watch; his fiscal policy eradicated the budget surplus and created massive deficits. Those who thought the economy was the most important issue voted overwhelmingly for Senator John Kerry. Yet Bush was reelected with 51 percent of the vote because people put their concern about terrorism and the war in Iraq ahead of their anxiety about poor economic and fiscal performance. And his party again gained seats in the House and Senate.

Current Issues

Though debates over tax policy may seem arcane, and sometimes are, tax policy says a lot about who the winners and losers in society are.

Tax Reform

Tax policy is always on the agenda. There are many reasons for trying to revise or reform the tax code: to simplify it, to achieve greater fairness, to increase revenue to pay for new spending or to balance the budget, or to decrease revenue as a way of downsizing government or to stimulate the economy in periods of sluggish growth. Reagan's huge tax cuts of the early 1980s were intended to stimulate the economy and to decrease government spending in favor of private investment. Clinton's tax legislation targeted fairness and deficit reduction. George W. Bush focused on cutting taxes primarily for the rich, but a little for other income groups as well. None of these tax policies—Reagan's, Clinton's, and Bush's—made the system simpler.

President Franklin D. Roosevelt once said that our tax code "might as well have been written in a foreign language," and the laws are dozens of times more complex now. The complexity occurs because tax policy is used to achieve a variety of social goals. Congress wants to help families with both parents working to have adequate care for their children, so it allows credits for child care; it wants to encourage business growth, so it gives credits and deductions for investment. (A *deduction* is the amount taxpayers have spent for some item, such as mortgage interest or business equipment, that they are allowed by law to subtract from their income before

Domestic issues can take a back seat to foreign policy when the nation is at war. The war in Iraq and against terrorism overshadowed economic issues in the 2004 election. Here, members of the 101st Airborne Division wait to be deployed for the attack on Iraq in 2003.

AP/Wide World Photos

figuring their tax liability.) Congress believes that voluntary giving to charitable organizations is good, so it creates deductions for that, too. Congress wants to encourage people to buy homes and to stimulate new housing construction, so deductions are allowed for interest on mortgage payments. Though each of these and hundreds of other exemptions and deductions may be desirable, together they create a tax code that is difficult to understand and which favors wealthier Americans who are able to take advantage of more loopholes.

Tax Fairness

In tax language, "fairness" means spreading the tax burden among households according to their ability to pay. A tax structure based on the principle of wealthy and middle-income households paying higher percentages of their income in taxes than poorer households is called a **progressive tax.** A tax that requires the poor to pay proportionately more than those in middle- and upper-income brackets is a **regressive tax.**

The wealthiest Americans pay the largest share of income tax revenue because they have the largest share of the country's wealth. The top 1 percent, who account for about 17 percent of earned income, pay about 36 percent of all income taxes. The bottom 80 percent, who account for about 41 percent of earned income, pay about 17 percent of all income taxes.

However, payroll taxes are regressive. That is, the lower income groups have a larger proportion of their income withheld. The reason that payroll taxes disproportionately hit lower- and middle-income taxpayers is that earned income above $90,000 is not subject to the Social Security tax. Interest and dividend income is not taxed either, and this is primarily earned by wealthier

Americans. Social Security and Medicare taxes take, on average, about 9 percent of income (but much less for the wealthy) and are now almost as large a share of federal revenues as personal income taxes (see Figure 1). However, on retirement, the majority of workers get benefits well in excess of what they have had withheld in payroll taxes.

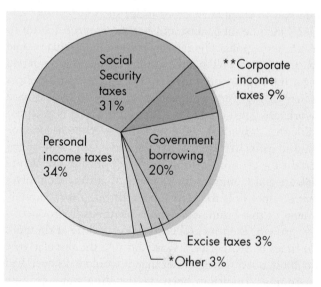

FIGURE 1 ■ Estimated Federal Revenue Sources, 2005† ($2 trillion)

*Customs duties; fines; penalties, Federal Reserve earnings, gift and estate taxes.

**Estimates made prior to 2004 corporate tax cuts.

†Does not include revenue from business activities such as park fees. This is subtracted from spending.

SOURCE: Derived from figures in the *Budget of the United States Government, Fiscal Year 2005* (Washington, D.C.: Government Printing Office, 2004). Note that these are all estimates. Overall spending is estimated to be slightly over $2 trillion, excluding the cost of the war in Iraq.

TABLE 1	Average After-Tax Income Gains, 1979–1997
The income gap between rich and poor has grown significantly in the past two decades.	
Top 1 percent	$414,200
Middle fifth	$3,400
Bottom fifth	−$100

SOURCE: Congressional Budget Office (analysis of data at www.cbpp.org).

By the end of the 1990s, the upper-income groups were receiving a larger percentage of (before-tax) national income than at any time since 1936.[24] Even while paying a higher percentage of their income in income taxes than less well off Americans, the after-tax income of the wealthiest 1 percent still grew by 157 percent from the late 1970s to the late 1990s, while that of the middle fifth grew by only 10 percent.[25] (See Table 1.) The impact of the Bush tax cuts made that inequality even greater, since those cuts favored the highest income groups.

Tax Burden

Americans think they are highly taxed, but compared to citizens in other developed countries, they are not. The *federal income* tax burden for most Americans has been falling since the 1990s. In 2001, a household with a median income of $64,600 paid about 7 percent of it in *income* taxes, the lowest amount since 1957.[26] Overall, in 2001, federal personal income, payroll, and other taxes (such as taxes on alcohol, gasoline, and cigarettes) took an average of 16.3 percent of the income of the middle fifth of American taxpayers.[27] This is the lowest percentage since the CBO began publishing such data.[28] Of course, most households pay state and local taxes in addition to federal taxes.

Tax Simplification

Many politicians talk about tax reform but few propose any significant changes. The Reagan and Clinton changes altered rates but not the basic code, and because they did not reduce deductions and loopholes, their changes offered no simplification of the system. George W. Bush's tax cuts were more radical in their size and their targeting of upper-income groups, but they made the code even more complex because of a vast array of new deductions and credits. Because Bush's estate, personal, and corporate tax cuts are phase in programs, they will require taxpayers to deal with different numbers and rules each year until 2010. Furthermore, Congress regularly approves "extenders" or special, limited-time tax breaks for business groups or other special categories of taxpayers. Each year Congress has to either suspend or renew them. All of this piecemeal legislating adds

thousands of pages to the tax code. To get a good idea of just how complex our tax system is, go to the IRS Web site (www.irs.gov), click on "Forms and Publications," and scroll through the vast array of forms that must be filed when claiming deductions.

Tax reform targeting simplification will have to come to grips with the system of deductions and not just focus on changes in the rate structure. There are four nominal personal income tax rates (not counting zero) ranging from 10 to 35 percent. The corporate tax rate is 34 percent. Sometimes people talk about these rates as if they do, in fact, reflect the share of income paid to the government. However, virtually no individual or corporation pays the nominal rates because of credits, exemptions, and deductions. We have already seen that the effective federal income tax rate (after deductions and exemptions) for the average household is about 7 percent. Similarly, no wealthy household pays 35 percent of its gross income in income tax. According to the 2003 tax returns released by President Bush and Vice President Cheney, both of whom are in the highest tax bracket, George and Laura Bush had $822,126 in taxable income and an effective tax rate of 27.7 percent, and Dick and Lynn Cheney had taxable income of $1,900,339 and an effective tax rate of 12.7 percent.[29] Other people in the top tax bracket have even lower effective tax rates because of the skill of their accountants and lawyers in sheltering their income. This is the complex part of the tax code—how taxable income is computed and what write-offs are available to which people. No reform that deals only with rates and ignores deductions can simplify that tax code or make it fairer (see Figure 2).

The same generalization applies to corporations. Many (perhaps as high as 61 percent) pay no tax at all, and others pay effective rates from 5 percent to 33 percent, depending on how they are able to use tax law to shelter or exempt profits.[30]

As long as there are deductions and loopholes to lower taxable income, the tax code, with its 17,500 pages of explanation for filling out more than 650 different forms, will continue to grow. In 1988 the average taxpayer spent seventeen hours and seven minutes filing a tax return; in 2004 it took twenty-eight hours and thirty minutes.[31] The rules are so Byzantine that a 2003 Treasury Department survey of IRS walk-in services found 43 percent of the questions received no answer or were answered incorrectly.[32]

Members of Congress seem happy with the complicated tax system, despite what many of them say. The complexity of the system and the tens of thousands of pages of tax codes mean that they can provide tax benefits to favored corporate and personal donors without much public scrutiny. Every budget bill contains hundreds of special exemptions, sometimes to individuals or individual corporations, or sometimes to a small class of them.

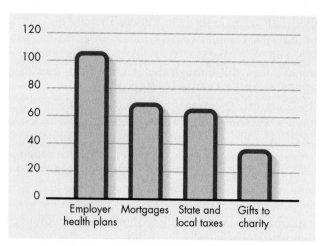

FIGURE 2 ■ Tax Deductions Mostly Benefit Middle- and Higher-Income Families *Billions of tax revenue dollars are lost through deductions, largely benefiting middle- and upper-class families. The figure shows total cost, in billions, of 2005 deductions for each category.*

SOURCE: "Estimates of Total Income Tax Expenditures," in *Analytic Perspectives on FY 2005 Budget of the United States* (Washington, D.C.: Government Printing Office, 2004), Table 18-1.

These giveaways are seldom debated, and each of them makes the tax code more complicated and less equitable.

Sixty percent of Americans favor a progressive tax system but the public also appears to favor a simple, more straightforward system. This is the attraction of single rate or form-free reform proposals.

Flat Tax

One set of proposals under consideration would abolish our present tax code and replace it with a **flat tax**—that is, a single rate for all income groups. One version of the flat tax proposed by a former member of the congressional leadership calls for a single rate of 17 percent for all Americans and the elimination of all deductions except for one large standard deduction of about $35,000 for a family of four. Its supporters argue that it would simplify the tax code, cut millions from the federal budget for IRS administration, and reduce the present U.S. 1040 form to a single-page or a postcard-sized form. Flat tax advocates believe that a progressive tax policy punishes people for earning more and creating wealth. They argue that fairness can be better achieved by requiring all Americans to pay the same proportion of their income to the government. Supporters also claim that with the large personal exemption, lower-income individuals would pay a smaller percentage of their income in taxes than under the present system and that there would be a *de facto* zero tax rate for an estimated ten million of the poorest Americans.

Though the tax rate is flat in theory, in practice it could be modestly progressive. For example, using a flat rate of 17 percent, those making less than $35,000 would

pay nothing; those making $135,000 would pay $17,000 (17 percent on $135,000 minus the $35,000 deduction), an effective rate of about 12.5 percent, and those making $1,035,000 would pay $170,000, or 17 percent of $1 million, an effective rate of 16.4 percent. Megamillionaires would pay close to the 17 percent rate. Middle-income taxpayers, those making $50,000 to $75,000, would pay effective rates of 5 percent to 9 percent. Most of the lowest income households are not subject to income tax now and, in fact, can qualify for an earned income tax credit. They could be worse off with a flat rate.

Moreover, many wealthy households would likely pay even less than their current effective tax rate and, depending on the flat rate set, the middle class could end up paying more. This is true because under the existing system, every taxpayer receives a standard deduction and a personal exemption amounting to more than $22,000 for a family of four, *without* itemizing any deductions. Since most middle-class families can deduct their home mortgage interest, health insurance and medical expenses, and IRA contributions, and claim education and child-care credits, they may have deductions greater than the single deduction allowed under some flat rate plans. And everyone would continue to have Social Security and Medicare taxes withheld, and also have to pay state and local taxes.

One major problem with the flat rate approach is that it is highly unlikely that Congress or the president would refrain from adding exemptions and deductions to the basic rate. All the special interests that now have a place in a tax code that is nominally progressive will also want a place in a code that is nominally flat. And exemptions and deductions would soon make a flat tax more regressive.

National Sales Tax

Another proposal is to replace the personal income tax with a national sales, or consumption, tax. Under this tax regime, our current tax code would be abolished and taxes would be levied on what we buy, not on what we earn. All but five states currently have their own sales tax, usually ranging from 4 to 7 percent. With a national sales tax, there would be no need to file a tax return because taxes would be paid as one spends, as with the state sales taxes.

A sales tax is very regressive because poor people spend a higher proportion of their income than do wealthy people, who can afford to invest a significant portion of their incomes. Purchases such as clothing, appliances, and cars take a much higher proportion of the incomes of poor and middle class than of wealthy families. And a regressive federal tax would compound the regressivity of state and local taxes. Citizens for Tax Justice estimates that the state and local tax burden for the richest families, nationwide, is 7.9 percent of their income; for middle-income families, 9.8 percent; and for the poorest families, 12.5 percent.[33] To reduce the regressivity of the tax, basic necessities, such as food, on which the lowest-income groups spend a high proportion of their earnings, would have to be exempt, as they are in many states.

A proposal for adoption of a national sales tax is now before Congress. It would abolish income, Social Security, Medicare, corporate, and estate taxes and replace them with a 30 percent tax on retail sales and many services, such as banking. As a replacement for all major sources of current revenue, a sales tax would have to produce staggering amounts to cover all federal outlays, which in 2005 were over $2 trillion.

Some analysts doubt that a 30 percent sales tax would produce the revenue needed. Such a tax might well need to be more than 50 percent of the purchase price or cost of service to recover all of the tax revenue eliminated by abolishing other taxes.[34] Remember that it would have to raise enough to cover Social Security payments at a time when millions of baby boomers will be retiring. If required to pay a tax on every purchase and many services, the bottom 80 percent of taxpayers could pay as much as 51 percent more than they are now paying in federal taxes.[35]

One solution to the regressivity of a sales tax is to adopt the approach taken in Great Britain and other European countries, where a value-added tax (VAT) is added to the purchase price of most goods and services, but in return citizens receive a vast array of government-funded social services, including health care, which reduces every household's out-of-pocket expenses. Because it would be difficult here to get approval for an increase in government services, it has been proposed that the sales tax be adopted in combination with an income tax on the highest earners. Income tax would be abolished for everyone else.[36] This is what income tax looked like before it was expanded to everyone to raise the money needed to fight World War II.

Progressivity, simplification, and balancing the budget without major cuts in social spending will be the focus of the battle over tax reform. At the outset of his second term, Bush said he was committed to reforming the tax code and was open to consideration of both flat and national sales tax proposals. But he has also said that certain deductions, such as for home mortgage and charitable contributions, are untouchable. He also said that he wants to eliminate income tax on capital gains and dividend income. Under these conditions, and with the rates proposed, flat tax and sales tax would almost certainly be too low to recover revenues that would be lost by abolishing the current tax code. Democrats would like to see the code simplified as well, but their primary objective in reform is to keep the tax structure progressive.

"The economy's never been better. Here's another potato!"

Income Distribution

One of the most contested areas of fiscal policy is the extent to which it should be used to redistribute wealth among income groups. The principal argument is whether government should help those at the lower end of the income spectrum through progressive taxation (placing a lower tax burden on middle- and lower-income families than on the wealthy), or through spending policies that provide heavily subsidized services to those who otherwise could not afford them.

Those who believe private property is the preeminent right in a capitalist society tend to oppose the use of fiscal policy to redistribute wealth downwards. Those who see a society of haves and have-nots, with relatively few in the middle, as inherently unstable and a threat to democracy are more supportive of taxing and spending to prevent extreme maldistribution of income. Since the passage of civil rights and affirmative action laws, the general perception is that our society is becoming progressively more democratic. But while the gap in equality before the law and access in the marketplace has been closing, the distribution of wealth is more unequal than at any time since World War II. What has caused income distribution to become so unbalanced and have government policies contributed to it?

The transition made in the 1980s and 1990s from a manufacturing economy toward one based on high-tech service industries is one reason for the growing gap between the rich and the rest. This transition had less to do

The American postwar economy lifted millions of families into middle-class status. At left is thirty-two-year-old Florence Thompson and her three daughters in 1936 after drought and the Depression drove them from Oklahoma to look for a better future in California. The family was living in a migrant labor camp and surviving on vegetables dug up from fields and birds the children killed. Publication of the photo prompted the government to send twenty thousand pounds of food to the camp, but by then the Thompsons had moved on. At right is the same family forty-three years later in Modesto, California, where Mrs. Thompson's children eventually were able to buy her a home. But before her last illness and death in 1983, they had to solicit contributions to pay for her medical care.

with government policy than with economic transition and globalization. It may be as important a transition as the one in the late nineteenth century from agriculture to manufacturing. Joseph Schumpeter, the famous twentieth-century economist, called such transitions "creative destruction" because they can produce great dislocation, including severe job loss and changes in the wage and salary structure, but over the long term can lead to a stronger economy.[37]

The transition period from the mid-1970s to the mid-1990s was a hard time for blue-collar workers. It had been a different story for their parents. From the post–World War II decades into the 1970s, family income grew over 3 percent a year.[38] Indeed, in 1966, a fifty-year-old man could look back over a ten-year period in the workforce and see that his income had risen over 30 percent. At the end of the 1980s, his son could look back over the same number of years and find his income had risen only 10 percent.[39] In real terms, blue-

collar workers were earning less than their parents did at a comparable age, and growth in living standards had nearly stopped.

There were fewer well-paying jobs for blue-collar workers than there had been twenty years earlier because heavy industries that traditionally paid high wages to unionized workers fell on hard times. Wage concessions were made by workers worried about job security and the unionized segment of the labor force dropped from 47 percent, where it had been in the postwar years, to 13 percent.[40] The decline of unions not only meant that workers lost economic clout, but it also meant that they lost political clout, since unions were an important part of the political coalition supporting progressive policies such as civil rights, health care reform, support for education, and other policies tied closely with equality and well-being.

During the last decade of the twentieth century it appeared that the country had completed the difficult transition. The United States experienced a remarkable nine years of low unemployment, economic growth, and low inflation. But the recovery was a song in two keys. From the standpoint of a job hunter, the economy looked good; jobs were plentiful, but income inequality increased dramatically and working people lost benefits. By 1995, of all men between the ages of twenty-five and thirty-four, 32 percent earned "less than the amount necessary to keep a family of four above the poverty line." Families needed two wage earners to maintain the old standard of living.[41] To the millions of uninsured Americans in low-paying jobs, a million immigrants, many of them poorly educated, were being added to the labor pool each year.

In 2000, families' net worth fell for the first time in fifty-five years.[42] Except for the most highly educated, the *lifetime* earnings of men have been declining for thirty years, while lifetime earnings' inequality between low- and high-skill workers has continued to increase over the same period.[43]

One development making it harder to narrow the wealth gap is that, even as the gap in lifetime earnings between high school– and college-educated workers continues to widen, it is becoming increasingly more difficult for poorer families to send their children to college. Education is the key to getting ahead in this economy, but aid for lower-income students is declining while tuition costs are rising in both public and private universities. The percentage of household income required to send a child to a four-year state school rose far faster for the poorest fifth of Americans than for middle- and upper-income groups. Yet in the competition for students, many universities no longer consider need as the primary factor in awarding grants and scholarships and the share of grants going to middle- and upper-income students is increasing. And government, too, is giving more student aid to rich, private colleges than to public institutions. In 2003, government's median aid per student to support low-interest college loans was $14.38, but Stanford got $211 and Dartmouth $174.[44]

As real wages were stagnating and the average income of the poorest fifth was falling, the average corporate executive was paid $11.9 million per year, earning more in one day than the average American worker earned in a year.[45] This is why the 1990s was labeled the "decade of greed." Yet the difference in total wealth is far greater than wages alone suggest, because those in the highest income brackets had money to save, invest in the stock market, and buy homes, which made it possible for them to take advantage of the real estate and stock booms of the 1990s in ways unavailable to those with little capital. The concentration of wealth and privilege (especially access to higher education in elite institutions) has become so pronounced that one observer refers to the formation of an "overclass."[46]

These trends deepened after Bush came to office, in large part due to tax policies, the failure to address health costs, and policies directed at increasing corporate rather than worker income. Health costs were rising far faster than inflation and businesses could not afford to pay as large a share of the premiums or they could not offer insurance at all.

In 2003, as the economy started to come out of the recession, median household income did rise but only enough to recover the losses of the two previous years. The share of GDP going to wage and salary income fell for fourteen straight quarters, something that has not happened since World War II. At the same time, the share of GDP going to corporate profits has been increasing.[47] Income losses in the private sector were compensated for by money from government. Sixty-two percent of income growth in 2002 and 2003 came from government in the form of tax cuts, Social Security, Medicare, veterans' benefits, unemployment insurance, and other subsidies. (This compares to 19 percent of income growth coming from government during Clinton's first term.)[48] Government is clearly not a sustainable source of income growth, even if we were not at war and the budget were not in deficit.

The Bush income tax cuts, which have been called "the most regressive in history," have also added to the income gap. The bottom 40 percent of taxpayers got 9 percent, while the top 1 percent got 34 percent of the benefits.[49] The rationale for this weighting of tax cuts is the standard supply-side argument that they will lead to greater business investment and stimulate growth. Early evidence suggests this did not happen. Overall, tax payments fell by $1.2 trillion dollars between 2001 and 2004, but investment increased by only $200 billion.[50] Economic growth picked up but very few jobs were created.

While the tax cuts did not produce any great increase in private sector jobs, it did further the twenty-two-year trend of after-tax income increasing much more rapidly for the wealthiest Americans than for middle- and lower-income households. The after-tax income of the top 1 percent of income earners rose 139 percent, for the middle fifth of income earners by 17 percent, and the bottom fifth of income earners by 8 percent (see also Table 1).[51]

The share of wealth (that is, all assets not just income) moving toward the top quintile has also increased. In 1973, the top one-fifth of households had 44 percent of U.S. income; in 2002, they had 50 percent. The share for the bottom fifth dropped from 4.2 percent to 3.5 percent.[52] We continue to have the most unequal distribution of wealth of any industrialized democracy.

Health insurance, higher education, and mortgages take increasingly larger shares of disposable income and many households have assumed huge debt burdens to provide health care and college educations for their children.[53] In 2004, Americans' collective debt ($8.8 trillion) was greater than the national debt and they spent a

"The Money Tree" © Winston Smith. Reprinted by permission

The booming economy of the late 1990s gave the illusion that money grows on trees, but many people were left in the dirt. The stock market crash of 2002 brought the rest back to reality.

higher percentage of their income on interest than the government does servicing its debt. Every 15 seconds, 24 hours a day, 365 days a year, someone files for bankruptcy. In 2004, more children lived through their parents' bankruptcies than lived through their divorces.[54]

Deficit and Debt

Another crucial economic issue is whether government should be allowed to spend more than it takes in. Should the government be required, as many states are, to balance its budget? If not, at what point does indebtedness become a drag on the economy?

A **budget deficit** occurs when federal spending exceeds federal revenues. The accumulation of money owed by the government from all budget deficits over time is the **national debt.** In the first quarter of fiscal 2005, the national debt stood at $7.5 trillion and was rising rapidly because of record-setting deficits in Bush administration budgets.

A balanced budget is generally regarded as sound policy in ordinary times. But the importance of a balanced budget fades during war and other hard times, such as recession or depression. The United States has weathered extraordinary periods of overspending—the Revolutionary, Civil, and Second World Wars all left the

country with huge debts that it managed to pay down. During the twelve years of the Reagan and George H. Bush administrations (1981–1992), $2.4 trillion dollars was added to the national debt. With the record spending in George W. Bush's first term, $1.5 trillion was added to the national debt.

The debt will continue to increase rapidly if the Bush tax cuts are made permanent, the war in Iraq continues, and discretionary social spending is not cut. In fact, the annual budget deficit is projected to reach $1.2 trillion in 2014. (See the box "Taxing and Spending Policies during Wartime" on page 576)

How Do We Get Such Huge Deficits?

Government officials typically project a rosy picture of revenues that exceed spending. Some of the gap between the projected surplus and the actual deficit is due to wishful thinking about revenues, or as it is called, errors in revenue projection. Another factor is unforeseen changes in the economy or external events, such as war, that may produce more spending than projected.

Predicting revenue is not a science, as much as we would like to think otherwise; it is rooted in political as well as economic considerations. To estimate accurately what revenues are likely to be and what outlays will be needed, budget writers have to project future rates of economic growth, inflation, unemployment, and productivity. With economic growth comes greater revenue from taxes. With economic slowdown, factories are idle, workers are laid off, tax revenues fall, and more money is needed for unemployment insurance, welfare support, crime control, and even mental health care. Projecting growth and revenues more than a few years out is very difficult and even small errors in predictions make an astoundingly large difference. For example, underestimating unemployment by 1 percent can mean a multibillion-dollar error in budgeting because unemployment reduces revenue and increases expenditures.

Presidents usually use the estimates of economic growth, inflation, and unemployment that work best to justify their economic policies: this is where the wishful thinking comes in. President Reagan's projections were especially far off the mark. David Stockman, Reagan's first budget director, described, in what has become a classic statement on budgetary politics, how such estimates were made for the first budget he prepared. To justify a huge tax reduction and show a balanced budget, significant economic growth and low inflation had to be projected. The administration's initial figures included a 2 percent projected inflation rate, a figure far below the existing rate. The chair of the Council of Economic Advisers, Murray Weidenbaum, said, "Nobody is going to predict 2 percent inflation on my watch. We'll be the laughingstock of the world."[55] So Stockman and Weidenbaum bargained over what the forecasts would be; Weidenbaum selected an inflation figure he could live with, and Stockman raised the economic growth projections. Of course, both were horribly wrong, and that is why the real deficit was a hundred times bigger than projected.

In preparing its first multiyear budget forecast, George W. Bush's staff was able to come up with much more optimistic projections than the CBO by not factoring in the long-term costs of tax cuts and by using lower estimates of increases in mandatory spending for Medicare. The CBO, because it serves both parties and the political agenda of neither, is not compelled to accept the most or the least rosy estimates of economic performance, and thus its projections are usually more reliable than those of the White House. While Bush's OMB predicted a return to a balanced budget in 2005, the CBO saw deficits running into 2006 and well beyond if the tax cuts were made permanent. And, in fact, the CBO forecast was much more accurate; in 2004 the Bush budget had a deficit that was the third highest (as a percentage of GDP) since World War II, with 2005's deficit projected to be only slightly smaller.[56]

Omitting the cost of tax cuts alone from budget projections could account for a difference of $4 to $5 trillion in long-term revenues. Even though the administration's intent from the beginning was to make the cuts permanent, writing in a sunset (termination) provision made it easier to pass the legislation by not having to acknowledge the long-term losses. And while the administration talked about $1 trillion in surpluses over the next decade, all of that surplus was from Social Security taxes, money that is off-budget and supposedly reserved (or, as candidate Al Gore repeated many times in 2000, put in a lockbox) for future payments to retirees. The Bush administration's budget projections, minus the Social Security offset, showed a $1.5 trillion deficit.[57] After studying these projections one economist said, "No company, other than Enron, would think of counting its pension funds as surplus operating funds."[58]

This is a sleight of hand used by all presidents. Their annual budget messages always contain two deficit estimates, one for the regular, or unified, budget that reduces the deficit by the amount of the Social Security surplus, and a second that is closer to the actual deficit. The difference can be several hundred billions of dollars, but the larger number is rarely mentioned. No chief executive wants to predict a decade of red ink. (See Figure 3.)

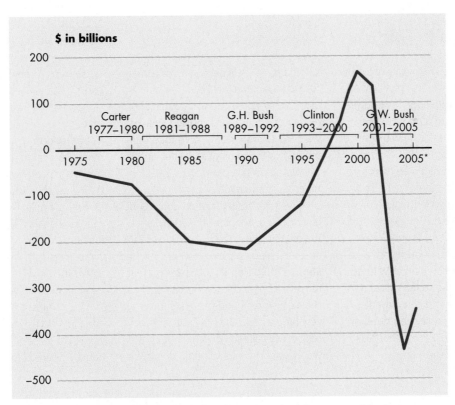

FIGURE 3 ■ The Deficit Returns *The country had four years of budget surpluses in the latter years of the Clinton administration and the first year of the George W. Bush administration before the combination of the recession, the 2001 tax cuts, and increases in military spending sent the budget back into deficit in 2002. It is projected to stay there indefinitely.*

*Numbers for 2004 and 2005 are Congressional Budget Office estimates (September 2004) and do not include all costs of the war with Iraq.

TAXING AND SPENDING POLICIES DURING WARTIME

No country's resources are infinite, so when a government is faced with multiple crises it has to start making choices between what it can and cannot afford to do. Governments face such choices during economic hard times and during war, both of which place new and often heavy burdens on revenues. Typically, leaders have to choose to raise taxes or cut spending.

The United States has been in one of these make-a-choice situations since 2001. When terrorists attacked the World Trade Center on September 11, the economy had already been in a mild recession for five months. By the end of the year, more than a million jobs had been lost, and at least a million more were expected to disappear before the economy improved. The initial cost of the attacks was $95 billion, not counting the $60 to $80 billion to pay for the first phase of the military response. After four years of surpluses, the budget was heading toward a major deficit. New economic woes came with a major stock market crash in 2002, and the 2003 decision to invade Iraq, which added billions to the defense budget. The government was in the position of having to revitalize the airline industry and New York City's economy, while fighting a recession, domestic terrorist threats, and a foreign war, all with declining revenues due to tax cuts and the increasing number of unemployed. State revenues also shrank, leaving states and localities with huge budget shortfalls and in need of federal help.

Historically, the government has responded to recession and war in different ways: in bad economic times it often tries to stimulate growth with tax cuts, while in wartime it raises taxes to pay for increased military spending. In the post–9/11 world, however, the Bush administration chose to increase military *and* social spending while continuing to cut taxes. This was a radical fiscal departure; until the Iraq war there had never been a tax cut during wartime. In fact, with the exceptions of the Mexican-American War and the first Gulf War, there have been tax increases to pay for every war.[1] Even the first Gulf War was not really an exception; a tax increase had passed the year before and went into effect just as the war began. In addition, our allies paid for most of the war.

When the war in Iraq began, Treasury Secretary John Snow told Congress, "The costs . . . will be small. We can afford the war, and we'll put it behind us."[2] Snow's predictions follow a long history of underestimating the price of war. The Civil War cost more than thirteen times the original estimates and the Vietnam War cost eleven to fifteen times more than first projections.[3]

The Bush administration addressed only the direct costs of the Iraq war—the money requested to pay for military and support operations—which reached about $200 billion in 2005. But budget requests do not convey the indirect costs of the war, and these are, in fact, very hard to calculate. Because the budget was already in deficit when the war began, the invasion and reconstruc-

tion were financed completely with borrowed money. Borrowing means that we pay the cost of interest on this new debt in future budgets.

As government continues to borrow larger and larger amounts to cover revenue shortfalls, there is less money available for private borrowing and this, in turn, slows economic growth. By some estimates the GDP was a full point lower in the year after the invasion than it would have been without the war. And every point lost in growth means $400 billion lost in tax revenues.[4]

The war also increased the cost of oil, both by driving up demand and by decreasing output (because of war and instability, Iraq's oil production stalled). To this must be added unforeseen costs for a lengthy occupation, nation building, and humanitarian assistance. Much of the reconstruction work was outsourced to private firms on no-bid contracts, further driving up costs.

Before the Iraq war began, one estimate put its cost at $1.9 trillion if it did not go smoothly.[5] This figure was almost identical to revenue lost from the tax cuts passed from 2001 to 2003. As the postwar insurgency dragged on and the military could not stop the sabotage against Iraq's oil industry and infrastructure, reconstruction costs climbed sharply. And as casualties rose, so did the need for medical care and rehabilitation for veterans.

The only fiscal adjustments the Bush administration made to waging the war were to increase defense spending and to borrow billions of dollars to pay for it. The

Presidents are inclined to accept the rosiest projects because they all come to office with taxing and spending policies they want to put in place. Achieving those goals is usually seen as politically more important than balancing the budget. There is no room in any budget for crisis—war, recession, or natural disaster. Costs incurred by these events are typically paid for by supplemental budget requests that drive up existing deficits.

tax cutting he began in his first year continued throughout his first term. Furthermore, he increased social spending. He supported huge increases in farm subsidies and put intense pressure on congressional leadership to get his controversial half-trillion-dollar prescription drug benefit bill passed before the 2004 election.

Congress played the same game as the president. As cynical as it may seem, national crises offer golden opportunities for Congress to get funding for pet projects for their districts. A month after the 9/11 attacks, for example, a $20 billion antiterrorism package was attached to a Pentagon appropriations bill, and senators added 103 amendments with $400 million earmarked for pet projects, most of which had little or nothing to do with the military or national security. The head of a lobbying association said it was "a free-for-all . . . It's like squirrels running around finding acorns and putting them in the ground for winter."[6] Senator John McCain (R-Ariz.) said the defense bill would "have more Christmas tree goodies on it than the North Pole."[7]

Even with his own party in control of Congress, the president did little to stop any of the massive pork-barrel spending bills that passed in the first three years after the 9/11 attacks. During his first term Bush never vetoed a spending bill and he never withdrew a tax cut proposal. In 2004, even as it was clear the Iraq war would be neither quick nor easy and the budget deficit was ballooning toward a half trillion dollars, a huge corporate tax cut passed and additional personal tax cuts were

proposed. By the end of Bush's first term, Citizens for Tax Justice estimated that if Bush succeeded in making his tax cuts permanent and did nothing to curb spending, the U.S. Treasury would have to borrow $10 trillion to cover the revenue shortfalls through 2014.[8]

1. On the relationship between tax policy and war see W. Elliot Brownlee, *Federal Taxation in America: A Short History* (New York: Cambridge University Press, 2004).
2. David E. Rosenbaum, "Tax Cuts and War Have Seldom Mixed," *New York Times*, March 9, 2003, 13.
3. William D. Nordhaus, "The Economic Consequences of a War with Iraq," in Carl Kaysen, et al., *War With Iraq: Costs, Consequences, and Alternatives,* (Cambridge, Mass.: American Academy of Arts and Sciences, Committee on International Security Studies, 2002), 52.
4. Miles A. Pomper, with Niels C. Sorrels, "War: Deficit-Maker Supreme," *CQ Weekly*, January 11, 2003, 71.
5. Nordhaus, "The Economic Consequences of a War with Iraq," 56–57. Nordhaus was revising his estimate in 2004. Estimates of total costs are in dispute, some arguing the $2 trillion figure is too high and others saying it is too low, but, in any case, it is difficult to assess with the war still in progress. The paper is available at www.amacad.org, or at Nordhaus's Web site at www.econ.yale.edu/~nordhaus/homepage/homepage.htm.
6. Leslie Wayne, "So, Friend, It's Time for That Tax Cut," *New York Times,* November 18, 2001, sec. 3, 1.
7. "Senators Put Pet Projects into Defense Bill," *Champaign-Urbana News-Gazette,* December 15, 2001, A5.
8. Citizens for Tax Justice, "Bush Still on Track to Borrow $10 Trillion by 2014 According to Latest Official Estimates." Paper issued January 30, 2004, 1 (www.ctj.org). This estimate is "conservative" next to the Laurence J. Kotlikoff and Scott Burns's $51 trillion estimate of total indebtedness in *The Coming Generational Storm: What You Need to Know about America's Economic Future* (Cambridge, Mass.: MIT Press, 2004).

Are Deficits and Debt a Problem?

Despite the widespread conviction that moderate deficits are sometimes needed to stimulate the economy, most experts agree that the huge recurring deficits of the 1980s and the early 1990s impaired the country's long-term health, and that today's even larger deficits are in danger of doing the same. When government borrowing reaches a high level, it crowds out private borrowing and, therefore, private investment. And the intense competition for investment dollars drives up interest rates.

Consumers add to the competition for money. In 2004 Americans held $2 trillion in credit-card debt, $8.8 trillion with mortgage and other debts included.[59] With government and consumers competing for money, domestic sources become exhausted and government has to turn to foreign sources. Collectively, our indebtedness to foreign institutions and individual investors (Japanese, Chinese, and Europeans, principally) is equivalent to roughly 28 percent of our GDP. The outflow of dollars in interest payments made by our government to foreign investors contributes to our trade deficit, weakens the dollar, and makes us even more vulnerable to the uncertainties of international markets. If foreign investors decided that our fiscal irresponsibility makes investment here risky and withdrew their investments in government bonds, then interest rates would rise sharply and our economy could be thrown into a serious recession.

The amount of the national debt owned by government agencies is also a potential time bomb. The Social Security Trust Fund, for example, is required by law to invest its surplus (money paid in each year by workers and employers in excess of what is needed to meet outlays to Social Security recipients) in government securities. Just as you, a private investor, might loan the government money by buying a Treasury bond, so does the Social Security Trust Fund. The interest paid on these securities stays in the Trust Fund along with the bonds. The government uses the cash received from the Trust Fund purchase of securities, just as it uses the cash you spend to buy a bond, to offset the budget deficit. It means less money has to be borrowed from banks and other institutions at higher interest rates. When the securities held by the Trust Fund mature, the government must find the money to pay them off or else default on its commitments to retiring workers. This latter option is not likely because of the clout of the millions of Americans to whom Social Security payments are owed. Finding the cash to pay off notes held by the Trust Fund could mean tax increases of significant magnitude.

When the government holds a huge debt, part of every tax dollar must be earmarked for interest payments. Both the economy and the public suffer from the government's reduced fiscal flexibility. There is less money in the budget to meet urgent needs in education, health care, research, and the infrastructure improvements necessary to economic growth. In the single year between 1998 and 1999 as the budget went into surplus, money spent on net interest payments on the debt dropped by $13 billion; if the budget had stayed in surplus in the de-cade from 1998 to 2009, as then projected, annual interest payments would have declined from $243 billion to $71 billion instead of being on the increase, as they are now. Even to Bill Gates, a savings of $172 billion is a lot of money. In terms of policy needs, $172 billion could provide a lot of health care for children or need-based aid for college students, to take only two examples.

Clinton's last budget contained a plan for paying off all of the publicly held debt by 2013. But economists disagree about how urgent it is to pay it down. Those who support reducing debt level point to the amount of money tied up in annual interest payments. Those who believe there is no urgency in paying off the debt include some conservatives who believe cutting taxes is important for continued economic growth, and some liberals who believe it is more important to spend on education, training future workers, and improving the infrastructure necessary for industrial growth and increased productivity.

What Can Be Done?

With budget shortfalls projected for at least the next de-cade, the debate over paying down the national debt is moot. The effort now is to stop the growth of the debt by eliminating budget deficits.

Because the Treasury Department cannot borrow beyond limits set by Congress, one obvious option is for Congress to refuse to approve an increase in the debt ceiling and force the Treasury Department to stop borrowing money. Congress has done this a few times, but when the government runs out of operating funds, it must shut down.

Hypothetically, the government could print more money or stop making interest payments when budget shortfalls occur. Defaulting would destroy the government's financial credibility at home and abroad with the banks and corporations who help finance the debt, and it would betray millions of private citizens who invest in government bonds individually or through their pension plans. If the Treasury Department simply printed more money, the market would be flooded with dollars, setting off an inflationary spiral.

For years, many saw the solution to recurring deficits as amending the Constitution to require a balanced budget. The most recent call for a constitutional convention to pass such an amendment won support in thirty-two states in 1990, just two short of the minimum needed. But changing the Constitution is usually regarded as a last-ditch alternative, and shepherding an amendment through to ratification can take years. Therefore, many in Congress look to legislative action as a quicker and surer route to deficit reduction.

Congress *has* tried to discipline itself by passing budget enforcement laws intended to prevent deficit spending. The Balanced Budget and Emergency Deficit Control Act of 1985, more commonly referred to by its cosponsors' names—the Gramm-Rudman-Hollings (GRH) Act—was supposed to trigger automatic cuts in most programs if annual goals for deficit reduction were not met. All it produced were accounting tricks. The deficit was artificially reduced by selling off public land and public enterprises, a one-shot infusion of money that did nothing to solve any long-range spending problems (it is like selling your house to pay off a vacation), and by gimmicks such as delaying military pay raises for a day. Spending items were put into an "off-budget category" and not counted in the estimate of the deficit.

As deficits and debt continued to soar, Congress adopted much tougher rules that set caps on spending and barred any bill that increased spending without offsetting spending cuts or new revenue to support it. If a program had a net cost—that is, if new spending was not matched by a revenue increase—the funds were sequestered. This provision is called the pay-as-you-go system, or simply **pay-go.** If the president or Congress wanted to pass a tax cut or increase spending on an entitlement program, they had to pair it with offsetting spending cuts or provide a new revenue source.

These temporary rules were first adopted in 1990 in an agreement between George H. Bush and the Democratic majority in Congress. They divided federal spending into two categories: discretionary, and direct or mandatory (see Figure 4). **Discretionary spending** is set by annual appropriations bills passed by Congress and, as the label suggests, amounts are established at the discretion of members of Congress in any given year. Included in this category of spending are items such as government operating expenses and salaries for many federal employees. Spending on each item is limited by the dollar ceilings, or caps, that Congress authorizes for the year.

Mandatory spending, in contrast, is mandated by permanent laws. Even though some of these outlays are provided for by annual appropriation bills, Congress *must* spend the money because there are laws that order it to do so. Examples of mandatory spending are payments made for Medicare and Medicaid, various government subsidies such as farm price supports, and unemployment insurance. In 2005, discretionary spending is expected to account for 38 percent of all budgetary outlays, and mandatory spending for 62 percent.

As its name implies, mandatory spending is harder for Congress to control than discretionary spending. Yet mandatory spending is not uncontrollable in every instance. In considering the president's budget, Congress cannot simply refuse to fund Medicaid, for example, nor can it decide to drastically lower its funding level. But it can amend the law that created Medicaid to change eligibility, or it can repeal the law and remove any need for appropriations. Most mandatory spending then, while not controllable through the budgetary

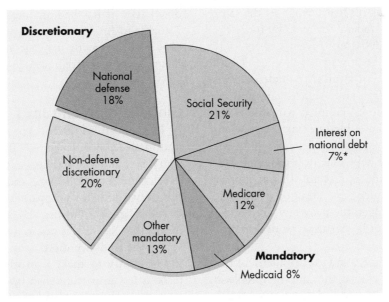

FIGURE 4 ■ **Estimated Federal Spending, 2005 ($2.1 trillion)**

*Does not include interest paid on government securities held by the Social Security Trust Fund.

SOURCE: *Budget of the United States Government, Fiscal Year 2005* (Washington D.C.: U.S. Government Printing Office, 2004), Table S-12, 386.

process alone, can be altered by legislation. This is what happened with federal welfare programs in 1995; the laws that made spending mandatory were rewritten and most of the program responsibilities devolved to the states. An expenditure such as interest on the national debt, however, is truly mandatory and can be reduced only by paying down the debt.

In 1993, against the wishes of many Democrats, Clinton supported renewal of the spending caps and the pay-go principle and a few years later committed to achieving a balanced budget by 2002. In combination with continued economic growth and low unemployment that produced greater-than-anticipated federal revenues, spending caps and pay-go rules put the 1998 unified budget in surplus and produced a balanced budget three years ahead of schedule. However, the budget surpluses were achieved through the accounting device of offsetting revenue shortfalls in the regular budget with the surplus in Social Security. Fiscal 2001 was the only year with a genuine surplus and Clinton's last budget actually proposed spending 9 percent *less* than it expected to receive in revenues.

Once the budget went into surplus, however, Congress immediately began modifying the rules that had constrained spending. It has been raising caps annually since 1999, and the pay-go rule was all but discarded.[60] Moderate Republicans and Democrats fought to restore pay-go and caps to the 2005 budget as the only way to stop rising deficits, but the administration resisted.[61]

After reductions in discretionary spending under Reagan and Clinton, George W. Bush increased it by an amazing 36 percent during his first term.[62] At the same time, his tax cuts reduced federal revenues by twice the amount of Reagan's. In 2004, tax revenues were only 15.8 percent of GDP, the lowest level since World War II.[63] The current level of spending on defense, wars and nation building in Iraq and Afghanistan, and on Social Security and Medicare, coupled with the estate and personal and corporate income tax cuts means there is no immediate prospect that deficits will disappear or that the national debt will stop growing. Because there are no nonpartisan forecasts that economic growth alone can produce the additional revenue needed to balance the budget, there are few alternatives to increased deficits except higher taxes or drastic program cuts.[64]

It is easy to blame Congress and the president for this fiscal recklessness, and, of course, they are responsible in the last resort, but they are responding to the public's desire to have everything: lower taxes, government programs to benefit them and their families, and massive military spending.

Economic Growth and Job Creation

The role government plays in fostering growth and creating jobs has to change over time if it is to be responsive to public needs and to structural changes in the economy. As we have shown, the American economy is changing faster than the ability of many of its citizens to keep pace in education and training. Even if an American economy has been supplanted by a global economy, there is little evidence to suggest that Americans have stopped thinking that there is an economy contiguous with the country's borders and that their government is responsible in some way for its performance.

As the U.S. economy's position in the global economy has changed, so has the government's ability to affect economic change. The days when the board chairman of General Motors could say, "What is good for GM is good for the country and what is good for the country is good for GM" are over. The American economy is now a region of the global economy, and both business and labor must compete in an international market. Japan, the European Union, China, Taiwan, Hong Kong, South Korea, Singapore, and several Latin American countries are now major rivals in world trade. We cannot dominate markets with our manufactured or agricultural products, and we cannot keep jobs within our borders when it is more profitable for businesses to operate elsewhere. The competition is good in that it forces us to become more efficient and brings greater prosperity to the citizens of other countries (who are potential consumers of the goods and services we produce). But it has had an impact on the kinds of jobs available to Americans and the wages paid: 20 to 25 percent of the growth in wage inequality in the United States has been attributed to labor competition in a global market.[65]

Globalization and Jobs

At least one-third of world production is controlled by multinational corporations.[66] This international dispersion of economic activity—investment, research and development, production, and distribution—through the networking of companies across national borders is called **globalization.** By definition, globalization means that business is not as nation centered today as it was in the mid-twentieth century. Because business exists primarily to make a profit, loyalty to a particular place is less important than favorable economic conditions for production and distribution. Thus corporations are continuously scouting for those locations where, for example, labor costs are cheapest and regulation is least burdensome. To trade unions and environmental and consumer groups, it means that U.S. cor-

Danziger © 2004 The Washington Post.

porations are becoming less dependent on and less responsive to American workers and consumers. It also means that they may be moving beyond the reach of government regulation that was adopted to safeguard workers' and consumers' rights and to protect the public against environmental abuses or other negative consequences of business activity.

We may still jealously guard our territorial boundaries, but today no border can contain financial and intellectual activities. The revolution in technology—computers, telecommunications, and transportation—brought us to this new era. Money can be transferred to foreign banks instantaneously through computerized accounts, making competition for investment international. The most highly paid workers—scientists, systems planners and analysts, lawyers, and entertainers, for example—are very mobile; modern transportation makes it feasible to travel to employment opportunities anywhere in the world, and telecommunications makes it easy to transmit their ideas. They are part of an international labor pool.

Businesses do not make decisions on relocating to another city or country based on how their departure will affect the local economy. Those with new ideas do not worry (unless restricted by national security laws) about whether the company they sell their invention, new software, or design idea to is an American-based or a foreign company as long as they get the highest possible price for their services or product.

Transferring jobs abroad for competitive advantage is called **outsourcing** or **offshoring.** Businesses have long outsourced part of the work they could not do in-house because they did not have the right personnel or equipment, but most outsourcing was domestic, subcontracted to companies also located in the United States. Today jobs move by the millions from country to country in search of the best labor for the cheapest wage as companies look for an edge against competitors and to increase profits for shareholders. The jobs are not headed to any one place. Many U.S. manufacturing jobs went first to Mexico, and then on to a more highly educated and even cheaper labor force in China, where there is no chance for independent unions to organize. Many higher-skilled jobs have gone to India, and now India is outsourcing to China.

No one is certain how many American jobs have been offshored because most of the data are self-reports from businesses and they are not always forthright in providing numbers. One estimate is that about four hundred thousand jobs went overseas in 2004, and that up to fourteen million Americans are now in jobs (financial analysts, medical technicians, paralegals, mathematicians, and computer technologists) that are at risk of being offshored.[67] The major dilemma presented for workers is that for most there are no replacement jobs because the economy is not producing them fast enough. Those who have found others jobs are earning far less than in the positions they lost.

What Can Government Do?

There are deep divisions among experts over what government should or can do to foster job growth or assist workers displaced during economic transitions. Some say government should stay out of the way, taxing and regulating business as little as possible, and wait for new job growth. Others believe government should take an active role in providing retraining and income support during these periods of transition when there is serious job loss. Every administration takes basic steps to protect American jobs where it can, by monitoring trade practices to see that foreign markets are open to American products, subsidizing the educational system and research and development, funding repair and upgrading of the country's infrastructure, and targeting new technologies and industries for tax subsidies or other support. Politically, it is almost impossible for government to look like it is doing nothing.

The loss of old jobs to outsourcing and the slowness of the economic recovery to create new jobs were major issues in the 2004 presidential campaign. Private sector job losses during Bush's first term were offset in small part by new jobs created in the public sector. Government grew about 5 percent during Bush's first term as thousands of new jobs were added to the public payroll, many related to defense and homeland security. Historically, government has established new programs expressly to put the unemployed back to work during a severe recession or a depression, usually on public works programs such as building roads and bridges or conservation projects. But our economy has moved beyond that time when government is seen as a major source of new jobs, so the new public sector jobs created under Bush are not an answer to the substantial loss of jobs due to the decline of the manufacturing sector and job outsourcing. To some extent, new government hiring is a problem in that it adds to budget deficits.

Government can use tax policy to discourage the offshoring of jobs and to attract foreign investors here. Under current policy, the right to defer taxes on profits earned abroad rewards businesses for investing abroad. (Deferral is not permitted on domestic earnings.) A change in this policy might discourage the movement of some business activity abroad, but the savings from the tax break are a tiny portion of the savings from cheaper labor, which are estimated to range as high as 50 percent.[68]

There is almost nothing that will stop businesses from putting their investments where they can make the greatest profit. That means government should do what it can to make it profitable for foreign investors to come here. Being part of a global economy means that jobs flow here as well as migrate out; 6.4 million Americans worked for foreign companies in 2001, both in manufacturing and service jobs. Many "Japanese" cars are manufactured in the United States, for example, just as parts for some "American" cars are manufactured abroad. The number of jobs that were outsourced between 1986 and 2001 (one guesstimate is about ten million) is greater than those created by foreign companies in the United

States, but some argue that taking any precipitous action to slow outsourcing will only interfere with job creation by foreign investors here.[69]

Given its great university system and leadership in high technology, the United States is better prepared than many countries to train workers for a high-tech, service-oriented economy. But doing this means continuing to upgrade the educational system so that it does an equally good job for people in all income groups. Declining college enrollments among children from low- and lower-middle-income families is a serious problem, not just for them and for our society's commitment to equal access, but also for our future economic competitiveness. Government policies do address some access issues. Individuals can claim tax deductions for computers purchased for use as educational and job tools, and government levies a surcharge on telephone service that has paid for the wiring of virtually all public schools and libraries for Internet service. This makes it possible for all children, regardless of their income group, to have access to new technology.

Immigration policies are another area where government can have an impact on the domestic labor pool. Just as our businesses export jobs, so they import foreign workers to fill jobs here. Every year business asks government to provide tens of thousands of special entry visas to highly skilled foreign workers. This includes universities, who must hire thousands of scientists from abroad to staff their programs, especially in mathematics, science, and engineering. This pressure will increase as economic forecasters predict a shortage of skilled workers in the coming decade.

One of the most important actions government can take is to adopt fiscal policies that will end this new cycle of huge budget deficits, thus freeing more money for private borrowing and investment. There is also widespread agreement that rising health care costs will continue to discourage job creation until government steps in to assume more of the burden.

Among the most significant consequences of globalization and offshoring are their potential for worsening the maldistribution of wealth. More than half of laid-off workers who found new jobs in 2004 took big pay cuts.[70] Congress took nominal action by providing two years of income support to workers over fifty who can show that trade had been the reason for their job loss and who take new jobs that pay less than their old job.[71] Government could also help if it tackles the health care issue, ensuring that workers and their families will have health insurance, and improves unemployment benefits for the involuntarily unemployed.

But something government can do little about is where the profits from outsourcing go. The largest shares of the benefits realized from offshoring are going to the

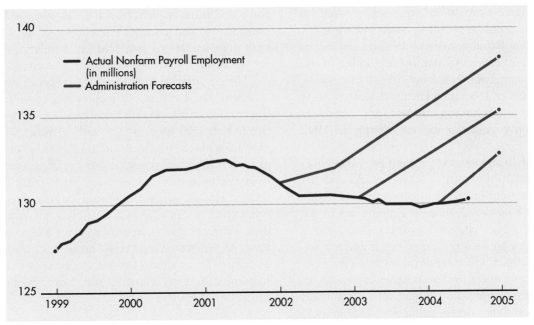

FIGURE 5 ■ **Job Creation Much Slower Than Predicted in Recent Years** *The George W. Bush administration has consistently overestimated future job growth.*
SOURCE: Bureau of Labor Studies; *Economic Reports of the President, 2002, 2003,* and 2004. Paul Krugman, *New York Times,* March 9, 2004, online article at www.NYTimes.com.

shareholders of the companies and to the consumers who buy the products.[72] While economists argue that over the long term the movement of jobs around the globe will lift all boats, in the short term, workers are struggling to stay afloat. (See Figure 5.)

Government could choose to do nothing to address these job and income issues and allow the market to set the terms of competition, the level of employment, and the distribution of wealth, but this option has not been chosen by any modern industrial country.

Conclusion: Is Our Economic Policy Responsive?

The health of any economy depends on many factors, only some of which government can influence and none of which it can completely control. Private spending accounts for close to 70 percent of our economy, so economic policies of the private sector and the consumption and saving habits of Americans play an enormous role in the state of the economy. But government can help protect us from recession and depression, create jobs, and guarantee minimum wages and safety conditions.

It should be evident now that our country passes through cycles of economic boom and bust. How we weather these cycles depends to a great extent on fiscal

and monetary policies. We expect fiscal policy, that is, taxing and spending, to be more directly responsive to the public because it is created by elected officials. Monetary policy, that is, setting of interest rates and controlling the supply of money, is made by individuals shielded to some extent from the short-term wishes of both the public and elected officials, except perhaps in crisis situations. The fact that fiscal policy is made in more open and democratic processes does not necessarily make it more responsible. Fiscal policy is, and has to be, more responsive to the voters, while monetary policymakers are freer to respond to macroeconomic conditions—*as they see them.*

Fiscal policymakers, while eager to give voters what they want, have not been especially good stewards of the American economy over the past several decades. Nor have voters held them accountable. During the 1970s and 1980s, economic policymakers, both government and private, were living for the short term. In the 1980s, corporate America improved its profit margin at the expense not only of investment but also of workers, many of whose real wages fell significantly. Government policymakers preferred politically popular tax cuts over balancing the budget or investing in programs to improve our nation's infrastructure, promote research, or upgrade human capital through education and training. Moreover, government was content to let income inequalities grow and even exacerbated them by cutbacks in social programs.

The 1990s were a time of taking stock of what the 1980s' private and public spending binge had wrought. Clinton and the Republican-led Congress reined in spending, and businesses that had overexpanded in the 1980s began cutting back their labor forces, eliminating unnecessary jobs and computerizing clerical work.[73] With fewer employees turning out more goods and services, productivity began to increase sharply in 1992 and 1993.

The mid-1990s also saw a movement away from policy geared toward short-term electoral results and toward long-term solutions to the problem of maintaining the country's economic vitality. Coming out of the transition to a high-tech, service-oriented economy, the United States began a period of economic growth and deficit reduction and entered the twenty-first century as the largest and most productive economy on earth. At the same time, government relaxed controls on large corporations, deregulating accounting standards and business behavior in fields such as telecommunications and energy. These policies allowed some corporate leaders to run free, accumulating personal wealth at the expense of investors and consumers.

The country has been divided over how government should respond to growing income disparity. The Clinton administration argued that a responsive government is one that uses fiscal policy both to foster economic growth and to regulate the distribution of income generated by that growth. George W. Bush and the Republican-controlled Congress argue that the country's economic difficulties stemmed precisely from this overresponsive, interventionist, Keynesian approach. In their view, the most responsive government is one that leaves an unfettered market to "grow" the economy and distribute its wealth. This is the essence of the long-standing debate in American politics over the proper relationship of government to the economy.

Murray Says No to a Permanent Tax Cut

espite her opposition to the estate tax, Senator Patty Murray voted against making its repeal permanent. The measure was stopped by a technicality in Senate rules that required sixty yea votes to bring the bill to the floor for a straight up or down vote. Only two Republicans defected, while nine Democrats crossed over to support the repeal, three of whom were up for reelection. On a straight up or down vote, if all had held their ground, the measure would have passed 54–44.

Why did Murray choose to stick with her party this time? Her reasons were both pragmatic and principled. Several things had changed since her earlier votes for repeal of the estate tax. When Clinton was in the White House, Murray knew he would veto it. She was able to vote for the Republicans' bill, pleasing some of her constituents, knowing that Clinton's opposition would send the bill to a reconciliation process. In the Clinton administration, any bill that emerged with the possibility of getting a presidential signature was likely to target tax reductions for small business owners and family farmers and smaller estates. But in 2002, Bush was a strong advocate of estate tax repeal. If the Senate passed the House version of the bill, it would sail through to enactment with permanent tax cuts that went entirely to the wealthiest people in the country.

Second, the original bill had passed during a time of budget surpluses when it was easy to make the case that some of those dollars should go back to taxpayers. With money to spend and voters to woo

during the presidential campaign, the timing was perfect. But in 2002, the budget was in deficit, the country was in a recession, and it was fighting a war on terrorism that had already cost billions and was threatening to spread to Iraq. When coupled with the double-digit increase in defense spending, disaster relief, and antirecession measures, the cumulative costs of all the new tax cuts would explode. Government borrowing would skyrocket and the amount of the budget devoted to interest payments would escalate. This could send the budget into the same downward spiral as in the 1980s when military spending coupled with tax cuts doubled the national debt. Such a situation would make it impossible to fund programs for the rural working class and poor that Murray supported.

Third, Democrats did not want to vote for tax cuts that overwhelmingly favored the wealthy at a time when we have the biggest inequality in income and wealth of any developed country. This would be a slap at the party's own voting base. Furthermore, during the Clinton administration, when balanced budgets and surpluses were achieved, the Democrats had cut into traditional Republican territory and were now regarded by the public as the better budget managers. Democrats were not eager to surrender this ground as they positioned themselves for the upcoming midterm and the next presidential election. They were happy to portray Bush as the *spend-but-don't-tax* president.

In voting against permanent repeal of the estate tax, Murray again

stated her complete opposition to it as bad for family-owned businesses, workers, and new job creation. She promised there would be future votes on estate tax repeal, and in better economic times she would again vote yes. But between now and then, she says, "Congress and the Administration need to reach agreement on a basic budget framework that makes room for estate tax repeal." Otherwise, she says, they will just be "playing politics."[74] But of course Murray, too, was playing politics.

Murray was right about there being occasion for another vote. The Republicans immediately announced their intention to regroup and present the measure again, after the summer recess when the Senate rule that prevented it from being considered in a straight up or down vote will have lapsed. The president's senior adviser, Karl Rove, said it should not be looked on as a defeat, but as one battle in a "war."[75] Furthermore, the president told Congress he had another new package of tax cuts he wanted to send to the Hill.

Murray's vote against permanent repeal did not diminish her popularity at home. She easily won reelection in 2004, and the Democratic leadership in the Senate named her assistant floor leader in the 109th Congress. This will make it very difficult for Murray to abandon the party position on repeal of the estate tax.

To learn more about the estate tax and contrasting views of its fairness, go to this chapter's "You Are There" exercises on the text Web site.

Key Terms

capitalist economy	monetary policy
socialism	progressive tax
mixed economy	regressive tax
depression	flat tax
inflation	budget deficit
recession	national debt
productivity	pay-go
fiscal policy	discretionary spending
Keynesian economics	mandatory spending
stagflation	globalization
supply-side economics	outsourcing (offshoring)

Further Reading

Greider, William, *Secrets of the Temple: How the Federal Reserve Runs the Country* (New York: Simon & Schuster, 1989). It is hard to imagine a book about the Federal Reserve Board being interesting, but this one is. It reveals the human face behind this most technical institution.

Hayek, Friedrich von, *The Road to Serfdom,* 50th anniversary ed. (Chicago: University of Chicago Press, 1994). The seminal statement of anti-Keynesian economics written by an Austrian economist and later championed by Milton Friedman and the University of Chicago school. Von Hayek argues that too much government intervention in the economy is dangerous and could turn people into slaves.

Heilbroner, Robert L., and Lester C. Thurow, *Economics Explained: Everything You Need to Know about How the Economy Works and Where It's Going* (New York: Simon & Schuster, 1998). This text is a readable discussion of major economic concepts and issues.

Johnston, David Cay, *Perfectly Legal: The Covert Campaign to Rig Our Tax System to Benefit the Super Rich—and Cheat Everyone Else* (New York: Portfolio, 2003). This text describes why the rich are getting richer and the middle and working classes are losing out.

Phillips, Kevin P., *Wealth and Democracy: A Political History of the American Rich* (New York: Broadway Books, 2002). A former Republican political operative explains why he is fed up with the economic policies of both major parties for doing so little to stop influence buying by the wealthy and growing income inequality. The main focus is on the negative impact on democracy of a maldistribution of wealth.

Sen, Amartya Kumar, *Development as Freedom* (New York: Oxford University Press, 2001). A Nobel laureate in economics and one of the world's leading authorities on development explains the relationship between income and well-being and between economic development and democracy.

Shipler, David K., *The Working Poor: Invisible in America* (New York: Knopf, 2004) A Pulitzer Prize–winning reporter for the New York Times looks at migrant farm laborers and other lower-income workers, explaining how their political and economic condition is linked to the overall health of the country.

Stockman, David A., *The Triumph of Politics: How the Reagan Revolution Failed* (New York: Harper & Row, 1986). Reagan's budget director tells all.

Weisman, Steven R., *The Great Tax Wars: Lincoln to Wilson, the Fierce Battles over Money and Power That Transformed the Nation* (New York: Simon & Schuster, 2002). A history of the long political battle to establish a permanent income tax. Among its many interesting facts: in 1939, only 7 percent of the labor force earned enough to pay income tax.

For Viewing

Farmingville (2004 entry at the Sundance Film Festival) This film documents the hostility of a Long Island community toward migrant farm workers from Mexico and Central America.

The Fountainhead (1949) A screen treatment of Ayn Rand's blockbuster novel. It is not often that a novel becomes a major tract in the wars between economic schools of thought. Rand's brand of libertarian capitalism inspired millions, including current Fed chair Alan Greenspan. The film stars Gary Cooper.

The Hudsucker Proxy (1994) This comedy by the Coen brothers is about a company that installed a moron as president in order to drive the company into the ground and carry out a stock scam.

Roger and Me (1989) Documentary filmmaker Michael Moore shadowed General Motors's CEO, Roger Smith, hoping to get him to visit his hometown, Flint, Michigan, so he could see firsthand how GM's factory closings led to the city's economic decline. This film made many of the ten-best lists for 1989.

Wall Street (1987) This film captured public disenchantment with the "Me Decade" obsession with personal enrichment at all costs.

Electronic Resources

www.oecd.org
The Web site of the Organization for Economic Cooperation and Development, whose membership comprises the world's most developed industrial democracies. It offers comparative data on tax structure, economic growth, distribution of wealth, and cost of living in these countries.

www.wsj.com
The Wall Street Journal *probably has the best coverage of economic news of any U.S. newspaper. However, if you want to see the Web edition, you must subscribe.*

www.whitehouse.gov/fsbr/esbr.html
An "Economic Statistics Briefing Room," with links to national economic statistics, GDP, income, unemployment, prices, and interest, in addition to international economic statistics.

www.omb.gov

The Web site of the Office of Management and Budget with links to all U.S. budget documents and supplemental appropriations.

www.whitehouse.gov/cea

Even the Council of Economic Advisers has its own Web page, with numerous links to economic statistics, budgets of the United States, and other useful information.

www.federalreserve.gov

This is the Web site of the Federal Reserve System with links to the regional banks. The site offers a history of the Fed, a description of the work of its constituent parts, testimony and reports to Congress, consumer information, and publications free to the public.

www.irs.gov

The Web site of the Internal Revenue Service offers a history of the agency and its work and provides help with personal income taxes. Users can download forms and publications and get information on the reform of the IRS passed by Congress in 1998.

www.cbpp.org

At the Web site of the Center for Budget and Policy Priorities, you can find reports on taxing and spending policy with a different perspective than that at government agencies.

 InfoTrac College Edition

Search for the following articles in the InfoTrac database:

Broaddus, Jr., and J. Alfred. "Macroeconomic Principles and Monetary Policy," *Economic Quarterly* (Winter 2004).

Gale, William G. and Peter R. Orszag. *"Fiscal Follies: The Real Budget Problem and How to Fix It,"* Brookings Review (Fall 2003).

Jones, George G., and Mark A. Luscombe. "Making Sense of the New Tax Legislation," *Journal of Accountancy* (September 2001).

Tager, Michael, and William Van Lear. "Fiscal and Monetary Policy Rules Revisited," *Social Science Journal* (January 2001).

For more articles, enter

"Monetary policy" in the Subject Guide, and then go to subdivision "United States";

"Fiscal policy" in the Subject Guide; and

"Tax reform" in the Subject Guide.

 American Government Resources

Visit the Public Policy section of the Wadsworth American Government Resources Web site (politicalscience.wadsworth.com/amgov) for a variety of tools to help you explore economic policy further. Included are simulations, video clips, Microcase exercises, and a wealth of other activities.

CHAPTER 17

SOCIAL WELFARE AND HEALTH POLICY

This 55,000-ton pile of raw sugar is part of the surplus that costs taxpayers $1.4 million a month to store. Sugar subsidy programs cost American consumers about $2 billion annually.

© Brad Doherty, Brownsville, TX

Should the Government Subsidize Corporate Farming?

The Political and Legal Bases of Social Welfare Policies

The Evolution of Social Welfare Policies

Income Support Programs
  Retirees and Their Dependents
  The Poor
  Farmers
  Veterans
  The Impact of Income Support Programs

Health Care Programs
  Health Care for Seniors
  Health Care for the Poor and Disabled
  Health Care for Veterans

Subsidized Services
  Education
  Housing
  Agriculture

Tax Subsidies
  Corporations
  Families and Homeowners

Current Issues
  Health Care
  Social Security
  Reforming Aid to the Poor

Conclusion: Are Social Welfare Programs Responsive?

ou are Tim Hutchinson (R-Ark.), nearing the end of your first term in the Senate. It is April 2002, and the Senate is facing a vote on a bill to provide price supports and other financial aid to farmers. The Republican majority in the House has already passed a version of the bill that you could have given wholehearted backing. But the Democrat-controlled Senate is bringing to the floor its own bill, one that sets a cap on the amount of support from the federal government that any farmer or corporate farm can receive in a given year. It also would increase the amount of money available to help small farmers and promote conservation. Your decision this election year is whether to *support* the bill that provides support for agriculture or to vote *against* it because it is opposed by corporate farmers in your state.

Like other senators standing for reelection in farm states, you have been pressing for additional relief for the country's struggling farmers. You represent one of the poorest states in the Union; per capita personal income is little more than half that of the wealthiest state. More than 40 percent of Arkansas is farmland, close to half its population is rural, and one-fifth of the state's employment is agriculture-related. In the past year, Arkansas farmers received $740 million in subsidies from the federal government, but you believe it was not enough.[1]

Because of your state's economic profile, you sought and won a seat on the Agriculture Committee. But farming is also a personal issue; before attending Bob Jones University and becoming a pastor and teacher at a Christian college, you lived and worked on your parents' farm. You see farmers as the bedrock of the country, economically and morally, and agriculture as "the first industry of America," essential to national security and economic well-being.[2]

Farm subsidies are a means by which government underwrites part of the cost of agriculture; they include direct payments to farmers or agribusinesses to reduce the economic risks of growing food and other crops. The original objective was to make it economically feasible for farmers to stay in business and guarantee the United States a domestic supply of cotton, sugar, and basic foodstuffs. More than 90 percent of subsidies are paid out in price supports; the government guarantees set prices—usually more than the market commands—for crops like corn, wheat, rice, cotton, and soybeans, to name the most heavily subsidized. If the market price falls below the guaranteed level, the government pays the difference while also purchasing and storing tons of surplus crops each year. Some of that surplus goes to federal programs such as food stamps and subsidized school lunches.

The government also pays farmers to withhold land from production, either to promote conservation or to reduce the production of crops or farm products (cheese, butter, dried milk) that the government holds in surplus. Collectively, these farm support programs have made agriculture the most subsidized industry in the United States.

The first farm subsidy legislation was adopted to protect family farms and marginal operations, and all of the rhetorical justification for continuing the program still focuses on family farms. But small farmers have been going out of business by the tens of thousands since the 1970s. By 1997, there were only two million farms left in the United States, and about half of these were hobby farms, having less than $10,000 in gross sales.[3] In reality, most of the subsidy money goes to large farm operations and agribusiness corporations. The media have had some fun calling attention to well-off subsidy recipients, like an heir to the Rockefeller fortune, basketball star Scottie Pippen, and the billionaire Ted Turner, founder of CNN and TNT, but they are not exceptions. By the 1980s, when farm subsidies accounted for half of all farmers' income, most of the payments were going to the wealthiest farmers. Just 10 percent of farm owners receive two-thirds of all subsidies.[4] From 1996 to 2001, the average payment for the top 1 percent of subsidy recipients was $558,698, while the average for the bottom 80 percent was $5,830.[5]

In principle, conservative Republicans have opposed farm subsidies and most other government income support programs. So when more ideological Republicans like Newt Gingrich seized the party leadership, they succeeded in passing the 1996 Freedom to Farm bill to phase out crop supports over a seven-year period. Gingrich vowed to return market forces to agriculture and to wean the industry from "East German socialist farm programs."[6] Not only did you agree with that goal; you cowrote the bill, which lifted government restrictions on acreage and crops and was

supposed to greatly reduce subsidies while promoting farm exports. But the effort failed when grain prices dropped abroad and U.S. crops were no longer competitive in the global marketplace. Producers asked for emergency payments, and a big bailout package passed in 2001. Now here you are a year later, looking at a bill that calls for spending even more on price supports and adds new crops—peanuts and apples—to the program. In fact, if this bill passes, direct payments to farmers will have increased sevenfold since the Republicans gained control of the House.[7]

Opponents of the ten-year, $171 billion bill passed by the House have been unsparing in their criticism of the program's size and cost. Two members argued that "it represents the most sweeping nonmilitary expansion of the federal government since the Great Society" of the 1960s, while a fellow Republican warned that "we are in danger of systematically turning farmers into dependent serfs of the federal government."[8]

This might have been your view when you were writing the Freedom to Farm bill. You won your Senate seat running on a platform of balanced budgeting, tax relief, and welfare and education reform. Nevertheless, you

want a farm subsidies bill passed. You justify your support, saying, "Unfortunately, a confluence of factors has crippled the ability of American farmers to compete internationally. High energy prices, closed markets, heavily subsided foreign competition, natural disasters, and burdensome federal environmental regulations have pushed many farmers to and over the brink of bankruptcy."[9]

You cannot afford to be against something so important to your state's economy and to some of your biggest campaign donors. Your problem is with the Senate version of the bill. The cap it places on how much an individual can receive in direct payments in any year would reduce the current support level from $460,000 to $275,000. The House version you favor retains the higher limit. The Senate bill also would channel more money to food subsidies for the poor and about $55 billion to smaller farmers, especially through increases to the conservation programs that pay for not planting or grazing on land that is depleted or eroding. In short, the Senate bill would reduce benefits for large-scale farming and redirect some of that money to smaller farm operations.

Family farmers are an important part of your political base, but agribusiness is preeminent in Arkansas. In fact, your state has three of the country's top ten recipients of farm payments: Tyler Farms, Riceland Foods, and Rice Mill all own multiple farms and collected millions in subsidies last year. Tyler Farms alone has received $24 million in various kinds of support over the past five years, but its CEO insists that "it's not like a welfare check."[10] Grain farms like Riceland's, along with cotton growers, are the most highly subsidized farmers in the United States.

If you vote for the Senate bill, you would send a message to small farmers that you are in favor of giving more aid to them and less to corporate operations. And if the bill does pass, it would go to a conference committee where you can be certain the compromise version will push the ceiling on payments closer to current levels. In this way, you could give something to both small and large farmers, and you would help push a farm support bill through to passage.

But do you want to cast a vote that will anger agribusiness, the source of some of your biggest campaign donations? Your reelection race in the fall is shaping up as an uphill battle; in fact, the White House is privately saying that your defeat is a strong possibility. It is not the best time to aggravate the most powerful economic interests in the state. But you have other constituents and campaign promises to consider. How will it look for a supporter of education reform to vote for a bill that proposes to spend three times the amount on farm subsidies that Congress voted to spend on President Bush's new education program?[11] How will you defend your position as a budget balancer if, after supporting big tax cuts, you vote for a bill that adds to the post–9/11 double-digit spending increases? And should you vote to support the wealthiest farmers when you just voted for a welfare reform that will lower income support for the poor? Though recipients of federal farm subsidies are quick to deny that their program is welfare, income support payments to farmers dwarf welfare payments to poor nonfarm families.

Should you vote against the Senate bill and protect the higher payment caps for large farm interests, perhaps alienating small farmers and damaging your image as a fiscal conservative? Or should you risk antagonizing the agribusiness lobby and vote for a bill that will give more benefits to small farmers and the poor? How should you vote?

In almost all areas of American politics, it is those who vote, give the most to candidates, belong to the most influential interest groups, and are politically active in other ways who have the most impact on government policies. It should come as no surprise, then, that these are the same people who benefit most from social welfare policies. All the same, it probably *will* come as a surprise because the term *social welfare* usually brings to mind images of welfare mothers, elderly people in nursing homes, and indigents receiving surplus food and living in shelters or public housing, not images of the wealthy farmers, shareholders, and CEOs who benefit from billions of dollars in tax subsidies every year.[12]

Americans tend to view welfare as largesse for the other guy, and their own benefits—scholarships and guaranteed loans for students; price supports and credit assistance to farmers; preferred mortgage rates to veterans; retirement benefits and medical care for seniors; billions in annual tax deductions for savings plans, home ownership, education, private health care, and charitable giving—as their tax dollars at work. Although federal social welfare programs aid almost all groups—rich, poor, and almost everyone in between—more social welfare spending is targeted at the well-off than at the poor.

In this chapter, we will discuss the political and legal bases for social welfare policies, briefly review how they have evolved, and then describe programs and tax policies adopted to serve the needs of specific groups of Americans.

The Political and Legal Bases of Social Welfare Policies

Imagine for a minute that you are a farmer in a chronically drought-stricken African country. If your cattle die or your crops fail, the chances of malnutrition and even starvation are fairly high. There is no crop insurance, no agricultural extension service, no income support or food vouchers, no public health service, and perhaps no schools to teach your children skills other than farming. Governments often do not have the reach, the resources, or sometimes even the will to provide a safety net. This is what pure capitalism without a social welfare program would be like. It is closer to what our system was like in the early 1930s when American farmers fled the Dust Bowl states trying to find work to allow them to feed their children. There were religious and other private charities, and state and local governments provided some services, but all their resources combined could not cope with the dislocation and needs created by the Great Depression. The federal government's response to the Depression was the beginning of large-scale federal welfare and social insurance programs.

We use the term *social welfare policy* to refer broadly to direct or indirect government subsidies for individuals and families, who are often grouped by category such as "the poor," "the disabled," and "the elderly."

Most developing nations do not have a set of social programs to protect citizens against poverty and famine, provide health care, or make education available to all. Here malnourished Sudanese children wait for aid from international relief agencies.

same time, we give even more support to the middle class and the rich because policymakers could not get elected if they were not responsive to the expectations of their most powerful supporters and constituents.

Few people in any industrialized country today think they should be left completely at the mercy of natural or market forces. They look to social welfare policies to take the worst risks out of living in a capitalist system, offering protection for the ill, disabled, elderly poor, and unemployed while also providing a sturdy safety net for businesses.

Where does the authority come from to do all this? The Preamble to the Constitution says that promotion of the general welfare was one purpose for creation of the Union, and Article I assigns the responsibility of providing for the general welfare to Congress, but the scope of the formal powers granted to Congress is a topic of continuing debate. Congress's authority to enact social welfare programs stems from powers implied by the "general welfare" phrase and from its formal power to tax. Government's taxing authority allows it to accumulate the resources needed to provide social services as well as a means for taking income from some people and redistributing it to others. This is not unidirectional, however; sometimes government redistributes money from the rich to the poor and sometimes from the less well off to the wealthy.

Direct subsidies are payments government makes to individuals by checks, vouchers, or credits. Social Security payments, price support payments, cash assistance to the poor, and food vouchers are direct subsidies. *Indirect subsidies* are goods or services provided by the government to the public or to a specified group at below market value—for example, public education, health care, and public housing. If you are enrolled at a state college or university, chances are that your tuition and fees cover no more than half of real costs, possibly less—taxpayers pick up the difference.

Why does government do it—and should it be doing it? Whether it should be providing so many benefits is a philosophical question on which there will never be agreement. But there are many motivations for adopting such a wide variety of support programs. A political system like ours is predicated on equality of opportunity. The sick, the poor, the disabled, and the systemically discriminated against need assistance to put them on anything close to an equal footing. This support in turn helps foster economic growth because every country's development is dependent on a healthy, educated population. As government has grown and become involved in all segments of society, we have come to rely on its help to cushion life's blows for the least well off. At the

The Evolution of Social Welfare Policies

At the time the Constitution was written, no level of government was involved in providing aid to families and individuals. Local governments were responsible for the poor but gave little aid. Orphaned or destitute children were apprenticed to better-off families, where they worked as servants. Workhouses were established for the able-bodied poor, and some minimal aid was given to the old or sick.[13] Churches and other private charities helped the "deserving" poor and unfortunate. Those thought to be undeserving were treated harshly. These attitudes reflected the belief that individuals bore the primary responsibility for their own fate.

While government took little responsibility for the well-being of individuals, it was involved in the economic development of the country and the creation of jobs. In at least one case (the Homestead Act, passed during the Civil War), this resulted in direct benefits to families and individuals: To encourage settlement of the western states, the government gave away 246 million acres of land, in 160-acre allotments, to 1.5 million homesteaders. If settlers stayed on the land for five years and developed it, they received title free and clear.

Government also encouraged development through its immigration policies, although it did little to help new residents after their arrival. The great waves of immigration at the end of the nineteenth century and the beginning of the twentieth generated a desperate need for health care, housing, and education in the big cities, but what there was came primarily from private charities or settlement houses, such as Chicago's Hull House, or from local political party organizations. Settlement houses taught literacy and work skills and provided lessons in hygiene and rudimentary health care for infants and children. New arrivals got help finding housing and jobs from ward heelers for the big cities' political machines, who were looking to trade favors for votes.

The idea that government should provide extensive public services such as education, hospitals, and asylums developed in the nineteenth century. But the concept of paying individuals benefits is a twentieth-century idea. Gradually, the belief grew that government has a responsibility to help at least some of those at the bottom of the ladder. These changed attitudes led to the enactment of state laws, beginning in 1911, to establish aid programs for poor children and their mothers. Fifteen years later, most states had such laws, freeing many children from apprenticeships and poorhouses.

Most of our major federal social welfare programs were developed in the 1930s as part of the New Deal's response to the Great Depression. These programs provided support to farmers, poor families, and the elderly poor. During the 1960s' War on Poverty, old programs were expanded, and major new ones to assist with health care—Medicare and Medicaid—were added.

Over the decades, the United States has amassed a large number of social welfare programs (see Figure 1), but that does not make us a "welfare state." Welfare states have a coordinated set of income support programs to ensure access to basic necessities in a uniform way, not just for those in need but for the population as a whole. These are governments that accept the premise that jobs, health care, education, and the basic material necessities of life are entitlements or human rights, and some may even have that principle incorporated into their constitutions. In contrast, our social welfare programs are largely uncoordinated efforts designed to solve the particular problems of specific groups (for example, college students, the poor, farmers, the elderly) on a piecemeal basis. We shall look at some of these programs by category: income support programs, health care and other subsidized services, and tax subsidies.

Income Support Programs

Today the federal government has programs providing income support to retirees and their dependents, the disabled and their dependents, farmers, poor families, and the unemployed, in addition to pension plans for its civilian and military personnel.

Retirees and Their Dependents

The earliest and the most comprehensive of income support programs is the Old Age Survivors Disability and Health Insurance Program, adopted in 1935 to ensure that the elderly would not live in poverty after retirement. President Roosevelt and the other New Dealers who initiated the program would be astounded at its current magnitude. **Social Security** has evolved into a government-managed retirement fund for American workers from all income groups, a life insurance pro-

Hull House helped new immigrants develop employable skills. This photo from the 1920s or 1930s shows a sewing class for women.

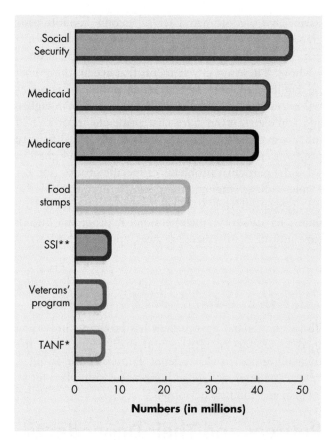

FIGURE 1 ■ **Direct Federal Aid** *More than eighty million Americans receive direct federal aid. This figure does not include indirect subsidies or tax subsidies. (The numbers in this figure add up to more than eighty million because some people benefit from more than one federal program.)*

*Temporary Assistance for Needy Families, the program that replaced Aid to Families with Dependent Children.

**Supplemental Security Income, the aid program for the needy elderly and disabled.

SOURCE: *Budget of the United States, Fiscal Year 2005*, 69, 154, 157, 282 [Centers for Medicare and Medicaid Services (www.cms.hhs.gov/researchers)].

gram for surviving dependents and spouses, and an income support program for people with disabilities. Participation is not voluntary, and over the decades, the program has grown to cover 96 percent of all workers. Nearly one of every six individuals now receives a Social Security payment, and seven in ten can expect to be covered in the future. Social Security covers so many Americans that each of us is issued a Social Security identification number at birth.

Social Security is financed through a payroll tax on employees and employers. The employee's contribution, slightly over 6.2 percent (7.65 percent, including Medicare) of the first $90,000 of earnings, is withheld from wages; employers contribute an equal amount. As with income tax, this is a nominal rate because taxes are paid on adjusted gross income; therefore, the effective rate is lower for some. Self-employed workers must pay

both the workers' and employers' share (with the Medicare tax, 15.3 percent of their adjusted gross income) and send payments to the IRS with their annual income tax return. Social Security taxes are credited to a special off-budget trust fund and invested in government securities until they are needed to cover benefit payments. In other words, Social Security benefits are not paid out of the general revenue funds that come from personal and corporate income or excise taxes. They are paid entirely from contributions made to the trust fund by employers, their employees, and the self-employed, plus the accrued interest.

Social Security taxes produced 31 percent of all federal revenues in 2005, and payments to beneficiaries accounted for just over 21 percent of federal spending. It is the single largest expenditure in the federal budget. Lower-income workers are hardest hit by these taxes because all their earnings are subject to the tax. Earnings above $90,000 are not subject to Social Security tax so the wealthiest Americans have a smaller proportion of their income withheld in payroll taxes.

Lower-income retirees receive more benefits relative to their earnings than do wealthier participants. But 60 percent of Social Security payments do go to individuals living above the poverty line.[14] For this reason, and also to shore up the trust fund, middle- and upper-income beneficiaries are required to pay taxes on 85 percent of their Social Security income at the same rate at which the rest of their income is taxed.

The size of the monthly stipend received by beneficiaries is determined by how many years they worked, how much they earned, and whether they are alone or have dependents. Currently, a retiree born in 1939 can qualify for full benefits at age sixty-five years and four months and can request payments as early as age sixty-two at a lower stipend. The age of eligibility for full benefits increases by small increments with birth year. For each year up to age seventy that retirement is postponed, the monthly stipend increases.

Social Security is categorized as social insurance rather than a welfare program because it is inclusive— for people of all income groups—and because only those who have paid into the program, or their survivors, can collect benefits. Since people do not have to show financial need to participate, everyone can accept it without the public stigma of being on welfare. This aspect of the program increases its political popularity. Yet it is a mistake to think that beneficiaries are only getting back what they and their employers paid into the program through payroll deductions, plus accumulated interest. This is true for some short-lived people. But given today's longer life spans, Social Security pays most of its recipients more than they paid in, something no private insurance program would do. In 1940, a sixty-five-year-old was expected to collect benefits for

One of the success stories of American public policy, Social Security gives most elderly the freedom to swim in society's mainstream. However, some changes are needed to maintain its benefits for the next generation.

twelve and a half years; by 2004, that had increased to seventeen and a half years.

Social Security has grown from about 220,000 recipients in 1940 to 47 million in 2004. Ninety percent of Americans sixty-five years of age or older are currently receiving Social Security benefits. They account for about 72 percent of all beneficiaries; their survivors, dependents, and the disabled account for the remainder. The average monthly benefit to a retired worker has risen from a mere $13 in 1940, when many fewer people were covered and withholding was much less, to $926 in 2004.[15]

In 1950, Social Security accounted for only 3 percent of all retirement income. It is now 35 percent of the income of elderly couples, 38 percent for an unmarried elderly male, and 52 percent for an elderly single woman. It forms a larger part of elderly women's income because women earn less over the life course and have fewer private pensions, savings, or other investments.[16] (The median income of a woman working full time in 2002 was $9,000 less than that of a man.)[17] Without Social Security, almost half of our senior citizens would be poor, whereas today the poverty rate for those sixty-five and older is at a historic low of 10.2 percent.[18] To the extent that continued payments from the fund keep people above the poverty line, they are doing what Social Security was intended to do.

Social Security has stayed afloat because of ever-increasing numbers of people paying in at steadily rising rates. The taxes withheld from the paychecks of today's workers provide the payouts to current retirees just as they supported the generation before them. The aging of the population and the declining ratio of workers to retirees does present a threat to the long-term solvency of the system. (We return to this in the "Current Issues" section.)

The Poor

Federal income support programs for the poor began as part of the original Social Security legislation, which established, along with the retirement program for seniors, a national program of unemployment insurance. This legislation was passed to combat the effects of the Great Depression, when nearly a quarter of the workforce was unemployed and state and local programs did not have the resources to meet demand. Except for Social Security itself, which is funded and managed entirely at the federal level, most income support programs have been run jointly by federal, state, and local governments. In most cases, state programs of assistance to the poor and unemployed predated federal programs; federal money was sent to bolster these programs, sometimes with new guidelines set by Congress.

Eligibility

A major difference between beneficiaries of an inclusive program like Social Security and one that exclusively targets the poor is that qualification for participation requires a **means test.** Participants must periodically demonstrate eligibility by showing that they are poor—they must have both limited income and few assets.

The definition of who is poor is revised each year by the Census Bureau, which makes adjustments to account for changes in inflation and the cost of living. It does not set a single income level but many, depending on age and household composition. In 2003, for example, a single person under sixty-five years of age was considered poor if his or her income was below $9,573; the comparable figure for a family of four was $18,660 (see Figure 2). Not everyone agrees with the Census Bureau's poverty estimates because they do not take into account many "in kind" benefits poor people receive, such as food and housing subsidies and medical care. If these were added to income, critics of the threshold say, the poverty rate would be reduced by about 4 percent. Others argue that the Census Bureau *understates* the amount of poverty by using 1960s standards that focused on the price of food and underestimate the cost of housing, fuel, education, and health care. A common alternative estimate for a family of four is $30,000 to $34,000.[19]

The Elderly and the Disabled

One of the first grant-in-aid programs established under Social Security authority, **Supplemental Security Income (SSI),** provides income support for the blind and people with disabilities and for the elderly not covered by Social Security or whose Social Security benefits are not large enough to lift them out of poverty. For 20 percent of seniors, Social Security is their *only* income, which may be insufficient to meet their basic

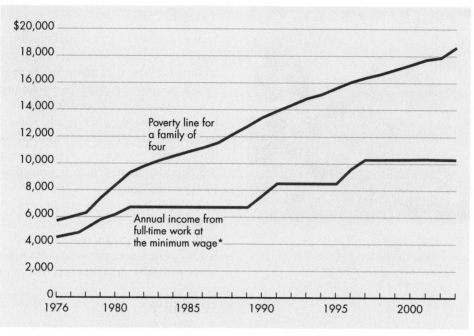

FIGURE 2 ■ The Poverty Line and the Minimum Wage *The U.S. Census Bureau adjusts the poverty line annually. Congress sets the minimum wage for working Americans, which was last raised in 1997 to $5.15 per hour. As this figure shows, a person working full-time at the minimum wage does not earn enough to provide a family of four with a minimum standard of living.*

*Assumes a minimum wage of $5.15 per hour for forty hours a week, fifty weeks a year. Some states have set their own minimum wage above the federal level.

2003 poverty threshold from the U.S. Census Bureau.

living costs. Other SSI recipients are workers or survivors of workers who were not covered by the Social Security program (something unlikely to happen much in the future given the expansion of Social Security to virtually all jobs). Although created by Social Security legislation and run by the same agency, SSI is funded from general tax revenues, not Social Security payroll taxes.

In 2004, about seven million Americans received SSI; about one-third were Social Security recipients whose benefits were too low to meet basic needs, and most of the remainder were people under age sixty-five with disabilities.[20] Payments to those receiving only SSI range from $552 per month for an individual to $829 for a couple.

To qualify for SSI, a individual cannot have more than $2,000 or a couple more than $3,000 in assets (cash or stocks and bonds; personal home and car do not count). SSI recipients are automatically eligible under federal standards for food stamps and health insurance (discussed later), but states have considerable leeway to change eligibility standards.

Poor Families

Aid to Families with Dependent Children (AFDC) was another grant-in-aid program that grew out of Social Security legislation. The purpose was to strengthen maternal and child welfare services being provided by the states (see Figure 3). Coverage was soon extended to mothers as well as their dependent children and later to both fathers and mothers with dependent children. Because AFDC was a joint federal-state program administered at the state level, eligibility and benefits varied from state to state.

Despite the success that AFDC had in providing food and shelter to dependent children, critics argued that it fostered dependency instead of encouraging independence and hard work. For example, although the number of AFDC recipients was fairly stable from the mid-1970s to the late 1980s, it shot up in the recession of the late 1980s and early 1990s. In contrast to the common stereotype, however, the increase in welfare recipients was not tied to the size of welfare stipends, which in real terms (adjusted for inflation) began a steady decline in the 1970s.

The largest growth in number of recipients came when economic times were hard; but when the economy improved, the rolls did not always fall back to their previous level. Part of the reason is that even in years when the economy was growing, many of the new jobs being created did not pay enough to meet basic living costs. Welfare rolls also grew because of the increase in the number of births to unmarried women without

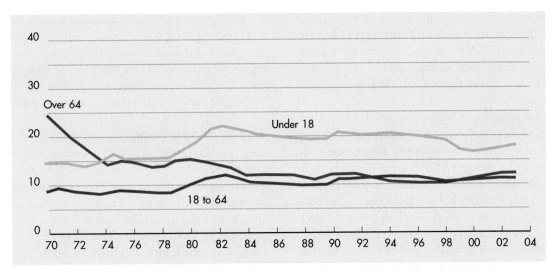

FIGURE 3 ■ **Profile of the Poor** *The number of children living in poverty has increased in the past three years. Children are considerably more likely to be poor than any other age group.*

SOURCE: U.S. Census Bureau, "2003 Poverty Tables" (www.census.gov). The poverty threshold for a single person under age sixty-five in 2003 was $9,578; for a family of four, it was $18,660.

job skills who were often still children themselves (see Table 1). It is extremely difficult for a single parent with no job skills to support children, especially without child-care support, so many turned to AFDC. The number of births to single women continues to be high: 68 percent of all African American, 27 percent of all white, and 42 percent of all Hispanic births are to unmarried women. And more than 80 percent of these

TABLE 1	Families Living in Poverty

Poverty is much more common in female-headed and minority families.

	Percentage in Poverty
All families	**11**
White	9
Black	23
Hispanic	22
Asian	10
Married-couple families	**6**
White	6
Black	9
Hispanic	17
Asian	8
Female-headed families, no husband present	**30**
White	26
Black	39
Hispanic	38
Asian	24

SOURCE: U.S. Census Bureau, "2003 Poverty Tables" (www.census.gov).

unwed mothers go on the welfare rolls for at least some time. Even so, the number of unmarried teenage women giving birth has been declining since 1996.[21]

Our society makes it difficult for women to choose low-paid work over welfare. They are often worse off because of child-care costs and the loss of medical benefits that come with AFDC but not with most low-paying jobs. Nevertheless, the majority of AFDC recipients collected benefits for a relatively short time.[22] They found a job or married someone who earned more than poverty wages (or both). But nearly one-quarter of the women who went on AFDC stayed for ten years or more, and another 20 percent stayed for six to nine years. Though most AFDC recipients were white, long-term recipients were more likely to be black or Hispanic unmarried teenage mothers with no high school diploma (see Figure 4).

AFDC became the main target for critics of cash assistance to the poor. Its cost was much lower than other income support programs, but to its critics, it appeared to be rewarding the wrong kind of behavior while getting no results. They saw AFDC as discouraging work, encouraging out-of-wedlock births, and allowing fathers to take no responsibility for their children. While a consensus grew that the welfare system needed to be reformed, there were strong differences over how to do it.

In 1993, President Clinton took office promising to end welfare "as we know it." In the 1994 elections, the Republican "Contract with America" promised even more dramatic reform. After heated debate, in 1996 Congress passed, and the president signed, a welfare reform bill that abolished AFDC and with it the concept of welfare as an entitlement to all those who met federal guidelines. Instead, in the new **Temporary Aid to Needy Families (TANF)** program, states were mandated to set up their own welfare systems under loose federal guidelines, to be funded by block grants from the federal government.

TANF is a results-oriented program that sets time limits on eligibility and requires participants to move "from welfare to work," the signature slogan of the reform bill. States receiving TANF funds were to have, at minimum, 30 percent of the people on their welfare rolls working at least thirty hours a week during the program's initial five years. "Work" included job training, community service, and continuing education. TANF recipients are required to hold jobs within two years of entering the program, and working families can receive assistance for a lifetime maximum of five years. States were allowed to exempt up to 20 percent of the people receiving assistance from this requirement (for example, people who are physically or mentally unable to hold a job or parents with young children and no child care).

Initially, people who feared the impact of TANF on children and welfare recipients unable to find employment severely criticized the program. In response, some modifications were made to allow recipients to receive child care, transportation, and other noncash assistance beyond the two-year cutoff. These modifications were designed to help those who took low-paying jobs and who needed such additional assistance to keep their families intact.[23] However, states have the authority to enact more stringent limits.

One dark trend in the first five years of reform was that forcing women with dependent children into the labor force caused an increase in no-parent families. The reasons are unclear, but more mothers left their children with relatives. Possibly it is because of the burden of holding down jobs, often with irregular hours, combined with the demands of child care and a loss of benefits. Hardest hit were African American children in inner cities, where the number living without a parent more than doubled after the welfare-to-work reforms.[24]

Another dark side to reform was the reduction in state spending for welfare. Whereas in the early years, spending in some states increased dramatically as they offered job training and other assistance to move people from welfare to work, after the decline in welfare rolls (by as much as two-thirds in midwestern states), spending also declined. That may seem logical, since there are fewer clients, but in most states, 70 percent or more of welfare recipients still need training and other assistance if they are to find jobs. Although Congress set a requirement that states must spend at least as much as they were spending in 1996 to qualify for block grant money to cover income support, 2001 spending by most states was only 75 percent of the 1996 level.[25]

Part of the decrease in spending can be attributed to Congress's giving states considerable flexibility in how they use a certain portion of block grant money, allowing them to create "rainy day funds." States can reserve for later use money they are entitled to receive for TANF, or they can divert it to other purposes.[26]

The Working Poor

As criticism grew of paying welfare benefits to the chronically unemployed, more emphasis was placed on rewarding the working poor. The **earned income tax credit (EITC),** which has been in place since 1975, may sound like a tax subsidy, but it can result in a direct payment to the claimant. The EITC is a negative income tax, which gives both single and married individuals, with and without dependent children, credits against their tax liability. The credit can be used to reduce taxes owed, but for families whose income is so low that they have no income tax liability, the credit is returned as a direct payment from the government. Claims for the credit are filed on a form attached to one's annual income tax report. In 2003, more than nineteen million families and individuals—about one of every seven tax returns filed—claimed the credit. An estimated five million of these families were lifted above the official poverty threshold by an EITC payment.[27]

This approach to poverty rewards work and allows poor families to receive government aid without becoming a client of the welfare bureaucracy. President Reagan called the EITC the "best antipoverty, best pro-family, best job creation measure to come out of Congress." That both the Clinton and Bush administrations were able to expand EITC is a measure of its bipartisan support. But it is still a frequent target of budget cutters.

The working poor can also qualify for help with the cost of job training and, in many states, for help with child care. Poor families receiving TANF benefits can apply for such assistance when they move off welfare and into jobs. Welfare reform authorized states to give assistance to any family earning up to 85 percent of the state's median income. More than two million children were receiving day care in federal- and state-funded child-care centers in 2002.[28]

Food Subsidies

Another major supplement to the income of the poor comes from the Department of Agriculture's food stamp program. Until 2004, **food stamps** were paper coupons that served as vouchers redeemable in grocery stores for food. Now this food subsidy is issued in the form of an electronic credit accessed by a debit card. The credit may be used only to purchase unprepared food and cannot be used for dining out or for liquor or tobacco. Their average dollar value per household ranges from about $160 to $350 a month depending on

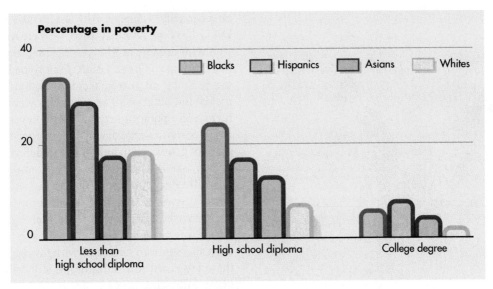

Percentage in poverty

Blacks   Hispanics   Asians   Whites

Less than high school diploma

High school diploma

College degree

FIGURE 4 ■ Percentage of Families in Poverty, by Education Level and Ethnicity of Head of Household, 2003

SOURCE: U.S. Census Bureau, *Statistical Abstract of the United States, 2003* (Washington, D.C.: Government Printing Office, 2003), tab. 707.

the state. Because of the move from paper coupons to electronic credits, the program is expected to undergo a name change in the near future.

The food stamp program began as a temporary measure of support during the last years of the Great Depression, but was revived and made permanent as part of Lyndon Johnson's War on Poverty. Its coverage expanded during the early 1970s in response to an investigation that revealed that tens of thousands of Americans suffered from malnourishment, resulting in retarded growth, anemia, protein deficiencies, high rates of infant mortality, scurvy and rickets (from insufficient vitamin C, vitamin D, and milk), and an impaired ability to learn. In the first years of the program, malnutrition among the poor decreased, as did the incidence of diseases caused by poor nutrition.

Even though the food stamp program was pared back during the 1980s, one of every ten Americans was receiving the coupons in the years just before the 1996 welfare reforms. One of the objectives of those reforms was to reduce the size of the program by eliminating fraud and abuse. To that end, Congress established fines for states that make too many errors in determining eligibility for the program. Most states now require recertification of eligibility every three or four months. The 1996 law also made most legal immigrants ineligible for food stamp assistance. In the two years following adoption of the new certification procedures, participation in the program declined by 25 percent.[29] This led the Department of Agriculture (DoA) to call for increased participation. Food stamps have always been seen as a constructive means for reducing food surpluses (which are warehoused by the DoA), as well as for fighting

hunger. The 2002 Farm Bill restored coverage to legal immigrants who have been in the country at least five years, and it encouraged greater participation by the working poor. The rising poverty rate has also had an impact on the number of recipients, which was expected to jump from twenty-one million in 2001 to twenty-five million in 2005.[30] This would still be only about three-fifths of those believed to be eligible nationwide.[31]

The government provides an additional food subsidy to pregnant women and preschool children through the Special Supplemental Nutritional Program for Women, Infants, and Children. Because poorly nourished mothers have more sickly babies and because poorly nourished children do not learn as well as children with adequate diets, the government now provides support for mothers-to-be and new mothers who cannot afford to buy the kinds or amounts of foods necessary for good nutrition for themselves and their infants. These women and children are also eligible for a pre-preschool program that provides family services from before birth until the infants become eligible for Head Start (discussed later in this chapter) at age three.[32]

Farmers

Income support programs for farmers were described in "You Are There" at the start of this chapter. Direct federal aid has accounted for almost half of total farm income since the 1980s, and it has been as high as 70 percent in some farm states. Farming is the most heavily subsidized occupation in the United States. Ninety percent of all farmers still earn less than $20,000 a year,

In the 1930s, homelessness was largely caused by the Great Depression. Here is photographer Dorothea Lange's historic photo of a homeless Oklahoma family during that era.

Library of Congress

while the top 1 percent account for more than half of all farm income.

Like Social Security, income support for farmers was motivated by the urgent needs and dire living conditions of one segment of the American population. Because food self-sufficiency is regarded by many as essential to national security and because many farmers were being forced off the land, providing federal aid took on a special urgency. But also like Social Security, farm aid has evolved into an income support program not for poor or marginal family farms but for all farming enterprises, including the largest and most profitable. Unlike Social Security, where even the top payments are modest and all participants get some minimum payments, farm aid provides staggeringly large sums to the wealthiest farmers while 60 percent of farmers receive no subsidies at all.[33] In 2000, of 1.6 million receiving farm aid, about 57,500 got more than $100,000; at least 154 got more than $1 million. Fully $17 million went to farms operated by government agencies, and millions more to university farms.[34] Almost 85 percent of the subsidies are received by fewer than one-quarter of the country's two million farmers.

At least twenty *Fortune* 500 companies received checks from federal programs in 2000, as did eleven members of Congress. They included the speaker of the House, the ranking Democrat on the House Agriculture Committee, and the chair of the Senate Finance Committee, Charles Grassley. Grassley, who claims to be primarily a farmer and not to live in Washington, D.C., "except Monday through Fridays," has received payments as large as $110,936—mailed to his Washington residence. The senator's claim to be living and farming in Iowa may stretch credulity, but his explanation that all but $20,000 of his payments went to meet equipment and operating expenses is believable.[35] The operating costs of large farms are staggering, and a good share of government aid is used to defray these expenses. The question is whether taxpayers' money should make the difference between agribusinesses' and corporate farms' staying in or going out of business.

Richard Lugar (R-Ind.), another Agriculture Committee member who receives subsidy payments for a corn and soybean farm and who says he could not grow these crops without subsidies, is still critical of the program. Subsidies, he says, "distort markets by encouraging overproduction to drive prices lower in a self-perpetuating cycle."[36]

In 1996, Congress made a halfhearted attempt to phase out income supports for certain crops over a seven-year period, but instead payments quadrupled from $7.3 billion in 1995 to $32.2 billion in 2000. As American farmers lost their competitiveness in the global marketplace, Congress ramped up the subsidies. Agriculture and the "family farm" hold a special place in the American identity—they represent the country's breadbasket, its Corn and Bible Belts, conjuring up images of waving fields of grains, pioneers, and an "authentic" America that politicians love to be associated with.

But current programs are not well regarded by the small family farmers whom politicians like to claim they are saving. By 2001, fully 73 percent of rural Nebraskans polled believed that caps should be set on the amount of subsidies any individual can receive.[37] In Congress, the main division on this issue is more along regional than party lines. Senators from states where agriculture is dominated by family farms are in favor of the lower caps and shifting more of the money to small farmers. Senators from states with huge farms run by agribusinesses favor retaining the higher payment limit.

The commitment of Congress to continue business as usual in farm policy was made clear in its approval of large increases in subsidies in the 2002 farm bill. Even more impressive was that it was done during a period of recession, tax cuts, budget deficits, and rising farm income. Between 2002 and 2004, farm income doubled yet farm subsidies still rose 40 percent during the same period.[38]

If farm subsidies are to be reformed, the pressure will probably come from abroad. Continued spending on price supports for agricultural commodities conflicts with the U.S. commitment to free trade and its obligations as a member of the World Trade Organization (see

Chapter 19). The United States is a party to international trade agreements that, to ensure fair competition among the world's farm exporters, limit how much a government can pay in price supports. If the WTO rules against the United States in grievances filed by other member countries, payments to farmers would have to be cut if we want to be in compliance with international obligations.

Veterans

Through the Department of Veterans Affairs, the federal government provides income support to veterans with disabilities. To qualify for a disability pension, a veteran must be able to prove that the disability was acquired while on active duty. The level of support, whether full or partial, depends on the severity of the disability. In 2005, some 2.7 million veterans will receive about $25 billion in disability pensions.[39]

The government also funds a retirement program for career servicemen and servicewomen at a cost of close to $34 billion annually.[40] It would be hard to justify not having a pension system for military personnel, but the plan's eligibility standards have many critics. Because so many career service personnel retire at an early age, they are able to hold down full-time jobs while drawing full military pensions. As a result, most military pensions are paid to individuals with above-average incomes who will also be eligible to receive Social Security.

The Impact of Income Support Programs

Income support programs for the elderly, disabled, and dependent children played a major role in reducing poverty rates in the United States from their highs in the 1930s. Due in part to the Great Society programs of the 1960s, the proportion of families in poverty dropped from 21 percent in 1959 to 10 percent in 1973, the lowest point ever achieved in the United States.[41] It then increased steadily, reaching a high of 14 percent in 1993, before the booming economy of the 1990s sent it downward. On the rise again, it stood at 12.5 percent in 2003. That year, one of every three poor persons was a child, and fifteen million people were living in extreme poverty (below one-half the poverty line).[42]

Income support programs for the poor and disabled draw much more attention from budget cutters than support programs for the middle- and upper-income beneficiaries, such as many recipients of Social Security payments and farm subsidies. Collectively, these programs account for the largest outlay of government revenues, but the majority of these payouts by far go to those enrolled in social insurance programs and to owners of industrial farms rather than to the poor and unemployed.

Health Care Programs

In the United States, government aid for health care is a social benefit for some people in all income groups but not for all people. Nonetheless, health care is by far the most costly indirect government subsidy. Half of all federal, state, and local spending on means-tested programs is for medical care.[43] Through Medicare, Medicaid, and Veterans Affairs, the government is the largest health care provider in the country.

The federal government has been involved in some aspects of health care for decades, but before 1965, there was no general federal support for individual health care. In 1965, after years of debate over government's responsibility, concern about the problems of millions of Americans who could not afford adequate health care prompted President Johnson to propose and Congress to pass two programs, Medicare (for the elderly) and Medicaid (for low-income people).

Health Care for Seniors

Medicare is a public health insurance program that funds many medical expenses for the elderly and disabled. It includes hospital insurance, and additional voluntary coverage helps pay for physicians' services, outpatient hospital services, and some other costs.

Hospital insurance is paid for by the Medicare payroll tax, while the elective portion is financed through general revenues and monthly premiums paid by participants. Everyone eligible for Social Security benefits is eligible for Medicare, and over 90 percent of Social Security recipients buy the optional insurance. In 2005, the program will cover more than forty million people at a cost of $290 billion.

There are many factors that explain the improved health profile of the elderly over the past forty years, including scientific breakthroughs in the treatment of some diseases, but Medicare is responsible for many of the gains. Compared to the period before 1965, more seniors are able to see doctors now, and the elderly have more but shorter hospital stays. There have been declines in death rates from diseases affecting the elderly, such as heart attacks and strokes, and a decrease in the number of days of restricted activity that older people experience.[44]

In spite of these substantial accomplishments, Medicare has not been a complete success. It is expensive, and many of those who need it have trouble paying their portion of the costs. There has been extensive fraud in

Individuals depend on government for many health services including mass vaccination programs. In 2004, a shortage of flu shots occurred because the government contracted with only two suppliers of vaccine, and one defaulted. Here people wait in line for flu shots in Roanoke, Virginia.

the program, especially overbilling by doctors and HMOs.

The maximum fees the government has set for services are lower than some doctors have been willing to accept, and as a consequence, they refuse to treat Medicare patients. Patients themselves have been criticized for driving up costs by making unnecessary doctor or hospital visits and having unrealistic expectations about what medical care can do to resolve their health problems. Experts of all political persuasions continue to predict that the Medicare program will go broke within the next few decades unless changes are made in the program or a national health care system is put in place. A similar cost problem afflicts the other major federal health care program, Medicaid.

Health Care for the Poor and Disabled

Medicaid is a federal-state program that pays for medical care for disabled and unemployed people as well as some of the working poor who do not have coverage and cannot afford to buy it. States set their own Medicaid eligibility standards, within federal guidelines. Nationwide, 11 percent of Americans receive health coverage through Medicaid, with some variation among states.[45] Medicaid pays for one-third of all births, two-thirds of nursing home stays, and provides nearly half of the public funds for AIDS patients.[46]

Medicaid has now surpassed Medicare as the second most expensive entitlement program (after Social Security). It will cover about forty-two million people in 2005 and cost over $322 billion. It is an indication of how much of the responsibility the federal government has devolved on the states that in 2005, the federal share of Medicaid costs will be about $182 billion, compared to $140 billion for the states.[47] On average, states spend 22 percent of their budgets on Medicaid and due to its rapid growth in a revenue-short period, it is crowding out spending for education and other needs.[48]

Even with Medicare, Medicaid, and private health insurance provided through the workplace, almost forty-five million Americans remain without health insurance, two-thirds from wage-earning families whose income is above the poverty line. And as we have pointed out, the loss of health insurance discourages parents from leaving welfare to take low-income jobs. In five states, over 20 percent of the population remains uninsured. Uninsured individuals are more common in the southern states and less common in New England and the Midwest.[49]

To ensure greater coverage of children, in 1997 the government created the State Children's Health Insurance Program (SCHIP). Working through existing state programs, it set a goal of insuring all children whose parents do not qualify for Medicaid and who cannot afford private insurance. Covering all children who are eligible has been difficult because many families remain

Like most individuals in middle-class families, this young man gets good medical treatment for chronic illnesses such as asthma. However, the uninsured and the poverty stricken are much more likely to die from lack of treatment of such diseases.

unaware of the program. And some states have done little to make them aware of their eligibility, instead diverting to other programs federal money allocated for SCHIP. But more than five million children who would otherwise not have health insurance are now covered by SCHIP.

Health Care for Veterans

In addition to Medicare, Medicaid, and SCHIPS the government also funds a national system of hospitals, outpatient clinics, nursing homes, and psychiatric clinics, run by the Department of Defense (DoD) and Veterans Affairs (VA), that provide health care to about four million veterans. (The VA also maintains a national system of cemeteries for veterans and their families.) The wars in Afghanistan and Iraq are creating a new generation of combat veterans and an increased need for health care and rehabilitation. The DoD and VA are two of the country's largest providers of medical services, yet nearly 1.7 million veterans have no health insurance or access to government hospitals and clinics for veterans.[50]

Subsidized Services

Other subsidized services reach a broad swath of the American public. Virtually everyone who relies on a municipal bus system or intercity trains or who drives on a highway, for example, benefits from federally subsidized mass transit and support for highway construction. Other federal aid mostly benefits middle- and high-income Americans.

Education

Elementary and secondary education in the United States is primarily in the hands of local governmental

units and funded largely through state and local taxes. Because the No Child Left Behind program's testing mandate has imposed significant new costs on public schools, the federal government has increased the level of aid to elementary schools, although not by nearly as much as promised.

The federal government *is* a major funder of higher education through grants and guaranteed loans to undergraduates and fellowships and low-interest loans to graduate students. Almost every American college student is aware of Pell grants, but the granddaddy of all student support programs, and the most successful in terms of overall impact on the country, is the GI Bill of Rights (see the box "The GI Bill of Rights").

Government also funds an early-learning program for children from poor households. Head Start provides preschool education, with the objective of teaching children from poor families skills they will need to succeed in primary school. It also encourages parents to become involved in their children's education and to read to them at home. Head Start has been a widely supported program from its inception in the 1960s, but it is still underfunded in terms of the number of students who could benefit from it. With funding of $6.8 billion in 2005, it will accommodate only a small percentage of eligible children, even though studies show that preschoolers with Head Start experience do better in school than other poor children without preschooling.[51]

Housing

The federal government has many programs to support home ownership and has several agencies that help veterans, farmers, and low-income families obtain mortgage loans at subsidized rates. However, most spending is to help middle-class Americans, not those at lower income levels struggling to find housing.

The Federal Housing Finance Board, which supervises twelve Federal Home Loan Banks, (the best known of which are known by their nicknames, Fannie Mae and Freddie Mac) make it easier for lower- and middle-income families to obtain mortgages. They do not issue mortgages but buy them from other lenders, freeing those lenders to issue more mortgages. Through these banks, the government underwrites more than three-fourths of all mortgages on single-family homes.[52]

One of the Bush administration's priorities is fostering what it calls "an ownership society." Home ownership has been encouraged, even in the face of record debt held by consumers. The Fed has helped this policy along by keeping interest rates low during a period of massive government and consumer borrowing. Home purchases have been increasing, especially of larger homes with bigger mortgages. About 40 percent of the mortgages have variable, rather than fixed, rates

It has been called the "greatest piece of legislation Congress ever passed," a "Marshall Plan for America," and "a magic carpet to the middle class." Virtually all Americans have heard of the GI Bill of Rights, but few realize how broad its impact was. When it was signed into law in 1944, just two weeks after D-Day, neither President Roosevelt nor Congress thought they were passing a transformative piece of legislation. They just wanted to help the millions of veterans who would be returning from the war in Europe and Asia reintegrate into civilian life and the labor force.

Since the earliest days of the Republic, the national government has provided benefits to veterans for military service during wartime, but only after veterans organized to demand compensation for lost time and wages. Veterans of the Revolutionary and Civil Wars were promised a land bonus and eventually did receive a pension, but only after threatening revolt. Civil War veterans were extremely well connected in Congress, getting it to authorize pensions that by 1888 accounted for 20 percent of the federal budget.

Partly in reaction to this excess, World War I veterans received a tiny cash payment on mustering out but were promised a small annuity to be paid near retirement age. This was too long a wait for those who fell on hard times in the early years of the Great Depression. But in 1932, when they marched on Washington to demand early payment of their "bonuses," their demonstration was violently suppressed by U.S. Army units under the command of General Douglas MacArthur.

The spectacle of the military assaulting veterans may have been on the mind of Congress when it approved benefits for the twelve million men and women returning from service in World War II. No one was looking for another march on Washington.

A comprehensive assistance package was opposed by all the powerful leaders in Congress and by President Roosevelt. Some were opposed to providing cash assistance for fear it would encourage soldiers not to look for jobs, while others were against a bonus bill because it would single out for benefits only one group of people who contributed to the war effort. But some kind of bonus was supported by an overwhelming majority of the American public. In the end, the compromise bill—called the Bill of Rights for GI Joe and Jane—was written by a member of the American Legion. Its congressional sponsors were relatively unknown Republicans and conservative Southern Democrats, some of whom supported the bill primarily as a way to

A federal law passed during World War II, the GI Bill of Rights, transformed American society by granting each veteran educational benefits and loans to buy homes and start businesses. Returning veterans flooded America's universities by the millions, changing the face of higher education. The facilities at Indiana University, like those of so many other schools, were soon overtaxed, forcing relocation of student registration to its field house.

Courtesy: Indiana University Archives

of interest. Should an inflationary spiral be set in motion by the current level of public and private borrowing, the interest on many of these mortgages will be adjusted upward and add significantly to the debt load already being carried by consumers.[53] Much of this buying has been made possible by the government-backed mortgage giants, whose debt load of $4 trillion was sufficiently large in 2004 to cause Fed Chair Alan Greenspan to warn Congress to restrict the level of debt that Fannie Mae and Freddie Mac can carry.[54]

By comparison, the government spends about $30 billion a year to pay for shelters for the homeless and to provide vouchers to defray housing costs for poor families whose rent exceeds 30 percent of their income.

prevent class warfare. Among the principal players was one woman, Edith Nourse Rogers, a liberal Republican from Massachusetts and the ranking minority member of the Veterans Affairs Committee, who had helped create the Women's Army Corps. She went on to become the first woman to chair a major House committee.

The GI Bill—officially titled the Serviceman's Readjustment Act—contained three major benefits: a living stipend and tuition vouchers for college, low-interest mortgages for purchase of a first home, and loans for starting new businesses. These measures set off a chain reaction that helped shape modern America. To understand how one bill could have such an impact, one has to keep in mind what the economic situation of the average GI was like when we entered World War II.

In 1940, the average soldier was twenty-six, had only one year of high school, and came from a family for whom college was financially out of reach.[1] Had these young men and women not served in the war and received the GI benefit, most could never have gone back to school. Many educators and college presidents opposed the voucher program, arguing that they would have to lower their standards and admit students with poor educational backgrounds. But veterans returned to school in record numbers, more than a million in 1946 alone, when they accounted for almost half of all college enrollments in the United States. In 1950, almost a quarter of all college students were still veterans.[2]

The GI Bill thus stimulated a tremendous growth in higher education, creating the need to hire more faculty and build new facilities, eventually giving rise to a new system of state colleges in many states.

In the first years after the war, however, most veterans chose private schools, since at the time vouchers provided enough to cover tuition in the Ivy League. By 1946, the influx of veterans almost doubled Harvard's enrollment, and they "hogged the honor rolls,"[3] there and throughout the Ivy League. With college educations, many working-class families moved into the middle class, making it possible for them to afford to send their children to college and continue the families' upward mobility. With federally guaranteed mortgages, many vets were also able to leave rental housing in the cities for homes in the outlying areas. So many new homeowners entered the market that it prompted the building of housing developments like Levittown and began the suburbanization of America. This in turn fostered the building of highways and schools and the whole infrastructure necessary to support new towns.

The bill did not work equally well for everyone, in part because African Americans did not have the same choices as whites in using their benefits. Because housing was segregated in most new suburban areas, including Levittown, the route out of the city to affordable housing was less possible for blacks than for whites. Although black vets got the same educational benefits, they did not have the

range of choices in schools, given segregation in some universities and the use of a quota system in others. But thousands did get to college, among them many of those who would become leaders of the modern civil rights movement.

What was so significant about this legislation was that its purpose was to provide financial help that made it possible for young men and women to become more productive citizens for the remainder of their lives. The GI Bill provided education vouchers to eight million veterans. It doubled home ownership, from one in three before the war to two in three afterward. According to a 1986 government study, "each dollar invested in the bill yielded $5 to $12 in tax revenues."[4] The GI Bill was such a success that it was renewed in 1956 with scaled-back benefits for those who had served in Korea and later for Vietnam vets. Overall, the bill's single most important contribution may have been in its extraordinary expansion of higher education because it "signaled the shift to the knowledge society"; for this reason, its passage may in the future be seen "as one of the most important events of the twentieth century."[5]

1. Doris Kearns Goodwin, on "Remembering the GI Bill," *NewsHour with Jim Lehrer*, PBS, July 4, 2000.
2. Michael J. Bennett, *When Dreams Come True: The GI Bill and the Making of Modern America* (Washington, D.C.: Brassey's, 1996), 18.
3. Ibid., 19.
4. Spencer Michaels, on "Remembering the GI Bill," *NewsHour with Jim Lehrer*, PBS, July 4, 2000.
5. Peter Drucker, *Post-Capitalist Society* (New York: HarperBusiness, 1993), 3.

Agriculture

The government has established separate loan agencies to help farmers buy homes, retain land, or expand operations. Like farm subsidy programs, which were designed to help the average farm family hang on to their farms, these programs provide more help to the well-off than to struggling family farmers. Moreover, though termed "loans," the funds spent might more accurately be called grants. Between 1988 and 1992, the Farmers Home Administration (FmHA) wrote off $11.5 billion in bad loans and still carries about $5.2 billion in delinquent loans.[55]

Agriculture support also includes subsidized land and water. Ranchers are subsidized by a Bureau of Land

Federal support for housing is largely targeted to middle-income groups. Hundreds of thousands of poorer Americans remain homeless. Here a shelter provides dinner for the homeless in New York City.

Management policy that allows them to graze their cattle on 270 million acres of public land at a cost per animal of $1.35 (private landowners charge an average of $9.26 per animal). Despite many attempts to revise these fees upward, ranchers believe they are entitled to use of these public lands, even though some land has been completely denuded and is eroding from overgrazing.

The federal government also offers ranchers and farmers billions of dollars in subsidized water. Most water project costs are never repaid. For example, the water brought to California by the $8.8 billion California Central Valley Irrigation Project has created wealth for huge corporate as well as family farms. But of the $36,000-per-acre cost of irrigation, only $527 per acre is returned to the government.

Because of federal subsidies, water is cheap, and farmers grow water-intensive crops even in naturally arid areas. The most water used by California farmers is for pasturing cows and sheep and for growing crops that can be grown more economically elsewhere, such as alfalfa, cotton, and rice, which normally are grown only in very wet climates. These crops use far more water than the grapes, nuts, oranges, strawberries, and tomatoes we associate with California farming.[56]

Tax Subsidies

In addition to direct payments, such as farm subsidies and Social Security benefits, and indirect subsidies, such as for education and Medicare, a third type of federal subsidy is provided through tax breaks. The biggest government subsidies for the well-off take this form, distinguishing them from the direct payment programs that characterize aid to the poor. The cost of these programs is counted in lost revenues rather than cash outlays. A tax subsidy permits some people and corporations to pay much less in taxes than the assessed rate for their income level.

Corporations

The biggest winners in the tax subsidies for the well-off category are corporations. The usual reason cited for extending so many tax incentives to business is to encourage economic and job growth that will benefit the population at large. Although some tax breaks do lead to the creation of jobs, many do not, or at least not domestically.

The vast array of current tax breaks for business are seen by their critics as a form of welfare. **Corporate welfare** has been defined as "any action by local, state, or federal government that gives a corporation or an entire industry a benefit not offered to others." The benefit can be in the form of services, low-interest loans, grants, concessions of land, or tax exemptions, deferrals, or lowered rates.[57] Mining and logging companies, for example, lease federal land at bargain-basement prices. Tax write-offs for capital gains cost the taxpayer more than SSI, and deductions for charitable contributions cost the Treasury about one-third more than it spends on food stamps (see Figure 5). The corporate tax exemption for income earned on exports is estimated to have resulted in $2.3 trillion in lost revenues since it was adopted thirty years ago.[58]

It would be easy to go on at length listing costs of various business tax breaks, but they only count as welfare if taxpayers get nothing in return for the subsidies.

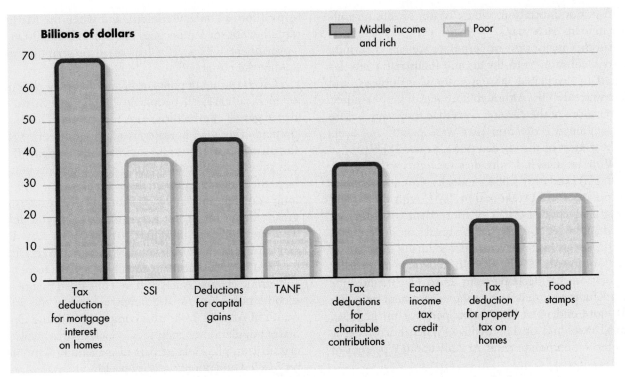

FIGURE 5 ■ The Cost of Federal Programs for the Poor and Tax Breaks for the Middle Income and Rich

SOURCE: Office of Management and Budget, *Budget of the United States Government, Fiscal Year 2005* (Washington, D.C.: Government Printing Office, 2004), 69, 154, 356; Office of Management and Budget, *Analytical Perspectives* (Washington, D.C.: Government Printing Office, 2004), tab. 18-1.

In many instances, this seems to be the case. During the 1990s, when AT&T, Bechtel, Boeing, General Electric, and McDonnell Douglas were awarded 40 percent of all loans and grants made by the Export-Import Bank, employment by those firms dropped by 38 percent. During a period in the late 1980s and early 1990s when General Electric was buying up other companies, including RCA, it received several billion dollars in tax breaks while reducing its workforce by 165,000.[59] And while Enron was receiving government subsidies for developing oil fields, it was bilking shareholders out of billions of dollars.

In addition to subsidies from the federal government, corporations get huge tax breaks and grants from state and local governments. In the competition to attract new jobs, state governments try to outbid one another in offering financial aid to corporations. The town of Albert Lea, Minnesota, for example, gave $3.3 million in tax breaks to Seaboard Corporation to keep its meatpacking plant in operation, and the state provided millions more. Seaboard lowered wages, brought in migrant labor, let its waste overwhelm the city's sewage treatment plant, and four years later relocated to another town that offered even greater subsidies. Many of the migrant laborers who moved to Minnesota could not afford to live there and went on welfare, and the

state spent hundreds of thousands of dollars retraining workers.[60]

In Galesburg, Illinois, six different taxing entities offered incentives to help keep the Maytag refrigerator plant in their town. After getting $2.8 million in sales tax revenue to retrofit its plant, $5.8 million in aid from the state, and ten years of property tax abatements worth more than $2 million, Maytag moved its plant to Mexico.[61] The mayor wanted to sue to get some of the subsidies back but found little support from other citizens fearful that doing so would make their town unattractive to new businesses at a time when they desperately need jobs. Yet as these businesses move their operations offshore, they are rewarded with another subsidy from the federal government—the right to defer taxes on their foreign income, a subsidy they could not have claimed had they kept their jobs in the United States.

One estimate is that state, local, and federal tax breaks offered to attract businesses to relocate cost taxpayers from $44,000 to $29 million per job created.[62] Policymakers continue to subscribe to the argument that tax breaks for corporations will produce new jobs despite the fact that most job growth in the United States has long come from small businesses. (They have their own government support agency—the Small

Business Administration, which writes or sells off millions in loans each year.)

Another major cost of corporate welfare is cleanup of toxic emissions into the air and industrial waste deposited in municipal sewage systems, waterways, and toxic waste dumps. Although corporations are required to bear more of the cleanup costs than they were before environmental protection laws were passed, taxpayers still bear most of the burden (see Chapter 18).[63]

With business tax subsidies currently costing between $125 and $150 billion annually, Congress continues to extend old breaks and in 2004, with the budget facing a revenue shortfall of more than $400 billion, passed a new set of corporate tax breaks on the grounds that they were necessary incentives during a period of slow job growth. As the share of federal taxes paid by corporations has declined from 25 to 11 percent since the 1960s, the burden for funding government spending falls more and more heavily on personal income and payroll taxes and on borrowing. (When borrowing is factored in, corporate taxes are only about 9 percent of total revenues.)

Families and Homeowners

Corporations may be the biggest winners of tax subsidies, but the government has not neglected mainstream America. It is "working families" that Congress most likes to cite as the beneficiaries of tax breaks and tax cuts, and indeed, some are not trivial. In 2003, the tax deduction for mortgage interest, for example, cost the U.S. Treasury more than four times as much as payments to TANF recipients[64] (see Figure 5). Families also receive tax credits for child care, adoption costs, school and college tuition, out-of-pocket health care costs, and tax deferrals for private savings plans.

Direct aid for the poor often produces outrage; even Medicare and Social Security and other largely middle-class programs are often subject to scathing criticism. But subsidized services and tax breaks for the middle class and the well-off are subjected to much less scrutiny, perhaps because these benefits are more hidden and different in kind than benefits for the poor. It may also be because the most well off, through their campaign contributions, have a greater say in the content of public debates.

Current Issues

Health Care

Some $1.8 trillion was spent on health care in the United States in 2004, or about $6,000 per person.[65] The cost of health care is increasing at twice the rate of economic growth.[66] In all, 40 percent of all health care

is paid for by the government, and when the Medicare drug benefit for seniors goes into full effect in 2006, the government will pay for half of all prescription drugs sold in the country.[67]

Given the aging population and the increasing price of medical care, all people in the United States will never get all the medical care they want. Though we pretend otherwise, in reality we have a rationing system for medical care; it is rationed by ability to pay. If you can afford it or if you have the right insurance, you can have the most expensive treatment, even if it will prolong your life only a few days or make you only marginally better off or not better off at all. If you do not have the money or insurance coverage, you may die at an early age even though you have a treatable condition.

Medical care is also not equally accessible to all racial and ethnic groups. Analysts have concluded that neither income nor educational differences explain the poorer health of African Americans compared with the United States population overall; they conclude that racial discrimination plays a large part in explaining why blacks receive less and poorer-quality health care than others.[68]

Medical care is also not well rationed over the life cycle; we spend a very large proportion of health care resources on people in the last year of their lives. Thirty percent of all Medicare costs are incurred for last-year care, much of it for the last month of treatment.

Other nations also ration medical care, but they do it in a different way. In Canada, which has a government-funded national health care system, greater effort is spent on preventive medicine. And expensive tests are reserved for those with a high probability of benefiting from them. People sometimes have to wait for elective surgery, imposing an inconvenience but ensuring that facilities will be used more efficiently. In several European countries, rationing is done by making decisions about who gets first priority for expensive procedures. For example, except in life-threatening circumstances, priority for an elective hip replacement would be given to a middle-aged working person over an elderly person.

In 2004, almost eight thousand U.S. doctors (about 1 percent of all practicing physicians) published a letter in the *Journal of the American Medical Association* arguing that private sector solutions have failed and calling for the elimination of for-profit hospitals and **health maintenance organizations (HMOs).** HMOs are groups of doctors who agree to provide full health care for a fixed monthly charge. The physicians who signed the letter advocate a government-financed health insurance system covering every American. They said it would save billions.[69]

The Irrationality of the Existing System

We spend twice as much, per capita, than the country that ranks second to us in health spending. But we have

"Kids, your mother and I have spent so much money on health insurance this year that instead of vacation we're all going to go in for elective surgery."

less to show for it. In a ranking of countries of the world, we are tied with Malaysia for thirty-fourth in child mortality under age five.[70] We rank twenty-ninth in life expectancy, between Portugal and Slovenia.[71] A study by the Institute of Medicine and the National Academy of Science concluded that from forty-five thousand to ninety-five thousand deaths a year—more than due to breast cancer, car accidents, or AIDS—are due to hospital and medical staff errors.[72]

Despite our extremely high spending, forty-five million Americans remain uninsured. About eighteen thousand adults between the ages of twenty-five and sixty-four die every year for lack of health coverage, and the economy loses $65 to $130 billion in productivity and other costs.[73]

The high cost and lack of access that are central to our medical system have many other negative effects. Health care costs are a burden on corporations as well as families. After corporate income taxes, employee benefits are the largest structural cost to business. Many employers find themselves not only unable to compete with developing countries because of the low cost of labor in those countries but also unable to compete with developed economies because in Canada, Western Europe, and Japan, taxpayers, not employers, assume most of the burden for providing health care. In the United States, a disproportionate part of the employers' cost falls on large manufacturers; in 2002, for example, General Motors spent $4.5 billion on health care for its employees.[74] This not only drives U.S. businesses abroad looking for employees who will work for lower wages and no benefits, but it makes the U.S. unattractive as a location for foreign businesses.

In fact, the impact of rising health care costs on declining competitiveness seems to have large businesses

rethinking their opposition to government-financed health care. Though the fear of "socialized" medicine has prevented thorough health care reform for decades, the irrationality and cost of the existing system is changing the opinions of some powerful interests.

Health care costs also stress household budgets and the ability of families to save, especially for college educations. Health premiums rose by more than 11 percent in 2004, four times the rate of inflation and five times the increase in workers' salaries. Although families are spending proportionately less on food and clothing than they did thirty years ago, they are spending much more on housing and health care.[75] For families who cannot afford health insurance, a major illness can lead to bankruptcy. By comparison, a patient in Sweden never has to spend more than $118 a year out of pocket for visits to the doctor, and the state pays all medical costs above $236 a year. In Belgium, where the "right to health" is an article in the constitution, a three-day treatment for a cancer patient costs only $2,000, and the patient pays only $36.[76]

Figure 6 presents an interesting picture of the relationship of costs to outcomes in several areas of the United States. Spending, by itself, has no overall effect on quality of care.

Why High Costs?

Two decades ago, when government rejected publicly financed universal health care coverage in favor of the profit model as the way to keep down health costs, health care spending was about 10.5 percent of GDP. It is now closing in on 16 percent and is expected to rise to 18.4 percent of GDP by 2013.[77] Waste and inefficiency account for 10 to 20 percent of the cost,[78] and hospital costs are rising because more than one of every four health care dollars goes to administration.[79] But the principal driving forces are thought to be new drugs and new medical technology that make it possible to do more for more people.[80] In 2003, for example, drug costs rose more than 9 percent, but only one-third of the rise came from price increases. The rest came because "more people are using more drugs in more expensive combinations."[81]

The aging population is another reason for higher costs. One out of six people can now expect to live to the age of one hundred. The elderly have more health problems than younger people, so as their numbers increase, the demand for medical services rises. The growing reliance on high technology such as CT scanners, MRI, dialysis, and laser equipment, intensive care units, and other sophisticated medical tools costs billions of dollars. High technology has made possible organ transplants and other procedures unheard of a few years ago available today, but at a huge cost.

Hospitals all want the most sophisticated equipment, which drives up overall costs and results in duplication

Region	Medicare Spending Annual per capita costs, adjusted for regional differences.	Specialist Visits In last six months of patient's life.	Hospital Stays Inpatient days, last six months of life.	Care Index* Percentage of patients who received effective treatment. U.S. mean: 47.1%
Portland, OR	$3,898	3.7	5.3	47.8%
Minneapolis	$3,663	3.8	6.6	52.6%
Orange County, CA	$5,968	20.1	9.0	50.0%
Miami	$7,847	25.1	14.1	49.9%
	Spending on Medicare patients in Miami is double that of Minneapolis . . .	. . . Miami patients see specialists six times as often . . .	. . . and Miami patients are hospitalized twice as long . . .	. . . but the difference in effectiveness of care is negligible

FIGURE 6 ■ More Spending, More Treatment, Similar Results *Medicare spending varies widely between regions, but evidence suggests that the extra money has little or no beneficial effect for the overall population.*

*Care index includes the following measures: vaccination for pneumococcal pneumonia; screening for breast and colon cancer; eye examinations for diabetics; HgA1c and blood lipid monitoring for diabetes; and for heart attack victims, the prescription of aspirin therapy, beta blockers, ACE inhibitors, and reperfusion with thrombolytic agents or PTCA.

SOURCE: Gina Kolata, "Research Suggests More Health Care May Not Be Better," *New York Times,* July 21, 2002, 20.

and underutilization. Many Americans have become obsessed with state-of-the-art technology and do not want to drive long distances to have access to it. If one hospital has a sophisticated machine, others nearby also want it, even if there are not enough patients in the vicinity to use the extra machines. The resulting competition for patients encourages marketing to persuade doctors to use the equipment so that it can be paid for. The public—as patients, insurance buyers, and taxpayers—picks up the bill.

High-technology medicine also creates new demands for medical procedures even though higher spending for more treatments does not produce significantly better results than lower spending and fewer treatments.[82] When better procedures become available, more people want them, so even if the new procedures are cheaper than the old, the total cost is higher. Surgery for cataracts, an eye disease affecting many elderly, is an example. Until two decades ago, surgery was painful and often ineffective. Now new techniques and materials allow plastic lenses to be inserted into the eye surgically, greatly improving vision. As a consequence, many more people receive the surgery, at a greatly increased total cost, even though the individual procedures cost less.[83]

The financial and even legal pressure to perform many unnecessary procedures also drives up costs. One-quarter to one-third of all medical procedures are unneeded or are actually harmful.[84] For example, delivery of babies by cesarean (c-section) is the most common

surgical procedure in the United States, and experts estimate that twice as many are done as are necessary. Doctors can charge more for cesareans than for a "normal" delivery, and a c-section can be done at the doctor's and the patient's convenience.[85]

The fact that government insurance programs cover many of the people most likely to be sick—the elderly and the poor—while private health insurers cover those at least risk—the young, the well, and the well-off—means that it is very hard to hold down costs of publicly funded programs. To compensate, state governments, which bear a large share of the costs, are tightening access to Medicaid while the federal government limits the amount it pays on bills that doctors and hospitals submit to Medicare and Medicaid. But these are stopgap solutions that have led to doctors' refusing to take patients covered by Medicare.

Although there is greater recognition that government will have to take some action to contain health care costs if economic growth is to continue and U.S. businesses are to remain competitive, the current legislative proposals are for either passive or indirect government involvement. Ever since it defeated the Clinton administration's attempt to mandate employers to provide health insurance to all workers, Congress has continued to show little interest in major reform. It has approached each health care issue on a piecemeal basis. In recent years, the dominant issue has been holding down drug costs for seniors, but even on this issue, Congress was deeply split, and the leadership managed

THEN CAME THE SCARE TV ADS. "...THE GOVERNMENT WANTS TO TEAR DOWN OUR HEALTH CARE SYSTEM AND FORCE US TO HAVE SURGERY PERFORMED BY MOTOR VEHICLE BUREAU CLERKS!

OH NO!   NEVER!

to squeak through a bill only with parliamentary tactics and heavy arm twisting. No reform was achieved and there will be savings only for the lowest-income groups and those with the greatest use of prescription drugs. It is estimated that one senior in four will actually have to pay more for their drugs than before the benefit bill was passed.[86] Health care is approached much like all other social welfare issues: with changes and benefits targeted at specific groups. There is no commitment to an overall policy on health care and no consensus on who is responsible for providing it.

The Bush administration has continued this piecemeal approach, advocating tax credits for the purchase of private health insurance. This in itself will do nothing to address rising costs, and it will do little for low-income families who do not have the money to buy insurance and therefore cannot get any benefit from the tax credit.

John Kerry, the Democratic presidential candidate in 2004, proposed relieving both individuals and businesses of some health care costs by creating a government insurance program to cover the cost of catastrophic illnesses. Because these illnesses are by far the most expensive to treat, the plan would have reduced health insurance premiums for corporations and individuals. To pay for it, Kerry would have rolled back tax reductions for those making $200,000 and more.

Advocates of the privatized system are quick to label big solutions "socialized medicine" or "government control of medicine." At some point, the cost and ineffectiveness of the existing system will outweigh the leverage of these special-interest groups, but not until more of the public sees health care as a major issue.

Social Security

As a retirement program for everyone, Social Security continues to be politically popular among all groups, save the very young, because it alleviates some of the economic risks of growing old. It is a great public policy success story, but the program does have problems. The aging of the population in combination with the heavy borrowing from the trust fund to pay current expenses has left the program in need of reform. Its popularity, however, makes a frank discussion of basic changes in the fundamental nature of the program politically risky. There is also serious disagreement over how much trouble the system is in and whether it needs another rules adjustment, such as it received in the 1970s and 1980s, or a radical overhaul.

There is agreement on the two major problems facing the Social Security system. One is that the ratio of active workers to retirees is decreasing. Even though immigration keeps us from zero growth, there will be only 2.2 active workers for each Social Security beneficiary in 2031, compared to 3.3 in 2004.[87] This is because the number of people over age sixty-five is growing and is expected to almost double from thirty-six million in 2004 to seventy-four million in 2034. The second problem is the fact that presidents and Congress continue to use Social Security trust fund surpluses to offset budget deficits. In 2004, the fund was still collecting 50 percent more than it needed to make payments to current retirees. The overcollection was by design, in anticipation of the drain on the trust fund that will occur as the baby boom generation (those born between 1946 and 1964) reaches retirement age. Reforms passed in the 1980s increased payroll tax rates and the amount of income taxed and forced virtually all U.S. workers into the program. The intention was to lock down this surplus so that as the population aged and the number of younger workers paying into the program declined, the surplus would be there to cover payouts to the growing number of retirees. But during years when general revenue funds are insufficient to cover government spending, budget makers in the White House and Congress borrow from the Social Security trust fund to reduce deficits.

When that money is needed to pay benefits, will the government be able to repay what it has borrowed from the trust fund? It is hard to believe that government would fail to make good on this commitment to millions of Americans, although one poll showed that young people were more likely to believe in flying saucers than in the viability of the Social Security system.[88]

Some of their concern is undoubtedly fed by politicians' repeated predictions that the Social Security trust fund will go broke "in the next few years" unless changes are made. Some elected officials are advocates of privatizing the system and want to spread doubt and even panic about its stability. The program's trustees say that Social Security will be financially able to make full payments to all beneficiaries until 2018 and payments of about three-fourths of the current benefit level from then until 2042 if no changes are made in the program.

But changes are already being phased in; one is a gradual raising of the retirement age—something that makes sense given how much longer people are living and working. Other tweaking would reduce the automatic annual cost-of-living increases recipients get (the 2003 increase was the lowest in four years) and increase the share of earnings subject to payroll tax. The ceiling on taxable income was raised to $90,000 in 2005 and could easily be raised again. If the income tax cut for the highest income earners were reversed instead of being made permanent as the Bush administration wants, it would go a long way toward ending budget deficits and the need to borrow from the Social Security trust fund.

Those who are opposed to the idea of a government-managed retirement system tend to favor restructuring Social Security. The most significant and persistent of these proposals involve some degree of privatization of the payroll withholding tax. The Bush administration favors this approach, although it refuses to call it *privatization* because that word does not play well in polls. The Bush plan would allow people who want to invest some of the money now withheld from their paychecks for Social Security in stocks, bonds, or funds of their choosing to take part of the money withheld for the trust fund and set up their own retirement accounts. Just over 6 percent of each paycheck (up to the income ceiling) is now withheld for Social Security; the Bush plan would allow 2 percent, or almost one-third of the withholding, to be invested by individual workers as they see fit, assuming as much or as little risk as they want. The re-

maining portion of the payroll tax obligation would be paid into the Social Security trust fund just as it is now.

But reductions in contributions in even these small percentages would put the fund in an even more tenuous financial position as the number of beneficiaries explodes over the next few decades and the ratio of active workers declines. However, supporters of this approach believe that those who invest on their own will be able to get a much higher rate of return than the government does on its investment of money in the trust fund, which invests solely in low-risk, low-interest government securities.

There are two formidable obstacles to the partial privatization plan. If the stock market falters or if bad investment decisions are made, millions of seniors may end up having insufficient retirement income. Most people have no special expertise in investment strategies, and whereas putting the money in stocks and bonds or mutual funds will provide a windfall in commissions for investment firms, there is no guarantee that the money will earn a higher rate of return or even that it will not be lost. The stock market and mutual funds were rocked by fraud and corruption from 2001 to 2004, and private pension plans have been failing at an alarming rate, leaving taxpayers to pay part of the bill for bankrupt companies. When retirement arrives and an individual has lost the money invested or earned less of a return than Social Security could have provided, would they have the right to turn to the government to supplement their lower Social Security benefits, and if so, where would government get the money?

The larger and more immediate problem is where the trust fund will get the money to pay benefits to baby boomer retirees if it allows younger workers to take up to a third of their contributions into the private market.

"My pension has been renegotiated, and in lieu of a monthly check I'll receive a crateful of seasonal fruit."

Some Bush advisers say the answer is to borrow the money that would be needed—anywhere from $800 billion to $2 trillion—to pay retiree benefits.[89] With 40 percent of the national debt already held by foreigners and no ready domestic sources with the amount of money needed, the question is where the government would find enough lenders to fund Social Security and to cover the rest of the shortfall in spending. Critics in Bush's own party say the borrowing scheme is unrealistic and that partial privatization cannot happen without raising taxes, reducing benefits, or both.

Reducing benefits would present another set of problems because 53 percent of the workforce has no private pension coverage to supplement Social Security benefits and 32 percent of Americans have no retirement savings other than what they have paid into Social Security.[90] For more than two million of these retirees, Social Security payments are already insufficient to meet the cost of living, so a further reduction could cause an even greater number to look to supplemental payments from the SSI program. And because SSI is funded by general revenues, not the trust fund, any large jump in the number of beneficiaries would further increase budget deficits.

Reforming Aid to the Poor

Most analysts agree that the TANF program was a success from the standpoint of getting people off welfare and into the labor force. The new time limits and work requirements forced many states to reorient their efforts toward helping clients develop job and life skills instead of passive assistance to see that they had food and shelter. By 2003, the number of people on welfare rolls had dropped by 60 percent.

TANF has shown that at least in good economic times, welfare rolls can be reduced and more people employed. For people healthy and skilled enough to hold down jobs and lucky enough to find them, "welfare to work" has been successful in ending dependency on cash assistance.

But we should not overstate the success of TANF. Most welfare recipients who left the program have not been lifted out of poverty. Average incomes of the newly employed were $12,000 in Iowa and Ohio and $14,000 in Indiana and Michigan.[91] Other problems add to the job-seeking difficulties of welfare recipients. Lack of suitable skills for today's economy is a significant problem. Sizable proportions of welfare recipients suffer from mental or physical disabilities, learning disabilities, and substance abuse problems. Any one of these conditions makes finding and keeping a job difficult, and many unemployed have more than one of these problems.[92]

When the welfare reform bill came up for reauthorization in 2002, Congress and the White House could not agree on whether to reauthorize the original program or to reform it. The Bush White House has demanded that the program be amended to increase the work requirement to forty hours a week, sixteen of which could be in education and skills training, but only for a period of three months. Opponents in Congress and in state government say this is unrealistic given the job market and the decline in funding available for child care. Unable to reach agreement with the White House, Congress has kept TANF operating by passing temporary extensions.

Impact of Reform

One reason for the lack of agreement on what is needed for reauthorization is that there is still no clear understanding of how reductions in welfare rolls have been achieved or what has happened to families who have left the program. Riding the improvements in the economy, the decline in welfare enrollments began two years before the 1996 overhaul bill was passed and three years before it went into effect in most states. The initial drop in enrollees is attributed to rule changes in local programs that began in 1994, after a number of states received waivers from the federal government to experiment with reform.[93] Then, just as the overhaul bill went into effect, the economy started to boom, creating twenty-three million jobs by 2000. This opened up the labor market to new job seekers as employers, facing a worker shortage, hired the relatively unskilled and inexperienced. In addition, after devolution of welfare to the states, there was another downward shift of responsibilities to the county level. As the eligibility and conditions of enrollment changed, varying from one locality to another, many enrollees dropped out of welfare programs.

Early estimates attributed one-third of the reduction in welfare clients to the federal overhaul legislation.[94] But the highly unusual coincidence of mutually reinforcing economic conditions and program reforms makes it difficult to know if further reforms will produce a similar contraction in welfare programs. TANF supporters who attribute the decline in number of welfare clients during the first six years after the reform primarily to work requirements and fixed years of eligibility believe that tightening these standards further will produce another round of significant reductions. Those who credit the unusually good economic conditions for most of the reduction believe that Bush's demand for an increase in the work requirements to forty hours a week will remain unrealistic as long as the economic recovery produces too few jobs to meet the demand for work.

Bush's proposal also requested $1 billion in 2005 to encourage welfare recipients to marry, on the assumption that children do better in two-parent households and that child care would be more workable and less costly.[95] It is a fact that the poverty rates in two-parent households are significantly lower than in single-parent households (see Table 1). Women earn on average 75 cents for every dollar earned by a man (down from 76 cents in 2003), so single-parent households headed by women are doubly disadvantaged.

Devolution to the States

The other major push in the Bush proposals is to continue the process of devolution to the states. The most significant tool in this process is the **superwaiver,** blanket exemptions that would free states from federal poverty program standards and requirements so that they would have much greater latitude to set standards and eligibility for a wide range of poverty programs, including TANF, food stamps, child care, employment and job-training services, and public housing.[96] States have long been able to obtain from federal agencies waivers freeing them from requirements for a specific program, but superwaivers would allow for exemptions on all federally mandated poverty programs.

The superwaiver encapsulates the Bush approach to welfare reform in that it signals an intent to withdraw the federal government from such programs as far as possible. Many members of Congress are very critical of superwaivers because they believe they will concentrate authority for program decisions in the executive branch.

Governors could go to a cabinet secretary (of health and human services, for example) or an agency head and get a super waiver that would allow them to escape congressionally mandated standards for providing income, educational, and health services to the poor and disabled.[97]

Increases in Welfare Enrollments

By 2003, after several years of net job losses in the private sector and a rising poverty rate, welfare enrollments started to move up again. In the years after the reform, about two million families left the welfare rolls and joined another twenty million low-income families to compete for low-skill jobs. One-third of those who left the rolls have no jobs, and no one is sure how they are surviving.[98] Another ominous sign is that the employment level for single mothers declined at a higher rate than for other groups.[99] With insufficient federal or state revenue to support needed child care and job training and an economy that is not producing enough new jobs to keep pace with demand, it remains to be seen if the first round of reductions in welfare rolls can be expanded on or if one welfare researcher was correct when he said the huge drop in welfare rolls in the 1990s was "a once-in-a-hundred-years coming together of policies that pushed people off of welfare and pulled people into jobs."[100]

Why Welfare Reform?

Although the cost to taxpayers is a frequently stated goal of reform and was one of the forces driving the 1996 welfare reform, it was probably not the primary objective. Income support for the poor pales in comparison to income support and indirect subsidies to millions of far better off Americans. And no meaningful reform will cost less than the old AFDC program. It is likely that playing to the distaste people have for "welfare" and the idea that some recipients are getting something for nothing were at least as important a motivation for reform as saving money.

Improving program performance and getting results for the individual are far more compelling reasons than cost reduction for trying to reform welfare. This would be better not only for the individual clients but also for the economy and society as a whole. In America, we like to think that everyone can have a chance to achieve to the best of his or her ability and that parents can have a reasonable hope that their children's lives will be better than their own. Moreover, democracies function better when there are no permanent classes of "haves" and "have-nots" (see Table 2). People who must worry about how to feed and house their families are not going to be full participants in the political process. By helping sustain an underclass, we undermine the political system itself.

TABLE 2	Distribution of Household Income in the United States, 1980–2000

Income distribution in the United States is becoming more lopsided.

	Percentage of Income Earned		
Percentage of Households	**1980**	**1990**	**2000**
Lowest 20%	4.3	3.9	3.6
Next lowest 20%	10.3	9.6	8.9
Middle 20%	16.9	15.9	14.9
Next highest 20%	24.9	24.0	23.0
Highest 20%	43.7	46.6	49.2
Top 5%	15.8	18.6	21.0

SOURCE: U.S. Census Bureau, "Historical Income Table: Households," 2004 (www.census.gov/hhes/income/histinc/h02.html).

But there will never be agreement among welfare reformers on what kinds of reforms are necessary because there is no basic agreement on why people are poor. Those who think that poverty is the fault of the poor because they are deficient in character or effort are far less likely to support government help for the poor than are those who believe that poverty is a product of the economic system, bad luck, and parentage (the wealth of your parents determines a lot about your own opportunities to get ahead).

Conclusion: Are Social Welfare Programs Responsive?

Looking at our vast array of social welfare benefits, it would be easy to conclude that government is not only responsive to the American public but hyperresponsive. Through income support programs, subsidized services, and tax breaks, social welfare provides something for everyone while reflecting government's greater responsiveness to individuals and groups who wield political influence. The poor, although comprising more than 12 percent of the population, do not have the influence, organization, or access to win public support for programs benefiting them. In hard times, when support is most needed, programs for the poor often take the brunt of budget cuts. But not all Americans view politics solely in terms of what *they* get, and some have learned that the growth of an underclass harms everyone.

Most taxpayers define themselves as middle income, and they support services for themselves and others like them. Benefits to the upper classes are tolerated to a large extent because they often take the form of technical or specially tailored tax breaks that most of the public has never heard of. When they do catch the public's attention, often because of abuse—such as offshore tax shelters or business deductions for stock options given to CEOs—they can trigger resentment and reform.

The making of social welfare policy also illustrates our government's lack of an overarching policy or philosophy about its responsibilities for ensuring basic human services. Instead, it responds in piecemeal fashion to crises or to pressure from the most influential interest groups and lobbyists and gives far too little attention to long-term planning. While Americans worry about the viability of the country's healthcare system, Congress is too often preoccupied with responding to short-term demands to hold down drug costs or to cap jury awards in malpractice suits.

Finally, it is clear that Congress has established a massive tangle of support programs to protect individuals and businesses from the risks of the same marketplace whose self-regulating properties it loves to praise. Two of the central questions about social welfare policies today have to be whether government assumes too much risk for individuals and for business and whether it assumes more risk for the powerful than for the weak.

Hutchinson Votes to Subsidize Big Farmers

Tim Hutchinson voted against the Senate version of the farm bill. He said that he preferred the House bill because it provided "the safety and certainty our farmers need. That safety and certainty was wiped out of the Senate bill by a misguided amendment that arbitrarily limits payments to farmers with high production costs." He added that the bill did "not reflect Arkansas priorities" and would be devastating for agriculture in his state.[101]

By the time the bill came to the floor, it was clear it would pass without Hutchinson's vote, so he knew that farm subsidies would be approved without his having to go on record as supporting lower income support payments. The bill was sent to conference committee, where it took three months to negotiate a final report. Hutchinson, like most farm state senators who had voted against the Senate bill, voted yes on the conference report. It provides for $45 billion in new spending during the first five years, a 27 percent increase over existing programs. The ceiling on payments was lowered to a midway point between the House and Senate bills ($360,000) but "with enough exceptions to make it a symbolic compromise."[102]

Hutchinson said that the final version provides the "safety net" farmers need until new markets open up abroad. He cited President Bush's description of farm and ranch families as embodying "some of the best values of our nation: hard work and risk taking."[103] He did not add that farm subsidies reduce, if not eliminate, risk taking primarily for the wealthiest farm industries, not for the average family farmer. This is why some in rural America call it "farming the government, not farming the land."[104]

Hutchinson's vote, like that of many other subsidy supporters, is another example of why government continues to grow. We expect liberals to vote for agricultural price supports because they believe in government spending for social welfare. But government also grows as a result of corporate welfare, and much of its support comes from conservatives who decry big government even while voting to expand it when it is beneficial to their constituents and campaign donors. The farm support bill is an example of how government welfare policies are most responsive to the lobbying influence of the well-off.

In the end, Hutchinson's decision to stand by Arkansas agribusiness did not help him at the polls. He had won his seat running as a social and fiscal conservative, loosely aligned with the Christian Right. After divorcing his wife to marry a young member of his staff, Arkansas voters deserted him, and he went down to defeat in 2002. His successor, however, is no less a supporter of farm subsidies.

For all the benefits extended to wealthy farmers, many farm families remain in need. The ink was barely dry on the $171 billion farm support bill when Congress approved an additional $6 billion in drought relief.

To learn more about this farm bill and the nature of agricultural subsidies, go to this chapter's "You Are There" exercises on the text Web site.

Key Terms

farm subsidies
Social Security
means test
Supplemental Security Income (SSI)
Aid to Families with Dependent Children (AFDC)
Temporary Aid to Needy Families (TANF)

earned income tax credit (EITC)
food stamps
Medicare
Medicaid
corporate welfare
health maintenance organizations (HMOs)
superwaiver

Further Reading

Robert Coles, *The Youngest Parents: Teenage Pregnancy as It Shapes Lives* (New York: Norton, 1997). Based on several years of intensive interviews with a diverse group of teenage parents, this book illuminates their lives, largely by letting them speak for themselves.

Jason DeParle, *American Dream: Three Women, Ten Kids, and a Nation's Drive to End Welfare* (New York: Viking, 2004). A veteran *New York Times* reporter whose beat is the inner city followed three single welfare mothers for a decade and set down their stories within a short history of welfare policy.

Barbara Ehrenreich, *Nickel and Dimed: On (Not) Getting By in America* (New York: Metropolitan Books, 2001). Ehrenreich, a well-known writer and women's rights activist (and a biologist by training), tells about her experience doing blue-collar work to find out what it would be like for a woman to try to support herself at minimum-wage jobs. She found that many who worked full time, some holding several jobs, still could not afford both food and housing.

Ronald Jager, *The Fate of Family Farming: Variations on an American Idea* (Hanover, N.H.: University Press of New England, 2004). A philosophy professor who grew up on a family farm discusses the link between agriculture and democracy and looks at how four different types of family farms have adapted to high-tech agriculture, global markets, and government subsidies.

Laurence J. Kotlikoff and Scott Burns, *The Coming Generational Storm* (Cambridge, Mass.: MIT Press, 2004). Boston University economists give a worst-case scenario of the economic burden facing the next generation from accumulated budget deficits and indebtedness to government entitlement and insurance programs.

For Viewing

Dark Days (2000) An award-winning documentary at the Sundance Film Festival, this film looks at the lives of homeless people who live in the train tunnels beneath Manhattan.

The Farmer's Wife (1998) This PBS documentary watched by millions explores what one farm couple had to do to survive economically and the impact on family life. The first hour can be viewed online at www.pub.org/frontline. Compare this documentary treatment of a real farm family to two commercial films released in 1984 inspired by the despair in farming communities during the wave of farm foreclosures in the 1970s and 1980s, *The River,* with Sissy Spacek and Mel Gibson, and *Country,* with Jessica Lange and Sam Shepard.

Harvest of Shame (1960) This CBS documentary, narrated by Edward R. Morrow, at the time one of the country's most respected newscasters, generated public awareness of malnutrition and poverty among migrant workers in the United States and helped build support for the war on poverty.

The Hospital (1971) Chaos in a hospital—or as it was once billed, "Madness, Murder, and Malpractice"—was never so entertaining as in this Oscar-winning black comedy.

Wall Street Fix (2004) This *Frontline* documentary focuses on offshore tax shelters that are on the margins of legality. It can be viewed at the website www.pbs.org/frontline.

America's War on Poverty (1995) This is a History Channel series on the 1960s legislative program to eradicate poverty in America.

 ## Electronic Resources

www.aphsa.org
This page of the American Public Human Services Association has information on and analyses of all welfare programs. It is a useful site for tracking the progress of welfare reform.

www.ncsl.org
As part of its responsibility to state legislative bodies, the National Conference of State Legislatures provides assessments of changes in

federal welfare law. In addition, this is a source of information on the welfare and Medicaid programs of individual states.

www.ssa.gov
Like all other government agencies, the Social Security Administration has its own Web site, providing a broad array of information on its history and programs. Here employers can find out how to comply with laws governing Social Security taxation, and parents of disabled children can learn how to avoid losing SSI benefits.

www.hhs.gov
This page links to the agencies of the Department of Health and Human Services, including the Food and Drug Administration, the Administration for Children and Families, and the Centers for Disease Control and Prevention.

www.ewg.org
This Web site is maintained by the Environmental Working Group to make public farm subsidy disbursements. If you want to know who gets how much, this is the place to look.

 ## InfoTrac College Edition

Search for the following articles in the InfoTrac database:

Jencks, Christopher. "Liberal Lessons from Welfare Reform: Why Welfare-to-Work Turned out Better Than We Expected," *American Prospect* (July 15, 2002).

Rank, Mark R., and Thomas A. Hirschl. "Welfare Use as a Life Course Event: Toward a New Understanding of the U.S. Safety Net," *Social Work* (July 2002).

Vartanian, Thomas P. and Justine M. McNamara. "The Welfare Myth: Disentangling the Long-term Effects of Poverty and Welfare Receipt for Young Single Mothers," *Journal of Sociology & Social Welfare* (December 2004).

Williamson, John B., Tay K. McNamara, and Stephanie A. Howling. "Generational Equity, Generational Interdependence, and the Framing of the Debate over Social Security Reform," *Journal of Sociology & Social Welfare* (September 2003).

For more articles, enter

"Social Security" in the Subject Guide;

"Welfare reform" in the Subject Guide;

"Medicare" in the Subject Guide.

 ## American Government Resources

Visit the Public Policy section of the Wadsworth American Government Resources Web site (politicalscience.wadsworth.com/amgov) for a variety of tools to help you explore social welfare and health policy further. Included are simulations, video clips, Microcase exercises, and a wealth of other activities.

CHAPTER 18

REGULATION AND ENVIRONMENTAL POLICY

Coal-burning plants are changing our environment, but whether government should regulate them is a source of controversy.

© Tom Bean, 1997/DRK Photo

Do You Belong Inside Government, or Outside?

Reasons for Regulation

Damage to Common Property

Inefficient Competition

Lack of Necessary Coordination

Unacceptable Inequities

Kinds of Regulation

The Regulatory Process

Writing Regulations

Regulatory Oversight

Implementing and Enforcing Regulations

Cycles of Regulation

Deregulation

ReRegulation

Deregulation: The Current Round

Keeping Pace with Change

**Regulatory Politics and
Environmental Politics**

Evolution of Government's Role

Implementing Environmental Regulations

Science, Policy, and Environmental
Protection

Benefits and Costs of Regulation

**Conclusion: Is Regulatory Policy
Responsive?**

ou are Eric Schaeffer, a twelve-year veteran of the Environmental Protection Agency (EPA). For the past five years you have been the director of the Office of Regulatory Enforcement, or the EPA's "top cop" as the position is sometimes called. One of your major jobs is to negotiate industry compliance with clean air standards. If industries have emitted more pollutants into the air than allowed, you negotiate with them about how they can fix the problem and the fine they will have to pay.

It is February 2002, thirteen months into George W. Bush's first term and your enforcement job is becoming very difficult because of the president's opposition to the clean air rules as they are currently written. You are beginning to believe that you will not be allowed to complete the settlement agreements you are negotiating with power companies and oil refineries because of the administration's decision to rewrite the very rules you are now trying to enforce. A committed environmentalist, you have to decide whether to stay on the job and get the best settlements you can before weaker enforcement rules go into effect or to resign and try to work for enforcement of the Clean Air Act from outside government.

The proposed rule changes are focused on a provision in the Clean Air Act called the New Source Review. "New Source" refers to new sources of air pollution that might be created when power plants upgrade

and expand their facilities, such as building new smokestacks. The provision has been around since the landmark Clean Air Act of 1970 was renewed in 1977, and was retained in the 1990 version, signed into law by George H. Bush. It requires that whenever utilities or refineries expand or upgrade their plants they must also improve pollution controls so the plants will emit lower amounts of pollutants into the air than before the upgrade. Those plans are subject to review by regulators. New Source was a compromise that acknowledged the financial burden placed on older plants by the cost of equipment and remodeling necessary to meet clean air standards. With New Source, the EPA was essentially saying to industry: Since you have decided to upgrade your plant, you must use this opportunity to upgrade pollution controls as well. Nonetheless, many industries, especially coal plants, opposed the New Source provision, arguing that it would inhibit expansion and remodeling or add significantly to the costs of upgrading.

At first, the New Source provision was ignored by businesses and regulators alike, but in the mid-nineties the attorneys general of several Northeastern states started suing companies that had upgraded their plants without investing in the required pollution controls. The Clinton administration joined in some of these suits, and threatened to sue other industries, so by the end of his term you were negotiating settlements with a number of oil refineries and nine utilities.

The Clinton administration had taken a new approach by consolidating all of the EPA's enforcement programs—for clear air, water, and toxic waste management—in a single office, the one you now head. Furthermore, instead of pursuing compliance on a company-by-company basis, the EPA began reviewing performance by industry sectors (all utilities or oil refineries in a certain region of the country for example) to gain across-the-board industry compliance by the industry.[1] You have been very successful in this. In fact, just six months ago, John Ashcroft presented you with the Justice Department's John Marshall Award for your cooperation with DoJ attorneys in reaching massive cleanup settlements with one-third of the country's oil refineries.[2]

Negotiations with another third of all refineries and a number of big utilities were underway in 2001 when George W. Bush entered the White House. Because Bush had made it clear that he supported more industry-friendly enforcement rules, you and your fifteen-member staff worked fourteen-hour days trying to reach settlements before his inauguration.[3] But most companies held off entering into agreements, believing that they would escape the fines or be able to negotiate a more lenient plan for compliance with the new administration.

You are not concerned with the president's party affiliation; as a federal bureaucrat your job is to implement the laws passed by Congress and to do so with neutral competence, serving Republicans and Democrats alike. Although you are a registered Democrat, you began working at the EPA in 1990, when George H. Bush was president, and before that you worked on environmental issues for several years as a staff assistant to a Republican member of the House. The EPA was founded in 1970 by a Republican president, Richard Nixon, and led by Republican appointees. It is staffed by hundreds of career bureaucrats of varying political views and party

registration and its work has had more bipartisan support than perhaps any other major government agency. But, as with any agency or cabinet department, the top policymaking positions are political appointments and the Bush administration has filled the top jobs at the EPA and other agencies key to environmental regulation—the Departments of Interior, Agriculture, and Justice—with lawyers and lobbyists from industries regulated by those agencies.

Just four months after taking office, Bush asked the EPA's enforcement division to reassess the New Source provision and Vice President Cheney pressured EPA administrators to write new rules, even while publicly saying that investigations begun under the old rule would not be affected. In June 2002, the assistant EPA administrator who was put in charge of writing the new rules also assured the Senate that there would be no "negative impact on enforcement cases."[4]

But, well aware that Mr. Bush's EPA would be more industry friendly than Clinton's had been, some of the utilities and industries being sued for compliance immediately sought relief from the new administration. They had reason to believe they would get it. At the outset of Bush's run for the presidency, the head of the Edison Electric Institute, one of Bush's biggest fundraisers and a former Yale classmate, had sent a confidential letter to energy industry leaders suggesting that they bundle (roll together) their contributions to "ensure that our industry is credited" for its generosity to Bush's campaign.[5] Now some of Bush's biggest campaign contributors have come to collect.

You find yourself in a position of trying to conduct negotiations with industry representatives who seem certain you have no White House backing for the settlements you are trying to cut. You know that representatives of the very industries you are negotiating with have been invited to participate in rewriting the rules because you have seen memos from industry lobbyists to regulators circulating within the EPA.

Two of the companies that had signed consent decrees on settlements now refuse to sign the final settlements and others have stopped negotiating, believing they will get a better offer in the near future. You know it is impossible to enforce a rule that everyone knows has no support in the White House.[6]

You see your position as further weakened by an administration budget proposal that will cut two hundred staff members from the civil enforcement program at a time when you think the office is already seriously understaffed. But a great deal is at stake. The small number of power companies you are negotiating with "are responsible for two-thirds of the sulfur dioxide and one quarter of the nitrogen oxides emitted from all sources in the U.S." More than twenty thousand early deaths each year are attributed to fine particle pollution from power plants. And the same plants also account for one-third of all the airborne mercury emissions that end up contaminating waterways and fish consumed by humans.[7]

On the one hand, maybe you can do more by staying in your job and working to get as much enforcement as possible under the new rules. You have fifteen years of experience working on environmental policy whereas political appointees to government agencies come and go rather quickly and many never master the substance of the issues. It is also true that some come into an agency hostile to its work but, once they get involved, end up being captured by it. You could stay and try to lobby the new policy appointees and perhaps win over some of them to support retention of the strong enforcement rules.

But on the other hand, you feel like a "doormat" and wonder how you can enforce provisions of a law while the White House and Bush's EPA appointees are "constantly telegraphing 'the law is stupid.'"[8] Perhaps you can do more by leaving government and finding another venue from which to lobby those members of Congress who want the law it passed to be enforced.

What should you do?

Adam Smith believed the "invisible hand" of the marketplace works to increase production and make individual firms more efficient.[9] As each tries to maximize its profit, market forces push it toward increasing efficiency and productivity as the only means of staying competitive. In the process, in Smith's view, the greater good of society is served; jobs are created, economies grow, and the rising tide lifts all boats. If the economy did work this way and if everyone in business were honest and played by the unwritten rules, we would have little regulation. But unfortunately, the economy goes awry in ways that threaten the public good because market forces are not sufficient to protect us from the intended or unintended consequences of economic activity. So government regulates to limit or correct these effects: exploitation of labor, dangerous consumer products, unsafe foods and drugs, monopolies, insider trading, and pollution to name a few.

The crucial question in the debate over government's role in regulation can be stated simply, but it cannot be answered simply. How can we define standards that protect society's interest in having a clean and healthy environment, safe food and prescription drugs, and a level playing field for businesses and consumers in the marketplace and, at the same time, not unreasonably impede economic growth and job creation? How much risk should government protect us from? How should the benefits of regulation be weighed against the costs of those regulations to business and industry? The public gives no clear-cut answer to these questions. Regulation that is seen as beneficial by one group is regarded by another as wasteful and unnecessary red tape. This is why there is continuing controversy over what should be regulated, how much regulation is needed, and the regulatory mechanisms that should be used.

In this chapter, we look at the evolution of government's regulatory authority, identify types of regulation and their objectives, and describe the standards used to measure their effectiveness. Then we look at how we cycle through periods of regulation and deregulation depending on the political climate in Washington. Finally, we look at one of the most strongly supported, yet controversial, areas of regulatory policy: environmental law.

Reasons for Regulation

Regulation is necessary for several reasons: (1) the damage to common property that would occur without regulation, (2) inefficient competition, (3) a lack of necessary coordination, and (4) unacceptable inequities.

Damage to Common Property

One reason for regulation has been called the **tragedy of the commons**.[10] The "commons" refers to the air

we breathe and the water we drink, which belong to us all. The "tragedy" is that some individuals may seek to exploit them for their own uses to the detriment of the common good. To maximize their profits, farmers pump as much irrigation water as they need from rivers or aquifers, even in water-short areas, and industries spew toxic chemicals into the air or bury them in the soil. They are acting in accordance with the profit motive. Indeed, most individuals who exploit the commons gain economically and thus have considerable incentive to do so. But when many people exploit the commons, the community as a whole suffers.

Consider the case of Los Angeles and General Motors (GM). Los Angeles once had a low-pollution electric railway system. In the 1930s, GM bought the system and then destroyed it, because GM wanted to sell cars, trucks, and buses. The company replaced the electric system with noisy, polluting diesel buses, so uncomfortable and unreliable that Los Angelenos were given a great incentive to rely on private autos.

In 1949, after buying and destroying electric railway systems in more than one hundred cities, GM was fined a paltry five thousand dollars by the government for illegally conspiring to replace municipal services with its own. Meanwhile, the company made millions of dollars. Due in large part to reliance on cars, smog in Los Angeles became a major health hazard. Some studies claimed that children who grew up in Los Angeles lost up to 50 percent of their lung capacity from breathing in the polluted air.[11] Obviously, it is absurd to charge GM with creating the entire automobile culture of Los Angeles, but clearly its drive for private profits did not contribute to the common good.

When GM or any other entity, such as a chemical company that disposes of its toxic wastes in an unsafe way, imposes a cost on the public, it has created an **externality.** Externalities are costs or benefits that are not reflected in market prices. Environmental degradation is a negative externality because the social costs, the burdens imposed on society, are not reflected in the cost of the goods whose production caused the damage. For example, when a coal-burning utility emits sulfur dioxide into the air the company is essentially disposing of a by-product at no cost by simply burning it off and releasing it into the air. This places an unfair burden on the public, both in terms of the health risks and the costs of environmental cleanup.

This emission also leads to inefficiency in the marketplace because the utility is not made to bear the true cost of generating electricity. If companies are allowed to externalize costs in this way, they will produce more of a product than is economically or environmentally sound. But if they have to absorb or internalize the cost of emitting pollutants and add it to the price consumers pay for the service or product, then utilities and manufacturers

Houston, a center of the petrochemical industry, vies with Los Angeles as the smog capital of the United States.

have "an incentive to reduce production to acceptable levels or to develop alternative technologies."[12] It also prevents consumers from making decisions on purchasing or use that are based on real costs. Instead, costs that are hidden—deferred payments that taxpayers will make much later for environmental cleanup or health care—encourage consumption.

To make the market more efficient and to get companies to stop producing goods and services whose real costs are not reflected in the prices charged for those goods and services (for example, to get a petrochemical plant to stop releasing toxins into the air), the government can set standards for how much of the pollutant can be emitted and set the recovery costs through penalties and fines from violators. Alternatively, it can impose taxes on emissions or discharges and charge for pollution up front (more on this later in the chapter).

Inefficient Competition

In a capitalist system, government intervention is also justifiable when competition is inefficient. Adam Smith believed that in an open market, goods and labor would be used in a way that would limit costs and maximize profits. The competition among manufacturers trying to sell the same products to consumers would force them to make goods as cheaply as possible.

But sometimes competition does not work to drive down prices or increase efficiency. The large capital outlays required to build the infrastructure for public utilities—laying water pipes and gas lines, or building power grids—means that it is not cost effective for every community to have more than one company. Thus utilities (such as gas and electricity producers) have long been "controlled monopolies" regulated by state governments. A utility is allowed to be the only provider of a service in a given geographic area, but a state utility board regulates rates because people do not have a choice

of sellers of electricity or gas. Smith himself agreed that this form of government intervention was appropriate.

However, the drive toward privatization of public services has led some states to deregulate electric utilities, to encourage the most efficient and cost-effective use of power by transmitting it across the country to wherever it was most needed at any point in time. Consumers, who, in the era of controlled monopolies could count on the states to regulate prices and order local plants to maintain reserves strictly for local use, found themselves without this protection.

This was especially true in California, where electricity prices skyrocketed and there were frequent blackouts. California deregulated its utilities differently than other states. It kept the plants that distributed electricity to consumers and the authority to set consumer prices, but it sold all of its generating plants to private companies. It also sold the right to regulate the wholesale price of electricity that the generating plants still provided to the state-owned distribution plants. During a heat wave in the summer of 2000, prices spiked and stayed high even in times of low use. It turned out that the now privately owned generating plants that California had contracted with were producing enough electricity to cover demand even during high-use periods, but they were withholding electricity to drive up prices in a captive market. The state spent more than $9 billion purchasing electricity from other states to end the blackouts and dampen consumer rage. Essentially, California had sold off public utilities to private companies that then held the state ransom to exorbitant prices. Electric bills increased fivefold, and state-owned power distribution plants went bankrupt.[13]

In the end, California reinstated price controls and sued energy providers for price gouging. California's electrical utilities have become a model of how not to deregulate, leading other states to put their deregulation plans on hold. The deregulation of electricity illustrates that in some areas of economic activity privatization does not lead to greater efficiencies, more competition, or lower prices.

Lack of Necessary Coordination

Another reason for regulation is that sometimes the free market produces an unacceptable lack of coordination. An obvious example is regulation of airline flights. The free market is not well suited to determine which airline will have priority to schedule a departure at 2:00 P.M. on a certain runway at Kennedy International Airport in New York. Competition could lead to disaster. Thus the Federal Aviation Administration (FAA) has been empowered to coordinate takeoffs, landings, and travel routes. Some of this authority has been privatized by allowing airlines to sell or trade their airport slots. But air traffic control remains a federal function.

Unacceptable Inequities

Another reason for regulation is to promote equity. Equity in this context does not refer to equality in outcome but rather to ensuring fair conditions for participation in the marketplace. Sometimes individuals or groups are severely disadvantaged by the private marketplace. For example, legislation setting minimum wages, banning child labor, protecting workers' rights to organize, and defining minimum standards for workplace health and safety is intended to redress the inequity in power between individual workers and employers. But government also protects employers from workers who organize for bargaining power. The conditions under which workers can unionize and the timing and conditions of strikes, or work stoppages, in certain sectors of the economy are also restricted by federal law.

Regulations forbidding race and gender discrimination are also designed to enhance equity. Consumer protection laws, such as those forbidding false advertising, and laws licensing pharmacists, physicians, lawyers, and public accountants are based on the assumption that consumers will often not have sufficient information to evaluate the competence of those selling the service or product. Government seeks to remedy an inequity in information between the buyer and the seller of a product or service.

Regulating Monopolies

The first major attempt to reduce inequities by regulation was **antitrust law**, which prohibits monopolies. A **monopoly** exists when one or a few firms control the sale of a product or service in a particular market. Where a monopoly exists, the producer(s) can fix prices, setting them well above the cost of production, or they can sell below cost to drive small businesses out of the market. The Sherman Antitrust Act of 1890 and the

Children working in a vegetable cannery. At the turn of the century, many young children worked twelve-hour days in unhealthy conditions. New Deal–era regulations outlawed most child labor, but abuse of child labor laws is increasing in some urban areas.

© The Ganger Collection, New York

Clayton Act of 1914 made uncontrolled monopolies and price rigging illegal. One firm may use antitrust laws to sue others or the government itself may initiate antitrust actions. The enforcement of antitrust legislation has waxed and waned over the years.

Mergers can lead to monopolies as competitors combine forces to control a larger share of the market. Therefore, when large companies want to merge or acquire their competitors, they are required to submit their proposals for review to the Department of Justice or the Federal Trade Commission (FTC) so that government regulators can determine whether their combination would adversely affect competition and prices.

Our economy has experienced five major waves of business mergers: at the turn of the twentieth century and in the 1920s, the 1960s, the 1980s, and the 1990s. The number of merger proposals tripled during the 1990s with more than seventy thousand deals worth nearly $6 trillion during the Clinton years alone.[14] Some see this trend as a repeat of the corporate mergers that swept the American economy at the turn of the century, when GM was created from more than two dozen car companies, and U.S. Steel was formed by combining many small steel companies. In these situations, government regulators have to decide whether the mergers will make the economy more efficient and

Reprinted with permission of Steve Kelley/*The Times-Picayune*, New Orleans.

competitive or whether they will create monopolies and lead to price fixing.

Ninety-five percent of the merger proposals made during the Clinton years went unchallenged by the Department of Justice. A notable exception, on which it was joined by many state governments, was antitrust action against Microsoft, alleging it tried to corner the market in computer software. Although the case revealed that Microsoft made a 90 percent pretax profit on its Windows operating system, the government's case did not rest on the price-fixing standard. Instead, government lawyers established a new basis for challenging monopolies—constraint of innovation or technological change.[15]

Correcting Inequities in the Marketplace

Correcting inequities in the marketplace is one of the most controversial types of regulation. Conservatives often argue that this type of regulation is unnecessary because they believe a free market is self-regulating. They reason that unsafe or ineffective products will sooner or later end up unwanted: pizza eaters can stop buying pizza with artificial cheese; unions can protect workers from unreasonable demands of corporations. But some opponents of regulation are against unions, too, believing they interfere with the free market for labor.

Defenders of equity-based regulations point out that the market works too slowly in providing vital information. People have been killed and injured before information about defective products became widely known. In the mid-1960s, many children were born with serious deformities because of the prescription drug thalidomide, which their mothers took during pregnancy to prevent miscarriages. This incident caused Congress to set higher standards for drug safety and the Food and

Drug Administration (FDA) to tighten its drug-testing rules. Before 1972, twenty million consumers were injured each year by unsafe products and, of those, thirty thousand were killed and more than one hundred thousand were permanently disabled. This prompted Congress to establish the Consumer Product Safety Commission (CPSC), an independent regulatory agency mandated to establish safety standards for consumer products.

Some people believe education campaigns, not regulation, are the best way to protect people. But education campaigns are not cheap, especially over a long period of time, and they are not always effective either. The government's campaign to educate the public about the health hazards of smoking has had a significant impact, but the campaign has cost tens of millions of dollars, and about one-quarter of Americans still smoke.

Congress does not regulate to remedy the effects of every inequity. Sometimes the costs are seen as greater than the gains; in other cases, resistance by politically powerful groups—the banking and telecommunications industries, for instance—is stronger than lobbying by potential beneficiaries of regulation.

Kinds of Regulation

There are several types of regulation:

1. *Requiring information.* Government may regulate by requiring that an employer, lender, or other entity provide certain kinds of information to employees or consumers. For example, credit-card companies must provide cardholders with information about interest rates and how to appeal erroneous charges. Manufacturers of many food products must list in-

gredients on the label and give their nutritional content. This requirement allows consumers to see whether their peppermint ice cream, for example, is colored with beet juice or red dye number 2, a potentially dangerous additive, and how many calories come from fat and sugar. This requirement is called **truth in labeling.** Manufacturers sometimes oppose labeling the contents of their goods because, as one said, "If you label, you're telling consumers there is something wrong with this product."[16]

The FDA also requires that when information *is* provided, it should be accurate. Many manufacturers have taken advantage of a new public awareness of the relationship between health and nutrition by labeling their products as "health" foods. The FDA has forced manufacturers to remove words such as *fresh* from processed juices and *no cholesterol* from food products that are high in vegetable fats that could contribute to heart disease. It is also demanding that manufacturers remove false claims that their products are "organic," "biodegradable," or have other attributes they do not possess.

2. *Licensing.* Government may regulate by requiring people to obtain licenses to practice certain trades or professions or to operate certain businesses. For example, the federal government licenses radio and television stations, and states license doctors, beauticians, dentists, and many others. This reassures clients and patients that those providing the services have met minimum qualifications for their professions. But licensing is also valuable for those receiving a license because it allows them to make money while keeping others out.

3. *Setting standards.* Manufacturers must meet certain standards for content, quality, environmental cleanliness, workplace safety, and employee wages and working conditions. A product called chicken soup must have a minimum amount of chicken in it, and hot dogs cannot include more than a certain proportion of bone, hair, insects, and other extraneous material. The FDA requires manufacturers of condoms to test them for leaks and to destroy an entire batch of one thousand if more than four are defective. Failure to maintain the standards can result in fines or other legal penalties, if convicted.

4. *Providing economic incentives.* Higher taxes may be imposed on goods or activities viewed as less beneficial than on those deemed more beneficial. Examples are a tax on cars that use fuel inefficiently or on an industry that emits toxic chemicals into the air. Some people, particularly conservatives, believe taxation is a better way to achieve regula-

tory goals than setting mandatory standards because it gives individuals or businesses an incentive to comply and the choice not to (and to pay for the damage).

5. *Limiting liability.* Some regulations are designed to encourage the availability of certain products or services by having government assume some of the market risks. Congress has passed laws limiting the ability of patients to sue their HMOs and is trying to set ceilings on the amount of monetary damages that can be claimed in medical malpractice and other civil suits. Federal law prohibits citizens from filing suits against nuclear power plants for personal or property losses resulting from a nuclear accident.

Similarly, drafters of the homeland security bill sneaked in a provision exempting drug manufacturers from liability for the mercury content of vaccines, a provision having nothing to do with homeland security but a lot to do with protecting the financial interests of campaign donors. In these cases, the taxpayers, not the industries, assume the financial burden.

The Regulatory Process

Many Americans blame federal bureaucrats when they are stymied by Byzantine rules or endless paperwork to get government approval for some activity. But regulation is a many-layered process with at least five different aspects: passing the legislation that defines regulatory goals, writing rules to achieve those goals, overseeing the rule writers, implementing and enforcing the rules, and keeping pace with change after the standards are set and rules are written. Here we discuss rule writing, oversight, and implementation, leaving the discussion of reforming rules to keep pace with change until the next section.

Writing Regulations

Most regulatory activity stems from very general, even vaguely stated, mandates because passing legislation, especially in a divided government, requires compromise. If bill writers were too specific, legislation would probably never get passed. When a bill is passed establishing some regulatory goal, such as driver safety, child-labor protection, safe food, or clean air, its content rarely includes specifics on how the goals are to be achieved. Instead, as discussed in Chapter 12, after a bill becomes law, it is up to executive branch specialists to write the rules necessary to achieve these goals. Because most regulations are implemented at the state level, federal regulators often work with their state counterparts in writing these rules.

Laws granting regulatory authority often require public input, so citizens and interest groups also get involved in rule writing. This has been true since the beginning of the twentieth century for areas of regulatory policy such as food safety and fair labor practices. But historically, much of the public's input came from the interest groups and industries that would be affected by the rules being written. In fact, interest groups and industry lobbyists work so closely with regulators in writing rules that there is always concern, as discussed in Chapter 12, that agencies can be "captured" by those they are supposed to be regulating.

Kenneth Lay, then CEO of Enron, had a direct hand in selecting the man George W. Bush named to replace the head of the Federal Energy Regulatory Commission (FERC), the agency that was supposed to regulate Enron. Lay had opposed the reappointment of the former head after he set limits on power prices and refused Enron greater access to the national power grid.[17] Congressional investigators found that FERC knew for at least a year that energy companies were withholding electricity supplies to drive up prices, yet the new head of FERC took no action against them.

In the 1960s, when the participation and procedural "revolutions" swept through government, Congress began placing more emphasis on citizen participation in rule writing. The Consumer Product Safety Act even authorized nongovernmental groups and organizations to submit their own versions of rules to agencies.[18] This movement to democratize the process by providing more public hearings and extended periods for public comment on regulations had advocates among both pro- and antiregulatory groups in Congress. It was a way to open up the process and make it more accountable, but it was also a way of slowing down the issuance of new rules by allowing many opportunities for rule opponents to impede the process. Where citizens see an immediate impact of rules, such as those on handling toxic waste in their communities, ensuring clean drinking water, defining safe foods, or placing restrictions on the use of public lands, a surprising number of people attend hearings or submit written comments. Using the Web sites of regulatory agencies to solicit comments has also greatly increased the public's role in writing rules.

Standards of Evaluation

No matter how many individuals and groups get involved in the process, writing effective regulations requires guidelines beyond the policies and goals stated in the authorizing legislation. One of the standards by which the effectiveness of any regulation is judged is whether it results in a net benefit for society. It is easy for both the average citizen and the bureaucrat to see

that it is not cost effective to enforce a rule requiring all workplace toilet seats to be horseshoe shaped. No one fought to prevent the rule's abolition. But in most cases, it is far more difficult to decide whether a rule has more negative than positive effects. How do we decide whether the risk involved in using a particular chemical or product, or working in a hazardous environment, is great enough to regulate? There is no agreement on which standard of evaluation should be used.

In authorizing new regulations, Congress uses different standards of risk. One is the "no-risk" standard: if a substance is found to cause cancer or present any life-threatening risk, it cannot be used—even in amounts well below the danger level. Sometimes called the "better-safe-than-sorry" rule, it is often applied to regulations on food and drug safety.

In other cases, the "margin of safety" criterion is used. The regulatory agency establishes a reasonable standard and then allows an extra margin of safety. For example, standards for clean air mandate the EPA to declare how much lead, sulfur, and other materials can be in the air before it is judged unsafe. Then the agency is supposed to set the standards a little higher to allow the extra margin of safety.[19]

Sometimes Congress mandates a standard whereby cost of the regulation is to be weighed against the risk. The process of making this evaluation is called **cost-benefit analysis.** Today, any rule that will have an economic impact greater than $100 million must be submitted for cost-benefit analysis. A rule governing consumer product safety, for example, would not be adopted unless the benefits outweigh the costs to business of complying with the rule. Generally, proregulation groups prefer the no-risk or margin of safety standards, while antiregulation forces prefer cost-benefit analysis.

Applying Standards

Deciding which standard to apply and assigning values to these standards inevitably involve both science and politics. For example, critics of cost-benefit analyses have charged that these analyses are not done fairly or competently.[20] They believe that costs are concrete and easily calculated, while benefits are often more difficult to put in dollar terms. How do you quantify saving human lives? If a particular rule is likely to save five lives per year at a cost of $5 million, does the regulation offer a net cost or a net benefit? Ultimately, it depends on what monetary value is placed on a life, but it also depends on whether every life is treated as of equal or different monetary worth.

Cost-benefit analysis is not for the fussy idealist. One of the measures used to determine the value of a life is earning power. So, for example, the life of a man with a college degree would be worth more than that of a

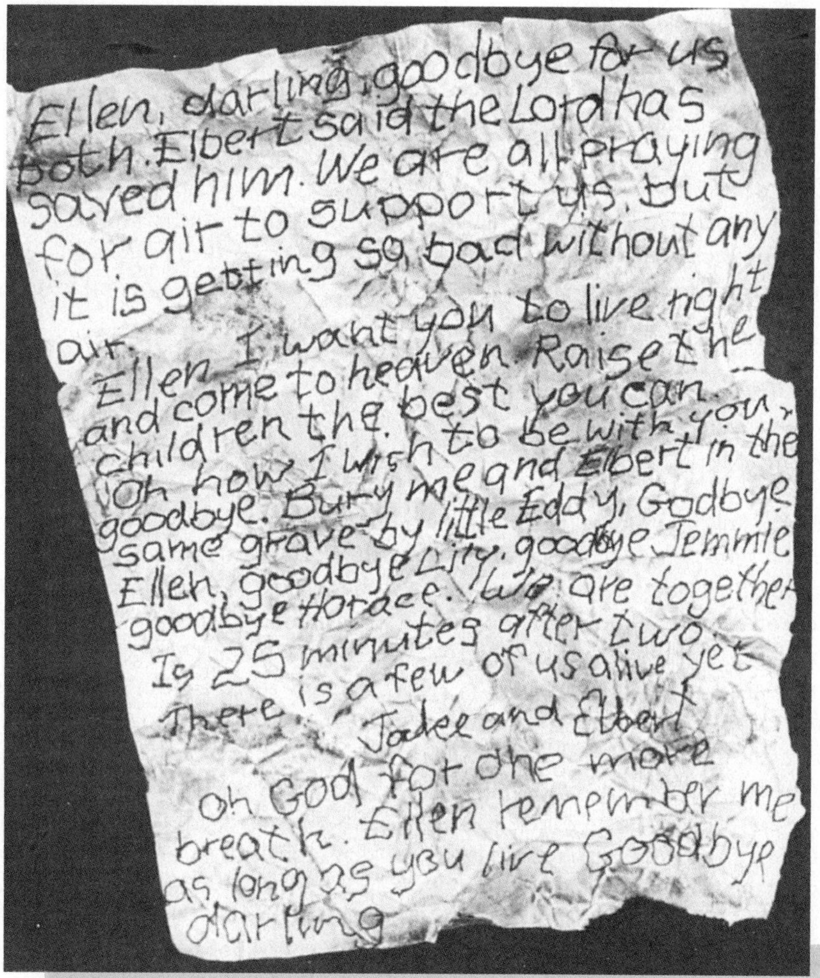
Ellen, darling, goodbye for us
both. Elbert said the Lord has
saved him. We are all praying
for air to support us, but
it is getting so bad without any
air.
Ellen I want you to live right
and come to heaven. Raise the
children the best you can.
Oh how I wish to be with you,
goodbye. Bury me and Elbert in the
same grave by little Eddy, Godbye
Ellen, goodbye Lily, goodbye Jemmie
goodbye Horace. We are together
Is 25 minutes after two.
There is a few of us alive yet.
Jacee and Elbert
Oh God for one more
breath. Ellen remember me
as long as you live Goodbye
darling

United Mineworkers of America

Jacob Vowell wrote this letter shortly before dying of suffocation in a mine disaster in Fraterville, Tennessee, in 1902. Such disasters eventually prompted government regulation of mining, which has since saved many lives, including the Pennsylvania miners rescued in the summer of 2002.

woman with a high school diploma, and either life would be worth more than a child's or an older person past the peak of maximum earning power.

The ugliness of this type of calculation was brought home when private charities were making decisions on how much to compensate families of victims lost in the terrorist attacks on the World Trade Center. Because of their greater earning power, stockbrokers were deemed worthy of far more compensation than those of the firefighters who died trying to save them. The life of a thirty-three-year-old equities trader, for example, was valued at $6.3 million and that of a forty-year-old firefighter was valued at $1.3 million.[21] This is everyday decision making for insurance companies, but many citizens believe government should value lives equally and, where lives are at risk, should not use cost-benefit analysis in writing rules.

A more stringent variation of cost-benefit analysis, called **risk assessment,** was put in place in 1995 when the Gingrich Republicans assumed control of Congress. This standard for determining whether a rule is needed requires that the risks to the public of a particular product or act be assessed using rigid standards of scientific proof. In essence, risk assessment requires that the methods and data an agency presents to show proof of risk must be replicable in independent research by outside scientists. Risk assessment is the standard currently applied by regulatory overseers in the Bush administration.

Risk assessment is used by some agencies, including the EPA—which at one time placed the same value on all lives—to calculate the cost effectiveness of environmental cleanup programs. Risk assessors determine the "value of a statistical life" by calculating how much categories of individuals would be willing to pay for increased safety or to be free of the symptoms caused by exposure to pollutants.[22] This method assumes that older people, for example, having lived most of their lives, would be less risk averse and, therefore, less willing to pay for safety. Hence in calculating the cost effectiveness of a pollution control program, the dollar value of a life saved is set lower for an older American (this is sarcastically referred to as the "senior death discount").[23]

Once in final form, rules are published in the *Code of Federal Regulations* and updated each year. Divided into more than three hundred categories, or titles, each representing a regulatory area, they total tens of thousands of pages. Title 40 alone—environmental protection rules—required twenty-seven volumes by 2002. But rule writing is just the beginning of the process.

Regulatory Oversight

Rule writing is overseen primarily by Congress and the president, but the federal courts have a role when an aggrieved party challenges the legality of rules or the interpretation of congressional intent. The public's oversight role, as discussed earlier, has been steadily increasing over the past thirty years.

The president has several ways to exercise oversight. Since the Carter administration, a principal means has been to issue executive orders that identify an overall rationale for rule writing that is in keeping with the political philosophy and goals of the administration. With Carter, it was rational management and public participation; with Reagan and George H. Bush, it was cost-benefit analysis or, more specifically, eliminating rules whose implementation was costly to business. Clinton's executive orders stressed public participation and openness as well as cost effectiveness.

Presidents also exercise oversight through their appointment powers, since all agency heads are presidential appointees. Most are selected on the basis of policy agreement with the president, but the head of the EPA is under more pressure to follow presidential preferences than ones on fixed-term appointments. Furthermore, a presidential appointee heads the Office of Management and Budget (OMB), which is the principal oversight agency for the executive branch and which must approve agency budget requests.

The OMB's authority to review agency rules derives from an executive order issued by President Reagan as part of his efforts in administrative deregulation. This innovation was designed to give the OMB the authority to identify and eliminate duplicate rules and to develop procedures for cost-benefit analysis. Reagan gave the OMB the job of reviewing rules from more than fifty federal agencies. Many argued that giving this power to the OMB would erode the independence of regulatory agencies. This was, no doubt, partly the intent of the change. Regulations developed by agencies under formal rules and according to due process could be killed by the OMB without any public hearings or advance notification. This violated the spirit of the Administrative Procedure Act, which requires openness in rulemaking, and it diminished governmental responsiveness to the general public. For example, EPA rules for limiting the amount of toxic chemicals that industries could dump in municipal sewage systems were killed three months after they were issued. This undoing of the rules followed extensive lobbying of the OMB by chemical manufacturers and other producers of toxic wastes.[24]

Each new administration can set different guidelines, often by executive order, for writing rules or for the standards of evaluation written into rules. (See the "You Are There" section for this chapter.) Just as an agency starts carrying out a directive—sometimes even before it has had the chance to do so—administrations change, or control of Congress changes hands, and all the proceeding guidelines are overridden by new legislation or executive orders. Just as regulatory policy changed when George H. Bush left office and Clinton entered, there were also sharp differences between Clinton's last directives to regulatory agencies and those sent by George W. Bush.

Shortly after entering office, Bush rescinded a Clinton rule lowering the amount of arsenic allowable in drinking water. The action provoked such a negative public response that Bush reversed himself and restored the standard. It was one in a series of Clinton rules Bush had overridden, but the sharp reaction to this one caused him to pay more attention to public perception of his deregulatory program, leading one watchdog group to refer to his policies as "before arsenic and after arsenic."[25] But working much more quietly, Bush changed rules on timber management and snowmobile use in national forests and parks, ocean polluting, and dumping in rivers by mining operations, among others.

Although regulatory agencies are frequently criticized for waste and inefficiency, they have to work under this burden of constantly shifting directions. Ultimately, it is Congress that has the broadest powers of oversight because, at the beginning of the process, it can influence the ways rules are written by the clarity of direction it writes into the enabling legislation. Congress can also amend the original law, change budget authorization for agencies, or attach riders to appropriations bills that effectively kill agency-written rules.

Like presidents, members of Congress also try to impose their political agendas on regulatory agencies. The Gingrich Republicans were zealously committed to deregulation and insisted on the use of the risk-assessment standard to determine whether a rule was necessary. They also supported opening the process of rule writing further to peer and judicial review, hoping proposed regulations would die while tied up in administrative and court challenges. The process was likened

to injecting Arnold Schwarzenegger with steroids, "in hopes he soon will be so muscle-bound he can't move at all."[26]

Congressional oversight can also affect the regulatory process when committees become captured by lobbyists. The wave of corporate corruption scandals from 2001 to 2003, for example, had as much to do with the failure of congressional oversight as it did with the laxness of regulatory agencies. Taking just one aspect of the scandals, the misrepresentation of corporate earnings, it is clear that Congress prevented regulatory agencies from doing their job. In the late 1990s, the Financial Accounting Standards Board (FASBE, pronounced "fasby") proposed a new rule that would prohibit corporations from giving their employees stock options without counting them as a business expense. These options cost companies hundreds of millions of dollars, yet corporations were not required to subtract them from their earnings. The effect of this was to greatly inflate the annual earnings reports and mislead investors into thinking the companies were in much better shape than they were.

FASBE's proposed rule had the support of the chairman of the Securities and Exchange Commission (SEC), but it did not go over well among powerful members of Congress who collectively had received millions of dollars in campaign contributions from accounting firms. Senators Christopher Dodd and Joseph Lieberman, both Democrats from Connecticut (the site of many corporate headquarters), led a successful fight for a Senate resolution repudiating FASBE's proposed rule. FASBE retreated, as did the SEC chair, Arthur Levitt Jr., who later said it was the worst decision he made at the SEC.[27]

Congress also balked when Levitt proposed a new SEC rule to restrict accounting firms from acting as con-sultants to the corporations they audited. House Energy and Commerce Committee chair, Billy Tauzin (R–La., now a lobbyist for the pharmaceutical industry), sent Levitt a four-page list of detailed questions about the rule and also told him that an appearance of conflict of interest was not enough; he must provide proof that auditors' objectivity was undermined by serving in the dual role of consultant. Soon Levitt received similar letters of objection from forty-six other congressmen. And, at the request of industry lobbyists, Henry Bonilla (R–Tex.), a member of the House Appropriations Committee, threatened to cut the SEC's budget. Levitt fought back by organizing a nationwide series of public hearings, but Congress delayed the rule on procedural grounds knowing Levitt's term was near an end.[28]

These abuses of the oversight function to win concessions for political supporters and campaign contributors are a huge challenge to effective rule writing and enforcement, and they are not likely to go away. There are seventy-five lobbyists in Washington for every member of Congress; many have deep pockets.[29] The defeat of the FASBE and SEC rules contributed to investor losses in excess of $60 billion, the bankruptcy of Enron and other corporations, and the collapse of the Arthur Anderson accounting firm. And the corporate malpractice that led to these failures was then investigated by the very oversight committees whose members thwarted the rules that might have prevented it.

Implementing and Enforcing Regulations

Federal and state regulatory agencies share the responsibility for the implementation and enforcement of those rules not killed in the oversight process, but the overwhelming burden of enforcement falls on the state agencies. After standards and general rules are set by federal agencies, the specific plans for implementing them are designed by state regulators. Because state bureaucracies often divide functional authority differently than the federal government, responsibility for implementing rules on worker safety, fair labor practices, toxic emissions into the air and water, or disposal of hazardous waste may be spread over multiple agencies, each of which may have played some role in writing or refining the rules as well as in their enforcement. The challenges to effective implementation are enormous due to the number of agencies, scientists, legislators, and regulated parties involved and the political and technical differences among them. Moreover, divided government, court challenges, and federal and state disagreement over jurisdiction also present obstacles to effective implementation.

We have already seen how divided government can impede the implementation of rules if the president and the majority in Congress have different views on regulation. But the regulators themselves are often divided on policy issues. The directors of federal agencies might be from a different party than the heads of state agencies and their views on regulation and commitment to enforcement can vary considerably. Furthermore, the scientists and technicians who staff regulatory agencies likely are guided more by professional competence than by the policy preferences of an agency head or elected official.

Regulated industries often refuse to comply with rules or the standards on which they are based. They frequently challenge the jurisdiction of the agencies, the constitutionality of rules, and the reasonableness of standards in federal courts. Every health standard ever issued by OSHA has been challenged in court. And each year hundreds of EPA rules are subjects of lawsuits.[30] Federal regulators also find that, in practice, some rules are nitpicking and not worth enforcing or that enforcement costs more than any benefit that might be gained. Other rules are based on standards that end up not working well to achieve the goal. In the current era of rapid technological change, some rules, and the standards they are based on, become obsolete soon after they are written. This is especially true for the regulation of telecommunications and biotechnology.

Then there are the inevitable disagreements over jurisdiction between federal and state rulemakers. For example, some states have resisted implementing rules that they think will endanger their ability to attract industry or that they believe give federal authorities too much say over their state resources (for example, conservation of wetlands and wilderness areas or protection of animals on the endangered species list). Governors and other state officials are far closer to the electorate in

their states than Washington bureaucrats are and more likely to listen to them than to an EPA, OSHA, or FDA administrator.

One recent example of state regulators resisting federal jurisdiction comes from the deregulation of electric utilities. In the 1990s, twenty-four states deregulated their utilities, leaving them free to buy and sell electricity wherever they could get the best price, from independent companies and peaker plants (companies that generate electricity for sale just during peak periods of use) rather than from in-state plants. This approach required transmitting electricity around the country from generating plants to wherever it was most needed at any point in time. So the deregulated power plants could purchase electricity from sources hundreds and even a thousand miles away. As new plants entered the market, the demand for use of the national grid system to transmit electricity increased, leading to regional electricity shortages and brownouts. Congress ordered monopoly utilities in regulated states to allow other companies to use their grids, but the states believed they should retain the regulatory authority they had always had over utilities. Congress argued that power transmitted across a national grid system is interstate commerce, and only Congress has the authority to regulate it. The result was a tug-of-war between Congress and the states over the regulation of utilities.[31]

Thus as we have seen, every phase of the regulatory process is open to influence by parties affected by the content of regulations. Those with a direct stake in a particular type of regulation can give testimony and lobby influential legislators while legislation is being written. They can lobby bureaucrats who write the rules mandated by legislation, agency heads responsible for implementation of rules, or members of congressional committees with oversight functions. Rules, and the ways they are or are not enforced, can be appealed to the agencies issuing them and, in some cases, challenged in federal courts. Powerful interest groups have opportunities to pressure the White House on the appointment of agency heads and the content of specific rules.

Because regulation does incur costs as it bestows benefits, it is inevitable that those who sustain the costs will compete with those seeking benefits to influence the process of writing and implementing rules. All of this competition between pro- and antiregulation forces, between regulators and the regulated, and among the regulators themselves slows the implementation and enforcement of rules designed to achieve regulatory goals established by Congress. Effective implementation is also slowed by weak enforcement powers. Although agencies are authorized to assess penalties for noncompliance, these punishments are usually negligible. In the face of these obstacles, it is amazing how much federal and state regulators have been able to achieve in protecting lives, safeguarding the environment, and promoting equity and competitiveness in the marketplace.

Cycles of Regulation

Like other government activity, the push for government regulation comes in fits and starts. The first spurt came in the late 1800s, when a poor economy led to charges, especially by farmers, that the large corporations of the day were exploiting the public. In 1890 with the Sherman Antitrust Act, Congress prohibited firms from conspiring to set prices or restrain trade in other ways. It also declared monopolies illegal and established the Interstate Commerce Commission to regulate the railroads.

The next burst of regulatory activity came after the turn of the twentieth century, in the Progressive Era. Demands for consumer protection arose largely because industrialization and railroad transportation created national markets for goods formerly produced and consumed locally. In these new national markets, consumers had little recourse if the products they bought from distant companies were not safe or reliable. Consumer fraud became endemic. Businesses engaged in deceptive advertising, food products often contained harmful substances (Coca-Cola contained cocaine; formaldehyde was used to preserve milk), and popular patient medicine usually contained alcohol or addictive drugs, such as opium.[32] Reformers also pointed to unsafe and unsanitary conditions in the meatpacking industry. After the media and so-called muckrakers highlighted these scandals, Congress banned certain food additives, prohibited false claims about products, and gave the Department of Agriculture power to inspect meat sold in interstate commerce.

The New Deal era spurred further regulatory activity. After one hundred people died from an unsafe drug, Congress passed an act mandating that the FDA declare a drug safe before it could be marketed. In the activist 1960s and 1970s, reformers were again influential in pressuring Congress to undertake new regulatory activity.

Agencies were established to regulate consumer product safety (the CPSC), the environment (the EPA), and industrial safety (OSHA). The powers of older agencies, such as the Federal Trade Commission (FTC), were strengthened.

Deregulation

As long as there has been regulation, there have been demands for **deregulation**—that is, ending or paring back regulation in a particular area. Although deregulation has had broad bipartisan support since the 1970s, there are partisan differences in the nature of this support. Democrats tend to support deregulation to the extent that it makes business activity more efficient and less cumbersome. Republicans are more likely to see this as a starting point and go further by opposing, in principle, certain kinds of regulation—working conditions, product safety, and a minimum wage, for example—as interference with market competition.

Deregulation can be carried out legislatively—that is, by an act of Congress—or administratively—by executive orders, appointments to policy positions in regulatory agencies, and through the oversight function of the OMB. One method of administrative deregulation is to strip regulatory agencies of personnel and budgets. This was a favored tactic of President Reagan; it was not until the last year of his administration that regulatory agencies (with the exception of the EPA) recovered to the level of funding they had when he entered office.

Another way to deregulate administratively is to appoint agency heads who favor either little regulation or self-regulation by industry. This will almost ensure that the number of regulations proposed and enacted will decrease, and that enforcement will slow. Reagan used this means to deregulate at the EPA and OSHA in particular, and George W. Bush has taken this approach to almost every area of rule making. To regulate the energy industry, he appointed a man recommended by leaders of the industries he would be regulating. Similarly, to head the SEC and regulate the stock market, Bush chose Harvey Pitt, a corporate lawyer whose career had been spent representing some of Wall Street's most powerful firms and who immediately said he would make the SEC an "accountant-friendly" place. To deal

"I've deregulated Arthur, but he still doesn't run very efficiently."

with possible conflicts of interest created by stock analysts rating stocks in which they had a financial stake, Pitt proposed, as an alternative to writing new rules, an honor system that would require brokers to sign a statement denying they benefited financially from their ratings.[33] When Pitt chose a man who had chaired the audit committee of an accounting firm under investigation for fraud to head a new accounting oversight board, he finally became a liability to the Bush administration and was forced to resign. Hostile public reaction to corporate corruption forced Bush to accept publicly, and even to campaign for, regulations he had earlier opposed. Out of the public spotlight, however, he sent more business-friendly directives to regulatory agencies, telling them how he expected the new rules on auditing corporate finance to be implemented.

In addition to his appointment powers, a president can also use executive orders to deregulate—just as he can to regulate—by sending directives to agencies changing evaluation standards or implementation and enforcement procedures. This is one way for a president to bypass Congress—and perhaps the only way when Congress is controlled by an opposing party—to pursue some of his objectives. But, as noted earlier, these actions do not have the permanence of legislative measures. The next president can revoke existing guidelines by issuing his own countermanding executive orders.

Types of Deregulation

Legislative and administrative deregulators may cast a narrow net, targeting individual rules, industries, or specific agencies, or a broad net, targeting the entire regulatory apparatus.

Eliminating Rules Presidents Carter, Reagan, and Clinton promoted regulatory reform through the elimination of unnecessary rules. During the Carter administration, OSHA abolished more than eleven hundred of its ten thousand rules; many, such as the horseshoe-shaped toilet seat rule, had been severely criticized as nitpicking. OSHA paperwork requirements, particularly for small businesses, were reduced, and safety inspections were concentrated on the industries with the worst safety records. The Reagan administration continued this pattern.

But at the outset of the Clinton administration, federal statutes and formal rules still totaled about one hundred million words. OSHA's remaining four thousand major regulations specified "everything from the height of railings to how much a plank can stick out from a temporary scaffold," although most of its 140 regulations on wooden ladders had been eliminated.[34] From those examples it is easy to see why rule elimination is a logical target for a deregulator: not only is it costly and inefficient to monitor and enforce rules on the grain of

wood in ladders, it is also impossible. There are not enough inspectors to enforce even those rules that are essential to worker and consumer health and safety.

Deregulating by Industry Many proponents of deregulation argue that it is not enough to streamline, eliminate the more trivial rules, and make regulators more accountable; in some areas, regulators simply should not be regulating at all.

Deregulating by industry began in the Carter administration with trucking, the railroads, and the airlines, and it had strong bipartisan support. The advantage to industry of less regulation is transparent, but it is also meant to benefit consumers by providing greater choice and lower prices or fares due to increased competition and greater efficiency in the marketplace. Not everyone agrees that these goals have been achieved by wholesale deregulation of industries. For an example of industry deregulation see the box "Deregulation and Re-Regulation: The Case of the Airlines" on page 634.

Reregulation

In politics as in physics, actions usually produce reactions. Actions to deregulate bring cries for a resumption of regulatory activity, or **reregulation.** Airline deregulation is an example of this cycle of action and reaction, as are electric utilities and corporate accounting practices.

Banking is still another example of how industry deregulation led to re-regulation, but only after it had cost taxpayers $150 billion. Traditionally, banks and savings and loan (S&L) institutions were heavily regulated and protected from competition. But during the 1970s and early 1980s, interest rates rose rapidly, and banks and S&Ls competed fiercely to retain their depositors and attract new ones. They were also in competition with the federal government for investors' money as interest rates on treasury notes continued to rise. In the bipartisan deregulatory mood of the time, Congress adopted a series of measures, beginning in 1980, to deregulate many aspects of the banking industry. Both banks and S&Ls were given more freedom to decide what financial services to offer. Within days, interest was being paid on checking accounts; credit card companies raised their interest rates; brokerages, insurance firms, and even department stores got into the banking business; and S&Ls offered a new range of services and made new types of investments that were formerly prohibited.

Some S&Ls attracted new depositors by paying interest rates that were more than double the interest rates their mortgage holders were paying. With these policies, it was only a matter of time before the S&Ls would go broke, unless they made windfall profits from their investments. As a result, many S&Ls, big and small,

The bank failures of the 1930s, which wiped out the life savings of ordinary and wealthy citizens alike, led the government to provide insurance for depositors at banks and savings and loans. This program meant that the taxpayers in general, and not individual depositors, paid the bill when reckless and sometimes illegal actions of banks and savings and loans caused a new round of failures after deregulation in the 1970s.

made increasingly risky investments to survive and profit in the now highly competitive atmosphere. Banks, too, made high-risk loans to farmers and foreign governments, while some S&Ls made shaky real estate investments and then saw the bottom drop out of their investments when real estate prices plummeted.

During this period, federal scrutiny of bank and S&L activities fell drastically, even though the government, through its deposit insurance program, guaranteed each deposit (of up to $100,000) that the banks and S&Ls used for their risky investments. Charles E. Schumer (D-N.Y.) said the government "behaved like a fire insurance company that said to its customers: 'Go ahead, play with matches. We'll cover you if anything goes wrong.'" Congress repeatedly denied requests from the Federal Home Loan Bank Board, which regulates S&Ls, for more examiners and auditors. In the last half of the 1980s, one thousand banks failed, including the nation's eighth largest, Continental Illinois. Thanks to the federal deposit insurance program, few individuals lost their savings, but it took an additional $4 billion loan from the government to restore Continental Illinois to solvency.

The S&L crisis proved much more costly; 27 percent of all thrifts failed. Covering the losses, the federal insurance company for S&Ls, the Federal Savings and Loan Insurance Corporation (FSLIC), went broke. By 1996, about $150 billion of taxpayers' money had been committed to the bailout of failed S&Ls.

In short, deregulation in the financial industry led to disaster. Proponents of deregulation argue that a truly free market would be more efficient because consistently bad business decisions would bring failure without benefit of a taxpayer rescue. But, in the case of Continental Illinois and the hundreds of insolvent S&Ls, the government believed—as it did with the major air carriers—that the nation could not afford to let them go under. Huge banks defaulting and millions of people losing their savings would send shock waves throughout the nation, so the federal government stepped in to save them. Thus critics of banking deregulation argue that since banks have the luxury of Uncle Sam's pocketbook when things go wrong, they should be forced by Uncle Sam to conduct themselves in a prudent manner. The S&L bailout reflected this view by imposing tougher new regulations that S&Ls must now meet.

Deregulation: The Current Round

Reregulation, especially by industry, is often a response to a transparent failure of deregulation, sometimes of

From 1938 to 1978, commercial airlines were heavily regulated by the Civil Aeronautics Board (CAB) and needed its approval to select routes and set fares. Originally, regulations were designed to help the struggling airline industry by protecting it from competition. This worked so well for existing air carriers that after forty years of federal rule-making, it was almost impossible for new airlines to enter the industry. In the mid-1970s, however, when the oil crisis had caused fares to skyrocket and several airlines were in economic difficulty, Congress decided to deregulate. In 1978, President Carter signed a bill phasing in deregulation. The CAB was abolished and regulation was left to the Federal Aviation Administration (FAA), which oversees air safety.

By opening up competition among the airlines, proponents of deregulation hoped the airlines would seek ways to become more efficient and then lower fares. Airlines were allowed to fly new routes without CAB approval and were permitted flexibility in setting their fares. But Congress also provided subsidies to carriers serving small communities to ensure they did not abandon unprofitable routes.

In its early years, deregulation did increase competition; the number of airlines nearly tripled between 1978 and 1983, and the number of people choosing to travel by air doubled by the 1990s. But deregulating airlines does not change the fact that big capital outlays are necessary for a new company to break into the market. The first carriers were protected from competition by the CAB, but for the post-deregulation startups, there was no such protection. Many airlines folded or sold out during the recession of the early 1980s. By 1990, the eight largest airlines controlled about 90 percent of all commercial air travel in the United States. Deregulation had reduced rather than increased competition.

Competition was also diminished when the airlines divided up the nation into regional turfs. In ten major cities, two-thirds of the air traffic fell under the control of one airline, such as TWA in St. Louis and Northwest in Minneapolis and Detroit. In the huge hub airports at Chicago and Atlanta, two airlines, United and American, gained control of three-fourths of the traffic.

The special twenty- to thirty-year leasing arrangements major carriers made with large airports gave a single airline control over much of the traffic and a *de facto* veto power over expansion projects that would provide new gates for potential competitors.[1]

At these airports, the daily number of allowable landings and takeoffs is set by the federal government. When the Department of Transportation allocated those slots, they were divided among all carriers, but after 1986, when carriers were freed to buy, sell, lease, or trade their landing and take-off slots, the major carriers gained control of 98 percent of airport slots.[2] Not surprisingly, a Government Accountability Office study showed that at concentrated or "fortress" hubs, the fares of the dominant airlines were consistently higher than the fares at other airports.[3] And trying to route most passengers through hub airports to make connecting flights led to enormous inefficiencies. Although the country had 429 airports, 70 percent of all air traffic was being routed through just 31 of them.[4] That made most of the nation's flights dependent on the weather in hub cities, and when flights were grounded there, traffic backed up around the country. By 2000, the busiest airports were plagued by flight delays, canceled flights, and angry passengers.

After deregulation, comparatively little money went into expanding airports, upgrading air traffic control equipment, or building new airports. Only six new runways were built at the largest airports during the 1990s, and the Denver International Airport is the only major airport to have been built since 1976. Travelers had more flights to choose from, but planes became more crowded. Passenger complaints and lost baggage claims skyrocketed. Although average airfares dropped 36 percent after deregulation, passengers had to contend with a Byzantine system for setting fares. On one 1997 United Airlines domestic flight, for example, twenty-nine passengers with identical coach accommodations paid twenty-three different fares, ranging from $87 to $728.[5]

Deregulation had a much stronger downside for small and midsize cities that often were left with a single carrier and monopoly prices.[6] Since the lowest fares went to travelers who could plan well ahead or fly standby, business travelers with fixed appointments made at short notice were the hardest hit economically; in 2000, they were paying 50 percent more than they had in 1996.[7]

In 2001, with major carriers entering into alliances to control huge chunks of the market and passenger dissatisfaction growing, Congress was considering a variety of reregulatory measures. The largest airlines were already losing money at alarming rates when the hijacking of commercial airliners by terrorists for use as weapons dealt another tremendous blow to the financial health of major carriers. Given the carriers' economic distress and airports' very lax safety procedures, Congress believed it had no choice but to provide a financial bailout and begin a process of reregulation.

Congress delegated authority to a new Air Transportation Stabilization Board (ATSB), with Fed Chair Alan Greenspan as chair. The panel was to grant loans to airlines with the strongest business plans and to deny help to any airline that looked as if it was going to fail. In return, airlines receiving aid were asked to give the government an equity stake in their companies.[8]

Congress also tightened regulation to try to prevent future hijackings. The lapses that allowed the terrorists to board the flights that crashed on 9/11 were due both to inadequate federal safety standards and to indifferent airline enforcement. The standard security questions directed at passengers had long since become a joke. At electronic check-ins, passengers were allowed to answer the questions on the whereabouts and packing of their luggage just by pressing options offered on a computer screen. One reporter said it was as if airport security expected travelers to ask one another, "Dear, did we pack the nuclear waste in your suitcase or mine?" or, "Honey, is the plutonium in your purse or the black duffel?"[9]

Although it provoked a furious debate between deregulators and re-regulators, Congress decided to end privatization and make all airport screeners federal employees, requiring citizenship and a high school diploma, upgrading pay and benefits, and imposing more rigorous training standards. Congress also required airports to purchase new, much more sensitive screening equipment, screen all check-in luggage, and thoroughly search all carry-on bags and passengers. As added protection, Congress reinstated the old sky marshal program, putting security guards on passenger flights. Among the most controversial changes was the authorization of pilots to carry guns and limitations on the legal liability of airlines for injuries caused by those pilots.

The dire state of the industry after 9/11 led to many operational changes to improve the efficiency and overall performance of the big airlines. With travel down, airlines permanently elimi-nated flights to cities already well served by other carriers. And competition increased as small no-frills airlines stepped into the breach and won over many passengers who had relied on the large carriers. A year after 9/11, low-fare airlines were carrying more than 20 percent of all air passengers in the United States.[10] They fly point-to-point without connecting flights, avoiding hub airports. Some lines fly only a single type of aircraft, cutting down on training and maintenance costs, and many have no food service or frequent-flier plans. Businesses that had begun cutting travel budgets well before 9/11 started flocking to the discount airlines, a big blow to the major carriers, which make most of their profits from business travelers.[11]

Since 1978, 137 carriers have filed for bankruptcy. Three of the ten largest are in bankruptcy; together, the big carriers have lost $30 billion since 2000, and they continue to lose. And in the years from the end of World War II until 1994, "the sum of the industry's profits and losses was less than zero."[12] This led investment analyst Warren Buffet to suggest that it might have been "a blessing for shareholders if someone had thought to shoot down Orville Wright at Kitty Hawk."[13]

As the newer airlines like South-west and JetBlue capture the domestic market, the bigger airlines are turning to international flights to try to stay in business. Delta's CEO told his employees, "The harsh reality is that our world has permanently changed, and we must change with it."[14]

Some industry analysts say the continued dominance of megacarriers is inevitable because the industry, like information technology or telecommunications, evolves "toward heavy concentrations among a few players because of the high barriers to entry and heavy capital costs."[15] This is the view of those who see the airline industry as a combination public-private enterprise that should be treated like a controlled monopoly and exempt from antitrust rules. They believe the benefits to consumers (low fares, more routes, standardized service) are worth it. But deregulation advocates say government should leave it to the marketplace to determine which carriers will survive the industry crisis.[16]

1. Kirk Victor, "Hub Cap," *National Journal,* May 12, 1990, 1145.
2. "Demise of 'Regs' Threw Airlines into Tailspin," 15.
3. Kathy Koch, "Can Congress Prevent Aviation Gridlock?" *Congressional Quarterly Outlook,* October 16, 1999, 7.
4. James C. Benton, "Hill Ready to Wrest Control in America's Frustrated Skies," *Congressional Quarterly Weekly Report,* June 23, 2001, 1488.
5. Matthew L. Wald, "So, How Much Did You Pay for Your Ticket?" *New York Times,* April 12, 1998, sec. 4, 2.
6. Micheline Maynard, "A Nation of Airport Haves and Have-Nots, *New York Times,* September 26, 2004, sec. 3, 1.
7. Koch, "Can Congress Prevent Aviation Gridlock?" 7; Jeff Plungis, "Lawmakers Wary of Unfriendly Skies Weigh Revisiting Airline Regulation," *Congressional Quarterly Weekly Report,* July 8, 2000, 1675.
8. Laurence Zuckerman, "Do All Airlines Deserve a Taxpayer Rescue?" *New York Times,* October 21, 2001, sec. 3, 1.
9. Thomas L. Friedman, "Naked Air," *New York Times,* December 26, 2001, A29.
10. David Leonhardt and Micheline Maynard, "Troubled Airlines Face Reality: Those Cheap Fares Have a Price," *New York Times,* August 18, 2002, 1.
11. "Bargain Airlines," *News Hour with Jim Lehrer,* PBS, September 17, 2002.
12. Roger Lowenstein, "Into Thin Air," *New York Times Magazine,* February 17, 2002, 40–42.
13. Warren Buffet quoted in Lowenstein's "Into Thin Air."
14. Michelene Maynard, " Survival of Fittest and Leanest Becomes Strategy for the Airlines," *New York Times,* October 30, 2004, A1.
15. Stephen Labaton, "Airlines and Antitrust: A New World. Or Not." *New York Times,* November 18, 2001, sec. 3, 1.
16. Ibid., 13.

crisis proportions, as with S&L failures, power shortages, airline security, and corporate bankruptcies. For the most part, support for reregulation has remained industry specific. Where there are no crises looming, the default rhetorical position for most elected officials is to favor deregulation wherever possible.

The principle of deregulation has been gaining momentum ever since the Carter administration. In the Reagan years, it became an ideological position. In the early 1990s, as the country faced huge budget and trade deficits and an economy that was barely growing, there was near unanimous support for reducing the regulatory burden on both private and public entities to see whether it would help speed up the economic recovery. During the long period of economic expansion that followed, sentiment for deregulation did not decrease but continued to gain momentum.

At least four factors have contributed to continued deregulatory zeal. The first stems from the general policy approach of the Clinton administration, which was to find the middle ground in every policy dispute. Although Clinton favored health-based regulations, he opposed overconcentration of rulemaking in the federal government and was sympathetic to the complaints of both business and state governments about the cost of implementing regulations.

A second factor was the strong deregulatory policy of the Republican leadership that took control of both houses of Congress in 1995. Divided government kept in check, or overrode, Clinton administration tendencies to come down on the side of regulation when a middle ground could not be found.

A third factor sustaining deregulatory momentum was structural change in the global economy. Advances in transportation and telecommunications have changed the "balance between government and international markets" and the terms of business competition.[35] Global competition for market share has allowed businesses, including the heavily regulated banking and utilities industries, to argue that to have the freedom to reorganize on a scale necessary to maintain competitiveness in international markets, they must be deregulated. This argument found broad bipartisan support in Congress and in both the Clinton and George W. Bush administrations.

In 1999, for example, Congress essentially dismantled the Glass-Steagall Act that had separated the banking, insurance, and securities industries since the Great Depression. Commercial banks, already the second most profitable of all industries, are now free to engage in securities trading and to handle the title insurance of your new home as well as to give you a home mortgage and handle your checking account. Congress even sanctioned the creation of banks for large depositors, where accounts will not be protected by deposit insurance.

Within the new, bigger-companies-for-bigger-markets rationale, the number of mergers mushroomed, with only token opposition from the Department of Justice's antitrust division or from the FTC, even though the 1990s saw the twenty largest mergers in U.S. history.[36] There has been consolidation in the pharmaceutical, oil, telecommunications, and freight and shipping industries. Similar consolidation is being attempted by cable companies, even though no cable merger has ever resulted in a price decrease for consumers. (In fact, cable prices have increased three times faster than inflation.)[37]

Many in government see the 1990s wave of mergers as inevitable, necessitated by global competition. But critics of "merger mania" argued that too little thought is being given to the consequences of corporate consolidations—namely, that the more assets companies acquire through mergers, the more resources they have to buy still other companies. One member of Congress warned, "We've got to have the [antitrust] resources that prevent this society from turning from a capitalist society into an oligarchy."[38]

A fourth stimulus to deregulation is the power of large corporations to influence the political process. Through their key role in financing the campaigns of candidates of both major parties (see Chapter 9), they are guaranteed at least a symbolic hearing for their arguments for deregulation. Currently, the balance of power in Washington is heavily skewed toward corporations, with labor unions, consumer groups, and others who favor regulation in decline.

Corporate financial power resulting from consolidations—for example, Adelphia and WorldCom—gave political access and protection from congressional oversight. Several regulations of the financial industry, rolled back in the 1990s, allowed CEOs and their auditors to cook their books, and eventually led to a stock market crash. This, in turn, led to investor (voter) rage and to legislation reregulating accounting firms and the ways corporations compensate their CEOs and report company earnings.

However, at the same time that limited reregulation was taking place, deregulation continued at a stepped-up pace in other sectors of the economy, including energy, mining and logging, telecommunications, worker safety, product liability, and, as we will discuss later, environmental protection. George W. Bush shares the deregulatory fervor of the Gingrich Republicans and, with a divided Congress in his first two years, employed Reagan's approach of appointing antiregulation agency heads and cutting agency budgets.

Keeping Pace with Change

Rapid advances in technology over the past decade have challenged government's regulatory powers. One of the most difficult issues has emerged from advances in biotechnology: should government or the marketplace decide whether science should engineer human life, and should business market it?

Some argue that cloning, for example, could save thousands of lives by providing healthy tissue, bone marrow, or organs needed by people with illnesses that require grafts or transplants from a genetically matched person. Some make a straightforward argument for genetic engineering; they see nothing wrong with procedures that could eliminate the risk of disabling diseases or birth deformities in unborn children. Cloning might also allow infertile couples to have children. In fact, some see cloning as a reproductive freedom issue, and just as they do not want government to regulate whether a woman can terminate a pregnancy, they do not believe government should prevent the cloning of offspring.

To what standard does government look to determine whether cloning is good or bad for the public, and what is the legal basis for this regulatory authority? Typically, government regulates to promote public health and safety and equal access in the marketplace. Should regulatory decisions on cloning be made by committees of scientists, doctors, clergy, and ethicists? If so, who would choose the committee members, and how would they be accountable to the public?

Consumer concern about the safety of genetically engineered foods has also brought demands for new regulation. Lawsuits have been filed against the federal government and biotech companies demanding that the foods grown from genetically altered seeds (called "frankenfoods" by their critics) be more carefully studied before being declared safe. In some cases, opponents have demanded the removal of food already on the market. While the FDA insists that genetically altered foods are safe, it has written new rules requiring manufacturers to inform the FDA of their intent to market such products and has drawn up guidelines for those who want to label contents voluntarily. But food safety is not the only issue. About half the soybeans and a third of the corn planted in the United States are grown from genetically altered seed stocks, creating the potential for emergence of pesticide-resistant insects.[39] In this area, too, government has begun to act, ordering farmers to grow at least 20 percent of their corn and soybeans from nongenetically altered seed.

Communications technology is another area where changes are occurring more rapidly than regulators can keep pace. In 2003, 55 percent of all Americans had home access to the Internet, and online commerce was booming. Many of its supporters see the Internet as the model of a free market, open to all and completely unregulated, and they believe it should stay that way. Advocates of greater government oversight believe that excitement over the development of e-commerce, the

Most scientists and even the United Nations have indicated that genetically altered foods are safe, but, nonetheless, many are skeptical and worry about the long-term effects on both humans and agriculture.

new ease in rapid global communication, and the emergence of global markets have caused people to forget the dangers of an unfettered market.[40]

For example, an unregulated Internet has resulted in consumer and credit card fraud, illegal online securities trading, criminal solicitation, access of children to pornography, and public dissemination of personal credit and medical histories and other invasions of personal privacy. Congress has yet to adopt measures to regulate in most of these areas, but more than seventy-five bills dealing with issues of privacy, access, and content on the Internet were under consideration before 9/11.[41] After the 9/11 terrorist attacks, legislative attention shifted to *removing* privacy protections, allowing (under the PATRIOT Act) intelligence and law enforcement agencies unprecedented access to individual e-mail accounts and records of Internet activity.

Regulating high-tech requires scientific study and time for assessment and it also requires members of Congress to familiarize themselves with the intricacies of a multitude of new technologies and their applications before they write legislation. But changes are occurring with such rapidity it seems impossible that government regulation will be able to keep pace with their application in the market.

Regulatory Politics and Environmental Protection

In this section we use the example of environmental protection to illustrate how legislators, regulators, and interest groups have contributed to the politicization of the regulatory process.

Everyone breathes the air and drinks the water, and one in four Americans lives or works in proximity to a hazardous waste site.[42] Therefore, environmental protection has a huge constituency. A majority of the public supports spending for environmental protection, even when agreeing with the statement that government should regulate less. Government action to safeguard public health through protection of the environment has had broader public and more bipartisan legislative support than almost any area of regulation. For three decades, the importance of this type of regulatory activity has been proclaimed by leaders from Richard Nixon—who called a clean environment the "birthright" of every American—to Al Gore, who wrote a best-selling book based on the notion that safeguarding the environment should be "the central organizing principle for civilization."[43]

Nevertheless, neither widespread support for regulatory activity nor its real achievements have been able to prevent a strong backlash from developing against the environmental activism of federal agencies and interest groups. This is reflected in federal funding, which peaked in 1980, fell sharply during Reagan's deregulatory push, then grew by modest increments during the George H. Bush and the Clinton administrations before beginning to fall again during the presidency of George W. Bush.

Evolution of Government's Role

How can we define standards that protect society's interest in having a clean and healthy environment and at the same time not unreasonably handicap business and individual producers of pollution? Historical and current debates over environmental policy revolve around this issue.

The Constitution contains no hint of concern about preserving and protecting the environment. Indeed, the Founders' and our own orientation to the environment is rooted in the Western, Judeo-Christian tradition that the physical world exists to serve human needs.[44] This sentiment was reinforced during the eighteenth-century period known as the Enlightenment, which led people to believe that through science and learning, we could conquer almost any obstacle to human progress.[45] Awareness of the negative consequences of science and technology for the environment was a long way away.

But in the nineteenth century, concern grew about the effect that the Industrial Revolution, coupled with rapid population growth, might have on the environ-

ment. Late in that century, a conservationist movement to preserve some of the natural environment from farmers, ranchers, and loggers who were clearing the land resulted in the creation of the national forests and a national park system.[46]

Along with concern about saving some forests and other areas of scenic beauty came an awareness of pollution. The first effort to combat water pollution was an 1899 law requiring that individuals dumping waste into navigable waters get a permit from the Army Corps of Engineers. In 1924, Congress banned oceangoing ships from dumping oil in coastal waters. Neither of these acts was enforced very well, but the legislation did indicate an embryonic concern with pollution.

The modern environmental movement probably stems from a book, Rachel Carson's *Silent Spring,* originally published in 1962. Carson argued that pesticides used in agriculture find their way into the air and water and harm crops, animals, and people. Moreover, she demonstrated that scientists and engineers did not know the extent of these harmful effects, nor did they seem particularly concerned. The chemical industry immediately attacked Carson, accusing her of hysteria and misstatement of facts. The industry's attacks created widespread publicity for her views and raised the environmental consciousness of millions of Americans. President Kennedy cited Carson's work as his reason for ordering a review of government regulation of pesticides.

The decade and a half following the publicity over Carson's book was characterized by a burst of new regulatory activity. Public concern peaked, too. Huge oil spills, rivers catching fire, and the growing impact of the automobile on air quality lent substance to these concerns. By 1970, opinion polls showed that the most frequently cited public problem was protecting the environment, which was surprising in light of the continuing protest against the Vietnam War.[47] In April 1970, Earth Day was inaugurated, and hundreds of thousands of citizens across the nation demonstrated to show their concern about the environment. Every year since, one day in April has been set aside to celebrate the planet's resources and to heighten environmental awareness.

In 1970, Congress gave citizens a more formal way to affect environmental policy. New legislation, the **National Environmental Policy Act,** or **NEPA,** as it is usually called, mandated government agencies to prepare **environmental impact statements** for internal projects or projects they fund. Impact statements require justification for projects or actions proposed as well as a list of all the people and agencies consulted. Most important, these analyses must detail the effect, including any negative consequences, that a project or other activity would have on the environment. No new buildings, dams, sewers, pipelines, or highways were to be built, nor any research or other government projects initiated, until this statement had been filed.

Not only did the law give federal agencies the power to comment on each other's environmental impact statements, but it also gave citizens access. Early environmental legislation was the first to incorporate the 1960s ethic of public involvement and "full disclosure of the information on which government bases its decisions."[48] These provisions became an important device for organizations interested in protecting the environment, giving them a real opportunity to influence environmental policies. Within a few years, more than four hundred legal suits were filed to force the government to comply with the act's provisions; by 1980, thousands had been filed.[49]

Another landmark move marking the growing federal involvement in environmental protection was the 1970 creation of the **Environmental Protection Agency (EPA)** by President Nixon.[50] Recognizing that responsibilities for pollution control were spread throughout the executive branch, Nixon, with congressional approval, brought them together in one regulatory agency with a single head who reported to the president. During the EPA's first years, three foundational pieces of environmental protection legislation were passed by Congress: the Clean Air Act (1970), the Clean Water Act (1972), and the Endangered Species Act (1973). During the 1970s, the EPA received extensive new mandates to regulate hazardous waste, pesticides, and noise pollution.

An Earth Day celebrant illustrates a possible future scenario if air pollution is not curbed.

AP/Wide World Photos

Implementing Environmental Regulations

Passing laws is one thing, enforcing them another. Congress mandated the EPA to achieve certain goals, but the EPA had to write the rules for reaching them and then monitor their implementation by the states. For example, under the Clean Air Act, the EPA was ordered to establish air quality standards for major pollutants, a task the EPA estimated would require writing three hundred to four hundred rules. States were mandated to draw up plans that would bring local air quality into compliance with these new federal standards. In keeping with the commitment to public involvement in the regulatory process, the Clean Air Act also permitted citizens to sue to enforce its provisions.[51] Of course, the industries and public utilities subject to the new rules also had the right to challenge them.

Regulating Air Pollution

Though, in theory, the EPA can have a noncompliant company closed down, this move is simply not politically feasible or economically wise. Generally, the agency is reluctant to enforce standards against large companies with political clout or small profit margins, especially industries crucial to the nation's economic health. To take action against a large industry requires significant political will all the way to the White House. That kind of commitment is rarely evident.

The standard approach to rule writing provided few incentives for industry to comply. Penalties were often not assessed, and when they were, the fines were usually far less than the cost of complying with the standards. Furthermore, sometimes cheaper solutions could be found to pollution than the regulations specified.

The Carter administration adopted the policy of allowing compliance in some industries to be based on the **bubble concept.** This policy allowed companies to meet an overall standard for emission of pollutants. Imagine that a bubble has been placed over a factory with ten smokestacks, each emitting pollutants. Under the old rules, each smokestack would have to meet EPA standards. Under the bubble concept, one or more smokestacks might exceed the limits on emissions as long as the total emissions within the bubble met the standard. Rather than bringing all ten smokestacks into compliance, the company might find it cheaper to install equipment on five smokestacks if doing so would reduce total emissions to the required level. The bubble concept provided greater flexibility in determining how a standard would be met and reduced the cost of compliance.

From the bubble concept, a more flexible system evolved, allowing for a multifactory bubble. A limit or cap is placed on the amount of a pollutant that can be emitted in a geographic area, and factories within that area are allowed to buy, sell, or trade rights to pollute as long as collective emissions do not exceed the cap. For example, the EPA sets a limit on how much sulfur dioxide (the chemical that causes acid rain) can be emitted into the air in a particular area; then state environmental agencies sell permits to pollute. Utility companies, which emit a great deal of sulfur dioxide, can then decide whether it is cheaper for them to buy and install scrubbers to reduce plant emissions or to buy permits that allowed them to pollute. This policy, called **cap-and-trade,** allows industries some flexibility in meeting pollution standards, but if they do pollute, they have to pay in advance.

The bubble concept was hardly a panacea, however. It still required the EPA to set standards for each particular type of pollutant. Since the petrochemical industry was founded during World War II, tens of thousands new chemicals have been manufactured, and of the three thousand that are in high production, just over 40 percent have been even minimally tested for health effects.[52] During its first twenty years, the EPA set standards for only seven of the most toxic chemicals. Believing that it would be impossible to set standards for each separate chemical, the EPA replaced the pollutant-by-pollutant approach with a more comprehensive industry-by-industry approach.[53] Now limits are set on all toxic emissions combined, and, following the cap-and-trade policy, industries with emission levels below allowable limits earn credits that they can "bank," sell, or trade to other industries whose emission levels are above the standard.

Regulation of air quality is a good illustration of how industry and public responses to the implementation of rules can influence reassessment and revision. The goals of the original Clean Air Act were not weakened but strengthened by subsequent amendments and reauthorizing legislation because the rules to reach goals were revised in ways that make them less cumbersome and more cost effective to administer. The cap-and-trade approach has been adopted by international environmental agencies as a means for achieving worldwide reductions in the emissions of carbon dioxide and other gases linked to global warming, with nations, rather than businesses, buying and trading permits to pollute.

Water Quality

Before 1972, at least eighteen thousand communities regularly dumped their untreated raw sewage into rivers and lakes. Food, textile, paper, chemical, metal, and other industries discharged twenty-five trillion gallons of wastewater each year.

These activities occurred despite federal attempts to improve water quality. A 1948 law authorized the federal government to give funds to local governments to build sewage treatment plants. Thousands of communities used the grants for this purpose, and the program was seen as a welcome pork-barrel project as much as a regulatory one. In 1965, Congress mandated that states establish clean water standards in order to get these sewage treatment grants. But the law was not effective. States did not want to establish stringent quality standards because they were afraid industries would leave.

In 1972, the federal government tried again. It set as goals to achieve "fishable and swimmable" waters by 1983 and zero discharges into water by 1985. Industries were to have permits to discharge wastes; they were to use the "best practicable" technology by 1977 and the "best available" technology by 1983 to make sure the pollutants discharged were the smallest amounts possible. The EPA set uniform national standards for discharge control for each type of industry so states did not have to compete to attract industries or to keep them from moving away by setting the most lax standards.

It took years to implement water quality standards effectively for many of the same reasons that confounded air quality enforcement: rules were not correctly written, inadequate monitoring, industry resistance, and foot dragging in Congress. A substantial number of industries and municipalities did not meet the standard of technology necessary to clean up waste.[54] Some sewage treatment facilities were built inadequately and others were operated improperly because they lacked trained technicians. The EPA and state environmental agencies did not have the personnel to monitor carefully how local governments spent their sewage grants. Local governments also resisted the standards set by the Clean Water Act because of the cost to municipal budgets. Most towns and cities, especially during the bad economic times of the 1970s, did not have the resources to pay for what was essentially an unfunded mandate. Even today, one-third of all EPA spending is on grants to the states to build and maintain water and sewage facilities.

Congress yielded to political pressure from local governments and industry. In 1977, it weakened some of the provisions of the Clean Water Act and granted exemptions and extensions. Thus polluters had reason to believe they need not comply with standards or deadlines because Congress would come to their rescue.

Congress also dragged its feet on enforcement of the Safe Drinking Water Act (1974), waiting a dozen years before imposing a timetable on the EPA for issuing safety standards. Finally, in 1991, Congress did pass new and more stringent safety standards for tap water, requiring more frequent testing for lead levels in municipal water supplies, only to see them threatened by a new round of deregulation.

But the difficulty achieving the goals of clean water legislation was not all due to resistance to regulation and its costs. Part of the problem was with the rules themselves: when the first rules were written, not enough was known about the sources of water pollution to determine which sources to target first. Industries and municipal sewage plants accounted for only part of the water pollution problem. Other contributors were not being regulated. For example, what are called "nonpoint sources" (that is, discharges that do not come from a specific pipe) account for as much as half of all water pollution. Runoff of fertilizer from farmlands is a big source of nonpoint pollution and is difficult to control. So are the sewers connecting drains and grates in city streets. Storm sewers collect gas, oil, fertilizers, pesticides, animal excrement, and other unpleasant substances and then deposit them directly into the nearest waterway.

Current rules written to achieve clean water goals stress pollution from these nonpoint sources. For example, the EPA has told states that they have to develop plans for controlling pesticide runoff from farms and for limiting urban sprawl. This will create a new set of enforcement problems. Cracking down on farmers and construction firms or local land developers is much more difficult politically than attacking huge corporations that dump toxic waste in public waterways. In the Grain Belt states, local politicians may find it hard to tell cash-strapped family farmers that if they do not alter their use of pesticides (changes that could lower production), they may have to help pay for pesticide cleanup.

Despite all of these problems, today's drinking water is much safer than it was before the clean water laws were enacted, and 60 percent of all rivers and lakes are now safe for swimming and fishing.

Hazardous Waste

Most hazardous waste—toxic chemicals—is generated by government agencies and private industry. From 1976 to 1980, Congress passed legislation designed to clean up hazardous waste sites created by industry, and assigned financial responsibility to the companies doing the dumping. It also levied a tax on industry to create a **Superfund** to take care of hazardous waste left by companies long defunct or other waste with sources unknown.

Hazardous waste sites created by the government, especially in the development of nuclear weapons and nuclear power, have already exacted enormous health costs. No one warned the citizens of Nevada about radioactivity, even though the government exploded more than one thousand bombs in their state. Atomic Energy Commission documents refer to people living in the fallout area as "a low-use segment of the population."[55] According to a study by the Centers for Disease Control and Prevention (CDC), eleven thousand people died because of exposure to radioactive fallout from above-ground weapons testing, and it contributed to a minimum of twenty-two thousand cancers.[56]

Thousands of others suffered health problems as a result of working in or living near weapons industries or serving as subjects in weapons research. Six hundred thousand people in thirty-seven states worked in the nuclear weapons industry during the Cold War. In the 1940s, when government engineers recruited Navajo men and boys living near Cove, Arizona, to mine the uranium necessary for new atomic weapons programs, no one mentioned the dangers of radon exposure. In a government study of how irradiated nutrients are metabolized (paid for by the Quaker Oats Company), boys in a state home were fed oatmeal laced with radioactive isotopes. In other experiments, terminal cancer patients were radiated to toxic levels, hospital patients were injected with plutonium, and at least two hundred thousand military personnel were exposed to radioactive materials to test the consequences of exposure to atomic weapons and bomb blasts.

Not until the 1990s did Congress hold hearings on the "human radiation experiments" and appropriate money to compensate for injuries and deaths to uranium miners, participants in nuclear testing, and victims of radioactive fallout.[57]

The nuclear weapons plant in Hanford, Washington, knowingly released into the air massive amounts of radioactive materials, including iodine, for test purposes. Downwind, near Mesa, Washington, in an area known as the "death mile," 14 of 108 residents became ill with or died of cancer, and several children died or were born with disabilities.[58] Researchers from the CDC believe that twenty thousand children in eastern Washington may have been exposed to unhealthy levels of this iodine by drinking milk from cows grazing in contaminated pastures.[59]

In Fernald, Ohio, a red-and-white checkerboard design on a water tower and the name "Feed Materials Production Center" led some residents to believe a local firm produced animal feed. Instead, it made uranium rods and components for warheads. Residents were stunned to find out that, for thirty-five years, the plant had dumped radioactive refuse into pits in the ground that regularly overflowed when it rained. The plant also discharged 167,000 pounds of nuclear waste into a local river and released about twice that much into the air. Though these actions were taken by the private company that ran the plant, they were approved

Since 9/11, government officials have often warned Americans that an attack on the United States by terrorists armed with biological, chemical, or nuclear weapons is all but inevitable. Much attention has been paid to the possibility of terrorists acquiring such weapons, or the materials to make them, from so-called rogue nations (North Korea, Iran, Libya, and Iraq, for example) or stealing materials from poorly secured weapons and waste storage facilities in Russia and the former republics of the Soviet Union. In their presidential debates in 2004, both George W. Bush and John Kerry labeled the threat of weapons of mass destruction in terrorists' hands one of the most serious challenges facing the United States.

We are cooperating with Russia and its former republics to destroy weapons of mass destruction, and the materials for making them, that are stored in poorly secured facilities. We are also trying to recover highly enriched uranium shipped to other countries for use in their nuclear energy or research programs. In earlier years, the United States "loaned, leased or sold" highly enriched uranium—enough to make one thousand nuclear bombs—to forty-three countries. Some of the material has been returned but much remains out of U.S. control.[1]

While the government legislates, negotiates, and cajoles to get foreign governments to destroy or better safeguard their weapons and materials stockpiles, it has not done that well getting its own agencies to clean up domestic weapons and energy plants and hazardous waste storage sites. The environmental and health hazards posed by the Department of Defense (DoD) and Department of Energy (DoE) sites have long been an issue. Now the exis-

tence of mass quantities of radioactive materials and agents used in chemical and biological weapons at multiple sites across the country has become a major security problem. At the DoE's Washington State Hanford site alone there are fifty-five *million* gallons of high-level radioactive waste awaiting disposal.[2] Four other sites in Idaho, South Carolina, and Tennessee contain "substantial quantities of nuclear material . . . in the form of assembled nuclear weapons and test devices, major nuclear components, and other high-grade materials such as solutions and oxides." An attack on any one of these sites, the Government Accountability Office (GAO) says, would have "devastating consequences."[3]

After 9/11, weapons plants and testing and storage sites were ordered to develop plans for securing their facilities against theft or attacks from outside, or by insiders working with terrorists groups. Sites at highest risk—those where nuclear weapons are assembled or disassembled—are required to develop more complex security plans, including protection against a large scale terrorist attack. The ultimate risk at these plants is that a breach in security could result in a nuclear detonation. However, it will be years before acceptable security plans will actually be put in place. Most now exist only on paper.

One problem is budgetary; work at some of the sites is substantially underfunded. Some of the most dangerous materials need to be transported to other, safer sites, yet the DoE says it does not have the funding to do it.[4] Decontaminating and decommissioning the nation's uranium enrichment plants alone will cost in the billions and take decades. Moreover, we must dispose not only of our own nuclear wastes, but also those materials being reclaimed from foreign governments as well. Then,

too, the government is developing and testing new nuclear weapons (such as the Bush administration's bunker bomb program) and every year is piling up more radioactive waste at research and testing sites.

There are many other munitions and hazardous waste sites to be cleaned up as well—including an estimated fifteen million acres of shutdown military ranges—and huge reserves of chemical and biological weapons to be destroyed. At just one site in Anniston, Alabama, the government had stored 660,000 chemical weapons (such as mustard gas and sarin) before it began incinerating them in 2003.[5] At the current level of spending, the GAO estimates that cleanup for all of the chemical and other hazardous waste sights created by the military will take seventy-five to three hundred years.

In addition to budgetary problems, the government faces significant popular opposition to parts of its plans that deal with cleanup. For example, Washington voters passed an initiative to stop the shipment of any more radioactive materials to the Hanford site (a court ruling blocked the initiative).[6]

1. Joel Brinkley and William J. Broad, "U.S. Lags in Recovering Fuel Suitable for Nuclear Arms," *New York Times,* March 7, 2004, 8.
2. Government Accountability Office, "Nuclear Waste: Absence of Key Management Reforms on Hanford's Cleanup Project Adds to Challenges of Achieving Cost and Schedule Goals," GAO Report no. GAO-04-611 (June 9, 2004), 1. There is an archive of reports on nuclear waste at the GAO Web site (www.gao.gov).
3. Government Accountability Office, "Nuclear Security: Several Issues Could Impede the Ability of DoE's Office of Energy, Science and Environment to Meet the May 2003 Design Basis Threat," GAO Report no. GAO-04-894T (June 22, 2004) 3.
4. Ibid., 8.
5. Jeffrey Gettleman, "Army Begins Burning Biological Weapons in Alabama Town," *New York Times,* August 10, 2003, 12.
6. Larry Copeland, "Alabamians Fear Chemical Disaster," *USA Today,* August 18, 2003, 3A.

and even encouraged by the supposed regulators, the Atomic Energy Commission. Senator John Glenn (D-Ohio) said, "We are poisoning our people in the name of national security."[60]

To add insult to injury, the government backed federal contractors challenging the findings of the medical panels who ruled on the eligibility of nuclear weapons workers to receive financial aid for medical care. In 2002, President Bush reversed this policy and told the Department of Energy (DoE) to help twelve thousand workers file claims for compensation.

An EPA report estimates that the number of hazardous waste sites needing cleanup is growing by twenty-eight per year, and that as many as 355,000 hazmat (hazardous materials) sites will require cleanup over the next three decades at a cost of more than $250 billion. In spite of this, the Superfund budget has not been increased since 2001, and more than half its budget is spent on nine major sites.[61]

Science, Policy, and Environmental Politics

A former EPA director once said that the EPA's mission is like trying to give someone an appendectomy while the person is running the hundred-yard dash.[62] The agency is always shooting at a moving target: just as regulators establish rules for dealing with a pollutant, research reveals new dimensions to the problem or identifies other toxins from new sources. Public pressures also vacillate and sometimes public opinion is not consistent with the way the public acts. Elected officials also change, and their views on regulation can be dramatically different. So it is not surprising that it is difficult to make and enforce environmental policy.

In this section we take a brief look at the chief forces making environmental regulation difficult: changing science, public pressures, interest groups, and lack of consensus among policymakers.

Changing Science

Sound regulatory policy has to be based on good science and the scientific process is not always fast. Rapid changes in high technology and the massive changes brought by globalization have made it very difficult for policy to keep pace with change.

Sometimes scientific findings of one era are overridden by later research, and policies based on the earlier findings are not valid. Of course, science, like technology, is an ever-developing human enterprise and it is hardly surprising that better techniques and insights lead to improvements in scientific understanding. Nonethe-

less, regulations based on premature or faulty science can lead to expensive regulatory solutions.

Policies on toxic waste and hazardous substances are singled out by critics as the worst examples of wasteful spending and misguided priorities. They point to studies by the National Cancer Institute that claim that only 1 to 3 percent of the nation's half-million yearly cancer deaths result from exposure to environmental pollutants.[63] Yet regulations to control these pollutants often force businesses and government to spend billions of dollars to restore contaminated sites to a pristine state. Reformers cite as examples the unsafe standard for dioxin presence in water, which is equivalent to one drop in Lake Michigan, and the so-called dirt-eating rules, or standards of safety determined by how much chemical-contaminated soil a child could consume without becoming ill.[64] Opponents of the no-risk standard ask whether it is cost effective to clean up all toxic waste sites to the point that dirt is safe to eat or the water is safe to drink, especially if the amount of chemical contained in that soil or water presents no significant risk through normal exposure.

In too many cases, critics argue, the evidence used to support policy decisions has been unsound. Laws are made and standards mandated, only to have researchers revise the findings on which the laws were based. Scientists studying dioxin and DDT toxicity, for example, have said that early estimates of the danger level for human exposure were faulty. Much of the research on toxicity has been based on animal studies using the method of administering a "maximum tolerance dose" of the substance being studied. Researchers say that two-thirds of the chemicals such studies showed to be carcinogenic would be benign if ingested at lower levels. In addition, there is not a direct correspondence between rodent and human body chemistry, so we cannot be certain that humans will be affected in the same way rats are when exposed to the same chemicals. Arsenic, for example, is highly toxic to humans but not to rats.[65]

At other times, policymakers deliberately ignore or misuse scientific findings in pursuit of their own ideological ends. While the EPA employs hundreds of scientists, their attempts to research and report on environmental problems in a neutrally competent manner are at times undone by political opposition to their conclusions. The Bush White House has become known for its tendency to delete from agency reports conclusions that do not have political support in the administration. Of course, these revisions rarely escape public attention because they are leaked by disgruntled bureaucrats.

One prominent example of such political editing of scientific reports was the deletion of conclusions from an EPA report on global warming. The scientists' findings reflect a consensus that global warming exists and is a serious problem. Bush ignored this and claimed that there is no scientific consensus on the issue and that more research is needed before remedial action is taken. In this case, scientific findings were overridden by politics.

Clinton had accepted the science on global warming, but there was so much opposition in Congress to his environmental initiatives that he did not even submit the Kyoto Treaty, an international agreement on global warming that he had signed, to the Senate because he knew he could not get the needed votes for ratification. Global warming is *the* poster issue for how politics can trump scientific research on environmental issues.

Public Pressures

Trying to formulate policy based on sound science is complicated by pressures from the public. With the information explosion on how exposure to toxic substances in our food, water, land, and air may be linked to cancer and other illnesses, Americans have become increasingly health conscious. Heightened awareness of environmentally related diseases has led to increased pressure on government to protect us from toxic substances.

Sometimes this creates "politics of panic" and makes government too responsive to public pressure.[66] For example, in 1989, Congress passed a law in the wake of a public outcry that summer over the littering of East Coast beaches with medical and human waste and dead sea life. After cities spent billions to comply with the law, some experts said the beaches had not been contaminated by toxic waste dumped in the ocean after all, but by overtaxed storm sewer systems. While limiting the use of oceans as dumping grounds is a good thing in itself, it is extremely expensive to regulate, and the danger it presents is less than that from inadequate sewage systems.

The public's behavior is also not entirely consistent with the goals it claims to support. We want clean air and water, but we do not want to give up gas-guzzling cars and SUVs, plastic containers, energy-consuming conveniences, and other pollution-causing aspects of our lifestyles. We use far more energy per person than do the people of any other nation except Canada, and with energy use comes pollution. And emissions from vehicles now cause more pollution than emissions from industrial smokestacks. Part of this heavy consumption is due to our level of economic development and to consumer wealth, but part is plain wastefulness. High oil prices in the 1970s curbed energy use for a while, but we have returned to our high-consumption ways, despite a renewed interest in curbing our dependence on Middle Eastern oil. It is unrealistic to expect the EPA to control pollution when we do not police ourselves.

Interest Groups

Interest groups on both sides of the regulatory issue often exaggerate their claims, thus making it difficult to sort out likely implications of regulation or lack of regulation. Both sides play on public fears. Environmental groups at times make unreasonable demands for setting safety standards. Their critics say this has caused billions to be spent to achieve unrealistic and unnecessary goals, while more threatening hazards are ignored. The National Cancer Institute (NCI), for example, thinks priority should be given to public education on diet and other behavior that puts people at greater risk for cancer than exposure to environmental pollutants. City governments would rather spend federal grants on repairing sewer systems than on trying to restore brownfields (contaminated urban sites) to the safety thresholds prescribed by Congress.

Environmental interest groups counter by asking whether we really want to risk people's lives by waiting until we get better evidence. They support low- and no-risk standards and believe it is better to err on the side of safety and not wait to regulate until people start dying. They take issue with the NCI findings and claim environmental pollutants are responsible for up to 15 percent of all cancer deaths.

Environmentalists have also been criticized for being unwilling to admit their successes for fear of losing financial support for their organizations and momentum for the movement. These successes, coupled with what has been characterized as "compassion fatigue" among the American public, has led to an intense competition among environmental groups for membership and

It might be partly OPEC's fault, for using its cartel to limit supplies.

It might be partly the oil companies' fault, for using tight supplies to gouge on profits.

And just possibly it's partly your fault, for buying that ridiculous vehicle that gets what, 12 miles per gallon?

NOTHING IS EVER MY FAULT.

I'M AN AMERICAN MOTORIST.

MY MISTAKE.

financial support.[67] This, in turn, the groups' critics argue, has led them to make "apocalyptic prophecies to further their political objectives." One fundraising letter from the National Audubon Society, for example, claimed that it could "project with some accuracy the eventual end of the natural world as we know it."[68]

But antiregulatory forces play equally to public fears and, in recent years, have had more success. Business and industries being regulated try to scare the public with visions of the huge costs of regulating while ignoring the benefits. But most of these costs are passed on to consumers in the form of higher prices. According to Bush's 2003 budget message, consumers pay, mostly through higher prices, $50 to $60 billion each year—almost ten times the EPA's entire budget.

But all dollar estimates of the cost of environmental regulation are controversial because of the disagreement over what monetary value to put on intangibles such as human health, comfort, appreciation of clean air, or loss of individual liberties or over whether it is even possible to put a price on them. The best estimates show that air pollution control, for example, has been a large net benefit not only to the nation's air quality but to its economy. Although industries must pay employees to deal with federal regulations, and some pollution control equipment costs millions, pollution devices improve health and ultimately mean fewer days lost from sickness, reduced medical costs, and longer life for materials less damaged by corrosion.[69] Cleaning up the air also increases agricultural output. Some people are laid off when factories choose to close rather than install pollution control devices, but even more people are employed making, distributing, and educating people about air pollution devices.

In addition, sixty thousand public and private companies are engaged in environmental activities, employing almost one and a half million people and generating annual revenues in the billions.[70] Ecotourism is also developing as a major industry, helping to revive small towns and rural areas bypassed by development. Today the number of birdwatchers is greater than that of hunters and fishermen combined, and birders spend an estimated $20 billion a year on travel to festivals and on gear and seeds.[71] Whale watching has also become a huge industry.

Lack of Consensus among Policymakers

Regulatory policy is controversial because we do not have a consensus on how we should regulate. Many people have also criticized the command and control approach to regulatory policy that lays down rules and orders people and industries to comply.[72] To force compliance with rules requires monitoring by a large, expensive, and unwanted bureaucracy. When rule breakers are caught, they are assigned penalties that realistically cannot be enforced, even after huge sums are spent on legal fees to force compliance. Reformers stress the need to make greater use of economic incentives to encourage desired behavior and to reduce the cost of enforcing regulations. Instead of trying to control their behavior after the fact, individuals and businesses should be made to "face up to the full costs and consequences" of harmful actions at the time they make their decisions."[73]

The objective of the proposed reforms is to discourage environmentally or other socially harmful behavior by driving up its cost and thereby putting the individual or business engaging in it at a competitive disadvantage in the marketplace. This approach tries to eliminate a negative externality by bringing the polluter's incentives in line with the social costs imposed on the public. Disincentives could take the form of high-cost pollution permits for companies that decide to pollute and taxes on manufacturing or purchasing environmentally harmful products, waste disposal processes, and energy use. Environmental groups support heavy "green" taxes on "products and activities that pollute, deplete, or otherwise degrade natural systems."[74] Such taxes would help pay for mounting cleanup costs and, at the same time, would provide a market incentive to avoid actions that endangered the public.

Market-based incentives have been proposed by those deregulation advocates who, in almost every instance, place individual and private property rights above the obligation to protect the commons (that is, mineral resources, waterways, the air, and parklands) for the public good. They assume that the marketplace is the only arena for resolving what is rational and appropriate economic behavior. But the marketplace is no more or less than the people who operate within it, precisely because it is a place where individuals and businesses pursue private gain. There is no guarantee that the cumulative effect of these actions will benefit the common good.

Other supporters of regulatory reform believe it is possible for the government to set standards for health and safety and environmental protection while limiting its role in rule writing. This view was expressed in Philip Howard's best-selling book on regulatory law, *The Death of Common Sense: How Law Is Suffocating America*. Much cited by both Republicans and Democrats, Howard argues that the federal government has gone too far in its belief that science and technology make it possible to protect against every public danger and that this has led to an excessive number of rules that try to anticipate every eventuality. This approach,

Howard says, has left the economy suffocating under the weight of countless picky and unnecessary rules. Howard's solution was to decentralize the rule-writing process while leaving federal standards in place, a policy generally in line with Clinton deregulation policy.

In accordance with the Clinton-Gore "reinventing government" policy, the EPA proposed a Common Sense Initiative (CSI) to revise unrealistic, costly standards and to eliminate unnecessary rules.[75] George W. Bush, who supports deregulation, called Clinton's CSI ineffective because it lacked clear goals and was without legal authority.[76] His policy favors reliance on voluntary compliance by business and application of the risk assessment standard to spur deregulation. In the case of clean air standards, for example, Bush has argued that the economic demands of meeting standards impedes economic growth and discourages businesses from modernizing. When he weakened the enforcement rules he promised that his approach, as embodied in his Clear Skies Initiative, would significantly reduce the amount of pollutants emitted into the air while being much less onerous for industry. While the weaker enforcement rules went into effect, the Clear Skies bill never made it out of committee. However, Bush's approach is similar to Clinton's in that both give the states primary responsibility for enforcement.

Every state has its own EPA, and almost 90 percent of all environmental enforcement is in the hands of the states. As the federal government has reduced its spending on environmental protection, it has expected the states to pick up the tab. But with their own revenue shortfalls to cope with, the states spent less (as a percentage of overall spending) in 2003 than at any time in the previous seventeen years.[77]

Industries are not necessarily better off dealing with the state agencies. Instead of dealing with one EPA, they have to deal with the EPAs of every state they operate in, and keep abreast of rules and procedures as they vary from state to state. But because states are trying to attract both foreign and domestic industries, it could encourage a competition among them to provide relaxed enforcement, just as states compete to give tax breaks to industries that will relocate. This should not be possible as long as federal standards are in place and states are charged with the responsibility of seeing that industries and utilities are in compliance. But under the Bush administration, federal standards have been relaxed as regulated industries have been invited to help write the very rules that will regulate their activities.

Defending environmental protection in principle has remained good politics, but forcing *implementation* of EPA rules is not always seen as good politics. When Congress held hearings in the early 1990s to consider renewing several major pieces of environmental legislation and to evaluate the implementation process, deregulators particularly targeted the Clean Water Act, which is extremely costly to implement, and the Endangered Species Act, which many western farmers and ranchers believe interferes with their property rights. While the Republican-controlled Congress did not revoke the major clean air and water statutes, it did little to compel state governments to enforce them.

Changing human behavior is at the center of the current debate over how much progress has been made in environmental protection and how much remains to be done. The optimists point to real achievements in improving air and water quality, reforestation, and cleaning up toxic waste, and they believe it is possible to control or limit ecological damage through adjustments in human behavior. A different school of optimists believes that science will provide the technology needed to combat the environmental damage that is an inevitable by-product of economic development and they remind us of the importance to our economic security of continued growth.

The pessimists acknowledge the achievements made in rolling back damage from pollution and other consequences of our current lifestyles. But they argue that the major ecological threats cannot be addressed without fundamental change in human behavior. Representing this outlook, Al Gore has said, "The maximum that is politically feasible, even the maximum that is politically *imaginable* right now, still falls short of the minimum that is scientifically and ecologically necessary."[78]

Benefits and Costs of Regulation

Regulation has many acknowledged successes but they are produced at a cost.[79] Some are trivial, such as depriving hunters of the satisfaction of shooting eagles. But some are significant. Businesses and environmentalists differ wildly about what the net cost of improvements in the environment, public safety, and other areas have been, although it is indisputable that regulation requires industry to increase its costs to relieve the larger community of the burden of pollution, unsafe products, hazards to workers, or other negative aspects of business activity.

How much was it worth, for example, to have dramatically reduced the lead content in air by mandating unleaded and lower-leaded gasoline? When testing began, measurable levels of lead in children were eight times higher than they are today and, consequently, the level of brain damage in children from airborne lead has also dropped dramatically.[80] Was it worth the cost to clean up Los Angeles's air to the point that city smog alerts dropped from 122 in 1978 to zero in 2001?

It is how costs are calculated that brings values, and therefore politics, into the regulatory process. Those against regulation minimize the value of health, life, and a clean environment, and look only (or mostly) at the costs of achieving those aims. In fact there is no way for science or accounting alone to place a value on a human life that everyone will agree on any more than regulators can put a dollar value on the preservation of the bald eagle or of wilderness areas within national parks that will be acceptable to everyone. Many do not even accept the idea that quantitative values can be placed on human life or on the intrinsic satisfactions that exist above and beyond the economic value of protecting endangered species and their habitats.

Even some environmentalists argue that the cost of preserving a wilderness area must be offset by its "existence value" or "contingent value," the price the public is willing to pay just for the sake of keeping a pristine area in existence. But how does one determine the dollar value people will place on a wilderness area? Some environmentalists worry that putting a dollar value on nature sets a bad precedent. Former interior secretary Bruce Babbitt, for example, has said that we have reached the point where "[w]e know the cost of everything and the value of nothing . . . you can't just cost this stuff out." He argues that economics should not drive a debate that is about something much deeper.[81]

Although environmental regulation retains a high level of public support, regulation of business activity remains controversial. Some continue to believe that its cost is too high and that it leads to crushing paperwork, endless litigation, loss of jobs, and diminishment of the rights of business and individual property owners. Americans want government to anticipate problems and to proscribe behavior by businesses and individuals that endangers public health. But we do not want to force unnecessary, costly regulations on business that will drive up prices for consumers, slow the economy, and increase unemployment. Is our national economic condition such that we must pick our poisons and regulate to protect public health and safety only when it is "cost effective"?

Conclusion: Is Regulatory Policy Responsive?

Americans have called on government to protect them from unsafe workplaces, unclean air and water, fraudulent advertising, hazardous highways and drunk drivers, dangerous drugs, and many of life's other perils. But then we turn around and say we want government "off our backs." We resent the rules, regulations, and red tape. We want government protection, but we are uncertain about how much and what we are willing to give up in return.

Most Americans share the belief that the private sector can do many things better than government and have a general distaste for red tape and in-your-face government. But it was the federal government, not industry, that took the initiative on environmental protection and workplace health and safety. Even though to some Americans there is no such thing as a good regulation, many would agree that the majority of federal environmental regulations, most administered by state governments—to preserve forests and wilderness areas; clean up the air and waterways, drinking water, and toxic waste sites; and to protect the habitats of endangered species—*are* examples of responsive regulation. And regulating for worker, product, and food and drug safety has saved millions of lives. The benefits have not come cheap, but all have been realized through government regulatory activity and not from business or individual consumers regulating their own behavior.

Most businesses do favor regulations that bring sufficient order in the marketplace to support public confidence because, without it, business—certainly publicly traded companies—cannot function. Some may even lobby for the kind of regulation that protects them from domestic or foreign competitors. But when a regulation does not benefit a specific business, then it, too, wants government off its back, complaining that regulation decreases autonomy and increases operating costs.

Complaints about overregulation provoke legislative attempts to deregulate and to cut money for enforcement by both federal and state regulatory agencies. But the subsequent laxness in enforcement can lead to abuses and provoke calls for reregulation. All of these actions and reactions are responsive, in the sense of giving the public and business community at least some of what they want. But elected officials may respond to their political base first and to the larger public only when pressured.

Regulators have a hard job because they have to be responsive to the president and his political appointees in their agencies as well as to Congress and the political agendas of its members. In addition, they must be responsive to the thousands of inquiries about, and challenges to, rules posed by the public, including powerful interest groups and lobbyists who may be aligned with members of congressional oversight committees. Theirs is no easy road to walk.

In forming our opinions about government regulations and regulators, it is sometimes easy to forget that regulators are carrying out presidential orders and congressional acts. While bureaucrats may be overly zealous or overly lax in enforcing laws they are mandated to enforce, ultimately it is Congress that decides what is to be regulated and that calls an agency to heel when they are overregulating or neglecting to regulate.

Regulatory policy is a good example of fluctuations in government responsiveness to the public. In general, regulation exists because influential groups—sometimes representing a majority, other times not—demand government action to protect their interests. At times, regulatory effort is directed primarily toward protecting business. At times of heightened public awareness of finite natural resources and the health risks of environmental degradation, consumer and environmental groups have succeeded in getting government to better regulate business and itself.

The public generally approves of deregulation up to the point where it affects them negatively. But a majority has long opposed efforts to get government completely out of the business of protecting health, safety, and the environment.

Schaeffer Resigns to Work outside Government

In late February 2002, Eric Schaeffer resigned as the EPA's director of the Office of Regulatory Enforcement, saying he was tired of fighting a White House that "seems determined to weaken the rules that we are trying to enforce."[82] The new rules were not completed until November 2002 and the announcement was made at a Friday afternoon EPA news conference where no cameras were allowed; the EPA director declined to be present and Bush made no public statement.

The new rules made it easier for utilities to expand without installing new pollution control equipment by allowing industries to replace up to 20 percent of their plants and still call it routine repair or maintenance rather than an upgrade. This would exempt them from the requirement of adding new pollution controls and allow them to dump thousands of tons of new pollutants into the air.[83] Schaeffer's reaction was incomprehension at why they "were so greedy. Five percent would have been too high, but 20? I don't think the industry expected that in its wildest dreams."[84]

Although the New Source Review provision had been effectively gutted, EPA Director Christie Todd Whitman said the revisions would make it easier for plants to modernize and still result in improved air quality. In May 2003, she resigned, although she denied any policy clashes with the Bush administration.[85] But others quoted Whitman as saying that in meetings with other Bush appointees, she was often in a ten to two minority. Former Secretary of State Colin Powell, who also spent most of his tenure in a policy minority, described Whitman's role at the EPA as a "wind dummy," referring to "the buffeting she took for the administration's unpopular initiatives."[86]

Not all opponents of the new policies resigned; Nikki Tinsley, a Clinton appointee, stayed on as the EPA's inspector general and in a report on the rule changes requested by the Senate, charged the Bush administration with "misinforming Congress about the potential impact of [the new rules] on the government's ability to enforce the law." Tinsley's report claimed that the rule change undermined the government's ability to enforce old cases and to pursue new ones. It said the investigation by her office "could find no basis for the new rule in science or law," and urged restoration of the New Source provision.[87]

The Government Accountability Office found that the reasons provided for weakening New Source Review by the Bush administration were based mainly on anecdotes provided by regulated industries. And the *Washington Post* revealed early in 2004 that some of the wording in the EPA's new rule on mercury emissions had been lifted almost word-for-word from a proposal submitted by the lawyers for power companies.[88]

In 2003, the amount of sulfur dioxide emitted into the air increased by 4 percent, all of it from coal-fired plants.[89] The EPA and the DoJ continued to negotiate the cases Schaeffer had begun and, in 2004, settled with more oil refineries. The coal companies continued to hold out.[90]

The month after his resignation, Eric Schaeffer, with backing from the Rockefeller Family Fund, founded his own nonprofit, nonpartisan policy group, the Environmental Integrity Project, to lobby for enforcement of environmental protection laws. All but giving up on lobbying federal regulators for enforcement of clean air provisions, Schaeffer's group turned its focus on state governments, trying to develop "a trickle-up strategy."[91]

Key Terms

tragedy of the commons

externality

antitrust law

monopoly

truth in labeling

cost-benefit analysis

risk assessment

deregulation

reregulation

National Environmental Policy Act (NEPA)

environmental impact statement

Environmental Protection Agency (EPA)

bubble concept

cap-and-trade

Superfund

Further Reading

Rachael Carson, *Silent Spring* (New York: Fawcett Crest, 1964). This book, and industry's reaction to it, spurred the development of the modern environmental movement.

Mark Dowie, *Losing Ground: American Environmentalism at the Close of the Twentieth Century* (Cambridge, Mass.: MIT Press, 1995). Here, a former publisher of *Mother Jones* argues that the environmental movement has become weak and irrelevant by catering to Washington and losing touch with its grassroots supporters.

Gregg Easterbrook, *A Moment on the Earth: The Coming Age of Environmental Optimism* (New York: Viking, 1995). An environmental reporter gives an upbeat assessment of the achievements of environmentalism and argues that the movement needs to acknowledge its successes and redefine its priorities and tactics.

Carole Gallagher, *American Ground Zero: The Secret Nuclear War* (Cambridge, Mass.: MIT Press, 1993). This is a photojournalistic study of the victims of radioactive fallout from nuclear testing in Nevada.

Shepard Krech III, *The Ecological Indian: Myth and History* (New York: W. W. Norton & Company, 1999). An environmental anthropologist examines the stereotype of the ecologically correct American Indian and shatters some myths about the relationship between Indian cultures and the environment.

Derek Leebaert, *The Fifty-Year Wound: The True Price of America's Cold War Victory* (Boston: Little, Brown, 2002). Here is a cost-benefit analysis of the Cold War that looks at both the dollar and human costs of defeating the Soviet Union.

Walter A. Rosenbaum, *Environmental Politics and Policy,* 3rd ed. (Washington, D.C.: CQ Press, 1995). This is probably the best overview of environmental policymaking.

Eric Schlosser, *Fast-Food Nation: The Dark Side of the All-American Meal* (Boston: Houghton Mifflin, 2001). Here is an account of how America's indulgence in fast foods can affect health and nutrition. It tells you things you may not want to know about such as how much fat is in McDonald's French fries and the lax standards regulating the raising and slaughter of the cattle that gave their lives for your hamburger.

Upton Sinclair, *The Jungle.* (1906; new annotated edition, New York: Norton, 2003). A graphic story of the Chicago stockyards, which helped create the demand for regulation of food processing.

For Viewing

Bigger than Enron (2002). This *Frontline* documentary from PBS on how the failure of congressional and regulatory oversight led to corporate fraud can be viewed online at www.pbs.org/frontline.

The China Syndrome (1979). This Oscar-winning film focuses on a reactor meltdown in a fictional nuclear power plant accident that threatened surrounding areas with radiation poisoning. Part of the film's popularity was due to the real-life threats posed by the Three-Mile Island accident in the United States.

Dangerous Prescriptions (2003). This is another *Frontline* documentary on regulatory failures, in this case, the FDA's carelessness in allowing inadequately tested prescription drugs on the market. It can be viewed online at www.pbs.org/frontline.

Erin Brockovitch (2000). This Hollywood film is a highly fictionalized account of a real case of toxic waste pollution in California.

Immigration by the Numbers (1998). This is a PBS documentary made by environmentalists who argue that the scale of immigration, in combination with the concentration of immigrants in a small number of populous states, has been a major contributor to suburban sprawl.

Silent Running (1971) and *Soylent Green* (1973). Apocalyptic visions of ecological disaster have inspired many books and movies. Both of these films are cult classics and *Silent Running* is considered by many critics to be one of the greatest of all sci-fi films. It is about the removal to outer space of the remnants of the Earth's forests after the planet's ecological collapse. *Soylent Green* is a detective story set in 2022 after overpopulation and pollution have created a massive food shortage on Earth.

Silkwood (1983). This is an Oscar-winning film based on the life of Karen Silkwood, a nuclear power plant worker in Oklahoma who died mysteriously in a car accident after challenging safety conditions in the plant.

Super Size Me (2004). This documentary made for theatrical release looks at the health impact of a month of eating every meal at a fast-food chain (McDonald's). The public attention garnered by this comic treatment of a serious problem increased public discussion of whether government should require consumer warnings on fast and junk foods.

 Electronic Resources

www.epa.gov
The home page of the EPA offers information on issues, organization, and regulations. You can also find a guide to all major environmental protection projects in your state.

www.ftc.gov
The home page of the Federal Trade Commission provides information on antitrust action, consumer credit privacy, and business guidance. You can also file a complaint online.

www.cpsc.gov
The home page of the Consumer Product Safety Commission offers updates on product safety problems and each month posts a list of recalled products, such as a McDonalds's giveaway for children (a bobble-headed figurine with high lead content in its paint).

www.hanford.gov
Here is a toxic waste site with its own Web page! You can see photos of the site and get progress reports on cleanup and on the work of the Superfund.

www.sierraclub.org
This is the home page of the Sierra Club, one of the largest and most influential environmental interest groups. From this page, you can check on the environmental voting records of your members of Congress and see where they received their campaign contributions.

www.fda.gov
The Web site of the Food and Drug Administration contains information on all major areas of the agency's work in food and drug safety, reports on current research, and pending regulations and legislation.

InfoTrac College Edition

Search for the following articles in the InfoTrac database:

Easterbrook, Gregg. "Air Condition: Bush, Pollution, and Hysteria," *New Republic,* July 1, 2002.

Kane, Tim D. "Deregulation California Style," *USA Today* (magazine) (July 2001).

Kjellen, Bo. "A U.S. Dialogue Heard Around the World: A Climate Policy Framework: Balancing Policy and Politics," *Environment* (December 2004).

Vocino, Thomas. "American Regulatory Policy: Factors Affecting Trends Over the Past Century," *Policy Studies Journal* (August 2003).

For more articles, enter

"Deregulation" in the Subject Guide;

"George W. Bush" in the Subject Guide, and then go to the subdivision "environmental policy"; and

"Clean Air Act" in the Subject Guide.

 American Government Resources

Visit the Public Policy section of the Wadsworth American Government Resources Web site (politicalscience.wadsworth.com/amgov) for a variety of tools to help you explore regulation and environmental policy further. Included are simulations, video clips, Microcase exercises, and a wealth of other activities.

CHAPTER 19

FOREIGN POLICY

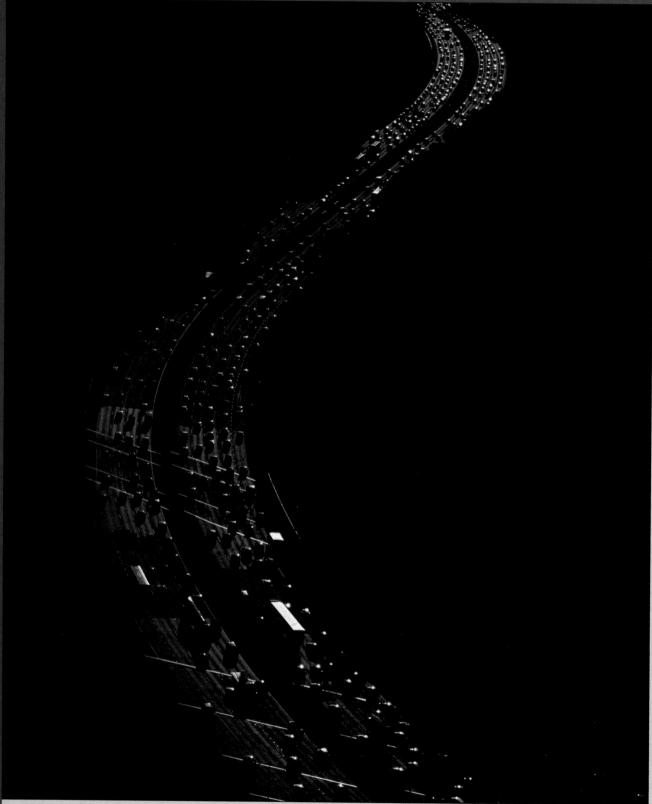

© Sarah Leen/National Geographic Images

Americans' reliance on cars and their love affair with SUVs and other heavy autos and trucks make the United States more reliant on Middle Eastern oil, and also create huge environmental issues.

Should You Give the President a Blank Check to Invade Iraq?

Foreign Policy Goals

Making Foreign Policy in a Democracy
The President and His Inner Circle
Specialists
Congress
Interest Groups and Lobbyists
Public Opinion

Changing Approaches to U.S. Foreign Policy
Isolationism
Containment
Détente
Cold War Revival and Death
Merchant Diplomacy and Multilateralism
Homeland Security and Preemption

Instruments of Foreign Policy
Diplomacy
Intelligence Gathering
Military Instruments
Economic Instruments

Defining Security in the Global Age

Conclusion: Is Our Foreign Policy Responsive?

ou are Richard Lugar, Republican senator from Indiana and senior member of the Foreign Relations Committee.[1] It is September 2002. You are considering a congressional resolution that would give President Bush authority to take whatever action he deems necessary to force Saddam Hussein, president of Iraq, into compliance with the UN resolutions that forbid him to have programs for manufacturing weapons of mass destruction (WMD). Although not spelled out in the resolution, U.S. action in Iraq would almost certainly include removing Saddam from power, a goal Bush set early in his administration.

You were a supporter of the first President Bush when he launched Operation Desert Storm, the military campaign to liberate Kuwait after it had been invaded by Saddam Hussein in 1991. But when he had said that as commander in chief he did not need congressional approval, you had advised him that it would be foolhardy to undertake such a mission without congressional support. The elder Bush gave in, winning approval of his resolution by just five votes. After the younger Bush announced his intentions to launch a military strike against Iraq, he, too, said that although he was willing to consult Congress, he did not need its approval.

You gave the son the same advice you gave his father: send a resolution to Congress and build an international coalition. But unlike the elder Bush, George W. has shown little interest in working through the United Nations or trying to build an international alliance.

You are troubled by Bush's willingness to use military force unilaterally. You are considered one of the Senate's leading foreign policy experts and a "cardinal" of the realist school.[2] Realists, as the name suggests, are neither ideologues nor idealists. Your group believes the United States must take a hard-nosed view of what it can and cannot accomplish in the world and that it should not undertake what it cannot afford to do or cannot finish.

Realists are at odds with the Senate's neoconservatives, who want to go it alone and assert America's unmatched military power wherever the president thinks it is in our national interest to do so. Realists like you also differ, although less frequently, with the more idealistic "Wilsonians" like current Foreign Relations Committee chair Joseph Biden (D-Del.). Wilsonians put faith in international law and organizations and believe that the United States, wherever possible, should try to work through the UN and other multilateral arrangements. You are a sometime ally of the Wilsonians because they are also cautious about committing U.S. resources to achieve goals that are not shared by our allies or others in the international community who could help share the burden.

One reason you think invading Iraq may be overreaching is the unfinished war in Afghanistan. We have not accomplished our objective of finding Osama bin Laden and driving al-Qaeda from the country. Though the capital, Kabul, seems relatively peaceful, in other parts of the country, warlords and pockets of al-Qaeda sympathizers are still in control, and some of the organization's leaders, including bin Laden, could still be in the border areas. In addition, although you believe Iraq is an "acute problem," you see it "as one proliferation problem among many,"[3] including the two other countries in Bush's "axis of evil," North Korea and Iran.

As the senior Republican on the Foreign Relations Committee, you joined forces with Biden to write an op-ed piece for the *New York Times* urging the president to build public support, seek congressional approval, and try to work through the UN before undertaking unilateral action. And Bush did it: he went to the UN and made a speech outlining all the reasons Saddam was a danger and why the UN should take action to force compliance with its sanctions. With Biden, you wrote to the president commending the speech, urging him to keep the American public informed, and reminding him again that he must seek congressional approval for any military action.[4]

Now congressional hearings have been held, and the president has submitted a resolution. But like many in both parties in Congress, you are worried about its sweeping language: he is asking for authority "*to use all means that he determines to be appropriate, including force,* in order to enforce the United Nations Security Council resolutions . . . , defend the national security interests of the United States against the threat posed by Iraq, and *restore international peace and security in the region*"[5] (italics added).

Voting yes on this resolution would be giving the president a blank check to wage war throughout the entire Middle East and to undertake any measures necessary to ensure stability after a military victory. Almost everyone in Congress agrees with the president that Saddam is a dangerous man willing to use weapons of mass destruction against us, just as he has already used chemical weapons against his own people. Like most members of Congress, you want to support the president on this national security issue. But you are not convinced that a military invasion is the only option.

Yet with the midterm election just six weeks away, many in Congress, both Democrats and Republicans, but especially Democrats, are unwilling to speak out on Iraq for fear of appearing critical of the president on an issue of national security and being labeled unpatriotic in an election season. And many Democrats want to pass the resolution quickly and get the campaign focused on the domestic issues important to voters. The election is of huge importance to both parties because of the narrow margins of the majorities in both chambers. The president has made support for his Iraq policy the main issue at virtually every fundraiser he has attended.

The public seems divided; opinion polls show a majority supportive of invasion, but support drops significantly for a war where there might be a significant number of American deaths. Yet Americans do want to strike back at those who attacked on 9/11, and despite the lack of any evidence, the president continues to link Iraq and al-Qaeda. In such a situation, every president has a huge advantage in leading public opinion and setting the agenda. He is the chief foreign policymaker and has access to information that the public, and even Congress, does not.

You have the stature and the bipartisan respect to question the president's approach. No one is going to accuse you of turning this into a partisan issue. Now in your fifth term, you do not have to stand for reelection this year, and your seat is as safe as any seat in the Senate. Moreover, you are one of the Senate's experts on terrorism and WMD. After the breakup of the Soviet Union, you took a special interest in reducing stockpiles of nuclear and chemical weapons left over from the Cold War. You were especially concerned about terrorists getting access to the weapons or material to make them and staging an attack on the United States. You even made a series of campaign commercials for television in which you tried to raise public awareness of the dangers.

As a realist, you want answers to the nagging questions: how many troops does Bush want to send to Iraq, how much will it cost, where will the money come from, what will the region look like after an invasion, and what will our commitment be to a post-Saddam Iraq? You also want to know whether we will be engaging in nation building as we are in Afghanistan, how much that will cost, and how the operation will affect the success of the war against al-Qaeda. Many realists believe that al-Qaeda is a more immediate threat to the United States than Iraq, which, since the Gulf War in 1991, has had its weapons programs under near constant surveillance by the UN. At this point, no one is certain how much success the UN arms inspection team has had in dismantling Saddam's weapons programs. Even if forthcoming evidence convinces you war is necessary, you are not certain that Congress should sign the blank check the president has asked for.

You must decide: Do you trust the president's judgment as commander in chief and vote to give him the blanket authority he wants to use force in the Middle East? Or should you work with those Democrats and Republicans who think Congress should assert its authority as the only body with constitutional power to declare war and define the terms under which the president can wage a war on Iraq?

In an unusual delivery of foreign aid, the United States dropped packets of food during the early weeks of military action in Afghanistan. In addition to providing some modest humanitarian relief, this aid drop was designed to influence public opinion in the United States, Afghanistan, and around the world.

The foreign policy of the United States has a substantial impact on the world, yet we are not all-powerful. We are one of many nations; decisions about war and peace and about trade and diplomacy are made by people in all nations. In this sense, public expectations about what we can achieve have often been unrealistically high.

Yet we are the world's most powerful nation in terms of both military and economic strength.[6] Thus our power, and how we use it, has a tremendous impact on people throughout the world.

In the 1990s, many of the resources that had been devoted to competition with the former Soviet Union were redirected toward other goals. We suffered from a sense of uncertainty because the Cold War with Communist countries, which had defined much of our foreign policy since the late 1940s, was over. The nature of international cooperation and competition changed, and we were forced to rethink the means we use to pursue our foreign policy objectives. During the unprecedented period of peace and prosperity at the end of the century, we were more inward looking and less willing to devote as much of our energies and resources to foreign policy as we had in the past. As we shifted from a world divided between East and West to one increasingly linked by the forces of globalization, much of the world left behind the great power struggles of the Cold War and immersed itself in trade rivalries and economic competition.

At the outset of the twenty-first century, as the sole remaining superpower, we settled into a kind of triumphalism grounded in a belief that the Western ideals of democracy, capitalism, and free trade had become the world's agenda. In this atmosphere of unrivaled military power, the United States experienced the first attack on its territory since the Japanese bombed Pearl Harbor in 1941 and the first attack on the continental United States since the War of 1812.

In this chapter, we examine past and present foreign policy goals, how foreign policy decisions are made, and how foreign policy concerns have changed over time. Then we describe the major military and economic instruments of foreign policy and the challenges policymakers face in an era of globalization and a post–September 11 world.

Foreign Policy Goals

The goals any nation has and the means it uses to pursue them are influenced by its traditions, core values,

International trade has created a global economy and new challenges for foreign policymakers. Here a Beijing bicyclist delivers computer monitors.

tional weaponry or biological, chemical, or nuclear weapons of mass destruction—physical security must be defended against both external and internal attacks. (See the box "Fighting the War at Home.") Since September 11, 2001, greater emphasis has been placed on how to prevent terrorist attacks from within and how to stop the proliferation of weapons of mass destruction. As we will discuss later, how we provide for our physical security in an age of high technology and globalization is undergoing serious rethinking.

A second goal is to help protect the physical security of our neighbors and major democratic allies. Since World War II, we have committed ourselves, through the North Atlantic Treaty Organization (NATO), to join in the defense of Canada and Western, Southern, and now even some Eastern European nations. We also have treaty commitments to Japan, South Korea, and the nations of South and Central America and a bilateral agreement on defense with Taiwan.

A third goal is to protect our economic security. Although the United States is blessed with many natural resources, we must purchase such essential resources as oil, manganese, and tin elsewhere. Safeguarding access to these resources may include stabilizing the governments of producing nations or protecting the sea lanes in which goods are shipped. Our economic well-being is equally dependent on selling our goods abroad, which in turn depends on how cheaply we can manufacture or grow products desired in other parts of the world and how willing our trading partners are to buy them.

Economic self-interest is almost always a factor in foreign policy, even in dealings with our closest allies, because they do not always want to import U.S. goods that compete with their own. Thus trade missions and participation in the international organizations that govern trade relations are crucial to achieving our foreign policy goals, even though the public paid scant attention to them before the 1990s. Today the electronic flow of capital into and out of the country is also essential to our economic viability, so ensuring the privacy of information transfers, including financial transactions, and securing computer systems against hackers are becoming as important to national security as protecting sea lanes.

A fourth overlapping goal is to extend our sphere of influence. Historically, this has meant keeping foreign powers out of the Caribbean and Latin America. In the 1780s, Thomas Jefferson said he hoped Spain would hold on to its territory in South America until "our population can be sufficiently advanced to gain it from them piece by piece."[7] Since the beginning of the nineteenth century, we have warned off foreign powers from meddling in the affairs of any country in the Americas, and there is still a tendency to see Latin America as "our turf."

Since World War II, our sphere of interest has extended around the world. We have sought to influence

ideology, and geopolitical situation (that is, the advantages and limitations imposed by geographical location, size, and wealth relative to other nations). Foreign policies are the strategies adopted and actions taken by a government to achieve its goals in its relationships with other nations. These actions range from informal negotiations to waging war, from writing position papers to initiating trade boycotts. They may require economic, political, cultural, or military resources.

The art of foreign policymaking includes choosing means suitable to the objective sought. Due to our size and great wealth, huge diplomatic corps, military forces, and intelligence establishment, we have the fullest possible range of foreign policy instruments at our disposal. Sometimes the possession of so many means of pursuing foreign policy objectives affects the setting of the objectives themselves; that is, the more a country is able to do, the more it may try to do.

Our primary foreign policy goal, like that of every other nation, is to protect our physical security. Until the era of long-range bombers and ballistic missiles, achieving this goal meant preventing land invasions, and in this we have been successful. Our success was due largely to our separation from the other major powers by two oceans and being bounded on the north and south by two friendly countries. In the nuclear era, when we could be attacked by air by long-range bombers and intercontinental ballistic missiles launched by land or sea, we had to develop an air as well as a ground defense.

In today's era of terrorist attacks—with conven-

FIGHTING THE WAR AT HOME

Responsibility for defending U.S. soil has always been divided among the various commanders of the military's regional theaters of war, such as the Pacific, European, and Southern (South American) commands, and by NORAD, the agency responsible for detecting attacks by air or space. It is illegal for the U.S. military to play a role in domestic law enforcement and has been since 1878, when a law, the Posse Comitatus Act, was implemented to stop federal troops from being used to enforce civilian laws (such as supervising elections in states of the former Confederacy).

The attacks of September 11, 2001, precipitated two major organizational changes in this arrangement: the establishment of the Department of Homeland Security and the creation of a new regional defense theater, the U.S. Northern Command (NorthCom) on U.S. soil. NorthCom places under a single command the responsibility for defense against attacks on U.S. soil by land, air, space, or sea.

It was designed to prevent the confusion that arose on 9/11 over who was in charge of what. That day, after the hijacked planes were detected, fighter planes scrambled, but there was confusion over areas of responsibility and the chain of command. Even when fighter planes caught up with the flight over Pennsylvania, there was uncertainty over who had authority to approve shooting down a civilian aircraft. The orders eventually came from Vice President Cheney, who may or may not have had prior approval from President Bush. The chaos in the White House and in communication between the traveling president and his cabinet was well documented in the report of the 9/11 Commission.[1]

The establishment of NorthCom has raised concerns about the relationship between military and civilian authority in times of national emergency. Historically, federal courts have allowed the military to play the indirect role of providing as-

sistance but not taking a direct or active role in any matter under the jurisdiction of domestic law enforcement. But the existence of NorthCom could make it difficult to limit the military's role and keep it subordinate to civilian authority because of the now overlapping responsibilities for responding to terrorist attacks.[2] NorthCom's mission is not only to defend against foreign invasion or internal terrorist attacks but also to help Homeland Security and the Federal Emergency Management Agency (FEMA) deal better with natural disasters and other civil problems. Will military officers from NorthCom have the authority to take control of civilian functions in these emergencies, supplanting local law enforcement, the FBI, and Homeland Security personnel? The specter of military officers in civilian roles has raised concerns among civil libertarians who believe that we must maintain strict boundaries around the military's role, limiting it to national defense and restricting its involvement in civilian affairs.

Pentagon officials and NorthCom's commander see no conflict. They say that their role is one of coordination and providing backup to civilian authorities. NorthCom's commander calls it "one-stop shopping."[3] In the event of an attack, and at the request of local officials or FEMA, NorthCom could supply people trained to respond to chemical, biological, and nuclear attacks; equipment; and supplies. Or it could provide intelligence or other assistance to law enforcement agencies. And NorthCom can do some things no domestic law enforcement can do, such as flying occasional combat air patrols over U.S. cities.

Civil libertarians are especially worried about the potential for the kind of domestic surveillance of leftist and antiwar groups the military engaged in during the 1960s. They say that NorthCom's responsibility for defense against terrorist attacks means it will have to be actively engaged in monitoring domestic

events and collecting intelligence within the United States. NorthCom will have 150 to 200 people working in intelligence, although the commander says they will collect intelligence only from other agencies, like the FBI, state militia, and the National Guard Bureau, and send it on to the Defense Intelligence Agency for analysis. But NorthCom *will* have responsibility for passing along intelligence information from one civilian agency to another. And in a not altogether reassuring description, NorthCom's commander said, "We are not going to be out there spying on people. We get information from people who do."[4]

Verbal guarantees are not enough for the ACLU, which claims that the Posse Comitatus Act has loopholes that with "creative interpretation" would allow the military to be involved in domestic law enforcement.[5] They want Congress to establish guidelines that will guard against any domestic law enforcement role for the military. Although the Pentagon has not asked for changes in the Posse Comitatus Act, the White House did ask that the law be reviewed to see whether it interferes with the military's role in homeland security.[6] The Bush administration insists that the military will continue to be "outward-looking," but in 2005 there were commando units (code named Power Geyser) working with civilian agencies on counterterrorism missions inside the U.S.[7]

1. *The 9/11 Commission Report: Final Report of the National Commission on Terrorist Attacks upon the United States* (New York: Norton, 2004), 38–46.
2. "Guarding the Homeland," *NewsHour with Jim Lehrer,* PBS, September 27, 2002.
3. Interview with General Ralph E. Eberhart, commander of NorthCom, by Dan Sagalyn. Portions were aired on *NewsHour with Jim Lehrer,* PBS, September 27, 2002.
4. "Guarding the Homeland."
5. Ibid.
6. Eric Schmitt, "Military Role in U.S. Gains Favor," *New York Times,* July 21, 2002, 16.
7. Eric Schmitt, "In Terror Fight, Domestic Role for U.S. Troops," *New York Times,* January 23, 2005, 1.

security arrangements on all continents. Even after the post–Cold War base closures, we still have more military bases and more troops outside our borders than any other country in the world. We also try to spread our influence by promoting democracy, capitalism, and Western cultural values. Our State Department maintains a system of public libraries around the world to disseminate information on our government, economy, and popular culture and also funds thousands of cultural and academic exchanges between American and foreign artists and scholars each year. At optimum we offer our political and economic systems as models of development, and at minimum try to foster a favorable attitude toward the United States that will make it easier for us to achieve our foreign policy goals.

Our specific foreign policy objectives, such as protecting access to oil in the Middle East, drying up funding sources for terrorist operations, removing trade barriers and increasing U.S. exports, are almost always related to achieving one or more of these four general goals.

Making Foreign Policy in a Democracy

Alexis de Tocqueville was one of the first to remark that it is difficult to have a coherent foreign policy in a democracy. His sentiments have been echoed thousands of times since. Why, when there has been basic agreement on the broad goals of our foreign policy, has the United States had such difficulty articulating a coherent and consistent set of objectives?

Some of the confusion in foreign policymaking arises because we elect new leaders every four or eight years. Inconsistencies within a single administration can also be partly explained by the sheer number of organizations and individuals who in some way influence the process of making and implementing foreign policy: the president, members of Congress, heads of relevant cabinet departments and independent agencies, chiefs of the armed services, White House staff and other political advisers, interest groups, lobbyists, the media, and the public. Leaders and citizens from other countries may also have some influence when they are crucial to the successful pursuit of an objective. (For example, when he made the decision to invade Iraq, President Bush told the Saudi Arabian ambassador, Prince Bandar—whose country he would need to use as a staging area—before he informed his own secretary of state.) Which groups and individuals have an impact on policy varies greatly with the issue and the decision-making style of the president.

Historically, inconsistencies in our foreign policy were rarely caused by differences among policymakers over fundamental goals but rather over whether action was necessary in a specific situation and what that action should be. But between the end of the Cold War and the September 11 attacks—that is, between the disappearance of the old imminent threat and the appearance of a new one—there was disagreement even over the fundamentals. Of course, policymakers still believed that physical and economic security were primary goals, but there was more confusion than at any time in the past over what constituted the primary threats to national security and exactly who and what we should be protecting ourselves from. The direct attack on U.S. soil crystallized our foreign policy focus, perhaps even more strongly than during the Cold War, but after a year, disagreements again emerged over strategy. Americans agreed on the goal of destroying al-Qaeda's terrorist network, just as they had agreed on containing Soviet influence during the Cold War. But once again there is disagreement on how much intervention in the internal affairs of another country is justifiable or on what form that intervention should take (as noted in "You Are There" at the start of this chapter).

Here we will look at some of the groups and individuals who influence the foreign policymaking process and how division and conflict among them can affect the content and execution of U.S. policy.

The President and His Inner Circle

As head of state and commander in chief of the armed forces, the president is in control of the nation's diplomatic and military establishments. In addition, as the nexus of the vast diplomatic and military communications and intelligence networks, he has the most complete and privileged access to information of anyone in the policymaking network. In times of crisis, without immediately available alternative sources of reliable information, members of Congress and the public have historically almost always relied on the president's sources. The Clinton years of divided government were a partial exception to this rule; with no overt foreign policy crises, presidential decisions, even those made in response to attacks on U.S. facilities and forces abroad, were constantly challenged by an especially contentious Congress.

Given the central role of the president in foreign policymaking and the fact that most presidents enter office with very little foreign policy expertise, it is important to know who advises him. No firm rules dictate whom the president must consult on foreign policy, but usually he gives at least a perfunctory hearing to people who head departments and agencies involved with making or implementing policy. The government officials best positioned to advise the president on foreign policy

President George W. Bush seeks the advice of his associates after the 9/11 attacks. To the left of Bush is Colin Powell, then secretary of state, Donald Rumsfeld, secretary of defense, and Condoleezza Rice, then national security adviser and now secretary of state. To the right is Vice President Richard Cheney.

include the secretaries of defense and state, the national security adviser, and the head of the CIA. The president also frequently consults the Joint Chiefs of Staff, the U.S. ambassador to the United Nations, the secretary of the treasury, the U.S. trade representative, and influential members of Congress.

These individuals represent a wide range of experience and bring different perspectives to the analysis of foreign policy issues. The secretary of state is usually concerned with the nation's diplomatic relations and the use of diplomatic channels to implement the president's policies. The secretary of defense (a civilian) is primarily concerned with military and security issues and the use of the military to pursue foreign policy goals. Members of the Joint Chiefs of Staff are military professionals who give advice to the president on both the readiness of their service arms and the appropriateness of their use in specific situations. Members of Congress may be consulted because they are political allies of the president, because they are in leadership positions crucial for mobilizing support on an issue, or because they have developed expertise in military or foreign policy issues through their committee assignments.

The president may also consult his wife or friends and advisers outside government, not because of their policy expertise but because he trusts in their good judgment and wants the perspective of people close to him who may have no organizational interests or policy agenda to further. In recent years, it has become common for presidents to call on private citizens to negotiate disputes, a practice that has been dubbed the franchising or subcontracting of foreign policy. These freelancers are often retired diplomats, but individuals with little foreign policy experience, such as former presidential candidate Jesse Jackson, have also been used.

The most noted of these private diplomats is former president Jimmy Carter, who heads a center, affiliated with the Carter presidential library, devoted to international mediation. Carter has gone, sometimes at his own initiative, to many trouble spots, including North Korea, Bosnia, and Haiti. For his efforts mediating conflicts and monitoring elections in some of the world's newer democracies, Carter received the Nobel Peace Prize in 2002. But sitting presidents have not always been happy with Carter's high-profile visits or his comments about them, believing that the former president has appeared at times to be conducting an independent policy line.

Who the president draws into his inner circle of advisers depends in large part on his experience and decision-making style. President Kennedy, who had almost no foreign policy experience, assembled a committee of cabinet heads and close advisers to help him construct his response to the Soviets during the Cuban Missile Crisis. But during the Persian Gulf crisis, the first President Bush reportedly made the decision to send troops to Saudi Arabia relying almost exclusively on his own judgment and that of a few close advisers.

If a president comes to office with a foreign policy

agenda and expects to make his political reputation and leave his mark on history in this policy area, as Richard Nixon and the first George Bush did, he will surround himself with like-minded people and replace those who disagree with him or ignore their advice. Bush appointed both members of the foreign policy establishment who had held high positions in previous administrations and several associates from his tenure as CIA director, an organizational tie that made many in Congress uncomfortable.

Ex-governors like Carter, Reagan, Clinton, and George W. Bush can compensate for their lack of foreign policy experience when they become president by surrounding themselves with experts. Nevertheless, Carter and Reagan chose foreign policy advisers with limited experience and had difficulty maintaining unity among them. In contrast, Clinton appointed an experienced team of advisers, including a number from the Carter administration, but was himself more focused on domestic policy and less decided on foreign policy goals early in his presidency.

George W. Bush came to office with even less international experience than Clinton and a pronounced disinterest in international politics. He chose his entire first-tier foreign policy advisers, and part of the second tier, from those who had served in his father's and earlier Republican administrations. Collectively they were, arguably, the most experienced group of foreign policy advisers assembled by any president since the end of World War II. But some came with predetermined worldviews and in a few cases, such as that of Donald Rumsfeld, their own policy agendas. For all their experience, they were unable to see in warnings from intelligence reports the likelihood of a terrorist attack on U.S. soil or to plan an effective postinvasion strategy for Iraq.

Specialists

The process of formulating long-term policy usually involves more people than the number involved in decision making in crisis situations. The State Department, with twenty-six thousand employees, has experts on every region of the globe and on substantive policy issues such as economic assistance, trade, political affairs, and arms control.

Political officers in Washington and in our embassies and consulates abroad write daily summaries of important political and economic events in the countries to which they are assigned. This information is used to provide daily briefings for higher-level officials, but almost none of it ever reaches the president's desk, and only a small portion of it can be read even by the secretary of state. Specialists in other cabinet departments and independent agencies, such as Defense, Treasury,

Commerce, Agriculture, and Justice, do research and write reports, and the work of intelligence gatherers is also extremely important.

We should not assume that these experts present neutral information that is somehow mechanically cranked out as public policy. Even if the experts do their best to provide the most accurate information and most comprehensive policy alternatives possible, top policymakers see the information through their own perceptual and ideological lenses. Our Vietnam policies failed in part because many of our best Asia experts had been purged from the State Department during the McCarthy era. The Reagan administration ignored advisers who cautioned against its covert policies in Nicaragua and Iran and replaced State Department experts who disagreed with its Central America policies. More than most presidents, Reagan made appointments to key positions in the State Department based on political considerations rather than on career expertise. The Bush administration ignored both intelligence reports and advice from experts in the State Department in its rush to war in Iraq. High turnover in specialist positions has at times put us at a disadvantage relative to our adversaries and allies. Almost all of the policymaking positions within the foreign policy establishment are held by political appointees who usually stay only a few years. This turnover compounds the loss of expertise that comes from maneuvering specialists out of career positions when their recommendations do not support the preferred policies of a particular administration. During the Cold War, for example, the former Soviet Union had much the same team of arms control negotiators for many years. Our negotiating teams changed, on average, every three to four years. Since arms control is an extremely complex field, our negotiators were continually in the process of learning.

There are, however, career specialists in the federal bureaucracy who are not political appointees, such as the staff of intelligence agencies, area specialists in the State and Defense Departments, and almost all members of the Foreign Service. Their briefings may simply be ignored if they do not support policy choices preferred by their superiors. And turf battles can result in incomplete or inaccurate information reaching the highest levels. Agency separation, competition, and even antagonism led to many of the failures and misuses of intelligence prior to and after the September 11 attacks.

Experts outside government who are associated with various think tanks are also sometimes influential in foreign policymaking. Primarily located in Washington, close to decision makers and the national media, these institutions—such as the Institute for Policy Studies on the left of the political spectrum, the Libertarian Cato Foundation and the conservative Heritage Foundation on the right, and the Brookings Institution, the American Enterprise Institute, and the Council on Foreign Relations in the middle—conduct and publish research on policy issues. By writing articles for national newspapers and journals and being interviewed on news and public affairs programs, experts in these institutions "wage perpetual war against each other" trying to determine the course of American foreign policy.[8]

Congress

The leading members of congressional committees on foreign affairs and armed services and of the oversight committees for intelligence agencies play a larger role in foreign policy than the average member plays. But Congress as a whole has specific constitutional authority to act as a check on the president's policies through its power to declare and fund wars and the requirement for Senate ratification of treaties and confirmation of ambassadorial and high-level State and Defense Department and intelligence agency officials. Because Congress appropriates all money for carrying out foreign policy, the president is limited in the scope of the actions he can take without congressional approval.

Rivalry between the White House and Congress in foreign policymaking intensifies or diminishes with the issue in question. Nowhere is conflict greater than over the use of the military to achieve foreign policy goals. (This subject is discussed in greater detail in Chapter 11.) Politicians and scholars have been arguing for more than two hundred years about how Congress's constitutional authority to "declare war" limits the president's authority as commander in chief. The Founders, believing it too dangerous to give war powers to the president alone, were also unwilling to accept wording that would have given Congress the power to "make war." Instead, they gave Congress the power to "declare war," leaving the president, according to James Madison's notes on the debate, "the power to repel sudden attacks."[9] This left Congress and the president to struggle over what constitutes an attack on the United States and when a military intervention is a war.

There have been more than two hundred occasions when the president has sent troops into combat situations without congressional approval. In fact, Congress has exercised its power to declare war only five times, and on only one of those occasions, the War of 1812, did it conduct a debate before issuing the declaration. Yet the two undeclared wars in Korea and Vietnam alone produced almost one hundred thousand American deaths, more than the combined losses of all of our declared wars, except World War II and the Civil War.[10]

The War Powers Resolution, which was intended to curb what Congress believes is presidential usurpation of its authority, has been opposed by every president since Lyndon Johnson. No prior approval was sought for sending troops to Lebanon, Grenada, or Panama, and both Presidents Bush sought it for their actions in Iraq only under pressure. During the Clinton administration, Democrats tried to strengthen the act and Republicans to repeal it; neither effort was successful. As one supporter of the act commented, "Every president finds Congress inconvenient, but we're a democracy, not a monarchy."[11]

Whatever their differences with Congress, presidents in the postwar era have usually proclaimed their desire to have a "bipartisan" foreign policy; that is, they want support from both parties in order to present a united front to the world. Presidents will often try to frame policies in a national security context as a way to pressure Congress into accepting their position, but Congress's role is not simply to rubber-stamp executive branch policies. Presidents especially need bipartisan support when treaties are to be ratified because it is rare for one party to have the necessary two-thirds majority in the Senate or for members of each party to be united in their ranks.

Presidents like to say that in facing the rest of the world, Americans are all on the same side. But this view is too simplistic. Policies shaping how we deal with the rest of the world are controversial and complex. Party positions do differ on these as on most other issues, as shown in roll call votes.[12] Democrats tend to favor lower levels of military spending and higher levels of foreign aid than Republicans and to support interest group demands for worker and environmental protection restrictions on trade agreements, the funding of international agencies, and working multilaterally to achieve goals. Republicans are more likely to support unrestricted trade and military intervention to protect U.S. economic interests and to oppose family planning aid to poor countries. They are also more likely than Democrats to oppose placing U.S. troops under foreign command as part of multilateral forces.[13]

Differences between the two major parties on foreign policy are usually apparent in the national platform each party issues in presidential election years. Even so, it often seems that the opposition party has no coherent alternative to the president's policy. This is probably because under normal circumstances, most members of Congress spend their time on the domestic issues that are so important to their constituents (especially at election time). In times of crisis, as when U.S. troops are committed to combat, the opposition party usually rallies in support of administration policy so that the country can present a united front to the world.

Once these troops are actually engaged in battle, those who continue to oppose the president's actions can find themselves in the position of appearing to give higher priority to their policy preferences than to the safety of U.S. troops. At this point, it is very difficult for the opposition party to oppose the president's policy effectively. Despite George H. Bush's narrow margin of congressional support for the use of force in the Persian Gulf, once the air war began there was virtually no criticism of administration policies by members of Congress. There are notable exceptions, such as bipartisan criticism of Johnson's and Nixon's Vietnam policies, but this dissent came late in the course of the fighting, when public opinion was turning against the war and administration policies did not seem to be working. Even then, Congress approved virtually all expenditures requested to wage the war. And even as criticism of George W. Bush's handling of the Iraq war mounted, very few Republicans or Democrats voted against supplemental funding to pay the costs. Most members are fearful that their vote will be seen not as opposition to policy but as a refusal to support U.S. troops, and the president's party loyalists are eager to paint a dissenting vote that way.

In Congress, members of the opposition party are more likely to state policy alternatives on an *ad hoc* basis, acting as individuals, not for the party. The public may be confused when it hears a half dozen or more policy alternatives presented by members of the same party, and it may even conclude that they are "lone rangers" trying to gain political advantage in a situation that seems to call for national unity.

Interest Groups and Lobbyists

A multiplicity of interest groups are concerned with foreign policy issues: international businesses; public interest groups, such as those that lobby on environmental and human rights issues; veterans' organizations; farmers who grow crops for export; labor unions; and ethnic groups interested in their ancestral lands, such as African, Jewish, Arab, Irish, Cuban, Mexican, and Polish Americans.

In general, it is harder for interest groups to affect foreign policy than to influence domestic policy. Part of the reason for this is that the president and the executive branch have greater weight than Congress in day-to-day foreign policy decision making. But interest group activity has always been effective in some policy areas, especially those related to containing communism and regulating trade and foreign investment. For example, electronics industries lobby against national security restrictions that keep them from exporting computer equipment and software that have military applications. Farm and business organizations lobby on behalf of import quotas and tariffs to protect their domestically produced goods and against trade restrictions and embargoes that prevent them from selling their products abroad.

Americans have a long history of trying to win favorable U.S. policy for their countries of birth or ancestry.

Some have even undertaken private action in support of home countries: Irish Americans have sold guns to the Irish Republican Army and Jewish Americans to Jews in Palestine trying to establish an independent Israel; Cuban Americans have trained a military force on U.S. soil to overthrow the Castro government in Cuba (even though it is illegal to do so under U.S. law).

Perhaps no other nationality group has had as much success in setting the foreign policy agenda for their homeland as Cuban Americans. The strength of their lobby is due in part to a predisposition in Congress for their policy preference and in part to the concentration of their population in one state with a large number of electoral votes (Florida). The Cuban American lobby has been the driving force behind preferential treatment for Cuban immigrants and the maintenance of an economic embargo against the Castro government. In recent years, however, the Cuba lobby has seen its influence decline. U.S. farm and business lobbies, afraid of losing export and investment opportunities on the island to Canada and Europe, succeeded in getting Congress to lift the sanctions on food exports and lighten travel restrictions. As indication of how important an electoral force Cuban Americans are in Florida, Bush toughened sanctions on travel and humanitarian aid before the 2004 election. He did not, however, interfere with agricultural trade deals.

During the past quarter century, three factors have opened up the foreign policy decision-making process to greater influence by interest groups. The first is the growing importance of campaign spending and the rise of political action committees (PACs). Both the president and members of Congress depend on large campaign contributions from interest groups and are thus more vulnerable to a wide range of their demands.

Second, the personal presidency, in combination with the rise of identity politics, has increased the need of presidents to serve a multitude of constituencies and interests. Under pressure from African American interest groups, Clinton gave U.S. policy toward Africa a prominence it had never had previously. His twelve-day trip to six African nations in 1998 was the first by a U.S. president in twenty years and the most extensive ever. Women's and religious interest groups have also become important lobbies, affecting policies on foreign aid, family planning, abortion, immigration, and women's rights. Women's groups found an advocate in Madeleine Albright, the first woman to serve as secretary of state; she identified international women's rights as one of the Clinton administration's priority issues.

Third, the globalization of economic activity has intensified interest groups' efforts to influence trade policy because of their concern about its impact on wages, job opportunities, child labor, worker safety, and the environment. This has led to new and very vocal alliances among trade unions and environmental and human rights groups who oppose some aspects of current trade policy. During a conference of the world's top trade officials in Seattle in 1999, thousands of protesters took to the streets and managed to shut down parts of the city and interrupt the proceedings, and at each succeeding summit meeting, they have launched similarly high-profile attacks on international monetary policy. This has driven summit organizers to move the meetings to ever more remote locations.

Private citizens who are part of Washington's elite also play a role in foreign policy.[14] For example, Henry Kissinger, former secretary of state; Brent Scowcroft, former national security adviser; and Lawrence Eagleburger, former undersecretary of state, formed a consulting business. They advised some of the world's largest corporations about foreign affairs and how international developments might affect the world economic climate in general and their corporations in particular. At the same time, Kissinger and his associates provided advice to government through their service on various influential advisory boards.

A quasi-governmental advisory group of former State and Defense Department officials, the Defense Policy Board, also has had considerable impact on foreign policy, especially during the George W. Bush administration, as has the neoconservative group Project for the New American Century (PNAC), which wrote the first policy brief on invading Iraq in 1995.

Some former members of Congress and high-level political appointees have become registered agents (lobbyists) for foreign governments after leaving office. Some who are public officials one day are private citizens the next and public officials again a few years later.[15] Rules about what constitutes a conflict of interest in such cases are unclear.

Public Opinion

Overall, the views of the public on foreign policy are not that different from those of elected policymakers. When they do vary, public opinion has little direct effect except on high-profile issues that could make a difference at the polls. One reason is that much of our foreign policy is made incrementally over a long period of time and out of public view. Other decisions are made in "crisis" situations or in secrecy for national security reasons.

Another factor limiting the public's ability to influence foreign policy decisions is that only a minority of Americans know much about even the most publicly discussed issues, and many have no opinion about them. The public has always been more interested in domestic issues that impinge directly on daily life, such as the availability of jobs and the cost of consumer goods. Although there is growing awareness of the impact of foreign policy, especially trade issues, on daily life, it is difficult for the public to be well informed on the technical problems involved in trade and tariff negotiations.

Network television news programs, responding to their viewers' primary interest in domestic issues, cut back international coverage substantially during the 1990s. People who rely on television as their main news source, as a majority of Americans do, see only a few minutes of foreign coverage each day. After 9/11, when viewers began expressing more interest in foreign policy and information about other countries, especially those with Muslim populations, television news programs increased their coverage of international affairs. But in polls taken one month after the attacks, Americans were saying again that their primary concerns were jobs and the economy.

In general, the public is more likely to concede its ignorance on a wider range of issues in foreign policy than in domestic policy and to accept the judgments of decision makers. Therefore, on most issues, it is easier for the president to influence public opinion on foreign

Art Collection, Harry Ransom Humanities Research Center, The University of Texas at Austin

In World War I, government rhetoric and propaganda shaped public opinion by portraying German opponents as bloodthirsty gorillas. This army enlistment poster was printed in 1917.

affairs through use of the media than it is for public opinion to change the president's foreign policy. President Bush's consistent linking of al-Qaeda and Iraq were hugely successful in convincing the public that Iraq had had a role in the 9/11 attacks. Three years later, well after the president and secretary of defense conceded publicly that there was no evidence for such a link, 40 percent of Americans continued to believe that Saddam Hussein had been "personally involved" in the attacks.[16] That belief appeared to be an important factor in support for the reelection of the president in 2004.

Sometimes, however, public opinion resists attempts to change it. It is more likely to remain firm when the public holds the administration in low repute or when the government is divided, as it was on Vietnam. Deeply held opinions are also more resistant to administration pressure.

In the long term, the public always has the option of voting out of office those who disagree with majority views on foreign policy issues. However, it is difficult to use the vote to mandate that a president take a specific action, since, as we saw in Chapter 8, people vote on the basis of many different issues.

Trade policy provides a good illustration of the limits on the ability of public opinion to change the president's position on a foreign policy issue. Interest group opposition to the North American Free Trade Agreement (NAFTA), which eliminated trade barriers between Mexico, Canada, and the United States, was so strong that it led most Democrats, who were then the majority in Congress, to openly oppose their own party's president on this issue. One member said, "All of the traditional groups we count on to reelect us [Democrats] are against NAFTA."[17] Despite this opposition from his own party's leadership and from traditional Democratic constituencies, Clinton never wavered in his support for NAFTA because increasing trade was the cornerstone of both his domestic and his foreign policies.

Ultimately, without some public support, foreign policy objectives that require substantial commitments of time and resources will prove unsuccessful. The necessity of public support for large-scale undertakings is evident in attempts to manipulate public access to information. This is most common during wartime, when the government can justify press censorship on national security grounds. Withholding negative information (for example, high casualty rates, slow progress, civilian losses) can help keep public support high. The Persian Gulf War was fought with keen attention to public opinion. The short air war preceding the ground attack was calculated not only to minimize military casualties and the length of the ground war but also to maintain public support for the president's policies. Moreover, the restricted press coverage, which did not allow casualties to be shown, enhanced that support.

In the Iraq war, reporters were embedded with the troops, partly on the assumption that living with the troops and taking fire with them in combat zones would be a bonding experience and lead to less distanced, more sympathetic coverage. The Defense Department also prohibited the photographing of soldiers' coffins as they were returned to the United States for burial. They said it was to protect family privacy, but it was also a way to divert public attention from the rising body count. In addition, official casualty counts issued by the Department of Defense included only troops wounded in combat, not those who were wounded in the line of duty but outside of combat. This policy understated the actual casualty count by thousands.

In general, because of the revolution in information technology, it is becoming harder for the president, or the president and Congress together, to appeal for public support based on a claim of privileged information. Even though the president and Congress may have more reliable information and better analyses of it, the press, interest groups, and the general public now have many more sources of information on foreign policy issues than they had a decade ago. The story of prisoner abuse in the Abu Ghraib prison camp—which became known to the International Red Cross and government officials some months earlier—broke because digital photos taken by troops at the site were e-mailed to friends and relatives and circulating on the Internet.

More Americans are in e-mail contact with people in other countries and have access to the Web sites of foreign newspapers, governments, and think tanks, as well as to declassified documents in electronic archives. In fact, private firms here and abroad, including former Soviet intelligence operatives, will even sell satellite reconnaissance photography to order.[18]

Changing Approaches to U.S. Foreign Policy

Isolationism

Historically, noninvolvement with other nations outside the Americas was a principal goal of our foreign policy. This policy is called **isolationism.** In the nineteenth and early twentieth centuries, Americans generally stayed aloof from European conflicts and turned inward, busy with domestic expansion and development.

One important exception was our continuing military and political involvement in Latin America, which was justified by the **Monroe Doctrine** of 1823. In articulating this doctrine, President James Monroe warned European powers that were not already in Latin America

Millions of Russian civilians and soldiers were killed in World War II. In this photo, grieving Soviets search for their loved ones after Nazi murder squads massacred a village in the Crimea in 1942.

to stay out. This was a brazen move because we were a minor power challenging the major powers of the time.

As European powers withdrew from the region in the late nineteenth and early twentieth centuries, the United States began to play an increasingly active and at times interventionist role. With little regard for national sovereignty, we sent troops to protect U.S. citizens or business interests and to replace existing governments with those more sympathetic to our wishes. Paradoxically, the Monroe Doctrine derived primarily from isolationist, not interventionist, sentiment. By keeping foreign powers on their side of the ocean and out of our hemisphere, we believed we would be less likely to be drawn into conflicts abroad.

During this time, Americans did not think it appropriate to intervene in the problems of Europe or to keep a large standing army at home. This attitude was an offshoot of the predominant mood in domestic affairs: preoccupation with economic growth and fear of a strong central government. Isolationism was also a realistic position in the sense that the United States was not yet a world power. Another source of isolationist sentiment was the belief that the United States was unique and that the more entangling alliances it entered into with foreign countries, the more likely it would "be corrupted and its unique nature . . . subverted."[19]

This isolationist sentiment lapsed briefly in 1917–1919, when America entered World War I on the side of the British and French against Germany but rapidly revived at its close. Despite the wishes of President Woodrow Wilson, the U.S. Senate refused to join the League of Nations, the ill-fated precursor to the United Nations. Although we have no public opinion polls from these early years, with hindsight, 70 percent of Americans polled in 1937 thought it had been a mistake to enter World War I.

Yet the United States was never truly isolationist in its actions. Throughout the whole early isolationist era, we frequently intervened diplomatically and militarily in the Caribbean and Central America and consistently sought to expand U.S. commercial and cultural influence throughout the world. Even President McKinley, who was labeled an "imperialist" by Democrats for his military adventures in the Caribbean and the Philippines, was easily reelected. And his successor, Theodore Roosevelt, is better characterized as an interventionist than an isolationist. Polls from the post–World War I era show that Americans overwhelmingly favored joining an international peacekeeping body like the League of Nations. And historians have pointed out that there were enough votes in the Senate to ratify participation in the League had President Wilson been willing to accept amendments to the treaty agreement.[20]

Americans have almost always been willing to participate in world affairs to defend our national interests. But we are often slow to recognize just what is at stake. In 1939, we refused to join Britain in its war to stop Nazi Germany's attempted conquest of Europe. It was not until the December 1941 Japanese attack on Pearl Harbor, Hawaii, that the public was willing to support entry into World War II. When Germany and Italy then declared war on the United States, we fought in Europe alongside Britain, the Soviet Union, and remnant armies from the occupied nations of Europe.

Containment

The Allied victory in 1945 brought a split between the Soviet Union and its Western allies. The Soviet Union lost twenty million people in the war (the United States lost four hundred thousand). Given these losses in a German invasion that was only one of many invasions of Russian territory over the centuries, the Soviet government was determined, especially as a protection against Germany, to have friendly neighbors in Europe, just as we wanted them in Latin America. To ensure this, the Soviet Union was willing to use any means, including intervention, to secure Communist governments in the ring of nations surrounding it—Poland, Czechoslovakia, Romania, Hungary, and Bulgaria. Our wish for free elections in these nations was seen by the Soviet Union as an attempt to isolate it. The Russians believed we wanted to surround them with anti-Soviet governments, thus making their sacrifices in World War II futile. Many of our policymakers saw the subversion of Eastern European governments as the beginning of a Soviet effort to conquer Europe.

As the only major power not decimated by the war, the United States was unable to return to its isolationist prewar stance. In 1947, the Truman administration formulated a policy to limit the spread of communism by meeting any action taken by the Soviet Union to spread its influence with counterforce or a countermove by the United States. Known as **containment** (also called the Truman Doctrine), this policy led U.S. decision makers to see most of the world's conflicts in terms of rivalry between the Soviet Union and the United States. The Soviet coup d'état in Czechoslovakia in 1948 and the rise to power of the Chinese Communist government of Mao Zedong in 1949 fueled U.S. fears that the Communists would try to expand the area under their control as far as possible. Consequently, when Communist North Korea attacked South Korea in 1950, we intervened as the nucleus of a United Nations force, believing we had to stop the spread of communism in Korea before the Soviets undertook further expansion.

Just as isolationism began as a defensive posture to keep European conflicts out of the Americas, containment was aimed at limiting the Russians to their post–World War II reach and out of our sphere of influence. Instead of trying to roll back Soviet power, containment was designed to keep it from expanding to a point that changed the global power balance or dragged the United States into unwanted conflicts. The chief instruments of containment policy were economic and military aid to developing countries, cultural exchanges, covert activity, alliance building, nuclear deterrence, and as in Korea and Vietnam, limited war fought with conventional weaponry.

Containment philosophy was at work in the Marshall Plan, which provided economic relief to the nations of Western Europe in 1947 (aid was offered to some Eastern European governments, but they refused it). In addition, the United States entered into military alliances with friendly nations in Europe and Asia to stop the spread of Soviet influence or even to roll it back. The most important of these was **North Atlantic Treaty Organization,** which in 1949 joined the United States, Canada, and their Western European allies in a mutual defense pact against Soviet aggression in Europe. Building these military alliances to compete with the Soviet Union and its Eastern European allies was a response to the **Cold War** era that we had now entered. We were not in military battle with the Russians, but the deep hostility between the two nations threatened to turn any conflict into a major armed confrontation.

Nuclear Deterrence

The nuclear era began in 1945, when the United States dropped atomic bombs on the Japanese cities of Hiroshima and Nagasaki. Although the debate on the necessity and ethics of dropping these bombs still continues, Japan surrendered, bringing the war in the Pacific to an end and making an invasion of the island by the Allies unnecessary.

At the close of the war, the United States was the only nuclear power. The Soviet Union exploded its first bomb in 1949, but it did not have an operational warhead until the mid-1950s and for a while thereafter had no intercontinental bombers or missiles to deliver the bombs. Despite our nuclear superiority, we found our power limited. Nuclear weapons were of little use in the pursuit of most foreign policy objectives because the threat of inflicting mass destruction to achieve a nonvital objective was not credible to opponents. Hence during the period of nuclear superiority, the United States saw its Chinese Nationalist allies lose to Communists in China, its French allies lose to Ho Chi Minh in Indochina (Vietnam), and an anti-Communist uprising in Hungary in 1956 crushed by Soviet tanks.

In 1955, the Soviet Union and its Eastern European satellites formed the Warsaw Pact, a military alliance to counter NATO. People began to see all international relations as part of the bipolar competition between a Western bloc of countries united under the U.S. nuclear umbrella and an Eastern bloc of nations operating under the protection of the Soviet nuclear umbrella.

American nuclear dominance began to erode in the late 1950s. *Sputnik,* the Soviet satellite that was the first to orbit the Earth, showed that the Soviet Union had successfully built large rockets capable of firing missiles that could reach the United States. The fear of Soviet rocketry advances led to a program to build and

©John Van Hasselt/CORBIS SYGMA

Fifty years after the bombing of Hiroshima, the city appears fully restored. But the U.S. decision to use atomic weapons is still so controversial that the Smithsonian Institution had to withdraw a planned fiftieth anniversary exhibit that presented arguments on both sides of the issue. Other assaults on cities, such as the U.S. firebombing of Tokyo and Japan's "Rape of Nanjing," caused at least as many deaths, but the use of the atomic bomb stands out in public memory because it opened the door to a new kind of warfare.

deploy nuclear-tipped intercontinental ballistic missiles (ICBMs) to supplement our bomber force.

Even with Soviet advances, American nuclear superiority was maintained for another decade. Yet everyone agreed that neither side could attack the other without the certain knowledge that both the attacker and the attacked would suffer enormous damage. No sane leader would risk so much damage by striking first.[21] This capability is called **mutual assured destruction,** referred to by the fitting acronym **MAD.**

Despite public frustration with the Cold War—being neither totally at war nor at peace—successive administrations found that "rolling back" communism in the nuclear age was not possible without the kind of risk and commitment of resources most Americans were unwilling to assume. Although the Kennedy administration did risk nuclear war over Soviet placement of nuclear weapons in Cuba, ninety miles from our shores, we stood by and avoided such risks when the Soviet Union invaded Hungary in 1956, Czechoslovakia in 1968, and Afghanistan in 1979. And the Soviet Union stood down when we tried to overthrow Castro in 1961 and when we forced the removal of Russian missiles from the island in 1962, and avoided confrontation when we sent military forces to oppose a Russian-backed nationalist movement in Vietnam.

One of the basic premises of containment was that all Communist nations were controlled by the Soviet Union. But as the 1950s progressed, it became clear that this was not true. Both Albania and Yugoslavia spurned Moscow's control. The Chinese became increasingly independent and in the early 1960s broke with the Soviet Union, declaring that "there are many paths to socialism." Despite this, we continued to define most international events in terms of Communists versus anti-Communists, no matter how poorly the characterization fit. This conviction formed the basis of the **domino theory,** the proposition that if one country fell to Communist rule, it would set off a chain reaction in neighboring countries, just as a long line of dominoes standing on end will fall in sequence when the first one is toppled. If U.S. intervention could prevent the first country to come under attack from falling, others would stand firm. This rationale led us into Vietnam, our longest war to date.

Vietnam

Early Period If one were ranking the landmark events of the twentieth century, surely World War II would rank at the top. We live in a completely different world than would have existed had Hitler not been defeated. Fighting alongside Britain and the Soviet Union, the United States achieved its greatest military victory and forged the alliance with Western Europe that led to our most important treaty relationship. Yet the Vietnam War has had a far greater impact on U.S. military policy since its end in 1975. We will try to explain why.

When we became involved in Vietnam, it was still part of the French colonial territory of Indochina. After the defeat of the Japanese occupying forces in World War II, the Indochinese Communist Party, led by Ho Chi Minh, engaged the returning French forces in a war for independence. Ho appealed several times to the United States—a critic of both British and French colonial policies—for support in this effort but was rebuffed. As the war in Indochina dragged on, the Cold War settled in, and containment became the organizing concept in American foreign policy. By 1954, when Ho's troops defeated the French in a major battle, the United States was underwriting 80 percent of the cost of the French effort in Vietnam. But after considerable deliberation, the Eisenhower administration refused to provide troops or air support to save the French because Eisenhower believed this could bog us down in a long war requiring many troops, certainly a prescient view.

At a conference in Geneva in 1954, a temporary boundary was established separating the territory of Ho's government in the North from that of the French- and U.S.-backed government in the South until elections could be held to choose leaders for all of Vietnam. The new prime minister in the South, Ngo Dinh Diem, was a staunch anti-Communist Catholic with influential friends in the U.S. Catholic community and Congress. Diem's government refused to participate in the elections scheduled for 1956, and the United States backed him because it feared that Ho's Communist government would win the election. The temporary partition between the North and South continued, and after the assassination of Diem in 1963, it soon became clear that the South Vietnamese government would collapse without more U.S. intervention.

In a march on Washington, antiwar protesters put flowers in the guns of military police to symbolize peace.

President Johnson listens in anguish to a tape sent by his son-in-law (Charles Robb, then an officer in Vietnam and later a U.S. senator from Virginia), talking about the men lost in battle in Vietnam.

Armed Intervention In 1964, President Johnson won congressional approval for massive intervention in Vietnam. In an August television address to the American public, Johnson claimed that two U.S. destroyers had been attacked by North Vietnamese torpedo boats while on routine patrol in international waters near the Gulf of Tonkin. He announced his intention to retaliate by bombing sites in North Vietnam. The next day, after presenting misleading information about the role of the U.S. destroyers in initiating the attack, he asked Congress to endorse the Gulf of Tonkin Resolution authorizing him "to take all necessary measures to repel any armed attack against the forces of the U.S. and to prevent further aggression."

Presidents Johnson and Nixon used the Tonkin Resolution to justify each act of escalation in the war. This deception laid the groundwork for the gradual erosion of congressional support for the war effort.

In early 1965, Johnson sent in U.S. troops in the belief that the war would be over "in a matter of months." After all, the United States had sophisticated equipment and training and complete air superiority. But three years later, after a half million U.S. troops had been committed to combat, the Vietcong—North Vietnam's southern allies—were able to launch a major offensive that demonstrated that all our military efforts had not

made one square foot of Vietnam truly secure. When the Joint Chiefs of Staff requested more than two hundred thousand additional troops, a stunned President Johnson decided to undertake a review of Vietnam policy. Even the Joint Chiefs were not sure how many years and troops it might take to win. As public opposition to the war grew, Johnson called for peace talks and announced that he would not run for reelection in 1968. The talks began in May 1968 and dragged on through the administration of Johnson's successor, Richard Nixon.

President Nixon wanted to leave Vietnam without appearing to have lost the war. To accomplish this, he tried "Vietnamizing" the war by forcing the South Vietnamese government to give more responsibility to its own army. He authorized the massive bombing of Hanoi and began withdrawing U.S. troops.

Nixon's most controversial war policy was his decision to expand the war into neighboring Cambodia, supposedly to destroy a huge underground headquarters of the North Vietnamese army near the Vietnamese border. In addition to igniting the largest public protests of the war, the invasion finally led to significant congressional opposition. The Gulf of Tonkin Resolution was repealed, and a resolution was passed prohibiting the president from using budgeted funds to wage a ground war in Cambodia. Nixon had planned to withdraw the troops from Cambodia anyway and did so quickly. But bombing in Cambodia continued until 1973, when Congress forbade the use of funds for this purpose. This was the only time Congress actually blocked presidential policies in the war.

In 1973, the United States and North Vietnam signed a peace agreement. We might have reached the same agreement in 1969, but President Nixon had believed this would jeopardize his reelection chances in 1972 and perhaps other foreign policy goals, too.[22] The victory of the Vietcong and North Vietnamese finally occurred in 1975 as the South Vietnamese army disintegrated in the face of a Communist attack.

Lessons from Vietnam Much of our thinking about the use of the military today is still informed by the lessons of policy failures in Vietnam.[23] Even though at its peak in 1968–1969 our military force in Vietnam exceeded half a million, had sophisticated equipment and training, and had complete air superiority, we were eventually defeated. Why did we fail?

- *We did not have clear goals.* Policymakers never agreed on whether we were fighting China, the Soviet Union, North Vietnam, or rebels in the South (the Vietcong). It was not clear what or whom we were trying to defend or what Vietnam was supposed to look like after the North was defeated.

This photo of a naked South Vietnamese girl screaming after a napalm attack by "friendly" forces became one of the most famous photographs of the war and a major incitement to antiwar protest. The girl, Kim Phue, survived, despite enduring pain and long-term treatment for her wounds. Now living in Canada, she is pictured at right with her son, Huan (his name means "prospects"). She notes, "I know my picture did something to help stop the war. I have to show [my son] what happened to his mom, to her country, and that there should never be war again."

- *We did not understand the political aspects of the war.* Supporting a series of unpopular South Vietnamese governments, we were at first oblivious to the vast indigenous opposition to the South Vietnamese government from Communists, other nationalists, and Buddhists. Our inability to construct an effective policy for "winning the hearts and minds" of the domestic opposition to the South Vietnamese government appears to have been a fatal weakness of policymakers from Eisenhower through Nixon.

    In 1995, on the twentieth anniversary of the war's end, Robert McNamara, secretary of defense in the Kennedy and Johnson administrations and a principal architect of early Vietnam policy, wrote a book publicly stating for the first time that by 1967 he had come to the conclusion that the war was a mistake and could not be won. Principal among his eleven reasons for the loss were the incompetence of the South Vietnamese government and armed forces and American underestimation of the North Vietnamese.[24] President Johnson's refusal to accept this conclusion led McNamara to leave—or be made to leave—the cabinet in 1968. But as revealed by the release of the tapes of Johnson's phone calls, at the very time he was making large troop commitments, Johnson was saying, "I don't see any way of winning."[25]

- *We did not understand the nature of guerrilla warfare.* For much of the war, we did not fight against a standing army dressed in the uniform of an enemy force. It was often impossible for our troops to tell soldier from civilian or enemy from ally. Although

we inflicted heavy casualties on the Vietcong and North Vietnamese forces, we killed thousands of civilians in the process. Our opponents were able to demonstrate to the people of the South that their government and its ally, the United States, could not protect them or their villages. In fact, the Vietcong were able to dominate much of the rural South. Our policies—to "destroy villages in order to save them" and to take people from their own villages to "strategic hamlets," where presumably they were safe from the Vietcong—were bitterly resented by many South Vietnamese.

- *We were impatient with the war and were unwilling to devote unending resources to winning it.* We knew from the British experience in defeating Communist guerrillas in Malaysia that we would need at least ten soldiers to the guerrillas' one and that we might need ten years to win the war, but no leader dared tell the public that we must commit ourselves for that long. We were unwilling to invest the resources or time needed to defeat a guerrilla enemy. Since the goals were unclear, few wanted to risk use of the ultimate weaponry that could have destroyed the North. Although this stance was rational, it did not seem to lead to the obvious question of whether our objectives were worth the effort we were making.

- *We did not have public support.* Although public opinion was generally supportive during the first years of the war, support eroded as it became clear that we were bogged down in an interminable and indecisive conflict. Only about 20 percent of the public favored an immediate withdrawal in 1965,

Mobs of South Vietnamese civilians scale the walls of the U.S. embassy in Saigon, trying to hitch a ride on the evacuation helicopters as the North Vietnamese enter the city and the last Americans leave in 1975.

but by mid-1969, support for withdrawal began to increase and reached 50 percent within the next year. By 1971, public support for withdrawal grew to overwhelming proportions.[26]

The United States persisted in Vietnam for nearly eleven years because most policymakers believed in standing firm against what they saw as Communist aggression and because no president wanted to be responsible for losing a war. But Vietnam shattered the belief in containment and U.S. illusions that it could serve as the world's police force. Many Americans believed that both our aims and tactics in Vietnam were immoral. Others believed that our aims were just but unachievable. Still others thought that we should have stayed until we won. All these sentiments led to a good deal of public self-examination about the war.

The failure of our Vietnam policy produced the **Vietnam syndrome,** an attitude among the public and officials of uncertainty about our foreign policy goals and our ability to achieve them through military means. Decision makers became more reluctant to commit troops to combat situations or to threaten military action to pursue containment goals. Some people regarded this new caution as a positive development that would keep us from becoming involved in new military entanglements we could not win. But many others believed that this national self-doubt tied the hands of decision makers and prevented them from using the full range of our capabilities to pursue national interests abroad.

These differences persist among policymakers today. Colin Powell, former chairman of the Joint Chiefs of Staff and George W. Bush's first secretary of state, did two tours of duty in Vietnam. His experience there was the basis of what is now called the *Powell doctrine:* never commit U.S. forces to combat abroad without clear goals and an exit plan. It led to Powell's initial opposition to committing troops to the Persian Gulf War in 1991 and to unilateral military action against Iraq in 2002.

Détente

Richard Nixon came to office after public opinion had begun to turn against the war, and he immediately began looking for ways to shape international relations in the post–Vietnam War era. As a man whose career was built on making political hay out of his staunch anticommunism, President Nixon was well placed to make diplomatic overtures to the Soviet Union without fear of being attacked by any but the most die-hard Cold Warriors. Thus Nixon and his national security adviser and later secretary of state, Henry Kissinger, developed a policy called **détente,** which was designed to deescalate Cold War rhetoric and to promote the notion that relations with the Soviet Union could be conducted in ways other than confrontation.

With a policy of détente, we could reward the Soviet Union for "good behavior" on the international scene and at the same time reduce our own military expenditures, slow the arms race, and perhaps step back from the brink of war. The détente doctrine recognized that although the Soviet Union would remain our adversary, it, too, had legitimate interests in the world. Détente also recognized the growing military strength of the Soviet Union and the fact that it was in our interests to pursue bilateral agreements, such as on arms control, that would try to limit this strength.

Among the most notable achievements of the détente policy were the treaty agreements limiting the number of defensive antiballistic missile (ABM) launchers that each side could possess and freezing the number of offensive missiles in each side's stockpile.

During this era of new diplomacy with the Soviet Union, President Nixon also sent out feelers to see whether China was interested in reestablishing diplomatic ties. Even though it was home to one-fifth of the world's population, China had been shut out of the mainstream diplomatic community, largely due to U.S. pressure, since the Communist victory in 1949. After two years of negotiations through third parties, the first cultural exchange (a visit by the U.S. Ping-Pong team) was arranged in 1971. By the time of President Nixon's visit in 1972, many nations had resumed diplomatic relations with China, and it had regained its seat in the United Nations Security Council. Full diplomatic recognition by the United States, however, did not come until the Carter administration.

The resumption of diplomatic relations between China and the United States was one of the most remarkable achievements of Nixon's and Kissinger's attempts to break the Cold War stalemate. Nonetheless, it was consistent with their balance-of-power approach to foreign policy. By making this effort during a period of hostility in relations between the Soviet Union and China, Nixon was probably hoping to gain leverage in dealings with the Soviet Union (what some referred to as "playing the China card").

The Nixon-Kissinger visits to China were all the more remarkable because they occurred while U.S. troops were still fighting in Vietnam. It had been the specter of a Sino-Soviet-led Communist bloc and a near paranoid fear of "yellow hordes" (in the racist parlance of the time) advancing throughout Asia that led us to fight in Korea and Vietnam. Within a few short years, China's image was recast from dreaded enemy to friendly ally, and Cold War fears of world Communist domination were greatly diminished.

The doctrine of détente complemented the mood of isolationism and weariness that grew in the wake of the Vietnam War. Public and elite opinion after the war was divided. Isolationist, go-it-alone sentiment peaked immediately after the war but then declined.

A new spirit of **cooperative internationalism** characterized the early Carter administration.[27] Carter and his advisers saw the world as far more complex than Cold War rhetoric suggested. They believed that problems of global poverty, inequitable distribution of wealth, abuse of human rights, and regional competitiveness were substantial threats to world order and that

One of the first major achievements of the Nixon-Kissinger policy of détente was to reestablish normal relations with the People's Republic of China, governed by the Communist Party since 1949. Here Nixon attends a state banquet in Beijing with then premier Zhou Enlai.

the United States should work with other nations to solve these problems.

In 1979, Carter signed a new agreement with the Soviet Union placing limits on offensive missiles. But the Soviets' stunning invasion of Afghanistan that same year ended the chance of gaining Senate approval for the treaty. Public and elite opinion shifted, and Cold War views, never completely abandoned, became much more respectable again.

Cold War Revival and Death

The Reagan administration took office in 1981 determined to challenge the Soviet Union in every way possible. During his first term, Reagan totally renounced the Nixon-Kissinger principle of détente and labeled the Soviet Union an "evil empire." He and his advisers continued to view the world largely in light of a U.S.-Soviet competition. They painted a simple picture of an aggressive, reckless, and brutal Soviet Union and a peace-loving and virtuous United States. Despite the rhetoric, however, the administration did not risk direct confrontation.

Reagan's approach differed from containment because it was more ideologically than strategically driven; he sought not just to contain the Soviets but to undo the status quo. One method Reagan endorsed was stepping up the arms race and, by forcing them to keep pace, drive the Soviets into economic ruin. The centerpiece of this policy was his plan to build an antimissile defense system, the Strategic Defense Initiative (SDI), derisively known as Star Wars. The plan was based on a laser technology that did not yet exist but that was supposed to intercept and destroy nuclear-tipped ballistic missiles before they reached their targets in the United States. Its projected cost was tens of billions of dollars. Reagan's SDI and military buildup programs increased military spending to record peacetime levels.

Though the election of Reagan put a Cold Warrior in the White House, the public was not willing to buy Cold War arguments wholeheartedly. By Reagan's second term, a dramatic drop in public support for increased military spending and growing public pressure for progress on arms control helped push the administration toward a less belligerent stance. Violent rhetoric was toned down, and conciliatory gestures multiplied.[28] Washingtonians believed that President Reagan wanted to reach some agreement with the Soviets in order to be remembered as a peacemaking president.

The moderation in Reagan's rhetoric was also a response to changes in the Soviet Union. In 1985, Mikhail Gorbachev, the new general secretary of the Communist Party of the Soviet Union, called for "new thinking" and began to shake up Soviet society as it had not been shaken since the Russian Revolution in 1917.[29] Faced with a stagnating economy and an antireform Soviet leadership, Gorbachev encouraged competition in the economy, criticism of corruption and inefficiencies by government agencies, and free elections of some government legislative bodies.

In addition to his domestic reforms, Gorbachev challenged the status quo in the international community with his policy of *glasnost,* or opening to the outside world. He encouraged foreign investment and requested foreign aid to help rebuild the Soviet economy; he made it easier for Soviet citizens to emigrate, pulled Soviet troops out of Afghanistan, and reduced aid to Soviet-backed governments in Nicaragua and Cuba.

Gorbachev also took the initiative in resuming arms control negotiations with President Reagan. In 1987, the two men reached an agreement on intermediate-range nuclear forces (INF). To ensure compliance, the United States sent inspectors or monitors to the Soviet Union, and the Soviets sent them to Western Europe and the United States to observe production facilities and the dismantling and removal of the missiles.

During the first two years of George H. Bush's administration, the Soviet empire in Eastern Europe disintegrated with such rapidity that all policymakers were caught off-guard. The Soviet-dominated governments were dismantled, Communist parties changed their names, opposition parties formed, and free multiparty elections were held.

In late 1989, demonstrators assaulted the most visible symbol of the Cold War, the Berlin Wall (built by the Soviets in 1961 to divide Soviet-occupied East Berlin from NATO-occupied West Berlin), and began tearing it down. A year later, the reunification of Germany marked the end of the post–World War II power alliance in Europe.

Then, in 1991, after a brief, unsuccessful coup against him, Gorbachev resigned as head of the Communist Party and stripped the party of its role in government. Facing massive restructuring problems, he made major foreign policy concessions to Western governments in order to obtain economic aid. Among them was an agreement to remove Soviet military forces from Cuba, the last vestige of Cold War competition in the Western Hemisphere.

With no strong center left in Moscow, the non-Russian states of the Soviet Union declared their independence. Gorbachev was left with no country to lead, his power supplanted by the presidents of the fifteen newly independent republics. As the Soviet Union passed from the scene, all nations had to adjust to a realignment of the world order.

Early in the 1990s, the first President Bush spoke of a "new world order," although no one was quite certain what it meant in terms of concrete foreign policies, other than the absence of U.S.-Soviet military competition. In the new order, foreign policies would presumably be less dependent on military capabilities. Still, some Americans feared that as the world's sole remaining military superpower, the United States would feel freer to use its military advantage in pursuit of its foreign policy goals. However, without the Soviet threat to justify expenditures, the United States began to shrink its military. There was also strong public pressure to avoid new foreign entanglements. With the Cold War over, Americans seemed weary of trying to understand and change the world. They were more impressed by the failures of foreign aid, military intervention, and diplomacy than by foreign policy successes, more weighed down by problems at home than by those in other countries. Bush found that he could justify intervention in the Persian Gulf, and later in the civil war in Somalia, only through cost sharing and participation in an international force under UN auspices.

Merchant Diplomacy and Multilateralism

Bill Clinton took office as the first president born after World War II and one of twelve never to have served in the military. He was a self-described child of the Cold War, an opponent of the Vietnam War, and more shaped by the skepticism of that era than by memories of the Allied victory in World War II. In his campaign, he reminded voters that we had not defeated the Soviet Union in battle but that it had collapsed from within due to "economic, political, and spiritual failure." The lesson, Clinton said, was clear: "Given the problems we face at home, we must first take care of our own people and their needs." He believed that the best foreign policy is to have a strong economy.[30]

With this as his theme, Clinton signaled a change in approach to foreign policy. Befitting the end of the Cold War, greater emphasis would be given to economic than to military instruments of foreign policy, and more attention would be paid to using our economic strength to achieve political goals, such as promotion of democracy and human rights, which Clinton said we had neglected in our pursuit of strategic interests.

Clinton's foreign policy was so rooted in the pursuit of national economic interests that almost all issues were discussed in terms of their value to U.S. trade relations. (Clinton's second-term national security adviser was an international trade lawyer.) This led some observers to label his foreign policy "merchant diplomacy."[31] De-emphasizing military in favor of economic diplomacy suited the public mood, which, although not one of withdrawal from world affairs, was leery of new political entanglements.

Despite the deemphasis on military force, there were many occasions during Clinton's administration when its use was deemed necessary. But unlike previous presidents, Clinton was reluctant to rely on the unilateral use of force. When he ordered troops to Haiti in 1994 to oust a military dictatorship and restore the elected president, it was only after gaining UN backing. It marked the first time an American president had sought prior international approval for a military intervention in the Caribbean. To some, it was a radical departure from, or even an end to, the Monroe Doctrine.[32] But it was compatible with Clinton's view of the post–Cold War world as a community of nations becoming increasingly linked through the forces of globalization and in which every country should assume part of the burden for maintaining international peace and security. Avoiding costly military entanglements also helped end the huge budget deficits run up by the military spending and tax cuts of the Reagan era.

The difficulty with a multilateral approach to achieving foreign policy goals is that the national interests (and therefore the motivation for intervening) that each country has at stake in any international dispute vary. This can paralyze the policy process and make military cooperation to resolve a conflict impossible to achieve. Reluctance to act alone kept the United States on the sidelines when its intervention might have saved hundreds of thousands of lives. Clinton did not intervene to stop ethnic cleansing in the breakaway republics of Yugoslavia until thousands had died. When we did get involved, it was as part of a NATO force, with shared costs and troop commitments, but one could argue that it was with greater legitimacy and a more effective force than the United States could have provided by acting on its own in Europe. The most glaring failure of multilateralism during Clinton's administration was the decision to follow the UN's lead in not intervening to stop the genocide in Rwanda, a conflict that cost an estimated eight hundred thousand lives. Both Clinton and the intervention-shy UN leadership later admitted this as a drastic failure of preventive diplomacy and international peacekeeping.

Homeland Security and Preemption

When he campaigned for the presidency, George W. Bush advocated a foreign policy that was even less interventionist than Clinton's had been. He opposed any long-term or open-ended commitment of U.S. troops to international combat units or peacekeeping missions. He said that we had to be "humble" about our role in the world and that we should not be engaged in nation building in countries where our troops were committed. Selecting Colin Powell, the former chair of the Joint Chiefs of Staff and a man famously reluctant to commit U.S. troops to combat, as his secretary of state suggested that Bush might follow a very cautious approach to American military involvement around the world.

Bush's early actions also indicated a shrinking back from diplomatic engagement, and he soon established himself as someone who preferred going it alone. The United States did not withdraw from international organizations, but Bush's rhetoric suggested that he would only *consult* with other countries, not deal with them as equals. He announced his opposition to a number of treaty arrangements. He withdrew U.S. involvement in the Kyoto agreements on global warming, which Clinton had signed, because he thought it placed unreasonable burdens on American businesses; he refused to renew the ABM treaty because it would keep him from pursuing the development of the space-based antimissile defense system (SDI) Reagan had begun; and he refused to agree to U.S. participation in an international court to try war crimes and human rights abuses because he thought it would make American peacekeeping troops subject to false accusations.

These early actions contributed to the view that Bush's foreign policy approach would shift the U.S. stance from multilateralism to unilateralism. The terrorist attacks of September 11, 2001, reinforced certain aspects of this approach but changed others. Bush did organize a multinational force before taking military action in Afghanistan, suggesting an accommodation with multilateralism. But laying claim to Reagan's "evil empire" terminology, he labeled three nations—Iraq, Iran, and North Korea—as an "axis of evil" and agents of state-sponsored terrorism. The conviction that an international ring of state-sponsored terrorists was lying in wait to launch other attacks led to a major redefinition of U.S. defense policy. Whereas historically the United States had maintained a posture of defensive response, striking only after being attacked, the Bush national security team endorsed a strategy of **preemption,** or striking

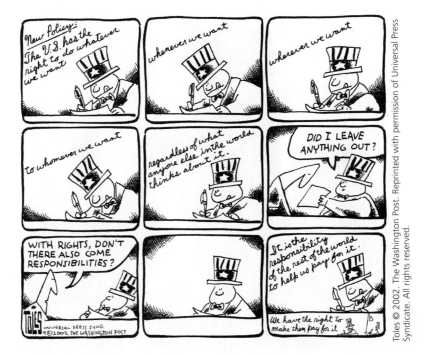

first.[33] In a much-quoted speech delivered at West Point after 9/11, Bush said, "The war on terrorism will not be won on the defensive. . . . We must take the battle to the enemy, disrupt its plans, and confront the worst threats before they emerge." Reinforcing this point, Vice President Cheney added, "We have enemies with nothing to defend. . . . For that reason, this struggle will not end with a treaty or accommodation of terrorists [but] with complete and utter destruction" of terrorist networks.[34]

Preemption is not a new idea in U.S. foreign policy; it has always been there as an option in defense policy. John Kennedy, for example, had General Maxwell Taylor write a paper outlining a strategy for a nuclear first strike against the Soviet Union.[35] It is unlikely that any president would fail to strike first in a situation where it was certain it would prevent a lethal attack on the United States. The distinctive aspect of the Bush position is his use of preemption as a guiding principle of defensive strategy rather than as a policy option.

Bush put his policy into effect shortly after announcing it by calling for a preemptive strike against Iraq. If the administration had argued that it had proof that an attack on the United States was imminent, probably few analysts would have seen preemption as a policy shift. But Bush's Iraq policy was based not on known capabilities or actual plans but on assumed *intent*. And it was unclear whether it was to be a unique operation or just the first in a series of strikes against the "axis of evil." Congressional critics argued that invoking the policy to invade a sovereign nation with thousands of combat troops encroached on Congress's constitutional prerogative to declare war.

After less than two years in office, Bush's approach to foreign policy had been drastically revised from a pas-

sive unilateralism to an interventionist unilateralism. For reasons of both principle and cost (human and economic), many in Congress expressed a reluctance to accept preemption as a principle of foreign policy, if not rejecting it as a necessary option in specific situations. Its opponents believe that the idea of attacking a country only to prevent the possibility that it might attack us sets a frightening precedent for international rules of engagement, legitimizing preemptive military or nuclear strikes by other countries against their enemies.

Bush did put together a "coalition of the willing" to participate in the invasion of Iraq, but of the more than thirty countries signing on, only Great Britain contributed any serious contingent of combat troops. Troops and civilian personnel from other countries served mainly in support and humanitarian roles. And Great Britain's contribution of nearly thirty thousand troops for the invasion was immediately reduced to eight thousand after U.S. troops reached Baghdad and therefore were gone when the major fighting began.

Although Clinton's multilateralism slowed U.S. response to situations where lives could have been saved had we acted more quickly, it was an approach that rationed the use of U.S. military force and spending, maintaining the bulk of strength for response to vital national security threats. It was also an approach that tried to augment our worldview and to inform the administration's policy analyses by factoring in our allies' assessments of foreign policy crises. This can slow response time, but it can also prevent precipitous entry into situations we do not fully understand. Bush's preemptive unilateralism (or token multilateralism) has pushed U.S. military strength to its limits so that there is no ready reserve for responding to other substantial

McDonald's is a ubiquitous reminder of American power, and all over the world, anti-Iraqi war protesters demonstrated against America by staging protests at McDonald's. Here protesters climb the McDonald's sign in Seoul, South Korea.

threats; it also has left the United States to pick up the entire military costs of the war and much of the cost of reconstruction. And all of this is being paid for with borrowed money. In its execution, unilateralism has led back to multilateralism because of our need for economic and military help from allies to stabilize and reconstruct Iraq.

Bush's unilateral policies also unleashed a wave of anti-Americanism throughout Europe and parts of Asia as well as the Middle East. After 9/11, world opinion was almost entirely sympathetic, but the U.S. decision to invade Iraq triggered fear and hatred in many parts of the world. Even among our closest allies, including Britain, Canada, and Australia, public opinion was against the war and especially hostile to the Bush administration. Negative public opinion can have serious consequences if it encourages people to pressure their governments to refuse to help the United States achieve its objectives. It is a consequence of living in an intensely interdependent world that the leaders of activist governments must court world, as well as domestic, opinion.

Instruments of Foreign Policy

The United States, because of its size and wealth, has enormous capabilities for pursuing its foreign policy ob-

jectives. In this section we describe some of them, beginning with diplomacy, the universal means for the conduct of state-to-state relationships.

Diplomacy

As head of state, the president serves as chief diplomat. The principal office for carrying out his foreign policy is the State Department. The United States has relations with 180 of the world's 191 nations. Unlike many other countries that automatically recognize every government accepted by its own people, the United States's decisions on formal recognition are made on political grounds. That is why it was years before we recognized the governments of the Soviet Union and the People's Republic of China, and we still do not recognize the government established by Fidel Castro in Cuba in 1959.

In addition to its permanent Washington-based civil service bureaucracy, the State Department maintains 260 embassies, consulates, and missions to international organizations in countries around the world. They are staffed by nine thousand Foreign Service officers and about thirty thousand local nationals.

Directing each embassy is the president's personally appointed emissary, or ambassador. Ambassadors are often career Foreign Service officers, but in some of the largest and most important embassies and in some of the smaller but very desirable posts, the ambassador may be a political appointee chosen from among the president's friends or campaign contributors. Ambassadors not only represent the president's policy to officials in the countries where they are posted but also act as intermediaries, carrying policy messages back to the president or secretary of state from their host countries.[36] The United States also has ambassadors or emissaries attached to regional and international organizations such as the UN, NATO, and the World Trade Organization.

The work of other Foreign Service officers is divided by function—cultural and military attachés, trade representatives, aid specialists, and consular and political officers, for example. It is common in the most strategically important countries for one or more of these individuals to be an undercover CIA officer.

For the huge tasks assigned it, the State Department is a very small organization, tenth in size among cabinet departments. And it must make do with a very small budget—about 1 percent of total spending, which, when adjusted for inflation, is about 50 percent less than we spent twenty years ago.[37]

Intelligence Gathering

One of the important components in formulating foreign and military policy is economic, military, and diplomatic information gathered by operatives of the government's fifteen intelligence agencies. The best known of these is, of course, the Central Intelligence Agency (CIA), but several cabinet departments (Treasury, State, and Energy) also have intelligence-gathering offices, and Justice has the FBI. Historically, the FBI has been devoted to domestic law enforcement, policing international drug trafficking, and fighting organized crime, but its mission was overhauled after 9/11, and counterterrorism work is now its main function. (See the "You Are There" in chapter 12.)

The Pentagon has its own Defense Intelligence Agency (DIA), and each of the service arms (Army, Navy, Air Force, Marines) also has its own intelligence office. And there are three separate agencies for high-tech intelligence gathering, such as satellite reconnaissance and aerial mapping. The National Security Agency is so secret that its employees cannot be photographed; its funding is part of the "black budget," unknown to the public and to much of Congress. In fact, total annual spending on intelligence gathering and analysis—about $40 billion—is a guesstimate, since some part of it is not included in the published budget.

The CIA also has a covert operations division, about whose activities little is ever made public. Agents sign lifetime agreements prohibiting them from public discussion of their work; manuscripts must be vetted by the agency prior to publication, and publication can be prevented or book royalties impounded if material is published without agency permission. However, most of the work done by intelligence agencies, including the CIA, involves routine fact collecting, research, and report writing rather than covert operations. And the scope of action for covert operations, such as assassinations of foreign heads of government (now illegal without presidential authorization) and recruiting local collaborators of dubious character, was drastically curtailed in the 1970s.

Despite the many operations and independent agencies, about 80 percent of the intelligence budget has been under the control of the Secretary of Defense, even while the head of the CIA held the official title of director of intelligence. Under Donald Rumsfeld's tenure at Defense, budgetary controls became an issue because of his known distrust of CIA intelligence gathering and analysis. Under Rumsfeld, the DIA, historically more involved in analysis than gathering information, became a more independent intelligence-gathering operation. This added to the existing agency turf and policy battles that came under scrutiny after 9/11.

It is difficult for the public to assess the overall contributions of intelligence agencies. Over the past several decades, we have heard of many failures, some spectacular, but we rarely hear about successes, so it is hard to put the failures into context. But since the later years of the Cold War, public accounts of our intelligence-gathering capability have revealed increasing ineptness: years of overestimating Soviet military and economic strength, counterproductive undercover activities in Vietnam, and failure to detect moles working in our agencies—failures that led to the deaths of many U.S. agents. The failures surrounding the September 11 attacks were so great that they led to the first major reassessment of our intelligence-gathering capabilities since the 1970s. Almost all of the initial criticism fell on the CIA and the FBI. It may not be a coincidence that these two are usually headed by political appointees rather than career professionals.

The joint inquiry of the House and Senate concluded that intelligence agencies are very good at gathering information but very poor at timely translations and analysis and disastrous at interagency information sharing.[38] The rivalry and turf wars between the FBI and CIA in particular contributed to inefficiencies in data sharing and analysis. Although the FBI was reorganized, the principal foreign intelligence agencies remain untouched by post–9/11 reforms, except for improvements in interagency coordination, renewed efforts at recruiting more highly skilled area specialists, and greater flexibility for covert operations. Critics of the post–9/11 reorganization believed that by leaving the FBI and CIA outside the Department of Homeland Security, intelligence gathering and analysis would become even more decentralized. Some were concerned that policymakers would be able to go "analysis shopping," choosing whichever agency's data best supported their policy preferences. This kind of competition between agencies, critics charged, would further politicize intelligence work.[39]

Fuel was added to this fire when Bush named the head of the House Intelligence Committee and former CIA agent Porter Goss to head the CIA. Goss took with him several members of his congressional staff with no experience inside the agency to replace the CIA's own personnel managers. Veteran agents began resisting, leaking information to the press about Goss's management style and about their differences with the Bush administration's political use of intelligence. In response, Goss issued a memo to agency employees that their purpose was to serve the president and his policy, not to oppose them. A number of high-level veteran agents, most of whom believed the directive violated their mandate to exercise neutral competence, resigned or were forced out.[40]

Intelligence operations were cited by the bipartisan 9/11 Commission as one of the most serious institutional failures leading to 9/11. The commission's report concluded that intelligence problems could be fixed only by consolidation of all operations under a single directorate.[41] The commission cochairs traveled around the country lobbying for support of a new law to establish a national director of intelligence, to be appointed by the president with cabinet status, who would have control over the intelligence budget and coordination of the work in all agencies. In the face of open opposition from the Defense Department (Rumsfeld) and deep divisions in Congress, a bill was passed at the end of 2004. Some of the opposition came from those who believe the fundamental problem lies not in coordination at the top but in how intelligence is gathered, specifically the lack of agents on the ground, especially those who can infiltrate terrorist organizations. It will be some time before we know whether the creation of a new directorate will bring more coherence to U.S. intelligence gathering and assessment.

Military Instruments

Defense policy evolves in rough correspondence with changing approaches to foreign policy and perceptions of security threats. Formulating policy on how to use the country's military capabilities is the work of the secretary of defense, the president's national security team, and the Joint Chiefs of Staff.

For more than forty years, we thought our military strength was our most important asset in our effort to keep the world "free." Relying on the strategy of mutually assured destruction, we built up an arsenal of nuclear-tipped missiles and bombers capable of delivering nuclear warheads. But the effectiveness of nuclear weapons as an instrument of foreign policy depended on their not being used. The nuclear arsenal helped achieve the ultimate goal of avoiding defeat or destruction by a foreign power, but it was not a flexible instrument of policy. In the first decades of the Cold War, we relied so heavily on nuclear deterrence that we neglected other aspects of our military capability, including the capacity to fight limited wars with conventional weaponry. Yet conventional fighting forces have always been more important than nuclear weapons in pursuing containment and other foreign policy goals.

In the 1960s, our military planners thought we should be strong enough to fight two and a half wars at the same time. As the Vietnam War demonstrated what a drain on our economic and military resources a limited war could be, the Nixon administration lowered our goal to waging one major war and one smaller war. Our defeat in Vietnam, combined with the growing likelihood that containment would be more dependent on conventional limited wars than on strategic nuclear warfare, led the Carter and Reagan administrations to place greater emphasis on improving combat readiness and building a new arsenal of high-tech weaponry.

Spending on nuclear preparedness itself became an instrument of foreign policy in the 1980s, as Reagan vowed to crush the Soviets economically by forcing them into a spending war in a race to acquire an antiballistic missile system. The arms race added to the Soviets' economic woes but also endangered our own economic security by contributing to huge budget deficits and robbing the civilian economy of many of our best scientists and engineers. In total, an estimated $5.1 trillion (not counting cleanup costs) was spent on nuclear preparedness, consuming from one-fourth to one-third of all military spending and producing about seventy thousand warheads and weapons.[42]

The end of the Cold War removed the need to prepare for a major nuclear confrontation with the Soviet Union. The arsenal of warheads, ICBMs, and nuclear bombers was drastically cut, and many domestic and foreign bases closed. After the Persian Gulf War, the size of the military was cut by a third, and base closings continued. We also reached tentative agreement with Russia to reduce our stockpile of 10,400 operable nuclear weapons to 3,000. (By later agreement between George W. Bush and Russian president Vladimir Putin, this number was lowered to 2,000.) By the turn of the century, military spending was at its lowest level—3 percent of GDP—since before World War II.

But questions were being raised about whether military training and armaments were appropriate for twenty-first-century warfare. The Clinton administration determined that the major security threats, such as terrorism, could not be dealt with by traditional warfare. And early in the Bush administration, military planners called for a shift to give the military a "richer set of military options."[43]

Today, the primary objective of reform is to make the military more mobile, capable of a quick response and armed with lighter, more flexible high-tech weaponry. A major showdown over this change came at the outset of Secretary Donald Rumsfeld's tenure. Rumsfeld wanted to kill new heavy-weapons programs and transfer the funds to weapons to outfit a mobile light infantry more suitable to counterterrorism. He won despite opposition by some of the Army's top leadership.

In 2001, in response to the 9/11 attacks, the Pentagon began to prepare the armed forces for **asymmetrical warfare**—conflict between combatants of very unequal strength. In this type of warfare, the weaker antagonist, knowing that direct military confrontation would lead to certain defeat, identifies and attacks a weak spot in the armor of the stronger opponent. Al-Qaeda identified a security vulnerability in one of our strengths—openness and access in American society—and used it to its advantage in organizing the attack, training the operatives, and eventually gaining control of commercial airliners to use as weapons against American citizens.

Transforming the military to fight this new kind of warfare requires a break with strategies, weaponry, training, traditions, and career paths established in the armed forces over a period of decades. It has not been easy for civilian leaders to win acceptance among military professionals, most of whom have prepared for everything from guerrilla and limited warfare to all-out nuclear confrontation, and some of whom believe we have not seen the last of traditional ground warfare. Rumsfeld forced out those who resisted, including the Army's chief of staff and others who opposed an Iraq invasion plan that was based on the new thinking—fewer troops, with lighter-weight, more mobile equipment. The top leaders argued that Rumsfeld was asking for fewer troops than needed to carry out the mission, especially for stabilizing Iraq after Saddam Hussein's overthrow. In addition, many of the lightweight, unarmored vehicles that troops had to use to patrol postinvasion Iraq and to transport supplies became death traps. Nearly two years into the war, despite all evidence to the contrary, Rumsfeld insisted that the war plan had succeeded. However, when the Iraqi elections scheduled for early 2005 were threatened by the level of instability in the country, Rumsfeld relented and sent more troops.

Proposals to reinstate the draft, which Nixon abolished in 1971 to quell antiwar protests, have garnered almost no official or public support. The conversion to all-volunteer armed services more than thirty years ago produced enough enlistees to meet the military's combat needs until the Iraq war required a large-scale commitment of troops for a prolonged period. The National Guard and the reserves now account for more than 40 percent of all troops in Iraq, and many have had their tours extended multiple times. In addition, the Army has reactivated its stop-loss program, which prevents active-duty personnel from mustering out when their term limits are up. It has also called back to service individuals who thought they had completed their obligations years ago but who are technically still considered reserves. And hundreds of noncitizens have also been recruited on the understanding that they will receive automatic citizenship when their tours of duty are completed.

Many Americans may not realize that we have been outsourcing some of our military activities for years. The armed services bolster service personnel with military contractors—private citizens—to help train recruits and do other combat-related work. In Bosnia in 1996, one of every ten Americans in the peacekeeping force was a civilian under contract to the Pentagon.[44] The numbers are at least as high in Iraq, where low-paid infantry officers can be assigned to protect civilian employees earning three to four times as much and who are not subject to the same rules, discipline, or chain of command as regular military personnel.

The president's military options are now limited—should he want to undertake another preemptive action using ground troops, the military could not deliver without a draft.

Military Intervention

Over the course of American history, the military has been used less often to wage total or limited warfare than to intervene in small countries whose affairs have been seen as linked to U.S. economic or security interests.

Through much of the Cold War, we were somewhat more reluctant to intervene with U.S. troops for fear of escalation to a nuclear conflict. But the Reagan and Bush administrations demonstrated a renewed willingness to pursue U.S. objectives with military force, especially in situations where we had unrivaled military superiority. Still, there were strong indicators that the military was ill prepared to carry out an interventionist role to achieve primarily political objectives. For example, the seven thousand troops the elder President Bush sent into Panama in 1989 had mixed success. We did remove Panamanian president Manuel Noriega from power and install a new government, but we killed more Panamanian civilians than soldiers.

The military performed better in the Persian Gulf War. This war was short, fought largely from the air with high-tech weaponry, well planned from the standpoint of minimizing American casualties, and the troops functioned according to or above expectations. From the standpoint of personnel (training and morale), the military appeared to be more battle ready in the early 1990s than it had been in the 1970s and early 1980s. Although some of the highly touted weaponry did not perform as well as initially claimed, it did serve to limit American casualties.

To judge the success of a military intervention, we have to be able to identify its objectives. In many cases, these are not made clear, or the real goals are hidden behind more palatable objectives. For example, the Persian Gulf War was fought, according to the president, to make the world unsafe for dictators and to restore Kuwaiti independence. After the deaths of thousands of Iraqis, Kuwait did regain its independence, but the Gulf region had no fewer dictators than it had before the war. The intervention was also successful in achieving the less openly stated goal of keeping a large part of the world's oil supply in the hands of governments sympathetic to the United States and other wealthy, oil-dependent countries.

Intervention can also give rise to new expectations and demands. Our intervention with European allies in Bosnia and Kosovo helped save lives and keep those conflicts from spreading to other countries, but it did little to solve the underlying political problems. The stated goal of intervening in Afghanistan was to defeat the Taliban, capture Osama bin Laden, and liberate the Afghan people. We did defeat the Taliban and liberated some people, women especially, but the small number of troops we committed to the operation were insufficient, after liberation, to protect freedoms for anyone living outside a few key cities. Where warlords resumed control of their old territories, many of the same restrictions, including those on women, were put back in place. Furthermore, free of the Taliban's religious restrictions, many farmers returned to growing poppies as their main crop, and by 2004, Afghanistan was the source of the great majority of heroin coming into the United States. And in the midst of the country's political instability and on top of our commitments elsewhere, we had created a demand for nation building that we were not able to fund.

Military intervention is a high-risk (and in some cases unlawful) tool of foreign policy; it requires great planning and skill, as well as luck and good timing, for it to be successful. When intervention does not achieve what it was supposed to, either from the standpoint of U.S. policymakers or in the eyes of the populace of the target country, everyone knows whom to hold accountable.

However, due to the capabilities of our military establishment, our desire to play a world leadership role, and the expectations of other world leaders about our role in world peacekeeping, American presidents cannot ignore the uses of the military in the pursuit of foreign policy goals.

Military Alliances

For decades, the United States gave highest priority to security relationships with Great Britain and the nations of Western Europe. This was due in large part to shared heritage, commitment to democratic government, and in the postwar years, common membership in NATO.

Since its beginnings in 1949, NATO has acquired a much broader strategic focus than its original purpose of deterring Soviet aggression in Europe. Despite the unity of purpose among the founding members, there were always internal differences. In the early years of the alliance, the United States was by far the strongest power in the West. Britain and France had been shattered by World War II, but as the years passed, these nations regained their economic power. West Germany also recovered and joined the alliance in 1954. As these states became stronger, they wanted to assume a more powerful role in the alliance. They feared that the United States, with its Asian interests and adventures, could drag them into wars they did not wish to fight. They also worried that they might be vulnerable to Soviet military power because the United States would not think it worthwhile to risk all-out war. France, which never accepted U.S. domination of NATO, withdrew from some military aspects of the alliance.

The end of the Cold War defused the long-standing differences of the alliance partners over the nature of the Soviet threat and the control and use of American nuclear weapons deployed in Europe. The United States agreed to remove its nuclear weapons from European soil and to reduce the number of troops stationed in Germany.

In the post–Cold War years, the alliance has continued to address problems of stability in Europe, including ethnic warfare in the disintegrating Yugoslavia and separatist movements in the successor states of the Soviet Union. Today the principal strategy for maintaining regional political stability is integrating new states militarily and politically into the Western alliance. By 2004, NATO's original dozen members had expanded to twenty-six, encompassing most of the countries of Eastern as well as Western Europe. How NATO will evolve remains to be seen. But its original singularity of purpose no longer exists.

The United States's relationships with the countries of Asia have also had a strong military component, including military agreements with China and Taiwan, defense treaties with both Japan and South Korea, and large military contingents in both countries. Since the end of the Allied occupation of Japan, we have assumed a large part of the responsibility for Japan's defense by including Japan under our "nuclear umbrella." To protect U.S. security and trade routes, the Seventh Fleet has been based in Japan since the end of World War II, and the United States continues to maintain military bases throughout the island nation.

Military Aid

Another means of pursuing foreign policy goals is to provide grants, credits, or loans to countries with whom we have common defense interests to enable them to purchase armaments and other military equipment. In

"With the whole world in NATO, we won't have to take any more crap from Mars."

equip and train the terrorists who planned the 9/11 attack on the United States.

Economic Instruments

We have several economic instruments of foreign policy: trade, economic sanctions, and foreign aid. Much of our economic diplomacy is carried out by the State Department and its Agency for International Development (USAID). Other cabinet departments, Commerce and Treasury especially, devote increasing amounts of time to the pursuit of international economic goals, and American ambassadors now receive training in how to promote American businesses.[47]

Achieving the economic goals of foreign policy is not simply a matter of negotiating the technical details of trade or aid agreements. Their pursuit often involves pressuring the governments of other countries to change internal policies. When the United States demands that a country remove trade barriers on certain products that we want to export, such as rice, meat, or auto parts, it often amounts to asking them to negate long-standing political agreements they have with domestic producers. And when we make loans or give aid, the agreements are often conditional on the recipient countries' adopting domestic policies that we dictate. Thus the aggressive pursuit of economic goals can lead to extensive intervention in the affairs of other countries.

Trade

Negotiating sound trade agreements is essential to the economic health of a large importing and exporting country such as the United States. At the end of World War II, the United States was the world's greatest trading power; half of all world trade passed through our ports. Today that figure has fallen to 14 percent, and we have lost much of the power we once had to regulate the flow of trade.[48] This is especially significant because trade now accounts for about a quarter of our GDP and one-third of our economic growth.[49]

We import far more goods from other countries than they import from us, creating a trade deficit. For years, our trade deficit has been climbing, reaching a new high with virtually each successive quarter of financial reporting. Business and labor leaders want government protection from imports, and as a result, political support for protectionist policies grows. **Protectionism** is government intervention to protect domestic producers and their employees against competition from foreign producers of manufactured and agricultural goods. Protectionist policies can take the form of a ban on goods from abroad, quotas on imports, or taxes (tariffs) on imports to make them more expensive and therefore less competitive in the United States. We have used protectionist policies to help American

addition, we often send American forces abroad to train soldiers or bring foreign officers to the United States to study in our military schools. One-third to two-thirds of all U.S. foreign aid is spent on military support. We extend aid in the hope that greater military preparedness of allies will reduce the likelihood of our having to intervene to defend mutual security interests. Aid also supports U.S. defense industries and arms dealers, since "virtually all military assistance is spent on U.S. goods and services."[45] (The United States is the world's largest arms dealer, accounting for almost half of all arms delivered to other countries.)

Since the 1960s, one of the principal recipients of military aid has been Israel, a country that shares many of our political and cultural values and has been our strongest ally in the Middle East. However, a great deal of our military aid has gone to countries like Egypt and Jordan, whose ties to us are far less stable and whose governments are not democracies.

Sometimes we build up the armed forces of countries that after a change in leadership or foreign policy have used those forces to work against our national interests. The most spectacular case in recent years was our support for the military buildup in Iraq when it was at war with Iran (which we had also armed). When Iraq threatened our interests by seizing oil-rich Kuwait, we went to war against an army that we and our allies had helped supply and train.

In intelligence work, this phenomenon of an unintended spillover is called "blowback."[46] For example, when Afghanistan fought against the Soviet Union in the late 1970s and 1980s, we provided Afghan fighters, including the militant Islamic Taliban, training and equipment. Some of the leaders of the Taliban used equipment and training received from U.S. forces to

farmers and the manufacturers of automobiles, textiles, steel, clothing, computer chips, and other goods.

Protecting American industries sounds patriotic. Supporters of protectionism argue that these policies protect new industries until they can get established and support old industries essential to our defense and basic self-sufficiency. They also say that protectionist policies can save American jobs and maintain our standard of living by placing tariffs on imported goods manufactured by foreign workers who are paid subsistence wages. They even claim that protection can help make domestic industries more efficient and competitive.

Protectionist policies usually result in higher consumer prices because of the elimination of competition from foreign labor and the products they produce. Opponents of protectionism argue that is cheaper to compensate displaced domestic workers and retrain them for other jobs than it is to pay the higher cost for protected goods and labor.

Increased cost is just one of the criticisms of protectionism made by advocates of free trade. **Free trade** is a policy of minimum intervention by governments in trade relations. Its advocates, or free traders, believe that government regulation of trade, for economic or political reasons, reduces the efficiency of the world economy, thus preventing countries from maximizing their income.[50] Free trade, like capitalism, is relative; all countries place some restrictions on trade to protect domestic labor and business interests. In fact, forms of protection historically applied to 30 to 40 percent of all trade.

Free traders claim that in addition to increasing prices, protectionism also discourages industry efficiency and competitiveness. They argue that opening U.S. markets to Japanese cars in the 1970s gave Americans the choice of a superior product, and to stay competitive, the American auto industry was forced to improve its efficiency and its cars. By the 1990s, American autoworkers were able to turn out a car for significantly less money than Japanese workers, and they had a product far superior to their 1970s models.

Finally, critics of protectionism say that imposing quotas or tariffs on other nations' goods just leads them to respond in kind, limiting our export markets. Retaliatory measures can spiral into a trade war, and trade wars have the potential to expand into military competition to protect market access.

Despite these dangers, pressure for protectionist legislation continues because job retention and creation are major issues in all industrialized countries. Former Senator Ernest Hollings (D-S.C.) said everyone in Congress continues to tout free trade even "when they know free trade is like dry water. There is no such thing."[51] George W. Bush elevated free trade to a "moral principle," but this did not keep him from imposing quotas

or tariffs on steel, textiles, beef, and other goods to satisfy the demands of a number of interest groups.[52]

The ability of any government to adopt protectionist measures and have them stick is limited by membership in the World Trade Organization (WTO). The WTO, headquartered in Geneva, Switzerland, was founded in 1995 to remove barriers to free trade and to mediate trade disputes between member countries. WTO policies are set primarily by consensus of its member countries, represented by their trade ministers. All members belong to the general council, which is empowered to resolve trade disputes. However, there is an appellate body, and countries can be sanctioned for not abiding by WTO decisions.[53]

The near-universal membership of the WTO includes many smaller and poorer countries that do not have the legal infrastructure or the political freedoms that exist in the United States. This has created concern among U.S. interest groups that membership in the WTO will cause a rollback in regulatory standards to the lowest level existing in any member country. Unions worry they will lose well-paying jobs with benefits to nonunionized workers in poorer countries who will work for low wages, no benefits, and few safety protections and who in some cases lack the freedom to unionize. And environmental activists fear that none of the

Carol Guzy/ The Washington Post. Reprinted with permission.

A demonstrator refuses to give way to a police horse during protests against economic policies toward developing nations.

regulations applied to food production and distribution in the United States will be enforced for foodstuffs imported from countries without a commitment to environmental protection. They claim that globalization and free trade are hastening the relocation of industry to countries where there are no limitations on toxic emissions into the air and water or regulation of the dumping and storing of hazardous waste. Human rights groups claim that free trade is adding to the already widespread abuse of child labor, unequal pay for women, and the exploitation of prison labor. They oppose the removal of barriers to trade and investment in countries controlled by dictatorships, fearing that by helping build up these economies, we will strengthen their governments and contribute to even greater human rights abuses.

The strongest free trade area is the **European Union (EU).** Formerly called the European Economic Community or European Common Market, the EU was formed in 1957 to foster political and economic integration in Europe. The very countries that have served as our staunchest military allies are at the same time among our strongest economic competitors. In 1992, the EU removed all internal economic barriers and customs posts for member nations, and in 2002 it began phasing in a common currency (the euro). The membership of the EU has expanded to twenty-five from its original six members, with four more awaiting entry (see Table 1). The EU, with a single trade policy, a single agricultural policy, and a single market of 440 million people, is the world's biggest trading bloc. The euro, the object of some skepticism when it was introduced, is now substantially stronger than the dollar and threatening to replace it as the international currency standard.

Trade problems in East Asia also loom large in our foreign policy. The U.S. business community has long coveted access to China's consumer market of 1.3 billion people, and developing export and investment opportunities in that massive market is a constant priority in our relations with China. That was evidenced by the token actions taken against that government for its brutal repression of the prodemocracy movement in 1989 and Clinton's decision in 2000 to grant China permanent normal trade relations. We have pressured China far more on the issue of protecting the copyrights of American artists, musicians, and writers than on human rights. Jeopardizing access to Chinese consumers to defend a principle is a bigger risk than U.S. policymakers are willing to take, even though imports from China account for much of our trade deficit. Our position of exporting raw materials to China and importing finished goods—which cost much less than if manufactured here—has, some argue, placed us in the position of a developing country.[54]

TABLE 1	European Union		
Austria	France*	Latvia	Portugal
Belgium*	Germany*	Lithuania	Slovakia
Cyprus	Greece	Luxembourg*	Slovenia
Czech Republic	Hungary	Malta	Spain
Denmark	Ireland	Netherlands*	Sweden
Estonia	Italy*	Poland	United Kingdom
Finland			
Applicants			
Bulgaria	Croatia	Romania	Turkey

*Original member when founded as the European Economic Community (Common Market) in 1957. For more on the European Union, go to www.eu.int.

Despite the near complete focus on the war on terrorism, trade will continue to be a—if not *the*—central foreign policy issue for most Americans because of what it means for job security and the cost of goods. Our huge trade deficit has greatly weakened the dollar. Although that should improve our trade imbalance (because it makes American goods cheaper to buy abroad), it has not. Americans continue to buy massive quantities of imported goods because they are so much cheaper than American-produced goods, and American investors continue to take their money abroad looking for cheaper labor and less government regulation. (See Chapter 16 for a discussion of outsourcing.)

Economic Sanctions

Economic sanctions are policies designed to get a state to change its behavior or to take some action or set of actions by refusing to engage with it in the conventional range of international economic relations (for example, trade, aid, or loans) or by denying it access to specific economic goods or services. Economic sanctions are generally regarded as middle-of-the-road measures.[55] They are stronger than talking diplomacy but weaker than military confrontation. No country in the world has imposed them as often as the United States.

Those who believe that economic sanctions can work under the right circumstances point to their use against the government of South Africa. South Africa, one of the largest countries in Africa, was governed by a white minority of five million in a nation of about thirty million. Due to the system of apartheid, the huge black majority had no say in government and lacked all civil and economic rights. After rising public protests in the United States had pressured corporations to remove their businesses from South Africa and forced colleges, churches, cities, and foundations to "divest"—sell stocks in companies that had investments in South Africa—and refuse to do business with companies that operated in South Africa, the United States imposed mild economic sanctions. In this case, it might be said that government policy was co-opted by the private sector. Divestiture occurred on an international scale, with corporations from all parts of the world pulling out of South Africa. These actions, coupled with sanctions placed on South Africa by the United Nations, undoubtedly played a role in the elimination of all remaining apartheid laws and the end of white minority rule.

In situations where the international community cannot achieve such widespread consensus as it did on South Africa, economic sanctions have not been as effective in attaining their objectives. One study of 103 instances of economic sanctions dating from World War I found a success rate of 36 percent. Sanctions were most effective when the goals were modest or when the sanctions were used to destabilize a government; they were least effective in damaging a country's military capacity or in effecting some major change in a state's behavior.[56] Sanctions are much more likely to be successful when a large state targets a much smaller, weaker state, but even then there is not a high likelihood of success if the goals are too ambitious.

Rarely does the United States target a large or powerful country, unless it is to achieve a very limited objective, such as by using trade sanctions to force the former Soviet Union to allow the emigration of Jews. The United States elects not to impose an embargo on China, even though democracy and human rights are at the very least as scarce as in Cuba, against which we have had a trade embargo for forty years. China is an economically powerful country, and recent administrations have concluded that sanctions would achieve nothing while hurting the United States economically.

The Cuba example shows that even against a much smaller country, which was once quite dependent on the United States as a trading partner, sanctions will not necessarily be effective. Even the most severe form of sanction, a trade embargo, has not achieved its goal of effecting significant political and economic reform or destabilizing the Castro government. Sanctions likely contributed to a lower standard of living for Cubans, but they did little to change the leadership's policies (or lifestyle). Many other countries are willing to trade with Cuba, and meanwhile, the Cuban government has been able to use the U.S. embargo to deflect criticism from its own economic failures.

Foreign Aid

Extending economic assistance to other countries is another tool of American foreign policy. Since the end of World War II, the United States has spent more than $500 billion on foreign aid, about two-thirds of which was given in military assistance. Aid can also take the form of grants, technical assistance, or guaranteed loans,

for example. The primary object of the aid is to promote development and stability, but indirectly it is a means for influencing the direction of other countries' development, expanding export markets for U.S. goods, and spreading our sphere of influence. Most of the money earmarked for economic assistance has been channeled through USAID, and 80 percent of its contracts and grants are used to purchase American goods.[57]

Whereas economic sanctions operate by denying a state goods or services until it changes its behavior, foreign aid is used as an incentive to change behavior or as a reward for actions taken. After the dissolution of the Soviet Union, the United States paid millions of dollars in aid to the Ukraine and other republics in the Russian Federation to destroy nuclear weapons inherited from the Soviet arsenal, and the Clinton administration promised $4.6 billion to North Korea to pay for the development of alternative energy sources if it gave up its nuclear program.

Loans and credits to help bail out countries suffering from recession or financial collapse became a common form of foreign aid in the 1980s and 1990s. Though Congress and the public have been reluctant to help pay for the financial failings of other countries, especially when they are strong trade competitors, in the global economy we are all swimming in the same financial sea, and a regional economic crisis can quickly become a world crisis. If it foments political instability, such an economic crisis may even lead to larger security crises. The technology that has allowed money to move almost instantaneously from one country to another has also, as Fed chair Alan Greenspan warns, "enhanced the ability of the system to rapidly transmit problems in one part of the globe to another."[58] To prevent or minimize the impact on our economy, we have to help pay for other governments' mistakes—just as they may have to help pay for ours.

The greatest success ever achieved with foreign aid was the rebuilding of Europe after World War II under the Marshall Plan. Since that time, major successes have been rare, and in recent years, disillusionment with economic aid as an effective means for achieving our goals has grown. How to use aid to help the world's poorest countries remains one of our most perplexing foreign policy problems. Our relations with developing countries are important, yet in most cases, military aid, military intervention, and economic aid have not worked very well in promoting economic progress, democratic government, or positive attitudes toward the United States. One major reason is that we often targeted aid to countries that were politically important but not necessarily democratic or stable. During the Cold War era, when we were trying to woo countries from the Soviet sphere of influence, aid money ended up in the bank accounts of corrupt leaders—as in Haiti, Zaire, and Panama, for example—or was spent on showy construction projects that did little to further development. Such failures led to congressional and public disillusionment with the effectiveness of foreign aid, both as a tool of foreign policy and as a spur to economic development. But today it is far less likely that aid money would find its way into the hands of a corrupt leader. Aid programs are now often funded and administered through humanitarian agencies and other independent nongovernmental organizations (NGOs).

Another reason for poor results is that we do not give much aid; our foreign budget is dwarfed (as a percentage of GDP) by those of Japan and Western Europe. Foreign aid accounts for less than one half of 1 percent of the federal budget and costs the average taxpaying family about $32 per year.[59] Our aid to the world's poorest countries costs about $6 per U.S. citizen annually.[60] We do have a history, however, of being more generous than any other country in providing emergency aid for disaster relief (floods, earthquakes, droughts and other natural disasters). This is why President Bush's initial token pledge of financial support for victims of the 2004 tsunami in the Indian Ocean, many of whom were Muslim countries, provoked immediate negative reaction. The pledge was quickly increased tenfold, exclusive of significant military support.

Some people wonder why we bother at all to aid governments with poor human rights records, that have made little effort to improve the lot of the average person, and that are sometimes militantly anti-American in their foreign policy rhetoric. In terms of our national interests, it is not good that half of the world's population is unable to buy the agricultural and industrial goods we export. For many years, the world's largest economies have been one another's principal trading partners. With the populations of these countries stabilizing, their economies may not be able to continue to grow without parallel growth in developing economies and the new markets that will open to trade.

About a quarter of the world's population lives in "extreme poverty" (defined as living on less than $1 per day), while the world's richest three billionaires own more of the world's wealth than the poorest six hundred million people combined.[61] The fear is that globalization will exacerbate this already lopsided division of the world's wealth, leaving behind anyone without educational or technological resources. Aid can be seen as an investment that will pay off in stability and friendly governments, which will translate into more exports and reduced military spending for us.

The Clinton administration, not surprisingly, put most of its effort into trade policy, believing "that open markets and rules-based trade are the best engine we know to lift living standards, reduce environmental destruction and build shared prosperity."[62] In other words, increasing trade with Africa creates jobs in the United States and raises living standards in Africa while costing the American taxpayer virtually nothing in aid.

The Bush administration has proposed increasing foreign aid by 50 percent. However, any new U.S. aid was to go only to the poorest countries, and only if they commit to democracy, free trade, open markets, and deregulation.[63] Bush's initiative was gutted by Congress before it ever got off the ground, a victim of huge budget deficits and spending on the war in Iraq, and the bulk of foreign aid is now directed toward nation building in Afghanistan and Iraq.

The irony of the reliance on trade, and free trade at that, to build the economies of the poorest nations is that American and European protectionist policies on agricultural products are some of the most economically damaging policies that farmers in these countries face. As one World Bank official noted, "The average cow is supported by three times the level of income of a poor person in Africa."[64]

Defining Security in the Global Age

Globalization and the end of the Cold War have required a redefinition of national security and a reassessment of how prepared we are to meet the new challenges. At the end of the twentieth century, one-third of the world's nations were waging war, many of them conflicts that Cold War alignments had kept from erupting. In addition, new threats arose from independent or state-sponsored terrorism. This instability in the international system has made the threat from weapons of mass destruction much more uncertain.

Today, the most difficult security challenge is preventing terrorist groups, acting alone or in concert with a state hostile to the United States, from gaining access to missile technology and to the materials needed to make biological, chemical, or nuclear weapons. During the Cold War, only five nations (the United States, the Soviet Union, Britain, France, and China) produced and stockpiled nuclear weapons. Two of those powers were our allies in NATO, and with the Soviet Union, we at least had diplomatic relations and the capacity to negotiate treaties on testing, stockpiling, and even use (as in the no-first-strike agreements). The mutual assured destruction (MAD) strategy was rooted in, and dependent on, the conviction that the fairly small number of people who were in a position to make decisions about the use of nuclear weapons were sane and rational and had something to lose if their countries were destroyed and that the threat of mutual destruction would keep any leader from launching a first strike.

As the number of states that have or are trying to gain nuclear capability has increased, the materials and technology to make nuclear weapons have proliferated across the globe. When India and Pakistan conducted tests in 1998, the number of nuclear-ready countries increased to seven. At least thirteen nations—and perhaps as many as thirty—have the capacity to produce warheads.

After its defeat in the Persian Gulf War in 1991, Iraq was forced to dismantle its weapons programs and submit to United Nations monitoring, and based on inspections after the 2003 invasion, it appears that these programs were never reinstated. Most of the nation's chemical and biological weapons appear to have been destroyed by UN inspectors during the 1990s.

The largest stores of enriched uranium and plutonium needed to make nuclear weapons are in the United States (see the box "Cleaning Up Nuclear Waste" in Chapter 18) and the successor states of the Soviet Union, mainly Russia. In addition to the amounts produced for research and continuing weapons production, large reservoirs are accumulating from the dismantling of thousands of warheads as required by disarmament agreements between the United States and Russia. All of this material has to be disposed of or stored, and Russian storage sites are scattered and poorly secured. A major aspect of the U.S. response to the new security threat has been to assist Russia and its neighbors with transporting, storing, and safeguarding these materials.

The production and storage of enriched uranium and plutonium are supposed to be carefully recorded and monitored, but record keeping has been so inade-quate, especially at Russian sites, that no one is sure exactly how much material is missing. Substantial black market trafficking in these materials is well documented.[65] Once the material is acquired, the technology necessary to build a simple uranium bomb like the one dropped on Hiroshima in 1945 is available to "anyone with a personal computer."[66]

With technology and expertise moving across borders and available in books or on the Internet, the breakdown of security measures in Russia, and the deliberate dissemination of restricted technology by states interested in increasing the number of nuclear powers, the likelihood that nuclear weapons will fall into the hands of "rogue" states or terrorist groups continues to grow. The head of Pakistan's nuclear program has admitted selling materials and parts to China and Iran and perhaps other countries as well (perhaps with tacit official consent, since he was not punished). Both President Bush and presidential candidate John Kerry agreed that unsecured nuclear material and its potential access by terrorist groups constituted the primary threat to world peace.

A few years ago, it was hard to imagine that we might look back at the Cold War as a simpler and even safer time, yet today's world is more complex than it was in the days of MAD. Nuclear proliferation makes defense against nuclear strikes exceedingly difficult because it is no longer sufficient just to monitor national defense establishments. It is less certain from where or from whom a strike might come. The CIA's failure to predict India's nuclear tests, despite years of surveillance of its arms program, is not reassuring about our ability

"I miss the Commies."

to determine when independent actors have gained access to nuclear, chemical, and biological weapons or missile technology.

Globalization has also intensified the threat from terrorist attacks. International exchanges of people and goods are ubiquitous, and there are so many points of vulnerability, including the computer systems on which international business and finance, as well as national security systems, are now completely dependent. Globalization means that foreign problems left unattended find their way to our door, not only armed conflicts but also financial and environmental crises and epidemic diseases that can spread rapidly from one country to another.

For this reason, the Clinton administration declared health, education, and environmental protection in developing countries as primary U.S. foreign policy goals, linking them to U.S. national security. Almost everyone can see the worldwide AIDS epidemic as an urgent humanitarian and health issue, but many in Congress were stunned by Clinton's characterization of the AIDS epidemic in Africa as a national security issue. Of nearly forty million people infected with the human immunodeficiency virus (HIV) worldwide, two-thirds are in Africa. It is spreading most rapidly among women and from them to their newborns. The United Nations estimates that in six sub-Saharan nations, the average child born in 2004 will not live to forty years of age.[67] Adding to the potential for instability is the rising incidence of AIDS in the armies of some African nations; one in four South African soldiers is reportedly infected with HIV/AIDS.[68]

A 2002 CIA report reinforced the view of the AIDS epidemic as an international security problem; it identified five "major regional or global players," including China and Russia, whose political and economic stability are endangered by surging rates of HIV and AIDS.[69] Money to teach AIDS prevention and pay for health care is now an important aspect of foreign aid. This is just one of the new meanings of security in a very interdependent world.

Conclusion: Is Our Foreign Policy Responsive?

As the head of the world's largest military and economic power and a partner in major military and trade alliances, the president has a constituency larger than the American public. He is often called on to be responsive to the needs of other people or countries—victims of famines, civil wars, natural disasters, and human rights abuses or countries in need of military and economic assistance.

But is the direction of our foreign policy responsive to the American public? Public attitudes can constrain the general policy directions of the president and Congress, but presidents can do a lot to shape these attitudes. Over the long term, as in Vietnam, the administration must be somewhat responsive to public sentiment that intensely opposes administration policy. But it is far harder for the public to have a short-term impact on military policy. Because everyone agrees on the general goal of protecting the nation from external attack, the public is far less inclined to be critical of military policy than it is of other areas of foreign policy. But this free rein has led to excessive secrecy, inefficiencies, and extravagant spending that are surely not in the public interest.

After 9/11, there was no need to convince the public that a threat existed, and the public gave the president unprecedented support for military action against al-Qaeda. As long as the public believed in a connection between Iraq and the 9/11 attacks, there was substantial backing for President Bush's preemptive war policy. But when evidence for such a connection failed to materialize and the war turned into an occupation characterized by urban warfare, public support waned. But it is difficult for a government to respond to public opinion shifts once troops are engaged in combat. The commitment has been made, and responsiveness to public mood has to wait.

In other areas of foreign policy, the public has more opportunity for influence than in the past, even on more technical issues like trade, immigration, and human rights. The rise of powerful lobbies on trade issues and the voting blocs of "hyphenated" Americans, for example, can have a significant impact on policy decisions. The information revolution also has given the public a much greater opportunity to be informed on the whole range of foreign policy issues, even, on occasion, on classified war policy. Without the dissemination of photographs showing prisoner abuse at the Abu Ghraib prison in Iraq, public pressure might never have been brought to bear to end the practices.

Because of our greater connectedness to all parts of the world through the Internet and because of globalization in general, Americans are far more aware of the relationships between foreign policy and their everyday lives and standard of living. In the day-to-day world of diplomacy, Foreign Service officers work tirelessly to promote American agricultural and other exports and American business interests in general. The State Department's own description of its work cites creating jobs and opening markets as central to its mission. Representing American policy as a vehicle for the promotion of individual economic interests is in itself an indication of how necessary policymakers feel it is to at least have the appearance of being responsive to the public.

Lugar Votes to Fill in Some of the Blanks

ugar did not vote for the resolution as worded by the White House. He wanted to vote for some resolution to support action against Iraq but did not want to give the president a blank check to make war. Lugar made several suggestions for compromise wording, but the president resisted them all, including one circulated by Lugar and Biden that would have required that any use of force be sanctioned by the UN Security Council.[70]

Bush said that weakening the original language would "tie his hands." He also chided the Democrat-controlled Senate by saying it was putting special interests above national security and that if Congress waited to vote until they knew what action the UN was going to take, the American people would think they were signing over the country's most pressing national security interests to international organizations. While Congress continued to negotiate compromise wording, Iraq agreed to let UN inspectors back into the country to search for weapons of mass destruction. This took some steam out of the urgency for military action and helped convince Bush that he would have to accept a more specifically worded resolution.

But members of the House wanted to get the issue out of the way so that they could get out on the campaign trail without leaving the president empty-handed or looking like they had avoided the issue. So a bipartisan group in the House, led by then Minority Leader Richard Gephardt, drafted its own version of the resolution and got White House support. This left the Biden-Lugar version, which required a UN resolution approving the use of force before troops

were committed to Iraq, dead in the water. All Biden and Lugar could do was offer their terms as an amendment to the House resolution. But once Bush had signed on to it, the momentum was all with the House version and the Biden-Lugar amendment was defeated. After Bush called Lugar and promised to "push diplomacy to the maximum degree," Lugar gave in and voted for the resolution.[71] Only one Republican defected from the party, but twenty-one Democrats voted no.

The House version did accomplish some of what Lugar wanted, including restricting the use of military force to Iraq, requiring the president to exhaust all diplomatic means before turning to force, setting a schedule for congressional briefings, and making it clear that all of the authority being given to the president was limited to his powers as defined in the War Powers Resolution. Bush got his check, but some of the blanks had been filled in.

By refusing to do what its predecessors had done for Lyndon Johnson—passing the Gulf of Tonkin Resolution with little debate or dissent—Congress exercised its checking power on the president's role as commander in chief but not its authority to declare war. Leaving the timing and the final decision to the White House, Congress become a bystander on

Iraqi policy after the invasion was under way. Once troops are in combat, the conduct of war rests in the hands of the president and the military.

When postinvasion inspections and investigations concluded that Saddam had no nuclear weapons program and that the UN weapons inspectors may have destroyed his cache of chemical and biological weapons and his ability to make more, Congress found that it had given authority for war based on faulty intelligence or intelligence distorted by the White House in order to win congressional approval. Because Congress is controlled by the Republicans, who were not eager to make the president look bad, this revelation triggered more consternation in intelligence agencies than in Congress.

The congressional vote of support for the invasion of Iraq is just one more example of how the modern presidency has siphoned warmaking power from Congress. We cannot say what Congress would have done if all of the divergent views within the intelligence community on the nature of the Iraqi threat had been made available

before the vote. But much, if not all, of this information could have been made available, especially to members of the select committees on intelligence in the House and Senate, if they had wanted to contest the president's case. A president who is willing to put his authority behind a foreign policy action involving use of the military or the commitment of troops, especially in the kind of political climate created by 9/11, is very likely to find a pliant Congress—even more so when he claims to have access to intelligence available to no one else. It is a virtual certainty in an election year when there is enormous public support for the president's position.

The cards were stacked against the go-slower and only-go-with-allies approach of Senator Lugar. But he did move into a position of greater leverage on other foreign policy issues. When the Republicans retook control of the Senate in 2003, Lugar finally got the chair of the Foreign Relations Committee that he had been seeking for years.

To learn more about this important vote and its implications, go to this chapter's "You Are There" exercises on the text Web site.

Key Terms

isolationism

Monroe Doctrine

containment

Cold War

North Atlantic Treaty Organization (NATO)

mutual assured destruction (MAD)

domino theory

Vietnam syndrome

détente

cooperative internationalism

preemption

asymmetrical warfare

protectionism

free trade

European Union (EU)

Further Reading

Anonymous (Michael Scheurer), *Imperial Hubris: Why the West Is Losing the War on Terror* (Washington, D.C.: Brassey's, 2004). A veteran CIA intelligence analyst and expert on Osama bin Laden and al-Qaeda explains why he resigned his position over policy differences with CIA leadership and the White House on how the war on terror is being waged. Although he published anonymously, his identity was revealed almost immediately.

Richard A. Clarke, *Against All Enemies: Inside America's War on Terrorism* (New York: Free Press, 2004). This best-selling book was written by the head of the counterterrorism unit in the first Bush and the Clinton administrations and it tells almost all about why he left government during the second Bush administration. Clarke describes his frustration over his inability to get the national security staff to take the al-Qaeda and Osama bin Laden threats seriously.

Louis Fisher, *Presidential War Power* (Lawrence: University of Kansas Press, 1995). A staff member of the Congressional Research Service reviews presidential use of the military from the first days of the Republic to the present and concludes that congressional warmaking powers have been usurped by the executive branch.

James Mann, *The Rise of the Vulcans: Bush's War Cabinet* (New York: Viking, 2003). This study of key members of George W. Bush's cabinet and national security staff explains how they came to be so influential in setting the direction of foreign policy.

Robert S. McNamara, *In Retrospect: The Tragedy and Lessons of Vietnam* (New York: Times Books, 1995). The former secretary of defense and a principal architect of Vietnam War policy gives eleven reasons why he thinks the Vietnam War was a mistake, rejecting the domino theory and placing a preponderance of blame on the incompetence of South Vietnamese forces and U.S. underestimation of the North Vietnamese.

Joseph Nye, *The Paradox of American Power: Why the World's Only Superpower Can't Go It Alone* (New York: Oxford University Press, 2002). A political science professor and former Clinton Defense Department official explains why he believes that unilateralism cannot work in the era of globalization.

David Remnick, *Lenin's Tomb: The Last Days of the Soviet Empire* (New York: Random House, 1993). This is a critically acclaimed account of the demise of the Soviet Union.

Neil Sheehan, *A Bright Shining Lie* (New York: Random House, 1988). The Vietnam War is seen through its effect on a young American officer.

Joseph E. Stiglitz, *Globalization and Its Discontents* (New York: Norton, 2002). A Nobel Prize–winning economist and supporter of globalization argues there are too many inequities in trade relations between rich and poor countries and criticizes the International Monetary Fund for forcing policies on poorer countries that undermine democracy.

For Viewing

Ambush in Mogadishu (1998) This PBS *Frontline* documentary on the incident that came to known as Blackhawk Down—the killing of eighteen American soldiers in Somalia—won the Edward R. Murrow journalism prize.

It contains gripping footage of the shootout between Marines and Somalia warlord gangs and shows how a humanitarian mission can draw American troops into conflict. View it online at www.pbs.org/wgbh/pages/frontline/shows/ambush, and compare with the popular commercial film on the same event, *Blackhawk Down,* 2001.

The Best Years of Our Lives (1946) Winner of seven Academy Awards including Best Picture, this film was one of first to deal seriously with the problems war veterans have reacclimating to civilian life. It emphasizes the solidarity among World War II vets of different ages and backgrounds by focusing on three from the same town who meet on the return journey at war's end—one from the working class, a second from the middle class, and the third a wealthy banker. The middle-class teen was played by a nonactor and real-life double amputee veteran. Compare this to a film about the reintegration of a Vietnam War vet such as *Coming Home* (1978) or *Born on the Fourth of July* (1989), and note what a difference forty years and public perception of the Vietnam War made in film treatments of the issue of returning vets. *Coming Home* starred noted antiwar activist Jane Fonda.

The Fog of War (2003) This is less a documentary than an arty filmic treatment of interviews with former defense secretary and Vietnam war planner Robert McNamara on the foreign policy of the Kennedy and Johnson administrations.

Hearts and Minds (1975) This is a polemic against the Vietnam War, reissued in 2004. When the government attempts to mold public opinion in support of a controversial foreign policy goal or an unpopular war, it usually produces a counterreaction in the world of art and film. Compare *Hearts and Minds* as both film and argument with *Fahrenheit 9/11,* Michael Moore's 2004 polemic against the Iraq war.

Is Wal-Mart Good for America? (2004) This *Frontline* documentary looks at the impact of Wal-Mart's merchandising strategy on America's trade imbalance and the decline of its manufacturing sector. It can be viewed online at www.pbs.org/wgbh/pages/frontline/shows/walmart.

On the Beach (1959) The film version of Neville Shute's novel about nuclear war depicts the last group of survivors in Australia as they wait for the radioactive cloud to roll in and end their lives and, with them, life on the planet. Another cup of cheer from the good old days.

Tinker, Tailor, Soldier, Spy (1979) and its sequel, *Smiley's People,* 1982. The story of the archrivalry between the world-weary head of Britain's MI-5 and the brilliant mastermind of Russian intelligence is drawn from the novels by John Le Carré, himself a former British intelligence officer. There is no better portrait of the dedicated but jaded combatants in the spy wars between the free world and the Iron Curtain countries.

The Trials of Henry Kissinger (2002) Based on Christopher Hitchens's shoot-to-kill book on one of most controversial national security advisers and secretaries of state in the postwar era, this documentary raises questions about the effectiveness and the morality of Kissinger's realist, balance of power approach to foreign policy during the Nixon administration.

Rumsfeld's War (2004) This PBS *Frontline* documentary examines Secretary of Defense Donald Rumsfeld's battle with the Pentagon hierarchy—the "war" of the title—to make over the U.S. military into a smaller, more mobile force equipped with lighter weapons. It explores the split this caused among Pentagon brass and its effects on planning and strategy in the Iraq War. It can be viewed online at www.pbs.org/wgbh/pages/frontline/shows/pentagon.

Dr. Strangelove, or How I Learned to Stop Worrying and Love the Bomb (1964) This classic black-and-white film from the Cold War era takes the fear of nuclear war with the Soviet Union and the MAD strategy that dominated nuclear weapons programs and works them into comic hysteria.

The War Behind Closed Doors (2003) This PBS *Frontline* documentary looks at the policy differences among Bush's top advisers about the wisdom of invading Iraq. It can be viewed online at www.pbs.org/wgbh/pages/frontline/shows/iraq.

 Electronic Resources

usinfo.state.gov
This site has the United States Information Agency's daily briefings and news on a variety of international issues from the official U.S. government perspective. It includes links to several foreign-language sources and a searchable database from archived material.

www.state.gov
The home page of the State Department contains links to information on the department itself and on a variety of international issues, organized by region and by issue.

www.nytimes.com
The home page of the New York Times *provides the most thorough coverage of international news by any U.S. newspaper.*

www.economist.com
The home page of The Economist, *an international magazine that specializes in in-depth articles on important international and political issues and provides a foreign perspective on the news.*

www.cwihp.si.edu
The Cold War International History Project at the Smithsonian's Woodrow Wilson Center makes available new information and perspectives on the history of the Cold War, especially findings from previously inaccessible sources from former Communist countries.

www.loc.gov/rr/international/portals.html
Portals to the World, a site managed by the Library of Congress, offers in-depth information and annotated Internet resources for selected countries of Europe, Africa, North and South America, and Asia.

www.gwu.edu/~nsarchiv
This site, maintained by an independent research institute at George Washington University, makes available declassified international affairs and national security documents obtained under the Freedom of Information Act.

InfoTrac College Edition

Search for the following articles in the InfoTrac database:

Brooks, Stephen G., and William C. Wohlforth. "American Primacy in Perspective," *Foreign Affairs* (July–August 2002).

Fisher, Louis. "Deciding on War Against Iraq," *Perspectives on Political Science* (Summer 2003).

Hirsch, Michael. "Bush and the World," *Foreign Affairs* (September–October 2002).

Lindsay, James M. "Deference and Defiance: The Shifting Rhythms of Executive-Legislative Relations in Foreign Policy," *Presidential Studies Quarterly* (September 2003).

For more articles, enter

"International relations" in the Subject Guide

"National security" in the Subject Guide

"Terrorism" in the Subject Guide

 ## American Government Resources

Visit the Public Policy section of the Wadsworth American Government Resources Web site (politicalscience.wadsworth.com/amgov) for a variety of tools to help you explore foreign policy further. Included are simulations, video clips, Microcase exercises, and a wealth of other activities.

THE DECLARATION OF INDEPENDENCE*

In Congress, July 4, 1776.

A Declaration by the Representatives of the United States of America, in General Congress assembled.

When in the Course of human Events, it becomes necessary for one People to dissolve the Political Bonds which have connected them with another, and to assume among the Powers of the Earth, the separate and equal Station to which the Laws of Nature and of Nature's God entitle them, a decent Respect to the Opinions of Mankind requires that they should declare the causes which impel them to the Separation.

We hold these Truths to be self-evident, that all Men are created equal, that they are endowed by their Creator with certain unalienable Rights, that among these are Life, Liberty, and the Pursuit of Happiness—That to secure these Rights, Governments are instituted among Men, deriving their just Powers from the Consent of the Governed, that whenever any Form of Government becomes destructive of these Ends, it is the Right of the People to alter or to abolish it, and to institute new Government, laying its Foundation on such Principles, and organizing its Powers in such Forms, as to them shall seem most likely to effect their Safety and Happiness. Prudence, indeed, will dictate that Governments long established should not be changed for light and transient Causes; and accordingly all Experience hath shewn, that Mankind are more disposed to suffer, while Evils are sufferable, than to right themselves by abolishing the Forms to which they are accustomed. But when a long Train of Abuses and Usurpations, pursuing invariably the same Object, evinces a Design to reduce them under absolute Despotism, it is their Right, it is their Duty, to throw off such Government, and to provide new Guards for their future Security. Such has been the patient Sufferance of these Colonies; and such is now the Necessity which constrains them to alter their former Systems of Government. The History of the present King of Great Britain is a History of repeated Injuries and Usurpations, all having in direct Object the Establishment of an absolute Tyranny over these States. To prove this, let facts be submitted to a candid World.

He has refused his Assent to Laws, the most wholesome and necessary for the public Good.

He has forbidden his Governors to pass Laws of immediate and pressing Importance, unless suspended in their Operation till his Assent should be obtained; and when so suspended, he has utterly neglected to attend to them.

He has refused to pass other Laws for the Accommodation of large Districts of People, unless those People would relinquish the Right of Representation in the Legislature, a Right inestimable to them, and formidable to Tyrants only.

He has called together Legislative Bodies at Places unusual, uncomfortable, and distant from the Depository of their Public Records, for the sole Purpose of fatiguing them into Compliance with his Measures.

He has dissolved Representative Houses repeatedly, for opposing with manly Firmness his Invasions on the Rights of the People.

He has refused for a long Time, after such Dissolutions, to cause others to be elected; whereby the Legislative Powers, incapable of Annihilation, have returned to the People at large for their exercise; the State remaining in the mean time exposed to all the Dangers of Invasion from without, and Convulsions within.

He has endeavoured to prevent the Population of these States; for that Purpose obstructing the Laws for Naturalization of Foreigners; refusing to pass others to encourage their Migration hither, and raising the Conditions of new Appropriations of Lands.

He has obstructed the Administration of Justice, by refusing his Assent to Laws for establishing Judiciary Powers.

He has made Judges dependent on his Will alone, for the Tenure of their offices, and the Amount and payments of their Salaries.

He has erected a Multitude of new Offices, and sent hither Swarms of Officers to harass our People, and eat out their Substance.

He has kept among us, in times of Peace, Standing Armies, without the consent of our Legislatures.

He has affected to render the Military independent of, and superior to the Civil Power.

He has combined with others to subject us to a Jurisdiction foreign to our Constitution, and unacknowledged by our Laws; giving his Assent to their Acts of pretended Legislation:

For quartering large Bodies of Armed Troops among us:

For protecting them, by a mock Trial, from Punishment for any Murders which they should commit on the Inhabitants of these States:

---

*The spelling, capitalization, and punctuation of the original have been retained here.

For cutting off our Trade with all Parts of the World:

For imposing Taxes on us without our Consent:

For depriving us, in many cases, of the Benefits of Trial by Jury:

For transporting us beyond Seas to be tried for pretended Offences:

For abolishing the free System of English Laws in a neighbouring Province, establishing therein an arbitrary Government, and enlarging its Boundaries, so as to render it at once an Example and fit Instrument for introducing the same absolute Rule into these Colonies:

For taking away our Charters, abolishing our most valuable Laws, and altering fundamentally the Forms of our Governments:

For suspending our own Legislatures, and declaring themselves invested with Power to legislate for us in all Cases whatsoever.

He has abdicated Government here, by declaring us out of his Protection and waging War against us.

He has plundered our Seas, ravaged our Coasts, burnt our towns, and destroyed the Lives of our People.

He is, at this Time, transporting large Armies of foreign Mercenaries to compleat the works of Death, Desolation, and Tyranny, already begun with circumstances of Cruelty and Perfidy, scarcely paralleled in the most barbarous Ages, and totally unworthy the Head of a civilized Nation.

He has constrained our fellow Citizens taken Captive on the high Seas to bear Arms against their Country, to become the Executioners of their Friends and Brethren, or to fall themselves by their Hands.

He has excited domestic Insurrections amongst us, and has endeavoured to bring on the Inhabitants of our Frontiers, the merciless Indian Savages, whose known Rule of Warfare is an undistinguished Destruction, of all Ages, Sexes and Conditions.

In every state of these Oppressions we have Petitioned for Redress in the most humble Terms: Our repeated Petitions have been answered only by repeated Injury. A Prince, whose Character is thus marked by every act which may define a Tyrant, is unfit to be the Ruler of a free People.

Nor have we been wanting in Attentions to our British Brethren. We have warned them from Time to Time of Attempts by their Legislature to extend an unwarrantable Jurisdiction over us. We have reminded them of the Circumstances of our Emigration and Settlement here. We have appealed to their native Justice and Magnanimity, and we have conjured them by the Ties of our common Kindred to disavow these Usurpations, which would inevitably interrupt our Connections and Correspondence. They too have been deaf to the Voice of Justice and of Consanguinity. We must, therefore, acquiesce in the Necessity, which denounces our Separation, and hold them, as we hold the rest of Mankind, Enemies in War, in Peace, Friends.

We, therefore, the Representatives of the UNITED STATES OF AMERICA, in General Congress Assembled, appealing to the Supreme Judge of the World for the Rectitude of our Intentions, do, in the Name, and by Authority of the good People of these Colonies, solemnly Publish and Declare, That these United Colonies are, and of Right ought to be, Free and Independent States; that they are absolved from all Allegiance to the British Crown, and that all political Connection between them and the State of Great Britain, is and ought to be totally dissolved; and that as Free and Independent States, they have full Power to levy War, conclude Peace, contract Alliances, establish Commerce, and to do all other Acts and Things which Independent States may of right do. And for the support of this declaration, with a firm Reliance on the Protection of divine Providence, we mutually pledge to each other our Lives, our Fortunes, and our sacred Honor.

CONSTITUTION OF THE UNITED STATES OF AMERICA*

We the people of the United States, in Order to form a more perfect Union, establish Justice, insure domestic Tranquility, provide for the common defence, promote the general Welfare, and secure the Blessings of Liberty to ourselves and our posterity, do ordain and establish this Constitution for the United States of America.

Article I

Section 1. All legislative Powers herein granted shall be vested in a Congress of the United States, which shall consist of a Senate and House of Representatives.

Section 2. The House of Representatives shall be composed of Members chosen every second Year by the People of the several States, and the Electors in each State shall have the Qualifications requisite for Electors of the most numerous Branch of the State Legislature.

No person shall be a Representative who shall not have attained to the Age of twenty-five Years, and been seven Years a Citizen of the United States, and who shall not, when elected, be an Inhabitant of that State in which he shall be chosen.

Representatives and direct [Taxes]¹ shall be apportioned among the several States which may be included within this Union, according to their respective Numbers [which shall be determined by adding to the whole Number of free Persons, including those bound to Service for a Term of Years, and excluding Indians not taxed, three fifths of all other Persons].² The actual Enumeration shall be made within three Years after the first Meeting of the Congress of the United States, and within every subsequent Term of ten Years, in such Manner as they shall by Law direct. The Number of Representatives shall not exceed one for every thirty Thousand, but each State shall have at Least one Representative; and until such enumeration shall be made, the State of New Hampshire shall be entitled to chuse three, Massachusetts eight, Rhode Island and Providence Plantations one, Connecticut five, New-York six, New Jersy four, Pennsylvania eight, Delaware one, Maryland six, Virginia ten, North Carolina five, South Carolina five, and Georgia three.

When vacancies happen in the Representation from any State, the Executive Authority thereof shall issue Writs of Election to fill such Vacancies.

The House of Representatives shall chuse their Speaker and other Officers; and shall have the sole Power of Impeachment.

Section 3. The Senate of the United States shall be composed of two Senators from each State [chosen by the Legislature thereof],³ for six Years; and each Senator shall have one Vote.

Immediately after they shall be assembled in Consequence of the first Election, they shall be divided as equally as may be into three Classes. The Seats of the Senators of the first Class shall be vacated at the Expiration of the second year, of the second Class at the Expiration of the fourth Year, and of the third Class at the Expiration of the sixth Year, so that one third may be chosen every second Year [and if Vacancies happen by Resignation, or otherwise, during the Recess of the Legislature of any State, the Executive thereof may make temporary Appointments until the next Meeting of the Legislature, which shall then fill such Vacancies.]⁴

No Person shall be a Senator who shall not have attained to the Age of thirty Years, and been nine Years a Citizen of the United States, and who shall not, when elected, be an Inhabitant of that State for which he shall be chosen.

The Vice President of the United States shall be President of the Senate, but shall have no Vote, unless they be equally divided.

The Senate shall chuse their other Officers, and also a President pro tempore, in the Absence of the Vice President, or when he shall exercise the Office of President of the United States.

The Senate shall have the sole Power to try all Impeachments. When sitting for that Purpose, they shall be on Oath or Affirmation. When the President of the United States is tried, the Chief Justice shall preside: And no Person shall be convicted without the Concurrence of two thirds of the Members present.

Judgment in Cases of Impeachment shall not extend further than to removal from Office, and disqualification to hold and enjoy any Office of honor, Trust or Profit under the United States; but the Party convicted shall nevertheless be liable and subject to Indictment, Trial, Judgment and Punishment, according to Law.

---

*The spelling, capitalization, and punctuation of the original have been retained here. Brackets indicate passages that have been altered by amendments to the Constitution.

1. Modified by the Sixteenth Amendment.
2. Modified by the Fourteenth Amendment.

3. Repealed by the Seventeenth Amendment.
4. Modified by the Seventeenth Amendment.

Section 4. The Times, Places and Manner of holding Elections for Senators and Representatives, shall be prescribed in each State by the Legislature thereof; but the Congress may at any time by Law make or alter such Regulations, except as to the Places of chusing Senators.

[The Congress shall assemble at least once in every Year, and such Meeting shall be on the first Monday in December, unless they shall by Law appoint a different Day.][5]

Section 5. Each House shall be the Judge of the Elections, Returns and Qualifications of its own Members, and a Majority of each shall constitute a Quorum to do Business; but a smaller Number may adjourn from day to day, and may be authorized to compel the Attendance of absent Members, in such Manner, and under such Penalties as each House may provide.

Each House may determine the Rules of its Proceedings, punish its Members for disorderly Behaviour, and, with the Concurrence of two thirds, expel a Member.

Each House shall keep a Journal of its Proceedings, and from time to time publish the same, excepting such Parts as may in their Judgment require Secrecy; and the Yeas and Nays of the Members of either House on any question shall, at the Desire of one fifth of those present, be entered on the Journal.

Neither House, during the Session of Congress, shall, without the Consent of the other, adjourn for more than three days, nor to any other Place than that in which the two Houses shall be sitting.

Section 6. The Senators and Representatives shall receive a Compensation for their Services, to be ascertained by Law, and paid out of the Treasury of the United States. They shall in all Cases, except Treason, Felony and Breach of the Peace, be privileged from Arrest during their Attendance at the Session of their respective Houses, and in going to and returning from the same; and for any Speech or Debate in either House, they shall not be questioned in any other Place.

No Senator or Representative shall, during the Time for which he was elected, be appointed to any civil Office under the Authority of the United States, which shall have been created, or the Emoluments whereof shall have been encreased during such time; and no Person holding any Office under the United States, shall be a Member of either House during his Continuance in Office.

Section 7. All Bills for raising Revenue shall originate in the House of Representatives; but the Senate may propose or concur with Amendments as on other Bills.

Every Bill which shall have passed the House of Representatives and the Senate, shall, before it become a Law, be presented to the President of the United States; If he approves he shall sign it, but if not he shall return it, with his objections to that House in which it shall have originated, who shall enter the Objections at large on their Journal, and proceed to

reconsider it. If after such Reconsideration two thirds of that House shall agree to pass the Bill, it shall be sent, together with the Objections, to the other House, by which it shall likewise be reconsidered, and if approved by two thirds of that House, it shall become a Law. But in all such Cases the Votes of both Houses shall be determined by yeas and Nays, and the Names of the Persons voting for and against the Bill shall be entered on the Journal of each House respectively. If any Bill shall not be returned by the President within ten Days (Sundays excepted) after it shall have been presented to him, the Same shall be a Law, in like Manner as if he had signed it, unless the Congress by their Adjournment prevent its Return, in which Case it shall not be a Law.

Every Order, Resolution, or Vote to which the Concurrence of the Senate and House of Representatives may be necessary (except on a question of Adjournment) shall be presented to the President of the United States; and before the Same shall take Effect, shall be approved by him, or being disapproved by him, shall be repassed by two thirds of the Senate and House of Representatives, according to the Rules and Limitations prescribed in the Case of a Bill.

Section 8. The Congress shall have Power To lay and collect Taxes, Duties, Imposts and Excises, to pay the Debts and provide for the common Defence and general Welfare of the United States; but all Duties, Imposts and Excises shall be uniform throughout the United States;

To borrow Money on the credit of the United States;

To regulate Commerce with foreign Nations, and among the several States, and with the Indian Tribes;

To establish a uniform Rule of Naturalization, and uniform Laws on the subject of Bankruptcies throughout the United States;

To coin Money, regulate the Value thereof, and of foreign Coin, and fix the Standard of Weights and Measures;

To provide for the Punishment of counterfeiting the Securities and current Coin of the United States.

To establish Post Offices and post Roads;

To promote the Progress of Science and useful Arts, by securing for limited Times to Authors and Inventors the exclusive Right to their respective Writings and Discoveries;

To constitute Tribunals inferior to the supreme Court;

To define and punish Piracies and Felonies committed on the high Seas, and Offences against the Law of Nations;

To declare War, grant Letters of Marque and Reprisal, and make Rules concerning Captures on Land and Water;

To raise and support Armies, but no Appropriation of Money to that Use shall be for a longer Term than two Years;

To provide and maintain a Navy;

To make Rules for the Government and Regulation of the land and naval Forces;

To provide for calling forth the Militia to execute the Laws of the Union, suppress Insurrections and repel Invasions;

To provide for organizing, arming, and disciplining the Militia, and for governing such Part of them as may be employed in the Service of the United States, reserving to the

---

5. Changed by the Twentieth Amendment.

States respectively, the Appointment of the Officers, and the Authority of training the Militia according to the discipline prescribed by Congress;

To exercise exclusive Legislation in all Cases whatsoever, over such District (not exceeding ten Miles square) as may, by Cession of particular States, and the Acceptance of Congress, become the Seat of the Government of the United States, and to exercise like Authority over all Places purchased by the Consent of the Legislature of the State in which the Same shall be, for the Erection of forts, Magazines, Arsenals, dock-Yards, and other needful Buildings;—And

To make all Laws which shall be necessary and proper for carrying into Execution the foregoing Powers, and all other Powers vested by this Constitution in the Government of the United States, or in any Department or Officer thereof.

Section 9. The Migration or Importation of such Persons as any of the States now existing shall think proper to admit, shall not be prohibited by the Congress prior to the Year one thousand eight hundred and eight, but a Tax or duty may be imposed on such Importation, not exceeding ten dollars for each Person.

The Privilege of the Writ of Habeas Corpus shall not be suspended, unless when in Cases of Rebellion or Invasion the public Safety may require it.

No Bill of Attainder or ex post facto Law shall be passed.

[No Capitation, or other direct, Tax shall be laid, unless in Proportion to the Census or Enumeration herein before directed to be taken.][6]

No Tax or Duty shall be laid on Articles exported from any State.

No Preference shall be given by any Regulation of Commerce or Revenue to the Ports of one State over those of another; nor shall Vessels bound to, or from, one State, be obliged to enter, clear, or pay Duties in another.

No Money shall be drawn from the Treasury, but in Consequence of Appropriations made by Law; and a regular Statement and Account of the Receipts and Expenditures of all public Money shall be published from time to time.

No Title of Nobility shall be granted by the United States; and no Person holding any Office or Profit or Trust under them, shall, without the Consent of the Congress, accept of any present, Emolument, Office, or Title, of any kind whatever, from any King, Prince, or foreign State.

Section 10. No state shall enter into any Treaty, Alliance, or Confederation; grant Letters of Marque and Reprisal; coin Money; emit Bills of Credit; make any Thing but gold and silver Coin a Tender in Payment of Debts; pass any Bill of Attainder, ex post facto Law, or Law impairing the Obligation of Contracts, or grant any Title of Nobility.

No State shall, without the Consent of the Congress, lay any Imposts or Duties on Imports or Exports, except what may be absolutely necessary for executing its inspection Laws; and the net Produce of all Duties and Imposts, laid by any State on Imports or Exports, shall be for the Use of the Treasury of the United States; and all such Laws shall be subject to the Revision and Controul of the Congress.

No State shall, without the Consent of Congress, lay any duty of Tonnage, keep Troops, or Ships of War in time of Peace, enter into any Agreement or Compact with another State, or with a foreign Power or engage in War, unless actually invaded, or in such imminent Danger as will not admit of delay.

Article II

Section 1. The executive Power shall be vested in a President of the United States of America. He shall hold his Office during the Term of four Years, and, together with the Vice President, chosen for the Same Term, be elected, as follows.

Each State shall appoint, in such Manner as the Legislature thereof may direct, a Number of Electors, equal to the whole Number of Senators and Representatives to which the State may be entitled in the Congress; but no Senator or Representative, or Person holding an Office of Trust or Profit under the United States, shall be appointed an Elector.

[The Electors shall meet in their respective States, and vote by Ballot for two Persons of whom one at least shall not be an Inhabitant of the same State with themselves. And they shall make a List of all the Persons voted for, and of the Number of Votes for each; which List they shall sign and certify, and transmit sealed to the Seat of the Government of the United States, directed to the President of the Senate. The President of the Senate shall, in the Presence of the Senate and House of Representatives, open all the Certificates, and the Votes shall then be counted. The Person having the greatest Number of Votes shall be the President, if such Number be a Majority of the whole Number of Electors appointed; and if there be more than one who have such Majority, and have an equal Number of Votes, then the House of Representatives shall immediately chuse by Ballot one of them for President; and if no Person have a Majority, then from the five highest on the List the said House shall in like Manner chuse the President. But in chusing the President, the Votes shall be taken by States, the Representation from each State having one Vote; A quorum for this Purpose shall consist of a Member or Members from two thirds of the States, and a Majority of all the states shall be necessary to a Choice. In every Case, after the Choice of the President, the Person having the greatest Number of Votes of the Electors shall be the Vice President. But if there should remain two or more who have equal Votes, the Senate shall chuse from them by Ballot the Vice President.][7]

The Congress may determine the Time of chusing the Electors, and the Day on which they shall give their Votes; which Day shall be the same throughout the United States.

No person except a natural born Citizen, or a Citizen of the United States, at the time of the Adoption of this Constitution, shall be eligible to the Office of President; neither shall

---

6. Modified by the Sixteenth Amendment.

7. Changed by the Twelfth Amendment.

any Person be eligible to that Office who shall not have attained to the Age of thirty five Years, and been fourteen Years a Resident within the United States.

[In Case of the Removal of the President from Office, or of his Death, Resignation, or Inability to discharge the Powers and Duties of the said Office, the same shall devolve on the Vice President, and the Congress may by Law provide for the Case of Removal, Death, Resignation or Inability, both of the President and Vice President, declaring what Officer shall then act as President, and such Officer shall act accordingly, until the Disability be removed, or a President shall be elected.][8]

The President shall, at stated Times, receive for his Services, a Compensation, which shall neither be encreased nor diminished during the Period for which he shall have been elected, and he shall not receive within that Period any other Emolument from the United States, or any of them.

Before he enter on the Execution of his Office, he shall take the following Oath or Affirmation:—"I do solemnly swear (or affirm) that I will faithfully execute the Office of President of the United States, and will to the best of my Ability, preserve, protect and defend the constitution of the United States."

Section 2. The President shall be Commander in Chief of the Army and Navy of the United States, and of the Militia of the several States, when called into the actual Service of the United States; he may require the Opinion, in writing, of the principal Officer in each of the executive Departments, upon any Subject relating to the Duties of their respective Offices, and he shall have Power to grant Reprieves and Pardons for Offences against the United States, except in Cases of Impeachment.

He shall have Power, by and with the Advice and Consent of the Senate, to make Treaties, provided two thirds of the Senators present concur; and he shall nominate, and by and with the Advice and Consent of the Senate, shall appoint Ambassadors, other public Ministers and Consuls, Judges of the supreme Court, and all other Officers of the United States, whose Appointments are not herein otherwise provided for, and which shall be established by Law; but the Congress may by Law vest the Appointment of such inferior Officers, as they think proper, in the President alone, in the Courts of Law, or in the Heads of Departments.

The President shall have Power to fill up all Vacancies that may happen during the Recess of the Senate, by granting Commissions which shall expire at the end of their next Session.

Section 3. He shall from time to time give to the Congress Information of the State of the Union, and recommend to their Consideration such Measures as he shall judge necessary and expedient; he may, on extraordinary Occasions, convene both Houses, or either of them, and in Case of Disagreement between them, with Respect to the Time of Adjournment, he may adjourn them to such Time as he shall think proper; he shall receive Ambassadors and other public Ministers; he shall take Care that the Laws be faithfully executed, and shall Commission all the Officers of the United States.

Section 4. The President, Vice President and all civil Officers of the United States, shall be removed from Office on Impeachment for, and Conviction of, Treason, Bribery, or other high Crimes and Misdemeanors.

Article III

Section 1. The judicial Power of the United States, shall be vested in one supreme Court, and in such inferior Courts as the Congress may from time to time ordain and establish. The Judges, both of the supreme and inferior Courts, shall hold their Offices during good Behaviour, and shall, at stated Times, receive for their Services, a Compensation, which shall not be diminished during their Continuance in Office.

Section 2. The judicial Power shall extend to all Cases, in Law and Equity, arising under this Constitution, the Laws of the United States, and Treaties made, or which shall be made, under their Authority;—to all Cases affecting Ambassadors, other public Ministers and Consuls;—to all Cases of admiralty and maritime Jurisdiction;—to Controversies to which the United States shall be a Party;—to Controversies between two or more States;—[between a State and Citizens of another State;][9]—between Citizens of different States,—between Citizens of the same State claiming Lands under Grants of different States, [and between a state, or the Citizens thereof, and foreign States, Citizens or Subjects.][10]

In all cases affecting Ambassadors, other public Ministers and Consuls, and those in which a State shall be Party, the supreme Court shall have original Jurisdiction. In all the other Cases before mentioned, the supreme Court shall have appellate Jurisdiction, both as to Law and Fact, with such Exceptions, and under such Regulations as the Congress shall make.

The Trial of all Crimes, except in Cases of Impeachment, shall be by Jury; and such Trial shall be held in the State where the said Crimes shall have been committed; but when not committed within any State, the Trial shall be at such Place or Places as the Congress may by Law have directed.

Section 3. Treason against the United States, shall consist only in levying War against them, or in adhering to their Enemies, giving them Aid and Comfort. No Person shall be convicted of Treason unless on the Testimony of two Witnesses to the same overt Act, or on Confession in open Court.

The Congress shall have Power to declare the Punishment of Treason, but no Attainder of Treason shall work Corruption of Blood, or Forfeiture except during the Life of the Person attainted.

---

8. Modified by the Twenty-fifth Amendment.

9. Modified by the Eleventh Amendment.
10. Modified by the Eleventh Amendment.

Article IV

Section 1. Full Faith and Credit shall be given in each State to the public Acts, Records, and judicial Proceedings of every other State. And the Congress may by general Laws prescribe the Manner in which such Acts, Records and Proceedings shall be proved, and the Effect thereof.

Section 2. The Citizens of each State shall be entitled to all Privileges and Immunities of Citizens in the several States.

A Person charged in any State with Treason, Felony, or other Crime, who shall flee from Justice, and be found in another State, shall on Demand of the executive Authority of the State from which he fled, be delivered up, to be removed to the State having Jurisdiction of the Crime.

[No Person held to Service or Labour in one State under the Laws thereof, escaping into another, shall, in Consequence of any Law or Regulation therein, be discharged from such Service or Labour, but shall be delivered up on Claim of the Party to whom such Service or Labour may be due.][11]

Section 3. New States may be admitted by the Congress into this Union; but no new State shall be formed or erected within the Jurisdiction of any other State; nor any State be formed by the Junction of two or more States, or Parts of States, without the Consent of the Legislatures of the States concerned as well as of the Congress.

The Congress shall have Power to dispose of and make all needful Rules and Regulations respecting the Territory or other Property belonging to the United States; and nothing in this Constitution shall be so construed as to Prejudice any Claimes of the United States, or of any particular State.

Section 4. The United States shall guarantee to every State in this Union a Republican Form of Government, and shall protect each of them against Invasion, and on Application of the Legislature, or of the Executive (when the Legislature cannot be convened) against domestic Violence.

Article V

The Congress, whenever two thirds of both Houses shall deem it necessary, shall propose Amendments to this Constitution, or on the Application of the Legislatures of two thirds of the several States, shall call a Convention for proposing Amendments, which, in either Case, shall be valid to all Intents and Purposes, as Part of this Constitution, when ratified by the Legislatures of three fourths of the several States, or by Conventions in three fourths thereof, as the one or the other Mode of Ratification may be proposed by the Congress; Provided that no Amendment which may be made prior to the Year One thousand eight hundred and eight shall in any Manner affect the first and fourth Clauses in the Ninth Section of the first Article; and that no State, without its Consent, shall be deprived of its equal Suffrage in the Senate.

Article VI

All Debts contracted and Engagements entered into, before the Adoption of this Constitution, shall be as valid against the United States under this Constitution, as under the Confederation.

This Constitution, and the laws of the United States which shall be made in Pursuance thereof; and all Treaties made, or which shall be made, under the Authority of the United States, shall be the supreme Law of the Land; and the Judges in every State shall be bound thereby, any Thing in the Constitution or Laws of any State to the Contrary notwithstanding.

The Senators and Representatives before mentioned, and the Members of the several State Legislatures, and all executive and judicial Officers, both of the United States and of the several States, shall be bound by Oath or Affirmation, to support this Constitution; but no religious Text shall ever be required as a Qualification to any Office or public Trust under the United States.

Article VII

The Ratification of the Conventions of nine States, shall be sufficient for the Establishment of this constitution between the States so ratifying the Same.

Done in Convention by the Unanimous Consent of the States present the Seventeenth Day of September in the Year of our Lord one thousand seven hundred and Eighty seven and of the Independence of the United States of America the Twelfth. IN WITNESS whereof we have hereunto subscribed our Names.

Go. WASHINGTON
Presid't. and deputy from Virginia

Attest
William Jackson
Secretary

Delaware
Geo. Read
Gunning Bedford jun
John Dickinson
Richard Basset
Jaco. Broon

Massachusetts
Nathaniel Gorham
Rufus King

Connecticut
Wm. Saml. Johnson
Roger Sherman

New York
Alexander Hamilton

New Jersey
Wh. Livingston
David Brearley

Wm. Paterson
Jona. Dayton

Pennsylvania
B. Franklin
Thomas Mifflin
Robt. Morris
Geo. Clymer
Thos. FitzSimons
Jared Ingersoll
James Wilson
Gouv. Morris

Virginia
John Blair
James Madison Jr.

North Carolina
Wm. Blount
Richd. Dobbs Spaight
Hu. Williamson

---

11. Repealed by the Thirteenth Amendment.

South Carolina

J. Rutledge

Charles Cotesworth Pinckney

Charles Pinckney

Pierce Butler

Georgia

William Few

Abr. Baldwin

New Hampshire

John Langdon

Nicholas Gilman

Maryland

James McHenry

Dan of St. Thos. Jenifer

Danl. Carroll

Amendment I[12]

Congress shall make no law respecting an establishment of religion, or prohibiting the free exercise thereof; or abridging the freedom of speech, or of the press; or the right of the people peaceably to assemble, and to petition the Government for a redress of grievances.

Amendment II

A well regulated militia, being necessary to the security of a free State, the right of the people to keep and bear arms, shall not be infringed.

Amendment III

No Soldier shall, in time of peace be quartered in any house, without the consent of the owner, nor in time of war, but in a manner to be prescribed by law.

Amendment IV

The right of the people to be secure in their persons, houses, papers, and effects, against unreasonable searches and seizures, shall not be violated, and no warrants shall issue, but upon probable cause, supported by oath or affirmation, and particularly describing the place to be searched, and the persons or things to be seized.

Amendment V

No person shall be held to answer for a capital, or otherwise infamous crime, unless on a presentment or indictment of a Grand Jury, except in cases arising in the land or naval forces, or in the militia, when in actual service in time of war or public danger; nor shall any person be subject for the same offence to be twice put in jeopardy of life or limb; nor shall be compelled in any criminal case to be a witness against himself, nor be deprived of life, liberty, or property, without due process of law; nor shall private property be taken for public use, without just compensation.

Amendment VI

In all criminal prosecutions, the accused shall enjoy the right to a speedy and public trial, by an impartial jury of the State

and district wherein the crime shall have been committed, which district shall have been previously ascertained by law, and to be informed of the nature and cause of the accusation; to be confronted with the witnesses against him; to have compulsory process for obtaining witnesses in his favor, and to have the assistance of counsel for his defence.

Amendment VII

In Suits at common law, where the value in controversy shall exceed twenty dollars, the right of trial by jury shall be preserved, and no fact tried by a jury, shall be otherwise reexamined in any Court of the United States, than according to the rules of the common law.

Amendment VIII

Excessive bail shall not be required, nor excessive fines imposed, nor cruel and unusual punishments inflicted.

Amendment IX

The enumeration in the Constitution, of certain rights, shall not be construed to deny or disparage others retained by the people.

Amendment X

The powers not delegated to the United States by the Constitution, nor prohibited by it to the States, are reserved to the States respectively, or to the people.

Amendment XI
(Ratified February 7, 1795)

The Judicial power of the United States shall not be construed to extend to any suit in law or equity, commenced or prosecuted against one of the United States by Citizens of another State, or by Citizens or Subjects of any Foreign State.

Amendment XII
(Ratified June 15, 1804)

The Electors shall meet in their respective states, and vote by ballot for President and Vice-President, one of whom, at least, shall not be an inhabitant of the same state with themselves; they shall name in their ballots the person voted for as President, and in distinct ballots the person voted for as Vice President, and they shall make distinct lists of all persons voted for as President, and of all persons voted for as Vice-President, and of the number of votes for each, which lists they shall sign and certify, and transmit sealed to the seat of the government of the United States, directed to the President of the Senate;—The President of the Senate shall, in the presence of the Senate and House of Representatives, open all the certificates and the votes shall then be counted;—The person having the greatest number of votes for President, shall be the President, if such number be a ma-

---

12. The first ten amendments were passed by Congress on September 25, 1789, and were ratified on December 15, 1791.

jority of the whole number of Electors appointed; and if no person have such majority, then from the persons having the highest numbers not exceeding three on the list of those voted for as President, the House of Representatives shall choose immediately, by ballot, the President. But in choosing the President, the votes shall be taken by states, the representation from each state having one vote; a quorum for this purpose shall consist of a member or members from two-thirds of the states, and a majority of all the states shall be necessary to a choice. [And if the House of Representatives shall not choose a President whenever the right of choice shall devolve upon them, before the fourth day of March next following, then the Vice-President shall act as President, as in the case of the death or other constitutional disability of the President.][13]—The person having the greatest number of votes as Vice-President, shall be the Vice-President, if such number be a majority of the whole number of Electors appointed, and if no person have a majority, then from the two highest numbers on the list, the Senate shall choose the Vice-President; a quorum for the purpose shall consist of two-thirds of the whole number of Senators, and a majority of the whole number shall be necessary to a choice. But no person constitutionally ineligible to the office of President shall be eligible to that of Vice-President of the United States.

Amendment XIII
(Ratified on December 6, 1865)

Section 1. Neither slavery nor involuntary servitude, except as a punishment for crime whereof the party shall have been duly convicted, shall exist within the United States, or any place subject to their jurisdiction.

Section 2. Congress shall have power to enforce this article by appropriate legislation.

Amendment XIV
(Ratified on July 9, 1868)

Section 1. All persons born or naturalized in the United States, and subject to the jurisdiction thereof, are citizens of the United States and of the State wherein they reside. No State shall make or enforce any law which shall abridge the privileges or immunities of citizens of the United States; nor shall any State deprive any person of life, liberty, or property, without due process of law; nor deny to any person within its jurisdiction the equal protection of the laws.

Section 2. Representatives shall be apportioned among the several States according to their respective numbers, counting the whole number of persons in each State, excluding Indians not taxed. But when the right to vote at any election for the choice of electors for President and Vice Presi-

dent of the United States, Representatives in Congress, the Executive and Judicial officers of a State, or the members of the Legislature thereof, is denied to any of the male inhabitants of such State, being [twenty-one][14] years of age, and citizens of the United States, or in any way abridged, except for participation in rebellion, or other crime, the basis of representation therein shall be reduced in the proportion which the number of such male citizens shall bear to the whole number of male citizens twenty-one years of age in such State.

Section 3. No person shall be a Senator or Representative in Congress, or elector of President and Vice President, or hold any office, civil or military, under the United States, or under any State, who having previously taken an oath, as a member of Congress, or as an officer of the United States, or as a member of any State legislature, or as an executive or judicial officer of any State, to support the Constitution of the United States, shall have engaged in insurrection or rebellion against the same, or given aid or comfort to the enemies thereof. But Congress may by a vote of two-thirds of each House, remove such disability.

Section 4. The validity of the public debt of the United States, authorized by law, including debts incurred for payment of pensions and bounties for services in suppressing insurrection or rebellion, shall not be questioned. But neither the United States nor any State shall assume or pay any debt or obligation incurred in aid of insurrection or rebellion against the United States, or any claim for the loss or emancipation of any slave, but all such debts, obligations and claims shall be held illegal and void.

Section 5. The Congress shall have power to enforce, by appropriate legislation, the provisions of this article.

Amendment XV
(Ratified on February 3, 1870)

Section 1. The right of citizens of the United States to vote shall not be denied or abridged by the United States or by any State on account of race, color, or previous condition of servitude.

Section 2. The Congress shall have power to enforce this article by appropriate legislation.

Amendment XVI
(Ratified on February 3, 1913)

The Congress shall have power to lay and collect taxes on incomes, from whatever source derived, without apportionment among the several States, and without regard to any census or enumeration.

13. Changed by the Twentieth Amendment.

14. Changed by the Twenty-sixth Amendment.

Amendment XVII
(Ratified on April 8, 1913)

The Senate of the United States shall be composed of two Senators from each State, elected by the people thereof, for six years; and each Senator shall have one vote. The electors in each State shall have the qualifications requisite for electors of the most numerous branch of the State legislatures.

When vacancies happen in the representation of any State in the Senate, the executive authority of such State shall issue writs of election to fill such vacancies: *Provided,* That the legislature of any State may empower the executive thereof to make temporary appointments until the people fill the vacancies by election as the legislature may direct.

This amendment shall not be so construed as to affect the election or term of any Senator chosen before it becomes valid as part of the Constitution.

Amendment XVIII
(Ratified on January 16, 1919)

Section 1. After one year from the ratification of this article the manufacture, sale, or transportation of intoxicating liquors within, the importation thereof into, or the exportation thereof from the United States and all territory subject to the jurisdiction thereof for beverage purposes is hereby prohibited.

Section 2. The Congress and the several States shall have concurrent power to enforce this article by appropriate legislation.

Section 3. This article shall be inoperative unless it shall have been ratified as an amendment to the Constitution by the legislatures of the several States, as provided in the Constitution, within seven years from the date of the submission hereof to the States by the Congress.[15]

Amendment XIX
(Ratified on August 18, 1920)

The right of citizens of the United States to vote shall not be denied or abridged by the United States or by any State on account of sex.

Congress shall have power to enforce this article by appropriate legislation.

Amendment XX
(Ratified on January 23, 1933)

Section 1. The terms of the President and Vice President shall end at noon on the 20th day of January, and the terms of Senators and Representatives at noon on the 3rd day of January, of the years in which such terms would have ended if this article had not been ratified, and the terms of their successors shall then begin.

15. The Eighteenth Amendment was repealed by the Twenty-first Amend-

Section 2. The Congress shall assemble at least once in every year, and such meeting shall begin at noon on the 3rd day of January, unless they shall by law appoint a different day.

Section 3. If, at the time fixed for the beginning of the term of the President, the President elect shall have died, the Vice President elect shall become President. If a President shall not have been chosen before the time fixed for the beginning of his term, or if the President elect shall have failed to qualify, then the Vice President elect shall act as President until a President shall have qualified; and the Congress may by law provide for the case wherein neither a President elect nor a Vice President elect shall have qualified, declaring who shall then act as President, or the manner in which one who is to act shall be selected, and such person shall act accordingly until a President or Vice President shall have qualified.

Section 4. The Congress may by law provide for the case of the death of any of the persons from whom the House of Representatives may choose a President whenever the rights of choice shall have devolved upon them, and for the case of the death of any of the persons from whom the Senate may choose a Vice President whenever the right of choice shall have devolved upon them.

Section 5. Sections 1 and 2 shall take effect on the 15th day of October following the ratification of this article.

Section 6. This article shall be inoperative unless it shall have been ratified as an amendment to the Constitution by the legislatures of three-fourths of the several States within seven years from the date of its submission.

Amendment XXI
(Ratified on December 5, 1933)

Section 1. The eighteenth article of amendment to the Constitution of the United States is hereby repealed.

Section 2. The transportation or importation into any State, Territory, or possession of the United States for delivery or use therein of intoxicating liquors, in violation of the laws thereof, is hereby prohibited.

Section 3. This article shall be inoperative unless it shall have been ratified as an amendment to the Constitution by conventions in the several States, as provided in the Constitution, within seven years from the date of the submission hereof to the States by the Congress.

Amendment XXII
(Ratified on February 27, 1951)

No person shall be elected to the office of the President more than twice, and no person who has held the office of President, or acted as President, for more than two years of a term to which some other person was elected President shall be elected to the office of the President more than once. But this Article shall not apply to any person holding the office of President when this Article was proposed by the Congress, and shall not prevent any person who may be holding the office of President, or acting as President, during the term within which this Article becomes operative from holding the office of President or acting as President during the remainder of such term.

Amendment XXIII
(Ratified on March 29, 1961)

Section 1. The District constituting the seat of Government of the United States shall appoint in such manner as the Congress may direct:

A number of electors of President and Vice President equal to the whole number of Senators and Representatives in Congress to which the District would be entitled if it were a State, but in no event more than the least populous State; they shall be in addition to those appointed by the States, but they shall be considered, for the purposes of the election of President and Vice President, to be electors appointed by a State; and they shall meet in the District and perform such duties as provided by the twelfth article of amendment.

Section 2. The Congress shall have power to enforce this article by appropriate legislation.

Amendment XXIV
(Ratified on January 23, 1964)

Section 1. The right of citizens of the United States to vote in any primary or other election for President or Vice President, for electors for President or Vice President, or for Senator or Representative in Congress, shall not be denied or abridged by the United States or any State by reason of failure to pay any poll tax or other tax.

Section 2. The Congress shall have power to enforce this article by appropriate legislation.

Amendment XXV
(Ratified on February 10, 1967)

Section 1. In case of the removal of the President from office or of his death or resignation, the Vice President shall become President.

Section 2. Whenever there is a vacancy in the office of the Vice President, the President shall nominate a Vice President who shall take office upon confirmation by a majority vote of both Houses of Congress.

Section 3. Whenever the President transmits to the President pro tempore of the Senate and the Speaker of the House of Representatives his written declaration that he is unable to discharge the powers and duties of his office, and until he transmits to them a written declaration to the contrary, such powers and duties shall be discharged by the Vice President as Acting President.

Section 4. Whenever the Vice President and a majority of either the principal officers of the executive departments or of such other body as Congress may by law provide, transmit to the President pro tempore of the Senate and the Speaker of the House of Representatives their written declaration that the President is unable to discharge the powers and duties of his office, the Vice President shall immediately assume the powers and duties of the offices as Acting President.

Thereafter, when the President transmits to the President pro tempore of the Senate and the Speaker of the House of Representatives his written declaration that no inability exists, he shall resume the powers and duties of his office unless the Vice President and a majority of either the principal officers of the executive department or of such other body as Congress may by law provide, transmit within four days to the President pro tempore of the Senate and the Speaker of the House of Representatives their written declaration that the President is unable to discharge the powers and duties of his office. Thereupon Congress shall decide the issue, assembling within forty-eight hours for that purpose if not in session. If the Congress, within twenty-one days after receipt of the latter written declaration, or, if Congress is not in session, within twenty-one days after Congress is required to assemble, determines by two-thirds vote of both Houses that the President is unable to discharge the powers and duties of his office, the Vice President shall continue to discharge the same as Acting President; otherwise; the President shall resume the powers and duties of his office.

Amendment XXVI
(Ratified on July 1, 1971)

Section 1. The right of citizens of the United States, who are eighteen years of age or older, to vote shall not be denied or abridged by the United States or by any State on account of age.

Section 2. The Congress shall have the power to enforce this article by appropriate legislation.

Amendment XXVII
(Ratified on May 7, 1992)

No law, varying the compensation for the services of the Senators and Representatives, shall take effect, until an election of Representatives shall have intervened.

FEDERALIST PAPER 10

Among the numerous advantages promised by a well-constructed Union, none deserves to be more accurately developed than its tendency to break and control the violence of faction. The friend of popular governments never finds himself so much alarmed for their character and fate as when he contemplates their propensity to this dangerous vice. He will not fail, therefore, to set a due value on any plan which, without violating the principles to which he is attached, provides a proper cure for it. The instability, injustice, and confusion introduced into the public councils have, in truth, been the mortal diseases under which popular governments have everywhere perished, as they continue to be the favorite and fruitful topics from which the adversaries to liberty derive their most specious declamations. The valuable improvements made by the American constitutions on the popular models, both ancient and modern, cannot certainly be too much admired; but it would be an unwarrantable partiality to contend that they have as effectually obviated the danger on this side, as was wished and expected. Complaints are everywhere heard from our most considerate and virtuous citizens, equally the friends of public and private faith and of public and personal liberty, that our governments are too unstable, that the public good is disregarded in the conflicts of rival parties, and that measures are too often decided, not according to the rules of justice and the rights of the minor party, but by the superior force of an interested and overbearing majority. However anxiously we may wish that these complaints had no foundation, the evidence of known facts will not permit us to deny that they are in some degree true. It will be found, indeed, on a candid review of our situation, that some of the distresses under which we labor have been erroneously charged on the operation of our governments; but it will be found, at the same time, that other causes will not alone account for many of our heaviest misfortunes; and, particularly, for that prevailing and increasing distrust of public engagements and alarm for private rights which are echoed from one end of the continent to the other. These must be chiefly, if not wholly, effects of the unsteadiness and injustice with which a factious spirit has tainted our public administration.

By a faction I understand a number of citizens, whether amounting to a majority or minority of the whole, who are united and actuated by some common impulse of passion, or of interest, adverse to the rights of other citizens, or the permanent and aggregate interests of the community.

There are two methods of curing the mischiefs of faction: the one, by removing its causes; the other, by controlling its effects.

There are again two methods of removing the causes of faction: the one, by destroying the liberty which is essential to its existence; the other, by giving to every citizen the same opinions, the same passions, and the same interests.

It could never be more truly said than of the first remedy that it was worse than the disease. Liberty is to faction what air is to fire, an aliment without which it instantly expires. But it could not be a less folly to abolish liberty, which is essential to political life, because it nourishes faction than it would be to wish the annihilation of air, which is essential to animal life, because it imparts to fire its destructive agency.

The second expedient is as impracticable as the first would be unwise. As long as the reason of man continues fallible, and his is at liberty to exercise it, different opinions will be formed. As long as the connection subsists between his reason and his self-love, his opinions and his passions will have a reciprocal influence on each other; and the former will be objects to which the latter will attach themselves. The diversity in the faculties of men, from which the rights of property originate, is not less an insuperable obstacle to a uniformity of interests. The protection of these faculties is the first object of government. From the protection of different and unequal faculties of acquiring property, the possession of different degrees and kinds of property immediately results; and from the influence of these on the sentiments and views of the respective proprietors ensues a division of the society into different interests and parties.

The latent causes of faction are thus sown in the nature of man; and we see them everywhere brought into different degrees of activity, according to the different circumstances of civil society. A zeal for different opinions concerning religion, concerning government, and many other points, as well of speculation as of practice; an attachment to different leaders ambitiously contending for pre-eminence and power; or to persons of other descriptions whose fortunes have been interesting to the human passions, have, in turn, divided mankind into parties, inflamed them with mutual animosity, and rendered them much more disposed to vex and oppress each other than to cooperate for their common good. So strong is this propensity of mankind to fall into mutual animosities that where no substantial occasion presents itself the most frivolous and fanciful distinctions have been sufficient to kindle their unfriendly passions and excite their most violent conflicts. But the most common and durable source of factions has been the various and unequal distribution of property. Those who hold and those who are without property have ever formed distinct interests in society. Those who are creditors, and those who are debtors, fall under a like discrimination. A landed interest, a manufacturing interest, a mercantile interest, a moneyed interest, with many lesser interests, grow up of necessity in civilized nations, and divide them into different classes, actuated by different sentiments and views. The regulation of these various and interfering interests forms the principal task of modern legislation and involves the spirit of party and faction in the necessary and ordinary operations of government.

No man is allowed to be a judge in his own cause, because his interest would certainly bias his judgment, and, not improbably, corrupt his integrity. With equal, nay with greater reason, a body of men are unfit to be both judges and parties at the same time; yet what are many of the most important acts of legislation but so many judicial determinations, not indeed concerning the rights of single persons, but concerning the rights of large bodies of citizens? And what are the different classes of legislators but advocates and parties to the causes which they determine? Is a law proposed concerning private debts? It is a question to which the creditors are parties on one side and the debtors on the other. Justice ought to hold the balance between them. Yet the parties are, and must be, themselves the judges; and the most numerous party, or in other words, the most powerful faction must be expected to prevail. Shall domestic manufacturers be encouraged, and in what degree, by restrictions on foreign manufacturers? are questions which would be differently decided by the landed and the manufacturing classes, and probably by neither with a sole regard to justice and the public good. The apportionment of taxes on the various descriptions of property is an act which seems to require the most exact impartiality; yet there is, perhaps, no legislative act in which greater opportunity and temptation are given to a predominant party to trample on the rules of justice. Every shilling with which they overburden the inferior number is a shilling saved to their own pockets. It is in vain to say that enlightened statesmen will be able to adjust these clashing interests and render them all subservient to the public good. Enlightened statesmen will not always be at the helm. Nor, in many cases, can such an adjustment be made at all without taking into view indirect and remote considerations, which will rarely prevail over the immediate interest which one party may find in disregarding the rights of another or the good of the whole.

The inference to which we are brought is that the *causes* of faction cannot be removed and that relief is only to be sought in the means of controlling its *effects*.

If a faction consists of less than a majority, relief is supplied by the republican principle, which enables the majority to defeat its sinister views by regular vote. It may clog the administration, it may convulse the society; but it will be unable to execute and mask its violence under the forms of the Constitution. When a majority is included in a faction, the form of popular government, on the other hand, enables it to sacrifice to its ruling passion or interest both the public good and the rights of other citizens. To secure the public good and private rights against the danger of such a faction, and at the same time to preserve the spirit and the form of popular government, is then the great object to which our inquiries are directed. Let me add that it is the great desideratum by which alone this form of government can be rescued from the opprobrium under which it has so long labored and be recommended to the esteem and adoption of mankind.

By what means is this object attainable? Evidently by one of two only. Either the existence of the same passion or interest in a majority at the same time must be prevented, or the majority, having such coexistent passion or interest, must be rendered, by their number and local situation, unable to concert and carry into effect schemes of oppression. If the impulse and the opportunity be suffered to coincide, we well know that neither moral nor religious motives can be relied on as an adequate control. They are not found to be such on the injustice and violence of individuals, and lose their efficacy in proportion to the number combined together, that is, in proportion as their efficacy becomes needful.

From this view of the subject it may be concluded that a pure democracy, by which I mean a society consisting of a small number of citizens, who assemble and administer the government in person, can admit of no cure for the mischiefs of faction. A common passion or interest will, in almost every case, be felt by a majority of the whole; a communication and concert results from the form of government itself; and there is nothing to check the inducements to sacrifice the weaker party or an obnoxious individual. Hence it is that such democracies have ever been spectacles of turbulence and contention; have ever been found incompatible with personal security or the rights of property; and have in general been as short in their lives as they have been violent in their deaths. Theoretic politicians, who have patronized this species of government, have erroneously supposed that by reducing mankind to a perfect equality in their political rights, they would at the same time be perfectly equalized and assimilated in their possessions, their opinions, and their passions.

A republic, by which I mean a government in which the scheme of representation takes place, opens a different prospect and promises the cure for which we are seeking. Let us examine the points in which it varies from pure democracy, and we shall comprehend both the nature of the cure and the efficacy which it must derive from the Union.

The two great points of difference between a democracy and a republic are: first, the delegation of the government, in the latter, to a small number of citizens elected by the rest; secondly, the greater number of citizens and greater sphere of country over which the latter may be extended.

The effect of the first difference is, on the one hand, to refine and enlarge the public views by passing them through the medium of a chosen body of citizens, whose wisdom may best discern the true interest of their country and whose patriotism and love of justice will be least likely to sacrifice it to temporary or partial considerations. Under such a regulation it may well happen that the public voice, pronounced by the representatives of the people, will be more consonant to the public good than if pronounced by the people themselves, convened for the purpose. On the other hand, the effect may be inverted. Men of factious tempers, of local prejudices, or of sinister designs, may, by intrigue, by corruption, or by other means, first obtain the suffrages, and then betray the interests of the people. The question resulting is, whether small or extensive republics are most favorable to the election of proper guardians of the public weal; and it is clearly decided in favor of the latter by two obvious considerations.

In the first place it is to be remarked that however small the republic may be the representatives must be raised to a certain number in order to guard against the cabals of a few; and that however large it may be they must be limited to a certain number in order to guard against the confusion of a multitude. Hence, the number of representatives in the two cases not being in proportion to that of the constituents, and being proportionally greatest in the small republic, it follows that if the proportion of fit characters be not less in the large than in the small republic, the former will present a greater option, and consequently a greater probability of a fit choice.

In the next place, as each representative will be chosen by a greater number of citizens in the large than in the small republic, it will be more difficult for unworthy candidates to practice with success the vicious arts by which elections are too often carried; and the suffrages of the people being more free, will be more likely to center on men who possess the most attractive merit and the most diffusive and established characters.

It must be confessed that in this, as in most other cases, there is a mean, on both sides of which inconveniencies will be found to lie. By enlarging too much the number of electors, you render the representative too little acquainted with all their local circumstances and lesser interests; as by reducing it too much, you render him unduly attached to these, and too little fit to comprehend and pursue great and national objects. The federal Constitution forms a happy combination in this respect; the great and aggregate interests being referred to the national, the local and particular to the State legislatures.

The other point of difference is the greater number of citizens and extent of territory which may be brought within the compass of republican than of democratic government; and it is this circumstance principally which renders factious combinations less to be dreaded in the former than in the latter. The smaller the society, the fewer probably will be the distinct parties and interests composing it; the fewer the distinct parties and interests, the more frequently will a majority be found of the same party; and the smaller the number of individuals composing a majority, and the smaller the compass within which they are placed, the more easily will they concert and execute their plans of oppression. Extend the sphere and you take in a greater variety of parties and interests; you make it less probable that a majority of the whole will have a common motive to invade the rights of other citizens; or if such a common motive exists, it will be more difficult for all who feel it to discover their own strength and to act in unison with each other. Besides other impediments, it may be remarked that, where there is a consciousness of unjust or dishonorable purposes, communication is always checked by distrust in proportion to the number whose concurrence is necessary.

Hence, it clearly appears that the same advantage which a republic has over a democracy in controlling the effects of faction is enjoyed by a large over a small republic—is enjoyed by the Union over the States composing it. Does this advantage consist in the substitution of representatives whose enlightened views and virtuous sentiments render them superior to local prejudices and to schemes of injustice? It will not be denied that the representation of the Union will be most likely to possess these requisite endowments. Does it consist in the greater security afforded by a greater variety of parties, against the event of any one party being able to outnumber and oppress the rest? In an equal degree does the increased variety of parties comprised within the Union increase this security. Does it, in fine, consist in the greater obstacles opposed to the concert and accomplishment of the secret wishes of an unjust and interested majority? Here again the extent of the Union gives it the most palpable advantage.

The influence of factious leaders may kindle a flame within their particular States but will be unable to spread a general conflagration through the other States. A religious sect may degenerate into a political faction in a part of the Confederacy; but the variety of sects dispersed over the entire face of it must secure the national councils against any danger from that source. A rage for paper money, for an abolition of debts, for an equal division of property, or for any other improper or wicked project, will be less apt to pervade the whole body of the Union than a particular member of it, in the same proportion as such a malady is more likely to taint a particular county or district than an entire State.

In the extent and proper structure of the Union, therefore, we behold a republican remedy for the diseases most incident to republican government. And according to the degree of pleasure and pride we feel in being republicans ought to be our zeal in cherishing the spirit and supporting the character of federalists.

To what expedient, then, shall we finally resort, for maintaining in practice the necessary partition of power among the several departments as laid down in the Constitution? The only answer that can be given is that as all these exterior provisions are found to be inadequate the defect must be supplied, by so contriving the interior structure of the government as that its several constituent parts may, by their mutual relations, be the means of keeping each other in their proper places. Without presuming to undertake a full development of this important idea I will hazard a few general observations which may perhaps place it in a clearer light, and enable us to form a more correct judgment of the principles and structure of the government planned by the convention.

In order to lay a due foundation for that separate and distinct exercise of the different powers of government, which to a certain extent is admitted on all hands to be essential to the preservation of liberty, it is evident that each department should have a will of its own; and consequently should be so constituted that the members of each should have as little agency as possible in the appointment of the members of the others. Were this principle rigorously adhered to, it would require that all the appointments for the supreme executive, legislative, and judiciary magistracies should be drawn from the same fountain of authority, the people, through channels having no communication whatever with one another. Perhaps such a plan of constructing the several departments would be less difficult in practice than it may in contemplation appear. Some difficulties, however, and some additional expense would attend the execution of it. Some deviations, therefore, from the principle must be admitted. In the constitution of the judiciary department in particular, it might be inexpedient to insist rigorously on the principle: first, because peculiar qualifications being essential in the members, the primary consideration ought to be to select that mode of choice which best secures these qualifications; second, because the permanent tenure by which the appointments are held in that department must soon destroy all sense of dependence on the authority conferring them.

It is equally evident that the members of each department should be as little dependent as possible on those of the others for the emoluments annexed to their offices. Were the executive magistrate, or the judges, not independent of the legislature in this particular, their independence in every other would be merely nominal.

But the great security against a gradual concentration of the several powers in the same department consists in giving to those who administer each department the necessary constitutional means and personal motives to resist encroachments of the others. The provision for defense must in this, as in all other cases, be made commensurate to the danger of attack. Ambition must be made to counteract ambition. The interest of the man must be connected with the constitutional rights of the place. It may be a reflection on human nature that such devices should be necessary to control the abuses of government. But what is government itself but the greatest of all reflections on human nature? If men were angels, no government would be necessary. If angels were to govern men, neither external nor internal controls on government would be necessary. In framing a government which is to be administered by men over men, the great difficulty lies in this: you must first enable the government to control the governed; and in the next place oblige it to control itself. A dependence on the people is, no doubt, the primary control on the government; but experience has taught mankind the necessity of auxiliary precautions.

This policy of supplying, by opposite and rival interests, the defect of better motives, might be traced through the whole system of human affairs, private as well as public. We see it particularly displayed in all the subordinate distributions of power, where the constant aim is to divide and arrange the several offices in such a manner as that each may be a check on the other—that the private interest of every individual may be a sentinel over the public rights. These inventions of prudence cannot be less requisite in the distribution of the supreme powers of the State.

But it is not possible to give to each department an equal power of self-defense. In republican government, the legislative authority necessarily predominates. The remedy for this inconveniency is to divide the legislature into different branches; and to render them, by different modes of election and different principles of action, as little connected with each other as the nature of their common functions and their common dependence on the society will admit. It may even be necessary to guard against dangerous encroachments by still further precautions. As the weight of the legislative authority requires that it should be thus divided, the weakness of the executive may require, on the other hand, that it should be fortified. An absolute negative on the legislature appears, at first view, to be the natural defense with which the executive magistrate should be armed. But perhaps it would be neither altogether safe nor alone sufficient. On ordinary occasions it might not be exerted with the requisite firmness, and on extraordinary occasions it might be perfidiously abused. May not this defect of an absolute negative be supplied by some qualified connection between this weaker department and the weaker branch of the stronger department, by which the latter may be led to support the constitutional rights of the former, without being too much detached from the rights of its own department?

If the principles on which these observations are found be just, as I persuade myself they are, and they be applied as a criterion to the several State constitutions, and the federal Constitution, it will be found that if the latter does not perfectly correspond with them, the former are infinitely less able to bear such a test.

There are, moreover, two considerations particularly applicable to the federal system of America, which place that system in a very interesting point of view.

First. In a single republic, all the power surrendered by the people is submitted to the administration of a single government; and the usurpations are guarded against by a division of the government into distinct and separate departments. In the compound republic of America, the power surrendered by the people is first divided between two distinct governments, and then the portion allotted to each subdivided among distinct and separate departments. Hence a double security arises to the rights of the people. The different governments will control each other, at the same time that each will be controlled by itself.

Second. It is of great importance in a republic not only to guard the society against the oppression of its rulers, but to guard one part of the society against the injustice of the other part. Different interests necessarily exist in different classes of citizens. If a majority be united by a common interest, the rights of the minority will be insecure. There are but two methods of providing against this evil: the one by creating a will in the community independent of the majority—that is, of the society itself; the other, by comprehending in the society so many separate descriptions of citizens as will render an unjust combination of a majority of the whole very improbable, if not impracticable. The first method prevails in all governments possessing an hereditary or self-appointed authority. This, at best, is but a precarious security; because a power independent of the society may as well espouse the unjust views of the major as the rightful interests of the minor party, and may possibly be turned against both parties. The second method will be exemplified in the federal republic of the United States. Whilst all authority in it will be derived from and dependent on the society, the society itself will be broken into so many parts, interests and classes of citizens, that the rights of individuals, or of the minority, will be in little danger from interested combinations of the majority. In a free government the security for civil rights must be the same as that for religious rights. It consists in the one case in the multiplicity of interests, and in the other in the multiplicity of sects. The degree of security in both cases will depend on the number of interests and sects; and this may be presumed to depend on the extent of country and number of people comprehended under the same government. This view of the subject must particularly recommend a proper federal system to all the sincere and considerate friends of republican government, since it shows that in exact proportion as the territory of the Union may be formed into more circumscribed Confederacies, or States, oppressive combinations of a majority will be facilitated; the best security, under the republican forms, for the rights of every class of citizen, will be diminished; and consequently the stability and independence of some member of the government, the only other security, must be proportionally increased. Justice is the end of government. It is the end of civil society. It ever has been and ever will be pursued until it be obtained, or until liberty be lost in the pursuit. In a society under the forms of which the stronger faction can readily unite and oppress the weaker, anarchy may as truly be said to reign as in a state of nature, where the weaker individual is not secured against the violence of the stronger; and as, in the latter state, even the stronger individuals are prompted, by the uncertainty of their condition, to submit to a government which may protect the weak as well as themselves; so, in the former state, will the more powerful factions or parties be gradually induced, by a like motive, to wish for a government which will protect all parties, the weaker as well as the more powerful. It can be little doubted that if the State of Rhode Island was separated from the Confederacy and left to itself, the insecurity of rights under the popular form of government within such narrow limits would be displayed by such reiterate oppressions of factious majorities that some power altogether independent of the people would soon be called for by the voice of the very factions whose misrule had proved the necessity of it. In the extended republic of the United States, and among the great variety of interests, parties, and sects which it embraces, a coalition of a majority of the whole society could seldom take place on any other principles than those of justice and the general good; whilst there being thus less danger to a minor from the will of a major party, there must be less pretext, also, to provide for the security of the former, by introducing into the government a will not dependent on the latter, or, in other words, a will independent of the society itself. It is no less certain than it is important, notwithstanding the contrary opinions which have been entertained, that the larger the society, provided it lie within a practicable sphere, the more duly capable it will be of self-government. And happily for the *republican cause,* the practicable sphere may be carried to a very great extent by a judicious modification and mixture of the *federal principle.*

ABRAHAM LINCOLN'S GETTYSBURG ADDRESS

Four score and seven years ago our fathers brought forth on this continent a new nation, conceived in liberty and dedicated to the proposition that all men are created equal. Now we are engaged in a great Civil War, testing whether that nation or any nation so conceived and so dedicated can long endure. We are met on a great battlefield of that war. We have come to dedicate a portion of that field as a final resting place for those who here gave their lives that that nation might live. It is altogether fitting and proper that we should do this. But in a larger sense, we cannot dedicate—we cannot consecrate—we cannot hallow this ground. The brave men, living and dead, who struggled here have consecrated it far above our poor power to add or detract. The world will little note nor long remember what we say here, but it can never forget what they did here. It is for us the living, rather, to be dedicated here to the unfinished work which they who fought here have thus far so nobly advanced. It is rather for us to be here dedicated to the great task remaining before us—that from these honored dead we take increased devotion to that cause for which they gave the last full measure of devotion—that we here highly resolve that these dead shall not have died in vain, that this nation, under God, shall have a new birth of freedom, and that government of the people, by the people, for the people shall not perish from the earth.

NOTES

Chapter 1

1. Robin Toner, "Voters are Very Settled, Intense, and Partisan, and It's Only July," *New York Times,* July 25, 2004, 1.

2. Ibid.

3. Marco R. della Cava, "Just Vote," *USA Today,* August 3, 200, D1.

4. Ibid.

5. U.S. Census Bureau, *Statistical Abstract of the United States, 2003* (Washington, D.C.: Government Printing Office, 2004), tab. 419.

6. Poll conducted by the Institute of Politics at Harvard, April, 2004. Bill Straub, "The Sleeping Giants," *Champaign-Urbana News-Gazette,* May 2, 2004, B1.

7. Poll conducted by the Leon and Sylvia Panetta Institute. "Campus Apathy," *Champaign-Urbana News-Gazette,* June 13, 2004, A7.

8. The most infamous episode was in November 1917 at the Occoquan Workhouse in Virginia.

9. See John Hibbing and Beth Theiss-Morse, *Congress as Public Enemy: Public Attitudes toward American Political Institutions* (Cambridge: Cambridge University Press, 1995); John Hibbing and Beth Theiss-Morse, "Civics Is Not Enough: Teaching Barbarics in K–12," *PS,* March 1996, 57–62.

10. Hibbing and Theiss-Morse, *Congress.*

11. *Federalist Paper* 2.

12. Gore Vidal, "Coached by Camelot," *New Yorker,* December 1, 1997, 88.

13. Walt Whitman, Preface to *Leaves of Grass* (1855), in *Leaves of Grass and Selected Prose,* ed. Lawrence Buell (New York: Random House, 1981), 449.

14. Edward Countryman, *Americans: A Collision of Histories* (New York: Hill & Wang, 1996).

15. John Sugden, *Tecumseh: A Life* (New York: Holt, 1998).

16. U.S. Immigration and Naturalization Service, *2000 Statistical Yearbook of the Immigration and Naturalization Service* (Washington, D.C.: Government Printing Office, 2000). These are estimates; the government has not collected emigration data since 1957.

17. Census Bureau, *Statistical Abstract, 2003,* tab. 51.

18. U.S. Census Bureau, "The Foreign-Born Population in the United States," March 2000, 1 (www.census.gov).

19. U.S. Office of Immigration Statistics, "Immigrants," in *2002 Yearbook of Immigration Statistics* (Washington, D.C.: Department of Homeland Security, 2002), tab. 3 (uscis.gov); Nancy F. Rytina, *Estimates of the Legal Permanent Resident Population and Population Eligible to Naturalize in 2003* (Washington, D.C.: Department of Homeland Security, 2004), tab. 3 (uscis.gov).

20. Office of Immigration Statistics, "Immigrants," tab. 6.

21. George F. Will, "Buchanan Takes Aim," *Washington Post National Weekly Edition,* December 16, 1991, 28

22. *The Christian American,* quoted in Dick Kirschten, "Building Blocs," *National Journal,* September 26, 1993, 2173.

23. James Q. Wilson, "The History and Future of Democracy," lecture delivered at the Ronald Reagan Presidential Library, November 15, 1999.

24. "Religion and the Founding of the American Republic. Part I: America as a Religious Refuge: The Seventeenth Century," Library of Congress exhibit (lcweb.loc.gov/exhibits/religion).

25. Nicholas von Hoffman, "God Was Present at the Founding," *Civilization* (April–May 1998), 39–42.

26. Michael J. Sandel, *Democracy's Discontent: America in Search of a Public Philosophy* (Cambridge, Mass.: Belknap Press, 1997), 56–57.

27. Sarah Mondale and Sarah B. Patton, eds., *School: The Story of American Public Education* (Boston: Beacon Press, 2001), 36.

28. Elizabeth Becker, "All White, All Christian, and Divided by Diversity," *New York Times,* June 10, 2001, sec. 4, 7. Becker was writing about her hometown.

29. Census Bureau, *Statistical Abstract, 2003,* tabs. 79, 80. These numbers are derived from self-reports because the Census Bureau does not collect data on religious affiliation.

30. On identity politics, see Walter Benn Michaels, *Our America: Nativism, Modernism, and Pluralism* (Durham, N.C.: Duke University Press, 1997).

31. Census Bureau, *Statistical Abstract, 2003,* tab. 62.

32. U.S. Census Bureau, *General Social and Economic Characteristics :U.S. Summary* (Washington, D.C.: Government Printing Office, 1990), pt. 1, tab. 12.

33. Michael Lind, "The Beige and the Black," *New York Times Magazine,* August 16, 1998, 38; Randall Kennedy, *Interracial Intimacies* (New York: Pantheon, 2003).

34. The origins of governmental systems are discussed by John Jay in *Federalist Paper* 2.

35. Garry Wills, *Lincoln at Gettysburg: The Words That Remade America* (New York: Simon & Schuster, 1992), 145.

36. Carl F. Kaestle, "Introduction," in *School,* ed. Mondale and Patton, 13.

37. Ibid., 16.

38. Brian Friel, "Don't Know Much about History," *National Journal,* August 2, 2003, 2500–2501.

39. "The Educated Citizen," in *School,* ed. Mondale and Patton, 22.

40. Robert Reinhold, "Resentment against New Immigrants," *New York Times,* October 26, 1986, 6E.

41. Michael Thompson, Richard Ellis, and Aaron Wildavsky, *Cultural Theory* (Boulder, Colo.: Westview, 1990), 216.

42. For a discussion of the Declaration of Independence's origins in pragmatism versus the political philosophy of the Founders, see Pauline Maier, *American Scripture: Making the Declaration of Independence* (New York: Knopf, 1997).

43. Wilfred M. McClay, "Communitarianism and the Federal Idea," in *Community and Political Thought Today,* ed. Peter Augustine Lawler and Dale McConkey (Westport, Conn.: Praeger, 1998), 102.

44. Alexis de Tocqueville, *Democracy in America* (New York: Knopf, 1945; originally published 1835).

45. Quoted in Anthony Lewis, "Hail and Farewell," *New York Times,* December 15, 2001, A31.

46. This discussion draws on Sidney Verba and Norman Nie, *Participation in America* (New York: Harper & Row, 1972), and Stephen Earl Bennett and Linda L. M. Bennett, "Political Participation," in *Annual Review of Political Science,* ed. Samuel Long (Norwood, N.J.: Ablex, 1986).

47. E. J. Dionne Jr., *Why Americans Hate Politics* (New York: Simon & Schuster, 1991).

48. Robert D. Putnam, *Bowling Alone: The Collapse and Revival of American Community* (New York: Simon & Schuster, 2000).

49. Robert A. Dahl, *A Preface to Democratic Theory* (Chicago: University of Chicago Press, 1956), 142.

50. These ideas are at the core of rival bodies of theory in political science. See especially Robert A. Dahl's classic *Who Governs? Democracy and Power in an American City* (New Haven, Conn.: Yale University Press, 1961) on pluralism; C. Wright Mills, *The Power Elite* (New York: Oxford University Press, 1956); and Michael Parenti, *Democracy for the Few,* 7th ed. (Belmont, Calif.: Wadsworth, 2001), on permanent losers.

51. See Arthur F. Bentley, *The Process of Government* (Chicago: University of Chicago Press, 1908), and David Truman, *The Governmental Process* (New York: Knopf, 1951).

52. Theda Skocpol, *Diminished Democracy: From Membership to Management in American Civic Life* (Norman: Oklahoma University Press, 2003).

53. The modern statement of this idea began with Robert Michels, who formulated the "iron law of oligarchy" in *Political Parties: A Sociological Study of the Oligarchical Tendencies of Modern Democracy,* trans. Eden and Cedar Paul (New York: Hearst International, 1915; originally published 1911).

54. Parenti, *Democracy for the Few.*

55. The classic work is Mills's *Power Elite.*

56. Louis D. Brandeis, "The Opportunity in the Law," address to the Harvard Ethical Society, May 4, 1905.

57. Russell Baker, "That Insolent Weld," *New York Times,* August 26, 1997, A19. *Champaign-Urbana News-Gazette,* August 29, 1997, A4.

58. Robert Wright, "Hyper Democracy," *Time,* January 23, 1995, 18.

59. David S. Broder, "Can We Govern?" *Washington Post National Weekly Edition,* January 31, 1994, 23.

60. Hedrick Smith, *The Power Game: How Washington Works* (New York: Random House, 1988) ch. 17.

61. For example, see Theodore J. Lowi, *The End of Liberalism,* 2nd ed. (New York: Norton, 1979).

62. Joseph Schumpeter, *Capitalism, Socialism, and Democracy* (New York: Harper Bros., 1950).

63. E. E. Schattschneider, *The Semisovereign People* (New York: Holt, Rinehart and Winston, 1960), 141.

64. League of Conservative Voters poll, March 2002.

65. Theda Skocpol, "Will 9/11 and the War on Terror Revitalize American Civic Democracy?" *PS,* September 2002, 537.

66. E. J. Dionne Jr., "Preferring Policies over Politics," *Washington Post National Weekly Edition,* February 7, 2000, 22.

67. Alan Wolfe, "Couch Potato Politics," *New York Times,* March 15, 1998, sec. 4, 17.

68. Polls conducted by the Harwood Institute and by *Time* and the Cable News Network, January 2002.

69. Skocpol, "Will 9/11 . . . ?" 539; Putnam, *Bowling Together.*

Chapter 2

1. Nixon hoped he might be considered an American Disraeli. Benjamin Disraeli was a British prime minister in the nineteenth century known for his progressive ideas. Nixon admired Robert Blake's biography of Disraeli, and mentioning this to a Attorney General Elliot Richardson in 1971, Richardson replied, "The similarities are great, Mr. President, but what a pity that Blake could not quote Disraeli's conversations." That Nixon did not destroy the tapes even after they became a liability can appar-

ently be attributed to this reason. Sidney Blumenthal, "The Longest Campaign," *New Yorker,* August 8, 1994, 37.

2. *United States v. Reynolds,* 345 U.S. 1 (1953).

3. The Indians, of course, had their own governments, and the Spanish may have established Saint Augustine, Florida, and Santa Fe, New Mexico, before the English established Jamestown. The Spanish settlements were extensions of Spanish colonization of Mexico and were governed by Spanish officials in Mexico City.

4. This is not to suggest that the Pilgrims believed in democracy. Apparently, they were motivated to draft the compact by threats from some on the *Mayflower* that when the ship landed they would "use their owne libertie; for none had power to command them." Thus the compact was designed to bind them to the laws of the colony. Richard Shenkman, "*I Love Paul Revere, Whether He Rode or Not*" (New York: HarperCollins, 1991), 141–142.

5. David Hawke, *A Transaction of Free Men* (New York: Scribner, 1964), 209.

6. William H. Riker, *Federalism* (Boston: Little, Brown, 1964), 18–20.

7. For an account of the foreign affairs problems under the Articles of Confederation, see Frederick W. Marks III, *Independence on Trial: Foreign Affairs and the Making of the Constitution* (Baton Rouge: Louisiana State University Press, 1973).

8. Louis Fisher, *President and Congress* (New York: Free Press, 1972), 14.

9. The government under the Articles, however, could boast one major accomplishment: the Northwest Ordinance, adopted in 1787, provided for the government and future statehood of the land west of Pennsylvania (land that would become most of the Great Lakes states). The law also banned slavery in this territory.

10. Gordon S. Wood, "The Origins of the Constitution," *This Constitution: A Bicentennial Chronicle,* Summer 1987, 10–11.

11. Eric Black, *Our Constitution* (Boulder, Colo.: Westview Press, 1988), 6.

12. For development of this idea, see Kenneth M. Dolbeare and Linda J. Medcalf, "The Political Economy of the Constitution," *This Constitution: A Bicentennial Chronicle,* Spring 1987, 4–10.

13. Black, *Our Constitution,* 59.

14. The Constitution would, however, retain numerous positive aspects of the Articles. See Donald S. Lutz, "The Articles of Confederation as the Background to the Federal Republic," *Publius* 20 (Winter 1990), 55–70.

15. Robert McCloskey, *The American Supreme Court* (Chicago: University of Chicago Press, 1960), 29.

16. Fred Barbash, "James Madison: A Man for the '80s," *Washington Post National Weekly Edition,* March 30, 1987, 23.

17. Robert A. Dahl, *A Preface to Democratic Theory* (Chicago: University of Chicago Press, 1956), 5. Yet according to a poll in 1987, the bicentennial of the Constitution, only 1 percent of the public identified Madison as the one who played the biggest role in creating the Constitution. Most—31 percent—said Thomas Jefferson, who was a diplomat in France during the convention. Black, *Our Constitution,* 15.

18. Some argue that Hamilton, rather than Madison, was the driving force behind the Constitution, especially if his efforts after ratification—as an influential member of Washington's cabinet and later—are taken into account. Kenneth M. Dolbeare and Linda Medcalf, "The Dark Side of the Constitution," in *The Case Against the Constitution: From the Antifederalists to the Present,* ed. Kenneth M. Dolbeare and John F. Manley (Armonk, N.Y.: Sharpe, 1987), 120–141.

19. Robert A. Dahl, *How Democratic Is the American Constitution?* (New Haven, Conn.: Yale University Press, 2001), 7.

20. Gouverneur Morris, of Pennsylvania. Dahl, *How Democratic,* 11–12.

21. Dahl, *How Democratic,* 11–12.

22. Ibid., 14.

23. Paul Finkelman, "Slavery at the Philadelphia Convention," *This Constitution: A Bicentennial Chronicle* (1987), 25–30.

24. Ibid., 29.

25. Ibid., 18.

26. Quoted in Thomas G. West, *Vindicating the Founders: Race, Sex, Class, and Justice in the Origins of America* (Lanham, Md.: Rowman & Littlefield, 1997), 15.

27. Theodore J. Lowi, *American Government* (Hinsdale, Ill.: Dryden, 1976), 97.

28. Quoted in C. Herman Pritchett, *Constitutional Law of the Federal System* (Englewood Cliffs, N.J.: Prentice Hall, 1984), xi.

29. Quoted in Richard Hofstadter, *The American Political Tradition* (New York: Random House, 1948), 13.

30. Quoted in Richard Hofstadter, The American Political Tradition (New York: Vintage, 1948), 6-7.

31. *Federalist Paper 51.*

32. *Federalist Paper 47.*

33. Max Farrand, *The Framing of the Constitution of the United States* (New Haven, Conn.: Yale University Press, 1913).

34. Charles O. Jones, *The Presidency in a Separated System* (Washington, D.C.: Brookings Institution, 1994), 14.

35. Charles O. Jones, *Separate but Equal Branches* (Chatham, N.J.: Chatham House, 1995), 12.

36. *Federalist Paper 51.*

37. Jones, *Presidency in a Separated System,* 16, thus modifying Neustadt's classic definition of "a government of separated institutions sharing powers." Richard E. Neustadt, *Presidential Power and the Modern Presidents* (New York: Macmillan, 1990), 29.

38. For elaboration, see Dahl, *How Democratic Is the American Constitution?* 24–25.

39. Ibid.

40. Seymour Martin Lipset, "Why No Socialism in the United States?" in *Sources of Contemporary Radicalism,* ed. Seweryn Bialer and Sophis Sluzar (Boulder, Colo.: Westview Press, 1977), 86.

41. These were not the only reasons people migrated to America, of course, but these were the primary ones. For development of this idea, see John W. Kingdon, *America the Unusual* (Boston: Bedford St. Martin's, 1999), 58–63. After the Revolutionary War, many Americans who were sympathetic to England and more comfortable with authority moved to Canada. At the same time, some Canadians who were more individualistic moved to the United States, thus reinforcing the original migration pattern.

42. For elaboration, see West, *Vindicating the Founders,* 43–54.

43. Donald S. Lutz, "The Relative Influence of European Writers on Later Eighteenth-Century American Political Thought," *American Political Science Review* 78 (1984), 139–197.

44. Alpheus T. Mason and Richard H. Leach, *In Quest of Freedom: American Political Thought and Practice,* 2nd ed. (Englewood Cliffs, N.J.: Prentice Hall, 1973), 51.

45. For development of this idea, see Martin Landau, "A Self-Correcting System: The Constitution of the United States," *This Constitution: A Bicentennial Chronicle* (Summer 1986), 4–10.

46. John P. Roche, "The Founding Fathers: A Reform Caucus in Action," *American Political Science Review* 56 (1962), 799–816.

47. Benjamin F. Wright Jr., "The Origins of the Separation of Powers in America," in *Origins of American Political Thought,* ed. John P. Roche (New York: Harper & Row, 1967), 139–162.

48. John R. Roche, "The Founding Fathers: A Reform Caucus in Action," *American Political Science Review* 55 (December, 1961), 805.

49. James MacGregor Burns, *The Vineyard of Liberty* (New York: Knopf, 1982), 33.

50. Bernard Bailyn, *Voyagers to the West* (New York: Knopf, 1982), 20.

51. The Boston Tea Party, contrary to myth, was not prompted by higher taxes on British tea. Parliament lowered the taxes to give the British East India Company, facing bankruptcy, an advantage in the colonial market. This threatened American shippers who smuggled tea from Holland and controlled about three-fourths of the market. The shippers resented Parliament's attempt to manipulate the economy from thousands of miles away. Shenkman, "*I Love Paul Revere,*" 155.

52. *Federalist Paper 10.*

53. Black, *Our Constitution,* 21.

54. For elaboration, see Dolbeare and Medcalf, "Dark Side of the Constitution."

55. Calvin C. Jillson and Cecil L. Eubanks, "The Political Structure of Constitution Making," *American Journal of Political Science* 29 (1984), 435–458.

56. Jonathan Elliot, *The Debates in the Several State Conventions on the Adoption of the Federal Constitution as Recommended by the General Convention at Philadelphia, in 1787,* 2nd ed., 5 vols. (Philadelphia, 1896), 2: 102.

57. On Anti-Federalist thinking, see William B. Allen and Gordon Lloyd, eds., *The Essential Antifederalist,* 2nd ed. (Lanham, Md.: University Press of America, 2002); John F. Manley and Kenneth M. Dolbeare, *The Case against the Constitution* (Armonk, N.Y.: Sharpe, 1987).

58. Richard S. Randall, *American Constitutional Development,* vol. 1, *The Powers of Government* (New York: Longman, 2002), 54.

59. "A Fundamental Contentment," *This Constitution: A Bicentennial Chronicle* (Fall 1984), 44.

60. Quoted in Charles Warren, *The Making of the Constitution* (Boston: Little, Brown, 1928), xiv. Jefferson made this observation from afar, as he was serving as ambassador to France at the time of the Constitutional Convention.

61. Keith Perine, "Congress Shows Little Enthusiasm for Bush's Marriage Amendment," *CQ Weekly* (February 28, 2004), 533.

62. Alan P. Grimes, *Democracy and the Amendments to the Constitution* (Lexington, Mass.: Lexington Books, 1978). Grimes also shows how the adoption of new amendments reflects the rise of new power blocs in society.

63. This discussion borrows heavily from George P. Fletcher, *Our Secret Constitution: How Lincoln Redefined American Democracy* (New York: Oxford University Press, 2001); Bruce Ackerman, *We the People,* vol. 2, *Transformations* (Cambridge, Mass.: Belknap Press, 1998); and Garry Wills, *Lincoln at Gettysburg* (New York: Simon & Schuster, 1992). For a complementary view, see Charles Black, *A New Birth of Freedom: Human Rights, Named and Unnamed* (New York: Grosset/Putnam, 1997). For a somewhat different view about the impact of the New Deal, see G. Edward White, *The Constitution and the New Deal* (Cambridge, Mass.: Harvard University Press, 2001).

64. Historian James McPherson, quoted in Fletcher, *Our Secret Constitution,* 57; Ackerman, *We the People,* 10.

65. Many of Lincoln's prejudicial comments came in response to more blatant racist remarks by his opponents. Lincoln abandoned his support for black emigration before he was elected to a second term as president. For a critical perspective on Lincoln's racial views, see Lerone Bennett Jr., *Forced into Glory: Abraham Lincoln's White Dream* (Chicago: Johnson, 2000). For a positive perspective, see William Lee Miller, *Lincoln's Virtues: An Ethical Biography* (New York: Knopf, 2002).

66. Fletcher, *Our Secret Constitution,* 24.

67. John Hope Franklin, *From Slavery to Freedom,* 3rd ed. (New York: Vintage, 1969), 283.

68. The proclamation also prompted European workers, who were attracted to the idea of laborers

around the world gaining more freedom, to rally to the Union's cause. Ibid., 283.

69. These paragraphs rely on the interpretations of Wills, *Lincoln at Gettysburg,* and Fletcher, *Our Secret Constitution.*

70. Fletcher, *Our Secret Constitution,* 53.

71. A precursor of this view was the era of Jacksonian democracy in the 1830s.

72. A contemporary celebration of the nation as an entity can be seen in the poetry of Walt Whitman.

73. Wills, *Lincoln at Gettysburg,* 38. Wills insists that this was not a coincidence, and he debunks the notion that Lincoln hastily dashed off his remarks while on his way to the town or to the speech itself (27–31).

74. Fletcher, *Our Secret Constitution,* 35, 4. Others might nominate Lincoln's second inaugural address, in which he offered reconciliation to the South, or Martin Luther King Jr.'s "I Have a Dream" speech.

75. The *Dred Scott* case is explained in Chapters 13 and 15.

76. The equal protection clause is covered fully in Chapter 15, and the due process clause is covered fully in Chapter 14.

77. Fletcher, *Our Secret Constitution,* 25.

78. In this vein, Congress first experimented with an income tax during the war. It would return to this tax in the decades after the war.

79. There was a debate about the validity of the Thirteenth Amendment and especially the Fourteenth, much as there had been about the validity of the Constitutional Convention and the Constitution for bypassing the procedures for amendment established by the Articles of Confederation. Congress conditioned the slave states' reentry into the Union upon their ratification of the Fourteenth Amendment. Otherwise, not enough states would have ratified the amendment. Yet one legal scholar argues that Congress served as a quasi constitutional convention in which members, like Lincoln before them, sensed that they were reinventing rather than following the Constitution. Their actions would have been thwarted if the public had opposed them. Ackerman, *We the People,* ch. 6–8.

880. For example, the abolitionist movement and the Fifteenth Amendment would fuel the drive for women's suffrage, as explained in Chapter 15.

81. This section borrows heavily from Ackerman, *We the People,* and Theodore J. Lowi, *The Personal President* (Ithaca, N.Y.: Cornell University Press, 1985).

82. We never had a pure laissez-faire approach—there always was some governmental regulation—but this is the term most associated with the attitudes of the time.

83. At least one legal scholar dismisses the notion that the Court's "old men" were reactionaries or fools. Although today people consider them mistaken, at the time they were following established doctrine. Ackerman, *We the People.*

84. Elaboration of and sources for these statements can be found in Chapter 13.

85. The Court said he did affect the market slightly because he did not buy the twelve acres' worth of wheat that he would have needed if he had obeyed the order. The Court's main point, however, was that Congress has the authority to pass such laws. *Wickard* v. *Filburn,* 317 U.S. 111 (1942).

86. Lowi, *Personal President,* 49. Writers during the Depression and in the decades after it also recognized this as a revolution. Ernest K. Lindley, *The Roosevelt Revolution, First Phase* (New York: Viking, 1933); Mario Einaudi, *The Roosevelt Revolution* (New York: Harcourt, Brace & World, 1959).

87. Karl Vick, "A President Who Woke Up Washington," *Washington Post National Weekly Edition,* April 28, 1997, 8.

88. Ibid., 9.

89. Lowi, *Personal President,* 44.

90. Ibid., xi.

91. This era also saw a shift to a more presidency-centered government that persists to a significant degree today. Lowi, *Personal President.*

92. President Ronald Reagan in the 1980s and congressional Republicans in the early 1990s mounted the biggest challenges to the changes initiated by the Depression and the New Deal, as will be discussed in later chapters.

93. Of course, the process was evolutionary; the changes did not spring solely from these two crises. Moreover, some might maintain that the Supreme Court under the leadership of Chief Justice Earl Warren in the 1950s and 1960s also remade the Constitution because of its rulings expanding the Bill of Rights. Yet the changes brought about by the Warren Court probably had less impact overall than those wrought by Reconstruction or the New Deal.

94. For a discussion of the role played by the philosophy of pragmatism in resolving these conflicts, see Fletcher, *Our Secret Constitution,* ch. 11.

95. West, *Vindicating the Founders,* xi.

96. Parts of the Constitution have been copied by some Latin America countries, Liberia (founded by Americans), and the Philippines (formerly an American territory).

97. "South Africa Looks at U.S. Constitution," *Lincoln Journal-Star,* October 7, 1990; David Remnick, " 'We, the People,' from the Russian," *Washington Post National Weekly Edition,* September 10, 1990, 11.

98. European countries, Australia, Canada, Costa Rica, Israel, Japan, and New Zealand.

99. Dahl, *How Democratic . . . ?* tabs. 1 and 2, 164–165. Dahl counts only countries that have "strong" federalism, bicameralism, and judicial review.

100. Jones, *Presidency in a Separated System,* xiii.

101. Dahl, *How Democratic . . . ?* 115.

102. Jones, *Presidency in a Separated System,* 3.

103. Kingdon, *America the Unusual,* 7–22. Exceptions include education and regulation of civil rights and the environment. They also include a massive national defense establishment and an extensive criminal justice system. In these aspects, our government is bigger than in many other advanced industrialized countries.

104. Richard Morin, "Happy Days Are Here Again," *Washington Post National Weekly Edition,* August 25, 1997, 38.

105. About 25 percent split their ticket between candidates for president and representative. In addition, others split their vote between candidates for president and senator or between candidates for representative and senator. For an examination of the research about divided government, see Morris Fiorina, *Divided Government,* 2nd ed. (Boston: Allyn & Bacon, 1996), 153.

106. Lewis Lapham, "Get Me Rewrite!" *New York Times Book Review,* February 4, 1996, 11.

107. 418 U.S. 683 (1974).

108. For a contemporary analysis of executive privilege, see Mark J. Rozell, *Executive Privilege,* 2nd ed. (Lawrence: University of Kansas, 2002).

109. Jeffrey Toobin, *A Vast Conspiracy* (New York: Touchstone, 1999), 333–334.

110. Jeb Stuart Magruder. "Ex-Aide: Nixon Ordered Watergate Break-In," *Lincoln Journal Star,* July 27, 2003.

111. Tip O'Neill with William Novak, *Man of the House* (New York: Random House, 1987). The tapes did contain some useful advice for future presidents. Unfortunately, this advice, on tapes not released until 1999, came too late for President Clinton: "Frankly, we shouldn't have had those interns. They're a pain in the ass." "Verbatim," *Time* October 18, 1999 35.

112. Bob Woodward and Carl Bernstein, *The Final Days* (New York: Simon & Schuster, 1976), 343, 403–404, 423.

113. "Tapes Confirm Nixon Approved Hush Money," *Lincoln Journal-Star,* June 5, 1991. For a survey of presidents' efforts to record their conver-

sations, see William Doyle, *Inside the Oval Office: White House Tapes from FDR to Clinton* (New York: Kodansha, 1999).

Chapter 3

1. The battle between Nevada and Washington over Yucca Mountain is recorded in state and federal documents, press releases, and newspaper stories archived at the state of Nevada Web site (*www.nv.gov*) . Part of this section is based on those materials, including archived articles from the *Las Vegas Review-Journal.*

2. From a position paper issued by the state of Nevada, "Why Does the State Oppose Yucca Mountain?" (www.state.nv.us/nucwaste).

3. See for example, Carole Gallagher, *American Ground Zero: The Secret Nuclear War* (Cambridge, Mass.: MIT Press, 1993).

4. This summary of Guinn's career is from Michael Barone, Richard E. Cohen, Charles E. Cook, and National Journal Group, *Almanac of American Politics, 2002* (Washington, D.C.: National Journal Group, 2001), 943–944.

5. Statement of Governor Kenny C. Guinn before the U. S. Senate Energy and Natural Resources Committee, May 22, 2002, 3-4 (www.state.nv.us/nucwaste).

6. Interview on the *NewsHour with Jim Lehrer,* PBS, July 10, 2002.

7. Barone et al., *Almanac of American Politics, 2002,* 940.

8. Shawn Zeller, "Gambling Millions on Anti-Yucca Lobbying," *National Journal,* June 15, 2002, 1797.

9. William H. Riker, *The Development of American Federalism* (Boston: Kluwer Academic, 1987), 6.

10. The delegate was George Read of Delaware. See William H. Riker, *Democracy in America,* 2nd ed. (New York: Macmillan, 1965).

11. *Federalist Paper* 39.

12. Vernon L. Parrington, *Main Currents in American Thought* (New York: Harcourt, Brace, 1927).

13. David Truman, "Federalism and the Party System," in *Federalism: Mature and Emergent,* ed. Arthur W. MacMahon (New York: Russell & Russell, 1962), 123.

14. Daniel Elazar, *American Federalism: A View from the States,* 3rd ed. (New York: Harper & Row, 1984).

15. U.S. Census Bureau, *Statistical Abstract of the United States, 2003* (Washington, D.C.: Government Printing Office, 2004), tab. 34.

16. All figures in this paragraph from U.S. Census Bureau, *Statistical Abstract of the United States, 2001* (Washington, D.C.: Government Printing Office, 2002), tabs. 20, 23, 24, and 652.

17. Robert S. Erikson, Gerald C. Wright, and John McIver, *Statehouse Democracy: Public Opinion and Policy in the American States* (New York: Cambridge University Press, 1993).

18. See Madison's discussion of this in *Federalist Paper* 39.

19. See Forrest McDonald, *States' Rights and the Union: Imperium in Imperio, 1776–1876* (Lawrence: University Press of Kansas, 2000).

20. A 1976 Supreme Court decision (*National League of Cities* v. *Usery,* 426 U.S. 833) used the Tenth Amendment as a reason to forbid the federal government to extend minimum wage and hour laws to state and local government employees. (This decision was partly overruled in 1985 (in *Garcia* v. *San Antonio Metropolitan Transit Authority,* 469 U.S. 528).

21. Political scientist Howard Gillman, quoted in Linda Greenhouse, "At the Court, Dissent over States' Rights Is Now War," *New York Times,* June 10, 2002, sec. 4, 3.

22. Part of this discussion is drawn from Richard Leach, *American Federalism* (New York: Norton, 1970), ch. 1. See also Christopher Hamilton and

Donald Wells, *Federalism, Power and Political Economy: A New Theory of Federalism's Impact on American Life* (Englewood Cliffs, N.J.: Prentice Hall, 1990).

23. *McCulloch v. Maryland*, 4 Wheat. 316 (1819).

24. *Niles' Register*, May 13, 1819.

25. Alfred Kelly and Winfred Harbeson, *The American Constitution: Its Origins and Development* (New York: Norton, 1976).

26. Daniel Elazar, *The American Partnership* (Chicago: University of Chicago Press, 1962).

27. Perhaps because he is a sociologist, Theodore Caplan did not fully appreciate the extent of federal involvement in Muncie, even in 1924—the support of veterans, schools, roads, and hospitals by federal land grants. Nevertheless, his major point is valid: The federal presence was low-profile in the 1920s. Caplan is quoted in Daniel Walker, *Toward a Functioning Federalism* (Cambridge, Mass.: Winthrop, 1981), 3–4.

28. Timothy Conlan, *From Federalism to Devolution: Twenty-Five Years of Intergovernmental Reform* (Washington, D.C.: Brookings Institution, 1998), 6.

29. John Maggs, "Sorry States," *National Journal*, August 9, 2003, 2538.

30. On Nixon's managerial approach to federalism, see Lawrence D. Brown, *New Policies, New Politics: Government's Response to Government's Growth* (Washington, D.C.: Brookings Institution, 1983). The comparative discussion of Lyndon Johnson's, Richard Nixon's, and Ronald Reagan's federalism policies draws on Conlon, *From New Federalism to Devolution*, ch. 1, 6, and 13.

31. Conlon, *From New Federalism to Devolution*, 109.

32. See, for example, William J. Clinton, "Federalism," Executive Order 13132, *Federal Register* 54, no. 163 (August 10, 1999): 43255–43259. Clinton discussed his views on state activism and federalism in general with the historian Gary Wills in "The War between the States and Washington," *New York Times Magazine* (July 5, 1998): 26–29.

33. Quoted in Conlon, *From New Federalism to Devolution*, 1.

34. Grover Norquist, arguably the most powerful lobbyist in Washington quoted in Philip Gourevitch, "Fight on the Right," *The New Yorker*, April 12, 2004, 37.

35. Dan Carney, "Latest Supreme Court Rulings Reinforce the Federalist Trend," *Congressional Quarterly*, June 26, 1999, 1528; Linda Greenhouse, "High Court Faces Moment of Truth in Federalism Cases," *New York Times*, March 28, 1999, 20.

36. David Broder, "Take Back the Initiative," *Washington Post National Weekly Edition*, April 10, 2000, 6.

37. James W. Brosnan, "Not Taxing Internet Sales Hurts," *Champaign-Urbana News-Gazette*, February 21, 2000, A6.

38. Barney Frank (D-Mass.), quoted in Michael Grunwald, "Everybody Talks about States' Rights," *Washington Post National Weekly Edition*, November 1, 1999, 29. Frank was referring to Republicans only, but the quote fits Democrats as well.

39. Wills, "War between the States and Washington," 26.

40. Sheryl Gay Stolberg, "As Congress Stalls, States Pursue Cloning Debate," *New York Times*, May 26, 2002, 1, 19.

41. Stephen Labaton, "Washington's Deregulatory Mood Finds Its Opposite in Vexed States," *New York Times*, January 13, 2002, 1.

42. Kirsten Downley Grimsley, "Where Congress Fears to Tread," *Washington Post National Weekly Edition*, August 21, 2000, 18.

43. Ibid., 19.

44. U.S. Census Bureau, *Statistical Abstract of the United States, 2001* (Washington, D.C.: Government Printing Office, 2002), tabs. 449 and 640.

45. Alice Rivlin, *Reviving the American Dream: The Economy, the States, and the Federal Government* (Washington, D.C.: Brookings Institution, 1992).

46. Jia Lynn Yang, "States: Battling Cleanup," *National Journal*, August 9, 2003, 2544.

47. See Mary Ann Glendon, *Abortion and Divorce in Western Law* (Cambridge, Mass.: Harvard University Press, 1987), 87–88; see also Susan Welch, Sue Thomas, and Margery Ambrosius, "Family Policy," in *State Politics and Policy*, 5th ed., ed. Virginia Gray and Herbert Jacob (Boston: Little, Brown, 1995).

48. For a review of the politics surrounding the law, its provisions, and limitations, see Conlon, *From New Federalism to Devolution*, ch. 13.

49. Neil Berch, "Why Do Some States Play the Federal Aid Game Better than Others?" *American Politics Quarterly* 20 (1992), 366–377.

50. Enid F. Beaumont and Harold Hovey, "State, Local, and Federal Development Policies: New Federalism Patterns, Chaos, or What?" *Public Administration Review* 45 (1985), 327–332; Barry Rubin and C. Kurt Zorn, "Sensible State and Local Development," *Public Administration Review* 45 (1985), 333–339.

51. Thomas Hargrove, "How Taxes Affect Population Growth," *Champaign-Urbana News-Gazette*, March 24, 2002, B1.

52. John Tierney, "New York Wants Its Money Back, or at Least Some of It," *New York Times*, June 27, 2004, WK4.

53. Broder, "Take Back the Initiative," 6; John Maggs, "Ballot Boxing," *National Journal*, July 1, 2000, 2147.

54. Wills, "War between the States . . . and Washington," 27.

55. Richard Cohen, "States Aren't Saints Either," *Washington Post National Weekly Edition*, April 3, 1995, 28; R. W. Apple, "You Say You Want a Devolution," *New York Times*, January 29, 1995, sec. 4, 1.

56. B. Drummond Ayres Jr., "Louisiana Apathy: The Ebb and Flow," *New York Times*, November 18, 2001, A20.

57. Katherine Sullivan, "In Defense of Federal Power," *New York Times Magazine*, August 18, 1996, 36.

58. Richard Neustadt, *The American Presidency*, episode 5, PBS, April 2000.

59. NBC News poll, January 2002.

60. ABC News poll, January 2002.

61. NBC News/*Wall Street Journal* poll, December 2001; both CBS and Gallup polls in June 2002 showed declining approval levels for Congress and the Supreme Court.

62. Shawn Zeller, "Gambling Millions on Anti-Yucca Lobbying," *National Journal*, June 15, 2002, 1797.

63. Statement issued by the office of the governor of Nevada, July 9, 2002.

64. Steve Tetreault. "Yucca Mountain: State Seeks Money to Fight Repository," *Las Vegas Review-Journal*, July 23, 2004 (www.state.nv.us/nucwaste).

65. Zeller, "Gambling Millions," 1797.

Chapter 4

1. Richard Morin and Claudia Deane, "Thumbs Up for the USA," *Washington Post National Weekly Edition*, December 3, 2001, 34.

2. Richard Morin and Dana Milbank, "Bush and GOP Enjoy Record Popularity," *Washington Post*, January 29, 2002, A01.

3. Mike Allen, "A War Strategy at Home," *Washington Post National Weekly Edition*, January 14, 2002, 15.

4. Morin and Milbank, "Bush and GOP Enjoy Record Popularity," A01.

5. Allen, "A War Strategy at Home," 15.

6. Richard Morin, "The Ups and Downs of Political Poll-Taking," *Washington Post National Weekly Edition*, October 5, 1992, 37.

7. Timothy E. Cook, "The Bear Market in Political Socialization and the Costs of Misunderstood Psychological Theories," *American Political Science Review* 79 (1985), 1079–1093.

8. S. W. Moore et al., "The Civic Awareness of Five- and Six-Year-Olds," *Western Political Quarterly* 29 (1976), 418.

9. R. W. Connell, *The Child's Construction of Politics* (Carlton, Australia: Melbourne University Press, 1971).

10. Fred I. Greenstein, *Children and Politics* (New Haven, Conn.: Yale University Press, 1965), 122; see also Fred I. Greenstein, "The Benevolent Leader Re-visited: Children's Images of Political Leaders in Three Democracies," *American Political Science Review* 69 (1975), 1317–1398; Robert D. Hess and Judith V. Torney, *The Development of Political Attitudes in Children* (Chicago: Aldine, 1967).

11. Hess and Torney, *The Development of Political Attitudes in Children*; Connell, *The Child's Construction of Politics*.

12. Greenstein, *Children and Politics*; Greenstein, "The Benevolent Leader Revisited: Children's Images of Political Leaders in Three Democracies"; and Hess and Torney, *The Development of Political Attitudes in Children*.

13. Connell, *The Child's Construction of Politics*.

14. F. Christopher Arterton, "The Impact of Watergate on Children's Attitudes toward the President," *Political Science Quarterly* 89 (1974), 269–288; see also P. Frederick Hartwig and Charles Tidmarch, "Children and Political Reality: Changing Images of the President," paper presented at the 1974 Annual Meeting of the Southern Political Science Association; J. Dennis and C. Webster, "Children's Images of the President and Government in 1962 and 1974," *American Politics Quarterly* 4 (1975), 386–405; Robert Hawkins, Suzanne Pingree, and D. Roberts, "Watergate and Political Socialization," *American Politics Quarterly* 4 (1975), 406–436.

15. Gallup Organization, "Public Trust in Federal Government Remains High," January 8, 1999.

16. Michael Delli Carpini, *Stability and Change in American Politics: The Coming of Age of the Generation of the 1960s* (New York: New York University Press, 1986), 86–89.

17. Richard M. Merelman, *Political Socialization and Educational Climates* (New York: Holt, Rinehart and Winston, 1971), 54; more recently, the percentage of liberals among college freshman and the public is about the same.

18. Roberta Sigel and Marilyn Hoskin, *The Political Involvement of Adolescents* (New Brunswick, N.J.: Rutgers University Press, 1981).

19. John R. Hibbing and Elizabeth Theiss-Morse, *Congress as Public Enemy: Public Attitudes toward American Political Institutions* (Cambridge: Cambridge University Press, 1995). It is plausible to assume that the content of early political socialization influences what is learned later, but the assumption has not been adequately tested. Thus, we might expect the positive opinions toward government and politics developed early in childhood to condition the impact of traumatic events later in life; David Easton and Jack Dennis, *Children in the Political System: Origins of Regime Legitimacy* (New York: Mc-Graw-Hill, 1969); Robert Weissberg, *Political Learning, Political Choice, and Democratic Citizenship* (Englewood Cliffs, N.J.: Prentice Hall, 1974). See also Donald Searing, Joel Schwartz, and Alden Line, "The Structuring Principle: Political Socialization and Belief System," *American Political Science Review* 67 (1973), 414–432.

20. Jack Citrin, "Comment: The Political Relevance of Trust in Government," *Washington Post National Weekly Edition* 68, September 1974, 973–1001; Jack Citrin and Donald Green, "Presidential Leadership and the Resurgence of Trust in Government," *British Journal of Political Science* 16 (1986), 431–453.

21. Dean Jaros, Herbert Hirsch, and Frederic J. Fleron Jr., "The Malevolent Leader: Political So-

cialization in an American Subculture," *American Political Science Review* 62 (1968), 564–575.

22. Kent Tedin, "The Influence of Parents on the Political Attitudes of Adolescents," *American Political Science Review* 68 (1974), 1579–1592.

23. M. Kent Jennings, *Generations and Politics* (Princeton, N.J.: Princeton University Press, 1981).

24. Kathleen Dolan, "Attitudes, Behaviors, and the Influence of the Family: A Re-examination of the Role of Family Structure," *Political Behavior* 17 (1995), 251–264.

25. On the impact of the public schools and teachers on political socialization, particularly with respect to loyalty and patriotism, see Hess and Torney, *The Development of Political Attitudes in Children.*

26. Gabriel A. Almond and Sidney Verba, *The Civic Culture: Political Attitudes and Democracy in Five Nations, an Analytic Study* (Boston: Little, Brown, 1965); John R. Hibbing and Elizabeth Theiss-Morse, "Civics Is Not Enough: Teaching Barbarics in K-12," *PS: Political Science and Politics* (1996), 12; Norman H. Nie, Jane Junn, and Kenneth Stehlik-Barry, *Education and Democratic Citizenship in America* (Chicago: University of Chicago Press, 1996).

27. Nie, et al., *Education and Democratic Citizenship in America.*

28. Hibbing and Theiss-Morse, *Congress and Public Enemy: Public Attitudes toward American Political Institutions.*

29. Richard G. Niemi and Jane Junn, *Civic Education: What Makes Students Learn* (New Haven, Conn.: Yale University Press, 1998). See also Richard G. Niemi and Julia Smith, "Enrollments in High School Government Classes: Are We Short-changing Both Citizenship and Political Science Training?" *PS: Political Science and Politics* 34 (2001), 281–288. Honors and advanced placement (AP) programs, along with active learning, can improve student understanding and achievement in American history.

30. Stephen Bennett, Staci Rhine, and Richard Flickinger, "Reading's Impact on Democratic Citizenship in America," *Political Behavior* 22 (2000), 167–195.

31. Nie, et al., *Education and Democratic Citizenship in America.*

32. Alfonso Damico, M. Margaret Conway, and Sandra Bowman Damico, "Patterns of Political Trust and Mistrust: Three Moments in the Lives of Democratic Citizens," *Polity* 32 (2000), 377–400.

33. Joel Westheimer and Joseph Kahne, "Educating the 'Good' Citizen: Political Choices and Pedagogical Goals," *PS: Political Science and Politics* 2 (2004), 241–247.

34. Richard M. Merelman, "Democratic Politics and the Culture of American Education," *American Political Science Review* 74 (1980), 319–332, Hibbing and Theiss-Morse, "Civics Is Not Enough: Teaching Barbarics in K-12"; Nie, et al., *Education and Democratic Citizenship in America.*

35. Material for this section is drawn from Everett C. Ladd and Seymour M. Lipset, *The Divided Academy: Professors and Politics* (New York: McGraw-Hill, 1975); Charles Kesler, "The Movement of Student Opinion," *National Review,* November 23, 1979, 29; Ernest L. Boyer, *College: The Undergraduate Experience in America* (New York: Harper & Row, 1987); "Fact File: Attitudes and Characteristics of This Year's Freshman," *Chronicle of Higher Education,* January 11, 1989, A33–A34; General Social Survey, *National Opinion Research Center,* 1984, 87. During the early 1970s, more college freshmen identified themselves as liberal compared to the public at large.

36. Alexander W. Astin, William S. Korn, and Linda Sax, *The American Freshman: Thirty Year Trends* (Los Angeles: Higher Education Research Institute, Graduate School of Education and Information, 1997).

37. Rebecca Trounson, "Poll Says College Freshmen Lean Left," www.commondreams.org/headlines02/0128-01.htm.

38. Thomas Bartlett, "Evaluating Student Attitudes Is More Difficult This Year," *Chronicle of Higher Education,* February 1, 2002, A35–A38. See also Linda Sax, Alexander W. Astin, and William S. Korn, *The American Freshman: National Norms for Fall 1998* (Los Angeles: Higher Education Research Institute, Graduate School of Education and Information Studies, 1998).

39. "College Freshman More Politically Liberal Than in the Past, UCLA Survey Reveals," 2001 CIRP Press Release: CIRP Freshman Survey, January 28, 2001.

40. Linda Sax, Alexander W. Astin, William S. Korn, and Kathryn M. Mahoney, *The American Freshman: National Norms for Fall 1999* (Los Angeles: Higher Education Research Institute, Graduate School of Education and Information Studies, 1999).

41. "Attitudes and Characteristics of Freshmen," *Chronicle of Higher Education,* August 27, 2004, 19.

42. M. Kent Jennings and Richard G. Niemi, *The Political Character of Adolescence: the Influence of Families and Schools* (Princeton, N.J.: Princeton University Press, 1974), 243.

43. Maxwell McCombs and Donald Shaw, "The Agenda Setting Function of the Media," *Public Opinion Quarterly* 36 (1972), 176–187.

44. Benjamin I. Page, Robert Y. Shapiro, and Glenn R. Dempsey, "What Moves Public Opinion?" *American Political Science Review* 81 (1987), 23–44.

45. Herbert F. Weisberg, "Marital Differences in American Voting," *Public Opinion Quarterly* 51 (1987), 335–343.

46. Michael A. Fletcher, "On Campus, a Patriotic Surge," *Washington Post National Weekly Edition,* December 10, 2001, 31.

47. Paul R. Abramson, *Political Attitudes in America: Formation and Change* (San Francisco: W. H. Freeman, 1983), 150, 213; see also Paul R. Abramson, *The Political Socialization of Black Americans: a Critical Evaluation of Research on Efficacy and Trust* (New York: Free Press, 1977).

48. Philip E. Converse, Aage R. Clausen, and Warren E. Miller, "Electoral Myth and Reality: The 1964 Election," *American Political Science Review* 59 (1965), 321–326.

49. John P. Robinson, "The Press as Kingmaker: What Surveys Show from the Last Five Campaigns," *Journalism Quarterly* 49 (1974), 592.

50. See jacob@jacbian.org; also Nick Anderson, "Kerry Wins the Paper Endorsement Derby, for What It's Worth," *Los Angeles Times,* October 29, 2004, A5.

51. Susan Herbst, *Numbered Voices: How Opinion Polling Has Shaped American Politics* (Chicago: University of Chicago Press, 1993); Benjamin Ginsberg, "How Polling Changes Public Opinion" in *Manipulating Public Opinion: Essays on Public Opinion as a Dependent Variable,* ed. Michael Margolis and Gary A. Mauser (Pacific Grove, Calif.: Brooks/Cole, 1989).

52. For a review of the history of polling, see Bernard Hennessy, *Public Opinion,* 4th ed. (Monterey, Calif.: Brooks/Cole, 1983), 42–44, 46–50. See also Charles W. Roll and Albert H. Cantril, *Polls: Their Use and Misuse in Politics* (New York: Basic Books, 1972), 3–6.

53. Peverill Squire, "Why the 1936 Literary Digest Poll Failed," *Public Opinion Quarterly* 52 (1988), 125–133; see also Don Cahalan, "The Digest Poll Rides Again," *Public Opinion Quarterly* 53 (1989), 107–113.

54. Hennessy, *Public Opinion,* 4th ed., 46.

55. "Consulting the Oracle," *U.S. News and World Report,* December 4, 1995, 52–55; Joshua Green, "The Other War Room," *Washington Monthly,* April 2002, 11–16.

56. Green, "The Other War Room."

57. Joe Klien, *The Natural* (New York: Doubleday, 2002), 7.

58. John E. Harris, "Presidency by Poll," *Washington Post National Weekly Edition,* January 8, 2001, 9–10.

59. Green, "The Other War Room."

60. Harris, "Presidency by Poll."

61. Steven Mufson and John E. Harris, "Clinton's Global Growth," *Washington Post National Weekly Edition,* January 22, 2001, 8–9.

62. Green, "The Other War Room."

63. Ibid., 11.

64. Ibid., 12.

65. Lawrence R. Jacobs and Robert Y. Shapiro, *Politicians Don't Pander: Political Manipulation and the Loss of Democratic Responsiveness* (Chicago: University of Chicago Press, 2000).

66. Bill Kovack and Tom Rosensteil, "Campaign Lite," *Washington Monthly,* January-February 2001, 31–38.

67. Claudia Deane, "And Why Haven't You Been Polled?" *Washington Post National Weekly Edition,* January 18, 1999, 34; Richard Morin, "The Election Post Mortem," *Washington Post National Weekly Edition,* September 30, 1996, 37.

68. Real Clear Politics, www.realclearpolitics.com/polls.html; see also "Pre-Election Polls Largely Accurate," *The Pew Research Center for the People and the Press,* November 23, 2004, www.people-press.org/commentary/display.php3?AnalysisID=102.

69. "All Things Considered," National Public Radio, October 30, 1992.

70. "Consulting the Oracle," 53.

71. Ibid., 53.

72. Richard Morin, "Surveying the Surveyors," *Washington Post National Weekly Edition,* March 2, 1992, 37.

73. David Broder, "Push Polls Plunge Politics to a New Low," *Lincoln Journal-Star,* October 9, 1994, 5E.

74. *New Yorker,* March 20, 1999, 18.

75. Richard Morin, "When the Method Becomes the Message," *Washington Post National Weekly Edition,* December 19, 1994, 33.

76. Richard Morin, "Tuned Out, Tuned Off," *Washington Post National Weekly Edition,* February 5, 1996, 6–8.

77. Ibid., 8

78. Ibid., 8

79. Richard Morin, "They Know Only What They Don't Like," *Washington Post National Weekly Edition,* October 3, 1994, 37.

80. Center for Political Studies, 1986 National Election Study, University of Michigan, "Wapner Top Judge in Recognition Poll," *Lincoln Journal-Star,* June 23, 1989, 1.

81. Michael Delli Carpini and Scott Keeter, "Stability and Change in the U.S. Public's Knowledge of Politics," *Public Opinion Quarterly,* (1991), 583–612.

82. Richard Morin, "We Love It—What We Know of It," *Washington Post National Weekly Edition,* September 22, 1997, 35.

83. Morin, "They Know Only What They Don't Like," 35.

84. Ibid., 35.

85. Richard Morin, "Foreign Aid: Mired in Misunderstanding," *Washington Post National Weekly Edition,* March 20, 1995, 37.

86. Richard Morin, "What Informed Public Opinion?" *Washington Post National Weekly Edition,* April 10, 1995, 36.

87. Vladimer Orlando Key, *The Responsible Electorate* (Cambridge, Mass.: Harvard University Press, 1966); Norman H. Nie, Sidney Verba, and John R. Petrocik, *The Changing American Voter* (Cambridge, Mass.: Harvard University Press, 1976), ch. 18; Samuel L. Popkin, *The Reasoning Voter: Communication and Persuasion in Presidential Campaigns* (Chicago: University of Chicago Press, 1994).

88. Gallup Organization, poll conducted April 6, 2004.

89. Popkin, *The Reasoning Voter: Communication and Persuasion in Presidential Campaigns.*

90. Morin, "Tuned Out, Turned Off," 8.

91. Gallup Organization, poll conducted June 16, 2003.

92. *Newsweek,* poll conducted September 2–3, 2004.

93. Harold Meyerson, "Fact-Free News," *Washington Post National Weekly,* October 10-26, 2003, 26.

94. Andrew Sullivan, article found on www .andrewsullivan.com/main_article.php? artnum=20040126.

95. General Social Survey, 2002.

96. Ibid.

97. Ibid.

98. NPR/Kaiser/Harvard, February 2001 from the Web at www.publicagenda.org.

99. General Social Survey, 2002.

100. Herbert Gans, *The War against the Poor* (New York: Basic Books, 1995).

101. Gallup Organization, poll conducted April 5, 2004.

102. Ibid.

103. Data here are from Peter Hart Research Associates Survey for the Council for Excellence in Government, March 16–18, 1995.

104. Pew Research Center, poll conducted March 7, 2002.

105. David Broder and Richard Morin, "A Question of Values," *Washington Post National Weekly Edition,* January 11, 1999, 6–7.

106. This section draws heavily on Howard Schuman, Charlotte Steeh, and Lawrence Bobo, *Racial Attitudes in America* (Cambridge, Mass.: Harvard University Press, 1985); Howard Schuman, Charlotte Steeh, Lawrence Bobo, and Maria Krysan, *Racial Attitudes in America,* rev. ed. (1997); Data summaries are drawn from the General Social Surveys of the National Opinion Research Center, University of Chicago, and National Elections Studies of CPS, University of Michigan; see also Lee Sigelman and Susan Welch, *Black Americans' Views of Racial Inequality* (Cambridge, Mass.: Cambridge University Press, 1991).

107. General Social Survey, 1996; Richard Morin, "Polling in Black and White: Sometimes the Answers Depend on Who's Asking the Questions," *Washington Post National Weekly Edition,* October 30, 1989, 37.

108. General Social Survey, 1996; "Whites Retain Negative Views of Minorities, a Survey Finds," *New York Times,* January 10, 1991, C19; Mary R. Jackman, "General and Applied Tolerance: Does Education Increase Commitment to Racial Inequality?" *American Journal of Political Science* 25 (1981), 256–269; Donald Kinder and David Sears, "Prejudice and Politics: Symbolic Racism versus Racial Threats to the Good Life," *Journal of Personality and Social Psychology* 40 (1981), 414–431.

109. Jon Hurwitz and Mark Peffley, *Perception and Prejudice: Race and Politics in the United States* (New Haven, Conn.: Yale University Press, 1998).

110. Richard Morin, "We've Moved Forward, but We Haven't," *Washington Post National Weekly Edition,* October 5, 1998, 34.

111. "Whites Retain Negative Views of Minorities, a Survey Finds," C19.

112. General Social Survey, 1998; see also Donald Kinder and Lynn Saunders, *Divided by Color: Racial Politics and Democratic Ideals* (Chicago: University of Chicago Press, 1996); Howard Schuman and Lawrence Bobo, "Survey-Based Experiments on White Attitudes toward Residential Integration." *American Journal of Sociology* 94 (1988), 519–526; see also Schuman et al., *Racial Attitudes in America,* rev. ed.

113. General Social Survey, 1998.

114. Richard Morin, "It's Not as It Seems," *Washington Post National Weekly Edition,* July 16, 2001, 34.

115. Ibid., 34.

116. Richard Morin, "No Place for Calm and Quiet Opinion," *Washington Post National Weekly Edition,* April 24, 1994, 34.

117. Martin Gilens and Paul Sniderman, "Affirmative Action and the Politics of Realignment," paper presented at the Midwest Political Science Association Meeting, Chicago, 1995.

118. Morin, "It's Not as It Seems"; ABC/Washington Post poll, 1981 and 1986.

119. General Social Survey, 1998.

120. Robert Putnam, "Bowling Together," *American Prospect* 13 (2002), online article.

121. Ibid.

122. John Sullivan, George Marcus, Stanley Feldman, and James Pierson, "Sources of Political Tolerance: A Multivariate Analysis," *American Political Science Review* 75 (1981), 92–106.

123. Samuel A. Stouffer, *Communism, Conformity, and Civil Liberties* (New York: Wiley, 1954).

124. Robert W. Jackman, "Political Elites, Mass Publics, and Support for Democratic Principles," *Journal of Politics* 34 (1972), 753.

125. Herbert McClosky and John Zaller, *The American Ethos: Public Attitudes toward Capitalism and Democracy* (Cambridge, Mass.: Harvard University Press, 1986).

126. Clyde Z. Nunn, Harry J. Crockett Jr., and J. Allen Williams, *Tolerance for Nonconformity* (San Francisco: Jossey-Bass, 1976).

127. "Polls Find Americans Angry, Anxious, Less Altruistic," *Lincoln Journal-Star,* September 21, 1994, 9.

128. Richard Morin and Claudia Deane, "A Thumbs Up for the USA," *Washington Post National Weekly Edition,* December 3, 2001, 34.

129. Mary Beth Sheridan, "Report Says Bias against Muslims in U.S. up 70 Percent," *Lincoln Journal-Star,* May 4, 2004, 9A.

130. Judith Shklar, quoted in Paul Taylor, "In Watergate's Wake: The Good, the Bad, and the Ugly," *Washington Post National Weekly Edition,* June 22, 1992, 25.

131. Almond and Verba, *The Civic Culture: Political Attitudes and Democracy in Five Nations, an Analytic Study,* 64–68.

132. Arthur H. Miller, "Political Issues and Trust in Government, 1964–1970," *American Political Science Review* 68 (1974), 951–972.

133. Arthur H. Miller and Stephen A. Borrelli, "Confidence in Government during the 1980s," *American Politics Quarterly* 19 (1991), 147–173.

134. Steven Langdon, "Clinton's High Victory Rate Conceals Disappointments," *Congressional Quarterly Weekly Reports,* December 31, 1994, 3619–3623.

135. David Broder and Dan Balz, "Who Wins?" *Washington Post National Weekly Edition,* February 15, 1999, 6–7.

136. Alexander Stille, "Suddenly, Americans Trust Uncle Sam," *New York Times,* November 3, 2001, A13

137. CBS News/New York Time Poll, July 11–15, 2004.

138. Theodore J. Lowi, *The Personal President* (Ithaca, N.Y.: Cornell University Press, 1995).

139. Seymour M. Lipset and William Schneider, *The Confidence Gap: Business, Labor, and Government in the Public Mind* (New York: Free Press, 1983).

140. Hibbing and Theiss-Morse, *Congress as Public Enemy.*

141. Miller, "Political Issues and Trust in Government, 1964–1970," 951–972.

142. Richard Morin, "Less Than Meets the Eye," *Washington Post National Weekly Edition,* March 16, 1998, 35.

143. Richard Morin, "Is Anyone Listening?" *Washington Post National Weekly Edition,* February 14, 1999, 34.

144. Benjamin I. Page and Robert Y. Shapiro, "Effects of Public Opinion on Policy," *American Political Science Review* 77 (1983), 175–190.

145. Sidney Verba and Norman H. Nie, *Participation in America: Political Democracy and Social Equality* (New York: Harper & Row, 1972), ch. 15.

146. State of the Union Address, *New York Times,* January 30, 2002.

147. Ibid.

148. Gallup Organization, poll conducted October 6, 2004.

149. American Research Group Poll, October 5, 2004, at www.americanresearchgroup.com.

Chapter 5

1. The source for information in this vignette is Nick Kotz, "Breaking Point," *Washingtonian,* December 1996, 94–121.

2. James David Barber, *The Pulse of Politics* (New York: Norton, 1980), 9.

3. Kevin Phillips, "A Matter of Privilege," *Harper's,* January 1977, 95.

4. Richard Harwood, "So Many Media, So Little Time," *Washington Post National Weekly Edition,* September 7, 1992, 28.

5. Thomas R. Dye and L. Hannon Zeigler, *American Politics in the Media Age* (Monterey, Calif.: Brooks/Cole, 1983), 123–124.

6. Edwin Diamond, *The Tin Kazoo* (Cambridge, Mass.: MIT Press, 1975), 13.

7. According to the first nationally representative study, conducted by the Henry J. Kaiser Family Foundation in 1999. "Media Use Almost a Full-Time Job for American Youth, Study Finds," *Lincoln Journal-Star,* November 18, 1999.

8. Doris A. Graber, *Mass Media and American Politics* (Washington, D.C.: Congressional Quarterly Press, 1980), 2.

9. William Lutz, *Doublespeak* (New York: Harper & Row, 1989), 73–74.

10. Robert W. McChesney and John Nichols, "It's the Media, Stupid," in *Voices of Dissent,* 5th ed., ed. William F. Grover and Joseph G. Peschek (New York: Longman, 2004), 116–120.

11. Shanto Iyengar, *Is Anyone Responsible? How Television Frames Political Issues* (Chicago: University of Chicago Press, 1991), 1.

12. "Ticker," *Brill's Content,* May 1999, 128.

13. Elizabeth Gleick, "Read All about It," *Time,* October 21, 1998, 66. See also Tom Rosenstiel, *The State of the News Media, 2004* (Washington, D.C.: Project for Excellence in Journalism, 2004).

14. "Ticker," 128.

15. Scott Althaus, "American News Consumption during Times of National Crisis," *PS,* September 2002, 517–521.

16. Thomas E. Patterson, *The Mass Media Election* (New York: Praeger, 1980), 58–60, 62–63.

17. Michael J. Wolf and Geoffrey Sands, "Fearless Predictions," *Brill's Content,* July-August 1999, 110. For a discussion of the future impact of the Internet on media concentration and diversity, see Robert W. McChesney, *The Problem of the Media* (New York: Monthly Review Press, 2004), 211–217.

18. Eve Gerber, "Divided We Watch," *Brill's Content,* February 2001, 110–111.

19. Harwood, "So Many Media," 28.

20. Donald Kaul, "Effects of Merger between AOL, Time Warner Will Be Inescapable," *Lincoln Journal-Star,* January 18, 2000; Ken Auletta, "Leviathan," *New Yorker,* October 29, 2001, 50.

21. McChesney, *Problem of the Media,* 182–183.

22. McChesney and Nichols, "It's the Media," 120. Antitrust laws provide few restrictions on these activities. McChesney, *Problem of the Media,* 235–240.

23. For examination of this development, see Lawrence Lessing, *The Future of Ideas* (New York: Random House, 2001). For an alternative view, see McChesney, *Problem of the Media,* 205–209.

24. Benjamin M. Compaine, *Who Owns the Media?* (White Plains, N.Y.: Knowledge Industry Publications, 1979), 11, 76–77; Michael Parenti, *Inventing Reality* (New York: St. Martin's Press, 1986), 27; Paul Farhi, "You Can't Tell a Book by Its Cover," *Washington Post National Weekly Edition,* December 5, 1988, 21; Andrews, "A New Tune for Radio."

25. Robert McChesney, "AOL–Time Warner Merger Is Dangerous and Undemocratic," *Lincoln Journal-Star,* January 17, 2000.

26. Rosenstiel, *State of the News Media,* 9.

27. Daren Fonda, "National Prosperous Radio," *Time,* March 24, 2003, 50; Marc Fisher, "Sounds All Too Familiar," *Washington Post National Weekly Edition,* May 26, 2003, 23.

28. McChesney, *Problem of the Media,* 178.

29. Ibid., 188.

30. Mary Lynn F. Jones, "No News Is Good News," *American Prospect,* May 2003, 39.

31. "Clear Channel Growth the Result of 1996 Deregulation," *Lincoln Journal Star,* October 5, 2003.

32. David Gram, "Opponents of War Have Trouble Getting Message Out," *Lincoln Journal Star,* February 25, 2003.

33. "Broadcaster: *Nightline* Won't Air on Its Stations," *Lincoln Journal Star,* April 30, 2004.

34. http://money.cnn.com/2004/10/11/news/newsmakers/sinclair_kerry/index.htm?cnn=yes

35. Frank Rich, "Will We Need a New 'All the President's Men'?" *New York Times,* October 17, 2004, AR1.

36. Elizabeth Lesly Stevens, "Mouse.Ke.Fear," *Brill's Content,* December 1998–January 1999, 95. For other examples, see Jane Mayer, "Bad News," *New Yorker,* August 14, 2000, 30–36.

37. Jim Hightower, *There's Nothing in the Middle of the Road but Yellow Stripes and Dead Armadillos* (New York: HarperCollins, 1997), 121.

38. Rifka Rosenwein, "Why Media Mergers Matter," *Brill's Content,* December 1999–January 2000, 94.

39. Dean Alger, *Megamedia: How Giant Corporations Dominate Mass Media, Distort Competition, and Endanger Democracy* (Lanham, Md.: Rowman & Littlefield, 1998). ABC did address it once—at 4 A.M.

40. The Project for Excellence in Journalism, affiliated with Columbia University's Graduate School of Journalism, concluded after a five-year study that newscasts by stations owned by smaller companies were significantly higher in quality than newscasts by stations owned by larger companies. "Does Ownership Matter in Local Television News?" February 17, 2003 (www.journalism.org).

41. Neil Hickey, "Money Lust," *Columbia Journalism Review,* July-August 1998, 28.

42. *Now, with Bill Moyers,* PBS, April 11, 2003.

43. Ted Turner, "Break Up This Band!" *Washington Monthly,* July-August, 2004, 35.

44. Victor Navasky, "Is Big Really Bad? Well, Yes," *Time,* January 24, 2000, 52.

45. Howard Kurtz, "Welcome to Spin City," *Washington Post National Weekly Edition,* March 16, 1998, 6. See also Roger Parloff, "If This Ain't Libel . . . ," *Brill's Content,* Fall 2001, 95–113.

46. Elizabeth Kolbert, "For Talk Shows, Less News Is Good News," *New York Times,* June 28, 1992, E-2.

47. Times Mirror Center for the People and the Press, *The Vocal Minority in American Politics* (Washington, D.C.: Times Mirror Center for the People and the Press, 1993).

48. In addition, she received $50,000 for a book elaborating on her story, $250,000 for posing nude for *Penthouse* magazine, and about $20,000 for appearing on German and Spanish television shows. "Flowers Says She Made Half Million from Story," *Lincoln Journal-Star,* March 21, 1998.

49. Ernest Tollerson, "Politicians Try to Balance Risk against Rewards of Reaching Talk-Radio Audiences," *New York Times,* March 31, 1996, 12.

50. McChesney, *Problem of the Media,* 96; Paul Taylor, "The New Political Theater," *Mother Jones,* November-December 2000, 30–33.

51. David Halberstam, "Preface," in Bill Kovach and Tom Rosenstiel, *Warp Speed: American in the Age of Mixed Media* (New York: Century Foundation Press, 1999), x.

52. Tom Rosenstiel, *The Beat Goes On: President Clinton's First Year with the Media* (New York: Twentieth Century Fund, 1994), 35. For an extensive examination of this incident, see Dan E. Moldea, *A Washington Tragedy* (New York: Regnery, 1998). A similar pattern occurred when a conservative magazine, *Insight,* charged that the Clinton administration was "selling" burial plots in Arlington National Cemetery to "dozens of big-time political donors or friends of the Clintons." Because the cemetery is reserved for military veterans, anonymous officials were quoted as saying this was "corruption of the worst kind." The charge was repeated on talk radio and then aired in Congress when some members demanded an investigation. Within forty-eight hours, it was reported in the mainstream media. Yet there was no truth to it. Howard Kurtz, "The Story That Wouldn't Stay Buried," *Washington Post National Weekly Edition,* December 1, 1997, 12.

53. Kurtz, "Welcome to Spin City," 6.

54. Quoted in Richard Corliss, "Look Who's Talking," *Time,* January 23, 1995, 25.

55. Kurt Anderson, "The Age of Unreason," *New Yorker,* February 3, 1997, 42.

56. Lev Grossman, "Meet Joe Blog," *Time,* June 21, 2004, 66.

57. Ibid.

58. Nicole Devenish, Communications Director of President Bush's reelection campaign in 2004, quoted in Nancy Gibbs', "Blue Truth, Red Truth," *Time,* September 27, 2004, 30.

59. Dom Bonafede, "Press Paying More Heed to Substance in Covering 1984 Presidential Election," *National Journal,* October 13, 1984, 1923.

60. Seth Mnookin, "Advice to Ari," *Brill's Content,* March 2001, 97.

61. Ken Auletta, "Fortress Bush," *New Yorker,* January 19, 2004, 53.

62. Thomas M. De Frank, "Playing the Media Game," *Newsweek,* April 17, 1989, 21.

63. Charles Peters, *How Washington Really Works* (Reading, Mass.: Addison-Wesley, 1980), 18.

64. Auletta, "Fortress Bush," 54.

65. William Greider, "Reporters and Their Sources," *Washington Monthly,* October 1982, 13–15.

66. See, for example, Jeffrey Toobin, *A Vast Conspiracy: The Real Story of the Sex Scandal That Nearly Brought Down a President* (New York: Simon & Schuster, 1999), 310.

67. When a spy's identity becomes public, foreign governments try to retrace the spy's movements and determine his or her contacts to see how the CIA operated in their country.

68. Reporters, however, are not liable for reporting information that officials disclosed. Following their journalistic standards, they refused to reveal the identity of their sources.

69. Howard Kurtz, "Lying Down on This Job Was Just Fine," *Washington Post National Weekly Edition,* April 19, 1999, 13.

70. Ann Devroy, "The Republicans, It Turns Out, Are a Veritable Fount of Leaks," *Washington Post National Weekly Edition,* November 18, 1991, 23.

71. Daniel Schorr, "A Fact of Political Life," *Washington Post National Weekly Edition,* October 28, 1991, 32.

72. Howard Kurtz, "How Sources and Reporters Play the Game of Leaks," *Washington Post National Weekly Edition,* March 15, 1993, 25.

73. Steven Brill, "Pressgate," *Brill's Content,* July-August 1998, 123–151; Steven Brill, "At Last, a Leakless Investigation," *Brill's Content,* December 1998–January 1999, 31–34.

74. Brill, "Pressgate," 149.

75. James Poniewozik, "Down by Law," *Time,* December 25, 2000–January 1, 2001, 79.

76. Samuel Kernell, *Going Public: New Strategies of Presidential Leadership* (Washington, D.C.: Congressional Quarterly Press, 1986), 59. Woodrow Wilson also tried to cultivate correspondents and host frequent sessions, but he did not have the knack for this activity and so scaled back the sessions. Kernell, *Going Public,* 60–61. He did perceive that "some men of brilliant ability were in the group, but I soon discovered that the interest of the majority was in the personal and the trivial rather than in principles and policies." James Bennet, "The Flack Pack," *Washington Monthly,* November 1991, 27.

77. Dwight Eisenhower was actually the first president to let the networks televise his press conferences, but he did not do so to reach the public. When he wanted to reach the public, he made a formal speech. The networks found his conferences so untelegenic that they stopped covering the entire session each time. Kernell, *Going Public,* 68.

78. Ibid., 104.

79. Bennet, "The Flack Pack," 19.

80. Dom Bonafede, "'Mr. President,'" *National Journal,* October 29, 1988, 2756.

81. Garry Wills, "But Don't Treat It as a Game," *Lincoln Journal,* March 26, 1993.

82. James Fallows, *Breaking the News: How the Media Undermine American Democracy* (New York: Pantheon, 1996), 196.

83. Charles Hagen, "The Photo Op: Making Icons or Playing Politics?" *New York Times,* February 9, 1992, H28.

84. Frank Rich, "Operation Iraqi Infoganda," *New York Times,* March 28, 2004, AR21.

85. "The Man behind the Curtain Award," *Mother Jones,* September-October 2002, 67.

86. Kiku Adatto, cited in Howard Kurtz, "Networks Adapt to Changed Campaign Role," *Washington Post,* June 21, 1992, A-19. See also Diana Owen, "Media Mayhem: Performance of the Press in Election 2000," in *Overtime! The Election 2000 Thriller,* ed. Larry J. Sabato (New York: Longman, 2002), 123–156.

87. Lance Morrow, "The Decline and Fall of Oratory," *Time,* August 18, 1980, 78.

88. David Halberstam, "How Television Failed the American Voter," *Parade,* January 11, 1981, 8.

89. George E. Reedy, *The Twilight of the Presidency* (New York: New American Library, 1970), 112.

90. Quoted in Thomas Griffith, "Winging It on Television," *Time,* March 14, 1983, 71.

91. "Talking about the Media Circus," *New York Times Magazine,* June 26, 1994, 63.

92. Auletta, "Fortress Bush," 61–62.

93. W. Lance Bennett, *News: The Politics of Illusion,* 2nd ed. (White Plains, N.Y.: Longman, 1988).

94. Larry J. Sabato, *Feeding Frenzy: How Attack Journalism Has Transformed American Politics* (New York: Free Press, 1991).

95. Deborah Tannen, *The Argument Culture* (New York: Ballantine, 1998), 81.

96. Ibid., 55.

97. Robert J. Bennett, "We Should Scuttle the Partisanship," *Washington Post National Weekly Edition,* March 24, 1997, 21.

98. Fallows, *Breaking the News,* 62–63.

99. Joan Konner, "Diane 'Got' Gore. But What Did We Get?" *Brill's Content,* September 1999, 59–60.

100. Joseph N. Cappella and Kathleen Hall Jamieson, *Spiral of Cynicism* (New York: Oxford University Press, 1997), 31.

101. Mary Matalin and James Carville, *All's Fair* (New York: Random House, 1994), 184–185.

102. See Sabato, *Feeding Frenzy,* for additional reasons for this increase.

103. "Ticker," *Brill's Content,* July-August 1998, 152, citing the Project for Excellence in Journalism, "Changing Definitions of News: A Look at the Mainstream Press over 20 Years," March 6, 1998.

104. Fallows, *Breaking the News,* 196.

105. An examination of 224 incidents of criminal or unethical behavior by Reagan administration appointees found that only 13 percent were uncovered by reporters. Most were discovered through investigations by executive agencies or congressional committees, which then released the information to the press. Only incidents reflecting personal peccadilloes of government officials, such as sexual offenses, were exposed first by reporters. John David Rausch Jr., "The Pathology of Politics: Government, Press, and Scandal," *Extensions* (University of Oklahoma), Fall 1990, 11–12. For the Whitewater scandal, reporters got most of their tips from a Republican Party operation run by officials from Republican presidential campaigns. Regarding sexual matters, reporters got most of their tips from prosecutors for the independent counsel, lawyers for Paula Jones, or a book agent for Linda Tripp. See Brill, "Pressgate," 134.

106. William Rivers, "The Correspondents after 25 Years," *Columbia Journalism Review* 1 (Spring 1962), 5.

107. Coolidge, in his reelection campaign, was actually the first president to use radio as a means of addressing the public directly.

108. James David Barber, *Presidential Character* (Englewood Cliffs, N.J.: Prentice Hall, 1992), 238.

109. Reagan got his start in show business as a radio sportscaster in Des Moines, Iowa, announcing major league baseball games "live." Of course, he was not actually at the games: he got the barest details—who was at bat, whether the pitch was a strike or a ball or a hit—from the wireless and made up the rest to create a commentary that convinced listeners that he was watching in person.

110. Hedrick Smith, *The Power Game* (New York: Random House, 1988), 403.

111. Timothy J. Russert, "For '92, the Networks Have to Do Better," *New York Times,* March 4, 1990, E23.

112. Smith, *Power Game,* 420.

113. Steven K. Weisman, "The President and the Press," *New York Times Magazine,* October 14, 1984, 71–72; Dick Kirschten, "Communications Reshuffling Intended to Help Reagan Do What He Does Best," *National Journal,* January 28, 1984, 154.

114. Sidney Blumenthal, "The Syndicated Presidency," *New Yorker,* April 5, 1993, 45.

115. Brit Hume, of NBC News.

116. For an extensive examination of this phenomenon, see Toobin, *Vast Conspiracy.*

117. John F. Harris, "Bush's Lucky Break," *Washington Post National Weekly Edition,* May 14, 2001, 23.

118. For examination of coverage during Clinton's early days in office, see William Glaberson, "The Capitol Press vs. the President: Fair Coverage or Unreined Adversity?" *New York Times,* June 17, 1993, A11; Christopher Georges, "Bad News Bearers," *Washington Monthly,* July-August 1993, 28–34; and Toobin, *Vast Conspiracy,* 247–248.

119. Tannen, *Argument Culture,* 54.

120. Howard Kurtz, "Assessing—and Controlling—the Damage to the Presidency," *Washington Post National Weekly Edition,* February 2, 1998, 21.

121. Auletta, "Fortress Bush," 60.

122. Steven Thomma and William Douglas, "Bush: U.S. Must 'Stay the Course,'" *Lincoln Journal Star,* April 14, 2004.

123. Auletta, "Fortress Bush," 54, 57, 64.

124. Ibid., 55.

125. John F. Harris, "On the World Stage, Bush Shuns the Spotlight," *Washington Post National Weekly Edition,* April 23, 2001, 11; Ronald Brownstein, "Bush Forced into Role He May Not Want:

Communicator," *Lincoln Journal-Star,* September 15, 2001.

126. John F. Harris and Dan Balz, "A Well-Oiled Machine," *Washington Post National Weekly Edition,* May 14, 2001, 6.

127. James Carville, quoted in John F. Harris, "Bush's Lucky Break," *Washington Post National Weekly Edition,* May 14, 2001, 23.

128. Aides claimed that *Air Force One* was a target, but it was revealed that this claim was an exaggeration to parry the criticism that Bush received. Eric Pooley and Karen Tumulty, "Bush in the Crucible," *Time,* September 24, 2001, 49.

129. Calvin Woodward, "Warrior Bush: It Doesn't Come Naturally," *Lincoln Journal-Star,* October 6, 2002.

130. Michael Duffy, "Marching Alone," *Time,* September 9, 2002, 42.

131. Presidential historian Henry Graff, cited in Ron Fourier, "President Stumbles with Mideast Rhetoric," *Lincoln Journal-Star,* April 20, 2002.

132. Joe Klein, "Why the 'War President' Is Under Fire," *Time,* February 23, 2004, 17.

133. David L. Greene, "Bush Often Great Miscommunicator," *Lincoln Journal-Star,* October 6, 2002.

134. Philip Gourevitch, "Bushspeak," *New Yorker,* September 13, 2004, 38.

135. For a reporter's perspective on the difference this makes, see Harris, "Bush's Lucky Break." As Harris observes, imagine the reaction if Clinton had been in office when that American surveillance plane was forced down in China. Could he have gotten away with insisting as Bush did that the detained personnel were not actually hostages and then cutting a deal to get them, but not our plane, back by apologizing for being in international airspace?

136. Stephen Hess, *Live from Capitol Hill!* (Washington, D.C.: Brookings Institution, 1991), 62; Timothy E. Cook, *Making Laws and Making News: Media Strategies in the U.S. House of Representatives* (Washington, D.C.: Brookings Institution, 1989), 2.

137. Hess, *Live from Capitol Hill!* 102.

138. Hendrik Hertzberg, "Comment: The Pot Perplex," *New Yorker,* January 6, 1997, 4–5. For an interesting article about medical uses of marijuana and about a club of marijuana users, see Evelyn Nieves, "Half an Ounce of Healing," *Mother Jones,* January-February 2001, 49–53.

139. Joe Klein, *The Natural* (New York: Doubleday, 2002), 109.

140. Robert Schmidt, "May It Please the Court," *Brill's Content,* October 1999, 74.

141. For analysis, see Rorie L. Spill and Zoe M. Oxley, "Philosopher Kings or Political Actors? How the Media Portray the Supreme Court," *Judicature,* July-August 2003, 22–29.

142. Schmidt, "May It Please the Court," 73.

143. Ibid.

144. During the invasion of Grenada in 1983, the military excluded all journalists, even turning away at gunpoint those who reached the island on their own. During the invasion of Panama in 1989 and the Persian Gulf War in 1990, the military created press pools with some journalists who were escorted to selected sites and who reported the news for media organizations in the pools. Censorship also reduced coverage.

145. Michael Tomasky, "Breaking the Code: Or, Can the Press Be Saved from Itself?" in Cynthia Brown, ed., *Lost Liberties* (New York: New Press, 2003), 151–152.

146. Auletta, "Fortress Bush," 62.

147. Hampton Sides, "Unembedded," *New Yorker,* March 24, 2003, 31.

148. Robert Jensen, "The Military's Media," *Progressive,* May 2003 (www.progressive.org). For an oral history based on interviews with journalists, see Timothy Carlson, *Embedded: The Media at War in Iraq* (Guilford, Conn.: Lyons Press, 2003).

149. Howard Kurtz, "Situation Coverage," *Washington Post National Weekly Edition,* May 5, 2003, 6.

150. Edward Jay Epstein, *News from Nowhere* (New York: Random House, 1973), 13.

151. Graber, *Mass Media and American Politics,* 62.

152. Milton Coleman, "When the Candidate Is Black like Me, *"Washington Post National Weekly Edition,* April 23, 1984, 9.

153. Roper Organization, "A Big Concern about the Media: Intruding on Grieving Families," *Washington Post National Weekly Edition,* June 6, 1984. See also Cappella and Jamieson, *Spiral of Cynicism,* 210.

154. McChesney, *Problem of the Media,* 116.

155. Karen Tumulty, "I Want My Al TV," *Time,* June 30, 2003, 59.

156. Liddy, who was convicted in the Watergate scandal, instructed listeners where to aim when shooting agents of the Bureau of Alcohol, Tobacco, and Firearms to kill them.

157. Tony Blankley, "Radio Show Goes On," *Washington Times,* October 10, 2002.

158. McChesney, *Problem of the Media,* 117.

159. For a history of the origins of Fox News, see David Carr, *Crazy like a Fox* (New York: Portfolio, 2004).

160. For analysis, see Ken Auletta, "Vox Fox," *New Yorker,* May 26, 2003, 58.

161. Genever Overholser, "It's Time for News Networks to Take Sides," *Lincoln Journal-Star,* August 26, 2001.

162. Robert S. Boynton, "How to Make a Guerrilla Documentary," *New York Times Magazine,* July 11, 2004, 22. See also the documentary "Outfoxed" (2004).

163. Auletta, "Vox Fox," 63–64.

164. Overholser, "It's Time"; David Plotz, "Fox News Channel," *Slate,* November 22, 2000 (slate.msn.com).

165. Jeff Cohen and Jonah Goldberg, "Face-Off: Beyond Belief," *Brill's Content,* December 1999–January 2000, 54.

166. Edith Efron, *The News Twisters* (Los Angeles: Nash, 1971); L. B. Bozell and B. H. Baker, "And That's the Way It Isn't," *Journalism Quarterly* 67 (1990), 1139; Bernard Goldberg, *Bias* (New York: Regnery, 2002); Alterman, *What Liberal Media?*

167. S. Robert Lichter, Stanley Rothman, and Linda S. Lichter, *The Media Elite* (Bethesda, Md.: Adler & Adler, 1986), 21–25. See also Hess, *Live from Capitol Hill!* app. A, 110–130.

168. John Johnstone, Edward Slawski, and William Bowman, *The Newspeople* (Urbana: University of Illinois Press, 1976), 225–226.

169. Stanley Rothman and S. Robert Lichter, "Media and Business Elites: Two Classes in Conflict?" *Public Interest* 69 (1982), 111–125; S. Robert Lichter and Stanley Rothman, "Media and Business Elites," *Public Opinion,* October-November 1981, 44.

170. Stephen Hess, *The Washington Reporters* (Washington, D.C.: Brookings Institution, 1981), 89; see also Lichter et al., *Media Elite,* 127–128.

171. James Fallows, "The Stoning of Donald Regan," *Washington Monthly,* June 1984, 57. Most individual reporters also probably care more about their career than ideology, but this could lead to bias. In 1976, one media analyst ran into an old friend, an NBC correspondent. When the analyst asked how she was doing, she answered, "Not so great. My candidate lost." That is, the candidate she had covered during the presidential primaries lost his bid for the nomination. Because reporters often follow "their" presidential candidate into office, she lost her chance to become NBC's White House correspondent. Graeme Browning, "Too Close for Comfort?" *National Journal,* October 3, 1992, 2243.

172. One Pittsburgh publisher interjects his views into news stories. Kimberly Conniff, "All the Views Fit to Print," *Brill's Content,* March 2001, 105.

173. Howard Kurtz, *Media Circus* (New York: Random House, 1994), 48.

174. Russell J. Dalton, Paul A. Beck, and Robert Huckfeldt, "Partisan Cues and the Media: Information Flows in the 1992 Presidential Election," *American Political Science Review* 92 (March 1998), 118.

175. C. Richard Hofstetter, *Bias in the News* (Columbus: Ohio State University Press, 1976); Graber, *Mass Media and Politics*, 167–168; Michael J. Robinson, "Just How Liberal Is the News?" *Public Opinion*, February-March 1983, 55–60; Maura Clancy and Michael J. Robinson, "General Election Coverage: Part I," *Public Opinion*, December 1984–January 1985, 49–54, 59; Michael J. Robinson, "The Media Campaign, '84: Part II," *Public Opinion*, February-March 1985, 43–48.

176. Dave D'Alessio and Mike Allen, "Media Bias in Presidential Elections: A Meta-Analysis," *Journal of Communication* 50 (2000), 133–156.

177. Clancy and Robinson, "General Election Coverage"; Robinson, "Media Campaign, '84"; Michael J. Robinson, "Where's the Beef? Media and Media Elites in 1984," in *The American Elections of 1984*, ed. Austin Ranney (Durham, N.C.: Duke University Press, 1985), 184; Michael J. Robinson, "News Media Myths and Realities: What Network News Did and Didn't Do in the 1984 General Campaign," in *Elections in America*, ed. Kay Lehman Schlozman (Boston: Allen & Unwin, 1987), 143–170; Kim Fridkin Kahn and Patrick J. Kenney, *The Spectacle of U.S. Senate Campaigns* (Princeton, N.J.: Princeton University, 1999), 126–129.

178. Ken Auletta, "Inside Story," *New Yorker*, November 18, 1996, 55. Most journalists—89 percent according to one poll—voted for Clinton over Bush, but after the election, the media gave Clinton more negative coverage than they had given Bush in his first eighteen months. "Dealing with Bias in the Press," *Civilization*, February-March 1997, 24–27.

179. Robert Shogan, *Bad News: Where the Press Goes Wrong in the Making of the President* (Chicago: Dee, 2001), 231.

180. It helped the Democrat Carter in 1976 but hurt him in 1980. It helped the Republican Bush in 1988 but hurt him in 1992. Thomas E. Patterson, *Out of Order* (New York: Vintage, 1994), 131. It helped the Democrat Clinton in 1996, and at different stages of the campaign, it helped the Republican Bush or the Democrat Gore in 2000.

181. Shogan, *Bad News*, 204–245; Clymer, "Better Campaign Reporting."

182. Robert Parry, "He's No Pinocchio: How the Press Has Exaggerated Al Gore's Exaggerations," *Washington Monthly*, April 2001, 23–28.

183. Fewer than one in ten stories on the 2000 debates focused on policy differences; seven in ten focused on candidates' performance or strategy. Bill Kovach and Tom Rosenstiel, "Campaign Lite," *Washington Monthly*, January-February 2001, 31–32. For a perceptive analysis, see Clymer, "Better Campaign Reporting."

184. The media, however, did pay a lot of attention to Ross Perot's presidential bid in 1992 because he said he would spend $100 million on his campaign and because polls showed he could compete with Bush and Clinton.

185. For a recounting of his 2000 campaign, see Ralph Nader, "My Untold Story," *Brill's Content*, February 2001, 100.

186. "Clinton Gains More Support from Big Papers," *Lincoln Journal-Star*, October 25, 1992. Newspapers insist that there is little relationship between their editorial endorsements and their news coverage or even their political columns. An endorsement for one candidate does not mean more positive coverage or columns for that candidate because American media have established a tradition of autonomy in the newsroom. Dalton et al., "Partisan Cues," 118. However, some research shows that when papers endorse candidates, the papers show a small bias toward the candidates in their news stories (if the candidates are incumbents). Kim Fridkin Kahn and Patrick J. Kenney, "The Slant of the News: How Editorial Endorsements Influence Campaign Coverage and Citizen's Views of Candidates," *American Political Science Review* 96 (June 2002), 381–394.

187. Hofstetter, *Bias in the News*; Hess, *Live from Capitol Hill!* 12–13.

188. Robinson, "Just How Liberal . . . ?" 58; Arthur H. Miller, Edie N. Goldenberg, and Lutz Erbring, "Type-Set Politics," *American Political Science Review* 73 (January 1979), 69; Patterson, *Out of Order*, 6; Charles M. Tidmarch and John J. Pitney Jr., "Covering Congress," *Polity* 17 (Spring 1985), 463–483.

189. Richard Morin, "The Big Picture Is out of Focus," *Washington Post National Weekly Edition*, March 6, 2000, 21.

190. Steven Brill, "Quality Control," *Brill's Content*, July-August 1998, 19–20.

191. Patterson, *Out of Order*, 25, 245.

192. Stanley Rothman and S. Robert Lichter, "The Nuclear Energy Debate," *Public Opinion*, August-September 1982, 47–48; Stanley Rothman and S. Robert Lichter, "Elite Ideology and Risk Perception in Nuclear Energy Policy," *American Political Science Review* 81 (June 1987), 383–404; Lichter et al., *Media Elite*, ch. 7; Sabato, *Feeding Frenzy*, 87; and sources cited therein. But a study examining twenty years' coverage of governors and their states' unemployment and murder rates shows no bias toward Democratic or Republican governors. David Niven, "Partisan Bias in the Media?" *Social Science Quarterly* 80 (December 1999), 847–857.

193. Goldberg, *Bias*, ch. 5; Alterman, *What Liberal Media?* ch. 7.

194. Alterman, *What Liberal Media?* 104–117.

195. Ibid., 118–138. For an analysis of the coverage of the economy in the booming 1990s, see John Cassidy, "Striking It Rich: The Rise and Fall of Popular Capitalism," *New Yorker*, January 14, 2002, 63–73.

196. Bruce Nussbaum, "The Myth of the Liberal Media," *Business Week*, November 11, 1996; Fallows, *Breaking the News*, 49.

197. Further, the media give scant attention to labor matters, except when strikes inconvenience commuters. Mark Crispin Miller, "The Media and the Bush Dyslexicon," in Grover and Peschek, *Voices of Dissent*, 137–146. In 2001, the three main television networks used representatives of corporations as sources thirty times more often than representatives of unions. McChesney, *Problem of the Media*, 70–71.

198. McChesney, *Problem of the Media*, 106.

199. Robinson, "Just How Liberal . . . ?" 59

200. Parenti, *Inventing Reality*, ch. 7–11; Charles E. Lindblom, *Politics and Markets* (New York: Basic Books, 1977); J. Fred MacDonald, *One Nation under Television: The Rise and Decline of Network TV* (New York: Pantheon Books, 1990); Dan Nimmo and James E. Combs, *Mediated Political Realities* (White Plains, N.Y.: Longman, 1983), 135; Benjamin I. Page and R. Y. Shapiro, *The Rational Public* (Chicago: University of Chicago Press, 1992); John R. Zaller and Dennis Chiu, "Government's Little Helper: U.S. Press Coverage of Foreign Policy Crises, 1945–1991," *Political Communication* 13 (1996), 385–405.

201. John R. MacArthur, *Second Front: Censorship and Propaganda in the Gulf War* (New York: Hill & Wang, 1992); James Bennet, "How They Missed That Story," *Washington Monthly*, December 1990, 8–16; Christopher Dickey, "Not Their Finest Hour," *Newsweek*, June 8, 1992, 66.

202. In the 1950s and early 1960s, newspapers, magazines, and television networks sent few correspondents to Vietnam, so most accepted the government's account of the conflict. Susan Welch, "The American Press and Indochina, 1950–1956," in *Communication in International Politics*, ed. Richard L. Merritt (Urbana: University of Illinois Press, 1972), 207–231; Edward J. Epstein, "The Selection of Reality," in *What's News?* ed. Elie Abel (San Francisco: Institute for Contemporary Studies, 1981), 124. When they did dispatch correspondents, many filed pessimistic reports, but their editors believed the government rather than the correspondents and refused to print these reports. Instead, they ran articles quoting optimistic statements by government officials. See David Halberstam, *The Powers That Be* (New York: Dell, 1980), 642–647. In 1968, the media did turn against the war, but rather than sharply criticize it, they conveyed the impression that it was futile. Daniel C. Hallin, *The "Uncensored War": The Media and Vietnam* (New York: Oxford University Press, 1986).

203. "Return of Talk Show Is Healthy Sign," *Lincoln Journal Star*, October 6, 2001.

204. Alterman, *What Liberal Media?* 202.

205. Anthony Collings, "The BBC: How to Be Impartial in Wartime," *Chronicle of Higher Education*, December 21, 2001, B14.

206. Alterman, *What Liberal Media?* 29; Todd Gitlin, "Showtime Iraq," *American Prospect*, November 4, 2002, 34–35.

207. McChesney, *Problem of the Media*, 122–123.

208. "The *Times* and Iraq," *New York Times*, May 26, 2004, A10; Daniel Okrent, "Weapons of Mass Destruction? Or Mass Distraction?" *New York Times*, May 30, 2004, WK1.

209. Jim Thompson, "Letters to the Public Editor," *New York Times*, June 6, 2004, WK2.

210. James Poniewozik, "What You See vs. What They See," *Time*, April 7, 2003, 68–69. For example, that U.S. searches caused considerable damage to Iraqi homes and that these raids swept up many innocent family members. *Morning Edition*, National Public Radio, May 4, 2004. Also, that in the run-up to the war, U.S. agents had bugged the homes and offices of United Nations Security Council members who had not proclaimed support for the war. Camille T. Taiara, "Spoon-Feeding the Press," *San Francisco Bay Guardian*, March 12, 2003 (www.sfbg.com/37/24/x_mediabeat.html).

211. Frank Rich, "The Spoils of War," *New York Times*, April 13, 2003, AR1; Paul Janensch, "Whether to Show Images of War Dead Is Media Dilemma," *Lincoln Journal Star*, March 31, 2003.

212. Terry McCarthy, "Whatever Happened to the Republican Guard?" *Time*, May 12, 2003, 38.

213. Todd Gitlin, "Embed or in Bed?" *American Prospect*, June 2003, 43.

214. Leon V. Sigal, *Reporters and Officials* (Lexington, Mass.: Heath, 1973), 120–121; Lucy Howard, "Slanted 'Line'?" *Newsweek*, February 13, 1989, 6. See also Hess, *Live from Capitol Hill!* 50. Trivia buffs might wonder who has been the subject of the most cover articles in *Time* magazine—the answer is Richard Nixon (fifty-five). "Numbers," *Time*, March 9, 1998, 189.

215. Cook, *Making Laws and Making News*, 8.

216. W. Lance Bennett, "Toward a Theory of Press-State Relations in the United States," *Journal of Communication* 40 (1990), 103–125.

217. Three times as many people believe the media are "too liberal" than believe they are "too conservative" (45 percent to 15 percent). McChesney, *Problem of the Media*, 114.

218. M. D. Watts, D. Domke, D. V. Shah, and D. P. Fan, "Elite Cues and Media Bias in Presidential Campaigns: Explaining Public Perceptions of a Liberal Press," *Communication Research* 26 (1999), 144–175.

219. William Kristol, quoted in Alterman, *What Liberal Media?* 2–3.

220. Robert Vallone, Lee Ross, and Mark R. Lepper, "The Hostile Media Phenomenon," *Journal of Personality and Social Psychology* 49 (1985), 577–585; Roger Giner-Sorolla and Shelly Chaiken, "The Causes of Hostile Media Judgments," *Journal of Experimental Social Psychology* 30 (1994), 165–180.

221. Dalton et al., "Partisan Cues and the Media."

222. W. Phillips Davison, "The Third-Person Effect in Communication," *Public Opinion Quarterly* 47 (1983), 1–15.

223. Dave D'Alessio, "An Experimental Examination of Readers' Perceptions of Media Bias," unpublished manuscript, University of Connecticut, n.d.; Mark Peffley, James M. Avery, and Jason E. Glass, "Public Perceptions of Bias in the News Media," paper presented at the annual meeting of the Midwest Political Science Association, Chicago, April 19–22, 2001.

224. According to a statement by a CNN producer in the documentary "Outfoxed."

225. First CBS postponed the documentary during the summer of 2004. Then the network postponed the documentary after it was embarrassed by the discovery that it had displayed a forged letter about George W. Bush's National Guard service. Conservatives believed that the CBS report was an intentional falsification. It is far more likely that the report was the result of a feverish desire for a scoop and an inadequate investigation into the letter's authenticity.

226. Jeff Cohen, senior producer of *Donahue*, MSNBC, quoted in McChesney, *Problem of the Media*, 108.

227. Goldberg, *Bias*, 92.

228. Theodore H. White, *America in Search of Itself* (New York: Harper & Row, 1982), 186.

229. Goldberg, *Bias*, 92.

230. "Anchorwoman Verdict Raises Mixed Opinions," *Lincoln Journal-Star*, August 9, 1983.

231. Kovach and Rosenstiel, *Warp Speed*, 64.

232. Hess, *Live from Capitol Hill!* 34; Rosenstiel, *State of the News Media*, 21.

233. Molly Ivins, "Media Conglomerates Profit at Expense of News, Public," *Lincoln Journal-Star*, October 26, 2001.

234. James Fallows, "On That Chart," *Nation*, June 3, 1996, 15.

235. Maureen Dowd, "Flintstone Futurama," *New York Times*, August 19, 2001, WK 13.

236. "Poll: Reporters Avoid, Soften Stories," *Lincoln Journal-Star*, May 1, 2000; David Owen, "The Cigarette Companies: How They Get Away with Murder, Part II," *Washington Monthly*, March 1985, 48–54. See also Daniel Hellinger and Dennis R. Judd, *The Democratic Facade*, 2nd ed. (Belmont, Calif.: Wadsworth, 1994), 59. Through the 1920s, newspapers refrained from pointing out that popular "patent medicines" were usually useless and occasionally dangerous because the purveyors bought more advertising than any other business. Mark Crispin Miller, "Free the Media," *Nation*, June 3, 1996, 10.

237. Roger Mudd, quoted in *Television and the Presidential Elections*, ed. Martin A. Linsky (Lexington, Mass.: Heath, 1983), 48.

238. "Q&A: Dan Rather on Fear, Money, and the News," *Brill's Content*, October 1998, 117.

239. Barry Sussman, "News on TV: Mixed Reviews," *Washington Post National Weekly Edition*, September 3, 1984, 37.

240. Bill Carter, "Networks Fight Public's Shrinking Attention Span," *Lincoln Journal-Star*, September 30, 1990.

241. Epstein, *News from Nowhere*, 4.

242. William A. Henry III, "Requiem for TV's Gender Gap," *Time*, August 22, 1983, 57.

243. Richard Morin, "The Nation's Mood? Calm," *Washington Post National Weekly Edition*, November 5, 2001, 35.

244. For an examination of how the media exaggerated the Whitewater scandal, see Gene Lyons, *Fools for Scandal* (New York: Franklin Square Press, 1996).

245. The third and final special prosecutor concluded that there might be some evidence of wrongdoing in the law firm records of Hillary Clinton but that there was not enough evidence to justify prosecution.

246. Fallows, *Breaking the News*, 133.

247. Peggy Noonan, quoted in Jeffrey Klein, "News Value, Not Values," *Brill's Content*, July–August 2000, 54.

248. "Naked News Program Taken Off Air," *Lincoln Journal-Star*, January 15, 2002.

249. The pope was making a historic visit to Cuba. The networks had considered this so important that they had sent their anchors to Havana. At the same time, renewed violence in Northern Ireland threatened to scuttle the peace talks between Catholics and Protestants, and continued refusal from Iraq to cooperate with United Nations biological and chemical weapons inspectors threatened to escalate to military conflict.

250. Eric Pooley, "Monica's World," *Time*, March 2, 1998, 40.

251. Quoted in Fallows, *Breaking the News*, 201.

252. Samuel G. Freedman, "Fighting to Balance Honor and Profit on the Local News," *New York Times*, September 30, 2001, sec. 2, 26.

253. Lawrie Mifflin, "Crime Falls, but Not on TV," *New York Times*, July 6, 1997, E3. According to one researcher, crime coverage is also "the easiest, cheapest, laziest news to cover" because stations just listen to the police radio and then send a camera crew to shoot the story.

254. Heather Maher, "Eleven o'Clock Blues," *Brill's Content*, February 2001, 99.

255. Molly Ivins, "Don't Moan about the Media, Do Something," *Lincoln Journal-Star*, November 1999.

256. David S. Broder, "Can We Govern?" *Washington Post National Weekly Edition*, January 31, 1994, 23.

257. Newspaper ads were placed in college papers by Holocaust deniers, claiming that there is no proof that gas chambers actually existed. The editor of one paper justified accepting the ad by saying, "There are two sides to every issue and both have a place on the pages of any open-minded paper's editorial page." Tannen, *Argument Culture*, 38. For examination of this phenomenon, see Deborah E. Lipstadt, *Denying the Holocaust: The Growing Assault on Truth and Memory* (New York: Plume, 1993).

258. Kathleen Hall Jamieson, *Dirty Politics: Deception, Distraction, Democracy* (New York: Oxford University Press, 1992), 184–185.

259. Tannen, *Argument Culture*, 286.

260. Howard Kurtz, quoted in Tannen, *Argument Culture*, 29.

261. Patterson, *Out of Order*, 53–59.

262. Lee Sigelman and David Bullock, "Candidates, Issues, Horse Races, and Hoopla: Presidential Campaign Coverage, 1888–1988," *American Politics Quarterly* 19 (January 1991), 5–32. So was emphasis on human interest. In 1846, the *New York Tribune* described the culinary habits of Representative William "Sausage" Sawyer (D-Ohio), who ate a sausage on the floor of the House every afternoon: "What little grease is left on his hands he wipes on his almost bald head which saves any outlay for Pomatum. His mouth sometimes serves as a finger glass, his shirtsleeves and pantaloons being called into requisition as a napkin. He uses a jackknife for a toothpick, and then he goes on the floor again to abuse the Whigs and Making the British party." Cook, *Making Laws and Making News*, 18–19.

263. Patterson, *Out of Order*, 74; Marion R. Just, Ann N. Crigler, Dean E. Alger, Timothy E. Cook, Montague Kern, and Darrell M. West, *Crosstalk: Citizens, Candidates, and the Media in a Presidential Campaign* (Chicago: University of Chicago Press, 1996); Mathew Robert Kerbel, *Remote and Controlled* (Boulder, Colo.: Westview Press, 1995); Bruce Buchanan, *Electing a President* (Austin: University of Texas Press, 1991).

264. Owen, "Media Mayhem," 127.

265. Richard Morin, "Toward the Millennium, by the Numbers," *Washington Post National Weekly Edition*, July 7, 1997, 35.

266. Patterson, *Out of Order*, 81–82.

267. Fallows, *Breaking the News*, 162, 27.

268. Epstein, *News from Nowhere*, 179, 195.

269. Rosenstiel, *State of the News Media*, 18.

270. John Horn, "Campaign Coverage Avoids Issues," *Lincoln Journal-Star*, September 25, 1988. Another survey found that 28 percent of women and 40 percent of men change channels every time during commercial breaks. "Ticker," *Brill's Content*, September 1999, 128.

271. John Eisendrath, "An Eyewitness Account of Local TV News," *Washington Monthly*, September 1986, 21.

272. Michael Deaver, "Sound-Bite Campaigning: TV Made Us Do It," *Washington Post National Weekly Edition*, November 7, 1988, 34.

273. Fred Friendly, quoted on *All Things Considered*, National Public Radio, March 4, 1998.

274. Thomas E. Patterson, *The Vanishing Voter* (New York: Knopf, 2002), 92.

275. The extent of the media's impact has been debated over the years. See Lawrence Bartels, "Messages Received: The Political Impact of Media Exposure," *American Political Science Review* 87 (June 1983), 267–285; John R. Zaller, "The Myth of Massive Media Impact Revived: New Support for a Discredited Idea," in *Political Persuasion and Attitude Change*, ed. Diane Mutz, Paul Sniderman, and Richard Brody (Ann Arbor: University of Michigan Press, 1996).

276. Donald L. Shaw and Maxwell E. McCombs, *The Emergence of American Political Issues: The Agenda-Setting Function of the Press* (Saint Paul, Minn.: West, 1977). For a review of agenda-setting research, see Everett M. Rogers and James W. Dearing, "Agenda-Setting Research: Where Has It Been, Where Is It Going?" in *Communication Yearbook 11* (Newbury Park, Calif.: Sage, 1988), 555–594.

277. Lutz Erbring, Edie N. Goldenberg, and Arthur H. Miller, "Front-Page News and Real-World Clues: A New Look at Agenda-Setting by the Media," *American Journal of Political Science* 24 (February 1980), 16–49.

278. Michael Bruce MacKuen and Steven Lane Coombs, *More than News* (Beverly Hills, Calif.: Sage, 1981), 140; Rogers and Dearing, "Agenda-Setting Research," 572–576; Gladys Engel Lang and Kurt Lang, *The Battle for Public Opinion* (New York: Columbia University Press, 1983), 58–59.

279. Richard Morin, "Public Enemy No. 1: Crime," *Washington Post National Weekly Edition*, January 24, 1994, 37; Molly Ivins, "Hard Questions, Easy Answers," *Lincoln Journal*, July 7, 1994; Richard Morin, "A Public Paradox on the Drug War," *Washington Post National Weekly Edition*, March 23, 1998, 35.

280. Erbring et al., "Front-Page News," 38; MacKuen and Coombs, *More than News*, 128–137.

281. Shanto Iyengar and Donald R. Kinder, *News That Matters* (Chicago: University of Chicago Press, 1987), 42–45.

282. Rogers and Dearing, "Agenda-Setting Research," 569; MacKuen and Coombs, *More than News*, 101; Erbring et al., "Front-Page News," 38.

283. Rogers and Dearing, "Agenda-Setting Research," 577, citing Jack L. Walker, "Setting the Agenda in the U.S. Senate," *British Journal of Political Science* 7 (1977), 423–445. See also Cook, *Making Laws and Making News*, 116, 130–131.

284. Michael J. Robinson and Margaret A. Sheehan, *Over the Wire and on TV* (New York: Russell Sage Foundation/Basic Books, 1983); Robinson, "Media Campaign, '84," 45–47.

285. Thomas Griffith, "Leave Off the Label," *Time*, September 19, 1984, 63.

286. He did own property in the district, so he did satisfy the residency requirement.

287. Charles Krauthammer, "We Conservatives Had a Dream: His Name Was Howard Dean," *Lincoln Journal Star*, January 24, 2003.

288. Although Dean's campaign had started declining before this speech, he would have done better in the New Hampshire primary and then could have hung on longer. The speech received so much attention because it confirmed for reporters their be-

lief that he said inappropriate things and was "not presidential."

289. Doris A. Graber, "Kind Pictures and Harsh Words: How Television Presents the Candidates," in *Elections in America,* ed. Kay Lehman Schlozman (Boston: Allen & Unwin, 1987), 141.

290. Ibid., 116.

291. Anthony Lewis, quoted in Larry J. Sabato, "Open Season: How the News Media Cover Presidential Campaigns in the Age of Attack Journalism," in *Under the Watchful Eye,* ed. Mathew D. McCubbins (Washington, D.C.: CQ Press, 1992), 146.

292. Tannen, *Argument Culture,* 79–83.

293. See the excellent summary found in Stephen Ansolabehere, Roy Behr, and Shanto Iyengar, "Mass Media and Elections," *American Politics Quarterly* 19 (January 1991), 109–139.

294. Bruce Buchanan, *Electing a President: The Markle Commission Report on Campaign '88* (Austin: University of Texas Press, 1990); Montague Kean, *30-Second Politics* (New York: Praeger, 1989); Marion Just, Lori Wallach, and Ann Crigler, "Thirty Seconds or Thirty Minutes: Political Learning in an Election," paper presented at the annual meeting of the Midwest Political Science Association, Chicago, April 1987.

295. In the Democratic race in 1976, Jimmy Carter finished second to "uncommitted" in the Iowa caucuses. This was enough to give him twenty-three times more coverage in *Time* and *Newsweek* and five times more coverage on network television than any of his rivals. Finishing first by just 4 percent in the New Hampshire primary landed him on the covers of *Time* and *Newsweek* and brought him twenty-five times more coverage on network television than the runner-up. David Paletz and Robert Entrum, *Media—Power—Politics* (New York: Macmillan, 1981), 35ff.

296. Patterson, *Out of Order,* 44.

297. Ansolabehere et al., "Mass Media and Elections," 128–129; Christine F. Ridout, "The Role of Media Coverage of Iowa and New Hampshire in the 1988 Democratic Nomination," *American Politics Quarterly* 19 (January 1991), 45–46, 53–54; Marc Howard Ross, "Television News and Candidate Fortunes in Presidential Nomination Campaigns," *American Politics Quarterly* 20 (January 1992), 69–98.

298. Henry Brady, "Chances, Utilities, and Voting in Presidential Primaries," paper delivered at the annual meeting of the Public Choice Society, Phoenix, 1984, cited in Ansolabehere et al., "Mass Media and Elections"; Bartels, *Presidential Primaries and the Dynamics of Public Choice* (Princeton, N.J.: Princeton University Press, 1988).

299. Lee Sigelman and Carol K. Sigelman, "Judgments of the Carter-Reagan Debate," *Public Opinion Quarterly* 48 (1984), 624–628.

300. Theodore H. White, *The Making of the President, 1960* (New York: Atheneum, 1961), 333.

301. The clearest examples occurred in 1976 and 1984. In the 1976 debate between Gerald Ford and Jimmy Carter, Ford erroneously said that there was "no Soviet domination of Eastern Europe." People surveyed within twelve hours of the debate said they thought Ford won. But the media zeroed in on this slip, and people surveyed later said they thought Carter had won. In the first debate in 1984, Reagan appeared tired and confused. By a *modest margin,* people polled immediately after the debate said they thought Walter Mondale had won. But the media focused on Reagan's age and abilities, and by *increasingly large margins,* people polled in the days after the debate said Mondale had won. Perhaps viewers did not catch Ford's statement or, due to selective perception, notice Reagan's doddering, but the media called attention to them, which prompted many viewers to reconsider and reverse their verdict.

302. John R. Zaller, "Monica Lewinsky's Contribution to Political Science," *PS,* June 1998, 182–189.

303. MacKuen and Coombs, *More than News,* 222.

304. For a review, see ibid., 147–161.

305. Robert S. Erickson, "The Influence of Newspaper Endorsements in Presidential Elections," *American Journal of Political Science* 20 (1976), 207–233; Dalton et al., "Partisan Cues." Also see Kahn and Kenney, "Slant of the News."

306. David Barker, "The Talk Radio Community," *Social Science Quarterly* 79 (1998), 261–272; C. Richard Hofstetter, "Political Talk Radio, Situational Involvement, and Political Mobilization," *Social Science Quarterly* 79 (1998), 273–286.

307. Benjamin I. Page, Robert Y. Shapiro, and Glenn R. Dempsey, "What Moves Public Opinion?" *American Political Science Review* 81 (1987), 23–43. Critical news and commentaries about presidents seem to lower their popularity. Darrell M. West, "Television and Presidential Popularity in America," *British Journal of Political Science* 21 (1991), 199–214. Even television's "framing" of events, as isolated incidents or parts of patterns, affects viewers' opinions about these events. Shanto Iyengar, *Is Anyone Responsible? How Television Frames Political Issues* (Chicago: University of Chicago Press, 1991). See also Thomas E. Nelson, Rosalee A. Clawson, and Zoe M. Oxley, "Media Framing of a Civil Liberties Conflict and Its Effect on Tolerance," *American Political Science Review* 91 (1997), 567–583.

308. Iyengar, *Is Anyone Responsible?* ch. 6 and 8.

309. Kathleen Hall Jamieson, quoted in Howard Kurtz, "Tuning Out the News," *Washington Post National Weekly Edition,* May 29, 1995, 6; William Raspberry, "Blow-by-Blow Coverage," *Washington Post National Weekly Edition,* November 6, 1995, 29.

310. Michael J. Robinson, "Public Affairs Television and the Growth of Political Malaise," *American Political Science Review* 70 (1976), 409–432; Miller et al., "Type-Set Politics."

311. "Study: Public More Cynical than Media," *Champaign-Urbana News-Gazette,* May 22, 1995.

312. Fallows, *Breaking the News,* 202–203.

313. See Cappella and Jamieson, *Spiral of Cynicism.*

314. Fallows, *Breaking the News,* 247.

315. Graber, *Mass Media,* 244; Doris Graber, *Processing News: How People Tame the Information Tide* (White Plains, N.Y.: Longman, 1984). A 1993 survey concluded that almost half of Americans over sixteen have such limited reading and math skills that they are unfit for most jobs. One task the survey included was to paraphrase a newspaper story. Many people could scan the story but not paraphrase it when they finished it. Paul Gray, "Adding Up the Under-Skilled," *Time,* September 20, 1993, 75. For a critique, claiming that the oligopolistic structure of the media makes it impossible to know if people are getting what they actually want, see McChesney, *Problem of the Media,* 198–202.

316. Reuven Frank, quoted in Neil Hickey, "Money Lust," *Columbia Journalism Review,* July-August 1998, 35.

317. The idea for this paragraph came from James Fallows, "Did You Have a Good Week?" *Atlantic Monthly,* December 1994, 32, 34.

318. Iyengar, *Is Anyone Responsible?*

319. James Poniewozik, "Don't Blame It on Jayson Blair," *Time,* June 9, 2003, 90.

320. Times Mirror Center for the People and the Press, "The New Political Landscape" (poll), October 1994.

321. Joe Klein, "Dizzy Days," *New Yorker,* October 5, 1998, 45.

322. Marta W. Aldrich, "Support for Media Freedoms Waning," *Lincoln Journal-Star,* July 4, 1999.

323. Stephen Earl Bennett, "Trends in Americans' Political Information," *American Politics Quarterly* 17 (October 1989), 422–435; Richard Zoglin, "The Tuned-Out Generation," *Time,* July 9, 1990, 64.

324. Robert N. Entman, *Democracy without Citizens: Media and the Decay of American Politics* (New York: Oxford University Press, 1989), 17.

325. See McChesney, *Problem of the Media,* 96–97.

326. Peters, *How Washington Really Works,* 32.

327. The source for the epilogue, except where noted otherwise, is Kotz, "Breaking Point."

328. Tannen, *Argument Culture,* 82.

329. Ibid., 74.

330. Yet when journalists themselves come under occasional attack from other media, they do not like it any more than officials do. They are just as "thin-skinned" as officials are. Issues of *Brill's Content* provide numerous examples. Another example comes from Toobin, *Vast Conspiracy,* 268. After the 1992 election, Linda Bloodworth-Thomason, a Hollywood supporter of Bill Clinton, produced a short film for the inauguration. The film included a series of sound bites from Washington journalists during the campaign, dismissing Clinton as "unelectable" and "dead meat." Although Thomason apparently regarded the film as "a harmless needle at some puffed up egos," some of the journalists regarded it as "an act of war." In Toobin's view, the controversy over the film, which poisoned the relationship between the president and the press from the beginning, reflected the thin skins of the press corps.

Chapter 6

1. "Gray Power," *Time,* January 4, 1988, 36.

2. "Our Footloose Correspondents," *New Yorker,* August 8, 1988, 70.

3. "Is Bush Abusing Seniors with Medicare Rx Benefit?" Factcheck.org, January 9, 2004, www.factcheck.org/article125.html.

4. March Kaufman and Bill Brubaker, "Drug Prices Soar in 4 Years," *Lincoln Journal-Star,* May 26, 2004, 3A.

5. Jim Drinkard, "Drug Bill a Well-Financed Victory for Industry," *USA Today,* July 6, 2003, A04.

6. Jeffrey H. Birnbaum, *The Lobbyists: How Influence Peddlers Get Their Way in Washington* (New York: Times Books, 1993), 32.

7. Mark A. Peterson and Jack. L. Walker Jr., "Interest Group Responses to Partisan Change: The Impact of the Reagan Administration upon the National Interest Group System," in *Interest Group Politics,* 2nd ed., ed. Allan J. Cigler and Burdett A. Loomis (Washington, D.C.: CQ Press, 1987), 162.

8. Alexis de Tocqueville, *Democracy in America* (New York: Knopf, 1945), 191. (Originally published 1835)

9. Gabriel Almond and Sidney Verba, *Civil Culture* (Boston: Little, Brown, 1965), 266–306.

10. David Truman, *The Governmental Process* (New York: Knopf, 1964),25–26.

11. Ibid., 59.

12. Ibid., 26–33.

13. James Q. Wilson, *Political Organizations* (New York: Basic Books, 1973), 198.

14. Graham. K. Wilson, *Interest Groups in America* (Oxford: Oxford University Press, 1981), ch. 5; see also Graham K. Wilson, "American Business and Politics," in *Interest Group Politics,* 2nd ed., ed. Cigler and Loomis, 221–235.

15. Kay Lehman Schlozman and John T. Tierney, "More of the State: Washington Pressure Group Activity in a Decade of Change," *Journal of Politics* 45 (1983), 335–356.

16. Christopher H. Foreman Jr., "Grassroots Victim Organizations: Mobilizing for Personal and Public Health," in *Interest Group Politics,* 4th ed., ed. Allan J. Cigler and Burdett A. Loomis (Washington, D.C.: CQ Press, 1994), 33–53.

17. William Brown, "Exchange Theory and the Institutional Impetus for Interest Group Formation," in *Interest Group Politics,* 6th ed., ed. Allan J. Cigler and Burdett A. Looms (Washington, D.C.: CQ Press, 2002), 313–329; William Brown, "Benefits and Membership: A Reappraisal of Interest Group Activity," *Western Political Quarterly* 29 (1976), 258–273; Terry M. Moe, *The Organization of Interests: Incentives and the Internal Dynamics of Political Interest*

Groups (Chicago: University of Chicago Press, 1980).

18. Jack L. Walker Jr., "The Origins and Maintenance of Interest Groups in America," *American Political Science Review* 77 (1983), 398–400.

19. Robert. H. Salisbury "An Exchange Theory of Interest Groups," *Midwest Journal of Political Science* 13 (1969): 1–32.

20. Jeffrey M. Berry, *The Interest Group Society* (Boston: Little Brown, 1984), 26–28.

21. Ibid.

22. Wilson, *Political Organizations*, ch. 3.

23. Alex Kuczynski, "New AARP Magazine Courting Younger Readers," *New York Times*, January 22, 2001, C1.

24. Clyde Brown, "Explanations of Interest Group Membership over Time," *American Politics Quarterly* 17 (1989), 32–53.

25. Nicholas Babchuk and Ralph V. Thompson, "The Voluntary Associations of Negroes," *American Sociological Review* 27 (1962), 662–665; see also Patricia Klobus-Edwards, John N. Edwards, and David L. Klemmack, "Differences in Social Participation of Blacks and Whites," *Social Forces* 56 (1978), 1035–1052.

26. Robert D. Putnam, *Bowling Alone* (New York: Simon & Schuster, 2000). See also Robert D. Putnam, "Bowling Alone: America's Declining Social Capital," *Journal of Democracy* 6 (1995), 65–78, and Robert J. Samuelson, "Join the Club," *Washington Post National Weekly Edition*, April 15, 1996, 5.

27. Theda Skocpol, "The Narrowing of Civic Life," *American Prospect*, June 2004, A5–A7.

28. Samuelson, "Join the Club."

29. Richard Stengel, "Bowling Together," *Time*, July 22, 1996, 35.

30. Theda Skocpol, "Associations without Members," *American Prospect*, July-August 1999, 66–73.

31. Mark T. Hayes, "The New Group Universe," in *Interest Group Politics*, 2nd ed., ed. Cigler and Loomis, 133–145.

32. Calvin Tomkins, "A Sense of Urgency," *New Yorker*, March 27, 1989, 48–74.

33. Walker, "Origins and Maintenance of Interest Groups"; E. E. Schattschneider, *Semi-Sovereign People* (New York: Holt, Rinehart and Winston, 1960), 118.

34. David S. Broder and Michael Weisskopf, "Finding New Friends on the Hill," *Washington Post National Weekly Edition*, October 3, 1994, 11.

35. Charles E. Lindblom, "The Market as Prison," *Journal of Politics* 44 (1982), 324–336; Michael Genovese, *The Presidential Dilemma: Leadership in the American System* (New York: HarperCollins, 1995).

36. Steven Greenhouse, "Labor Is Forced to Reassess as Union Leaders Convene," *New York Times*, March 9, 2004, A12.

37. Steven Greenhouse, "Union Membership Rose in '98, but Unions' Percentage of Workforce Fell," *New York Times*, January 20, 1999, A22; Paul E. Johnson, "Organized Labor in an Era of Blue-Collar Decline," in *Interest Group Politics*, 3rd ed., ed. Allan J. Cigler and Burdett A. Loomis (Washington, D.C.: CQ Press, 1991), 33–62.

38. Harold Myerson, "Organize or Die," *American Prospect*, September 2003, 39–42.

39. Steven Greenhouse, "Report Faults Laws for Slowing Growth of Unions," *New York Times*, October 24, 2000, A14.

40. Steven Greenhouse, "Union Membership Slides Despite Increased Organizing," *New York Times*, March 22, 1998, A8.

41. "Poll Indicates Unions Gaining Favor with Public," *Champaign, Illinois, News-Gazette*, August 30, 2001, C10.

42. David S. Broder, "The Price of Labor's Decline," *Washington Post*, September 9, 2004, A27. See also Lawrence Mishel, Jared Bernstein, and Sylvia Allegretto, *The State of Working America* (Washington, D.C.: Economic Policy Institute, 2004).

43. Broder, "Price of Labor's Decline."

44. Frank Swoboda, "A Healthy Outcome for Organized Labor," *Washington Post National Weekly Edition*, March 8, 1999, 18; Steven Greenhouse, "In Biggest Drive since 1937, Union Gains a Victory," *New York Times*, February 26, 1999, A1.

45. Steven Greenhouse, "The Most Innovative Figure in Silicon Valley? Maybe This Labor Organizer," *New York Times*, November 14, 1999, 26.

46. Steven Greenhouse, "Angered by HMOs' Treatment, More Doctors Are Joining Unions," *New York Times*, February 4, 1999, A1, A25.

47. Steven Greenhouse, "Graduate Students Push for Union Membership," *New York Times*, May 15, 2001, A18.

48. Undergraduate resident hall advisers at the University of Massachusetts recently voted to affiliate with the United Auto Workers. The issue is job security. A residence hall assistant was fired for missing a staff meeting. Richard Corliss, "RAs of the World Unite!" *Time*, March 25, 2002, 56; Daniel J. Fitzgibbons, "Administration Opposes Union Bid by RAs," *University of Massachusetts, Campus Chronicle*, April 13, 2001.

49. Steven Greenhouse, "Labor Federation Looks beyond Unions," *New York Times*, July 11, 2004, 18.

50. Allan J. Cigler and John M. Hansen, "Group Formation through Protest: The American Agriculture Movement," in *Interest Group Politics*, 1st ed., ed. Allan J. Cigler and Burdett A. Loomis (Washington, D.C.: CQ Press, 1983), 84–109; Allan J. Cigler, "Organizational Maintenance and Political Activity on the Cheap: The American Agriculture Movement," in *Interest Group Politics*, 3rd ed., ed. Allan J. Cigler and Burdett A. Loomis (Washington, D.C.: CQ Press, 1991), 81–108.

51. Information on annual expenditures is found in U.S. Census Bureau, *Statistical Abstract of the United States, 2003* (Washington, D.C.: Government Printing Office, 2003), tab. 812.

52. Dick Lugar, "The Farm Bill Charade," *New York Times*, January 21, 2002, A15.

53. Andrew S. McFarland, *Common Cause: Lobbying in the Public Interest* (Chatham, N.J.: Chatham House, 1984); see also Andrew S. McFarland, *Public Interest Lobbies: Decision Making on Energy* (Washington, D.C.: American Enterprise Institute, 1976).

54. Ronald G. Shaiko, "More Bang for the Buck: The New Era of Full-Service Public Interest Groups," in *Interest Group Politics*, 3rd ed., ed. Cigler and Loomis, 109.

55. Ibid., 120.

56. For a discussion of the evolution of NOW and its success in lobbying Congress, see Anne N. Costain and W. Douglas Costain, "The Women's Lobby: Impact of a Movement on Congress," in *Interest Group Politics*, ed. Cigler and Loomis.

57. EMILY'S List home page, www.emilyslist.org.; Jeffrey H. Birnbaum and Eric Pooley, "New Party Bosses," *Time*, April 8, 1996, 28–32.

58. Richard Morin and Claudia Deane, "The Administration's Right-Hand Women," *Washington Post National Weekly Edition*, May 7, 2001, 12.

59. Eric M. Uslaner, "A Tower of Babel on Foreign Policy," in *Interest Group Politics*, 3rd ed., ed. Cigler and Loomis, 309.

60. Kenneth D. Wald, *Religion and Politics* (New York: St. Martin's Press, 1985), 182–212.

61. Sidney Blumenthal, "Christian Soldiers," *New Yorker*, July 18, 1994, 36.

62. James L. Guth, John C. Green, Lyman A. Jellstedt, and Corwin E. Struck, "Onward Christian Soldiers: Religious Activist Groups in American Politics," in *Interest Group Politics*, 3rd ed., ed. Cigler and Loomis, 57; Charles Levendosky, "Alternative Religious Voice Finally Being Raised," *Lincoln Journal-Star*, March 3, 1996, 7B.

63. Michael Lind, "The Right Still Has Religion," *New York Times*, December 9, 2001, Section 4, 13; Blumenthal, "Christian Soldiers."

64. "Citing 'Moral Crisis,' a Call to Oust Clinton," *New York Times*, October 23, 1998, A1, A8.

65. Richard Parker, "On God and Democrats," *American Prospect*, March 2004, 40.

66. Richard Berke, "Falwell Is Raising Money to Press Conservative Family Agenda," *New York Times*, December 14, 2001, A1, A9.

67. David Firestone, "Evangelical Christians and Jews Unite for Israel," *New York Times*, June 9, 2003, 25.

68. Malcolm Foster, "Christian Zionists See Bush Peace Plan as Biblical Betrayal," *Lincoln Journal-Star*, July 26, 2003, 3C.

69. Parker, "On God and Democrats."

70. Levendosky, "Alternative Religious Voice."

71. Lynette Clemetson, "Clergy Group to Counter Conservatives," *New York Times*, November 17, 2003, A15.

72. Stephanie Simon, "Atheist Organization Jubilant over Ruling on Pledge," *San Francisco Chronicle*, July 1, 2002, A2.

73. Elisabeth Bumiller, "On Gay Marriage, Bush May Have Said All He's Going To," *New York Times*, March 1, 2004, A15.

74. Shawn Zeller, "Marching On, but Apart," *National Journal*, January 12, 2002, 98–103.

75. Sheryl Gay Stolberg, "Vocal Gay Republicans Upsetting Conservatives," *New York Times*, June 1, 2003, A15.

76. "Gender Rights: Helping Men, Women, Etc.," *Time*, June 18, 2001, 72.

77. Ibid.

78. Christopher J. Bosso, "Adaptation and Change in the Environmental Movement," in *Interest Group Politics*, 3rd ed., ed. Cigler and Loomis, 155–156.

79. Ibid., 162.

80. Ibid., 169.

81. Andrew Goldstein, "Too Green for Their Own Good?" *Time*, August 26, 2002, A58.

82. Katharine Q. Seelye, "Bush Team Still Reversing Environmental Policies," *New York Times*, November 18, 2001, A20.

83. John Mintz, "Would Bush Be the NBA's Point Man in the White House?" *Washington Post National Weekly Edition*, May 8, 2000, 14; Mike Doming, "NRA Promises an All-Out Assault on Al Gore's Presidential Campaign," *Lincoln Journal-Star*, May 21, 2000, 2A; Thomas B. Edsall, "Targeting Al Gore with $10 Million," *Washington Post National Weekly Edition*, May 29, 2000, 11.

84. Linda Greenhouse, "U.S., in a Shift, Tells Justices Citizens Have a Right to Guns," *New York Times*, May 8, 2002, A1.

85. Ibid.

86. Ibid.

87. "Echoes of Tobacco Battle in Gun Suits," *New York Times*, February 21, 1999, 18.

88. Bob Herbert, "The NRA Is Naming Names," *New York Times*, October 13, 2004, A21.

89. Robin Toner, "Abortion's Opponents Claim the Middle Ground," *New York Times*, April 25, 2004, Section 4, 1.

90. Kate Zernike, "30 Years after Abortion Ruling, New Trends but the Old Debate," *New York Times*, January 20, 2003, A1, A16.

91. Sam Howe Verhovek, "Creators of Antiabortion Web Site Told to Pay Millions," *New York Times*, February 3, 1999, A11.

92. Charles Lane, "Ruling Curbs Abortion Foes' Tactics: Court Says 'Wanted' Posters and Web Site Are Intimidation," *Washington Post*, May 17, 2002, A2.

93. Alissa Rubin, "Interest Groups and Abortion Politics in the Post-Webster Era," in *Interest Group Politics*, 3rd ed., ed. Cigler and Loomis, 249–251; *Congressional Quarterly Weekly Report*, March 27, 1993, 755–757; "More than a Million March in Washington for Reproductive Rights," press release, Planned Parenthood Federation of American, April 25, 2004.

94. David S. Broder, "Let 100 Single-Issue Groups Bloom," *Washington Post,* January 7, 1979, C1–C2; see also David S. Broder, *The Party's Over: The Failure of Politics in America* (New York: Harper & Row, 1972).

95. Wilson, *Interest Groups in America,* ch. 4.

96. Ed Henry, "It's the '90s: Old Dogs, New Tricks," *Roll Call Monthly,* November 1997, 1.

97. Diana M. Evans, "Lobbying the Committee: Interest Groups and the House Public Works and Transportation Committee in the Post-Webster Era," in *Interest Group Politics,* 3rd ed., ed. Cigler and Loomis, 257–276.

98. Berry, *Interest Group Society,* 188.

99. Birnbaum, *Lobbyists,* 40.

100. Leslie Wayne and Michael Moss, "A Nation Challenged: The Airlines; Bailout for Airlines Showed the Weight of Mighty Lobby," *New York Times,* October 10, 2001, Al, B10.

101. Ibid., B10.

102. Ibid., B10.

103. Ibid., B10.

104. Robert Pear, "Lobbyists Seek Special Spin on Federal Bioterrorism Bill," *New York Times,* December 11, 2001, A1, A18.

105. Ernest Wittenberg and Elisabeth Wittenberg, *How to Win in Washington* (Cambridge, Mass.: Blackwell, 1989), 24.

106. Elizabeth Drew, *Politics and Money: The New Road to Corruption* (New York: Macmillan, 1983), 78.

107. Ibid.

108. Lowell Bergman and Jeff Gerth, "Power Trader Tied to Bush Finds Washington All Ears," *New York Times,* May 25, 2001, A1.

109. Ibid.

110. Eric Schmitt, "Nomination for FDA Post Nears Approval in Senate," *New York Times,* October 21, 1998, A13.

111. Rebecca Adams, "Harvard Professor Faces Tough Questions but Is Expected to Win Confirmation as Head of Regulatory Affairs Office," *CQ Weekly,* May 19, 2001, 1166.

112. Sheryl Gay Stolberg, "Bush in Political Hot Spot in Picking an FDA. Chief," *New York Times,* February 8, 2002, A17; Sheryl Gay Stolberg, "Deputy Is Appointed to Direct Food and Drug Agency as Impasse Continues," *New York Times,* February 26, 2002, A22.

113. Evelyn Nieves, "Civil Rights Groups Suing Berkeley over Admissions Policy," *New York Times,* February 3, 1999, A11.

114. William Glaberson, "Groups Gird for Long Legal Fight on New Bush Antiterror Powers," *New York Times,* November 30, 2001, Al, B7.

115. James Dao, "Environmental Groups to File Suit over Missile Defenses," *New York Times,* August 28, 2001, A10.

116. For more on interest group litigation at the district court level, see Lee Epstein and C. K. Rowland, "Debunking the Myth of Interest Group Invincibility in the Courts," *American Political Science Review* 85 (1991), 205–220.

117. Samuel Kernell, *Going Public: New Strategies of Presidential Leadership* (Washington, D.C.: CQ Press, 1986), 34.

118. Richard Harris, "If You Love Your Grass," *New Yorker,* April 20, 1968, 57.

119. Alison Mitchell, "A New Form of Lobbying Puts Public Face on Private Interest," *New York Times,* September 30, 1998, Al, A14.

120. Ibid.

121. Evans, "Lobbying the Committee," 269.

122. Michael Weisskopf, "Letting No Grass Roots Grow under Their Feet," *Washington Post National Weekly Edition,* October 24, 1993, 20–21.

123. Sandra G. Boodman, "Health Care's Power Player," *Washington Post National Weekly Edition,* February 14, 1994, 6.

124. Ibid., 7.

125. Ibid., 7.

126. Ibid., 7.

127. "MoveOn's Big Moment," *Time,* November 24, 2003, 32.

128. George Packer, "Smart-Mobbing the War," *New York Times Magazine,* March 9, 2003, 46–49.

129. Boodman, "Health Care's Power Player," 7.

130. James Dao, "The 2000 Campaign: The Grassroots," *New York Times,* October 21, 2000, Section 1, 18.

131. Ibid.

132. Michael Towle, "Ad for Fighter Plan Aimed at Congress," *Lincoln Journal-Star,* May 2, 1997, 7A.

133. Greenpeace, *Denial and Deception: A Chronicle of ExxonMobil's Efforts to Corrupt the Debate on Global Warming* (Washington, D.C.: Greenpeace, 2002).

134. Birnbaum, *Lobbyists,* 40.

135. Steven Greenhouse, "Carnival of Derision to Greet the Princes of Global Trade," *New York Times,* November 11, 1999, A12.

136. Ibid.

137. Cary Goldberg, "How Political Theater Lost Its Audience," *New York Times,* September 21, 1997, 6; "Greenpeace Protest Shipload of Newsprint," *Lincoln Journal-Star,* October 21, 1999, 3; "15 Antimissile Protesters Face Felony Charges," *New York Times,* August 12, 2001, A16.

138. Dan Balz and David S. Broder, "Take Two Lobbyists and Call Me in the Morning," *Washington Post National Weekly Edition,* October 18, 1993, 10–11.

139. Rebecca Adams, "Intense Lobbying Gets under Way over Whether to Block Ergonomics Rules," *CQ Weekly,* February 10, 2001, 328.

140. R. Kenneth Godwin and Barry J. Seldon, "What Corporations Really Want from Government: The Public Provision of Private Goods," in *Interest Group Politics,* 6th ed., ed. Allan J. Cigler and Burdett A. Loomis (Washington, D.C.: CQ Press, 2002), 205–224.

141. Much of the information in this section is from Burdett A. Loomis, "Coalitions of Interests: Building Bridges in the Balkanized State," in *Interest Group Politics,* 2nd ed., ed. Cigler and Loomis, 258–274.

142. Birnbaum, *Lobbyists,* 83.

143. David Segal, "Bob Dole Leads the Cast of Rainmakers," *Washington Post National Weekly Edition,* September 27, 1997, 20.

144. Deborah L. Acomb, "Poll Track," *National Journal,* January 5, 2002, 58.

145. Godwin and Seldon, "What Corporations Really Want."

146. Dan Clawson, Alan Neustadt, and Denise Scott, *Money Talks* (New York: Basic Books, 1992), 91.

147. Schattschneider, *Semi-Sovereign People,* ch. 2.

148. Ibid., 35.

149. Kevin Phillips, "Fat City," *Time,* September 26, 1995, 51.

150. Christopher Jencks, "On Unequal Democracy," *American Prospect,* June 2004, A2–A4; see also Katherine Neckerman, *Social Inequality* (New York: Russell Sage Foundation, 2004).

151. Robert Pear and Robin Toner, "Medicare Plan Covering Drugs Backed by AARP," *New York Times,* November 18, 2003, A16.

152. Ibid.

153. Gary Rotstein, "Members Give AARP Earful for Backing GOP Plan," *Pittsburgh Post-Gazette,* Nov 19, 2003, A1.

154. Ibid.

155. David S. Broder and Amy Goldstein, "How the GOP Wooed AARP," *Washington Post National Weekly Edition,* November 24, 2003, 11; Mark Sherman, "Angry Members Leave AARP," *Lincoln Journal-Star,* January 17, 2004, 3A.

156. "A Seniors Moment," *New York Times Magazine,* December 7, 2003, 28.

157. Sherman, "Angry Members."

158. Barbara T. Dreyfuss, "The Seduction," *American Prospect,* June 2004, 18–23.

159. "Seniors Moment."

160. Ibid.

161. Sheryl Gay Stolberg and Milt Freudenheim, "AARP Support for Medicare Bill Came as Membership Grew 'Younger,'" *New York Times,* November 26, 2003, A1.

162. Ibid.

Chapter 7

1. Jonathan Franzen, "The Listener," *New Yorker,* October 6, 2003, 85–90.

2. Background information from Brian Nutting and H. Amy Stern, eds., *CQ's Politics in America, 2002: The 107th Congress* (Washington, D.C.: CQ Press, 2001).

3. Dana Milbank and David S. Broder, "Can't They Just Get Along?" *Washington Post National Weekly Edition,* January 26, 2004, 6–7.

4. Theda Skocpol, "A Bad Senior Moment," *American Prospect,* January 2004, 26–29.

5. Charles Babington, "Scorched-Earth Politics," *Washington Post National Weekly Edition,* January 5, 2004, 22.

6. Sheryl Gay Stolberg, "The High Costs of Rising Incivility on Capitol Hill," *New York Times,* November 30, 2003, 10.

7. According to Norm Ornstein, cited in Paul Glastris, "Perverse Polarity," *Washington Monthly,* June, 2004, 22.

8. E. E. Schattschneider, *Party Government* (New York: Holt, Rinehart and Winston, 1960), 1.

9. Jack Dennis, "Trends in Public Support for the American Party System," in *Parties and Elections in an Anti-Party Age,* ed. Jeff Fishel (Bloomington: Indiana University Press, 1978).

10. Frank J. Sorauf, *Political Parties in the American System,* 4th ed. (Boston: Little, Brown, 1980).

11. Maurice Duverger, *Political Parties* (New York: Wiley, 1963). See also Edward R. Tufte, "The Relationship between Seats and Votes in Two-Party Systems," *American Political Science Review* 67 (1973), 540–554.

12. Theodore J. Lowi, in *The Personal President: Power Invested, Promise Unfulfilled* (Ithaca, N.Y.: Cornell University Press, 1985), notes that the two-party system survived in the United States despite the use of multimember districts in elections for Congress in the nineteenth century.

13. *CQ Weekly,* January 12, 2002, 136; *CQ Weekly,* January 2, 2004, 53.

14. Robert S. Erikson, Gerald C. Wright, and John P. McIver, *Statehouse Democracy: Public Opinion and Policy in the American States* (New York: Cambridge University Press, 1993), ch. 5.

15. Frank Bruni, "Bush Signaling Readiness to Go His Own Way," *New York Times,* April 3, 2000, A1–A15.

16. Robert G. Kaiser, "Hindsight Is 20/20," *Washington Post National Weekly Edition,* February 19, 2001, 11. Nader's support in Florida and New Hampshire prevented Gore from winning those states.

17. Barbara Ehrenreich, "Don't Blame Me," *Time,* November 20, 2000, 69.

18. "Republicans Helping Nader," NewsMax.com, July 12, 2004 (www.newsmax.com/archives/articles/2004/7/11/160540.shtml). This amounted to about $50,000 of the $1 million Nader had raised at the time.

19. Ralph Nader, "My Untold Story," *Brill's Content,* February 2001.

20. Richard Hofstadter, *The Idea of the Party System: The Rise of Legitimate Opposition in the United States, 1780–1840* (Berkeley: University of California Press, 1969).

21. Lowi, *Personal Presidency.*

22. James MacGregor Burns, *The Vineyard of Liberty* (New York: Knopf, 1982).

23. In 1820, there had been around 1.2 million free white men over twenty-five years of age; by 1840,

there were 3.2 million white men of over the age of twenty.

24. Robert A. Dahl, *How Democratic is the American Constitution?* (New Haven: Yale University Press, 2003), 30.

25. Ibid.

26. William L. Riordon, *Plunkitt of Tammany Hall* (New York: E.P. Dutton, 1963) 28.

27. Milton L. Rakove, *Don't Make No Waves, Don't Back No Losers* (Bloomington: Indiana University Press, 1975), 112.

28. Kevin Phillips, *The Emerging Republican Majority* (New York: Doubleday, 1969).

29. In contrast, European parties do have members, who pay dues and sign a pledge that they accept the basic principles of the party. The percentage of voters who are members ranges from 1 or 2 percent in some countries to over 40 percent in others. 30. National Election Study, 2002.

31. James L. Sundquist, *Dynamics of the Party System: Alignment and Realignment of Political Parties in the United States* (Washington, D.C.: Brookings Institution, 1973).

32. Phillips, *Emerging Republican Majority.*

33. Tali Mendelberg, *The Race Card,* (Princeton, N.J.: Princeton University Press, 2001).

34. Ibid., 97.

35. Ibid., 3.

36. Thomas F. Shaller, "Forget the South," *Washington Post National Weekly Edition,* November 24, 2003, 21.

37. Thomas B. Edsall, "The Fissure Running through the Democratic Party," *Washington Post National Weekly Edition,* June 6, 1994, 11.

38. John R. Petrocik and Frederick T. Steeper, "The Political Landscape in 1988," *Public Opinion,* September-October 1987, 41–44; Helmut Norpoth, "Party Realignment in the 1980s," *Public Opinion Quarterly* 51 (1987), 376–390.

39. Edsall, "Fissure," 11.

40. Thomas B. Edsall, "The Shifting Sands of America's Political Parties," *Washington Post National Weekly Edition,* April 9, 2001, 11.

41. Mary Agnes Carey, "Democrats Want Women: Party Targets Single Female Voters," *CQ Weekly,* March 6, 2004, 567.

42. Gebe Martinez and Mary Agnes Carey, "Erasing the Gender Gap Tops Republican Playbook," *CQ Weekly,* March 6, 2004, 565.

43. Ibid.

44. David Sarasohn, "Wall Falls on Reagan Coalition," *Lincoln Sunday Journal-Star,* February 18, 1990, 1C.

45. David Von Drehle, "The Left Invigorated," *Washington Post National Weekly Edition,* July 14, 2003, 13.

46. Steven Roberts, "Near-Death Experience," *U.S. News and World Report,* November 6, 1996, 28.

47. National Election Studies, Center for Political Studies, University of Michigan, 1952–2000 (www.umich.edu/~nes).

48. Ibid.

49. Everett Carill Ladd, *Where Have All the Voters Gone?* (New York: Norton, 1982).

50. Martin P Wallenberg, *The Rise of Candidate-Centered Politics* (Cambridge, Mass.: Harvard University Press, 1991).

51. Thomas E. Patterson, *The Vanishing Voter* (New York: Knopf, 2002).

52. Walter Dean Burnham, *Critical Elections and the Mainstream of American Politics* (New York: Norton, 1970); Helmut Norpoth and Jerrold Rusk, "Partisan Dealignment in the American .Electorate," *American Political Science Review* 76 (1982), 522–537; David W Rhode, "The Fall Elections: Realignment and Dealignment," *Chronicle of Higher Education,* December 14, 1994, 131–132.

53. John R. Petrocik, "Realignment," *Journal of Politics* 49 (1987), 347–375; George Rabinowitz, Paul-Henri Gurian, and Stuart MacDonald, "The Structure of Presidential Elections and the Process of Realignment," *American Journal of Political Science* 28 (1984), 611–635; David S. Broder, "The GOP Plays Dixie," *Washington Post National Weekly Edition,* September 12, 1988, 4; Thomas B. Edsall, "A Serious Case of White Flight," *Washington Post National Weekly Edition,* September 10, 1990, 13.

54. *CQ Weekly,* January 3, 2004, 53–55.

55. For a discussion of party influence on voting in Congress, see William R. Shaffer, *Party and Ideology in the United States Congress* (Lanham, Md.: University Press of America, 1980).

56. Bruce I. Oppenheimer, "The Importance of Elections in a Strong Congressional Era," in *Do Elections Matter?* ed. Benjamin Ginsberg and Alan Stone (Armonk, N.Y.: Sharpe, 1996), 120–138.

57. David S. Broder, "Polarization a Growing Force for Political Parties," *Lincoln Journal-Star,* January 22,1995, 4B.

58. Dan Carney, "As Hostilities Rage on the Hill, Partisan-Vote Rate Soars," *Congressional Quarterly Weekly Report,* January 27, 1996, 199–200.

59. Mary Lunn F. Jones, "Rock and a Hard Place," *American Prospect,* June 2003, 18–19.

60. *Congressional Quarterly Weekly Report,* December 11, 1999, 2993–2994; *CQ Weekly,* January 3, 2004, 48.

61. Lloyd Grove, "A Good Ol' Boy Going in for the Kill," *Washington Post National Weekly Edition,* August 22, 1998, 12–13.

62. Frank J. Sorauf, *Money in American Elections* (Glenview, Ill.: Scott, Foresman, 1988), 121–153; Paul Herrnson, *Party Campaigning in the 1980s* (Cambridge, Mass.: Harvard University Press, 1988).

63. Federal Election Commission, *Campaign Finance Reports and Data: Party Activity, 2002* (www.fec.gov).

64. Anthony Corrado and Heitor Gouvea, "Financial Presidential Nominations under the BCRA," in *The Making of the Presidential Candidate, 2004,* ed. William G. Mayer (Lanham, Md.: Rowman & Littlefield, 2003).

65. Xandra Kayden, "The Nationalization of the Party System," in *Parties, Interest Groups, and Campaign Finance Laws,* ed. Michael Malbin (Washington, D.C.: American Enterprise Institute, 1980).

66. Stanley Kelley Jr., *Interpreting Elections* (Princeton, N.J.: Princeton University Press, 1983); Stanley Kelley Jr., Richard Ayres, and William G. Bower, "Registration and Voting: Putting First Things First," *American Political Science Review* 61 (1967), 359–379.

67. Marjorie Connelly, "Who Voted," *New York Times,* November 12, 2000, 4.

68. Gallup Poll, "Public Divide on Bush: Great Partisan Difference in Job Approval," March 10, 2004.

69. Data from "Portrait of an Electorate," *New York Times,* November 10, 1996, 28; Lee Sigelman, "If You Prick Us, Do We Not Bleed? If You Tickle Us, Do We Not Laugh? Jews and Pocketbook Voting," paper prepared for presentation at the 1990 American Political Science Meeting; Susan Welch and Lee Sigelman, "The Politics of Hispanic Americans," *Social Science Quarterly,* 1991; New York Times, November 5, 1992, B9.

70. Paul Abramson, John H. Aldrich, and David Rohde, *Change and Continuity in the 2000 Elections* (Washington, D.C.: CQ Press, 2003).

71. Ibid.

72. In recent elections, the percentages able to identify correctly general differences between the major party candidates varied between 26 and 55 percent.

73. Abramson, Aldrich, and Rohde, *Change and Continuity, 2000.*

74. Ibid.

75. Paul Abramson, John H. Aldrich, and David Rohde, *Change and Continuity in the 1996 Elections* (Washington, D.C.: CQ Press, 1998).

76. Morris Fiorina, *Retrospective Voting in American National Elections* (New Haven, Conn.: Yale University Press, 1981).

77. Edward R. Tufte, *Political Control of the Economy* (Princeton, N.J.: Princeton University Press, 1978); Douglas Hibbs, "The Mass Public and Macroeconomic Performance," *American Journal of Political Science* 23 (1979), 705–731; John Hibbing and John Alford, "The Electoral Impact of Economic Conditions: Who Is Held Responsible," *American Journal of Political Science* 25 (1981), 423–439.

78. Robert Kaiser, "Deeply Divided We Stand— and That's No Surprise," *Washington Post National Weekly Edition,* November 20, 2000, 22.

79. "Medicare," *CQ Weekly,* January 3, 2004, 39.

80. Ibid.

81. Robert Pear and Robin Toner, "A Final Push in Congress," *New York Times on the Web,* November 23, 2003 (www.nytimes.com).

82. John Cranford, "'Key Votes' Highly Partisan," *CQ Weekly,* January 3, 2004, 24.

Chapter 8

1. Roger Simon, "Turning Point," *U.S. News & World Report,* July 19, 2004, 44.

2. Mark Singer, "Running on Instinct," *New Yorker,* January 12, 2004, 43–59. This article, written a week before the caucuses, predicted, like most other journalists, a Dean victory and speculated whether he could go all the way to beat Bush in the November election.

3. Simon, 38.

4. William H. Flanigan, *Political Behavior of the American Electorate,* 2nd ed. (Boston: Allyn and Bacon, 1972), 13. See also Chilton Williamson, *American Suffrage from Property to Democracy 1760–1860* (Princeton, N.J.: Princeton University Press, 1960).

5. James MacGregor Burns, *Vineyard of Liberty* (New York: Knopf, 1982), 363.

6. August Meier and Elliot M. Rudwick, *From Plantation to Ghetto: An Interpretive History of American Negroes* (New York: Hill & Wang, 1966), 69.

7. Robert Darcy, Susan Welch, and Janet Clark, *Women, Elections, and Representation* (Lincoln: University of Nebraska Press, 1994).

8. Ralph G. Neas, "The Long Shadow of Jim Crow: Voter Intimidation and Suppression in America Today," *People for the American Way Foundation,* August 2004, or online at www.naacp.org/inc/pdf/jimcrow.pdf.

9. Grandfather clause: *Guinn* v. *United States, 238 U.S.* 347 (1915); white primary: *Smith* v. *Allwright, 321 U.S.* 649 (1944).

10. Data on black and white voter registration in the southern states are from the Statistical Abstract of the United States (Washington, D.C.: U.S. Bureau of the Census, various years).

11. California, Florida, Michigan, New Hampshire, New York, and South Dakota.

12. Richard J. Timpone, "Mass Mobilization or Government Intervention? The Growth of Black Registration in the South," *Journal of Politics* 57 (1995), 425–442.

13. *City of Mobile* v. *Bolden,* 446 U.S. 55 (1980).

14. *Thornburg* v. *Gingles,* 478 U.S. 301 (1986).

15. Bob Benenson, "Arduous Ritual of Redistricting Ensures More Racial Diversity," *Congressional Quarterly Weekly Report,* October 24, 1992, 3385. For a very thorough review of the legal and behavioral impact of the Voting Rights Act, see Joseph Viteritti, "Unapportioned Justice: Local Elections, Social Science, and the Evolution of the Voting Rights Act," *Cornell Journal of Law and Public Policy* (1994), 210–270.

16. *Shaw* v. *Reno,* 125 L.Ed.2d 511, 113 S.Ct. 2816 (1993); *Miller* v. *Johnson,* 132 L.Ed.2d 762, 115 S.Ct. 2475 (1995); *Bush* v. *Vera,* 135 L.Ed.2d 248, 116 S.Ct. 1941 (1996).

17. Darcy et al., *Women, Elections, and Representation.*

18. Speech in 1867 by George Williams cited in Peter Pappas' "Re-defining the Role of Women in Industrial America" at www.peterpappas.com/journals/industry/women3.pdf.

19. The discussion in this paragraph is drawn largely from Lois W. Banner, *Women in Modern America: A Brief History* (New York: Harcourt Brace Jovanovich, 1974), 88–90; Glenn Firebaugh and Kevin Chen, "Vote Turnout of Nineteenth Amendment Women," *American Journal of Sociology* 100 (1995), 972–996.

20. Mississippi, Alabama, Florida, and Virginia, plus Iowa, Nebraska, and Kentucky.

21. Nicholas Thompson, "Locking Up the Vote: Disenfranchisement of Former Felons was the Real Crime in Florida," *Washington Monthly* (January-February 2001), 17–21; see also Amanda Ripley, "Barred from the Ballot," *Time,* January 21, 2001, 63. Data cited are from a forthcoming book by Jeff Manza and Christopher Uggen, *Locking Up the Vote* (New York: Oxford University Press, 2005).

22. Thompson, ibid., 18.

23. Thompson, ibid., 20.

24. Tom Fiedler, "The Perfect Storm," in *Overtime!: The Election 2000 Thriller,* ed. Larry J. Sabato (New York: Longman, 2002), 11.

25. Liz Krueger, "Budgeting for Another Florida," *New York Times,* February 8, 2004, 14.

26. Dale Keiger, "E-lective Alarm," *Johns Hopkins Magazine,* February 2004, 50.

27. Ibid.

28. See report of Electionline.org on voting law changes at www.electionline.org/site/docs/pdf/2004.Election.Preview.Final.Report.pdf.

29. See www.Tallahassee.com/mld/tallahassee/news/9202503.htm

30. Richard Jensen, "American Election Campaigns: A Theoretical and Historical Typology," paper delivered at the 1968 Midwest Political Science Association Meeting, quoted in Walter Dean Burnham, *Critical Elections and the Mainsprings of American Politics,* (New York: Norton, 1970), 73.

31. Frances Fox Piven and Richard A. Cloward, *Why Americans Don't Vote,* (New York: Pantheon Books, 1988), 30.

32. Part of the explanation for declining voting rates is that the number of citizens who are ineligible to vote has increased, which depresses voter turnout statistics. Immigrants, other noncitizens, and, in some states, convicted felons are not eligible to vote. When those individuals are removed from the calculation of proportion voting, the proportion voting is increased by about five points, and most of the turnout decline occured in the 1960s. See Michael P. McDonald and Samuel Popkin, "The Myth of the Vanishing Voter," *American Political Science Review* 95 (2001), 963–974.

33. *Statistical Abstract of the United States 2001,* Table 401. This self-report is probably an overestimate.

34. *Statistical Abstract of the United States 2001,* Table 404.

35. Daniel J. Elazar, *American Federalism: A View from the States* (New York: Crowell, 1972); *Statistical Abstract of the United States 2003,* Table 422.

36. Piven and Cloward, *Why Americans Don't Vote,* 162; *Statistical Abstract of the United States 2001,* Table 401; Piven and Cloward, *Why Americans Still Don't Vote: And Why Politicians Want It That Way* (Boston: Beacon Press, 2001).

37. G. Bingham Powell, "American Voter Turnout in Comparative Perspective," *American Political Science Review* 80 (1986), 30; Piven and Cloward, *Why Americans Don't Vote,* 119; Arend Lijphart, "Unequal Participation: Democracy's Unresolved Dilemma," *American Political Science Review* 91 (1997), 1–14.

38. Steven Hill and Rashad Robinson, "Demography vs. Democracy: Young People Feel Left out of the Political Process," *Los Angeles Times,* November 5, 2002, 2. Posted by the Youth Vote Coalition (www.youthvote.org/news/newsdetail.cfm?newsid=6). The survey cited was conducted by Harvard University.

39. Eric Plutzer, "Becoming a Habitual Voter: Inertia, Resources, and Growth in Young Adulthood," *American Political Science Review* 96 (2002), 41–56.

40. Anna Greenberg, "New Generation, New Politics," *American Prospect,* October 1, 2003, A3.

41. These examples are from Editorial, "Barriers to Student Voting," *New York Times,* September 28, 2004, 26.

42. George F. Will, "In Defense of Nonvoting," *Newsweek,* October 10, 1983, 96.

43. Richard Morin, "The Dog Ate My Forms, and, Well, I Couldn't Find a Pen," *Washington Post National Weekly Edition,* November 5, 1990, 38.

44. Lawrence R. Jacobs and Robert Y. Shapiro, *Politicans Don't Pander:* Political Manipulation and the Loss of Democratic Responsiveness (Chicago: University of Chicago Press, 2000).

45. Priscilla L. Southwell, "Voter Turnout in the 1986 Congressional Elections," *American Politics Quarterly* 19 (1991), 96–108; Stephen Ansolabehere, Shanto Iyengar, Adam Simon, and Nicholas Valentino, "Does Attack Advertising Demobilize the Electorate?" *American Political Science Review* 88 (1994), 829–838.

46. Richard Lau, Lee Sigelman, Caroline Heldman, and Paul Babbitt, "The Effects of Negative Political Advertisements," *American Political Science Review* 93 (1999), 851–875; Steven E. Finkel and John Geer, "A Spot Check: Casting Doubt on the Demobilizing Effect of Attack Advertising," *American Journal of Political Science* 42 (1998), 573–595. Research on turnout is found in Stephen Ansolabehere and Shanto Iyengar, *Going Negative* (New York: Free Press, 1996). In her book *Packaging the Presidency: A History and Criticism of Presidential Campaign Advertising* (New York: Oxford University Press, 1984), Kathleen Jamieson also argues that there are checks on misleading advertising, but later ("Is the Truth Now Irrelevant in Presidential Campaigns?"), she notes that these checks do not always work well. See Jamieson, *Dirty Politics: Deception, Distraction, and Democracy* (New York: Oxford University Press, 1992).

47. Thomas E. Patterson, *The Vanishing Voter* (New York: Knopf, 2002). Curtis B. Gans, "The Empty Ballot Box," *Public Opinion* 1 (September-October 1978), 54–57; Curtis Gans, quoted in Jack Germond and Jules Witcover, "Listen to the Voters—and Nonvoters," *Minneapolis Star Tribune,* November 26, 1988. This effect was foreshadowed by Michael J. Robinson, "American Political Legitimacy in an Era of Electronic Journalism," in *Television as a Social Force: New Approaches to TV Criticism,* eds. Douglass Cater and Richard Adler (New York: Praeger, 1975). See also Austin Ranney, *Channels of Power: The Impact of Television on American Politics* (New York: Basic Books, 1983); and Richard Boyd, "The Effect of Election Calendars on Voter Turnout," paper presented at the Annual Meeting of the Midwest Political Science Association, April 1987, Chicago.

48. Boyd, "The Effect of Election Calendars on Voter Turnout," 43. See Piven and Cloward, *Why Americans Don't Vote,* 196–197, for illustrations of these kinds of informal barriers, and Piven and Cloward, *Why Americans Still Don't Vote: And Why Politicians Want It That Way,* for further examples.

49. Ibid.

50. Ruy Texeira, *Why Americans Don't Vote: Turnout Decline in the United States 1960–1984* (Boulder, Colo.: Greenwood, 1987); Texeira, *The Disappearing American Voter* (Washington, D.C.: Brookings Institute, 1992); and Peverill Squire, Raymond Wolfinger, and David Glass, "Residential Mobility and Voter Turnout," *American Political Science Review* 81 (1987), 45–66.

51. Piven and Cloward, *Why Americans Don't Vote,* 17.

52. For a review of these studies, see Bill Winders, "The Roller Coaster of Class Conflict: Class Segments, Mass Mobilization, and Voter Turnout in the United States, 1840–1996," *Social Forces* 77 (1999), 833–860.

53. Ibid.

54. Raymond E. Wolfinger and Steven J. Rosenstone, *Who Votes?* (New Haven, Conn.: Yale University Press, 1980), Table 6-1.

55. Steven J. Rosenstone and Raymond E. Wolfinger, "The Effect of Registration Laws on Voter Turnout," *American Political Science Review* 72 (1978), 22–45; Glenn Mitchell and Christopher Wlezien, "Voter Registration Laws and Turnout, 1972–1982," paper presented at the Annual Meeting of the Midwest Political Science Association, April 1989, Chicago; Mark J. Fenster, "The Impact of Allowing Day of Registration Voting on Turnout in U.S. Elections from 1960 to 1992," *American Politics Quarterly* 22 (1994), 74–87.

56. Kim Quaile Hill and Jan E. Leighley, "Racial Diversity, Voter Turnout, and Mobilizing Institutions in the United States," *American Politics Quarterly* 27 (1999), 275–295.

57. Piven and Cloward, *Why Americans Don't Vote,* 230–231.

58. Stephen Knack, "Does 'Motor Voter' Work?" *Journal of Politics* 57 (1995), 796–811.

59. Michael Martinez and David Hill, "Did Motor Voter Work?" *American Political Quarterly* 27 (1999), 296–315; Piven and Cloward, *Why Americans Still Don't Vote: And Why Politicians Want It That Way.*

60. Squire et al., "Residential Mobility and Voter Turnout." See also Samuel C. Patterson and Gregory A. Caldeira, "Mailing in the Vote: Correlates and Consequences of Absentee Voting," *American Journal of Political Science* 29 (1985), 766–788.

61. These examples are drawn from Raymond Wolfinger, Benjamin Highton, and Megan Mullin, "How Postregistration Laws Affect the Turnout of Blacks and Latinos," paper presented at the 2003 Annual Meeting of the American Political Science Association, Philadelphia, Pennsylvania, August 28–31.

62. Jo Becker, "Voters May Have Their Say Before Election Day," *Washington Post,* August 26, 2004, A01.

63. Texas, Minnesota, Louisiana, and Missouri are the only states west of the Mississippi not allowing unrestricted absentee voting; Florida, North Carolina, Vermont, and Maine are the only states east of the Mississippi who do. See Michael Moss, "Parties See New Promise When Ballot Is in the Mail," *New York Times,* August 22, 2004, 12; R. W. Apple, Jr. "Kerry Pins Hopes in Iowa on Big Vote from Absentees," *New York Times,* September 28, 2004, 18.

64. Apple, Jr., ibid.

65. More recent studies of turnout include Richard J. Timpone, "Structure, Behavior and Voter Turnout in the United States," *American Political Science Review* 92 (1998), 145–158; Henry Brady, Sidney Verba, and Kay Lehman Schlozman, "Beyond SES: A Resource Model of Political Participation," *American Political Science Review* 89 (1995), 271–294.

66. Winder, "The Roller Coaster of Class Conflict: Class Segments, Mass Mobilization, and Voter Turnout in the United States, 1840–1996" For a review of this literature, see John Petrocik, "Voter Turnout and Electoral Preference," in *Elections in America,* ed. Kay Lehman Schlozman (Boston: Allen & Unwin, 1987). See also Bernard Grofman, Guillermo Owen, and Christian Collet, "Rethinking the Partisan Effects of Higher Turnout," *Public Choice* 99 (1999), 357–376.

67. Paul Farhi, "Politics Enters the Information Age," *Washington Post National Weekly Edition,* July 26, 2004, 13.

68. Kim Quaile Hill, Jan Leighley, and Angela Hinton-Anderson, "Lower-Class Mobilization and Pol-

icy Linkage in the U.S. States," *American Journal of Political Science* 39 (1995), 75–86.

69. Anthony Downs, *An Economic Theory of Democracy* (New York: Harper, 1957).

70. Morin, "The Dog Ate My Forms, and, Well, I Couldn't Find a Pen."

71. Kay Lehman Schlozman, Sidney Verba, and Henry Brady, "Participation's Not a Paradox: The View from American Activists," *British Journal of Political Science* 25 (1995), 1–36.

72. Norman H. Nie, Sidney Verba, Henry Brady, Kay Lehman Schlozman, and Jane Junn, "Participation in America: Continuity and Change," presented at the Midwest Political Science Association, April 1988. The standard work, though now dated, on American political participation is Sidney Verba and Norman H. Nie, *Participation in America: Political Democracy and Social Equality* (New York: Harper & Row, 1972).

73. Brady et al., "Beyond SES: A Resource Model of Political Participation."

74. Nie et al., "Participation in America: Continuity and Change"; Verba and Nie, *Participation in America: Political Democracy and Social Equality.*

75. Paul Allen Beck and M. Kent Jennings, "Political Periods and Political Participation," *American Political Science Review* 73 (1979), 737–750; Nie et al., "Participation in America: Continuity and Change"

76. The following discussion draws heavily upon John H. Aldrich, *Before the Convention: Strategies and Choices in Presidential Nomination Campaigns* (Chicago: University of Chicago Press, 1980).

77. Ibid. See also David W. Rohde, "Risk Bearing and Progressive Ambition: The Case of Members of the United States House of Representatives," *American Journal of Political Science* 23 (1979), 1–26.

78. Quoted in Audrey A. Haynes, Paul-Henri Gurian, Stephen M. Nichols, "The Role of Candidate Spending in Presidential Nomination Campaigns," *Journal of Politics* 59 (February 1997), 213–225.

79. Ibid.

80. "Political Grapevine," *Time*, February 8, 1988, 30.

81. Hendrick Hertzberg, "This Must Be the Place," *New Yorker*, January 31, 2000, 36–39.

82. "The Fall Campaign," *Newsweek Election Extra*, November–December 1984, 88.

83. B. Drummond Ayres Jr., "It's Taking Care of Political Business," *New York Times*, July 18, 1999, 22.

84. Bruce Babbitt, "Bruce Babbitt's View from the Wayside," *Washington Post National Weekly Edition*, February 24, 1988, 24. The one thousand days figure is from the *Congressional Quarterly Weekly Report*, February 1, 1992, 257.

85. Katharine Q. Seelye and Marjorie Connelly, "Republican Delegates Leaning to Right of G.O.P. and the Nation," *New York Times*, August 29, 2004, 13.

86. Gerald M. Pomper and Susan S. Lederman, *Elections in America: Control and Influence in Democratic Politics* (New York: Longman, 1980), ch. 7.

87. Quote from Gerald M. Pomper in Adam Nagourney, "What Boston Can Do for Kerry," *New York Times*, July 18, 2004, 5.

88. David Carr, "Whose Convention is It? Reporters Outnumber Delegates 6 to 1" *New York Times*, July 27, 2004, E1.

89. Lee Sigelman and Paul Wahlbeck, "The 'Veepstakes': Strategic Choice in Presidential Running Mate Selection," *American Political Science Review* 94 (1997), 855–864.

90. Ibid.

91. Ibid.

92. Robert L. Dudley and Ronald B. Rapaport, "Vice-Presidential Candidates and the Home State Advantage: Playing Second Banana at Home and on the Road," *American Journal of Political Science* 33 (1989), 537–540.

93. *New York Times*, July 11, 2004, 16.

94. Associated Press, "Nader Denied Spots on Several State Ballots," October 14, 2004. Article online at www.firstamendmentcenter.org/news.aspx?id=14192.

95. Daron Shaw, "A Study of Presidential Campaign Event Effects from 1952 to 1992," *Journal of Politics* 61 (1999), 387–422.

96. See *Congressional Quarterly*, July 23, 1988, 2015; Thomas M. Holbrook, "Campaigns, National Conditions and U.S. Presidential Elections," *American Journal of Political Science* 38 (1994), 973–998.

97. E. J. Dionne, Jr., "One Nation Deeply Divided," *Washington Post*, November 7, 2004, A31, quoted in Morris P. Fiorina with Samuel J. Abrams and Jeremy C. Pope, *Culture War? The Myth of the Polarized America* (New York: Pearson Longman, 2005), 6.

98. Matthew Dowd, quoted in Fiorina, ibid., 6.

99. Fiorina, ibid., 21.

100. Editorial, "A Polarized Nation?" *Washington Post*, November 14, 2004, 6. Several of these ideas were summarized nicely in this article.

101. Benjamin I. Page and Richard A. Brody, "Policy Voting and the Electoral Process: The Vietnam War Issue," *American Political Science Review* 66 (1972), 979–995.

102. The discussion of the functions of the media relies heavily on the excellent summary found in Stephen Ansolabehere, Roy Behr, and Shanto Iyengar, "Mass Media and Elections," *American Politics Quarterly* 19 (1991), 109–139.

103. Kathleen Hall Jamieson, "Ad Wars," *Washington Post National Weekly Edition*, October 4, 2004, 22.

104. Robert MacNeil, *People Machine: The Influence of Television on American Politics* (New York: Harper & Row, 1968), 182.

105. Elisabeth Bumiller, "Selling Soup, Wine and Reagan," *Washington Post National Weekly Edition*, November 5, 1984, 6–8.

106. Jim Rutenberg, "Seeking Voters Through Habits in TV Viewing," *New York Times*, July 18, 2004, 1.

107. Data are drawn from Rutenberg, ibid. See Thomas E. Mann, "Elections and Change in Congress," in *The New Congress*, eds. Thomas E. Mann and Norman J. Ornstein (Washington, D.C.: American Enterprise Institute for Public Policy Research, 1981), 32–54; David Mayhew, *Congress: The Electoral Connection* (New Haven, Conn.: Yale University Press, 1974); Glenn R. Parker and Roger H. Davidson, "Why Do Americans Love Their Congressmen So Much More Than Their Congress?" *Legislative Studies Quarterly* 4 (1979), 53–62.

108. Daron Shaw, "The Methods behind the Madness: Presidential Electoral College Strategies, 1988–1996," *Journal of Politics* 61 (1999), 893–913 shows the evolution of advertising focus during these three elections.

109. Dana Milbank and Jim VandeHei, "The Mean Season is in Full Bloom," *Washington Post National Weekly Edition*, June 7, 2004, 13. Both campaigns agreed the figures were accurate.

110. John Theilmann and Allen Wilhite, "Campaign Tactics and the Decision to Attack," *Journal of Politics* 60 (1998), 1050–1062.

111. The study of negative advertising research was done by Richard Lau, Lee Sigelman, Caroline Heldman, and Paul Babbitt, "The Effects of Negative Political Advertisements," *American Political Science Review* 93 (1999), 851–875.

112. Howard Kurtz, "The Ad-Slingers in the TV Corral," *Washington Post*, October 10, 2004, A06.

113. Ibid.

114. Democratic consultants are more likely to find negative advertising distasteful than Republican consultants. However, this does not necessarily translate into partisan differences in use.

115. Paul Taylor, "Pigsty Politics," *Washington Post National Weekly Edition*, February 13, 1989, 6.

116. Eileen Shields West, "Give 'Em Hell These Days Is a Figure of Speech," *Smithsonian* (October 1988), 149–151. The editorial was from the Connecticut Courant.

117. Charles Paul Freund, "But Then, Truth Has Never Been Important," *Washington Post National Weekly Edition*, November 7, 1988, 29.

118. Quoted in Freund, "But Then, Truth Has Never Been Important," 29.

119. Ansolabehere and Iyengar, *Going Negative.*

120. Jamieson, *Packaging the Presidency: A History and Criticism of Presidential Campaign Advertising.*

121. Thomas E. Patterson, *The Mass Media Election: How Americans Choose Their President* (New York: Praeger, 1980), 3.

122. Martin Schram, *The Great American Video Game: Presidential Politics in the Television Age* (New York: Morrow, 1987).

123. Mike Allen, "Bush's Isolation from Reporters Could be a Hindrance," *Washington Post*, October 8, 2004, A09.

124. For example, see Norman J. Ornstein and Thomas E. Mann, ed., *The Permanent Campaign and Its Future* (Washington, D.C.: American Enterprise Institute and the Brookings Institution, 2000).

125. See Thomas E. Mann, "Elections and Change in Congress," in *The New Congress;* Mayhew, *Congress: The Electoral Connection;* Parker and Davidson, "Why Do Americans Love Their Congressmen So Much More Than Their Congress?"

126. See Paul Feldman and James Jondrow, "Congressional Elections and Local Federal Spending," *American Journal of Political Science* 28 (1984), 152; Glenn R. Parker and Suzanne Parker, "The Correlates and Effects of Attention to District by U.S. House Members," *Legislative Studies Quarterly* 10 (1985), 239.

127. Christopher Buckley, "Hangin' with the Houseboyz," *Washington Monthly* (June 1992), 44.

128. Linda L. Fowler and Robert D. McClure, *Political Ambition: Who Decides to Run for Congress?* (New Haven, Conn.: Yale University Press, 1989), 47. John Hibbing and Sara Brandes, "State Population and the Electoral Success of U.S. Senators," *American Journal of Political Science* 27 (1983), 808–819. See also Glenn R. Parker, "Stylistic Change in the U.S. Senate, 1959–1980," *Journal of Politics* 47 (1985), 1190–1202.

129. Thomas E. Mann, *Unsafe at Any Margin: Interpreting Congressional Elections* (Washington, D.C.: American Enterprise Institute for Public Policy Research, 1978).

130. "Women, Minorities Join Senate," *CQ Almanac* (1992), 8A–14A; "Wave of Diversity Spared Many Incumbents," *CQ Almanac* (1992), 15A–21A, 24A; "The Elections," *Congressional Quarterly*, November 12, 1994, 3237.

131. These examples are drawn from David S. Broder, "What Democracy Needs: Real Races," *Washington Post*, October 31, 2004, B7.

132. See Gary C. Jacobson, *The Politics of Congressional Elections*, 2nd ed. (Boston: Little, Brown, 1987), 51 for a discussion of financial needs in the 1980s.

133. Ibid.

134. Barbara Hinckley, "The American Voter in Congressional Elections," *American Political Science Review* 74 (1980), 641–650; Barbara Hinckley, "House Reelections and Senate Defeats: The Role of the Challenger," *British Journal of Political Science* 10 (1980), 441–460.

135. John Alford and John R. Hibbing, "The Disparate Electoral Security of House and Senate Incumbents," paper resented at the Annual Meeting of the American Political Science Association, September 1989, Atlanta, 107.

136. A good review of these arguments is found in John R. Hibbing and Sara L. Brandes, "State Population and the Electoral Success of U.S. Senators," *American Journal of Political Science* 27 (1983), 808–

819. See also Eric Uslaner, "The Case of the Vanishing Liberal Senators: The House Did It," *British Journal of Political Science* 11 (1981), 105–113; Abramowitz, "A Comparison."

137. Hibbing and Brandes, "State Population and the Electoral Success of U.S. Senators." See also Glenn R. Parker, "Stylistic Change in the U.S. Senate, 1959–1980," ibid.

138. Edie N. Goldenberg and Michael W. Traugott, *Campaigning for Congress* (Washington, D.C.: CQ Press, 1984); Gary C. Jacobson and Samuel Kernell, *Strategy and Choice in Congressional Elections.* (New Haven, Conn.: Yale University Press, 1981).

139. Edward Walsh, "Wanted: Candidates for Congress," *Washington Post National Weekly Edition,* November 25, 1985, 9.

140. See Gerald C. Wright Jr. and Michael B. Berkman, "Candidates and Policy in United States Senate Elections," *American Political Science Review* 80 (1986), 567–588; Robert S. Erikson and Gerald C. Wright, "Voters, Candidates, and Issues in Congressional Elections," in Lawrence C. Dodd and Bruce I. Oppenheimer, eds., *Congress Reconsidered,* 7th ed. (Washington, D.C.: CQ Press, 2001), 67–95.

141. See James Campbell, "Explaining Presidential Losses in Midterm Elections," *Journal of Politics* 47 (1985), 1140–1157. See also Barbara Hinckley, "Interpreting House Midterm Elections," *American Political Science Review* 61 (1967), 694–700; Samuel Kernell, "Presidential Popularity and Negative Voting," *American Political Science Review* 71 (1977), 44–66; Edward Tufte, "Determinants of the Outcomes of Midterm Congressional Elections," *American Political Science Review* 69 (1975), 812–826; Alan Abramowitz, "Economic Conditions, Presidential Popularity and Voting Behavior in Midterm Elections," *Journal of Politics* 47 (1985), 31–43.

142. Data on voters' issue preferences on Election Day can be found in the article "41% Said National Security Issues Most Important," *Rasmussen Reports,* November 2, 2004 at www.rasmussenreports.com/Issue%20Clusters_Election%20Night.htm.

143. Editorial, "A Polarized Nation?" *Washington Post,* November 14, 2004, 6. Several of these ideas were summarized nicely in this article.

144. Benjamin I. Page and Robert Y. Shapiro, "Effects of Public Opinion on Policy," *American Political Science Review* 77 (1983), 175–190.

145. Arthur Schlesinger Jr., *Wall Street Journal,* December 5, 1986. But see also Jacobs and Shapiro, *Politicians Don't Pander: Political Manipulation and the Loss of Democratic Responsiveness.*

146. Roger Simon, 75.

147. Ibid.

Chapter 9

1. Senator Charles E. Schumer, New York, schumer.senate.gov; Michael Barone with Richard Cohen and Grant Ujifusa, *The Almanac of American Politics, 2002* (Washington, D.C.: National Journal, 2001), 1038.

2. Ibid.

3. Paul Krugman, "Everyone Is Outraged," *New York Times,* July 2, 2002, 21.

4. Quoted in Kenneth Jost, "Accountants under Fire," *CQ Researcher,* March 22, 2002, 255.

5. Richard Dunham, "The Vindication of Arthur Levitt," *Business Week Online,* February 18, 2002, businessweekonline.com.

6. Jost, "Accountants under Fire," 255.

7. Daniel J. Parks, "Fuzzy Battle Lines Complicate Effort to Overhaul Financial Services," *CQ Weekly,* February 27, 1999, 491.

8. Jimmy Breslin, *How the Good Guys Finally Won: Notes from an Impeachment Summer* (New York: Ballantine, 1974), 14.

9. Robert E. Mutch, "Three Centuries of Campaign Finance Law," in *A User's Guide to Campaign Finance Reform,* ed. Gerald C. Lubenow (Lanham, Md.: Rowman & Littlefield, 2001).

10. Congressional Quarterly, *Dollar Politics,* 3rd ed. (Washington, D.C.: CQ Press, 1982), 3.

11. Haynes Johnson, "Turning Government Jobs into Gold," *Washington Post National Weekly Edition,* May 12, 1986, 6–7.

12. Quoted in Richard Hofstadter, *The American Political Tradition* (New York: Vintage, 1958), 165.

13. Congressional Quarterly, *Dollar Politics,* 3.

14. Larry J. Sabato, *Feeding Frenzy* (New York: Free Press, 1991).

15. Kevin Phillips, "How Wealth Defines Power," *American Prospect,* Summer 2003, A9. The U.S. Constitution defines a quorum as a majority of senators currently in office.

16. Elizabeth Drew, *Politics and Money* (New York: Collier, 1983), 9.

17. *Buckley* v. *Valeo,* 424 U.S. 1 (1976).

18. Glen Justice, "Irrelevance Stalks a Post-Watergate Invention," *New York Times,* November 16, 2003, 3.

19. Glen Justice, "Kerry's Campaign Finances Soar," *International Herald Tribune,* June 28, 2004, 7.

20. See Larry J. Sabato and Glenn Simpson, *Dirty Little Secrets: The Persistence of Corruption in American Politics* (New York: Times Books, 1996); Marick Masters and Gerald Keim, "Determinants of PAC Participation among Large Corporations," *Journal of Politics* 47 (1985), 1158–1173; and J. David Gopoian, "What Makes PACs Tick?" *American Journal of Political Science* 28 (1984), 259–281.

21. See Kevin Grier and Michael Mangy, "Comparing Interest Group PAC Contributions to House and Senate Incumbents," *Journal of Politics* 55 (1993), 615–643.

22. J. David Gopoian, "Change and Continuity in Defense PAC Behavior," *American Politics Quarterly* 13 (1985), 297–322; Richard Morin and Charles Babcock, "Off Year, Schmoff Year," *Washington Post National Weekly Edition,* May 14, 1990, 15.

23. Thomas Romer and James M. Snyder, "An Empirical Investigation of the Dynamics of PAC Contributions," *American Journal of Political Science* 38 (1994), 745–769.

24. Alison Mitchell, "Time Passes, Money Flows," *New York Times,* June 16, 1996, E5.

25. Mike Allen, "Does an Embassy Trump the Lincoln Bedroom?" *Washington Post National Weekly Edition,* May 7, 2001, 14.

26. Mike Allen, "The Mother of All Fundraisers," *Washington Post National Weekly Edition,* May 20, 2002, 13.

27. *Federal Election Commission* v. *National Conservative PAC,* 470 U.S. 480 (1985).

28. David S. Broder, "Both Major Parties Abuse Soft Money Loophole," *State College* (Pa.) *Centre Daily Times,* May 30, 2000, 6A.

29. Paoul Farhi, "A Team Effort," *Washington Post National Weekly Edition,* March 29, 2004, 12.

30. Quoted in Nancy Gibbs and Karen Tumulty, "A New Day Dawning," *Time,* April 9, 2001, 50.

31. Bradley Smith, *Free Speech: The Folly of Campaign Finance Reform* (Princeton, N.J.: Princeton University Press, 2001); Russ Lewis, "Foreign to the First Amendment," *Washington Post,* July 2, 2002, A15.

32. Thomas Byrne Edsall, "Campaign Reform Boomerang," *American Prospect,* September 2003, 61.

33. Ibid.

34. Paul Taylor, "TV's Political Profits," *Mother Jones,* May-June 2000, 32.

35. *Washington Post,* February 24, 2002, B7. The statement is based on a study of 146 countries.

36. David S. Broder, "Where the Money Goes," *Washington Post National Weekly Edition,* March 26, 2001, 4.

37. Jeff Leeds, "TV Stations Balk at Free Air Time for Candidates," *Lincoln Journal-Star,* May 14, 2000, 3A.

38. Ibid.

39. Ibid.

40. "Public Order in the Courts," *American Prospect,* November 18, 2002, 8. See also Harold Stanley and Richard Niemi, *Vital Statistics on American Politics, 2001-02* (Washington, D.C.: CQ Press, 2002), tab. 2-3.

41. Mark Twain, "Pudd'nhead Wilson's New Calendar."

42. Quoted in *New York Times,* June 13, 1998, A7.

43. Ibid.

44. Stanley and Niemi, *Vital Statistics on American Politics,* tab. 2-4.

45. "Numbers," *Time,* February 28, 2000, 27.

46. Quoted in Gary Jacobson, *Money in Congressional Elections* (New Haven, Conn.: Yale University Press, 1980), 61.

47. David S. Broder, "The High Road to Lower Finance?" *Washington Post National Weekly Edition,* June 29, 1987, 4; see also Diane Granat, "Parties' Schools for Politicians or Grooming Troops for Election," *Congressional Quarterly Weekly Report,* May 5, 1984, 1036.

48. Diana C. Mutz, "Effects of Horse-Race Coverage on Campaign Coffers: Strategic Contributing in Presidential Primaries," *Journal of Politics* 57 (1995), 1015–1042.

49. Audrey A. Haynes, Paul-Henri Gurian, and Stephen M. Nichols, "The Role of Candidate Spending in Presidential Nomination Campaigns," *Journal of Politics* 59 (1997), 220. See also Gary Orren, "The Nomination Process," in *The Elections of 1984,* ed. Michael Nelson (Washington, D.C.: CQ Press, 1986), ch. 2, and Wayne Parent, Calvin Jillson, and Ronald E. Weber, "Voting Outcomes in the 1984 Democratic Primaries and Caucuses," *American Political Science Review* 81 (1987), 67–84.

50. Haynes, Gurian, and Nichols., "Role of Candidate Spending," 223.

51. Nelson Polsby and Aaron Wildavsky, *Presidential Elections* (New York: Scribner, 1984), 56.

52. David Nice, "Campaign Spending and Presidential Election Results," *Polity* 19 (1987), 464–476, shows that presidential campaign spending is more productive for Republicans than for Democrats.

53. John Alford and David Brady, "Person and Partisan Advantages in U.S. Congressional Elections, 1846-1990," in *Congress Reconsidered,* ed. Larry Dodd and Bruce Oppenheimer, 5th ed. (Washington, D.C.: Congressional Quarterly, 1993).

54. David Epstein and Peter Zemsky, "Money Talks: Deterring Quality Challengers in Congressional Elections," *American Political Science Review* 89 (1995), 295–308.

55. Robert S. Erickson and Thomas R. Palfrey, "Campaign Spending and Incumbency: An Alternative Simultaneous Equations Approach," *Journal of Politics* 60 (1998), 355–373; Alan Gerber, "Estimating the Effect of Campaign Spending on Senate Election Outcomes Using Instrumental Variables," *American Political Science Review* 92 (1998), 401–411.

56. Jacobson, *Money in Congressional Elections;* Gary Jacobson, "The Effects of Campaign Spending in House Elections," *American Journal of Political Science* 34 (1990), 334–362; Christopher Kenny and Michael McBurnett, "A Dynamic Model of the Effect of Campaign Spending on Congressional Vote Choice," *American Journal of Political Science* 36 (1992), 923–937; Donald Green and Jonathan Krasno, "Salvation for the Spendthrift Incumbent," *American Journal of Political Science* 32 (1988), 884–907; Gary Jacobson, *The Politics of Congressional Elections,* 2nd ed. (Boston: Little, Brown, 1987), ch. 4; Stephen Ansolabehere and Alan Gerber, "The Mismeasure of Campaign Spending," *Journal of Politics* 56 (1994), 1106–1118; Alan Gerber, "Estimating the Effect of Campaign Spending."

57. Federal Elections Commission, 2001–2002 database, www.fec.gov; Common Cause, report of November 6, 2002, www.commoncause.org.

58. "Scandal Shocks Even Those Who Helped It Along," *New York Times,* February 3, 2002, 7.

59. See Woodrow Jones and K. Robert Keiser, "Issue Visibility and the Effects of PAC Money," *Social Science Quarterly* 68 (1987), 170–176. Janet Grenzke, "PACs and the Congressional Supermarket," *American Journal of Political Science* 33 (1989), 1–24, found little effect of PAC money on a series of votes that were not obscure. Laura Langbein, "Money and Access," *Journal of Politics* 48 (1986), 1052–1064, shows that those who received more PAC money spend more time with interest group representatives.

60. Jean Reith Schroedel, "Campaign Contributions and Legislative Outcomes," *Western Political Quarterly* 39 (1986), 371–389; Richard L. Hall and Frank Wayman, "Buying Time: Moneyed Interests and the Mobilization of Bias in Congressional Committees," *American Political Science Review* 84 (1990), 797–820.

61. Thomas Downey (D-N.Y.), quoted in "Running with the PACs," *Time,* October 25, 1982, 20.

62. "Congress Study Links Funds and Votes," *New York Times,* December 30, 1987, 7.

63. John Frendreis and Richard Waterman, "PAC Contributions and Legislative Behavior: Senate Voting on Trucking Deregulation," *Social Science Quarterly* 66 (1985), 401–412. See also W. P. Welch, "Campaign Contributions and Legislative Voting," *Western Political Quarterly* 25 (1982), 478–495.

64. Diana Evans, "Policy and Pork: The Use of Pork Barrel Projects to Build Policy Coalitions in the House of Representatives," *American Journal of Political Science* 38 (1994), 894–917; Laura Langbein, "PACs, Lobbies, and Political Conflict: The Case of Gun Control," *Public Choice* 75 (1993), 254–271; Laura Langbein and Mark Lotwis, "The Political Efficacy of Lobbying and Money: Gun Control in the House, 1986," *Legislative Studies Quarterly* 15 (1990), 413–440; Schroedel, "Campaign Contributions and Legislative Outcomes."

65. Adam Clymer, "'84 PACs Gave Much to Senate Winners," *New York Times,* January 6, 1985, 13.

66. Quoted in Drew, *Politics and Money,* 79.

67. See Grenzke, "PACs and the Congressional Supermarket"; also see Frank Sorauf, *Money in American Elections* (Glenview, Ill.: Scott, Foresman, 1988).

68. Grenzke, "PACs and the Congressional Supermarket"; John Wright, "Contributions, Lobbying, and Committee Voting in the U.S. House of Representatives," *American Political Science Review* 84 (1990), 417–438; Henry Chappel Jr., "Campaign Contributions and Voting on the Cargo Preference Bill," *Public Choice* 36 (1981), 301–312.

69. Digital History, *Hypertext History,* "The Progressive Era," October 30, 2004, www.digital history.uh.edu/database/hyper_titles.cfm.

70. John Alford and David Brady, "Person and Partisan Advantages in U.S. Congressional Elections, 1846–1990," in *Congress Reconsidered,* ed. Larry Dodd and Bruce Oppenheimer, 5th ed. (Washington, D.C.: CQ Press, 1993); Peter Slevin, "Postwar Contracting Called Uncoordinated," *Washington Post,* October 31, 2003, A23.

71. "Study: Bush Donors Get Government Favors," *Lincoln Journal-Star,* May 28, 1992.

72. "Clinton Regrets Rich Pardon," March 31, 2002, CBSNEWS.com/stories/2002/03/31/politics/main505042.shtml; BBC News World Edition, "Rich's '$450,000' for Clinton Library," news.bbc.co.uk/hi/English/world/Americas/newid_1163000/1163917.stm. George H. W. Bush's last-minute pardon of a convicted $1.5 million heroin trafficker got much less publicity; John Monk and Gary Wright, "Why Did Bush Free Smuggler? Mystery Lingers in Charlotte Case," *Charlotte Observer,* March 27, 1993, 1A.

73. Charles Lewis, quoted in "Book Details Candidates' Extensive Financial Alignments," *Lincoln Journal-Star,* January 12, 1996, 5A.

74. Tom Kenworthy, "The Color of Money," *Washington Post National Weekly Edition,* November 6, 1989, 13.

75. Kevin Phillips, "How Wealth Defines Power," *American Prospect,* Summer 2003, A9; U.S. Census Bureau, *Statistical Abstract of the United States, 2003* (Washington, D.C.: Government Printing Office, 2003), tab. 688.

76. Gary Wasserman, "The Uses of Influence," *Washington Post National Weekly Edition,* January 11, 1993, 35.

77. Larry Makinson and Joshua Goldstein, *Open Secrets: The Cash Constituents of Congress,* 2nd ed. (Washington, D.C.: CQ Press, 1994), 23.

78. Amy Dockser, "Nice PAC You've Got There . . . A Pity if Anything Should Happen to It," *Washington Monthly,* January 1984, 21.

79. Juliet Eilperin, "'The Hammer' DeLay Whips Lobbyists into Shape," *Washington Post National Weekly Edition,* October 25, 1999, 8.

80. Jeff Leeds, "TV Stations Balk at Free Air Time for Candidates," *Lincoln Journal-Star,* May 14, 2000, 3A.

81. Walter Lippmann, "A Theory about Corruption," in Arnold J. Heidenheimer, ed. *Political Corruption* (New York: Holt, Rinehart and Winston, 1970), 294–297.

82. Susan Welch and John Peters, "Private Interests in the U.S. Congress," *Legislative Studies Quarterly* 7 (1982), 547–555; see also John Peters and Susan Welch, "Private Interests and Public Interests," *Journal of Politics* 45 (1983), 378–396.

83. "Having It All, Then Throwing It Away," *Time,* May 25, 1987, 22.

84. Elizabeth Drew, "Letter from Washington," *New Yorker,* May 1, 1989, 99–108; see also Dan Balz, "Tales of Power and Money," *Washington Post National Weekly Edition,* May 1, 1989, 11–12.

85. Quoted in Drew, "Having It All," 22.

86. Hank Paulson, CEO of Goldman Sachs, quoted in Joseph Nocera, "System Failure," *Fortune,* June 24, 2002, 62ff.

87. Keith Bradsher, "How to Pooh-Pooh $70 Million War Chests," *New York Times,* April 30, 2000, 6.

88. Richard Stevenson and Jeff Gerth, "Web of Safeguards Failed as Enron Fell," *New York Times,* January 20, 2002, 1.

89. Paul Krugman, "A System Corrupted," *New York Times,* February 18, 2002, A25.

90. Ibid.

91. Jonathan Alter, "Which Boot Will Drop Next?" *Newsweek,* February 4, 2002, 25.

92. "Enron and Other 'Bumps,'" *Washington Post,* June 23, 2002, B6.

93. "An 'Accounting Opportunity,'" *Washington Post,* June 18, 2002, A18; Nocera, "System Failure."

94. Michael Kinsley, "Blame the Accountants for Crooked Companies," *Lincoln Journal-Star,* June 4, 2002, 4B; Molly Ivins, "What Took So Long?" *Fort Worth Star-Telegram,* June 6, 2002.

95. Paul Krugman, "Fool Me Once," *New York Times,* October 8, 2002, 31.

Chapter 10

1. Justin Pritchard, "Mapping the Democrats' Future," *Champaign-Urbana News-Gazette,* January 5, 2002, B1.

2. Sources for this summary of Pelosi's political background include David Hawkings and Brian Nutting, eds., *CQ's Politics in America: The 108th Congress* (Washington, D.C.: CQ Press, 2003), 83–85; Michael Barone and Richard E. Cohen, *The Almanac of American Politics, 2004* (Washington, D.C.: National Journal, 2003), 186–188; and Mary Lynn F. Jones, "House Rules," *American Prospect,* January 13, 2002, 10–11.

3. Susan Ferrechio, "Rep. Nancy Pelosi," *CQ Weekly,* December 28, 2002, 55.

4. James R. Chiles, "Congress Couldn't Have Been This Bad, or Could It?" *Smithsonian,* November 1995, 70–80.

5. Susan Webb Hammond, "Life and Work on the Hill: Careers, Norms, Staff, and Informal Caucuses," in *Congress Responds to the Twentieth Century,* ed. Sunil Ahuja and Robert Dewhirst (Columbus: Ohio State University Press, 2003), 74.

6. David S. Broder, "Dumbing Down Democracy," *Lincoln Journal-Star,* April 5, 1995, 18.

7. Quoted in Kenneth J. Cooper and Helen Dewar, "No Limits on the Term Limits Crusade," *Washington Post National Weekly Edition,* May 29, 1995, 14.

8. "Congress of Relative Newcomers Poses Challenge to Bush, Leadership," *Congressional Quarterly Weekly Review,* January 20, 2001, 179–181.

9. "Datafile," *Congressional Quarterly Weekly Review,* February 21, 2004, 456.

10. Ibid., 476.

11. *Baker v. Carr,* 369 U.S. 186 (1962).

12. *Wesberry v. Sanders,* 376 U.S. 1 (1964).

13. Bruce Cain and Janet Campagna, "Predicting Partisan Redistricting Disputes," *Legislative Studies Quarterly* 12 (1987), 265–274.

14. See the report on *Miller v. Johnson,* 515 U.S. 900 (1995); see *New York Times,* July 2, 1995, E1, E4.

15. Hanna F. Pitkin, *The Concept of Representation* (Berkeley: University of California, 1967), 60.

16. Ibid., 60–61.

17. Ibid., 61.

18. Leslie Laurence, "Congress Makes Up for Neglect," *Lincoln Journal-Star,* December 5, 1994, 8.

19. ABC News poll, November 4, 2003, www.abcnews.com.

20. Roger H. Davidson and Walter J. Oleszek, *Congress and Its Members,* 9th ed. (Washington, D.C.: CQ Press, 2004), 132–134; Richard Fenno, *Home Style: House Members in their Districts,* 2nd ed. (New York: Longman, 2003), 232–247.

21. Roger H. Davidson and Walter J. Oleszek, *Congress and Its Members,* 7th ed. (Washington, D.C.: CQ Press, 2000), 114.

22. John Alford and John Hibbing, "The Disparate Electoral Security of House and Senate Incumbents," paper presented at the annual meeting of the American Political Science Association, Atlanta, September 1989.

23. Fenno, *Home Style.*

24. These numbers are projected from those given for 1998 and 2000 in Davidson and Olezsak, *Congress and Its Members,* 9th ed. (Washington, D.C.:CQ Press, 2004), 142.

25. Ibid., 145.

26. *Budget of the United States, Fiscal 2005* (Washington, D.C.: Government Printing Office, 2004), 22.

27. Robert Sherill, "Squealing on Porcine Politics," *Washington Post National Weekly Edition,* September 7, 1992, 35; the quote is by Alan Schick from Brian Kelly, "Pigging Out at the White House," *Washington Post National Weekly Edition,* September 14, 1992, 23.

28. Jeffrey Brainard and Ron Southwick, "A Record Year at the Federal Trough: Colleges Feast on $1.67 Billion in Earmarks," *Chronicle of Higher Education,* August 10, 2001, A20.

29. Citizens Against Government Waste, "Pig Book," www.cagw.org/site/PageServer?page name=reports_pigbook2004.

30. Ibid.

31. "Congress's Embarrassment of Pork," *New York Times,* June 19, 2004, 16.

32. Quoted in Kenneth Shepsle, "The Failures of Congressional Budgeting," *Social Science and Modern Society* 20 (1983), 4–10. See also Howard Kurtz, "Pork Barrel Politics," *Washington Post,* January 25, 1982.

33. Congressional Quarterly, *The Origins and Development of Congress* (Washington, D.C.: CQ Press, 1976).

34. Neil McNeil, *Forge of Democracy* (New York: McKay, 1963), 306–309.

35. Mark Hankerson, "Participation Hits Record," *Congressional Quarterly Weekly Review,* December 11, 1999, 2979.

36. Jackie Koszczuk, "Master of the Mechanics Has Kept the House Running," *Congressional Quarterly Weekly Review,* December 11, 1999, 2963.

37. Michael Barone, Richard E. Cohen, and Charles E. Cook Jr., *Almanac of American Politics, 2002* (Washington, D.C.: National Journal, 2002), 46.

38. Ibid.

39. For a review of all congressional committees and subcommittees, see the *Congressional Quarterly* special edition *CQ Guide to the Committees,* March 16, 2002.

40. Davidson and Oleszek, *Congress and Its Members,* 198.

41. See Roger Davidson, "Subcommittee Government," in *The New Congress,* ed. Thomas E. Mann and Norman J. Ornstein (Washington, D.C.: American Enterprise Institute for Public Policy Research, 1981), 110–111. Some of this occurs because members of Congress tend to be wealthy, and the wealthy make investments in corporations. It also occurs because members' financial interests are often similar to the interests in their districts (for example, representatives from farm districts are likely to be involved in farming or agribusiness).

42. Sara Brandes Crook and John Hibbing, "Congressional Reform and Party Discipline: The Effects of Changes in the Seniority System on Party Loyalty in the U.S. House of Representatives," *British Journal of Political Science* 15 (1985), 207–226.

43. Congressional Quarterly, *Congress from A to Z* (Washington, D.C.: CQ Press, 1999), 378.

44. Davidson and Oleszek, *Congress and Its Members,* 204.

45. Richard E. Cohen, "Best Seats in the House," *National Journal,* March 4, 2000, 682; Karen Foerstel, "House Offers Mixed Reviews for Committee Term Limits," *Congressional Quarterly Weekly Review,* June 22, 2002, 1653–1655.

46. For a review of how the task force has been used, see Walter J. Oleszek, "The Use of Task Forces in the House," Congressional Research Service Report No. 96-843-GOV, 1996, www.house.gov/rules/96-843.htm.

47. *Budget of the United States, 2005,* 19–32.

48. Ronald Moe and Steven Teel, "Congress as a Policy-Maker: A Necessary Reappraisal," *Political Science Quarterly* 85 (1970), 443–470.

49. Bruce Oppenheimer, "The Rules Committee," in *Congress Reconsidered,* ed. Lawrence Dodd and Bruce Oppenheimer (New York: Praeger, 1977), 96–116.

50. Thomas Geoghegan, "Bust the Filibuster," *Washington Post National Weekly Edition,* July 12, 1994, 25.

51. Michael Malbin, "Leading a Filibustered Senate," in *Extensions* (Carl A. Albert Center, University of Oklahoma), Spring 1985, 3.

52. Clinton aide Chuck Brain, quoted in Richard E. Cohen, "The Third House Rises," *National Journal,* July 28, 2001, 2395.

53. David J. Vogler, *The Third House: Conference Committees in the United States Congress* (Evanston, Ill.: Northwestern University Press, 1971); see also Lawrence D. Longley and Walter J. Oleszek, *Bicameral Politics* (New Haven, Conn.: Yale University Press, 1989).

54. Morris Ogul, "Congressional Oversight: Structures and Incentives," in *Congress Reconsidered,* ed. Dodd and Oppenheimer; see also Loch Johnson, "The U.S. Congress and the CIA: Monitoring the Dark Side of Government," *Legislative Studies Quarterly* 5 (1980), 477–501.

55. Joseph Califano, "Imperial Congress," *New York Times Magazine,* January 23, 1994, 41.

56. Richard E. Cohen, Kirk Victor, and David Bauman, "The State of Congress," *National Journal,* January 10, 2004, 104–105.

57. Quoted in ibid., 105.

58. Henry A. Waxman, "Free Pass from Congress," *Washington Post,* July 6, 2004, A19.

59. Joseph J. Schatz, "Appropriations Chairman: Hill's New Hardship Post," *Congressional Quarterly Weekly Review,* May 15, 2004, 1127.

60. Cohen, Victor, and Bauman, "State of Congress," 96.

61. Herbert Asher, "Learning of Legislative Norms," *American Political Science Review* 67 (1973), 499–513. Michael Berkman points out that freshmen who have had state legislative experience—who now account for more than half of all House members—adapt to the job faster than other members. See "Former State Legislators in the U.S. House of Representatives: Institutional and Policy Mastery," *Legislative Studies Quarterly* 18 (1993), 77–104.

62. *Minot* (N.D.) *Daily News,* June 17, 1976.

63. Rep. Jim DeMint (R-S.C.), quoted in Davidson and Oleszek, *Congress and Its Members,* 264.

64. Samuel Kernell, *Going Public* (Washington, D.C.: CQ Press, 1986).

65. Viewer statistics are available at C-SPAN's Web site (www.c-span.org). These are from July 2002.

66. For a list see Hawkings and Nutting, *CQ's Politics in America,* 1138–1139.

67. Michael Wines, "Washington Really Is in Touch. We're the Problem," *New York Times,* October 16, 1994, 4:2.

68. Richard Fenno, quoted in ibid.

69. Gallup poll, June 2004, www.gallup.com.

70. "Poll Track," *National Journal,* January 5, 2002, 58.

71. The information in this paragraph comes from Karen Foerstel, "Grass Greener after Congress," *Congressional Quarterly Weekly Review,* March 11, 2000, 515–519.

72. Rep. George Miller (D-Calif.), quoted in Harold Meyerson, "How Nancy Pelosi Took Control," *American Prospect,* June 2004, 36.

73. Ibid.

74. Meyerson, "How Nancy Pelosi Took Control," 38.

75. Ibid.

76. Ibid., 35.

Chapter 11

1. This effort was led by Richard Scaife, a millionaire and former owner of the *Washington Times* newspaper. With others, he funded the production and distribution of a video making the case that Clinton had had Vincent Foster murdered, despite the fact that three separate police and special prosecutor investigations concluded that Foster's death had been, beyond any doubt, a suicide. Activists on the Christian Right, including Pat Robertson, advocated for the case made in the video.

2. Quoted in Bill Clinton, *My Life* (New York: Knopf, 2004), 835.

3. Quoted in Allen Cowell, "Impeachment: What a Royal Pain," *New York Times,* February 7, 1999, 4:5.

4. "George Mason: Forgotten Founder," *Smithsonian,* May 2000, 145.

5. Clinton, *My Life,* 835.

6. Woodrow Wilson, *Congressional Government: A Study in American Politics* (New Brunswick, N.J.: Transaction, 2002). Originally published in 1885.

7. Theodore Lowi, *The Personal President: Power Invested, Promise Unfulfilled* (Ithaca, N.Y.: Cornell University Press, 1985).

8. Arthur M. Schlesinger Jr., *The Imperial Presidency* (Boston: Houghton Mifflin, 1973). Schlesinger has published an updated version based on the presidency of George W. Bush: *War and the American Presidency* (New York: Norton, 2004).

9. Harold M. Barger, *The Impossible Presidency* (Glenview, Ill.: Scott, Foresman, 1984).

10. Jefferson's management of the presidency is described in Joseph J. Ellis, *American Sphinx: The Character of Thomas Jefferson* (New York: Knopf, 1997), 186–228.

11. David Stout, "Presidential Candidates Seem Indifferent to a Salary Rise," *New York Times,* May 30, 1999, 16; Daniel J. Parks, "Prospective Presidential Pay Raise, First in 30 Years, Would Also Ease Other Officials' Salary 'Compression,'" *Congressional Quarterly Weekly Review,* May 29, 1999, 1264.

12. Information on all three impeachments proceedings can be found at www.historyplace.com.

13. These terms were popularized by Clinton Rossiter in *The American Presidency* (New York: Harcourt, Brace & World, 1956), a political science classic.

14. *United States v. Curtiss-Wright Export Corporation,* 299 U.S. 304 (1936).

15. See the discussion in *Federalist Paper 69,* written by Alexander Hamilton.

16. Quoted in "Notes and Comment," *New Yorker,* June 1, 1987, 23.

17. Ibid.

18. Thomas F. Cronin, *The State of the Presidency* (Boston: Little, Brown, 1975), 118.

19. Congress's anger at Roosevelt's court-packing scheme held up the reorganization for two years; see Chapter 13.

20. Charles O. Jones, *The Presidency in a Separated System* (Washington, D.C.: Brookings Institution Press, 1994), 56–57.

21. For more on Bush's White House staff and method of making appointments, see G. Calvin Mackenzie, "The Real Invisible Hand: Presidential Appointees in the Administration of George W. Bush," and Martha Joynt Kumar, "Recruiting and Organizing the White House Staff," *PS: Political Science and Politics* 1 (2002), 27–40.

22. "Hell from the Chief: Hot Tempers and Presidential Timber," *New York Times,* November 7, 1999, 4:7.

23. Quoted in Richard Pious, *The American Presidency* (New York: Basic Books, 1979), 244.

24. Public Broadcasting System, *The American President,* episode 10..

25. Ann Reilly Dowd, "What Managers Can Learn from Manager Reagan," *Fortune,* September 15, 1986, 32–41.

26. See John H. Kessel, "The Structures of the Reagan White House," *American Journal of Political Science* 28 (1984), 231–258.

27. Hillary Rodham Clinton, quoted in Carol Gelderman, *All the Presidents' Words: The Bully Pulpit and the Creation of the Virtual Presidency* (New York: Walker, 1997), 160.

28. A good description of Clinton's relationship to his White House staff can be found in Joe Klein, *The Natural: The Misunderstood Presidency of Bill Clinton* (New York: Doubleday, 2002).

29. For more on Bush's management style, see the several articles in the special section "C.E.O. U.S.A.," *New York Times Magazine,* January 14, 2001, 24–58.

30. Ron Suskind, *The Price of Loyalty: George W. Bush, the White House, and the Education of Paul O'Neill* (New York: Simon & Schuster, 2004).

31. Michael Nelson, ed., *The Presidency A to Z* (Washington, D.C.: CQ Press, 1998), 487–488.

32. For a review of the backgrounds of men who have served in the vice presidency and the roles they have played, see L. Edward Purcell, *Vice Presidents* (New York: Facts on File, 2001); Michael Nelson, *A Heartbeat Away* (New York: Priority, 1988); Paul C. Light, *Vice-Presidential Power: Advice and Influence in the White House* (Baltimore: Johns Hopkins University Press, 1984); and George Sirgiovanni, "The 'Van Buren Jinx': Vice Presidents Need Not Beware," *Presidential Studies Quarterly* 18 (1988), 61–76.

33. Purcell, *Vice Presidents,* 380.

34. Ron Suskind, "Without a Doubt," *New York Times Magazine,* October 17, 2004, 49.

35. Richard E. Neustadt, *Presidential Power: The Politics of Leadership from FDR to Carter* (New York: Wiley, 1980).

36. Samuel Kernell, *Going Public: New Strategies of Presidential Leadership* (Washington, D.C.: CQ Press, 1986), 15.

37. Charles O. Jones, *Separate but Equal Branches* (Chatham, N.J.: Chatham House, 1995).

38. Lowi, *Personal President,* xi.

39. Quoted in Dick Kirschten, "Reagan Warms Up for Political Hardball," *National Journal,* February 9, 1985, 328.

40. Nicholas Lemann, "The Quiet Man," *New Yorker,* May 7, 2001, 68.

41. Morris Fiorina, *Divided Government* (New York: Macmillan, 1992), 7.

42. "Bush Starts a Strong Record of Success with the Hill," *Congressional Quarterly Weekly Review,* January 12, 2002, 112.

43. John Barry, "What Schwarzkopf 's Book Leaves Out," *Newsweek,* September 28, 1992, 68.

44. A good overview of Rumsfeld's attempts to transform the military and his role in planning and directing the war in Iraq can be found in the transcript of the PBS program *Rumsfeld's War,* broadcast October 26, 2004, available at www.pbs.org/wgbh/pages/frontline/shows/pentagon.

45. *Youngstown Sheet and Tube Co. v. Sawyer,* 343 U.S. 579 (1952).

46. Nelson, *Presidency A to Z,* 12.

47. For discussion of the president's removal powers in light of a 1988 Supreme Court decision regarding independent counsels, see John A. Rohr, "Public Administration, Executive Power, and Constitutional Confusion," and Rosemary O'Leary, "Response to John Rohr," *Public Administrative Review* 49 (1989), 108–115.

48. Jones, *Presidency in a Separated System,* 53.

49. Alexander Simendinger, Sydney J. Freedberg Jr., and Siobhan Gorman, "The Experiment Begins," *National Journal,* June 15, 2002, 1775–1787.

50. Nelson, *Presidency A to Z,* 169.

51. The Bush White House provides a link to all executive orders issued by the president at the White House home page (www.whitehouse.gov).

52. Nelson, *Presidency A to Z,* 170.

53. Jeffrey K. Tulis, *The Rhetorical Presidency* (Princeton, N.J.: Princeton University Press, 1987).

54. Quoted in Garry Wills, *Lincoln at Gettysburg* (New York: Simon & Schuster, 1992), 31.

55. David Halberstam, *The Powers That Be* (New York: Dell, 1980), 30.

56. "Travels of the President," *New York Times,* August 8, 2004, 18.

57. Michael Waldman, Clinton's former chief speechwriter, on *Morning Edition,* National Public Radio, January 1, 2002.

58. Lowi, *Personal President.*

59. "Poll Shows Americans Want a Strong Leader," *Lincoln Journal-Star,* June 16, 1992, 5.

60. Thomas Friedman, "Addicted to 9/11," *New York Times,* October 14, 2004, p. A 29.

61. "A Talk with Clinton," *Newsweek,* January 25, 1993, 37.

62. Carl M. Cannon, "Judging Clinton," *National Journal,* January 1, 2000, 23.

63. Klein, *The Natural,* 208.

64. Kernell, *Going Public,* 15.

65. Ari Fleischer, quoted in *CQ Today News,* May 19, 2003, www.cq.com.

66. "The Presidency," *Newsweek,* December 20, 1993, 46.

67. Geoffrey Nunberg, "The Curious Fate of Populism: How Politics Turned into Prose," *New York Times,* August 15, 2004, WK7; Philip Gourevitch, "Bushspeak," *New Yorker,* September 13, 2004, 36–43.

68. Nicholas Lemann, "Remember the Alamo," *New Yorker,* October 18, 2004, 153.

69. Bruce Miroff, "The Presidency and the Public: Leadership and Spectacle," in *The Presidency and the Political System,* 5th ed., ed. Michael Nelson (Washington: CQ Press, 1998), 320.

70. Lonnie G. Bunch III et al., *The American Presidency: A Glorious Burden* (Washington, D.C.: Smithsonian Institution, 2000), 19.

71. George C. Edwards III, *The Public Presidency* (New York: St. Martin's Press, 1983), 253.

72. John Mueller, *War, Presidents, and Public Opinion* (New York: Wiley, 1970).

73. For example, see Edwards, *Public Presidency,* 239–247.

74. *National Journal,* December 8, 1990, 2993; January 19, 1991, 185; February 16, 1991, 412.

75. For more on the Gulf War's impact on Bush's ratings, see John A. Krosnick and Laura A. Brannon, "The Impact of the Gulf War on the Ingredients of Presidential Evaluations: Multidimensional Effects of Political Involvement," *American Political Science Review* 87 (1993), 963–975.

76. "Opinion Outlook," *National Journal,* February 18, 1995, 452.

77. See, for example, the comments of Arthur M. Schlesinger Jr. in Cannon, "Judging Clinton," 22; Steven A. Holmes, "Losers in Clinton-Starr Bouts May Be Future U.S. Presidents," *New York Times,* August 23, 1998, 18; and Adam Clymer, "The Presidency Is Still There, Not Quite the Same," *New York Times,* February 14, 1999, 4:1.

78. See, for example, David S. Broder and Dan Balz, "Who Wins?" *Washington Post National Weekly Edition,* January 15, 1999, 6–7, and Cannon, "Judging Clinton," 22–23.

79. Richard E. Neustadt, *Presidential Power: The Politics of Leadership from FDR to Carter* (New York: Wiley, 1980).

80. A classic study on this topic is James David Barber's *Presidential Character: Predicting Performance in the White House* (Englewood Cliffs, N.J.: Prentice Hall, 1989), originally published in 1973.

81. Quoted in Arthur M. Schlesinger Jr., "The Ultimate Approval Rating," *New York Times Magazine,* December 18, 1996, 50.

82. Ibid.

83. Ibid.

84. The full text of Starr's report to Congress appeared in the *New York Times,* September 12, 1998, B1–B18. The transcript of Clinton's grand jury testimony was reprinted in the *New York Times,* September 22, 1998, B1–B8. You can review impeachment documents, hear sound bites from trial testimony, and look at the principal participants at www.pbs.org/newshour/impeachment.

85. Much of the information recounted here is based on Jeffrey L. Katz, "Exit Strategies Divide Senate," *Congressional Quarterly Weekly Review,* January 30, 1999, 249.

86. Carroll J. Doherty, "Senate Acquits Clinton," *Congressional Quarterly Weekly Review,* February 13, 1999, 361–362.

87. Quoted in Michael Barone and Richard E. Cohen, *Almanac of American Politics, 2002* (Washington, D.C.: National Journal, 2001), 693.

88. Dan Carney, "Impeachment's Long Shadow," *Congressional Quarterly Weekly Review,* January 2, 1999, 10.

Chapter 12

1. The account of Edmonds's FBI assignments, her on-the-job-discoveries, and her complaints to supervisors are detailed in various interviews posted on the Internet, including "Lost in Translation," Ed Bradley's interview with Sibel Edmonds on CBS's *60 Minutes,* broadcast October 27, 2002 (CBSNews.com); interview of Edmonds by Amy Goodman, April 29, 2004 (www.democracynow.org); interview by Amy Goodman and Juan Gonzalez of Coleen Rowley and Sibel Edmonds, April 9, 2004 (www.democracynow.org); interview with Sibel Edmonds by Christopher Deliso, July 1, 2004 (www.balkanalysis.com); and "Whistleblowers from Vietnam to 9/11: A Conversation," interview by Amy Goodman and Juan Gonzalez, with Daniel Ellsberg and Sibel Edmonds, April 29, 2004 (www.democracynow.org/article.pl?sid=04/04/29/1513230).

2. Sibel Edmonds, quoting her FBI supervisor, *60 Minutes,* October 27, 2002.

3. Nancy Gibbs, "Botching the Big Case," *Time,* May 21, 2001, 36.

4. George Lardner Jr., "The Rest of the Ruby Ridge Story," *Washington Post National Weekly Edition,* August 13, 2001, 30; Dan Eggen, "More FBI Blunders in the Lee Probe," *Washington Post National Weekly Edition,* September 3, 2001, 29. In 2001, the press revealed that numerous FBI offices did not turn over relevant evidence and paperwork for the Oklahoma City bombing prosecution; and in 2002, there were more humiliations as hundreds of FBI computers and guns were found to be missing and the agency could not account for them.

5. Eric Lichtblau, " FBI Said to Lag on Translations of Terror Tapes," *New York Times,* September 28, 2004, 1.

6. Bruce Adams, "The Frustrations of Government Service," *Public Administration Review* 44 (1984), 5. For more discussion of public attitudes about the civil service see Herbert Kaufman, "Fear of Bureaucracy: A Raging Pandemic," *Public Administration Review* 41 (1981), 1.

7. The classic early work on western bureaucracy is Max Weber's. See H. H. Gerth and C. Wright Mills, trans., *From Max Weber: Essays on Sociology* (New York: Oxford University Press, 1946), 196–239. 8. On distinctions between public and private bureaucracies see Barry Bozeman, *All Organizations Are Public: Bridging Public and Private Organizational Theories* (San Francisco: Jossey-Bass, 1987).

9. "Federal Executives' Bonuses Scrutinized," *Champaign-Urbana News-Gazette,* January 23, 2002, A4.

10. From a letter to W. T. Barry, quoted in "A Citizen's Guide on Using the Freedom of Information Act and the Privacy Act of 1974 to Request Government Records," report to the U.S. House of Representatives 50 (1999), 2.

11. Reported in Sam Archibald, "The Early Years of the Freedom of Information Act, 1955–1974," *PS: Political Science and Politics,* December 1993, 730.

12. Debra Gersh Hernandez, "Many Promises, Little Action," *Editor and Publisher,* March 26, 1994, 15.

13. Government Accounting Office, *Freedom of Information Act: State Department Request Processing* (Washington, D.C.: Government Printing Office, 1989).

14. "President Declassifies Old Papers," *Omaha World-Herald,* April 18, 1995, 1.

15. Clinton administration policy on compliance with FOIA can be found in Federation of American Scientists, Project on Government Secrecy, "Clinton Administration Documents on Classification Policy," 2003, www.fas.org/sgp/clinton/index.html.

16. Memo from Attorney General John Ashcroft, October 12, 2001. The text of this memo and all major Bush administration statements and documents regarding its FOIA and openness in government policies are posted at the Federation of American Scientists Web site, www.fas.org. Also see openthegovernment.org.

17. Eric Lichtblau, "Government by, and Secret from, the People," *New York Times,* September 5, 2004, WK5.

18. Evan Hendricks, *Former Secrets: Government Records Made Public through the Freedom of Information Act* (Washington, D.C.: Campaign for Political

Rights, 1982); "Behind the Freedom of Information Act," *Now with Bill Moyers,* PBS, April 5, 2002.

19. Joyce Appleby, "That's *General* Washington to You," *New York Times Book Review,* February 14, 1993, 11, a review of Richard Norton Smith, *Patriarch* (Boston: Houghton Mifflin, 1993). See also James Q. Wilson, "The Rise of the Bureaucratic State," *Public Interest* 41 (1975), 77–103.

20. Wilson, "Rise of the Bureaucratic State."

21. Leonard D. White, *Introduction to the Study of Public Administration,* 4th ed. (New York: Macmillan, 1955), 4.

22. David H. Rosenbloom, "'Whose Bureaucracy Is This Anyway?' Congress's 1946 Answer," *PS: Political Science and Politics,* December 2001, 773.

23. Paul C. Light, *Thickening Government: Federal Hierarchy and the Diffusion of Accountability* (Washington, D.C.: Brookings Institution, 1995).

24. Office of Management and Budget, *Special Analyses: Budget of the United States, Fiscal Year 1990* (Washington, D.C.: Government Printing Office, 1989), 1–13; Office of Management and Budget, *Historical Tables: Budget of the United States, Fiscal Year 1996* (Washington, D.C.: Government Printing Office, 1995), 245.

25. U.S. Census Bureau, *Statistical Abstract of the United States, 2001,* (Washington, D.C.: Government Printing Office, 2001), tab. 450.

26. Richard E. Stevenson, "Bush Budget Links Dollars to Deeds with New Ratings," *New York Times,* February 3, 2002, 1, 23; Eric Schmitt, "Is This Any Way to Run a Nation?" *New York Times,* April 14, 2002, WK4. Agency evaluations can be viewed at the OMB Web site, www.omb.gov.

27. "Federal Government Found to Have Gotten Bigger," *Champaign-Urbana News-Gazette,* January 23, 2004, A3.

28. Paul C. Light, "Fact Sheet on the Continued Thickening of Government," Brookings Institution, July 23, 2004, www.brookings.edu/views/papers/light/20040723.htm.

29. Ibid. Light does an "inventory" of senior positions in cabinet departments every six years.

30. Jim Hoagland, "Dissing Government," *Washington Post National Weekly Edition,* December 8, 2003, 5.

31. Paul C. Light, "What Federal Employees Want from Reform: Reform Watch Brief No. 5," Brookings Institution, March 2002, www.brookings.edu/comm/reformwatch/rw05.htm.

32. For a discussion of these issues, see Peter T. Kilborn, "Big Change Likely as Law Bans Bias toward Disabled," *New York Times,* July 19, 1992, 1, 16.

33. Jill Smolows, "Noble Aims, Mixed Results," *Time,* July 31, 1995, 54.

34. Theodore Lowi, *The End of Liberalism* (New York: Norton, 1969).

35. Woodrow Wilson, "The Study of Administration," *Political Science Quarterly* 56 (1941), 481–506. Originally published in 1887.

36. See David H. Rosenbloom, "Have an Administrative Rx? Don't Forget the Politics!" *Public Administration Review* 53 (1993), 503–507.

37. "Hatch Act Revamped," *PA Times,* November 1, 1993, 3; "Hatch Act Political Curbs Retained for Some Workers," *Lincoln Journal-Star,* July 16, 1993, 3.

38. This was revealed by the head of the Clinton and Bush counterterrorism unit, Richard A. Clarke, who spoke with Bush on September 12, 2001, in the war room and recounted the event in *Against All Enemies* (New York: Free Press, 2004) and in public testimony before the televised 9/11 Commission hearings in 2004.

39. Public testimony before the televised 9/11 Commission hearings, 2004.

40. Report issued by the chief U.S. arms inspector, Charles A. Duelfer, October 2004.

41. Charles Peters, *How Washington Really Works* (Reading, Mass.: Addison-Wesley, 1980), 46–47.

42. Nicolas Thompson, "Finding the Civil Service's Hidden Sex Appeal," *Washington Monthly,* November 2000, 31.

43. Terry More, "Regulators' Performance and Presidential Administrations," *American Journal of Political Science* 26 (1982), 197–224; Terry More, "Control and Feedback in Economic Regulation," *American Political Science Review* 79 (1985), 1094–1116.

44. More, "Control and Feedback."

45. Use of the term *capture* by political scientists studying regulation seems to have originated with Samuel Huntington, "The Marasmus of the ICC," *Yale Law Journal* 61 (1952), 467–509; it was later popularized by Marver Bernstein, *Regulating Business by Independent Commission* (Princeton, N.J.: Princeton University Press, 1955).

46. See "C-5As with Wing Modifications Planned for September Delivery," *Aviation Week and Space Technology,* December 22, 1969, 13; and "Whatever Happened to the C-5A 'White Elephant'?" *U.S. News and World Report,* June 19, 1972, 63.

47. David C. Morrison, "Extracting a Thorn, Air Force–Style," *National Journal,* March 7, 1987, 567. For more on Fitzgerald's experiences, see A. Ernest Fitzgerald, *The Pentagonists: An Insider's View of Waste, Mismanagement, and Fraud in Defense Spending* (Boston: Houghton Mifflin, 1989).

48. W. John Moore, "Citizen Prosecutors," *National Journal,* August 18, 1990, 2006–2010.

49. Fred Alford, quoted in Barbara Ehrenreich, "All Together Now," *New York Times,* July 15, 2004, A23.

50. Steve Fainaru and Dan Eggen, "Chief among the Charges," *Washington Post National Weekly Edition,* June 10, 2002, 30.

51. Robert Pear, "Congress Moves to Protect Federal Whistleblowers," *New York Times,* October 3, 2004, 21.

52. Eric Schmitt, "The Rube Goldberg Agency," *New York Times,* March 24, 2002, WK5.

53. Charles T. Goodsell, *The Case for Bureaucracy: A Public Administration Polemic,* 2nd ed. (Chatham, N.J.: Chatham House, 1985), 140.

54. Schmitt, "Is This Any Way to Run a Nation?"

55. Letter from Senators Patrick Leahy and Charles Grassley to Department of Justice Inspector General Glenn A. Fine, June 19, 2002; letter from Senators Patrick Leahy and Charles Grassley to Attorney General John Ashcroft, August 13, 2002. Both are posted at www.thememoryhole.org/spy/edmonds_letters.htm.

56. Interview on CBS's *60 Minutes,* October 27, 2002.

57. Edmonds was angry that her testimony was not mentioned in the report or that FBI procedures were not criticized. See her letter to Thomas Kean, cochair of the 9/11 Commission, August 1, 2004, posted at www.scoop.co.nz/mason/stories/HL0408/S00012.htm.

58. Interview of Coleen Rowley and Sibel Edmonds by Amy Goodman and Juan Gonzalez, April 9, 2004; transcript at www.democracynow.org.

59. Interview on CBS's *60 Minutes,* October 27, 2002. Also see the letter from Senator Grassley to FBI Director Robert Mueller, October 28, 2002, posted at www.thememoryhole.org/spy/edmonds_letters.htm.

60. Statement of Robert S. Mueller at FBI press conference, May 29, 2002.

61. Lichtblau, "FBI Said to Lag."

62. Eric Lichtblau, "Whistle-Blowing Said to Be Factor in an FBI Firing," *New York Times,* July 29, 2004, A1.

63. The revamped mission of the FBI is posted at the agency's Web site, www.fbi.gov. See the section titled "FBI Priorities."

Chapter 13

1. The vote tallies here are approximate numbers rather than actual numbers.

2. Harris was eventually forced to resign her position as secretary of state for failing to follow the election laws that she was responsible for enforcing. She then capitalized on her newfound notoriety by running for and winning a seat in the U.S. House of Representatives.

3. This ruling applied to ballots for which the machines did not detect a vote ("undervotes"). The order did not include ballots for which the machines detected more than one vote ("overvotes"), disqualifying them.

4. Samuel Issacharoff, "Political Judgments," in *The Vote: Bush, Gore, and the Supreme Court,* ed. Cass R. Sunstein and Richard A. Epstein (Chicago: University of Chicago Press, 2001), 64. For an analysis of relevant portions of Florida's election law, see Larry D. Kramer, "The Supreme Court in Politics," in *The Unfinished Election of 2000,* ed. Jack N. Rakove (New York: Basic Books, 2001), 105–157.

5. Richard A. Epstein, "'In Such Manner as the Legislature Thereof May Direct': The Outcome in *Bush* v. *Gore* Defended," in *The Vote,* ed. Sunstein and Epstein, 13–37; Michael W. McConnell, "Two-and-a-Half Cheers for *Bush* v. *Gore,*" in ibid., 98–122.

6. David A. Strauss, "*Bush* v. *Gore:* What Were They Thinking?" in *The Vote,* ed. Sunstein and Epstein, 203.

7. For example, it did not force Miami-Dade County to resume the recount it had stopped, it did not force Republican counties where officials improperly treated absentee ballots to reassess them, and it did not declare the infamous and confusing "butterfly ballot" of Palm Beach County unlawful. For further discussion, see ibid., 202–203.

8. Six were Democratic appointees; one was a compromise choice.

9. This is not to say that they were clearly nonpartisan. We do not know. They issued a mixed bag of rulings, with more going against Gore's campaign than for it.

10. Justice Felix Frankfurter in *Colegrove* v. *Green,* 328 U.S. 549, 556 (1946).

11. The liberal is Justice John Paul Stevens, who some consider a moderate liberal. In any event, he is not an archliberal like past Justices William O. Douglas, William Brennan, or John Marshall or even a less consistent liberal such as Chief Justice Earl Warren.

12. Jeffrey Rosen, "A Majority of One," *New York Times Magazine,* June 3, 2001, 34.

13. *Planned Parenthood* v. *Casey,* 505 U.S. 833 (1992).

14. The Court could declare the case a "political question," although this designation is normally reserved for cases involving separation of powers on the federal level.

15. Issacharoff, "Political Judgments," 56.

16. Rosen, "Majority of One," 64.

17. Bush's lawyers considered this their weakest argument, though it would attract the most justices. Another argument could be based on an interpretation of Article II, Section 1, of the Constitution. According to this interpretation, the Florida court cannot exercise judicial review of any Florida legislation affecting the presidential election. Discussion of this interpretation gets quite complex for an introductory text, and ultimately this interpretation attracted only three justices.

18. The Rehnquist Court has also used it in cases addressing racial legislative redistricting. For an intriguing argument that the Court is altering equal protection doctrine in these cases, see Pamela S.

Karlan, "The Newest Equal Protection: Regressive Doctrine on a Changeable Court," in *The Vote,* ed. Sunstein and Epstein, 77–97.

19. Cass R. Sunstein, "Order without Law," in *The Vote,* ed. Sunstein and Epstein, 213.

20. Ibid., 218.

21. Frank I. Michelman, "Suspicion, or the New Prince," in *The Vote,* ed. Sunstein and Epstein, 130 and 136, n. 34.

22. *McCleskey* v. *Kemp,* 481 U.S. 279 (1987). All of the justices in the majority in *Bush* v. *Gore* were in the majority in *McCleskey,* except Clarence Thomas, who was not yet on the Court.

23. Alan M. Dershowitz, *Supreme Injustice: How the High Court Hijacked Election 2000* (New York: Oxford University Press, 2001), 133–134.

24. John Hibbing and Elizabeth Theiss-Morse, *Congress as Public Enemy: Public Attitudes toward American Political Institutions* (New York: Cambridge University Press, 1995), ch. 2 and 3.

25. John R. Schmidhauser, *Justices and Judges* (Boston: Little, Brown, 1979), 11.

26. *Federalist Paper* 78.

27. Henry J. Abraham, *Justices and Presidents* (New York: Oxford University Press, 1974), 74.

28. Henry J. Abraham, *The Judicial Process,* 3rd ed. (New York: Oxford University Press, 1975), 309.

29. Drew Pearson and Robert S. Allen, *The Nine Old Men* (New York: Doubleday/Doren, 1937), 7; Barbara A. Perry, *The Priestly Tribe: The Supreme Court's Image in the American Mind* (Westport, Conn.: Praeger, 1999), 8–9.

30. *Federalist Paper* 78.

31. 5 U.S. 137 (1803). Technically, *Marbury* was not the first use of judicial review, but it was the first clear articulation of judicial review by the Court.

32. Jefferson was also angry at the nature of the appointees. One had led troops loyal to England during the Revolutionary War. Eric Black, *Our Constitution: The Myth That Binds Us* (Boulder, Colo.: Westview Press, 1988), 66.

33. Debate arose over whether the four should be considered appointed. Their commissions had been signed by the president, and the seal of the United States had been affixed by Marshall, as secretary of state. Yet it was customary to require commissions to be delivered, perhaps because of less reliable record keeping by government or less reliable communications at the time.

34. Marbury had petitioned the Court for a writ of mandamus under the authority of a provision of the Judiciary Act of 1789 that permitted the Court to issue such a writ. Marshall maintained that this provision broadened the Court's original jurisdiction and thus violated the Constitution. (The Constitution allows the Court to hear cases that have not been heard by any other court before—if they involve a state or a foreign ambassador. Marbury's involved neither.) Yet it was quite clear that the provision did not broaden the Court's original jurisdiction—so clear, in fact, that Marshall did not even quote the language he was declaring unconstitutional. Furthermore, even if the provision did broaden the Court's original jurisdiction, it is not certain that the provision would violate the Constitution. (The Constitution does not say that the Court shall have original jurisdiction *only* in cases involving a state or a foreign ambassador.) Many members of Congress who had drafted and voted for the Judiciary Act had been delegates to the Constitutional Convention, and it is unlikely that they would have initiated a law that contradicted the Constitution. And Oliver Ellsworth, who had been a coauthor of the bill, then served as chief justice of the Supreme Court before Marshall. But these interpretations allowed Marshall a way out of the dilemma.

35. Quoted in Walter F. Murphy and C. Herman Pritchett, *Courts, Judges, and Politics,* 3rd ed. (New York: Random House, 1979), 4.

36. John A. Garraty, "The Case of the Missing Commissions," in *Quarrels That Have Shaped the Constitution,* ed. John A. Garraty (New York: Harper & Row, 1962), 13.

37. *Fletcher* v. *Peck,* 10 U.S. 87 (1810); *Martin* v. *Hunter's Lessee,* 14 U.S. 304 (1816); *Cohens* v. *Virginia,* 19 U.S. 264 (1821).

38. *Gibbons* v. *Ogden,* 22 U.S. 1 (1824).

39. *Scott* v. *Sandford,* 60 U.S. 393 (1857).

40. *Ex parte Merryman,* 17 Fed. Cas. 144, no. 9487 (1861).

41. *Ex parte McCardle,* 74 U.S. 506 (1869).

42. For examination of the ways in which the Civil War and Reconstruction fomented a constitutional "revolution," see Bruce Ackerman, *We the People: Transformations* (Cambridge, Mass.: Harvard University Press, 1998). Ackerman offers a similar examination of the significance of the New Deal period.

43. *Hammer* v. *Dagenhart,* 247 U.S. 251 (1918).

44. *Lochner* v. *New York,* 198 U.S. 45 (1905).

45. *Adkins* v. *Children's Hospital,* 261 U.S. 525 (1923).

46. *Adair* v. *United States,* 208 U.S. 161 (1908); *In re Delis,* 158 U.S. 564 (1895).

47. *United States* v. *E. C. Knight Co.,* 156 U.S. 1 (1895).

48. Lawrence Baum, *The Supreme Court,* 8th ed. (Washington, D.C.: CQ Press, 2004).

49. C. Herman Pritchett, *The American Constitution,* 2nd ed. (New York: McGraw-Hill, 1968), 166.

50. For convenience, scholars and journalists refer to the Supreme Court by the name of the chief justice, although the Court's doctrine is determined by all of its justices.

51. However, the Warren Court may not have been as out of step with the political branches as often believed. See Lucas A. Powe, *The Warren Court and American Politics* (Cambridge, Mass.: Harvard University Press, 2000), 160–178.

52. One legal scholar says the most striking feature about Supreme Court decision making in the 1990s was the effort by five justices to resolve most issues as narrowly as possible, shunning sweeping pronouncements for case-by-case examination. Cass R. Sunstein, *One Case at a Time: Judicial Minimalism on the Supreme Court* (Cambridge, Mass.: Harvard University Press, 2001).

53. For an analysis, see John T. Noonan, *Narrowing the Nation's Power* (Berkeley: University of California Press, 2002).

54. Ray Kurzweil, quoted in Joel Garreau, "The Second Evolution of the Species," *Washington Post National Weekly Edition,* May 6, 2002, 11.

55. Occasionally, for important cases, the entire group of judges in one circuit will sit together, "en banc." (In the large Ninth Circuit, eleven judges will sit.)

56. If at least $75,000 is at stake, according to congressional law.

57. Quoted in Henry J. Abraham, "A Bench Happily Filled," *Judicature* 66 (1983), 284.

58. For elaboration on the Senate's role, see Stephen B. Burbank, "Politics, Privilege, and Power: The Senate's Role in the Appointment of Federal Judges," *Judicature* 86 (2002), 24.

59. Victor Navasky, *Kennedy Justice* (New York: Atheneum, 1971), 245–246.

60. Harry P. Stumpf, *American Judicial Politics,* 2nd ed. (Upper Saddle River, N.J.: Prentice Hall, 1998), 175. After Taft nominated a Catholic to be chief justice, the speaker of the House cracked, "If Taft were Pope, he'd want to appoint some Protestants to the College of Cardinals." Henry J. Abraham, *Justices and Presidents: A Political History of Appointments to the Supreme Court,* 2nd ed. (New York: Oxford University Press, 1985), 168.

61. Elliot E. Slotnick, "A Historical Perspective on Federal Judicial Selection," *Judicature* 86 (2002), 13.

62. For an analysis of internal documents that established this process in the Reagan administration, see

Dawn Johnsen, "Tipping the Scale," *Washington Monthly,* July-August 2002, 1–18.

63. Robert A. Carp, Ronald Stidham, and Kenneth L. Manning, *Judicial Process in America,* 6th ed. (Washington, D.C.: CQ Press, 2004), 164.

64. Marilyn Nejelski, *Women in the Judiciary: A Status Report* (Washington, D.C.: National Women's Political Caucus, 1984).

65. Sheldon Goldman, "Reagan's Second-Term Judicial Appointments," *Judicature* 70 (1987), 324–339.

66. Sheldon Goldman, Elliott E. Slotnick, Gerard Gryski, Gary Zuk, and Sara Schiavoni, "W. Bush Remaking the Judiciary: Like Father like Son?" *Judicature* 86 (2003), 304, 308.

67. Ibid.

68. David Greenberg, "Actually, It is Political," *Washington Post National Weekly Edition,* July 26–August 1, 2004, 23.

69. One of President Reagan's nominees, Douglas Ginsburg, withdrew his nomination due to widespread opposition in the Senate, so officially his nomination was not denied.

70. Nixon's nomination of G. Harold Carswell was a notable exception. At his confirmation hearing, a parade of legal scholars called him undistinguished. Even his supporters acknowledged that he was mediocre. Nixon's floor manager for the nomination, Senator Roman Hruska (R-Nebr.), blurted out in exasperation, "Even if he is mediocre, there are a lot of mediocre judges and people and lawyers. They are entitled to a little representation, aren't they, and a little chance? We can't have all Brandeises, Cardozos, and Frankfurters, and stuff like that there." Abraham, *Justices and Presidents,* 6–7.

71. For an examination of the relationship between ethical lapses and ideological reasons, see Charles M. Cameron, Albert D. Cover, and Jeffrey A. Segal, "Senate Voting on Supreme Court Nominees: A Neoinstitutional Model," *American Political Science Review* 84 (1990), 525–534.

72. The heat of the battle obscured the fact that when the vacancy occurred, President Reagan was spoiling for a fight. His reputation had been tarnished by the Iran-Contra affair, and he wanted to demonstrate that he could still dominate Congress as he had during his first term. Aides gave the Senate Judiciary Committee a list of possible nominees and asked if any would pose problems. The Democrats said Bork would pose the greatest problem, so Reagan nominated Bork.

73. For some time, the Senate confirmed fewer nominees to the lower courts in the fourth year of a president's term when the Senate's majority was from the other party. The senators hoped their candidate would capture the White House in the next election. They delayed confirmation so there would be numerous vacancies for their president and, through senatorial courtesy, for themselves to fill as well. Jeffrey A. Segal and Harold Spaeth, "If a Supreme Court Vacancy Occurs, Will the Senate Confirm a Reagan Nominee?" *Judicature* 69 (1986), 188–189.

74. For an objective measure of obstruction and delay, see Sheldon Goldman, "Assessing the Senate Judicial Confirmation Process: The Index of Obstruction and Delay," *Judicature* 86 (2003), 251.

75. Al Kamen, "Switching Sides to Court Victory," *Washington Post National Weekly Edition,* July 14, 1997, 15.

76. Quoted in Savage, "Clinton Losing Fight for Black Judge," *Los Angeles Times,* July 7, 2000, A1.

77. Scherer, "Judicial Confirmation Process," 240–250.

78. Goldman et al., "W. Bush Remaking the Judiciary," 304, 308.

79. Schmidhauser, *Justice and Judges,* 55–57.

80. Merle Miller, *Plain Speaking* (New York: Berkeley/Putnam, 1974), 121.

81. Harold W. Chase, *Federal Judges* (Minneapolis: University of Minnesota Press, 1972), 189.

82. John Gruhl, "The Impact of Term Limits for Supreme Court Justices," *Judicature* 81 (1997), 66–72.

83. The fourth, Rehnquist, disqualified himself because he had worked on the administration's policy toward executive privilege.

84. *Jones v. Clinton,* 137 L.Ed.2d 945, 117 S. Ct. 1636 (1997).

85. Martin Shapiro, "The Supreme Court: From Warren to Burger," in *The New American Political System,* ed. Anthony King (Washington, D.C.: American Enterprise Institute, 1978), 180–181.

86. Robert Seigliano, *The Supreme Court and the Presidency* (New York: Free Press, 1971), 147–148.

87. Quoted in Abraham, *Justices and Presidents,* 62.

88. Earl Warren, *The Memoirs of Earl Warren* (Garden City, N.Y.: Doubleday, 1977), 5.

89. Quoted in Abraham, *Justices and Presidents,* 63.

90. "How Much Do Lawyers Charge?" *Parade,* March 23, 1997, 14.

91. Lois G. Forer, *Money and Justice* (New York: Norton, 1984), 9, 15, 102.

92. Karen O'Connor and Lee Epstein, "The Rise of Conservative Interest Group Litigation," *Journal of Politics* 45 (1983), 481. See also Richard C. Cortner, *The Supreme Court and the Second Bill of Rights* (Madison: University of Wisconsin Press, 1981), 282.

93. The dentist agreed to fill the cavity only in a hospital, where the procedure would be far more expensive. *Bragdon v. Abbott,* 141 L.Ed.2d 540 (1998).

94. *Sutton v. United Air Lines,* 144 L.Ed.2d 450 (1999).

95. The Court ruled the same in a case involving a man with high blood pressure who could not get a job driving trucks. *Murphy v. United Parcel Service,* 144 L.Ed.2d 484 (1999).

96. *Toyota Motor Manufacturing v. Williams,* 151 L.Ed.2d 615 (2001).

97. Robert Bork, *The Tempting of America* (New York: Touchstone/Simon & Schuster, 1990).

98. James Madison's notes from the Constitutional Convention and the *Federalist Papers* are considered the most authoritative sources, but relying on them is fraught with problems. Because Madison edited his notes many years after the convention, his experiences in government or lapses of memory might have colored his version of the intentions of the delegates. Because Madison, Hamilton, and Jay published the *Federalist Papers* to persuade New York to ratify the Constitution, their motive may have affected their account of the intentions of the delegates.

99. Lawrence Tribe, *On Reading the Constitution* (Cambridge, Mass.: Harvard University Press, 1992).

100. *Osborn v. U.S. Bank,* 22 U.S. 738 (1824), at 866.

101. Abraham, *Judicial Process,* 324.

102. *United States v. Butler,* 297 U.S. 1, at 94.

103. Murphy and Pritchett, *Courts, Judges, and Politics,* 586.

104. *Furman v. Georgia,* 408 U.S. 238 (1972). Blackmun did vote against the death penalty later in his career.

105. Quoted in Alexander Bickel, *The Morality of Consent* (New Haven, Conn.: Yale University Press, 1975), 120.

106. "Judicial Authority Moves Growing Issue," *Lincoln Journal,* April 24, 1977.

107. Jeffrey A. Segal and Albert D. Cover, "Ideological Values and the Votes of U.S. Supreme Court Justices," *American Political Science Review* 83 (1989), 557–564. For different findings for state supreme court justices, see John M. Scheb II, Terry Bowen, and Gary Anderson, "Ideology, Role Orientations, and Behavior in the State Courts of Last Resort," *American Politics Quarterly* 19 (1991), 324–335.

108. Harold Spaeth and Stuart Teger, "Activism and Restraint: A Cloak for the Justices' Policy Prefer-

ences," in *Supreme Court Activism and Restraint,* ed. Stephen P. Halpern and Clark M. Lamb (Lexington, Mass.: Lexington Books, 1982), 277.

109. *Engel v. Vitale,* 370 U.S. 421 (1962).

110. *Abington School District v. Schempp,* 374 U.S. 203 (1963).

111. *Stone v. Graham,* 449 U.S. 39 (1980).

112. *Lee v. Weisman,* 120 L.Ed.2d 467 (1992).

113. *Santa Fe Independent School District v. Doe,* 147 L.Ed.2d 295 (2000).

114. *Burnet v. Coronado Oil and Gas,* 285 U.S. 293 (1932), at 406.

115. *Denver Area Educational Telecommunications Consortium v. Federal Communications Commission,* 116 S.Ct. 2374 (1996).

116. *United States v. Butler,* 297 U.S. 1 (1936), at 79.

117. Some might say that judges, rather than make law, mediate among various ideas that rise to the surface, killing off some and allowing others to survive. Robert Cover, "Nomos and Narrative," *Harvard Law Review* 97 (1983), 4.

118. Quoted in Murphy and Pritchett, *Courts, Judges, and Politics,* 25.

119. *Gratz v. Bollinger,* 156 L.Ed.2d 257 (2003); *Grutter v. Bollinger,* 156 L.Ed.2d 304 (2003).

120. Quoted in David J. Garrow, "The Rehnquist Reins," *New York Times Magazine,* October 6, 1996, 70.

121. Quoted in Robert Wernick, "Chief Justice Marshall Takes the Law in Hand," *Smithsonian,* November 1998, 162.

122. Joan Biskupic, "Here Comes the Judge? Maybe Not," *Washington Post National Weekly Edition,* February 14, 2000, 30.

123. Jeffrey A. Segal and Harold J. Spaeth, *The Supreme Court and the Attitudinal Model* (New York: Cambridge University Press, 1993), 262–264.

124. Jeffrey Rosen, "Rehnquist's Choice," *New Yorker,* January 11, 1999, 31.

125. *Morning Edition,* National Public Radio, March 5, 2004.

126. Michael S. Serrill, "The Power of William Brennan," *Time,* July 22, 1985, 62.

127. Ibid.

128. David J. Garrow, "One Angry Man," *New York Times Magazine,* October 6, 1996, 68–69.

129. *Webster v. Reproductive Health Services,* 492 U.S. 490 (1989).

130. *United States v. Virginia,* 135 L.Ed.2d 735, 787–789 (1996).

131. Quoted in Alpheus T. Mason, *Harlan Fiske Stone* (New York: Viking, 1956), 308.

132. Charles Evans Hughes, *The Supreme Court of the United States* (New York: Columbia University Press, 1928), 68.

133. Interview with Justice Ruth Bader Ginsburg, *Morning Edition,* National Public Radio, May 2, 2002. Ginsburg said that foreign jurists admit they disagree with each other but do not make it public.

134. Linda Greenhouse, "The High Court and the Triumph of Discord," *New York Times,* July 15, 2001, sec. 4, 1.

135. Alexis de Tocqueville, *Democracy in America* (1832).

136. *Roe v. Wade,* 410 U.S. 113 (1973).

137. Baum, *Supreme Court,* 170, 173.

138. Craig R. Ducat and Robert L. Dudley, "Federal Appellate Judges and Presidential Power," paper presented at the Midwest Political Science Association meeting, April 1987.

139. Baum, *Supreme Court,* 158.

140. Sheldon Goldman, "How Long the Legacy?" *Judicature* 76 (1993), 295.

141. The Eleventh Amendment overturned *Chisholm v. Georgia* (1793), which had permitted the federal courts to hear suits against a state by citizens of another state. The Fourteenth overturned the Dred Scott case, *Scott v. Sandford* (1857), which had held that blacks were not citizens. The Sixteenth overturned *Pollock v. Farmers' Loan and Trust* (1895), which had negated a congressional law authorizing

a federal income tax. The Twenty-Sixth overturned *Oregon v. Mitchell* (1970), which had negated a congressional law allowing eighteen-year-olds to vote in state elections.

142. *Goldman v. Weinberger,* 475 U.S. 503 (1986).

143. William N. Eskridge Jr., "Overriding Supreme Court Statutory Interpretation Decisions," *Yale Law Journal* 101 (1991), 338.

144. Thomas R. Marshall, "Public Opinion and the Rehnquist Court," in *Readings in American Government and Politics,* 3rd ed. (Boston: Allyn & Bacon, 1999), 115–121.

145. Richard Morin, "A Nation of Stooges," *Washington Post,* October 8, 1995, C5.

146. Gregory A. Caldeira, "Neither the Purse nor the Sword," paper presented at the American Political Science Association meeting, August 1987.

147. Quoted in Abraham, *Justices and Presidents,* 342–343.

148. Robert G. McCloskey, *The American Supreme Court* (Chicago: University of Chicago Press, 1960), 225.

149. *Bush v. Gore,* 531 U.S. 98 (2000).

150. Two dissenting justices did express concerns about the absence of statewide standards, but in all other respects they disagreed with the majority.

151. Three justices in the majority also objected to the Florida Supreme Court's interpretation of Florida law. They said that Article II of the Constitution allows the U.S. Supreme Court to invalidate a state supreme court's interpretation of its own law that applies to presidential elections.

152. The majority misconstrued the "safe harbor" provision of federal electoral law as an actual deadline. McConnell, "Two-and-a-Half Cheers" 118. In fact, twenty states failed to submit their electors by this supposed deadline in 2000. "Numbers," *Time,* December 25, 2000, 53.

153. And by preventing the state from trying specific standards, the Court disregarded its customary practice of announcing the law and then allowing the losing litigant to fix the problem.

154. Dershowitz, *Supreme Injustice,* 37; George P. Fletcher, *Our Secret Constitution* (New York: Oxford University Press, 2001), 247; Strauss, "Bush v. Gore," 193; Sunstein, "Order without Law," 209.

155. Jeffrey Toobin, *Too Close to Call* (New York: Random House, 2001), 184. The minority was apparently just as stunned as the legal scholars. Ibid., 249.

156. Sunstein, "Order without Law," 207.

157. Richard Epstein, quoted in Dershowitz, *Supreme Injustice,* 83.

158. A. E. Dick Howard, quoted in David G. Savage, "The Vote Case Fallout," *ABA Journal* 87 (2001). 32.

159. Elizabeth Garrett, "Leaving the Decision to Congress," in *The Vote,* ed. Sunstein and Epstein, 46; Michelman, "Suspicion," 129–130; Sunstein, "Order without Law," 212. No identifiable group was singled out for discriminatory treatment, and there was no intentional discrimination.

160. Karlan, "Newest Equal Protection," 95.

161. Dershowitz, *Supreme Injustice,* 230, n. 34.

162. Karlan, "Newest Equal Protection," 90–91. The older punch card machines are more likely to fail to detect a vote on some ballots *and* to mistakenly detect more than one vote on other ballots, causing these latter to be disqualified. Thus these machines have a poorer record for both undervotes and overvotes.

163. Dershowitz, *Supreme Injustice,* 82.

164. For an extended examination, see Dershowitz, *Supreme Injustice,* ch. 4. Also see Michelman, "Suspicion," 126–137. For a somewhat contrary view, see Stephen Holmes, "Afterword: Can a Coin-Toss Election Trigger a Constitutional Earthquake?" in *Unfinished Election,* ed. Rakove (New York: Basic Books, 2001), 235–251.

165. Strauss, "Bush v. Gore," 187.

166. Ibid., 189–191; Bruce Ackerman, quoted in Dershowitz, *Supreme Injustice,* 175; Jamin B. Raskin, "Bandits in Black Robes," *Washington Monthly,* March 2001, 25–28.

167. Terrance Sandalow, quoted in Linda Greenhouse, "Collision with Politics Risks Court's Legal Credibility," *New York Times,* December 11, 2000, A1.

168. Quoted in Dershowitz, *Supreme Injustice,* 94. For an extended discussion, see 95–120.

169. Evan Thomas and Michael Isikoff, "The Truth behind the Pillars," *Newsweek,* December 25, 2000, 46.

170. Dershowitz, *Supreme Injustice,* 162–163; Rosen, "Majority of One," 73.

171. Sunstein, "Order without Law," 205–222; McConnell, "Two-and-a-Half Cheers" 107.

172. For a discussion, see Garrett, "Leaving the Decision to Congress," 38–54.

173. John F. Harris, "A Muddled Outcome," *Washington Post National Weekly Edition,* November 19, 2001, 11.

174. Unpublished study by James L. Gibson, Gregory A. Caldera, and Lester K. Spence, cited in John C. Yoo, "In Defense of the Court's Legitimacy," in *The Vote,* ed. Sunstein and Epstein, 226–227, n. 21.

175. Study by Wendy W. Simmons, cited in Yoo, "In Defense," 226, n. 19.

176. Rosen, "Majority of One," 37.

Chapter 14

1. Ian James, "Importance of Gitmo Questioned," *Lincoln Journal-Star,* June 26, 2004.

2. The administration has announced that some will be tried in military tribunals. These few will be charged, will receive counsel, and will gain access to military tribunals, of course.

3. When the Supreme Court agreed to take the case, the government released the two Britons.

4. *Johnson v. Eisentrager,* 339 U.S. 763 (1950).

5. A related argument is that the military has discretion on the battlefield, and in the war on terrorism, all American territory, including foreign bases, is part of the battlefield.

6. Joseph Margulies, "At Guantanamo Bay, a Year in Limbo," *Washington Post National Weekly Edition,* January 6, 2003, 22.

7. Michael Ratner, "Moving Away from the Rule of Law," *Cardozo Law Review* 24 (2003), 1518.

8. Richard Morin, "The High Price of Free Speech, "*Washington Post National Weekly Edition,* January 8, 2001, 34.

9. Poll for the First Amendment Center and the *American Journalism Review,* conducted by the Center for Survey Research and Analysis at the University of Connecticut, June and July 2002. Reported in Ken Paulson, "Too Free?" *American Journalism Review,* September 2002, available at www.ajr.org/Article.asp?id=2621.

10. The states did not ratify a proposed amendment that would have required at least one representative in Congress for every fifty thousand people. That amendment would have put about five thousand members in today's Congress. The states also did not ratify, until 1992, another proposed amendment that would have prohibited a salary raise for members of Congress from taking effect until after the next election to Congress.

11. *Reid v. Covert,* 354 U.S. 1 (1957).

12. *Barron v. Baltimore,* 32 U.S. 243 (1833).

13. Also, many states had their own bill of rights at the time, and other states were expected to follow.

14. *Gitlow v. New York,* 268 U.S. 652 (1925). *Gitlow* is usually cited as the first because it initiated the twentieth-century trend. However, *Chicago, Burlington and Quincy R. Co. v. Chicago,* 166 U.S. 266 (1897), was actually the first. It applied the Fifth Amendment's just compensation clause, requiring

government to pay owners "just compensation" for taking their property.

15. *Argersinger v. Hamlin,* 407 U.S. 25 (1972).

16. Even Justice Black, who claimed that he interpreted it literally. To do so, he had to define some speech as "action" so that it would not be protected.

17. *Milk Wagon Drivers Union v. Meadowmoor Dairies,* 312 U.S. 287 (1941).

18. Quoted in Deborah Tannen, *The Argument Culture* (New York: Ballantine, 1998), 25.

19. Thomas I. Emerson, *The System of Freedom of Expression* (New York: Random House/Vintage, 1971), 6–8.

20. For a history of speech cases between the Civil War and World War I, see David M. Rabban, *Free Speech in Its Forgotten Years* (New York: Cambridge University Press, 1997).

21. Zechariah Chafee Jr., *Free Speech in the United States* (Cambridge, Mass.: Harvard University Press, 1941), 51–52.

22. *Schenk v. United States,* 249 U.S. 47 (1919); *Frohwerk v. United States,* 249 U.S. 204 (1919); *Debs v. United States,* 249 U.S. 211 (1919); *Abrams v. United States,* 250 U.S. 616 (1919); *Gitlow v. New York,* 268 U.S. 652 (1925); *Whitney v. California,* 274 U.S. 357 (1927).

23. *Gitlow v. New York.*

24. David Cole, "The Course of Least Resistance: Repeating History in the War on Terrorism," in *Lost Liberties,* ed. Cynthia Brown (New York: New Press, 2003), 15.

25. Novelist Philip Roth observes, "McCarthy understood better than any American politician before him that people whose job was to legislate could do far better for themselves by performing; McCarthy understood the entertainment value of disgrace and how to feed the pleasures of paranoia. He took us back to our origins, back to the seventeenth century and the stocks. That's how the country began: moral disgrace as public entertainment." *I Married a Communist* (New York: Vintage, 1999), 284.

26. *Dennis v. United States,* 341 U.S. 494 (1951).

27. In the cases of *Yates v. United States,* 354 U.S. 298 (1957), and *Scales v. United States,* 367 U.S. 203 (1961), among others.

28. Earl Warren, *The Memoirs of Earl Warren* (Garden City, N.Y.: Doubleday, 1977), 6.

29. Johanna McGeary, "McCarthy's First Slander," *Time,* April 7, 2003, A28. There were, of course, some active Communists, and there was a spy network in the 1940s. See Ted Morgan, *Reds: McCarthyism in Twentieth-Century America* (New York: Random House, 2003).

30. Cole, "Course of Least Resistance," 1.

31. *Brandenburg v. Ohio,* 395 U.S. 444 (1969). In more recent cases, a cross was burned at a Ku Klux Klan rally in a privately owned field and another was burned in the yard of an African American family. The Supreme Court ruled that states can ban cross burning with an intent to intimidate because this amounts to a threat. Thus it upheld the conviction in the latter case but struck down the conviction in the former case. *Virginia v. Black,* 155 L.Ed.2d 535 (2003).

32. *Brandenburg v. Ohio.*

33. Attorney General Tom Clark quoted in *Esquire,* November 1974.

34. Jean E. Jackson, "ACTA Report Criticizes Professors," *Anthropology News,* March 2002, 7.

35. Gia Fenoglio, "Is It 'Blacklisting' or Mere Criticism?" *National Journal,* January 19, 2002, 188.

36. For some examples, see Michael Tomasky, "Dissent in America," *American Prospect,* April 2003, 22. See also Ann Coulter, *Treason: Liberal Treachery from the Cold War to the War on Terrorism* (New York: Crown Forum, 2003), and Sean Hannity, *Deliver Us from Evil* (New York: Regan Books/HarperCollins, 2004).

37. *Jeannette Rankin Brigade v. Chief of Capital Police,* 409 U.S. 972 (1972); *Edwards v. South Carolina,* 372 U.S. 229 (1963).

38. *United States v. Grace,* 75 L.Ed.2d 736 (1983).

39. *Grayned v. Rockford,* 408 U.S. 104 (1972); *Tinker v. Des Moines School District,* 393 U.S. 503 (1969).

40. *Brown v. Louisiana,* 383 U.S. 131 (1966).

41. *Southeastern Promotions v. Conrad,* 420 U.S. 546 (1975).

42. *Adderley v. Florida,* 385 U.S. 39 (1966).

43. *Greer v. Spock,* 424 U.S. 828 (1976).

44. *Amalgamated Food Employees v. Logan Valley Plaza,* 391 U.S. 308 (1968).

45. *Lloyd v. Tanner,* 407 U.S. 551 (1972); *Hudgens v. NLRB,* 424 U.S. 507 (1976).

46. Leonard Pitts Jr., "Intolerance Meets Its Nemesis at an Albany Mall," *Lincoln Journal-Star,* March 10, 2003.

47. *Rosenfeld v. New Jersey,* 408 U.S. 901 (1972); *Brown v. Oklahoma,* 408 U.S. 914 (1972).

48. *Cohen v. California,* 403 U.S. 15 (1971).

49. *Gooding v. Wilson,* 405 U.S. 518 (1972); *Lewis v. New Orleans,* 408 U.S. 913 (1972).

50. C. Herman Pritchett, *The American Constitution,* 2nd ed. (New York: McGraw-Hill, 1968), 476, n. 2. However, police in some places continue to arrest for swearing. Judy Lin, "ACLU Fights Police on Profanity Arrests in Pittsburgh Area," *Lincoln Journal-Star,* July 11, 2002.

51. *FCC v. Pacifica Foundation,* 438 U.S. 726 (1968).

52. Jonathan D. Salant, "FCC Wants to Up Fine for Cursing," *Lincoln Journal-Star,* January 15, 2004.

53. *Wilkinson v. Jones,* 480 U.S. 926 (1987).

54. *Cox v. Louisiana,* 379 U.S. 536 (1965).

55. *Schenk v. Pro-Choice Network,* 137 L.Ed.2d 1 (1997).

56. *Collin v. Smith,* 447 F.Supp. 676 (N.D. Ill., 1978); *Collin v. Smith,* 578 F.2d 1197 (7th Cir., 1978).

57. *United States v. Schwimmer,* 279 U.S. 644 (1929).

58. *Frisby v. Schultz,* 101 L.Ed.2d 420 (1988).

59. *United States v. O'Brien,* 391 U.S. 367 (1968).

60. *Tinker v. Des Moines School District.*

61. *Smith v. Goguen,* 415 U.S. 566 (1974); *Spence v. Washington,* 418 U.S. 405 (1974).

62. *Texas v. Johnson,* 105 L.Ed.2d 342 (1989).

63. *United States v. Eichman,* 110 L.Ed.2d 287 (1990).

64. However, in 1995, after Republicans became the majority in Congress, they renewed efforts to adopt a constitutional amendment but fell just three votes short in one house.

65. *Hurley v. Irish-American Gay, Lesbian and Bisexual Group of Boston,* 515 U.S. 557 (1995).

66. *Boy Scouts of America v. Dale,* 147 L.Ed.2d 554 (2000).

67. *Roberts v. U.S. Jaycees,* 468 U.S. 609 (1984); *Board of Directors of Rotary International v. Rotary Club of Duarte,* 481 U.S. 537 (1987).

68. The Court has also invalidated racial discrimination in labor unions and private schools and sexual discrimination in law firms, despite claims of freedom of association. *Railway Mail Association v. Corsi,* 326 U.S. 88 (1945); *Runyon v. McCrary,* 427 U.S. 160 (1976); *Hison v. King & Spalding,* 467 U.S. 69 (1984)6957.

69. Quoted in David Halbertstam, *The Best and the Brightest* (Greenwich, Conn.: Fawcett, 1969), 769.

70. From Watergate tapes released in 1996. For transcripts of tapes made public in 1996, see Stanley Kutler, ed., *Abuse of Power: The New Nixon Tapes* (New York: Free Press, 1998).

71. *New York Times v. United States,* 403 U.S. 713 (1971). In addition to seeking injunctions, the Nixon administration sent a telegram to the *New York Times* demanding that it cease publication of the excerpts, but the FBI had the wrong telex number for the newspaper, so the telegram went first to a fish company in Brooklyn. R. W. Apple, "Lessons from the Pentagon Papers," *New York Times,* June 23, 1996, E5.

72. Actually, the Pentagon Papers did include some current information, regarding ongoing negotiations and the names of CIA agents in Vietnam, but

Ellsberg had not passed this information to the newspapers. However, the government and the Court were unaware of this, so the government argued that publication could affect national security, and the Court decided the case with this prospect in mind. Thus the Court's ruling was stronger than legal analysts realized at the time. Erwin N. Griswold, "'No Harm Was Done,'" *New York Times,* June 30, 1991, E15.

73. *United States v. Progressive,* 467 F.Supp. 990 (W.D., Wisc., 1979).

74. *Hazelwood School District v. Kuhlmeier,* 98 L.Ed.2d 592 (1988).

75. Then radio and television stations used actors with Irish accents to dub the comments made by IRA members. In 1994, the government lifted the ban.

76. *Branzburg v. Hayes,* 408 U.S. 665 (1972).

77. *Cox Broadcasting v. Cohn,* 420 U.S. 469 (1975).

78. This was not a Supreme Court case.

79. *Time v. Hill,* 385 U.S. 374 (1967).

80. *Wilson v. Layne,* 143 L.Ed.2d 818 (1999); *Hanlon v. Berger,* 143 L.Ed.2d 978 (1999).

81. *New York Times v. Sullivan,* 376 U.S. 254.

82. Harry Kalven, "The *New York Times* Case: A Note on 'the Central Meaning of the First Amendment,'" *Supreme Court Review* (1964): 221.

83. *Monitor Patriot v. Roy,* 401 U.S. 265 (1971).

84. *Associated Press v. Walker,* 388 U.S. 130 (1967).

85. *Greenbelt Cooperative Publishing v. Bresler,* 398 U.S. 6 (1970).

86. *Curtis Publishing v. Butts,* 388 U.S. 130 (1967).

87. *Gertz v. Robert Welch,* 418 U.S. 323 (1974), and *Time v. Firestone,* 424 U.S. 448 (1976).

88. Eric Press, "Westmoreland Takes on CBS," *Newsweek,* October 22, 1984, 62.

89. William A. Henry III, "Libel Law: Good Intentions Gone Awry," *Time,* March 4, 1985, 94.

90. Ibid., 71.

91. *Roth v. United States,* 354 U.S. 476 (1957); *Manual Enterprises v. Day,* 370 U.S. 478 (1962); *Jacobellis v. Ohio,* 378 U.S. 184 (1964); *A Book Named "John Cleland's Memoirs of a Woman of Pleasure" v. Attorney General of Massachusetts,* 383 U.S. 413 (1966).

92. *Miller v. California,* 413 U.S. 15 (1973).

93. *Jenkins v. Georgia,* 418 U.S. 153 (1974).

94. "Project: An Empirical Inquiry into the Effects of *Miller v. California* on the Control of Obscenity," *New York University Law Review* 52 (1977): 810–939.

95. Eric Schlosser, "Empire of the Obscene," *New Yorker,* March 10, 2003, 61.

96. *New York v. Ferber,* 458 U.S. 747 (1982). The Court left open the question of whether child pornography with serious literary or artistic value would be protected. *Osborne v. Ohio,* 495 U.S. 103 (1990).

97. The Pilgrims, who had experienced religious toleration in Holland (after persecution in England), left because they wanted a place of their own, not because they could not worship as they pleased. The Dutch were so tolerant that the Pilgrims' children had begun to adopt Dutch manners and ideas. Richard Shenkman, *"I Love Paul Revere, Whether He Rode or Not"* (New York: HarperCollins, 1991), 20–21.

98. The only religious reference in the Constitution occurs in the date when the document was written: "Year of our Lord one thousand seven hundred and eighty-seven." And that may have been mere convention; "year of our Lord" is the English equivalent of A.D.

99. Apparently Roger Williams, a clergyman and the founder of Rhode Island, was the first to use this metaphor. Lloyd Burton, "The Church in America," *New Yorker,* September 29, 2003, 10. James Madison was another of the Founders who pioneered our religious freedom. For an analysis of his views, see Vincent Phillip Munoz, "James Madison's Principle of Religious Liberty," *American Political Science Review,* 97 (2003), 17–32.

100. Gary Wills, quoted on *Thomas Jefferson,* PBS, February 18, 1997.

101. *Torcaso v. Watkins,* 367 U.S. 488 (1961).

102. *Pierce v. Society of Sisters,* 268 U.S. 510 (1925).

103. *Cooper v. Pate,* 378 U.S. 546 (1963); *Cruz v. Beto,* 405 U.S. 319 (1972).

104. *Church of the Lukumi Babalu Aye v. Hialeah,* 124 L.Ed.2d 472 (1993).

105. *Reynolds v. United States,* 98 U.S. 145 (1879). Most Mormons, however, did not approve of polygamy. Even when polygamy was most popular, perhaps only 10 percent of Mormons practiced it. Shenkman, *"I Love Paul Revere,"* 31. Yet today reports indicate that polygamy is still flourishing among Mormons, perhaps more than ever. Lawrence Wright, "Lives of the Saints," *New Yorker,* January 21, 2002, 43.

106. *Sherbert v. Verner,* 374 U.S. 398 (1963).

107. Although a congressional statute mandates "reasonable accommodation," the Court interpreted it so narrowly that it essentially requires only minimal accommodation. *Trans World Airlines v. Hardison,* 432 U.S. 63 (1977). For analysis, see Gloria T. Beckley and Paul Burstein, "Religious Pluralism, Equal Opportunity, and the State," *Western Political Quarterly* 44 (1991): 185–208. For a related case, see *Thornton v. Caldor,* 86 L.Ed.2d. 557 (1985).

108. *Wisconsin v. Yoder,* 406 U.S. 205 (1972).

109. *United States v. Lee,* 455 U.S. 252 (1982).

110. *United States v. American Friends Service Committee,* 419 U.S. 7 (1974).

111. *Goldman v. Weinberger,* 475 U.S. 503 (1986); *O'Lone v. Shabazz,* 482 U.S. 342 (1986).

112. *Employment Division v. Smith,* 108 L.Ed.2d 876 (1990).

113. American Indian Religious Freedom Act of 1994.

114. Ruth Marcus, "One Nation, under Court Rulings," *Washington Post National Weekly Edition,* March 18, 1991, 33.

115. *Boerne v. Flores,* 138 L.Ed.2d 624 (1997).

116. William Lee Miller, "The Ghost of Freedoms Past," *Washington Post National Weekly Edition,* October 13, 1986, 23–24.

117. *Church of Holy Trinity v. United States,* 143 U.S. 457 (1892).

118. *Engel v. Vitale,* 370 U.S. 421 (1962); *Abington School District v. Schempp,* 374 U.S. 203 (1963).

119. *Stone v. Graham,* 449 U.S. 39 (1980). The Ten Commandments themselves have been divisive. In 1844, six people were killed in a riot in Philadelphia over which version of the Ten Commandments to post in the public schools. E. J. Dionne Jr., "Bridging the Church-State Divide," *Washington Post National Weekly Edition,* October 11, 1999, 21.

120. George W. Andrews (D-Ala.), quoted in C. Herman Pritchett, *The American Constitution,* 3rd ed. (New York: McGraw-Hill, 1977), 406.

121. Kenneth M. Dolbeare and Phillip E. Hammond, *The School Prayer Decisions* (Chicago: University of Chicago Press, 1971).

122. Robert H. Birkby, "The Supreme Court and the Bible Belt," *Midwest Journal of Political Science* 10 (1966): 304–315.

123. Julia Lieblich and Richard N. Ostling, "Despite Rulings, Prayer in School Still Sparks Debate, Still Practiced," *Lincoln Journal-Star,* January 16, 2000.

124. "Five Schools Get Ten Commandments," *Lincoln Journal-Star,* August 12, 1999.

125. J. Gordon Melton, quoted in Jon D. Hull, "The State of the Union," *Time,* January 30, 1995, 55.

126. Peter Cushnie, "Letters," *Time,* October 15, 1984, 21.

127. The Supreme Court invalidated Alabama's law that authorized a moment of silence "for meditation or voluntary prayer" because the wording of the law endorsed and promoted prayer. But most justices signaled approval of a moment of silence without such wording. *Wallace v. Jaffree,* 86 L.Ed.2d 29 (1985).

128. *Lee v. Weisman,* 120 L.Ed.2d 467 (1992).

129. *Jones v. Clear Creek,* 977 F.2d 965 (5th Cir., 1992).

130. *Moore v. Ingebretsen,* 88 F.3d 274 (1996).

131. *Santa Fe Independent School District v. Doe,* 530 U.S. 290 (2000).

132. Anna Quindlen, "School Prayer: Substitutes for Substance," *Lincoln Journal-Star,* December 8, 1994.

133. Quoted in ibid.

134. A current guide for public school teachers, addressing practices that are permissible and those that are advisable in various situations, is Charles C. Haynes and Oliver Thomas, *Finding Common Ground* (Nashville, Tenn.: First Amendment Center, 2002).

135. *Widmar v. Vincent,* 454 U.S. 263 (1981). The law requires high schools that receive federal funds to allow meetings of students' religious, philosophical, or political groups if the schools permit meetings of any "noncurriculum" groups. Schools could prohibit meetings of all noncurriculum groups. A Salt Lake City high school banned all nonacademic clubs rather than let students form an organization for homosexuals in 1996. Interviews with teachers and students two years later indicated that as a result of the ban on clubs, school spirit declined and class and racial rifts expanded. Clubs no longer brought students together, and clubs such as Polynesian Pride and the Aztec Club, for Latinos, no longer provided a link between these students and their school. "Club Ban Aimed at Gays Backfires," *Lincoln Journal-Star,* December 6, 1998.

136. *Board of Education of the Westside Community Schools v. Mergens,* 496 U.S. 226 (1990).

137. David Van Biema, "Spiriting Prayer into School," *Time,* April 27, 1998, 28–31.

138. Harriet Barovick, "Fear of a Gay School," *Time,* February 21, 2000, 52.

139. *Rosenberger v. University of Virginia,* 132 L.Ed.2d 700 (1995). Yet the Rehnquist Court later ruled that states that provide scholarships for students at colleges and universities don't have to provide them for students preparing for the ministry. *Locke v. Davey,* 158 L.Ed.2d 21 (2004).

140. For the nation's first celebration of Columbus Day in 1892, Francis Bellamy wrote, "I pledge allegiance to my flag and the republic for which it stands, one nation indivisible, with liberty and justice for all." For Bellamy, the key words were "indivisible," which referred to the Civil War and emphasized the Union over the states, and "liberty and justice for all," which emphasized a balance between freedom for individuals and equality between them. During the Cold War in the 1950s, Americans feared "godless communism." Some objected to communism as much because of the Soviet Union's official policy of atheism as because of its totalitarianism. A religious revival swept the United States as preachers such as Billy Graham warned that Americans would perish in a nuclear holocaust unless they opened their arms to Jesus Christ. Congress replaced the traditional national motto— "E Pluribus Unum" ("Out of Many, One")—with "In God We Trust," and it added this new motto to our paper money. Fraternal organizations, especially the Catholic Knights of Columbus, and religious leaders campaigned to add "under God" to the Pledge of Allegiance. The Presbyterian pastor of President Eisenhower's church in Washington urged the addition in a sermon as the president sat in a pew. With little dissent, Congress passed and the president signed a bill to do so in 1954. The legislative history of the act stated that the intent was to "acknowledge the dependence of our people and our government upon . . . the Creator . . . [and] deny the atheistic and materialistic concept of communism." The president stated that "millions of our school children will daily proclaim in every city and town . . . the dedication of our nation and our people to the Almighty." Thus the phrase was adopted

expressly to endorse religion. David Greenberg, "The Pledge of Allegiance: Why We're Not One Nation 'under God,'" *Slate,* June 28, 2002, http://slate.msn.com/?id_2067499 S.

141. *Elk Grove Unified School District* v. *Newdow,* 159 L.Ed.2d 98 (2004).

142. *Lynch* v. *Donnelly,* 79 L.Ed.2d 604 (1984).

143. *Allegheny County* v. *ACLU,* 106 L.Ed.2d 472 (1989).

144. Dirk Johnson, "Schools Seek to Skirt Rules on Religion," *New York Times,* February 27, 2000, 16.

145. *Epperson* v. *Arkansas,* 393 U.S. 97 (1968).

146. Some groups use the more sophisticated-sounding term *creation science.* Although these groups do address the science of evolutionary theory, the courts consider creation science religion in the guise of science. Other groups use the term *intelligent design,* which is similar to creation science, although it is not based directly on the Bible.

147. *Edwards* v. *Aguillard,* 482 U.S. 578 (1987). The Kansas Board of Education tried to circumvent these rulings by simply deleting evolution from the state's science curriculum in 1999. A lower court also invalidated a Louisiana school district's policy that evolution be taught only with a disclaimer mentioning the biblical version of creation, and the Supreme Court denied certiorari over the objections of Justices Scalia and Thomas. *Tangipahoa Board of Education* v. *Freiler,* 147 L.Ed.2d 974 (2000).

148. Peter Applebome, "Seventy Years after Scopes Trial, Creation Debate Lives," *New York Times,* March 10, 1996, 1, 12.

149. For examination of these trends, see Jeffrey Rosen, "Is Nothing Secular?" *New York Times Magazine,* January 30, 2000, 40–45.

150. *Everson* v. *Board of Education of Ewing Township,* 330 U.S. 1 (1947); *Board of Education* v. *Allen,* 392 U.S. 236 (1968); *Meek* v. *Pittinger,* 421 U.S. 349 (1975).

151. *Lemon* v. *Kurtzman,* 403 U.S. 602 (1971); *Committee for Public Education and Religious Liberty* v. *Nyquist,* 413 U.S. 756 (1973).

152. For example, striking down tax credits but upholding tax deductions to reduce tuition costs for parents. Ibid.; *Mueller* v. *Allen,* 463 U.S. 388 (1983).

153. *Zelman* v. *Simmons-Harris,* 153 L.Ed.2s 604 (2002).

154. The city of Milwaukee and the state of Florida also had voucher programs at this time.

155. Wendy Kaminer, "The God Bullies," *American Prospect,* November 18, 2002, 9.

156. *Rochin* v. *California,* 342 U.S. 165 (1952).

157. Seymour Wishman, *Confessions of a Criminal Lawyer* (New York: Penguin, 1981), 16.

158. *Stein* v. *New York,* 346 U.S. 156 (1953).

159. Wendy Kaminer, *It's All the Rage* (Reading, Mass.: Addison-Wesley, 1995), 78.

160. *Weeks* v. *United States,* 232 U.S. 383 (1914).

161. *Mapp* v. *Ohio,* 367 U.S. 643 (1961).

162. This exception applies when police use a search warrant that they did not know was invalid. *United States* v. *Leon,* 82 L.Ed.2d 677 (1984); *Massachusetts* v. *Sheppard,* 82 L.Ed.2d 737 (1984).

163. *Olmstead* v. *United States,* 277 U.S. 438 (1928).

164. *Katz* v. *United States,* 389 U.S. 347 (1967).

165. "Numbers," *Time,* June 14, 1999, 41.

166. *Brown* v. *Mississippi,* 297 U.S. 278 (1936).

167. *McNabb* v. *United States,* 318 U.S. 332 (1943); *Mallory* v. *United States,* 354 U.S. 449 (1957); *Spano* v. *New York,* 360 U.S. 315 (1959).

168. *Ashcraft* v. *Tennessee,* 322 U.S. 143 (1944).

169. *Miranda* v. *Arizona,* 384 U.S. 436 (1966).

170. *Dickerson* v. *United States,* 530 U.S. 428 (2000).

171. Jan Hoffman, "Police Tactics Chipping Away at Suspects' Rights," *New York Times,* March 29, 1998, 35.

172. *Johnson* v. *Zerbst,* 304 U.S. 458 (1938).

173. *Powell* v. *Alabama,* 287 U.S. 45 (1932).

174. *Gideon* v. *Wainwright,* 372 U.S. 335 (1963).

175. *Argersinger* v. *Hamlin,* 407 U.S. 25 (1972); *Scott* v. *Illinois,* 440 U.S. 367 (1974).

176. *Alabama* v. *Shelton,* 152 L.Ed.2d 888 (2002).

177. *Douglas* v. *California,* 372 U.S. 353 (1953).

178. Wendy Cole, "Death Takes a Holiday," *Time,* February 14, 2000, 68.

179. Jill Smolowe, "Race and the Death Penalty," *Time,* April 29, 1991, 69.

180. Peter Applebome, "Indigent Defendants, Overworked Lawyers," *New York Times,* May 17, 1992, E18.

181. Alan Berlow, "Texas, Take Heed," *Washington Post National Weekly Edition,* February 21, 2000, 22.

182. Richard Carelli, "Death Rows Grow, Legal Help Shrinks," *Lincoln Journal-Star,* October 7, 1995.

183. The Burger Court did rule that the right to counsel entails the right to "effective" counsel, but the Court set such stringent standards for establishing the existence of ineffective counsel that few defendants can take advantage of this right. See *Strickland* v. *Washington,* 466 U.S. 668 (1984), and *United States* v. *Cronic,* 466 U.S. 640 (1984).

184. *Baldwin* v. *New York,* 339 U.S. 66 (1970); *Blanton* v. *North Las Vegas,* 489 U.S. 538 (1989).

185. *Duncan* v. *Louisiana,* 391 U.S. 145 (1968).

186. *Taylor* v. *Louisiana,* 419 U.S. 522 (1975).

187. *Swain* v. *Alabama,* 380 U.S. 202 (1965).

188. The Court implicitly upheld the death penalty in *Wilkerson* v. *Utah,* 99 U.S. 130 (1878), and *In re Kemmler,* 136 U.S. 436 (1890).

189. *Furman* v. *Georgia,* 408 U.S. 238 (1972).

190. *Gregg* v. *Georgia,* 428 U.S. 153 (1976).

191. *Woodson* v. *North Carolina,* 428 U.S. 289 (1976).

192. *Coker* v. *Georgia,* 433 U.S. 584 (1977).

193. *McCleskey* v. *Kemp,* 95 L.Ed.2d 262 (1987). Studies of Florida, Illinois, Mississippi, and North Carolina have found similar results. Fox Butterfield, "Blacks More Likely to Get Death Penalty, Study Says," *New York Times,* June 7, 1998, 16.

194. Leonard Pitts Jr., "Fate of 100 Innocent Men Casts Doubt on Capital Punishment," *Lincoln Journal-Star,* April 13, 2002.

195. Adam Liptak, "Juries Reject Death Penalty in Nearly All Federal Trials," *New York Times,* June 15, 2003, 12; Alex Kotlowitz, "In the Face of Death," *New York Times Magazine,* June 6, 2003, 34.

196. *Atkins* v. *Virginia,* 153 L.Ed. 2d 335 (2002).

197. *Penry* v. *Lynaugh,* 106 L.Ed.2d 256 (1989).

198. *Brady* v. *United States,* 397 U.S. 742 (1970).

199. *Griswold* v. *Connecticut,* 38 U.S. 479 (1965).

200. For a rare exception, see *Time* v. *Hill,* 385 U.S. 374 (1967).

201. *Griswold* v. *Connecticut.*

202. *Eisenstadt* v. *Baird,* 405 U.S. 438 (1972); *Carey* v. *Population Services International,* 431 U.S. 678 (1977).

203. *Eisenstadt* v. *Baird.*

204. Lloyd Shearer, "This Woman and This Man Made History," *Parade,* 1983.

205. *Roe* v. *Wade,* 410 U.S. 113 (1973).

206. Bob Woodward, "The Abortion Papers," *Washington Post National Weekly Edition,* January 30, 1989, 24–25.

207. All but New York's. Three other states allowed abortion on demand, though not quite as extensively as *Roe,* so the ruling also invalidated their laws. Jeffrey A. Segal and Harold J. Spaeth, *The Supreme Court and the Attitudinal Model* (New York: Cambridge University Press, 1993), 333.

208. *Akron* v. *Akron Center for Reproductive Health,* 76 L.Ed.2d 687 (1983).

209. "The Supreme Court Ignites a Fiery Abortion Debate," *Time,* July 4, 1977, 6–8.

210. *Beal* v. *Doe,* 432 U.S. 438 (1977); *Maher* v. *Roe,* 432 U.S. 464 (1977); *Poelker* v. *Doe,* 432 U.S. 519 (1977); *Harris* v. *McRae* 448 U.S. 297 (1980).

211. Benjamin Weiser, "The Abortion Dilemma Come to Life," *Washington Post National Weekly Edition,* December 25, 1989, 10–11.

212. Alan Guttmacher Institute, *Facts in Brief: Abortion in the United States* (New York: Alan

Guttmacher Institute, 1992); Stephanie Mencimer, "Ending Illegitimacy as We Know It," *Washington Post National Weekly Edition,* January 17, 1994, 24.

213. *Webster* v. *Reproductive Health Services,* 106 L.Ed.2d 410 (1989).

214. *Planned Parenthood of Southeastern Pennsylvania* v. *Casey,* 120 L.Ed.2d 674 (1992). Justice Anthony Kennedy changed his mind after the justices' conference, from essentially overturning *Roe* to reaffirming it. His was the fifth vote to reaffirm, as it would have been to overturn.

215. William Booth, "The Difference a Day Makes," *Washington Post National Weekly Edition,* November 23, 1992, 31.

216. *Planned Parenthood of Southeastern Pennsylvania* v. *Casey,* 120 L.Ed.2d 674 (1992).

217. *Hodgson* v. *Minnesota,* 111 L.Ed.2d 344 (1990); *Ohio* v. *Akron Center for Reproductive Health,* 111 L.Ed.2d 405 (1990); *Planned Parenthood Association of Kansas City* v. *Ashcroft,* 462 U.S. 476 (1983).

218. *Hodgson* v. *Minnesota,* 111 L.Ed.2d 344 (1990).

219. Margaret Carlson, "Abortion's Hardest Cases," *Time,* July 9, 1990, 24.

220. Butch Mabin, "Supreme Court Says Teen Seeking Abortion Too Immature," *Lincoln Journal-Star,* December 13, 1997.

221. *Stenberg* v. *Carhart,* 530 U.S. 914 (2000).

222. Barry Yeoman, "The Quiet War on Abortion," *Mother Jones,* September-October 2001, 46–51.

223. "Survey Reveals U.S. Views on Abortion to Be Contradictory," *Lincoln Journal-Star,* June 19, 2000.

224. For an analysis of the political dynamics that produced this moderate result, see William Saleton, *Bearing Right: How Conservatives Won the Abortion War* (Berkeley: University of California Press, 2003). The title is an exaggeration.

225. Alissa Rubin, "The Abortion Wars Are Far from Over," *Washington Post National Weekly Edition,* December 21, 1992, 25.

226. Richard Lacayo, "One Doctor Down, How Many More?" *Time,* March 22, 1993, 47.

223. Rebecca Mead, "Return to Sender the Usual Hate Mail," *New Yorker,* October 29, 2001, 34.

228. Douglas Frantz, "The Rhetoric of Terror," *Time,* March 27, 1995, 48–51.

229. Dan Sewell, "Abortion War Requires Guns, Bulletproof Vests," *Lincoln Journal-Star,* January 8, 1995.

230. "Blasts Reawaken Fear of Domestic Terrorism," *Lincoln Journal-Star,* January 17, 1997.

231. Richard Lacayo, "Abortion: The Future Is Already Here," *Time,* May 4, 1992, 29; Jack Hitt, "Who Will Do Abortions Here?" *New York Times Magazine,* January 18, 1998, 20.

232. Randall Terry, quoted in Anthony Lewis, "Pro-Life Zealots 'Outside the Bargain,'" *Lincoln Journal-Star,* March 14, 1993.

233. Joseph Scheidler, quoted in Sandra G. Boodman, "Bringing Abortion Home," *Washington Post National Weekly Edition,* April 15, 1993, 6.

234. Stanley K. Henshaw, "Abortion Incidence and Services in the United States, 1995–1996," *Family Planning Perspectives,* November-December 1998.

235. For further analysis of the role of abortion in our legal and political debates since *Roe,* see Alan M. Dershowitz, *Supreme Injustice* (New York: Oxford University Press, 2001), 191–194, 201.

236. For an elaboration of this history, see "In Changing the Law of the Land, Six Justices Turned to Its History," *New York Times,* July 20, 2003, WK7.

237. Four states at this time revised their statutes to bar sodomy only between homosexuals: Kansas, Missouri, Oklahoma, and Texas.

238. *Bowers* v. *Hardwick,* 92 L.Ed.2d 140 (1986); see also *Doe* v. *Commonwealth's Attorney,* 425 U.S. 901 (1976).

239. *Lawrence and Garner* v. *Texas,* 539 U.S. 558 (2003).

240. "Gays Getting More Acceptance as They're More Open, Poll Says," *Lincoln Journal-Star,* April 11, 2004.

241. Paul Gewirtz, quoted in Joe Klein, "How the Supremes Redeemed Bush," *Time,* July 7, 2003, 27.

242. The courts apply the clause to "adversarial proceedings," such as lawsuits, including divorces.

243. The House sponsor of the act, Robert Barr (R-Ga.), said the act was necessary because "the flames of hedonism, the flames of narcissism, the flames of self-centered morality are licking at the very foundation of our society, the family unit." At the time he was protecting the family unit, he was in his third marriage. Margaret Carlson, "The Marrying Kind," *Time,* September 16, 1996, 26.

244. For elaboration, see David Von Drehle, "Same-Sex Unions Take Center Stage," *Washington Post National Weekly Edition,* December 1, 2003, 29.

245. John Cloud, "1,138 Reasons Marriage Is Cool," *Time,* March 8, 2004, 32. A few go in the opposite direction, such as eligibility for Medicaid, which takes into account a spouse's income.

246. Advisory Opinion on Senate No. 2175, Supreme Judicial Court of Massachusetts, February 3, 2004.

247. David J. Garrow, "Toward a More Perfect Union," *New York Times Magazine,* May 9, 2004, 54.

248. Senator Wayne Allard (R-Colo.); Senator Rick Santorum (R-Pa.); James Dobson. Andrew Sullivan, "If at First You Don't Succeed . . . ," *Time,* July 26, 2004, 78.

249. Alan Cooperman, "Anger without Action," *Washington Post National Weekly Edition,* June 28, 2004, 30.

250. Garrow, "Toward a More Perfect Union," 57.

251. The Supreme Court did invalidate a Colorado constitutional amendment prohibiting laws barring discrimination against homosexuals, saying that the amendment singled out homosexuals and denied them the opportunity enjoyed by others to seek protection from discrimination. This put the brakes on a drive to adopt similar provisions in other states. *Roemer v. Evans,* 134 L.Ed.2d 855 (1996).

252. President Clinton also ordered the FBI to end policies that made it difficult for homosexuals to be hired.

253. The policy was originally based on psychoanalytic theory, which considered homosexuality a mental illness. This conclusion was rejected by the American Psychiatric Association some years later.

254. Israel drafts every eighteen-year-old man and woman. It does consider homosexuality in the assignment of jobs. Gays who admit their orientation to their superiors confidentially are restricted from security-sensitive jobs for fear they are susceptible to blackmail. But gays who acknowledge their orientation openly could not be blackmailed, so they are treated the same as straights. Randy Shilts, "What's Fair in Love and War," *Newsweek,* February 1, 1993, 58–59; Eric Konigsberg, "Gays in Arms," *Washington Monthly,* November 1992, 10–13;"Canada Had No Problems Lifting Its Military Gay Ban," *Lincoln Journal-Star,* January 31, 1993. See also Randy Shilts, *Conduct Unbecoming: Gays and Lesbians in the U.S. Military* (New York: St. Martin's Press, 1993).

255. Philip Shenon, "New Study Faults Pentagon's Gay Policy," *New York Times,* February 26, 1997, A8.

256. Ibid.; "Group Says Gays Worse Off in Military since New Policy," *Lincoln Journal-Star,* February 28, 1996. Pentagon officials say many discharges result from recruits who decide that they do not like the military and who then volunteer that they are homosexual as a way of getting discharged. Dana Priest, "The Impact of the 'Don't Ask, Don't Tell' Policy," *Washington Post National Weekly Edition,* February 1, 1999, 35. As a result of the increase in discharges, the Clinton administration tried to bolster the policy by having the services discourage harassment, from threats to derogatory jokes aimed at gays, and by requiring low-ranking officers to consult with senior legal advisers before beginning an investigation into alleged homosexual conduct.

257. Mark Thompson, "How to Meet the Troop Need? Don't Ask," *Time,* July 19, 2004, 18.

258. Charles Peters, "Tilting at Windmills," *Washington Monthly,* May 2001, 4.

259. Al Kamen, "When Exactly Does Life End?" *Washington Post National Weekly Edition,* September 18, 1989, 31; Alain L. Sanders, "Whose Right to Die?" *Time,* December 11, 1989, 80.

260. *Cruzan v. Missouri Health Department,* 111 L.Ed.2d 224 (1990).

261. Otto Friedrich, "A Limited Right to Die," *Time,* July 9, 1990, 59.

262. Tamar Lewin, "Ignoring 'Right to Die' Directives, Medical Community Is Being Sued," *New York Times,* June 2, 1996, 1.

263. *Washington v. Glucksberg,* 138 L.Ed.2d 772 (1997); *Vacco v. Quill,* 138 L.Ed.2d 834 (1997).

264. David E. Rosenbaum, "Americans Want a Right to Die—or So They Think," *New York Times,* June 8, 1997, E3.

265. Ibid.

266. Dershowitz, *Supreme Injustice,* 189.

267. *Rasul v. Bush,* 159 L.Ed.2d 548 (2004).

268. *Ex parte Milligan,* 71 U.S. 2 (1866).

269. *Hamdi v. Rumsfeld,* 159 L.Ed.2d 578 (2004).

270. "All Things Considered," *NPR,* September 23, 2004.

Chapter 15

1. John W. Dower, *War without Mercy* (New York: Pantheon, 1986), 112.

2. Peter Irons, *Justice at War* (New York: Oxford University Press, 1983), 269.

3. Dower, *War without Mercy,* 92.

4. John Hersey, "Behind Barbed Wire," *New York Times Magazine,* September 11, 1988, 120.

5. Russell Nye, *Fettered Freedom* (Lansing: Michigan State University Press, 1963), 187, 227–229. Note that the 1860 census shows eighteen slaves in New Jersey, the one exception to the statement that northern states abolished them.

6. *Scott v. Sandford,* 60 U.S. 393 (1857).

7. Despite the ruling, Taney considered slavery "a blot on our national character." Three decades before the case, he had freed his own slaves, whom he had inherited from his parents. When the South seceded, Taney remained with the Union. Richard Shenkman, *"I Love Paul Revere, Whether He Rode or Not"* (New York: HarperCollins, 1991), 168.

8. Slavery became so much a part of the southern economy that the paper money of some Confederate states featured pictures of slaves harvesting cotton. *Fresh Air Weekend,* National Public Radio, August 18, 2002.

9. The Emancipation Proclamation, issued during the Civil War in 1863, was apparently a tactical move to discourage European countries from aiding the Confederacy. It gave the Civil War a moral purpose, making foreign intervention less likely. The proclamation could not free southern slaves at the time because the Union did not control the southern states, which had seceded.

10. Bruce Ackerman, *We the People: Transformations* (Cambridge, Mass.: Harvard University Press, 1998); George Fletcher, "Unsound Constitution: Oklahoma City and the Founding Fathers," *New Republic,* June 23, 1997, 14–18. These conclusions make dubious the arguments that judges should be guided only by the intentions of the original Founders as they resolve contemporary cases. Ignoring the transformation that occurred as a result of the Civil War and these amendments amounts to using a highly selective and self-serving version of history.

11. Civil Rights Act of 1866; Civil Rights Act of 1871; Civil Rights Act of 1875.

12. See Eric Foner, *Reconstruction: America's Unfinished Revolution* (New York: Harper & Row, 1988).

13. The name Jim Crow came from a white performer in the 1820s who had a vaudeville routine in which he blackened his face with burnt cork and mimicked black men. He sang "Wheel About and Turn About and Jump, Jim Crow." This routine led to minstrel shows in high schools and colleges, with students portraying and satirizing blacks. The shows were popular into the 1960s.

14. Kenneth Karst, "Equality, Law, and Belonging: An Introduction," in *Before the Law,* 5th ed., ed. John J. Bonsignore et al. (Boston: Houghton Mifflin, 1994), 429.

15. C. Vann Woodward, *The Strange Career of Jim Crow,* 2nd ed. (London: Oxford University Press, 1966), 44.

16. *Civil Rights Cases,* 109 U.S. 3 (1883).

17. C. Herman Pritchett, *The American Constitution,* 3rd ed. (New York: McGraw-Hill, 1977), 486.

18. *Plessy v. Ferguson,* 163 U.S. 537 (1896). The Court's ruling prompted states to expand their Jim Crow laws. Before *Plessy,* states segregated just trains and schools.

19. *Cumming v. Richmond County Board of Education,* 175 U.S. 528 (1899). Then the Court enforced segregation in colleges. It upheld a criminal conviction against a private college for teaching blacks together with whites. *Berea College v. Kentucky,* 211 U.S. 45 (1908).

20. Woodward, *Strange Career of Jim Crow,* 113. Before the Civil War, northern states had passed some Jim Crow laws, which foreshadowed the more pervasive laws in southern states after the war. Leon F. Litwack, *Trouble in Mind: Black Southerners in the Age of Jim Crow* (New York: Knopf, 1998).

21. Jacqueline Jones, *The Dispossessed: America's Underclasses from the Civil War to the Present* (New York: Basic Books, 1992), 83. And they were still being cheated. One sharecropper went to the landowner at the end of the season to settle up but was told he would not receive any money that year because the landowner needed it to send his son to college. The sharecropper moved to the North. Interview with the sharecropper's son on *The Best of Discovery,* Discovery television channel, June 11, 1995.

22. Richard Kluger, *Simple Justice* (New York: Knopf, 1976), 89–90.

23. Philip Dray, *At the Hands of Persons Unknown* (New York: Random House, 2002).

24. Ibid.

25. Woodward, *Strange Career of Jim Crow,* 114.

26. Yet talk of the riot was banished from newspapers, textbooks, and everyday conversations. After some years, most Oklahomans were unaware of it, except those who lived through it. In the 1990s, newspaper articles prompted the state to establish a commission to investigate the riot, leading to more awareness. Jonathan Z. Larsen, "Tulsa Burning," *Civilization,* February-March 1997, 46–55; Brent Staples, "Unearthing a Riot," *New York Times Magazine,* December 19, 1999, 64–69. For an examination, see James S. Hirsch, *Riot and Remembrance: The Tulsa Race War and Its Legacy* (New York: Houghton Mifflin, 2002).

27. "Torn from the Land," Associated Press, wire.ap.org. The Web site offers an investigative report with numerous stories. For an illuminating look at the lives and status of black people in the Deep South in the 1920s, see Nan Woodruff, *American Congo: The African American Freedom Struggle in the Delta* (Cambridge, Mass.: Harvard University Press, 2003).

28. Wilson apparently opposed segregation in government but still allowed it to appease southerners who were a major portion of his Democratic Party and whose support was essential for his economic reforms.

29. *Guinn v. United States,* 238 U.S. 347 (1915). This clause had been written into election laws to

make it more difficult for freed blacks and their children to qualify to vote (their grandfathers having been illiterate slaves) while effectively exempting whites from having to submit to literacy testing.

30. *Buchanan v. Warley*, 245 U.S. 60 (1917).

31. In 1939, the NAACP established the NAACP Legal Defense and Educational Fund as its litigation arm. In 1957, the Internal Revenue Service, pressured by southern members of Congress, ordered the two branches of the NAACP to break their connection or lose their tax-exempt status. Since then, they have been separate organizations, and further references in this chapter to the NAACP are in fact to the NAACP Legal Defense and Educational Fund.

32. Juan Williams, "The Case for Thurgood Marshall," *Washington Post*, February 14, 1999, W16.

33. Kluger, *Simple Justice*, 134.

34. *Missouri ex rel. Gaines v. Canada*, 305 U.S. 337 (1938).

35. *Sweatt v. Painter*, 339 U.S. 629 (1950).

36. *McLaurin v. Oklahoma State Regents*, 339 U.S. 637 (1950).

37. Esther Brown, a white woman from a Kansas City suburb, had a black maid who lived in nearby South Park. In 1948, when Brown saw the decrepit school for black students in South Park, she complained to the board of education in the town. At a meeting, she said, "Look, I don't represent these people. One of them works for me, and I've seen the conditions of their school. I know none of you would want your children educated under such circumstances. They're not asking for integration—just a fair shake." From the audience, Brown received catcalls and demands to go back where she came from. A woman behind her tried to hit her. The school board responded by gerrymandering the black neighborhood out of the South Park school district. Kluger, *Simple Justice*, 388–389.

38. Earl Warren, *The Memoirs of Earl Warren* (Garden City, N.Y.: Doubleday, 1977), 291.

39. Kluger, *Simple Justice*, 656.

40. *Brown v. Board of Education of Topeka*, 347 U.S. 483 (1954).

41. *Holmes v. Atlanta*, 350 U.S. 879 (1955); *Baltimore v. Dawson*, 350 U.S. 877 (1955); *Schiro v. Bynum*, 375 U.S. 395 (1964); *Johnson v. Virginia*, 373 U.S. 61 (1963); *Lee v. Washington*, 390 U.S. 333 (1968).

42. *Brown v. Board of Education II*, 349 U.S. 294 (1955).

43. Justice Tom Clark later told a political science conference that one justice had proposed desegregating one grade a year, beginning with kindergarten or first grade, but this concrete standard was rejected because the other justices felt it would take too long. In retrospect, it might have been quicker, and easier, than the vague standard used.

44. *Griffin v. Prince Edward County School Board*, 377 U.S. 218 (1964); *Norwood v. Harrison*, 413 U.S. 455 (1973); *Gilmore v. Montgomery*, 417 U.S. 556 (1974); *Green v. New Kent County School Board*, 391 U.S. 430 (1968).

45. Quoted in James F. Simon, *In His Own Image* (New York: McKay, 1974), 70.

46. *All Things Considered*, National Public Radio, December 10, 2003.

47. William Cohen and John Kaplan, *Bill of Rights* (Mineola, N.Y.: Foundation Press, 1976), 622.

48. *Swann v. Charlotte-Mecklenburg Board of Education*, 402 U.S. 1 (1971); *Columbus Board of Education v. Penick*, 443 U.S. 449 (1979); *Dayton Board of Education v. Brinkman*, 443 U.S. 526 (1979); *Keyes v. School District 1, Denver*, 413 U.S. 921 (1973).

49. Lee A. Daniels, "In Defense of Busing," *New York Times Magazine*, April 17, 1983, 36–37.

50. White flight began after World War II as affluent families moved to the suburbs. Although white flight continued for economic reasons, it increased because of busing as well.

51. *Milliken v. Bradley*, 418 U.S. 717 (1974).

52. For example, some suburbs of Kansas City, Missouri, did not allow black students to attend high schools. Some black families, then, moved back to the city, aggravating both school segregation and residential segregation. James S. Kunen, "The End of Integration," *Time*, April 29, 1996, 41.

53. *Board of Education of Oklahoma City v. Dowell*, 112 L.Ed.2d 715 (1991). The Court said that school districts could stop busing when "the vestiges of past discrimination had been eliminated to the extent practicable." See also *Freeman v. Pitts*, 118 L.Ed.2d 108 (1992).

54. *Missouri v. Jenkins*, 132 L.Ed.2d 63 (1995).

55. Anjetta McQueen, "Desegregation Waning," *Lincoln Journal-Star*, May 16, 1999.

56. FBI director J. Edgar Hoover ordered wiretaps that he hoped would link King with communists. When the taps failed to reveal any connection, Hoover had agents bug a hotel room, where they heard King having extramarital sex. Taylor Branch, *Pillar of Fire: America in the King Years, 1963–65* (New York: Simon & Schuster, 1998).

57. Woodward, *Strange Career of Jim Crow*, 186.

58. This incident occurred in 1961. Nicholas Lemann, "The Long March," *New Yorker*, February 10, 2003, 88.

59. *Norris v. Alabama*, 294 U.S. 587 (1935); *Smith v. Texas*, 311 U.S. 128 (1940); *Avery v. Georgia*, 345 U.S. 559 (1952).

60. An excellent collection of articles is presented in *Reporting Civil Rights: American Journalism, 1941–1973* (New York: Library of America, 2003).

61. Henry Louis Gates Jr., "After the Revolution," *New Yorker*, April 29 and May 6, 1996.

62. Louis Menand, "He Knew He Was Right," *New Yorker*, March 26, 2001, 95.

63. Lemann, "Long March," 86.

64. Patrick Reddy, "Why It's Got to Be All or Nothing," *Washington Post National Weekly Edition*, October 18, 1999, 23.

65. This was true for national elections. The transformation took longer for state and local elections.

66. *Heart of Atlanta Motel v. United States*, 379 U.S. 421 (1964).

67. For discussion of organized labor's ambivalence toward enactment and enforcement of the employment provisions of the act, see Herbert Hill, "Black Workers, Organized Labor, and Title VII of the 1964 Civil Rights Act: Legislative History and Litigation Record," in *Race in America*, ed. Herbert Hill and James E. Jones (Madison: University of Wisconsin Press, 1993), 263–341.

68. *Griggs v. Duke Power*, 401 U.S. 424 (1971).

69. *Washington v. Davis*, 426 U.S. 229 (1976). When the Burger Court held that standards must relate to the job, it placed the burden of proof on employers. (They had to show that their requirements were necessary.) In *Wards Cove Packing v. Atonio*, 490 U.S. 642 (1989), the Rehnquist Court shifted the burden of proof to workers. This technical change had a substantial impact; it made it hard for victims to win in court. In 1991, Congress passed new legislation to override the ruling and clarify its intent that employers should bear the burden of proof.

70. *Shelley v. Kraemer*, 334 U.S. 1 (1948).

71. Less directly, the numerous national and state policies that encouraged urban sprawl provided the opportunity for middle-class whites to flock to the suburbs, leaving the cities disproportionately black.

72. For more extensive examination, see Andrew Hacker, *Two Nations: Black and White, Separate, Hostile, Unequal* (New York: Scribner, 1992).

73. Richard Morin, "Southern Discomfort," *Washington Post National Weekly Edition*, July 15, 1996, 35.

74. Gary Orfield, quoted in Mary Jordan, "Separating the Country from the *Brown* Decision," *Washington Post National Weekly Edition*, December 20, 1993, 33. See also Maia Davis, "Harvard Study

Finds New Segregation," *Lincoln Journal-Star*, January 20, 2003.

75. Adam Cohen, "The Supreme Struggle," *New York Times*, January 18, 2004, E22.

76. Thomas M. Shapiro, *The Hidden Cost of Being African American* (New York: Oxford University, 2004), 170–179.

77. Jordan, "Separating the Country from the *Brown* Decision."

78. Mary Jordan, "On Track toward Two-Tier Schools," *Washington Post National Weekly Edition*, May 31, 1993, 31.

79. J. Harvie Wilkinson, *From Brown to Bakke* (New York: Oxford University Press, 1979), 118–125; "School Segregation Worsens, Study Says," *Lincoln Journal*, December 14, 1993; William Celis III, "Forty Years after *Brown*, Segregation Persists," *New York Times*, May 18, 1994, A1.

80. Kunen, "End of Integration," 39.

81. Jonathan Kozol, *Savage Inequalities: Children in America's Schools* (New York: HarperPerennial, 1992), 4.

82. Ibid., 3.

83. Ibid., 35. However, only three public schools in Alabama are named after King, a native of the state. "Numbers," *Time*, January 24, 2000, 23.

84. Rob Gurwitt, "Getting off the Bus," *Governing*, May 1992, 30–36; Jervis Anderson, "Black and Blue," *New Yorker*, April 29 and May 6, 1996.

85. Shapiro, *Hidden Cost*, 144–145.

86. "That's Quite a Range," *Lincoln Journal*, January 21, 1993.

87. In addition, cities have numerous nonprofit institutions—colleges, museums, hospitals—that benefit the entire urban area but do not pay property taxes. According to one estimate, 30 percent of the cities' potential tax base is tax-exempt, compared with 3 percent of the suburbs'. Kozol, *Savage Inequalities*, 55. There are a few exceptions. Jordan, "On Track," 31.

88. Kozol, *Savage Inequalities*, 155–156.

89. Ibid., 53, 84.

90. Ibid., 123–124. Researchers debate the extent to which more resources lead to more learning. The results are mixed, though most studies show that resources do improve learning. Larry V. Hedges, Richard D. Laine, and Rob Greenwald, "Does Money Matter? A Meta-Analysis of Studies of the Effects of Differential School Inputs on Student Outcomes," *Educational Researcher* 23 (1994), 5–14; Kevin B. Smith and Kenneth J. Meier, "Politics, Bureaucrats, and Schools," *Public Administration Review* 54 (1994), 551–558; David Card and Alan B. Krueger, "Does School Quality Matter?" *Journal of Political Economy* 100 (1992), 1–40; Ronald F. Ferguson, "Paying for Public Education: New Evidence on How and Why Money Matters," *Harvard Journal of Legislation* 28 (1991), 465–498; Keith Baker, "Yes, Throw Money at the Schools," *Phi Delta Kappan* 72 (1991), 628–631. For an earlier contrary view, see Eric A. Hanushek, "The Economics of Public Schooling: Production and Efficiency in Public Schools," *Journal of Economic Literature* 24 (1986), 1141–1177.

91. Steve Lopez, "Money for Stadiums but Not for Schools," *Time*, June 14, 1999, 54.

92. Jay Mathews, "A Confirmation of Bias," *Washington Post National Weekly Edition*, March 19, 2001, 34; Robert England and Kenneth Meier, "From Desegregation to Integration: Second-Generation School Discrimination as an Institutional Impediment," *American Politics Quarterly* 13 (1985), 227–247; Charles Bullock and Joseph Stewart, "Incidence and Correlates of Second-Generation Discrimination," in *Race, Sex, and Policy Problems*, ed. Marian Palley and Michael Preston (Lexington, Mass.: Lexington Books, 1979); Stephen Wainscott and J. David Woodard, "Second Thoughts on Second-Generation Discrimination," *American Politics Quarterly* 16 (1988), 171–192.

93. Kenneth Meier and Robert England, "Black Representation and Educational Policy," *American Political Science Review* 78 (1984), 392–403; Kenneth Meier, Joseph Stewart, and Robert England, *Race, Class, and Education: The Politics of Second-Generation Discrimination* (Madison: University of Wisconsin Press, 1989).

94. Although lower-class students are disproportionately disciplined, and African Americans are disproportionately lower-class, African Americans are even more disproportionately disciplined than their class status would indicate.

95. Beverly Cross, quoted in Jodie Morse, "Learning while Black," *Time,* May 27, 2002, 50.

96. Suits claiming discrimination fell 51 percent from 1975 to 1984. Marc Galanter, "Beyond the Litigation Panic," in *New Directions in Liability Law: Proceedings of the Academy of Political Science,* vol. 37 (New York: Academy of Political Science, 1988), 21, 23.

97. Richard Morin and Michael H. Cottman, "The Invisible Slap," *Washington Post National Weekly Edition,* July 2, 2001, 7.

98. Edward Barnes, "Can't Get There from Here," *Time,* February 19, 1996. 33.

99. Hacker, *Two Nations,* 48–49.

100. William A. Henry III, "The Last Bastions of Bigotry," *Time,* July 22, 1991, 66–67.

101. "Employers' Replies to Racial Names," *NBER Digest,* September 2003, 1.

102. David Wessel, "Studies Suggest Potent Race Bias in Hiring," *Wall Street Journal,* September 4, 2003, A2.

103. Earl G. Graves, *How to Succeed in Business without Being White* (New York: HarperBusiness, 1997).

104. Reed Abelson, "Anti-Bias Agency Is Short of Will and Cash," *New York Times,* July 1, 2001, BU1.

105. Jerry De Muth, "Fair-Housing Suits: Color Them Gold," *Washington Post National Weekly Edition,* August 11, 1986, 34.

106. "Hispanics Face More Bias in Housing," *Lincoln Journal-Star,* November 8, 2002. Another study found similar discrimination in fairly progressive northern cities. "Professional Should Address Discrimination," *Lincoln Journal-Star,* April 24, 2002.

107. *All Things Considered,* National Public Radio, August 5, 2001.

108. Jerry Knight, "Coloring the Chances of Getting a Mortgage," *Washington Post National Weekly Edition,* October 28, 1991, 26; "Racial Disparities Seen in Home Lending," *Lincoln Journal,* October 22, 1991.

109. Nina Burleigh, "The Suburbs Won't Vouch for This," *Time,* May 13, 1996, 43. Yet Presidents Nixon and Ford instituted a small-scale program for housing vouchers, and President Reagan also supported the idea.

110. Sarah Cohen and D'Vera Cohn, "Continental Shift," *Washington Post National Weekly Edition,* April 9, 2001, 6.

111. James Traub, "The Year in Ideas," *New York Times Magazine,* December 9, 2001, 94.

112. Hacker, *Two Nations,* 35–38. For information on why blacks do not want to live in white neighborhoods, see Maria Krysan and Reynolds Farley, "The Residential Preferences of Blacks: Do They Explain Persistent Segregation?" *Social Forces* 80 (2002), 937–980.

113. According to the Supreme Court's interpretation of Fourth Amendment search and seizure law, police can stop and frisk individuals who officers have a "reasonable suspicion" to believe are committing a crime. But officers must have more than a hunch to meet the standard of "reasonable suspicion" (though less than the "probable cause" required to obtain a search warrant). A person's race is not a valid criterion, except when the person's race and physical description match those of a particular suspect being sought.

114. John Lamberth, "DWB Is Not a Crime," *Washington Post National Weekly Edition,* August 24, 1998, 23.

115. Michael A. Fletcher, "May the Driver Beware," *Washington Post National Weekly Edition,* April 8, 1996, 29.

116. Jake Tapper, "And Then There Were None," *Washington Post National Weekly Edition,* January 13, 2003, 9.

117. Jeffrey Goldberg, "The Color of Suspicion," *New York Times Magazine,* June 20, 1999, 53.

118. David Cole and John Lamberth, "The Fallacy of Racial Profiling," *New York Times,* May 13, 2001, sec. 4, 13.

119. Pierre Thomas, "Bias and the Badge," *Washington Post National Weekly Edition,* December 18, 1995, 6–9.

120. Henry Louis Gates Jr., "Thirteen Ways of Looking at a Black Man," *New Yorker,* October 23, 1995, 59; Anderson, "Black and Blue," 64.

121. Tammerlin Drummond, "Coping with Cops," *Time,* April 3, 2000, 72–73.

122. Laura M. Markowitz, "Walking the Walk," *Networker,* July-August 1993, 22.

123. William Raspberry, "The Little Things That Hurt," *Washington Post National Weekly Edition,* April 18, 1994, 29. See also Ellis Cose, *The Rage of a Privileged Class* (New York: HarperCollins, 1993).

124. Morin and Cottman, "Invisible Slap," 6.

125. Kozol, *Savage Inequalities,* 179–180.

126. Juan Williams, "Why Segregation Seems So Seductive," *Washington Post National Weekly Edition,* January 24, 1994, 24. For an extended examination, see Derrick Bell, *Faces at the Bottom of the Well: The Permanence of Racism* (New York: Basic Books, 1992).

127. Stephan Thernstrom and Abigail Thernstrom, *America in Black and White: One Nation, Indivisible* (New York: Simon & Schuster, 1997), especially part 3. Some improvement began before the civil rights movement, when southern blacks migrated to northern cities in the 1940s.

128. Andrew Tobias, "Now the Good News about Your Money," *Parade,* April 4, 1993, 5.

129. James Smith and Finis Welch, "Race and Poverty: A 40-Year Record," *American Economic Review* 77 (1987), 152–158.

130. Joel Garreau, "Candidates Take Note: It's a Mall World after All," *Washington Post National Weekly Edition,* August 10, 1992, 25.

131. However, their rate of home ownership—48 percent—is the same as the national rate was in the 1940s. Whites' rate is 74 percent now. Deborah Kong, "Strides Made, but Still Much Disparity between Blacks, Whites," *Lincoln Journal-Star,* July 22, 2002.

132. Thernstrom and Thernstrom, *America in Black and White,* 500.

133. Ibid., 507.

134. Ibid., 506.

135. Orlando Patterson, quoted in ibid., 507.

136. Orlando Patterson, quoted in Anderson, "Black and Blue," 62.

137. From 1967 to 1987, according to calculations by William Julius Wilson. David Remnick, "Dr. Wilson's Neighborhood," *New Yorker,* April 29 and May 6, 1996.

138. Sociologist William Julius Wilson develops this idea extensively in *The Truly Disadvantaged* (Chicago: University of Chicago Press, 1987).

139. U.S. Census Bureau, *Statistical Abstract of the United States, 2001* (Washington, D.C.: Government Printing Office, 2001), tab. 38.

140. Wilson, *The Truly Disadvantaged.*

141. Remnick, "Dr. Wilson's Neighborhood," 98.

142. Samuel Walker, *Sense and Nonsense about Crime and Drugs,* 3rd ed. (Belmont, Calif.: Wadsworth, 1994), xviii, 3.

143. Thernstrom and Thernstrom, *America in Black and White,* 533.

144. Peter Reuter, "Why Can't We Make Prohibition Work Better? Some Consequences of Ignoring the Unattractive," in *Perspectives on Crime and Justice, 1996–1997 Lecture Series* (Washington, D.C.: National Institute of Justice, 1997), 30–31.

145. "Doctor: Harlem's Death Rate Worse than Bangladesh's," *Lincoln Journal,* January 18, 1990.

146. Connie Cass, "More Young Black Men in Trouble with Law," *Lincoln Journal-Star,* October 5, 1995.

147. Donald Kaul, "Only Surprise Is That Riots Didn't Happen Sooner," *Lincoln Journal,* May 19, 1992.

148. Drummond Ayres, Jr., "Decade of Black Struggle: Gains and Unmet Goals," *New York Times,* April 2, 1978, sec. 1, 1.

149. See Veronica Chambers, *Having It All?* (New York: Doubleday, 2003).

150. Harold Meyerson, "A Tale of Two Cities," *American Prospect,* June 2004, A8.

151. According to the most recent research, in 2002, Hispanics might face somewhat more discrimination in housing than blacks. Hispanics who tried to buy a house faced discrimination 20 percent of the time, and those who tried to rent an apartment did so 25 percent of the time. "Hispanics Face More Bias in Housing."

152. Tammerlin Drummond, "It's Not Just in New Jersey," *Time,* June 14, 1999, 61.

153. John Bowe, "Nobodies," *New Yorker,* April 21, 2003, 106.

154. Guadalupe San Miguel, "Mexican American Organizations and the Changing Politics of School Desegregation in Texas, 1945–1980," *Social Science Quarterly* 63 (1982), 701–715.

155. Ibid., 710.

156. Leo Grebler, Joan W. Moore, and Ralph C. Guzman, *The Mexican-American People* (New York: Free Press, 1970), 157.

157. Even children of illegal aliens have been given the right to attend public schools by the Supreme Court. The majority assumed that most of these children, although subject to deportation, would remain in the United States, given the large number of illegal aliens who do remain here. Denying them an education would deprive them of the opportunity to fulfill their potential and would deprive society of the benefit of their contribution. *Plyler v. Doe,* 457 U.S. 202 (1982).

158. Luis Ricardo Fraga, Kenneth J. Meier, and Robert E. England, "Hispanic Americans and Educational Policy: Structural Limits to Equal Access and Opportunities for Upward Mobility," unpublished paper, University of Oklahoma, 1985, 6.

159. Luis Ricardo Fraga, Kenneth J. Meier, and Robert E. England, "Hispanic Americans and Educational Policy: Limits to Equal Access," *Journal of Politics* 48 (1986), 850–873.

160. *San Antonio Independent School District* v. *Rodriguez,* 411 U.S. 1 (1973).

161. Anjetta McQueen, "Dual-Language Schools Sought," *Lincoln Journal-Star,* March 16, 2000.

162. *Lau* v. *Nichols,* 414 U.S. 563 (1974).

163. McQueen, "Dual-Language Schools Sought."

164. Lynne Duke, "English Spoken Here," *Washington Post National Weekly Edition,* December 21, 1992, 37.

165. Eloise Salholz, "Say It in English," *Newsweek,* February 20, 1989, 23.

166. Joel Kotkin, "Can the Melting Pot Be Reheated?" *Washington Post National Weekly Edition,* July 11, 1994, 23.

167. James Traub, "The Bilingual Barrier," *New York Times Magazine,* January 31, 1999, 34–35.

168. Ibid., 33–34.

169. Margot Hornblower, "No Habla Español," *Time,* January 26, 1998, 63.

170. "Bilingualism's End Means a Different Kind of Change," *Champaign-Urbana News-Gazette,* June 7, 1998.

171. Hornblower, "No Habla Español."

172. Jacques Steinberg, "Test Scores Rise, Surprising Critics of Bilingual Ban," *New York Times,* August 20, 2000, Y1.

173. U.S. Census Bureau, "Social and Economic Characteristics," *2000 Census of the Population* (http://factfinder.census.gov/servlet/QTTable?_bm=y&-geo_id=D&-qr_name=DEC_2000). Four percent of Asian language speakers do not speak English.

174. Nancy Landale and R. S. Oropesa, "Schooling, Work, and Idleness among Mexican and Non-Latino White Adolescents," working paper, Pennsylvania State University, Population Research Institute, 1997.

175. Thomas Boswell and James Curtis, *The Cuban American Experience* (Totowa, N.J.: Rowman & Allanheld, 1983), 191.

176. Kevin F. McCarthy and R. Burciaga Valdez, *Current and Future Effects of Mexican Immigration in California—Executive Summary* (Santa Monica, Calif.: RAND Corp., 1985), 27.

177. Ruben Navarrette Jr., "Hispanics See Themselves as Part of United States," *Lincoln Journal-Star,* December 23, 2002.

178. Ibid.

179. "Survey: Hispanics Reject Cohesive Group Identity," *Lincoln Journal,* December 15, 1992.

180. Lynne Duke, "English Spoken Here," *Washington Post National Weekly Edition,* December 21, 1992, 37.

181. Darryl Fears, "The Power of a Label," *Washington Post National Weekly Edition,* September 1, 2003, 29.

182. Gregory Rodriguez, "Finding a Political Voice," *Washington Post National Weekly Edition,* February 1, 1999, 22–23.

183. Karen Tumulty, "Courting a Sleeping Giant," *Time,* June 11, 2001, 74.

184. *Cherokee Nation v. Georgia,* 30 U.S. 1 (1831); *Worcester v. Georgia,* 31 U.S. 515 (1832).

185. Alfonso Ortiz, *The Pueblo* (New York: Chelsea House, 1994), 10.

186. Vine Deloria Jr. and Clifford M. Lytle, *American Indians, American Justice* (Austin: University of Texas Press, 1983), 221.

187. Ibid., 222–225.

188. Michael Lieder and Jake Page, *Wild Justice* (New York: Random House, 1997).

189. Indian Self-Determination Act (1975).

190. Ellen Nakashima and Neely Tucker, "A Fight over Lost Lands, Money Owed," *Washington Post National Weekly Edition,* April 29, 2002, 30.

191. According to the Indian Gaming Regulatory Act (1988), tribes can establish casinos if their reservation lies in a state that allows virtually any gambling, including charitable "Las Vegas nights."

192. Kathleen Schmidt, "Gambling a Bonanza for Indians," *Lincoln Journal-Star,* March 23, 1998.

193. Felicity Barringer, "Ethnic Pride Confounds the Census," *New York Times,* May 9, 1993, E3.

194. W. John Moore, "Tribal Imperatives," *National Journal,* June 9, 1990, 1396.

195. Quoted in Ruth B. Ginsburg, *Constitutional Aspects of Sex-Based Discrimination* (Saint Paul, Minn.: West, 1974), 2.

196. Karen De Crow, *Sexist Justice* (New York: Vintage, 1975), 72.

197. Nadine Taub and Elizabeth M. Schneider, "Women's Subordination and the Role of Law," in *The Politics of Law: A Progressive Critique,* rev. ed., ed. David Kairys (New York: Pantheon, 1990), 160–162.

198. *Bradwell v. Illinois,* 83 U.S. 130 (1873).

199. From an amicus curiae (friend of the court) brief by 281 historians filed in the Supreme Court case, *Webster v. Reproductive Health Services,* 106 L.Ed.2d 410 (1989).

200. Donna M. Moore, "Editor's Introduction" in *Battered Women,* ed. Donna M. Moore (Beverly Hills, Calif.: Sage, 1979), 8.

201. Barbara Sinclair Deckard, *The Women's Movement,* 2nd ed. (New York: Harper & Row, 1979), 303.

202. In the early 1960s, a board game for girls—What Shall I Be?—offered these options: teacher, nurse, stewardess, actress, ballerina, and beauty queen. David Owen, "The Sultan of Stuff," *New Yorker,* July 19, 1999, 60.

203. Reprinted in "Regrets, We Have a Few," *Time Special Issue: 75 Years of Time,* 1998, 192.

204. For an examination of Betty Friedan's role in the movement and the political dynamics among the various factions in the movement, see Judith Hennessee, *Betty Friedan: Her Life* (New York: Random House, 1999). For an examination of women's views toward feminism, see Elinor Burkett, *The Right Women* (New York: Scribner, 1998).

205. Robert Alan Goldberg, *Enemies Within* (New Haven, Conn.: Yale University Press, 2002).

206. De Crow, *Sexist Justice,* 119.

207. This is why Betty Friedan later felt compelled to write a book espousing the concept of motherhood: *The Second Stage* (New York: Summit, 1981).

208. For a discussion of these points, see Jane Mansbridge, *Why We Lost the ERA* (Chicago: University of Chicago Press, 1986); Mary Frances Berry, *Why ERA Failed* (Bloomington: Indiana University Press, 1986); Janet Boles, "Building Support for the ERA: A Case of 'Too Much, Too Late,'" *PS: Political Science and Politics* 15 (1982), 575–592.

209. Shenkman, *"I Love Paul Revere,"* 136–137.

210. *Reed v. Reed,* 404 U.S. 71 (1971).

211. *Hoyt v. Florida,* 368 U.S. 57 (1961).

212. *Taylor v. Louisiana,* 419 U.S. 522 (1975).

213. *Stanton v. Stanton,* 421 U.S. 7 (1975).

214. "White Men Still First," *Lincoln Journal-Star,* April 1, 1995.

215. "Gender Wage Gap Still an Issue," *Champaign-Urbana News-Gazette,* April 3, 2001.

216. Lisa McLaughlin, "In Brief," *Time,* October 9, 2000, G12.

217. U.S. Census Bureau, *Statistical Abstract of the United States, 1997* (Washington, D.C.: Government Printing Office, 1997), tab. 645.

218. This view is according to a survey of women in three countries. Women in Canada and Great Britain had these same complaints. Carol Kleiman, "Study Examines Barriers to Women Climbing Ladder," *Lincoln Journal-Star,* April 2, 2001.

219. Susan Benesch, "The Birth of a Nation," *Washington Post National Weekly Edition,* August 4, 1986, 12.

220. The act also requires employers to continue health insurance coverage during the leave and to give the employee the same job or a comparable one upon her or his return.

221. Lisa Genasci, "Many Workers Resist Family Benefit Offers," *Lincoln Journal-Star,* June 28, 1995.

222. Nancy R. Gibbs, "Bringing Up Father," *Time,* June 28, 1993, 55–56.

223. Ann Crittenden, "Parents Fighting Back," *American Prospect,* June 2003, 22.

224. Joyce Gelb and Marian Lief Palley, *Women and Public Policies* (Princeton, N.J.: Princeton University Press, 1982), 102. The author of Title IX, Representative Patsy Mink (D.-Hawaii), had applied to medical schools but was not considered because she was a woman. Mink intended Title IX to open the doors. She said it was "never intended to mean equal numbers or equal money" in athletics. Susan Reimer, "Title IX Has Unintended Consequences," *Lincoln Journal-Star,* April 9, 2000.

225. "Women's Determination Has Evened Playing Fields," *State College* (Pa.) *Centre Daily Times,* May 1, 2004.

226. Welch Suggs, "Uneven Progress for Women's Sports," *Chronicle of Higher Education,* April 7, 2000, A52–A56; Bill Pennington, "More Men's Teams Benched as Colleges Level the Field," *New York Times,* May 9, 2002, A1.

227. Suggs, "Uneven Progress for Women's Sports," A52.

228. Michele Orecklin, "Now She's Got Game," *Time,* March 3, 2003, 57.

229. Mary Duffy, quoted in E. J. Dionne Jr., "Nothing Wacky about Title IX," *Washington Post National Weekly Edition,* May 19, 1997, 26.

230. *Mississippi University for Women v. Hogan,* 458 U.S. 718 (1982).

231. *Orr v. Orr,* 440 U.S. 268 (1979).

232. *Michael M. v. Sonoma County,* 450 U.S. 464 (1981).

233. *Rostker v. Goldberg,* 453 U.S. 57 (1981).

234. A simplified version of this scenario was used by President Johnson in support of affirmative action.

235. Early decisions include *University of California Regents v. Bakke,* 438 U.S. 265 (1978); *United Steelworkers v. Weber,* 443 U.S. 193 (1979); and *Fullilove v. Klutznick,* 448 U.S. 448 (1980).

236. Two critics include Thomas Sowell, *Preferential Policies: An International Perspective* (New York: Morrow, 1990), and Dinesh D'Souza, *Illiberal Education* (New York: Free Press, 1991).

237. *United Steelworkers v. Weber; Sheet Metal Workers v. EEOC,* 92 L.Ed.2d 344 (1986); *Firefighters v. Cleveland,* 92 L.Ed.2d 405 (1986); *United States v. Paradise Local Union,* 94 L.Ed.2d 203 (1987).

238. *Firefighters v. Stotts,* 467 U.S. 561 (1985);*Wygant v. Jackson Board of Education,* 90 L.Ed.2d 260 (1986).

239. *Richmond v. Croson,* 102 L.Ed.2d 854 (1989); *Adarand Constructors v. Pena,* 132 L.Ed.2d 158 (1995). The perception that minorities are taking over is also reflected in a peculiar poll finding: The average American estimated that 32 percent of the U.S. population was black and 21 percent was Hispanic at a time when they were just 12 percent and 9 percent. Richard Nadeau, Richard G. Niemi, and Jeffrey Levine, "Innumeracy about Minority Populations," *Public Opinion Quarterly* 57 (1993), 332–347.

240. Quoted in Robert J. Samuelson, "End Affirmative Action," *Washington Post National Weekly Edition,* March 6, 1995, 5.

241. James E. Jones, "The Genesis and Present Status of Affirmative Action in Employment," paper presented at the annual meeting of the American Political Science Association, Washington, D.C., September, 1984; Robert Pear, *New York Times,* June 19, 1983; Nelson C. Dometrius and Lee Sigelman, "Assessing Progress toward Affirmative Action Goals in State and Local Government," *Public Administration Review* 44 (1984), 241–247; Peter Eisinger, *Black Employment in City Government* (Washington, D.C.: Joint Center for Political Studies, 1983); Milton Coleman, "Uncle Sam Has Stopped Running Interference for Blacks," *Washington Post National Weekly Edition,* December 19, 1983.

242. This "is one of the better kept secrets of the debate." Alan Wolfe, "Affirmative Action, Inc.," *New Yorker,* November 25, 1996, 107. See also the numerous sources cited there.

243. Gertrude Ezorsky, *Racism and Justice: The Case for Affirmative Action* (Ithaca, N.Y.: Cornell University Press, 1991), 48–49, 63–65.

244. Wilson, *The Truly Disadvantaged.*

245. Donald Kaul, "Privilege in Workplace Invisible to White Men Who Enjoy It," *Lincoln Journal-Star,* April 9, 1995; Richard Morin and Lynne Duke, "A Look at the Bigger Picture," *Washington Post National Weekly Edition,* March 16, 1992, 9.

246. Eisinger, *Black Employment in City Government.*

247. Thomas J. Kane, "Racial and Ethnic Preference in College Admissions," paper presented at the Ohio State University College of Law Conference, "Twenty Years after *Bakke,*" Columbus, April 1998.

248. Stephen Carter, quoted in David Owen, "From Race to Chase," *New Yorker,* June 3, 2002, 54.

249. For example, low test scores, poor writing sample, lack of college prep courses, or letters of recommendation with serious reservations. Jeffrey Rosen, "How I Learned to Love Quotas," *New York Times Magazine,* June 1, 2003, 54; Lee Hockstader, "The Texas 10 Percent Solution," *Washington Post National Weekly Edition,* November 11, 2002, 30. A major effect on the University of California system has been "cascading," with minority enrollments dropping at the most competitive UC campuses but increasing at the less competitive ones. Minorities have been cascading from the top tier to the next tiers, where their academic records more closely match those of the other students. Traub, "The Class of Prop. 209," *New York Times Magazine,* May 2, 1999, 51.

250. Jacques Steinberg, "The New Calculus of Diversity on Campus," *New York Times,* February 2, 2003, WK3.

251. *Gratz v. Bollinger,* 156 L.Ed.2d 257; *Grutter v. Bollinger,* 156 L.Ed.2d 304.

252. Traub, "Class of Prop. 209."

253. John Larew, "Why Are Droves of Unqualified, Unprepared Kids Getting into Our Top Colleges?" *Washington Monthly,* June 1991, 10–14; Theodore Cross, "Suppose There Was No Affirmative Action at the Most Prestigious Colleges and Graduate Schools," *Journal of Blacks in Higher Education,* March 31, 1994, 47, 50.

254. For an examination of the *Bakke* ruling and its impact on graduate schools, see Susan Welch and John Gruhl, *Affirmative Action and Minority Enrollments in Medical and Law Schools* (Ann Arbor: University of Michigan Press, 1998).

255. Kluger, *Simple Justice,* 90.

256. Dick Kirschten, "Not Black-and-White," *National Journal,* March 2, 1991, 496–500.

257. *Korematsu v. United States,* 323 U.S. 214 (1944).

258. Peter Irons, "Race and the Constitution: The Case of the Japanese American Internment," *This Constitution,* Winter 1986, 23.

259. William O. Douglas, *The Court Years* (New York: Random House, 1980), 279.

260. Irons, *Justice at War,* vii–ix, 186–218.

261. Ibid., vii, 367; Hersey, "Behind Barbed Wire," 73.

262. *Korematsu v. United States,* 584 F.Supp. 1406 (1983).

263. In 1948, Congress passed a law providing $37 million to settle damage claims by internees, but this was less than one-tenth of the amount that the government estimates internees had lost.

264. Tom Zeller, "In Every Mind the Memory, in Every Building a Threat," *New York Times,* September 30, 2001, WK4.

Chapter 16

1. Richard W. Stevenson, "House Approves a Bill to Repeal the Estate Tax," *New York Times,* June 10, 2000, A12.

2. Senator Patty Murray, statement in Favor of the Estate Tax Elimination Act (S. 1128). Murray's Web site maintains an archive of press releases (www.murray.senate.gov/news).

3. John Godfrey, "Though Tax Writers Are Busy, House and Senate Far Apart in Follow-Up to Last Year's Cut," *Congressional Quarterly Weekly Review,* May 25, 2002, 1384.

4. See Senator Patty Murray's Web site at http://www.murray.senate.gov/ruralhealth/index.cfm.

5. Stevenson, "House Approves a Bill to Repeal the Estate Tax," A12; Joel Friedman and Andrew Lee, "Permanent Repeal of the Estate Tax Would be Costly, Yet Would Benefit Only a Few, Very Large Estates," Report of the Center on Budget and Policy Priorities, June 20, 2002, 1 (www.cbpp.org).

6. John Godfrey and Jeremy Torobin, "Senate Thwarting of Estate Tax Repeal Blunts GOP's Leg-

islative Offensive," *Congressional Quarterly Weekly Review,* June 15, 2002, 1592.

7. Senator Patty Murray, statement on Marriage Penalty Tax Relief. Murray's Web site maintains an archive of press releases (www.murray.senate.gov/news).

8. Adam Smith, *Inquiry into the Nature and Causes of the Wealth of Nations* (1776; reprinted in several editions, including Indianapolis: Bobbs-Merrill, 1961).

9. James K. Galbraith, *Balancing Acts: Technology, Finance, and the American Future* (New York: Basic Books, 1989); Robert L. Heilbroner and Lester C. Thurow, *Five Economic Challenges* (Englewood Cliffs, N.J.: Prentice Hall, 1981), 62.

10. Quoted in John Greenwald, "Knitting New Notions," *Time,* January 30, 1989, 46.

11. John Maynard Keynes, *The General Theory of Employment, Interest and Money* (New York: Harcourt, Brace, 1935).

12. The FOMC is made up of a board of governors including five Federal Reserve Bank heads.

13. Ben Wildavsky, "Atlas Schmoozes," *National Journal,* May 17, 1997, 974–977.

14. For a brief review of the Fed's work, see James L. Rowe Jr., "Holding the Purse Strings," *Washington Post National Weekly Edition,* June 28, 1999, 6–8.

15. William Greider, *Secrets of the Temple: How the Federal Reserve Runs the Country* (New York: Simon & Schuster, 1987), 461. Grieder's analyses of the Reserve Board's anti-inflation policies in the early 1980s are revealing and compelling.

16. Robert D. Auerbach, "That Shreddin' Fed," *Barrons,* December 10, 2001, 36. Auerbach was an economist for the House Banking Committee for eleven years.

17. Louis Uchitelle, "He Didn't Say It. But He Knew It," *New York Times,* April 30, 2000, sec. 3, 1.

18. "Spoils to GOP Victors," *Champaign-Urbana News-Gazette,* August 6, 2002, 1.

19. Edward R. Tufte, *Political Control of the Economy* (Princeton, N.J.: Princeton University Press, 1978).

20. Steven Greenhouse, "Brady Sought Greenspan Policy Pledge," *International Herald Tribune,* September 25, 1992, 13.

21. Paul Krugman, "The Maestro Slips Out of Tune," *New York Times Magazine,* June 6, 2004, 80.

22. "Poll: Citizens OK about Money, Glum on Future," *Champaign-Urbana News-Gazette,* April 12, 1995, B8.

23. Paul Krugman, "Dynamo and Microchip," *New York Times,* February 20, 2000, sec. 4, 13.

24. Isaac Shapiro, "Are We Soaking the Rich?" Center on Budget Policy and Priorities Report, April 16, 2002, 1 (www.cbpp.org).

25. Isaac Shapiro, "Overall Federal Tax Burden–Including Middle Income Families–at Lowest Levels in More Than Two Decades," Center on Budget and Policy Priorities Report, April 10, 2002, 3–4 (www.cbpp.org).

26. The government raises small amounts of revenue by taxing consumption through the levies it places on the sale or manufacture of some luxury and nonessential items such as liquor and cigarettes, as well as on a few essential products such as gasoline. These excise taxes are designed not only to raise revenue, but also to limit or discourage use of scarce or dangerous products, which is why they are sometimes called "sin taxes."

27. Shapiro, "Overall Federal Tax Burden on Most Families—Including Middle-Income Families—at Lowest Levels in More Than Two Decades," 2.

28. Data are from the Center on Budget and Policy Priorities Report (www.cbpp.org), quoted in "Middle-Class Tax Blow Hits Lowest Level Since 1957," *Champaign-Urbana News- Gazette,* April 15, 2002, A8.

29. David Cay Johnston, "A Taxation Policy to Make John Stuart Mill Weep," *New York Times,* April 18, 2004, WK14.

30. Jill Barshay, "Business Lobby Storms Senate to Shape Corporate Tax Bill," *CQ Weekly,* May 8, 2004, 1073.

31. "Government Says Americans Spending More Time on Taxes," *Champaign-Urbana News-Gazette,* April 15, 2004, 1.

32. "Problems Cited at IRS Help Centers," *Champaign-Urbana News-Gazette,* September 4, 2003, 1.

33. Citizens for Tax Justice, "State and Local Taxes Hit Poor and Middle Class Far Harder than the Wealthy." Report issued June 26, 1996. See the report online at www.ctj.org/html/whopays.htm.

34. Institute on Taxation and Economic Policy, "The Effects of Replacing Most Federal Taxes with a National Sales Tax: A State-by-State Distributional Analysis." Paper issued September 2004, 2.

35. Ibid., 3.

36. This is a proposal made by Yale law professor Michael J. Graetz, "To the Point of No Returns," *New York Times,* November 15, 2004, A23.

37. Joseph A. Schumpeter, *Business Cycles: A Theoretical, Historical, and Statistical Analysis of the Capitalist Process* (New York: McGraw-Hill, 1939).

38. John Berry, "The Legacy of Reaganomics," *Washington Post National Weekly Edition,* December 19, 1988; Spencer Rich, "Are You Really Better Off Than You Were Thirteen Years Ago?" *Washington Post National Weekly Edition,* September 8, 1986, 20; Levy, "We're Running Out of Gimmicks to Sustain Our Prosperity," *Washington Post National Weekly Edition,* December 29, 1986, 18–19.

39. Editorial, "Two Trillion Dollars Is Missing," *New York Times,* January 8, 1989, E28.

40. Louis Uchitelle, "For Employee Benefits, It Pays to Wear the Union Label," *New York Times,* July 16, 1995, F10.

41. Lester C. Thurow, "Companies Merge; Families Break Up," *New York Times,* September 3, 1995, E11.

42. "Family Wealth Down for 1st Time in 55 Years," *Champaign-Urbana News-Gazette,* March 14, 2001, A8.

43. Stephanie Aronson, "The Rise in Lifetime Earnings Inequality among Men," Federal Reserve Board Staff Report, Finance and Economics Discussion Series, March 2002, 4 (www.federalreserve.gov).

44. Greg Winter, "Rich Colleges Receiving Richest Share of U.S. Aid," *New York Times,* November 9, 2003, 1.

45. David Leonhardt, "Why Is This Man Smiling? Executive Pay Drops Off the Political Radar," *New York Times,* April 16, 2000, sec. 4, 5. For a survey of executive salaries, see David Leonhardt, "Will Today's Huge Rewards Devour Tomorrow's Earnings?" *New York Times,* April 2, 2000, sec. 3, 1.

46. Michael Lind, *The Next American Nation: The New Nationalism and the Fourth American Revolution* (New York: Free Press, 1995), 139–216.

47. Isaac Shapiro and David Kamin, "Share of Economy Going to Wages and Salaries Drops for Unprecedented 14th Straight Quarter." Report issued by the Center on Budget and Policy Priorities, October 29, 2004, 1–3 (www.cbpp.org).

48. John Maggs, "Winners and Losers in the Bush Economy," *National Journal,* May 15, 2004, 1501.

49. Ibid., 1495.

50. Ibid., 1501.

51. "Census Data Show Poverty Increased, Income Stagnated, and the Number of Uninsured Rose to Record Levels in 2003." Report issued by the Center on Budget and Policy Priorities, August 27, 2004, 8 (www.cbpp.org)

52. Census Bureau data from "Income Gap Rose in Past Two Decades," *Champaign-Urbana News-Gazette,* August 17, 2004, 1, A8.

53. On the heath care and mortgage debt burden see Elizabeth Warren and Amelia Warren Tyagi,

The Two-Income Trap: Why Middle-Class Mothers and Fathers Are Going Broke (New York: Basic Books, 2003), 84–87 and 129–137.

54. Elizabeth Warren of the Harvard Law School, interview by Bill Moyers, *Now,* PBS, February 6, 2004.

55. David Alan Stockman, *Triumph of Politics: How the Reagan Revolution Failed* (New York: Harper & Row, 1986).

56. Citizens for Tax Justice, "Bush Still on Track to Borrow $10 Trillion by 2014 According to Latest Official Estimates," Paper issued January 30, 2004, 1 (www.ctj.org).

57. Robert Greenstein, "President's Budget Uses Accounting Devices and Implausible Assumptions to Hide Hundreds of Billions of Dollars in Costs," Center for Budget and Policy Priorities, February 5, 2002, 2 (www.cbpp.org).

58. Mark Murray, John Maggs, et al., quoting Brookings' analyst William G. Gale in "The Deficit Difference," *National Journal,* February 9, 2002, 384.

59. Maggs, "Winners and Losers in the Bush Economy," 1496.

60. Victor Allred, "PAYGO Goes by the Wayside," *Congressional Quarterly Weekly Report,* January 13, 2001, 96.

61. Andrew Taylor, "Deal on Pay-As-You-Go Rules a Must for Budget Resolution," *Congressional Quarterly Weekly Report,* April 17, 2004, 897–900.

62. Maggs, "Winners and Losers in the Bush Economy," 1495.

63. Ibid., 1496.

64. For a worst-case scenario see Laurence J. Kotlikoff and Scott Burns', *The Coming Generational Storm: What You Need to Know about America's Economic Future* (Cambridge, Mass.: MIT Press, 2004). Kotlikoff estimates the government will have a gap of $51 trillion between revenues and obligations over the coming decade.

65. David E. Sanger, "Look Who's Carping Most about Capitalism," *New York Times,* April 6, 1997, E5. This estimate has been accepted by the former chair of the Council of Economic Advisers, Laura D. Tyson.

66. According to United Nations statistics.

67. Lael Brainard and Robert E. Litan, "'Offshoring' Service Jobs: Ban or Boon and What to Do?" *Brookings Policy Brief #132,* April 2004, 2.

68. Ibid., 4.

69. Ken Nelson, "Outsourcing, Turned Inside Out," *New York Times,* April 11, 2004, sec. 3, 1.

70. Louis Uchitelle, "It's Not New Jobs. It's All the Jobs." *New York Times,* August 29, 2004, 3, 6.

71. Brainard and Litan, "'Offshoring' Service Jobs: Ban or Boon and What to Do?" 7.

72. Ibid., 4.

73. Louis Uchitelle, "Fewer Jobs Filled as Factories Rely on Overtime Pay," *New York Times,* May 16, 1993, 18.

74. Murray's press release explaining her vote against repeal of estate tax, June 12, 2002.

75. Godfrey and Torobin, "Senate Thwarting of Estate Tax Repeal Blunts GOP's Legislative Offensive," 1592.

Chapter 17

1. Gebe Martinez, "Playing the Blame Game on Farm-Friendly Politics," *Congressional Quarterly Weekly Review,* April 20, 2002, 1010.

2. Press release from the office of Senator Tim Hutchinson, May 13, 2002.

3. U.S. Census Bureau, *Statistical Abstract of the United States, 2001* (Washington, D.C.: Government Printing Office, 2001), tab. 801.

4. John Kelly, "Ag Subsidies; Rich Get Richer, Rest Get By," *Champaign-Urbana News-Gazette,* September 23, 2001, A1.

5. Elizabeth Becker, "As House Prepares Farm Bill, Question of Who Needs Help, and How Much," *New York Times,* September 9, 2001, 22.

6. Ibid.

7. "Spoils to GOP Victors," *Champaign-Urbana News-Gazette,* August 6, 2002, A7.

8. Gebe Martinez, "Free-Spending Farm Bill a Triumph of Politics," *Congressional Quarterly Weekly Review,* May 4, 2002, 114. The first quote is from John Boehner (R-Ohio) and Cal Dooley (D-Calif.), the second from Patrick Toomey (R-Pa.).

9. Press release from the office of Senator Tim Hutchinson, February 13, 2002.

10. Philip Brasher, "Big Farms Hog Much of Subsidies," *Champaign-Urbana News-Gazette,* August 2, 2001, C6.

11. Martinez, "Playing the Blame Game," 1008.

12. Donald L. Barlett and James B. Steele, "Corporate Welfare," *Time,* November 9, 1998, 35.

13. Patricia Dunn, "The Reagan Solution for Aiding Families with Dependent Children: Reflections of an Earlier Era," in *The Attack on the Welfare State,* ed. Anthony Champagne and Edward Harpham (Prospect Heights, Ill.: Waveland, 1984), 87–110.

14. Melinda Upp, "Relative Importance of Various Income Sources of the Aged, 1980," *Social Security Bulletin,* January 1983, 5.

15. All of the statistics on Social Security recipients are from Social Security Administration, "Social Security Online" (www.ssa.gov).

16. Social Security Administration, "Social Security Information for Women" (www.ssa.gov/women).

17. Ibid.

18. U.S. Census Bureau, "2003 Poverty Tables" (www.census.gov).

19. Barbara Ehrenreich, who writes on working-class life, is one who believes that the poverty level is set too low. Swanee Hunt, "Number of Poor May Be Far Higher Than Government Statistics Indicate," *Champaign-Urbana News-Gazette,* December 7, 2003, B1.

20. Social Security Administration, "Monthly Statistical Snapshot," September 2004, 1 (www.ssa.gov).

21. U.S. Census Bureau, *Statistical Abstract of the United States, 2003* (Washington, D.C.: Government Printing Office, 2003), tab. 91.

22. Greg J. Duncan, *Years of Poverty, Years of Plenty: The Changing Economic Fortunes of American Workers and Families* (Ann Arbor: Survey Research Center, Institute for Social Research, University of Michigan, 1984); Spencer Rich, "Who Gets Help and How," *Washington Post National Weekly Edition,* May 15, 1989, 37.

23. Department of Health and Human Services, Temporary Assistance for Needy Families (TANF) Program, Administration for Children and Families, final rule summary (www.acf.dhhs.gov/programs/ofa/exsumcl.htm); Liz Schott, Ed Lazere, Heidi Goldberg, and Eileen Sweeney, "Highlights of the Final TANF Regulations," Center on Budget and Policy Priorities, April 29, 1999 (www.cbpp.org/4-29-99wel.htm).

24. Nina Bernstein, "Side Effect of Welfare Law: The No-Parent Family," *New York Times,* July 29, 2002, 1, 14.

25. Mark Murray, Marilyn Werber Serafini, and Megan Twohey, "Untested Safety Net," *National Journal,* March 10, 2001, 687.

26. Ibid.

27. Nicholas Johnson, Joseph Llobrera, and Bob Zahradnik, "A Hand Up: How State Earned Income Tax Credits Help Working Families Escape Poverty in 2003," Center on Budget and Policy Priorities, March 3, 2003 (www.cbpp.org/3-3-03sfp.htm). Seventeen states also offer the EITC against state income taxes.

28. Murray et al., "Untested Safety Net," 687.

29. Ibid., 690.

30. Office of Management and Budget, *Budget of the United States Government, Fiscal Year 2005* (Washington, D.C.: Government Printing Office, 2004), 69.

31. Robert Pear, "Electronic Cards Replace Coupons for Food Stamps," New York Times, June 23, 2004, 1.

32. Jay Mathews, "Study Shows Early Head Start Gains," *State College* (Pa.) *Centre Daily Times,* June 5, 2002, 1.

33. Nicholas Kristof, "Farm Subsidies That Kill," *New York Times,* July 5, 2002, A21.

34. John Kelly, "Lion's Share of Farm Subsidies Going to a Select Few," *State College* (Pa.) *Centre Daily Times,* September 10, 2001, 1.

35. John Lancaster, "Our Farm-Friendly Lawmakers," *Washington Post National Weekly Edition,* September 10, 2001, 11.

36. Quoted in ibid.

37. Becker, "As House Prepares Farm Bill."

38. Timothy Egan, "Big Farms Reap Two Harvests with Aid as Bumper Crop," *New York Times,* December 26, 2004, sec. 1, 36.

39. *Budget of the United States, Fiscal Year 2005,* 285.

40. U.S. Census Bureau, *Statistical Abstract of the United States, 2003* (Washington, D.C.: Government Printing Office, 2004), tab. 545.

41. Richard B. Freeman, "Labor Market Institutions and Earnings Inequality," *New England Economic Review,* May-June 1996, 158; U.S. Census Bureau, "Current Population Survey," March 1960 to 2001 (www.census.gov).

42. U.S. Census Bureau, "2003 Poverty Tables." For an analysis of the data in these tables, see "Census Data Show Poverty Increased, Income Stagnated, and the Number of Uninsured Rose to a Record Level in 2003," Center on Budget and Policy Priorities, August 27, 2004 (http://www.cbpp.org/8-26-04pov.htm).

43. Murray et al., "Untested Safety Net," 691.

44. Clarke E. Cochran et al., *American Public Policy,* 6th ed. (New York: St. Martin's/Worth, 1999), 282.

45. Rebecca Adams, "America's Unraveling Safety Net," *Congressional Quarterly Weekly Review,* May 22, 2004, 1225.

46. Ibid., 1226.

47. *Budget of the United States, Fiscal Year 2005,* 148.

48. Erin Heath, "Medicaid: The Pendulum Swings," *National Journal,* August 9, 2003, 2546.

49. Chris L. Peterson, "Health Insurance: Uninsured by State, 2003" (www.pennyhill.com/healthpolicy/96-979epw.html).

50. "Many Vets Found without Insurance," *Champaign-Urbana News-Gazette,* October 19, 2004, A2.

51. Lawrence J. Schweinhart et al., *Lifetime Effects: The High/Scope Perry Preschool Study through Age 40* (Ypsilanti, Mich.: High/Scope Press, 2004).

52. "Greenspan Warns about Mortgage Giants' Debt," *Champaign-Urbana News-Gazette,* February 24, 2004, C8.

53. Timothy L. O'Brien and Jennifer Lee, " Seismic Shift under the House of Fannie Mae," *New York Times,* October 3, 2004, sec. 3, 1, 9.

54. "Greenspan Warns," C8.

55. Sharon La Franiere, "Though They Owe, Still They Reap," *Washington Post National Weekly Edition,* February 28, 1994, 10–11.

56. "Nature Humbles a State of Mind," *New York Times,* February 10, 1991, E3; Marc Reisner, "The Emerald Desert," *Greenpeace,* July-August 1989, 7.

57. Barlett and Steele, "Corporate Welfare," 38.

58. Donald L. Barlett and James B. Steele, "Fantasy Island," *Time,* November 16, 1998, 84.

59. Ibid., 87.

60. Donald L. Barlett and James B. Steele, "The Empire of the Pigs," *Time,* November 30, 2002, 53–54.

61. Timothy Egan, "Towns Hand Out Tax Breaks, Then Cry Foul as Jobs Leave," *New York Times,* October 20, 2004, A18.

62. See Donald L. Barlett and James B. Steele, "Paying a Price for Polluters," November 23, 1998, 77, and "Corporate Welfare," 39.

63. For some sample costs of cleanup of industrial waste, see Barlett and Steele, "Paying a Price for Polluters," 72–80.

64. *Budget of the United States, Fiscal Year 2005; Analytical Perspectives,* tab. 18-1.

65. Steve Lohr, "Health Care Costs Are a Killer, but Maybe That's a Plus," *New York Times,* September 26, 2004, WK5.

66. David Cutler, *Your Money or Your Life: Strong Medicine for America's Health Care System* (New York: Oxford University Press, 2004).

67. Gardiner Harris, "As Doctors Write Prescriptions, Drug Companies Write Checks," *New York Times,* June 27, 2004, 19.

68. Harrell R. Rodgers Jr., *The Cost of Human Neglect: America's Welfare Failure* (Armonk, N.Y.: Sharpe, 1982), 91. Recent studies show that this continues to be true. See Peter Kilborn, "Racial Health Gap Remaining a Reality," *Lincoln Journal-Star,* January 26, 1998, 3A.

69. Mark Sherman, "Doctors Call for National Coverage," *Lincoln Journal-Star,* August 13, 2003, p. 1.

70. Holly Sklar, "Rolling the Dice on Our Nation's Health Care," *Champaign-Urbana News-Gazette,* December 22, 2002, B4.

71. Donald L. Barlett and James B. Steele, "The Health of Nations," *New York Times,* October 24, 2004, WK11; Hillary Rodham Clinton, "Now Can We Talk about Health Care?" *New York Times Magazine,* April 18, 2004, 29.

72. Lohr, "Health Care Costs Are a Killer."

73. Institute of Medicine study, cited in Clinton, "Now Can We Talk?"

74. Daniel Gross, "Whose Problem Is Health Care?" *New York Times,* February 8, 2004, BU6.

75. Elizabeth Warren and Amelia Warren Tyagi, *The Two-Income Trap: Why Middle-Class Mothers and Fathers Are Going Broke* (New York: Basic Books, 2003).

76. "Europe Mulls Private Medical Care," *Champaign-Urbana News-Gazette,* November 29, 2003, A3.

77. Barlett and Steele, "Health of Nations."

78. Lohr, "Health Care Costs Are a Killer."

79. Clinton, "Now Can We Talk?" 30.

80. Lohr, "Health Care Costs Are a Killer"; Malcolm Caldwell, "High Prices," *New Yorker,* October 25, 2004, 88.

81. Caldwell, "High Prices," 88; see also John Abramson, *Overdosed America* (New York: HarperCollins, 2004).

82. Gina Kolata, "More May Not Mean Better in Health Care, Studies Find," *New York Times,* July 21, 2002, sec. 1, 20.

83. Ibid.

84. Erik Eckholm, "Those Who Pay Health Costs Think of Drawing Lines," *New York Times,* March 28, 1993, 1.

85. Nancy Watzman, "Socialized Medicine Now—without the Wait," *Washington Monthly,* October 1991, 45–46. In Canada, doctors cannot collect as much per cesarean if the frequency with which they do the procedure exceeds the percentage considered reasonable. Thus the economic incentive to do cesareans disappears.

86. Robert Pear, "Study Finds Savings in Medicare Drug Benefit," *New York Times,* November 23, 2004, A16.

87. Social Security Administration, "Fact Sheet Social Security, 2004," 2 (www.ssa.gov/pressoffice/factsheets/basicfact-alt.htm).

88. Robert Pear, "AARP Opposes Bush Plan to Replace Social Security with Private Accounts," *New York Times,* November 12, 2004, A19.

89. Richard W. Stevenson, "Bush's Social Security Plan Is Said to Require Vast Borrowing," *New York Times,* November 28, 2004, 1, 22.

90. Social Security Administration, "Fact Sheet Social Security, 2004."

91. Somini Sengupta, "Living on Welfare: A Clock Is Ticking," *New York Times,* April 29, 2001, 26.

92. Eileen P. Sweeney, "Recent Studies Indicate That Many Parents Who Are Current or Former Welfare Recipients Have Disabilities," Center on Budget and Policy Priorities, February 29, 2000 (www.cbpp.org/2-29-00wel.pdf); Erica Goode, "Childhood Abuse and Adult Stress," *New York Times,* August 2, 2000, A22.

93. Corine Hegland, "What Works for Welfare?" *National Journal,* January 10, 2004, 107.

94. Pamela Loprest, "Long Ride from Welfare to Work," *Washington Post,* August 30, 1999, A19.

95. On Bush's marriage initiative and work requirements, see Bill Swindell, "Welfare Reauthorization Becomes Another Casualty in Congress's Partisan Crossfire," *Congressional Quarterly Weekly,* April 3, 2004, 805–806.

96. Pietro S. Nivola, Jennifer L. Noyes, and Isabel V. Sawhill, "Welfare and Beyond," Policy Brief No. 29, Brookings Institution, March 2004, 2.

97. Ibid., 3–6.

98. Hegland, "What Works for Welfare?" 109–110.

99. Arloc Sherman, Shawn Fremstad, and Sharon Parrott, "Employment Rates for Single Mothers Fell Substantially During Recent Period of Labor Market Weakness," Center on Budget and Policy Priorities, June 22, 2004 (www.cbpp.org/6-22-04ui.htm).

100. Gordon Berlin, vice president of MDRC, a non-partisan research group, quoted in Hegland, "What Works for Welfare?" 108.

101. Press release from the office of Senator Tim Hutchinson, February 13, 2002.

102. Elizabeth Becker, "Accord Reached on a Bill Raising Farm Subsidies," *New York Times,* April 2, 2002, 11.

103. Press release from the office of Senator Tim Hutchinson, May 13, 2002.

104. Kristof, "Farm Subsidies That Kill."

Chapter 18

1. Eric Schaeffer, "Clearing the Air: Why I Quit Bush's EPA," *Washington Monthly,* July-August 2002, 21; Samantha Levine, "Portrait: Eric Schaeffer, At the Top of His Lungs," *US News & World Report,* December 2, 2002, 28–29.

2. Seth Borenstein, "EPA Enforcer Quits, Saying Lobbyists Now Write the Rules," *Philadelphia Inquirer,* March 1, 2002, A16.

3. Levine, "Portrait: Eric Schaeffer, At the Top of His Lungs."

4. Editorial, "Cover-Up on Clean Air," *New York Times,* October 6, 2004, A28.

5. Thomas R. Kuhn quoted in Bruce Barcott, "Changing All the Rules," *New York Times Magazine,* April 4, 2004, 43.

6. Letter of resignation from Eric Schaeffer to EPA Director Christie Todd Whitman, February 27, 2002. The letter was released to the public.

7. Testimony of Eric Schaeffer before the Senate Democratic Policy Committee, February 6, 2004, 1. (www.cleanairtrust.org/testimony.schaeffer.html) The data Schaeffer quotes was collected by the EPA.

8. Levine, "Portrait: Eric Schaeffer, At the Top of His Lungs."

9. Adam Smith, 1776, *An Inquiry into the Nature and Causes of the Wealth of Nations* (New York: Bantam Classics, 2003; or any edition).

10. See discussion in William Ophuls, *Ecology and the Politics of Scarcity; Prologue to a Political Theory of the Steady State* (San Francisco: W. H. Freeman, 1977), 145–147.

11. NBC News Special Report on the 20th Anniversary of Earth Day, April 22, 1991.

12. William P. Cunningham et al., eds., *Environmental Encyclopedia,* 2nd ed.(Detroit: Gale Research, 1998), 395; Ruth A. Eblen and William R. Eblen, eds., The Encyclopedia of the Environment (Boston: Houghton Mifflin, 1994), 243.

13. Steven Pearlstein, "The Disaster of Deregulation," *Washington Post National Weekly Edition,* September 10, 2001, 6.

14. Kirk Victor and Michael Posner, "Merger Mania," *National Journal,* July 15, 2000, 2282; Stephen Labaton, "Oligopoly," *New York Times,* June 11, 2000, sec. 4, 1.

15. Steve Lohr, "The New Math of Monopoly," *New York Times,* April 9, 2000, sec. 4, 1. Excerpts from the federal court ruling against Microsoft appeared in *New York Times,* April 4, 2000, C14–C15.

16. Margaret Kriz, "Global Food Fight," *National Journal,* March 4, 2000, 689.

17. Neela Banerjee, "Who Will Needle Regulators Now That Enron's Muzzled?" *New York Times,* January 20, 2002, sec. 3, 1.

18. Cornelius M. Kerwin, *Rulemaking: How Government Agencies Write Law and Make Policy* (Washington, D.C.: CQ Press, 1994), 171.

19. See the discussion in Walter A. Rosenbaum, *Environmental Politics and Policy,* 3rd ed. (Washington, D.C.: CQ Press, 1985), 90–95.

20. See Susan J. Tolchin and Martin Tolchin, *Dismantling America: The Rush to Deregulate* (Boston: Houghton Mifflin, 1983), esp. chap. 4. For an assessment of cost savings under Reagan's regulatory policies, see George C. Eads and Michael Fix, *Relief or Reform? Reagan's Regulatory Dilemma* (Washington, D.C.: Urban Institute Press, 1984), 241–245.

21. David W. Chen, "What's a Life Worth?" *New York Times,* June 20, 2004, sec. 4, 4; Elizabeth Kolbert, "The Calculator," *New Yorker,* November 25, 2002, 42–49.

22. For examples of what people would be willing to pay to be free of various problems caused by air pollution see Jim Holt, "The Human Factor," *New York Times Magazine,* March 28, 2004, 13–14.

23. John Tierney, "Life: The Cost Benefit Analysis," *New York Times,* May 18, 2003, sec. 4, 14.

24. Tolchin and Tolchin, *Dismantling America: The Rush to Deregulate.*

25. Rebecca Adams, "GOP, Businesses Rewrite the Regulatory Playbook," *Congressional Quarterly Weekly Report,* May 5, 2001, 995.

26. Denis Hayes, "Earth Day Plus 25 Years: Things Are Looking Up for the Earth," *Champaign-Urbana News-Gazette,* April 23, 1995, B1.

27. Arthur Levitt Jr., SEC chair during the Clinton administration, interview by Bill Moyers, *Now with Bill Moyers,* PBS, June 20, 2002.

28. Jane Mayer, "The Accountants' War," *New Yorker,* April 22, 2002, 64–72.

29. Ibid., 68.

30. Kerwin, *Rulemaking: How Government Agencies Write Law and Make Policy,* 264.

31. Margaret Kriz, "Electric Power Play," *National Journal,* June 3, 2000, 1744–1748.

32. Kenneth J. Meier, *Regulation: Politics, Bureaucracy, and Economics* (New York: St. Martin's Press, 1985), 78–80.

33. Joseph Nocera, "System Failure," *Fortune,* June 24, 2002, 3.

34. Philip K. Howard, *The Death of Common Sense: How Law Is Suffocating America* (New York: Random House, 1994), 12.

35. Daniel Yergin and Joseph Stanislaw, *Commanding Heights: The Battle between Government and the Marketplace That Is Remaking the Modern World* (New York: Simon & Schuster, 1998), 11.

36. Victor and Posner, "Merger Mania," 2281.

37. "Mergers and Monopolies," *Now with Bill Moyers,* PBS, April 26, 2002. Transcript is online at www.pbs.org/now/transcript/transcript_cable.html.

38. Victor and Posner, "Merger Mania," 2289.

39. Kriz, "Global Food Fight," 688.

40. Richard W. Stevenson, "Playing Catch-Up with Monopolies," *New York Times,* November 14, 1999, sec. 4, 16.

41. "Internet Bills Multiply," *Congressional Quarterly Weekly Report,* September 4, 1999, 2033. Research for this article contributed by these *CQ* staff members: M. Jessie Barczak, Sandra Basu, Sheryl Henderson Blunt, Leila Corcoran, Lantie Ferguson, Robert Levine, and Alan K. Ota.

42. Al Gore, "Earth Days Have Become Earth Years," *New York Times,* April 23, 1995, E17.

43. Al Gore, *Earth in the Balance: Ecology and the Human Spirit* (Boston: Houghton Mifflin, 1992), 294.

44. Lynn White Jr., "The Historical Roots of Our Ecological Crisis," *Science* 155 (1967), 1203–1207.

45. See Robert A. Nisbet, *History of the Idea of Progress* (New York: Basic Books, 1980) for an interesting examination of the idea of progress from antiquity to the present.

46. See Meier, *Regulation: Politics, Bureaucracy, and Economics,* chap. 6, for an overview of early attempts by the federal government to protect the environment.

47. James E. Anderson, David W. Brady, and Charles Bullock III, *Public Policy and Politics in America* (North Scituate, Mass.: Duxbury, 1978), 74.

48. Kerwin, *Rulemaking: How Government Agencies Write Law and Make Policy,* 171.

49. Meier, *Regulation: Politics, Bureaucracy, and Economics,* 145; Norman J. Vig and Michael E. Kraft, "Environmental Policy from the Seventies to the Eighties," in *Environmental Policy in the 1980s: Reagan's New Agenda,* eds. Vig and Kraft (Washington, D.C.: CQ Press, 1984), 16.

50. Information about the founding of the EPA is drawn from Steven A. Cohen, "EPA: A Qualified Success," in *Controversies in Environmental Policy,* eds. Sheldon Kamieniecki, Robert O'Brien, and Michael Clarke (Albany: State University of New York Press, 1986), 174–199; Meier, *Regulation: Politics, Bureaucracy, and Economics,* 142–146.

51. Meier, *Regulation: Politics, Bureaucracy, and Economics,* 147.

52. "Kids and Chemicals," *Now with Bill Moyers,* PBS, May 10, 2002. Transcript is online at www .pbs.org/now/transcript/transcript117_full.html.

53. Quoted from the U.S. Environmental Protection Agency's 2000 long-term mission statement, "Preparing for a New Era of Environmental Protection," at www.epa.gov.

54. Helen Ingram and Dean Mann, "Preserving the Clean Water Act," in *Environmental Policy in the 1980s: Reagan's New Agenda,* eds. Vig and Kraft, 260.

55. Carole Gallagher, *American Ground Zero: The Secret Nuclear War* (Cambridge, Mass.: MIT Press, 1993), xxiii.

56. "Cold War Testing Could Have Killed 11,000," *Champaign-Urbana News-Gazette,* March 2, 2002, A5.

57. U.S. Senate Committee on Government Affairs, hearings on *The Human Subject Radiation Experiments,* 103rd Cong., 2nd sess., 1994, S.Hrg. 103-1060; U.S. Senate Committee on Government Affairs, hearings on *The Human Subject Radiation Experiments,* 104th Cong., 2nd sess., 1996, S.Hrg. 104-588.

58. Tom Morganthau with Mark Miller, Ginny Carroll, and Janet Huck, "Nuclear Danger and Deceit," *Newsweek,* October 31, 1988, 28–30.

59. Ed Magnuson, "They Lied to Us," *Time,* October 31, 1988, 64.

60. Ibid., 61.

61. Michael Janofsky, "Changes May Be Needed in Superfund, Chief Says," *New York Times,* December 5, 2004, 24.

62. William D. Ruckelshaus, the EPA's first director, quoted in David Bollier and Joan Claybrook, *Freedom from Harm: The Civilizing Influence of Health, Safety and Environmental Regulation* (Washington, D.C.: Public Citizen and Democracy Project, 1986), 95.

63. Keith Schneider, "Second Chance on Environment," *New York Times,* March 26, 1993, A17.

64. Keith Schneider, "New View Calls Environmental Policy Misguided," *New York Times,* March 21, 1993, 16.

65. Joel Brinkley, "Many Say Lab-Animal Tests Fail to Measure Human Risk," *New York Times,* March 23, 1993, A16.

66. Much of the discussion in this section is based on a series of articles on environmental policy written by Keith Schneider, Michael Spector, and Joel Brinkley that ran in the *New York Times* from March 21st to March 26th, 1993.

67. Keith Schneider, "For the Environment, Compassion Fatigue," *New York Times,* November 6, 1994, E3.

68. National Audubon Society fundraising letter cited by Keith Schneider, "Big Environment Hits a Recession," *New York Times,* January 1, 1995, F4. Other critical assessments of the environmental movement's pessimistic outlook can be found in Martin W. Lewis, *Green Delusions: An Environmentalist Critique of Radical Environmentalism* (Durham, N.C.: Duke University Press, 1992); Bill McKibben, "An Explosion of Green," *Atlantic Monthly,* April 1995, 61–83; Evan J. Ringquist, "Is 'Effective Regulation' Always Oxymoronic? The States and Ambient Air Quality," *Social Science Quarterly* 76, no. 1 (1995), 69–87.

69. See Rosenbaum, *Environmental Politics and Policy,* 3rd ed., 126–127; Bollier and Claybrook, *Freedom from Harm: The Civilizing Influence of Health, Safety and Environmental Regulation,* 116.

70. U.S. Census Bureau, *Statistical Abstract of the United States, 1999,* Table 415.

71. Jonathan Rosen, "Birding at the End of Nature," *New York Times Magazine,* May 21, 2000, 66.

72. David Osborne and Ted Gaebler, *Reinventing Government: How the Entrepreneurial Spirit Is Transforming the Public Sector* (New York: Plume Books / Penguin, 1992), 299–305.

73. Ibid., 302.

74. Philip Shabecoff, "Tax Proposed on Products and Activities That Harm Environment," *New York Times,* February 10, 1991, 1.

75. Budget of the U.S. Government, *U.S. Budget for Fiscal Year 1996* (Washington, D.C.: U.S. Government Printing Office, 1995), 81–90.

76. Budget of the U.S. Government, *U.S. Budget for Fiscal Year 2003* (Washington, D.C.: U.S. Government Printing Office, 2002), 305.

77. Jia Lynn Yang, "States: Batting Cleanup," *National Journal,* August 8, 2003, 2544.

78. Al Gore quoted by Bill McKibben, "Not So Fast," *New York Times Magazine,* July 23, 1995, 25.

79. See research by Nicholas Ashford reported in U.S. Senate Governmental Affairs Committee, 96th Congress, "Benefits of Environmental, Health, and Safety Regulation" (Washington, D.C.: U.S. Government Printing Office, March 25, 1980); Gregg Easterbrook, *A Moment on the Earth: The Coming Age of Environmental Optimism* (New York: Viking, 1995).

80. "Kids and Chemicals."

81. Bruce Babbitt quoted in Sam Howe Verhovek, "They Exist. Therefore They Are. But, Do You Care?" *New York Times,* October 17, 1999, sec. 4, 5.

82. Letter of resignation from Eric Schaeffer to EPA Director Christie Todd Whitman.

83. Testimony of Eric Schaeffer before the Senate Democratic Policy Committee, 2.

84. "Changing All the Rules," 77.

85. Ibid.

86. Felicity Barringer, "Bush's Record: New Priorities in Environment," *New York Times,* September 14, 2004.

87. Editorial, "Cover-Up on Clean Air."

88. Testimony of Eric Schaeffer before the Senate Democratic Policy Committee, 3.

89. "Acid Rain Pollution Goes Up in 2003," *Champaign-Urbana News-Gazette,* September 23, 2004, A2.

90. Michael Janofsky, "E.P.A. Cuts Pollution Levels With Refinery Settlements," *New York Times,* October 10, 2004, sec. 1, 22.

91. Levine, "Portrait: Eric Schaeffer, At the Top of His Lungs," 29. The Web site for Schaeffer's foundation is www.environmentalintegrity.org.

Chapter 19

1. The representation of Senator Lugar's views is based on press releases and biographical material posted at his Senate Web site and interviews on the *NewsHour with Jim Lehrer,* PBS, August 1, 2002, and September 19, 2002.

2. Miles A. Pomper, "Philosophical Conflicts Complicate Iraq Debate," *Congressional Quarterly Weekly Review,* August 3, 2002, 2096–2100.

3. "Lugar Statement on '10110 over 10' at Senate Foreign Relation Committee Hearing," press release from Lugar's office, October 9, 2002.

4. The September 10, 2002, Lugar-Biden letter to President Bush can be found at Lugar's Web site under the "press releases" link (lugar.senate.gov/091202.htm). Their op-ed letter can be linked at Biden's Web site (biden.senate.gov).

5. Joint resolution submitted to Congress September 19, 2002.

6. Office of Management and Budget, *Budget of the United States, Fiscal 1996* (Washington, D.C.: Government Printing Office, 1995), 121.

7. Walter LaFeber, "Marking Revolution, Opposing Revolution," *New York Times,* July 3, 1983, sec. 4, 13.

8. I. M. Destler, Leslie H. Gelb, and Anthony Lake, *Our Own Worst Enemy: The Unmaking of American Foreign Policy* (New York: Simon & Schuster, 1984), 115–116.

9. Madison's notes from *Documents Illustrative of the Formation of the Union of the American States,* quoted in Joan Biskupic, "Constitution's Conflicting Clauses Underscored by Iraqi Crisis," *Congressional Quarterly Weekly,* January 5, 1991, 34.

10. Ronald D. Elving, "America's Most Frequent Fight Has Been the Undeclared War," *Congressional Quarterly Weekly Report,* January 5, 1991, 37.

11. Representative Toby Roth (R-Wis.), quoted in Katharine Q. Seelye, "House Defeats Bid to Repeal 'War Powers,'" *New York Times,* June 11, 1995, A7.

12. Barry B. Hughes, *The Domestic Context of American Foreign Policy* (San Francisco: Freeman, 1978), ch. 5.

13. Robert Weissberg, *Public Opinion and Popular Government* (Englewood Cliffs, N.J.: Prentice Hall, 1976).

14. Information in this paragraph is based on Jeff Gerth with Sarah Bartlett, "Kissinger and Friends and Revolving Doors," *New York Times,* April 30, 1989, 1ff.

15. For a discussion of the foreign policy establishment, see Walter Isaacson and Evan Thomas, *The Wise Men: Six Friends and the World They Made* (New York: Simon & Schuster, 1986).

16. Tom Zeller, "The Iraq-Qaeda Link: A Short History," *New York Times,* June 20, 2004, WK4.

17. Carl M. Cannon, "Judging Clinton," *National Journal,* January 1, 2000, 21.

18. Robert Wright, "Private Eyes," *New York Times Magazine,* September 5, 1999, 50–54; William J. Broad, "Snooping's Not Just for Spies Any More," *New York Times,* April 23, 2000, sec. 4, 6.

19. Historian Michael Hogan, quoted in John M. Broder, "Gentler Look at the U.S. World Role," *New York Times,* October 31, 1999, 14.

20. Paul Johnson, "The Myth of American Isolationism," *Foreign Affairs,* May-June 1995, 162.

21. Bruce Russett, *The Prisoners of Insecurity* (San Francisco: Freeman, 1983).

22. See James Nathan and James Oliver, *United States Foreign Policy and World Order,* 2nd ed. (Boston: Little, Brown, 1981), 359–361.

23. For one view of the impact of Vietnam on the thinking of today's high-ranking officers, see H. R. McMaster, *Dereliction of Duty* (New York: Harper-Collins, 1997).

24. Robert S. McNamara, *In Retrospect: The Tragedy and Lessons of Vietnam* (New York: Times Books, 1995).

25. Michael Beschloss, *Reaching for Glory: Lyndon Johnson's Secret White House Tapes, 1964–1965* (New York: Simon & Schuster, 2001), 166.

26. Weissberg, *Public Opinion and Popular Government,* 144–148.

27. Ole Holsti, "The Three-Headed Eagle," *International Studies Quarterly* 23 (1979), 339–359; Michael Mandelbaum and William Schneider, "The New Internationalisms," in *The Eagle Entangled: U.S. Foreign Policy in a Complex World,* ed. Kenneth Oye, Donald Rothchild, and Robert J. Lieber (New York: Longman, 1979), 34–88.

28. For an analysis of U.S.-Soviet relations in the Reagan era, see Alexander Dallin and Gail Lapidus, "Reagan and the Russians," and Kenneth Oye, "Constrained Confidence and the Evolution of Reagan Foreign Policy," in *Eagle Resurgent?* ed. Kenneth Oye, Robert Lieber, and Donald Rothchild (Boston: Little, Brown, 1987), and John Newhouse, "The Abolitionist" (pts. 1 and 2), *New Yorker,* January 2 and 9, 1989.

29. See George F. Kennan, "After the Cold War," *New York Times Magazine,* February 5, 1989, 32ff.

30. Bill Clinton, "A Democrat Lays Out His Plan," *Harvard International Review,* Summer 1992, 26.

31. Thomas Friedman, "What Big Stick? Just Sell," *New York Times,* October 2, 1995, E3.

32. Elaine Sciolino, "Monroe's Doctrine Takes Another Knock," *New York Times,* August 7, 1994, E6. For a discussion of the U.S. turn to multilateralism, see Stanley Hoffmann, "The Crisis of Liberal Internationalism," *Foreign Policy* 98 (1995, 159–177.

33. "National Security Strategy of the United States," September 2002. The president's annual report to Congress is posted at www.whitehouse.gov.

34. "Bush Plans 'Strike First' Military Policy," *Champaign-Urbana News-Gazette,* June 10, 2002, A-3.

35. Fred Kaplan, "JFK's First-Strike Plan," *Atlantic Monthly,* October 2001, 81–86.

36. To get an idea of an ambassador's work, look at "Ambassador: Under Fire Overseas" at www.pbs.org.

37. U.S. Department of State, "Diplomacy: The State Department at Work," 2 (www.state.gov).

38. The findings of the congressional investigation into intelligence failures prior to and after 9/11 can be read at the Web site for the Senate Select Intelligence Committee (intelligence.senate.gov). See transcripts of the testimony of Eleanor Hill, director of the Joint Inquiry staff.

39. James Bamford, "How to (De-)Centralize Intelligence," *New York Times,* November 24, 2002, sec. 4, 3.

40. For an account of one CIA veteran's reasons for resignation see Anonymous, *Imperial Hubris: Why the West Is Losing the War on Terror* (Washington, D.C.: Brassey's, 2004). Anonymous is Michael Scheurer, who was the CIA's leading expert on Osama bin Laden and al-Qaeda. His identity was quickly exposed by the subject matter in the book.

41. See the chapter "How to Do It–A Different Way of Organizing Government," in *The 9/11 Commission Report: Final Report of the National Commission on Terrorist Attacks on the United States* (New York: W. W. Norton, 2004), 399–428.

42. Brookings Institution estimate, cited in Tom Cohen, "The NATO Connection," *Champaign-Urbana News-Gazette,* March 14, 1999, B5. A lower estimate of the costs of nuclear preparedness can be found in David C. Morrison, "Putting a Price Tag on the Arms Race," *National Journal,* May 13, 1995, 1171.

43. U.S. Department of Defense, *Quadrennial Defense Review Report* (Washington, D.C.: Government Printing Office, 2001), 17. The full report is at the Pentagon's Web site (www.dod.gov/pubs/qdr2001.pdf).

44. Leslie Wayne, "America's For-Profit Secret Army," *New York Times,* October 13, 2002, sec. 3, 10.

45. "Diplomacy: The State Department at Work," 2.

46. Jim Hoagland, "What Goes Around . . . ," *Washington Post National Weekly Edition,* January 24, 2000, 5.

47. Joan Spero, an undersecretary of state, quoted in David E. Sanger, "How Washington Inc. Makes a Sale," *New York Times,* February 19, 1995, sec. 3, 1.

48. "Diplomacy's New Hit Man: The Free-Market Dollar," *New York Times,* May 24, 1998, sec. 4, 5.

49. Julie Kosterlitz, "Trade Crusade," *National Journal,* May 9, 1998, 1054–1055.

50. For a concise summary of the advantages and disadvantages of protectionism and free trade, see Paul Krugman, *The Age of Diminished Expectations* (Cambridge, Mass.: MIT Press, 1992), 101–113.

51. Quoted in David E. Rosenbaum, "Free Trade Is Like Dry Water, Y'All," *New York Times,* December 19, 2004, sec. 4, 2.

52. "National Security Strategy of the United States," 18.

53. For a description of WTO structure, membership, and activities, see "WTO: Special Report," *Congressional Quarterly Weekly Report,* November 27, 1999, 2826–2838.

54. This was an argument made in *Frontline*'s documentary on Wal-Mart's marketing strategy, which is heavily dependent on the importation of cheap goods from China. "Is Wal-Mart Good for America?" *Frontline,* PBS, November 16, 2004 (www.pbs.org/wgbh/pages/frontline/shows/walmart).

55. Gary Clyde Hufbauer and Jeffrey J. Schott, with Kimberly Ann Elliot, *Economic Sanctions Reconsidered: History and Current Policy* (Washington, D.C.: Institute for International Economics, 1985), 10.

56. Ibid, 80.

57. "Diplomacy: The State Department at Work," 2.

58. Quoted in David E. Sanger, "Strategies in a Market Era," *New York Times,* January 4, 1998, sec. 4, 4.

59. Joseph Kahn, "The World's Bankers Try Giving Money, Not Lessons," *New York Times,* October 1, 2000, sec. 4, 5.

60. Missy Ryan, "Arrested Development," *National Journal,* June 10, 2000, 1822.

61. Tom Walker, "Planet of Riches Still Blighted by Poverty," *London Sunday Times,* January 2, 2000, 16.

62. Bill Clinton, quoted in Jane Perlez, "At Conference on Trade, Clinton Makes Pitch for Poor," *New York Times,* January 30, 2000, 6.

63. David E. Sanger, "Bush Plan Ties Foreign Aid to Free Market and Civic Rule," *New York Times,* November 26, 2002, A12.

64. *Congressional Quarterly Daily Monitor,* August 28, 2002.

65. Material in this section is drawn from Michael R. Gordon, "A Whole New World of Arms Races to Contain," *New York Times,* May 3, 1998, sec. 4, 1; John Kifner and Jo Thomas, "Singular Difficulty in Stopping Terrorism," *New York Times,* January 18, 1998, 16; Keith Easthouse, "The Stewardship Debate," *Champaign-Urbana News-Gazette,* June 14, 1998, B1, B4–B5; and Michael R. Gordon, "Russian Thwarting U.S. Bid to Secure a Nuclear Cache," *New York Times,* January 5, 1997, 1, 4.

66. "What Does It Take to Make a Bomb?" *Frontline,* PBS, 1998 (www.pbs.org/wgbh/pages/frontline/shows/nukes/stuff/faqs.html).

67. Michael Wines and Sharon LaFraniere, "Hut by Hut, AIDS Steals Life in a Southern Africa Town," *New York Times,* November 28, 2004, 1.

68. Henri E. Couvin, "Stability of Africa Is Threatened as AIDS Gains Foothold in Armies," *New York Times,* November 24, 2002, 11.

69. "AIDS Threatens Global Security," *NewsHour with Jim Lehrer,* PBS, October 1, 2002.

70. *Congressional Quarterly Daily Monitor,* October 1, 2002.

71. "Lugar Statement on Iraq Resolution," press release from Senator Lugar's office, October 3, 2002.

527 groups Tax-exempt groups, named after the provision in the tax code, that are organized to provide politically relevant advertising, usually with the aim of helping particular candidates or parties. Technically they are supposed to be independent but in reality are often closely linked to the candidates.

Abscam A 1981 FBI undercover operation in which six House members and one senator were convicted of taking bribes.

Activist judges Judges who are not reluctant to overrule the other branches of government by declaring laws or actions of government officials unconstitutional.

Administrative Procedure Act (APA) Legislation passed in 1946 that provides for public participation in the rule-making process. All federal agencies must disclose their rule-making procedures and publish all regulations at least thirty days in advance of their effective date to allow time for public comment.

Adversarial relationship A relationship in which the parties are constantly in conflict with each other.

Affirmative action A policy in job hiring or university admissions that gives special consideration to members of traditionally disadvantaged groups.

Agents of political socialization Sources of information about politics; include parents, peers, schools, the media, political leaders, and the community.

Aid to Families with Dependent Children (AFDC) A program that provides income support for the poor.

American Civil Liberties Union (ACLU) A nonpartisan organization that seeks to protect the civil liberties of all Americans.

Americans with Disabilities Act Passed to protect those with disabilities from discrimination in employment and public accommodations, such as stores, restaurants, hotels, and health care facilities.

Amicus curiae In Latin, "friend of the court." A third party that gives advice in a legal case to which it is not a party.

Antifederalists Those who opposed the ratification of the U.S. Constitution.

Antitrust law Laws that prohibit **monopolies**.

Appropriations Budget legislation that specifies the amount of authorized funds that will actually be allocated for agencies and departments to spend.

Articles of Confederation The first constitution of the United States; in effect from 1781 to 1789.

Asymmetrical warfare Conflict between combatants of very unequal strength.

Authorizations Budget legislation that provides agencies and departments with the legal authority to operate; may specify funding levels but do not actually provide the funding (the funding is provided by **appropriations**).

Baker v. Carr A 1962 Supreme Court decision giving voters the right to use the courts to rectify the malapportionment of legislative districts.

Balanced budget amendment A proposed constitutional amendment that would require balancing the federal budget.

Balanced government Refers to the idea that the different branches of government all represent different interests, forcing the various factions to work out compromises acceptable to all.

Bandwagon effect The tendency of voters to follow the lead of the media, which declare some candidates winners and others losers, and vote for the perceived winner. The extent of this effect is unknown.

Battleground states Also known as "swing states." During a presidential election, these are states whose Electoral College votes are not safely in one candidate's pocket; candidates will spend time and money there to try to win the state.

Bay of Pigs invasion The disastrous CIA-backed invasion of Cuba in 1961, mounted by Cuban exiles and intended to overthrow the government of Fidel Castro.

Behavioral approach The study of politics by looking at the behavior of public officials, voters, and other participants in politics, rather than by focusing on institutions or law.

Bible Belt A term used to describe portions of the South and Midwest that were strongly influenced by Protestant fundamentalists.

Bilingual education Programs where students whose native language is not English receive instruction in substantive subjects such as math in their native language.

Bill of Rights The first 10 amendments to the U.S. Constitution.

Bills of attainder Legislative acts that pronounce specific persons guilty of crimes.

Black Codes Laws passed by Southern states following the **Civil War** that denied most legal rights to the newly freed slaves.

Blockbusting The practice in which realtors would frighten whites in a neighborhood where a black family had moved by telling the whites that their houses would decline in value. The whites in panic would then sell their houses to the realtors at low prices, and the realtors would resell the houses to blacks, thereby resegregating the area from white to black.

Block grants A system of giving federal funds to states and localities under which the federal government designates the purpose for which the funds are to be used but allows the states some discretion in spending.

Boll Weevils Conservative Democratic members of Congress, mainly from the South, who vote more often with the Republicans than with their own party.

Brownlow Committee Appointed by Franklin Roosevelt in 1935, the committee recommended ways of improving the management of the federal bureaucracy and increasing the president's influence over it.

Brown v. Board of Education The 1954 case in which the U.S. Supreme Court overturned the **separate-but-equal doctrine** and ruled unanimously that segregated schools violated the Fourteenth Amendment.

Bubble concept A policy that permits flexibility in meeting pollution standards by allowing a company to meet an emissions standard if total emissions from all smokestacks at a factory or from all factories in a given area (under an imaginary bubble) meet the standard, even though emissions from individual smokestacks or factories fail to comply.

Budget and Accounting Act of 1921 This act gives the president the power to propose a budget and led to presidential dominance in the budget process. It also created the **Bureau of the Budget,** changed to the **Office of Management and Budget** in 1970.

Budget deficit Occurs when federal spending exceeds federal revenues.

Bureaucratic continuity The stability provided by career-oriented civil servants, who remain in government for many years while presidents, legislators, and political appointees come and go.

Bureau of the Budget Established in 1921 and later changed to the **Office of Management and Budget,** the BOB was designed as the president's primary means of developing federal budget policy.

Burger Court The U.S. Supreme Court under Chief Justice Warren Burger (1969–1986). Though not as activist as the **Warren Court,** the Burger Court maintained most of the rights expanded by its predecessor and issued important rulings on abortion and sexual discrimination.

Bush v. Gore U.S. Supreme Court case in 2000 where the Supreme Court set aside the Florida Supreme Court's order for a manual recount of the presidential votes cast in the state. The Court's decision meant that Bush got Florida's electoral votes, giving him a majority of all electoral votes and, thus, the election.

Canadian health care plan A single-payer system in which individuals choose their own doctors and the province pays the doctors for services performed; fees are strictly regulated.

Cap-and-trade Policy where a limit or cap is placed on the amount of a pollutant that can be emitted in a geographic area. Factories within that area are allowed to buy, sell, or trade rights to pollute as long as collective emissions do not exceed the cap.

Capitalist economy An economic system in which prices, wages, working conditions, and profits are determined solely by the market.

Captured agencies Refers to the theory that regulatory agencies often end up working on behalf of the interests they are supposed to regulate.

Casework The assistance members of Congress provide to their constituents; includes answering questions and doing personal favors for those who ask for help. Also called **constituency service**.

Caucus Today, a meeting of local residents who select delegates to attend county, state, and national conventions where the delegates nominate candidates for public office. Originally, caucuses were limited to party leaders and officeholders who selected the candidates.

Central Intelligence Agency (CIA) Created after World War II, the CIA is a federal agency charged with coordinating overseas intelligence activities for the United States.

Checks and balances The principle of government that holds that the powers of the various branches should overlap to avoid power becoming overly concentrated in one branch.

City-state In ancient Greece, a self-governing state such as Athens or Sparta, consisting of an independent city and its surrounding territory.

Civil case A case in which individuals sue others for denying their rights and causing them harm.

Civil disobedience Peaceful but illegal protest activity in which those involved allow themselves to be arrested and punished.

Civil Rights Act of 1964 Major civil rights legislation that prohibits discrimination on the basis of race, color, religion, or national origin in public accommodations.

Civil Rights Act of 1968 Civil rights legislation that prohibits discrimination in the sale or rental of housing on the basis of race, color, religion, or national origin; also prohibits **blockbusting, steering,** and **redlining.**

Civil Service Commission An agency established by the **Pendleton Act of 1883** to curb **patronage** in the federal bureaucracy and replace it with a merit system.

Civil War The war between the Union and the Confederacy (1861–1865), fought mainly over the question of whether the national or state governments were to exercise ultimate political power. Slavery was the issue that precipitated this great conflict.

Classical democracy A system of government that emphasizes citizen participation through debating, voting, and holding office.

Closed primary A primary election where participation is limited to those who are registered with a party or declare a preference for a party.

Cloture A method of stopping a **filibuster** by limiting debate to only 20 more hours; requires a vote of three-fifths of the members of the Senate.

Coalition A network of **interest groups** with similar concerns that combine forces to pursue a common goal; may be short-lived or permanent.

Coalition building The union of **pressure groups** that share similar concerns.

Cold War The era of hostility between the United States and the Soviet Union that existed between the end of World War II and the collapse of the Soviet Union.

Commercial bias A slant in news coverage to please or avoid offending advertisers.

Committee of the Whole Refers to the informal entity the House of Representatives makes itself into to debate a bill.

Commodity groups Interest groups that represent producers of specific products, such as cattle, tobacco, or milk producers.

Comparable worth The principle that comparable jobs should pay comparable wages.

Concurrent resolutions Special resolutions expressing the sentiment of Congress, passed by one house with the other concurring, but not requiring the president's signature.

Confederal system A system in which the central government has only the powers given to it by the subnational governments.

Conference committee A committee composed of members of both houses of Congress that is formed to try to resolve the differences when the two houses pass different versions of the same bill.

Conflict of interest The situation when government officials make decisions that directly affect their own personal livelihoods or interests.

Conscientious objectors Persons who oppose all wars and refuse military service on the basis of religious or moral principles.

Conservative A person who believes that the domestic role of government should be minimized and that individuals are responsible for their own well-being.

Constituencies The persons a member of Congress represents. For a senator, all the residents of the state; for a member of the House, all the residents of the member's district.

Constituency service The assistance members of Congress provide to residents in their districts (states, if senators); includes answering questions and doing personal favors for those who ask for help. Also called **casework.**

Constitution The body of basic rules and principles that establish the functions, limits, and nature of a government.

Constitutional Convention The gathering in Philadelphia in 1787 that wrote the U.S. Constitution; met initially to revise the **Articles of Confederation** but produced a new national **constitution** instead.

Containment A policy formulated by the Truman administration that aimed to limit the spread of communism by meeting any action taken by the Soviet Union with a countermove; led U.S. decision makers to see most conflicts in terms of U.S.-Soviet rivalry.

Contras Rebels who fought to overthrow the Sandinista government of Nicaragua.

Contribution limits Regulation of the overall amount of money that individuals and groups give to candidates.

Cooperative federalism The continuing cooperation among federal, state, and local officials in carrying out the business of government.

Cooperative internationalism The belief that problems of global poverty, inequitable distribution of wealth, abuse of human rights, and regional competitiveness are substantial threats to world order, and thus that the United States should work with other nations to solve these problems.

Corporate welfare Tax breaks or financial subsidies given by government to corporations.

Cost-benefit analysis The process of evaluating a **regulation** by weighing its cost against the risk of harm if it is not implemented.

Cost overruns The amount by which the cost of a certain project exceeds the expected cost.

Cost-plus project A project for which the contractor is reimbursed for all of its costs in addition to a set, agreed-upon profit rate.

Court-packing plan President Franklin D. Roosevelt's attempt to expand the size of the U.S. Supreme Court in an effort to obtain a Court more likely to uphold his New Deal legislation.

Courts of appeals Intermediate courts between trial courts (**district courts** in the federal system) and the supreme court (the U.S. Supreme Court in the federal system).

Cracking, stacking, and packing Methods of drawing district boundaries that minimize black representation. With cracking, a large concentrated black population is divided among two or more districts so that blacks will not have a majority anywhere; with stacking, a large black population is combined with an even larger white population; with packing, a large black population is put into one district rather than two so that blacks will have a majority in only one district.

Cradle-to-grave regulations for dealing with hazardous wastes that require the wastes to be identified as toxic and handled in an environmentally sound manner from the time of creation until disposition.

Credentials committee A body responsible for examining the credentials of political convention delegates.

Criminal case A case in which a government (national or state) prosecutes a person for violating its laws.

Cruel and unusual punishment Torture or any punishment that is grossly disproportionate to the offense; prohibited by the Eighth Amendment.

Cuban Missile Crisis The 1962 stand-off between the United States and the Soviet Union over an offensive missile buildup in Cuba. The Soviets finally agreed to remove all the missiles from Cuban soil.

Cumulative voting A proposed reform to increase minority representation; calls for members of Congress to be elected from at-large districts that would elect several members at once. Each voter would have as many votes as the district had seats and could apportion the votes among the candidates as he or she wished, such as giving all votes to a single candidate.

Dealignment Term used to refer to the diminished relevance of political parties.

De facto **segregation** Segregation that is based on residential patterns and is not imposed by law; because it cannot be eliminated by striking down a law, it is more intractable than **de jure segregation.**

Deficit A condition in which expenditures exceed revenues.

De jure **segregation** Segregation imposed by law; outlawed by *Brown v. Board of Education* and subsequent court cases.

Delegated legislative authority The power to draft, as well as execute, specific policies; granted by Congress to agencies when a problem requires technical expertise.

Demagogue A leader who obtains political power by appealing to the emotions and biases of the populace.

Democracy A system of government in which authority resides in the people.

Departments Executive divisions of the federal government, such as the Departments of Defense and Labor, each headed by a cabinet officer.

Depression A period of prolonged high unemployment.

Deregulation Ending **regulation** in a particular area.

Detente A policy designed to deescalate **Cold War** rhetoric and promote the notion that relations with the Soviet Union could be conducted in ways other than confrontation; developed by President Richard M. Nixon and Secretary of State Henry Kissinger.

Devolution Allowing lower units of government (such as at the state and local level) to make and implement policy.

Direct democracy A system of government in which citizens govern themselves directly and vote on most issues; e.g., a New England town meeting.

Direct lobbying Direct personal encounters between lobbyists and the public officials they are attempting to influence.

Direct primary An election in which voters directly choose a party's candidates for office.

Discretionary spending Spending by the federal government where the amount is set by annual **appropriations** bills passed by Congress; includes government operating expenses and salaries of many federal employees.

District courts The trial courts (lower-level courts) in the federal system.

Divided government The situation when one political party controls the presidency and the other party controls one or both houses of Congress.

Dixiecrat A member of a group of southern segregationist Democrats who formed the States' Rights Party in 1948.

Domino theory The idea that if one country fell under communist rule, its neighbors would also fall to communism; contributed to the U.S. decision to intervene in Vietnam.

Dred Scott case An 1857 case in which the U.S. Supreme Court held that blacks, whether slave or free, were not citizens and that Congress had no power to restrict slavery in the territories; contributed to the polarization between North and South and ultimately to the **Civil War.**

Dual federalism The idea that the Constitution created a system in which the national government and the states have separate grants of power with each supreme in its own sphere.

Due process The guarantee that the government will follow fair and just procedures when prosecuting a criminal defendant.

Earned income tax credit (EITC) A negative income tax. Instead of paying tax, persons with low incomes receive a payment from the government or a credit toward their taxes.

Education Amendments of 1972 These forbid discrimination on the basis of sex in schools and colleges that receive federal aid.

Electoral College A group of electors selected by the voters in each state and the District of Columbia; the electors officially elect the president and vice president.

Emancipation Proclamation Abraham Lincoln's 1863 proclamation that the slaves "shall be . . . forever free." At the time, applied only in the Confederate states, so had little practical impact, because the Union did not control them. However, it had an immense political impact, making clear that the Civil War was not just to preserve the Union but to abolish slavery.

Environmental impact statement An analysis of a project's effects on the environment; required from government agencies under the National Environment Policy Act of 1970 before any new projects could be carried out.

Environmental Protection Agency (EPA) The regulatory agency with responsibility for pollution control; created in 1970 by President Richard M. Nixon.

Equal Credit Opportunity Act This act forbids discrimination on the basis of sex or marital status in credit transactions.

Equal Employment Opportunity Commission (EEOC) The EEOC enforces the **Civil Rights Act of 1964,** which forbids discrimination on the basis of sex or race in hiring, promotion, and firing.

Equal Pay Act A statute enacted by Congress in 1963 that mandates that women and men should receive equal pay for equal work.

Equal protection clause The Fourteenth Amendment clause that is the Constitution's primary guarantee that government will treat everyone equally.

Equal Rights Amendment (ERA) A proposed amendment to the Constitution that would prohibit government from denying equal rights on the basis of sex; passed by Congress in 1972 but failed to be ratified by a sufficient number of states.

Establishment clause The First Amendment clause that prohibits the establishment of a church officially supported by government.

European Union (EU) A union of European nations formed in 1957 to foster political and economic integration in Europe; formerly called the European Economic Community or Common Market.

Exclusionary rule A rule that prevents evidence obtained in violation of the Fourth Amendment from being used in court against the defendant.

Executive leadership The president's control over the bureaucracy in his capacity as chief executive; achieved through budgeting, appointments, administrative reform, lobbying, and mobilizing public opinion.

Executive orders Rules or regulations issued by the president that have the force of law; issued to implement constitutional provisions or statutes.

Executive privilege The authority of the president to withhold information from the courts and Congress.

Exit polls Election-day poll of voters leaving the polling places, conducted mainly by television networks and major newspapers.

Ex post **facto law** A statute that makes some behavior illegal that was not illegal when it was done.

Externality A cost or benefit of production that is not reflected in the product's market price. **Regulation** attempts to eliminate negative externalities.

Faithless elector A member of the **Electoral College** who votes on the basis of personal preference rather than the way the majority of voters in his or her state voted.

Farm subsidies Government payments to farmers to raise the price they receive for crops to above-market prices.

Federal Communication Commission (FCC) A regulatory agency that controls interstate and foreign communication via radio, television, telegraph, telephone, and cable. The FCC licenses radio and television stations.

Federal Election Campaign Act A 1974 statute that regulates campaign finance; provided for public financing of presidential campaigns, limited contributions to campaigns for federal offices, and established the **Federal Election Commission,** among other things.

Federal Election Commission Created in 1975, the commission enforces federal laws on campaign financing.

Federalism A system in which power is constitutionally divided between a central government and subnational or local governments.

Federalist Papers A series of essays in support of the U.S. Constitution; written for New York newspapers by Alexander Hamilton, James Madison, and John Jay during the debate over ratification.

Federalists Originally, those who supported the U.S. Constitution and favored its ratification; in the early years of the Republic, those who advocated a strong national government.

Federal Register A government publication describing bureaucratic actions and detailing regulations proposed by government agencies.

Federal Reserve Board Created by Congress in 1913, the board regulates the lending practices of banks and plays a major role in determining **monetary policy.**

Felonies Crimes considered more serious than **misdemeanors** and carrying more stringent punishment.

Feminization of poverty The phenomenon that the majority of families living in poverty are headed by females.

Fifteenth Amendment An amendment to the Constitution, ratified in 1870, that prohibits denying voting rights on the basis of race, color, or previous condition of servitude.

Filibuster A mechanism for delay in the Senate in which one or more members engage in a continuous speech to prevent the Senate from taking action.

Fireside chats Short radio addresses given by President Franklin D. Roosevelt to win support for his policies and reassure the public during the Great Depression.

First Amendment The first amendment to the United States constitution, guaranteeing freedom of expression, which includes freedom of speech, religion, assembly, association, and freedom of the press.

Fiscal policy Government's actions to regulate the economy through taxing and spending policies.

Fixed-cost project A project that a contractor has agreed to undertake for a specified sum.

Flat tax A tax structured so that all income groups pay the same rate.

FOIA The Freedom of Information Act, passed in 1966 and amended in 1974, lets any member of the public apply to an agency for access to unclassified documents in its archives.

Food stamp program A poverty program that gives poor people coupons redeemable in grocery stores for food.

Franking The privilege of members of Congress that allows them to send free mail to their constituents.

Freedom of association Guarantees the right of an individual to join with others to speak, assemble, and petition the government for a redress of grievances. This right allows a minority to pursue interests without being prevented from doing so by the majority.

Freedom of speech The First Amendment guarantee of a right of free expression.

Free exercise clause The First Amendment clause that guarantees individuals the right to practice their religion without government intervention.

Free trade A policy of minimum intervention by government in trade relations.

Frontrunners Candidates whom political pros and the media have portrayed as likely winners.

Full faith and credit A clause in the U.S. Constitution that requires the states to recognize contracts that are valid in other states.

Fundraiser An event, such as a luncheon or cocktail party, hosted by a legislator or candidate for which participants pay an entrance fee.

Game orientation The assumption in political reporting that politics is a game and that politicians are the players; leads to an emphasis on strategy at the expense of substance in news stories.

Gender gap An observable pattern of modest but consistent differences in opinion between men and women on various public policy issues.

General revenue sharing A Reagan administration policy of giving states and cities federal money to spend as they wished, subject to only a few conditions.

Gerrymander A congressional district whose boundaries are drawn so as to maximize the political advantage of a party or racial group; often such a district has a bizarre shape.

Gettysburg Address Famous speech by President Lincoln to dedicate the battlefield where many had fallen during the Civil War. Lincoln used the occasion to advance his ideal of equality and promote the Union.

Glasnost Mikhail Gorbachev's policy of opening the Soviet Union to the outside world by encouraging foreign investment, allowing more Soviet citizens to emigrate, and permitting multiparty elections in eastern Europe.

Globalization The international dispersion of economic activity through the networking of companies across national borders.

Going public The process in which Congress or its members carry an issue debate to the public via the media; e.g., televising floor debates or media appearances by individual members.

GOP Grand Old Party or Republican Party, which formed in 1856 after the Whig Party split. The GOP was abolitionist and a supporter of the Union.

Grace Commission A special commission established by President Ronald Reagan to recommend ways of cutting government waste.

Grandfather clause A device used in the South to prevent blacks from voting; such clauses exempted those whose grandfathers had the right to vote before 1867 from having to fulfill various requirements that most people could not meet. Since no blacks could vote before 1867, they could not qualify for the exemption.

Grand jury A jury of citizens who meet in private session to evaluate accusations in a given **criminal case** and to determine if there is enough evidence to warrant a trial.

Grants-in-aid Federal money provided to state and, occasionally, local governments to establish programs to help people such as the aged poor or the unemployed; began during the New Deal.

Grassroots lobbying The mass mobilization of members of an **interest group** to apply pressure to public officials, usually in the form of a mass mailing.

Great Compromise The decision of the **Constitutional Convention** to have a bicameral legislature in which representation in one house would be by population and in the other house, by states; also called the Connecticut Compromise.

Habeas corpus Latin for "have ye the body." A writ of habeas corpus is a means for criminal defendants who have exhausted appeals in state courts to appeal to a federal **district court.**

Hatch Act A statute enacted in 1939 that limits the political activities of federal employees in partisan campaigns.

Head of state The president's role as a national symbol of collective unity and pride.

Health maintenance organization (HMO) A group of doctors who agree to provide full health care for a fixed monthly charge.

Home rule The grant of considerable autonomy to a local government.

Honoraria Legal payments made to legislators who speak before **interest groups** or other groups of citizens.

Horse race coverage The way in which the media reports on the candidates' polling status and strategies, rather than covering their positions on relevant issues.

Hyperpluralism The idea that it is difficult for government to arrive at a solution to problems because **interest groups** have become so numerous and so many groups have a "veto" on issues affecting them.

ICBM Intercontinental ballistic missiles, or land-based missiles.

Identity politics The practice of organizing on the basis of sex, ethnic or racial identity, or sexual orientation to compete for public resources and influence public policy.

Ideology A highly organized and coherent set of opinions.

Impeachment and removal A two-step process by which Congress may remove presidents, judges, and other civil officers accused of malfeasance. The House decides questions of impeachment; if a majority favors impeachment, the Senate decides whether to remove the accused from office.

Imperial presidency A term that came into use at the end of the 1960s to describe the growing power of the presidency.

Implied powers clause The clause in the U.S. Constitution that gives Congress the power to make all laws "**necessary and proper**" for carrying out its specific powers.

Impoundment A refusal by the president to spend money appropriated by Congress for a specific program.

Incrementalism A congressional spending pattern in which budgets usually increase slightly from year to year.

Independent A voter who is not aligned with any political party.

Independent agencies Government bureaus that are not parts of **departments.** Their heads are appointed by and responsible to the president.

Independent counsel See **Special prosecutor.**

Independent expenditures Campaign contributions made on behalf of issues or candidates, but not made directly to candidates or political parties.

Independent spending Spending on political campaigns by groups not under the control of the candidates.

Indirect democracy A system of government in which citizens elect representatives to make decisions for them.

Indirect lobbying Attempts to influence legislators through such nontraditional means as letter-writing campaigns.

Individualistic political culture One of three primary political cultures in the United States. One in which politics is seen as a way of getting ahead, of obtaining benefits for oneself or one's group, and in which corruption is tolerated. See also **moralistic** and **traditionalistic political cultures.**

Inflation The situation in which prices increase but wages and salaries fail to keep pace with the prices of goods.

Influence peddling Using one's access to powerful people to make money, as when former government officials use access to former colleagues to win high-paying jobs in the private sector.

Informal norms Unwritten customs that help keep Congress running smoothly by attempting to diminish friction and competition among the members.

Infotainment Television news stories that, without any sacrifice of probity or responsibility, display the attributes of fiction, of drama.

Injunction A court order demanding that a person or group perform a specific act or refrain from performing a specific act.

Inquisition A medieval institution of the Roman Catholic Church used to identify and punish heretics.

Institutional approach An investigation of government that focuses on institutions, such as Congress or the civil service, and their rules and procedures.

Institutional loyalty An **informal norm** of Congress that calls for members to avoid criticizing their colleagues and to treat each other with mutual respect; eroded in recent decades.

Interest groups Organizations that try to achieve at least some of their goals with government assistance.

Investigative reporting In-depth news reporting, particularly that which exposes corruption and wrongdoing on the part of government officials and big institutions.

Iroquois Confederacy An association of Native Americans in what is now New York State that was based on the principles of **checks and balances and federalism,** among other things.

Isolationism A policy of noninvolvement with other nations outside the Americas; generally followed by the United States during the nineteenth and early twentieth centuries.

Issue consistency The extent to which individuals who identify themselves as "**liberal**" or "**conservative**" take issue positions that reflect their professed leanings.

Issue voting Refers to citizens who vote for candidates whose stands on specific issues are consistent with their own.

Jeffersonian Republicans (Jeffersonians) Opponents of a strong national government. They challenged the **Federalists** in the early years of the Republic.

Jim Crow laws Laws enacted in southern states that segregated schools, public accommodations, and almost all other aspects of life.

Joint resolutions Measures that have the force of law and must be approved by both houses of Congress and signed by the president.

Judicial review The authority of the courts to declare laws or actions of government officials unconstitutional.

Junkets Trips by members of Congress to desirable locations with expenses paid by lobbyists; the trips are ostensibly made to fulfill a "speaking engagement" or conduct a "fact-finding tour."

Jurisdiction The authority of a court to hear and decide cases.

Justices of the peace Magistrates at the lowest level of some state court systems, responsible mainly for acting on minor offenses and committing cases to higher courts for trial.

Keating 5 Senators Alan Cranston, John McCain, Donald Riegle, John Glenn, and Dennis DeConcini, who were investigated by the Senate for ethics violations in connection with campaign contributions they received from financier/developer Charles Keating. All later intervened on his behalf with federal regulators.

Keynesian economics The argument by John Maynard Keynes that government should stimulate the economy during periods of high unemployment by increasing spending even if it must run **deficits** to do so; the deficits would be made up by higher employment and thus higher tax revenues during periods of prosperity.

Kitchen cabinet A group of informal advisers, usually longtime associates, who assist the president on public policy questions.

Know-Nothing Party An extreme right-wing party in mid-nineteenth-century America that opposed Catholics and immigrants.

Korematsu **v.** *United States* After the attack on Pearl Harbor during World War II, Fred Korematsu and many other Japanese Americans were relocated (by presidential order) to detention camps in inland states. Korematsu claimed that the order discriminated against him on the basis of his race and thereby violated his Fifth Amendment right to due process of law. On appeal, the U.S. Supreme Court upheld the order excluding 120,000 Japanese Americans from the West Coast. The majority held that the government could take precautions to prevent espionage and sabotage during wartime.

Lame duck An officeholder, legislature, or administration that has lost an election but holds power until the inauguration of a successor.

Landslide An election won by a candidate who receives an overwhelming majority of the votes, such as more than a 10-point gap.

Leaks Disclosures of information that some government officials want kept secret.

Legislative calendar An agenda or calendar containing the names of all bills or resolutions of a particular type to be considered by committees or either legislative chamber.

Legislative veto A congressional **oversight** tool that allows one or both houses to block agency actions. Though the legislative veto was held unconstitutional by the Supreme Court in 1983, legislation with provisions for legislative vetoes continues to be passed, and agencies continue to honor the vetoes.

Libel Printed or broadcast statements that are false and tarnish someone's reputation.

Liberal A person who believes in a national government that is active in domestic policies, providing help to individuals and communities in such areas as health, education, and welfare.

Limited government A government that is strong enough to protect the people's rights but not so strong as to threaten those rights; in the view of John Locke, such a government was established through a **social contract.**

Line-Item veto A proposal that would give a president the power to veto one or more provisions of a bill while allowing the remainder of the bill to become law.

Literacy tests Examinations ostensibly carried out to ensure that voters could read and write but actually a device used in the South to disqualify blacks from voting.

Litigation Legal action.

Lobbying The efforts of **interest groups** to influence government.

Majority leader The member of the majority party in the House of Representatives who is second in command to the **Speaker.** Also, the leader of the Senate, who is chosen by the majority party.

Majority-minority district A congressional district whose boundaries are drawn to give a minority group a majority in the district.

Managed competition An aspect of the Clinton health care plan that involved joining employers and individuals into large groups or cooperatives to purchase health insurance.

Mandamus, writ of A court order demanding government officials or a lower court to perform a specified duty.

Mandate A term used in the media to refer to a president having clear directions from the voters to take a certain course of action; in practice, it is not always clear that a president, even one elected by a large majority, has a mandate or, if so, for what.

Mandatory spending Spending by the federal government that is required by permanent laws; e.g., payments for **Medicare.**

Marble cake federalism The idea that different levels of government work together in carrying out policies; governments are intermixed, as in a marble cake.

Marbury **v.** *Madison* The 1803 case in which the U.S. Supreme Court enunciated the doctrine of **judicial review.**

Market share The number of members of an **interest group** compared to its potential membership; having a large market share is an advantage.

Markup The process in which a congressional subcommittee rewrites a bill after holding hearings on it.

McCain–Feingold Act Also known as the Bipartisan Campaign Finance Reform Act of 2001, this legislation was created to regulate campaign financing. It limited the amount of gifts and banned soft money contributions to the national parties but not to certain types of private groups.

McCarthyism Methods of combating communism characterized by irresponsible accusations made on the basis of little or no evidence; named after Senator Joseph McCarthy of Wisconsin who used such tactics in the 1950s.

McCulloch v. Maryland An 1819 U.S. Supreme Court decision that broadly interpreted Congress's powers under the **implied powers clause.**

McGovern–Fraser Commission A commission formed after 1968 by the Democratic Party to consider changes making convention delegates more representative of all Democratic voters.

Means test An eligibility requirement for poverty programs under which participants must demonstrate that they have low income and few assets.

Media event An event, usually consisting of a speech and a photo opportunity, that is staged for television and is intended to convey a particular impression of a politician's position on an issue.

Media malaise A feeling of cynicism and distrust toward government and officials that is fostered by media coverage of politics.

Medicaid A federal-state medical assistance program for the poor.

Medicare A public health insurance program that pays many medical expenses of the elderly and the disabled; funded through **Social Security** taxes, general revenues, and premiums paid by recipients.

Merit system A system of filling bureaucratic jobs on the basis of competence instead of **patronage.**

Minimum tax A proposed tax that would require corporations and individuals with high incomes to pay a certain minimum amount in federal taxes.

Minority leader The leader of the minority party in either the House of Representatives or the Senate.

Miranda rights A means of protecting a criminal suspect's **rights against self-incrimination** during police interrogation. Before interrogation, suspects must be told that they have a right to remain silent; that anything they say can be used against them; that they have a right to an attorney; and that if they cannot afford an attorney, one will be provided for them. The rights are named after the case *Miranda v. Arizona.*

MIRV Stands for multiple independently targeted reentry vehicles; an offensive missile system that uses a single rocket to launch a number of warheads, each of which could be aimed at a different target.

"Mischiefs of faction" A phrase used by James Madison in the *Federalist Papers* to refer to the threat to the nation's stability that factions could pose.

Misdemeanors Crimes of less seriousness than **felonies,** ordinarily punishable by fine or imprisonment in a local rather than a state institution.

Missouri Compromise of 1820 A set of laws by which Congress attempted to control slavery in the territories, maintaining the balance between slave and nonslave states.

Mixed economies Countries that incorporate elements of both capitalist and socialist practices in the workings of their economies.

Monetary policy Actions taken by the **Federal Reserve Board** to regulate the economy through changes in short-term interest rates and the money supply.

Monopoly One or a few firms that control a large share of the market for certain goods and can therefore fix prices.

Monroe Doctrine A doctrine articulated by President James Monroe in 1823 that warned European powers not already involved in Latin America to stay out of that region.

Moralistic political culture One of three political cultures in the United States. One in which people feel obligated to take part in politics to bring about change for the better, and in which corruption is not tolerated. See also **individualistic** and **traditionalistic political cultures.**

Most favored nation (MFN) Trade status granted to a trading partner that permits that nation to export goods to the United States under the most advantageous **tariff** arrangements that the United States allows.

Motor voter law A statute that allows people to register to vote at public offices such as welfare offices and drivers' license bureaus.

Muckrakers Reform-minded journalists in the early twentieth century who exposed corruption in politics and worked to break the financial link between business and politicians.

Multiparty system A type of political party system where more than two groups have a chance at winning an election.

Mutual assured destruction (MAD) The capability to absorb a nuclear attack and retaliate against the attacker with such force that it would also suffer enormous damage; believed to deter nuclear war during the **Cold War** because both sides would be so devastated that neither would risk striking first.

NAACP (National Association for the Advancement of Colored People) An organization founded in 1909 to fight for black rights; its attorneys challenged segregation in the courts and won many important court cases, most notably, ***Brown v. Board of Education.***

Nader's Raiders The name given to people who work in any of the "public interest" organizations founded by consumer advocate and regulatory watchdog Ralph Nader.

Nation-centered federalism The view that tthe Constitution was written by representatives of the people and and ratified by the people. Nation-centered federalists believe that the national government as the supreme power in the federal relationship. (Hamilton articulated this view in the *Federalist Papers*.) Nation-centered federalism was the view used by northerners to justify a war to prevent the southern states from seceding in 1861. The alternative view, state centered federalism, is the view that the Constitution was developed by states.

National chair The head of a political **party organization,** appointed by the **national committee** of that party, usually at the direction of the party's presidential nominee.

National committee The highest level of **party organization;** chooses the site of the national convention and the formula for determining the number of delegates from each state.

National debt The total amount of money owed by the federal government; the sum of all budget **deficits** over the years.

National Environmental Policy Act (NEPA) Legislation that mandates government agencies to prepare environmental impact statements for projects they fund.

National Organization for Women (NOW) A group formed in 1966 to fight primarily for political and economic rights for women.

NATO (North Atlantic Treaty Organization) A mutual defense pact established by the United States, Canada, and their western European allies in 1949 to protect against Soviet aggression in Europe; later expanded to include other European nations.

Natural rights Inalienable and inherent rights such as the right to own property (in the view of John Locke).

"Necessary and proper" A phrase in the **implied powers clause** of the U.S. Constitution that gives Congress the power to make all laws needed to carry out its specific powers.

Neutral competence The concept that bureaucrats should be uninvolved or neutral in policymaking and should be chosen only for their expertise—not their political affiliation.

New Deal A program of President Franklin D. Roosevelt's administration in the 1930s aimed at stimulating economic recovery and aiding victims of the Great Depression; led to expansion of the national government's role.

New Deal coalition The broadly based coalition of southern conservatives, northern liberals, and ethnic and religious minorities that sustained the Democratic Party for some 40 years.

New federalism During the Nixon administration, the policy under which unrestricted or minimally restricted federal funds were provided to states and localities; during the Reagan administration, a policy of reducing federal support for the states.

News release A printed handout given by public relations workers to members of the media, offering ideas or information for new stories.

Nineteenth Amendment An amendment to the Constitution, ratified in 1920, guaranteeing women the vote.

Nullification A doctrine advocated by supporters of state-centered federalism, holding that a state could nullify laws of Congress.

Obscenity Sexual material that is patently offensive to the average person in the community and that lacks any serious literary, artistic, or scientific value.

Obstruction of justice A deliberate attempt to impede the progress of a criminal investigation or trial.

Occupational Safety and Health Administration (OSHA) An agency formed in 1970 and charged with ensuring safe and healthful working conditions for all American workers.

Office of Management and Budget (OMB) A White House agency with primary responsibility for preparing the federal budget.

Open primary A primary election that is not limited to members of a particular party; a voter may vote in either party's primary.

Outsourcing (offshoring) Companies transfer of jobs abroad in order to increase their profit (because they pay foreign workers less).

Overlapping membership The term refers to the tendency of individuals to join more than one group. This tends to moderate a group's appeals, since its members also belong to other groups with different interests.

Oversight Congress's responsibility to make sure the bureaucracy is administering federal programs in accordance with congressional intent.

Parliamentary government A system in which voters elect only their representatives in parliament; the chief executive is chosen by parliament, as in Britain.

Party boss The head of a political "machine," a highly disciplined state or local **party organization** that controls power in its area.

Party caucus Meetings of members of political parties, often designed to select party nominees for office.

Party convention A gathering of party delegates, on the local, state, or national level, to set policy and strategy and to select candidates for elective office.

Party identification A psychological link between individuals and a political party that leads those persons to regard themselves as members of that party.

Party in government Those who are appointed or elected to office as members of a political party.

Party in the electorate Those who identify with a political party.

Party organization The "professionals" who run a political party at the national, state, and local levels.

Party system The configuration of parties in a political system. Usually noted in conjunction with the number of parties in the system—one party system, two party system, or multi party system.

Patronage A system in which elected officials appoint their supporters to administrative jobs; used by **political machines** to maintain themselves in power.

Pay-go ("pay-as-you-go") Budgetary rules adopted by Congress that set caps on spending and bars legislation to increase spending without offsetting cuts in spending or increases in revenue.

Pendleton Act of 1883 This act created the **Civil Service Commission,** designed to protect civil servants from arbitrary dismissal for political reasons and to staff bureaucracies with people who have proven their competence by taking competitive examinations.

Pentagon Papers A top-secret study, eventually made public, of how and why the United States became embroiled in the Vietnam War; the study was commissioned by Secretary of Defense Robert McNamara during the Johnson administration.

Permanent campaign The situation in which elected officials are constantly engaged in a campaign; fund-raising for the next election begins as soon as one election is concluded.

Personal presidency A concept proposed by Theodore Lowi that holds that presidents since the 1930s have amassed tremendous personal power directly from the people and, in return, are expected to make sure the people get what they want from government.

Photo op A "photo opportunity" that frames the politician against a backdrop that symbolizes the points the politician is trying to make.

Platform committee The group that drafts the policy statement of a political party's convention.

Plea bargain An agreement between the prosecutor, defense attorney, and defendant in which the prosecutor agrees to reduce the charge or sentence in exchange for the defendant's guilty plea.

Plebiscite A direct vote by all the people on a certain public measure. Theodore Lowi has spoken of the "Plebiscitary" presidency, whereby the president makes himself the focus of national government through use of the mass media.

Plessy v. Ferguson The 1896 case in which the U.S. Supreme Court upheld segregation by enunciating the **separate-but-equal doctrine.**

Pluralism The theory that American government is responsive to groups of citizens working together to promote their common interests and that enough people belong to **interest groups** to ensure that government ultimately hears everyone, even though most people do not participate actively in politics.

Pocket veto A legislative bill dies by pocket veto if a president refuses to sign it and Congress adjourns within 10 working days.

Policy implementation The process by which bureaucrats convert laws into rules and activities that have an actual impact on people and things.

Political action committee (PAC) A committee established by corporation, labor union, or **interest group** that raises money and contributes it to a political campaign.

Political bias A preference for candidates of particular parties or for certain stands on issues that affects a journalist's reporting.

Political culture A shared body of values and beliefs that shapes perceptions and attitudes toward politics and government and, in turn, influences political behavior.

Political equality The principle that every citizen of a democracy has an equal opportunity to try to influence government.

Political machines Political organizations based on **patronage** that flourished in big cities in the late nineteenth and early twentieth centuries. The machine relied on the votes of the lower classes and, in exchange, provided jobs and other services.

Political patronage Party leaders who, once in office, openly award government jobs and other benefits to their supporters.

Political socialization The process of learning about politics by being exposed to information from parents, peers, schools, the media, political leaders, and the community.

Political tolerance The willingness of individuals to extend procedural rights and liberties to people with whom they disagree.

Political trust The extent to which citizens place trust in their government, its institutions, and its officials.

Politics A means by which individuals and **interest groups** compete, via political parties and other extragovernmental organizations, to shape government's impact on society's problems and goals.

Poll tax A tax that must be paid before a person can vote; used in the South to prevent blacks from voting. The Twenty-fourth Amendment now prohibits poll taxes in federal elections.

Popular sovereignty Rule by the people.

Pork barrel Funding for special projects, buildings, and other public works in the district or state of a member of Congress. Members tend to support such projects because they provide jobs for constituents and enhance the members' reelection chances, rather than because the projects are necessarily wise.

Power to persuade The president's informal power to gain support by dispensing favors and penalties and by using the prestige of the office.

Precedents In law, judicial decisions that may be used subsequently as standards in similar cases.

Precinct The basic unit of the American electoral process—in a large city perhaps only a few blocks—designed for the administration of elections. Citizens vote in precinct polling places.

Preemption Military strategy of "striking first." Aggressively endorsed by the Bush national security team after the September 11, 2001 terrorist attacks.

Presidential immunity Immunity of the president from lawsuits for acts that occur during his term in office and are related to his official responsibilities.

Presidential preference primary A **direct primary** where voters select delegates to presidential nominating conventions; voters indicate a preference for a presidential candidate, delegates committed to a candidate, or both.

Presidential press conference A meeting at which the president answers questions from reporters.

Pressure group An organization representing specific interests that seeks some sort of government assistance or attempts to influence public policy. Also known as an **interest group.**

Pretrial hearings Preliminary examinations of the cases of persons accused of a crime.

Prior restraint Censorship by restraining an action before it has actually occurred; e.g., forbidding publication rather than punishing the publisher after publication has occurred.

Private interest groups Interest groups that chiefly pursue economic interests that benefit their members; e.g., business organizations and labor unions.

Probable cause In law, reasonable grounds for belief that a particular person has committed a particular crime.

Productivity The ratio of total hours worked by the labor force to total goods and services produced.

Professional association A **pressure group** that promotes the interests of a professional occupation, such as medicine, law, or teaching.

Progressive Movement Reform movement designed to wrest control from political machines and the lower-class immigrants they served. These reforms reduced corruption in politics, but they also seriously weakened the power of political parties.

Progressive reforms Election reforms introduced in the early twentieth century as part of the Progressive movement; included the secret ballot, primary elections, and voter registration laws.

Progressive tax A tax structured so that those with higher incomes pay a higher percentage of their income in taxes than do those with lower incomes.

Prohibition Party A political party founded in 1869 that seeks to ban the sale of liquor in the United States.

Proportional representation An election system based on election from multimember districts. The number of seats awarded to each party in a district is equal to the percentage of the total the party receives in the district. Proportional representation favors the multiparty system.

Protectionism Government intervention to protect domestic producers from foreign competition; can take the form of **tariffs,** quotas on imports, or a ban on certain imports altogether.

Public disclosure The requirement of names of campaign donors be made public.

Public forum A public place such as a street, sidewalk, or park where people have a First Amendment right to express their views on public issues.

Public interest A term generally denoting a policy goal, designed to serve the interests of society as a whole, or the largest number of people. Defining the public interest is the subject of intense debate on most issues.

Public interest groups Interest groups that chiefly pursue benefits that cannot be limited or restricted to their members.

Public opinion The collection of individual opinions toward issues or objects of general interest.

Pure speech Speech without any conduct (besides the speech itself).

Push poll A public opinion poll presenting the respondent with biased information favoring or opposing a particular candidate. The idea is to see whether certain "information" can "push" voters away from a candidate or a neutral opinion toward the candidate favored by those doing the poll. Push polls seek to manipulate opinion.

Quorum calls Often used as a delaying tactic, quorum calls are demands that all members of a legislative body be counted to determine if a quorum exists.

Racial profiling Practice that targets a particular group for attention from law enforcement based on racial stereotypes, A common occurrence is black drivers being stopped by police disproportionately.

Realignment The transition from one stable party system to another, as occurred when the **New Deal coalition** was formed.

Reapportionment The process of redistributing the 435 seats in the House of Representatives among the states based on population changes; occurs every 10 years based on the most recent census.

Recession Two or more consecutive three-month quarters of falling production.

Reciprocity An **informal norm** of Congress in which members agree to support each other's bills; also called logrolling.

Reconstruction The period after the **Civil War** when black rights were ensured by a northern military presence in the South and by close monitoring of southern politics; ended in 1877.

Reconstruction Amendments Three amendments (13th, 14th, and 15th), adopted after the Civil War from 1865 through 1870, that eliminated slavery (13), gave blacks the right to vote (15), and guaranteed due process rights for all (14)

Redistricting The process of redrawing the boundaries of congressional districts within a state to take account of population shifts.

Redlining The practice in which bankers and other lenders refused to lend money to persons who wanted to buy a house in a racially changing neighborhood.

"Red Scare" Prompted by the Russian Revolution in 1917, this was a large-scale crackdown on so-called seditious activities in the United States.

Reelection constituency Those individuals a member of Congress believes will vote for him or her. Differs from a geographical, loyalist, or personal constituency.

Regressive tax A tax structured so that those with lower incomes pay a larger percentage of their income in tax than do those with higher incomes.

Regulation The actions of regulatory agencies in establishing standards or guidelines conferring benefits or imposing restrictions on business conduct.

Rehnquist Court The U.S. Supreme Court under Chief Justice William Rehnquist (1986–); a conservative Court, but still has not overturned most previous rulings.

Religious tests Tests once used in some states to limit the right to vote or hold office to members of the "established church."

Republic A system of government in which citizens elect representatives to make decisions for them; an **indirect democracy.**

Reregulation The resumption of regulatory activity after a period of **deregulation.**

Responsible party government A term that implies a choice between politcal parties, voters who comprehend that choice, and elected officials who vote for their party's position.

Responsiveness The extent to which government conforms to the wishes of individuals, groups, or institutions.

Restrained judges Judges who are reluctant to overrule the other branches of government by declaring laws or actions of government officials unconstitutional.

Restrictive covenants Agreements among neighbors in white residential areas not to sell their houses to blacks.

Retrospective voting Voting for or against incumbents on the basis of their past performance.

Right against self-incrimination A right granted by the Fifth Amendment, providing that persons accused of a crime shall not be compelled to be witnesses against themselves.

Right to abortion U.S. Supreme Court ruling in *Roe v. Wade* (1973) established that women have a right to terminate a pregnancy during the first six months. States can prohibit an abortion during the last three months because at that time the fetus becomes viable—it can live outside the womb.

Right to a jury trial The Sixth Amendment's guarantee of a trial by jury in any **criminal case** that could result in more than six months' incarceration.

Right to counsel The Sixth Amendment's guarantee of the right of a criminal defendant to have an attorney in any **felony or misdemeanor** case that might result in incarceration; if defendants are indigent, the court must appoint an attorney for them.

Right to die Rehnquist court decision where individuals can refuse medical treatment, including food and water, even if this means they will die. Individuals must make their decision while competent and alert. They can also act in advance, preparing a "living will" or designating another person as a proxy to make the decision if they are unable to.

Right to privacy A right to autonomy—to be left alone—that is not specifically mentioned in the U.S. Constitution, but has been found by the U.S. Supreme Court to be implied through several amendments.

Risk assessment A cost–benefit analysis standard that weighs the benefits of a particular regulation (such as in lives saved) against the costs of implementation of the regulation by companies and agencies.

Rules Committee The committee in the House of Representatives that sets the terms of debate on a bill.

Sandinistas The name of the group that overthrew Nicaraguan dictator Anastasio Somoza in 1978 and governed Nicaragua until 1990.

Scientific polls Systematic, probability-based sampling techniques that attempt to gauge public sentiment based on the responses of a small, selected group of individuals.

Scoop To obtain information before another reporter; also the information so obtained.

Second Amendment "The right of the people to keep and bear arms." Some interpret this as an absolute right to own and use guns, others as only an indication that guns can be owned if one is part of a government militia.

Seditious speech Speech that encourages rebellion against the government.

Selective perception The tendency to screen out information that contradicts one's beliefs.

Senatorial courtesy The custom of giving senators of the president's party a virtual veto over appointments to jobs, including judicial appointments, in their states.

Senior Executive Service The SES was created in 1978 to attract high-ranking civil servants by offering them challenging jobs and monetary rewards for exceptional achievement.

Seniority rule The custom that the member of the majority party with the longest service on a particular congressional committee becomes its chair; applies most of the time but is occasionally violated.

Separate-but-equal doctrine The principle, enunciated by the U.S. Supreme Court in *Plessy v. Ferguson* in 1896, that allowed separate facilities for blacks and whites as long as the facilities were equal.

Separation of church and state Legal concept where government institutions are kept separate from religious ones.

Separation of powers The principle of government under which the power to make, administer, and judge the laws is split among three branches—legislative, executive, and judicial.

Setting the agenda Influencing the process by which problems are deemed important and alternative policies are proposed.

Sharecroppers Tenant farmers who lease land and equipment from landowners, turning over a share of their crops in lieu of rent.

Shays's Rebellion A revolt of farmers in western Massachusetts in 1786 and 1787 to protest the state legislature's refusal to grant them relief from debt; helped lead to calls for a new national **constitution.**

Shield laws Laws that protect news reporters from having to identify their sources of information.

Single-issue groups Interest groups that pursue a single public interest goal and are characteristically reluctant to compromise.

Single-member districts Where only one individual is elected from a particular electoral district.

Social choice An approach to political science based on the assumption that political behavior is determined by costs and benefits.

Social contract An implied agreement between the people and their government in which the people give up part of their liberty to the government in exchange for the government protecting the remainder of their liberty.

Social insurance A social welfare program such as **Social Security** that provides benefits only to those who have contributed to the program and their survivors.

Socialism An economic system in which the government owns the country's productive capacity—industrial plants and farms—and controls wages and the supply of and demand for goods; in theory, the people, rather than the government, collectively own the country's productive capacity.

Social issue An important, noneconomic issue affecting significant numbers of the populace, such as crime, racial conflict, or changing values.

Social Security A social welfare program for the elderly and the disabled.

Soft money Contributions to national party committees that do not have to be reported to the federal government (and sometimes not to the states) because they are used for voter registration drives, educating voters on the issues, and the like, rather than for a particular candidate; the national committees send the funds to the state parties, which

operate under less stringent reporting regulations than the federal laws provide.

Sound bite A few key words or phrase included in a speech with the intent that television editors will use the phrase in a brief clip on the news.

Speaker of the House The leader and presiding officer of the House of Representatives; chosen by the majority party.

Special interest caucuses Groups of members of the House of Representatives who are united by some personal interest or characteristic; e.g., the Black Caucus.

Specialization An **informal norm** of Congress that holds that since members cannot be experts in every area, some deference should be given to those who are most knowledgeable about a given subject related to their committee work.

Special prosecutor A prosecutor charged with investigating and prosecuting alleged violations of federal criminal laws by the president, vice president, senior government officials, members of Congress, or the judiciary.

Spectacle presidency Term used to describe presidents who are mostly seen by the public as actors in public spectacles, stage-managed photo ops, featuring the president in a dramatically staged event or setting.

Speech plus conduct Speech combined with conduct that is intended to convey ideas; e.g., a sit-in (conduct) where the protesters chant slogans (speech).

Spin What politicians do to portray themselves and their programs in the most favorable light, regardless of the facts, often shading the truth.

Split-ticket voting Voting for a member of one party for one office and another party for a different office, such as for a Republican presidential candidate but a Democratic House candidate.

Spoils system The practice of giving political supporters government jobs or other benefits.

Stagflation The combination of high inflation and economic stagnation with high unemployment that troubled the United States in the 1970s.

Standing committees Permanent congressional committees.

Standing to sue The principle that individuals or groups must themselves have lost rights and suffered harm before they can bring a lawsuit.

Stare decisis Latin for "stand by what has been decided." The rule that judges should follow **precedents** established in previous cases by their court or higher courts.

"Star Wars" The popular name for former President Reagan's proposed space-based nuclear defense system, known officially as the Strategic Defense Initiative.

State-centered federalism The view that our Constitutional system should give precedence to state sovereignty over that of the national government. State centered federalists argue that that the states created the national government and the states are superior to the federal government.

States' rights The belief that the power of the federal government should not be increased at the expense of the states' power.

Statistical Abstract Annual summary of reports published by the federal government.

Statutes Laws passed by the legislative body of a representative government.

Steering The practice in which realtors promoted segregation by showing blacks houses in black neighborhoods and whites houses in white neighborhoods.

Straw polls Unscientific polls.

Structural unemployment Joblessness that results from the rapidly changing nature of the economy, which displaces, for example, auto and steel industry workers.

Subcommittee bill of rights Measures introduced by Democrats in the House of Representatives in 1973 and 1974 that allowed members of a committee to choose subcommittee chairs and established a fixed jurisdiction and adequate budget and staff for each subcommittee.

Subgovernment A mutually supportive group comprising a **pressure group,** an executive agency, and a congressional committee or subcommittee with common policy interests that makes public policy decisions with little interference from the president or Congress as a whole and little awareness by the public. Also known as an iron triangle.

Subpoena A court order requiring someone to appear in court to give testimony under penalty of punishment.

Suffrage The right to vote.

Sunshine Act Adopted in 1977, this act requires that most government meetings be conducted in public and that notice of such meetings must be posted in advance.

Superdelegates Democratic delegates, one-fifth of the total sent to the national convention who are appointed by Democratic Party organizations, in order to retain some party control over the convention. Most are public officials, such as members of Congress.

Superfund Revenue from a tax imposed on industry, along with federal funds, that is used for cleaning up hazardous waste sites.

Super Tuesday The day when most southern states hold **presidential preference primaries** simultaneously.

Super waiver Blanket exemptions that free states from federal program standards and requirements and give them greater latitude to set standards and eligibility requirements. Has been applied to welfare programs.

Supplemental Security Income (SSI) A program that provides supplemental income for those who are blind, elderly, or disabled and living in poverty.

Supply-side economics The argument that tax revenues will increase if tax rates are reduced; supposedly, more money will be available for business expansion and modernization, which will stimulate employment and economic growth and result in higher tax revenues.

Supremacy clause A clause in the U.S. Constitution stating that treaties and laws made by the national government are to be supreme over state laws in cases of conflict.

Symbiotic relationship A relationship in which the parties use each other for mutual advantage.

Symbolic speech The use of symbols, rather than words, to convey ideas; e.g., wearing black armbands or burning the U.S. flag to protest government policy.

Tariff A special tax or "duty" imposed on imported or exported goods.

Tax deductions Certain expenses or payments that may be deducted from one's taxable income.

Tax exemptions Certain amounts deductible from one's annual income in calculating income tax.

Teapot Dome scandal A 1921 scandal in which President Warren Harding's secretary of the interior received large contributions from corporations that were then allowed to lease oil reserves (called the Teapot Dome); led to the Federal Corrupt Practices Act of 1925, which required reporting of campaign contributions and expenditures.

Temporary Assistance for Needy Families (TANF) A program that provides income support for the poor; successor to Aid to Families with Dependent Children (AFDC).

Tenth Amendment Constitutional amendment stating that powers not delegated to the federal government nor prohibited to the states are reserved to the states and to the people. This amendment has generally not had much impact, though a few recent Supreme Court cases have referred to it.

Third party A political party made up of independents or dissidents from the major parties, often advocating radical change or pushing single issues.

Three-fifths Compromise The decision of the **Constitutional Convention** that three-fifths of a state's slave population would be counted in apportioning seats in the House of Representatives.

Ticket splitting Voting for a member of one party for a high-level office and a member of another party for a different high-level office.

Title IX Equal Opportunity in Education Act that forbids discrimination on the basis of sex in schools and colleges that receive federal aid. The amendment was prompted by discrimination against women by colleges, especially in admissions and financial aid.

Trade association An **interest** or **pressure group** that represents a single industry, such as builders.

Traditionalistic political culture One of three political cultures in the United States. One in which politics is left to a small elite and is viewed as a way to maintain the status quo. See **individualistic** and **moralistic political cultures.**

Tragedy of the commons The concept that although individuals benefit when they exploit goods that are common to all such as air and water, the community as a whole suffers from the pollution and depletion of resources that occur; a reason for **regulation.**

Treason The betrayal of one's country by knowingly aiding its enemies.

Truth in labeling The requirement that manufacturers, lenders, and other business entities provide certain kinds of information to consumers or employees.

Turnout The proportion of eligible citizens who vote in an election.

Two-party system Only two parties have a realistic chance of winning most political offices. This system is rare among other nations of the world but common in America.

Unanimous consent agreements Procedures by which a legislative body may dispense with standard rules and limit debate and amendments.

Underdogs Candidates for public office who are thought to have little chance of being elected.

Unfunded mandates Federal laws that require the states to do something without providing full funding for the required activity.

Unitary system A system in which the national government is supreme; subnational governments are created by the national government and have only the power it allocates to them.

United Nations An international organization formed in 1945 for the purpose of promoting peace and worldwide cooperation. It is headquartered in New York.

Unreasonable searches and seizures Searches and arrests that are conducted without a warrant or that do not fall into one of the exceptions to the warrant requirement; prohibited by the Fourth Amendment.

Unscientific polls Unsystematic samplings of popular sentiments; also known as **straw polls.**

Vietnam syndrome An attitude of uncertainty about U.S. foreign policy goals and our ability to achieve them by military means; engendered among the public and officials as a result of the U.S. failure in Vietnam.

Voting Rights Act (VRA) A law passed by Congress in 1965 that made it illegal to interfere with anyone's right to vote. The act and its subsequent amendments have been the main vehicles for expanding and protecting minority voting rights.

War Powers Resolution A 1973 statute enacted by Congress to limit the president's ability to commit troops to combat.

Warren Court The U.S. Supreme Court under Chief Justice Earl Warren (1953–1969); an activist Court that expanded the rights of criminal defendants and racial and religious minorities.

Watergate scandal The attempt to break into Democratic National Committee headquarters in 1972 that ultimately led to President Richard M. Nixon's resignation for his role in attempting to cover up the break-in and other criminal and unethical actions.

Weber, Max German social scientist, author of pioneering studies on the nature of bureaucracies.

Whigs Members of the Whig Party, founded in 1834 by National Republicans and several other factions who opposed Jacksonian Democrats.

Whips Members of the House of Representatives who work to maintain party unity by keeping in contact with party members and attempting to win their support. Both the majority and the minority party have a whip and several assistant whips.

Whistleblower An individual employee who exposes mismanagement and abuse of discretion in an agency.

White primary A device for preventing blacks from voting in the South. Under the pretense that political parties were private clubs, blacks were barred from voting in Democratic primaries, which were the real elections because Democrats always won the general elections.

Whitewater investigation An investigation conducted by a **special prosecutor** into the activities of President Bill Clinton and Hillary Rodham Clinton in connection with an Arkansas land deal and other alleged wrongdoings.

Winner-take-all The outcome of an election where only one individual is elected from a district or state, the individual who receives the most votes. It is contrasted with multi member systems where more than one person wins seats in an election.

Wire services News-gathering organizations such as the Associated Press and United Press International that provide news stories and other editorial features to the media organizations that are their members.

Writ of *certiorari* An order issued by a higher court to a lower court to send up the record of a case for review; granting the writ is the usual means by which the U.S. Supreme Court agrees to hear a case.

Yuppies Young upwardly mobile professionals.

INDEX

Page numbers in boldface refer to photographs and tables

AAM (American Agriculture Movement), 169
AARP (American Association for Retired People), 22, 161, 162, 164, 176, 180, 195
ABC, Inc., 101, 122, 123
Abolitionist movement, 539
Abortion
   access to, 497
   and AMA, 539
   and issue voting, 228
   number of in U.S., **493**
   parental notification requirements, 494
   partial-birth abortions, 494
   pharmaceuticals used to induce, 498
   political parties' stances on, 202, 262
   as privacy right, 492–498
   pro-life groups, 179, 184, 189, 493, 494, 496–497, 501
   protest restrictions, 473
   public funding of, 493–494
   right to, 493
   Roe v. Wade, 179, 430, 456, 493–494, 497
   teenage rates of, 495
   waiting periods, 494
Abscam, 308
Absentee ballots, 244–245, 253
Accounting industry, 286–287, 311–313, 629
ACLU (American Civil Liberties Union), 184–185, 448, 657
ACT (America Coming Together), 254, 296
Activist judges, 430, 451–452
ADA (Americans with Disabilities Act), 73, 412, 449–450
Adams, Abigail, 366
Adams, Charles Francis, 33
Adams, Henry, 391
Adams, John
   appointment of Marshall to chief justice, 432
   on congressional representation, 319
   on democracy, 37
   election of 1796, 206, 271
   on political parties, 206
   speeches, 381
Adams, John Quincy, 97, 206, 273, 381
Adams, Louisa, 366
Adjudication, 413
Administration, of policy, 411–412
Administrative Procedure Act (APA) (1946), 403, 407, 413, 628
Adversarial relationship, between media and politicians, 131–133

Advertising
   political ads, 151, 251, 268, 270, 290, 294, 298
   and profit of media companies, 145
Advocacy groups, 165
Advocacy media, bias of, 139–140
AFDC (Aid to Families with Dependent Children), 596–597
Affirmative action, 112, 437, 547–550
Afghanistan war, 136, 654, 655, 680
AFL-CIO (American Federation of Labor-Congress of Industrial Organizations), 165, 167, 169, 187, 302
Africa, AIDS in, 687
African Americans. *See also* Civil rights movement; Race discrimination; Slaves and slavery
   abortions, 495
   affirmative action, 112, 437, 547–550
   "brown bag tests," 514
   census identification, 14, 15
   citizenship rights, 50
   in Congress, 320, 322
   congressional caucuses for, 345
   and congressional redistricting, 240–241
   current status of, 528–531
   federal employees, 400
   and Florida's 2000 election problems, 243
   Great Migration of, 512
   interest groups, 174
   Lincoln's view of, 48–49
   as national convention delegates, 261
   news media's portrayal of, 146
   party identification, 226
   as political officeholders, 240
   political participation of, 21
   political power, 550
   prejudice against, 530
   as presidential candidates, 257
   public opinion of, 109–112
   separatist movements, 528
   as slave owners, 509
   as Southern Democrats, 216
   teenage pregnancy rates, 495
   voting rights, 12, 50, 237–240, 510, 512, 514
Age
   and campaign participation, 255
   congressional eligibility requirements, 317
   and political orientation, 12
   and political participation, 21
   presidential eligibility requirements, 359
   and voter turnout, 250

Agencies and departments, 408–411. *See also* Bureaucracy; *specific departments and agencies*
Agency for International Development (USAID), 681, 684
Agenda, setting the, 150–151
Agents, of political socialization, 91–96
Agnew, Spiro, 141, 309, 360
Agriculture. *See* Farmers and farming
Agriculture Department, **409**, 413, 420, 599
AIDS, 150, 175, 183, 418–419, 499, 687
Aid to Dependent Children, 71
Aid to Families with Dependent Children (AFDC), 596–597
Air Force, 422, 457
Air Force One, 373
Airline industry, 170, 182, 623, 632, 634–635
Air pollution, 619–620, 621, 639–640, 646
Airport screening, 529, 635
Air Transportation Stabilization Board (ATSB), 635
Alabama
   affirmative action programs, 548
   right to counsel in, 490
Alaska Public Interest Research Group, 185
Albert Lea, Minnesota, Seaboard Corporation's tax breaks, 607
Albright, Madeleine, 662
Al-Jazeera, 154–155
Alliances, military, 680
Al-Qaeda, **144**, 150, 654, 664, 679
AMA (American Medical Association), 192, 539, 608
Amazon.com, **554**
Ambassadors, 363, 676–677
Amendments, to Constitution. *See also specific amendments*
   Bill of Rights, 44, 45, 48, 465, 466
   campaign finance proposal, 299
   flag burning proposal, 474
   process of, 45, 48
   during Reconstruction, 50–51
   same-sex marriage ban proposal, 174
   states' ratification of, 45
America Coming Together (ACT), 254, 296
American Agriculture Movement (AAM), 169
American Bar Association, 492
American Bus Association, 170
American Civil Liberties Union (ACLU), 184–185, 448, 657
American Farm Bureau Federation, 169

American Independent Party, 204
American Medical Association (AMA), 192, 539, 608
American people, demographic profile of, 6–12
American Psychiatric Association, 175
The American Rifleman, 165
Americans for Generational Equity, 176
American Shore and Beach Preservation Association, 170–171
Americans with Disabilities Act (ADA), 73, 412, 449–450
"American system" of democracy, 16–20
Amish, 481
Amnesty International, 172
Amtrak (National Railroad Passenger Corporation), 411
Anarchists, **189**
Anderson, John, 264
Anglican Church, 11
Anthony, Susan B., 242, 539
Anthrax scare, 147
Antiabortion groups, 179, 184, 189, 493, 494, 496–497, 501
Antiballistic missiles (ABMs), 672
Anti-Federalists, vs. Federalists, 43–44
Antitrust law, 623, 624, 631
Antiwar protests, 188
APA (Administrative Procedure Act) (1946), 403, 407, 413, 628
Appointments, political by president, 379, 408, 410, 420
Appropriations, 341–342
Arab Americans, 15, 528–529
Archer-Daniels-Midland (ADM), 172
Aristotle, 5
Arizona, voting rights of Native Americans, 536
Arkansas, farming in, 589, 591, 616
Armey, Dick, 225
Army of God, 179
Arsenic, 643
Arthur Andersen, 311–312
Articles of Confederation, 31–33, 37, 43, 45, 62, 317
Ashcroft, John, 179, 405, 425, 471, 620, **659**
Asian Americans
   in Congress, 320
   federal employees, 400
   internment of Japanese Americans, 10, 377, 507–508, 551
   as national convention delegates, 261
   party identification, 217, 227
   public opinion, 112
Assassinations, of presidents, 360
Assault weapons ban, 179

Assembly, freedom of, 472
The Assembly on Federal Issues, 81
Assimilation, of Native Americans, 536
Assisted suicide, 501–502
Associated Press (AP), 122
Association, freedom of, 474–475
Asymmetrical warfare, 679
Atheists, 174
Atomic Energy Commission, 641
Atomic weapons. *See* Nuclear weapons
ATSB (Air Transportation Stabilization
    Board), 635
Attorneys
    members of congress as, 320
    right to, 490–491
    women as, 538–539
Auditing firms, 286, 311
Authoritarian governments, 62
Authorizations (budgeting), 341–342
Automobile industry, 184, 192, 303, 582

Babbitt, Bruce, 261, 647
Baker, James, 368
Baker v. Carr, 319
Bakke, University of California v., 548–549
Balanced budget, 574, 578–579, 580
Balance of power, 24
Baldwin, Tammy, 248–249
Ballots, **212,** 240, 243, 244–245, 247
Bank of the United States, 67
Bankruptcy, 574
Banks and banking
    Equal Credit Opportunity Act (1974),
        543
    Federal Reserve System, 410, 420,
        563–565, 566
    Glass-Steagall Act, 636
    and inflation, 560
    mortgages to blacks, 526
    redlining, 521
    regulation, 632–633, 636
    reserve requirements, 564
    S&L crisis, 632–633
Barbour, Haley, 182, 303
Battleground states, 265, 270
Bauer, Gary, 258
Bedford, Gunning, 35
Belgium, health care system, 609
Belknap, Jeremy, 37
Benham, Flip, 497
Berlin Wall, 673
Bernstein, Carl, 29, **30**
Bertelsmann, 122
BIA (Bureau of Indian Affairs), 536, 537
Bias, of news media, 138–150, 158
Biden, Joseph, 332, 653, 654, 688
Bilingual education, 533–534
Bill of Rights, 44, 45, 48, 465, 466
Bills. *See also* Legislation
    appropriations, 341–342
    authorizations, 341–342
    becoming law, 338
    committee action, 336, 339
    conference committees, 338
    debates over, 336–337
    introduction of, 336
    presidential vetoes, 338–339, 373–
        374
    scheduling of, 336
    voting on, 338
Bills of attainder, 465
Bin Laden, Osama, 150, 154
Bionda, Carole, 295
Biotechnology, 183, 437, 637
BIPAC (Business Industry Political action
    Committee), 191
Bipartisan Campaign Finance Reform
    Act, 291–292
Bipartisanship, 224–225, 383
Birdwatchers, 645
Birth control, 492, 493, 498
Black, Hugo, **436,** 447, 466, 467, 482–
    483, 516
Black Caucus, 345
"Black Codes," 510
Blackmun, Harry, 441, 451, 455, 493

Black power movement, 520
Blacks. *See* African Americans
Blair, Tony, 252
Block-busting, 521
Block grants, 71
Blogs, 126, 297
"Blowback," 681
Blue-collar workers, 216, 320, 572
"Blue" states, 265–267
BOB (Bureau of the Budget), 365, 420
Bonauto, Mary, **176**
Bonilla, Henry, 629
Bonoir, David, 315
Boorda, Mike, 119–120, 158
Border patrol, 488, 532
Bork, Robert, 442, 520
Bosnia, 680
Bowling Alone, 21, 165
Boxer, Barbara, 182
Boycotts, Montgomery bus boycott,
    190–191, 518
Boy Scouts, 475
Bradley, Bill, 125
Bradley, Joseph, 538–539
Bradwell, Myra, 538
Brandeis, Louis, 20, 451, 452, 454, 492
Braun, Carol Mosely, 235
Brennan, William, 455, 474, 477, 492
Brewer, David, 482
Breyer, Stephen, 444, 453
Bribery, 288–290, 309
Briefs, submissions to Supreme Court,
    453
Bristol-Myers Squibb, 168
Britain. *See* Great Britain
"Brown bag tests," 514
Brownlow Committee, 420
Brown University, and Title IX, 545
Brown v. Board of Education, 515–516
Bryan, William Jennings, 210, **256,** 386
Bubble concept, 639–640
Buchanan, James, 208, **390**
Buchanan, Patrick, 10, 205, 245
Buddhists, number in U.S., 11
Budget and Accounting Act (1921), 372
Budget deficits, 563, 574–580, 611
Budgets and budgeting
    balanced budget amendment, 574,
        578–579, 580
    of Bush (George W.) administration,
        575
    congressional duties and powers, 340,
        341–342, 372, 578–579
    deficits, 563, 574–580, 611
    and inflation, 574–575
    presidential duties and powers, 341,
        372, 574–576
    of Reagan administration, 574–575
Bumpers, Dale, 187
Bureaucracy. *See also* Federal employees
    access to public documents, 403–406
    as big government symbol, 399
    cabinet departments, 408, **409**
    citizens' influence over, 422
    congressional oversight of, 339–340,
        399, 420–421, 423
    court actions, 421
    duties and responsibilities, 411–413
    features of, 401
    Founding Fathers' vision of, 406
    goals of, 401–402
    government corporations, 410–411
    growth of, 406–408
    independent agencies, 408–409,
        412–413
    independent regulatory boards and
        commissions, 409–410, 413
    interest groups' influence over, 421–
        423
    meetings, 406
    merit system, 415–417
    openness of, 401, 403–406, 421
    performance standards, 402–403
    presidential oversight of, 380, 417,
        420, 423
    presidents' criticism of, 399

vs. private sector, 401, 403
responsiveness of, 423–424
role of, 399
rule making, 403, 412, 413
stereotypes, 399, 401
structure of, 401
Bureau of Indian Affairs (BIA), 536, 537
Bureau of Land Management, 605–606
Bureau of the Budget (BOB), 365, 420
Burger, Warren, 55, 437, 441, 447, 487
Burger Court
    abortion, 493
    affirmative action, 549
    Brennan's influence over, 455
    busing, 517–518
    capital punishment, 491
    characteristics of, 437
    and civil liberties, 502
    First Amendment rights, 472
    Miranda rights, 489
    news source confidentiality, 476
    obscenity ruling, 478
    public school funding, 533
    religious freedom, 481, 485
    right to counsel, 490
    search and seizure, 488
    sex discrimination ruling, 541, 546
Burton, Dan, 405
Bush, Barbara, 366
Bush, George H. *See also* Persian Gulf
    War
    and access to public documents, 405
    approval ratings, 387, **388**
    bureaucracy under, 407
    campaign image (1992), 268
    and Congress, 374, 375
    congressional gains/losses for party
        during administration, **371**
    economic policy through persuasion,
        565
    election of 1980, 256
    election of 1988, 271
    election of 1992, 229
    e-mail as public record, 406
    environmental policy, 638
    and the Fed, 566
    flag burning amendment, 474
    foreign policy, 659, 660, 673
    Gulf War, 269, 373
    judicial appointments, 441
    national debt during administration,
        574
    and news media, 133
    Panama invasion, 378
    pardons of, 363
    pictures of, **358, 361, 378**
    presidential effectiveness, 391
    public opinion of, 91
    regulatory policy, 628
    Supreme Court appointments, 129,
        437, 442, 443–444
    vice presidency of, 361
    White House staff, 365
    and Willie Horton ad, 215
Bush, George W. *See also* Election of
    2000; Election of 2004; Iraq War
    and access to public documents after
        9/11, 404–405
    appointments of, 416
    approval ratings, 89, 91, 116
    bipartisanship efforts, 224
    budget projections, 575
    and bureaucracy, 399, 407–408, 420
    campaign financing, 291, 292, 295,
        297, 299
    and Cheney, 370
    conflicts of interest, 308
    and Congress, 203, 221, 224, 225,
        338, 350, 373, 374, 375, 383–
        383
    congressional gains/losses for party
        during administration, **371**
    and conservative Christians, 174
    conservative domestic agenda, 116
    debate style, 272–273
    economic policy, 567, 575

e-mail usage, 406
and Enron, 302–303
environmental policy, 167, 178, 620,
    638, 643–644, 646, 649
executive orders, 380, 383
executive privilege, 381, 383
expansion of presidential power, 382–
    383, 389
federalism view, 73
financial supporters of, 306
foreign policy, 378, 660, 674–676,
    685
gay issues, 81, 176
government growth under, 581–582
government spending under,
    580
Guantanamo Bay prisoners, 463–464
and Hispanic voters, 217
ideology of, 108
image of, 386
judicial appointments, 441, 442
late night show jokes about, 105
"Leave No Child Behind" program,
    75, 80
mandate of, 280
missile defense plan, 185
moderate positions, 203–204
"moral values," 267
national debt during administration,
    574
and news media, 131, 135, 139
and NRA, 178–179
on *Oprah Winfrey Show,* 125
and Patriot Act, 471
personality and style of, 228
personal tax rate, 569
picture of, **267, 358, 364, 370, 659**
polls, use of, 101
prescription drug proposal, 162, 195,
    199–200
presidency of, 369, 384, 392
and public opinion, 89–90, 116
regulatory policy, 628, 631–632, 636
Social Security privatization plan, 612
speeches, 135, 386
tax policy, 567, 571, 573
time spent away from Washington,
    381–382
welfare reform, 613, 614
White House staff, 368
Yucca Mountain nuclear waste storage
    facility, 85
Bush, Laura, 366, 367
Bush v. Gore, 129, 429–431, 458–460
Business cycles, 560–561, 583
Business Industry Political action Com-
    mittee (BIPAC), 191
Business organizations, 166–167, 193
Busing, 516–518
Byrd, Robert, 142

CAB (Civil Aeronautics Board), 634
Cabinet, 365, 379, 406, 408, **409,** 417
Cable television, 122, 123, 124, 636
CAGW (Citizens Against Government
    Waste), 325–326
Cahill, Mary Beth, 275
Calhoun, John, 67
California
    bilingual education, 534
    child custody, 546–547
    deregulation of utilities, 622
    and 2004 election, 274
    voting procedures, 247
California Central Valley Irrigation Pro-
    ject, 606
Cambodia, 669
Campaign finance
    and conflicts of interest, 307–309
    Congressional races, 278, 279
    contribution limits, 290, 292–293
    donor influence, 301–305
    election of 2004, 297–298
    527 groups, 294, 296
    impact of, 299–308
    independent spending, 296–297

Campaign finance (*continued*)
  McCain-Feingold Act, 291–292
  and PACs, 293–294
  public disclosure, 290, 297
  public financing, 292, 298–299
  public opinion, **307**
  reform issues, 290–291, 298–299
  soft money, 292, 294
Campaigns, generally. *See* Political campaigns
Canada, health care system, 608
Candidates. *See* Political candidates
Cannon, Joseph, 328
Cap-and-trade, 646
Capital punishment, 491–492
Capitalist economy, 557, 558
Card, Andrew, 368
Cardoza, Benjamin, 453
Cargill, 172
Carlin, George, 472
Carr, Baker v., 319
Carson, Rachel, 638
Carter, Jimmy
  and access to public documents, 405
  approval ratings, **388**
  bureaucracy cuts, 407
  and Congress, **375**
  congressional gains/losses for party during administration, **371**
  delegation of duties to vice president, 369
  deregulation of airline industry, 634
  as "diplomat," 659
  economic policy through persuasion, 565
  election of 1976, 213, 258, 272
  election of 1980, 272
  environmental policy, 639
  foreign policy, 660, 672
  judicial appointments, 442
  military experience, 377
  picture of, **361**
  presidency of, 368
  regulatory policy, 628, 632
  television, use of, 152
  White House staff, 365
Carter, Rosalynn, 367
Casework, 325
Catholics. *See* Roman Catholic Church
Cato Institute, 405
Catt, Carrie Chapman, 243
Caucuses, 258, 259
CBO (Congressional Budget Office), 341, 342, 372, 562, 575
CBS Broadcasting Inc., 122, 129, 138, 143, 145, 146, 478
CDF (Children's Defense Fund), 165, 176
Celebrities, 151–152, 183
Censorship, 123, 146, 475–476
Census Bureau, 7, 14–15
Centers for Disease Control and Prevention, 77, 641
Central Defense Intelligence Agency (DIA), 677
Central Intelligence Agency (CIA), 79, 128, 417, 677–678, 687
Chads, 243
Chafee, Zechariah, 467
Chamber of Commerce, 191
Chambliss, Saxby, 269
Charitable contributions, 568, **607**
Charlotte, North Carolina, desegregation of schools, **516**
Chávez, César, 534
Checks and balances, 40–41, 54, 55, 157
Cheney, Richard
  conflict of interest charges, 308
  and Congress, 329, 331, 373
  and energy policy task force, 303
  at Halliburton, 312
  influence of, 370
  after 9/11 attacks, 361
  personal tax rate, 569
  subpoena of energy industry meeting records, 381

on terrorists detained at Guantanamo Bay, 463
  vulgarity on Senate floor, 225, 344
  as Washington insider, 263
Chicago
  Daley era, 210
  Democratic National Convention (1968), 263
  manufacturing job loss, 530
  services available in ghettos, 531
Chicago Times, 50
Chicano movement, 534
Chicanos, 535. *See also* Hispanics
Childcare assistance, 109, 599
Child labor, 68, 435, **436,** 623
Child pornography, 479
Children
  federal health insurance aid, 602–603
  interest groups for, 176
  living in poverty, **597**
  political socialization of, 92–95
Children's Defense Fund (CDF), 165, 176
Child support, 80
China, 363, 666, 668, 672, 683
Chinese Americans, census identification, 14
Chinese immigrants, 10
Christian Coalition, 173–174
Christianity, 11, 18
CIA (Central Intelligence Agency), 79, 128, 417, 677–678, 687
Citizens Against Government Waste (CAGW), 325–326
Citizens and citizenship
  in ancient Greece, 19
  congressional requirements, 317
  vs. individual liberty, 18
  of Native Americans, 536
  presidential eligibility requirements, 359
  revocation of, 9
  role of in democracy, 20–24
  schools' role in creation of, 95
  of women, 538
Citizens for Tax Justice, 570–571, 577
Citizenship and Immigration Services (USCIS), 8, 9
City dwellers, 12
Civic education, 250
Civil Aeronautics Board (CAB), 634
Civil cases, 446
Civil disobedience, 188
Civil liberties. *See also* Privacy, right to
  in Bill of Rights, 465–466
  courts' responsiveness in interpretation, 502
  criminal defendants' rights, 46–47, 437, 486, 488–492
  definition of, 465
  freedom of association, 474–475
  freedom of expression, 467–479
  freedom of press, 475–479
  freedom of religion, 479–486
  freedom of speech, 467–474
  of Guantanamo Bay prisoners, 463–464, 503–504
  and NorthCom, 657
  public opinion of, 465
  vs. rights, 435–437
  of suspected terrorists, 46–47, 113, 184–185
Civil rights. *See also* Civil rights movement
  affirmative action, 112, 437, 547–550
  coalitions, 190–191
  definition of, 508
  and FDR, 213–214
  and government responsiveness, 550
  litigation tactics, 184
  of women, 475, 538–547
Civil Rights Acts
  (1964), 214, 516, 520, 521, 541, 547
  (1968), 520, 521, 526
Civil rights movement
  court decisions, 513–518
  and immigration, 8

legislation, 520–521
  protests, demonstrations, and boycotts, 190–191, 518–520
  splintering of, 520
  tactics of, 189, 518, 520
  and trust in government, 114
  violence against, 519
Civil servants. *See* Federal employees
Civil Service Commission, 415
Civil Service Reform Act (1978), 420, 422
Civil War, 48–50, 68, 377, 510
Clark, Wesley, 235
Class issues
  and bias of news media, 142
  campaign participation, 255
  overclass, 573
  underclass, 530, 531
  voter turnout, 250
Clay, Henry, 327
Clayton Act (1914), 623
Clean Air Act, 192, 619, 639, 640
Clean Water Act, 639, 640, 646
Clear Channel Communications, 123, 124
Clear Skies Initiative, 646
Cleland, Max, 199, 224, 269
Cleveland, Grover, **255,** 365
Clergy Leadership Network, 174
Clinton, Hillary Rodham
  as first lady, 366, 367
  PAC of, 345
  Senate campaign, 301, 317, 367
  Whitewater scandal, 308
Clinton, William Jefferson
  and access to public documents, 404, 405
  anti-smoking campaign, 151
  approval ratings, 387–388, 393
  on *Arsenio Hall Show,* 125
  bureaucracy under, 407
  Catholic voters, 226
  and Congress, 203, 337, 338, 373, 374, 375
  congressional gains/losses for party during administration, **371**
  election of 1992, 213, 258
  election of 1996, 101, 213, 229
  e-mail as public record, 406
  environmental policy, 620, 638, 644, 646
  executive orders, 380
  executive privilege, 380–381
  Family and Medical Leave Act, 542–543
  and the Fed, 566
  federalism view, 72, 73
  fiscal policy, 564
  foreign policy, 660, 662, 673–674, 687
  fundraising efforts, 295
  gay issues, 176, 500–501
  health care reform, 23, 185, 189
  ideology of, 108
  impeachment investigation and trial, 129, 343, 355–357, 388, 389, 393
  and Jennifer Flowers, 125
  judicial appointments, 440, 442
  moderate positions, 203
  Monica Lewinsky scandal, 148
  NAFTA support, 664
  and news media, 134–135, 385, 386
  pardons of, 304, 363
  and Paula Jones, **448,** 544
  picture of, **376**
  political appointees' in private sector, 416
  popularity of, 228
  presidency of, 358, 368–369, 384, 389, 392
  press conferences of, 130
  public opinion of, 91, 93, 109
  public's trust in, 114
  regulatory policy, 628, 632, 636
  and Republican Party, 224

speeches, 382
  "states as laboratories" approach to policy, 72
  Supreme Court appointments, 437, 444
  tax policy, 567
  trade policy, 685
  use of polls, 99–101
  welfare reform, 74, 100, 149, 597–598
  White House staff, 365, 368–369
  Whitewater scandal, 135, 136, 147, 308
  Yucca Mountain nuclear waste storage facility, 85
Cloning, regulation of, 76, 637
Cloture vote, 337
CNN, 101, 122, 123, 124, 143, 145, 147
Coalitions, 189–191, 212–213
Coca-Cola, 631
Code of Federal Regulations, 628
Cold War
  containment policy during, 666, 668
  détente policy during, 671–672
  end of, 655, 673, 678
  nuclear capabilities during, 685
  and Reagan, 672–673
Coleman, Norm, 269
Colleges and universities
  affirmative action, 548–550
  alumni "legacies," 550
  funding of religious organizations, 485
  GI Bill, 605
  liberalism of, 95
  Pell grants, 603
  pork barrel projects, 325
  sex discrimination, 184
  student aid, 573
  Title IX, 543–546
  tuition increases, 573
College students
  foreign students, 9
  loans, 177
  political participation of, 4
  political socialization of, 95–96
  voter registration, 250
Colonies, 7, 31–33
Columbine High School, 149
Comcast, 123
Commander in chief, president as, 364
Commerce Department, **409**
Commercial associations, 475
Commercial bias, of news media, 145–150, 158
Committees (Congress), 331–333, 335, 336, 339–340, 341–342
Common Sense Initiative (CSI), 646
Communism
  containment policy, 666–671
  domino theory, 668
  and freedom of speech, 467–469
  McCarthy's charges, 467–468
  "Red Scare," 10, 467
  vs. socialism, 557
Communist Party, 204
Communitarianism, 18
Comparable worth plans, 542
Comulus Media, 123
Confederacy, and Emancipation Proclamation, 49
Confederal system, 62
Conference committees, 338
Confidence, in political institutions, **347**
Conflicts of interest, 286, 307–309, 416
Congress. *See also* House of Representatives; Legislation; Senate
  Abscam incident, 308
  accessibility of public documents, 403
  alliances in, 344–345
  assault weapons ban, 179
  bipartisanship after 9/11, 224–225, 383
  budget making, 340, 341–342, 372, 578–579
  bureaucratic oversight, 339–340, 399, 420–421

and Bush (George W.), 203, 221, 224, 225
campaign fundraising and spending, 301, 305, 325
casework, 325
checks and balances, **40**
committees, 331–333
communication with constituents, 323
conflicts of interest, 307–308
constituencies, 318
and Constitutional amendments, 45, 48
Constitutional Convention debate over, 34–35
delegated legislative authority, 412
demographic profile of members, 320–321
duties and powers of, 50–51, 65, 67, 73, 316, 335–336, 364, 592
elections, 277–279, 280
emergency operating procedures, 334–335
and the Fed, 564–565
federalism position, 73
fiscal policy, 562
foreign policy, 659, 661–662
Founding Fathers on, 316
"going public," 345–346
Homeland Security Department approval, 380
impeachment power, 355–356, 445
incumbency, 323–326
informal norms of conduct, 342–344
and interest groups, 22, 23, 24, 422
and judiciary, 457
and "Leave No Child Behind" program, 75
legal quorum, 335
and lobbyists, 181–182, 185, 187, 192, 339, 348–349, 629
mailing privileges, 325
members of, 316–318
military policy, 377
and news media, 136, 325, 332, 345–346, 347
9/11 Commission and investigation, 128, 370, 383, 425, 678
organization of, 326–328
and PACs, 294, 301, 303–304, 325, 345
partisanship in, 222, 225, 231, **314,** 343–344, 350, 356
pay and perks of members, 324
and political parties, 203, 221, 223
pork barrel projects, 325–326, 566, 577
and president, 371–379
public opinion of, 346–350
reforms of, 328
regulatory oversight, 628–629, 632, 634, 635
representation, 319–323
residency requirements, 317
responsiveness of, 350
role of, 20
rules, 200
schedule of members, 346
and separation of powers, 38, **39,** 40
sexual harassment in, 545
and slavery, 35, 35095
special-interest caucuses, 344–345
"State of the Union" address to, 363
support staff, 333–335, 346
task forces, 333
tenure of members, 318
term limits, 317–318
unfunded mandates of, 80
veto overrides, 374
voting by party, 222, 343
voting process, 200
voting record, 323
war powers, 364, 377–378, 661, 688–689
and Watergate scandal, 55
women in, 246

Congressional Budget Office (CBO), 341, 342, 372, 562, 575
Congressional districts, 240–241, 318–319
Congressional hearings, 183–184
Congress of Racial Equality (CORE), 174, 519–520
Connecticut Compromise, 35
CONRAIL, 411
Conservatism and conservatives. *See also* Republican Party
core beliefs, 106, 108
definition of, 106
of judges, 451–452
of national convention delegates, **262**
news media, 122, 139–140, 144, 145
racial issues, 112
Republicans as, 217
social issues, 109, **110**
states characterized as, 65
Web sites, 226
Constituency, 318
Constituency services, 325
Constitution. *See also* Amendments, to Constitution
ambiguity of, 450
as basis for federalism, 65–67
changes to, 45, 48
Civil War's impact, 48–51
on core values, 17–18
and economy, 558
and environmental protection, 638
and executive orders, 380
features of, 36–41
founders' motives, 41–43
full faith and credit clause, 81
on government's function, 5
and government's responsiveness, 53–54
implied powers clause, 65, 67
interpretation of, 48, 66–67, 450
and interstate relations, 81
judicial review, 432–433, 456
national government's duties and powers, 65–66
"necessary and proper" clause, 65, 67
and New Deal programs, 51–53
presidential requirements, 359
ratification of, 43–44
rights granted by, 465
secular nature of, 480
signing of, 36
social welfare program justification in, 592
state government's duties and powers, 66
uniqueness of, 53
Constitutional Convention, 11, 33–36, 43
Consultants, 286, 311
Consumer debt, 573–574, 578, 603–604
Consumer Product Safety Act, 626
Consumer Product Safety Commission (CPSC), 624, 631
Consumer protection, 413, 624, 631
Containment, 666–671
Continental Congress, 31, 32
Continuity Committees, 335
Contracts, 81, 304, 308–309, 380, 402
Contribution limits, 290, 292–293
Conventions, political, 218, 256, 259, 260, 261–263
Convictions, reversal of, 488
Coolidge, Calvin, press conferences of, 387
Cooperative federalism, 77
Cooperative internationalism, 672
CORE (Congress of Racial Equality), 174, 519–520
Core values, 17–20
Corporate welfare, 606–608, 616
Corporations
campaign contributions, 301, 302
employee health care costs, 609
globalization of, 581–582

mergers and acquisitions, 623–624, 636
political power of, 636
regulation of, 623–624, 631
taxation of, 569, 570
tax subsidies, 606–608
Corruption, 210, 288–289, 309
Cost-benefit analysis, 626–627
Council of Economic Advisers, 562
Counsel, right to, 490–491
Counties, number of in U.S., **77.** *See also* Local government
Country clubs, 525
Counts, Dorothy, **516**
Court-packing plan, 435
Courts. *See* Judiciary
Courts of appeals, 438, 440, 448
CPSC (Consumer Product Safety Commission), 624, 631
Crack cocaine, 531
"Cracking, stacking, and packing," 240
Credentials committee, 262
Crime
black offenders, 531
federal-state cooperation, 77
mandatory sentencing, 76
news coverage, 148
Willie Horton ad, 215
Criminal cases, 446
Criminal defendants, rights of, 46–47, 437, 486, 488–492
Cronkite, Walter, 138, 151
Cruel and unusual punishment, 491–492
Cruzan, Nancy, 501
Cruz, Ted, 684
Cuban Americans, 227, 531–532, 533, 534, 662. *See also* Hispanics
Cuban missile crisis, 668
Culture, political, 16–17, 64–65
Curley, James, 210
A Current Affair, 125
Customs, U.S., 488
Cyberporn, 479
Cynicism, of public, 156, 306, **307**

Dahl, Robert, 34
Daley, Richard J., 210
D'Amato, Alphonse, 326
Daschle, Tom, 278, 330, 334, 555
Data collection, 413
Date growers, 171
Davis, John W., 261
Daylight saving time, 189
DDT, 643
Dealignment, 219–220
Dean, Howard
campaign financing, 292
Internet fundraising, 226, 284, 293
at Iowa caucuses, 236, 281
media coverage, 152
mobilization of Democrats, 225, 235, 249
picture of, **153**
The Death of Common Sense (Howard), 645–646
Death penalty, 491–492
Deaver, Michael, 308
Debates, congressional, 336–337
Debates, presidential, 153, 271–273
Debs, Eugene, **468**
Debt, consumer, 573–574, 578, 603–604
Debt, national, 563, 574, 578, 580
Declaration of Independence, 17–19, 31, 50, 508
De facto segregation, 517, 522, 532
Defense. *See also* Military
congressional role, 377
government contracts, 308–309
policy, 678–681
president's role, 376–379
state's role, 78–79
Defense Department, 401, 407, 408, **409,** 642, 664, 677

Defense industry, 187
Defense of Marriage Act, 81, 499
Defense Policy Board, 663
DeGette, Diana, 176
De jure segregation, 516–517
DeLay, Tom, 181, 305, 344, 345
Delegated legislative authority, 412
Delegates, to national conventions, 259, 260
Democracy
"American system" of, 16–20
and capitalism, 558–559
citizen's role in, 20–24
conflicts of, 5
definition of, 19
and Electoral College, 276
foreign policy challenges in, 658
Founding Father's view of, 36–37
and grass roots lobbying, 186–187
indirect vs. direct forms, 20
and political culture, 16
and political parties, 201, 202, 207–208, 208
symbols of, 5
and unitary systems, 62
Democratic Congressional Campaign Committee, 226
Democratic National Committee (DNC), 222, 223, 226, 249
Democratic National Conventions, 260, 261–263
Democratic Party
"blue" states, 265–267
and Bush's (George W.) prescription drug proposal, 162
and business, 167
campaign finance, 291–292, 293, 294, 295, 296
characteristics of those voting for, 223–228
corruption style, 309
creation of, 207
delegate selection process, 260, 261
deregulation policy, 631
economic policy, 565, 566
and election of 1968, 260
and election of 2000, 245, **266**
and election of 2004, **266**
estate tax, 555, 556, 585
foreign policy, 661
historical evolution of, **209**
House seats, **322**
ideology of, 108, 217, 218
Iraq War, 654
and lobbyists, 181
member demographics, **214**
mobilization of voters, 254, 265
and NAFTA, 664
number identifying with, 213
and PACs, 293, 306
policy approach, 202
rise of, 212–213
southern strategy, 265
split over civil rights, 214
Tammany Hall machine, 211
tax policy, 571
and war on terrorism, 269
and women, 217
Democratic Senatorial Campaign Committee, 226
Demographic profile, of American people, 6–12
Department of Agriculture, **409,** 413, 420, 599
Department of Commerce, **409**
Department of Defense, 401, 407, 408, **409,** 642, 664, 677
Department of Education, 407, **409**
Department of Energy (DOE), **409,** 642, 643
Department of Health and Human Services, **409,** 417, 420
Department of Homeland Security. *See* Homeland Security Department
Department of Housing and Urban Development, **409**

Department of Interior, **409**
Department of Justice (DOJ), **409,** 425, 439, 623, 624
Department of Labor, **409**
Department of State. *See* State Department
Department of Transportation, **409,** 634, 635
Department of Treasury, 406, **409,** 420, 562, 578
Department of Veterans Affairs, 407, **409,** 521, 603
Departments and agencies, generally. *See* Bureaucracy
Depressions, 7, 51–53, 69–71, 212, 560
Deregulation, 167, 285, 631–636
Desegregation, 514–518, 521–522
Des Moines Register, 132
Détente, 671–672
Devolution, 72, 77
Dewey, John, 467
DIA (Central Defense Intelligence Agency), 677
Dickens, Charles, 316
Die, right to, 501–502
Diem, Ngo Dinh, 668
Digital television broadcasts, 123–124
Dioxin, 643
Diplomacy, 676–677
Direct democracy, 20, 36–37
Direct primaries. *See* Primary elections
Direct subsidies, 592, **593.** *See also* Social Security
Disabled persons, 595–596, 602
Disclosure, 290, 297, 308
Discretionary spending, 579
Discrimination. *See also* Race discrimination
    federal employment cases, 400
    against gays and lesbians, 176
    against men, 546–547
    against Muslims, 113
    public opinion of, 109
    against women, 184, 475, 538–546
Disney, 122, 123
District courts, 438, 440, 448
Diversity, of American people
    age, 12
    census issues, 14–15
    economic background, 11–12
    and identity politics, 12
    immigration, 6–10
    regional differences, 12
    religion, 10–11
Divided government, 40, 54, 374
Divorce, 546–547
Dixie Chicks, 123
Dixiecrats, 214
Doctors, unionization of, 169
Dodd, Christopher, 339, 629
Dole, Bob
    on ads financed by soft money, 294
    as lobbyist, 192
    media coverage, 130, 141
    military experience, 377
    on public funding of digital technology transition, 298
    on Schumer, 285
Dole, Elizabeth, 299
Domino theory, 668
Donaldson, Sam, 131
Do-not-call registry, 77
Douglas, William O.
    on Communist Party, 468
    on criminal defendants' rights, 486
    and FDR, 447
    on First Amendment threats, 469
    Korematsu v. United States decision, 507–508, 551
    picture of, **436**
    on privacy rights, 492
Douglass, Frederick, **238,** 246
Downs, Anthony, 254
Draft, military, 546, 679
Dred Scott case, 433, 509
Drinking water, 640

Drudge Report, 124
Drug industry, 168, 183, 184, 231. *See also* Prescription drugs
Drugs, illegal, 531
Dual federalism, 67, 68
Du Bois, W. E. B., 513
Due process clause, of Fourteenth Amendment, 50, 450, 466
Due process rights, of criminal defendants, 486, 508
Dukakis, Michael, 215, 257, 268
Durbin, Richard, 348–349

Eagleburger, Lawrence, 663
Earned income tax credit (EITC), 598–599, **607**
Earth Day, 178, 638
Earth First!, 178
E-campaigning, 273
E-commerce, 73
Economic crises, 560–561
Economic diversity, 11–12
Economic growth, 580–582
Economic policy
    and budget deficits, 574–580
    fiscal policy, 561–563
    government regulation of business cycle, 565
    income distribution, 571–574
    for job growth, 580–582
    monetary policy, 563–565
    and national debt, 574, 578
    persuasion of consumers and businesses, 564, 565
    political goals, 565–567
    responsiveness of, 583–584
    tax reform, 567–571
    during wartime, 576–577
Economic rights, 19–20
Economic sanctions, 683–684
Economic systems, 557–559
Economy
    and foreign policy goals, 656
    government intervention, 559–560
    voting according to condition of, 228–229, 567
Ecotourism, 645
Edmonds, Sibel, 397–398, 423, 425
Education. *See also* Colleges and universities; Public schools
    bilingual programs, 533–534
    discrimination in, 521–524, 532–534
    Head Start, 603
    "Leave No Child Behind" program, 75, 80
    and party affiliation, 216
    and political culture, 16
    as political socialization tool, 93, 94–96
    state activism, 76
    state vs. federal control, 75–76
    voter turnout by level of, 250
    of women, 538, 543
Education Department, 407, **409**
Edwards, John, 235, 263, 264
EEOC (Equal Employment Opportunity Commission), 412, 541, 547
Eighth Amendment, 45, 466, 486, 491–492
Eisenhower, Dwight D.
    approval ratings, **388**
    on communists, 468
    and Congress, 375
    congressional gains/losses for party during administration, **371**
    election of 1952, 213
    election of 1956, 213
    government spending, 71
    image of, 386
    picture of, **362**
    presidency of, 357, **390,** 391
    on segregation, 515
    Vietnam policy, 668
    Warren appointment, 435, 446
EITC (earned income tax credit), 598–599, **607**

Elderly persons, 176, 594–596. *See also* Medicare; Social Security
Election of 2000
    affluent voters, 216
    Bush's image, 268
    debates, 272–273
    discrimination in, 243
    economy as factor in, 567
    Florida issues, 73, 243, 244–245
    Gore's campaign, 264
    Gore's win of popular vote, 213
    media's call of, 129
    Nader campaign, 204–205
    NRA's impact on, 178, 187
    partisanship in, 265
    polls, 101, 102–103
    primaries, 258
    religious voters, 217
    Supreme Court decision, 429–431
    voter registration, 4
    voter turnout, 4
Election of 2004
    Bush's win, 213
    campaign strategies, 268, 274
    debates, 273
    Democratic nomination, 235–236, 281
    economy as factor, 567
    e-mail usage, 274–275
    mobilization of voters, 248–249
    Nader campaign, 204–205
    negative ads, 270
    polarization of voters, 3
    polls, 101, 103
    "red" and "blue" states, 265–267
    voter registration, 3, 247, 253
    voter turnout, 26, 249, 254, 280
Election registrars, 238, 239
Elections. *See also* Election of 2000; Election of 2004; Primary elections; Voting
    of 1796, 206
    of 1800, 206
    of 1824, 97, 206, 273
    of 1828, **251**
    of 1840, 247
    of 1856, 208
    of 1860, 209
    of 1872, 288
    of 1876, 238
    of 1896, 210, 288
    of 1920, 243
    of 1936, 97–98
    of 1952, 213, 268
    of 1956, 213
    of 1968, 258, 264
    of 1976, 213
    of 1980, 264
    of 1992, 213, 264
    of 1996, 101, 213, 247, 264
    and government responsiveness, 279–280
    media coverage, 129, 140–141, 149, 151, 153, 156, 258
    nature of, 202–203
    and poll usage, 101, 102–104
    presidential vs. midterm elections, 279
Electoral College
    and campaign strategies, 265, 274
    election of 1824, 206
    election of 2000, 213, 273
    Founding Fathers' intentions for, 37, 41, 275–276
    outcome different from popular vote, 206, 213, 273, 276
    reform proposals, 276
    system of, 273
Electric utilities, 622, 630, 649
Electronic surveillance, 488–489
Elites
    and Electoral College, 275
    Founding Fathers as, 43
    lobbying powers, 193
    political participation of, 21, 22–23
    political tolerance, 112
Ellison, William, 509

Ellsberg, Daniel, 422, 475
E-mail, 273, 274–275, 406
Emancipation Proclamation, 49
Embassies, 676–677
Emerson, Jo Ann, 231
EMILY's List, 172–173
Employment. *See* Labor and employment
Endangered Species Act, 639, 646
Energy crisis (1970s), **559**
Energy Department, **409,** 642, 643
English language, and political culture, 16–17
The Enlightenment, 42
Enron, 89, 167, 184, 294, 301, 302–303, 311–312, 607, 626, 629
Enumerated powers, of Congress, 335
Environmental groups, 178, 184, 185
Environmental impact statements, 638–639
Environmental Integrity Project, 649
Environmental protection
    achievements of, 646
    air pollution, 619–620, 621, 639–640, 646
    Bush (George W.) administration, 167, 178, 620, 638, 643–644, 646, 649
    costs/benefits of, 645, 646–647
    difficulties in, 643–646
    financial burden, 80
    historical evolution of, 638–639
    and interest groups, 644–645
    lack of consensus on, 645–646
    nuclear waste, 59–60, 85–86, 641–643
    public pressures, 638, 644
    and scientific research, 643–644
    water quality, 640–641
    and WTO membership, 683–684
Environmental Protection Agency (EPA)
    air quality standards, 619–620, 626, 639–640, 649
    cabinet status, 408
    challenges of, 643
    during Clinton-Bush transition, 416–417
    Common Sense Initiative (CSI), 646
    creation of, 639
    deletion of data after 9/11, 404
    duties and powers of, 639
    global warming studies, 187
    and Reagan administration, 631
    scientific research, 643–644
    water quality standards, 640
EOP (Executive Office of the President), 365
EPA. *See* Environmental Protection Agency (EPA)
Episcopal Church, 11
Epsy, Mike, 308
Equal Credit Opportunity Act (1974), 543
Equal Employment Opportunity Commission (EEOC), 412, 541, 547
Equality, 18–19, 50, 508
Equal Pay Act (1963), 542
Equal protection clause, of Fourteenth Amendment
    application to women and minorities, 541
    as *Bush v. Gore* basis, 430, 458, 459
    description of, 50
    impact of, 510
    interpretation of, 450, 511
    passage of, 48
    segregation as violation of, 515
Equal Rights Amendment (ERA), 48, 262, 539, 540–541
Equal Rights Party, 246
ERA (Equal Rights Amendment), 48, 262, 539, 540–541
Ernst & Young, 287
Ervin, Sam, 344
Espionage Act (1917), 467
Establishment clause, 482–486
Estate tax, 555–556, 585

Ethical standards, 308–310
Ethics in Government Act (1978), 308, 416
Ethnic diversity. See Diversity, of American people
EU (European Union), 683
European immigrants, 7
European Union (EU), 683
Evangelical Christians, 173–174, 227
Evidence, exclusionary rule applied to, 488
Evolution, in schools, 485–486
Exclusionary rule, 488
Executive branch. See also Presidency
    agency reorganization, 380
    checks and balances, **40**
    president as head of, 362
    and separation of powers, 38, **39,** 40
Executive leadership, 417, 420
Executive Office of the President (EOP), 365
Executive orders, 380
Executive privilege, 30, 55, 380, 383, 389
Exit polls, 102–103
Experts, lobbyists as, 182–183
Export-Import Bank, 607
Ex post facto laws, 465
Expression, freedom of, 467–479
Expressive associations, 474
Externality, 621
Extremist groups, 189
ExxonMobil, 187

FAA (Federal Aviation Administration), 529, 623, 634, 635
Faction, mischiefs of, 63
Fairness Doctrine, 139
Faithless elector, 276
Falwell, Jerry, 174, 185
Families
    as agent of political socialization, 93–94
    financial condition of, 573
    living in poverty, **597**
    tongue in cheek proposals to protect, 500
Family and Medical Leave Act, 542–543
Fannie Mae, 603, 604
Farm Bill (2002), 599, 600
Farmer, James, 519–520
Farmers and farming
    government regulation of, 51–52
    immigrant farmworkers, 532
    interest groups, 169, 172
    Shay's Rebellion, 32
Farmers Home Administration (FmHA), 605
Farm Security Act (2001), 170
Farm subsidies, 170, 172, 589–591, 599–601, 605–606, 616
Farrakhan, Louis, 192
FBI (Federal Bureau of Investigation)
    Director qualifications, 409
    duties of, 677
    history of, 398
    under J. Edgar Hoover, 406
    9/11 investigation, 422–423, 425
    openness of, 404
    problems with, 397–398
    Surveillance Court, 439
    whistleblowers, 398, 422–423, 425
FCC (Federal Communications Commission), 139, 410, 413, 472
FDA (Food and Drug Administration), 184, 421, 624, 625, 631
FDIC (Federal Deposit Insurance Corporation), 411
FEC (Federal Election Commission), 290, 297
The Fed, 410, 420, 563–565, 566
Federal Aviation Administration (FAA), 529, 623, 634, 635
Federal budget. See Budgets and budgeting
Federal Communications Commission (FCC), 139, 410, 413, 472

Federal Corrupt Practices Act (1925), 289
Federal Deposit Insurance Corporation (FDIC), 411
Federal Election Commission (FEC), 290, 297
Federal Emergency Management Agency (FEMA), 657
Federal employees
    age of, 414
    average salaries, 414
    conflicts of interest, 308
    diversity of, 400
    merit-based hiring and appointments, 212, 218, 247, 415–417
    number of, 52, **61,** 407, 408
    removal of poor performers, 420
    unionization, 420
    views of, 410–411
    whistleblowing by, 422–423
Federal Energy Commission, 184
Federal Energy Regulatory Commission (FERC), 303, 626
Federal government. See also Bureaucracy
    aid to states, 70, 71, 78–79, 80, 82
    under Articles of Confederation, 31–32
    Constitutional Convention debate, 34
    Constitutional restrictions, 66
    and education, 75–76
    expansion under FDR's New Deal, 52–53
    land owned by, 80
    power of, 37–38, 50–51, 61, 66–67, 70
    public opinion of, 109
    relations with states, 77–81
    revenue sharing, 71–72, 77
    spending, **70,** 579–580
    unfunded mandates of, 80
    welfare reform, 74
Federal Home Loan Bank Board, 633
Federal Housing Authority, 521
Federal Housing Finance Board, 603
Federalism
    vs. confederal system, 62
    constitutional bases for, 65–67
    costs/benefits of, 63–64
    definition of, 37, 61–62
    Founding Father's creation of, 62–63
    and growth of government, 68–77
    new federalism of Nixon, Reagan, and Clinton, 71–72
    political bases for, 62–65
    practice of, 77–83
    reasons for, 62
    vs. unitary systems, 62
The Federalist Papers, 45, 63, 66, 206, 288, 356, 364, 431, 432
Federalists
    vs. Anti-Federalists, 43–44
    control over Judiciary, 432
    as first political party, 206
    vs. Jeffersonians, 131
    use of negative ads, 271
Federal Open Market Committee (FOMC), 563
Federal Register, 380, 403
Federal Register Act (1813), 403
Federal Reserve System (the Fed), 410, 420, 563–565, 566
Federal revenue sources, **568.** See also Taxation
Federal Savings and Loan Insurance Corporation (FSLIC), 633
Federal Trade Commission (FTC), 623, 631
Feingold, Russ, 291
Felons, and voting rights, 243
FEMA (Federal Emergency Management Agency), 657
The Feminine Mystique (Friedan), 539
FERC (Federal Energy Regulatory Commission), 303, 626
Fernald, Ohio, nuclear weapons plant, 641
Ferraro, Geraldine, 246, 264
Fertilizers, 641

Fifteenth Amendment, 48, 50, 51, 237, 510, 539
Fifth Amendment
    civil liberties granted by, 45, 450, 466
    due process rights for criminal defendants, 46–47, 486
    and Japanese internment during WWII, 508
    privacy rights under, 492
    and self-incrimination, 489
    suspected terrorists' rights, 46–47
Filibusters, 337
Fillmore, Millard, presidential effectiveness, **390**
Film industry, concentration in, 122
Financial Accounting Standards Board (FASBE), 629
Financial services industry, 285–287
Fireside chats, 133, 381
First Amendment
    campaign spending limitations as violation of, 292, 299
    civil liberties granted, 45, 466
    freedom of association, 474–475
    freedom of press, 475–479
    freedom of religion, 479–486
    freedom of speech, 467–474
    interpretation of, 450
    privacy of association, 492
    public opinion of, 465
First ladies, 365, 366–367
Fiscal policy, 561–563, 566, 571, 583. See also Taxation
Fiske, John, 241
Fitzgerald, Ernest, 422
Fitzgerald, Peter, 182
527 groups, 294, 296
Flag, and symbolic speech, 474
Flat tax, 570
Florida
    2000 election issues, 73, 102, 243, 244–245, 429–431, 458
    2004 voter registration, 247
    voting rights of felons, 243
Flowers, Jennifer, 125
Flynt, Larry, 125
FmHA (Farmers Home Administration), 605
Focus groups, 107
FOIA (Freedom of Information Act) (1966), 403–406, 421, 422
FOMC (Federal Open Market Committee), 563
Food and Drug Administration (FDA), 184, 421, 624, 625, 631
Food industry, 624–625, 631, 637
Food stamps, **593,** 599, **607**
Forbes, Steve, 258
Ford, Betty, 366, 367
Ford, Gerald
    approval ratings, **388**
    and Congress, **375**
    congressional gains/losses for party during administration, **371**
    election of 1976, 272
    pardon of Nixon, 56, 360
    picture of, **361**
    presidency of, 368
    southerners' support of, 216
    Supreme Court appointments, 437
    vice presidency of, 360
Foreign aid, 684–685
Foreign-born population, 9, 10
Foreign Intelligence Surveillance Court, 439
Foreign policy
    Bush (George H.) administration, 659, 660, 673
    Bush (George W.) administration, 378, 660, 674–676
    Carter administration, 660, 672
    Clinton administration, 660, 662, 673–674, 687
    and Congress, 659, 661–662
    containment, 666–671
    definition of, 656

détente, 671–672
diplomacy, 676–677
economic instruments, 681–685
formation of, 658–664
and globalization, 685–687
goals of, 655–656, 658
intelligence gathering, 677–678
isolationism, 664–665
Jefferson administration, 656
Kennedy administration, 659
military instruments, 678–681
multilateralism, 673–674
news media's coverage of, 142–143
Nixon administration, 660
preemption, 674–675
president's powers, 363–364, 372–373, 375–376, 658–660, 662
Reagan administration, 660, 672–673
responsiveness of, 687
unilateralism, 675–676
Vietnam War policy failures, 669–671
Foreign Service, 660, 677
Fortas, Abe, 447, 473
Foster, Vince, 125
Founding Fathers
    balance of power, 24
    bureaucracy, 406
    on Congress, 316, 371
    on democracy, 36–37
    Electoral College, 275–276
    federalism idea, 62–63
    impeachment mechanism, 356
    indirect democracy choice, 20
    and interest groups, 163
    judicial appointments, 439
    judiciary, 431
    motives of, 41–43
    political culture aspirations, 16
    on political parties, 206
    on presidency, 357, 364, 381
    and right to privacy, 492
Founding Mothers, 33
Fourteenth Amendment. See also Equal protection clause, of Fourteenth Amendment
    application to women, 539
    description of, 50, 510
    due process clause, 50, 450, 466
    passage of, 48, 51
Fourth Amendment, 45, 450, 466, 486, 488–489, 492
Fox, Michael J., 183
Fox News Channel, 139–140, 143
Frankfurter, Felix, 515
Franking privilege, 325
Franklin, Benjamin, 33–34, 35, 37, 319, 439
Franks, Trent, 231
Freddie Mac, 603, 604
Freedom from Religion Foundation, 174
Freedom of assembly, 472
Freedom of association, 474–475
Freedom of expression, 467–479
Freedom of Information Act (FOIA) (1966), 403–406, 421, 422
Freedom of press, 475–479
Freedom of religion, 479–486
Freedom of speech, 467–474
Freedom to Farm bill, 590
Free exercise clause, 480–482
Free trade, 682–683
Frick, Henry, 304
Friedan, Betty, 539
Fringe media, 125, 126
Frist, Bill, 330, 344
FSLIC (Federal Savings and Loan Insurance Corporation), 633
FTC (Federal Trade Commission), 623, 631
Fugitive Slave Act, 81
Fulbright, J. William, 112
Full employment, 563
Full faith and credit clause, 81

Galesburg, Illinois, Maytag's subsidies, 607

Gallup, George, 98–99
Gambling casinos, 537–538
Game orientation, 149
Ganske, Greg, 269
GAO (Government Accountability Office), 303, 339, 634, 642, 649
Garfield, James, 360, 415
Garner, John Nance, 369
Gates, Bill, 556
Gay Activist Alliance, 175
Gay and Lesbian Advocates and Defenders (GLAD), 174, **176**
Gay and Lesbian Alliance Against Defamation (GLAAD), 174
Gay Liberation Front, 175
Gays and lesbians
    employee benefits, 500
    history of public attitudes and treatment, 175
    interest groups, 174–176
    marriage, 81, 92, 174, 218, 498–500
    in military, 185, 500–501
    right to privacy protections, 498–501
    state restrictions, 76
GDP (gross domestic product), 561
Gender, and campaign participation, 255. See also Women
GenderPAC, 176
General Accounting Office (now Government Accountability Office) (GAO), 303, 339, 634, 642, 649
General elections. See Elections
General Electric, 122, 123, 183, 607
General Motors (GM), 580, 609, 621, 623
A General Theory of Employment, Interest and Money (Keynes), 562
Generic Pharmaceutical Association, 168
Genetically engineered food, 637
Gentleman's Agreement, 8
Georgia, right to counsel in, 490
Gephardt, Richard, 235, 258, 346, 351, 377, 688
German immigrants, 7, 10, 11, 16–17
Germany
    inflation after WWI, **560**
    political parties of, 202
Gerry, Elbridge, 241
Gerrymandering, 240–241, 319
Get-out-the vote efforts, 3, 254
Gettysburg Address, 49–50
Ghettos, 531
GI Bill, 604–605
Gideon v. Wainwright, 490
Gillespie, Ed, 222
Gingrich, Newt
    and Clinton, 355
    on Congress, 344
    on Medicare, 195
    resignation of, 199
    as Speaker of House, 328–329, 333, 343
    view of government, 72
Ginsburg, Ruth Bader, 444
GLAAD (Gay and Lesbian Alliance Against Defamation), 174
GLAD (Gay and Lesbian Advocates and Defenders), 174, **176**
Gladstone, William, 36
Glasnost, 673
Glass-Steagall Act, 636
Glenn, John, 299, 643
Globalization, 580–582, 636, 662–663, 683, 685–687
Global warming, 187, 643–644, 674
"Going public," 345–346, 385–386
Goldberg, Arthur, 473
Goldwater, Barry, 214, 265, 520
Gonzales, Elian, 148
Goodsell, Charles, 423
GOP. See Republican Party
Gorbachev, Mikhail, 673
Gore, Albert. See also Election of 2000
    announcement of candidacy (2000 election), 132

body language and mannerisms during 2000 debates, 273
    campaign finance reform, 291
    environmental protection, 638, 646
    exaggerations to media, 141
    military experience, 377
    and NRA, 178, 187
    vice presidency of, 369–370
    vice presidential nomination (1992), 263
Gore, Bush v., 129, 429–431, 458–460
Gorham, Nathaniel, 32
Goss, Porter, 678
Government
    advantages/disadvantages of American system, 54
    functions of, 5, 16
    growth of, 68–77
    indispensability of, 5
    responsiveness of, 24–25
    role toward individual, 108
    trust in, 113–115
Government, responsiveness of
    bureaucracy, 423–424
    and civil rights, 550
    Congress, 350
    and Constitution, 53–54
    and economic policy, 583–584
    and elections, 279–280
    and federalism, 84
    and interest groups, 193–194
    judiciary, 457, 502
    and money, 309–310
    and political parties, 208, 229–230
    presidency, 392
    to public opinion, 115
    and regulatory policy, 647–648
    and social welfare, 615
    state and local governments, 83
Government Accountability Office (GAO), 303, 339, 634, 642, 649
Government corporations, 410–411
Government regulation. See Regulation
Government waste, 402–403
Governors, 252, 256
Governors Conference, 81
Graft, 289
Gramm, Phil, 286, 332
Gramm-Rudman-Hollings (GRH) Act (1985), 579
Grandfather clause, 238, 239
Grant, Ulysses S., political cartoon depicting, **288**
Grant-in-aid programs, 70, 71, 595, 596
Grassley, Charles, 425, 600
Grass roots lobbying, 185–187
Great Britain
    elections in, 252
    freedom of press in, 476
    government system, 62
    House of Commons protocols, 343–344
    in Iraq War, 675
    political parties in, 202, 221
Great Compromise, 35
Great Depression, 7, 51–53, 69–71, 212
Great Migration, 512
Great Society, 71
Greeks, ancient, 18–19
Green Party, 204, 226
Greenpeace, 178, 185, 188
Greenspan, Alan, 563, 564, 565, 566–567, 635, 684
Greider, William, 127
Gridlock, 24, 374
Griswold, Roger, **327**
Gross domestic product (GDP), 561
Group membership, decline in, 165. See also Interest groups
Guantanamo Bay prisoners, 463–464, 503–504
Guerrilla warfare, 670
Guinn, Kenny C., 59, 85
Gulf of Tonkin Resolution, 668, 669
Gulf Wars. See Iraq War; Persian Gulf War

Guns and gun control, 178–179, 192, 487

Habeas corpus, 438–439, **440**, 463, 465
Hackworth, David, 120
Haiti, 674
Haldeman, H. R., 368
Halliburton, 180, 308, 312
Hamilton, Alexander
    at Constitutional Convention, 35
    as Federalist Papers author, 45
    vs. Jefferson, 206
    on judiciary, 431
    on nation-centered federalism, 66
    view of government, 34
Hanford, Washington, nuclear weapons plant, 641
Hanna, Mark, 288
Hanssen, Robert, 398
Harding, Florence, 366
Harding, Warren G., 280, 289, **291, 390, 468**
Harkin, Tom, 185, 269, 278
Harlan, John, 472, 511
Harrisburg Pennsylvanian, 97
Harrison, William Henry, **390**
Hart, Gary, 258–259
Hastert, Dennis, 130, 199, 231, **314,** 329, 334, 343
Hatch, Orrin, 136, 345, 440
Hatch Act (1939), 416
Hatcher, Richard, 240
Hawaii
    same-sex marriage, 498
    voter turnout in, 249
Hayes, Rutherford B., 238, 510
Head of state, president as, 362–363
Head Start, 603
Health and Human Services Department, **409,** 417, 420
Health care
    access to, 608
    cost of, 573, 608, 609–611
    public support for spending on, **108**
Health care reform, 23, 185, 189, 610–611
Health insurance. See also Medicare
    Americans without, 602, 609
    Medicaid, 493, 579, 593, 602–603
Health maintenance organizations (HMOs), 608, 625
Hearings, congressional, 336, 339
Helms, Jesse, 444
Henry, Patrick, 34
Heritage Foundation, 171
Heston, Charlton, 187
Hill, Anita, 544
Hindus, number in U.S., 11
Hiroshima, **667**
Hispanics
    abortion rates, 495
    census identification, 14, 15
    in Congress, 320
    discrimination against, 531–535
    education, 532–534
    farmworkers, 532
    federal employees, 400
    identity of, 534–535
    interest groups, 174
    as national convention delegates, 261
    party identification, 217, 226–227
    as percentage of U.S. population, 10
    as political officeholders, 240
    political participation of, 21
    political power, 535, 550
    population, 532
    public opinion, 112
Hobbes, Thomas, 18
Ho Chi Minh, 668
Hollings, Ernest, 682
Holmes, Oliver Wendell, 446, 451, 473
Holocaust, 100, 148
Homeland Security Department
    administration of, 408
    budget of, **409**

Citizenship and Immigration Services division, 8, 9
    congressional approval, 380
    creation of, 420, 423, 657
    photo ops during 2004 election, 130
    state coordination, 78
    unfunded mandates of, 80
Homeless persons, 604, **606**
Home ownership, 603–604, 605
Home rule, 82
Homestead Act, 592
Homosexuals. See Gays and lesbians
Hoover, Herbert, 381, 562
Hoover, J. Edgar, 406
Horse race coverage, 149
Horton, Willie, 215, 257
House Appropriations Committee, 342
House Budget Committee, 342
House of Representatives. See also Congress
    Cheney's working office, 373
    committees, 331–333
    constituencies, 318–319
    creation by Constitution, 35
    demographic profile of members, 320, 321
    eligibility requirements, 317
    Iraq War resolution, 688
    leadership positions, 315–316, 328–329, 351
    Lyon-Griswold fight in, **327**
    makeup by party, **322**
    organization of, 326–328
    power to decide in elections without Electoral College majority, 273, 276
    prescription drug benefit bill, 199–200, 231
    reapportionment, 318
    redistricting, 240–241, 318–319
    reelections, 277–278
    reforms of, 328
    residency requirements, 317
    Rules Committee, 327, 328, 336
    vs. Senate, **337**
    speaker of the House, 326, 327, 328–329, 332
    task forces, 333
    tenure of members, 318
    term, **39,** 40, 317
Housewife, 540
Housing and Urban Development Department, **409**
Housing issues, 521, 526
Housing vouchers, 526
Howard, Philip, 645–646
Howard University, 514
Hoyer, Steny, 315, 351
Hughes, Charles Evans, 435, 450, 455
Hughes, Karen, 368
Hull House, 593
Human nature, 37
Human Rights Campaign, 174
Humphrey, Hubert, 260
Hussein, Saddam, 107, 143, **144,** 376
Hustler, 125
Hutchinson, Tim, 589, 590, 616

ICC (Interstate Commerce Commission), 410
Identity politics, 12, 319
Ideology
    of American people, 108
    of college students, 95
    of current political parties, 217–218
    definition of, 106
    of judges, 451–452
    of national convention delegates, **262**
    types of, 106, 108
Illegal drug use, 531
Illegal immigrants, 10, 532
Illinois
    inmates released from death row, 492
    right to counsel, 490

Immigrants and immigration
contributions to society, 10
employment, 582
English language mastery, 534
food stamp program eligibility, 599
historical background, 6–7
after 9/11/01, 8–9
numbers (1900-2000), **7**
picture of, **6**
policy issues, 8–9
and political culture of state, 64–65
quotas, 8, 212
religious diversity of, 10–11
restrictions, 8–9
voting rights, 247, 248
Immigration and Naturalization Service
(INS), 8, 9, 423
Impeachment
Clinton trial, 129, 343, 355–357,
388, 389, 393
congressional power of, 355–356
definition of, 355
Johnson (Andrew), 360
of judges, 445
Nixon, 360
Implied powers clause, 65, 67, 335
Import quotas, 681, 682
Imus, Don, 126
Income
and party affiliation, 216
and voter turnout, 250
Income distribution, 304–305, 569,
571–574, 582, 584, **615**
Income inequality or gap, 569
Income support programs, 594–601
Income tax, 69, 82, 567–569. *See also* Tax
cuts
Incumbents, 259, 277–278, 301, 306,
323–326
Independent agencies, 408–409, 412–
413
Independent regulatory boards and com-
missions, 409–410, 413
Independents, **214**, 219, 264, 265
Independent spending, 290
Independent Women's Forum, 173
India, nuclear capabilities, 686
Indian Claims Commission, 537
Indian immigrants, 10
Indian Removal Act (1830), 536
Indians. *See* Native Americans
Indirect democracy, 20, 25, 34, 36–37
Indirect subsidies, 592
Individualistic political culture, 64
Individual liberty, 17, 18, 19
Industrialization, 68, 435, 638
Inflation
definition of, 560
history of, 560
and interest rates, 564
prediction for budget planning, 574–
575
and unemployment, 561, 562
Influence peddling, 308
Informal norms, of Congress, 342–344
Information technology, 437
Infotainment, 147
Initiatives, 20, 83
Inman, Bobby Ray, 152
Innocence, presumption of, 486, 488
INS (Immigration and Naturalization
Service), 8, 9, 423
Institute of Medicine, 609
Instrumental federalism, 72
Insurance industry, 170. *See also* Health
insurance
Intelligence gathering, 657, 677–678
Intercontinental ballistic missiles
(ICBMs), 668
Interest groups. *See also* Lobbying and
lobbyists
and bureaucratic decision making,
421–423
coalition-building, 189–191
and court access, 448
definition of, 163

as democracy, 21–24
and environmental protection, 644–
645
foreign policy, 662–663
formation of, 163–165
Founding Fathers' view of, 163
and government responsiveness, 193–
194
historical background, 164
increase in, 25
media usage, 125
and political parties, 208
private interest groups, 165–172
public interest groups, 172–180
reasons for, 163
and regulation, 626, 630
strategies of, 180
success of, 191–193
tactics of, 180–191
Interest rates, and monetary policy, 563,
564
Interfaith Alliance, 174
Interior Department, **409**
Intermediate-range nuclear forces (INF),
673
Internal Revenue Service (IRS), 406, 569
Internet
access to, 637
campaign fundraising on, 293
federal agencies' web sites, 413
Gore's "creation of," 141
and grass roots lobbying, 186
inaccurate reports, 126
news from, 121, 124, 664
and interest group formation, 164
political Web sites, 226
porn on, 479
regulation of, 637
as presidential campaign tool, 273
straw polls, 97
trends, 122
Internment, of Japanese Americans, 10,
377, 507–508, 551
Interpretation of law, 449–450
Interstate commerce, regulation of, 73
Interstate Commerce Commission (ICC),
410
Interstate compacts, 81
Interstate relations, 81–82
Interviews, 127, 135
Intimate associations, 474
Investigative journalism, 133
Iowa, absentee ballot usage, 253
Iowa caucus, 236, 258, 259, 261, 281
Iran-Contra affair, 280, 309, 363
Iran hostage crisis, 151
Iraq War
al-Qaeda linkage as reason for, 664
Bush's "Mission Accomplished" statement, **131**
casualties of, 664
coalition, 675
congressional authorization, 378
cost of, 576
funding of, 662
media coverage, **131**, 137–138, 139,
143, 664
National Guard use, 78
pictures of soldiers killed in, **354**
Powell's initial opposition to,
671
prisoner abuses, **340**, 664
protests against, **676**
public support of, 116, 386
Senate resolution, 653–654, 688–
689
strategy, 377, 679
taxation and spending during, 576–
577
troop deployment, **568**
weapons of mass destruction as reason
for, 128, 143, **144**, 376, 417,
686, 688
Irish immigrants, 10, 11
IRS (Internal Revenue Service), 406, 569
Islam, 11, 113, 173, 320

Isolationism, 664–665
Israel, 155, 174, 681
Issues, political. *See also specific issues*
election of 1968, 268
election of 2004, 268
influence on voters, 228–229
news media's role in setting the
agenda, 150–151
opinion of "red" vs. "blue" states,
266
terrorism, 269
Issue voting, 228
ITT Corporation, 290

Jackson, Andrew
and bureaucracy, 400, 414, **415**
election of 1824, 97, 206
election of 1828, 207, **251**
election of 1832, 271
on Marshall, 434
and newspapers, 131
picture of, **435**
presidency of, 358, **390**, 391
Jackson, Jesse, 256, 257
Jackson, Robert, 447, 551
Jamestown, 30
Japan
bombing of, 666, **667**
Gentleman's Agreement with, 8
U.S. military base in, 680
Japanese Americans
census identification, 14
internment of, 10, 377, 507–508, 551
Japanese immigrants, 10
Jawboning, of consumers and businesses,
564, 565
Jaworski, Leon, 30
Jay, John, 5, 45
Jaycees, 475
Jefferson, Thomas
cabinet of, 364
and congressional rules of conduct,
343
on Constitution, 45
on education, 16
election of 1796, 206, 271
election of 1800, 206
federalism position, 84
foreign policy, 656
and Marshall, 432, 433, 434
on power to declare war, 364
presidency of, **357**, 358, **390**, 391
on role of government, 206
on separation of church and state, 480
speeches, 381
on two-house legislature, 40
on women, 538
Jeffersonian Republicans, 131, 206–207,
209
Jeffords, James, 331
Jews
congressional representation, 320
interest groups, 173
number in U.S., 11
party identification, 225
presidential candidates, 257
in Skokie, 473
Jim Crow laws, 511, 525
Job creation, 573, 580–582, **583**
Johnson, Andrew, 360, **390**
Johnson, Frank, 451
Johnson, Lady Bird, 366, 367
Johnson, Lyndon
affirmative action requirements for
firms with federal contracts,
380
approval ratings, **388**
Civil Rights Act (1964), 214
civil rights support, 520
and Congress, **375**, 389
congressional gains/losses for party
during administration, **371**
economic policy through persuasion,
565
election of 1964, 265
election of 1968, 258

Great Society, 71
judicial appointments, 442
leaks to media, 129
and media, 127
picture of, **669**
presidency of, 358, 368, **390**
as Senate majority leader, 329–330,
373
and Vietnam War, 668–669, 670
Johnson, Tim, 269
Joint Chiefs of Staff, 659, 669
Joint committees (Congress), 333, 678
Jones, Paula, **448**, 544
Journalists. *See* News media
Journal of the American Medical Association,
608
Judges
appointment of, **39**, 40
courts of appeals, 438
district courts, 438
impeachment of, 445
independence of, 446, 447
qualifications of, 445–446
restraint vs. activism, 450–452
selection of, 439–445
tenure of, 445, 446
term, **39**
Judicial activism, 430, 451–452
Judicial restraint, 430, 450–452
Judicial review, 432–433, 456
Judicial Watch, 405
Judiciary. *See also* Judges; Supreme Court
access to, 446, 448
checks and balances, **40**
Founding Fathers' view of, 431
historical development of role, 431–
438
interpretation of Bill of Rights, 466
interpretation of Constitution, 450
interpretation of statutes, 449–450
jurisdiction of, 438–439
law making role, 453
power of, 456–457
precedents, 452–453
procedures, 448–449
regulatory oversight, 628
responsiveness of, 457
and separation of powers, 38, **39**, 40
structure of, 438
de Tocqueville on, 456
Judiciary Act (1789), 438
Judiciary Committee, 441
"Juice committees," 331
Jurisdiction, 438–439
Jury trial, right to, 491
Justice Department, **409**, 425, 439, 623,
624

Kean, Thomas, 405
Kelley, Stanley, 223
Kemp, Jack, 264
Kennedy, Anthony, 455, 459, 480, 498,
542
Kennedy, Edward, 200, 345
Kennedy, Jacqueline, 366, 367
Kennedy, John F.
approval ratings, **388**
civil rights support, 520
and Congress, **375**
congressional gains/losses for party
during administration, **371**
debate with Nixon, 271–272
economic policy through persuasion,
565
forced desegregation of University of
Mississippi, 515
foreign policy, 659, 675
image of, 386
judicial appointments, 440
news coverage of Vietnam, 131
presidency of, 357–358, 368, **390**
press conferences of, 129
racial discrimination in public housing, 380
Kerner Commission, 531
Kerrey, Bob, 377

Kerry, John. *See also* Election of 2004
  background of, 235
  campaign ads, 270
  campaign financing, 226, 292, 293, 297
  Catholicism of, 257
  debates with Bush, 273
  early primary wins, 258
  e-mail list usage, 273, 274–275
  financial supporters of, 306
  as "flip-flopper," 268
  friendship with McCain, 345
  health care reform plan, 611
  and Iowa caucus, 236, 281
  late night show jokes about, 105
  as moderate, 218
  personality of, 228
  values of, 267
  Vietnam War record, 123, 270, 297, 377
  Yucca Mountain nuclear storage facility, 85
Kerry, Teresa Heinz, 366
Keyes, Alan, 317
Keynes, John Maynard, 562
Keynesian economics, 562–563
King, Martin Luther, 190, 191, 518–519
King, Rodney, 531
Kissinger, Henry, 663, 671
Knowledge, of citizens about public issues, 104–105
Know-Nothing Party, 10, 11, 204
Kohl, Herbert, 203
Koop, C. Everett, 418, 419
Korea, Reagan's trip to, 133–134
Korean War, 377, 666
Korematsu V. United States, 507–508, 551
Kosovo, 680
K Street strategy, 181
Ku Klux Klan, 189, 469, 513, 530
Kuwait, 680
Kyoto Treaty, 644, 674

Labeling, truth in, 625
Labor and employment. *See also* Federal employees; Unions and unionization; Wages and salaries
  affirmative action, 547–548
  child labor, 68, 435, **436,** 623
  discrimination, 521, 525–526, 541–545
  full employment, 563
  job growth, 573, 580–582, **583**
  outsourcing, 581–582
  regulation of, 623
  sexual harassment, 544–545
  unemployment, 561, 562, 566
  of women, 538, 541–543
Labor Department, **409**
Laissez-faire economics, 51, 435
Lambda Defense Fund, 174
Language, and political culture, 16–17
Late night shows, political knowledge from, 105, 125
Latin America, and Monroe Doctrine, 664–665
Latinos. *See* Hispanics
Law enforcement
  confessions, 489
  Miranda rights, 489
  during national emergencies, 657
  racial profiling, 527, 528–529, 532
  unreasonable searches and seizures, 488
Law making. *See* Legislation
Lawrence v. Texas, 498
Lay, Kenneth, 184, 302, 303, 626
Lazio, Rick, 301
Lead, 646
Leadership Conference on Civil Rights, 190–191
League of Nations, 665
League of United Latin American Citizens (LULAC), 174
Leahy, Patrick, 425
Leaks, of information, 127–129

"Leave No Child Behind" program, 75, 80
Left wing. *See* Liberalism and liberals
Legislation. *See also* Bills
  Congress's authority, 65
  court's role, 453
  delegated legislative authority, 412
  drafting of, 183
  president's power over, 372–375
  process of, 336–339
  state activism, 76–77
  after Supreme Court rulings, 457
  and task forces, 333
  vagueness of, 421
Legislature. *See* Congress
"Lemon law," 192
Leno, Jay, 105, 152
Letterman, David, 105, 152
Levin, Carl, 170, 186–187
Levitt, Arthur, 286, 287, 629
Lewinsky, Monica, 148, 393
Libel, 477–478
Liberalism and liberals. *See also* Democratic Party
  core beliefs, 106, 108
  definition of, 106
  Democrats as, 217
  of judges, 451–452
  of national convention delegates, 262
  news media, 122, 139, 140, 144, 145
  racial issues, 112
  social issues, 109, **110**
  states characterized as, 65
  Web sites, 226
Liberty, 17, 18, 19. *See also* Civil liberties
Libraries, and USA Patriot Act, 470–471
Licensing, 413, 625
Liddy, G. Gordon, 56
Lieberman, Joseph, 235, 257, 339, 629
Life expectancy, 609
Limbaugh, Rush, 125, 139
Limited government, 42
Lincoln, Abraham
  election of 1860, 209
  Emancipation Proclamation, 49
  Gettysburg Address, 49–50
  and growth in government, 68
  national security during Civil War, 377
  picture of, **364**
  on popular sovereignty, 19
  presidency of, 358, 363, **390,** 391
  presidential staff, 364–365
  speeches, 381
  view of black people, 48–49
Lippmann, Walter, 306
Literacy tests, for voting, 238, 239
Literary Digest, 97–98
Litigation, lobbyists' role in, 184–185
Little Rock, Arkansas, school desegregation, 515
Livingston, Robert, 125
Loans, for college, 177
Lobbying and lobbyists
  of accounting industry, 286
  and bureaucratic decision making, 421–422
  and Congress, 181–182, 185, 187, 192, 339, 348–349
  corporations, 301
  definition of, 163
  direct techniques, 181–185
  environmental protection, 649
  former Congress members as, 349
  by group, **166**
  indirect techniques, 185–189
  as interest group strategy, 180
  at legislative hearings, 336
  after 9/11/01, 170–171
  pharmaceutical industry, 168
  in state legislatures, 83
  of states and localities, 80–81
  "Ten Commandments" of, 182
  types of, 181
  used as construction workers in photo op, 130

Local government
  education, 75
  employees, **61,** 77
  federal aid, 70, 71
  lobbyists for, 80–81
  number of units in U.S., **77**
  relations with state, 82–83
  responsiveness of, 83
  spending, **70,** 77
Locke, John, 18, 42
Lockheed Martin, 187
Los Angeles
  air pollution in, 647
  and GM, 621
  riots, 531
Los Angeles County, public schools in, 523
Los Angeles Times, 507
Lott, Trent, 126, 215, 330
Louisiana
  right to counsel, 490
  segregation in, 511
  state corruption survey, 83
Louisiana Purchase, 68
Lowi, Theodore, 383
LULAC (League of United Latin American Citizens), 174
Luntz, Frank, 107
Lugar, Richard, 600, 653–654, 688–689
Lynchings, 512–513
Lyon, Matthew, **327**

MacArthur, Douglas, 377, 604
Machines, political, 209–210, 211, 289
Madison, Dolley, 366
Madison, James
  as Bill of Rights author, 45, 465
  on checks and balances, 40–41
  on Congress, 316
  on Constitution, 45
  as Constitutional Convention delegate, 34, 36
  on factions, 63, 288
  on federalism, 63
  The Federalist Papers, 45, 63, 206, 288
  on government's role, 18
  on human nature, 37
  on impeachment article wording, 356
  on knowledge of government, 403
  picture of, **63**
  presidential effectiveness, **390**
  on president's war propensity, 364
  on property rights, 43
  on separation of powers, 38
Madison, Marbury v., 432–433, 503
MAD (mutual assured destruction), 668
Magazines, time spent reading, 121. *See also* News media
Maher, Bill, 105, 143
Majority leader, of House, 329
Majority leader, of Senate, 329–330
Majority-minority districts, 240–241
Majority rule, 19
MALDEF (Mexican American Legal Defense and Educational Fund), 174
Mandates, 279–280, 384
Mandatory sentencing, 76
Mandatory spending, 579–580
Manufacturing, regulatory requirements, 624–625
Mapplethorpe, Robert, 478
Mapp v. Ohio, 488
Marbury, William, 432, **433**
Marbury v. Madison, 432–433, 503
Marijuana, legalization of, 136
Marketing research, and emergence of scientific polling, 98
Market share, of interest groups, 192
Markup sessions, 331, 336
Marriage
  interracial, 12, 529–530
  promotion of, 614
  same-sex marriage, 81, 92, 174, 218, 498–500
Marshall, John, 67, 432–433, 434, **435,** 450, 454, 536

Marshall, Thomas R., 369
Marshall, Thurgood, 441, 442, 453, 494, 514, 516, 518
Marshall Plan, 666, 684
Marx, Karl, 557
Maryland, McCulloch v., 67, 433
Massachusetts, same-sex marriage, 499
Mayflower Compact, 31
Mayors, African Americans as, 240
Maytag, 607
McAuliffe, Terry, 222
McCain, John
  anti-tobacco legislation, 185
  campaign finance, 291, 297
  campaign fundraising efforts, 299
  friendship with Kerry, 345
  military experience, 377
  on post-9/11 defense bill, 577
  presidential campaign (2000), 102
  on Telecommunications Act, 123
McCain-Feingold Act, 291–292, 293, 296
McCarthy, Eugene, 256, 258
McCarthy, Joseph, 467–468
McCarthyism, 468
McCorvey, Norma, 492–493, 497
McCulloch v. Maryland, 67, 433
McDade, Joseph, 309
McDonald's, 146, **676**
McGovern, George, 280
McKinley, William, 210, 247, 665
McNamara, Robert, 475, 670
Means tests, 595
Media. *See also* News media
  as agent of political socialization, 96
  definition of, 120
  freedom of, 475–479
  offensive language, 472
Media conglomerates, 122–124
Media events, 130–131
Media Fund, 296
Media malaise, 156
Medicaid, 493, 579, 593, 602–603
Medicare
  description of, 601–602
  establishment of, 200, 593
  number of recipients, **593**
  prescription drug benefit, 162, 195, 199–200, 231
  regional differences in spending on, **610**
  whistleblowers, 423
Meetings, openness requirements, 406
Mehlman, Ken, 275
Melting pot, America as, 11–12, 16
Men, discrimination against, 546–547
Mercury emissions, 649
Mergers and acquisitions, 623–624, 636
Merit-based hiring and appointments, 212, 218, 247, 415–417
Mexican American Legal Defense and Educational Fund (MALDEF), 174
Mexican Americans, 14, 174, 532, 534. *See also* Hispanics
Mexican immigrants, 10
Microsoft, 624
Midterm elections, 279
Military
  aid to foreign countries, 680–681
  alliances, 680
  Articles of Confederation limitations, 32
  draft, 546, 679
  homosexuals in, 185, 500–501
  integration of, 214, 380
  interventions by, 679–680
  and news media, 136–138
  preparedness of, 678–679
  president as head of, 364, 376–379
  size of, 678
  spending on, 678
  strategies, 679
  war-making power, 364, 377–379
Miller, George, 182
Mills, John Stuart, 467
Mineta, Norman, 529

Minimum wage, 109, 435, **596**
Minnesota, voter turnout in, 249
Minorities. *See specific minority groups*
Minority leader, 329, 351
Minority rights, 19
Miranda rights, 489
"Mischiefs of faction," 63, 163
Misery index, 561
Missouri
    black law school, 515
    right to die case, 501
Missouri Compromise, 433
Mixed economies, 557–558
Mixed marriages, 12, 529–530
Mobility
    and low voter turnout, 250, 252
    and political culture, 64
Mobilization techniques, 185–187
Moderates, 203–204, 218
Mondale, Walter, 264, 272, 369
Monetarists, 564
Monetary policy, 563–566, 583
Money, influence over politics, 287–290,
    301–305, 309–310. *See also* Cam-
    paign finance
Money supply, 563, 564
Monopolies, regulation of, 623–624
Monroe, James, **390**
Monroe Doctrine, 664–665, 674
Montesquieu, Charles de, 42, 43
Montgomery bus boycott, 190–191, 518
Moore, Michael, 123, 140
Moralistic political culture, 64
Mormons, 320, 480
Morning-after pill, 498
Mortgage debt, 603–604
Mortgage interest, tax deduction for,
    607, 608
Motor voter law, 253, 491
Moussaoui, Zacarias, 422
MoveOn.org, 186, 254, 296
Moyers, Bill, 170
Moynihan, Daniel Patrick, 103
MSNBC, 143
MTV, 146
Muckrakers, 289
Mueller, Robert, 398, 422–423, 425
Multilateralism, 673–674, 675–676
Multiparty systems, 202
Multiple-issue groups, 172–178
"Multiracial category" (census), 14–15
Muncie, Indiana, 69
Municipalities, number of, **77.** *See also*
    Local government
Murray, Patty, 555–556, 585
Music industry, concentration in, 122
Muskie, Edmund, 258, 259
Muslims, 11, 113, 173, 320
Mutual assured destruction (MAD), 668

NAACP (National Association for the
    Advancement of Colored People),
    15, 174, 190, 192, 513–514
NAB (National Association of Broadcast-
    ers), 298
Nader, Ralph, 141, 148, 183, 204–205,
    264
NAFTA (North American Free Trade
    Agreement), 100, 142, 203, 664
Narragansett Indians, 11
Narrowcast, 139
NASA (National Aeronautics and Space
    Administration), 409
National Abortion Rights Action League,
    179
National Academy of Science, 609
National Association for the Advance-
    ment of Colored People (NAACP),
    15, 174, 190, 192, 513–514
National Association of Broadcasters
    (NAB), 298
National Audubon Society, 178, 645
National bank, 67
National Cancer Institute (NCI), 643,
    644
National committees, 222–223

National conventions, 256, 259, 260,
    261–263
National Council of Churches, 173
National Council to Control Handguns,
    192
National debt, 563, 574, 578, 580
National emergencies, 657
National Environmental Policy Act
    (NEPA) (1970), 638
National Farmers' Union, 169
National government. *See* Federal gov-
    ernment
National Guard, 78, 679
National Highway Safety Administration,
    184
National Intelligence, 425
National Labor Relations Board (NLRB),
    421
National Organization for Women
    (NOW), 172, 539
National parks, 80
National party chair, 222
National Republican Congressional Com-
    mittee, 226
National Republican Party, 207, **209**
National Republican Senatorial Commit-
    tee, 226
National Rifle Association (NRA), 164–
    165, 178–179, 185, 187, 192, 487
National Right to Life Committee, 179
National sales tax, 570–571
National security, as foreign policy goal,
    656
National Security Agency, 128, 677
National Security News Service, 120
National Smokers Alliance, 185
National Taxpayers Union, 170, 172
National Women's Party, 243
National Women's Political Caucus, 173
Nation-centered federalism, 66
Nation of Islam, 192
Native Americans
    census identification, 14
    in Congress, 320
    discrimination against, 535–538
    federal employees, 400
    government policy toward, 536–538
    interest groups, 174
    number of tribes, 7
    peyote use, 481
    political power, 550
    tribal restoration, 536–538
    voting rights, 12, 536
Nativism, 10
Nativity scenes, public displays of, 485
NATO (North Atlantic Treaty Organiza-
    tion), 656, 666, 674, 680
Natural Resources Defense Council, 178,
    184, 185
Natural rights, 42
Navy, Boorda incident, 119–120, 158
NBC, 122, 123, 145
NCI (National Cancer Institute), 643,
    644
"Necessary and proper" clause, 65, 67,
    335
Negative advertising, 270–271
NEPA (National Environmental Policy
    Act) (1970), 638
Net worth, 573
Neustadt, Richard, 370, 390
Neutral competence, 415–417, 419
Nevada, nuclear waste storage in, 59–60,
    85–86
New Deal, 51–53, 70–71, 435, 593, 631
New Deal coalition, 212–213
New federalism, 71–72
New Hampshire primary, 236, 258, 261,
    281
New Jersey Plan, 34–35
News Corporation, 122
News media
    atomization trend, 124–127
    bias of, 138–150, 158
    bribery of, 288
    and Bush (George W.), 135

civil rights movement coverage, 519
and Clinton, 134–135
confidentiality of sources, 476–477
conflict framework, 148–149
and Congress, 136, 325, 332, 345–
    346, 347
congressional campaign coverage, 279
election coverage, 129, 140–141,
    149, 151, 153, 156, 258
episodic coverage, 157
exposure to, 120–121
foreign coverage, 663
freedom of press, 475–479
fringe sources, 125, 126
game orientation, 149
industry concentration trend, 122–
    124
and infotainment, 147
Iraq War coverage, **131,** 137–138,
    139, 143, 664
muckrakers, 289
national party convention coverage,
    262–263
Persian Gulf War coverage, 138, 143,
    372–373
political activism and censorship, 123
political advertising, 251
political impact of, 150–156
politicians' use of, 127–133
polls, use of, 101, 102, 103
portrayal of African Americans, 146
presidential campaign coverage, 267–
    268
presidents' use of, 385–387
and public opinion, 156, 157
and Reagan, 129, 133–134, 152, 386
responsiveness to people, 156–157
roles of, 121–122
sensationalism of, 147–148
and Supreme Court, 136
Vietnam War coverage, 143
war reporting, 136–138
New Source Review, 619–620, 649
Newspapers. *See also* News media
    decline in readership after growth of
        TV, 61
    election coverage, 140
    endorsements of candidates, 97, 141,
        153, 156
    and FDR, 133
    industry concentration, 122
    of political parties, 151
    profitability of, 145
    time spent reading, 121
    use of straw polls, 97
Newsweek, 120, 121, 158
Newton, Isaac, 42
New York City
    manufacturing job loss, 530
    public schools, 523
    Tammany Hall machine, 211
New York Herald, 97
New York Post, 139
New York Times, 73, 128, 131, 137, 138,
    152, 422
New York Times v. Sullivan, 477
NGOs (nongovernmental organizations),
    685
Nickles, Don, 184
NIMBY (not in my backyard), 85
9/11/01
    access to public documents after,
        404–405
    airport security after, 635
    bipartisanship after, 224
    bureaucracy failures, 423–424
    Bush's popularity after, 269
    Congress's investigation of , 128,
        677–678
    defense against attacks on U.S. soil af-
        ter, 657
    economic impact, 576
    FBI actions, 398, 422–423
    immigration after, 8–9
    lobbying activity after, 170–171
    news media's coverage of, 143

patriotism after, 25, 269
and public opinion, 98–99
succession discussion, 361
surveillance after, 439
trust in government after, 114
valuation of lives lost in, 627
view of government after, 84
9/11 Commission, 370, 383, 425, 678
Nineteenth Amendment, 48, 539
Ninth Amendment, 66, 465
Nixon, Richard
    approval ratings, **388**
    bureaucracy cuts, 407
    and Burger, 437, 447
    China visit, 672
    and Congress, **375**
    congressional gains/losses for party
        during administration, **371**
    debate with JFK, 271–272
    election of 1960, 256
    environmental protection, 639
    foreign policy, 660
    judicial appointments, 437, 441, 442
    on leaks to media, 129
    new federalism of, 71–72
    and news media, 131, 386
    and Pentagon Papers, 475
    pictures of, **361, 672**
    presidency of, 358, 368
    resignation of, 55
    southern strategy, 214
    TV effectiveness, 130
    and Vietnam War, 668, 669
    Watergate scandal, 29–30, 55–56,
        309, 360, 388–389
    White House staff, 368
Nixon, U.S. v., 55
NLRB (National Labor Relations Board),
    421
Nongovernmental organizations (NGOs),
    685
NORAD, 657
The North
    Great Migration to, 512
    segregation in, 512, 519
North American Free Trade Agreement
    (NAFTA), 100, 142, 203, 664
North Atlantic Treaty Organization
    (NATO), 656, 666, 674, 680
North Carolina, racial gerrymandering,
    241
NorthCom (U.S. Northern Command),
    657
North Korea, 684
Northwest Airlines, 634
Northwest Territory, 32
Novelli, Bill, 195
NOW (National Organization for
    Women), 172, 539
NRA (National Rifle Association), 164–
    165, 178–179, 185, 187, 192, 487
Nuclear deterrence, 666
Nuclear waste, 59–60, 85–86, 641–643
Nuclear weapons
    capabilities of terrorists and rogue
        states, 642, 685–686
    Carter administration, 672
    post-Cold War agreements, 678, 685–
        686
    Cold War deterrence, 666, 668
    in former Soviet Union, 642, 684
    SDI, 672–673

Obama, Barack, 240, 267, **322,** 331
Obscenity, 478–479
Occupation, of congressional members,
    320, 321
Occupational Safety and Health Adminis-
    tration (OSHA), 630, 631, 632
O'Connor, Sandra Day
    abortion rights, 455, 494
    affirmative action, 549
    background of, 429–430
    Bush v. Gore decision, 429–431, 458,
        459
    ideology of, 443

O'Connor, Sandra Day (*continued*)
  motto of, 460
  pictures of, **428**
  religious meetings in public schools, 484
Office of Management and Budget (OMB), 341, 365, 372, 379, 408, 420, 562, 575, 628
Offshoring, 581–582
Ohio
  as battleground state, 265
  election of 2004, 247, 253
Ohio, Mapp v., 488
Oil, 644
Oklahoma City bombing, 189, 363, 387, 469
Old Age Survivors Disability and Health Insurance Program. *See* Social Security
OMB (Office of Management and Budget), 341, 365, 372, 379, 408, 420, 562, 575, 628
O'Neill, Tip, 210, 287
Openness laws, 401, 403–406, 421
Operation Rescue, 496, 497
Oregon, assisted suicide in, 501
Osborne, Tom, 151–152
OSHA (Occupational Safety and Health Administration), 630, 631, 632
Otter, C. L., 231
Outsourcing, 581–582
Overclass, 573
Overtime wages, 167

Packing, 240
Packwood, Bob, 545
PACs. *See* Political action committees (PACs)
Paine, Tom, 237
Pakistan, nuclear capabilities, 686
Palestinians, 155
Panama, invasion of, 378, 679
Pardons, presidential, 304, 363
Parks, Rosa, 190, 518
Partial-birth abortions, 494
Partisanship
  of civil servants, 416
  in Congress, 222, 225, 231, **314,** 343–344, 350, 356
  of president, 371
  of public, 225
  of Supreme Court justices in *Bush v. Gore* decision, 459
  of voters, **220,** 254
Party caucus, 328, 351
Party identification, 213–218, 219, 223–228, 279, 322–323
Party organization, 201, 222–223, 230
Party system, 208–209. *See also* Political parties
Paterson, William, 35
Patriot Act. *See* USA PATRIOT Act
Patriotism, 25, 98
Patronage system, 210, 212, 218, 414–415
Paul, Alice, 243
Pay-go system, 579, 580
Payroll taxes, 568, 594
Peers, as agent of political socialization, 96
Pell grants, 603
Pelosi, Nancy, 231, **314,** 315–316, 344, 345, 351
Pendleton Act (1883), 415
Pennsylvania
  as battleground state, 265
  Nader's failure to get on 2004 ballot, 264
Pentagon Papers, 475
Permanent campaigns, 276–277
Perot, Ross, 204, 205, 264
Persian Gulf War
  Bush's approval ratings during, 269, 387
  Bush's decision to start, 659
  Bush's direct involvement in, 377

congressional support for, 662
funding of, 576
media coverage, 138, 143, 372–373
military preparedness, 679
objectives, 680
Powell's initial opposition to, 671
public support of, 664
and War Powers Act, 378
Personal contacts, of lobbyists, 181–182
Personal presidency, 383–386, 389, 392, 662
Persuasion, 370–371, 564, 565
Pesticides, regulation of, 638, 641
Pharmaceutical industry, 168, 183, 184, 231
Philadelphia, Pennsylvania
  Constitutional Convention in, 33
  public school funding, 524
Phillips Petroleum, 193
Philosophical influences, on Founding Fathers, 41–42
Photo opportunities, 130–131
Physicians for Social Responsibility, 185
Pierce, Franklin, **390**
Pilgrims, 30–31
"Pink collar" jobs, 542
Pitt, Harvey, 416, 631–632
Planned Parenthood, 179
Platform committee, 262
Plea bargains, 492
Pledge of Allegiance, 94, 485
Plessy v. Ferguson, 511, 515
Plunkitt, George Washington, 210, 211, 289
PNAC, 663
Pocket veto, 374
Police. *See* Law enforcement
Policy, public opinion's influence over, 115. *See also specific type of policy*
Policy implementation, 411–413
Political action committees (PACs)
  accountability of, 166
  coalitions between, 191
  of Congress members, 345
  dependency of Democratic incumbents on, 306
  and foreign policy, 662
  fundraising, 166
  growth of, 184
  influence of, 301, 303–304, 305
  methods of, 293–294
  origins of, 293
  spending of, 296
Political bias, of news media, 138–145
Political campaigns. *See also* Campaign finance; Presidential campaigns and candidates
  Americans' dislike of, 21, 251
  congressional campaigns, 277–279
  media coverage, 153, 156
  and national committees, 222–223
  permanent campaigns, 276–277
  role of political parties, 218–219
  volunteers, 254–255
Political candidates
  news media's encouragement of, 151–152
  and party affiliation, 202
  personality and style, 228
  and political parties, 218–219, 221
Political conventions, 218, 256, 259, 260, 261–263
Political corruption, 210, 288–289, 309
Political culture, 16–17, 64–65
Political equality, 18–19
Political machines, 209–210, 211, 289
Political participation. *See also* Voting
  of college students, 96
  importance of, 4, 26
  lack of, 20–21
Political parties. *See also specific parties*
  American system of, 202–205
  birth of, 206–207
  caucuses, 328, 351
  components of, 201
  and congressional campaigns, 279

decline of, 218–220
definition of, 201
and democracy, 201, 202, 207–208, 208
Founding Fathers' view of, 206
and government responsiveness, 208, 229–230
historical evolution of, 208–213
identification with, 213–218, 219, 223–228, 279, 322–323
importance of, 204–208
and interest groups, 208
media's role in decline of, 151
organization of, 201, 222–223, 230
policymaking role, 221–222
and presidential nomination, 256, 261
president's role, 371
and Progressive reforms, 248
purposes of, 201–202, 220–222
realignments of, 209, 213–216
and voting behavior, 223–229
welfare function of, 210, 218
Political patronage, 210, 212, 218, 414–415
Political socialization
  of adults, 96
  agents of, 91–96
  of children, 92–96
  of college students, 95–96
  definition of, 91
  impact of, 96–97
  process of, 92–93
Political tolerance, 112–113
Politicians, Founding Fathers as, 34, 42–43
Politics, definition of, 5
Polls or polling
  difficulties and limitations of, 101
  early efforts, 97–98
  exit polls, 102–103
  misuse of, 101–102
  political impact, 99–104, 277
  scientific methods, 98–99
Poll tax, 238, 239
Polygamy, 480
Popular sovereignty, 19, 37
Popular vote, 206, 213, 273, 275–276
Populist Party, 204
Pork barrel projects, 325–326, 566, 577
Pornography, 478–479
Posse Comitatus Act, 657
Poverty, 19, 530, 595–599, 601
Poverty line, **596**
Powell, Colin, 14, 257, 649, **659,** 671, 674
Power
  balance of, 24
  checks and balances, 40–41, 54, 55, 157
  of Congress, 50–51, 65, 67, 73, 316, 335–336, 364, 592
  division between federal and state government, 63
  of president, 357–359, 361–364, 372, 382–383, 388–389, 464
  separation of, 38–40, 55
  of states, 37–38, 61, 63–64, 66–67, 68, 70, 237
  to wage war, 364, 377–379, 382, 464, 661, 688–689
  who holds, 23–24
Power to persuade, 370–371
Prairie View A&M University, 250
Prayer, in public schools, 452
Precedents, 430, 452–453
Preemption, 674–675
Prejudice, 530
Prescription drugs
  cost of, 609
  Medicare drug benefit, 22, 161–162, 195, 199–200, 231, 608
Presidency
  appointments, 379, 408, 410, 420
  and bureaucracy oversight, 417, 420
  character, 390–391

"chief" titles, 362–364
communication with public, 381–382, 385–386
and Congress, 371–379
correspondence as public record, 382
defense policy, 376–379
development and growth of, 358–359
duties and powers of, 357–359, 361–364, 372, 382–383, 388–389, 464
economic policy, 562, 565
elasticity, of, 392
eligibility, 359–360
evaluation of performance, 389–391
executive leadership power, 379–381
executive orders, 380
executive privilege, 30, 55, 380, 389
federal budget, 341, 372, 574–576
federalism position, 73
fiscal policy, 562
foreign policy, 363–364, 372–373, 376, 658–660, 662, 676
Founding Fathers' view of, 357, 364, 381
goals and vision of, 391
"going public," 385–386
independence from Congress and state legislatures, 65
judicial appointments, 439–444, **445,** 457
mandates, 279–280
and news media, 385–387
pay and perks, 360
personal presidency era, 383–386
and political party, 371
power to persuade, 370–371
and public opinion, 387–388
ranking of, 390
regulatory oversight, 628–629, 631
removal from office, 360
removal of appointees, 379
reputation, 389–390
responsiveness of, 392
signing of bills, 338
spectacle presidency, 386–387
staff of, 364–365, 368–369
succession, 360–361
term, **39,** 360
veto power, 338–339, 373–374
war-making power, 377–379, 382, 661, 688–689
Presidential campaigns and candidates
  advertising, 268, 270–271
  announcement of, 258
  debates, 271–273
  electronic communication, 273
  money spent on, 300–301
  organization of, 264
  strategies, 265–268
  tactics of, 258
  television appearances, 271
Presidential debates, 153, 271–273
Presidential nominations, 256, 258–264, 262. *See also* Primary elections
Presidential preference primaries, 259–261. *See also* Primary elections
Presidential press conferences, 129–130, 135, 387
Presidential Succession Act, 360
Press. *See* News media
Press conferences, 129–130, 135, 387
Presumption of innocence, 486, 488
Primary elections
  impact of money on outcome, 300
  importance of, 258, 276
  New Hampshire, 236, 258, 261, 281
  participation of young people in, 249
  and political parties, 218
  process of, 259–261
  Progressive era origins, 212, 247
  and voter turnout in general election, 252
  white primaries of South, 238, 239
Prior restraint, 475–476
Privacy, right to
  and abortion, 492–498

and birth control, 492, 493
and Bork nomination, 442
and freedom of press, 477
of homosexuals, 498–501
and right to die, 501–502
Supreme Court's doctrine, 492
Private interest groups, 165–172
Private schools, public funding of, 486
Privatization, of Social Security, 101, 612
Procter & Gamble, 146
Productivity, 561
Professionals, party affiliation, 216
Profiling, racial, 527, 528–529, 532
The Progressive, 475
Progressive movement, 210, 212, 247
Progressive reforms, 247–248, 631
Progressive taxes, 568, 570
Prohibition Party, 204
Pro-life groups, 179, 184, 189, 493, 494, 496–497, 501
Property ownership, and voting rights, 237, 242
Property rights, 42, 43, 44
Proportional representation (PR), 202, 203
Protectionism, 681–682
Protests, demonstrations, and boycotts, 187–191, 472–473, 518–520
Public accommodations, 521, 525
Public Citizen, 183, 184
Public defenders, 490–491
Public disclosure, 290, 297, 308
Public documents, access to, 403–406
Public employees, **61.** *See also* Federal employees
Public financing, of political campaigns, 292, 298–299
Public forum, 472
Public health insurance, 493, 579, 593, 602–603. *See also* Medicare
Public interest groups, 172–180
Public opinion. *See also* Polls or polling
and Bush (George W.) administration, 89–90, 116
campaign finance reform, **307**
and citizens' lack of knowledge, 104–106
civil liberties, 465
of college students, 95–96
confidence in government, **307**
Congress, 346–350
contradictions of, 90
definition of, 90
of federal employees, 410–411
and focus groups, 107
and foreign policy formation, 663–664
formation of, 91–97
government's responsiveness to, 115
Holocaust, 100
Iraq War, 654
issues, **266**
measurement of, 97–106
nature of, 90–91
news media's influence, 156
9/11/01 impact, 98–99
political tolerance, 112–113
president, 387–388
racial issues, 109–112
regulation, 647–648
same-sex marriage, 92, 500
social issues, 109
social welfare, 108–109
Supreme Court, 347, 431, 457
and trust in government, 113–115
Vietnam War, 670–671
Public relations, and grass roots lobbying, 186–187
Public schools
busing, 516–518
discrimination in, 521–524, 532–534
evolution, 485–486
freedom of speech in, 473–474
funding, 522–524, 533, 603
number of districts, **77**
and political culture, 16

prayer in, 482–484
religious meetings in, 484–485
segregation in, 511, 514–518, 524, 532–533
Puerto Ricans, 531. *See also* Hispanics
Pure speech, 472
Puritans, 7
Push poll, 102

Quakers, 7
Quotas, immigration, 8, 212

Race
and campaign participation, 255
and political participation, 21
and presidency, 257
public opinion, 109–112
Race discrimination. *See also* Civil rights movement; Segregation; Slaves and slavery
against African Americans, 491–492, 508–513, 521–528
and capital punishment, 491–492
against Hispanics, 531–535
against Japanese Americans, 10, 377, 507–508, 551
laws prohibiting, 520–521
against Native Americans, 535–538
Race riots, 512–513, 531
Racial categories and identification, 14–15
Racial diversity. *See* Diversity, of American people
Racial profiling, 527, 528–529, 532
Racial violence, 512–513
Radio
conservative talk radio shows, 139
impact on elections, 156
industry concentration, 122
number of homes having, 121
political activism and censorship, 123
and presidency, 359
Radon, 641
Raging Grannies, 188
Railroad regulation, 435
Rainmakers, 192
Rally events, 387
Randolph, Edmund, 31, 34
Rankin, Jeannette, 246
Rather, Dan, 129, 143, 147
Ratification, of Constitution and Constitutional amendments, 43–44, 45
Reagan, Nancy, 366, 367
Reagan, Ronald
and access to public documents, 405
AIDS programs, 418–419
appointments by, 417
approval ratings, **388**
and blue-collar voters, 216
budget projections, 574–575
and bureaucracy, 399, 407
Catholic voters, 226
and Civil Rights Act, 520
and Congress, 373, 374–375
congressional gains/losses for party during administration, **371**
economic policy, 562, 563, 565, 574–575
on EITC, 599
election of 1976, 256
election of 1984, 258, 268, 272
environmental policy, 638
and ERA, 541
and Fairness Doctrine elimination, 139
foreign policy, 660, 672–673
image of, 386
Iran-Contra affair, 280, 309
judicial appointments, 437, 441–442
and media, 129, 133–134, 152, 386
national debt during administration, 574
new federalism of, 72
pictures of, **361, 387**
powers given to Bush during surgeries, 361

presidency of, 358, 368–369, **390, 392**
public's trust in, 114
reasons for seeking presidency, 256
regulatory policy, 628, 632
southern strategy, 214–215
speeches, 382
Supreme Court appointments, 437, 441–442
White House staff, 365, 368
Real estate agents, discriminatory practices, 521
Realignments, of political parties, 209, 213–216
Reapportionment, 318
Recessions, 560–561
Reciprocity, in Congress, 344
Reconstruction Amendments, 50–51
Reconstruction era, 237–238, 510–511
Redistricting, 240–241, 318–319
Redlining, 521
"Red Scare," 10, 467
"Red" states, 265–267
Reed, Thomas, 327
Reeve, Christopher, 183
Regional issues, 12
Regressive taxes, 568, 570–571, 573
Regulation. *See also* Environmental protection
of accounting industry, 312–313
authority, 565
of cloning, 76
definition of, 413
expansion during New Deal era, 51
historical cycles of, 631–637
of interstate commerce, 73
process of, 625–630
reasons for, 621–624
reduction in, 167
responsiveness of, 647–648
types of, 413, 624–625
Rehnquist, William, 437, **441,** 454, 455, 474, 501, 503, 520
Rehnquist Court
abortion, 494
activism/restraint of, 451
affirmative action, 549
characteristics of, 430, 437
and civil liberties, 502
death penalty, 492
dissents and disagreements within, 455
freedom of press, 475–476
freedom of religion, 481–482
freedom of speech, 473, 474
homosexual practices rulings, 498
Miranda rights, 489
prayer in public schools, 484
private school aid, 486
right to counsel, 490
right to die, 501
school segregation, 518
schools' funding of religious organizations, 485
Reid, Harry, 85, 278, 330, 344, 351
Religion
conflicts over, 11
diversity of American people, 10–11
freedom of, 479–486
and party affiliation, 217
and presidential nomination, 257
and state's liberal or conservative rating, 65
Religious interest groups, 173–174
Religious Right, 217–218
Religious tests, for voting, 237
Reno, Janet, 379
Reporters. *See* News media
Republic, 20, 34, 36–37, 63
Republican House Conference, 226
Republican National Committee (RNC), 139, 222, 223, 226
Republican National Conventions, 261–263
Republican Party
and blue-collar workers, 216
bribery of reporters (1872), 288

and Bush's (George W.) prescription drug proposal, 162, 195
and business, 167
campaign finance, 291–292, 294, 295, 296
characteristics of those voting for, 223–228
and Christian Coalition, 173–174
after Civil War, 213
and Clinton, 224, 355, 393
corruption style, 309
creation of, 209
delegate selection process, 260, 261
deregulation policy, 631
dominance of, 209, 210
economic policy, 565–566
and election of 2000, 245, **266**
and election of 2004, **266**
environmental issues, 178
and ERA, 541
estate tax, 555, 585
focus group usage, 107
foreign policy, 661
gay issues, 176
House seats, **322**
ideology, 217–218
and immigration, 212
Iraq War, 654
and lobbyists, 181
member demographics, **214**
mobilization of voters, 254, 265
number identifying with, 213
and PACs, 293
policy approach, 202
polling, 99
"red" states, 265–267
southern strategy, 214–216
Re-regulation, 632–633
Research, of federal government, 413
Residential segregation, 521, 526
Responsible party government, 221
Restrained judges, 430, 450–452
Restrictive covenants, 521
Retrospective voting, 228–229
Revenue sharing, 71–72
Rhode Island, founding of, 11
Rice, Condoleezza, 368, 370, **659**
Rich, Denise, 304
Ridge, Tom, 78
Rights. *See also* Civil liberties; Civil rights vs. civil liberties, 435–437
Locke on, 42
public opinion, 465
Right to counsel, 490–491
Right to die, 501–502
Right to jury trial, 491
Right-to-life movement, 179, 184, 189, 493, 494, 496–497, 501
Right to privacy. *See* Privacy, right to
Right wing. *See* Conservatism and conservatives
Riots, race, 512–513, 531
Risk assessment, 627–628
RJ Reynolds, 185
Robber barons, 288
Roberts, Owen, 435, 453
Robertson, Pat, 173, 174, 258
Rockefeller, Jay, 170
Rockefeller, Nelson, 360, 369
Roe v. Wade, 179, 430, 456, 493–494, 497
Rogers, Edith Nourse, 605
Rogers, Will, 563
Roman Catholic Church
anti-Catholic groups, 11
Congress representation, 320
opposition to women's suffrage, 242
party identification of members, 225–226, 228
presidential candidates, 257
and settlement of Maryland, 7
Roosevelt, Eleanor, 366–367
Roosevelt, Franklin D.
Brownlow Committee, 420
and civil rights, 213–214
and Congress, 374

Roosevelt, Franklin D. (*continued*)
congressional gains/losses for party during administration, **371**
death of, **384**
EOP creation, 365
fireside chats, 133, 381
image of, 386
internment of Japanese Americans, 377, 507
letters from public, 381
New Deal, 51–53, 70–71, 212–213
and news media, 133
nomination acceptance speech, 262
Pearl Harbor speech, **363**
picture of, **362**
pictures of, **69, 152**
presidency of, 359, 368, 384, **390, 391**
press conferences of, 129
Supreme Court appointments, 280, 384, 435, 447
on tax code, 567
use of polls, 99
vetoes, 374
Roosevelt, Theodore
"bully pulpit" presidency, **381**
foreign policy, 665
and growth in government, 68
image of, 386
judicial appointments, 441
picture of, **69**
presidency of, 358, **390**
press conferences of, 129
and Supreme Court, 446
trust-busting efforts, 387
Rostenkowski, Daniel, 309
Rotary Club, 475
Rove, Karl, 368, 369, 585
Rowley, Coleen, 422–423, 425
Ruby Ridge, 398
Ruckus Society, 187
Rule making, 403, 412, 413, 625–628, 639
Rules Committee, 327, 328, 336
Rumsfeld, Donald, 377, 463, 660, 679
Russell, Benjamin, 241
Russia, 673, 684, 686. *See also* Soviet Union
Russian immigrants, 10
Rutherford Institute, 448
Rwanda, 674

Safe Drinking Water Act (1974), 640
Sales taxes, 570–571
Salinger, Pierre, 126
Sallie Mae, 177
Salon, 124
Same-sex marriage, 81, 92, 174, 218, 498–500
Sanctions, 683–684
Sanford, Edward, 467
Santeria, 480
Santorum, Rick, 340
Sarbanes-Oxley Act, 312
Savings and loan (S&L) institutions, 632–633
Sawyer, Diane, 132, 148
Scalia, Antonin, 447, 455, 458, 459, 481, 498, 503, 544
Scandals, political, 93, 133, 148–149
Schaeffer, Eric, 619–620, 649
Schattschneider, E. E., 193, 201
Schering-Plough, 168
SCHIP (State Children's Health Insurance Program), 602–603
Schmitt, Harrison, 151
Schools. *See also* Colleges and universities; Public schools
as agent of political socialization, 93, 94–96
public funding of private schools, 486
School vouchers, 75
Schumer, Charles, 285, 311, 633
Schumpeter, Joseph, 572
Schwarzenegger, Arnold, 151

Scientific findings, and environmental regulation, 643–644
SCLC (Southern Christian Leadership Conference), 518
Scoop, 129
Scowcroft, Brent, 663
SDI (Strategic Defense Initiative), 672–673, 674
Seaboard Corporation, 607
Sea Shepherds, 178
Secession, 63
Second Amendment, 48, 466, 487
Secretary of defense, 659
Secretary of state, 659
Securities and Exchange Commission (SEC), 285, 286, 311, 312, 410, 416, 629, 631–632
Sedition Act (1798), 131
Sedition Act (1918), 467
Seditious speech, 467–469, 472
Segregation
court decisions, 511, 513–518, 521
de facto form, 517, 522, 532
de jure form, 516–517
laws against, 521
in The North, 512, 519
public opinion on, 109–110
residential patterns, 521, 526
in schools, 511, 514–518, 524, 532–533
in The South, 511, 515–516
Selective perception, 153
Self-government, 30–31
Self-incrimination, 489
Selma, Alabama, civil rights march, 519
Senate. *See also* Congress
bribery in, 289
campaign fundraising requirements, 300, 301
Clinton's impeachment, 393
cloture vote, 337
committees, 331–333
creation by Constitution, 35
day in life of Senator, 348–349
demographic profile of members, 320, 321
direct-election of members, 328
eligibility requirements, 317
equal representation of states, 38–39
estate tax, 555–556, 585
farm subsidies, 589–591, 616
filibusters, 337
vs. House of Representatives, **337**
Iraq War resolution, 653–654, 688–689
judicial appointments, 185, 439–444
leadership positions, 329–330
majority/minority leaders, 329–330
organization of, 327–328
and presidential appointments, 379
president pro tempore, 329, 360
reelection chances, 277–278
as stepping stone to presidency, 256
term, **39**, 40, 317
Senate Appropriations Committee, 342
Senate Budget Committee, 342
Senate Judiciary Committee, 422, 425
Senatorial courtesy, 379, 440
Senior Executive Service (SES), 420
Seniority rule, 332
Sensationalism, 147–148
Separate-but-equal doctrine, 511, 515
Separation of church and state, 480
Separation of powers, 38–40, 55
September 11, 2001. *See* 9/11/01
Serviceman's Readjustment Act (GI Bill), 605
SES (Senior Executive Service), 420
Setting the agenda, 150–151
Seventeenth Amendment, 48
Seventh Amendment, 45, 466
Sewage treatment plants, 640
Sex discrimination, 184, 475, 538–547
Sexual harassment, 544–545
Sharecroppers, 510
Sharpton, Al, 235, 258

Shay's Rebellion, 32
Sherman Antitrust Act (1890), 623, 631
Sierra Club, 178, 188
Silent Spring (Carson), 638
Simpson, Alan, 132
Simpson, O. J., 147, 527
Sinclair Broadcast, 123
Single-issue groups, 178–180
Single-member districts, 202
Single-parent households, 530, 597
Sit-ins, 518
Sixth Amendment, 45, 466, 486, 490, 491
60 Minutes, 145, 425
Skokie, Illinois, Nazi demonstration, 473
Slaves and slavery
abolishment of, 50, 509
black slave owners, 509
Constitutional issues, 35–36, 41
Dred Scott case, 433, 509
Emancipation Proclamation, 49
of farmworkers, 532
historical background, 7, 508–509
Lincoln's view of, 49
Three-fifths Compromise, 35, 41
Slave trade, **36**, 509
Slepian, Barnett, 179
S&L (savings and loan) institutions, 632–633
Smith, Adam, 557, 621, 622
Smith, Howard, 540
Smith, Nick, 231
Smith Act (1940), 467, 468
Smoking, 151, 185, 624
Snow, John, 579
Snow, Olympia, 222
Social class. *See* Class issues
Social contract, 42
Social insurance, 595. *See also* Social Security
Socialism, 557, 558, 559
Social issues, public opinion, 109. *See also* specific issue
Socialization. *See* Political socialization
Social Security
Bush's (George W.) privatization plan, 101, 612
changes to, 612
Clinton's policy, 100
eligibility, 594–595
establishment of, 594
funding of, 594
growth of, 595
and Medicare eligibility, 601
number of recipients, **593**
problems facing, 611–613
public support for, 109
Social Security Administration, 420
Social Security Trust Fund, 578, 611
Social welfare. *See also* Medicare; Social Security
abortion funding, 493–494
Aid to Families with Dependent Children (AFDC), 596–597
definition of, 591–592
devolution to states proposal, 614
earned income tax credit (EITC), 598–599
for farmers, 599–601
health care programs, 601–603
historical evolution of, 592–594
income support programs, 594–601
means tests for, 595
Medicaid, 493, 579, 593, 602–603
as political party function, 210, 218
public opinion, 108–109, 109
reasons for, 592
reform of, 74, 100, 149, 597–598, 599, 613–615
responsiveness of, 615
state vs. federal control, 74
subsidized services, 603–606
Supplemental Security Income (SSI), **593**, 595–596
tax subsidies, 606–608

Temporary Assistance for Needy Families (TANF), **593**, 598
Sodomy laws, 498
Soft money, 292, 294
Sony, 122
Sound bites, 130
Souter, David, 443–444
The South
political culture, 64
segregation in, 511, 515–516
and state-centered federalism, 66–67
South Africa, 187, 683–684
South Carolina, abortion clinic requirements, 495
Southern Christian Leadership Conference (SCLC), 518
Southern Democrats, 213, 216
Southern Republicans, 265
Sovereignty, popular, 19, 37
Soviet Union. *See also* Cold War
end of, 673–674
glasnost, 673
nuclear capabilities, 666
recognition of, 363
World War II, **665**
Speaker of the House, 326, 327, 328–329, 332, 351
Special-interest caucuses, 344–345
Special interest groups. *See* Interest groups
Specialization, in Congress, 344
Special Supplemental Nutritional Program for Women, Infants, and Children, 599
Spectacle presidency, 386–387
Speech, freedom of, 467–474
Speeches, of politicians, 130–131, 135
Speech plus conduct, 472–473
Speechwriters, 130–131
Sphere of influence, 656–657
Spin, of media, 132
Split-ticket voting, 54, 219–220, 247, 279
Spoils system, 304
Sputnik, 666
SSI (Supplemental Security Income), **593**, 595–596, **607**
Stacking, 240
Stagflation, 562
Standing committees, 331–333, 341–342
Stanton, Elizabeth Cady, 242, 246, 539
Star, 125
Stare decisis, 452
Starr, Kenneth, 393
State-centered federalism, 66–67, 72–73, 77
State Children's Health Insurance Program (SCHIP), 602–603
State Department
budget of, **409**
career specialists in, 660
economic diplomacy, 681
embassies, consulates, and missions of, 676
leak to press about Iraq War, 128
presidential appointments, 379
president's control over, 420
public libraries of, 658
during Washington administration, 406
State government
under Articles of Confederation, 32–33
Bill of Rights applied to, 466
Constitutional restrictions, 66
cultural differences in, 64–65
defense role, 78–79
and education, 75–76
employees, **61**
environmental protection, 646
federal aid, 70, 71, 78–79, 80, 82
federalism position, 76–77
federal revenue sharing, 71–72, 77
interstate relations, 81–82
as laboratories for policy experimentation, 72

liberal or conservative rating, **65**
lobbying in, 83
lobbyists for, 80–81, 85
Medicaid spending, 602
power of, 37–38, 61, 63–64, 66–67, 68, 70, 237
public opinion, 109
ratification of Constitutional amendments, 45
regulatory implementation and enforcement, 629–630
relations with federal government, 77–81
relations with local governments, 82–83
responsiveness of, 83
same-sex marriage, 498–500
sodomy laws, 498
spending, **70**, 71, 77
and unfunded mandates, 80
unitary relationship with local governments, 62
and welfare reform, 74, 614
State judiciaries, 438, **440**
State legislatures, and redistricting, 319
"State of the Union," 363
States' Rights Party, 214
Statistical Abstract of the United States, 413
Statutes, interpretation of, 449–450
Steel industry, 170, 377
Steering, by real estate agents, 521, 526
Stevens, John Paul, 463, 464–465, 487, 503
Stevens, Ted, 305
Stevenson, Adlai, 263
Stewart, Jon, 105
Stewart, Potter, 491
Stockman, David, 127, 326, 574
Stock options, 629
Stone, Harlan Fiske, 447, 455
Stonewall raid, 175
Strategic Defense Initiative (SDI), 672–673, 674
Straw polls, 97
Stump speeches, **256**
Subcommittees (Congress), 332–333
Subsidies
    for agriculture, 170, 172, 589–591, 599–601, 605–606, 616
    for corporations, 606–608
    direct vs. indirect, 592
    food stamps, **593**, 599
Suburbs, 517, 531
Succession, 360–361
Suffrage
    of African Americans, 12, 50, 237–240, 510, 512, 514
    age of eligibility, 243
    definition of, 237
    early limits, 237
    felons, 243
    of Native Americans, 12, 536
    reforms under Jackson, 207
    threats to, 243, 246–247
    of women, 12, 237, 242–243, 539
Suicide, assisted, 501–502
Sulfur dioxide emissions, 649
Sullivan, New York Times v., 477
Sunshine Act (1977), 406
Super Size Me, 146
Super Tuesday, 261
Super waivers, 614
Supplemental Security Income (SSI), **593**, 595–596, **607**
Supply-side economics, 562–563
Supremacy clause, 66
Supreme Court. *See also* Burger Court; Rehnquist Court; Warren Court
    abortion, 492–494, 496
    affirmative action, 548, 549
    appeals to, **440**, 448–449
    appointments to, 129, 437, 440–441
    bilingual education, 533
    Bush v. Gore decision, 129, 429–431, 458–460

campaign finance rulings, 292
capital punishment, 491
censorship of school papers, 475–476
chief justice's power, 454
and civil liberties, 502
civil rights, 513–518, 550
clerks, **449**
confessions to police, 489
deciding cases, 453–455
early reputation, 432
election of 2000, 129
FDR's appointments, 280, 384, 435, 447
federalism position, 73
freedom of assembly, 472
freedom of association, 475
freedom of press, 477
Guantanamo Bay prisoners, 463–464, 503–504
homosexual practice, 498
independence of judges, 447, 459
Internet regulation, 479
internment of Japanese Americans, 551
interpretation of Constitution, 450, 502
interpretation of statutes, 449–450
libel rulings, 477–478
location of, 432
Marshall Court, 67, 432–433, 434, **435**, 450, 454, 536
New Deal rulings, 51–52, 70
and news media, 136
news story sources' confidentiality, 476
obscenity rulings, 478
opinions of, 454–455
Pentagon Papers ruling, 475
prayer in public school, 482–484
precedents, 452–453
privacy rights, 492
public opinion of, 347, 431, 457
redistricting, 319
removal of appointees by president, 379
right to counsel, 490–491
role of, 48
rulings against government growth, 68
school segregation, 515–516
seditious speech, 467
segregation, 511, 515–516
term limits, 318
Thomas nomination, 129
unreasonable searches and seizures rulings, 488
Surgeon General, 418, 419
Surveillance, 488–489
Surveillance Court, 439
Swearing, 472
Sweden, 62
Sweden, health care system, 609
Swift Boat Veterans for Truth, 270, 296–297
Swing (battleground) states, 265, 270
Symbiotic relationship, between media and politicians, 127–131
Symbolic speech, 473–474

Tabloids, 125
Taft, William Howard, 387
Tailhook scandal, 119
Taliban, 680
Talk radio, 139, 156
Tammany Hall machine, 211, 289
Taney, Roger, 433–434, 509
TANF (Temporary Assistance for Needy Families), **593**, 598, **607**, 613–614
Tariffs, 681, 682
Task forces, 333
Tauzin, Billy, 629
Taxation
    congressional authority over, 65
    Constitutional compromise, 36
    estate tax, 555–556, 585
    fairness of, 568–569
    flat tax, 570

income tax, 69, 82, 567–569
    and offshoring of jobs, 582
    payroll taxes, 568, 594
    progressive vs. regressive taxes, 568, 570–571, 573
    reform of, 567–571
    as regulatory tool, 625, 645
    religious objections to, 481
    sales taxes, 570–571
    state variation in, 82
Tax burden, 569
Tax code
    changes (1986), 193
    complexity of, 567, 570
Tax credits, 109, 567, 598–599, **607**
Tax cuts
    and budget projections, 575
    Bush's (George W.), 566, 569, 573, 576, 577, 580
    and supply-side economics, 562
Tax deductions, 567–568, **569**, 570, **607**, 608
Tax subsidies, 606–608
Taylor, Maxwell, 675
Teapot Dome scandal, 280, 289
Technology, access to, 582
Teenage pregnancy, 495
Telecommunications Act (1996), 123
Television. *See also* News media
    bias of, 150
    Bush's (George W.) uncomfortableness with, 135
    candidates' appearances on shows, 271
    election coverage, 129, 140
    importance of, 121
    indecent material, 472
    industry concentration, 122
    number of homes having, 121
    political activism and censorship, 123
    political advertising, 268, 270–271, 290, 298
    and presidency, 359
    presidential debates, 271–273
    Reagan's use of, 133
    trends, 121
Temperance movements, 242
Temporary Assistance for Needy Families (TANF), **593**, 598, **607**, 613–614
Tenant, George, 417
Ten Commandments, public display of, 483, 485
Tennessee Valley Authority (TVA), 410–411
Tenth Amendment, 66, 67, 465
Term limits, 317–318, 333
Terrorism. *See also* 9/11/01
    congressional emergency procedures, 334–335
    defense against domestic threats, 657
    as election issue, 269
    and weapons of mass destruction, 642, 685–686
Terror suspects, interrogation of, 46–47
Texas
    black law school, 515
    college enrollment of minorities, 549
    right to counsel, 490
Texas, Lawrence v., 498
Textbooks, and political socialization, 94
Think tanks, 660–661
Third Amendment, 48, 466, 492
Third-parties, 141, 204, 205, 264
Thirteenth Amendment, 48, 50, 51
Thomas, Bill, 231
Thomas, Clarence, 129, 442, 444, **452**, 459, 503, 544
Thompson, Florence, **572**
Three-fifths Compromise, 35, 41
Thurmond, Strom, 126, 214, **215**
Tilden, Samuel, 510
Tillman, Benjamin, 238
Time magazine, 128, 147, 477, 539–540
Time Warner, 122
Tinker, Mary Beth, 473
Tinsley, Nikki, 649

Title IX, 543–546
Tobacco industry, 185, 187, 403
Tocqueville, Alexis de, 19, 163, 316, 456, 658
Tolerance, 112–113
Torricelli, Robert, 103, 309
Torture, 46
Town meetings, 20
Towns and townships, number of, **77**. *See also* Local government
Trade
    Constitutional compromise, 36
    NAFTA, 100, 142, 203, 664
    policies, 681–683
    WTO, 187–188
Traditionalistic political culture, 64
Tragedy of the commons, 621
Transgender issues, 176
Transportation Department, **409**, 634, 635
Treasury Department, 406, **409**, 420, 562, 578
Treaties
    under Articles of Confederation, 32
    Kyoto Treaty, 644, 674
    NATO, 656, 666, 674, 680
    and supremacy clause, 66
Truman, Bess, 367
Truman, Harry S.
    approval ratings, **388**
    congressional gains/losses for party during administration, **371**
    decisive style of, 390
    on economic policy, 562
    election of 1948, **104**
    election of 1952, 268
    integration of military, 214, 380
    judicial appointments, 446
    picture of, **104**
    on presidency, 359
    presidential effectiveness, **390**
    seizure of steel mills during Korean War, 377
    style of, 152
    Supreme Court appointments, 447
    vice presidency of, 369
    "whistlestop" campaign, **260**
Truman Doctrine (containment), 666–671
Trust
    of government, 113–115
    of racial and ethnic groups, 112
Truth in labeling, 625
Tsunami (2004), 685
Tulsa, Oklahoma, race riot, 513
TVA (Tennessee Valley Authority), 410–411
TWA, 634
Twain, Mark, 299
Tweed, Boss, 256
Twenty-Fifth Amendment, 360–361
Twenty-Fourth Amendment, 48, 239
Twenty-Second Amendment, 360
Twenty-Seventh Amendment, 48
Twenty-Sixth Amendment, 48, 243
Twenty-Third Amendment, 48
Two-party system, 202
Tyler Farms, 591

Underclass, 530, 531
Unemployment, 561, 562, 566
Unfunded mandates, 80
Unilateralism, 675–676
Uninsured, 602, 609
Unions and unionization
    decline of, 572
    federal employees, 420
    lobbying activity, **166**, 193
    membership trends, 167–169
    Supreme Court rulings, 435
Unitary system, 62
United Airlines, 634
United Kingdom. *See* Great Britain
United Nations, 62
United States Postal Service (USPS), 411
Universal health care, 609

Universities, generally. *See* Colleges and universities
University of Arizona, registration of student voters, 250
University of California v. Bakke, 548–549
University of Illinois, depository library program, 404
University of Michigan, affirmative action, 549
University of Mississippi, forced desegregation, 515
Unreasonable searches and seizures, 488–489
Urbanization, 68
Urban League, 174
U.S. Census Bureau, 7, 14–15
U.S. Citizenship and Immigration Services (USCIS), 8, 9
U.S. Steel, 623
USAID (Agency for International Development), 681, 684
USA PATRIOT Act
  access to e-mail accounts and Internet records, 637
  and civil liberties, 113
  democrats' support of, 224–225
  and FBI surveillance, 439
  foreign student database, 528
  and growth in federal bureaucracy, 407
  library provisions, 470–471
  size and complexity of bill, 338
USA Today, 136
USDA (United States Department of Agriculture), **409,** 413, 420, 599
USPS (United States Postal Service), 411
Utah
  child support for daughters vs. sons, 541
  voting rights of Native Americans, 536
Utilities, 622, 630, 649

Value-added tax (VAT), 571
Values, ideological battles over, 109
ValuJet, 634–635
Vanderbilt, Cornelius, 288
Ventura, Jesse, 151
Vermont, civil unions in, 499
Veterans
  GI Bill of Rights, 604–605
  health care program, 603
  income support programs, **593,** 601
Veterans Affairs Department, 407, **409,** 521, 603
Veto power, 338–339, 373–374
VH1, 146
Viacom, 122
Vice presidency
  duties and powers of, 360–361, 369–370
  pay and perks of, 369
  and presidential succession, 360
  replacement of, 360
  selection of candidate, 263–264
  as Senate presiding officer, 329, 369
  as stepping stone to president, 256
Vidal, Gore, 5
Vietcong, 669
Vietnam syndrome, 671
Vietnam War
  armed intervention, 668–669
  college students' political identification during, 95
  Ellsberg's whistleblowing, 422, 475
  end of, 669
  events leading up to, 668

freedom of press during, 475
freedom of speech during, 468–469, 472, 473–474
lessons from, 669–671
media's coverage of, 143
president's war-making power during, 377
protests against, **669**
Vinson, Frederick, 447, 468, 515
Violence
  against African Americans, 512–513
  of interest groups, 189
Violence Policy Center, 179
Virginia Plan, 34
Visas, 9, 10
VNS (Voter News Service), 102, 103
Voinovich, George, 278
Voltaire, 10
Voluntary organizations, decline in, 165. *See also* Interest groups
Voter News Service (VNS), 102, 103
Voter registration
  barriers to, 252–253, 254
  on Election Day, 253
  election of 2000, 4
  election of 2004, 3, 247, 253
  establishment of, 212
  motor voter law, 253
  purges of list, 247, 253
  rates of, 252
  reforms (2002), 243
  in the South after passage of VRA, 239
  of students, 250
Voter turnout
  in 1840, 247
  in 1896, 210
  in 2004, 249, 254, 280
  and Election Day practices, 253
  factors in, 21, 250–254
  mobilization techniques, 3, 187, 248–249, 253–254, 265
  in presidential vs. congressional elections, 249
  after Progressive reforms, 248
  recent trends, 249
  registrations vs. percentage voting, 4
  of young people, 248–249, 250
Voting. *See also* Elections
  by absentee ballot, 244–245, 253
  ballots, **212,** 240, 243, 244–245, 247
  bribery, 288
  and candidate evaluations, 228
  as cornerstone of freedom, 4
  decision-making process, 223
  electronic, 186
  issues, 228–229
  nonvoters, characteristics of, 250
  and party identification, 223–228
  split-ticket voting, 54, 219–220, 247, 253
Voting equipment, 243, 246–247
Voting rights. *See* Suffrage
Voting Rights Act (VRA), 239–240, 520, 521
Vouchers, for housing, 526
Vouchers, for schools, 75
VRA (Voting Rights Act), 239–240, 520, 521

Waco, Texas incident, 398
Wages and salaries
  Congress members, 324
  corporate executives, 573
  minimum wage, 109, 435, **596**
  overtime, 167
  president, 360

union vs. nonunion labor, 167
vice president, 369
women vs. men, 542
Waivers, given to states, 614
Wallace, George, 204, 239, 264, 399, 515
Wall Street Journal, 139, 148, 222
War, taxation and spending during, 576–577. *See also specific wars*
War-making power, 364, 377–379, 382, 464, 661, 688–689
War on Poverty, 593, 599
War on terrorism
  Bush's communication of, 135
  and civil liberties, 113
  as congressional election issue (2002), 269
  congressional power, 379
  and economic security, 116
  Guantanamo Bay prisoners, 463–464, 503–504
  interrogation of suspected terrorists, 46–47
  preemption strategy, 675
  public's support of, 89, 90
  taxation and spending during, 576
War Powers Act (1973), 377–378, 661
Warren, Earl, 435, **436,** 446, 451, 473
Warren, Mercy Otis, 33
Warren Court
  activism of, 451
  birth control, 492
  Brennan's influence over, 455
  communism rulings, 468
  electronic surveillance, 489
  expansion of civil liberties, 502
  freedom of speech rulings, 472
  free exercise of religion, 480–481
  Gideon v. Wainright, 490
  impact of, 435–437
  libel, 477
  Miranda rights, 489
  obscenity, 478
  school segregation, 515
Warsaw Pact, 666
Washington, D. C., early picture of, **317**
Washington, George
  bribery of voters, 288
  bureaucracy under, 406
  as Constitutional Convention delegate, 34, 35
  on political parties, 201
  presidential effectiveness, **390,** 391
  presidential staff, 364
  speeches, 381
  on two-house legislature, 40
Washington, Martha, 366
Washington Post, 29, 131, 141–142, 147, 478, 545, 649
Washington Times, 139
Watergate scandal, 29–30, 55–56, 132, 309, 360, 388–389
Water quality, regulation of, 640–641
Watts, J. C., 527
Waxman, Henry, 340
Wealth and the wealthy, 19, 304, **305,** 446, 448. *See also* Elites
The Wealth of Nations (Smith), 557
Weapons of mass destruction, 128, 143, **144,** 376, 417, 686, 688. *See also* Nuclear weapons
Web sites, 226, 273, 413. *See also* Internet
Webster, Daniel, 16
Weidenbaum, Murray, 574–575
Welfare. *See* Social welfare
Wellstone, Paul, 269
Whig Party, 207, 209, **255**
Whips, 315–316, 329, 351

Whistleblowers, 398, 422–423, 425
"Whistlestop" campaign, **260**
"White flight," 517, 522
White House staff, 364–365, 368–369, 380
White primaries, 238, 239
Whitewater scandal, 135, 136, 147, 308
Whitman, Christie Todd, 649
Whitman, Walt, 6
Wilder, Douglas, 240
Williams, Roger, 11
Willkie, Wendell, **259**
Wilson, Edith, 366
Wilson, James, 35
Wilson, Joseph, 128
Wilson, Woodrow
  and bureaucracy, 415
  League of Nations, 665
  picture of, **362**
  presidency of, 358–359, 361, **390**
  stroke of, 366
  on Supreme Court, 48
  typing of speeches, 365
Winner-take-all system, 202
Wisconsin, direct primaries established in, 212
Women
  affirmative action, 547–548
  in Congress, 320, 322
  congressional caucuses for, 345
  discrimination against, 184, 475, 538–546
  education, 538, 543
  employment of, 538, 541–543
  as federal employees, 400
  interest groups for, 172–173
  judges, 441–442, 443
  as national convention delegates, 261
  PACs, 294
  party affiliation, 217
  as political officeholders, 246
  as presidential candidates, 257
  and Revolutionary War, 33
  social welfare programs, 596–598, 599
  Title IX, 543–546
  voting rights, 12, 237, 242–243, 539
Women's movement, 188, 539–546
Wood, Alastair, 184
Woodhull, Victoria Claflin, 246
Woods, Tiger, 14
Woodward, Bob, 29, **30**
Working America, 169
Working poor, 598–599
Works Progress Administration (WPA), 70
World Trade Organization (WTO), 187–188, 600–601, 682
World War I, 243, 665
World War II, 71, **540,** 665, 668
WPA (Works Progress Administration), 70
Wright brothers, news media's coverage of first flight, 138
Writ of certiorari, 448–449
WTO (World Trade Organization), 187–188, 600–601, 682
Wyoming, women's voting rights in, 242

Young, Milt, 344
Youth
  campaign participation, 255
  voter turnout, 248–249, 250
Yucca Mountain nuclear waste storage facility, 59–60, 85–86
Yugoslavia, 674

Presidents, Elections, and Congresses, 1789–2004 (cont.)

Year	President	Vice President	Party of President	Election Year	Election Opponent with Most Votes*
1889–1893	Benjamin Harrison	Levi P. Morton	Rep	(1888)	Grover Cleveland
1893–1897	Grover Cleveland	Adlai E. Stevenson	Dem	(1892)	Benjamin Harrison
1897–1901	William McKinley	Garret A. Hobart (to 1901)	Rep	(1896)	William Jennings Bryan
		Theodore Roosevelt (1901)		(1900)	William Jennings Bryan
1901–1909	Theodore Roosevelt	(No VP, 1901–1905)	Rep		Took office upon death of McKinley
		Charles W. Fairbanks (1905–1909)		(1904)	Alton B. Parker
1909–1913	William Howard Taft	James S. Sherman	Rep	(1908)	William Jennings Bryan
1913–1921	Woodrow Wilson	Thomas R. Marshall	Dem	(1912)	Theodore Roosevelt
				(1916)	Charles Evans Hughes
1921–1923	Warren G. Harding	Calvin Coolidge	Rep	(1920)	James Cox
1923–1929	Calvin Coolidge	(No VP, 1923–1925)	Rep		Took office upon death of Harding
		Charles G. Dawes (1925–1929)		(1924)	John Davis
1929–1933	Herbert Hoover	Charles Curtis	Rep	(1928)	Alfred E. Smith
1933–1945	Franklin D. Roosevelt	John N. Garner (1933–1941)	Dem	(1932)	Herbert Hoover
		Henry A. Wallace (1941–1945)		(1936)	Alfred Landon
		Harry S. Truman (1945)		(1940)	Wendell Willkie
				(1944)	Thomas Dewey
1945–1953	Harry S. Truman	(No VP, 1945–1949)	Dem		Took office upon death of Roosevelt
		Alban W. Barkley		(1948)	Thomas Dewey
1953–1961	Dwight D. Eisenhower	Richard M. Nixon	Rep	(1952)	Adlai Stevenson
				(1956)	Adlai Stevenson
1961–1963	John F. Kennedy	Lyndon B. Johnson	Dem	(1960)	Richard M. Nixon
1963–1969	Lyndon B. Johnson	(No VP, 1963–1965)	Dem		Took office upon death of Kennedy
		Hubert H. Humphrey (1965–1969)		(1964)	Barry Goldwater
1969–1974	Richard M. Nixon	Spiro T. Agnew	Rep	(1968)	Hubert H. Humphrey
		Gerald R. Ford (appointed)		(1972)	George McGovern
1974–1977	Gerald R. Ford	Nelson A. Rockefeller (appointed)	Rep		Took office upon Nixon's resignation
1977–1981	Jimmy Carter	Walter Mondale	Dem	(1976)	Gerald R. Ford
1981–1989	Ronald Reagan	George Bush	Rep	(1980)	Jimmy Carter
				(1984)	Walter F. Mondale
1989–1993	George Bush	J. Danforth Quayle	Rep	(1988)	Michael Dukakis
1993–2001	William J. Clinton	Albert Gore	Dem	(1992)	George Bush
				(1996)	Robert Dole
2001–	George W. Bush	Richard Cheney	Rep	(2000)	Albert Gore
				(2004)	John Kerry